ART AND MANKIND

LAROUSSE ENCYCLOPEDIA OF PREHISTORIC AND ANCIENT ART

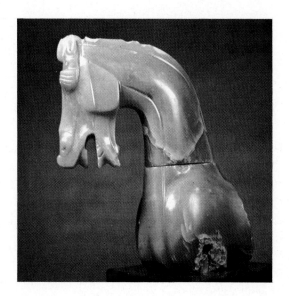

CHINESE. JADE HORSE'S HEAD. *Han Dynasty. Victoria and Albert Museum. Photo: Michael Holford.*
Frontispiece. MAGDALENIAN. *Cave painting at Lascaux. Photo: Colorphoto Hans Hinz.*

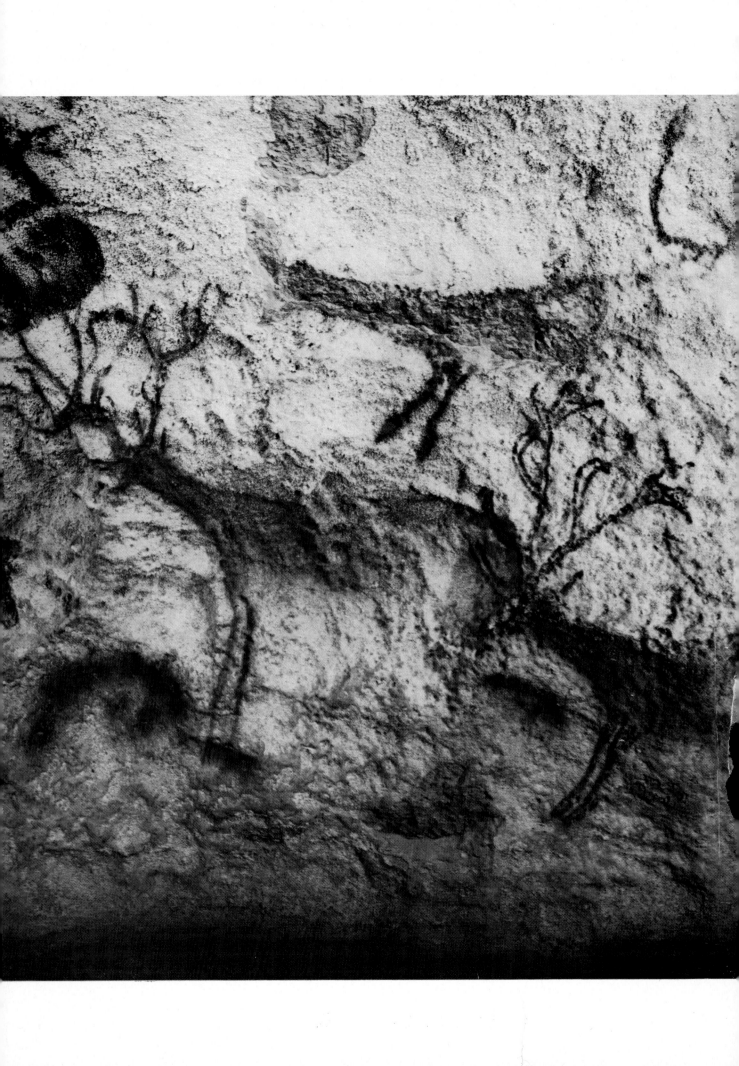

ART AND MANKIND

LAROUSSE ENCYCLOPEDIA OF

PREHISTORIC
AND ANCIENT ART

General Editor RENÉ HUYGHE

Member of the Académie Française
Professor in the Collège de France · Honorary Chief Curator of the Louvre

EXCALIBUR BOOKS

NEW YORK

Text prepared by Emily Evershed, Michael Heron,
Corinne Lambert, Hugh Newbury and Wendela Schurmann
from the French Original
L'ART ET L'HOMME

Copyright © 1957 Augé, Gillon, Hollier-Larousse, Moreau et Cie
(Librairie Larousse, Paris)

English-language edition © 1962 The Hamlyn Publishing Group Limited,
Astronaut House, Hounslow Road, Feltham, Middlesex, England.

Revised 1966
Second edition 1970

First published in USA 1981
by Excalibur Books
Excalibur is a trademark of Simon & Schuster

Distributed by Bookthrift
New York, New York

ISBN 0-89673-079-4
Printed in Singapore

CONTENTS

CONTRIBUTORS

JEANNINE AUBOYER, *Curator of the French national museums (Asiatic art, Musée Guimet)*

RAYMOND BLOCH, *Director of Studies at the Ecole des Hautes Etudes*

The late ABBÉ HENRI BREUIL, *member of the Institut de France, honorary Professor in the Collège de France*

FRANCOIS CHAMOUX, *Professor of Archaeology in the Faculty of Letters at Nancy*

GEORGES CONTENAU, *corresponding member of the Institut de France, honorary Chief Curator at the Louvre*

MADELEINE PAUL-DAVID, *Deputy Curator at the Musée Cernuschi, Paris*

PIERRE DEMARGNE, *Professor of Classical Archaeology at the Sorbonne*

CHRISTIANE DESROCHES NOBLECOURT, *Curator at the Louvre, adviser to UNESCO at the Centre de Documentation et d'Etudes sur l'Egypte Ancienne*

The late CHANOINE ETIENNE DRIOTON, *Professor in the Collège de France, Director General of the Service des Antiquités de l'Egypte, honorary Curator at the Louvre*

VADIME ELISSEEFF, *Curator of the Musée Cernuschi, Paris, Director of Studies at the Ecole des Hautes Etudes*

ROMAN GHIRSHMAN, *Director, French Archaeological Missions in Iran*

The late MARCEL GRIAULE, *adviser to the Assemblée de l'Union Française, Professor at the Sorbonne*

RAOUL D'HARCOURT, *late Director of Research at the Centre National de la Recherche Scientifique*

CHRISTOPHER HAWKES, F.S.A., *Professor of European Archaeology in the University of Oxford*

OLE KLINDT-JENSEN, *Curator at the National Museum at Copenhagen*

HENRY LAVACHERY, *of the Royal Belgian Academy, honorary Chief Curator of the Cinquantenaire Museum, Brussels, honorary Professor in the University of Brussels*

PIA LAVIOSA-ZAMBOTTI, *Professor of Palaeontology in the University of Milan, Primio dell'Accademia Nazionale dei Lincei*

ANDRÉ LEROI-GOURHAN, *Professor in the Faculty of Letters at Lyon, Director of the Centre de Recherches Préhistoriques at the Musée de l'Homme*

CHARLES PICARD, *member of the Institut de France, Director of the Institut d'Art et d'Archéologie in the University of Paris, honorary Professor at the Sorbonne*

GILBERT CHARLES PICARD, *Professor in the Faculty of Letters at Strasbourg, late Director of Antiquities in Tunisia*

MARGUERITE RUTTEN, *on the staff of the French national museums, Lecturer at the Ecole du Louvre*

CLAUDE F. A. SCHAEFFER, *member of the Institut de France, Professor in the Collège de France, Curator at the Musée des Antiquités Nationales*

PHILIPPE STERN, *Chief Curator of the French national museums (Asiatic art, Musée Guimet), Professor at the Ecole du Louvre*

ANDRÉ VARAGNAC, *Chief Curator of the Musée des Antiquités Nationales, Director of Studies at the Ecole des Hautes Etudes*

ERNEST WILL, *Professor in the Faculty of Letters at Lille, late member of the French School in Athens*

Simone Besques-Mollard, Desmond Collins, Jacques-Claude Courtois, Lydie Huyghe, Philippe Jean, Annie Masson-Detourbet, Henry Riechlen, and Marie-Louise Tisserant wrote the Historical Summaries

COLOUR PLATES

ACKNOWLEDGEMENTS

A.C.L., Brussels: 106, Acropolis Museum, Athens: 461. Aerofilms and Aero Pictorial Ltd: 20b, 188, 651. Aero-Photo: 637. Alinari: 466–8, 477, 483, 489, 496, 504, 532, 543a and c, 580–1, 594, 596, 598–9, 600, 603–4, 614, 655. American Museum of Natural History: 101. Anglo-Chilean Society: 124, 126. Antikensammlungen, Stuttgart: 294. Antikvarisk-Topografiska Arkivet, Stockholm: 375, 378, 381. Archaeological Museum, Ankara: 268. Archaeological Museum, Barcelona: 343. Archaeological Survey of India: 69, 82, 663–4, 682, 684–5, 688–9, 692–7. Archives Musée Guimet, Photo Chavannes: 699, 710; Photo Goloubev: 673, 680, 690–1; Photo Segalen: 701. Archives Photographiques, Paris: 30, 45–6, 48–9, 50, 54, 167, 176, 179b, 191, 193, 196, 204, 206, 216, 264, 267, 273, 278, 318, 431–2, 442, 453, 463, 512, 527, 530, 533, 541, 544a, 546, 564, 587, 619, 620, 638, 650. Art Institute of Chicago: 139, 423. Ashmolean Museum, Oxford: 169, 344a and b, 351, 352. Australia House, London: 100. L. Balsan: 66. Bardo Museum, Tunis: 565, 568, 570–1. Bildarchiv Foto Marburg: 257, 324, 486, 498. M. Bini: 347. E. Boudot-Lamotte: 177, 248, 253, 259, 283, 328, 340, 553, 560, 576. British Museum: 43, 76–7, 102, 107–110, 112–13, 119–20, 156, 165, 183, 190, 197–9, 207, 211–12, 240–1, 243, 245, 274–5, 277, 280, 298, 315–16, 349–50, 354, 362, 366, 368, 370, 441, 458, 493, 499, 502, 506, 515, 517–19, 521–2, 531, 536, 538, 563, 708, 721. J. Allan Cash: 114, 355, 424, 428, 440, 445, 464, 476, 478–80, 497, 624–5, 629, 632, 644, 654. Cernuschi Museum, Paris: 669. M. Chuzeville: 175, 181, 539, 549. R. Descharnes: 485. Directorate General of Antiquities, Baghdad: 79–80, 184, 189, 244, 272, 276. Directorate of Antiquities, Cairo: 249. Dominion Museum, New Zealand: 127, 134. Egyptian State Tourist Administration, Photo C. Zachary: 254, 262. Fogg Art Museum, Harvard University: 537. Fotofast, Bologna: 364. Foto-Grahl, Meissen: 534. Freer Gallery of Art: 403. French Government Tourist Office: 19, 20a, 26, 52–3. German Archaeological Institute, Athens: 481, 487. Giraudon: 178–9, 266, 271, 300–1, 309a, 311, 314, 334, 336, 367, 429, 457, 494–5, 547, 562, 579, 593, 636, 700. Gold Museum, Bogotá: 160. Government Museum, Madras: 674. P. Graziosi: 59. I. Groth-Kimball: 149. E. Hahn: 711. Hamlyn Group Photographic Library: 1, 3, 4, 7, 10–12, 40, 103, 116, 137, 148, 150, 202, 214, 217, 221, 279, 285, 319, 321, 330, 425–6, 433, 437, 447, 452, 462, 470, 472–4, 491, 513, 525, 544b, 555–6, 561, 567, 590, 605, 617, 621, 635, 641, 643, 647, 660, 665, 671, 679, 681, 703, 722, 724. Hassia: 291. Herakleion Museum: 320, 326, 331. Hermitage, Leningrad: 409, 413, 415, 422. H. Hinz: 16, 25. Hirmer Fotoarchiv, Munich: 170, 192, 200, 203, 213, 227, 261, 520. Historisches Museum, Berne: 363. M. Holford: 133. D. Hughes-Gilbey: 341. Independent Features: 81. Instituto Nacional de Antropología e Historia, Mexico: 146. Irish Tourist Board: 353. A. F. Kersting: 628, 645. E. Kusch: 87b, 142. Larousse: 2, 8, 13–15, 17, 21, 23, 28, 31, 33–4, 36, 41, 44, 56, 57, 58, 60, 63, 67, 70–3, 84–5, 87a, 88–92, 94, 96–7, 104, 115, 117–18, 121, 128, 135–6, 140–1, 158, 163, 166, 168, 182, 185, 186, 194–5, 201, 218–20, 223–6, 228–9, 231, 234–7, 239, 246–7, 250–1, 258, 260, 265, 270, 279, 281, 284, 289, 291–2, 295–7, 303–9b, 310a, 312–13, 316, 342, 360, 369, 383, 390–2, 395–7, 399, 400, 404, 407, 411, 414, 430, 438, 448–50, 455, 548, 558, 575, 597, 652, 667, 672, 675–8, 698, 702, 704, 707, 713, 725–7. J. A. Lavaud: 86, 388, 402, 406, 408, 418. Mansell-Alinari: 359, 434, 443–4, 460, 465, 482, 484, 501, 511, 528–9, 545, 578, 582, 585, 601–2, 606–9, 611, 616, 623, 627, 630–1, 633, 642, 653. Mansell-Anderson: 509b, 588, 591, 592, 610. Mansell Collection: 269, 436, 439, 446, 471, 488, 490, 492, 516, 526, 634. Mansell-Giraudon: 500. Metropolitan Museum of Art, New York: 111, 420, 454. Minneapolis Institute of Arts: 417, 705. Musée des Antiquités Nationales, Château de St Germain en Laye: 32, 35, 68, 361. Musée d'Aquitaine, Bordeaux: 24. Musée d'Archéologie Borély, Marseille: 371. Musée Guimet, Paris: 401, 656–9, 661–2, 666, 683, 686–7, 709, 723, 728. Musée de l'Homme, Paris: 6, 9, 22, 27, 38, 51, 57a, 62, 64, 93, 105, 122–3, 130–2, 144, 147, 151–3, 162. Musée de Sens: 646. Musée de la Ville, Haguenau: 427. Musées Royaux d'Art et d'Histoire, Brussels: 384. Museo Civico di Storia ed Arte, Trieste: 540. Museum of Fine Arts, Boston: 451, 524, 706, 718, 720. Narodni Muzej, Belgrade: 348, 357. National Anthropological and Archaeological Museum, Lima: 159. National Archaeological Museum, Athens: 238, 286, 333, 335, 510, 514. National Archaeological Museum, Madrid: 287, 507, 508, 566, 572. National Museum, Beirut: 232. National Museum, Copenhagen: 299, 358, 372–4, 376–7, 379–80, 382. National Museum, Helsinki: 61, 416. National Museum, Hungary: 356, 410. National Museum, Stockholm: 293. National Museum for Antiquities, Bucharest: 42, 288. National Museum of Anthropology, Mexico: 154. Ny Carlsberg Glyptotek, Copenhagen: 595. Ostasiatiska Museet, Stockholm: 419. Peabody Museum, Harvard University: 145. Picturepoint: 469 (John Baker). Pitt Rivers Museum, University of Oxford: 125. H. Plessis: 622. Paul Popper: 179c. J. Powell: 339. Prado, Madrid: 569. Prähistorische Abteilung, Naturhistorisches Museum, Vienna: 5. C. Ratton: 95. H. Roger-Viollet: 29, 65, 138, 161, 164, 187, 210, 222, 263, 282, 323, 325, 327, 475, 552, 557, 573, 574. Sabena: 155. Sakamoto Photo Research Laboratory: 668, 712, 714–17, 719. Sarajevo Museum: 344c. Service des Antiquités, Rabat: 639. Service Photographique, Réunion des Musées Nationaux, Paris: 74a and b, 75, 171–4, 180, 205, 208, 242. Soprintendenza alle Antichità, Florence: 365, 503, 577, 583. Soprintendenza alle Antichità, Rome: 509. Soprintendenza alle Antichità, Syracuse: 615. Soprintendenza alle Antichità-Egittologia, Turin: 230. Spanish National Tourist Office: 626. Staatliche Antikensammlungen und Glyptothek, Munich: 589. Staatliche Museen zu Berlin: 612–13. Teheran Museum: 387, 389, 393–4, 412, 421, 435, 550, 554, 559. Tropical Museum, Amsterdam: 129. University Museum, Philadelphia: 78, 143. Vatican Museum: 523, 535, 540, 584, 586, 618, 640, 649. Victoria and Albert Museum, London: 398. Walters Art Gallery, Baltimore: 456. William Rockhill Nelson Gallery of Art, Kansas: 405. R. Wood: 233, 252, 256, 322, 329, 337–8, 551. Yan: 37, 459.

INTRODUCTION

This book is not just another history of art of the traditional kind that merely sets out the facts, lists artists and their work, classifies schools and defines styles.

The study of the history of art, in fact, is subject to that universal law, the law of development. 19th-century positivism concentrated on hard facts, analysing them to the point of losing the overall picture in a mass of detail; but now there is a tendency everywhere to seek a more general understanding. To meet the new demands of today this book is designed to be both deeper and wider in scope–deeper because, behind the historical facts, it comes to grips with art itself by tracing the development of form and of aesthetic concepts; wider because it relates art to the general evolution of ideas and customs, of culture and civilisation, of humanity, in short.

The large number of discoveries in the last few years, coupled with the growth of public interest, has necessitated a study of the widest possible range which would sum up the present state of knowledge. This study will reach back to the remotest beginnings of prehistory and will carry the reader through classical Greece and Rome. It will cover not only our own Western tradition, but also those civilisations remotest from us in space or sophistication, in particular those of Asia.

But our aim is to synthesise the scholarship of these very diverse subjects. To do this we have had to use a radically new system which can be seen in the arrangement of each chapter. Firstly, the *facts*–dates, techniques, schools, artists–are set out chronologically and geographically in the traditional way, as comprehensively and concisely as possible. These 'Historical Summaries', at the end of each chapter, allow the specialist, student or amateur to find a fact without involving him in a tedious and chancy search; they constitute an encyclopedia in themselves. Secondly, the main body of each chapter consists of essays which, by breaking down the compartments into which art is usually confined so as to arrive at an overall view, present and comment on the general flow, the various influences and trends, and the way they react on each other, and thus give the reader a more complete *understanding* of the varied successive facets of art. Lastly the introductory sections, 'Art Forms and Society', bring out a *philosophy of art*. They show how art, whose outward appearance is continuously evolving, reflects and expresses the advance of man, whose ideas on life and the world keep pace with the change in the material conditions of his existence. This task has been assigned to the General Editor of the book who, however, has invited Monsieur Philippe Stern, the eminent Conservateur of the Musée Guimet in Paris, to assist in the sections referring to Eastern art, for which a specialist is essential.

So the reader will rapidly get his bearings and be able to find, according to his needs or tastes, food for thought or hard fact.

This book not only sets out to collect and summarise the body of knowledge that is usually grouped under the heading 'history of art'. It also aims at helping towards an understanding of art itself, its nature, its function and the role it has always played, and still plays, in the life of man.

There are many who regard art as only a pastime, a superior one, certainly, but still a pastime, an amusement. There are many who express an interest in art so as to be in the fashion and who are secretly contemptuous of it for being 'of no use'. Some come near to thinking it a luxury.

In fact, art is an essential function of man, indispensable to individuals and communities alike, for which they have found a need ever since the earliest period of prehistory. Art and mankind are indissolubly linked. There can be no art without mankind, and perhaps, too, no mankind without art. Through art, man expresses himself more fully, and thus understands and fulfils himself better. Through art, the world becomes closer and more comprehensible, more familiar. Art is the agency for a continual 'give and take' with our surroundings, a sort of spiritual respiration like the physical one without which our bodies cannot live. The individual or civilisation that exists withour art runs the risk of an asphyxia of the soul and a real moral breakdown.

The history of art fulfils man's deepest aspirations: to know what has gone before, what exists today and what might come in the future, and to create superbly–these are the characteristics of man and his greatness. Now, the history of art satisfies this twofold quest for knowledge and quality. Through it man learns to know himself better and to understand his nature throughout the centuries from the evidence, direct, irrefutable and still alive, of his works of art, for a work of art can, as nothing else, plumb the depths of man's sensibility and his soul.

But the history of art is also the best way of getting close to the dream that drives man to search for quality and understanding. Quality can be felt, but not defined or explained. One can only give it a name: in art it is called beauty. But in all the time that there have been artists and thinkers it has never been possible to pin it down in a 'theory of beauty'. In any given part of the world and at any given moment it can take a new, and often unexpected and disconcerting, form. Beauty is a will-o'-the-wisp: it goes where it pleases and cannot be confined. Any attempt to catch it merely extinguishes it.

So the double aim of this work is to help the reader to understand man better and to feel and share in man's ceaseless pursuit of quality. Its subtitle is not the traditional 'A History of Art' but 'Art and Mankind'. This is intended as a strong indication of our intentions in this book, not to pander to idle curiosity by publishing a mere catalogue of facts but to try to deepen our understanding of man through an understanding of art, and our understanding of art through an understanding of man.

Art is the joint responsibility of all men and thus differs from place to place and from century to century with as much variety and flexibility as the customs of different communities. So the history of art cannot be treated in isolation as a separate entity. The most radical differences are in man's ideas on reality and in his exploration of it. Everything in a particular period is dependent on them. It is not easy at first to see the connection between the scientist elaborating natural laws, the philosopher formulating theories, the writer putting his feelings and ideas on paper, the artist creating images and the musician organising sound. Each, however, in his own particular language, expresses the attitude of the period towards reality. A generation of men is like a ship steaming along the coast, with the passengers looking at the shore as it passes: one takes measurements, another a photograph, a third has a paint-box while a fourth records his impressions in a notebook. A superficial observer will see no relationship between these varied activities, but all without exception are looking at the same view from the same standpoint. Of course, it may happen that one passenger has decided to stand in the bows to see what may appear over the horizon, and that someone else, on the other hand, is in the stern to catch a last glimpse of the scene disappearing in the distance. All are, however, literally in the same boat, following the same course and moving at the same speed. The movement of the ship is the progress of a generation.

Thus the art of a particular period is directly related to the philoso philosophy of that period, to its literature, science and social and economic conditions. But it would be a mistake to think that art develops out of these factors. In reality it is itself one more factor and it, too, is an expression of contemporary society just as the others are, though differing from them in kind and, above all, in purpose. The writer expresses himself in words, while the artist uses images. But both translate into their own language the same stage of human evolution, from which one of them draws *ideas*, and the other creates *visions*. So the thinking and the art of a period always, at any rate deep down, run parallel.

If art is so closely linked with man, to the point of changing as man changes, it is because it is a reflection and an expression of him, almost an extension of him. But we must remember that 'man' can refer to either the individual or the community, and art reflects, and sometimes even reveals, the one as well as the other. Like a sensitive seismograph, it registers desires and fears, attitudes to life, ordinary feelings and the way they move us, common to men of the same faith, race, time, social group or culture.

However, an understanding of a historical, geographical and social situation is not enough to enable us infallibly to deduce the art which should result from these elements. To know the origin and geology of the stone an architect uses in a building is only to know the material with which he constructs it. But what is important is the unforeseeable result of his use of the material. This is in the domain not of history but of creation and quality.

Moreover, even though art is influenced by what creates it and by what surrounds it, it is nevertheless a world apart, with its own laws which it must obey. In the concert of human activities, art is an instrument that cannot be separated from all the others, but it has a place of its own in the orchestra; it has not only its own part in the score but also its own tone colour. Even more important, art has its own unique structure and obeys its own laws. It is, to a certain extent, dependent on the general history of mankind, in which it has its own place, and on the psychological make-up of the artist who creates it; but it must also, like a living organism, follow its own destiny. It has a way of evolving and transforming itself that is natural and necessary to it and which occurs in a similar manner everywhere in the world and in every age. Eminent thinkers have shown that art continually reproduces a 'life-cycle' from the primitive or experimental phase to the classical, then through the refined phase, a kind of mannerism, to end in the baroque phase, with its tendency towards exaggeration and confusion. It might be said, in fact, that form obeys a sort of biological law corresponding to the successive stages of youth, maturity and old age that, in the same way, are found among all living creatures, however unlike they may be in appearance and characteristics.

The work of art is the resultant of these infinitely varied forces that nevertheless come together to create its unity. One could say that a work is made up of three elements: the world of visible reality which is its starting-point and from which it takes its raw material, however much it may transform it; the plastic world, that is to say, the possibilities and limitations of the materials with which the work is made and of the way in which it is carried out; and the world of thoughts and feelings that impel and excite the artist and to which he tries to give concrete form.

We can now take a rather wider field of view in order to understand how this complex interplay of elements results in the unique amalgam of the eternal and the ephemeral that always exists in art. Throughout history, aestheticians have been sharply divided between two opposing views–that there is an absolute and inflexible yardstick of beauty or, on the other hand, that there is an infinite relativity of taste. Of the component parts that we have analysed, the appearance of nature, to all intents and purposes, does not change at all, and plastic problems remain practically the same. But the artist himself evolves continuously in the way he interprets the first of these and solves the second. But though he is carried along by the endless stream of human history, with the same rhythm and the same detours, the artist believes his goal to be a fixed point. This goal, to which he is drawn and to which he aspires and believes he is getting closer every day, is beauty. Sometimes he thinks he has reached it, and he stops and consolidates his advance. But not for long: soon he sets off again, still not satisfied.

Moreover, though everyone is making for the same goal, each thinks it is in a different direction, which leads to incessant argument. Only one thing is certain–that all are fired with the same ambition; and it is precisely this that creates the tension from which, when it is of high quality, beauty is born.

Of this journey, of its route and of the adventures on the way this book will try to give an account. But, for beauty it can do no more than introduce the reader into its presence.

That settles the plan of the book and its limits: we shall try to explain historically and psychologically the working of art; how each period offers it its raw material; how, in the way it treats the raw material, it obeys certain eternal laws, clings to some traditional habits and yields to some new impulses; and how it carries out a programme that may be imposed on it from outside. But these are just approaches. The result can only be felt: and this is up to the reader to do, by looking at the pictures in this book. There is no other way.

Is the history of art pointless, then, since it is enough merely to look? Certainly not, for through it one learns to approach the whole of art in an orderly manner and to recognise as valid all the infinite diversity of forms that man has invented down through the ages in every continent. Thus, by ridding the mind of the narrow formulas that can restrict one's judgment, the history of art forces us to seek beauty outside all those doctrines in which the dogmatist tries to imprison it.

RENÉ HUYGHE

1. *Right*. Drawings in the cave of Les Trois Frères: a sorcerer or hunter disguised as an animal is seen near the centre. *(Copy by Breuil.)*

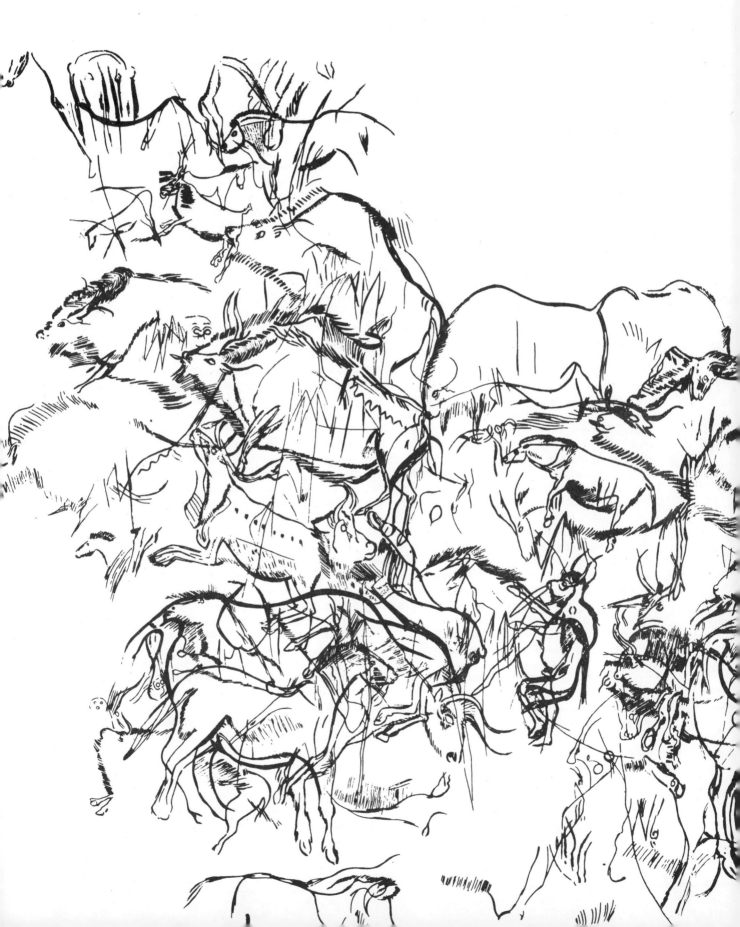

ART FORMS AND SOCIETY *René Huyghe*

Quite rightly our own age attaches particular importance to prehistoric art. We can indeed expect it to throw a unique light on the profound nature of art, because it shows art in its infancy, in its pure state, before the complications of civilisation transformed its scope.

THE FRANCO-CANTABRIAN PALAEOLITHIC AGE

The oldest information we possess comes from the Palaeolithic art of chipped stone, when the first implements fashioned by the will and hand of man appeared. In these utilitarian objects we can already see evidences of the principal laws of art, which emerge even more distinctly in those works whose intention was closer to what we mean by 'artistic'. The main source of these works is the extremely fertile zone known as the Franco-Cantabrian because it consists essentially of France, mainly present-day Languedoc, and the adjoining part of Spain situated to the north of the Cantabrian Mountains.

Art is primarily an act of taking possession. There seems no doubt that it is a means afforded man for attaching himself to the external world, for lessening the natural difference which separates him from it and the terror he experiences when confronted with it. Even the earliest examples of art show two aspects: in one man attempts to project himself on the universe, to make his mark on it, to put his name on it; in the other to annex it to himself, to make it his own. In both cases there is a struggle for possession, because he wants either to confirm his impress on the universe or to secure it in the form of an image, a carbon copy, which then becomes pliable and submissive. The first is a case of projection, the second of capture. The desire behind both is the same.

First let us examine man putting his mark on things, just as the owner of a herd puts his brand on his cattle. In the beginning the results were very elementary: man imitated the scratches made by bears on cave walls when sharpening their claws, and produced meandering parallel lines traced with his parted fingers. Soon primitive man improved his impress; he made coloured hand-prints or outlined his hand in colour (positive and negative hands), usually with red ochre or black. Abbé Breuil, who was, so to speak, the creator of prehistory as we know it today, has shown that children amuse themselves by planting their muddy hands on a white wall or lie down in the snow to see the marks left by their bodies.

The mark of possession becomes less symbolic and more effective if it is applied to an actual object, when it becomes a mark of ownership. Palaeolithic man reproduced on the bones he was going to make into tools the
8 hatchings he had first caused accidentally when scraping the meat from them. But we must note carefully that he transformed them instinctively. He may have imitated, but he also organised them. His mind came into play simultaneously with his hand. The hatchings lost the random character they had had when they came into being by chance: henceforth they obeyed inherent tendencies deeply embedded in our intelligence. They became regular, even symmetrical. In this way they ad-

umbrated what was later to become geometric and form decoration. As we shall see, we can already discern in them the fundamental laws which in the future were to govern all the forms invented by human genius.

The discovery of resemblance and symbolism

There is another aspect of possession in which man seizes things and captures them in the form of an image. He strives to make a copy which bears a sufficient resemblance to the alien beings or objects. According to a fundamental magical belief throughout the ages, the part is integral with the whole. Therefore a reproduction is binding on the original, except that unlike the original it can neither flee nor resist; it is at its owner's mercy.

But to make the operation effective there really must be duplication, i.e. resemblance. Even the higher animals such as the monkey have an inkling of what this means: they copy, they 'ape' things. In turn primitive man only had to organise this imitation and mould it to the laws of regularity peculiar to his mind, i.e. to rhythm, in order to create the dance. Thus the hunter and the sorcerer 4 mimicked the animal's walk and movements, completing and strengthening the illusion with some genuine animal-trappings, such as skins and skulls. This practice still exists among primitive peoples today, for example in certain ritual dances in South America. In such cases, the imitation and possession are effected by man's actual body and not as yet by the intermediary of an object fashioned by his hands. On the day when one of our ancestors had the idea of creating such an object, a sort of half-way house between himself and the animal because it was the image of the latter and the work of the former, he gave birth to the work of art. Thus from the very beginning we have confirmation of the character we confer on the image of being a dual reflection, on the one hand of the external world and on the other, of man.

Then comes sculpture, the simple reproduction of real forms translated into a material such as clay or bone, and after it, as the result of a bolder attempt, painting.

Since the likeness forms part of the model, it commits it; it makes it integral with the original. The fate of the original is bound up with the fate of the reproduction. Just as sorcerers in recent times believed that pricking a wax figure with a pin would affect the person represented, the Palaeolithic hunter believed that he was ensuring the effectiveness of his blows by adding facsimiles of spears to the painted bison or mammoth he 3, 6 intended to hunt.

This function of the facsimile, inherent in the origins of the work of art, remained active for a long time: in Egypt, drawings on the walls of the tomb were sometimes substituted for the actual foodstuffs and furniture needed for the dead person's life after death.

But the mental invisible link of the symbol could be substituted for the physical visible link. By a kind of transference, an image could be considered as the equivalent of a force or non-material power which prehistoric man recognised in nature. The most important for him was fertility, which enabled both men and the animals which were valuable for their flesh, skins, fur, etc., to

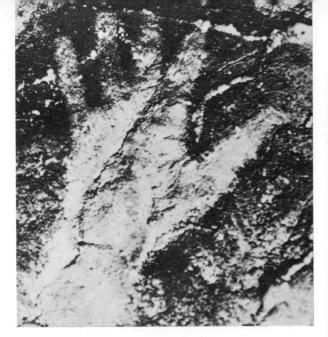

2. Hand surrounded by red ochre. Gargas.

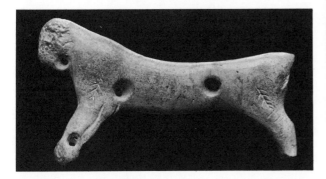

3. A feline carved from reindeer-horn. The holes and spears or arrows were believed to have given effectiveness to the hunter. Isturitz. *Musée de St Germain*.

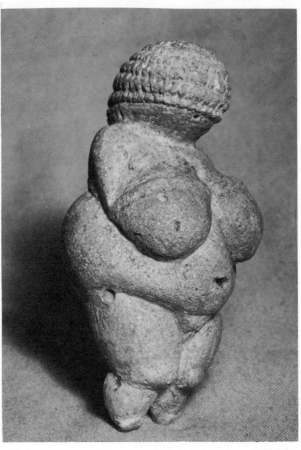

5. The Venus of Willendorf. *Naturhistorisches Museum, Vienna*.

MAGIC

Although its importance is controversial, magic is one of the basic elements of prehistoric art, from the hand imprints establishing a presence to the fecundity rites (Venuses) and sympathetic magic (wounded animals), not to mention figures of sorcerers incarnating animals.

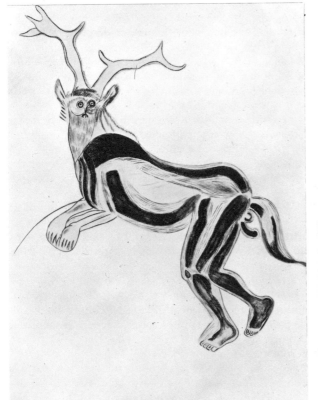

4. Sorcerer disguised as an animal. Les Trois Frères. *(After Breuil.)*

6. Horse traced on clay by a finger and pierced with holes, the holes simulating wounds caused by arrows or spears. Montespan.

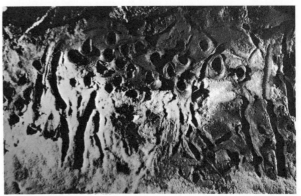

17

reproduce themselves. So the oldest known human figures represent women. They are known as 'Venuses', and the attributes of their sex are considerably emphasised or enlarged.

It is remarkable that these statuettes date from the Aurignacian period, the first age in which works of art appeared. It is obvious, then, that from that time the human brain was capable of generalising, of embracing in a single idea the feature common to a multitude of particular facts; furthermore, it knew how to embody that idea in an image borrowed from reality, that of woman, the source of the birth, continuity and increase of the species. The gift of abstraction and the symbol were already born!

Thus from the beginning man learnt how to represent things: either he reproduced animals to kill them via their likenesses, or he fashioned a rather stylised feminine body in order to master, through his possession of the model, the life force that it symbolised.

I should add that one is increasingly struck by the existence of drawings, or rather sketches, which in a much cruder way obviously represent human beings. They have been discovered recently in the cave of La Marche in Vienne, and previously at Laussel in the Dordogne, at Marsoulas in the Haute-Garonne, and in the Tarn; and mention should be made of the two sleeping women in the cave of La Magdeleine which have such life and elegance that they might almost be an anticipation of Modigliani. It seems that in many of these drawings the artist simply wanted to sketch 'human outlines' without attaching any ritual or magical significance to them. Perhaps we must also see in them a further stage of the need—already indicated at the beginning of this article —for projection on to a solid material: from imprints of hands primitive artists, impelled to reproduce animals, may have wanted to pass on to a more complete depiction of human beings, incised henceforth on rocks—just as present-day visitors to historic buildings cannot resist carving their names on the walls. These drawings are frequently clumsy, which seems to indicate a free, spontaneous activity, whereas the representation of animals, which had a considerable magical importance for the society of the epoch, was the product of an accomplished technique, a genuine science undoubtedly vested in and taught by the sorcerer-priests.

Realism, therefore, was established from the time of man's earliest artistic attempts.

First signs of a decorative art

But what we would call abstract art today, and which was then more simply a decorative art, had already begun to make progress and has continued to do so ever since.

The first hatchings made by man on bones differed, as we have said, from accidental scratches, because of his desire for order. In other words, man had already transferred to his handiwork the demands of his mind, which we now have to define. The universe baffles man because it is multiple and infinite, a chaos of constantly renewed sensations which exceed our powers of comprehension. Man, on the contrary, is essentially one; like every organism, he achieves physically and mentally the integration of everything which goes to make him up. He can only comprehend himself in the unity of his person, of his 'I'. The universe, in the form in which he sees it, appears as a kind of confused shimmer. He feels the need to rediscover himself in it, to have a clear-cut view of it, to apply to it the principle of simplification which is that of his own consciousness. The clarity and regularity which man instinctively wants to impose on everything around him, on everything which is not himself, are revealed in the first graffiti he made on a simple reindeer-bone. It is fascinating to follow his endeavours: where accidental hatchings ran in all directions, he undertook to make identical copies. This is how parallelism was born. It will be noted that the same instincts emerge in the dance, which consists at first in the disciplined repetition of the same type of step.

But here an obstacle arises: too strict or too absolute a unity, even if it corresponds to the aspirations of human nature, is so radically opposed to the lavish profusion of reality that it risks losing all contact with it. If, then, the work of art is by its nature a reflection of man, it is simultaneously the reflection of the reality around him. Here we have the emergence of one of the eternal rules of art: unity. But to avoid impoverishment or loss of vitality, it must include the greatest variety compatible with it. Symmetry provides an ideal solution to this need: the two elements it presupposes are identical but opposite. Where did man get this idea? Perhaps from the construction of his own body. How did he make use of it? By merely adding to a hatching on the slant its replica sloping the other way, he could obtain a V-shape. And in fact this shape made its appearance in the very first attempts at ornamentation, for example on the decorated bone from Laugerie-Basse. In the same way, in the dance the first method of 'varying a step' is to repeat it in the opposite direction, to retrace it.

Supposing that to the above V-shape the principle of repetition is applied in turn. Then the first continuous decorative motif is obtained: the sequence of Vs becomes a zigzag. We are still dealing with a single theme. Now let us suppose that in the quest for variety one of the V-shapes is combined with another decoration, for example with a simple dot: then a more complex unit is obtained, alternated to some extent and capable in its turn of being repeated. Rhythm is born. On certain engraved bones the following elementary combination can be seen: three dashes, one dot, three dashes, one dot, etc. It is the same with the dance: it would die of monotony if different steps were not combined which generate rhythm by their regular occurrence. What else had prehistoric man done but discover the principle which very much later would make possible the invention of the metopes of Greek temples such as the Parthenon?

We have seen the V-shape come to life. If instead of repeating it by juxtaposition an attempt is made to repeat it by symmetry, i.e. by folding it back on the pivot of its tip, an X is obtained. The bone from Laugerie-Basse exhibits this combination. The V-shape can also be repeated by folding it back on its two extremities. But then a new phenomenon comes to light: a lozenge is born, no longer an arrangement of lines but an organic figure enclosing a regular field of space. It could be said that geometry was founded at the same time. Both these possibilities are exploited on the bone from Laugerie-Basse. Another fact of importance also emerges: Palaeolithic man's consciousness of the appearance of a self-contained figure. Intuitively, he felt that his lozenge

AURIGNACIAN-PERIGORDIAN. The Venus of Savignano. Pigorini Museum, Rome. *Photo: Scala.*

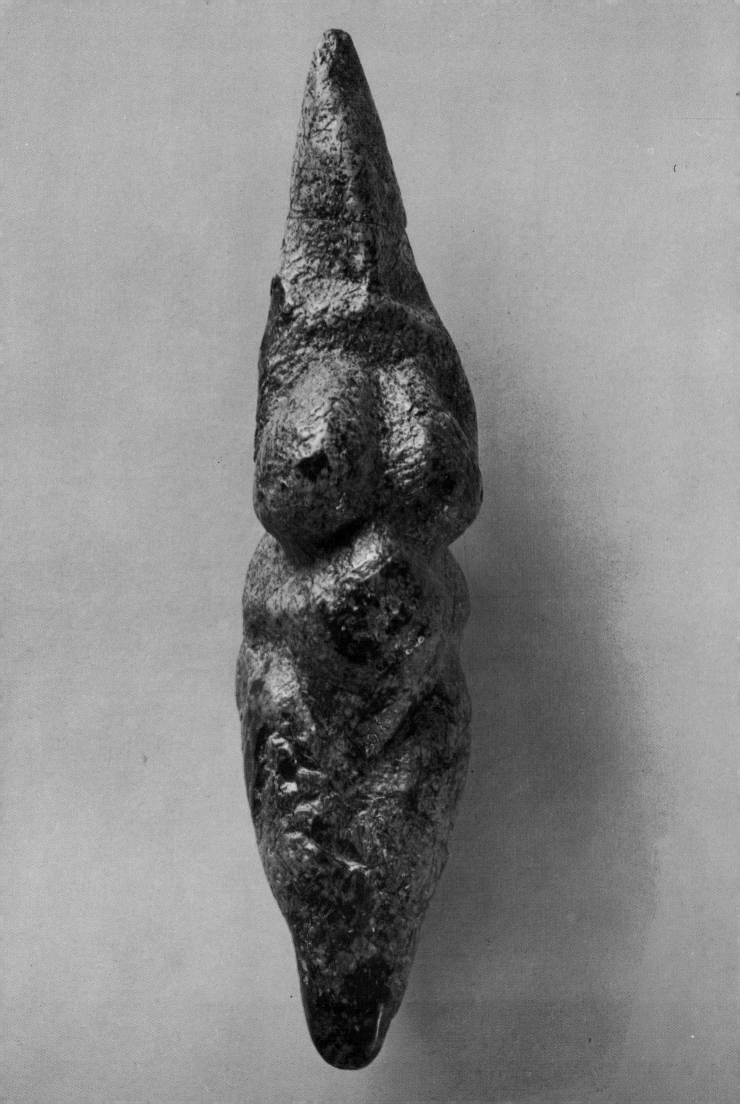

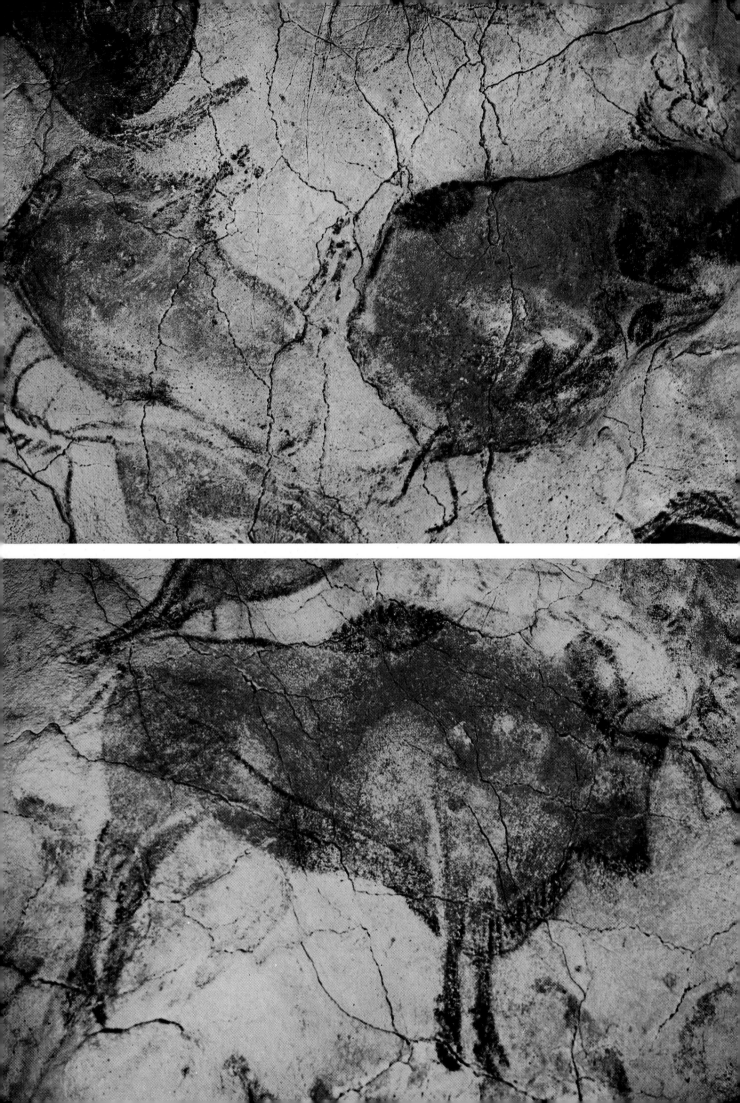

Sometimes, when depicting animals, or, more rarely, human beings, as in these astonishing figures from La Magdeleine [7], the artist shows a free sensitivity of observation which seems to anticipate Modigliani.

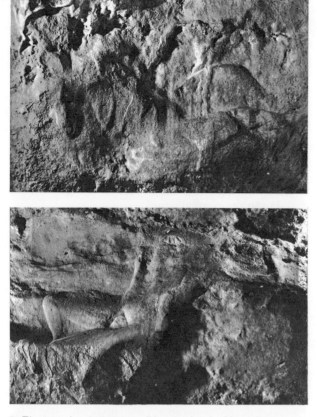

Other works start from the representation of nature; however, the same laws of regularity or symmetry are applied to them: a highly stylised female body also recalls a lozenge [9].

9. Venus carved in ivory. Found at Lespugue. (Actual size 5½ in.) *Musée de l'Homme, Paris.*

7. The two sleeping women (Venuses) at La Magdeleine.

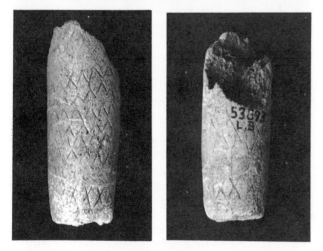

8. Two sides of an engraved bone found at Laugerie-Basse.

formed a whole, that it had its principle in a place which is the centre. He felt this so strongly that he found it necessary to mark it with a dot. With this gesture he opened up an entire new field to human thought.

Half-way between realism and abstraction

That is how the two major trends in art, realism and abstraction, were established. In one, man tries to render the appearance of the things he sees, to take hold of them; in the other, he strives to impose his own mental concepts on matter.

Is there no half-way house between these two tendencies? Paradoxically it is supplied by the most ancient creations of artistic genius, the Aurignacian Venuses, which were the work of a civilisation extending along the

edge of the northern glaciers from the Gulf of Gascony to the heart of Siberia. These Venuses represent the female body; they depict its appearance. But that appearance has been enormously modified by the application of the laws which had just manifested themselves in simple decoration. The artist developed everything which suggested regularity, symmetry and even geometry. That masterpiece the Venus of Lespugue conforms rigorously 9 to the lozenge-shape. Without ceasing to reflect its structure, the appearance of the human being is organised so as to be doubly symmetrical, not only in relation to its vertical axis, in the normal way, but also in relation to its horizontal axis, which is an arbitrary whim of the sculptor.

Is any better proof possible that art is stretched like a chain linking man at one end to the world at the other, and seeks to create a transition from the unity of the one to the infinite complexity of the other?

Do those works which are apparently most realistic also reveal this duality? Nature, even when she seems to be captured to perfection, as with the bison and reindeer of the Magdalenian period, always bears the marks of man's irresistible tendency to simplify. It is a physical and mental necessity; it is already implicit in the manual act of drawing. To see an animal is to be assailed by an endless multiplicity of visual sensations; in order to draw it, it is necessary to reduce these sensations to a shape which both embraces and signifies all of them. And this shape which our thought discovers and imposes has to be reduced to a single almost continuous line, the outline, in order that the hand may depict it on a wall or a reindeer-bone.

But the mind collaborates with the hand. When the Lascaux or Altamira painter captured the likeness of his model, he never represented a particular animal. From the limitless variety exhibited by individuals within

MAGDALENIAN. Bison. Cave paintings at Altamira.
Photo: Mas.

a species, he extracted the common factor which is also an abstraction: the type. The prehistoric artist never produced particular bison, horses or reindeer, but the bison, the horse or the reindeer. The generalisation was required in order to make the magic effective, for it would have been pointless to cast a spell on a specific animal which the hunter would have very little chance of meeting.

But there is another reason for this simplification: the law, so essential to man, of the least effort also drives him to seek a type which is formulated once and for all and only needs to be reproduced. It is an acquisition entrusted to the memory, almost a form of automatism. And incidentally it is the foundation of all academicism, the inevitable and ultimate end of any static art which continues to be taught. Prehistoric art has not escaped from this law, and it would be interesting to show how its masters copied an established model far more often than they observed directly from nature. Model drawings 10 carried on pebbles have been discovered and later re-12 discovered executed on a large scale in what are frequently distant places. This art may seem collective and anonymous to us, but undoubtedly it had its own great masters whose successful works were preserved and imitated.

The laws of evolution

Thus the art most apparently devoted to the reproduction of nature cannot escape from the law of manual or mental simplifications which tend in their extreme form to result in geometrical shapes. Prehistoric art already confirms a general rule which, as we shall see, is applicable to many subsequent civilisations. The need to simplify, which could be called the tendency to abstraction, first appears when an art is born: inability to follow nature in all her 11 unexpectedness leads to the substitution of equivalent elementary shapes.

Art tries next to overcome this inability and reaches a point of balance where the methods of execution render 12 a satisfactory account of what the eye sees. Then we have realism.

After this a new phase leading to stylisation begins. That is when art begins to refine on itself; the sophistication of artists and spectators removes the necessity of multiplying the evidence in order that the model in question be recognised; sometimes a simple allusion is enough. Art then experiences once again the temptation to substitute simple for complex shapes, since they are more satisfying to the mind's natural inclinations; the new shapes will gradually depart further and further from the model until they are no more than obscure signs for it.

Thus in mural art we first see the Aurignacian artist substituting a design with geometrical simplifications for the complicated shapes of his model. A child behaves in the same way when he is old enough to make a figure: in order to depict a man he begins by drawing circles, sticks and dots.

On the other hand, at the time of the great Magdalenian masterpieces simplification combined with richness of suggestion to form a marvellous innovation. The line was tremendously concentrated and at the same time was expressive. Then the artist was tempted to compete with the real and began to use trompe-l'œil; he made use of a bulge in the cave wall to suggest the hump of a bull.

But soon he was satisfied to repeat models already executed; he allowed himself to make simplifications which were more and more impoverishing until finally the original figure was reduced to a few shapes and a few lines, to a few allusions which were easy to repeat owing to their clarity. Once again, mental forms won the day over realistic forces. Abbé Breuil has introduced the term 'conceptual' realism, which differs widely from the sensory realism that strives to reproduce visual sensations as accurately as possible. Conceptual realism replaces them with more general shapes tending to the geometric.

The latter finally triumphed, and it has been possible to follow the transformation of a horse's head into a simple 17 oval which merely needed to be repeated indefinitely. In the eternal ebb and flow of art, man returned to the conceptions of his brain, to the detriment of sensations received from the external world.

That is an account of the civilisation of man the hunter; all the future developments of art were there in embryo: realism of observation; conceptual realism; abstraction verging on the decorative. Basically, contemporary art does not exhibit a more extensive range.

THE TRANSITION TO THE NEOLITHIC AGE: THE ART OF THE IBERIAN LEVANT

Even when Palaeolithic art managed to achieve a striking rendering of animals whose appearance it wanted to capture, it caught them within the bold despotism of an outline, in the generality of a type. This meant sacrificing the unexpected side of life which is life in motion. In this sort of rivalry, whose field was art and which went on between the unexpected driving force of vision and the forms extracted or imposed by the mind, the latter, however flexible they were, continued to endow the image with their own generality and immobility. Was it 54 possible to come still closer to life as it exhibits itself, to rejoin it in the impression of elusive mobility which it presents at first sight?

The appearance of an art of life

This achievement appeared with a new civilisation which had experienced the influence of the Franco-Cantabrian culture, in which it had sunk its roots, but which had primarily developed from the beginning of the transitional Mesolithic age. It continued not only into the Neolithic age of polished stone, but also, by a miraculous prolongation, into our own time among the Bushmen in Africa. The seeds of it can already be found in the famous Lascaux paintings, which nevertheless are numbered 16 among the earliest paintings of the Franco-Cantabrian culture, and in the numerous sketches of human figures which just because of their clumsiness lent themselves less to enclosure in a conceptual form.

But the art we are coming to belongs to another region, the Iberian Levant, the coast facing Africa with which it has even more connections than with the region to the north of the Pyrenees. These works open up a new chapter in the history of art.

One's feeling is not so much of the analysis of an observer being applied to the outline, to extract the main lines which will sum it up and define its essential structure, as of an entirely new gift for seizing the fleeting expression and retaining it in all its vividness.

The fact is that this art seems to pursue new ends.

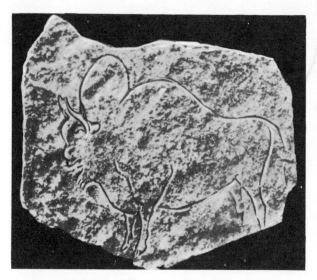

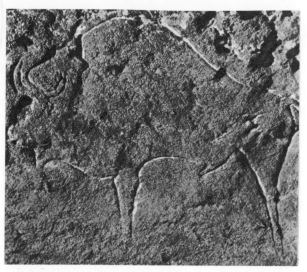

10. MAGDALENIAN. Bison engraved on a stone. La Genière.

11. AURIGNACIAN. Engraved bison. La Grèze.

EVOLUTION

We can follow the transformation of prehistoric art from the first attempts to complete and regularise the accidental resemblance of a pebble to an animal. After figures which were still simplified and arbitrary (only two feet, horns seen full-face on a head in profile [11], the exactness of observation increases (four feet), finally arriving at accurate modelling [12].
The apparent realism of prehistoric art should not conceal the existence of models which were repeated and copied, sometimes over vast distances [10, 12].

Apparently another interest, namely that of commemorating experience, succeeded to the symbolical magic of the sorcerer. In a society which begins to organise and stabilise itself, we could say that the main concern is to pass on to the future the principal activities of communal life, sometimes even to give permanence to the memory of an important action. The result is very different: previously the ritual act of the person making the drawing was what mattered most, and apparently no one worried much about looking at his work afterwards; succeeding

generations did not hesitate to superimpose drawings until they finally merged in an illegible network. In the same way, their animal representations were often found at the far end of gloomy caves which were inaccessible and where it was almost impossible to see them. Now the mural paintings, on the contrary, are no longer isolated from the spectator; they are situated at the entrances to the caves, in the light, and they are certainly primarily made to be looked at. Thus art gradually becomes conscious of its own value.

Moreover these paintings depict man in preference to animals, and man in his group life. The figures take part in communal activities—ceremonies, hunting, battles—and it is always the rendering of action which seems to concern the artist most. He is less interested in the outline than in the gesture, the movement. The revolution achieved is still more perceptible in technical processes: the outline no longer predominates, having given way to the suggestive spot of colour. (In the same way, later, the more intellectual Italian artist of the Renaissance was to express himself essentially through outline, whereas a

12. UPPER MAGDALENIAN. Bison partially painted in polychrome. Font-de-Gaume. *(After Breuil.)*

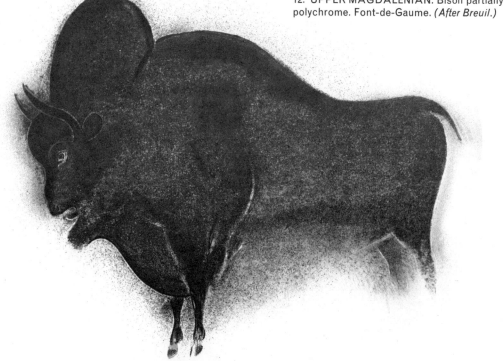

21

Rembrandt, anxious to translate the impression he received of life, mainly used the *tache*, or spot of colour.) It would be by no means ridiculous to talk of a kind of prehistoric impressionism.

But at the same time this art is expressionist in some aspects; the artist worries less about faithfully defining the essentials of a form than about increasing its mobility and suggesting its vividness or speed: a runner's legs are set impossibly far apart at the same time that, by a sort of emphasis, a stressed intonation of the visual language, they are made disproportionately long. The uppermost wish now is to put the evocative accent on the most striking sensation.

This art differs so clearly in spirit from Franco-Cantabrian that it develops in an entirely different direction. By dint of extracting the essential forms, the Franco-Cantabrian artist ended up by systematising them, by reducing them to a kind of geometry. Here, on the contrary, the image, attached above all to its suggestive force, is progressively summarised in a sign. It evolves into a kind of shorthand. One can see, for example, animals simplified to a horizontal line mounted on legs reduced to little sticks, the number of which, on the other hand, increases beyond all verisimilitude, the better to stress the ability to run. In the same way the warrior becomes a vertical stroke, broken up by cross-strokes for his arms, which are also multiplied in relation to the force attributed to him.

Here the final product was not an over-simplified geometry; rather a way was opened up at the end of which writing (pictographic in its first stages) would appear.

The causes of artistic change

What had happened? Subsistence by hunting was supplemented by the keeping of flocks, then by agriculture. Collective capital was established. With it came an enlargement of social groups, which seem always to have existed but on a much smaller scale. Robbery and warfare, which were unknown in the first societies, where people owned nothing and lived from day to day, came into existence and broke the monotonous pattern of life. Undoubtedly the people thought of preserving the memory of these events. Thus man crossed the threshold of history, however fragile and legendary it still was.

Is social evolution an adequate explanation of these transformations? Or should we introduce the confused and controversial concept of race? It does seem that the ethnic groups have intellectual characteristics and perceptible peculiarities which find expression in their art and the form they impose on it. There is no doubt that the new aesthetic trend was found only in places where there was considerable African influence. It is certain that a hunting scene appeared at Lascaux in the Dordogne particularly early, since the Perigordian was predominant there; it is also accepted that the Iberian Levant was in some aspects a product of the Franco-Cantabrian culture, but on the other hand the Spanish littoral certainly knew a more southerly people at a very early time. The art of this region was in fact to have echoes, sometimes very much later, in that of North Africa—the Atlas Mountains and the Sahara. Nor was it unconnected with the art which preceded Egyptian art proper in the lateral valleys of the Nile. It had a staggering counterpart in the art of southern Rhodesia, which was still being handed down

when the Boers arrived. Thus an immense 'province' emerges, stretching from north-east Spain (where the schematic pebbles from the Mas d'Azil in the south of France are echoed by the objects found beyond the Pyrenees) to South Africa.

THE NEOLITHIC AGE

The art of the Iberian Levant lasted much longer than Franco-Cantabrian art. It continued throughout the Mesolithic right up to the Neolithic, in which, moreover, it seems to have experienced its greatest development.

An art of expansion

The Neolithic, the age of polished stone following the age of chipped stone, was a new era of civilisation. Along the Nile and in Mesopotamia it soon reached the stage of cities and empires which marks the beginning of history. These empires will be studied in their logical if not their chronological place (Chapter 3). In order to understand the Neolithic properly, it must be examined in Europe (which was still prehistoric) where it developed, whereas the empires of Asia had already entered the historical phase centuries before. The Neolithic brought with it new means of spreading knowledge which ensured the diffusion of art forms over vast distances—trading along river valleys, the seasonal movement of flocks and in particular coastal navigation. The dolmen civilisation, which remains its major monument, seems likely, if one studies maps of its distribution, to have spread from India to Ireland by sea routes. (And even to America: we remember having seen on the Argentine pampa a large broken overturned menhir, originally several feet high, equal to the finest in Brittany.) Because of this, artistic motifs go beyond the frontiers of the groups which created them and are adapted and modified by human communities of quite different characters. The dolmen idol, often stylised into the face of an owl, as well as the rotunda constructions with an entrance corridor, such as the passage graves or tholoi, can be recognised, however deformed or debased, from one end of the Mediterranean to the other and even beyond, spreading northwards.

Admittedly the Aurignacian already extended over a considerable area, from the Atlantic to Siberia, as we have observed in connection with the Venuses, but undoubtedly we are dealing with slow dissemination by groups belonging to the same civilisation. What reflections gave birth to the strange abstract drawings of Gavr'inis in Brittany? The immense network of diffusion which was to hand on the plastic acquisitions of one civilisation to another, and even of one continent to another, began to fall into position.

New techniques made their appearance, undoubtedly not before that time—straw-plaiting, cloth-weaving, pottery-making. With them came new manual and visual habits which prepared the way for the future development of the decorative repertory. However, on the whole it remained faithful to the old forms—chevrons, zigzags, lozenges, chess-board patterns, etc. But it added more complex themes which were destined to last a long time: the 'meander', born of the random juxtaposition of pieces of striped material, and the spiral and its combinations, undoubtedly an imitation of the straps and slings of the first receptacles, were only the stylised reflections of

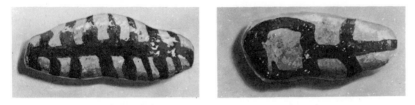

13. Group of running warriors. Teruel. *(After J. Cabré.)*

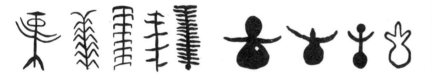

14. Painted pebbles from the Mas d'Azil.

15. Anthropomorphic petroglyphs from the Iberian Peninsula. *(After Obermaier and Cabré.)*

16. Hunting scene: wounded bison charging a man. Lascaux.

STYLISATION

A tendency to stylisation appeared at a very early date; it arose partly from an economy of effort on the artist's part. He tried to create a still recognisable figure with the minimum of lines. Consequently, stylisation is very common as an art grows old. A series can be reconstructed starting with a realistic figure and ending with a summary geometrical design.

Another form of stylisation, especially in Spanish and African art, used patches of colour—expressive because of their compressed vitality—instead of the geometrical pattern.

As from the extreme end of the Palaeolithic, these abbreviated figures become symbolic notations: the warrior's strength is expressed by the many arms on the body. In the Mesolithic, the pebbles from the Mas d'Azil show the final results of these curtailed figures which have become purely schematic, sometimes to the point of resembling letters.

17. Evolution of a horse's head.

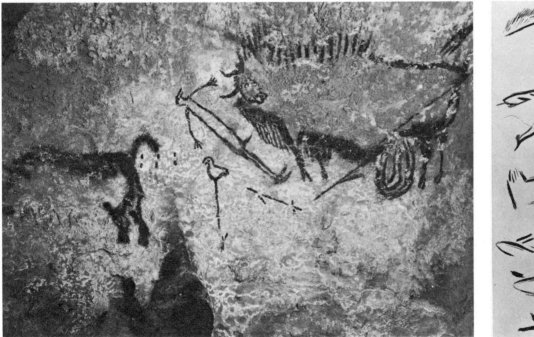

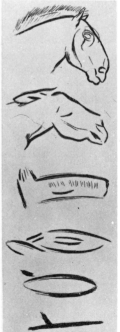

23

technical accidents. However, they were to inaugurate a new regime of decoration. The spiral especially, with its dynamic outline, appeared during the 3rd millennium in Danubian Neolithic pottery, and when the latter experienced its vast diffusion from the Rhine to the Dnieper, this new form went with it. In the metal ages Aegean art adopted it again as its favourite theme.

The beginnings of architecture

At this time a new and vitally important spirit had been breathed into art. One indication of this was the appearance of the monument, which approached architecture with the megaliths (which may also have been the forerunners of more advanced civilisations, such as Egypt in particular). Until that time man had worried only about his housing—huts, or later, at the beginning of the new age, lake-dwellings. He had made use of his artistic faculties only to satisfy, in everyday objects, his deeply rooted instinct for appropriation or to establish a higher communal art for ritual purposes, whether magical, religious or social.

Now he conceived the monument, in its turn an expression of the human group: he endowed it with a religious function, primarily by connecting it with the worship of the dead or divine powers. By making the structure larger than strict utility demanded, man wanted to solemnise it, to give it an exceptional character, a higher status. And the aesthetic faculty, inside the obscure instinct where it was still groping before it became conscious of its powers and its aims, started to function again. The aesthetic faculty was satisfied among primitive men by the vague notion that it conferred a higher status on anything it touched: it was therefore fitting for non-ephemeral things. It was already applied to the symbolical fertility statuettes which were the first idols and to the magical representations of animals. With the Neolithic age it turned to the commemoration of communal beliefs, either in the already extant form of rock paintings or in the first edifices of a sacred nature. Thus from the very beginning the age-old collaboration between art and religion was established.

In its simplest form the standing stone, or menhir, is the ancestor of the monument. Present-day thinking leans increasingly to the idea that it was intended to provide a permanent abode for the soul of a dead person. As it is always valuable to check up on theories about past ages through current ethnology, we may note that at the present time, in Madagascar for example, the standing stone continues this use: it is intended to serve as a receptacle for the wandering souls of the dead who could not be buried, usually those lost at sea. It should be pointed out that this new usage coincided with the appearance of the civilisation which spread by sea routes.

The menhir already expressed the fundamental function which we have designated in art: to create an intermediary between man and the universe. The menhir in fact consisted of a stone borrowed from the physical world. It came from nature; it formed part of it; but the stone was suddenly endowed by man with a meaning which it did not have on its own and was thus made into a symbol. It became the expressive sign of an inner life where the dead and the forces of nature (certainly including fire, which was to become of vital importance with the advent of metal) assumed the exclusive place which

had previously been occupied by the concept of fertility and, for the hunter, by animals.

The consequences of a new economy

Through the intermediaries of picking roots and berries and raising livestock the transition was gradually made from the mobile civilisation of the hunter to the sedentary culture of the farmer. The soil and its resources provided live foodstuffs in the form of cattle and vegetable foodstuffs in the form of crops, resulting in a surplus—impossible with game slain in the hunt, which would go bad.

That was the birth of collective capital, which supplies a cumulative reserve once immediate needs have been satisfied. It was the beginning of the city treasure, and in fact it foreshadowed the city. To collect, administer and protect this treasure a more highly developed, more hierarchical organisation was needed. The nomes (provinces) of Egypt are an example. This organisation, established by the products of agriculture, resulted from the interplay of the great natural forces, which were now appropriately revered in their turn. Consequently it was bound up with the new cosmic beliefs: the sun, the moon, the rain usurped the place once occupied by animals (although animal totems continued to survive). Sometimes by a sort of transference, which we often meet with (for even if man changes his beliefs, he never loses the images in which they are embodied but simply appropriates these to his new ideas), the animal becomes a symbol of the powers man worships. We shall hear of the lunar bull; by a further change, he could even become solar, as the lion usually is.

The farmer was to prove ready to meet not only his own needs but those of dwellers in the cities. Hence a supply of manpower was made available (as well as the means to pay for it) which could be earmarked for other tasks than the production of reserves of foodstuffs or provisions for immediate consumption. The worker and the craftsman were placed at the chief's disposal.

It was inevitable that the monument made by and for the community should develop at that time. Out of the menhir grew the dolmen and then the cromlech. At the same time the monument ceased to be directly given over to the dead, to be synonymous with the tomb; it was consecrated to the cult and its ceremonies, in which the collective soul of the community participated. Ultimately the regular and complex groups such as Stonehenge (c. 1500) confirmed that the creations of art were meant to be expressive of man: these arrangements of symbolic stones took on a significance that the individual stones did not have. Also, they were laid out according to plan; they represented forms in which were found once more, on what from now on was an architectural scale, the laws of regularity, repetition, symmetry and geometry which we have seen in the ornamental hatchings made on a bone by an unskilled hand. The menhir had already come under the sway of these laws in the gigantic undertaking of the alignments at Carnac. The later more complicated arrangements, such as Stonehenge, reflected the concepts of the centre, the circle, the axis, rhythm, etc., in which the signature of the human mind was recognisable.

At the moment, then, when with the appearance of the first great civilisations history was born, man without knowing it had already discovered all the basic ideas which were to be found in the future developments of art.

19

20b

20a

18

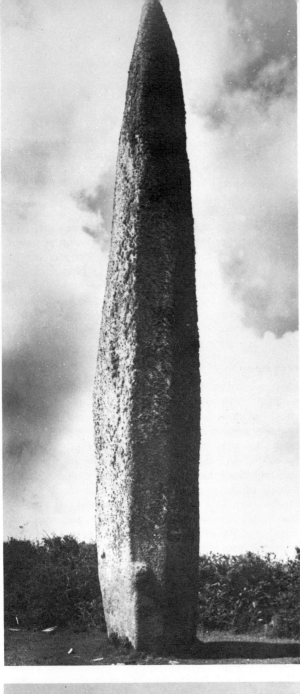

THE BIRTH OF ARCHITECTURE

With megaliths, prehistoric man learned the art of architecture: not only do the horizontal stones of the dolmens foreshadow the lintel [19], but an overall plan is visible in the alignments of menhirs [20a].

In late constructions such as Stonehenge, the circular shape of the cromlech shows great skill in the arrangement of its plan, elevation and solar orientation. Even so, the Egyptians had already been building their temples for over a thousand years.

18. Menhir at Kerloas (Finistère). Height *c.* 37 ft.

19. The dolmen known as the *Table des Marchands*, Locmariaquer.

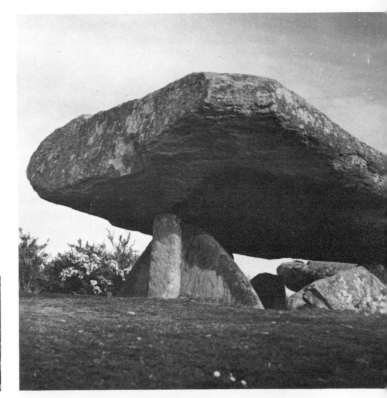

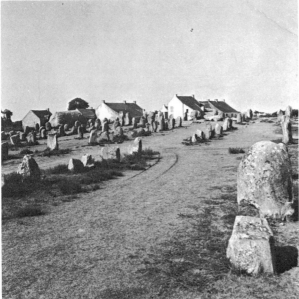

20a. Part of the stone alignments at Carnac.

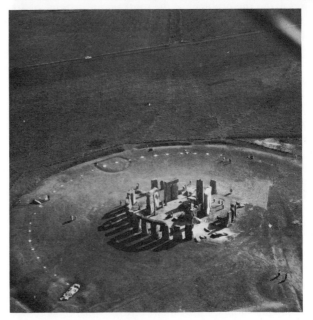

20b. Megalithic monument. Stonehenge. *c.* 1500 B.C.

25

THE BEGINNINGS OF ART *André Leroi-Gourhan*

Did man's first primitive tools already show signs of the obscure aesthetic drives which would later produce masterpieces, even before the appearance of prehistoric works of art proper? This section will deal with the precursors of these works of art.

The appearance of works of art in the Upper Palaeolithic is a recent phenomenon, if not in relation to prehistoric time—since they are credited with an age of some forty thousand years—at least in relation to biological time: nine-tenths of the history of mankind had unfolded when the ivory statuettes and the animals decorating the walls of caves suddenly appeared. Were there any true works of art before them?

Are eoliths the work of man?

The question of eoliths has been raised from the very beginning of the study of prehistory. They are most frequently nodules of rough flint whose shapes remind us of animals or of human heads. Some of them have been found in the same deposits as flints actually chipped into tools, but there are serious reasons for considering them very cautiously, for by and large they show no formal sign of human treatment. Moreover, identical examples are found at all epochs of prehistory, and, lastly, they are even found long before prehistoric times in large amounts of flint from all geological ages, although chance may throw up among thousands of stones of everyday shape only a single specimen whose outlines are surprisingly like some living thing. On the other hand, we shall refer later to a related phenomenon: the undeniable collection by men of relatively recent prehistoric periods of stones with strange shapes.

If we discard the dubious evidence provided by the eoliths, apparently mere freaks of nature, there remain very few material proofs of man's artistic activity before the Upper Palaeolithic and inadequate means of directly resolving the problem of the most remote origins of art. However, it is not impossible to tackle the subject indirectly by means of the evidence we do possess— human skeletons from various prehistoric periods and the chipped stone implements used by man. These are more or less our only material for research. We have no way of knowing whether primeval man drew circles in the sand with the tips of his fingers, whether he scratched silhouettes on the bark of trees or whether he striped his own body with long streaks of charcoal.

Besides, what do we mean by man? If we mean man identical with ourselves, Homo sapiens, the question is answered, because statuettes, engravings and paintings have been found in the vicinity of the oldest skeletons of Homo sapiens we possess. But science with its various theories is in general agreement today that other human forms (let us call them 'anthropian' forms) preceded our own. Much closer to us than monkeys were Pithecanthropus of Java, Sinanthropus of China, Atlanthropus of North Africa and Neanderthal man in Europe—creatures with low foreheads, deeply sunken eye-sockets and heavy jaw-bones. Pithecanthropus and Sinanthropus had much smaller brains than ours, although their size was already considerable. Although Neanderthal man's cerebral organisation may have differed from our own, the volume of his brain was equivalent to that of present-day man and he had a vertical posture identical with or very similar to our own.

They all used fire and chipped flint tools. These human beings who differed from us were much more varied than modern races; certain of these primitive anthropians had more developed characteristics than others, and we can tell that a particular one of them was Neanderthal in appearance and modern in brain, whereas another exhibits opposite characteristics. It is not unreasonable to attribute at least a rudimentary aesthetic activity to some of these anthropians, who exhibited an enormous number of nuances in their mental development.

When did art begin?

Here again we may well ask ourselves what we mean by art. In the following chapters this question would seem ridiculous, but it is quite pertinent before we pronounce our biased present-day judgment on the extremely scanty remains left by these early humans. When the first prehistoric works of art were found, scholars were immediately struck by their apparent affinities with the art of living primitive peoples, and a whole system of comparisons was drawn up which put these works on a mental plane which was not necessarily that of early man, nor even that of the 19th-century Australian aborigine. The anthropologists, like the historian of prehistoric art, have slowly dissociated themselves from the more obvious drawbacks of this course. Nevertheless, in an improved form it is still the only course. For insight into the art of the oldest anthropians research has been able to draw on anthropological documents, already tested by nearly a century of work, on the behaviour of the higher animals —work conducted by biologists without any preconceived idea of applying it to man, not even primitive man.

If we disregard everything which is generally agreed to be connected with deliberate aesthetic expression by man, there remain three fields to which our modern consciousness attaches an aesthetic significance: the balance of forms in nature, as in the perfection of a flower or a crystal; the expression of certain animal impulses through forms, as in the mating plumage of birds, the savage virility of the bull and the formidable beauty of the felines; the perfection of useful shapes in some of man's technical creations, such as the subtle curve of a sabre blade or the aerodynamic lines of an aircraft. These aesthetic fields are in fact the only ones through which we can hope to tackle the problem of art before its explicitly human expressions.

Apart from the great mural works of art, what aesthetic evidence are we offered by man of the Upper Palaeolithic, the last signpost we possess before facing the night of geological times? There is scarcely a single prehistoric site inhabited by the oldest representatives of Homo sapiens without its legacy of ammonite shells and fragments of rock crystal demonstrating Cro-Magnon man's sensitivity to the equilibrium of natural shapes; nor is there a site without its discoveries of the canine teeth of

21

26

animals, pierced as pendants, or figures of a sexual nature which show the lasting importance of the predatory or sexual impulses well known from observation of the animal kingdom. Lastly, in every site we always find pieces of exceptional quality among the flint implements, often treated in such a way that it is impossible not to admit the tool-maker's predilection for the shapes which come close to both aesthetic and functional perfection.

The first expressions of aesthetic feeling

Primitive man first gave rein to his rudimentary aesthetic needs by admiring flowers, sunsets and perhaps even the majesty of the great cliffs in which his caves were, and by collecting curious stones. Feelings leave no fossil remains behind but we do possess actual evidence of this last-mentioned tendency. We have evidence in the animal kingdom, also, of the collection of unusual objects. Quite apart from the magpie, whose acquisitive instinct is well known, the most striking example is that of the bowerbird of Australia and New Guinea, which constructs a bower of foliage and decorates its floor or entrances with stones and shells in specially selected colours. If we move on from birds to mammals, we might imagine that the gorillas and even more so the old anthropians would afford some splendid examples of 'natural' art. But this is not so, and the higher mammals exhibit the greatest indifference to everything outside the alimentary and sexual processes. There is no path leading by successive evolutionary stages from the bowerbird to Pithecanthropus. So aesthetic enjoyment of the natural world appears as a new aptitude peculiar to the anthropians.

Homo sapiens possesses this enjoyment, and we are entitled to conceive of his predecessors as possessing it, but we must beware of our judgment, for all the collections of natural oddities found among present-day primitive peoples—Amerindians, Melanesians, African Negroes—are in the witch-doctor's bag. He often regards them as tremendously valuable, but for reasons which have no direct connection with aesthetics. The same phenomenon existed during Antiquity and the Middle Ages and, until recent times, in Europe and the Far East, where natural oddities were housed with the alchemist and the apothecary. On the other hand, there is no doubt that visual satisfaction is often grafted on to the emotion which is born on the borders of the magic's wonders.

We have no reason to consider the quantities of crystals, fragments of lead and iron ore and fossilised shells—especially ammonites—which are found with the remains of Upper Palaeolithic man, as of different origin. The man who appreciated the value of the lines of a bison so much that he could render the striking images we know certainly also appreciated the perfect spiral of an ammonite.

When we leave the times of the first figurative works to return to earlier ages, we continue to meet such objects of curiosity until we no longer know whether we are in the presence of Homo sapiens or his predecessor; this obscure margin certainly seems to have been passed at some point during those early years, and we reach a period which is definitely prior to the age when Homo sapiens settled in our regions. Consequently we know that the last of the ancient anthropians—like modern man—possessed, even if it was in a rudimentary state, that appreciation of forms in which the aesthetic is certainly

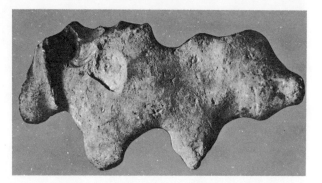

21. An unworked stone which suggests: *left.* a musk ox; *right.* a bear.

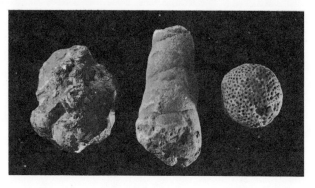

22. Stones collected by early man. *Musée de l'Homme, Paris.*

indivisible from a major part of magico-religious feeling. Beyond that, we know nothing about pre-Neanderthal man, Sinanthropus, Atlanthropus or Pithecanthropus, but it may be that their aesthetic behaviour was not given material expression in the objects which have reached us.

The 'animal aesthetic'

One of the keenest sources of our aesthetic satisfaction in the animal world is the direct issue of predatory or sexual incentives: the fangs and claws of the wild beast, the mating plumage of the bird, arouse an emotion which is not directly aesthetic. If we explicitly single out the beauty of forms or colours, it is because we are judging as modern men with whom aesthetic satisfaction has become, so to speak, the effect of a particular function. For Homo sapiens of primitive cultures, sensations of beauty were experienced through elementary physio-psychological impressions: it cannot have been otherwise for the anthropians who preceded him. The perception of the beauty of a lion is closely bound up with that of his power, with the superior power of the hunter who has killed him and wears the trophy of his canine tooth and with the magical efficacy of the tooth which guarantees its possessor all the virtues of the feline's strength and virility. The same is true of the beauty of the wild cow or mare, which are the sources of the hunter's livelihood and the symbols of an indispensable fertility. In the art of recent centuries it is not always easy to separate the aesthetic representation completely from the element which remains closely bound up with these primitive drives. If we start again from the last point fixed in time, i.e. from the period immediately preceding the first development of mural works in the Upper Palaeolithic, we are in an atmosphere which is perfectly consistent in this respect. Apart from all the flint or bone objects whose

27

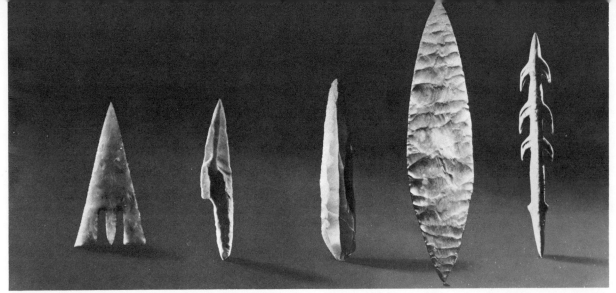

23. Examples of the perfection of prehistoric forms. *Left to right*. Tanged and winged flint arrowhead (Parc de Voudern, Morbihan). Shouldered point (Le Placard, Charente). Blade of Aurignacian type. Solutrean 'laurel leaf' (Volgu, Saône-et-Loire). Bone harpoon (Laugerie-Basse).

use is explicitly material, there remains a small heterogeneous collection consisting of teeth perforated at the roots, a few bone pendants—generally imitations of teeth —fragments of ferruginous ochre and the 'collectors' objects' which have just been mentioned.

The teeth are those of carnivores or, more frequently, the small atrophied canines of stags. The latter were extraordinarily popular for thousands of years, so much so that they were copied in any material which bore a slight resemblance to them—reindeer toe-joints, sawn horses'-teeth and fragments of cut up bone. Of all the game sought by the primitive hunter, the stag combined all the attributes which he wanted to appropriate for himself: it was the noblest of the herbivores; it was a rare animal, more difficult to find and strike down than the countless wild horses or reindeer; it was a passionate fighter in the mating season. As objects of ornamentation its canines must have been invested with an extraordinary potential, to judge by the attraction they exercised on prehistoric man.

The discovery of colour

The presence of ochre is no less revealing: the evidence of tooth pendants is lost when we go back to the times of the anthropians, but we continue to come across fragments of red ochre for quite a long time. The Upper Palaeolithic tells us about its use as a colour for mural paintings; we also know that a layer of it was placed around the dead man in burial places, which obviously gives it a religious significance; we know too that it was lavishly employed for other purposes, since in some dwelling places it finally formed a layer several inches thick on the ground. There are really only two hypotheses worthy of consideration, both, incidentally, confirmed by facts observed among recent primitive peoples: ochre could have been used to dye weapons and certain objects, or it could have been used to paint the body.

In any case, it is the most explicit sign we possess of an aesthetic activity, and it is important to note that it goes back beyond the limits of Homo sapiens to continue for some time among the anthropians. They have not yielded, up to the present at least, burial places with red ochre in them, but fragments of the colouring matter have been found in settlements.

The symbolism of the colour red, the pre-eminently beautiful colour, the symbol of blood and life, has also lasted throughout all ages and preserved its value among present-day humanity as it did in prehistoric times. Once more, this evidence which appears from the depths of the past concerns a domain in which the separation of the physical, the magical and the aesthetic is impossible.

The reassuring thing about this scanty inventory is that it constantly recurs in the facts relative to more recent prehistory and present-day primitive men as an extremely ancient basis on which conscious art has built and expanded as from the Upper Palaeolithic. Moreover this old substratum has continued to hold its own until the present day, never freed from the magical preoccupations and all the obscure resurgences of man's elementary behaviour.

Collection and ornamentation imply an act of consciousness and a desire for expression on man's part, however vague they may be. That is why it is not surprising to see them exhibited comparatively late and to observe their progressive enrichment. Future research may be able to trace the discovery of ochre to an even more remote age, but the hundreds of well-preserved sites which have been excavated during the last hundred years show that we can hardly expect to find genuine figurative works among Neanderthal men.

The functional aesthetic

There is one field in which, contrary to the preceding ones, the evidence of aesthetic activity is abundant: it is that of chipped stone implements. We have millions of objects at our disposal, ranging chronologically from the first millennia of prehistory, the age of Pithecanthropus, to the appearance of the first metal objects.

As regards the times which concern us here, the progress is striking: implements with more regular and improved outlines take the place of the irregular forms of the first period; many of them we could call beautiful in our own sense of the word. The search for pure forms appeared during the Acheulian, i.e. very early, two or three hundred thousand years before us; it grew, and reached its apogee during the Levalloiso-Mousterian, about one hundred thousand years ago, and ceased, with a few exceptions, to be as sensitive in our opinion at the beginning of the Upper Palaeolithic, around forty thousand years ago, at the very moment when art in the strict sense of the word began to make extraordinary progress.

As a result, the most beautiful forms of prehistoric tools developed in a totally different atmosphere from that of

23

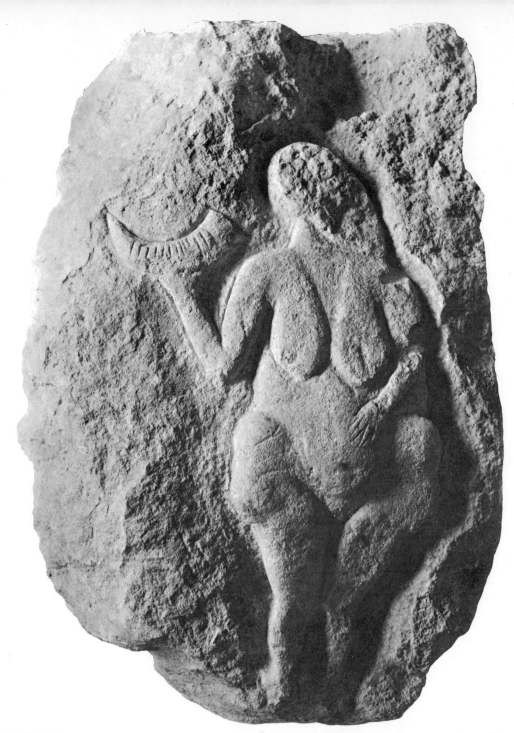

24. AURIGNACIAN. The Laussel Venus. She holds a horn in her hand. Bas-relief in stone. Les Eyzies. *Musée d'Aquitaine, Bordeaux.*

modern man. The admirable flint gravers, the long, delicately finished triangular points, the millions of objects (all showing remarkable technical skill) among which some masterpieces whose purity of form is disconcerting stand out, came from the hands if not of Sinanthropus at least of beings compared with whom Neanderthal man is 'modern'. It would seem very hard to maintain that these beings did not experience a certain aesthetic satisfaction, because they were excellent workmen who knew how to choose their material, come to terms with its faults, direct their strokes with absolute precision and produce from the block of undressed flint a form exactly corresponding to their intentions. Their work was not automatic; guided by a sequence of movements in a strict series, it induced reflection at every moment and certainly, in favourable circumstances,

resulted in the pleasure of creating a beautiful object.

This attitude is obvious, for, in the reality of the epoch, these implements did not exist of their own accord any more than did the polish of the canine tooth, the purity of the ammonite's spiral and the blinding vermilion of the ochre. The regularity of forms corresponded to the growing effectiveness of the cutting tool and an increasing economy in raw materials. The creator of forms was here a creator of implements, and just as we discovered the first gleams of aesthetic satisfaction in a psycho-physiological and magico-religious complex, it was in the techno-economic unfolding of the development of implements that the artistic satisfaction of the oldest anthropians showed through.

In any case, art in its primitive forms was indivisible from the total activity of the anthropian, as it is logical to suppose. An even more striking fact is that it continues to exist in the three forms we have emphasised throughout the evolution of human societies.

THE PALAEOLITHIC AGE *Abbé Henri Breuil*

*Although we are still in the dark night of time a new era
is opening: astonishing achievements begin to appear
in which, as we have shown, the fundamental laws of art are
already foreshadowed. It remains for us to place them
in relation to their civilisation. The most famous
of prehistorians and one of the founders of this new field
of study, Abbé Breuil, evokes this complex civilisation,
which flourished particularly in western Europe.*

When we think back to our early years, our recollections
soon run short; at the most a few facts and two or three
faces stand out in the mist of memories. The memory of
peoples is equally short. The length of geological human
time, the revolutions of the globe witnessed by ancient
man, the unceasing and profound changes in the earth's
scenery, the countless crowd of actors on its stage—they
have all been forgotten!

THE ORIGINS OF CIVILISATION

The fundamental data

The eye of ethnical memory is ill at ease as it plunges into
this dizzying perspective. All we have available to throw
light on the distant past is anonymous debris—chipped
and polished stones, broken shards, decorated and
fashioned bones, entombed skeletons or the scanty buried
remains of ancient men, rock panels decorated with
painted or engraved figures and lastly funerary monuments and ruined places of worship and fortified sites.

Such are the facts prehistory puts at our disposal to
mark the stages of human types and their civilisations,
from the obscure epoch when man emerged from among
the mammals of the end of the Tertiary period to the
time when the rudiments of our civilisation were organised with the domestication of cattle and with the beginnings of agriculture.

These first human groups are not unrelated to a great
number of present-day tribes in both hemispheres—the
Bushmen of South Africa, the Tasmanians, the Eskimos,
etc.—and their comparative study enables prehistorians
to understand fossil man better.

For its part, the geography of those early times shows
us (until a date quite close to our own from the geological
point of view) entire continents, such as the south Asian
shelf, today submerged beneath the waves, and continental bridges, now broken, between the two Mediterranean shores, between England and Europe and between
Anatolia and the Balkans.

On the other hand, at various times primitive man had
to overcome difficult obstacles of which we have only the
remotest idea. The Caspian extended much further
northward as a vast inland sea, and when the great
Scandinavian and Russian glaciers advanced, the gateway
to the East between western Europe and central Asia was
closed, and the Palaeolithic peoples could only penetrate
from Asia Minor and Africa into Europe by the south-
eastern and southern routes. The door did not open again
until much later to permit new migrations to the West.

That is why Europe, the only fully explored region
today, should be considered not as a self-sufficient unit

but as a peninsula attached to the north-west of the
prehistoric world, over which each new human wave
rolled in turn.

The presence of successive industries also poses racial
problems; although there is no doubt race and civilisation
are two things not to be confused, the introduction of
new civilisations in Europe normally coincides with the
appearance of new human types whose origin is not in
western Europe.

India, Asia Minor, western Europe, eastern, southern
and western Africa, and Java stand out as areas which
have gone through comparatively similar human phases.
In spite of the notable variations in industries, we can see
that they are related; even if the combinations are comparatively varied, the constituent elements reappear, and
in approximately the same order of succession. Moreover,
there seems to be little doubt that Siberia and even
northern China became, as from a certain moment at the
end of the Quaternary period, components of this
ensemble and probably the sources of the principal
variations.

The earliest social life

What were the first men—the most recent of whom, at
least, sometimes used to bury their dead—but a species
of ingenious brutes, well suited to launch the human
empire with flint and fire in a world of gigantic monsters?
Thanks to them, life was made possible for a more
refined type of human being who did not arrive in the
western part of the prehistoric world until the close of the
Ice Age. He reached there already formed into large
distinct races, consequently already ancient, and the
scholar's eye inevitably turns to the high plateau of Asia
and to the East Indies as the possible cradles of developments which remain mysterious. For was it not from
there that, hundreds of millennia before, the earliest men
came on the trail of the first elephants, horses and cows
which took this route at the end of the Tertiary?

Man was only belatedly forced to frequent caves
because of a cold phase towards the end of the last interglacial; then the curtain began to rise on his social life.
This more stable and preserving habitat reveals hearths
and sometimes tombs.

Engraved or carved bones and the mural decorations of
caves and shelters, apart from their great artistic interest,
pose many other problems concerning the magical and
perhaps religious aim of this earliest art. Strangely enough
the opulent women and sexual symbols of the Aurig-   24
nacian disappear later, giving way to the animal art
already in the course of development. Animals are represented pierced with symbolical arrows (bison and ibexes
at Niaux; horses at Lascaux), clay models are riddled   54
with spear marks (at Montespan, a headless lion and   6
bear, which seem to have received new skins at various
times)—facts which evoke the idea of sympathetic magic.
The numerous pregnant women and the men closely
pursuing their women suggest the idea of fertility magic.
The deliberate alteration of the essential features of
certain animals seems to indicate taboos. Human figures
dressed up in animal or grotesque masks evoke the   4

dancing and initiation ceremonies of living peoples or
represent the sorcerers or gods of the Upper Palaeolithic.
Later the painted rocks of eastern Spain enable us to
follow the natives of that time while hunting, waging
war, dancing and even in their family life.

Trade already existed in the Upper Palaeolithic, consisting of the export over long distances of marine or
fossil shells and the raw materials used to make tools.

The beginnings of artistic expression

The history of labour begins only with tools made from
stone at a time when their artificial nature was already
obvious enough to differentiate them from natural
fractures.

Tools were essential from the very beginning to rum-
mage in the soil and extract nourishing roots or the nodules of raw stone which were to be dressed. Hammers
and anvils were necessary to break them up, according to
techniques which underwent great changes down the
ages, from crude percussion on a lump of bare stone,
stone against stone, then wood against stone, to the fab-
rication of a bifacial or core tool intended to produce
longer and finer flakes and later long narrow blades by
procedures which are still obscure, although they undoubtedly included the use of a wooden wedge.

At all times tools fashioned by finishing the edges of
flakes were needed to work wood and bone. Weapons
were indispensable. At first they were massive. Held in
the hand or hafted, they were intended for striking with
the cutting edge, like an axe, or with the point, like a
halberd; later, preference was given to lighter types which
were used as daggers or as heads for lances, javelins and
arrows.

Cutting tools, too, were always necessary for dismem-
bering carcasses and for the preparation and making of
fur garments.

In the Magdalenian, the use of bony materials—ivory;
the bones or antlers of the deer tribe—became widespread; from these were made awls, spears, daggers,
smoothers, scissors, etc., and, towards the end, eyed
needles and barbed harpoons. In addition, painting with
mineral colours was used to decorate caves. Upper Palaeolithic man was capable of penetrating right to the end
of what were literally subterranean labyrinths, with lights
which could be relit in case of accidental extinction. This
presupposes a bold people, for in all countries the unsophisticated are terrified of the smallest dark caves.
These dark galleries (and perhaps other places as well)
were the theatres for magical ceremonial rites connected
with the increase of desirable and the disappearance of
dangerous animals and with the successful conclusion of
hunting expeditions.

As among the Eskimos, the winter was undoubtedly
a dead season for hunting; early man had to live largely
on the provisions he had accumulated. It was a time for
celebrating the rites of the tribe in the Eskimo manner:
the initiation of adolescents into traditions and beliefs and
the rights and duties of adults; ceremonies for the increase of useful animals, for the destruction of the biggest
wild beasts and for hunting magic; and appeals for these
ends to the higher powers who preside over these things,
to the souls of slain animals which they wanted to be re-
incarnated. All these customs, which still exist among the
Eskimos, may also have existed in the Upper Palaeolithic,

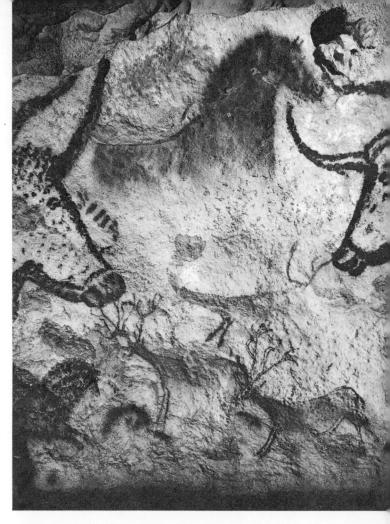

25. Reindeer and bulls painted on the cave walls at Lascaux.

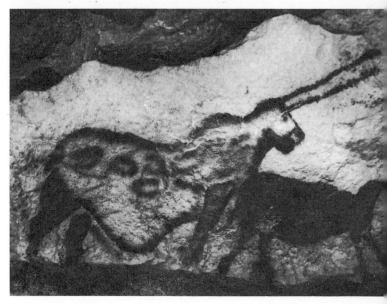

26. Imaginary bull-like animal. Lascaux.

and they would provide a satisfactory explanation of the
religious and magical nature of the figurative representations. A number of engraved or carved bones were probably fashioned to serve as hunting charms.

It is noteworthy that neither on the walls of decorated
caves nor on the painted rocks do we find any trace of the
geometrical or stylised decorations of portable art. Thus
notable variations in mental trends presided over each of
the branches of art.

31

THE ORIGINS OF ART

The vestiges which are so precious to the ethnographer are the only positive evidence of the origins of art, whether figurative or decorative.

The carved figures at the beginning of the Aurignacian and the engravings which also date from that time prove that art was not by any means in its infancy. Indeed, the statuettes from Brassempouy are evidence of a lengthy artistic past which is quite unknown to us.

Do we find artistic records in the Lower Palaeolithic? Boucher de Perthes was the first to think so, and others after him have held the same opinion; in the midst of smooth pebbles they have found nodules of flint with curious shapes which they have claimed were finished by Quaternary man. The fractures, which are supposed to be accentuated likenesses, were certainly caused by natural or mechanical agents which shattered the cavities or the more fragile projecting points. There are only a very few pieces to which the explanation of accidental resemblance might apply.

Later on, the development of the working of bone and the spread of this technique was the starting point of decorative art. Once it had produced utilitarian results, bone-working was to become an element of art; the rhythm of repeated incisions became appreciated and was copied, either to make a workaday or decorative object pleasing or to consecrate a magical or religious object.

But decorative art is not figurative art, which includes various elements: firstly, a mental element, which consists in recognising the resemblance given and taking pleasure in stating it, i.e. imitation; subsequently, a gesture of selection or reiteration, directed by the desire to preserve for oneself, to improve or to reproduce the image apprehended, i.e. duplication.

The sources of figurative art

Imitation is connected with deep psychological needs; every being tends to harmonise with its background by an unconscious mimetic urge. There is genuine imitation among the higher animals: two animals incite each other to reproduce their actions mutually by example. Some of them, parrots and monkeys for instance, even imitate types widely different from their own. This kind of aping is a spontaneous pantomime which in certain phases of existence can lead to a sort of game or drama: for example, the kitten which chases a dead leaf, the puppy which snatches at a stick as if it is his real prey.

Sexual selection leads to the establishment of some of these games; the preservation of the species determines others (such as that of the partridge imitating a wounded bird on the point of dropping, in order to distract the enemy from her defenceless brood).

In the same way children have an extraordinary propensity for mimicry, and even for drama.

The instinct of children and primitive peoples which drives them to imitate the walks and cries of various animals corresponds to the imitative phase of art, which presupposes an appreciation of the plastic likeness in action.

Hunting camouflage introduces another element: disguise, which may also spring from the desire to increase the resemblance to the animal. Such disguises have certainly played an enormous part among hunting peoples.

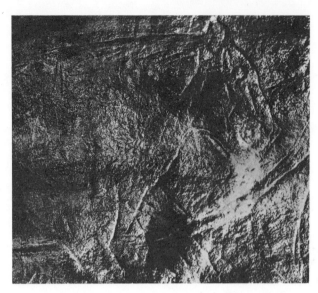

27. Engraved feline from Les Combarelles.

The animals' actual remains have supplied the raw material (for the Eskimos, the reindeer; for the North American Indians, the wolf; for the Bushmen, the ostrich).

The success of these stratagems has been interpreted in terms of hunting magic; the mask was considered to have supernatural power, and the imitative dances in which it was used were thought to confer power over the coveted animal.

The idea of likeness has other concomitant sources. Facial decoration has given rise in New Zealand to a closely parallel series; there, all figurative and even decorative art derives from the tattooed human face which has regenerated the other parts of the body. And there is another very rich source of the hunting peoples: the intentional observation and reproduction of the footprints of men or animals on the ground. The oldest engraved rocks of South Africa are sometimes covered with them. Other traces have been left by the human hand dipped in colour and pressed on a rock.

To bring out the hand use was also made of the stencil process: outlines of hands surrounded by colours. Then people began to draw hands directly, instead of using these primitive procedures.

From hand-prints to works of art

At the beginning of the Upper Palaeolithic men extracted the clayey deposit from the walls of certain caves. Their fingers as they plunged into the soft material left grooves of varying depth or holes side by side; these were not art —merely marks. The Aurignacians observed them; they noted the regularity of these imprints, the rhythm of the deep punctuations, of the parallel lines, and they reproduced them, no longer for the purpose of removing the clay but for themselves. They took pleasure in repeating them, complicating them and increasing their decorative value. That other ideas superimposed their influence on the preliminary step and transformed an aesthetic whim into ritual is quite possible and, indeed, probable here as it was for figurative art.

If art for art's sake had not been born, magical or religious art would never have existed; on the other hand, if magical or religious ideas had not made it possible to include art for art's sake among the more serious pre-

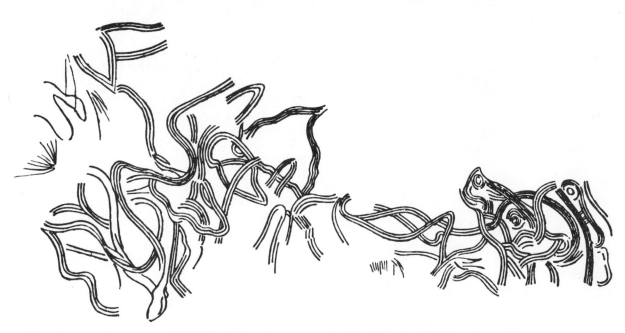

28. Meanders traced on a cave wall. A bull's head can be seen on the right. Altamira. *(After Breuil.)*

occupations of daily life it might never have got beyond the embryonic stage.

If the Aurignacians traced numerous decorative meanders on clay in the caves of Gargas (Pyrenees), Hornos de la Peña (Spain), etc., certain of their contemporaries made the same discoveries elsewhere. Fingers smeared with ochre or clay leave four parallel lines when they are trailed across a blank rock surface. This was the origin of the meandering decorations in the cave of La Pileta (near Málaga), the equivalent of the 'macaronis' of Gargas. If the idea of resemblance was born in the minds of the

29. Paintings from the ceiling of the great hall at Altamira. *(Composition by Gaston Ferré, after drawings by Breuil.)*

people who doodled like this, then, just as children do, they interpreted their marks on the spot and subsequently completed them to increase the likeness they had observed. Then they were able to reproduce the outline intentionally, and line drawing proper began. **28**

The transition must have been made quickly, for scarcely any definite examples have been found; the first figures are extremely simple but already frankly naturalistic. It is true that during the same period the Aurignacians were already carving remarkable statuettes of people **5, 9** in stone and ivory, and, soon after, were making bas-reliefs as well.

Once the idea of resemblance was implanted, the systematic interpretation of irregular rocks, stones and

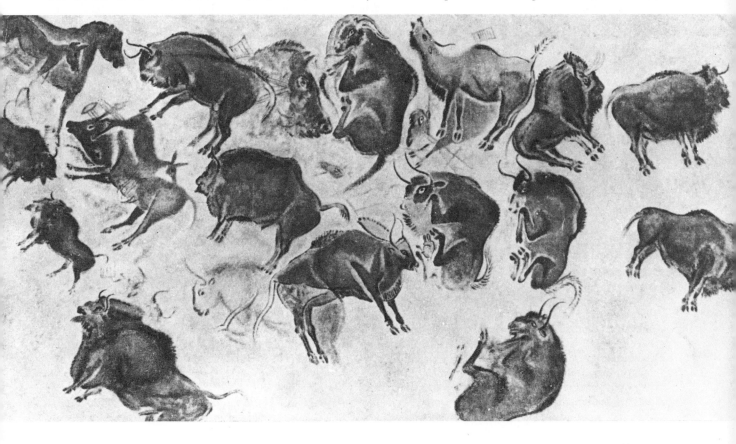

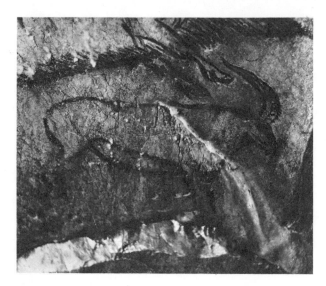

30. Ibex partially covered by a flow of calc-spar, proving the extreme age of the drawing. Niaux.

pieces of wood with natural forms could develop. We see numerous examples of this as from the Aurignacian.

The resemblances were accentuated by touching up or by adding lines. At first statuettes were made from clay, which was easy to handle, then from more durable materials.

Figurative art was by no means of one single origin. Starting from the instinct for the active imitation of the living by the living and from the feeling for likeness which is inherent in it, it developed first of all through dramatic art and disguises using animal remains, then from man-made masks which established their own autonomy.

When the mind was sufficiently evolved to interpret figuratively the imprints left by fingers trailed across walls, it passed on to the free representation which developed later in Palaeolithic drawing and painting.

While the figurative art which we saw in the mask, the tattooed face, and foot- or hand-print resulted only in highly conventional patterned creations, visual realism predominated in the drawings issuing from the interpretation of the smears which were later reproduced deliberately, and in the drawings and carvings stemming from accentuated natural irregularities, as well as in the subsequent figurines. It developed more particularly among peoples living by hunting, in which eyesight plays a vital role.

The great mural art

That is how the great mural art for which the prehistoric caves are famous would seem to have originated. It was independent of the art of small contemporary objects in which human statuary, derived from fur dolls, was already widespread. But graphic art at that time was only occasionally found in portable art. Engraved and painted slabs were the exception in Aurignacian art and, except at Parpalló in Spain, were still very rare in Perigordian and even Solutrean art. It was only in the Magdalenian that figurative art made big inroads on the decoration of small objects.

A profound knowledge of animal shapes formed the basis of this artistic reaction. In the course of their eventful lives, the hunters of mammoths, rhinoceroses, bears, big stags, etc., accumulated a wealth of powerful visual and dynamic impressions. They were the men who created and developed the mural art of the French caves, of the rock shelters of the Spanish Levant and of the engraved and painted rocks of the Sahara and South Africa: in every case it was big-game-hunting man who engendered naturalistic art.

Palaeolithic art, then, experienced an extraordinary flowering in western Europe. Its unfolding was almost identical in places considerable distances apart: from the Yonne to the Straits of Gibraltar and from Sicily to the Gulf of Gascony, but especially in the regions of Aquitaine and the French Pyrenees and in their western Cantabrian extension.

All these works of art can first be dated in relation to geological times. (It is obvious that drawings of extinct animals or animals which have moved elsewhere are contemporary with those animals or are modern forgeries. Partial or entire submergence in an untouched piece of ground and the existence of stalagmitic exudations covering them are adequate arguments for dismissing fraud.) 30

Their evolution can be followed with relative precision. After comparatively mediocre beginnings dominated by conventions (frontal horns on a body in profile; legs on 11 one side of the body only, concealing the other pair, etc.), 54 Quaternary art exhibited an increasingly lively feeling for animal forms. From the Perigordian onwards, in the painted silhouettes of Lascaux where the red, black or bistre patch applied with a kind of primitive air-brush 25, 26 was outlined in black, the development was astonishing.

After a break in our information corresponding to the first two-thirds of the Solutrean, we rediscover mural art with bas-reliefs reduced to incised outlines (Les 27 Combarelles), which easily led to shallow engraving on the over-hard rock of the Pyrenean and Cantabrian regions. Soon the latter became graffiti of no great importance—although the purity of outline is charming (Marsoulas, Teyjat, Font-de-Gaume)—and gave way to painting, which continued to develop. After the achievements of the Perigordian, mural art reverted to simple black line-drawings, as if in charcoal; later the line grew firmer and thicker; the down strokes and up strokes were differentiated. This was towards Magdalenian III. Then hatching developed; colours were modelled. The naive realism of the first phases tended to disappear before the calligraphic techniques of the various schools; this sometimes resulted in a search for violent attitudes which led to mannerism—at Altamira, for 29 example, where the painting makes use of the rock formations to convey the illusion better. From the beginning of Magdalenian VI genuine polychromy was established by surrounding, with a powerful black line, 12 modelled areas of various colours ranging from bistre to vermilion via purplish and orange tones. It was the culminating point of Magdalenian art, which was to die a sudden death.

In its final phases, this art resumed the linear style of the Aurignacian. The Mediterranean infiltration which was beginning was to give birth to the Azilian culture, but 14 these newcomers, primarily fishermen and collectors of snails and shellfish, did not have the powerful creative imagination of the great hunters.

It was not individual caprice which produced the painted caves. Even if a few outstanding individuals may have been needed at the very beginning to lay the ground-

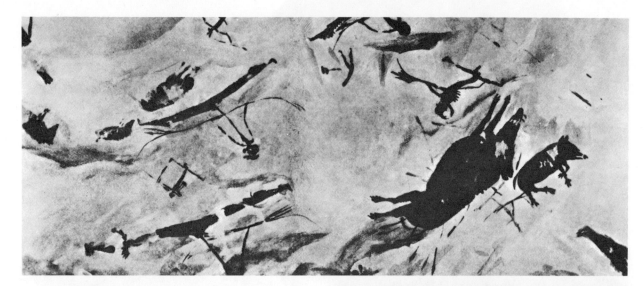

31a. Boar hunt. Painting in the cave of Remigia (Castile). (*After Obermaier and Breuil.*)

work for the discovery of artistic expression, the development of mural art was evidence of an exceptional collective interest and control.

The whole of western Europe was won over by the first illumination of beauty, born of the spark of genius of a few; but this upsurge was 'standardised' in rites considered as fundamental by all the Franco-Cantabrian tribes.

Nevertheless eastern Spain, almost isolated from France by the Pyrenees which were once again impassable as a result of glaciation, followed a different path and, probably owing to a mixture of Aurignacian traditions and an African source, the Capsian, ended up with a rock art in which pictures with several figures together are common; in which the human figure, hunting, making war or in his family or social life, is multiplied as in South African art.

It is not impossible that Western naturalistic art made contact with the Capsian and Neolithic pre-Egyptian world. We may also assume a parallel appearance in Africa of an art of hunters who, becoming pastoral in the north (see the decoration of the rock shelters in the Libyan desert and the Sahara), supplied the foundations for the development of proto-Egyptian and Cretan art. The existence of contacts between the Upper Palaeolithic men of Parpalló (Valencia) and the Africans is highly probable. The origin of Saharan naturalistic rock art—mostly Neolithic—and its relations with the Upper Palaeolithic art of western Europe remain open questions, as does that of its relations to the south-east with the rock art of Tanganyika and South Africa.

Geometrical decoration

Art in the Upper Palaeolithic developed with a keen observation of nature and an extraordinary degree of fidelity to it, but side by side with this development artists of varying efficiency and vitality copied and distorted the works from which they drew their inspiration. This resulted in the modification, destruction and sometimes even the reversal of the meaning of a naturalistic figure, until it was reduced to the role of an ornamental motif.

From Magdalenian IV onwards, and particularly dur-

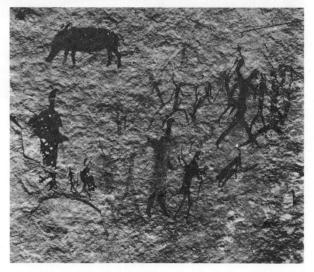

31b. Boar hunt. Rock painting from South Africa. Giant's Castle Game Reserve, Natal.

ing Magdalenian V and VI when sculpture was progressively abandoned, the ornamentation of everyday objects —perforators, spears, etc.—borrowed its elements increasingly from the naturalistic art of line engravings. The transposition of figures on to narrow surfaces could not take place without difficulty and waste. The law of least effort simplified these figures until they became mere diagrams. It is not uncommon to find on one and the same object all the transitions from a recognisable figure to a complete stylisation.

These valuable pieces give us the key to many others such as the head of a goat-like animal, from Massat, or the stick from La Madeleine decorated with horses' heads which gradually turn into ovals.

Nevertheless, these diagrams do not result only from the degeneration of better executed drawings. Stylised figurative art, as scholars have shown, springs from a genuine realism which is not visual but of the conceptual type observable among children. During the Upper Palaeolithic it existed side by side with and independent of the great naturalistic art. The significance of these simplified figures is not easy to define. The elements of this original stylised art greatly enriched ornamental art from the beginning of the Magdalenian, but especially at the end

35

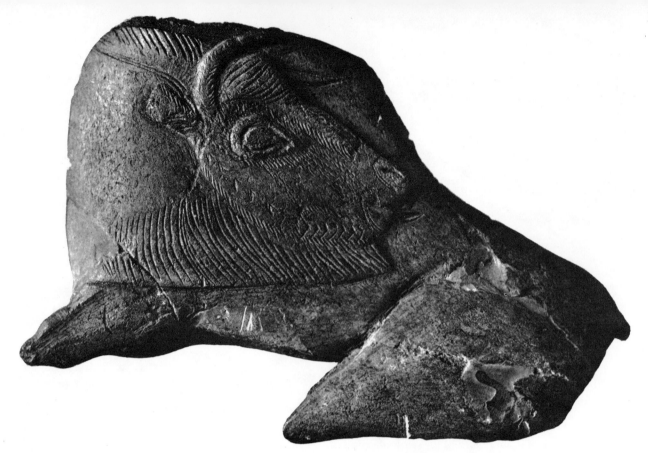

32. Bison carved in reindeer horn. La Madeleine. *Musée de St Germain*.

of its first third. A large number of Magdalenian bone blades exhibit very rich decorations which were obtained by grouping motifs of this origin—ellipses, zigzags, chevrons and fleurons. Among the figures there are representations of fish and animal heads and also of inanimate objects—various implements and even huts. Many of the designs were engraved or painted on cave walls.

But decorative art had still other sources. In the course of removing the meat from big game, man accidentally traced parallel lines on the bones by steady, successive blows with a flint. From the later Mousterian onwards, both at La Quina and at La Ferrassie, there have been occasional finds of bones incised with careful parallel lines which are evidence no longer of a chance result of butchery but of intentional work which transposed a fortuitous line into decoration.

When the working of bone, ivory and reindeer-horn developed widely in the Aurignacian and then in the Solutrean and Magdalenian, its technique became more accurate and to the accidental traces of dismemberment were added those caused by cutting up these raw materials to make narrow, elongated tools out of them.

Certain objects such as spears were meant to be fixed to a stave, either by bindings or by a single or double chamfer to which the extremity of the shaft was fixed. This produced other elements by which decoration profited—transverse incisions or flanges to ensure the firmness of the fastenings, incisions or grooves on the surfaces in contact with the shaft to make the adhesive substance stick more firmly. The habit of seeing a binding round a stick also resulted on various occasions in its being copied in a carved representation.

One of the most certain origins of the geometrical decoration of many Neolithic vases in both worlds comes from the first pots, often supported in baskets which were

destroyed by the firing and whose weaving left its trace on the belly. When the basket was superseded, the zigzags of its imprints were imitated by hand out of sheer force of habit.

Thus decorative art was born of the ornamental transposition of elements of technical origin; it was enriched with the residues of other elements, also technical, but fallen into disuse and ornamentalised, and by the decorative imitation of similar techniques; it made use of primitive designs by amalgamating and separating them; it reached its apogee by altering for its own enhancement elements borrowed from great art—mutilating, debasing, regrouping and dissociating them.

THE AFTERMATH OF PALAEOLITHIC ART

Stylised art and the Azilian culture

What was the fate of art after the great Magdalenian phase?

The years between the epoch when Upper Palaeolithic man hunted the last herds of reindeer in southwestern Europe and the age when semi-civilised invaders ploughed the first furrows there and put the first flocks out to pasture make up the Mesolithic, the period between the Palaeolithic, with extinct animals or animals which have moved to other climates, and the Neolithic, with our present-day fauna.

It must be admitted, however, that there were already pastoral and agricultural Neolithic men in Africa and Asia Minor at a time when Europe's Upper Palaeolithic was at its zenith.

The so-called Neolithic peoples were in reality the issue at the beginning of modern times of Upper Palaeolithic tribes which had migrated. Their migration was related to the improved climate in what were previously glacial regions. Also, the progressive drying-up of vast regions now deserted but where there once had been

36

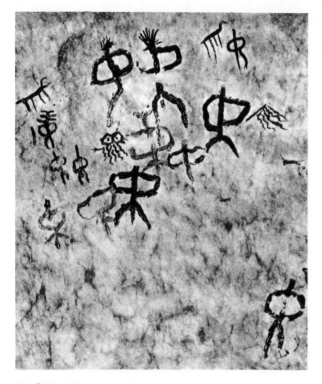

33. Stylised human figures and animals painted on the walls of the cave of La Graja. *(After Breuil.)*

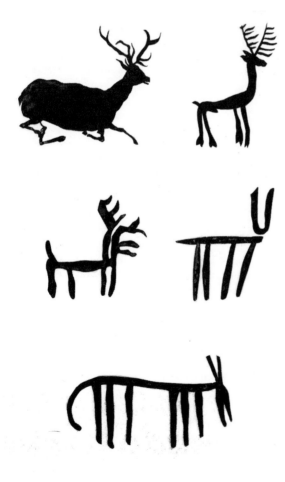

34. The evolution of the stylised figure of a stag, taken from the stag at Calapata (Teruel). *(After Carballo.)*

abundant rainfall forced the tribes which had formed at the end of the Quaternary and were already pastoral or agricultural to seek new lands for their flocks and crops.

In the classical regions of the Upper Palaeolithic, such as south-western France and north-western Spain, several successive cultural waves have been recorded, differing widely from one another in the evolution of art: the Azilian culture affords an instructive contribution.

In the cave of Mas d'Azil (Ariège), superimposed on a layer of Magdalenian IV there appears a category of characteristic objects, consisting of pebbles which are **14** either painted or engraved, or both. They are also found at the same level in other caves in the French Pyrenees and in Périgord; and others, possibly of an even earlier date, have been found in several caves in the north. It is quite possible that further careful research might disclose them at any level of the European Upper Palaeolithic, for the painted caves have on their walls groups of dots or bars and signs similar to those on the pebbles.

The caves of Castillo and Niaux enable us to observe that at an earlier epoch certain artists already possessed a large repertory of conventional signs from which the Azilian figures were derived. The origin of these painted pebbles, then, goes far back into the Upper Palaeolithic, especially into that of the Mediterranean region, where tribes lived along the littoral, existing mainly by collecting shellfish, a labour requiring little effort.

The painted motifs are most frequently dots or bars in different groupings: crosses with one or two arms, barred circles, fern-leaves, rectangles with two diagonals, circles with a central dot, and a few rare alphabetiform signs: E, F, etc. The painted pebbles mark a first stage in stylised art.

The Iberian rock paintings

When we first had the opportunity to study the paintings of the valley of Batuacas, we noted the striking similarity of the dots or bars aligned in series to the paintings on stones from the Mas d'Azil. In fact, H. Obermaier has established beyond doubt by twelve series of figures that it is possible to interpret the Mas d'Azil symbols in the light of the less stylised Spanish rock figures which **15** generally represent human forms: the double or triple chevron comes close to the diagram of a seated man; the single or two-armed cross and the ladder-shaped sign with a single vertical cutting through the middle of a large number of rungs recall an upright man. There are too many agreements between the series for their origins to be separate.

In our existing state of knowledge, prehistoric Iberian art seems to present the following picture: in Upper Palaeolithic times there existed in the Peninsula an Atlantic province, primarily Cantabrian, but which also spread into Castile and extended as far as southern Andalusia, to La Pileta, for example, and the neighbourhood of Málaga and Cadiz; its naturalistic art was the geographical extension of the Aurignacio-Magdalenian art of the Upper Palaeolithic in the south-west of France. Altamira is the most famous example. Nevertheless, at an **29** early date it yielded a profusion of schematic signs which are found again, only in very small numbers and at a late date, from the Pyrenees to the Dordogne, and more rarely in the latter. La Pileta is particularly rich in numerous and varied early signs.

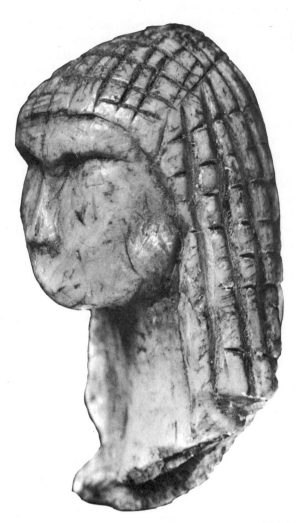

35. AURIGNACIAN. The Lady of Brassempouy. Ivory (Height *c.* 1 in.). *Musèe de St Germain*.

Estremadura, i.e. in the south-west.

Schematic art, in the form of coloured drawings on the one hand and rock engravings on the other, undoubtedly continued down to the beginning of the Bronze Age.

From schematic art to writing

It would be interesting to make a coordinative study of the signs and symbols derived from easily recognisable figures. Then the relative constancy of the superimpositions would be observed. Detailed comparisons from more remote places would enable us to follow the progress of schematic, or stylised, art towards Ireland and Scandinavia, where it rejoined another branch from central Asia. This last is the probable point of departure of schematic art, which radiated to the entire circumference of the Old World before writing came into being, giving the various Neolithic groups a complete collection of symbols which each group elaborated and adapted in its own way. Several extracted from these symbols the first elements of ideographic writing, whereas others, scattered far and wide throughout the world, continued to make use of these signs in the manner of their ancestors, who had not yet amalgamated them into phrases to express complexes of ideas.

Thus art, in its natural passage to a diagrammatic form, prepared the way for the birth of writing and provided the signs which would be needed. These signs are still not writing, but they lead up to it. The painted rocks are even more eloquent in their way than the inscribed tablets of Easter Island: at the two antipodes of our globe they form the ends of two chains, which perhaps linked up somewhere near the centre of Asia, at the foot of the mountains of eastern Siberia. In 1880 rubbings were taken of many rock engravings—some of which adopted highly simplified diagrams to render beings—which were interpreted with great pains. We can see in them a precursor of one of the human mind's greatest achievements, the symbol leading to writing. But its development was elsewhere. In the east, the south and the south-west the ingenuity of the Neolithic tribes of China, Chaldea, Egypt and north-west India was needed to organise these graphic signs, scanty at first, to add to them and elaborate them, in order finally to extract from them first ideographic and later phonetic script.

We have no doubt that this immense discovery was the result of the independent development by the various colonies dotted around the periphery of the 'Roof of the World' of the small stock of figure-symbols brought from their countries of origin.

But we have reached the time when the early peoples and races were settling into place; the material conditions of their lives were established. Prehistory in the strict sense of the word was finished. In spite of the absence of written documents, protohistory was beginning—history before writing, but by no means before traditions and legends.

We are, then—depending on the region in question— four to seven millennia behindhand, a very short phase if we compare it with the enormous period taken for the extraordinarily slow progress of humanity for hundreds of thousands of years.

The second artistic region of Palaeolithic Iberia was almost exclusively Mediterranean: it extended from Catalonia to the province of Almería. Although, through its splendid animal paintings, this Levantine art is a particular development of Upper Palaeolithic art and especially of Franco-Cantabrian Perigordian, it is distinguished from it, as we have already mentioned, by the abundance and the animated nature of equally realistic but summarily treated human figures—the product of complex figurative scenes of hunts and battles. It should be noted that certain stylised elements which preceded the realistic figures in some cases—at Minateda (Albacete) for example—are found in ever greater numbers towards the end of this art and appear to arise from a mixture with coastal Mediterranean influences, which become more and more numerous in relation to the original more northerly element. The influence of Saharan and even South African paintings seems undeniable, but, on the other hand, this influence could have come to Africa from the Mediterranean coast of Iberia.

The arrival, at the end of this period, of pastoral and agricultural Neolithic peoples enriched rock art with a number of new conventional elements, such as the representations of the 'owl-headed' female figures of the dolmen world and the rectangular and triangular idols of the Iberian Neolithic, among others. This new tendency was most widespread in Andalusia, the Sierra Morena and

31a
33

36

36. SAHARAN PREHISTORIC ART. Rock painting from the Haut-Mertouteh (Hoggar).

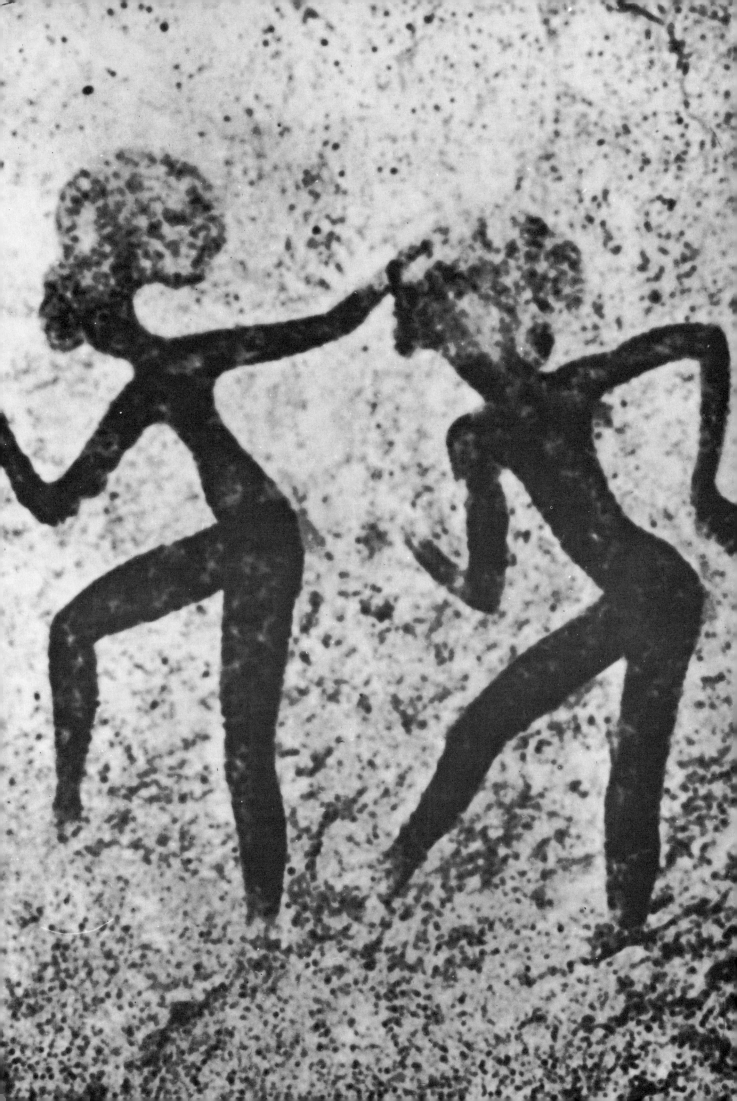

HISTORICAL SUMMARY: Prehistoric art

THE PLEISTOCENE

Over the last hundred years, evidence has come to light of deposits laid down in the latest divisions of geological time (the Pleistocene and Recent periods). Some of these indicate a colder climate than the present, since as far south as southern Europe the deposits contain bones of animals like the reindeer which now lives in cold tundra regions, as well as tundra plant remains. Such studies have often been dominated by the very wide occurrence in northern Europe of deposits actually laid down by once extensive ice sheets as far south as Weimar in central Germany and London. The ice sheets over Scandinavia must have been many thousands of feet thick.

But this does not represent the remains of one single glaciation, as some early workers believed. We know that the ice advanced several times, reaching different limits, and between these advances were periods just as warm as today. Some of these 'interglacial' periods were definitely a little warmer, for plants like rhododendron ponticum lived high in the Alps and in southern Ireland, far north of their natural limit today. The Montpellier maple was an important component of the forests of Britain during the last interglacial, and

hippopotamus ranged widely in the river estuaries and warm coastal regions. Even so the mean annual temperatures were probably not very different—perhaps 2°C. more in the warm interglacials and 7°C. colder at the glacial maxima.

When the tundra stretched across middle-latitude Europe, it must have been both a much larger area than now and much more congenial for life because the middle latitudes have nearly equal days and nights, quite different from the polar regions. Great herds not only of reindeer, but also of woolly mammoth, bison and horse were both a challenge and an abundant food supply for early man as he evolved sufficiently to take advantage of the situation.

Already during the last but one interglacial (Holstein) early man occupied favoured parts of Europe, hunting big game, elephants and rhinoceros, of species now extinct. But straightforward evolution on the spot was not to be his fate over the long period of time down to the present. The environment was forever changing and several times he was forced by ice advances to vacate northern Europe. The sea level fell as water was locked up in the icesheets and the Atlantic and Mediterranean coastal waters gave way to new land

areas and land bridges such as those from Britain to France and Italy to Sicily. Between other continents even more important land bridges developed like that of the Bering islands between Siberia and Alaska, and between southeast Asia and Indonesia. In the tropics the effects of climatic change and glacial advance were also marked— typical glaciation in the highest mountains and, for part at least of the time, heavier rainfall which allowed grassland to replace parts of the Sahara and similar deserts.

Unfortunately the details of the many climatic changes are difficult to reconstruct and there is no problem more perplexing than that of fixing the age of these periods in years. We can only make tentative estimates from the new techniques like radiocarbon (C.14) and the potassium-argon (K/Ar) method and hope that future work will confirm these estimates. Studies of the fossil pollen have proved the most informative approach to reconstructing the climatic sequence, for the tiny grains are well preserved in many deposits and numerous enough for us to estimate statistically the changes in vegetation. As a result we know that Europe had four main interglacial periods each with its own characteristic vegetation. The last we call Eem; the

EUROPE AND WESTERN ASIA IN PALAEOLITHIC TIMES
showing extent of glaciation and distribution of Aurignacian Venuses

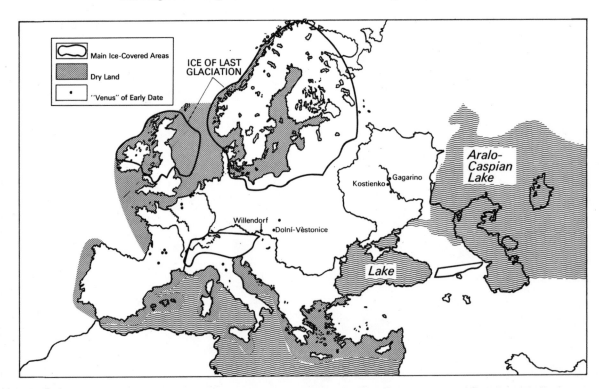

HUMAN CULTURAL AND PHYSICAL TYPES DURING THE PLEISTOCENE ICE AGE

PERIODS OF TIME	CULTURAL TYPES	AND THEIR CHARACTERISTIC TOOL FORMS	HOMINIDS (Identified by find locality)	BIOLOGICAL CLASSIFICATIONS (following Simpson)
? DONAU EARLY	**OLDOWAN**	CHOPPING TOOLS	**Olduvai Bed I** 4 Individuals ? Garusi and Kanam ?? Taungs, Sterkfontein, Makapan	*Australopithecus africanus*
PLEISTOCENE ? GÜNZ	EVOLVED **OLDOWAN**	CHOPPING TOOLS AND POLYHEDRICS	**Olduvai Lower Bed II** ? Sterkfontein Middle Breccia	
MINDEL GLACIATION	PRIMITIVE **ACHEULIAN**	HAND-AXES AND CLEAVERS	**Olduvai Upper Bed II** **Ternifine** ? Ubeidiyah and Mauer	*Homo*
	CHOPPING TOOL TECHNOLOGY cf. CLACTONIAN	CHOPPING TOOLS AND LARGE FLAKES	**Peking**—Chou k'ou-tien (Possibly Java man of Djetis and Trinil age)	*erectus*
HOLSTEIN INTERGLACIAL	TYPICAL **ACHEULIAN**	HAND-AXES AND FLAKE TOOLS (Notches, grattoirs and racloirs)	**Swanscombe** **Steinheim**	
RISS GLACIATION AND EEMIAN (LAST) INTERGLACIAL	**ACHEULIAN**		**Olduvai Bed IV** **Saldanha** ? Makapan Zuttiyeh and Lazaret	Early *Homo* *sapiens*
	VARIOUS NON-ACHEULIAN	?? CHOPPING TOOLS	**Saccopastore** **Solo River** **Ting Tsun** ? Taubach	
	CHARENTIAN	QUINA RACLOIRS, 'LIMACES' ETC.	**Ehringsdorf** **Teshik Tash**	
FIRST HALF LAST GLACIATION	**MOUSTERIAN COMPLEX** QUINA-FERRASSIE GROUP	FLAKE TOOL INDUSTRIES WITH RACLOIRS AND OTHER TOOLS IN VARYING PROPORTIONS ACCORDING TO TRADITION	**Neanderthals** (with large brow ridges) Classic group sensu lato La Chapelle La Quina, La Ferrassie· Monte Circeo, ? Spy, Regourdou and Marsal	Mainly *Neanderthal* or
	DENTICULATE, 'TYPICAL' AND ACHEULIAN TRADITIONS OF THE MOUSTERIAN	EUROPE AFRICA ASIA	Gibraltar, Veternica, Krapina, Broken Hill, Eyasi, Djebel Irhoud, Mt Carmel, Djebel Qafseh, Amud and Shanidar	*Gerontomorphic*
EUROPEAN EARLY LEPTOLITHIC SECOND HALF	**SZELETIAN** AND cf. **SZELETIAN** OF RUSSIA	LEAF POINTS	Brno, Zlaty Kun, (Pre-Szeletian Subalyuk) Sungir, Staroselje Kostenki Markina and Gorodsov site	*Modern form*
	W. EUROPE VARIOUS LEPTOLITHIC	BONE TOOLS BURINS, ETC.	Grimaldi Prognathous Female and Child Grimaldi 'Cromagnons' Pataud (Protomagdalenian)	*of* *Homo*
LATER LEPTOLITHIC	**PAVLOVIAN** **MAGDALENIAN**		Predmostí, Dolni Vestonice, Pavlov, Chancelade, Le Roc de Sers, St Germain and many others	*sapiens*

one before Holstein; and before that the Cromerian and Tiglian with no traces of man in most of Europe.

Between these warm periods the climate was cooler and fluctuated. There were ice advances; the last called Weichsel was not so extensive as the two ice advances between the Eem and Holstein which have been grouped under the name Saale; most extensive of all was the Elster, which preceded the Holstein. Ice advances before the Cromerian were probably much less extensive for all trace of them has been destroyed or buried. Only molluscs and vegetation typical of a cool climate identify two earlier cold periods which were complex and probably very long indeed. The names most usually used for the cold periods are those proposed by Penck and his associates from evidence on the northern slopes of the Alps. These names and those of the warmer periods are given above, and a very tentative estimate of their commencement, with the method used for its establishment, is given also. The only date which is well established is that of the rapid retreat of the last glacial ice from northern Europe, and its replacement by coniferous and more recently deciduous forests. The warmest time is not the present but the

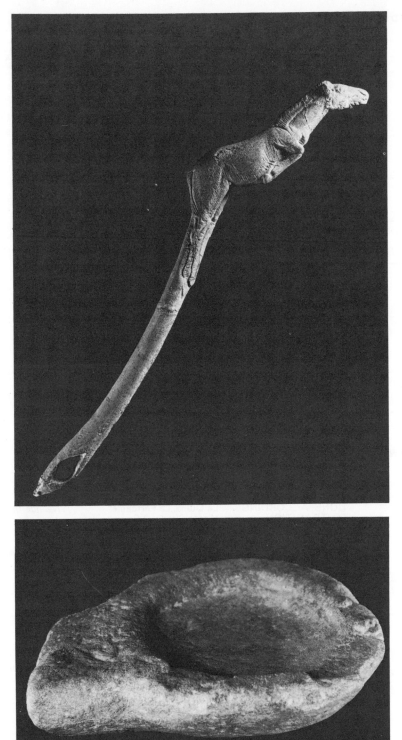

37. Bone spear-thrower with a carved horse. Bruniquel.

beginning of the so-called Atlantic period about 5000 B.C.

FOSSIL MAN AND RACES

The fossil remains of our ancestors and near ancestors are still very rare, usually fragmentary and difficult to date. Opinions about them are sharply divided, most frequently over the issue of whether individual specimens belong to extinct lines or to ancestral species. The Linnaean terminology is difficult to apply with confidence, and placing fossil finds in a new genus and species tends to prejudice their evolutionary position.

A typical example of such a controversy is over the remains from India called Ramapithecus. They and possibly identical fossils found in Europe and Asia date from some 5–15 million years ago, and an African fossil possibly of the same group dates back to 25 million years. Some authorities now believe these fossils to belong to a group ancestral to man but not to the living apes. This makes them into what we term hominids (or Hominidae). The hominids of the Pleistocene age are listed in the chart of physical types.

Prior to the Cromerian age the fossils are African, and Australopithecus africanus is the best known as a possible ancestor. A more numerous group called Australopithecus (Paranthropus) robustus is known to be part of a separate but related line specialising in the vegetable diet which is more normal for the apes. Human fossil finds from Olduvai Gorge probably date from well over a million years ago. The most abundant type here is almost certainly ancestral to modern races and according to some it belongs to the species Australopithecus africanus. From about 500,000 years ago hominids are found in Asia and Europe as well —the volcanic strata of Java and the fossil beds near Peking and Heidelberg being good examples. These fossils

38. MAGDALENIAN. Stone lamp in which animal fats were used. *Musée de l'Homme, Paris.*

CLIMATE	PERIOD	COMMENCEMENT (years ago)	MEANS OF ESTIMATION
Cold	**Donau**	2–2½ million	Potassium-Argon (abbrev. K/Ar)
Warm	**Tiglian**	Possibly about 1,200,000	Extrapolation and inferred K/Ar
Cold	**Günz**	Possibly about 950,000	Extrapolation
Warm	**Cromerian**	Possibly about 650,000	Extrapolation
Cold	**Mindel**	500–550,000	Potassium–Argon and faunal indications
Warm	**Holstein**	250–300,000	Amount of faunal and floral change
Cold	**Riss**	Possibly 200,000	Pa/Th
Warm	**Eem**	105,000	Pa/Th
Cold	**Würm (last) Glacial**	75,000	C.14 and Pa/Th
Warm	**Post-Glacial**	10,000	C.14 and varve (silt layer) counting

TEMPERATURE CURVE (Tentative Reconstruction) ←WARM COLD→	AGE in millennia	GLACIAL OR INTERGLACIAL PERIOD	MAIN CULTURAL GROUPS AND TRADITIONS
	250	**HOLSTEIN** Penultimate Interglacial	CLACTONIAN
	200		ACHEULIAN
			LEVALLOIS FLAKING INCREASES
	150	**RISS** Penultimate Glaciation	? CLACTONIAN DEVELOPING INTO CHARENTIAN TRADITION HIGH LODGE SURVIVING ACHEULIAN IN NORTH FRANCE AND BRITAIN
	100	**EEMIAN** Last Interglacial	EHRINGSDORF CHARENTIAN RARE ACHEULIAN FINAL ACHEULIAN
	50	**WÜRM** Last Glaciation	CHARENTIAN LA FERRASSIE AND LA QUINA AND CORDIFORM HAND-AXE MOUSTERIAN
			SZELETIAN AURIGNACIAN PERIGORDIAN SOLUTREAN MAGDALENIAN
	0		

have recently been grouped as Homo erectus.

By the time we reach Steinheim and Swanscombe man of the Holstein interglacial, the size of the brain has risen to that at the lower limit of modern populations and the tooth size has fallen also to near the modern size. They are often thought to mark the first Homo sapiens populations.

But fossil skulls remain varied in their appearance and in their frequency of occurrence down to the last glaciation. The best known group are the buried cave men of western Europe, sometimes called Neanderthals. Their position in human evolution is in dispute. Such features as heavy brow ridges and receding chins do not disappear from the record until after the middle of the last glaciation, and even then we are not sure how rapidly or why they disappeared.

Some workers believe that the beginning of the emergence of the major races is as early as Peking man. Others believe it is very recent indeed. The skulls associated with the Szeletian are the most reliably known early Leptolithic skulls and they appear to have European features already 30,000 years ago. Negroid and Eskimo affinities have been claimed for skeletons from Grimaldi and Chancelade, but most authorities are sceptical of the existence of such races in western Europe during the last glaciation.

Skeletal material is more frequent from the close of the last glaciation and from the post-glacial and this includes wide headed or brachycephalic peoples, possibly related to the so-called Alpine physical type of modern Europe. Nordic and Mediterranean physical types have also been identified tentatively, from this late period.

STAGES OF CULTURAL EVOLUTION

Archaeologists customarily divide Stone Age peoples into those who practise farming and food production (called Neolithic), and those who had not yet reached this type of economy and still lived by hunting and gathering food. Sometimes the latter people are subdivided into the post-glacial 'Mesolithic stage' peoples of the northern forests and the 'Palaeolithic stage' people of the preceding glacials and interglacials who more often hunted big game and herd animals. Now we know that farming began in some places about the time of the close of the last glaciation so that the Mesolithic stage, if we admit it at all, is only local.

The oldest well-defined stone tool cultural stage is the Oldowan of Africa, probably lasting more than a million years before tool making became well established in most of Europe and Asia. Because the bifacial handaxe was so characteristic of early man in western Europe this was once thought to be the mark of a Lower Palaeolithic stage, which gave way to a Middle Palaeolithic stage in which flake tools were rather commoner. This was best represented by the Mousterian culture or complex as we would now regard it— the material culture of the cave dwellers of the first half of the last glaciation.

Later in the last glaciation the manufacture of blades and highly characteristic stone points and chisels became common. This has been called Upper Palaeolithic or Leptolithic, and it is important because the evidence of art and magic become characteristic in some areas. Post-glacial peoples of Europe often made small barbs of flint called microliths, and these along with tree felling axes are the hallmark of the Mesolithic. Then the polishing of stone axes is one of the commonest features of the earliest farmers in the Neolithic stage which followed. Most of them in Europe had pottery and weaving also,

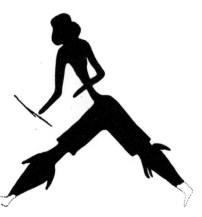

39. Women with plumed or feathered head-dresses. Valltorta.

40. A warrior wearing trousers. Painted in red. Cave of Secans (Teruel).

41. Frieze that includes women wearing skirts. Cogul (Lérida).

but the very earliest farmers (from about 8000 B.C.) were without pottery until its introduction about 5000 B.C.

SOCIAL AND ECONOMICAL LIFE

From early in the Pleistocene, man made tools of stone and probably of wood and bone as well. Fire seems to have been introduced about 300,000 years ago (in the Mindel phase). It was probably the widespread use of fire which made the occupation of caves feasible; certainly in the Riss period and very commonly in the last glacial period, they served as homes. No doubt when the coldness of the weather demanded it skin cloaks and shelters were made.

The wooden spear was in use in the Holstein period, and stone tipped spears probably from the Eem period onwards. Somehow or other big game was hunted even as early as the Mindel period. An important practice is found with the Neanderthal populations of the last glacial or of even earlier date, for they performed careful burials and left elementary grave offerings.

Although caves, when available, remained the main places of occupation throughout the last glacial period, simple open air dwellings, either tents or tent-like huts, were used as well from 30,000 years ago, and by about 25,000 B.C. some hunters of central Europe began to congregate at mammoth slaughter sites into aggregations of huts which we must call villages. Not long after we may be sure that skin clothing was already being sewn in the sophisticated manner of tailored fur suits still

being used by Arctic peoples, for we have found their needles and piercers. A rich diet of meat from wild herd animals probably kept the hunters healthy, supplemented in most cases by only a little vegetable food.

Fire was universally possessed by the later cave dwellers and we have lamps [38] used in penetrating the dark recesses of the cave. The spear thrower [37] was probably the most effective hunting device before the introduction of the bow [1, 13] at the close of the last glaciation.

During the Mesolithic, when the herd game was not usually available in Europe, some communities collected shell fish as their diet or took to fowling and fishing and other less spectacular forms of food gathering. They also domesticated the dog. Some idea of the clothes worn in the late Palaeolithic or Mesolithic can be gained from the charming rock paintings of Mediterranean Spain [39–41]; these included skirts and trousers. They however are not typical of the tundra hunters for they hunted animals of the temperate zone, and were partly naked like the American Indians.

The mode of life changed drastically when animal and plant domestication was discovered. The most important result was settled living in villages. Nowhere was the change earlier and of more consequence than in western Asia, for here the most suitable plants and animals for domestication occurred in their wild form. It probably began in some areas such as northern Iraq before 8000 B.C.

After some two million years of hunting the change to food production

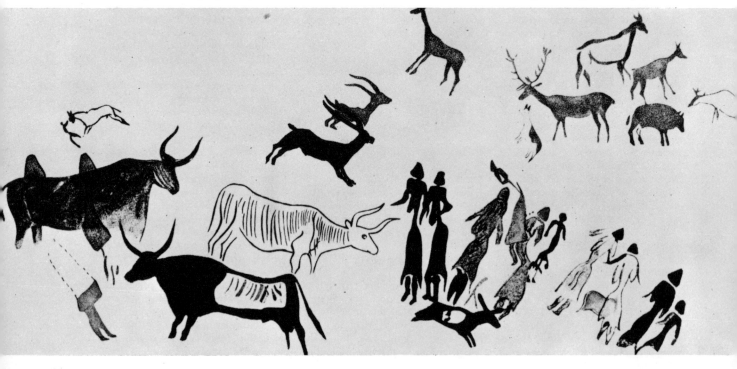

was final; there was to be no return to a hunting economy. Instead the tribal society with its respected chief began to disappear under the new conditions. The accumulation of domestic herds, surplus grain and household possessions made raiding and warfare profitable for the first time. Some farmers solved the problem of an expanding population by cultivating new lands, displacing the hunters and exploiting their territory many times more intensively. Others used the fertile plains of the dry subtropics and increased their yield by irrigation. But the irrigation had to be planned and the organiser wanted to ensure recognition of his services. Suddenly his natural allies were a new class of warriors or brigands. Fortified settlements like Jericho appeared in the valleys of the Levant, Turkey and Mesopotamia before 6000 B.C. A complicated and rigorously maintained hierarchy became the social pattern of suitable parts of Africa, Asia and later America. It was headed by the ruler, his warriors and the scribes essential for calculating the flood times, cataloguing the accumulating wealth and re-allocating the land after floods. Below these were the craftsmen, the farmers and lastly the slaves—more numerous than all the others together; but some fluidity of rank remained to meet the new and ever quickening developments which became the inevitable fate of a society suddenly geared to invention and technological advance. Civilisation had arrived. Its usual hallmarks, such as writing and monumental art, were in vogue by 3000 B.C.

THE ART OF HUNTING PEOPLES OF EARLY TIMES

THE CONTEXT OF THE ART OF THE LAST GLACIATION

Almost all of the famous cave paintings which date from the Ice Age, as well as many of the more significant art objects of comparable date, come from quite a small area of south-western France and northern Spain. In much thinner density evidence of Ice Age art is found elsewhere in western and central Europe including Italy, and it is well represented in certain parts of the U.S.S.R.

For reasons not entirely understood, but most probably related to a unique abundance of game, the richness of glacial age occupation in certain valleys of south-west France is unparalleled elsewhere and these peoples were the finest artists. In particular the occupation sites of a short stretch of the Vézère valley in the Dordogne département have revealed a series of superimposed culture strata sometimes totalling many feet thick, which have en-

abled a sequence of culture types to be established. Attempts to date Palaeolithic art have been largely directed to attaching art material to a particular culture stage in this sequence. As a result of modern work the sequence is recognised roughly as follows:

CULTURE TYPE	APPROXIMATE DATE OF END IN YEARS B.C.
Mousterian (various types)	35–40,000
Early Perigordian	30–35,000
Typical Aurignacian (4 stages)	c. 25,000
Later Perigordian (several types)	c. 20,000
Protomagdalenian	c. 19,000
Final Aurignacian (stage V)	c. 18,500
Solutrean (several stages)	c. 16,000
Magdalenian (6 stages)	c. 10,000
Azilian	7–8,000

The extent to which such a sequence is valid in other areas than the Vézère is not at present agreed; but as near as the Rhône valley and certainly in Czechoslovakia we find cultural types unrepresented in the Vézère. For the present, the actual age in years as estimated from radiocarbon or other indications is a better method of comparison of widely scattered art finds and styles. Since animals form a major part of the subject matter, deductions on the

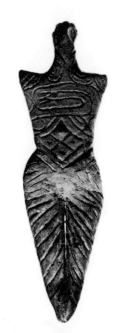

42. Terra-cotta figurine from Cucuteni (Rumania). *National Museum of Antiquities, Bucharest.*

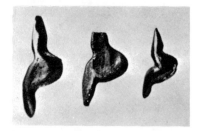

43. Mammoth carved on a spear-thrower. Bruniquel. *British Museum.*

44. Stylised female figures carved in lignite. The largest figure is 1¾ in. Petersfels.

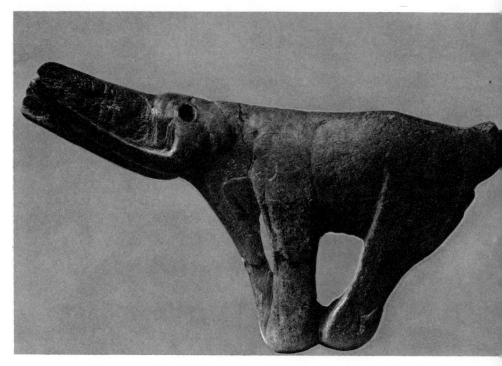

45

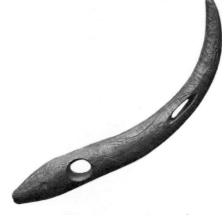

45. *Bâton de commandement* of reindeer-horn, decorated with a horse and masked figures. Teyjat.

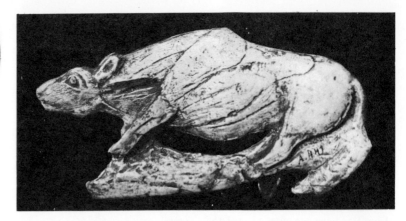

46. Hyena rampant. Fragments of an ivory spear-thrower. La Madeleine.

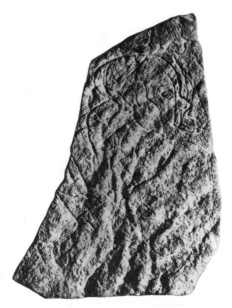

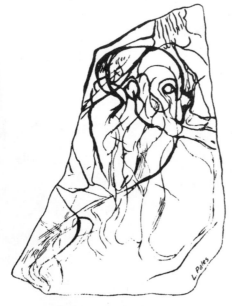

47. Profile of a man, engraved on schist. La Marche, Lussac-les-Châteaux. *Musée de l'Homme, Paris. Reproduction of the engraving by Dr Léon Pales.*

climate at the time the art was executed constitute a further possible line of approach. Finally several authorities have attempted to use the style of the art to build us a sequence of artistic development [**10, 11, 12, 17**]; the most famous of these was Breuil who has set out his views in an earlier section, and relies mainly on the assumption that satisfactory perspective was not at first achieved.

Two simple methods of establishing the Pleistocene antiquity of mural art exist, but both are very imprecise. Firstly there are unmistakable representations of animals which became extinct towards the close of the last glaciation; secondly a covering of stalactite may seal part of the picture [**30**]. The most reliable way to solve the problem of the antiquity of the earliest art comes from the recovery of small portable art objects sealed in place on living floors of known antiquity.

Analysis of the earliest occurrence of artistically carved objects does not entirely solve the problem of the birth of art. Some would regard the early stone tools of man as art, and the Neanderthal burials may well imply ritual of a kind which would normally qualify as art. Here we are up against the problem of the definition of art. Another case relevant in this context is that of body painting which is characteristic of surviving hunting peoples. In the closing stages of the Mousterian complex we find evidence for crayons of limonite ochre and manganese which have been used in colouring. By analogy it was probably in painting the human body that they were mainly employed. They are poor evidence for the beginning of art, but provide just the indications of a transitional stage to true art that one might expect.

DATED ART OBJECTS

On any interpretation of the meaning of art, some of the discoveries made in deposits of the earliest part of the Typical Aurignacian must qualify for inclusion. They are probably over 30,000 years old. A large stone from the Belcayre rock shelter has a shallow and crude engraving of a reindeer, and a similar rock from the Cellier shelter has the horns of an ibex engraved on it. By far the commonest and probably the earliest art motif is the subtriangular form with a pronounced cut across its narrower end, which has usually been interpreted as a vulvar symbol. Aurignacian sites in south-west France which have revealed such pieces are numerous: Castanet, Blanchard, Cellier, Poisson, Laussel, Les Rois, La Ferrassie are a few examples. The ibex and reindeer depictions quoted above are among only a few unquestionable pieces of representational art, and the animals from later Aurignacian stages at La Ferrassie do not bring the total of reliably dated Aurignacian animal representations very high. Accordingly it would probably be a mistake to attribute much undated wall art to this phase.

In central and eastern Europe where mural art is almost unknown the very earliest manifestations of art are probably as early as in western Europe. A carved ivory figure from Brno in Czechoslovakia, unfortunately broken, comes from a burial most probably of the Szeletian culture, and a painted horse from Sungir near Moscow is associated with a burial of a related culture type. Both are probably over 30,000 years old; both were found with burials over which red ochre had been strewn liberally. This demonstrates not only the collection of pigments, but also religious ritual, in all probability a cult directed at restoring vitality with the aid of life-giving blood, symbolically represented by the ochre. Again associated with both these burials and the earliest strata of the west is evidence of necklaces and other strings of shells, beads and pendants carved from bone, ivory and various stones.

The next horizon of the Vézère which has produced a characteristic art is a phase of the later Perigordian group, characterised by a special diminutive engraving tool, the de Noailles burin. This horizon is later than the 'Gravette' level called Perigordian IV and earlier than a final Perigordian level (VI). This is the horizon to which some of the famous female statuettes, called by archaeologists Venuses, belong—notably Tursac and Lespugue [**9**]. The very similar bas-relief carvings from Laussel [**24**] are probably the work of the same artists.

Venuses are commoner outside France, in Austria for example at Willendorf [**5**], and at the great mammoth hunters' camps of Dolní Věstonice in Czechoslovakia and Kostenki in south Russia. These examples span the time of the later Perigordian of the Vézère. As superbly exemplified in Willendorf, the female statuettes have the sexual regions, breasts, buttocks and stomachs accentuated, and other parts depicted smaller or not at all—the feet, arms and faces. Some have the fatty growth of the buttock region called steatopygia. Venuses have been found further east across Asiatic Russia at Buret and Malta, but the age of these may be later. They are considered in the section on Asia. Small models of animals similar to the Venuses are found at many of the central and east European sites. The ivories of Vogelherd are probably the earliest and include mammoth and horse. Mammoths are also known from Pavlov, Kostenki and other sites. Like the Venuses the raw material may be stone, ivory or even a kind of pottery.

Art objects have been found in strata of both the final Perigordian and Protomagdalenian at the important site of Laugerie Haute, but neither of these cultural types is at all frequent. A number of small engraved objects of Solutrean date from sites like Bade-

goule and Isturitz are important; but several examples of large scale bas-reliefs, once part of friezes along the cliffs, can be reliably included in the late Solutrean cultural province—notably Roc de Sers [**51**] and Fourneau du Diable [**53**]. Other cultural branches of the Solutrean group in south-east Spain at Parpalló and the Ardèche canyon of south-east France practised art.

By far the most abundant domestic art is that of the Magdalenian culture.

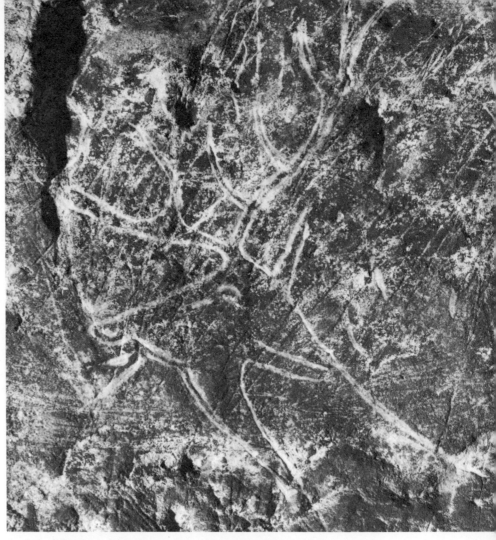

48. Engraved deer's head. Lascaux.

More specifically it is from the late part, stages Magdalenian IV–VI that such 'mobiliary' art is characteristic—in years about 13,000 to 10,000 B.C. Some of this is bone and ivory, engraved or carved in a purely decorative way; other objects are strictly functional like spear throwers [**37**, **43**], javelin heads as well as a variety of batons. Such material is abundant not only in the Vézère region but especially in the Pyrenees and the Charente, and further afield in the vicinity of Lake Constance

49. Bones carved with abstract motifs. Isturitz.

50. Carved fish. Abri Poisson, Gorge d'Enfer. Les Eyzies.

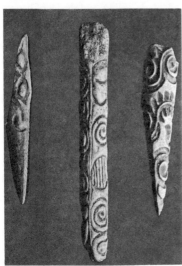

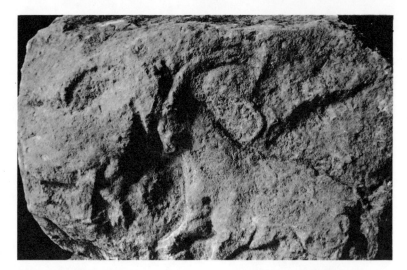

51. SOLUTREAN. Bas-relief showing two ibexes fighting. Roc de Sers. *Musée de l'Homme, Paris.*

52. MAGDALENIAN IV. Bison modelled in clay. Tuc d'Audoubert.

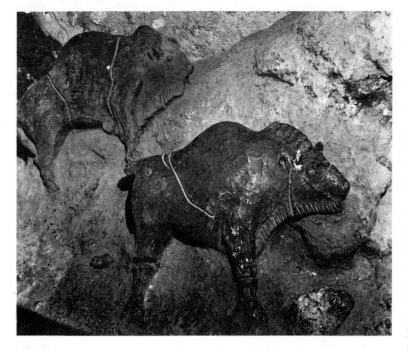

to the Solutrean. Wall art from rock shelters, but not hitherto from cave interiors, can be inferred as early as the Aurignacian from Castanet and La Ferrassie (paintings) as well as Belcayre and Cellier (carvings quoted above). It is also to be inferred from the de Noailles stage of the Perigordian on the evidence from fragments of paintings from Labattut and possibly the carved fish of Abri Poisson [**50**]. Many people believe that simple smeared lines [possibly **28**] and hand silhouettes from Pech-Merle and Gargas [**2**] in France, Castillo in northern Spain and a new discovery from Paglicci cave in Italy are pre-Solutrean. It has long been claimed that engravings at Pair-non-Pair were covered by deposits spanning the later Perigordian onwards, but this claim like similar ones over Hornos de la Peña lacks adequate assurance, and the strata are too imperfectly known for precise dating.

Nevertheless mural art is the most spectacular achievement of Palaeolithic man and much of it is regarded as Magdalenian. Bas-reliefs from Cap Blanc and Anglessur-l'Anglin are Magdalenian III; but mural paintings are outstandingly difficult to date. The Altamira paintings may well be contemporary with the 13,000 B.C. Magdalenian III culture strata adjacent and the Lascaux paintings may be contemporary with the 15,000 B.C. (and possibly Magdalenian II) strata from part of the cave interior. Fine engravings from Gabillou are probably of stage III from the associated cultural material. Indeed the distribution of large scale mural art and the Magdalenian III are so similar that it may be all attributable to this phase or the immediately adjacent periods.

The exceedingly fine engravings from Teyjat are apparently Magdalenian IV or early V since the stage V strata partly covered them. Some of the paintings are well preserved and include red, black, yellow and shades of brown and purple. When found together on the same animal as at Altamira this is called polychrome. Apart from animals no other recurrent motif is known except enigmatic symbols, possibly traps. Most authorities believe that the pictures are intended to be individual animals and not true composite scenes.

MASTERPIECES

Some sites such as Lascaux, Font de Gaume, Les Combarelles, Altamira and the east Pyrenean cave group are often classed apart as masterpieces.

Lascaux was discovered as recently as 1940 but has deteriorated in the last few years. The animal pictures are large and abundant—mainly aurochs, horse

between Switzerland and Germany. Portable art is not common in Magdalenian I or even stages II and III; but mural art is almost certainly characteristic of stage III.

The motifs vary. Curvilinear and spirals forms [**49**] are rare but significant; geometric forms [**8**] very rare indeed. Plant motifs are also rare. Zoomorphic motifs form the great majority where the subject matter can be identified. In the closing stages of the Magdalenian human figures, often male and badly drawn [**47**], again become frequent after a gap in western Europe of 10,000 years or so after the Venus period. Female figures reappear also in the Magdalenian VI of Couze and Lalinde. They are sufficiently distinctive not to be confused with the Venuses of earlier times. Further close

parallels are Fontales in southern France and Hohlenstein in Bavaria. It is to this phase that the Petersfels statuettes [**44**] should be referred; the treatment of the buttocks in silhouette is particularly characteristic. At its best the animal carving is superb [**32, 46**]. Some objects from this period [**3**] as well as supposedly late mural pictures may indicate hunting magic, specifically popular at this time.

EARLY MURAL ART

None of the painting and engraving on the walls of cave interiors as known today can be reliably dated to any specific phase before the Magdalenian III. The Solutrean bas-reliefs were presumably part of mural friezes, but no paintings can be dated beyond question

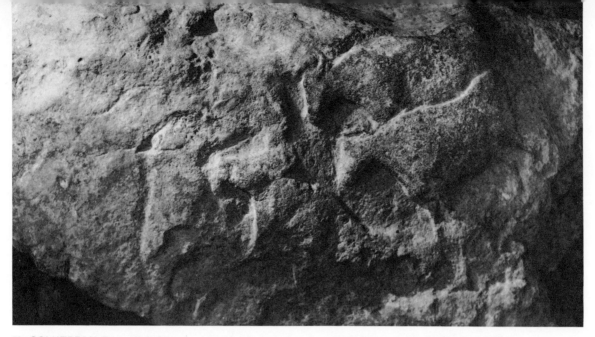

53. SOLUTREAN. Bas-relief of two bovine animals carved on limestone. Fourneau du Diable, Bourdeilles.

54. MAGDALENIAN. Bison wounded by arrows. Painted in black. Niaux.

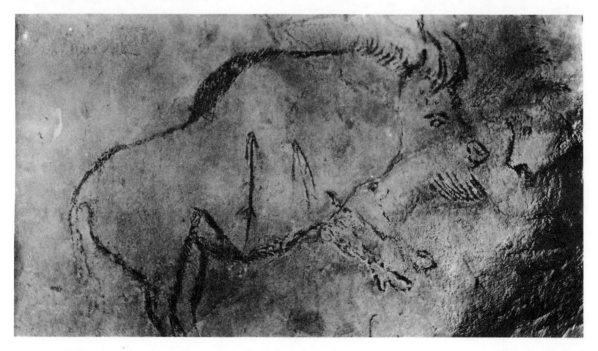

and deer [25]. An unidentifiable animal [26] sometimes called the unicorn may be seen among otherwise easily recognised animals. The unusual group of bison, rhinoceros and man [17], found in a shaft, is the nearest to a composite picture known. The animals have spears in or on them.

Les Combarelles contains very numerous but not easily seen engravings; horses are the commonest and bison second most frequent. The pictures have been known since 1901 and are usually regarded as Magdalenian [27].

Font de Gaume is characterised by polychrome bison and some mammoths. They are deep in the cave. Near the entrance of the cave archaeological material of many different periods has been found. The painting style is very

close to that of Altamira and usually regarded as Magdalenian.

Altamira is the painted cave which has been longest known. Bison are the most frequently depicted animals, but horse, deer, wolf and boar also occur. It is difficult to see the main series of paintings together adequately, since they stretch as much as 45 feet across the very low ceiling of the great hall [29]. Solutrean deposits are found here, as well as those of the Magdalenians, who were probably responsible for the paintings.

Niaux is the first of the Pyrenean group to be enumerated below. It has many black paintings, and as at Lascaux spears or arrows are commonly shown in the animals [54]. The pictures are especially far from the entrance of the cave and bison and horse are charac-

teristic. The clay floor has also been engraved in places and the inclusion of a fish here is rather special. The depiction of animals with spears on them is widely regarded as a form of hunting magic. Portable statuettes with spear holes as that from Isturitz [3] seem to fix this practice in Magdalenian times.

Les Trois Frères includes the painting of a man dressed in animal disguise [4], possibly a sorcerer—which does seem to confirm the notion of hunting magic, as do the speared horse from Le Portel [6] and the speared bear from Montespan found in nearby caves. Another sorcerer may be intended in the large panels of engravings from Les Trois Frères [1].

Tuc d'Audoubert is famed for its clay relief models of two bison [52] presumably of the same general age as

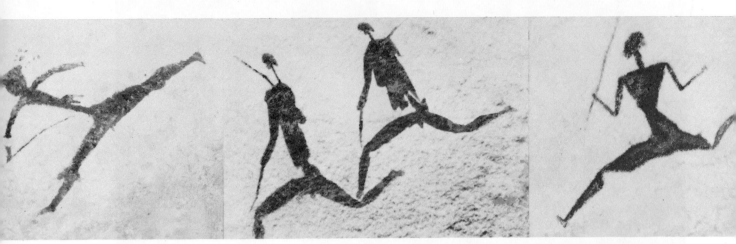

55. Painted figures of running men. *Left to right:* Valltorta Gorge; Ghat (Fezzan); painting by Bushmen (South Africa). All are in a similar style.

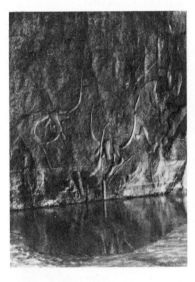

56. Bulls' heads engraved on rock. Tassili des Ajjers (Sahara).

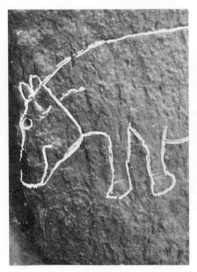

57a. Engraved hippopotamus. Tassili des Ajjers (Sahara).

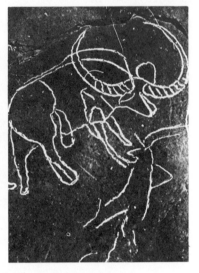

57b. Buffalo hunt. Rock engraving. Tassili des Ajjers (Sahara).

the other east Pyrenean cave art, and similar to bison carvings of known Magdalenian date. The bison seems to have been a favourite hunting animal of the Magdalenians.

EARLY MEDITERRANEAN ART

Two art styles originated by hunters living in the Mediterranean area are known. One in Italy is certainly as old as the end of the last glaciation, but the other found in Mediterranean Spain may be a little more recent. The engraved art of Italy and Sicily is the work of the Romanellian culture of about 9000 B.C. and includes large hunt animals like horse and aurochs. A large scene from Addaura consists of humans. The Romanellian style is characterised by very fine line engraving.

Possibly the most fascinating and informative of all art of prehistoric date is that of the Mediterranean provinces of Spain, notably Castellón, Albacete

and Teruel. This is called the Spanish Levant group. Some authorities believe that the art tradition here derived from the Magdalenian, but the general character of the painting is quite different, consisting of scenes—animals and humans together, usually silhouettes painted in red or black. These pictures [**13**, **31a**, **41**] are uniquely informative on such details as clothes and weapons. They include scenes which seem to be war dances and an execution. The Cogul woman frieze is one of the best known and as many as thirteen superimposed phases have been claimed from Minateda. A certain resemblance to African rock art [**55**] is often noted. A date as early as 8000 B.C. is possible.

Desmond Collins

AFRICAN ART

North Africa and the Sahara. Throughout the Sahara from Hoggar, Tassili and Tibesti to the Fezzan, and in

Libya, rock paintings and engravings are numerous [**56**, **57**, **59**]. One finds these subjects: animals such as elephants, giraffes and buffaloes, all abundant in this rich and humid region in prehistoric times; domestic animals such as sheep and cattle (sometimes with a circle between the horns); men, frequently disguised with horns, feathers, a tail. This art is essentially narrative, animated, even humorous. It describes the daily life of the buffalo-hunters—older than the Amratians of Egypt—and of the cattle-keepers. These longhorned cattle, painted in only slightly twisted perspective, similar to those of the Spanish Levant, originated, according to Abbé Breuil, in Abyssinia. The analogies between this Saharan art and Spanish rock art are important.

These paintings, at first markedly naturalistic (between 5000 and 3500 B.C.), gradually evolved towards a decadent stylisation. After a transitional period, a Libyan rock art appeared much later, evidence of a civilisation

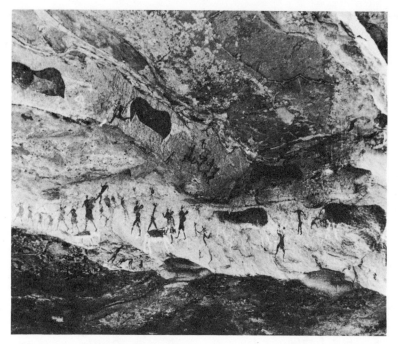

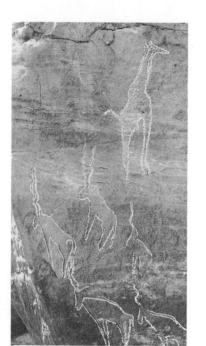

58. Large frieze painted on rock by Bushmen. Giant's Castle Game Reserve, Natal.

59. Engraved antelope and a giraffe. Wadi Mazanda (Fezzan).

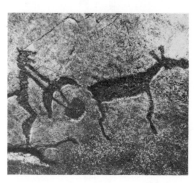

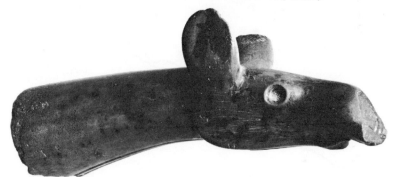

60. Figure of a sorcerer. Lake Onega (U.S.S.R.).

61. Head of an elk in stone. Sakkijärvi

acquainted with the horse and the chariot: for example, those astonishing engravings of a chariot 'at a flying gallop' at Tassili and Ahaggar (1300 B.C.?).

East Africa. There is a hiatus between Saharan art and the art of South Africa which the painted rocks of Lake Victoria, in northern Tanganyika, do not fill. Still not very well known, the most archaic paintings represent elephants, rhinoceroses and buffaloes. Subsequently human scenes appeared, but with no signs of livestock-raising. L.S.B. Leakey distinguishes eight stylistic series among them.

South Africa. The South African Neolithic continued until the arrival of the Europeans. In the 19th century the Bushmen were still making rock engravings and paintings according to archaic traditions.

This survival of a prehistoric art resembling that of southern Europe is one of the mysteries of prehistory. In southern Rhodesia archaeologists have

defined four series of paintings. In the Union of South Africa [58] Abbé Breuil has found sixteen series of paintings and four series of engravings. The problem remains of the relation of this art to the art of the cattle-keepers of the Sahara and North Africa, and beyond that to the paintings of the Spanish Levant [31a, 31b]. Undoubtedly they stem from a common tradition (Gordon Childe).

ARCTIC MURAL ART

In northern Scandinavia, Finland and the U.S.S.R. there are numerous mural paintings and engravings differing widely from the art of southern Scandinavia, which is stylised and dates from the later Bronze Age. In Scandinavia there are two groups of works: the more naturalistic and older group of the extreme north of Sweden and Norway; the group from eastern Norway and southern Sweden, with more stylised and more recent works.

In the U.S.S.R. there are two regions: in Karelia on the shores of Lake Onega [60]; in Siberia on the upper Yenisei.

This Arctic art, with a profusion of engravings but poorer in paintings (which are in red, violet and brown tones), has similarities to the art of the fisher-hunters of Palaeolithic Europe: fertility magic; sympathetic magic; siting on inaccessible rocks (in remote fjords, in this case). The animals represented (reindeer, elk, seals, fish, reptiles) are often of large dimensions. Men are rare and are sometimes masked (in the U.S.S.R.). Boats sometimes appear with an elk's head at the prow. Abstract signs and meandering parallel lines similar to those of Mezine and the eastern sites of the Aurignacian are found along with the animals. These last characteristics are evidence of origins not in Europe, but in the Oriental Upper Palaeolithic. Scandinavian authors place this belated Stone Age art between 5000 and 1500 B.C. [61].

Lydie Huyghe

51

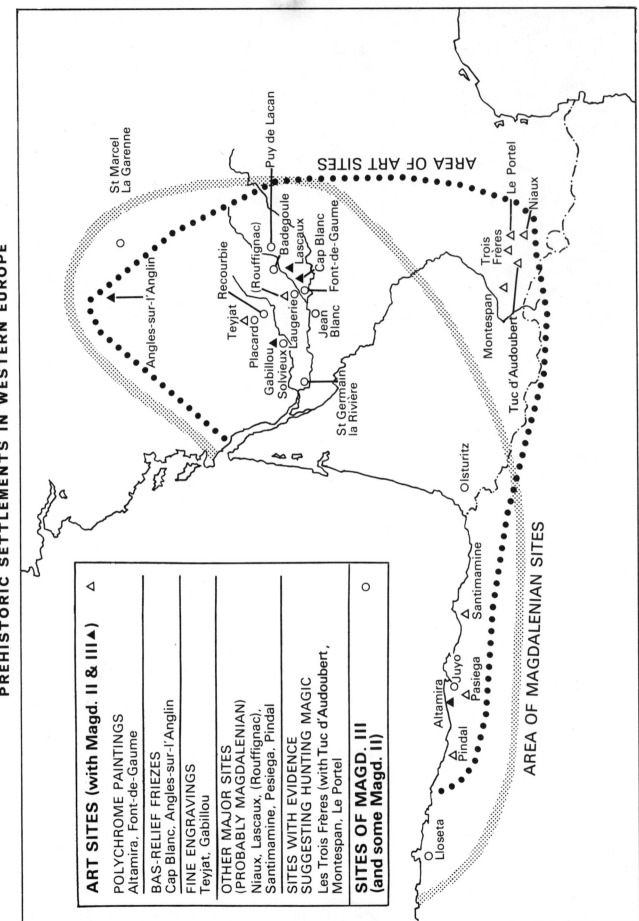

ART SITES (with Magd. II & III ▲)

POLYCHROME PAINTINGS
Altamira, Font-de-Gaume

BAS-RELIEF FRIEZES
Cap Blanc, Angles-sur-l'Anglin

FINE ENGRAVINGS
Teyjat, Gabillou

OTHER MAJOR SITES
(PROBABLY MAGDALENIAN)
Niaux, Lascaux, (Rouffignac),
Santimamine, Pesiega, Pindal

SITES WITH EVIDENCE
SUGGESTING HUNTING MAGIC
Les Trois Frères (with Tuc d'Audoubert,
Montespan, Le Portel

SITES OF MAGD. III
(and some Magd. II)

AREA OF ART SITES

AREA OF MAGDALENIAN SITES

St Marcel
La Garenne

Puy de Lacan

Le Portel
Niaux

Badegoule
Lascaux

(Rouffignac)

Cap Blanc
Font-de-Gaume

Recourbie

Trois
Frères

Teyjat

Placard

Jean
Blanc

Montespan

Angles-sur-l'Anglin

Gabillou
Solvieux

Laugerie

Tuc d'Audoubert

St Germain
la Rivière

Isturitz

Altamira

Juyo
Pasiega

Santimamine

Lloseta

Pindal

FROM THE NEOLITHIC TO
THE EARLY BRONZE AGE *André Varagnac*

*Europe's slower development enables us to follow the
progressive stages leading from the age of chipped stone
to that of polished stone and to the first appearance of
metal. Art forms change with the changes in society.*

It is a thankless task to write about Neolithic and Early
Bronze Age art in Europe: the subject disappears universally from general histories of art, so intense is the brilliance of the Near East and the eastern Mediterranean at
the same epochs.

Since all light comes from an irradiating source, we
look for the 'hearths' of civilisation and, paraphrasing the
language of elementary physics, we might suppose that
the degree of culture of different peoples is in inverse
proportion to the distance separating them from these
hearths. If this was so, why should we worry about the
faint gleams, the marginal flickers?

But there is another conception of the achievements of
civilisation and consequently of the arts. Ethnography,
associated with prehistory, has made us familiar with the
idea that since the appearance of Homo sapiens no human
activity has been totally devoid of aesthetic features, at
least not until the expansion of our industrial civilisations.
Mass production was needed to make ugliness our normal
background, for everything which is truly hand-made has
some aesthetic value, however slight.

Art and climate

Thus new problems arise, the first of which is whether
there is a link between art forms and climatic conditions.
In the 3rd millennium (the second half of which saw the
penetration of continental Europe by eastern and southern
cultures) Egypt and Mesopotamia had already produced
great figurative masterpieces, and the Minoan civilisation
was in full flower. But the arts of Neolithic Europe
63 showed a tendency to extreme geometrical stylisation and
to abstract compositions.

During the Mesolithic, Europe acquired the three
climates which it has today. They are distinguished by
their flora. North of Stockholm and Helsinki is the
coniferous forest, where the present-day Lapps still
follow a way of life recalling the Mesolithic; this line
winds through Russia and Siberia towards the mountains
of Mongolia, to end up at the Pacific near the top of
Sakhalin Island. Below this zone comes the temperate
zone with its forests of deciduous trees. It is bounded to
the south by the zone of trees which keep their leaves, of
which palm-trees are the most typical; this zone comprises the fringes of the Mediterranean, cuts Anatolia and
Iran in two, skirts the Himalayas, takes in Burma and
Tongking and turns north again from Canton to Shang-
hai.

Such is the climatic background against which the
great centres of Neolithic art were situated. European art
in the Neolithic was geometric nearly everywhere—the
Arctic zone alone held on to the style of the Upper
Palaeolithic. Representational art was mainly to arise in
the hot zone, whether in the Indies, the Near East or the
Mediterranean. Also, at the two extremities of Eurasia,
in China and the West, marginal influences periodically
introduced realistic styles; but even these figurative styles
were marked either by an abundance of geometrical
decoration or by a stylisation verging on the austere.

These peripheral influences were to prove extremely
important in Europe. It seems clear that primitive pastoral
and agricultural techniques reached northern China by
way of the neighbouring region of Lake Baikal: archaeological progress will tell us whether or not we can
attribute the origins of the curvilinear animal style (art
of the steppes) to this interpenetration of Neolithic men
and the Arctic hunters of Baikal. Nevertheless, it is true
that China was to set its definite mark on this style which
is recognisable in Western art both in the curvilinear and
animal ornamentation of the Celts and in the even more
figurative decoration of Romanesque capitals and illuminated manuscripts.

The Western contributions in the Neolithic were to
enrich Europe with an extremely stylised statuary, while 64–66
they were to establish for thousands of years the rectilinear
geometrical decoration of portable objects, which the
popular arts preserved up to the 20th century.

In the present chapter we are mainly going to discuss
art in the temperate zone of Eurasia. At first there were
relatively scattered populations with no urban agglo-
merations, of the type already existing in fairly large
numbers in the Near East during this second half of the
3rd millennium. The Mesolithic saw the progressive
disappearance in Europe of the rock art of the Upper
Palaeolithic; eventually nothing was left but the working
of bone and probably of wood together with the decoration of the painted pebbles. To this the Neolithic added 14
weaving and pottery, thus making up the group of
popular crafts whose primarily geometrical styles were
only to vary slightly up to the present day. But its main
contribution was the megalith, the first Western architectural style, in conjunction with which a new type of
sculpture was to appear.

The earliest European ceramics

It is important to realise the complexity of these phenomena in the Neolithic and the Early Bronze Age (whose
metal products, in most areas, were actually made of
copper). Undoubtedly the arts and crafts of these ages
came from the countries with a southern climate, but for
a real understanding of the history of European art we
should not be content merely to draw up a table of the
'spread of civilisation'. For this is the history of the reactions to such importations, of European originality—
an originality which would also be periodically reinforced
by Asian influences.

Towards the middle of the 2nd millennium, then, small
groups of crop-growers appeared in Europe in two
different sectors, while to the east of the Caspian and
Aral Seas, between Kazakhstan and Lake Baikal, other
pastoral and probably agricultural societies came on the
scene. Forest-clad Europe was attacked simultaneously

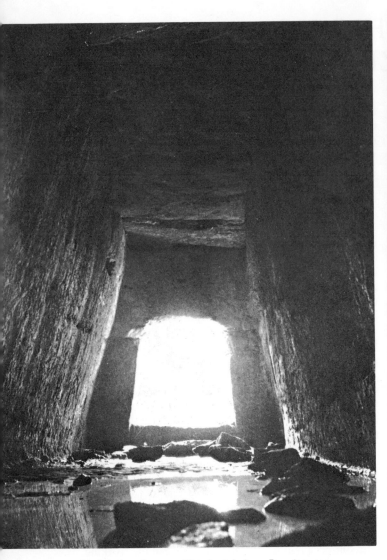

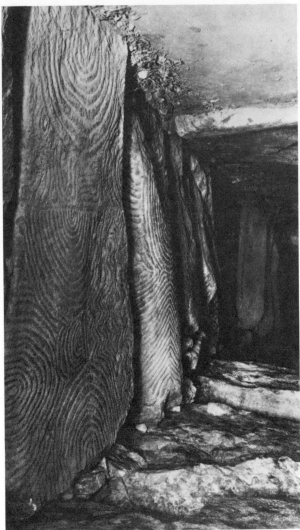

62. Interior of a megalithic burial place. Bounias, near Montmajour-lès-Arles.

63. Abstract designs engraved on the granite blocks of the tumulus at Gavr'inis (Morbihan).

from the south-east and the south-west. Ceramic techniques and decorations spread from Macedonia; some of them were diffused along the Black Sea towards the Ukraine in the direction of Kiev (the Tripolye culture), whereas others reached the central Danube and spread towards central Europe, the Rhine, and as far as Belgium 68 (the ribbon pottery culture). During this time, the Iberian Peninsula and probably Sardinia began to disseminate ceramics in the direction of French and Italian Liguria, some of which (the 'printed' pottery, with decorations made by the impressions of shells) were also native to North Africa, in particular to Mauretania, while others, of much finer materials and more elegant shapes, had hardly any forerunners except in the first agricultural settlements of pre-dynastic Egypt. This second type of pottery, which characterised the first Neolithic wave in the majority of French regions, has been called Chassey ware after the deposit at Camp de Chassey (Saône-et-Loire).

This over-all sketch calls for several observations. There were two ceramic families of quality—in the west, Chassey ware; in the east, a painted pottery which was found in a vast zone to the south and east of the Carpathians. The sweep of the curvilinear decorations of the

pottery of Cucuteni and Tripolye has been compared 67 with that of the first Chinese globular vases of Kansu and 85, 86 Honan. Possibly this may be accounted for by the advance of the steppe peoples, which was a prelude to Eurasian intercommunication.

The spread of the megalith civilisation

When we approach the study of megalithic monuments 18–20 we must bear in mind their original functions: dolmens were the houses of the dead; menhirs were erected to serve as receptacles for disembodied souls. Both are evidences of the first great religious civilisation, which was brought to the West from the East in the sailing ships which also brought the benefits of agriculture.

The detailed study of megaliths and their funerary 62 furniture is by no means completed. Specialists are only beginning to make out the general lines of the spread of megaliths in the West, at a time when it would be valuable to compare them with those of southern Russia and the Near East. At present we are probably right in thinking that a cultural penetration was primarily involved and only secondly a migration of peoples, for after linking together the stores of the Mediterranean, sailing ships, as from the end of the 3rd millennium, wove a network

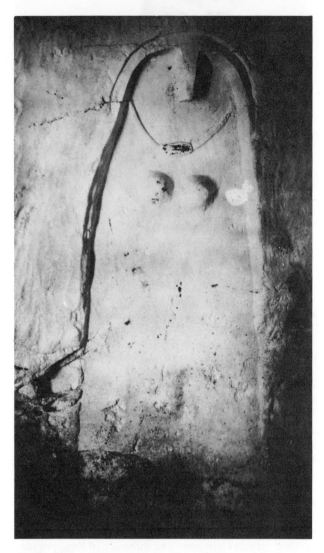

64. Neolithic goddess carved in the artificial sepulchral cave at Coizard (Marne).

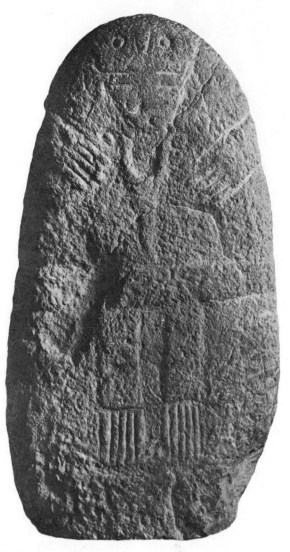

65. Female menhir statue. First half of the 2nd millennium. *Musée de St Germain.*

of exchange between Spain, the Atlantic coast of France, the British Isles, northern Germany and Scandinavia.

Dolmens are classified according to their architectural plan rather than to the objects composing their funerary furniture, for a religious edifice continues to be used and consequently periodically supplied with new religious objects. This method, advocated by Dr Glyn Daniel, leads us to summarise the development of Western megalithic architecture as follows.

A first cultural wave probably gave rise to the construction of dolmens consisting of one chamber, generally circular, preceded by a long narrower and lower corridor. This was the passage grave. It is extremely probable that it was spread by sea routes, for none of these momuments is more than sixty miles from the coast.

It seems that this first flowering was followed by a period of slow propagation, which was characterised by smaller monuments whose geographical distribution covered regions in the hinterland of the first districts. These small dolmens, consisting of a horizontal slab supported by others, are called simple dolmens, but, contrary to the theories of the first archaeologists, they were not elementary shapes but debasements of passage graves. Engraved or undecorated Chassey pottery is found along

with other ceramics in this type of megalith.

The third type, known as the gallery grave, is the only one not to yield any kind of funerary furniture: this time, therefore, a genuine migration was involved.

The menhir statues

These people were the creators of the sculptures to be found on a certain number of menhirs and in gallery graves or caves hollowed out of soft stone. Southern France has produced a fair number of menhir statues. The slabs of gallery graves from Brittany to Seine-et-Oise quite frequently exhibit a female effigy in bas-relief, a remarkably stylised face separated from the breasts by a 64 broad necklace with several rows of pearls. The funerary caves of the Marne afford similar representations. Certain engravings or carvings are purely geometrical. This is true of the Irish monument of New Grange and the slabs of the gallery grave at Gavr'inis (Morbihan). 63

The menhir statues represent human beings wearing ornaments and attributes which are mostly enigmatic. The face is carved in the upper ogive of the slab; the body is represented by projections standing out in low relief. The hands and feet are stylised to such an extent that the lower limbs were long interpreted as being stole flaps

55

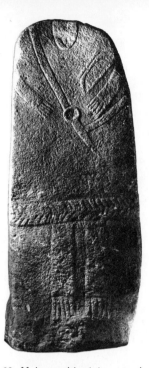

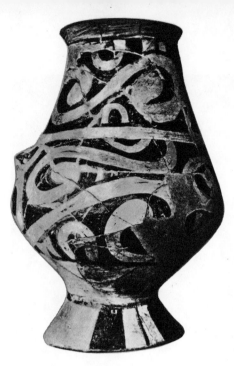

66. Male menhir statue carrying a fire-bow. *Musée Fénaille, Rodez.*

67. Pottery vessel showing a sweeping curvilinear design. Cucuteni (Roumania).

66 serving as a wide belt. Nearly all the male statues bear strange trappings which puzzled scholars for years and which are valuable evidence of one of the aspects of megalithic religion. They consist in fact of the elements of the fire-bow: on the person's left shoulder are the bow and the rod used as a drill, one extremity of which was to become incandescent; on the stomach there is a sort of cross-belt with a cup, sometimes fixed to the belt. The bow brace of the ancient French craftsmen's set of tools, still in use at the beginning of the century, included a similar disc (known as a *conscience*), on which the revolving drill was propped. The workman pressed on the drill, while his right hand worked the bow and his left hand the object to be pierced. Now, in a number of dolmens, the remains of ritual fires lit over the bones have been found. Fire, therefore, was associated with the worship of the dead.

The personage represented in this type of statue was perhaps a god, perhaps a sorcerer-priest, but more probably the king-priest-god, able to create fire and consequently to imitate lightning, which other bas-reliefs frequently represent in the form of one of those polished stone axes which are still called 'thunder stones' in Brittany. It is not impossible that the double rotation of the fire-bow inspired the motif of the double spiral which was absolutely predominant in the La Tène culture in the form of an S. Perhaps the engravings and sculptures representing labyrinths of overlapping spirals had the same origin: we know that their distribution is almost world-wide and that they are, in any case, one of the constants of the Eurasian domain.

Curvilinear and rectilinear decoration

We have already mentioned how interesting a comparison between Eastern and Western megalithic monuments would be. It is possible that their relations might enlighten us about certain sea routes by which a very special decoration, consisting of concentric hoops made with a blunt point, may have travelled. It appeared in Iran and Mesopotamia in the middle phase of the Tell Halaf epoch. The motif was very widespread in the West during the

Early Bronze Age. It is also found in the Late Bronze Age in Lusatian pottery. It is the elementary theme of the great Gavr'inis composition.

This decoration is one of the rare curvilinear motifs to be found in western European pottery. We have already noted the preference of eastern Europe for curved lines and of western Europe for rectilinear motifs. If we follow the progress of the Danubian cultures across central Europe, the passage from one style to another becomes apparent. During the Danubian I culture, decorations were in ribbon form, displaying considerable imagination 68 in the meanders unfolding on the bellies of vases. During the Danubian II culture, the semi-nomadic peasants reached central Germany. The influence of local populations apparently must be the explanation of the transformation of this decoration: a series of dashes or dots was substituted for the lines, while a geometrical arrangement favouring angular motifs replaced the curving meanders. These were the decorations of the Hinkelstein and the Rössen cultures.

Much later this preference was to triumph in the right-angled decoration of the Hallstatt culture and to continue in archaic Greece in the Dipylon vases. The same geometrical tendency was to inspire the first decorations of the continental workers in metal from the end of the Neolithic onwards.

From these few examples it can be seen that European protohistory owes as much to original developments as to foreign impulses. Influences coming from the Near East soon gave rise to autochthonous variants. This was the expression of a fundamental phenomenon of major importance. A strange complex of peoples matured on the great plains of the north, in contact with the Bohemian mountains which were rich in ore. Horsemen from the pontic regions probably brought them their language, while the western megalith-makers, the Danubian farmers and the Nordic Mesolithic men added and intermingled their traditions. It only needed the ironsmiths arriving in their turn from the south-east to install themselves in Bohemia for a new civilisation to arise—the Indo-European civilisation.

HISTORICAL SUMMARY: Neolithic art

The domestication of animals and the beginnings of stock-farming and agriculture initiated, in the Mesolithic, the new techniques: weaving, spinning, ceramics. The appearance of such important social features as stability of the habitat, division of the soil for agriculture, the development of trade and the beginning of urban civilisation, completely upset previous conceptions of art, which developed towards stylisation: for example, as with decorative art, a major art with the advent of pottery, and the menhir statues in western Europe. The appearance of megalithic monuments—the dawn of Western architecture—was the principal phenomenon.

Pottery. Some scholars have held the view that agriculture and pottery developed side by side. This is not so. It seems that Denmark had coarse pottery before it was familiar with crop-growing. Inversely, at Jericho in Palestine, and Jarmo in Kurdistan—settlements dating from about 5000 B.C., where the barley and wheat grown are close to the wild species—pottery is unknown.

Certain prehistorians would make ceramics the 'master fossil' which would enable us to follow racial migrations, and, in fact, the different types of pottery do seem to have spread over vast areas of civilisation. Thus the ribbon pottery of Danubian origin was typical of the agricultural peoples who invaded the black lands of central Europe during the 3rd millennium B.C.; this type of pottery moved up the valley of the Rhine as far as Alsace and the Low Countries and lasted until the Early Bronze Age in Bohemia, Poland and western Russia [68].

Smooth pottery of many different shapes was found in the palafittes. A particular type of pottery with an incised decoration of lozenges and chequer patterns was at its zenith in the Chasseyware style which characterised the end of the Neolithic in France and Italy.

Cord-ornamented pottery, decorated by the impress of cords on the raw clay, appeared a little later, with the advent of copper.

Pottery shaped like bells or chalices (that of the Beaker folk), originally from Spain, spread to France and Italy, and then to England, Holland and north Germany. Like the preceding kind, this pottery, contemporary with copper, was associated with a megalithic civilisation.

Lastly, the painted pottery of southeast Europe derived from Danubian

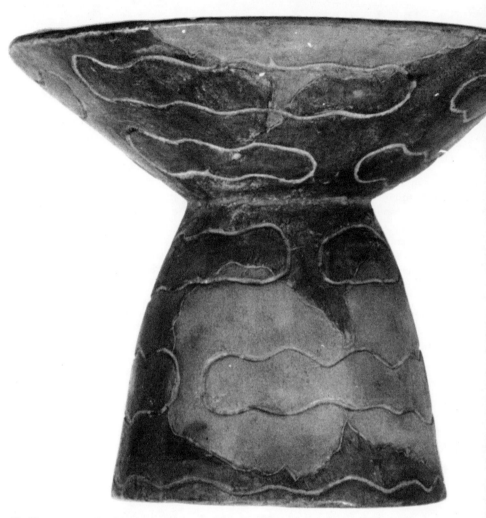

68. Stone vase with ribbon decoration. Tiszadada (Hungary). *A copy in the Musée de St Germain.*

pottery of the Tripolye type (Transylvania, Ukraine, Galicia), with spiral decorations which are sometimes black and sometimes black touched up with red on a white ground, is extremely beautiful and has its counterpart in China (Kansu [85], Honan) and in Turkestan.

Megaliths. These strange monuments are evidence of a highly organised social life. Menhirs, upright stones, are numerous in France, where the Locmariaquer menhir is the tallest (65 ft.). Menhirs may be grouped in 'alignments' (the longest is the one at Carnac, nearly two miles [20a]), or in a circle, in 'cromlechs'. The British Isles have the largest cromlechs, at Avebury and Stonehenge [20b].

Dolmens, composed of one or more horizontal slabs on top of upright stones, may form a gallery grave. They are numerous in Brittany (*Table des Marchands*, at Locmariaquer [19]) and in the Gard, Lozère, Ardèche and

Aveyron. The slabs of the gallery grave at Gavr'inis are covered with strange signs. The dolmens are collective burial places.

The menhir statues, often associated with representations of axes, are reminiscent of a religion of fire and lightning.

Megalithic monuments are extremely widespread (the British Isles, the Low Countries, southern Scandinavia, north Germany, southern Italy, the Balkans, Spain, North Africa, Syria, Palestine, the Caucasus, northern Persia, India, America, Japan and Polynesia).

During the last centuries of the 3rd millennium and up to the middle of the 2nd millennium, the megalithic peoples brought with them to Europe a religion, as well as the art of deep-sea navigation; the origin of these peoples is difficult to determine, but their role in the pre-Celtic cultures was very important.

Lidie Huyghe

THE AGRARIAN REVOLUTION

Pia Laviosa-Zambotti

The first great changes in art which accompanied the changes in civilisation were not confined to Europe. The transition from the Palaeolithic to the Neolithic and later periods corresponded everywhere with the appearance of agrarian, and later pastoral, life and produced a revolution in customs and beliefs which, in its turn, transformed art.

Man of the Lower and Middle Palaeolithic lived in small groups, leading a life very close to that of the wild beasts, in an atmosphere pregnant with terror. Hunger was a constant threat. Hundreds of thousands of years of this atmosphere filled with terrors of every kind had its effect on the spiritual formation of primitive humanity. The fear of enormous pachyderms and ferocious beasts gave rise to the worship of obscure animal powers. Man strove to identify himself with the animal. The magic of strength revealed to him the meaning of the divine.

The other problem which preoccupied him was the great mystery of birth and death. That is why he exalted woman in his art, especially her nudity, the organs of conception and sexual union.

At the end of the Palaeolithic, it is probable that a 'feminine world', a sketch of the matriarchal agrarian society, was in the slow process of formation. Woman was essentially the fecund procreator. Her mysterious prerogatives favoured her endowment with the magical powers which presided over the fertility of the earth.

Primitive agriculture, i.e. gardening, understood as a magico-religious activity, was therefore a feminine preserve, probably from the Palaeolithic onwards.

The agrarian matriarchy and its iconography

The agrarian revolution appeared in a zone where, at some time towards the end of the Palaeolithic, the harvest was considered definitely more important than the products of hunting. The Palestinian Natufian culture seems to exhibit this transitional process clearly. The Near East offered particularly favourable climatic conditions for the growth of wild grasses. The concentration of human groups of varied origins there encouraged an intense cultural interchange which led to a rapid expansion of civilisation and art.

Mesopotamia, subject to periodic floods which gave it a natural fertility, became, at the time when it was covered with a skilful network of canals, the zone of the biggest concentration of agrarian villages. Hence the increasingly rapid progress of its agriculture.

All the species of animals present in the Natufian were subsequently domesticated. Thus agriculture and stock-farming developed side by side, and the population grew.

In a civilisation where the harvest was organised as a regular activity, the progressive transfer of the authority of the male Palaeolithic hunter to the farming woman took place in the magico-religious spirit characteristic of primitive humanity. The procreative mother also knew how to fructify the earth, which would have remained barren without her magical intervention.

The mothers dominated the female agrarian community which was the basis of the new society. Their daughters had a pre-eminent role in it. A woman had to have several husbands whom she maintained and made use of for various tasks, especially stock-farming and the establishment and defence of the villages, which were constantly threatened by predatory nomads.

Conception was probably considered as a divine happening, by which the woman came into magical contact with the divinity; consequently her husband had no rights over her, the children or the landed property.

The first agrarian society was communal, as was that of the Palaeolithic. The problem of the independent family in a communal society only arose when material existence was finally assured and wealth had accumulated.

The matriarchal society was wholly under the sway of agrarian religiosity. Thus the mother was identified not only with the sacred bull, the serpent, the doves, the birds, etc., whose aspect she assumed, but also with the trees and plants in which divinity was implicit. All these themes are found in the art of Crete, where these religions continued for a long time. The emblem of the mother goddess was the serpent: its coils led to the centre of the earth, from which sprang the supreme generative activity of the mother goddess and into which the Tree of Life, symbol of the maternal religion, sank its deep roots.

Weaving and spinning must be considered as the two great feminine artistic achievements having a decisive bearing on the history of civilisation. Incidentally, mythology, too, attributes these inventions to woman. All the first ornamental pottery had a geometrical type of decoration; it was 'plectogenic', i.e. its paintings repeated the designs and colours of plaiting and weaving. Feminine art, then, was dominated by this patient technique, and by drawing her inspiration from geometrical art woman was exalting her own personality. She may have deprived this art of a lyrical quality and dynamic impulse, but she imbued it with a methodical, conservative spirit.

The only sculptures were terra-cotta figures of the nude goddess and the organs of fecundity, a theme already known in the Upper Palaeolithic. The moon, which regulates woman's monthly periods and the phases of agrarian activity, was conceived of as the male element and the lover of his mother; it became, therefore, along with the serpent, connected with the centre of the earth.

The pastoral revolution and the Erech civilisation

Under the influence of the agrarian revolution all the domestic animals—dogs, cows, goats, sheep and pigs—spread, eventually, throughout the zones dependent fairly directly on the Middle East (the Mediterranean lands, India, China). As a result, pastoral peoples appeared, especially in the desert areas adjoining Mesopotamia and in the mountains further north.

Undoubtedly the most ancient flock-keepers must be identified with the proto-Semites; they probably had their origins among the Palaeolithic hunters and cultivators (we have only to think of the Natufian culture). They must have preserved, along with the veneration of animals, the ancient masculine tribal institutions dominated by the elders and the sorcerer-chiefs. This pastoral civilisation, strengthening itself by contact with the agrarian world, was tempted at one point to supplant it by invasion. Thus the animal's high prestige was to remain constant in Eastern art, while the worship of the mother goddess of the agricultural peoples was to reappear very quickly—as early as Jemdet Nasr.

In Mesopotamia this pastoral revolution was given the name of the Erech (or Uruk) civilisation; in many ways it took the place of the matriarchal civilisation of the al 'Ubaid type. Pottery derived from basket-work and weaving then gave way to monochrome black-and-white pottery inspired by metal shapes.

The first writing was already established, and seals appeared marking the triumph of ownership and the importance of private property. In the matriarchal agrarian civilisation wealth was collective; in the Erech civilisation, on the contrary, we note the setting up of a personal masculine power. It was only able to impose itself after a long struggle with the established matriarchal power which owned the land. This struggle was clearly indicated in the Babylonian *Epic of the Creation*.

The first written history had a sacred character (secular history was an invention of the Greeks), and it was dominated by the religious concept which linked man intimately with the divinity. The adoration of animals evident in the Erech civilisation carried on the spirit of the Palaeolithic hunters.

But then transcendental religious tendencies appeared which conceived of an almost incorporeal divinity, endowed solely with the power of his look. Several eyes indicated that the god was all-seeing; an inner eye was evidence of his omniscience.

The *Epic of the Creation* recounted the fierce struggle of the sun god Marduk (chief Babylonian deity) when killing the female dragon Tiamat (a mother goddess) and told how he fashioned heaven and earth of her body. This universally current myth, which spread along with urban civilisation, even reached the Pacific and became basic to the Azteco-Incan civilisations of the Americas. Marduk's victory also led to the institution of the monarchical order and to the creation of absolute power. Before him, power belonged to a chief surrounded by other chiefs who were his equals and met in assembly to make the big collective decisions. The dynamic solar world of the heavens and light, based on the cult of the supreme god of lightning and the hammer, succeeded the static, lunar world of the polyandrous divinity Tiamat. The ziggurat, facilitating the ascent to heaven beyond the seven planets represented by its storeys, replaced the descent into the earth of the mother goddess. Then the first architecture of a sacred nature appeared, for the royal majesty was sacred.

The solar calendar replaced the lunar calendar. Myths were portrayed in art. Man discovered himself, along with his discovery of the heavens and the planetary system. He aspired to transcendency, weakening the matriarchal religion bound up with procreation and the earth. In this, Semitic thought was always to be opposed to that of the Eastern peoples who worshipped the terrestrial and animal principle.

As for Egypt, it experienced an agricultural development bordering on that of Mesopotamia. We can tell this by the primitive Mesopotamian agrarian civilisation of Hassuna, in which the simplest shapes of both monochrome and painted pottery appeared almost simultaneously. Even if painted pottery subsequently developed solely in the Babylonian sphere of al 'Ubaid-Eridu, monochrome pottery was originally almost exclusively of the Merimde and Badari types of the Egyptian civilisation. The Badarians of Egypt were pastoral people dominated by a 'cattle economy'. Everything leads us to assume that they were acquainted with matriarchal institutions, which are preserved up to the present day by the Berbers.

The spread of the agrarian revolution in Europe

When the Eastern agrarian revolution spread to Europe, the latter was in a decadent Palaeolithic phase, and, except in the extreme west, in Spain, the population was scanty. It was to increase considerably. The Danubian agrarian civilisation blossomed out in the Middle East after a delay of 1,500 years or more. It had a matriarchal character; its art was dominated by statuettes of the mother goddess, naked, or dressed in the Cretan manner, and by sacred animals.

In its pottery, geometrical decoration derived from basket-work was replaced by spirals and meanders— 67, 68 especially in the pottery between the Rhine and the Dnieper where Cretan influence of the Kamares type was felt. The Adriatic Illyrians, custodians of this world during protohistory, preserved the matriarchal institutions, as well as the pre-Indo-European language.

Iberia, which had received the agrarian civilisation from Cyprus and Egypt, had no pottery decorated with meanders and spirals. Shapes and decoration both remained plectogenic. However, the animal rock art of 47 Palaeolithic origin continued, renewing itself and gradually becoming more stylised. It became an intrinsic 33, 34 element of the new civilisation and, together with the megaliths, spread throughout the Atlantic countries.

Europe and the pastoral civilisation

The high Anatolian plateau was opened early to the pastoral revolution of the Erech type. Throughout this zone monochrome pottery based on metal shapes, with big handles and small spouts like the Erech prototypes, became standard, and shortly afterwards penetrated into the southern Balkans. It won the day over the pottery of matriarchal Cretan origin which was decorated with spirals and meanders.

In the Danubian Balkan region, this new influence helped to found the pastoral, warlike, Pannonian civilisation known as Vučedol-Baden.

At this epoch the most archaic Indo-European races (Hittites, Achaeans, proto–Latins) established themselves along the banks of the Danube and, at a later date, invaded the Mediterranean peninsulas (Anatolia, the Balkans, Italy).

In Spain, in Almería, the El Argar civilisation succeeded to the megalithic agrarian civilisation; there was evidence of Anatolian influence in its flourishing metal industry and its pottery, and also in the custom of interment in large jars. Dwelling places were built on hills defended by powerful stone bastions. The upper parts of these dwellings were reserved for the women. Thus the matriarchate was basic to early Iberian civilisation; it was also found in the islands colonised by the Iberians.

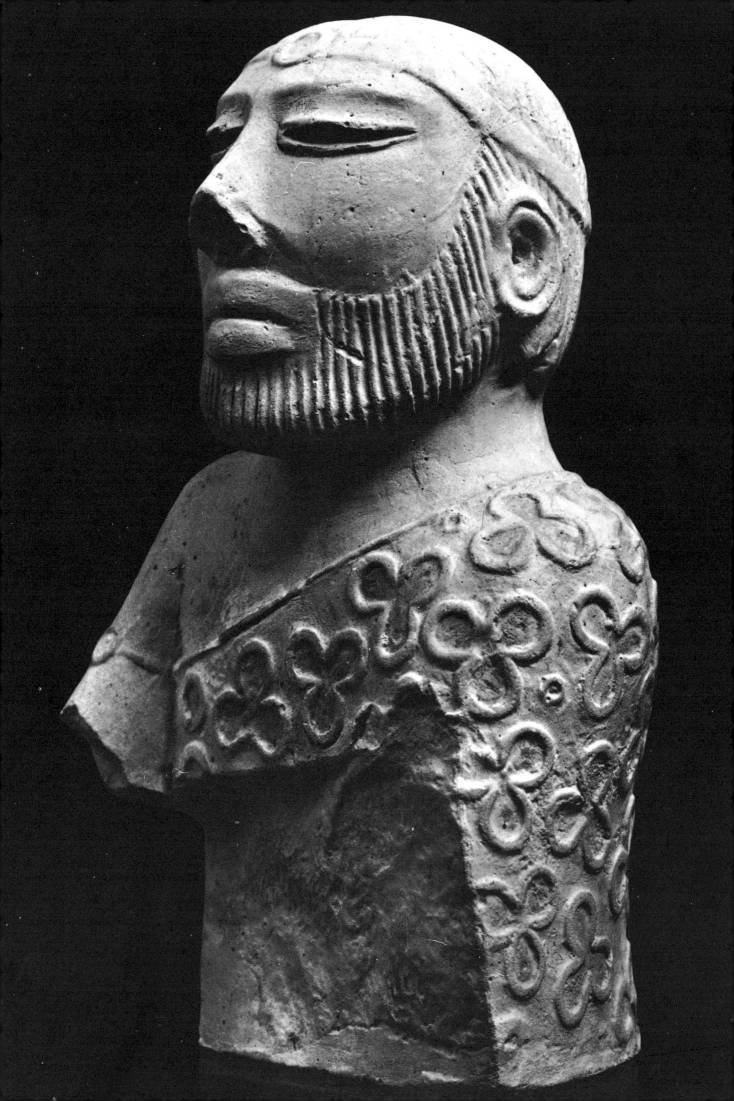

EARLY EMPIRES OF THE MIDDLE EAST

EGYPT—MESOPOTAMIA—THE INDUS *Georges Contenau*

*Although Europe's pre-eminence in the Palaeolithic age
compelled us to study the beginnings of art in that continent,
the more favourable climatic conditions in the Middle East
stimulated a more rapid appearance of the agrarian stage.
We must seek the germ of the historic civilisations there.*

Now we are going to tackle a vast territory—Egypt and
Mesopotamia, both of which rank as outstanding among
the oldest-known civilisations. We find there the conditions necessary for their flowering—a favourable
climate (somewhat similar in both areas owing to their
geographical situation) and the presence of the great
rivers, the Nile, the Tigris and the Euphrates, which
ensured their prosperity.

Egypt from its origins to the end of the pre-dynastic

Sometimes a great influence is attributed to the sites in
the Delta region; sometimes the Egyptian civilisation is
believed to have originated in the south. If there is general
agreement about the existence of influences which
modified its beginnings, scholars are less unanimous about
their nature and method of penetration.

The valley of the Nile was uninhabited until the waters
fell to roughly their present-day level; rock engravings
discovered by Winckler in the cliff caves, made by past
occupants who had left their traces behind, enabled him
to distinguish several groups of people, among them the
'primitive hunters' (engravings of animals), the 'primitive
inhabitants of the oases' (human figures), the 'autochthonous mountain-dwellers' (hunting scenes) and the 'invaders from the east'.

The representations of animals—elephants, horned
beasts, etc., some of which have gradually disappeared
from Egypt—bring us close again to the mural figures
of preceding ages and are undoubtedly inspired, in part at
least, by the same idea: the desire to capture the game.
But these magical figures indicate a more evolved stage.
70   The hunters are armed with large bows, and this advance
prevents us from attributing to them a too distant
antiquity. Also, the new desire to commemorate an
important event is added to the magical goal. The
presence of flat-bottomed boats with raised ends indicates,
as we shall see, the embarcations of the eastern invaders,
while the curved boats with elongated prows and sterns,
made of bundles of reeds, belong to the Egyptians. We
71, 72 may therefore conclude that several groups, some of
which were foreign, were already present in Egypt at the
time when its civilisation was taking shape.

These different population layers produced successive
types of civilisations which are named after the sites of
Upper Egypt where their characteristic features have
been found; they extend in a chronological order for
which, in the absence of reference dates, Sir Flinders
Petrie has proposed a system of 'sequence dating'. Those
of Tasa and Badari are placed before the date 30; that of
Nagada, from 30 to the beginning of history, includes the
Amratian and Gerzean sub-periods (first Naqada civilisation). Many sites in the north (Fayum, Merimde, el Omari

69. INDIAN. MOHENJO-DARO. Head of a bearded man.
c. 3rd millennium.

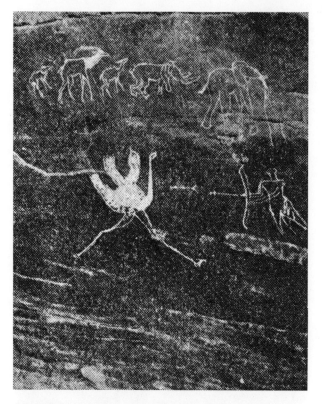

70. Graffiti by autochthonous mountain-dwellers in the
Egyptian desert. *(After J. Vandier.)*

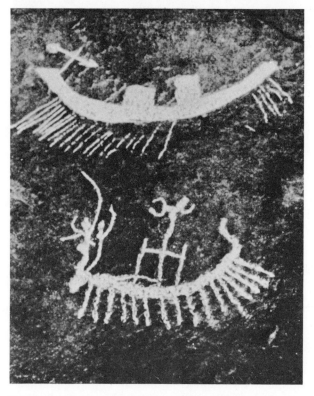

71. Boats of the early inhabitants of the Nile valley. Upper
Egypt, southern region. Engraving. *(After Winckler.)*

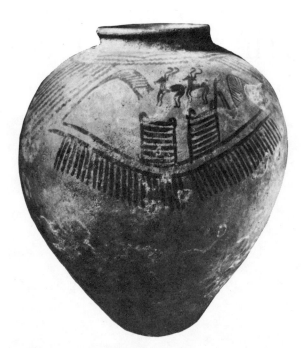

72. Gerzean pottery. The principal motif represents a boat. *Egyptian Museum, Cairo.*

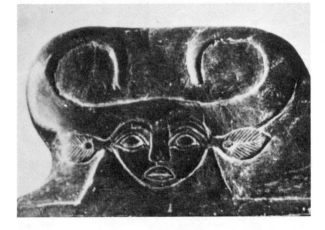

73. EGYPTIAN. Detail from the Narmer Palette. 1st Dynasty. *Egyptian Museum, Cairo.*

near Helwan, Maadi) are typical. If we disregard flint implements which verge on art at the end of the predynastic, the major artistic effort appears in pottery.

Some rare female figurines have been taken from the tombs; they have only rudimentary arms, and their joined legs finish in a point. Some animal tombs have suggested to certain scholars an already established zoolatry. Copper was known from the earliest periods, mainly in its natural state, but we must always distinguish between occasional use, which is the case here, and habitual employment, which did not come until very much later because of the rarity and great value of the metal. Professor Gordon Childe has asked whether we ought not seek the source of the ancient Egyptian culture, combined with African elements, in the Nigerian zone of the Sahara.

From the period of the prehistoric site of el Amrah comes a clay model of a rectangular house, taken from a tomb. Soon a number of small art objects appear (palettes and knives) as well as paintings like that in the tomb 73 at Hierakonpolis. The palettes for grinding make-up,

used from the earliest epoch, became votive objects; they 169, 170 were shaped like the oval bucklers of the Middle Ages. The ivory handles (once covered with burnished gold- 75 leaf) of chipped flint knives were of similar inspiration.

Protohistory in Mesopotamia

As in Egypt, the various periods have been named after their characteristic sites, but the original nomenclature has been modified in the light of later discoveries.

The sites of Hassuna, Samarra and Tell Halaf have yielded pottery which becomes progressively more developed. These three periods belong to the pottery of the north. But during this time another pottery was born in the south, passing through the same stages to spread in the north and supplant its predecessors. It came from al 'Ubaid (near Ur) and is well represented at Eridu, near the Persian Gulf, where the remains of important edifices have been found. The civilisation of this period was widespread in Mesopotamia and made outstanding progress; it had a genuine architecture and a knowledge of metals, and it made use of engraved seals with personal marks to denote ownership.

The Erech civilisation, which followed it, accentuated this progress; it was the time of the invention of writing, which at first, as in Egypt, consisted merely of the representation of objects. Frequent use, as well as the necessity of writing with a stylus on small clay slabs, debased it and led the scribes to break down their designs into a sequence of small lines. In this way cuneiform writing was produced.

At Susa, capital of Elam, in the south-east of the Mesopotamian plain, a necropolis has yielded funerary offerings (copper blades and pins, seals) and pottery of fine 74 clay decorated in the al 'Ubaid style. The animal motifs which adorn it tend to lapse into geometrical patterns. Nevertheless they are evocative of birds flying over the marshes, wild beasts near a water hole, etc., and these interpretations can be verified by following the successive debasements of the initial themes. Retaining something of the magical purpose of the rock paintings representing the game to be captured, they are almost a form of prewriting comparable to those Chinese paintings in which the landscape, its situation, the season and even the hour, are suggested by a few conventional accessories.

The Indus

Through his explorations in the Makran, Sir Aurel Stein rediscovered the route followed by protohistoric trade between the south of Mesopotamia and north-west India. Finds in the Indus basin have thrown some light on its civilisation before the arrival of the Aryans. In the various sites studied, the pottery shows apparent similarities to that of al 'Ubaid, especially at Amri (where it seems to come from a more ancient period) and at Mundigak. Harappa, in the Punjab, and Mohenjo-Daro, in Sind, have supplied square steatite seals with representations of animals (among them buffaloes and elephants) accompanied by writing as yet undeciphered. The last two sites include brick edifices arranged in a chess-board pattern, colonnaded buildings, baths, granaries, mills and communal ovens. Quite a number of ceramic figurines of women have been collected there, including statuettes of the mother goddess with a heavy and complicated coiffure. Some pieces are of quite exceptional interest,

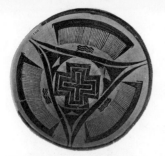

74a. SUSA. Interior of a painted terra-cotta cup. Before 3200. *Louvre.*

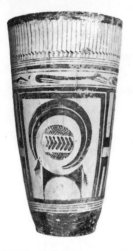

74b. SUSA. Painted terra-cotta vase. Before 3200. *Louvre.*

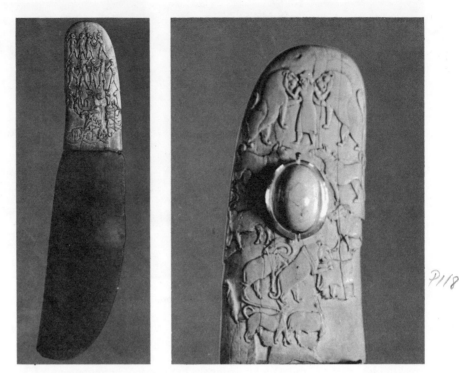

75. EGYPTIAN. Ivory knife from Jebel el Arak (front and back). Proto-dynastic epoch. *Louvre.*

69 especially the bust of a man (from Mohenjo–Daro) whose clothing is covered with trefoils (which also appear, in order to indicate animal fur, on a reclining bull with a human head, in the Louvre, dating from the Akkadian epoch). This personage, whose garment may be an animal skin, is normally considered as being of Semitic

81 type. Also worthy of notice are a stone torso (from Harappa) of masterly modelling which is unexpected at such a remote epoch and, in contrast, a copper figurine (from Harappa) which might easily be attributed to a much earlier period if its origin were not well established.

This Indus civilisation, which continued until the arrival of the Aryans, deserves, in spite of the little we know about it, to be mentioned side by side with those of Egypt and Mesopotamia. But any similarities can be explained by their mainly commercial contacts: there is no question of suggesting that there was a direct connection between Mesopotamia and the Indus valley; on the contrary, the influence of a common source is the most probable hypothesis.

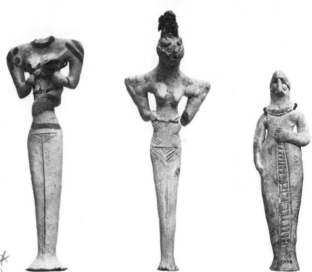

76. SUMERIAN. Figures in terra-cotta. *British Museum.*

Contacts between Egypt and Mesopotamia

The geographical situations of Egypt and Mesopotamia were similar; they were on almost the same latitude, with the same hydrographic system, and they had an incredibly fertile soil owing to the floods, for the rivers left an alluvial deposit when they withdrew. The political evolution of the two areas was comparable; they were communities of restricted size passing through the same phases of development, but with an apparent advance in Egypt, which was already divided into provinces or nomes, each obeying a chief and tending to group together —conditions necessary for progress. Mesopotamia seems more backward, a possible reason being that the basin experienced the shock of invaders whose traces we can see. But the delay was undoubtedly more apparent than

real. Some cities were prosperous: Eridu and Erech, to mention only two of them, were flourishing communities quite the equals of the capital of a nome. Nevertheless, we are reduced to conjectures about the exact structure of Mesopotamia at this period.

Both regions had very mixed populations; the shifting of important centres points to this in Mesopotamia. The substitution at the end of the al 'Ubaid period of the method of burying a corpse on its side with knees bent for that of a supine extended body is further confirmation.

It seems highly probable that if Egypt came under external influences these altered the continuity of her civilisation, even superficially, less than those which affected Mesopotamia; in comparison with the al 'Ubaid culture, the Erech culture exhibited profound changes which resulted in progress.

63

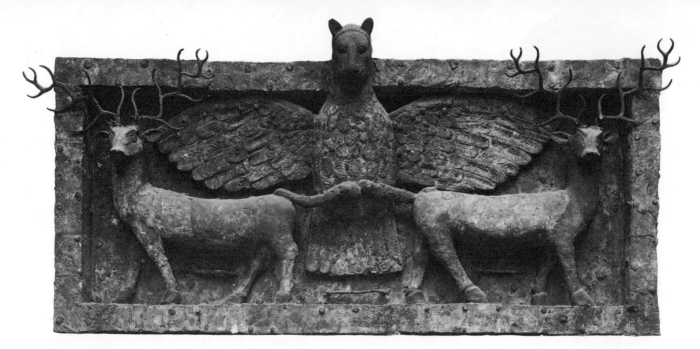

77. SUMERIAN. Copper panel representing a storm god.

Towards the end of the periods dealt with here certain lasting themes were already established in the sculpture of the two countries—hunting, the victorious chief breaking his enemy's head, fabulous animals. In the same way, especially in Mesopotamia, the taste for observation was already confirmed in animal representations.

Scholars have noted numerous similarities between Egypt and Mesopotamia in the shapes and ornamentation of stone and earthenware vases. Some of the decorations may possibly be peculiar to the beginnings of private ownership of pottery. Others are more confusing— friezes of stilt-birds around the edges of Susa I and Naqada II vases, silhouettes of female dancers in black on a lighter ground in Egypt and Persia.

The lion throwing a man to the ground (palette in the British Museum) has its counterpart at Ur on a fragment of a shield; the same holds true of the typical lion 73 in both countries. Hathor is represented on the Narmer

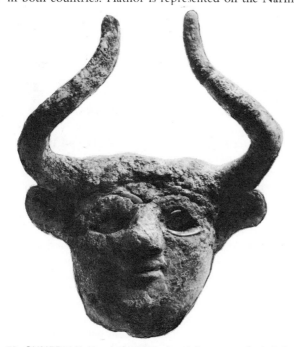

78. SUMERIAN. Head of a horned god, in copper. Early 3rd millennium. Royal Cemetery, Ur.

Palette by a cow's head with human features, and a horned head of a god comes from the tombs of Ur. 78

Excavations in protohistoric Mesopotamian sites have produced new, more comprehensive, information. The knife from Jebel el Arak (now in the Louvre) bears rep- 75 resentations of enemy boats together with Egyptian boats, the former having extremely high prows and sterns. The ancient Egyptians preserved these as the typical sacred ship. Both in the painting in the tomb at 166 Hierakonpolis and on the knife, a person is attacked by two lions which he is mastering; he is dressed in a long, belted tunic, wears a beard and has long hair, cut off at shoulder level, with a bandeau round it. The animals on the knife are of the same style as those of Erech and the palettes. Excavations, by restoring to us the culture of the Jemdet Nasr epoch, have supplied many specimens of this type.

Until the Mesopotamian chronology is established it remains difficult to specify how these relationships were effected. It would seem as if the resemblances come from Asia, since the motifs are, after all, comparatively sporadic in Egypt, whereas they abound and persist in Mesopotamia. It is quite possible that they are the result of military expeditions. The Jebel el Arak knife, which depicts a hand-to-hand combat, was found at the end of the Wadi Hammamat route which leads to the Red Sea and was undoubtedly still navigable at that time: we are entitled then to think of an expedition or of trade.

But might we not equally well imagine a common source? Until now the two areas have displayed an equal development and assured contacts. Present-day scholars think (and probably rightly) that the end of the predynastic coincided with the end of the Erech period, and the beginning of the Thinite with the Jemdet Nasr period, which is very plausible.

It is hardly possible to decide whether the matriarchal epoch postulated for the prehistoric periods recurred during the primitive phases of Egyptian and Mesopotamian civilisation. The small terra-cotta female figures with serpent-like heads found at Ur might be an echo of it, but the Mesopotamians did not remember it consciously, since they peopled the past with more or less mythical but always masculine royal dynasties. Moreover, for periods such as al 'Ubaid and Erech, the primitive phases were long since over.

EGYPT

Geography. Egypt, an immense oasis, stretches along the Nile valley for 1,250 miles; it has only 12,000 square miles available for cultivation (roughly the area of Belgium).

Since the beginnings of Egyptian civilisation there has been a distinction between the Nile valley, or Upper Egypt, and the Delta, or Lower Egypt.

Civilisation. The Egyptian Palaeolithic, like the European, was characterised by a chipped flint industry, first with core tools, then with flake tools.

In the Neolithic (5th millennium), the Tasian period is represented in the south at Tasa and Mostagedda, and in the north at Fayum, Merimde and el Omari, by hand-made pottery, stone implements, basket-work and the first woven cloths.

The Chalcolithic (4th millennium) begins with the Badarian culture (Badari, Matmar, Mostagedda). Copper appeared, pottery was improved, working in ivory developed (vases, one of which has an animal form) and the technique of glazed stone was discovered. Then followed the Naqada period, subdivided into the Amratian and Gerzean. The end of the last-named stage of civilisation coincided with the period immediately preceding the beginning of historic times, towards 2850 B.C. and the first pharaohs.

From the Tasian to the end of the Gerzean the tomb developed. At first merely a circular hole covered with a heap of stones, it became oval in the Amratian. Walls held either by laths or by a plastering of clay during the Gerzean, transformed the pit into a larger rectangular tomb capable of holding more abundant funerary material. In the dawn of history brick replaced the walls of wood or clay and the primitive heap of stones was organised into a rectangular solid mass built of brick which eventually became the mastaba of the Old Kingdom. The dead person, wrapped in either a linen cloth or a goat-skin or both, then in a reed mat replaced in the middle of the Gerzean by a ceramic or wooden coffin, lay in the pit, surrounded by funerary gifts and offerings of food, supposedly renewed magically, which enabled him to live indefinitely.

Art. The first works of art date from the end of the Gerzean: knife handles of gold (found at Jebel el Tarif, now in the Cairo Museum) and of ivory (the knife from Jebel el Arak, decorated on one side with a hunting scene and on the other with a fight between two

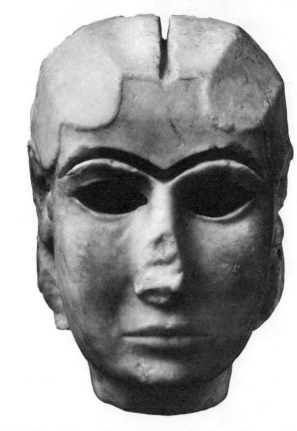

79. SUMERIAN. Alabaster head discovered at Warka. Jemdet Nasr period. c. 3000. *Baghdad Museum.*

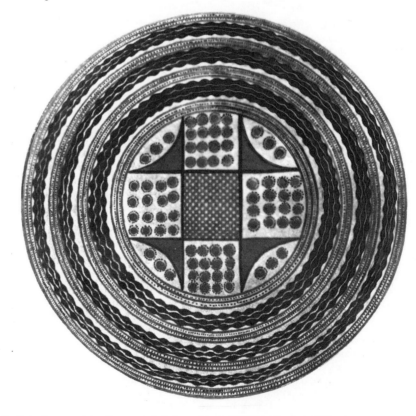

80. Polychrome plate discovered at Arpachiyah. Tel Halaf period. 4500 B.C. *Iraq Museum, Baghdad.*

65

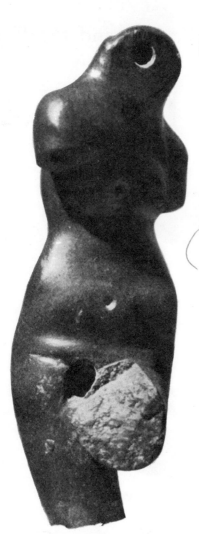

81. INDIAN. HARAPPA. Stuatuette of a dancer, in grey limestone. *c.* 2400–2000. *Museum of Central Asian Antiquities, New Delhi.*

groups of armed and naked men [**75**]).

Shield-shaped palettes of schist were also carved in bas-relief with hunting scenes (hunting palettes, Louvre and British Museum), battles (Palette of the Vultures, British Museum; palette in the Ashmolean Museum, Oxford), animals fighting (small palette from Hierakonpolis [**169**]) and scenes symbolical of triumph (palette with bulls, Louvre; Narmer Palette, Cairo Museum [**73**, **170**]).

PALESTINE

Geography. On the eastern coast of the Mediterranean, Phoenicia and Palestine, situated between Mesopotamia, the Aegean and Egypt, were destined to play an important role.

Civilisation. The two countries were inhabited from the most remote prehistoric times. Their Palaeolithic presents a variety of flint implements which is quite the equal of the Western industries, especially in the first phases. During the Mesolithic, the Natufian initiated agriculture in Palestine and perhaps helped to introduce it to the entire Neolithic world. The first buildings appeared; the dead were buried lying on one side. The immediate successor to this period was the Chalcolithic. Important remains have been recovered at Jericho: an abundance of pottery; painted and terra-cotta statuettes; traces of mud dwellings with walls and floors covered with reddish plaster. From the same epoch there have been finds at Megiddo of pottery decorated with stripes and incised geometrical motifs, and representations of men and animals, all skilfully executed. Brick or stone dwellings began to replace mud huts.

MESOPOTAMIA

Archaeology. For a quarter of a century now excavations, especially in Upper Mesopotamia, have brought our knowledge of the area's civilisation up to the beginning of the 4th millennium and have revealed the importance of the Sumerian contribution in the 3rd millennium.

Geography. Mesopotamia, like Egypt, has always lived on its oases and by the irrigation from its two great rivers, the Tigris and the Euphrates, which in the past used to flow separately into the Persian Gulf—which was less silted up around 4000 B.C. and still reached as far inland as Eridu. But it experienced terrible floods (the biblical Flood). Mesopotamia is embedded between two plateaux, Persia to the east and Asia Minor to the north-west.

Civilisation. The Palaeolithic in Mesopotamia is represented by finds of cave-dwellings hollowed in the sides of the lesser ranges of the Zagros Mountains (sites of Barda Balka, Hazer Mard, Zarzi, Karim Shahir and Jarmo). The transition from the Palaeolithic to the Neolithic, perhaps from the end of the 6th millennium onwards, is established at the Jarmo site, where, in a primitive village and not in a cave, traces of the continuation of the microlithic industry, and consequently proof of agriculture and stock-farming, have been found.

The earliest phase of the Neolithic is best studied at Hassuna and at Mattarah. Nomads who had settled down formed villages; their implements were stone, their pottery large and coarse. Polished pieces are rare. The dead were interred in jars. This archaic civilisation of Hassuna had relations with the area west of the Euphrates (Sakjegosu and Mersin) and with Palestine (Jericho and Megiddo).

In the 4th millennium, the civilisation of Samarra was characterised by the appearance of brick dwellings, following those of mud which succeeded the tent, then by the existence of a delicate elegant pottery, fashioned on the wheel, with monochrome decorations using geometrical elements and isolated subjects—birds, fish, etc.—and also central compositions of religious and symbolical significance. Implements were made of stone and bone. Metal was still unknown. Burial places were of sun-dried or of mud-brick.

The Tell Halaf civilisation followed that of Samarra. In addition to houses with several rooms, built of mud and brick, architecture appeared with circular constructions (tholoi) of mud on stone foundations (Arpachiyah X to VII; Tepe Gawra XX to XVII). The pottery, more technically skilful than the Samarran, showed less naturalism and exuberance in its polychrome animal decoration, but rather, a flexible geometrical tendency in which the wavy line played a part [**80**]; the oval existed side by side with chess-board patterns, with ornamental divisions encircling, in the decoration of plates, a large central rosette with many petals. Their improved implements were still of stone and bone. Copper, already known in Persia (Sialk I) since Hassuna II, made its appearance at the end of this period (Arpachiyah) at the same time as the seal and the terra-cotta figurines of mother goddesses.

The al 'Ubaid civilisation is the most important of the 4th millennium. It succeeded that of Halaf which in some sites it ended violently. As opposed to the preceding civilisations, whose initial home seems to have been situated in northern Mesopotamia, the al 'Ubaid civilisation appears to have first covered the whole of the south of the country. Architecture of sun-dried brick developed on high terraces (Eridu, Ur, Erech, Tepe Gawra). The temple consisted of a central hall with a table of offerings, surrounded by small chambers; it proved to be the prototype of later temples. Stone foundations and stepped walls appeared in the middle of this period, which must have been a very long one. The dead, generally laid on their sides with legs bent, were placed in rectangular chests of sun-dried brick.

The pottery is very delicate, of pale green, beige or pink, with black geometrical designs and stylised and geometricised figures of goats and birds towards the end of the period (Tello). Implements are of stone, bone and terra-cotta; obsidian is used for the first time. Carvings in button-seal form are more common in the north. While plump figurines of the mother goddess type reappear at Gawra and neighbouring sites, at Ur and Eridu snake-like statuettes with thin bodies and broad

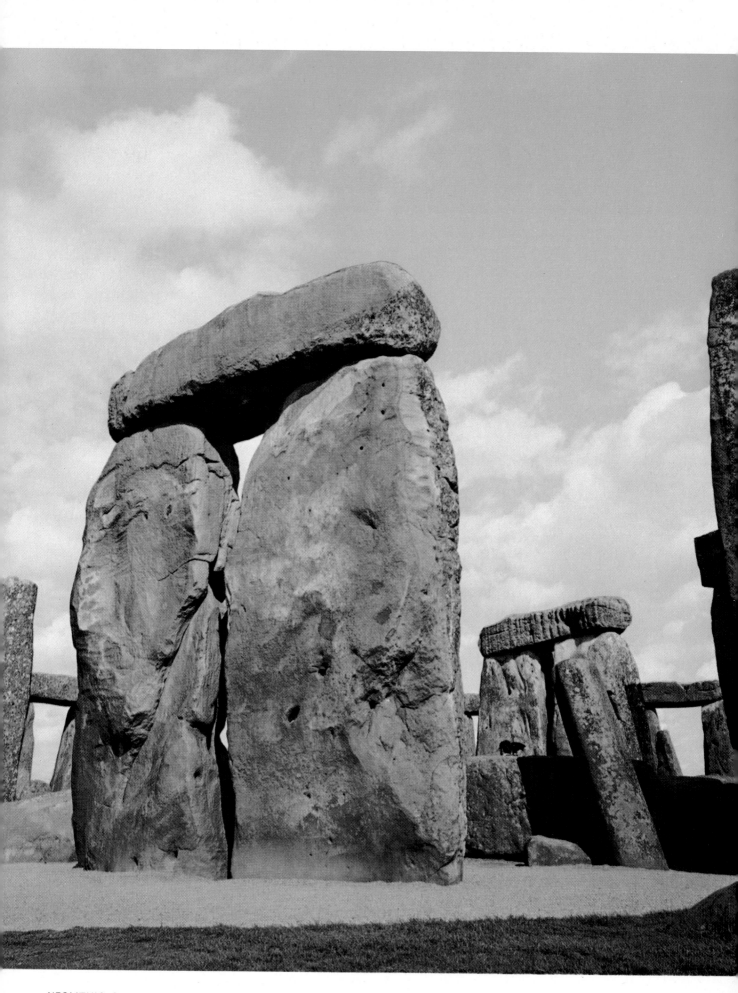

NEOLITHIC. Stonehenge. *c.* 1500 B.C. *Photo: A. F. Kersting.*

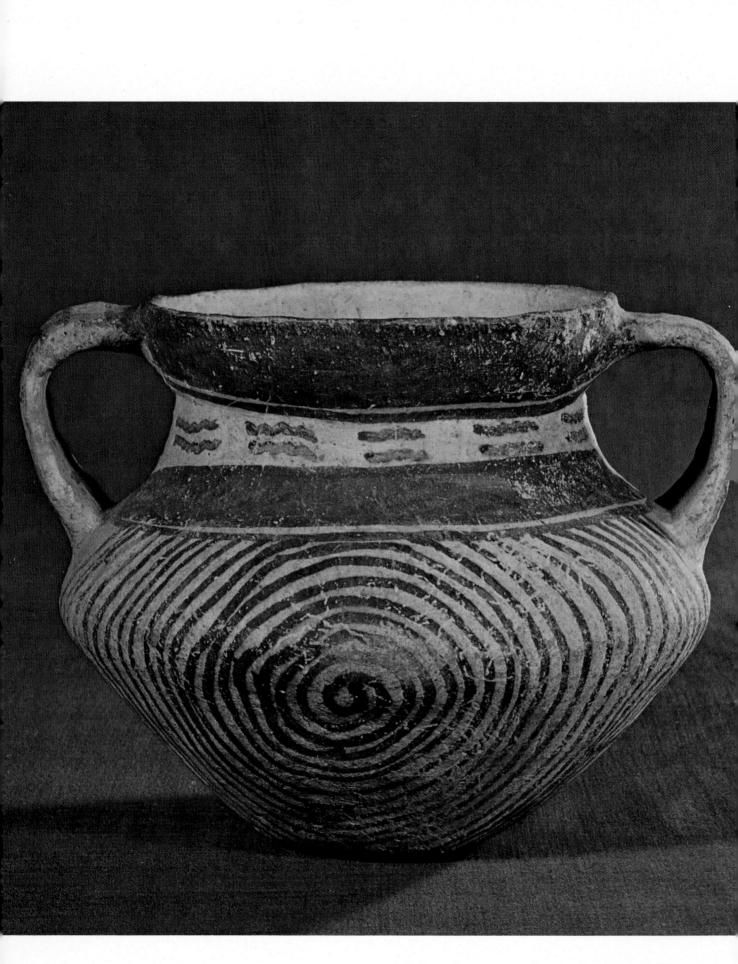

NEOLITHIC. Earthenware funerary jar. Kansu province, China.
c. 2000 B.C. *Photo: Michael Holford.*

shoulders punctuated with excrescences appear, but only in this layer of al 'Ubaid. Animals are coarsely modelled in clay.

Copper, used in the northern sites, has not been found in the south; perhaps it has not been preserved. Gold objects are discovered for the first time (Ur, Gawra).

In the first half of the 4th millennium, Sumerian invaders brought copper with them to Erech. The 'White Temple' (71 feet long, 39 feet high), the prototype of the ziggurat, was built of clay and bitumen; round it were constructed the 'Limestone Temple' and then the 'Red Temple' of brick. Pottery made on the wheel was grey. Reed cylinders have been found whose animal decoration with full and vigorous shapes shows an undeniable mastery. Tablets with pictographic signs appear, indicating the use of writing. In architecture, columns were embedded in sun-dried brick.

At Susa pottery from the 4th millennium with stylised decoration and an exquisite shape has been found in tombs alongside copper weapons and mirrors [74].

INDIA AND THE INDUS

Archaeology. The main result of the recent study of India's prehistory has been the discovery of pre-Aryan civilisation in the Indus valley, thanks to excavations undertaken separately in 1924 at Mohenjo-Daro in Sind and Harappa in the Punjab.

Geography. The basin of the Indus is situated to the north-west of India, near Persia, from which it is separated by Baluchistan; the river, with its source in the Himalayas, flows into the Arabian Sea via a vast delta.

Civilisation. From the Palaeolithic, bifacial tools of the Chelleo-Acheulian type had already been found in India, particularly near Madras. The excavations of 1935–1937 revealed the Palaeolithic of the upper Indus valley. Rock engravings and paintings have also been discovered in the caves of Singanpur.

The advent of the Neolithic seems to have been delayed, sometimes until well into historical times (until the 2nd century B.C. in the Deccan).

The northern regions, on the other hand, knew the use of metal very much earlier, and, towards the middle of the 3rd millennium B.C., there developed in the Indus valley a civilisation having a definite kinship with that of Mesopotamia, which is indicated in a variety of ways: in its architectural technique and its ornaments, and again in its seals. Important remains have been taken from the two sites of Harappa and

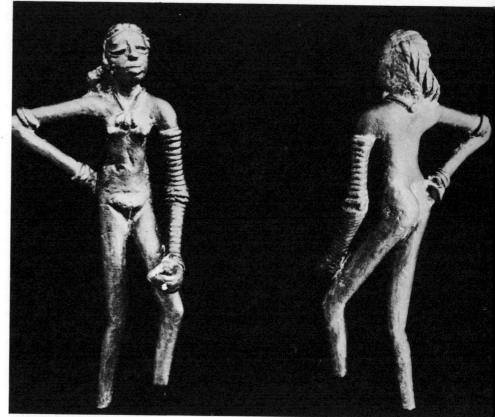

82. INDIAN. MOHENJO-DARO. Statuette of a dancing girl. *c. 2400–2000. Museum of Central Asian Antiquities, New Delhi.*

Mohenjo-Daro. We have proof of commercial exchanges with Mesopotamia. But since the writing is still undeciphered, we know nothing definite about this period [81, 82].

Between 1500 and 800 B.C., this civilisation was destroyed by Indo-European invaders, the Aryans, from the West, who gradually spread throughout India, bringing with them new social, political and religious insti-

tutions (Vedism, later transformed into Brahmanism).

Important remains of towns with brick buildings have been found at Harappa and Mohenjo-Daro. The public works (cisterns, sewers, etc.) were of a high standard.

Numerous seals have been found, mainly representing cattle in profile or a seated god [83].

Marie-Louise Tisserant

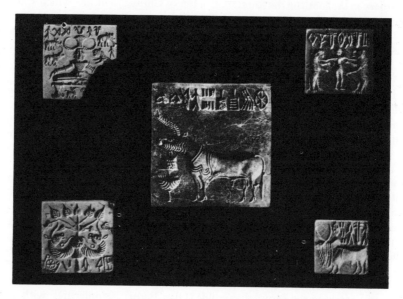

83. INDIAN. MOHENJO-DARO. Seals *c. 2400–2000* B.C. *National Museum of India, New Delhi.*

THE FIRST ASIATIC CIVILISATIONS

Vadime Elisseeff

*Asian art attracts much less attention during its initial
phase, which develops along with prehistory. Nevertheless
it underwent a similar gestatory period to that of the West,
but it was discovered more recently. We can only ignore early
Asian art at the risk of completely misunderstanding
its later developments.*

At the end of the Lower Palaeolithic, when Europe,
Africa and south Asia were being peopled with Neanderthal men, east and north Asia seemed to be forgotten
lands.

The forgotten lands

The settlements on the Chusovaya River in the Urals, and
at Teshik-Tash in the upper Oxus (Amu Darya) basin,
those of the Soan and Anyathian cultures of India and
Burma which resemble them, as well as the analagous
traces of the Patjitanian, diffused from Sumatra to the
Philippines, mark the far limits of the Mousterian industry
within the confines of the Sino-Siberian world. Admittedly the Scandinavian and Arctic glaciers, linked by
the Aralo-Caspian Sea, cut these territories off from the
Africo-European West, but there remained the southern
route and the Indo-Chinese passage. At the beginning of
the dispersal of mankind, this was the route to Peking
which must have been taken by Sinanthropus, that close
relation of the Javanese Pithecanthropus, who himself
came from an Indo-Chinese centre.

The human advance towards the East had already
reached the Yellow River in the Lower Pleistocene; it is
therefore possible that the southern cultures of the
Middle Pleistocene were diffused by the same route. But
in fact this stretch has yielded us no traces of Palaeolithic
culture similar to Western Mousterian cultures. A blank
patch, with a few rare traces of the beginning of the
Quaternary in the south on the southern frontier of China,
and in the north the remains of the Sinanthropus of
Chou-k'ou-tien—such is the physiognomy of eastern and
northern Asia on the eve of the Upper Palaeolithic.

The advance towards the West and the Palaeolithic

The last chipped stone industries reached these regions
and developed there. Three stages mark this development.

Sino-Siberian I is illustrated by the Chinese sites of
Chou-k'ou-tien (upper cave), Sjara-osso-gol and Chuei-
tong-ku and the Siberian sites of the neighbourhood of
Irkutsk, Malta, Buretj and Tchastinsk. The type of
industry is Moustero-Aurignacian.

Sino-Siberian II does not include a Chinese site but
comprises the Siberian sites of Afontova-gora II, Bisk,
Tomsk and Krasnoyarsk, with industries similar to
European Solutreo-Magdalenian.

The third stage covers an even greater area, stretching
from Lake Baikal (Selenga) to the Urals (Pereselentz) in
the north, as far as the middle basin of the Lena (Olek-
minsk) and reaching the Mongolian sands (Ulan Bator)
in the south. The cultures of this epoch still present
Magdalenian aspects, but are more closely akin to Western

Mesolithic cultures. The first artistic evidence from this
zone is very unequally distributed.

One single example of art appears in China: a fragment
of a chopper, incised with geometrical lines, found in a
cave at Kwangsi in the midst of a pebble industry. In
Siberia examples are more numerous; the Lake Baikal
region yields incised plaques of mammoth tusk with
animal or geometrical decorations already including the
spiral and the S-couchant motif, also roughly carved
birds and female statuettes which have often been compared with the European statuettes of Gagarino and
Willendorf. The origin of these last has been wrongly
attributed to Siberia, making them follow a westward
route which in eastern Europe branched off towards
Africa and western Europe. Even if the existence of these
statuettes proves similar religious concepts, nevertheless
these figures have differences which make it impossible
to ascribe the art of the European centres to that of the
Siberian sites.

The Sino-Siberian Palaeolithic cultures present a homogeneous character, in spite of certain local variations.
Coming from the south of China, while making their way
towards Europe they went through similar phases of
evolution with artifacts in which we find Mousterian,
Solutrean, Aurignacian and Magdalenian characteristics.
But none of these aspects enables us to fix an absolute
chronology, and it is highly probable that all this development took place in the last phase of the Upper Pleistocene.

The art of the first polished stone cultures

The Neolithic of these regions is also subject to marked
chronological differences in relation to Western Neolithic.
The great archaeological areas are four in number:
western Siberia, eastern Siberia, northern China and
southern China saw the flowering of the Kelteminar
culture which touched the pit culture of eastern Europe
to the west. There were also the Afanasievo culture to the
east and the Iranian cultures of Anau, Sialk and Susa
to the south. In them we find those geometrical motifs
common to all of the contemporary cultures. Eastern
Siberia had similar ornaments, and only slight variations
enable us to distinguish between the successive cultures
of Isakovo, Serovo and Kitoi. We are indebted to the
Serovo culture for the best examples of the local tradition
of animal art. Whether in the form of statuettes of elk
or in the medium of rock engravings, the assurance of
the Siberian artists grows and prepares the way for the
flowering in these regions of the future art of the steppes,
which was, therefore, only to be a new interpretation
of an already developed art.

Only China had the privilege of a genuinely artistic
Neolithic civilisation. This culture, known as the Yang-
shao, appeared in the 3rd millennium at the time when
the Kitoi culture flourished in the north and the Afanasievo and Kelteminar cultures in the west. In spite of
similarities with the Siberian and Mongolian centres,
nothing would have led us to foresee a magnificent and
richly decorated painted pottery considered by some

84

84

84

85, 86

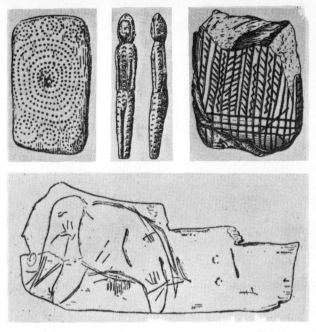

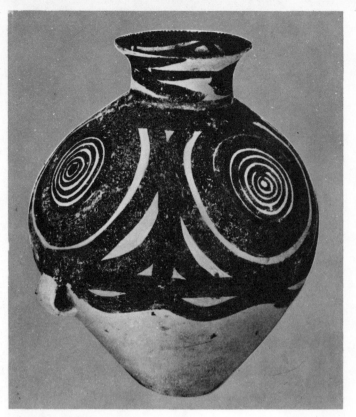

84. a. Incised plaque. Mammoth tusk. Upper Palaeolithic. Malta (Siberia). b. Female statue. Mammoth tusk. Upper Palaeolithic. Buretj (Siberia). c. Fragment of a chopper, incised with lines. Schist. Mesolithic. Kwangsi (China). d. Incised plaque. Mammoth tusk. Upper Palaeolithic. Malta (Siberia).

85. CHINESE. Neolithic painted pottery, from Ma-chang, Kansu. 1700–1300 B.C.

scholars as an Eastern branch of Western painted pottery. Admittedly there are many affinities, but no intermediate link confirms this origin. Stylistic studies have even led Professor J.G. Andersson to suppose, inversely, that there was a Chinese influence on Western painted pottery. But no trace of Chinese influence has been noted on the route from Eurasia during the Neolithic. The Yang-shao culture, therefore, may up to the present pass as having emerged fully equipped with a local proto-Neolithic culture, without any apparent attachment to those previous cultures by which it must nevertheless have been inspired.

In southern China the Neolithic is split into three cultures. That of Kwangsi is the most ancient and may be assimilated with the Mesolithic. Those of the Yangtze and of Si-kiang possess a grey monochrome pottery, but no painted ceramics. Some specialists have concluded from this that another Neolithic world existed beyond the Tsinling Mountains in contact with the Indo-Chinese Hoabinhian and Bacsonian cultures. There is no route entitling us to connect the painted pottery of northern China with the Neolithic block of southern China. Japanese excavations have, however, revealed painted pottery in Formosa which, in spite of the absence of bronze, has been attributed to a protohistoric period and has been considered as a southern expansion of the Yang-shao culture. The latter had already radiated northwards towards Manchuria, where painted pottery attributed to the beginning of the 2nd millennium has also been discovered. The absence of excavations in southern China does not definitely preclude the possibility of sites with painted pottery, and we are by no means sure that the old south-north route by which the Palaeolithic penetrated was not rediscovered by the bearers of this pottery. Admittedly, the road from the Yangtze to the Indus is long and we have no evidence, but we must not neglect this route, all the more so as the south may still have surprises in store for us with the rich agricultural centres of Bengal, Cochin-China and Tongking.

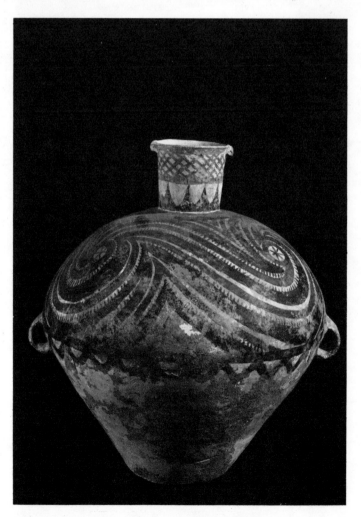

86. CHINESE. Neolithic painted pottery, from Pan Shan, Kansu. 3rd millennium B.C. *Cernuschi Museum, Paris.*

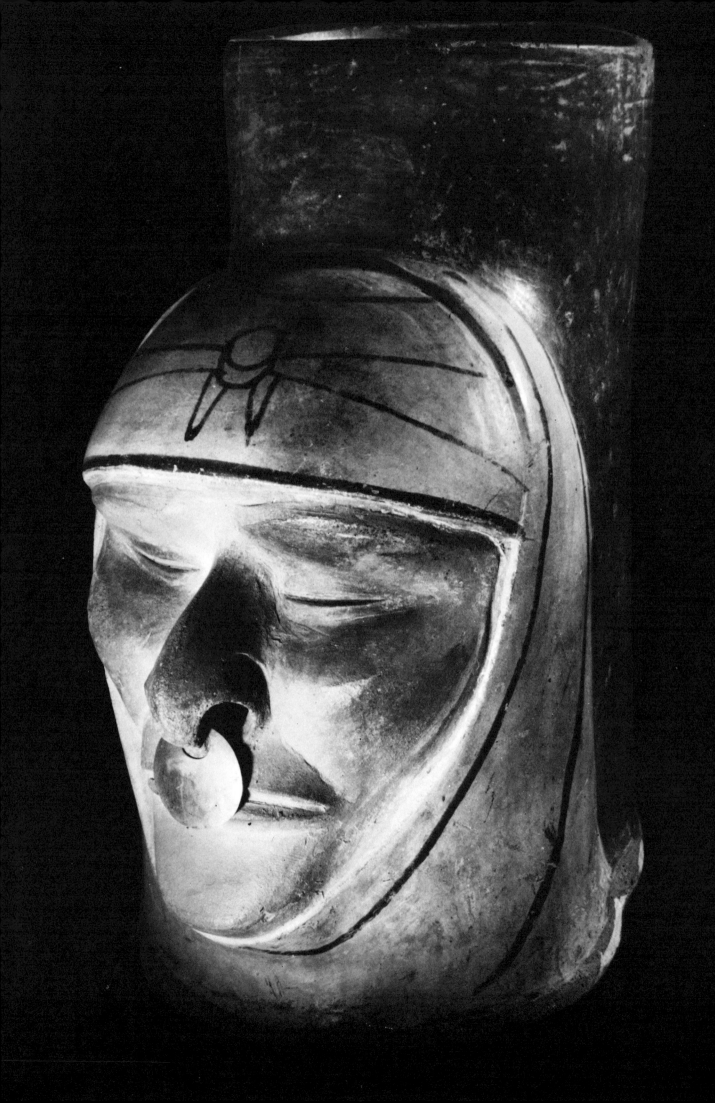

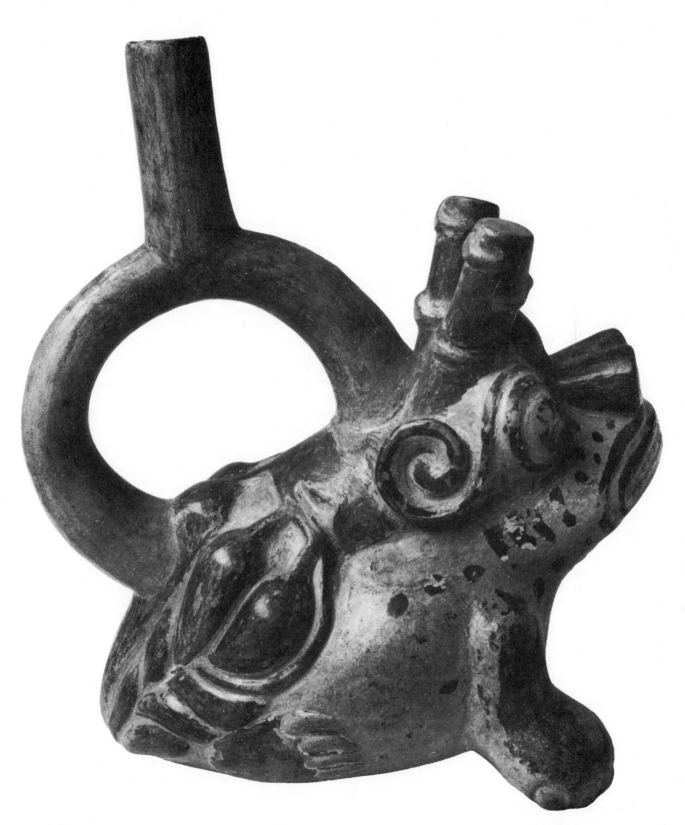

87. PERU. a. Fragment of Mochica anthropomorphic jar. The portrait-head, on the neck of the jar, has a gold nose-ring. *N. Cummings Collection, Chicago*. b. Frog-shaped vessel with 'stirrup-handle'. Mochica III. *Lambayeque Museum*.

ART FORMS AND SOCIETY *René Huyghe*

PRIMITIVE ART OUTSIDE PREHISTORY

When reconstituted by means of the evidence of pre-history the origins of art seem somewhat conjectural, with many gaps and mysteries counterbalancing a few expressive works. What man of those times has bequeathed to us can only yield its full meaning if we can cross-check it with the help of living, direct and observable proofs.

Fortunately they are within our reach: for some time now it has been pointed out how in a few years a child, all on its own, covers a condensed version of the path along which primitive man struggled so hard for thousands of years.

In addition comparatively recent, sometimes even contemporary, civilisations maintain patterns of life which have remained virtually unchanged since their beginnings. The thousand-year-old isolation of certain human groups, sometimes even scattered throughout whole continents, like North and South America or Australia, has favoured their relative stagnation at a human stage long since passed everywhere else.

Sometimes also (and this is a racial enigma) the deep-seated inability of a group has prevented it from advancing beyond a certain degree of development. If one day it finds itself in contact with men whose progress has followed a more normal course, it succumbs when faced with improved methods of aggression which it still has not dreamed of. This was so with the people of pre-Columbian America, the North American Indians and the Australian aborigines when the Europeans arrived and eventually crushed them. Sometimes tribes hidden in less fertile regions have been spared. This is the material which we must now compare with the evidence of prehistory.

Moreover, before we tackle the great empires which introduce the history of civilised art, the plan of the present work envisages the study at this point of all the evidence we possess of the passage from the primitive mentality to a more developed stage, closer to our own. For long disdained, this mentality enjoys a compensatory favour today, and it is sometimes considered fashionable to deny it the character of primitivism as implying a pejorative judgment. All we have to do is define the meaning of the word: although primitive art is capable of producing masterpieces as accomplished and as admirable as the others (for, as we have just seen, the fundamental laws of art operate from the very beginning), it is no less clear that it marks a preliminary stage, if only chronologically, on the way to future developments. So we shall preserve this perfectly justified term.

CHILDREN'S ART

The most immediate field of investigation is offered by childhood, in which we can rediscover the primordial endeavours of our species. Child psychologists have observed the phenomenon. The child begins by wanting to project his internal strength on the things which surround him. Between the ages of two and three, he looks for the chalk, pencil or even pebble which will enable him to put his mark, as yet incoherent, wherever he can. He scribbles on walls or paper; he covers them vehemently with a network of haphazard lines. Soon he is sketching more organised circular and spiral movements. It is only then that the notion of resemblance takes shape: at first it is fortuitous, random lines being interpreted after the event. 'It's a bow!' observed a three-year-old, seeing a line which he has impulsively scribbled; and then he deliberately adds an arrow.

He has only to take one more step in order to produce a conscious image. But just like prehistoric man with his succession of tentative efforts, the child begins with 'conceptual' realism. Mental equipment is innate, acquired directly; man brings it with him. Experience of the external world, on the other hand, is only acquired by a slow conquest, by an interpretation of sensations confused at first and elucidated as they become familiar. So the child first tries to replace the complexity of what he sees, which is beyond his ability to render, with simple shapes which his mind can grasp, the square, the circle, however irregularly his hand produces them. This diagram, scanty at first (a single circle for both body and head!), becomes more flexible, grows richer (two circles, one for the head, another for the body, on which he now begins to stick limbs, etc.). He makes increasing attempts to recapture everything his gaze takes in. But the mind continually acts as a screen, only retaining concentrated data, either simplified shapes or distinctive characteristics.

That was why prehistoric man of the Franco-Cantabrian period rendered the confused shapes of the animals 11 he saw by a clean line, while man of the Iberian Levant reduced them to the impression which had struck him 31 most and which he felt were the most charged with intensity and significance. In both cases, there was an effort to extract from the baffling complexity of reality concentrated elements, presenting that quality of unity which signifies the human mind and makes things intelligible to it.

In both cases, too, the procedures employed were radically different. We asked ourselves whether there were not 'families of minds' exhibiting opposite tendencies, different instinctive ways of solving the problems common to all men, the first of these families invoking more intellectual methods (shapes and their analysis) the second, more sensory methods (the impression and translation of the characteristic perceived). Now, these two families show themselves to be quite fundamental, because they are known to the child psychologist.

Psychiatrists working on the problem have shown that at the extremes there are an intellectual type with an abstract way of expression, and a sensory type with an objective way of expression. Between the two extends a whole range of intermediate types. This is the very same division which the Franco-Cantabrian and the Iberian thrust upon us. Although more recent researchers may have quibbled about this division, taking exception to its simplicity, nevertheless it corresponds to evidence which strikes every unprejudiced mind. We remember a visit to the art class of a primary school where great care had

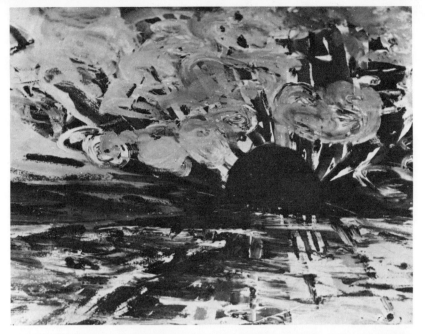

The attempt by modern artists to get back to first principles often leads them to adopt the simplest forms of expression. Here the expressionism of Vlaminck is matched by the spontaneity of a child of seven . . .

88. Sunset over the sea. Painting by a child aged 7.

. . . Analogies of the same kind can also be seen between modern art and the elementary 'uncomposed' structures conceived by mental patients. They are also to be found in the arts of primitive peoples [95].

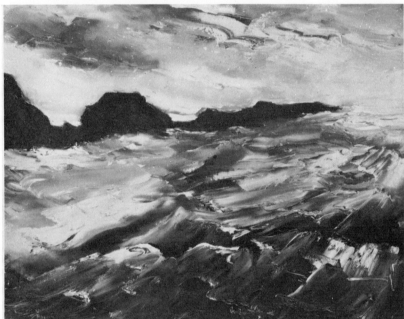

89. VLAMINCK. Seascape.

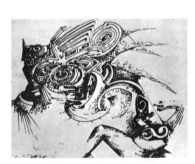

90. ANDRÉ MASSON. The Dream of Ariana, 1941.

91. The Birds. Painting by a mental patient suffering from depression with elements of paranoia. *Napsbury Collection.*

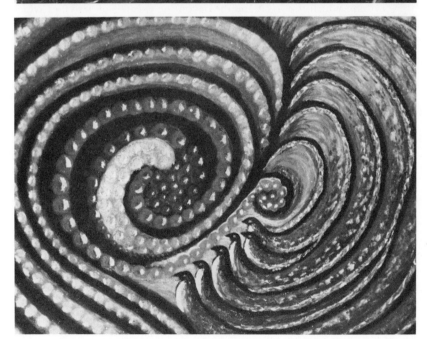

been taken to allow the young beginners absolute freedom of expression with pencil and brush. A dish of cherries served as a model. One of the infants, dominated by sensation, had smeared a roughly pyramidal patch of red, resting on a plate reproduced in a clumsy perspective. Another, on the other hand, had drawn as regular a circle as he was able, and inside it he had carefully arranged a series of small circles coloured red. Instinctively the latter painted the *idea* he formed of the sight before him; the other, the *sensation* he received from it, without trying to elucidate it. The two fundamental types of art were there, face to face. Without knowing it, two urchins revealed in individual temperaments what prehistory had already demonstrated in collective temperaments.

THE ART OF THE MENTAL PATIENT

There is another field of study, often drawn on by psychologists—insanity. Here the case is different: we hope to recapture the fundamental mechanism by observing destructive rather than constructive forces.

Our epoch, let us point out in passing, has for the first time attached great and often excessive importance to the artistic works of both mental patients and children. In this it is obeying the same propensity which has driven it to explore all the primitive, savage or archaic arts. This is because, unlike the epochs when the creative flow is imperious and asks itself no questions the better to assert its position, our own is gnawed by uncertainty. It investigates itself and man. It is hungry for a lost purity and freshness. It seeks to return to the sources of art or history, in the hope of rediscovering the secret of what is as yet untouched and undeformed by the frantic dialectics of our over-cultivated intelligence.

But the insane are less significant than one might think. The characteristic of insanity is, in fact, to destroy the balance, the basis of moral health, between the various tendencies by which man is tormented. It dislocates the unity which is the fundamental principle of the life of the mind, as of art. For unity through harmonious diversity the insane person substitutes, at best, the morbid unity of monomania, which, by the blind systematic elimination of everything which thwarts it and the devouring excess of its dominating impulse, becomes the very opposite, an element of disequilibrium.

So we shall certainly find the fundamental predispositions we have recognised already, repetition, regularity, etc., but they run in neutral like an engine accelerating madly with nothing to check it: they 'race'. In the dialogue, or rather chorus, of 'I' and 'the Other' which we have emphasised above all in art, it is 'the Other' which disappears: objective adherence to the real is diminished. Let us note that this adherence is also weakening and sometimes blotted out in modern art; inner creation no longer knows any restrictions. Hence perhaps the attraction felt by our age for the art of the mental patient.

As for the 'I', sometimes it is decomposed, sometimes it is absorbed by a single one of its principles which have become an obsession, transformed into an implacable cancer. Nevertheless, for the same reason, the art of mental patients may throw clearer light on the elements normally brought into play by art, like the magnifying glass which isolates and magnifies the point it aims at.

Sometimes we recognise the tendency to abstraction, submitting reality to its laws which have become mechanical, implacable; sometimes, on the other hand, the hypertrophy of an affective ruling passion which seizes the real, hands it over to its unbridled demands and devours it like a fire. From hyperabstraction to hyperexpressionism, we may occasionally find surprising accents which move us by their heart-rending and terrible sincerity. But the renewal of vision contributed by the art of mental patients, which has found favour in our time, is normally artificial, for it is based on destructive and no longer on constructive methods.

THE ART OF BACKWARD CIVILISATIONS

Such are the methods of investigation which our most direct experience suggests to us. What can those civilisations which we may call backward in the strict sense of the word teach us? Although it would be presumptuous to conclude from their many similarities that these civilisations are identical with the early ones they resemble most, they undoubtedly add force to the interpretations which have been placed on mankind's initial efforts. When, during a stay in Africa, Leo Frobenius, the German anthropologist, saw his hunting-companions drawing the outlines of animals on the ground and practising sympathetic magic on them, he was actually seeing a survival of the magical art postulated by prehistorians.

It is obvious that the age of the hunter is echoed in the society of the South African Bushmen which has continued to the present day; their rock paintings are almost identical with those of the Iberian Levant. But who could say whether their complicated mythology already existed in prehistory? Similarity is not identity.

The pre-Columbian, on the other hand, in America evokes the Neolithic age and the epoch of the agrarian empires. Tattooing, the use of masks and, in certain funerary rites, of ochre, proclaim links with the most ancient stages. Metal, copper and gold, were virtually unknown except in religious and ornamental objects. It would be easy to multiply such examples.

The vanished arts

The remains of prehistoric art are only the minutest traces of activities which were undoubtedly very much more diverse: there were certainly other forms of art which have disappeared for lack of a lasting medium. The Pueblo Indians, for example, still make what are sometimes admirable compositions on the ground with coloured sand. Ritual decrees that these 'sand paintings' must not survive the ceremonies which gave rise to them and they are effaced before sunrise.

Excluding such ephemeral manifestations in which destruction is deliberate, there is the example of fragile or perishable materials of which no trace remains. Thus there may well have been a 'wood civilisation' which would once have yielded as much evidence as the 'stone civilisations', but of which all traces have vanished. However we find its equivalents in certain backward societies. What remains of straw, cord and leather work? There is nothing ridiculous in the theory that during the Palaeolithic an art of a quite different, less religious character, practised more openly and thus more liable to destruction, may have existed side by side with the ritual works of the witch-doctor preserved in the depths of caves. What would remain of it? What are we to make of the two wonderfully supple and life-like women, discovered dur-

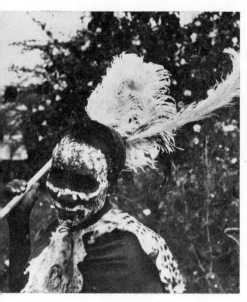

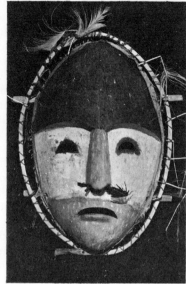

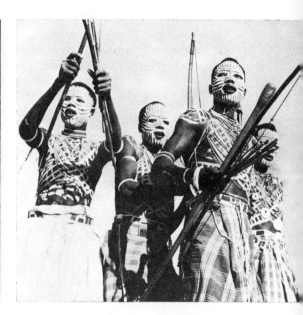

92. Karamajong warrior from Uganda painted for a ritual ceremony.

93. Eskimo mask from Alaska representing a mythical character. *Musée de l'Homme, Paris*.

94. Tattooed Turu dancers from East Africa.

95 *Right*. Baluba mask. *Ratton Collection*.

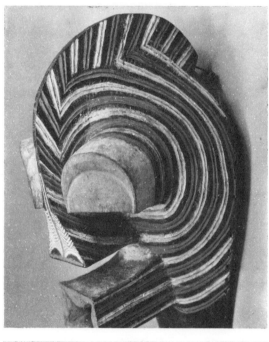

One of the most elementary forms of art, still practised among living primitives, is the decoration of the human body.
Masks often resemble this decoration.
By painting and tattooing, the entire human body becomes an ornamented surface, as can still be seen among peoples who have remained primitive.

96. Neolithic clay figures from Cucuteni (Roumania) with engraved patterns representing tattooing.

97. Examples of body painting by the Ona tribe of Tierra del Fuego.

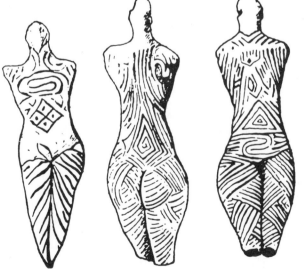

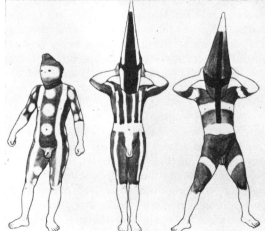

ing recent years in the cave of La Magdeleine in the Tarn? They pose a baffling problem. In the same way, the art of the Iberian Levant, also executed in the open air, but preserved by a favourable climate, is perhaps connected with earlier examples, unknown because they have vanished, from the Franco-Cantabrian.

Once again we find the magical idea at the basis of the dance: anyone who seizes the resemblance, the facsimile of the model, acquires actual possession of the model itself. Depending on the stage of evolution, this possession is for different ends: the hunter uses it to make himself master of the game he lives on. Certain Indians of the north-west coast of America imitate in mime the leaping of salmon, which is in fact their principal food.

The magical function of art

All this confirms the function which devolves upon art of representing either the visible or the invisible. In both cases, incidentally, it is always used to bring invisible forces into play. There is absolutely no cleavage between the 'animated' arts, such as dancing, and the 'figurative' arts, such as painting and sculpture. The dance is nearly
always accompanied by ritual painting of the face and
body; above all, it completes the illusion with the mask whose role is then of capital importance: the engravings of prehistoric sorcerers have confirmed the existence of disguises from the very earliest times. Take the engravings
in the cave of Les Trois Frères, for example. Now the mask is found in every continent; it still survives in certain popular European traditions. But to the primitive peoples it had the value of actual incarnation. Among certain North American Indians, a young man must first meet his guardian spirit in the forest and feel possessed by him, before making the mask which confirms and makes manifest this possession.

Everything goes to confirm what prehistoric art foreshadowed: the image incarnates what it represents; visible identity entails invisible identity. Art therefore is essentially a material means of reaching and demonstrating spiritual forces and even of introducing them into the world of the senses. Admittedly in a different way from our own and corresponding to another human stage, art nevertheless plays the same fundamental role which we have emphasised from the first. It serves to establish a connection between the two realities which split man in two, the physical reality which his body perceives and the immaterial reality in which his soul resides. Through art, he gives to the one the appearances of the other; he associates them and blends them.

Let us then summarise the conclusions drawn from the remains of prehistoric art and see how they can be verified in the art of living 'primitives'. Among them, art fulfils a function, on the one hand, and on the other satisfies a pure pleasure. First of all it is function: it realises, i.e. it makes the invisible enter into perceptible reality, the invisible which at the magical stage is composed of forces, tendencies, desires, and at the religious stage of an entire conception of the universe, as Negro art reveals. All this seems very remote from us. But did not art fulfil the same function for a community then as it does today for the individual? For what else does he himself demand but the realisation in images of what he dimly aspires to?

The Hopi Indians still represent the stage when art consists of mimic rituals: by movements of the body they symbolise the result they wish for and think they will ensure it in this magical way. But to sculpt or to paint is to give to an object the task of imitation, previously reserved for the body or its dances. Even in modern times in Africa, a barren woman has been seen carrying a doll on her back which in some way put her half-way towards the child she wanted. The magical double is no longer the dancer but an image manufactured with the hands.

It is clear then that realism is a condition of success. This is true in the Palaeolithic when the animal, subjected to enchantment by art, is represented with a suggestive skill, whereas the human figure, which does not assume such an essential role and is undoubtedly no more than an unimportant diversion, does not benefit from an elaborate technique and seems almost formless in comparison. This significant difference reappears in the 'primitive' arts of the Chibchas of Colombia.

But pure pleasure may be combined with the ritual function. The prehistoric artist's attempts to sketch his brothers certainly seems to have been a mere distraction, a kind of game. However the perfection of the animal representations also undoubtedly produced pleasure of an aesthetic nature. Perhaps it was not directly motivated by the actual act of depiction, but once perceived, it provoked it more or less unconsciously. The work and its characteristics were certainly primarily justified by a utilitarian end, since it was often executed in such conditions that, practically speaking, it could not be seen. Such is the case, where the drawings are superimposed, losing themselves in each other and finally becoming totally indecipherable. It is clear that in this case prehistoric men cheerfully sacrificed the beauty of their works of art to their practical role: in effect by this accumulation they believed that they were increasing the magical power.

Ritual power

It was because the work of art from the very beginning appeared as the custodian of animistic powers that it became the appointed receptacle of the souls of the dead, when society began to make them an object of worship. The prehistory of the Neolithic suggests that the standing stone, or menhir, was very probably a place for the soul's permanent repose. But this belief continues when the transition from the simple stone to the statue is made. The statue of the ancestor, whether in Africa, America or Oceania, is not merely an image; it is the habitat of the soul which is deemed to be immanent in it.

Primitive man is struck by the supernatural side of art, in which he is certainly prolonging the beliefs of prehistoric man. Here again, are we so very different, in spite of our new ideas? In the 19th century Baudelaire was still talking about art as supernaturalism like Heine before him. Melanesia was to contribute the term which expresses this power—the Mana. In fact it seems clear that resemblance alone (the relation with the visible world) is not enough to create the magical achievement; it needs the addition of a fluid (a complementary relation with the spiritual world).

Once again we have to acknowledge the proof that from the beginn ng the work of art is the meeting place of these two worlds, an intermediary, a 'third order', as we have called it, between that which exists in concrete reality and that which exists in spiritual reality. The latter is so important that sometimes, with fetishes for example, a 'consecration' ceremony is undertaken in order to introduce it into the work of art.

But when we meet a civilisation which we consider as much more developed, such as the Chinese or Tibetan, we rediscover the same fundamental conviction: their statues of the Buddha would have no valid existence unless the sacred texts were placed inside them and their eyes and mouth were painted.

Is this not another profound truth which we have merely adapted to suit our own mental processes? Do not we in our turn think that only inspiration, that spiritual force which inhabits the artist, gives him the power to create a worthwhile work?

Decorative art, which represents nothing, obeys the same law and is not so radically different from the figurative arts in this respect as one might suppose. When prehistoric man making his first attempts scratched a few vaguely organised hatchings on his bone implement, he was not only thinking of 'embellishing' it: he was inscribing it with the projection of himself, his mark of possession, his invisible presence. It was much more than the distinctive sign with which the present day owner brands his cattle; it was another magical act.

Primitive man often demonstrates that to him the fact of touching or taking hold of an object makes a portion of the person who made the movement pass into it and thus creates the beginning of possession. This obscure feeling, reinforced perhaps by traditional beliefs, is certainly one of the initial motives of decorative art.

Later, it developed: figures became signs and images. But they remained guardians of an invisible presence through the symbolical meaning they possessed. But that is merely a further extension of the resemblance: if an apparently purely geometrical figure is endowed with significance, it is because originally it was a representative image which has become progressively more and more stylised. Even when a pure geometrical shape is involved, it has been chosen for the relation it evokes with what the artist wants to suggest. The circle is connected with the sun or the thunder-wheel, the sinuous or zigzag line with water, etc. This remoter resemblance, less obvious than in a realistic work, implies the participation, the presence of the force thus evoked, one might almost say invoked.

The passage from magical to religious art does not change anything; it merely enriches this initial notion. Nor is the 'sacred' image limited to representing the divine being; it participates in him, contains him. The statue, to simple peoples, is not only a representation intended to evoke God, the Virgin or a saint: they adore a real incarnate presence in it. The Church, always on its guard against idolatry, is well aware of this.

Aesthetic pleasure

It is obviously difficult to make out, amid all these complicated feelings, how much aesthetic pleasure exists at this stage. Has beauty been perceived and intentionally sought? However obscure the notion may be, it is certainly dawning. The notion of talent and its price already existed: in America traces have been disclosed of artistic reputations spread over great distances and preserved in the memory for long periods; it happened in Africa, too, where they sometimes went so far as to deify the great creators, as was done in Egypt, at the very beginning of the IIIrd Dynasty, with Imhotep, the architect of the step pyramid of Zoser, at Sakkara. (In the same way Imhotep was the guardian of the Senets of the Royal Magic.) However, ethnographers have been able to quote cases where primitive man takes out the object on holidays and settles down to contemplate it, apparently experiencing pleasure in seeing and touching it.

In this way of thinking which is still incapable of self-analysis, the idea of magical or ritual value is hard to separate from an idea of quality, of prestige in the object's outward appearance. The pleasure felt in contemplation is the one which the artist instinctively seeks to provoke; it is the beginning of aesthetic feeling.

The laws of evolution

If primitive creations help us to verify the essential truth of what prehistory dimly shows us of the nature of art at its very beginnings, they also confirm the laws of evolution glimpsed at the same time. The most strictly geometrical decoration seems to be peculiar to the most developed tribes. We can observe this in the north-west of America. In Africa the admirable Ife bronzes, so much the expression of an advanced civilisation as to remind us, by their skilful balance between realism and the mastery of shapes, of Egypt—in particular of the 'replacement head' of the IVth Dynasty—are earlier than the Benin bronzes which derive from them. The process of stylisation from the first to the second is absolutely clear.

We can even ask ourselves whether the geometrical simplification in art so much appreciated today is not the sign of the culmination of an old civilisation rather than the mark of a culture in its infancy. Perhaps this is the case with African art as we know it. In the same way numbers of prehistoric works have only arrived at certain bold simplifications because they come at the end of a long previous evolution which we can sometimes reconstruct.

So once again art appears caught between the double tendency which makes it oscillate between the ambition to rival the real in its appearance and the desire, on the other hand, to reduce it to simplifications in which the geometrical spirit triumphs.

The observation of 'primitive' peoples throws new light on this point: for example, one often notes among the north-west American Indians that realistic figurative art is mainly the man's province and that abstract geometrical art is the woman's field. This is because weaving and pottery belong to household occupations, consequently to women. Now, these techniques lend themselves to geometrical ornament, to decoration. On the other hand, the magical power inherent in the likeness seems to reserve it for the exclusive attention of men. In New Guinea it has been noted that the carvers of statues of ancestors try to capture their characteristic features down to their tattoo marks, in order to retain the vital power of the dead man.

There we catch a glimpse of one of the possible reasons for the coexistence of a realistic art of representation and an art of abstract decoration, the first charged with effective religious power of a more sacred nature, the second only creating illusion by means of symbols, thus in a more indirect, more neutral manner and for this reason used in the simple decoration of everyday objects.

These brief observations suffice to show the lessons we may draw from a controlled comparison between the prehistoric and the 'primitive' arts.

THE ART OF LIVING PRIMITIVE PEOPLES *André Leroi-Gourhan*

*Some of the most ancient stages in the history of art,
lost in the obscurity of the past, may come alive
for us through surviving groups of people who have
remained more or less unchanged. Here we consider
those with the most archaic way of life.*

What do we mean by living primitives? It is difficult to
give the primitives a definite frontier, either in time or
geographically. The term is applied to living peoples
whose material culture corresponds to stages long since
passed by the men of the central regions of the two
land masses. These 'backward' peoples are obviously no
more primitive than we are in the historical sense, their
evolution being as long as that of the 'civilised' peoples.

The 'peoples beyond the third line'

The 'great arts' are situated in a chain round the world
running through the continental masses: from Peru to the
south of the United States, from Japan to Ireland and
North Africa (zone 1). Outside this vast geographical and
cultural ensemble are grouped the arts of Indonesia,
Polynesia, Melanesia, Africa, of the Lapps and Siberians,
of the Eskimos and the Indians of North and South
America (zone 2). Directly coupled with the areas of
development of the major civilisations, these are not
'primitive' arts; this misconception has long since disappeared. Each one of them developed with a varying
degree of independence, but from near or from far,
constantly or intermittently, they were influenced by the
great civilisations. Aesthetic analysis of the Lapps,
Samoyedes, Yakuts, Tunguses and Ainus, who form the
fringe of the 'hyperboreans' to the north of the ancient
continents (zone 2b), reveals the immediate influence of
Europe, central Asia, China or the combined influences
of several cultural entities; in the same way, Oceanic,
Eskimo and African art reveal the highly complex inter-

play of the components of an evolution which has gone
on for thousands of years over the accessible globe.

Consequently the primitives are the 'peoples beyond
the third line' and their archaism arises from fundamentally geographical causes. The only ones who stand
up to serious examination as primitives are the Bushmen
of the tip of South Africa, the Fuegians from the tip of
South America, and the Australian aborigines shut off in
their own continent (zone 3). But it is not possible to
credit even them with absolute isolation; the Australians
themselves had ancient contacts with New Guinea and
Asia. Primitives form small communities isolated from
the great human masses in which the development of
present-day societies goes on, communities moreover
whose members belong to archaic racial types. These
considerations do not imply that all the aspects of their
culture have slumbered for thousands of years to provide
us with a complete picture of prehistoric humanity. But
we must take into account the very special physical surroundings in which they live; their material life is deeply
affected by the climate and natural resources. They are
the lowest and most unfortunate of men in our present-
day world, whereas the prehistoric men of the ancient
world, who have been compared to them, were the leaders
of their time living in the most favourable regions.

In religious and aesthetic matters, it must be said that
their basic repertoire is in a state of constant modification.
The religious concepts and the figurative symbolism of
the Australians are very elaborate. At most, one might,
like Henri Bergson, consider that this evolution went on
by revolving indefinitely around a restricted number of
fundamental elements. The living 'primitive', then, is not
to be looked on as a 'living fossil', disregarding his status
as a man capable of personal intellectual development, his
ancient links with the central groups or the generally
miserable material conditions in which he lives.

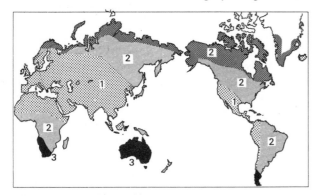

98. THE ZONES OF ARTISTIC PRODUCTION. In this
diagrammatic map of the main cultural areas in the world
between the 16th and 18th centuries, the smaller areas of
different structure are not represented. In general, however,
these large areas correspond with the areas of similar primitive character shown in map 99. It is fairly obvious that at the
present day, except for pockets of zone 2 existing in New
Guinea, Africa and South America and two or three minute
points of zone 3 in Australia, the whole of the map would be
incorporated in zone 1.

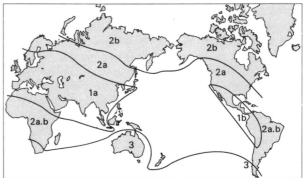

**99. POSITION OF PRIMITIVE ARTS THROUGHOUT THE
WORLD.** This map indicates the areas of persistent primitive
culture between the 15th and 19th centuries. Zone 1a
corresponds to the arts of the great Eurasian civilisations,
zone 1b to the great American civilisations. Note the central
position of zone 1. Zone 2a is occupied by those arts in direct
contact with the great civilisations, zone 2b by those with
indirect relations. Zone 3 covers the three groups, Bushmen,
Australian aborigines and Fuegians, who are outside the
areas of diffusion.

Is there such a thing as 'primitive' art?

Is it possible to extract a valid image from the primitives, taken en masse? It would be valuable, for if the Bushmen, Fuegians and Australian aborigines possessed a common fundamental aesthetic behaviour, it would not be unreasonable to apply the same behaviour to prehistoric man, and a general theory of the evolution of art would become possible. It does seem as if this common basis exists, and many studies have drawn on it, but we may ask if it does not simply represent human values in the widest sense; the primitives exhibit these values in a context which is often as elaborate as, but different from, our own, so that they become perceptible to us. If this was the only result it produced, the study of the aesthetic behaviour of the primitives would contribute a by no means negligible benefit.

What are the signs of a primitive art? In Chapter 1 we tried to explain the first stages of the figurative expression of elementary psycho-physiological impulses and we showed that these manifestations form a stratum later covered by manifestations further and further removed from the elementary common basis, even before cave art begins. Covered up and buried deeper and deeper, it continues to exist in all the arts, and part of modern aesthetic effort has consisted in exhuming it. This exhumation has found expression in a 'pilgrimage' to the true or supposed sources of 'primitive' art. But only the art of the Australians and the Fuegians can really be so considered. The latter are practically extinct, but what knowledge we do have of them shows little development in plastic representation, whereas the Australians, on the contrary, have abundantly developed this field, so that we prefer to make use of them for our demonstration.

We can leave aside the expression of genetic impulses: virility, fecundity and fertility lead to a figurative art whose resurgence is constant among the primitives as everywhere else. They are merely enveloped in a different context in each culture; perhaps their ultimate insipidity is the academic nude. So much has been written about the Palaeolithic statuettes, the pregnant mares of the caves and the mother goddesses that other important aspects of primitive art have been rather obscured.

Expressive symbolism

From the historian's point of view, art means essentially the work of art; in the eyes of the Australian aboriginal it is the inclusion of the personality in a figurative process.

Where we tend to see objects susceptible of aesthetic analysis, what the primitive feels above all is the rhythm of the figurative dramatisation. This explains why very frequently we cannot make him execute a 'work of art' outside the rhythmic whole in which it has its place. In other words, the work of art (mask, statuette or other object) is like a musical instrument, i.e. an effective and temporary element participating in the arrangement of a figurative structure. With us, opera, in the etymological and artistic sense, would best correspond to this attitude in which the mobilisation of all the various elements (instruments, voices, mime) determines the value of the artistic accessories, which may finally be reduced to mere symbols. Our aesthetic judgment of the primitive work, then, is applied to an image which is only the symbolical and partial projection of the whole figurative apparatus.

When we judge the plastic value of a mask by our own

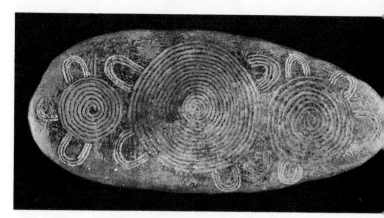

100. ABORIGINAL ART. AUSTRALIA. A tjuringa.

standards, it is as risky as if we judged the literary worth of a 15th-century poem by the initial illuminated letter.

In order to understand how the artist is included in the figurative process, let us imagine a group of Australian aborigines seated in a circle on the sand to take part in an incantation. The reciter pronounces words which are given a rhythmic accompaniment by the interjections and bust movements of the audience. As the recital unfolds, he traces in the sand with his finger-tip a perfect spiral, the centre of which corresponds to the end of a sentence. He adds progressively a second, a third and several more spirals, each one rhythmically integrated with the sentences of the recital.

Then, without stopping speaking, he connects the spirals by straight lines and finishes the design at the same time as the recital with a superb ease and mastery. The figurative drama is complete. Its raison d'être does not lie in the spiral drawings of which we can say that they have a symbolical decorative value, which, in a word, we can judge by our own standards. It is lived bodily by all its actors, and the plastic decoration, which may incidentally represent the most varied subjects, is only a projection of the figurative rhythm.

Moreover proof positive is supplied by the same aborigines. Among their works we possess small plaques of soft stone called tjuringas, engraved with the same groups of spirals or concentric circles. Considered individually, the image they bear has no significance of its own; it is merely potentially very expressive. Placed on the ground in the middle of the same circle of men, it sets the same figurative drama in motion: the reciter's finger follows the circles, turning like the needle on a gramophone record, the recital unfolds, the audience make their responses in a rhythmic ensemble identical with that of the first example. We are tempted to find out what the spirals mean, to what mysterious symbols they correspond, of what realistic themes they are the debased or secret representation, whereas the aboriginal is like a little girl who cannot skip or even see a skipping rope without singing in the appropriate tone: 'Salt—mustard—vinegar —pepper'.

Disguise and the mask

The artist, therefore, is also an instrument, and this emerges even more clearly in disguises. Body painting and disguise played an important role in prehistoric art, since red ochre is the first evidence of an aesthetic expression, and nearly all the representations of man in the

100

79

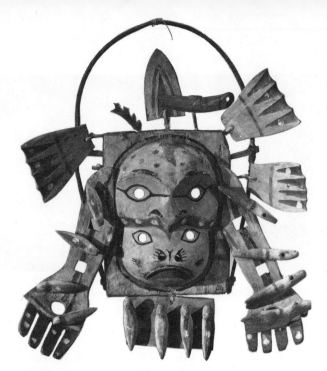

101. ESKIMO ART. ALASKA. Wooden dance mask.
American Museum of Natural History.

Upper Palaeolithic age are those of masked or disguised persons. It is probably no coincidence that living primitives obey the same aesthetic urges which lead them, too, to paint their bodies and the sides of cliffs and caves. Ochre, clay, charcoal, bird's down stuck on with blood, hair and beards dressed in strange ways are among the procedures which universally have the power to transform man himself into a figurative instrument. In the present-day world the Australians are masters of this technique, but it reappears at all stages of developed societies. The direct application to the skin of pastes and colouring matter leads to a representation which is all the more dramatic in that it is directly animated by the muscles of the actor's face and limbs. It is far more of a transfiguration than the mask.

Masks and disguises covering the whole body belong to a higher stage. The majority of the Australian aborigines know nothing of the mask and the Fuegians do not always seem to have known it, but it appears with uniform frequency in the intermediate cultures (zones 2 and 2a). Starting with the mask, the artist is completely enclosed in a figurative shell which acquires an individual existence. A dissociation between the actor and the character he represents begins to arise, whereas body painting effects the continuity between the world represented and the representing ego.

Incidentally it should be pointed out that the dissociation is still not complete in many cases; among the Eskimos, for example, the sculptor of the mask may be its user, the shape being inspired by the entity represented, and the division between this entity and the 'I' of the artist inappreciable. In developed societies (zone 1), facial painting and masks fall into various groups. They are found in popular festivals, the carnival for example, in the make-up of the Chinese, Japanese and European theatres, in feminine make-up, in theatrical masks, in the facial painting or masks symbolising religious characters. An equivalent progression could be noted in primitive body painting, popular fancy dress and the religious, military or civilian dress of developed groups corresponding to a status acquired by the individual who is recognised by

all as being 'dressed in the insignia of his office'.

When we attempt to bring out what is characteristic of the aesthetic behaviour of primitives, we rapidly perceive that it contains nothing which does not still exist in the more developed human groups.

Imaginative creation

With men, imaginative creation is of the same order as technical creation. During the physical and mental evolution of the higher primates, creative impulses were given expression by the creation of objects—weapons to kill game, tools for digging earth or for making weapons. The creation of a weapon is not a phenomenon independent of the physiological impulse; it prolongs and regulates a series of gestures which form a link between the hunter and the hunted. The tool, as we have seen further back, is also caught up in a current which leads it to aesthetic beauty through growing efficiency.

Aesthetic creation is of a very similar character; in the first manifestations the two terms are equivalent and indissociable. We are not going to deal here with the technical side of aesthetic realisation, the restrictions imposed by the quality of tools, the wood, earth, stone, metal, whose nature is sometimes a hindrance, sometimes an incentive, to creation; we are simply considering the relation between the function of the useful object and its shape, a relation which guides the evolution of forms. Over and above the elementary impulses of hunger and sex which give rise to extremely precocious expressions of aesthetic creation, we see the progressive materialisation of less directly practical attitudes, those which already in the animal world correspond to the free expenditure of surplus energy: exuberance and joy are channelled into more and more elaborate rhythmical arrangements. Anxiety about food and sexual impulses are at the most deeply intimate level of our souls.

The last part of prehistory saw the spread of an art which corresponded to new preoccupations—the search for man's place in the organised world, the imaginative creation of a natural and supernatural universe in which man finds security in proportion as he organises its structure. From this point onwards, the situation of living primitives is established: art has become a creation which mobilises, in different proportions, all the human aptitudes, technical procedures which help to master the materials and conduct which expresses the various urges. Art appears to us essentially in a religious form (the search for man's place in the world) expressing itself in a comparatively elaborate cosmogony (fitting the whole of Creation into a system which makes it 'manageable'), using all the resources at the disposal of the creative power of man (rhythmic gestures and sounds, plastic images) on a foundation where the elementary forces continually manifest themselves.

In the more developed societies, the growing requirements of technology and the increasingly intellectual form given to elementary impulses have progressively masked the fundamental relationship which exists between physiology, technology and art. To rediscover this link, we must go back to the rare groups whose development lags behind our own, to the few thousands of 'primitives' who are still living. Then we may understand, with the help of prehistoric records, some of the features of the beginnings of art.

AFRICAN ART *Marcel Griaule*

At first the study of African arts was confined to their surface appearance. Recently more ambitious scholars have sought to go still further: they have inquired into the secret motives and the states of mind of the African artists which give these works of art a meaning unfathomable by the average spectator. Marcel Griaule was the foremost of these innovators. The following section is one of the last articles written before his premature death and in it he condenses his valuable experience.

The motives which guide the hands of the sculptors and architects of Negro Africa, the strait jacket of ritual and symbolism in which the work of art is confined, the looser framework of institutions which surrounds it, the connections between some works themselves inside a society or from one people to another—all these factors should be as much subjects of study as the actual works themselves. For the arts of the Negroes, just like their ritual, their symbolism, and their social and political organisation, are a means of exhibiting a general conception of the universe, its origins, workings, goal and meaning.

We shall not attempt the classifications and syntheses so dear to the Western mind: they are still premature.

With a few rare exceptions, the regions actually known have only been superficially examined. More serious still is the fact that the white world has grown used to seeing the Negro world as unthinking, backward and incoherent. So much so that when the African peoples suddenly appear in a very different light it comes as a shock. And it is not so long ago that scholars themselves, undoubtedly worried by the latest revolutionary discoveries in the former French Sudan, did not dare define their positions. Today, Hellenists like P. M. Schuhl think in terms of possible relations between Greece and Africa south of the Sahara via intervening peoples; Egyptologists like Hans Hickmann are struck by the 'extraordinary resemblance' between Dogon customs and beliefs and the traditions of pharaonic Egypt; and Christiane Desroches Noblecourt is pursuing researches which take ample account of the enormous hinterland that tropical Africa forms in relation to the Nile valley.

This means that the Negro civilisations in their turn are becoming integrated into the world picture. But unlike so many others, they are not supported by a single written document, so that it is particularly difficult to establish an African chronology.

However this is not because the Negroes were ignorant of graphic processes: four Sudanese groups of varying sizes, the Mandingo, Bambara, Dogon and Bozo, had at their disposal, and to some extent still have, an imposing range of signs. The initiated Bambara know two hundred and sixty-four main symbols. The male Dogon possess a complicated system with 22 families of 12 elements, each of them covering a series of 22 pairs of signs. The women use a different, but probably equally rich, system. These signs are not only a means of expression: they have a value of their own, and they existed before the things they stand for, and brought them into being. Their system is a genuine art of writing and perhaps even of creating, applied to all the religious, social or natural

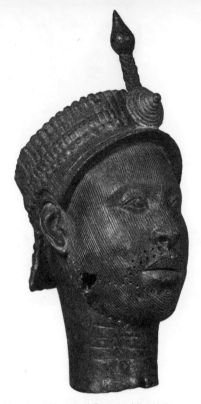

102. IFE. NIGERIA. Head said to be of Olokun (divine king or Oni) founder of the Yoruba Dynasty. Bronze. *British Museum.*

circumstances of life. It expresses that conception of the world to which the Sudanese have given permanence in a myth, and its 22 series reflect the 22 categories of things and beings as well as the various phases of the organisation of the cosmos.

The religious meaning of the images

The inclination to draw and paint goes back to very remote times, if we consider the profusion of engravings and paintings in the Sahara, open to Egyptian and Mediterranean influences, in East Africa, a transitional zone, and especially in South Africa. Few of these works have been explained.

In some Sudanese rituals rock paintings and signs play a vital role, such as, for instance, those in the Songo shelter in the Bandiagara cliffs, in Dogon country. These ideographs, laid out in bands and refurbished section by section at the time when the circumcision rites take place, reveal in sibylline figures the descent of an ark bringing order to the earth, and, in explicit figures, the masks of the society of men, as well as the material of the ceremonies every sixty years for the renewal of the cosmos.

The Keita of the Mandingo country also have similar rites at the time of the septennial re-making of the sanctuary of Kangaba, of 'international' fame, since numerous populations claim that they came from this 'vestibule of the Manda'. The meaning of the paintings outside the sanctuary had already been glimpsed: the rudimentary figures with limbs in the form of a cross, the outlines of hands and calabashes, the speckled areas, and the dotted lines in three colours which surrounded them contained a virtually static symbolism. But when one actually watched the figures being drawn, their deeper meaning appeared. First of all, the woman responsible for the work faced east and painted a black circle; then, turning to the north, she painted another circle at the top of a vertical line, followed by a similar figure, but including a transverse line forming the arms; in a fourth figure, another bar represented the legs. These four

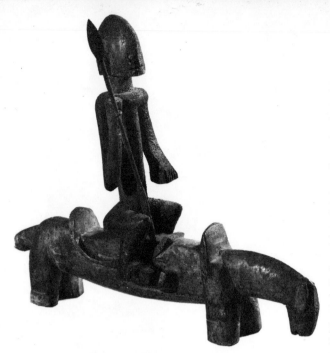

103. DOGON. MALI. Horseman from the sanctuary of Orosongo representing a minor deity. *Griaule Collection.*

works, finally, were finished off to represent people. The woman was actually representing on the wall the successive stages of the Creation: the explosion of the initial seed (the circle), the four cardinal points, that is to say the completion of the layout of the universe (the limbs in the form of a cross), next the lower limbs of the earthly beings, and lastly the sexual organs. For a few brief moments only, the figures preserve this unfinished aspect, which can never be recalled once the picture is finished; the sketches have become completed figures.

Now, these paintings are echoed in the sign of the 'man-universe' used 600 miles away by the Dogon, who it should be remembered take the name of Keita when staying in the Mandingo country. In its simplest form this sign is an ansate cross, named 'life of the world', a replica of an Egyptian hieroglyph with a similar name.

Like the Mandingo figures on the walls of the building used as a communal house, the Dogon sign is connected with the great family house whose plan resembles a man lying on his right side, throwing first on the altars, then through the open door into the universe, the male seed symbolised by the milk extracted from the unripe grains.

Parallel images could be found in the Cameroons, in the Fali granary whose eight chambers recall the bursting of the first seed, and in the Kotoko palace whose labyrinthine plan expresses the complexity of the world.

The symbolism of the minor arts

Each house in the village is in a particular district. The village itself is interpreted as a human being on the one hand, and as a heaven on the other, and in the guise of heaven it is associated with a 'twin' village which stands for the earth. This is why so many villages have 'Upper' or 'Lower' in their names.

The village in its turn is contained in a countryside laid out symbolically in which the crops were formerly sown in a spiral, punctuated by altars. At the centre of the spiral the first fields were divided into plots of land in a chess-board pattern. This pattern is also found in the design of their 'storey' house whose façade has eighty niches and in the pattern of their cotton bedspreads.

Weaving is the symbol of crop-growing; the weft is the water, so essential for agriculture, brought by man to the uncultivated lands represented by the warp. There is, in fact, by means of various combinations of patterns, a whole art woven into the cloth, that 'science of fabrics' of which the Bambara and the Samogo speak. The 'doctors' of all the Sudanese peoples give special names to each band of cloth according to its design. In the old days, there were 264 of these bands (the number of the written signs) and each one possessed its own meaning. Placed end to end they gave a succinct account of the mystery of the Creation and the adventures of the principal mythical beings.

Up to the present these various activities have been considered as minor ones, just like the brass objects which 108 embody the Baule method of counting: the weights for weighing gold from the Ivory Coast, which have recently been deciphered, exhibit, on the one hand, a system of plain geometrical signs and, on the other, animals representing numbers whose relation with the unit of measurement—two seeds—remains to be worked out.

Another minor art is wrought iron with which the 116 ironsmiths of all the tribes express the dramas of the formation and salvation of the earth. This is the case with the crucified figures found at Orosongo on the Dogon plateau. The man with outspread arms nailed to a lance-head is one of the disciples of the demiurge who has shed his blood and the seeds of his clavicles for the purification of humanity. Another figure, forged in the actual shaft of the lance, is the aquatic version of this disciple, the lower limbs having developed into fins.

A simplified replica has been found, in another village, of these two figures, with arms curving inwards, on an ordinary flat piece of iron. This expresses no more than the essence of the workings and results of this sort of redemption—the possession of the universe which has taken refuge in these open arms, and also the securing in their curves of all the good in the world to restore it to mankind.

Masks

These minor arts, neglected by Europe, express the same ideas as the larger works, for example the masks.

The mask should be studied not only in itself, but also in relation to everything which a society produces. It generally covers a part of the myth of the Creation and of the organisation of the world, but it also recalls, in succinct form, the other chapters in the story.

Thus, in the past, the Dogon mask shaped like a Cross 105 of Lorraine had one arm pointing upwards and the other downwards. It recalled the gesture of the creator indicating that his work was finished, one hand raised towards the sky, the other pointing to the earth. Later, a transverse axis was added to it so that it formed a sort of swastika symbolising the whirling of the demiurge, obliged to intervene in the world he had just created and which was already becoming disorganised. Subsequently, the mask took on its present-day form which also recalls by its seven constituent pieces the seven parts of the creative choreography of the being who 'set the world dancing'.

But in addition, this mask evokes the Creation itself, the top arm being the upper, the bottom arm the lower world, the central shaft the atmosphere. It also represents the descent to earth of an ark for the reorganisation of the

82

PERUVIAN. Clay vessel in the shape of a human head. Paracas. 1–500 A.D. Staatliches Museum für Völkerkunde, Munich. *Photo: Michael Holford.*

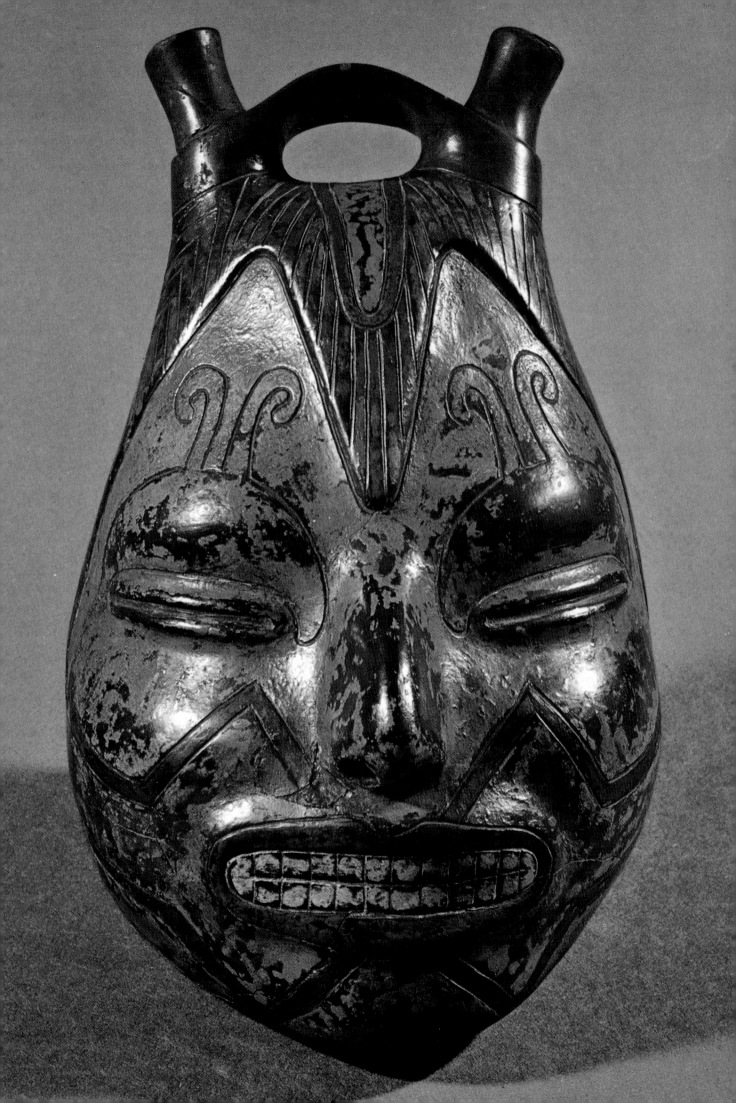

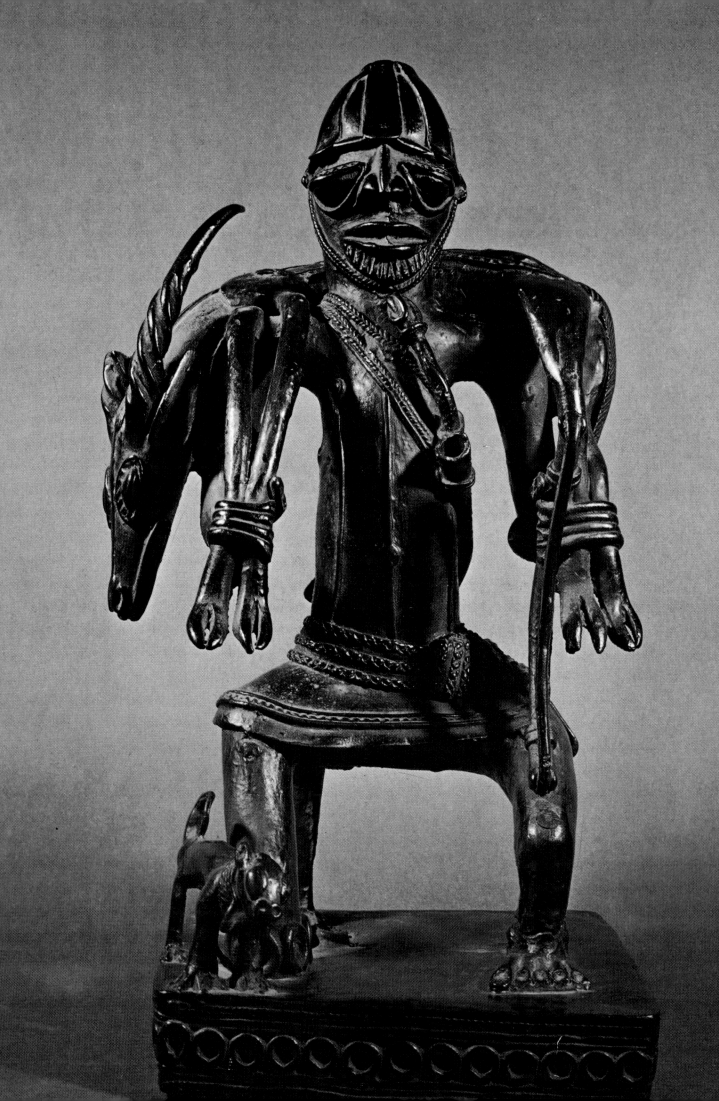

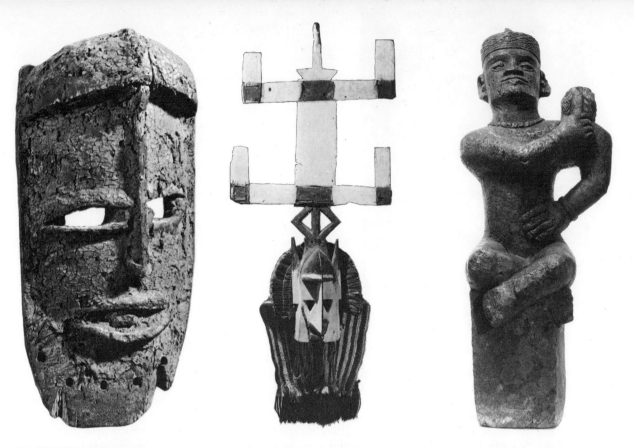

104. DOGON. MALI. Wooden mask representing the first dead ancestor. *Marcel Griaule Collection*.

105. DOGON. MALI. Dance mask in the shape of the Cross of Lorraine. *Musée de l'Homme, Paris*.

106. BAKONGO. CONGOLESE REPUBLIC. Stone statue of a chief. *Musées Royaux d'Art et d'Histoire, Brussels*.

world; the descent itself is the shaft and the vessel the face of the mask. Again, it symbolises the remains of the first dead human being in the world and by various details it alludes to other circumstances connected with the Creation.

The 'gateway-of-God' mask, whose two uprights enclose a line of chevrons terminating in a hollow hemisphere, also represents the spiral descent of the ark of the world. The hollow hemisphere, a calabash, is the personal symbol of a mythical female character who invented a method of agriculture.

A third mask, which, together with the two preceding ones, forms a series peculiar to the Dogon, is called a 'storey' mask. Its extremely high structure is made up of alternately solid and pierced grills which recall various phases of myths. But its principal meaning is the daily path of the sun, which its wearer expresses by bending his head backwards, from east to west. In addition, if there are seven solid and pierced grills, they represent the seven worlds; if there are eight, they recall the primordial ancestors; if ten or twelve, they mark the division of time. And whatever their number, the mask as a whole represents the house with eighty niches, while each of its details recalls a family house or a communal building in the village.

In addition to these three basic masks, modelled on signs traced, as we have seen above, on the rocks, there are masks of animals and men. Each of them, with the help of its accessories, the dances, songs and appropriate encouragements provided by the audience, translates an episode in the dramas of agriculture and social organisation or the material and moral environment. The sage Ogotemmeli, the first Sudanese to reveal the principles of Negro civilisation, used to say: 'The society of masked

men is the whole world. And when it moves in the public square, it mimes the movement of the world, it mimes the system of the world.' The better to demonstrate this role, he recalled that this choreography had a permanent replica in the paintings decorating the sanctuaries and representing the background of the life of mankind. The permanent works, bringing their constant aid to the functioning of the universe, correspond to the ephemeral movements and colours of the public square.

A similar role is played by the Bozo and Bambara societies of masked men. On the banks of the Niger, the Bozo groups of masks are vouched for as being the most ancient. The most numerous are composed of a sort of semicylindrical catafalque covered with fabrics falling to the ground. A head joined to the front of this mass is the mask in the strict sense of the word—the head of an antelope, ram or bull. On the top there are human or animal figures which are moved from inside like elementary puppets. When it appears in the public square, a mask of this sort is closely guarded by acolytes who, squatting round it, follow its movements and take care to hold the pieces of cloth down to ground level so that the wearer's feet remain invisible. Such a structure does not dance: it moves slowly, sways its head and waggles its puppets in time with the music.

Seeing it, one has a better understanding of what a mask means to the Bozo: a complex in which the form as a whole, the fabrics, the figures, the carved wood and the mime, however much reduced, contribute their ritual meaning and effectiveness. The head alone, the only object of interest to the average European art dealer or collector, is meaningless. But to observe the activity of the whole corps de ballet sheds new light on the order of the world. The rhythms of the drums are the actual

BENIN. S. NIGERIA. Hunter carrying an antelope. Probably late 19th century. Bronze. British Museum. *Photo: Michael Holford*

83

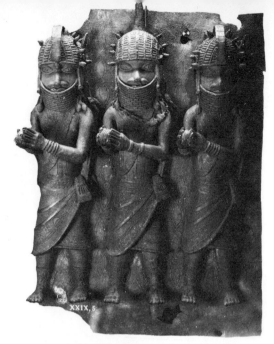

107. BENIN. NIGERIA. Bronze plaque. *British Museum.*

rhythms of the creation 'danced' by the demiurge. Their sound is the apotheosis of his voice which, according to the Bambara, was in the very beginning an 'inaudible' vibration. As for the characters who first appear on the scene, they are the crude beings dating back to the beginning of this first vibration, a period of disorder and obscurity. The wearers have simple face-masks and rags or costumes of undyed fibres, symbols of the absence of technical knowledge. Gradually their place is taken by the structures covered with fabrics, i.e. with light; their puppets personify the first mythical characters responsible for the initial disorder. They are prisoners and are integrated with the new order in spite of themselves. The animals summarily represented by the heads of the masks are those which were associated by the second demiurge with mankind's organisation of the earth and which have become totems. This task is represented by the fabrics, which are also fields. For the Bozo, primarily fishermen, nevertheless have ritual fields in the same way as the farmers, and their whirling dances symbolise the development of the creative vibration and the spread of agriculture.

Lastly the demiurge himself appears, a statuette with articulated arms, whose body, at first concealed in a wide-open cloth cylinder, emerges cautiously, then surges out of the hole, representing the life-giving water, his element on earth, which he summons with raised arms. He is followed by two masks with female faces, dressed in robes whose long fringed sleeves represent the rain; they are the twin daughters of the demiurge and act as deputies for the two stars presiding over the cosmic order.

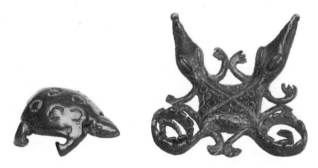

108. ASHANTI. GHANA. Weights. *British Museum.*

So much for the day masks. There is also a nocturnal corps de ballet, whose role is complementary to the other. A large part of the river-dwelling Bambara have imitated these masks and dances. Nocturnal and daytime ceremonies, with the same meaning as those of the Bozo, are celebrated annually. But we should also mention the agrarian masks which are familiar to all collectors and which represent highly stylised antelopes, the first mythical beings, in their attempts at agriculture. Their dance is the actual crop-growing, the initial superficial scraping of the soil, and it accompanies the weeding done by the young people. The ruin of these characters is also represented by the masked dances and visits of the children, who come to the threshing-floors and the yards where crops are garnered to beg the waste grain.

Art and the secrets of knowledge

What has been said about masks should also be said of the other forms of sculpture. The long series of carved wooden objects from the Congo, of which the Tervueren Museum, Belgium, has a unique collection—boxes, stools, figures, weapons—are all marked with an exuberant symbolism, scraps of which could possibly still be gathered from old initiates. This symbolism, incidentally, is expressed in objects of everyday use as in all the activities of the people. Thus there are good reasons for asking why a work of art excites a stronger emotion among the Negroes than any other object whose inner meaning is the same.

It is because the work of art expresses understanding with more freedom than technical or utilitarian articles; it has a more fluid ideal, one less directly connected with everyday activities. It gives man especial enjoyment and makes him feel more intimately linked with the cosmos because he understands it better intellectually. It is certainly more delightful to spin if one knows that the spindle, as it turns, is the sun, or to weave with the idea that the Word is being worked into the cloth.

But we risk forgetting the inner meaning if we concentrate solely on the technique. Thus it is more moving to dance carrying the symbol of a calendar system or the image in wood of a gesture by the demiurge on top of one's head, or to encourage a mask in a symbolic dance than it is to watch a weaver. In the former there is an escape from everyday life which, among these people, is nevertheless intimately bound up with the spiritual. A shuttle is both useful and significant; a mask is only significant. The shuttle has a mysterious side; the mask is all mystery.

Admittedly, the works of art are 'used', and we could describe them as useful; they are employed in regulated circumstances in which the life of the people is involved; but neither the shuttle nor the anvil, whose 'products' are palpable and immediate, would serve for this purpose. The aesthetic artifacts plunge emotions and labour into another atmosphere, which is not only religious, but also cosmogonic or metaphysical.

Thus the Negro creator, sculptor, decorator or ironsmith, whether he knows much or little of the esoteric extensions of his work, whether he works alone as an initiate or whether he is guided by the custodians of this knowledge, knows how to endow the volumes and lines with that power which can break through apparent cultural barriers to touch our own souls.

HISTORICAL SUMMARY: African art

HISTORY

The vast region which extends on both sides of the equator from the Sahara to Rhodesia gave birth to an art as original as that of the great civilisations. However it is premature to try to write its history, since Negro Africa has no archives and its ways of thinking and religions are almost unknown.

Originally, the population of Africa was constituted by an autochthonous element—the Negrillos—pushed back, then submerged by successive waves of black immigrants who reached the continent via the south-east. They were finally halted in their slow progress by the white invaders from the north and east, with whom they interbred.

The northern savannas were open to external influences from the earliest times. From the most remote antiquity close relations were established by the caravan routes of the Sahara, Egypt and Nubia with the Mediterranean and the Near East, and, during the ages, various currents from these regions—Jewish and Byzantine, among others—got as far as the Niger. Similar influences arrived via the eastern coast, whose gold mines were known from antiquity; they moved towards the interior, superimposing themselves or interpenetrating, and it is difficult to distinguish the effects of these multiple contributions.

However, it is certain that from the 4th century B.C. great states were established in the Sudan (West Africa) and an original civilisation developed along the Atlantic coast and south of the equator, although as from the 11th century iconoclastic Islam destroyed the forms of art connected with it. At the end of the 15th century, when the Portuguese navigators set foot in Africa, the majority of the kingdoms, Yoruba, Benin, Loango, Congo, Lunda, Luba, to mention only a few, were at their zenith. They could not withstand the pressure of the Europeans, who conducted the slave trade among their inhabitants for nearly four hundred years.

ANCIENT ART

The narratives of early authors, and the rare objects which they brought back, in addition to those discovered by archaeologists, are the only evidence of the past. Archaeology is a recent science in Africa, and systematic excavations have only been undertaken in isolated parts.

Nok culture. In the north of Nigeria, the recently discovered Nok culture (5th–1st centuries B.C.), revealed the most ancient specimens we know [**109**]. They consist of terra-cotta sculptures, human heads, a 'Janus' head, fragments of statuettes, animal figures.

Chad civilisation. The Lake Chad region and more especially the lower valley of the Logone and the Chari have yielded terra-cotta and bronze works attributed to the Sao (9th–16th centuries), a people who have disappeared today.

Nearly 15,000 pieces have been collected: funerary urns, vases, portraits consisting of the head alone, anthropomorphic and zoomorphic statuettes; ritual cups and bronze jewellery cast by the cire perdue, or 'lost wax', process (pendants, arm and ankle bracelets).

The Yoruba country (southern Nigeria). At Ife, religious centre of the region, human heads of brass and ceramics dating from the 12th century, in a style close to our own purest classical ideal, have been discovered. In spite of markedly African characteristics, this statuary poses problems of origin which have not yet been solved.

The stone statues and heads found at Esie are technically cruder.

Benin. We know of nearly 2,000 bronze sculptures from this ancient kingdom (13th–19th centuries): heads of kings and queens, animals (especially cocks and leopards), bas-reliefs, which once decorated the façades of the royal palaces, drums, cups, bracelets, swords, sticks, ivory statuettes, masks, carved tusks [**112–113**].

Following F. von Luschan and Struck, several periods are distinguished:

12th–15th centuries: influence of Ife, where the first artists from Benin are presumed to have learnt the cire perdue process.

15th–17th centuries: flowering of the art, representation of Europeans in the bas-reliefs.

18th century: beginning of the decadent period.

19th century: wooden sculptures covered with brass sheets, which no longer have anything in common with the ancient works.

Region of the Lower Congo. There have been recent discoveries of stone statuary dating from the 17th century, closely resembling that of Esie (Yoruba).

Zimbabwe civilisation. The hundreds of abandoned cities situated between the Zambezi and the Limpopo, especially Zimbabwe, belong to this culture. They are characterised by a monumental granite architecture (some walls of fitted stone are 12–15 ft thick)

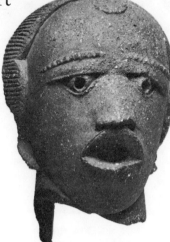

109. NOK. NORTHERN NIGERIA. Ceramic head. *Jos Museum.*

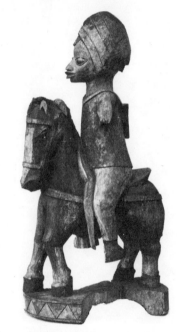

110. YORUBA. NIGERIA. Wooden horseman. Early 20th century. *British Museum.*

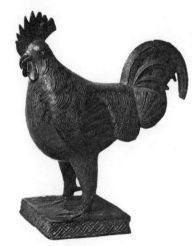

111. BENIN. NIGERIA. Bronze cockerel. *Metropolitan Museum of Art.*

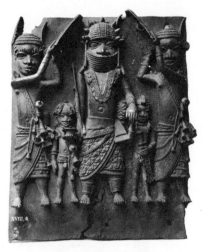

112. BENIN. NIGERIA. Bronze plaque, cast by the cire perdue process. *British Museum.*

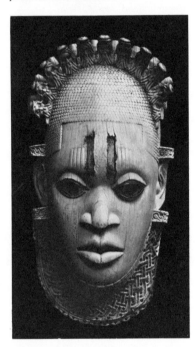

113. BENIN. NIGERIA. Ivory pendant. *British Museum.*

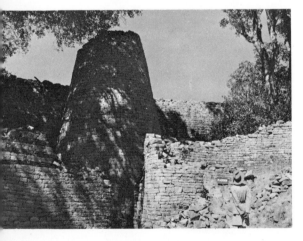

114. RHODESIA. The conical tower and part of the ruins at Zimbabwe.

linked with portable objects which include typically African pottery and fragments of Chinese porcelain of the Sung epoch. Although it is admitted that the cities were erected by the Negroes between the 6th and 12th centuries, some enigmas remain.

RECENT ART

In contrast, we possess enormous collections of objects of art made at the end of the last century, the chance results of travels or military expeditions, and more recently during scientific expeditions. They are limited to sculpture and it seems that the African genius showed its greatest brilliance in this form. From one end of the continent to the other, artists created a profusion of masks, statuettes, furniture and jewels. They are primarily wooden sculptures, the most ancient of which barely go back one hundred and fifty years; stone was rarely used (Mendi, Kissi); clay only produced artistic modelling in a few regions (Kinjabo, Bamum, Mangbetu); the art of metals nowhere reached the development which it had in the kingdoms of Guinea; carved ivory is also limited to this region and to the Congo among the Warega of Kivu.

In spite of its undeniable unity, this art presents not only wide differences which vary according to period and place, but also the alliance, within restricted limits, of apparently opposed conceptions.

PRINCIPAL ARTISTIC CENTRES

This list, based on Carl Kjersmeier's Centres de Style de la Sculpture Nègre Africaine, *only mentions the most important centres.*

Our ignorance of the social and religious context in which the objects existed makes any classification hypothetical. That of Melville J. Herskovits, based on the division of Africa into cultural regions, seems the least arbitrary to us, but it must be borne in mind that it is not rigid and that each area considered may exhibit an infinite variety of interpretations.

I The Sudanese region
The populations of the savanna, from the western coast of Lake Chad, have preserved a vigorous and sober art, depending on how successfully they were able to resist Islam. Sculpture in wood presents bare forms which tend towards geometry and abstraction. This style recurs among the peoples of the same origin whom distant migrations carried southwards, mainly the

Mangbetu and the Warega of the north-east of the Congo.

Mali: *Bambara.* Statuettes connected with fecundity, the worship of ancestors and twins. Anthropomorphic and zoomorphic masks (particularly of stylised antelopes).

Bozo (fishing peoples of the Niger living between Segu and Lake Debo). Anthropomorphic and zoomorphic masks decorated with puppets of all the characters specified in their religious system. Decorated dug-outs and paddles, musical instruments, furniture.

Dogon. Funerary statuettes, seven of which, 3 ft high, are exceptional works. Polychrome, often monumental masks. Everyday objects decorated with carved figures (cups, tobacco boxes, door shutters, and especially wooden locks similar to those which are very common among the Bambara and the Mossi [**103**].

Upper Volta: *Bobo.* Polychrome masks and wooden statuettes. Metal figurines. Carved footstools.

Senufo. Statuettes of ancestors. Masks with human faces often surmounted with horns. Seats and everyday objects.

Guinea: *Baga.* Statues of men and women. Polychrome anthropomorphic masks, tall bird masks. Drums and footstools supported by four human figures.

Kissi. Small steatite statues known by the name of *pomdo* (pl. *pomta*): 'images of the dead'.

Sierra Leone: *Mendi.* Male and female wooden statuettes; portrait heads, crouching statuettes in steatite, anthropomorphic masks entirely enclosing the dancer's head. 'Janus' (two-faced) and four-faced masks.

II The Guinea region
Along the Atlantic coast, art becomes more flexible and human. In addition to wood, work was done in metal, ivory and stone. The royal workshops gave a considerable impetus to the minor arts: the gold and silver ware from the royal treasures, weights for weighing gold dust, wood or ivory sceptres and batons.

This realistic living art, full of verve and dash, seems to be dominated by the influence of the Yoruba and of ancient Benin.

Ivory Coast: *Dan.* Great numbers of wooden masks of every sort from genuine portraits to representations of fabulous monsters.

Baule. Funerary statuettes placed on the tombs. Masks representing the principal divinities, men and animals, a few Janus masks.

Large numbers of everyday objects with carved figures: drums, weaving bobbins, spoons, combs, hairpins, fly-swatters, drum sticks, gong sticks, etc.

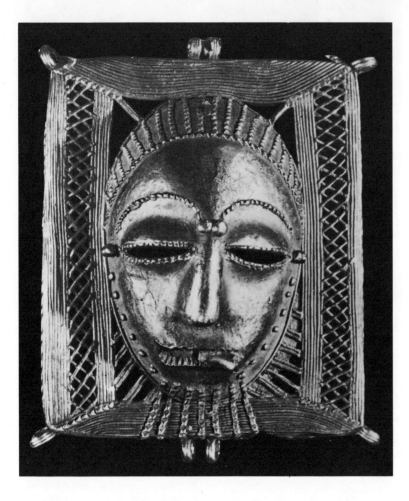

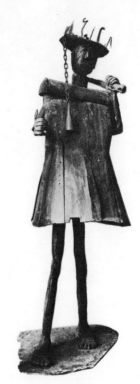

116. *Above.* DAHOMEY. Iron statue of the god of war, from Porto-Novo. *Musēe de l'Homme, Paris.*

115. *Left.* BAULE. IVORY COAST. Gold amulet. *Collection of the Institut Français d'Afrique Noire.*

Weights for weighing gold dust, gold amulets similar to those of the Ashanti [**115**].

Ghana: *Ashanti.* Clay figurines placed on the tombs, clay pipe bowls. Bronze weights for weighing gold dust, cast by the cire perdue process, reproducing scenes from popular life, flora, fauna, geometrical designs.

Receptacles for religious use, *kulluo*, also of metal. Use of gold leaf applied to everyday objects. Gold pendants (human masks).

Dahomey: *Fon.* Human or animal figures, often life-size, carved on wood and painted or cast in bronze, copper and iron. Clay bas-reliefs from the royal palace of Abomey (pictorial representation of the history of Dahomey).

Nigeria: *Yoruba.* Sculpture on wood, mainly comprising: statuettes connected with the worship of twins and fecundity; masks, very often polychrome; clubs used in dancing, and door shutters. Numbers of small everyday objects in ivory.

Ibo. Polychrome human figures in wood. Masks (especially of hippopotami).

Former British Cameroons: *Ekoi.* Tall masks with representations of human heads carved on wood and covered with skins. Numerous Janus heads.

Cameroun: *Bamilike.* Standing or seated human figures in wood, often covered with a coating of pearls. Masks and numerous everyday objects decorated with figures. Carved pillars and doors [**118**].

Bamum. A few scattered statuettes. Masks. Door-frames, window-frames, thrones supported by human or animal figures (especially leopards).

III The Congolese area

Throughout this region, the art of wood carving undergoes an extraordinary development. The artist chooses his species and gives them skilful patinas; extra-special care is given to the polishing and finishing of objects. Apart from the masks and statuettes, seats with caryatids, headrests, canes and figures bearing cups are equally works of art.

Generally speaking, a naturalistic and refined art developed more particularly in the ancient kingdoms (Loango, Congo, Lunda, Luba). The other peoples combine this realistic tendency, with considerable latitude, with a geometrical art which comes close to that of the Sudanese regions.

Central African Republic: *Fang.* Unornamented wooden statuettes of ancestors, masks, generally painted white.

Bakota. Highly stylised human figures one side of which is covered with copper sheeting.

Mpongwe. Polychrome masks of light wood.

Angola: *Batshioko.* Representations of ancestors. Wooden masks and masks of bark cloth stretched on a wooden frame, with their faces modelled in resin. Very numerous everyday objects: combs, snuffboxes, spoons, chiefs' thrones.

Congo: *Bakongo.* Figures of ancestors, kneeling women, motherhood. Figurines containing a cavity hollowed either in the head or the stomach, in which magical substances are placed. Studded figurines of humans and animals (dogs and leopards).

Bayaka. Large wooden polychrome figures. Figures of ancestors. Figures decorated with nails. Masks carved from one piece of wood, representing a human face surmounted by a human or animal representation.

Bakuba. Nine royal statuettes [**119**], seven of which have been identified (the most ancient probably dates from the beginning of the 17th century). Masks embellished with pearls, cowries and metal. Cups in the form of human figures. Small chests, boxes, goblets [**120**], drums, pipes, knives, carved

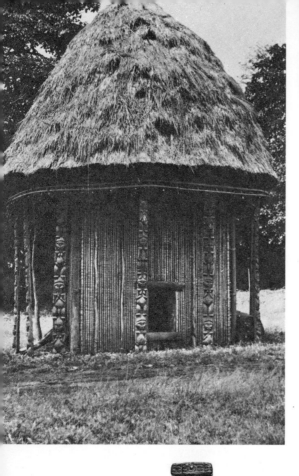

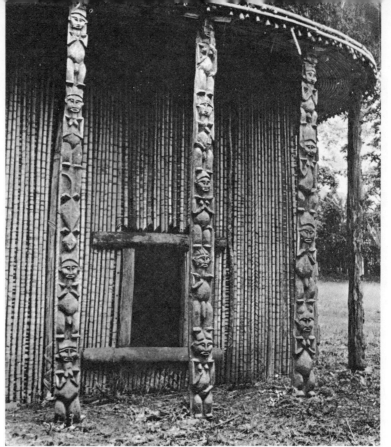

117. BAMILEKE. CAMEROONS. Hut with carved columns.

118. BAMILEKE. CAMEROUN. Detail of the façade of a hut.

119. BAKUBA. CONGO. Royal statuette: *British Museum*.

120. BAKUBA. CONGO. Wooden cups. *British Museum*.

hands symbolising those of slain enemies.

Bena Lulua. Statuettes of wood in a highly overloaded baroque style. Polychrome masks adorned with pearls. Drums and headrests.

Baluba. Figures of ancestors, Figures decorated with nails and having a magical role. Many sculptures representing a woman holding a cup known by the name of *The Beggar Woman*, used for collecting alms. Footstools supported by one, two or four caryatids or animals. Small ivory and bone statuettes.

Mangbetu. Clay sculpture. Pitchers surmounted by human figures.

Warega. Ivory statuettes and masks, whose eyes are frequently made of inlaid cowries.

Annie Masson-Detourbet

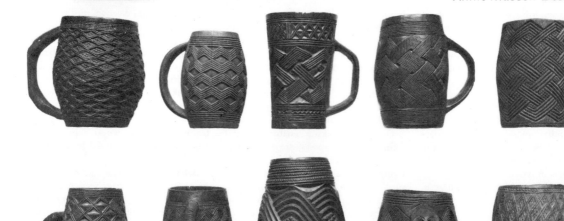

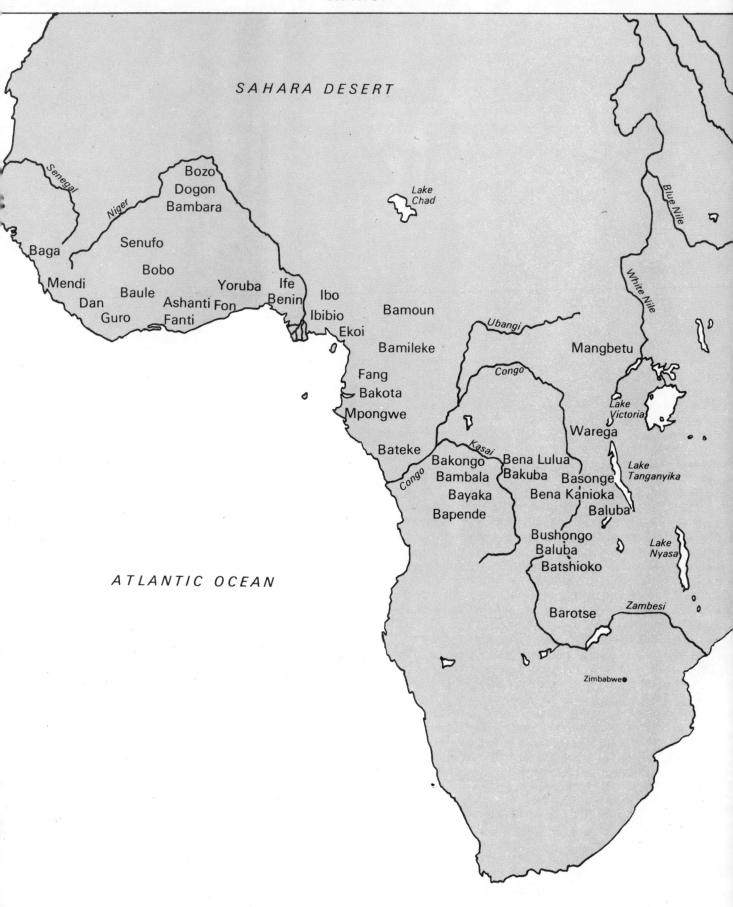

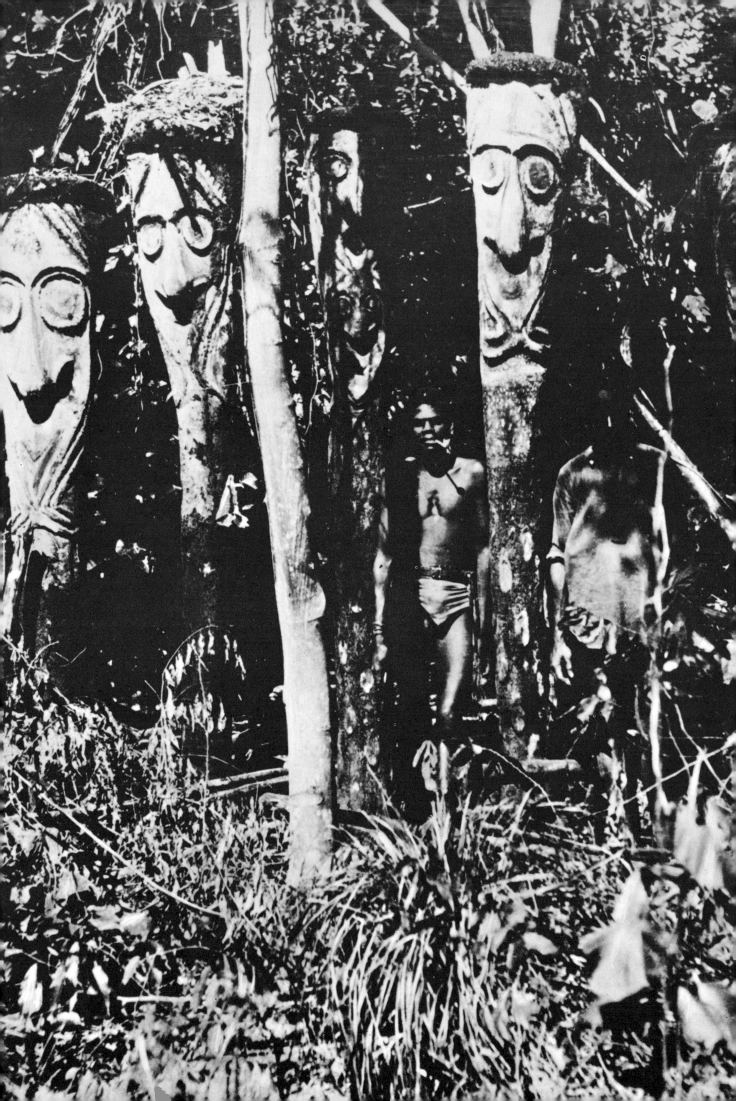

OCEANIC ART *Henry Lavachery*

The Pacific Ocean harbours innumerable islands where a relatively isolated archaic civilisation has perpetuated itself down to our own time, without its variety destroying its fundamental unity. In it we find confirmation of the magical and symbolical meaning of primitive arts.

The artists of Oceania were very imaginative in the creation of unusual forms and shapes. They expressed themselves most completely in sculpture, and sometimes in drawing. The Oceanians carved figures in relief or in the round, masks and a mass of other objects decorated with chiselling or inlays. The Melanesians added colour to them. Oceanic drawing is revealed in tattooing (strictly a Polynesian art), in the designs on tapas made of bark, in figurines engraved on wood and in rock carvings.

At first sight, Oceanic sculpture and drawing exhibit an extreme variety of styles. A closer scrutiny modifies this opinion, which, however, certain authors still hold.

Unity of feeling in the Oceanic arts

A primitive art—it is one of the essential features of its primitiveness—has a mission, which does not consist as it does with us in expressing the impressions of the creative artist, but rather the feelings of a group. Among the Oceanic peoples anxiety about the hereafter is predominant. Melanesian thought, like Australian, conceived of a world with no differentiation where dead and living, natural and supernatural, coexist in close association. The living have to defend themselves against the jealousy of the dead. As a result apparatus for magical precautions 133 has been created: images of the dead, mingled with those of the totemic animals, lizards, crocodiles, sea birds (which are the most ancient ancestors deified), ornament the assembly houses, serve as masks for the dancers of so-called 'secret' societies and sanctify a large number of everyday objects.

Works of art, by bringing the myths into everyday life, ensure the balance of society, but the chieftain is the link between this world and the supernatural world. His power is based on a genealogy which goes back to the creating gods, as well as on a freely spent and widely distributed fortune. This tradition is well suited to encourage creation, for the abundance of works of art and their brilliance are evidence of the same munificent generosity with regard to the dead (whom these works celebrate) as with regard to the living (who extract from them an additional amount of magical protection).

The great works of art are accomplished in a holiday atmosphere. The rich man who commissions them maintains the artists and sees to it that they are amply supplied with both necessities and luxuries. Parsimony over the cost would risk compromising the completion of the works and would put their mystical value in danger.

The Oceanic artists, and especially the sculptors in wood—to whom we owe the construction of canoes— are admired as a class; their position, both social and material, is comparable with that of the greatest chiefs. Magic, including the impeccable accomplishment of the

rites, is as indispensable to perfect creation, linked with the supernatural world, as manual skill or inventive genius.

The social position of Polynesian artists is just as high. They are credited with a special virtue called *Mana* which is a Melanesian conception. *Mana* is a force which extends from simple prestige to magical power. Among artists it is a question of establishing communion with the supernatural world. *Mana* is transmissible by contact. The tools of a great artist preserve his power, like an accumulator charged with electrical energy, and may transmit it to the man who is worthy of it. Representations of the deified dead, sometimes assembled in sanctuaries around the tombs, sometimes preserved in huts, are less numerous than in Melanesia. It is exceptional for these figures to adorn everyday objects, except those intended for sacred uses.

The beliefs of the Polynesian have evolved towards a cosmogony which is probably of Asiatic origin; it is dominated by the omnipotence of a few great divinities. Although the names of the gods vary according to the place and time, their functions remain clearly defined, and art has produced only a few representations of them.

Common features of the Oceanic style

To make himself understood by the community the primitive artist has to use formulas accessible to everyone. Hence quasi-permanent styles are indispensable as both a practical and a ritual necessity. Once more, art stands out as a language by which the artist addresses the community in forms acceptable to it. These 'acceptable forms' constitute a style.

In analysing a primitive style, it is advisable to distinguish the plastic 'terms' referring to the human figure in the strict sense from those referring to the figure's attributes, the tattoos, hair styles and body ornaments, characterising the being or group represented. These terms, which play no part at all in the plastic ensemble of the style, provide on the other hand precious indications about the origin of the work.

Apart from these adventitious details, the Oceanic styles are confined to a few principal types. Is it possible to determine their origins as well as the phases of their development? For we must not forget that the primitive arts evolve like our own so-called 'civilised' arts, although much more slowly for ritual and technical reasons.

Polynesian statuary has a common feature: the heads of its figures are exaggeratedly large. This peculiarity 121 appears in the majority of primitive imagery which thus naively emphasises the importance attributed to the seat of the personality. Among the Oceanians, notorious hunters of their enemies' heads, but also pious preservers of their parents' heads, there exists a pseudo-statuary in which the preserved head is modelled over with wax and 125 resin, and painted. Consequently a style is best revealed in its treatment of heads and masks. Among the primitives the body or bust is only a support for the head, and we can observe how the shape of the trunk and the other limbs undergoes few modifications. We shall classify the styles according to the different treatments of the head or

121. NEW HEBRIDES. Ancestral figures carved on tree trunks.

91

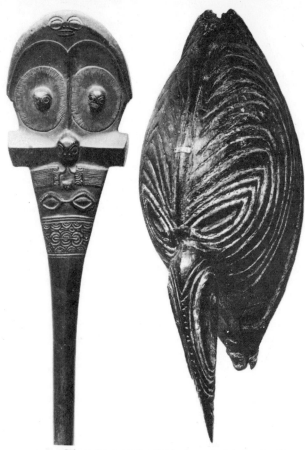

122. *Left.* MARQUESAS ISLANDS. Carved club-head with large disc-like eyes. *Musée de l'Homme, Paris.*

123. *Right.* URVILLE ISLAND (NEW GUINEA). Carved wooden dance mask. *Musée de l'Homme, Paris.*

face. Maurice Leenhardt (1947) has analysed the aesthetic mentality of the Oceanians to perfection; he emphasises the difficulty the New Caledonians have in conceiving of a world of more than two dimensions. This explains the door-frames or *Tale* of this region. The guardians of the entrance are ancestors stylised into a magnified flattened mask and a trunk reduced to a few geometrical signs. The same formula is applied to ridgepole figures. These 'two-dimensional' characteristics recur elsewhere: in the New Hebrides, in the masks from Ambrym, at Malekula, in the trunks of trees made into drums booming with the voices of the ancestors whose faces they bear. In the Gulf of Papua, among the Abelam, in New Guinea, images of ancestors look like cut-out drawings. Other figures from Ambrym are carved more deeply, cut, over-modelled (and painted) in the trunks of ferns. These

122 figures have large discs for eyes, a characteristic recurring in the equally 'two-dimensional' statuary of the Marquesas Islands and New Zealand.

This treatment of the mass in two dimensions may be confined to the face. Sometimes a flat face is contained in a rectangle (New Guinea, Gulf of Huon, Geelvink Bay), but more frequently in a triangle. Examples abound, from Lake Sentani to Polynesia (Tonga, Santa Cruz, Moorea, Raiavavae), and in Micronesia (the Carolines). Moreover the same formulas are applied in some statuaries of the Indian archipelago (Batak in Sumatra, Nias, Letti, the Philippines). According to Leenhardt these relations discovered on the path from Asia to Oceania enable us to credit the 'two-dimensional' style with a probably ancient Asiatic origin.

Figures in the round and masks in accentuated relief

are found, on the other hand, to the north of New Caledonia. The facial features are similar to those of the bas-reliefs on doors and their formal massing is akin to that of the Solomon Islands statues. This transition from two to three dimensions is almost imperceptible.

The basin of New Guinea

New Guinea and the string of islands which surrounds it have related arts. As the populations of the basin are complex and very mixed, the styles of their statuary provide valuable data for an anthropological classification.

The Swiss ethnologist Felix Speiser has proposed a nomenclature for the styles of the New Guinea basin. But we must remember that we shall often come across the primary two-dimensional style already defined with tribal variations.

To the south-east the first group of styles embraces the Massim district together with the Trobriand Islands. Comparable to the style of the Solomon Islands, it consists of sculpture in ebony or blackened wood, often inlaid with mother-of-pearl or powdered lime. The simple shapes are decorative rather than expressive. The artist's efforts are concentrated on the treatment of the face, hollowed out of the mass, with the nose forming a ridge. This predilection for hollows comes close to both the formulas of the Indian archipelago and those of the stone figures of Easter Island.

In the Massim area and its dependencies, such as the Admiralty Islands, we find large wooden cups of subtle elegance used at chiefs' banquets. The extremely sober decoration of the cups borrowed its motifs from the divine world of birds. In the Admiralty Islands, we see the appearance of the taste for polychrome work peculiar to the basin of New Guinea. Some figures recall the flat primary style, but they are embellished with red, black and white triangles.

The statuary of the Gulf of Papua and the valley of the Purari River, together with the Gulf of Huon, Tami Island, the Torres Strait and a part of Dutch New Guinea around Lake Sentani, forms a second Guinean group with the primary style. However, in addition to the flat figures engraved with white lines, the Gulf of Papua possesses masks in black and white tapa in which the artists' imagination runs riot: enormous eyes and mouth, devouring fangs—figures made to inspire terror. The wood carvings have less dramatic power.

The Sulka of the Gazelle peninsula, in New Britain, have invented fantastic masks which seem to have no terrestrial connection at all. They are immense 'scarecrows' assembled from bamboo, strips of stuck-on bone marrow and waving tapa. On certain days these figures come to life. Naked bodies, dripping with red make-up lead them solemnly round the orchards, whose fertility is bound up with this visit from the spirits. The magical dances, in which the figures wave and nod in movements regulated by the rhythm of wooden gongs, are the great moments in the aesthetic life of the primitives, the most vital and authentic expression of their art.

A third group, in New Guinea, unites the styles of the Sepik River, the Ramu, and, in Dutch New Guinea, those of Geelvink Bay, Humboldt Bay and the south-east (Merauke). Except among the Abelam whose plastic work is 'two-dimensional', shapes in the round predominate here and are freer. Plaques evoking ancestors, architec-

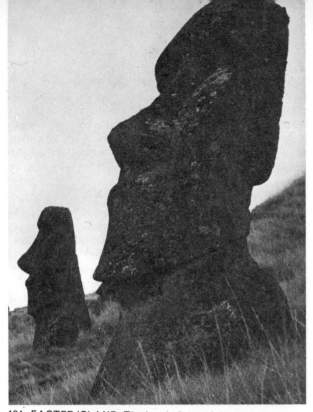

124. EASTER ISLAND. The head of one of the many statues to be found on Easter Island.

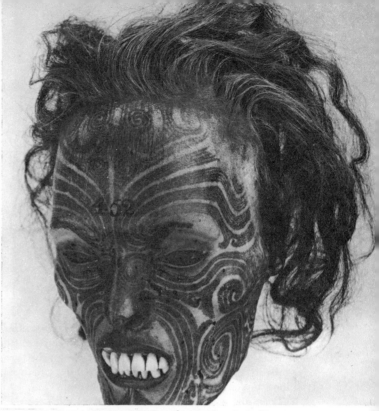

125. NEW ZEALAND. MAORI. Smoke-dried head of a Maori chief. *Pitt Rivers Museum, Oxford.*

tural ornaments and figures on houses, carved decorations on canoes—the artist's imagination is inspired by all the shapes provided by nature, and these masterful decorations seem like the works of a virtuoso. One of the strangest is undoubtedly the *Schnabelstil* ('beak style') practised by the tribe of Tchambuli at Speik. The near-by Mundkumor prefer more robust forms, and sometimes achieve a powerful naturalism.

123

The art of New Britain does not have the profusion of that of the main island. The most striking productions are the gigantic masks of the DukDuk Society, on which the social order rests. This poverty contrasts with the wealth of statuary in New Ireland, where the sculptors exhibit extraordinary virtuosity. In the centre of that island, the *Uli* figures represent the dead in immense shapes, in strong but subtle colours. In the north, the shapes diminish in size, while retaining the same simplicity. Often they disappear beneath a profusion of leaves, feathers, birds and fish which intermingle like the New Guinean ornaments, submerging the ancestor in their symbolism. Reds and whites, in violent contrast, a few blacks, a touch of blue, add to this confusion. On top of this the gill-covers of the molluscs endow the images with their glassy gaze and a kind of hallucinatory life. These figures are called *malanggan,* from the name of the feasts at which they are exhibited. Artists, supported by rich patrons who compete for their services, prepare the *malanggan* in secret. On the feast day, the images are revealed by collapsing part of the fence surrounding them. The crowd admires or criticises them. This 'salon' is a tribute to the deified dead. At it they are represented by dancers in delicately painted masks complete with hair and powerful profiles of supreme gravity. The worship of the dead, the ostentation of the patrons, the talent and rivalry of the artists, an expressive statuary loaded with mythical symbols, dancers with grandiose masks, the musical sympathetic magic, all contribute to make the *malanggan* feasts a synthesis of Melanesian culture.

A transitional zone

The zone between Melanesia and Polynesia, peopled with representatives from both regions (like Micronesia, which has recently included Malays as well), is poor in art.

Its wooden statuary reduces the human to the essential features. The two-dimensional face is akin to Melanesian conceptions, as well as the Polynesian Tonga and Samos. Of the first-named we know a few small-sized female figures. The face, without relief, is extended into a triangle; the rest of the body, with the exception of the arms, simple flat sticks, seeks to imitate nature. One image of a young girl, half reclining, is a symbol of idyllic Polynesian leisure. Sometimes, the primitive artists, for relaxation, abandon pure creation and imitate what they actually see. In the Santa Cruz Islands, some of which are

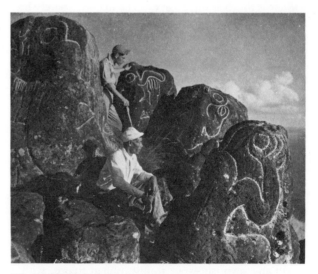

126. EASTER ISLAND. Rock carvings in the prehistoric village of Orongo. The carvings are connected with the cult of the Bird Man (Tangatu Manu). The carving in the foreground represents the Bird Man carrying the egg of the sacred bird (Manu Tara) in his right hand.

93

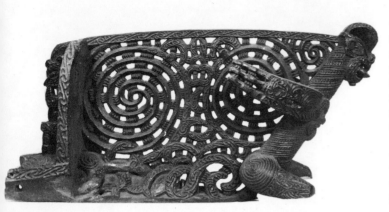

127. NEW ZEALAND. MAORI. Small carved canoe prow.
Dominion Museum.

peopled by black-skinned tribes, others by brown-skinned tribes from the west, the statues are akin to the Tongan style, in spite of their heaviness. Figurines of a similar type, probably modern, appear in the Fiji Islands, where the blood and cultures of the two Oceanic groups mingle.

Triangular faces, noses forming a cross with the eyebrows, the narrow arms of the Tongans, and bodies of extreme spareness characterise the statuary of the Carolines, at Nuku-manu and Takuu. The better-known figures of Nukor have more relief. The elongated mass of the heads of these *Tino* recur in certain figurines from Tahiti.

The Polynesian triangle

Let us approach the heart of the Polynesian triangle, from which sailed the tribes who colonised the islands of the South Seas. The Society Islands, the Cook Islands and the Austral Islands, all once in close relationship, provide evidence of related arts.

Here the masters are the carvers of stones for the sacred enclosures for the altars and also for the embankments on which some of the houses stand. Big stone statues are rare. The most massive are those from Raiavavae.

The stone images at Tahiti, Moorea and Raiatea are seldom as much as three feet tall, the majority barely half that. The shapes, dictated by the block which is merely penetrated by a few notches, verge on indigence. The tiny wooden images are ritual objects or were used to adorn canoes. These figures, the *Ti'l*, represent the dead, but the Polynesian religion also represented its higher gods. At Tahiti these are simple symbols. The god of war, Oro, is a fragment of wood the size of a child's arm, covered with a tightly laced network of fine coconut-fibre string (sennit). The scarlet feathers of the red-tailed tropic-bird are attached to it. By contact, they have become images of the god. Finally, all trace of art has evaporated.

At Mangaia, Tane, the patron of artists, is symbolised by an adze, with its blade fixed to a monumental handle. Some scholars see the stylisation of a human figure in the cross-pieces which ornament it. At Rurutu and Rarotonga, the images of Tangaroa, the god who created the world and men, show an almost human figure, with a cylindrical (Rurutu) or flat trunk, from which humanity emerges like young shoots bursting with sap. The Tangaroa from Rarotonga, in profile, have big elongated eyes with heavy eyelids like their mouths. At Raiavavae, some

wooden statues of great rarity exhibit a flat face with features in the form of a cross on minute geometrical masses. The war clubs, and the state oars with round or rectangular motifs, their handles engraved with human figures which are sometimes linear, are once again the most authentic works of art. On the blades we also rediscover the concave bodies and heads in the round of the style of Tahiti or Nukuor.

To the north of the triangle (Hawaiian Islands), a wooden statuary of great size developed towards the 12th century, it is believed, under the influence of Tahiti, with which island the Hawaiians had established relations. Still more ancient sculptures have left coarse stone remains on Necker Island, their faces akin to the primary substratum of Oceanic plastic art. The big Hawaiian figures represent the gods who guard the sanctuaries. The first white visitors made drawings of them. Distorted gestures to inspire fear, the ferocious grimace of the figure-for-eight mouths (recurring in New Zealand) contrast with the static statuary so far met with. Realism was pushed even further, as some recently discovered domestic statuettes prove.

Some figures of plaited rushes, decorated with the orange-red feathers of the *iiwi* bird, represented the god of war, Kukailimoku, whose terrifying image was carried in battle. Feather-work too, of great refinement, gave the kings splendid cloaks and provided them with headgear like Greek infantry. The Hawaiians also had a liking for plates and dishes and small pieces of furniture with pure lines, made of wood polished and grained with yellow.

At the south-west point of the triangle we find the Maoris of New Zealand. A harsh climate has toughened their character and sharpened their pride. Their somewhat rustic but essentially decorative art is often symbolical. Synthetic shapes are covered with the complicated and delicate arabesques of the Maori spiral possibly 127 derived from the heraldic tattooing (*moko*) of the warriors. 125 After death, the head, carefully smoked, is preserved among the family treasures. The spiral creates an apparent movement which is sometimes so lifelike that it tires the eye. The carved figures, which rarely have more than two dimensions, are contorted as if to avoid the decoration which invades all the objects, undulating around the 127 portals of the communal houses as well as the prows of the war canoes.

Is it possible to link these Maori ornaments with the ornamentation of the Melanesians? The latter make a sober arrangement on a plane surface of the natural motifs they transform. The Maoris, on the other hand, without actually leaving the plane surface, seem to be constantly escaping from it.

To the south-east the art of the Marquesas confirms the variety of the Polynesians' inspiration; however the variety of media is greater among the black peoples.

Like that of the Maoris, the art of the Marquesas is primarily graphic. Tattooing was its purest expression. The statuary is surface carving, touching lightly a very simple original shape. The open-air sanctuaries were peoples with large or small images, in stone or wood, of Tiki, the first man. His face, with its broad eyes, a sabre- 128 slash of a mouth and scrolls for nose and ears, recurs equally on men's skin and on the most insignificant utensils. He has some of the characteristics of that countenance which could be said to typify an art of the Pacific from Asia to Easter Island and sometimes even to pre-Columbian America.

Easter Island

The Tuamotu atolls on the route to Easter Island have perhaps known no art except that religious poetry in which the recently discovered grandiose and confused personality of Kiho, the greatest of all gods, appears.

At Mangareva (in the Gambier Islands) which contributed to the peopling of Easter Island, wooden images have been found with trunks and limbs imitating nature; they bear the flat face already encountered. Only one, it seems, combines curved and rectangular volumes, an example of those abstract conceptions which often attract the Polynesian sculptors.

At the southern extremity of this region is Easter Island, the Rapa-Nui of modern Tahitians. Its quantities of enormous statues of volcanic breccia were the first revelation of Polynesian art. Using this material, which is easily carved with stone burins, the Easter Islanders 124 erected more than five hundred images of their dead, with heights varying from nine to forty-eight feet. In the past they stood on the altar of the sanctuaries, which also served as tombs. Teams of specialists worked feverishly to carve them in a record time of three or four weeks. Brought down the slopes from the workshops, they were dragged to the edge of the ocean by hundreds of men and women.

The artists contributed very few variations to this 'mass-produced type'. They derive from the stele, and only their great narrow masks framed by long ears are more than two-dimensional. The bust, cut off at the navel, bears arms in bas-relief. The face occupies two-sevenths of the height. Shadows contrast strongly with the angular surfaces lit up by the ocean light.

Wood itself is rare and comes from a single species: the *Sophora toromiro*, with stunted scraggy trunks. Sometimes the sea throws up a floating tree. Thus, in the legends, treasures are always composed of wooden objects.

Wooden statuettes, which are quite unlike the monumental statues, represented the dead or spirits. They were in keen demand for exhibition around the sanctuaries on feast days. The works of specialists, some of the oldest have a finish and a delicacy which Cook noticed on his voyage. The best known, called *moai kavakava* (statues with many sides) by the natives, who still imitate them, represent emaciated and bearded old men with 133 macabre realism. The local version of the god Tane Make Make is ornamented with the beak of an albatross. Other sea birds play an important part in religious life. A being with the head of a sea bird, drawn with a free and accurate line, swarms over the rocks and lava. Hundreds of rock 126 engravings cover as much as several square yards of surface, representing the beings and plants of the island, everyday objects such as canoes, side by side, with figures combining animal and human elements. In the hundreds of minute signs engraved on wooden tablets some authorities think they see writing.

A comparative study of design in Oceania (with Australia) in all its forms would perhaps clear up the problem of the origins and development of this art. This account, however brief, brings out a 'two-dimensionalism' mainly imposed by a poorly developed technique. This 'primary style', often shown in the face, but also in the whole figure, recurs all the way along the route followed by the Oceanians from southern Asia and is proof of the fundamental unity of the arts in Oceania.

OCEANIA

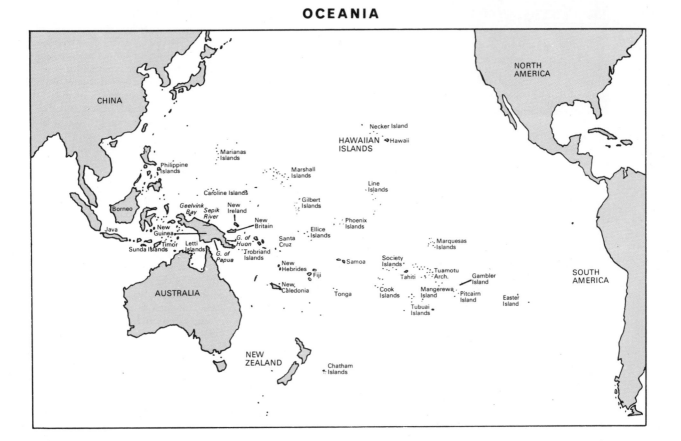

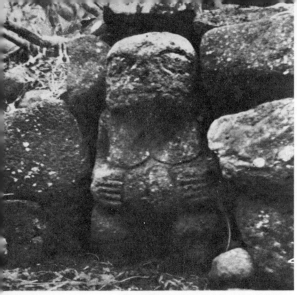

128. NOUKU-HIVA ISLAND (MAR-QUESAS ISLANDS). A figure of Tiki, the first man, in a sanctuary in Taipe Valley.

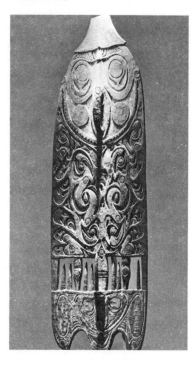

129. NEW GUINEA. Wooden plaque from a men's hut commemorating the dead. *Kon. Institut voor de Tropen, Amsterdam.*

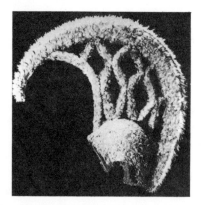

130. HAWAII. Wicker helmet covered with red and yellow feathers. *Musée de l'Homme, Paris.*

HISTORICAL SUMMARY:
Artistic geography of the Pacific

The Pacific Ocean, which covers twice the area of the Atlantic, touches both the Arctic and Antarctic Circles. To the south and west are found the islands which to the west suggest by their alignments the disappearance of slabs of a continent. On the other hand, beyond the Carolines-Kermadec line, the very much smaller islands clearly show their independent volcanic and coralline origin.

Melanesia. Approximately following the eastern and northern outlines of Australia, Melanesia, a chain of lofty volcanic islands, is extremely fertile, with semi-tropical vegetation. On the highest mountains some trees from the temperate zone have become acclimatised and their wood is used for sculpture.

The Melanesians, black peoples with curly hair, imported the pig. The symbolical and ceremonial importance of this animal is considerable. New Guinea has six hundred species of birds, often with splendid plumage, e.g. the bird of paradise. In Oceania feathers are much used in decoration and adornment. Some red feathers have even become divine symbols. The sea birds (albatrosses, frigate-birds) passed for messengers of the gods. They inspired all the Oceanic iconography.

The Melanesian dwelling varies from island to island, from the make-shift huts of the Admiralty Islands to the communal palaces of New Guinea. Their plan is circular in New Caledonia, the Santa Cruz Islands and New Ireland, oval in the Admiralty Islands and rectangular everywhere else. But nothing in these erections corresponds to what our civilisations understand by 'architecture', except perhaps the vast houses which serve as both a 'club' and a dormitory for the men of the village. In them take place the majority of the religious and social ceremonies. The art most rich in mystical significance decorates these edifices [**129**].

The sculptors use an adze with a stone or shell blade. The weight of the implement and the mediocre cutting edge of the blades, which have to be constantly resharpened, make the carving of wood or stone slow and difficult. But inexhaustible patience and a cheerful disregard for the passage of time triumph over these difficulties in the joy of creating [**131**, **132**].

Polynesia. A number of the foregoing remarks apply to the Polynesians, who left Asia much later than the black-skinned peoples. Originally from India—which has given them a quota of Caucasian blood—they stayed in Indonesia for a long time. As they were forbidden access to the islands occupied by the black-skinned peoples, the Polynesians reached Micronesia in their outrigger canoes which could sail the deep seas. These islands are poor and life in them was hard. Seeking other settlements, in the midst of the thousand and one adventures to which Polynesian mythologies have given poetic form, the first canoes penetrated into the heart of the South Sea island world. Undoubtedly the Society Islands were populated towards the beginning of the Christian era. Later, between the 5th and the 14th centuries, groups, some of which left from the centre, others from the new settlements, colonised the Polynesia which we know today.

The animal and vegetable resources of these countries are more meagre than those of the western islands. The colonisers enriched them with new plants. New Zealand and Easter Island, having different climates, escape from the general type of Polynesian culture which is closely dependent on its environment. But Maoris and Easter Islanders preserve the principal elements of the social and spiritual structure of central Polynesia.

Polynesian architecture, similar to that of Melanesia—with the exception of the communal houses reserved for the men—possesses megalithic constructions, raised stone enclosures, walls and piles of stones often supporting more flimsy materials. A large number of these constructions (*Mara'a*) were used for public social and religious ends. Stone carving predominates in the eastern and central regions. Sculpture in stone competes with wood carving. But in general the statuary in Polynesia is less abundant than in Melanesia. The absence of male 'clubs', the non-existence of polychromy, the small size of most of the images and also a certain proud reserve which overlies the Polynesian character make the art of these tribes less conspicuous.

Micronesia. In Micronesia, Polynesian culture wins the day. This region comprises six archipelagos of coral origin whose population recently underwent Malayan influence. The essence of their religion consists of fear of, and respect for, the dead. Plastic art is poor. It remains localised in the south of the Carolines and under the influence of the styles of the eastern boundaries of Polynesia. The richest art of this region is utilitarian and functional. The Micronesians are adept weavers of mats. Their real feeling for beauty is expressed in the patterns of interlaced fibres and the regularity of the notches which the adze makes in the wood. In the same way, the figures bring out the simple lines and volumes. We rediscover this tendency in Polynesia. The Samoans, the Tongans and the Fijians, apart from their poor statuary, carve bludgeons decorated with geometrical ornaments. A pleasing play of lines, protuberances and hollows, the cunning irregularity of features inspired by plaiting, the unexpectedness of delicately drawn animal or human outlines, the splendour of dark red or warm brown wood polished like an agate classify these Tongan bludgeons among the plastic arts. The tapa of marginal Polynesia are also among the most beautiful: delicacy, grandeur, thanks to a white tone 'broken' with orange, sober and geometrical black-red decoration contrasting with the tapa of New Guinea [132]. Princesses used to bring bundles of them as a dowry.

Everything which we have mentioned here belongs to the past. The Pacific, recently caught up in the orbit of vast world wars, has been submerged by modern civilisation.

Australia. Rock paintings and engravings, in the tradition of prehistory, have been made here until our own days (last example: 1936). Their conventional style, eschewing the search for movement, is pretty much the same throughout the country. The magical, religious or even simply narrative scope of these representations has been demonstrated.

Similar scenes recur as decorations on boats. Engraving is also done on shells and elongated oval stone or wooden plaques, called tjuringas [100]. These, which ensure liaison with the

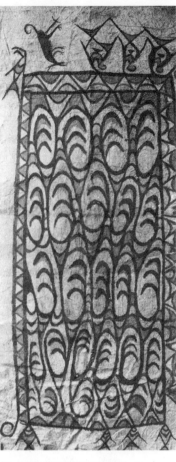

132. DUTCH NEW GUINEA. Tapa. *Musée de l'Homme, Paris.*

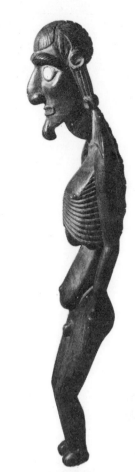

133. EASTER ISLAND. Wooden ancestor figure. *Staatliches Museum für Völkerkunde, Munich.*

ancestor totem, must not be seen by women. The drawings, in spite of their simplified and geometrical appearance, have a profoundly symbolical meaning. The Australian aborigines also practise painting on the skin.

The magical or religious paintings are often an integral part of a ritual outside which they lose all interest for the aborigines.

Henry Lavachery

131. SOLOMON ISLANDS. Carved wooden vase. *Musée de l'Homme, Paris.*

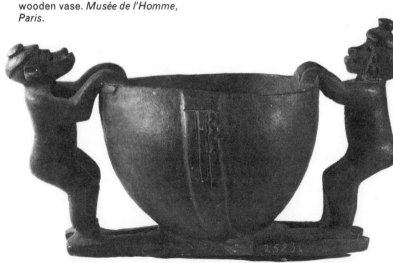

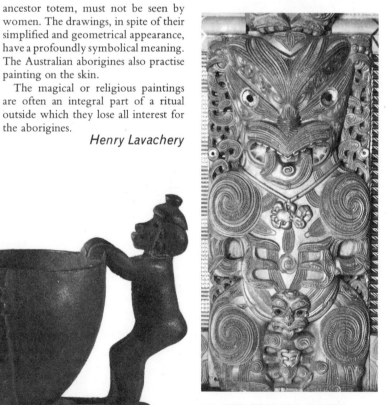

134. NEW ZEALAND. MAORI. Ancestral panel from ceremonial meeting-house. *Dominion Museum.*

NORTH AND SOUTH AMERICA

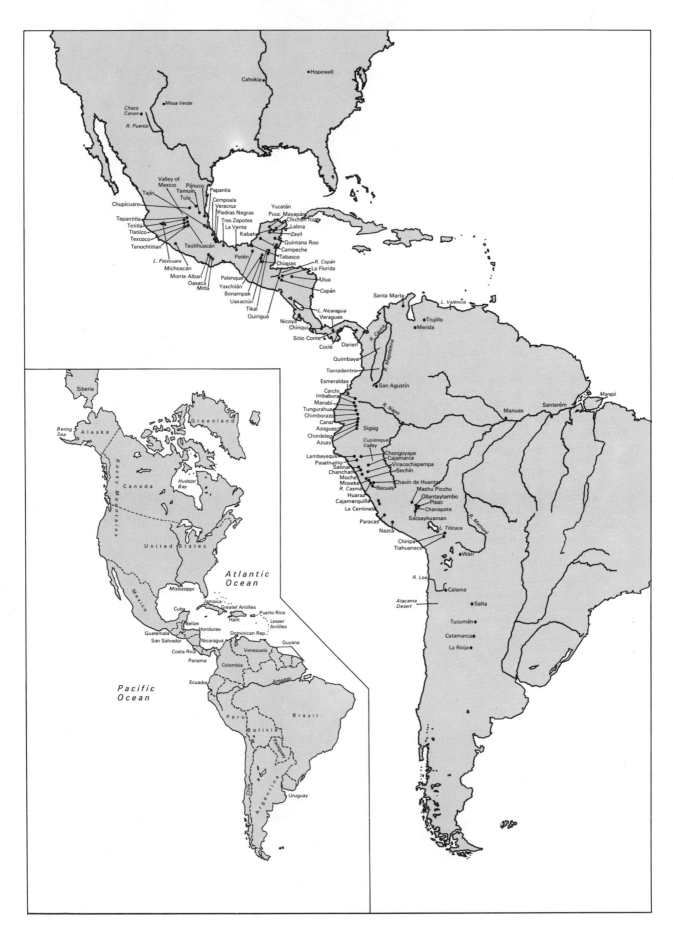

Hopewell
Cahokia
Mesa Verde
Chaco Canon
R. Puerco

Valley of Mexico
Pánuco
Tamuin
Papantla
Tula
Tajín
Cempoala
Veracruz
Chupícuaro
Piedras Negras
Yucatán
Puuc Mayapán
Tepantitla
Tres Zapotes
Chichén Itzá
Tetitla
La Venta
Labna
Tlatilco
Kabah
Zayil
Texcoco
Quintana Roo
Tenochtitlan
Teotihuacán
Campeche
L. Patzcuaro
Petén
Tabasco
Michoacán
Chiapas
R. Copán
Monte Alban
Palenque
La Florida
Oaxaca
Ulua
Mitla
Yaxchilán
Copán
Bonampak
Uaxactún
L. Nicaragua
Tikal
Veraguas
Quiriguá
Nicoya
Chiriquí
Sitio Conte
Coclé
Darien
Quimbaya
Tierradentro
Esmeraldas
San Agustín
Carchi
Imbabura
Manabí
Tungurahua
R. Napo
Chimborazo
Canar
Azogues
Sigsig
Chordeleg
Azuay
Cupisnique Valley
Lambayeque
Chongoyape
Pacatnamu
Cajamarca
Salinar
Viracochapampa
Chanchan
Sechín
Moche
Moxeke
Chavín de Huantar
R. Casma
Recuay
Machu Picchu
Huaraz
Ollantaytambo
Cajamarquilla
Pisac
La Centinela
Chanapata
Sacsayhuaman
Paracas
L. Titicaca
Nazca
Chiripa
Tiahuanaco
Wari

Santa Marta
L. Valencia
Trujillo
Merida
R. Cauca
R. Magdalena
Marajó
Manuas
Santarém
R. Mamoni
R. Loa
Calama
Atacama Desert
Salta
Tucumán
Catamarca
La Rioja

Siberia
Greenland
Bering Sea
Alaska
Canada
Rocky Mountains
Hudson Bay
United States
Atlantic Ocean
Mississippi
Mexico
Cuba
Jamaica
Greater Antilles
Puerto Rico
Belize
Haiti
Lesser Antilles
Guatemala
Honduras
Dominican Rep.
San Salvador
Nicaragua
Costa Rica
Guyana
Panama
Venezuela
Colombia
Pacific Ocean
Ecuador
Amazon
Peru
Brazil
Bolivia
Chile
Paraguay
Argentina
Uruguay

98

PRE-COLUMBIAN CIVILISATIONS

Raoul d'Harcourt

*The two Americas also provide the example of a continent
long virtually cut off from the rest of the world.
Nevertheless, the majority of the civilisations which
developed there had already reached a higher stage,
similar to that which we shall meet in the next chapter,
in our Western world, with the first great agrarian empires.*

Certain ethnic groups in America had reached a very
advanced degree of culture before the arrival of Columbus.

Without wishing to make too close a comparison
between the geographical situation of these groups and
that of the great civilisations of the Mediterranean basin,
whose waters encouraged interchanges, one cannot help
thinking that the most highly developed American
peoples were concentrated in much the same way, but in
their case on the slopes of an enormous mountain massif
between southern California and the high Chilean range:
the sea also bathed their coasts and made coastal navigation comparatively easy for them.

In these tropical regions, with low hot plains but temperate plateaux, two nuclei of peoples, one to the north,
the other to the south, created unified states in a historically similar manner. In both cases, a warlike tribe, as the
result of successive conquests, managed to impose its
will on the neighbouring tribes who were often more
civilised than it was. These warriors rapidly assimilated
the knowledge of the conquered and soon raised it to an
even higher level. This was true of the Aztecs in Mexico
and the Incas in Peru. Although American chronology as
a whole is by no means definitely established, we know
that these amalgamations, each of which gave birth to
a complex social organisation equivalent to a state, date
from the last centuries before the arrival of Columbus.

The arrival of the Spaniards, as much by the mere
contact with their civilisation as by the brutal methods
used to impose Christianity, shattered the fragile cultural
edifice erected during the two preceding millennia.

The problem of the origin of man on the new continent
will not be discussed in this article. Even if a few ships
from Oceania did land on the shores of the Pacific, their
small crews of primitive peoples could not have modified
a culture which was probably already stronger than their
own. The isolation in which the Indians lived makes the
study of their conception of the universe, their scientific
knowledge and their art particularly attractive.

Apart from the description of the first chroniclers, we
owe everything we have learnt to archaeological research
and excavations conducted with increasingly accurate
methods. They have thrown most light on the past. The
dry earth of the Peruvian littoral has made possible, as in
Egypt, the preservation of vivid evidence of the life of
long ago. In addition, the clearance of monuments
covered with sand, the replacing of worked stones strew-
ing the ground around the ruins have restored monuments
which had been thought destroyed for ever. Admittedly,
researches are far from complete: the forests of the
Chiapas and the high Andean valleys still conceal a great

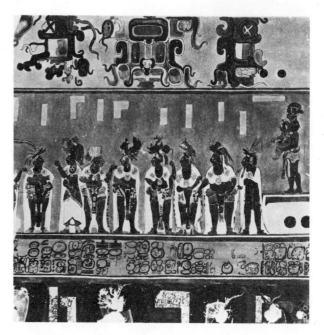

135. MEXICO. CHIAPAS BONAMPAK. Detail of a Mayan
fresco.

deal, but already we are beginning to put the past in order
and history is emerging. The epochs have been distinguished and with them their characteristic works. Clas-
sifying works of art is more difficult in America than elsewhere because of the differences of style or form they
exhibit, even when they belong to neighbouring regions.
For a long time these differences led archaeologists to
exaggerate the isolation in which the tribes lived. American chronology will only be established on firm foundations when a full radioactive carbon survey has been
carried out.

Duality of artistic conceptions

Works of art in America follow the universal law and
reflect the cosmogonic conceptions and beliefs of those
who executed them. The object born of art for art's sake
remains quite exceptional; the artist believed that he was
pursuing a utilitarian end while creating it, whether the
object concerned the living or the dead. The statuary,
with its representations of divinities, the funerary pottery,
whose prodigious diversity shows the interest the Indians
attached to it, the pyramid crowned with its sacrificial
altar and sometimes enclosing the tomb of an important
person, as at Palenque, are there to attest to it.

From our modern point of view, two different currents
dominate American art (quite independently of time and
place): one in the direction of realism, which seeks to copy
nature, and the other in the direction of stylisation, which
interprets it, or even breaks down its structure to rearrange it in a different way. These two currents are not
necessarily mutually exclusive and may coexist in the
same work.

The description of the works of art contained in two

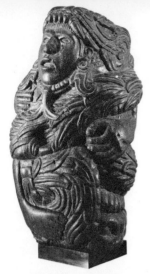

136. MEXICO. VALLEY OF MEXICO. Aztec porphyry statue of Quetzalcoatl in the form of a plumed serpent with a human head. *Musée de l'Homme, Paris.*

important regions, one in Central America, the other in South America, will bring out this aesthetic quality.

Painting and sculpture in Yucatán

Among the Mayas, realism is to be found primarily in paintings of social life and sculptured figures. The frescoes
135   of the temple of Bonampak, offered to the god of war undoubtedly to commemorate a victory, are executed on the whitewashed walls and show domestic scenes and processions in two bands, one above the other. The figures with normal proportions are in profile—not until a later period did the Mayas dare to place them facing the spectator—and their skulls bear the mark of deliberate deformation, while their noses, long and pronounced, are evidence of the artists' desire to represent the race; some musicians beat drums or blow long trumpets, warriors brandish their lances, servants bring objects of adornment, hold up feather parasols. These pictures represent everyday life without introducing any deliberate alteration, and the colours themselves are inspired by reality.

Let us take another example, the magnificent high relief No. 3 from Piedras Negras, dating from the 9th or 10th centuries, the epoch which saw the apogee of Mayan sculpture. The laws of perspective began to be applied in it. The figures, treated in relief, are almost separated from the background. The scene represents a chief seated on a sumptuous throne and leaning forward; three men on his right and three on his left, in different postures, with their arms folded on their chests, are watching him, while seven others, seated on the floor in the foreground, surround a low altar. The scene shows a perfect balance both in composition and technique; the arrangement of the group, the attitude of the figures (unfortunately several heads are missing), all contribute to make this panel the greatest masterpiece in America. It had no successors. The fall of what is wrongly known as the Ancient Empire involved the disappearance of the great sculptors.

In addition to these impressive groups, we must not neglect the representation of individuals, whether men or gods. Whether it be a statue or a simple medallion carved in bas-relief, the subject has the same qualities of strength, accuracy and style, and the same nobility.

Often the same monuments contain some decorative art, in which the imagination of the sculptor, given free rein for centuries, has created fictitious beings and ornamental motifs which however obey certain canons. Some-

times decoration begins with the framework of the main subject, usually in the form of series of hieroglyphs in lines and columns. They can be seen around a figure and also on certain parts of monuments, lintels or door-frames; they may even cover, as at Copán, the rises of a pyramid's steps. These hieroglyphs, absolutely personal to the Mayas, appear in the form of small reliefs carved in stone or modelled in stucco. They are of equal dimensions, except for some more important ones which play a part somewhat comparable to our capital letters. They are delicate carvings enclosed in ovals, rectangles or squares with rounded corners and containing lines, dots and curves, motifs arising from the scroll; others represent the head of an animal or a man with complicated outlines. These signs are the decorative twins of much more simple signs; thus numbers are composed of dots and bars, zero —for the Mayas invented it long before the Hindus— being represented by a small shell.

Although this feature is predominant, it is only one of the aspects of the decorative art of Yucatán. Let us follow, for example, the evolution of the rattlesnake motif, whose importance to the Mayas is possibly explicable in terms of remote totemic ideas. Originally represented by an artless outline produced by undulating parallel lines, it next assumed a more precise, more natural form, but it soon added to this whorls and spirals themselves taken from reptilian shapes. The position of the body crystallised in an S-shaped figure and the ornamental plumage of the quetzal, reserved for the head-dresses of the high dignitaries, began to decorate it here and there, near the tail or the head. The result is the famous plumed serpent. Then the animal became human; a man's head, recognisable by the nose and ears, even the whole face, seemed to issue from its gaping jaws. (Anthropomorphism was as highly   136
developed in America as in Egypt or Assyria.) Then the rattlesnake's head underwent the most unexpected transformations, the animal's features losing all traces of its natural appearance to become mere ornamental motifs; between the jaws open at right angles a tongue shoots out, divided into several forks with multiple scrolls. In a final transformation the animal became purely decorative. The serpent served as a subject, but it itself disappeared. On the decorated façades of monuments the undulating movements of the reptile, subject to the requirements of architectural style and the bonding of stones, assumed forms which break at right angles and finally gave birth to the staircase motif and even to the complete Greek fret   138
pattern.

Mochica naturalism and Nazca stylisation

We find these two opposite conceptions of art, in highly accentuated and geographically distinct forms, at the foot of the Andes, on the shores of the Pacific. In order to describe them, we shall take the Mochica peoples, at one time called the proto-Chimú, to the north of Lima, and the Nazca and Paracas, peoples to the south.

The art of South America is most perfectly expressed in its funerary ceramics. These vases, intended to contain the liquid necessary for men in their subterranean after-life, appear in the deepest archaeological layers, shortly after the first terra-cotta objects. At first simple shapes, with a globular belly, predominate, but the representation of man was rapidly incorporated. It became explicit and spread to animals, naive modellings of which are found

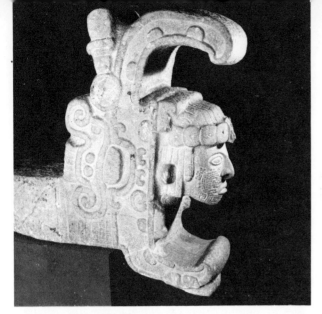

137. MEXICO. UXMAL (YUCATÁN). Mayan sculpture from the Temple of the Soothsayer.

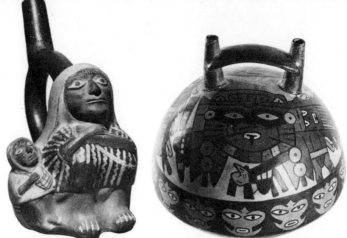

139. *Left.* CENTRAL ANDES. PERU. Classical Mochican 'stirrup' vase representing a mother and child. *W. Cummings Collection, Chicago.*

140. *Right.* CENTRAL ANDES. PERU. Nazca vase with two spouts. *R. H. Collection.*

in the Cupisnique and Salinar cultures. During the following centuries, the manner of the artist constantly seeking to render what he saw became still more precise; his hand became more skilful. To execute his work, he had at his disposal the belly of a vase the average size of a gourd. This belly was fitted with a hollow handle forming an arc surmounted by a vertical tube by which the liquid entered and was poured out ('stirrup handle'), or even by two parallel spouts. The artist could depict his subjects on the upper part of the belly, by transforming the aspect of the handles if necessary, or model the belly itself, by giving in the shape of the subject to be depicted. With such reduced surfaces and volumes, the Mochica potters managed to produce their most significant works. The zoomorphic and especially the anthropomorphic vases are the most interesting to us. The Indian is generally represented in his usual resting position, kneeling or squatting. The body is treated summarily, more sketched than modelled. The artist gives all his attention to the head whether it rises out of the belly or actually forms it. Thus the tombs of the Trujillo region contained thousands of funerary vases, *huacos*, reproducing an endless variety

of human figures, ranging from modelling which is still clumsy to the most finished works. The name 'portrait-vases' has been given to numerous pieces, so much do they give the impression of a definite individual. The artist has tackled every social class, from the chief to the old woman with a toothless chuckle; man has been caught in his daily occupations and even asleep. We also see him reduced to a skeleton still endowed with life, in spite of hollow eye-sockets and missing lips. The Mochica modeller was attracted by strange cases, pathological deformations of the head or body; we look at a procession of the sick, the one-eyed and the blind, cripples, delinquents or prisoners with arms or legs amputated, lacking both feet and dragging themselves along on their ankles sheathed in a sort of square clog. A piece of this kind in the Lima Museum bears the figure of a crouching blind man striking a tambourine, while a ring of dancers in light relief whirls headlong round the belly of the vase. In effect, there is no shortage of scenes with several figures, and painting is often allied with modelling.

Some scenes may merely be painted in monochrome on plain surfaces. The precision of the brush stroke and the

87a

138. MEXICO. ZAPOTEC CIVILISATION. Detail of the wall decoration in the palace of Mitla.

141. MEXICO. The traditional Greek fret motif is still found today in Mexico.

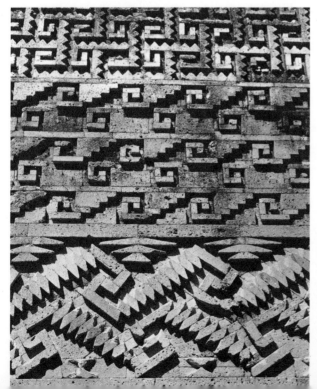

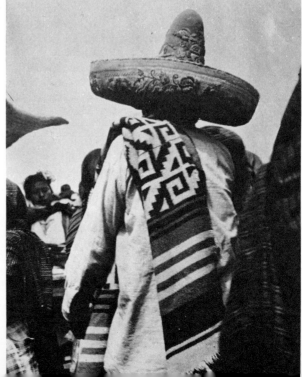

individuality of the style endow them with an interest equal to that obtained by modelling, but in another way. These scenes often deal with combats between enemy tribes; the conquerors are easily identified by their proud attitude, their rich clothing, their weapons and the treatment inflicted on their enemies. The struggle may take place between man and animal, which is always provided with human attributes in such cases. For anthropomorphism extends to all kinds of beings: carnivora, birds, fish, crustaceans or even shells. It may go as far as the humanisation of haricot beans, representing the newsbearers who themselves carried spotted beans in a small bag, to help them remember the news they had to transmit. The fights can equally well match a man and a jaguar as a bird and a crab, a stag and a serpent or even a hermit-crab stamping on a fish. Other examples are magnificently interpreted hunting scenes, fishing from rafts made of rushes, processions accompanying a chief carried in a litter, scenes of offerings and dances. All these designs with the brush comprise in their stylisation a veritable imaginative orgy combined with the most exact sense of observation and with lines reduced strictly to the essentials.

Further south, the ceramics of the Nazca region (with which the famous embroideries of Paracas are connected both in their colour and decoration) are still funerary pottery, but modelling moves into the background, replaced by painting. The simple shapes lend themselves to decoration: various kinds of cups, cylindrical vases with bell-mouthed edges, globular bellies with a low neck, or closed and surmounted by two narrow tubes close together and connected by a bridge. The rounded bottoms show that this pottery was meant to rest on loose soil. On some pieces the low relief representing a human being or an animal has been summarily indicated and the painting has been left to bring out the details. The Nazca civilisation, certainly a little earlier than the Christian era, later underwent the influence of Tiahuanaco, which is situated near Lake Titicaca, before finally merging with the Inca culture, a few centuries before the arrival of the Spaniards. The workmanship of the vases is excellent: regular thin well-fired sides covered with a layer of slip so fine as to appear glazed after firing. It is at Nazca that the potters have the widest range of colours in their palette; all the colours are represented in it, except blue: even if the red verges on violet and the yellow on the greenish, blue in the strict sense of the word was not established. In those archaeological layers judged the most ancient, the representations, although fairly clumsy, have very clear-cut realistic tendencies, but the artist, increasingly skilful with the centuries, interprets more, and his stylised art creates genuine laws. What does he represent? Fruits, roots, cactuses, some flowers; among the birds, sea-gulls, pelicans, parakeets, humming-birds, and among the quadrupeds, small rodents, foxes, llamas, or again snakes, fish and seals. Representations of the cat tribe, jaguars or pumas, are so stylised as to become doubtful.

As with the Mochicas, man's head occupies the first place; it is shown whole or mutilated, in the form of a bleeding trophy or a *tsantsa* (shrunken or dried head). It can be taken as typical of the transformations the Nazca people imposed on their subjects in order to fit them into their decorative system. The human head is first rep-resented separated from the body and bleeding, the lips closed and pierced by two long thorns; the hair is drawn back and the skull is threaded with a fine cord to hang it up by. Then the head breaks up, disintegrates; it seems to be partly concealed behind motifs shaped like tall battlements. All one can see is one eye, part of the mouth and a dark mass representing the hair. These features, isolated and repeated, appear in the decorative friezes, and the increasingly conventionalised head consists of nothing more than oval or triangular surfaces, on which three horizontal lines representing the eyes and the mouth are finally reduced to three dots.

Birds undergo similar transformations. An ear of corn becomes a rectangle placed at the end of a short stalk, surmounted by a group of dots with two crossed lines running through it. Only by studying the successive stages of simplification can we interpret the painter's thought accurately, since he no longer aims at more than the decorative effect, the well placed patch of colour.

The Nazcas also produced larger compositions in which these simplified motifs are incorporated. They created mythical beings, marine monsters: some seen in profile and still fish-like, probably representing *Orca gladiator*, the great killer whale of the seas; others, more numerous, whose enormous heads, in full face and with constant characteristics, leave only a minute space for the body. But they all have something human about them, facial features and accessories such as hair styles, earrings with multiple discs, nose-rings, batons, small reduced heads at the end of a paw or of a hand. There is no doubt that we have to do here with the representation of higher beings related to a mythology of which we know nothing. But here we are taking the aesthetic point of view and it must be admitted that, however strange and cruel they may seem, these compositions are excellent and well balanced, filling the surfaces allotted to them with flexibility; their colouring is warm and harmonious, and the black line which surrounds the motifs as in cloisonné work enhances their decorative value by separating the colours.

Relations between the two continents

We shall only allude here to the relations which may have existed between the peoples in each of the two continents of the New World.

A visitor examining pre-Columbian collections in a museum for the first time has the impression of a piecemeal production born of the most diverse aesthetic conceptions, of a veritable puzzle which could lead him to believe, in spite of a certain unity difficult to define, that each people lived in ignorance of its neighbours.

Nevertheless, after closer study, this impression of isolation disappears inside each continent. On the other hand it does continue from one continent to another. Some well known Americanists go so far as to deny the possibility, for example, of finding a Mexican piece, or a piece of clearly Mexican origin, in South America. This opinion is exaggerated: if the links between the two Americas are rare, it must be admitted that some do exist.

First let us see what each of these continents has in common. In the north, whether it is a question of mythology, agrarian gods, the calendar, hieroglyphic writing or the pyramid and its function, Mayan, Zapotec and Toltec sources, to name only the main ones, recur among the Aztecs, in their original state or modified, but always

140

easily recognisable. The monuments of Chichén Itza, which correspond to the so-called New Empire epoch, show clear echoes of these Toltec penetrations in their plans and decoration, which were felt as far as Central America.

In the southern continent the same thing holds good. For a long time Nazca underwent the influence of Tiahuanaco which spread along the coast to Pachacamac and beyond. The Chavín style made itself felt among the Mochica and we can follow the representation of shrunken heads along the Pacific (the custom of shrinking the head of the slain enemy still exists today among the Jivaros). As for the Incas, successive conquests enabled them to impose their social discipline, impregnated with communism, and to get sun worship accepted, superimposed on the worship of the preceding local pantheon; their *mitimaes*, or colonies od deportees, contributed to the mixing of customs and to a sort of perceptible unification, for the archaeologist, in the shapes and decoration of objects exhumed as far as the frontiers of the Argentine Chaco.

But the proofs of exchanges between the two continents are few and far between. The solar religion assumed very different forms in the two places; the mythologies taken as a whole are unlike. The languages, except the Chibcha dialects, which straddle the frontiers of both continents, have no affinity with each other; hieroglyphic writing, the privilege of a caste, did not even extend as far as the Isthmus of Panamá. The decimal system, adopted by the Incas, remained unknown to the Mexicans. It would be easy to multiply such examples.

However, we do know that coastal traffic carried Peruvian merchandise comparatively far north, using rafts, or *balsas*, similar to the celebrated *Kon-Tiki* which cruised the Pacific in 1946; a lieutenant of Pizarro's captured one of them during his first maritime expeditions to Peru. The complicated techniques of Peruvian and Colombian goldsmiths' work possibly penetrated Central America and Mexico by the same route.

Many of their customs are similar. Secondary burials in urns were practised both in the Chiapas and in the Amazon basin. The rite of cranial deformation, using compressive boards on young children, was observed equally in Yucatán, Central America and the Andes. Small clay female figurines of crude workmanship but with the same characteristics have been excavated throughout Mexico; they are also found in the whole southern part of South America as far as Marajo Island, at the mouth of the Amazon; with their different styles, they are undoubtedly connected with a very ancient cult of agrarian character. The Peruvian vases with twin tubular spouts connected by a thin bridge recur in Huasteca, near the Atlantic coast of Mexico. It is most unlikely that two independent creations were involved.

In any case, it is an acknowledged fact that the ancient pottery of the province of Esmeraldas, in Ecuador, exhibits a number of characteristics which indicate that a Mexican colony, bringing with it the aesthetic traditions of the high plateaux and also of Yucatán, stayed in the region. In Ecuador, a remarkable anthropomorphic vase of pure Mayan style was taken from a tomb; now, later an absolutely similar vase was found at Kaminalijuyu in Guatemala; in Ecuador it was not a question of an odd contribution by some old trader, but of a piece modelled

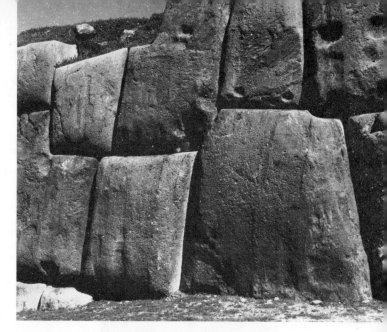

142. CENTRAL ANDES. PERU. Detail of the walls of Sacsayhuaman.

on the spot, as can be determined by small details.

We shall end these comparisons by the description of two decorative motifs which bring us back more especially to art and its sphere of influence.

The first consists of an incurved horn, a sort of question mark placed at the tip of the nose of mythical personages and fabulous beasts. It is a stylised highly artificial appendage found on no living animal in America even in embryonic state. In various forms deriving from each other, it is found in the paintings and sculpture of the tribes of the north-west, in Yucatán, in Central America and on the north coast of Peru as far as Chile.

The second and much more significant motif is the Greek fret pattern to which is joined laterally a regular broken line, placed obliquely. This motif is essentially American and is found nowhere in the ancient world. We can easily understand its formation: it is a sequence of scrolls, which, deformed by certain technical processes such as basket-work, mosaics and carved stone, have taken on an angular character. The actual scroll has become a simple key, while the line connecting two scrolls has been transformed into the profile of a staircase. The origin of the motif is not in doubt and the primitive scroll reappears from time to time under the artist's brush when he is no longer restrained in his interpretation by the technique. What is almost unique in the history of decoration art is the constant use of the Greek fret pattern and the dislocation of its elements which, while remaining associated, gave birth to infinitely varied combinations. Now, this motif is as abundant among the Pueblo Indians, in Mexico and Central America, as in the Andean civilisations and their Chilean and Argentinian extensions. How can we believe in the existence of several centres, each one giving birth to the same theme, which radiated out and met its counterparts in other regions, when a sequence of scrolls never gave rise to this motif in the Old World? We must rather admit that the Greek key-pattern, born at some point on American territory, perhaps beneath the fingers of a basket-worker, about two thousand years ago, gradually spread like a patch of oil; in any case, it is proof of intercontinental relations.

The two Americas, then, did not live in total ignorance of each other but one is still surprised that their interpenetration remained at such a superficial, limited stage.

HISTORICAL SUMMARY: The Americas

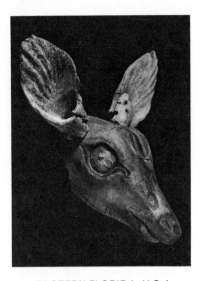

143. EASTERN FLORIDA, U.S.A. KEY MARCO. Wooden deer masquette. *University Museum, Philadelphia.*

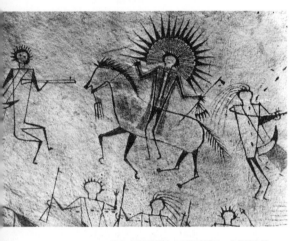

144. NORTH AMERICA. ARKANSAS. Detail of a Sioux chief's cloak, made of painted bison skin. *Musée de l'Homme, Paris.*

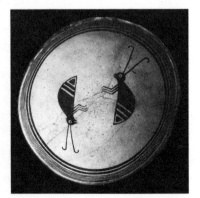

145. NEW MEXICO, U.S.A. MIMBRES VALLEY. Interior of a bowl decorated with stylised insects. *Peabody Museum, Harvard University.*

NORTH AMERICA

North America is only separated from Asia by the Bering Strait, which witnessed the passage of the first human groups who came to populate its new lands. The Eskimos were the only occupants of the desolate arctic regions and they never attempted to leave their specialised way of life to make contact with the Indians. The latter invaded the continent either by hugging the Pacific coasts, or by taking the high plateaux and the eastern slope of the Rocky Mountains. Until the European discovery the inhabitants of immense regions lived by picking roots and berries or by hunting. Only the plains of the middle west and east and semi-arid lands of the south-west had agricultural civilisations.

1. The arctic regions. The domain of the Eskimos (from the eastern coast of Siberia to Greenland). The economy is based on fishing and hunting the big marine mammalia (characteristic features: the oil lamp and the articulated harpoon). Eskimo culture has a long past; important archaeological remains have been uncovered, mainly to the west of Hudson Bay (Thule men, hunters of whales and bears, about the 8th century) and at Cape Orset (Bering Sea culture, more ancient than Thule, rich in forms and highly developed: curvilinear ornamentation on ivory objects, possibly influenced by the Neolithic of eastern Asia). The maximum development of Eskimo art is found on the coasts of Alaska: extremely expressive, often grotesque and humorous polychrome masks of carved wood [101]; ivory statuettes; utilitarian objects and ornaments of carved and engraved ivory (harpoon parts, straighteners and lugs, labrets, etc.). The finely engraved scenes constitute a veritable pictographic writing.

2. North-west coast. The civilisation of 'salmon-fishers' (Tlingit, Haida, Kwakiutl, Bella Coola, Chinook), installed from Cape Saint Eulalia (Alaska Bay) to the north of California. In this cold rainy and inaccessible region with many fjords rich in fish, the houses are made of wood, ornamented with totem poles carved out of cedar trunks (superimposed figures of fantastic animals often forming the history of a family with representations of ancestors). Masks, head ornaments and dancing-rattles of carved wood are painted bright colours and inlaid with mother-of-pearl. The canoes, chests, buckets, spoons and clubs for salmon-fishing are richly decorated with symbolical animals and marine monsters. There are few stone objects. Covers and blankets woven of vegetable fibres and wild goat's hair exhibit extraordinarily decorative compositions based on the same motifs as those used in sculpture.

3. The great central plains. This vast depression—from the foot of the Rocky Mountains to the Mississippi basin—rich in big game, attracted the nomadic tribes from the most remote times. From the 10th to the 18th centuries herds of bison multiplied, and horses and firearms appeared: the agricultural Indians (Sioux, Mandan, Pawnee, etc.) returned to a life based on hunting. A specialised art developed: the painted and embroidered decoration (porcupine-quills) of skins used for tents, cloaks, moccasins and bags [144]. These were often of the skins of bison and the deer tribe with geometrical red or black motifs, or large scenes (dances, hunting, religious ceremonies), with numerous stylised figures, in varied and symbolical colours.

4. The eastern plain and Florida. This is the region of the mound builders: heaps of earth of various kinds (10th–15th centuries), surrounded by works with geometrical shapes (Hopewell, Ohio); vast tumuli shaped like animals: tortoises, snakes, etc. (Wisconsin); a type of truncated pyramid, the bases of temples (Cahokia, Mississippi). Portable objects include ceramic vases (simple shapes, often with engraved decoration); bowls of carved stone (animal shapes); perforated engraved plaques of natural copper and shells; stone statuettes; wooden masks (heads of the deer tribe); large numbers of carved stone pipes (men and animals).

5. The south-west region. This is the civilisation of the Anasazi or Pueblos, farmers and potters influenced by Mexico. They took the place of the basket-makers. Their apogee was between the 11th and 13th centuries (Pueblo III) in three principal zones: New Mexico (stone constructions of Chaco Cañon); southern Colorado (the cliff-dwellings of Mesa Verde) and north-eastern Arizona. The architecture is remarkable: gigantic compartmented houses, using masonry, with ceremonial squares and temples (kiva). In a continuous development the pottery is decorated in black on white (Rio Puerco): stylised anthropomorphic and zoomorphic figures (Mimbres [145]); polychrome symbolical scenes.

MEXICO

The two Mexican cordilleras (the eastern and western Sierra Madre) are the extension of two chains of the Rocky Mountains, and the central Mexican plateau was open to migrations of nomadic hunters from the steppes of the north. This high plateau, especially the Valley of Mexico (7,345 ft), witnessed the development and disappearance of many brilliant civilisations (all based on maize, the main vegetable food of Mexico) before becoming the centre of the Aztec empire, destroyed in its turn by the Spaniards (execution of Montezuma II in 1519).

The mountainous regions which extend to the south of Mexico and as far as Chiapas are an absolute mosaic of languages and tribes. Some groups, owing to a better communal agrarian system, reached a high degree of cultural development.

As to the Atlantic slope of the eastern Sierra Madre and the humid zone of the coastal plain of the Gulf of Mexico (the Anahuac of the Aztecs), they have always attracted the civilised peoples of the high plateau.

What was the cause of the rapid decadence of the Maya civilisation (Yucatán peninsula), the highest native culture of the New World? Certain unfavourable conditions of the tropical environment and especially the general impoverishment of the cultivable land probably played a decisive role.

In many regions archaeological data are still inadequate to enable the establishment of a general chronological study applicable to the whole of Mexico.

1. The region of the high plateau. After the appearance of agriculture and pottery (towards the year 2000) came the so-called 'middle' civilisations, Copilco-Zacatenco (duration about 700 years) and Cuicuilco-Ticoman (about 300 years), with their pottery vases and statuettes: women with very well developed thighs, rudimentary arms and legs, lozenge-shaped decoration. Next came the *Tlatilco* phase: a highly developed art, with pottery comparable to that of the Olmecs (statuettes, nude torsos of young people, figures of babies).

The Teotihuacán civilisation. The monuments of the immense religious metropolis of Teotihuacán (truncated pyramids, including the Pyramid of the Sun: 195 ft high, about 47,000,000 cubic feet of filling [**155**]; stepped temples; palaces) were mainly constructed between the 3rd and 9th centuries. The art is sober and severe, characterised by monumental sculpture (goddess of water, 10 ft high; heads of

the rain god and plumed serpent god in the temple of Quetzalcoatl); funerary masks, combining realistic and stylised elements, of hard stone (porphyry, jade, jadeite, alabaster), sometimes covered with polychrome mosaics; admirable frescoes (Tepantitla; Tetitla). Great importance was attached to Tlaloc and the fire god, who appear repeatedly on the sculptures, frescoes, vases and ceramic statuettes.

The Toltec civilisation. From the 10th century, the Toltecs (Nahua) occupied Teotihuacán; their principal centre was Tula (other important sites: Xochicalco, Mayapán, Colhuacan). They had the calendar and a special system of writing, both different from those of the Mayas (the two systems of dates appear at Xochicalco). Their grandiose art—which recurs at Chichén Itza, in Yucatán [**148**]—is demonstrated on the principal stone monuments at Tula: a frieze of jaguars; plumed serpent and 'man-bird-serpent'; caryatids (15 ft high); pillars with armed warriors on their four sides; wall of serpents (devouring a man with a fleshless skull), painted and carved frieze.

The Aztec civilisation. The Aztecs, the last emigrants speaking the Nahuatl language, established themselves at various points on the Mexican plateau at the beginning of the 14th century (their capital, Tenochtitlan, was founded in 1325). For more than a century, they assimilated the art and culture of the Toltecs (especially at Colhuacan and Texcoco) whose influence remained particularly noticeable in architecture (pyramids, decorative friezes). The Aztecs demonstrate their originality in their religious statuary [**149**] (Coatlicue in Mexico Museum; Quetzalcoatl, in Musée de l'Homme), the bas-reliefs (Aztec calendar; Toecalli of the Holy War; Tizoc stone), the very austere secular statues (chief's head; seated men; animals), the masks and ornaments of hard stone, the objects of carved wood (drums), painted manuscripts.

2. The north-west region. Not very well known from the archaeological point of view. Consequently there is no chronology of the numerous interesting local cultures, of which the Colima and Nayarit are the principal ones. The Tarasco civilisation in the strict sense of the word was situated at Chupícuaro and around Lake Patzcuaro (Michoacán). Particularly noteworthy are the very expressive and often humorous pottery statuettes and figurines frequently painted in a naturalistic style: people and animals in various attitudes, groups of musicians and dancers, houses and domestic scenes.

3. The Gulf region. This region

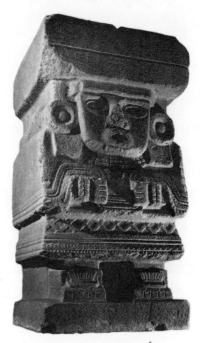

146. MEXICO. TEOTIHUACÁN. Sculpture supposed to represent the water goddess Chalchihuitlicue. *National Anthropological Museum, Mexico.*

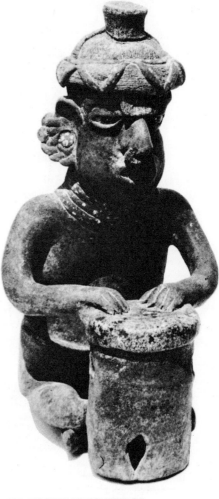

147. NORTH-WEST MEXICO. NAYARIT. Ceramic statuette of a musician. *Musée de l'Homme, Paris.*

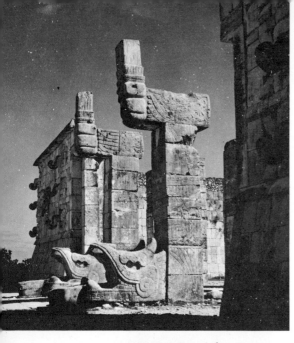

148. MEXICO. CHICHÉN ITZA. Columns at the entrance of the Temple of the Warriors.

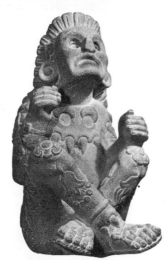

149. MEXICO. AZTEC CIVILISATION. Xochipilli, prince of the flowers and god of happiness, music and dancing. *National Anthropological Museum, Mexico.*

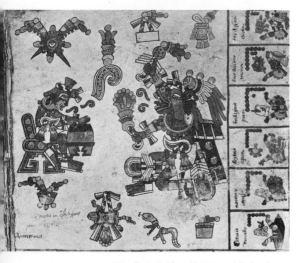

150. Detail of an Aztec calendar from the Codex Barbonicus. *Library of the Chamber of Deputies, Paris.*

contained three important civilisations: the Olmec, Totonac and Huaxtec. The art of the Olmecs (500–100 B.C.) is related to that of the ancient layers of Oaxaca (Monte Alban I and II) and the Valley of Mexico (Tlatilco). Main sites: La Venta (Tabasco) and Tres Zapotes (Veracruz). In addition to the monumental sculpture—monolithic statues, enormous human heads of basalt [151] (over 5 ft high, 15–18 ft in diameter) in a realistic style—there are the baby-like jade masks and statuettes, the divinity with a big stomach and the 'disdainful mouth'. The statue of a wrestler found at Uxpananan (26 in. high) is one of the masterpieces of Mexican sculpture.

The Totonac civilisation (approx. 400–1000) developed in the north of the State of Veracruz (Cempoala, Papantla). The characteristic monument is El Tajín (a pyramid with its four sides pierced with 365 niches). The art is original, the sculpture of high quality [152]: 'yokes' and 'palms' of hard stone; bas-reliefs; pottery statuettes with smiling faces [153].

The Huaxtec civilisation (Rio Pánuco) was situated to the north of the Totonac region. The present-day population continues to speak a Mayan dialect of very ancient origin. But the art, which developed late, is original (no obvious relation with the classical art of the Mayas). The stone statues (including the adolescent from Tamuín) often have a flattened surface, but are covered with finely carved ornamentation. The pottery differs from all the other Mexican styles; extremely varied shapes; vases with spout and handle decorated in black on a white ground.

4. The southern region. The principal archaeological site of the Zapotec civilisation, in the mountains of Oaxaca, is Monte Alban, where important excavations have revealed five periods of occupation. The earliest phase yields various monuments and sculptures strongly influenced by the Olmecs (particularly the slabs bearing the famous bas-reliefs of dancers). Towards the end of the 6th century A.D., the Zapotecs, imposing an original art and culture, built the biggest edifices of the Monte Alban terraces: stone stelae with figures and inscriptions, heads in relief decorating the walls; pendants and necklaces of jade and of other hard stones; countless pottery funerary urns, modelled to represent people and gods covered with rich ornaments.

In the 15th century the Mixtecs arrived, possibly the builders of the sober edifices of Mitla, decorated solely with geometrical motifs in relief [138]. They are especially known as painters and goldsmiths. The admirable gold

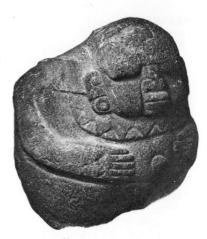

151. MEXICO. GULF REGION. Olmec statuette in stone from Tabasco. *Musée de l'Homme, Paris.*

objects from tomb 7 at Monte Alban (diadems, necklaces, various ornaments with semi-precious stones) show that they were the masters of many techniques probably imported from Colombia and Peru (laminating, chasing, casting by the cire perdue process, imitation filigree, soldering), and used them with the greatest virtuosity.

5. The Mayan region. This covered the west of Honduras, British Honduras, Petén and the highlands of Guatemala; in Mexico, Yucatán, a part of Chiapas, Campeche, Tabasco and Quintana Roo. At the present time some two million natives speaking Mayan dialects still live there. The pre-Mayan period and the beginnings of civilisation, towards 3000 B.C., it seems, remain obscure. Corn and pottery appeared towards 1000 B.C. The modelled vases and statuette of the Mamom type recall the most ancient pottery of the Mexican plateau. Then followed the period characterised by the Chicanel type pottery, contemporary with the first stone pyramids (350 B.C.–A.D. 300).

The Ancient Empire. The most ancient date—A.D. 320—inscribed on a jade plaque from the Tikal region (Leyden Museum) marks the beginning of the history of the Mayas. Its phases are known from stone stelae erected every twenty years (the first appeared at Uaxactùn, in 328). The 7th and 8th centuries marked the zenith of the classical period. The main centres were Copán, Quiriguá, Palenque, Piedras Negras, Yaxchilán. The sculpture, freed from the static style of the ancient period and applied to the decoration of stelae, lintels, altars, walls and the stairs of temples and palaces, produced matchless works of art. Wood, stone and stucco were used. The most extraordinary collections of monuments exist at Copán and Quirigua (stelae of colossal dimensions; richly clad priests

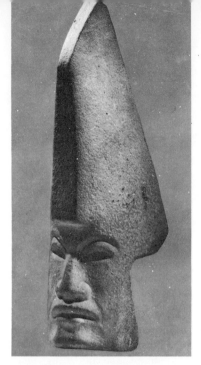

152. MEXICO. GULF REGION. Totonac head in stone. *Musée de l'Homme, Paris.*

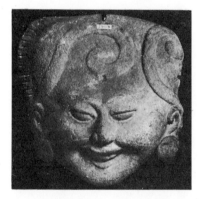

153. MEXICO. GULF REGION. Head of a Totonac terra-cotta statue. *Musée de l'Homme, Paris.*

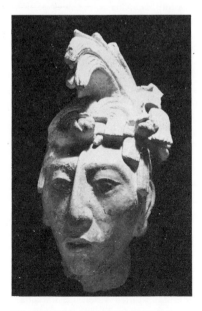

154. MEXICO. MAYAN CIVILISATION. Stucco head from Palenque. *National Anthropological Museum, Mexico.*

or chiefs; sumptuous flamboyant ornamentation). Palenque is famous for its stucco bas-reliefs (Temples of the Leaved Cross, the Sun, the Inscriptions [**157**]). The most beautiful frescoes were discovered in 1946 at Bonampak [**135**]: religious and secular scenes—chiefs, warriors, masked figures, musicians, ritual offerings, punishment of prisoners—executed in a realistic style and vivid colours on the walls of chambers (15 ft high). Painting was also used for the decoration of the codices and pottery vases.

The New Empire. From the 9th century onwards came the decadence of the civilisation and the abandoning of the classical sites of the south. Mayan groups (Itza) emigrated to Yucatán, where they were rejoined by the Toltecs, who left Tula under the leadership of their chief Kukulkan (Plumed Serpent): important towns such as Chichén Itza, Mayapán and Uxmal were founded; an artistic renaissance introduced the Mayan Puuc style, rich in geometrical and symbolical representations (palaces of Zayil, Labna, Kabah, Uxmal) and a style of Toltec origin, given its highest expression at Chichén Itza (Temples of the Warriors, the Plumed Serpent, the Jaguars) where we rediscover the characteristics of Tula art: Chac Mool, standard-bearer, telamones, felines, columns representing Quetzalcoatl [**148**], bas-reliefs with figures. Also found are pottery vases and statuettes, jade and jadeite objects, and turquoise mosaics. Goldsmiths' work was poorly developed.

CENTRAL AMERICA AND THE CARIBBEAN

In Central America proper, the distribution of the populations is closely bound up with the climate and the vegetation. The Pacific coast and particularly the dry highlands of the interior were the centre of gravity of the ancient civilisations. Archaeology is complicated in this transit and exchange zone, with its Mexican and Mayan elements, its Amazonian (Arawak) and Colombian (Chibcha dialects; Quimbaya goldsmiths' work) ingredients.

The West Indies, the first land discovered by Columbus (1492), were inhabited by two peoples from the South American continent, the Arawaks and the Caribs. The latter, last-minute immigrants, settled in the Lesser Antilles, where they partially exterminated the former Arawak population. The Taino civilisation of the Greater Antilles underwent the influence of Mexico at a recent period: maritime relations between the islands and Yuca-

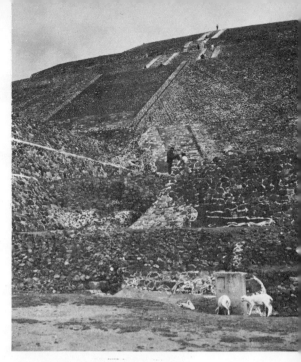

155. MEXICO. TEOTIHUACÁN CIVILISATION. The Pyramid of the Sun.

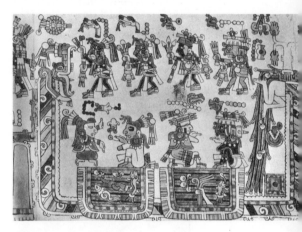

156. SOUTHERN MEXICO. MIXTEC. A page from the Codex Zouche-Nuttal. The scene probably represents the creation of the Mixtec people. Painted on deer skin. *British Museum.*

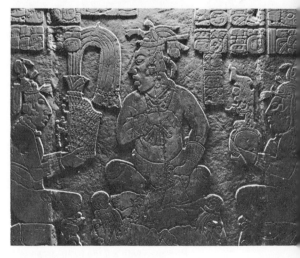

157. MEXICO. MAYAN CIVILISATION. Detail of a bas-relief in the courtyard of the palace at Palenque.

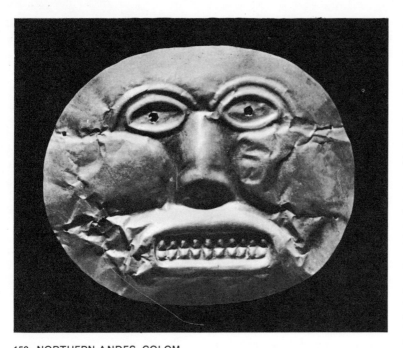

158. NORTHERN ANDES. COLOM-BIA. Quimbaya gold mask (compare the Mycenean mask [339]). *Gold Museum, Bogotá.*

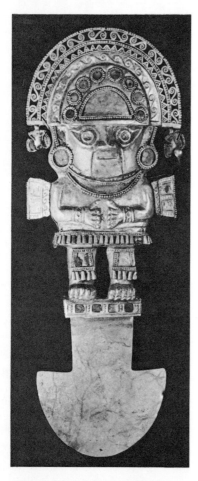

159. CENTRAL ANDES. PERU. Chimú gold ceremonial tranchet. Bird-man with a large head-dress. (Batan Grande, Lambayeque.) *National Anthropological and Archaeological Museum, Lima.*

tán still existed at the time of the European discovery. However, as in Central America—apart from the May-an sphere—there is no stone architec-ture.

1. Honduras. The valley of Ulua yields admirable marble vases with carved animals. Pottery of the same Mayan style has been found at Las Flores. At La Florida (Chamelicon), Ocopec and even at Copán: stone statues of an archaic character (non-Mayan). Felines on pillars; monkey-like figures surmounted by animal heads (height 30–50 in.).

2. Nicaragua. Zapatero and Ome-tepe Islands (Lake Nicaragua): varied archaeological material attributed to the Chorotegas. On these islands and the Pacific coast: stone statues with a columnar base (from 4 ft to 12 ft), figures with a 'guardian spirit'.

3. Costa Rica. The polychrome pottery of Nicoya is among the most exquisite in Central America: globular vases and tripods decorated with sil-houettes of symbolical serpents, croco-diles and jaguars. Zoomorphic stone mortars; gold figurines (warriors and head-trophies, crocodiles, birds: tech-niques of Chiriquí and Colombia). At Boruca and in the Guetar region: statues of men and animals in granular volcanic stone (12–24 in. high).

4. Panamá. The main centres are Chiriquí, Veraguas, Coclé and Darien. At Chiriquí (west): vases with painted or applied motifs (crocodiles, armadil-los); stone statues (including the Venus of Panamá, 31½ in.) and mortars shaped like jaguars or held up by figures of telamones, similar to the works of Costa Rica. The magnificent civilisa-tion of Coclé (a limited zone around the Gulf of Panamá) reached its fullest

development during the last two cen-turies before the conquest. Richest centre: Sitio Conte (Rio Grande) where the tombs of high dignitaries were uncovered: ceramics with curvilinear decorations, birds, mirrors, figurines and discs of gold and *tumbaga* (an alloy of gold and copper), decorations in repoussé work and imitation filigree, cut and set precious stones, ivory jewels covered with gold leaf.

5. The Taino civilisation (Greater Antilles). Main centres: Puerto Rico and Haiti. As sculptors, the Taino did admirable work in wood (*duho* or ceremonial seats) and stone (anthro-pomorphic idols, 'necklaces', stones with 3 points, monolithic axes, crush-ers). The less developed pottery pre-served the characteristics of the ceramics of the Arawak of the Lesser Antilles and the continent. The curious engravings on rocks found in various islands may be evidence of the first Arawak migra-tions.

SOUTH AMERICA

A. The Northern Andes (Venezuela, Colombia, Ecuador)

The Colombian massif is traversed by two great rivers, the Magdalena and the Cauca, excellent routes for pene-tration: hence the contacts between the developed civilisations of Colombia, Venezuela and Central America. The Ecuadorian Andes are high plateaux dominated by two chains of mountains and divided into a dozen basins with good agricultural land. As for the tropical region of the Ecuadorian coast, open to the influences of the north (Colombia, Mexico), it was particu-larly suitable for large human settle-ments.

Taken as a whole, the civilisations of the northern Andes—apart from those of the Taironas and San Agustín—have not left great public edifices behind but an extraordinary development of working in gold, the products and techniques of which were diffused far and wide (even to Mexico and the coast of Peru).

MAIN CENTRES OF ART

1. Venezuela. To the north, pottery of the Lake Valencia region: female statuettes with very large heads, short and massive limbs; decorated vases (modelled human and animal figures) recalling the pottery of Santarém (Am-azon). In the Andes of Trujillo and Merida: painted vases and statuettes; pendants cut out of thin stone plaques.

2. Tairona (Sierra Nevada of Santa Marta, Colombia). Houses on plat-forms, roads and bridges of stone slabs.

Gold work derived from that of Cauca and Panamá. Ceramics: cylindrical urns with covers, dishes with handles, vases with two spouts, 'appliqué' anthropo-zoomorphic motifs (Field Museum of Natural History, Chicago).

3. Chibcha (highlands of Bogotá, 8000–9000 ft). Rock paintings; figurines (funerary offerings) and ornaments of gold and *tumbaga*, thin plaques with filigreed decoration (cire perdue and soldering); painted vases and statuettes of pottery (decoration influenced by the metal techniques).

4. Quimbaya (valley of the Quindío and the Middle Cauca, Colombia). Ceramics in varied techniques (positive and 'reversed' painting, two or three colours, modelling, engraving, champlevé). The goldsmiths' work is one of the most precious in ancient America: helmets and discs (beaten and repoussé work), flasks and large hollow human figures in a realistic style, sceptres and massive ornaments (casting by the cire perdue process, soldering, plating, staining) are among the characteristic pieces common to Coclé (Panamá) and the Quimbaya zone. Only gold and copper, often alloyed, were used (Gold Museum of the Bank of the Republic, Bogotá [**158**, **160**]; Madrid Museum; University of Pennsylvania Museum).

5. San Agustín (Upper Magdalena, Colombia). Megalithic civilisation: temples constructed of blocks resembling the dolmens; sculptured rocks to the north of rivers (Lavapatas); important groups of realistic stone statues (warriors, animals) or stylised and symbolical (half-human, half-feline divinities). Statues of the same style have been found at Tierradentro (painted subterranean funerary chambers, guarded by big statues) and in the Popayan region (a more primitive type).

6. Esmeraldas and Manabí (Pacific coast, Ecuador). Monochrome vases with curvilinear engravings; countless realistic pottery statuettes (nude women, deformation of the skull, complicated hair styles, numerous ornaments—labrets, earrings, necklaces). Special type of goldsmiths' work: tiny ornaments of gold, gilded copper and hammered platinum. Stone sculptures exist at Manabi: slabs with bas-reliefs, statues of men, heavy U-shaped seats resting on crouching figures (Musée de l'Homme, Paris; University of Pennsylvania Museum).

7. Ecuadorian Andes. The principal centres of civilisation are, from north to south, Carchi, characterised by very large apodal vases with elongated bellies, and deep cups with a circular foot and painted decorations (geometrical motifs and stylised animals); Imbabura; Tungurahua-Chimborazo

(six successive periods); Azuay-Cañar, where extremely beautiful objects of gold and gilded copper have been excavated from tombs at Chordeleg, Azogues and Sigsig (pectoral plaques, crowns, pierced axes, applied ornaments for sceptres and throwers) (Rivet Collection, Musée de l'Homme, Paris).

B. The central Andes (Peru, Bolivia)

The coast of the Pacific is only a thin ribbon of deserts, broken up by the first spurs of the Andes and oasis-valleys at the river mouths. The Andes, which rapidly reach heights of 10,000 or 12,000 feet close to the coast, are divided in the interior by temperate or cold longitudinal valleys and high plateaux, which have all been centres of civilisation. From north to south:

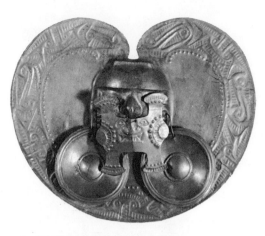

160. NORTHERN ANDES. COLOMBIA. Quimbaya gold pectoral. *Gold Museum, Bogotá.*

161. MEXICO. CHICHÉN ITZA. Temple of the Warriors.

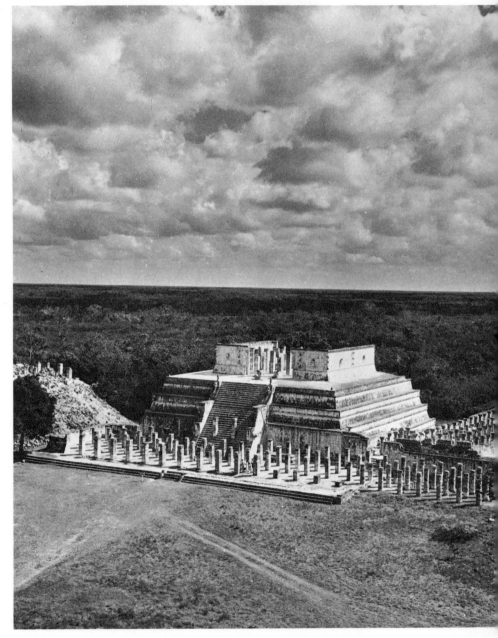

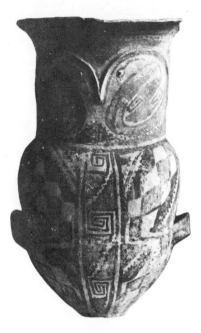

162. SOUTHERN ANDES. ARGENTINA (CALCHAQUÍ VALLEY). Painted Diaguite pottery. *Musée de l'Homme, Paris.*

163. CENTRAL ANDES. NORTHERN PERU. Chimú painted cotton fabric from Viru valley. Prisoners of war and series of stylised animals.

the valleys of the Cajamarca (8000–10,000 ft) and the Utcubamba (east of the Marañón); Callejón de Huaylas (at the foot of the Cordillera Blanca, highest point 21,996 ft); basin of the Mantaro (rising in the high plateau of Junín, 13,325 ft); basin of the Cuzco, centre of the empire of the Incas; basin of Titicaca, the biggest lake in the Andes (height 12,350 ft). In 1532, at the moment when Pizarro put an end to the development of the Indian civilisation of Peru, the Incas had succeeded in unifying the whole of this territory under their authority. It is this last cultural phase which was described by the chroniclers. But the work of archaeologists has brought to light the remains of civilisations which had flourished much earlier, in the mountains and on the coast. Thanks to recent discoveries and analyses by the carbon-14 method, we can go back more than 5,000 years (fishermen with the first signs of agriculture) and place the appearance of pottery on the coast at about 1200 B.C.

Period I (1000–200 B.C.). Chavín civilisation. Classical site: Chavín de Huantar (Ancash Andes). Temple constructed of quarried slabs; sculptures constituting the most important collection of stone works of art in South America. The best known: the so-called 'Lanzon' prismatic column, Raimondi stele (6 ft 6 in.), Tello obelisk (about 8 ft). Lintels treated in bas-relief and heads of men and felines in the round ornamented the city walls. The style is given homogeneity by its curvilinear drawing expressing volume and movement. The fundamental symbolical themes are the feline, the snake, the bird, in association with man and sometimes with plants.

Centres of art in the Cajamarca Andes: La Copa and Pacopampa (groups of statues akin to the San Agustín sculpture).

On the north coast: temple of Sechín, Casma (90 steles and blocks of granite: battle scenes and human sacrifices); temple of Moxeke (large figures of sun-baked clay); Cupisnique (monochrome pottery vases, decoration engraved and in relief in the style of the Chavín sculptures); Chongoyape (gold jewellery, decoration in repoussé work; carved stone vases).

Period II (200 B.C.–A.D. 400). Agriculture developed with the help of irrigation; there are numerous technical innovations in architecture, weaving, ceramics. Principal styles: Salinar, Huaraz (in the north); caves of Paracas, Chanapata and Chiripa (in the south).

Period III (400–1000). Classical local civilisations. North coast: Mochica, known especially for its countless naturalistic funerary vases. The subjects represented by modelling and painting (portraits, hunting, fishing and battle scenes, sacrifices, sexual customs) enable us to retrace the life of the people with great accuracy. Typical monument: the great truncated pyramid of Moche (Huaca del Sol), constructed of about 130 million adobes (bricks baked in the sun). South coast: necropolises of Paracas and Nazca with their wonderful fabrics and polychrome pottery vases, brilliantly decorated with symbolical and often complicated figures (birds, fish, plants, head-trophies, masked dancers, marine monsters). Northern Andes: Cajamarca (delicate pottery with a white clay, cups and spoons with painted 'cursive' decoration); Recuay (underground tombs; carved stone: lintels, slabs, statues of warriors and felines). Southern Andes: important centre of sculpture on stone (anthropomorphic statues, stelae with symbolical fish).

Period IV (1000–1300). The civilisation of Tiahuanaco extended at its height towards the south of Peru (Wari, Nazca), then up to the north (Lambayeque, Cajamarca); it also influenced the east of Bolivia and the north of Argentina and Chile. Main site: Tiahuanaco (12,675 ft, Bolivian shore of Lake Titicaca), which com-

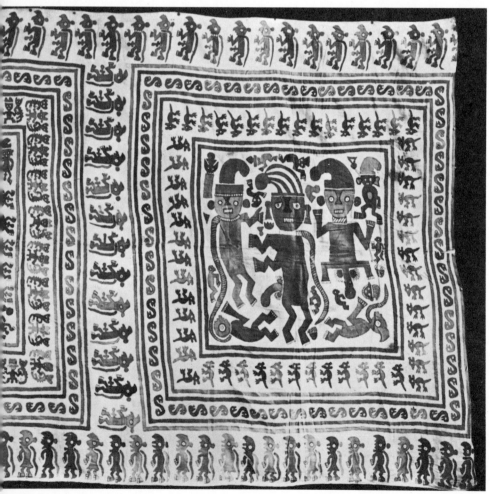

prised four groups of constructions made of enormous blocks of basalt and sandstone. The motifs (large frieze carved in relief, anthropo-zoomorphic divinity, felines, condors, snakes) of its numerous sculptures—in particular, the monolithic gates, including the Sun Gate—transcribed in brilliant colours on cloth and pottery, rapidly imposed themselves everywhere. The metallurgical techniques thrived: discovery of bronze, use of silver alloyed with copper and gold, soldering, gold and silver plating.

Period V (1300–1400). The renaissance of local cultures led to the constitution of kingdoms and confederations (the most important: the Chimú kingdom on the north coast) and great urban centres (Chanchan, Pacatnamú, Cajamarquilla, La Centinela) perfectly planned with streets, pyramids, terraces, city walls ornamented with adobe bas-reliefs, lakes, canals and reservoirs.

The pottery (styles: Chimú, Chancay, Ica) tends to industrial production, often to the detriment of art. On the other hand, weaving [**163**], feather work and particularly goldsmiths' work were maintained at a high artistic level. The tombs of Batan Grande (Lambayeque) yielded a fabulous quantity of objects of gold and silver alloy: cups, ceremonial knives [**159**], crowns, ear plugs, shirts made of gold leaf decorated in repoussé work.

Period VI (1440–1532). The Inca empire became organised. By its military conquests, it imposed a new economic, political and religious system (censuses by the *quipus*; roads; classes in hierarchical order). Their comparatively impoverished art was the domain of the stone carvers and constructors of towns, fortresses and agricultural terraces (Sacsayhuaman [**142**], Pisac, Ollantaytambo, Machu Picchu [**164**] are the classical sites around Cuzco, capital of the empire). The Incas carved only mortars, small ritual vases and a few rare statues (Viracochapampa; seated felines of Cuzco). The limited and utilitarian shapes of the pottery (vases, dishes, goblets) and the sober geometrical motifs preferred in its decoration influenced the art of various subject peoples.

ART COLLECTIONS. *Distributed between a number of European and American museums, they are mainly found in the National Museum at Lima (covering the whole of Peru, especially Chavín and Paracas), in the Larco Herrera Museum at Chiclín, near Trujillo (covering the civilisations of the north of Peru), in the Regional Archaeological Museum at Huaraz (Recuay civilisation) and in the Archaeological Museum at Cuzco (Inca).*

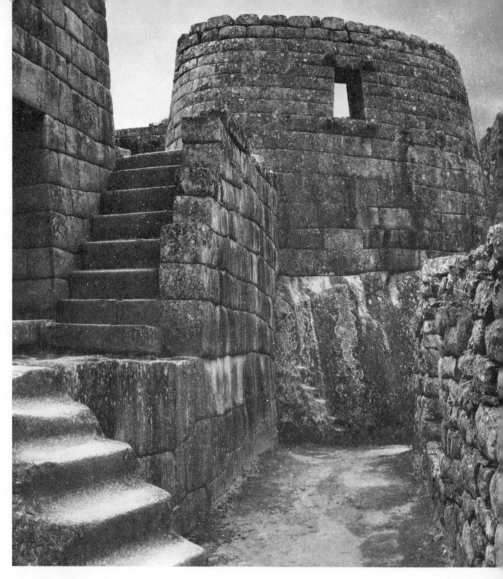

164. CENTRAL ANDES. PERU. The ruins of Machu Picchu.

C. The southern Andes (Chile, Argentina)

During their conquests in a southern direction, the Incas encountered various peoples settled in the cordilleras of Chile and Argentina, who had reached a certain cultural level, mainly under the influence of the Tiahuanaco civilisation. The oases in the Atacama desert (Rio Loa, Calama) have preserved rock engravings and paintings; carved wooden objects: knives, tablets and snuff tubes, goblets, and masks.

In the Andean valleys of north-west Argentina, the culture of the Barreales (Catamarca) seems to have been the most ancient: vases with simple shapes, of black and grey engraved pottery; urns decorated with polychrome 'dragons'; stone mortars and goblets. The Diaguite [**162**] or Calchaquí culture developed in the regions of Salta, Tucumán, Catamarca, La Rioja (moving belatedly into central Chile). Stone villages and fortresses; cemeteries of polychrome pottery urns (a feature of Amazonian origin); bronze plaques with figures and animals in relief.

D. The plains of the east

The ancient Arawak farmers of the tropical regions of the Amazon basin had acquired a comparatively high degree of civilisation in the pre-Colombian epoch; this is shown by the great artificial tumuli of the island of Marajó which have yielded sumptuous funerary urns (incised champlevé, modelled and painted decorations; stylised human and animal figures; curvilinear geometrical motifs). Other important centres: Santarém (vases overloaded with modelled ornaments); Mirakanguera and Manaus (middle Amazon); Rio Napo (anthropomorphic urns). Apart from the pottery, we know a few stone idols and statues (human figures crowned with an animal). Until the 18th century certain tribes of the Amazon basin made polychrome pottery of high quality and carved wooden objects inlaid with shells (horns, batons, clubs).

While the Tiahuanaco civilisation was flourishing in the central Andes, the Arawaks extended their civilisation (via the great rivers) as far as the eastern regions of Bolivia (Mojos, Rio Mamoré).

Henry Reichlen

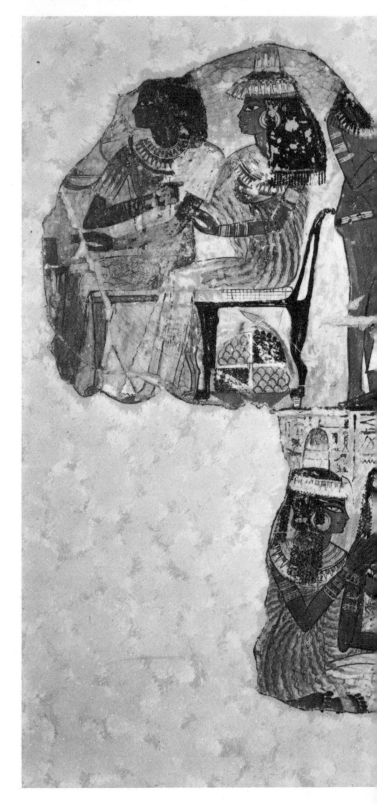

165. EGYPTIAN. Banquet scene. Wall painting. *British Museum*.

3 THE AGRARIAN EMPIRES

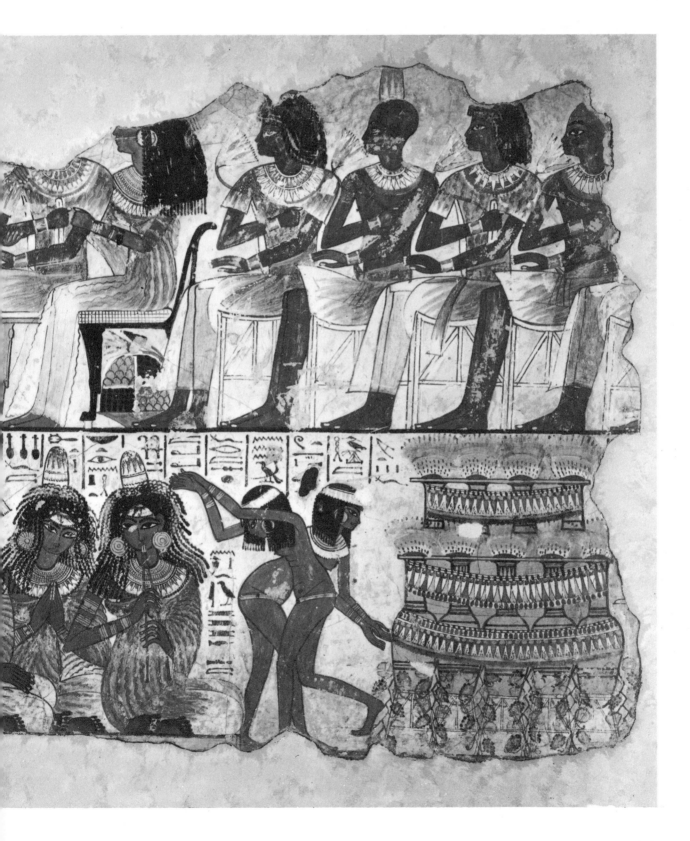

ART FORMS AND SOCIETY *René Huyghe*

With the emergence of the agrarian empires man entered history, but all he had really done was to pass on to a later stage of the agrarian era which had begun in the Neolithic. When the hunter (after various intermediate phases—pastoral, berry- and root-picking, etc.) made way for the cultivator, who was semi-nomadic at first, then permanently attached to the soil, it was the beginning of an epoch essential for the evolution of our species. We could say that this epoch has never ceased, merely enriching itself by new acquisitions, some of which, such as metal, have had tremendous consequences.

The Neolithic, then, inaugurated an era which was to last for thousands and thousands of years—almost the whole of what we call history. The village was born then, and soon afterwards the town, i.e. the city-state with its treasury and its chief, the priest-king—sometimes one and the same man, sometimes two different people. With the advent of these chiefs there arose palaces and temples; around them the aristocracies and élites developed.

Art had a thousand tasks before it. First of all it had to fulfil on a larger scale the responsibilities which had fallen to it since prehistoric times; to act as the accompaniment and instrument of religious life and to commemorate the events which marked the life of the community and, especially from now on, the life of its representative chief. But it acquired a completely new function: that of satisfying the growing taste for luxury which had taken hold of what we call today the 'ruling classes', and of meeting their need for prestige.

On the day when the city-state installed its hierarchical order, capable of indefinite extension, it began the progress towards the foundation of the empires. Climatic changes contributed to this. At the end of the glacial epoch in the Mediterranean zone, for example, there was a concentration of peoples in the great irrigated valleys as a result of the growing dearth of rivers. This concentration in a kind of oasis of a population constantly on the increase accelerated social development.

That is how the first civilisations grew: Egypt in the valley of the Nile, Mesopotamia in the conjoint valleys of the Euphrates and the Tigris, and, lastly, the Indus civilisations. All three of them formed a chain of relations, though it was often a loose one.

We could also add the pre-Columbian cultures in America, and China in Asia. The former, which remained isolated—for their original connection with China is debatable—have been studied in the previous chapter; they have at widely varying epochs maintained ways of life and art similar to those of pre- and protohistory. In fact, these civilisations have, as late as the 15th century, brought us into contact with the stage of the agrarian empires. China also went through this phase, but after emerging from prehistory it made such a rapid transition to the art of the Bronze Age that it will be dealt with in the next chapter, together with the other civilisations which were deeply affected by the discovery of that metal.

Consequently Egypt, Mesopotamia and the Indus will form the subject of the present chapter, because their ways of life and manners of expression were moulded by the agrarian system and bear its inescapable imprint. They owe their profound structure to it. Moreover, the first two civilisations are linked by the 'Fertile Crescent', the vast curve which stretches from the Nile to the Tigris, taking in Palestine, Phoenicia and Syria. Trade, diplomacy and war formed the relations which encourage us to study them simultaneously in order not to create the illusion of their 'splendid isolation', as is often done. They are all significant of the same phenomenon, the same moment in human history. Their arts are only distinguished by the characteristics, actually merely subsidiary, which give them individuality.

We shall see how from the beginning there were obvious artistic exchanges between the Nile basin and the basins of the Euphrates and the Tigris; how, during the centuries, aggressions, sometimes reciprocal attempts at annihilation or subjugation, led to military expeditions, mainly owing to Mesopotamian ambition; how the Egyptian hegemony, with its sights set barely beyond Syria, designated the latter as the essential point of contact and junction. Sargon I, the self-styled 'Master of the Region of Cedars (Lebanon) and of the Silver Mountains (Taurus)', dominated Amurru (Syria) as from the 26th century, and at the same time a pharaoh sent his warships to Byblos on the coast of Phoenicia. A thousand years later, Tuthmosis I was to extend his domination as far as the Euphrates. Consequently, the eastern coast of the Mediterranean was to be the scene of both brutal and peaceful encounters, the transit zone and connecting link of the ancient world. Soon it formed the principal route by which Crete, the newer civilisation, was able to draw on the arts of Egypt and Mesopotamia so as to unite the network of influences from which Greek art was to emerge.

The legacy of prehistory

In conformity with the spirit of synthesis in this work, our primary aim is to bring out the basic facts which distinguish this new stage of human society, and to assess its contribution.

But nothing is ever totally, absolutely, new; history does not so much replace prehistory as succeed to it; to a great extent it is the flowering of prehistory. Man would be revolving in a vacuum if he did not form a stock of acquired knowledge, a capital turned to different ends but constantly added to, in which the past is not lost even though it may be buried beneath later contributions: this artistic capital becomes a sort of humus.

In the present state of research, China marks an abrupt transition to the Neolithic after a very obscure Palaeolithic. America seems to have been even more effectively deprived of this primitive stage. Its peopling was probably effected via Asia and Oceania at the very end of this phase, and it almost immediately produced its empires of sun-worshippers—as were nearly all the agrarian empires. However, those around the Mediterranean had a rich and continuous basis of prehistory. Thus they have behind them in their 'artistic memory' the contribution of those first ages.

In Egypt, as in Palestine, we follow a development corresponding to that of the West since the Lower

OCEANIC. ADMIRALTY ISLANDS. Ancestor figure. Staatliches Museum für Völkerkunde, Munich. *Photo: Michael Holford.*

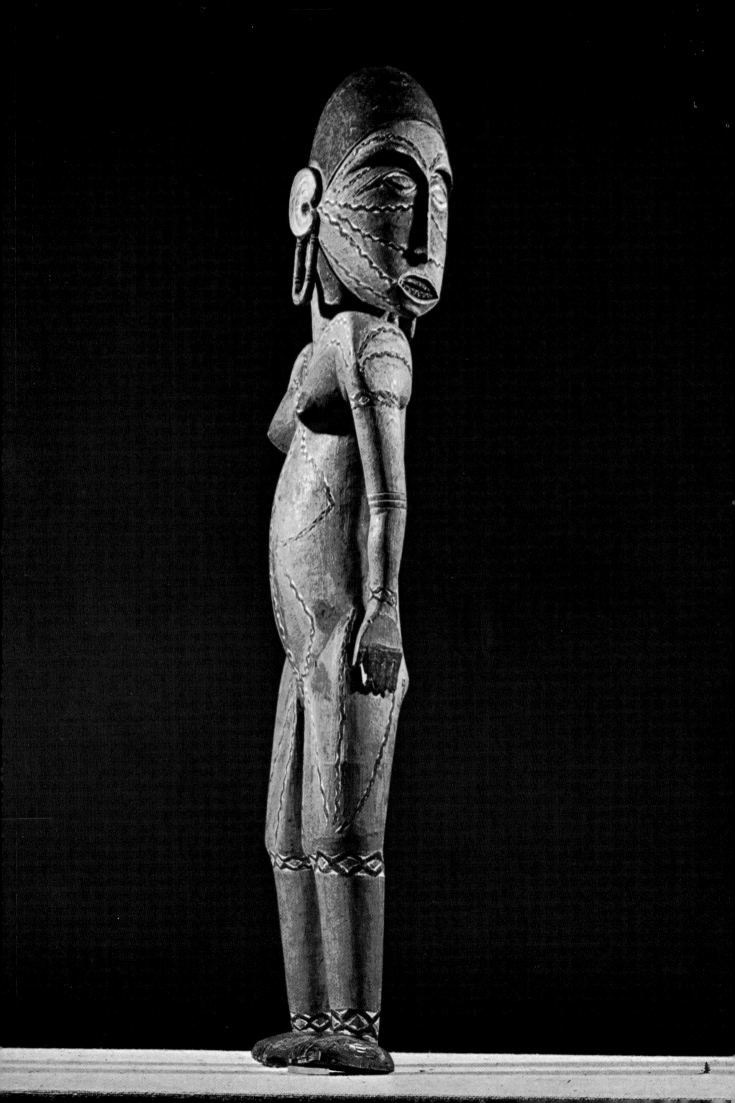

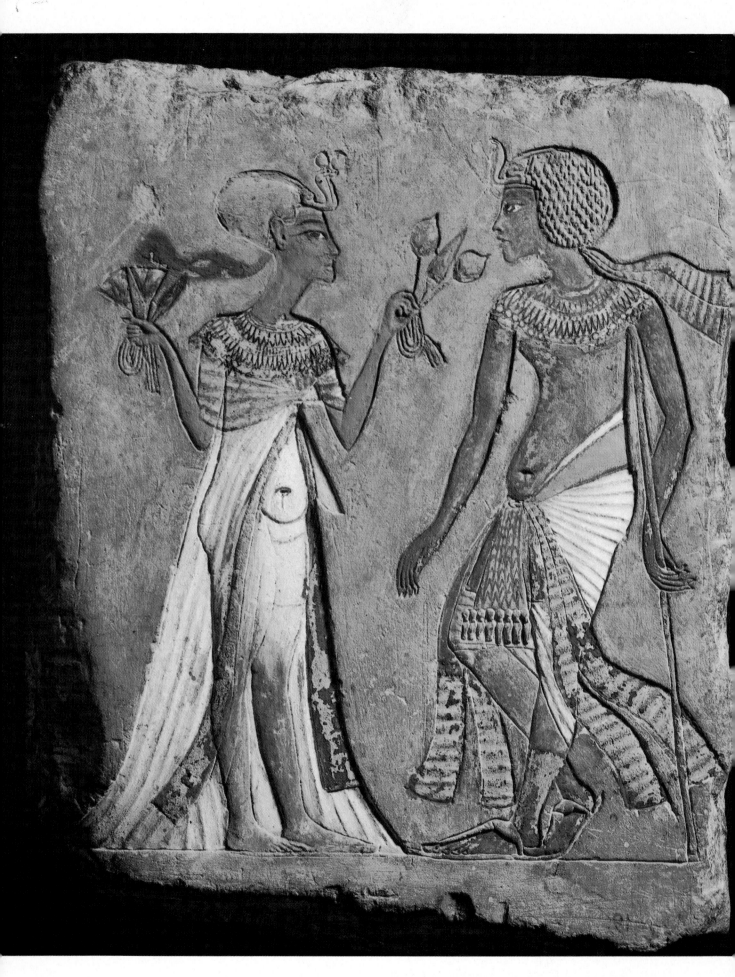

EGYPTIAN. Stele showing the Lady Ten-Chenat worshipping
Re-Harakhti. XXVIth Dynasty. Staatliche Museen, Berlin.
Museum photograph.

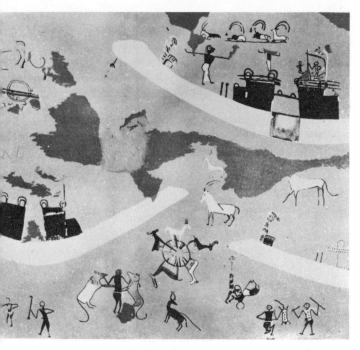

166. EGYPTIAN. PROTO-DYNASTIC. Fresco at Hierakonpolis. *Egyptian Museum, Cairo.*

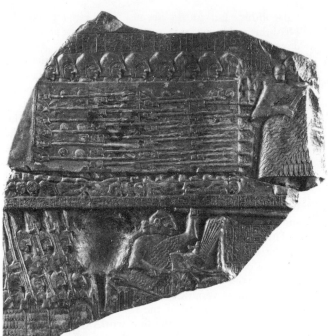

167. MESOPOTAMIAN. Stele of the Vultures, from Tello. 2nd side. 29th century B.C. *Louvre.*

COMPOSITION AND THE ORGANISATION OF SPACE

During the transition from prehistory to the stage of the great empires, art made considerable advances. It became devoted to organising the surface area to be decorated. In the most archaic works the prehistoric habit of juxtaposing the various figures indiscriminately still persists [166–169]. However, artists were already producing works consciously designed within a framework and dividing the surface by means of verticals, horizontals and symmetrical axes. [168–170.]

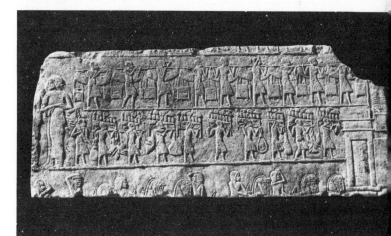

168. EGYPTIAN. OLD KINGDOM. Carrying of funerary offerings. Sakkara.

169. EGYPTIAN. PROTO-DYNASTIC. Small palette from Hierakonpolis (front and back). *Ashmolean Museum, Oxford.*

170. EGYPTIAN. OLD KINGDOM. Narmer Palette (front and back). *Egyptian Museum, Cairo.*

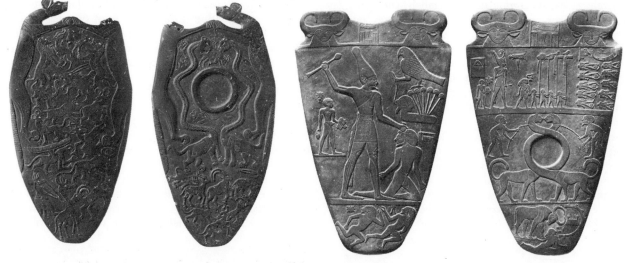

Palaeolithic, but in the second of these regions the Neolithic is skipped, as it were, because of the precocious development of the Natufian Mesolithic.

In Mesopotamia, excavations have shown that the future great cities were built on Neolithic foundations. Their memory has been kept so fresh that in present-day Iraq we can see huts of matting on a rush framework, the model for which existed in those early days. But this profound unity of growth, since the beginning of the Neolithic at least, was sustained in a particularly intensive manner in Egypt, which was nearer the great prehistoric centres of the West and Africa. Metal (copper, bronze and iron) took its place in a well-established and continuous line of evolution without disturbing this unity overmuch, although it did provide new means of expression.

The art of the agrarian empires is steeped in some way in the heritage of prehistory. The two essential conceptions of art which have revealed this to us—the magic image of the animal, as at Lascaux and Altamira, and the more impressionistic notation of human activities, as in the rock paintings of the Iberian Levant—seem to have left their traces in the first works found by H. A. Winkler in the lateral deserts of the Nile. There we find the processions of animals characterised by their profile —in direct descent from those created by the prehistoric Franco-Cantabrian hunters—and the more vivid works intended to catch the fleeting scene, similar to the paint-

70 ings of Spain, such as the ostrich flapping its wings as it flees from a hunter whose arrow is shown in the air.

These two conceptions, the one magical, the other commemorative, mingle and fuse in the first works which Egypt left on the threshold of its history: the knife handles of the last protohistoric phase—the Gerzean epoch of Naqada II. The tradition of the sacred magical animal resulted in its being made the symbol of totemic clans, adumbrated as from the previous Amratian period. Egypt remained faithful to this worship of the deified beast (Apis the bull, Hathor the cow, Horus the falcon, etc.). Moreover, these lions, bulls, gazelles and waders, evocative of the earliest political divisions of the nomes by

169 their totemic role, are sometimes depicted fighting. Then they give permanence pictorially to the memory of rivalries and primitive combats. Thus animal magic and visual narrative are combined in the works which mark the starting point of Egyptian art.

In addition, geometrical decoration also perpetuated itself: it is associated with other relics of prehistory. At Tasa and Badari the pottery shows the continuation of hatching and its combinations: parallels, chevrons, zigzags, chequer patterns, etc.—all the geometry born of man's first abstract efforts. These decorations are also

74 preserved on the vases of Susa I at Elam and at al 'Ubaid.

It is strange to see this geometrical tendency confronted with the tradition of the animal in profile and being affected by it. In Egypt, from the Amratian period onwards, silhouettes of hippopotamuses strike a compromise with the purely linear, diamond-shaped or square repertory. The artists made use of it in building up the outline and then in decorating the surface enclosed. Sometimes the same repertory is associated with scenes in which a hunter and his hounds or ritual dancers are depicted, recalling the patches in the notations of Ibero-African art, although with less vibrant dynamism.

The stenographic schematisations in which the art of

the Spanish Levant culminated are not the only ones to recur. From the 4th millennium onwards, the pottery of Susa I at Elam bore, instead of ibexes, the comb (pectiform) shapes which we are accustomed to find in Spanish 74 Levantine art, in which the animal is no more than a horizontal bar placed on vertical legs which are multiplied beyond all probability.

In the same decoration we find the purely geometrical regular outline united with the vivid being caught in an expressive silhouette and with those stylised animals which have a place half-way between these two positions. None of the directions taken by art since its beginnings has been abandoned.

The survival of magic and frontal representation

We have further evidence of this: two characteristic conceptions of prehistory, one of the role, the other of the scope of art, were perpetuated and developed.

The first conception makes the image a genuine double of its original and endows it, as such, with the same powers. Egypt was pre-eminently the country in which this notion of the magical double with the same value as its original asserted itself. In the tombs, mural paintings and statuettes repeat the scenes of everyday life to ensure that the dead man may have eternal use of them. In other 195 words, both magical art and narrative art finally serve the same purpose.

According to this belief, the statuettes of gods or humans in Egypt and Mesopotamia perpetuate a presence. The cylinder seal, when it depicts a libation, also gives it a lasting worth. Where the modern eye sees a purely anecdotal episode, the man of those times perceived in the painting or sculpture an effective surrogate for the being or action represented.

A conception of representation established from prehistoric times was also to be preserved in those arts destined to last, henceforth, for centuries. I refer to the well-known law of frontality. This fundamental convention of all the archaic arts requires that the body be depicted according to an arbitrary arrangement, more in conformity with logic than with appearances. It is really only a more systematic application of that conceptual realism (that is to say, more faithful to the idea which one has of a thing in principle than the aspect it presents to the spectator in fact) of which prehistory afforded the first examples and which is so different from our wholly sensorial and optical modern realism. In the Palaeolithic, horns were placed full face on an animal in profile. 11

We need only reflect an instant to understand that this way of representation is the corollary of the idea of the double. In point of fact, according to that idea the work of art is not limited to capturing what one may happen to see of a human being at the chance angle he presents to the artist. Far from it; it is the actual being; it duplicates him. It is equally true and real, but of another truth, another reality—that of the motionless image. It must therefore conform as closely as possible to its structure and not to its episodic fleeting appearance. Like an explanatory anatomical plate, then, it must display the outline of each part of the body as clearly as possible. In the same way, an architect prefers to have a plan and elevation of building rather than a photograph taken to suit the lens, the lighting, etc. That is why the law of frontality was now applied primarily and systematically

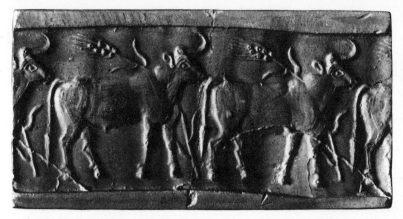

171. MESOPOTAMIAN. Hard stone cylinder seal and its impression. Erech period. Before 3000 B.C. *Louvre.*

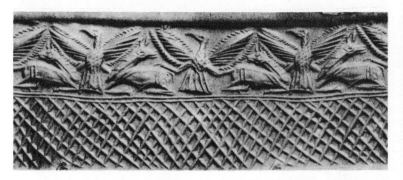

173. MESOPOTAMIAN. Impression of a cylinder seal made from a shell. Before 3000 B.C. *Louvre.*

INFLUENCE OF THE CYLINDER SEAL

A new enrichment of forms, and even their invention and composition, probably sprang from the use of the cylinder seal which was especially widespread in Mesopotamia. The eye of the artist grew used to seeing the same theme repeated indefinitely, and transposed the effect produced by this mechanical technique into large-scale decorations (the rhythm of repetition) . . .
. . . We may also assume that rigorously symmetrical composition and the combination of parts of animals, creating monsters, were stimulated by the reversed images and their division into sections produced by the cylinder seal.

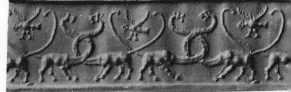

172. MESOPOTAMIAN. Jasper cylinder seal. Erech period. Before 3000 B.C. *Louvre.*

174. MESOPOTAMIAN. Bas-relief of the priest Dudu. From Tello. 28th century B.C. *Louvre.*

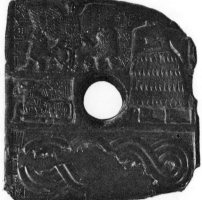

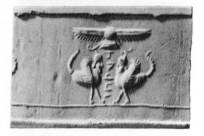

175. PERSIAN. Impression of a cornelian cylinder seal showing two scorpion-men under a solar disc. *Louvre.*

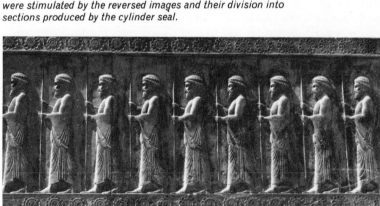

177. PERSIAN. Processional file of soldiers, Persepolis. 5th century B.C.

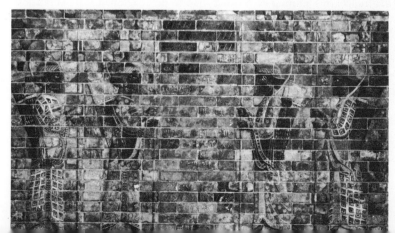

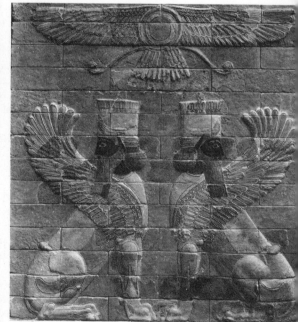

176. PERSIAN. Winged sphinxes from Susa. Glazed brick. *Louvre.*

178. PERSIAN. Procession of archers, from Susa. Glazed brick. 5th century B.C. *Louvre.*

to representations of man; the animal, for which similar preoccupations were not so essential, escaped it more easily in scenes where its role was anecdotal.

212   What has been called the 'block statue' satisfies the same needs. The reason the sculptor tried to enclose his over-all product in as simple a geometrical volume as possible was to reduce the chances of its breaking—because if the statue lost as much as a single fragment, the being it was equivalent to would suffer the same mutilation. Conceptual realism was applied everywhere, in both Egypt and Mesopotamia, until Greece renewed artistic vision and brought it more into conformity with sensations.

The creation of the frame and composition

So much for their share in continuity; but the agrarian empires also contributed and innovated. Their principal discovery was a new way of conceiving and organising the space in which the work was arranged. The new ideas of the frame and composition came to light and remained basic acquisitions for future centuries.

    It is quite remarkable that this transformation took place approximately at the beginning of history. It is even possible, in Egypt, to see its beginnings. In 1898 paintings were discovered at Kom el Ahmar coming

166 from a tomb of ancient Hierakonpolis and dating from late proto-dynastic times, i.e. the end of the 4th millennium. Unfortunately only a minute fragment of them remains since their transfer to the Cairo Museum. In their original state, one could see on the wall animals in profile, men fighting, bearers of vases, typical ships of the epoch and even a personage standing between two symmetrical wild beasts, just like the figure who first appeared in the 4th millennium in Mesopotamia and later became Gilgamesh between his lions. (Let us note in passing one of these many proofs of very ancient relations between the Nilotic and the Euphrates civilisations.) All the above-mentioned elements, of such differing natures and origins, were arranged as if at random on the wall. One could almost say that they had been thrown on it like confetti, regardless of whether the space was empty or was already filled. Prehistoric art has accustomed us to this disorder, which was the rule at that time.

    But let us take a work which is only slightly more recent, since it, too, belongs to an almost identical pre-dynastic

75 epoch—the knife from Jebel el Arak, found to the west of the Nile, near Denderah. Here order is suddenly revealed: the animals are arranged in vertical rows (aligned in each case on a horizontal base) forming 'registers'. The

167 same thing is true of the Stele of the Vultures (Louvre),
170 of the Narmer Palette, etc.

    From now on this arrangement remains unchanged; it recurs throughout Egyptian history in both paintings and

168 bas-reliefs. It goes hand in hand with a rectangular frame forming the limits of the decorated space, the 'field', to use a significant term. Suddenly the images accept a strict discipline—they are enclosed in spaces clearly divided by perpendicular borders, just like a page; they are arranged in rigorously parallel rows, like staves.

    This arrangement and constraint, hitherto unknown, also emerged in Mesopotamia. It appeared there constantly and naturally, instead of suddenly replacing an incoherent scattering, as in Egypt, so that it is tempting to seek its origin there. The vase from Warka (then Erech)

is an example from the Jemdet Nasr period, at the end of the protohistoric. The Standard of Ur and the front of 197 the harp from the same place, show how, from the threshold of history, i.e. first half of the 3rd millennium, this method of presentation was firmly established. Today it seems natural and elementary to us, yet then it brought about a considerable revolution. Before, the artist had thought only of the figure he was drawing; all he had asked for was something on which to draw it. But from that period onwards he conceived the work of art as a space (or a volume, in the case of sculpture), and he enclosed it within geometrical limits, or a frame. He felt obliged to arrange and organise his images within it by submitting them to certain principles of order which were those of composition. At first composition mainly obeyed the two principal axes, the vertical and horizontal, and their parallels.

    The above were notions which, however flexible, remained the basis of all works of art for thousands of years. They have only recently been questioned by the most daring modern researches. But did not the art born with the great agrarian civilisations inaugurate an immense phase in the history of art which perhaps is only coming to an end in our time, when, it would seem, a strange industrial, mechanical and atomic civilisation is establishing itself?

The influence of the agrarian mode of life

Where could these startlingly new ideas, the adumbration of which had been found exclusively, until then, in the art of pure geometrical decoration, have been born? It is necessary to consider the effect of the change in the way of life. The Palaeolithic hunter, used to watching animals, 'thought' art mainly in terms of outlines. The farmer had a different training and different mental habits. Seminomadic at first, then settled in increasingly restricted spaces owing to the growth of population and the limitation of irrigable land, he found himself confronted with the problem of dividing up the land and defining boundaries. He had to create surveying. For the first time he felt the need for a geometry which was no longer empiric and approximate but as precise and exact as calculation and instruments would allow. The strictness of these partitions of the land was all the greater since the divisions served as the basis for taxation. The trustees of this were none other than the priests. Diodorus Siculus and Herodotus were struck by the importance they assumed.

    The word of Greek origin *geometrein,* which designates geometry, has preserved a trace of the preoccupation which gave rise to it; it indicates that it is the measuring of land. In order to define the field and put it side by side with its neighbours, with regular surfaces which were easy to compose and apportion, the science of parallels, of segmentation into squares and rectangles exactly adjoining each other, had to be developed. The concept of the boundary was thus imposed; then, with the appearance of the plough, men became used to covering these cultivable fields with regular furrows.

    Art, the faithful reflection of mental and visual habits, could not but register these new usages. Their mark will be found in architecture (in the compact arrangement of quadrangular plans and in the structural disposition of the stones). Prehistoric constructions were made by piling up the building materials; from now on materials were

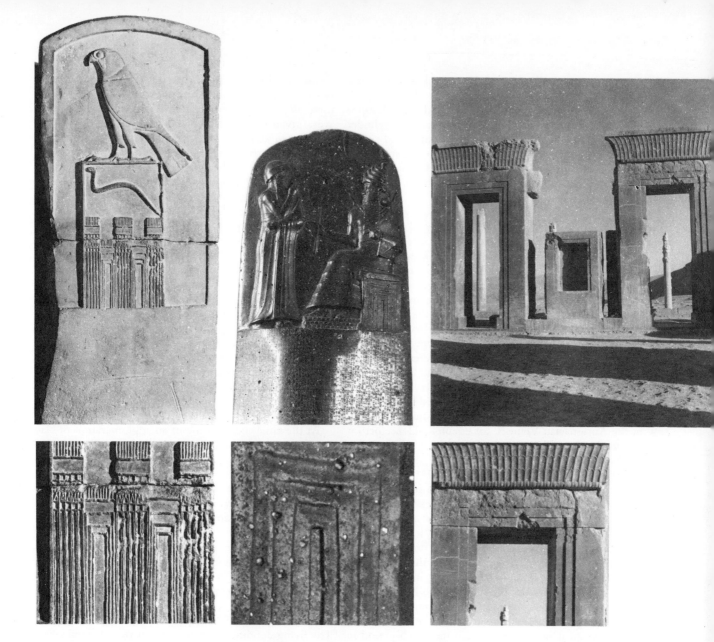

179a. EGYPTIAN. Stele of the
Serpent King. *c.* 3000 B.C. *Louvre.*

179b. MESOPOTAMIAN. Stele of
Hammurabi. *c.* 1700 B.C. *Louvre.*

179c. PERSIAN. Ruins of doorways
at the palace of Darius I, Persepolis.
Middle of the 1st millennium B.C.

BEGINNINGS OF THE RHYTHM OF GROWTH

*One of art's new and more subtle acquisitions was the substitution for
simple parallel lines [180] of a continuously amplified movement, like that
of a wave growing bigger [181 and 182]. It was the birth of plastic rhythm.
It appeared in architecture in the successive boxing of lines framing the
bays [179] . . .*

*. . . Although the preceding innovation mainly developed in Mesopotamia,
it was applied more effectively in Egypt, especially from the beginning of
the XVIIIth Dynasty. This confirms the general impression that inventive
power, particularly in the technical field, was predominant in Mesopotamia,
but that Egypt, perhaps more sensitive, made greater artistic use of it.*

182. EGYPTIAN. Isis protecting the
foot of Tutankhamen's second coffin.
XVIIIth Dynasty. *Egyptian Museum,
Cairo.*

180. MESOPOTAMIAN. Djinn with
two pairs of wings. 8th century B.C.
Louvre.

181. EGYPTIAN. PTOLEMAIC.
Draped female figure. *Louvre.*

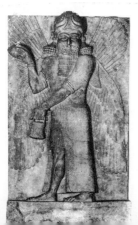

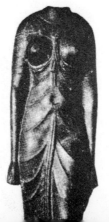

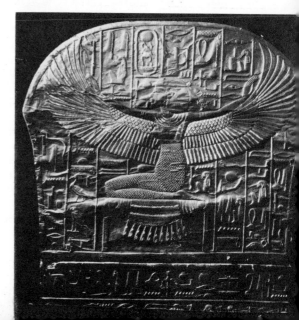

dressed geometrically so that they could be fitted into identical layers.

Another element appeared, particularly in Mesopotamia, to confirm these tendencies: the use of the cylinder seal which traders rolled on to the clay of closed jars to seal them with a continuous motif, so that any attempt at breaking them open would be detected. The cylinder seal, too, accustomed the eye to regular rows of subjects repeated in bands.

It must also have encouraged the symmetry of themes, which seems to have obsessed the Mesopotamian artist. The design the cylinder is to print appears on it in reverse. When rolled on to the chosen surface it keeps repeating the design up to its limit, as symmetrically as if reflected in a mirror. As soon as it has been printed, a lion facing right appears on the cylinder opposite the lion facing left whose counterpart it has just marked on the clay. This, I imagine, was one of the factors which led the art of Mesopotamia to create and spread, in Egypt for example, figures of a heraldic type, facing each other in pairs on either side of an axis, i.e. the Tree of Life between two members of the goat tribe, Gilgamesh between the two lions, etc. Symmetry had scarcely appeared in prehistoric art except when directly suggested by the human body—in the Aurignacian Venuses, for example. Henceforth it was used universally.

Technique and the invention of new themes

Innovations, particularly visual ones, are often born by chance: although interlacing as a decorative theme appeared quite naturally in the Neolithic as a result of basket-work, esparto-work and weaving, it was possibly not applied to figures until given the impetus of the cylinder seal. In the course of its motion, this continuous changing and cutting up of the printing image and the image printed afforded unexpected combinations, by their perpetual symmetric interplay. This may have given rise to the portrayals of animals with interlaced necks. These appear, it would seem, from the Erech period in Mesopotamian glyptics and pass from there to Egypt, but they are less common there. They are found, from the end of the 4th millennium, on the knife from Jebel el Tarif, and during the proto-dynastic period. Then they are seen in the Narmer Palette, in the 1st Dynasty.

Perhaps these chance combinations gave rise to the idea of the monster (which is strictly speaking Mesopotamian), that is to say, the idea of creating unreal beings by the juxtaposition of elements belonging to various real animal or even humans. This invention had an enormous success; starting at Sumer, it was perpetuated in an unbroken line up to medieval art. Egypt (with the sphinx, for example) and Greece joined the cavalcade en route.

Thus heterogeneous monsters, living interlaced forms and symmetry of figures may all have been brought to life by the new technique of the cylinder seal.

Another, older example—since it goes back to the genuine Neolithic—of visual innovation brought about by a technical accident is provided by pottery. When the craftsman decorates the edge of a bowl with the zigzag, he involuntarily creates a new figure which is only visible if he looks at his receptacle afterwards not in profile, but full face from underneath. In the circular form which he then sees, the zigzag forms a star.

It is our belief that all the variations of the radiating symmetrical shapes, from this star to the floral rose, are descendants of involuntary discovery which was made then. We must remember that resemblance and realism were given to man by evocative coincidences of lines, first traced at random by wandering fingers. Imagine, then, the contributions of the civilisations which received all the new crafts of weaving, plaiting, pottery, etc., from the Neolithic. The essential constituents of the formal and decorative repertory perpetuated until our own time were formed then. There was no further considerable contribution except for another technical revolution, that which brought about metallurgy.

This experience, at once manual and visual, not only supplied the eye with themes but it penetrated the sensibility. It was mainly because the Egyptian and Mesopotamian sensibilities were not identical that the arts created by them are separated by certain distinctive characteristics: the Egyptian worked solid, and even hard, materials; he liked clear, powerful shapes; he always came back to a grandiose sense of petrified monumentality. The Mesopotamian, virtually deprived of wood and stone and forced to use clay, had a much softer sense of form, which came out as much in his sculpture as in his architecture.

At the same time, his use of an agglomeration of clay which was solidified afterwards led him to discover and construct the vault or the cupola, while the Egyptian continued to prefer the hard horizontal lintel placed squarely on two uprights. Also, while the Egyptian drew his plastic effects from the articulation of clear solid places, the Mesopotamian developed on his always rather inconsistent masses the art of the sharp chiselling of details—making use of a resource offered him by the docile earth and refused the Egyptian by his recalcitrant material. This very special skill had another upsurge in Assyrian times in the carving of bas-reliefs on limestone.

Discovery of plant forms and rhythm

The living conditions offered by a particular civilisation are not only begetters of shapes. They are also begetters of subjects. The Palaeolithic hunter thought only of the animal; in the course of his rare incursions into the field of the human figure, he suddenly lost all the gifts which he had prodigiously perfected in order to dedicate them to animals. The artist of the great agrarian empires received his legacy and applied it to scenes of hunting (pastime of the kings and nobles) and to the depiction of animals found on the farm.

But he discovered another form, almost totally ignored until then—that of plants and flowers. He depicted them with flexibility and acuity, in a progression which led gradually and inevitably to landscape. Does not a cylinder seal from Ur of the 4th millennium already represent, with the stylisation peculiar to arts in their infancy, a hunt in the marshes among the reeds?

Nature even inspired the artist in architecture, more especially in decoration. The bundles of stalks forming columns suggested giving the capitals a floral appearance. In Egypt capitals were lotus-, palm- and papyrus-shaped, finally resulting in composite types. The arid geometry of primitive ornamentation was nourished and made more

183. MESOPOTAMIAN. Winged man-headed bull. 9th century B.C. *British Museum.*

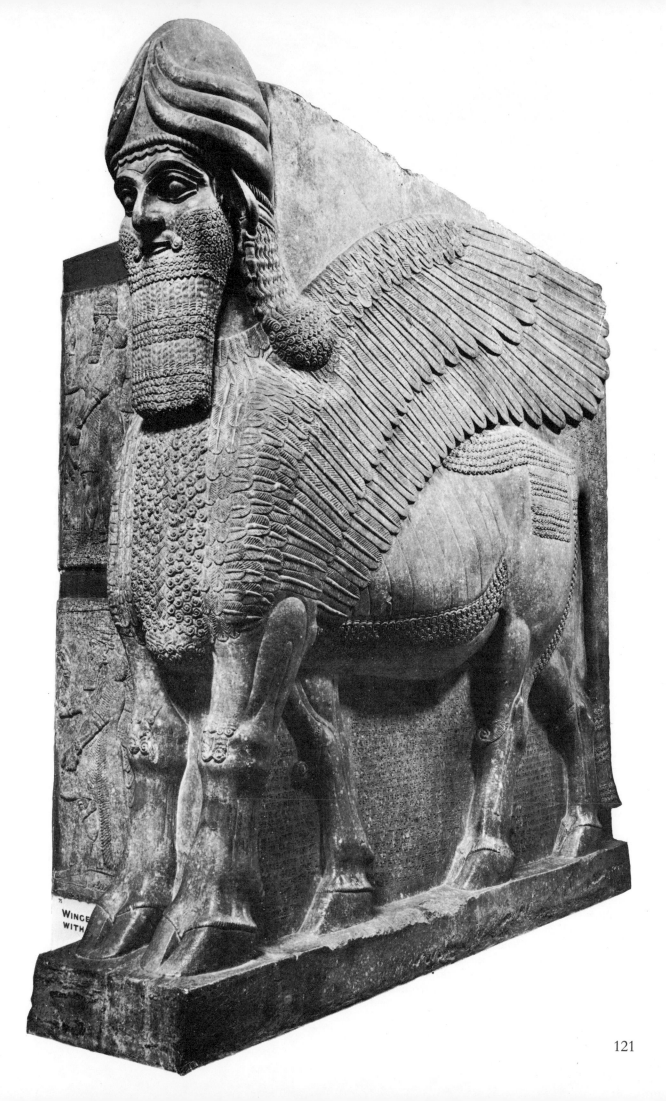

WINGE
WITH

121

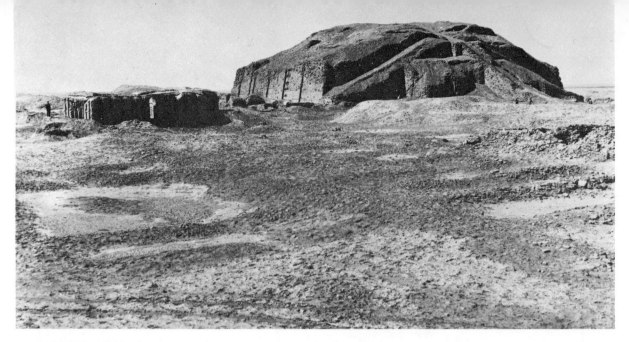

184. MESOPOTAMIAN. The ziggurat at Ur.

flexible by the assimilation of the living plant shapes. In Mesopotamia the star, which we saw in the circular decoration on pottery, changed into a rosette which resembled a flower with open petals, or a marguerite. Like all the acquisitions which gradually enrich the artistic repertory, this theme did not disappear. The law of stylisation helped to diversify decoration by reducing realistic themes to geometric ones. The enrichment of subject matter ended inevitably in the enrichment of forms.

Art was not content merely to increase this repertory. With the agrarian empires there arose a principle hitherto almost unknown: rhythm. Admittedly it had been hinted at in the elementary forms of repetition and alternation—

8 of which examples appeared from Palaeolithic times. But now the rhythms of progression were discovered, and conscious decorative use was made of them.

It would be possible to find the most elementary forms as early as the Neolithic. On Susa ceramics of the 4th millennium we can see an angle set in a similar, larger, angle which is crowned in the same way, and so on. This is the theme offered in the West by the concentric shapes which make up the mysterious ornamentation of the megalithic

63 steles of Gavr'inis, in Brittany. The same procedure is met with in Egypt in certain decorations: the frame of a door is lodged in another similar but larger shape, and the operation is repeated several times by successive

179 boxings. Thus the rhythm of growth was added to the simpler rhythms of repetition and alternation.

This new rhythm passed into the most typical archi-

187 tectural shapes, such as the step pyramid of the earliest times in Egypt, of the Sakkara type, and the ziggurat,

184 established in Mesopotamia from the 3rd millennium. The increasingly narrow storeys were sometimes of the same height, but elsewhere they were generally disposed in decreasing series.

There were more complicated rhythms: very early, in Egypt, the stylised folds of fabrics in bas-reliefs and paintings ceased to be rendered as monotonous parallels: the curve which was their origin opened up more and more, like a wave widening. This was not the simple and successive enlargement of the same shape but was the methodical transition from one shape to another by simplification of the curves—especially from the XVIIIth Dynasty onwards. The human spirit was enriched by an

experience hitherto unknown; agrarian society revealed to man the rhythms of life and those of natural phenomena —the days, the seasons and above all the plants—which added to repetition the cycle of growth and decrease, which is the most obvious biological law. This strikes the farmer when he watches both the progress of the stars and the periodicity of his crops.

In the general development of all the creative activities of a particular time, the sciences of numbers and geometry are at a stage parallel to that of the arts. We know that the Chaldeans solved problems corresponding to quadratic equations. Now, the problems which the amplification of curves sets in our time are within their province. At the time that the new, circular motifs—stars and rosettes— were being discovered, we should remember that Mesopotamian science, for its part, had learnt how to divide the circle into 360 parts. In other words, intellectual discoveries went together with visual discoveries, no doubt because they had the same initial causes.

The feeling for rhythms, then, became finer and was enriched at the same time that it found support in the parallel development of knowledge. It led inevitably to a comparison of the analogous factors of different dimensions belonging to one and the same series, to a seeking for the key to the relation which united and dominated them. Then the idea of proportion was discovered. Was it not an inevitable temptation for anyone faced with the enormous ziggurat, dominating all the constructions round it with its storeys of different colours glowing in the sun? Was not the calculation of its dimensions compulsory for the architect who had to create it? Thus the eye and the mind together made this discovery of proportion—a more conscious stage of the development of rhythms, which were at first almost purely instinctive and physical, like dancing, and were based essentially on 'repetition of the same theme'. It was to fall to Greece to reach the stage of conscious possession of this fundamental resource of art.

The arts of successive civilisations progress, leaving their heritage to the future. Each of the mainstreams we have just mentioned, increased by the contribution of the arts of the age of metals, proceeded, therefore, to the point of convergence where all their achievements were united: then the miracle of Greece sprang forth.

EGYPT AND MESOPOTAMIA *Georges Contenau*

The common conditions which brought into being the empires of Egypt and Mesopotamia created a close similarity between them which the normal method of studying the two countries separately tends to obscure. Dr Contenau, whose excavations and books have contributed so much to our knowledge of the ancient civilisations of the Near East, and who has already described their prehistoric phase (Chapter 1), brings out their fundamental similarities before going into details of their development up to the 2nd millennium B.C.

At the Thinite period in Egypt and at the beginning of the Jemdet Nasr epoch in Mesopotamia, civilisation as we conceive of it today already existed. The conditions for its flowering were all present: an abundance allowing of reserve stocks, tranquillity about the future and a spirituality without which techniques may flourish, but not a genuine culture. The prosperity of the two empires was assured by irrigation from the Nile, the Tigris and the Euphrates; the constant preoccupation and pride of the monarchs was to have a new canal dug or the old ones maintained. If the floods from the rivers were not controlled, they could have devastating consequences; the greater the network of canals, the larger the area of cultivable land. These canals were trade routes for an ever-increasing fleet of barges, and they further contributed to prosperity by the fish they contained.

Monarchy and religion

Security was assured by the establishment of a central monarchy with absolute power which controlled the ancient nomes. It was a lasting monarchy, and it accumulated reserve stocks. The benefits of such a productive government became all the more obvious when a revolution such as that which put an end to the Old Kingdom showed up the perils of consumer régimes. Then Egypt appeared to be ruined, but tradition prevailed and made good the damage done by the rule of the masses. In Mesopotamia (and that is undoubtedly the reason for its retarded development when Egypt was making great strides) the dynasties, of which we only know the names, succeeded each other from town to town as the chance result of local wars. It took the monarchy of Akkad to install powers capable of directing the whole country.

Eventually—and this provided the necessary spirituality —every human power had to recognise a divine power. There was in Mesopotamia and Egypt a demanding religion whose strength was allied with that of the sovereigns. The Egyptians recognised a god-king, all the more absolute for this reason, whose presence in the midst of his people gave them security in the future and helped to increase a fortunate characteristic, the optimism so obvious in their artistic productions.

The chief in Mesopotamia was not a god; he was merely his delegate. Very few kings were deified in the Tigris and Euphrates basins. The furthest these civilisations ever went was to claim a divinity as their foster-mother. And, as we shall see, this undoubtedly made the Mesopotamian less sure of tomorrow than his Nilotic neighbour who was reassured by the divine presence.

Let us take note of a fundamental difference between the two religions; the pharaohs of the Old Kingdom gave their intimates the benefits of their advantages in the hereafter, but the people had absolutely no share in these advantages. They did not begin to participate until the Middle Kingdom; as from that time every Egyptian had his share in the blessings of the after-life provided he was worthy of them. There was nothing comparable among the Mesopotamians, who had a miserable after-life. There is no doubt that this was one more reason for the sterner character of the Mesopotamians and their penchant for a more severe art. Lastly, we must take into account a people's natural propensity to seek beauty, as well as the feeling they may have for it. Neither the Egyptian nor the Mesopotamian rhapsodised over a particular object or landscape. Confronted with a wonderful spectacle, the Babylonian scribe could only find the following dry formula to express his enthusiasm: 'And it was beautiful to behold.' But the Egyptians were more sensitive to beauty and to charm, and they have transcribed them in works of a delicate elegance extremely rare among the Mesopotamians.

Thus we are led to analyse the arts of each of these two peoples and the conventions which governed them.

Material conditions and their effects on art

In Egypt and in Mesopotamia, as anywhere else, art was influenced by the potentialities in the soil and at the site where the monuments were erected. In both empires wood was rare; the palm-tree supplied trunks (which were not very resistant and which bent under weights) for roofs; all that could be extracted from them, however, were small panels. As it was a lengthy and expensive process to procure pine and cedar from Syria, the Mesopotamians were led to prefer rooms which were comparatively narrow in relation to their length, the breadth being limited by the weight which the palm trunks of the terrace could withstand without bending. The Egyptians, on the other hand, found in their quarries the material for columns suitable for supporting the roof beams.

Stone, the basic material for architecture, was found in abundance in Egypt, but it was lacking in Sumer. The Mesopotamians used clay, a common material, for brick architecture. But since fuel was scarce they used sun-dried brick, which is simply soft clay shaped to the required dimensions and laid out to dry in the open air. This was not very resistant, and the walls were constantly being repaired. The problem of transporting materials was easily solved by barge fleets which were highly developed in both countries. Boats with shallow draughts thronged their rivers, even in barely navigable spots. In Mesopotamia navigation was increased by the continuous extension of the canal system. When they had to go inland, the people of both countries had recourse to the caravan, for which paths and tracks were adequate. (These were caravans of donkeys, the horse and camel not being in common use until much later.)

For all these constructions, whose ruins still seem gigantic to us, the lack of mechanical means was replaced by slavery, without which the ancient world would have been incapable of carrying out the works whose remains we admire today. Major Lefebyre des Noëttes, who has studied the matter, has established that the use of the horse as a draught animal could not have spread until the collar which bore on its shoulders was invented. Before that, the collar enclosed the neck and withers, and the more the animal pulled the more it strangled itself. But even if they had had horse and collar at their disposal, I think that they would have still preferred the practice of slavery, because its yield was unlimited and its man-power could easily be renewed. The slaves of the state, prisoners of war or raids, cost nothing. All the difficulties of transporting materials were solved by increasing the number of workers; thanks to slaves, material progress in these civilisations largely anticipated the potentialities of machinery and industry.

The progress of techniques is an obvious condition of the evolution of art, and in this respect Egypt and Meso-potamia were not equally favoured. The absence of stone and its replacement by sun-dried clay bricks led Mesopo-tamia to produce a heavy, massive architecture, resistant only by its weight, with no possibility of any ornamenta-tion other than panels of the same material, applied to the walls—possibly a heritage from primitive wooden architecture. In such constructions the openings were reduced to a minimum for fear of collapse—however, this necessity suited the climate.

Egypt, on the other hand, was able from the beginning to build extensively in stone. For this reason it could use the column, which was not available to the Meso-potamians; but the scarcity of wood for roofs led the Egyptians to multiply the stone supports to which the weight of the roofs gave an exaggerated importance. There are two sorts of monuments which are special 187, 188 reflections of this structure by masses: the pyramid among 184, 186 the Egyptians, the ziggurat or storeyed tower (which was the type of the Tower of Babel) in Mesopotamia. The pyramid was stepped before being smooth, and the ziggurat remained stepped. But where the Egyptian was preparing a tomb for the god-king, the Mesopotamian only wanted a mass containing nothing but a small temple for the reception of the divinity. As a dependency it had at its feet a much larger sanctuary for the big ceremonies, in the same way that the pyramid was accompanied by temples. If, therefore, there were many features in com-mon in the shapes of these two monuments, they had no similarity of purpose. Perhaps this generally held opinion is rather rash. When Herodotus visited Babylon, he was told that the storeyed tower was the tomb of the god Bel (who was deemed to die, or rather to go into a winter sleep, every year, to reappear refreshed and full of life). Even if no cenotaph has yet been found in a Mesopota-mian ziggurat, R. Ghirshman has discovered several chambers in that of Choga Zambil, near Susa, and the excavations are by no means complete. It is hardly possible that the popular consensus of opinion was mis-taken when it informed Herodotus about a monument which was part of its religion for centuries. Perhaps the ziggurat of Choga Zambil, when completely excavated, will supply an answer in the sense which will appear most reasonable.

The ziggurats, the Mesopotamian palaces, appeared in massive shapes because of the friability of sun-dried brick, which was only resistant when in a great volume. These

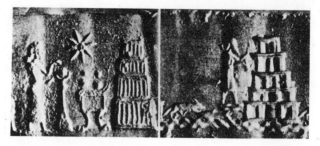

185. Religious scenes showing ziggurat. Impressions from Mesopotamian cylinder seals.

buildings were never made of anything but earth, and this fact greatly detracted from their aesthetic value. The material employed has its importance and makes itself felt. Schopenhauer put it very well in his *Aesthetics*: 'Suppose,' he says, in essence, 'that you are standing in front of a great monument of imposing proportions and volume, and you are informed that the monument is made of cork—your admiration will be considerably lessened.'

As for metal, it was known at an early date in both empires, through trade, and was skilfully worked. Before reaching the period of cast statues, Egyptians and Meso-potamians were content to cast the head, to which they joined a body composed of a core of tarred wood on which were adjusted thin, malleable sheets of copper, fixed with small nails (statues of Pepi I; bulls from the temple at al 'Ubaid; head from Nineveh). Many gold objects were made of comparatively thin gold leaf on a core of wood or metal; only very small objects were made of solid gold.

Painting was much more widely used than was at first thought (when it was not looked for in the excavations). Essentially decorative, it consisted of geometrical motifs in the interiors of dwellings or of large panels which replaced, in Mesopotamian provincial palaces, the bas-reliefs of the capitals and dealt with the same subjects. Often it consisted of pure patches of colour intended to heighten certain parts of scenes which were simply drawn (palace at Tell Ahmar). While it was used either on its own or on the religious or funerary bas-reliefs in the Egyptian tombs, it seems that painting was used in Meso-potamia only to touch up stone bas-reliefs.

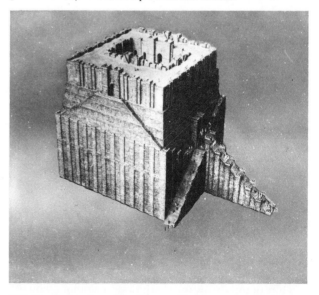

186. Reconstruction of the Tower of Babel. *Berlin Museum.*

124

The influence of religious beliefs

In all ancient societies art was deeply influenced by religion; one could say that at first it was solely devoted to its service in Egypt and Mesopotamia, for the civil power itself drew its source from religion. A brief summary of the distinctive features of the beliefs of the two peoples is equivalent to exposing the fields in which art had its outlet.

Egypt was a monotheistic country, but, owing to the way it was formed (from independent nomes united under a single will), superficial polytheism existed, resulting from the union of the various gods of the individual capitals under the aegis of the god-pharaoh who unified the country. We say superficial because each city honoured a god who was often akin to the god of the neighbouring city. The pharaoh was not only the religious head, the head chosen by god, he was the god himself—since the Egyptians believed that at the time of his conception the god had substituted his divinity for human nature in the features of the king his father. The worship of the god therefore extended to the king. When an Egyptian died he did not do so wholly, and it was accepted that his soul continued to live in the vicinity of his body; hence the care taken to preserve the body by mummification and hence the division of the tomb into two parts: a secret one for the body and its soul, another intended for funeral worship, to which the soul had access to enjoy the funerary offerings. But traces are also found of the belief that the soul could go to paradise where the god Osiris reigned; then the dead person was furnished with objects for the journey, and with statuettes, the 'guarantors' who would stand for him in the realms of the god.

The foregoing, which summarises the essentials and does not take the solar doctrine of Heliopolis into account, is enough to show the field in which art was practised: the temples and the gods and the king *per se* and in his relations with his divine ancestors—so much for life; as regards death, the building of the tomb and its decoration, a reminder of past life or a picture of what awaits the dead man in the hereafter. All this art, then, was primarily utilitarian, but how did the Egyptians come to give so much importance to these representations? Here we touch on one of the fundamental beliefs in Egypt and Mesopotamia which we shall comment on as it appeared in the former country, the 'doctrine of the name'.

This doctrine is not peculiar to Egypt and Mesopotamia; the Israelites knew it and Plato professed it, at least in part: a thing does not exist unless it has a name; to name it is to know it and take possession of it.

Starting with these premises, the consequences unfold with relentless logic; since knowing the name of a person confers power over him, the Egyptian and Mesopotamian gods were not slow to conceal theirs, and an Egyptian narrative tells us quite naturally: 'His real name was Imhotep, but they called him Petubastis.' Another text tells us how the magician Isis, having found out the name of the god Ra, who was ageing, made use of it to become a goddess. Voices had their value in the way they pronounced the name; hence the necessity for the person reciting the sacred formulas to have the 'right voice', the suitable tone. He also had to know the gesture which accompanies the voice or the formula—hence the dances of war and love. But to utter the name in a particular kind of voice while making a particular gesture had only

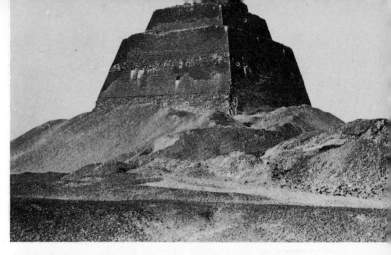

187. EGYPTIAN. The great pyramid at Medum. IVth Dynasty.

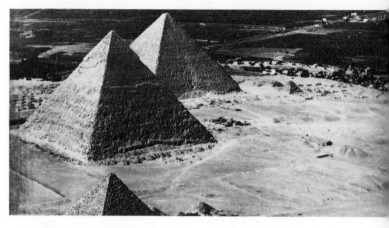

188. EGYPTIAN. Pyramids of Mycerinus, Chephren and Cheops.

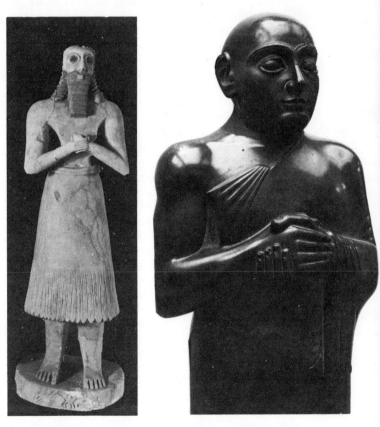

189. SUMERIAN. Statuette of a man. *Baghdad Museum.*

190. SUMERIAN. Votive figure dedicated by Gudea. *British Museum.*

125

a momentary value; to draw an action, to represent it, was a lasting act of taking possession—hence the cave paintings of the game which was hunted; the statue, whether large or small, guaranteed the existence of its original for as long as it itself existed; if the name of the person it represented was engraved on it, it was animated; if a prayer was engraved on the plinth or the clothing, then it became a facsimile of the devotee perpetually repeating its invocation to the gods to benefit its original.

There we have the explanation of Egyptian and Mesopotamian statuary and bas-reliefs. In all their works of art we shall find a similar desire: to honour the gods, but also to procure their favours. The art of archaic societies, then, is primarily utilitarian, since everything depends on the credit which the devotee obtains from the gods.

A number of the features encountered in the Egyptian religion recur in the Mesopotamian ritual; there was a principal god for each city and there were secondary gods, evil spirits tormenting the dead neglected by their descendants. But there are two fundamental differences between the religions. In Mesopotamia the king was not the god; he was merely his chosen one, the surrogate nominated by him. Also, there was no paradisal hereafter —only a sort of limbo of darkness and dust where the dead knew no happiness and might even suffer hunger if the living did not bring them offerings, while the Egyptian dead, by applying the power of the name, could animate all the representations of offerings which surrounded them, even if their families had forgotten them.

This was enough to create a profound difference between the two peoples; whereas the Egyptian felt sure of the future, the Mesopotamian felt his god remote and believed that nothing in the hereafter would console him for sufferings on earth.

Without even invoking a probable fundamental difference in character between the two peoples, these conditions were quite enough to appear clearly in their artistic productions. In any case, in its beginnings Mesopotamian art, like that of Egypt, was dominated by magico-religious considerations. Since religion continued to be the guiding principle, at least in theory, in the two countries, art retained this primitive point of view. Above all, it was in the service of the gods, for their glorification and intended for the protection of the faithful. Soon the great difference was established between the two countries: Egypt, from the nature of its soil, used tombs, caves or stone coverings for its burial places. It adorned them with figures glorifying the gods and intended to protect the dead; the fictions which represented a thing already endowed it with life. The Egyptians decorated the walls of tombs with the images of everything the dead person could hope for in the hereafter and provided him with funerary offerings and food; the Mesopotamians could only count on this last.

To a large extent the decoration of the Egyptian temples has survived; that of the Mesopotamian temples disappeared with the sanctuaries; however we can make suppositions about it from the few examples which remain. Our harvest is a rich one in the field of decorative art. Various objects and all the jewels were ornamented with motifs of religious origin—the lotus among the Egyptians, the marguerite-shaped rosette in Mesopotamia —and short religious scenes were used where bracelets, pendants and embroidery on dresses were concerned.

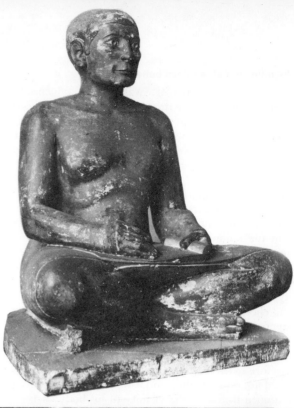

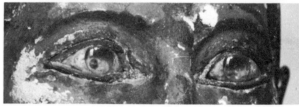

191. EGYPTIAN. The Seated Scribe. The detail shows the inset eyes. Vth Dynasty. *Louvre.*

Whereas in the West the decorative motifs were partially renovated at the same time as the styles, they remained constant in Mesopotamian and Egyptian art. Moreover, many of these motifs passed from one country to another through trade, particularly as far as the working of ivory was concerned. Some motifs were reproduced for ornamental reasons, without being understood.

Relations with spiritual life

If we divide what is known as civilisation into two parts, one dealing with material and technical progress, the other concerning the development of social and spiritual life, it is with the latter that art will be intimately linked.

We shall try to reconstitute it by the evidence; naturally, there can be no question of doing so for the periods in which civilisation was being formed. P. Gilbert has conducted an inquiry which began with records from the second half of the 3rd millennium B.C., the first being of a death mask of the (anonymous) owner of one of the Sakkara pyramids. It is a thinker's face, with a high forehead, indicating a refined race—such was the human type of the epoch. The quality of thought is revealed in the maxims of Ptahhotep, a sage among the contemporary rulers; his language was not that of a member of a hard and heartless society, but of a man who had experienced the evil which surrounds us and wants to avoid it, even to dissipate it by doing good. He extolled truth and justice. He recommended people to inspire affection, not fear; he believed in a moderate god, and added: 'If thy field prospers and the god heaps riches on you, do not go to other people's houses to eat.' His words were primarily

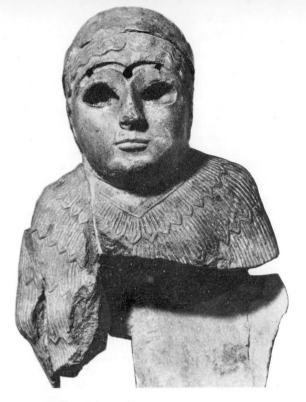

192. SUMERIAN. Bust of a woman.

addressed to those who were in positions of authority. 'Shun envy,' he said, 'it makes the most united quarrel.' Lastly he admonished: 'If you have risen in life, never forget your previous situation.' We quote one more phrase, which is thousands of years ahead of its time: 'Do not lift up your heart, that it be not humbled.'

After the turmoil which put an end to the Old Kingdom, another sage, towards 2100, was still uttering the same maxims and insisting on the duties towards the divinity, saying that he should be worshipped not only in himself but in his works: 'Venerate the god, whether he be made of bronze or precious stones, or of water replaced by water.' That was not enough; it was also necessary to think of one's neighbour, and the sage said: 'Console him who weeps.' The negative Egyptian attitude went even further; conscious of the definitive and irreparable nature of damage done to others, even if it is forgiven, the penitent later proclaimed: 'I have not made anyone weep.'

Such was the moral climate of the society (or at least of its élite) which produced the art of the Old and Middle Kingdoms.

Conventions of the human figure

While Egypt had at her disposal various kinds of stone suitable for carving statues, Mesopotamia was so short of raw materials that she even went so far as to use porous stone for this purpose; and as a result the Egyptians rapidly took to life- and larger than life-size statuary, while the Mesopotamians were confined to the statuette.

At first the two peoples adopted a fairly curtailed rule governing the proportions of the human body. The Egyptians soon freed themselves from it, but the Mesopotamians took longer, especially at the centre of Tello (ancient Lagash), where they adopted an improbably strict convention, using, as a measurement, four heads for the height of the body, whereas the average rule is seven to seven and a half heads. What inspired them to adopt an anomaly so much in contradiction with reality? These statues were made as ex votos and were dedicated

to the divinity; they were meant to replace the donor. The characteristic feature of a person is his head, and in these figures the body was a support, of no great interest. Moreover, if the person was of some standing the statue would bear his name so that the god was aware of it.

Ethnical features in sculpture were more pronounced in Mesopotamia than they were in Egypt, where the faces were generally well proportioned without any particular exaggeration. In the Sumerian epoch, in Mesopotamia, the nose was paradoxically accentuated into an eagle's beak; its curve was prolonged naturally with that of the low forehead crowned with a skull whose summit reached the occiput (which fell straight to the shoulders without bringing out the line of the neck). This appearance is not unconnected with the theory of F. von Luschan, who would have it that the first inhabitants of Mesopotamia were brachycephalics, with an aspect rather like that of the people of the Dinaric Alps. But the Sumerian skulls which have been subjected to analysis indicate that they are linked with the Mediterranean dolichocephalic race. The aspect given to their creations by the sculptors remains, therefore, rather disconcerting.

On the statues of the Egyptians—less frequently, incidentally, than on those of the Sumerians—the eyes were hollowed out and the sockets inlaid with an artificial eye intended to endow the expression with life; the Sumerians embedded the white of the eye (a sea-shell) and the pupil (lapis lazuli or bitumen) in a wide capsule of bitumen which was intended to imitate the eyelashes and which produces a strange effect. On the other hand, the eye of a statue such as the Egyptian one of the Seated Scribe, in the Louvre, with a pupil of crystal, is inset in **191** a thin capsule of copper which helps to obtain the effect sought for.

The statues are carved bald-headed or wearing wigs; they are upright and, according to the region, motionless (Tello) or with one foot forward (Tell Asmar). Among the Egyptians, the arms may be by the side of the body; but they are more often raised to the chest, with hands crossed, in Sumer. It was the attitude of respect for statues, whereas on bas-reliefs the forearm was flexed, the hand at mouth height. This came from the need to make the statue as invulnerable as possible to shocks, since the future safety of the individual depended on it.

The Egyptians had the same fear. They carved statues, which were seated on the ground with the knees drawn **212** up to the chin, forming a simple cube.

The main distinction between man and woman in Mesopotamian art was made by convention of dress; at first man was clad in a loin-cloth forming a skirt, and his torso was bare; woman wore a larger drape with which she covered her left shoulder, leaving the right shoulder and arm free; later, man adopted the female costume, and woman had a cloth which she draped in such a way as to cover both her shoulders. In the early times she had hair flowing down her back, tied up by a ribbon crossed X-wise. Later she wore a cloth on her hair, held by a sort of pad (the *agal* of the Bedouins). But no charm, no feminine aspect in the features, distinguished her. In the bas-relief of the ruler Ur-Nanshe, the long-haired person **193** is presumably the ruler's wife.

The very beautiful face of a fairly large-sized statue, found at Warka, has been catalogued as a woman's head, for the hair style, with small serrations held tightly

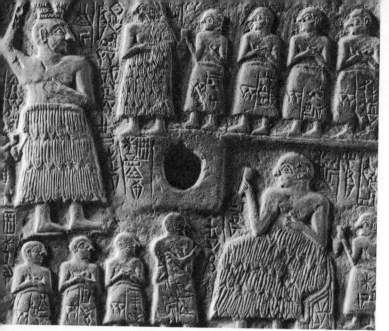

193. SUMERIAN. Bas-relief of Ur-Nanshe, from Tello. Middle of the 3rd millennium. *Louvre.*

against the forehead with a ribbon, is that of a woman (heads in the Louvre); without the ribbon and the big serrations, it would be the hair style of a man of the archaic dynastic epoch, as I believe it to be (Sumerian copper figure in the Louvre, and still later statuettes of King Lugalkisalsi in the Louvre and in Berlin).

There were just as many conventions governing bas-reliefs as statues. Bas-relief presented the artist with a new technical difficulty: the need to render three dimensions on a surface which only possessed two and to find stratagems to express the depth which the bas-relief could not reproduce.

Apparently the primitive artist faced with this obstacle reacted in the same way everywhere, since the archaic
193, 196 works of Egypt and Sumer resolved the problem in similar ways. The body was, so to speak, dissociated—each part being represented in the way which was most expressive (or perhaps easiest) for the sculptor. Thus the head, the legs and the feet were represented in profile; the upper part of the body, on the other hand, was frontal; it only acquired a three-quarters view with time. Then a literal distortion of the neck and the pelvis took place so as to make these disparate parts agree. The position of the feet, one behind the other on the same level, led to an uneven balance. Details exhibited just as great oddities. The eyes were frontal in a profile face, undoubtedly because of the importance of the look, which betrayed the emotions. But the sculptor drew in profile the long square beard which fell down to the chest, making a part of the mouth disappear. In the same way gods wearing horned tiaras and warriors with their helmets ornamented with lateral horns wore their head-dress frontally on a head in profile. The bas-relief in the
193 Louvre from Tello represents the ruler Ur-Nanshe (once transcribed Ur-Nina) and his family. It is an excellent example of these conventions. On the lower register of the relief the artist has got round the difficulty of depicting Ur-Nanshe seated by dressing him in a woollen skirt which covers the lower part of his body.

After the archaic period in Mesopotamia, when the faithful were represented naked before god, this dress remained common only among prisoners of war. Women were never represented naked. Much the same held good

in Egypt, with a few fine exceptions, but the female body was often merely covered with a cloth showing up the shapes, particularly a single breast which projected across the bas-relief beneath the fabric, something unknown to Mesopotamian custom. During the archaic period, it has been noted that the Mesopotamians depicted spindly muscles: for example, among the prisoners on a bas-relief from Akkadian times; among the bearers of offerings in the procession on the Warka vase. The tradition, therefore, was kept up for several centuries. Much later, in the Assyrian epoch, the muscles of arms and legs left visible by the clothing were always represented contracted in an effort, in a rather unnatural, sometimes unreal, manner. Egypt avoided these extremes.

And this leads us to point out a defect in the bas-reliefs which Mesopotamia and, to a lesser degree, Egypt were unable to overcome: the inability to reproduce correctly the articulation of the shoulder farthest from the spectator. In the bas-reliefs of prisoners from Akkad, the arms of one of them are bound behind his back. The artist has deliberately suppressed any possible link with the arm furthest away; on the Assyrian stele from Bel Harran Bel Utsur, on the other hand, the articulation of the shoulder is thrust forward in a pitiful way. In Egypt the sculptor was more skilful at avoiding the difficulty.

The study of attitudes in Mesopotamia, which owes a great deal to Flavigny, shows us many conventions which are difficult to explain at first sight: the depiction of a person on both sides of a scene, so that he is seen both from the left and from the right; person or objects placed one behind the other, which must be understood as being situated side by side. On some cylinders a two-faced god is seen between the principal god and the worshipper; some scholars interpret this anticipatory representation of Janus as a way of depicting intercession —the secondary god addressing himself alternately to the principal god and to the worshipper.

The breaking down of movement and attitudes was the subject of research in both countries. Egypt, in a series of sketches at Beni Hasan, showed wrestlers at various **194** moments of the fight which followed very close upon one another, but often preoccupation with preserving the combattants' dignity diminished the vigour of these works. The most decisive moment of the action was not chosen, for example, on the Stele of the Vultures, when the god is about to fracture the skulls of the conquered; there was more verve, a better choice of the vital moment, in Egyptian bas-reliefs.

Both the Egyptians and the Mesopotamians had an acute sense of the observation of animals and have left masterpieces behind. Perhaps the Mesopotamians were at their best in the Erech period and later in the Assyrian period, while the Egyptians, in such works as the geese from Medum and the animal scenes from el Amarna, were incomparable.

Spatial conventions

Certain conventions were adopted by the two empires to express several objects in line. The fashion current in Mesopotamia for depicting an animal with horns was to presume a strict profile so that only one was visible; the animal became, in a sense, single horned. Another procedure, for showing a team pulling a chariot, for example, consisted in superimposing the horses in space,

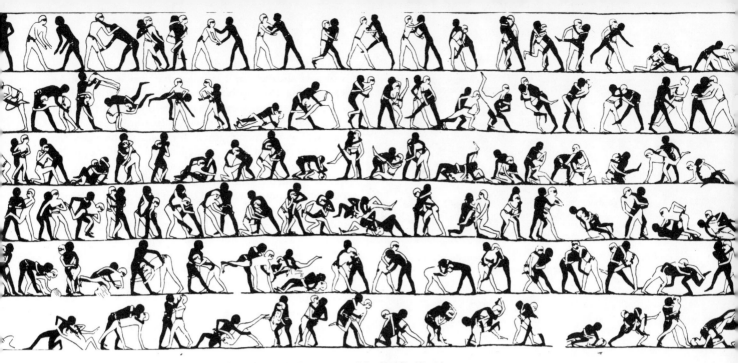

194. Wrestlers from tomb 15 at Beni Hasan (detail). Beginning of the Middle Kingdom.

far from one another, and connecting them to the chariot by their reins which describe an exaggerated curve. Or again, as children do, the artist added contour lines to the upper outline of the animal and to its feet. But animals and people were soon seen from a three-quarters view and overlapping each other, among both the Egyptians and the Mesopotamians.

195   The arrangement of scenes on a bas-relief brought up the problem of perspective, which archaic artists did not render as we do. They limited themselves to staggering the various elements of the composition one above the other, drawing them all the same size: the spectator had to re-establish the values and translate the thought of the sculptor. On some cylinder seals this is particularly clear. Thus the artist shows us oxen, their heads seen in strict profile, grouped around their stable made of plaited reeds. There again we see the rise of a convention also respected by the Egyptians. In order to show the contents of the stable the artist had drawn on either side of the edifice the forequarters of an animal which appears to be emerging through the wall, the door remaining free. In actual fact these animals are not emerging from the stable; they

are indicating its contents. At Thebes, in the tomb of Rekhmire, vizier of Tuthmosis III, men of Keftiu (Crete) were represented bringing gold vases in tribute. The vases were decorated internally with motifs in repoussé work. The artist drew them aligned on the edge of the vase as if they were coming out of it, a conventional way of showing the inside—at least according to some scholars, for this explanation is not unanimously accepted.

But from the remotest epochs the artist also used another procedure to get round the problem of perspective; he composed his scenes in registers, separated   193, 196 from one another by a clay line. This method of creation reduced the number of cases in which perspective had to be employed. Handsome examples are afforded by the Egyptian palettes, the Warka vase at Baghdad and the Stele of the Vultures in the Louvre.

Should we attribute these various procedures used by the Eastern sculptors to a genuine lack of skill? The artists invite us to examine their bas-reliefs, not with a single glance but by moving in front of each one of the motifs to be considered. It would seem more logical, one might say, to depict an ensemble of the type normally

195. Counting the flocks. Detail from the tomb of Tit at Sakkara. Vth Dynasty.

196. EGYPTIAN. The official Nefer receiving funerary offerings. Bas-relief from his mastaba. Vth Dynasty. *Louvre*.

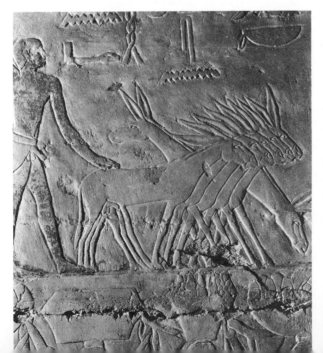

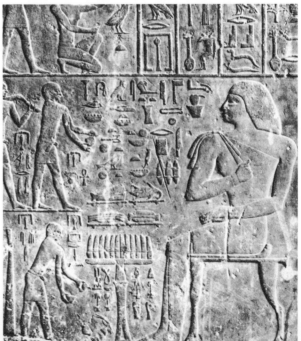

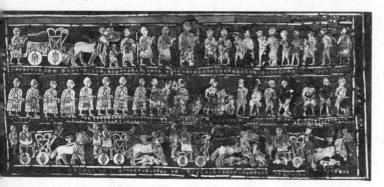

197. SUMERIAN. Standard of Ur. Mosaic depicting the king at war. First half of the 3rd millennium. *British Museum.*

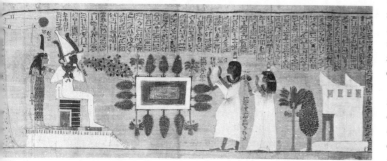

198. EGYPTIAN. Nakht and his wife Tuyu worshipping Osiris and Maat. Papyrus. XVIIIth Dynasty. The perspective of the pool is replaced by an abstract projection. *British Museum.*

taken in by our eyes from the spot where we stand; but a general view is rarely adequate. We approach or change our position to appreciate the details, the 'close-up'. We are more superficial in our way of expressing things; these ancient peoples exhibited more curiosity. In the same way, when we superimpose our figures in order to express perspective by diminishing the size of those that are supposed to be farther away, we are only using a subterfuge which is neither more nor less illogical than that of the Sumerians when they applied the same procedure to express the hierarchy of their personages. Their point of view was subjective; ours is objective, and a lengthy period of visual education has accustomed us to it. We have simply substituted one convention for another.

Here are a few examples. It is not uncommon that an observer can only see one side of a building. The artists of this epoch frequently depicted the short and the long side of a building on the same plane. This, presumably, led the Sumerians to a curious way of representing a war chariot. On the Stele of the Vultures and on the Standard 197 of Ur it is depicted with apparently four wheels, of which only one in front and one behind are visible; the front of the chariot with its grooves for the reins to pass through is presented full face, and behind the driver—an unusual feature—is the javelin thrower. Now, the small terra-cotta chariots which have been discovered—mostly with two wheels, rather like the chariot of Antiquity— put us on the right track. Since the Mesopotamians were unacquainted with the movable front axle, these four-wheeled chariots would have been virtually useless. In fact, they were two-wheeled; the artist, in the same way that he represented the front of the chariot face on, depicted its two wheels one beside the other, and the javelin thrower was really beside, not behind, the driver.

In a landscape, for example, if it was a question of representing a marsh bordered by trees on its four sides, the artist sometimes extended it before us as if it were 198 a box with its sides, represented by the trees, opened outwards and flattened down—or at least three sides, the one closest to and facing the spectator sometimes being flattened down inwards on the water.

If he wanted to show the interior of a property or a town, everything was spread out on the ground; we have to re-erect it all mentally, and where the interior of a building is concerned, the façade is removed and we see inside it as if looking into an open cupboard.

Many museums contain curious examples of this: in the Louvre there is a Mesopotamian bas-relief of Tiglath Pileser III, in which, in a town whose circular wall is seen from the top, there arises the side view of a castle. A cylinder from Susa depicts a winding river where the spectator, presumed to be in the middle of the water among the fish, sees the trees flattened down outwards on either bank.

In the British Museum, an Assyrian bas-relief shows a fortified camp seen from the top and divided into 199 quarters, each section displaying the inhabitants at their daily tasks; two sides of a tent are shown next to each other and without the covering, so that the tent's use as a stable is brought out. This bas-relief is an excellent example of possible combinations of perspectives.

Egypt, too, generally applied this procedure; some properties from the time of el Amarna are offered to our view like cupboards without doors, showing all their contents.

The conventions enumerated above in Egyptian and Mesopotamian art created an identical aesthetic climate for the two empires which was to last until the end of their political existence. These conventions were the result of a long past from which one does not normally break free, whereas those of the West came from Greece. Applied to a basically religious art and taking their part in sacred matters, these traditions could not undergo more than modifications of detail; moreover, they satisfied the dogmatic intention of all religious iconographies meant for the people, who would have been deprived of their teaching if too much imagination had been introduced.

But it is remarkable that Egypt and Mesopotamia, starting from such similar points of view, followed two roads so increasingly different. That was where the characters of the two peoples and their potentialities played a part.

The personality of Egyptian art

The Egyptian artist based his work on reality; he wanted a likeness for the utilitarian reasons we have mentioned. But he followed his own temperament in portraiture, which led him to idealise his models; he refined and ennobled them. The regularity of the features and the calm of the face were combined with the astonishing gaze with which the sculptor endowed the statue; we feel by-passed, seen through, by this look which ignores us to stare into the infinite. Several statues of the ruler Chephren 201 are known—potential spare bodies in case they were needed during his life beyond the grave; all of them have this piercing look.

All the officials and all the courtesans of the pharaohs of

XVIIIth Dynasty. Staatliche Museen, Berlin. *Museum photograph.*

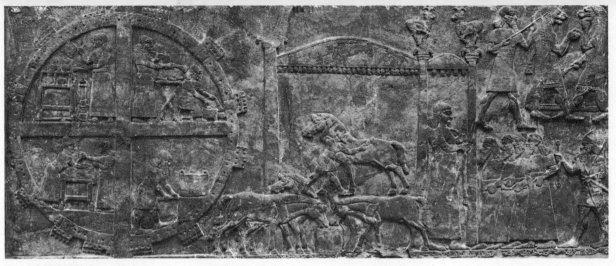

199. ASSYRIAN. Bas-relief showing a fortified camp. Period of Assurnasirpal. 9th century B.C. An example of abstract projection taking the place of perspective. *British Museum*.

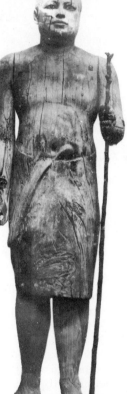

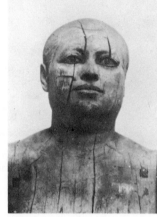

200. *Below*. EGYPTIAN. The Sheikh el Beled. Wood. Vth Dynasty. *Egyptian Museum, Cairo*.

201. Statue of Chephren, builder of the Second Pyramid at Gizeh. IVth Dynasty. *Egyptian Museum, Cairo*.

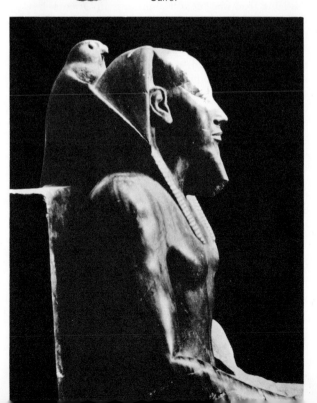

the Old Kingdom have their own particular physiognomy, but a vulgar feature is never seen on any of their faces. Even those who do not form part of the family or the court of the god-king have a calm certitude, as if they were assured of the future. Take, for example, the Seated

191 Scribe, in the Louvre, to whom the artist has added a lively, alert look by giving the statue eyes made of small fragments of crystal. And when it was a question merely of rendering good nature combined with dignity, what could surpass the wood statue known as the Sheikh el

200 Beled (or Ka-aper), in the Cairo Museum?

What more wonderful monument than the pyramid could house the tomb of the pharaoh, son of Ra, the sun god, whose rays were symbolised by the lines and sides of the monument. The most perfect is the Pyramid of Cheops, but all those of the pharaohs of the period do honour to the mathematicians who planned them.

And yet they were not enough for the pharaohs of the Vth Dynasty, who, proclaiming themselves sons of Ra, dedicated solar temples to their god in imitation of the Temple of the Sun at Heliopolis (the city of the sun), whose essential feature was an obelisk on a substructure, massive ancestor of the fine obelisks of later periods, the pyramidal top of which was one more link between the divinity and the god-king.

The scenes on mastabas were treated in the same spirit as the statuary. Often in very low relief, and naked, the sculptures were frequently given flat tints with the most pleasing effect. They copied life: scenes showing hunting, fishing, harvesting, tilling of the soil—but always with a kind of movement which did not go as far as effort. Man was always master of his material in these scenes, and optimism, the basis of the Egyptian character, was very evident. During the course of work jokes were exchanged and pleasant little scenes took place. Undoubtedly the life of the ancient Egyptian was not a permanent holiday, and he was beaten more than once, but his character, imbued with justice and truth, must have preserved him from the excesses which are portrayed in Mesopotamian monuments, which gloried in the terror they inspired. Even the funerary furniture (for example, that of Hetep-heres, mother of Cheops) and the everyday utensils in Egypt had a certain nobility of line.

Does this mean that Egypt did not have its periods of bad taste, in our sense at least? Certain elaborate vases from the tomb of Tutankhamen only make us appreciate those of the Old and Middle Kingdoms the more, in spite

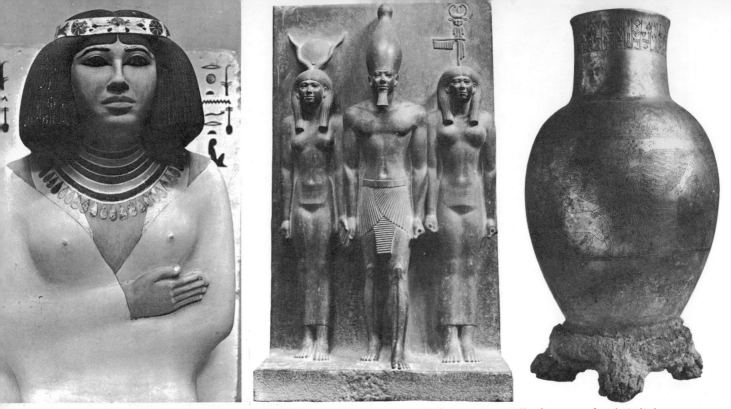

202. EGYPTIAN. The Lady Nofret. IVth Dynasty. *Egyptian Museum, Cairo.*

203. Mycerinus group. IVth Dynasty. *Egyptian Museum, Cairo.*

204. SUMERIAN. Silver vase from Entemena. Middle of the 3rd millennium. *Louvre.*

of the presence of some dubious shapes (vases shaped like two coupled ducks).

This noble period of the Memphite kingdom ended in revolution.

The Middle Kingdom renewed the tradition. Tombs which were veritable funerary apartments were substituted for the pyramids, while the governors of the nomes, the owners of domains in Upper Egypt, no longer wishing to be grouped around the pharaoh in death to gain his protection, hollowed out their tombs in the cliffs along the banks of the Nile. The decoration remained the same; it ornamented the sides of the wooden sarcophagi or mummy cases of the period. We have a plan of a chief's residence from the site of Kahun. It is an Oriental house, with no view giving on to the outside and with halls having roofs supported by columns.

Changes in sculpture were slight. Art was under the tutelage of the sacred; it could not change more than religion did. But frequently the expressions of the statues were different. It seemed that even if society had recovered its forms, it no longer had the same unshakable confidence in its monarchs that it had once had. It remembered the past and felt that what it had just experienced could easily not be unique; in this it was not mistaken, for the invasion by the Hyksos was still to come.

And the royal statuary reproduced disillusioned, bitter features. We find this in the portrait of King Sesostris III and in those sphinxes which were once believed to be Hyksos works but which are really in the tradition of the Middle Kingdom.

The bas-reliefs remained dynamic, like the one of Sesostris I in his ritual course before the god Min.

Goldsmiths' work and jewellery, if somewhat ornate, were exquisite, especially the crowns of Princess Khnu-

met, which were essentially funerary, for their lightness would have made them unsuitable for regular use.

To finish with the preoccupation with charm which we find in Egyptian art, let us recall those statues simply clad in a light veil: an ivory 'concubine' of the Ist Dynasty, having delightful proportions but still adhering too closely to the convention of a very short neck; the bust of Princess Nefer-hetep-s; the women in the Mycerinus group from the Old Kingdom; the charming bearers of offerings of the First Intermediate period; the young girls playing with a ball, from a tomb at Beni Hasan, a cheerful group in the main, in spite of the awkwardness of the positions of the arms. Here is one of the things which strikes us about Egyptian art; some of the figures do not bear analysis, although their elegance conceals their imperfections. Let us take a good look at them. We shall rarely find their equal in Mesopotamia (an exception being the small neo-Sumerian head from Ur).

203
205

The personality of Mesopotamian art

The aims of art in Mesopotamia were the same as in Egypt, but the potentialities were less from the very beginning. When Egypt had inaugurated the Thinite period under a united monarchy, Mesopotamia was entering on the Jemdet Nasr epoch, which was still protohistoric and was filled with internal conflicts. It did, however, produce fine works of art, although of a less pronounced style than the works from the beginning of historic times. Temples were built of which, as in contemporary Egypt, only traces remain. Bas-reliefs were carved on small stelae and vases. Glyptics flourished. The cylinder seals of this period were, of course, for religious purposes.

At the time of the beginning of the Old Kingdom in Egypt, with the IIIrd Dynasty, Mesopotamia entered on the epoch of the archaic dynasties, about which we know virtually nothing. It was only during the second part of this period, with the beginning of the Ist Ur Dynasty and the princes of Lagash (Tello) that genuine history began in Sumer; then Egypt entered on her Vth Dynasty and was able to pride herself on the pharaohs who built the

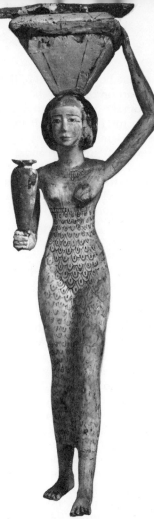

205. EGYPTIAN. Woman bearing an offering. Stuccoed and painted wood. XIth Dynasty. *Louvre.*

206. Votive statue of Gudea. 3rd millennium. *Louvre.*

Gizeh pyramids: Cheops, Chephren and Mycerinus.

Then came a veritable artistic flowering in Mesopotamia, although it was expressed in minor forms. The excellent copper and stone statuettes, while the artist has not been able to give them a feeling of animation, show that the conventions included variations. The abbreviated canon of Lagash was less strict in the Baghdad region. We notice that the statuettes which have lost the incrustation from their eye-sockets often give a more marked impression of life than those which have preserved it. A statuette, from the end of the period, of the administrator of Mari, on the Euphrates, is in the Sumerian style. Another, from Lagash (now in the Istanbul Museum), in the Sumerian style, is that of a bald-headed, clean-shaven, worshipper standing in an attitude of prayer. In my opinion it is the best specimen of Sumerian art which has come down to us.

The bas-reliefs which have been preserved are generally small. They are commemorative religious plaques with superimposed registers, and are of great archaeological interest. From the end of the period, the elaborately 167 carved Stele of the Vultures, arranged in the same way, is a very beautiful piece of decorative art. At this time Egypt had produced, besides the pyramids at Gizeh, the statues of the pharaohs, their constructors. But the two civilisations were by then on the same level in metalwork; 204 such works as the silver vase from Entemena bear comparison with objects of the Egyptian Vth Dynasty.

Sumer, which, in addition to its dynastic wars, had already undergone an upheaval which appeared total with the reforms of the ruler Urukagina, was then conquered

by the Semites of the Akkadian Dynasty. A marked progress in the arts is noticeable at this time, manifested 272 in half life-size statuary (only a few rather heavy fragments remain). A magnificent bas-relief of this period is the triangular Stele of Victory of the ruler Naram Sin, 217 in which the figures lead up in an ascending movement to that of the ruler, who is larger than life-size (a convention of respect which also existed in Egypt) and who is facing the top of a mountain. This work is treated as a baetylus, i.e. a stone in which a divinity is immanent; the canon of proportion is almost normal, and the somewhat exaggerated spindle-shaped musculature has a pleasing effect. This monument provides a transition from one formula to another which we miss in Egyptian art with its continuous development. Also in this period the linear writing of Mesopotamia, on its way to becoming cuneiform, became a decorative motif in its own right, as on the obelisk of King Manishtusu. However, the triumph of the new formula was not complete. The provinces were not won over by this new art. At Susa, the capital of Elam, a bust has been found of Manishtusu which is done in the most barbarous style imaginable.

The era of revolutions and invasions was not over. The wild mountain-dwelling Guti from the Zagros range occupied Babylon for nearly a hundred and twenty years. The country shook off their yoke and the Sumerians returned. They will now be referred to as neo-Sumerians, for although they preserved the principles of Sumerian art, the lessons of Akkad were not lost.

The IIIrd Ur Dynasty was founded, and under its first kings the town of Lagash produced its final works—but

133

what powerful ones they were!

One governor of the town, Gudea, with leisure, material resources and artists at his disposal, transformed it. He rebuilt the temples; he placed his votive statues, seated or upright, in them. All these statues were less than life-size except for one, which for this reason has been called 'colossal'. The statues were carved out of diorite, one of the hardest varieties of granite. Those in the Louvre, from regular excavations, are identified by an inscription. They are mutilated, but it has been possible to reconstruct the smallest one with certainty. The turbaned head exhibits a rather determined, serious physiognomy, with prominent chin and cheeks. The draping of the fabric (left smooth so as to create a space on which to engrave the prayer) enables us to make out the body beneath the garment; the modelling of the shoulder and arm is obvious.

These statues are disconcerting, for nothing previous in Mesopotamian art, except, perhaps, Akkadian sculpture, foreshadowed them, at least from the point of view of general progress. They may possibly have had some influence on Egypt, as P. Gilbert has observed, for at the same epoch, in the XIIth and XIIIth Dynasties, short statues in Egypt had similar clothing and drapery. But the statuary from the time of Gudea is all the more surprising since it was not followed up.

The works of the IIIrd Ur Dynasty can be placed, in spirit and technique, next to those we owe to Gudea. Following the usual fate, this dynasty was replaced by two dynasties at Isin and Larsa and later by a third at Babylon which remained master of the field. All three drew their inspiration, in their religious stelae, from the epoch of Gudea and the IIIrd Ur Dynasty. The Babylonian Dynasty has given us a work which derives from both Akkadian and Ur sources: Hammurabi's Code of Laws, which shows a representation of the king before his god carved in relief at the top of a stele bearing superlatively beautiful writing (as on the obelisk of Manishtusu).

Glyptics took the place, in Mesopotamia, of the funerary paintings of the Egyptian mastabas. Devotees before their deity and motifs borrowed from religious myths formed repertoires which were sometimes varied and sometimes identical, and which we know from hundreds of examples.

For some time now we have lost sight of possible links between Egypt and Mesopotamia. This is the place to recall one. The treasure found at the temple of Tod near Thebes, and dating from Amenemhat II, towards 1937 B.C., contained a number of Babylonian cylinders, of which the most recent can be attributed to the Larsa Dynasty (2023–1761) and also to the beginning of the Babylonian Dynasty. The latter had been synchronous with that of Larsa for one hundred and thirty-three years before conquering that kingdom under Hammurabi (1792–1750). Moreover, this link was not new, but it has been confirmed by these cylinders even though it cannot be defined more accurately.

Temples and palaces of later Mesopotamia have been found; they are ruins of crumbled earth, of which we can only make out the lower parts. At first the temple consisted of a single rectangular room with the image of the divinity. Later we find a court followed by a hall preceding the antecella and the cella. The palace was an assemblage of rooms arranged on the model of the private house, with a central court on to which the rooms gave. The most important from the time of Hammurabi is that of Mari, a kingdom on the frontiers of Babylonia and conquered by her under Hammurabi. In this palace and the adjacent temples statues of governors and divinities in a rather heavy style have been found. However, their style contrasts strongly with that of the small amount of statuary coming from Babylonia. A greater wealth of ornament is found in the costume than on the Babylonian statues and bas-reliefs.

The persistence of tradition

During the thousand years which have elapsed between the Romanesque period and our own day, how many variations there have been in Western art, including the many and frequently immoderate ones of our time! During the three thousand years of Egyptian and Mesopotamian civilisation some ups and downs and some progress have been noted but they always had definite limits. This was due to the innate conservatism of the East, reinforced by its religious beliefs. To the Babylonians all civilisation was a gift of the gods, revealed by their emissaries and leaving little room for progress. Hence the preoccupation with tradition. In Egypt, when a statue of a god was to be carved, the pharaoh had the 'old books' consulted. In the neo-Babylonian period, when a collapsed temple was reconstructed the king would say that he had built according to the ancient measurements, 'not a thumb more, not a thumb less'. A minor example will demonstrate the Assyrians' conservatism. In the palace of Til Barsip (at Tell Ahmar), discovered by F. Thureau-Dangin, King Tiglath Pileser III (8th century) had the walls covered with paintings. These are quite characteristic of the epoch, with court and state scenes and scenes of solemn processions. In the throne room, beneath a coat of plaster, we find a painting of Assyrian lancers charging at full gallop, rendered without perspective so that they look like some fantastic 'Ride of the Valkyries'. This work, far in advance of its time and foreshadowing the end of Sargon's dynasty, undoubtedly met with the hostility of the conformists, which is all the more reason today for us to give the unknown artist his due.

This rapid review of artistic developments in the basins of the Nile and the Tigris and Euphrates gives rise to a few reflections. Here were two peoples caught at a moment in their history when they had a common artistic and cultural patrimony. From then on and up to the middle of the 2nd millennium B.C.—the epoch we have reached—their art consisted solely of variations on the same theme. The advantage remained with Egypt, it would appear. It was more favoured by its location which made it less exposed to external attacks, by its policy of stability and by the materials its soil provided. Mesopotamia, on the other hand, sheltering various tribes, was only able to impose unity for short periods and was subject to foreign invasions. Lacking stone, it was not able to do itself full justice in architecture and sculpture. Lastly, Mesopotamia's rougher character kept it at a distance from emotion, from the instinctive search for the beautiful, and made it lean towards power. On the other hand, it is generally thought to have been ahead of Egypt in the scientific field.

THE RIVALRY AND THE ACHIEVEMENTS
OF THE EMPIRES *Etienne Drioton*

As we approach our own era, contacts, both belligerent and peaceful, weave an ever closer web between the countries of the Near East. Etienne Drioton, who was director of the Egyptian Archaeological Services for many years, continues the story of the development of the art of these countries within the framework of a fiercely conservative continuity of which traces survived in Egypt until a very late date.

The two great centres of civilisation in this part of the world, Egypt and Mesopotamia, had not, as we have seen, remained absolutely without contact before this time. From the beginning of the Old Kingdom, Byblos, which was very much under the influence of Egypt even down to its administration, had spread artistic formulas from the Nile valley to the neighbourhood of the Euphrates basin. At the time of the XIIth Dynasty political refugees, such as Sinuhe and the Egyptians mentioned by him as residing at the court of the Syrian ruler Amunenchi, passed on many of the elements of their culture to those around them. But these relations did not have a widespread effect because they were episodic.

With the advent of the New Kingdom in Egypt, new customs were established which resulted in more permanent contacts between the peoples and the arts of the two empires. Almost immediately after her liberation from the domination of the Hyksos, Egypt embarked on a policy of Asiatic conquests in order to prevent any recurrence of invasion from those parts. But instead of limiting himself to punitive expeditions, as had previous pharaohs, Tuthmosis III pushed on as far as the Euphrates, imposing an administrative tutelage on the conquered countries. Egyptian governors were put in command of garrisons quartered in strongholds, or commissioners of the pharaoh controlled the petty rulers who were left in power on condition that they paid tribute. In either case, the presence throughout the Near East of Egyptian families of high rank, accompanied by their household staffs and ordering from Egypt everything necessary for their comfort, must inevitably have set the fashion for the local aristocracies and made them familiar with the Nilotic civilisation, even if it did not make them adopt it.

On the other hand, the policy of foreign marriages, inaugurated by pharaohs of the XVIIIth Dynasty (and continued under the succeeding dynasties) to consolidate their policy of conquests, introduced the taste for Asiatic fashions into Egypt. The princesses—Mitannian and Babylonian in the XVIIth Dynasty, Hittite in the XIXth —who entered the harems of the kings of Egypt brought their retinues with them. The scarab which Amenhotep III had made to commemorate the arrival of the daughter of the king of Mitanni, enumerated her three hundred and seventeen retainers. At the same time, the prisoners of war who had been brought back from Asia in their thousands and put to work either on building or as servants in the temples, finally fused with the population. Foreign diplomatic correspondence drafted in cuneiform necessitated the presence in the palace archives of Babylonian personnel, references to whom have been found.

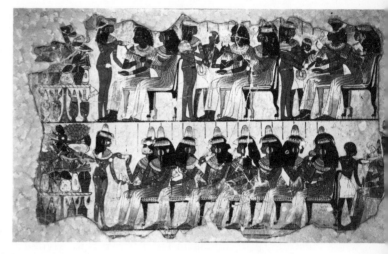

207. EGYPTIAN. Banquet scene. Wall painting. *British Museum.*

The palace schools received, side by side with children from the noblest families in Egypt, the sons of Asiatic rulers destined to govern under the tutelage of the pharaoh. The many embassies gave the strollers through the streets of Thebes the chance to observe the luxury of the Eastern courts. All these contacts made the Egyptians familiar with Asiatic culture and even inspired an esteem for it, since the scribes of the Ramesside period often used words borrowed from the languages of Canaan or Babylon to embellish their style.

Egypt and western Asia were not the only regions to establish regular contacts in the 2nd millennium B.C. Five tombs of the time of Tuthmosis III, among the most richly decorated of the Theban necropolis, depict Cretan embassies bringing the products of their industries to Egypt. The Minoan objects found in Syria and certain motifs adopted by Phoenician decorators lead us to think that there were active exchanges with the Aegean.

Assyria was to repeat, during the dynasties of Sargon and Sennacherib, what Egypt had done at the height of her territorial expansion. She deported to her court the sons of conquered monarchs in order to educate them in the principles of their masters so as to place them later as docile vassals on the thrones of their fathers. But the political measures which had led to a certain diffusion, earlier, of Egyptian art in the ancient Orient did not perform the same service for Assyrian art.

Moreover, the contacts between peoples were not as effective in the ancient Near East as they would be in the present-day Western world. With us the arts draw their vigour from the private inspiration of the artists. There, all the arts were controlled, because they were aulic arts created for the royal court by artists working according to the tastes of that court. They might contain, especially at the points where influences met, accidental borrowings, particularly in ornamentation. But these fancies only represented minute details, accidental grace-notes in relation to the whole. Both in Babylonia and Egypt art formed the traditional language of the civilisation incarnate in a particular monarchy, and no one ever dreamt of giving up his native tongue. Thus control tended to turn naturally towards purism. We can see this clearly in Egypt, where the national revival which came with the XXVIth Dynasty, immediately after the Assyrian occupation, adopted an archaistic art renewed from the age of the pyramids in order to assert the personality of renascent Egypt in the Eastern world.

Nevertheless, at the end of the period now being studied, Achaemenian art, even if it was essentially an aulic product like those which preceded it, aimed at being, through the deliberate will of its inventors, a mixture of the best of all the achievements of those peoples reduced to satrapies of the new state. In order to produce this imperial art, the Persian architects, as Darius relates in his dedicatory inscription in his palace at Susa, recruited Medes, Egyptians and Ionians, whom they set to work under their direction. But the Persian empire collapsed at the battle of Issus, and Hellenistic art took the place of Achaemenian in this attempt to unify the arts of the Near East.

The development of Egyptian taste in the New Kingdom

There are no remains of Hyksos monuments in Egypt, at least not in the Delta where they settled—if, indeed, these conquerors from Asia ever built any. It is possible that the Egyptians, after having driven out the Hyksos, devoted themselves to removing every trace of the hated domination. It may also be that the choice of sites for excavation has not yet fallen on the right places.

The expulsion of the Hyksos opened up for Egypt a new era, fertile in every field. At first nothing was changed in the artistic heritage from the Middle Kingdom, the tradition of which was preserved at Thebes, the capital of the weak kings of the XIIIth and XIVth Dynasties, vassals of the Hyksos. The resemblance between the works of this period and those of the XVIIIth Dynasty indicates that the divergence between them was not very great, except that the reviving power of the Theban monarchs restored to the arts the media they had lost. Instead of reproducing old stereotypes on used stones, the sculptors of the beginning of the XVIIIth Dynasty used handsome new stone for their stelae and recaptured the tone of the best works of the XIIth Dynasty. The same held good for sculpture in the round: the statuette of Tuthmosis III offering vessels of wine and the colossal group of Amenhotep III and Queen Tiy, from Medinet Habu, gave fresh vigour to the best traditions of the Middle Kingdom.

The consequences of the campaigns conducted in Asia by the first pharaohs of the XVIIIth Dynasty soon made themselves felt and effected a fundamental change in Egyptian aesthetics. The paintings of the time of Tuthmosis III—the ones in the tomb of Rekhmire, for example —exhibit a simplicity of taste which shows that they are still linked with the Middle Kingdom. But under Tuthmosis IV a new tendency appeared in funerary painting (which was always rather behind lay art) and flowered during the reign of Amenhotep III. There was a change of costume: abandoning the simple loin-cloth for men and the tight sheath for women, the Egyptians henceforth were draped in long veils of pleated muslin, whose transparency on the skin caused shadings from which the artists extracted new effects. The tributes of gold from Asia had enriched the whole country, from the royal treasury to the lowest officials. In this society, which still was ignorant of money, the precious metal was preserved in jewellery and other goldsmiths' work. A new type of ornamentation, with wealth as its keynote, served as a framework for Egyptian life.

In this atmosphere of opulence taste grew more refined. The austere strength of the art of the Old Kingdom, with the art of the Middle Kingdom as its academic phase, was regarded as a kind of antiquated simplicity and even poverty. The concept of physical beauty appeared. Admittedly there had been representations of women of great grace and purity, especially in the Old and Middle Kingdoms. But they were effects which were not consciously sought for. As from the middle of the XVIIIth Dynasty, however, beauty was cultivated for its own sake. It became the supreme ideal and rule of Egyptian art. Naturally its highest achievements were in the representation of women, whose charm was now communicated down to the slightest details. In its early phases Egyptian art had been a masculine art, so much so that a face detached from a statue or a relief always gave the impression of being a man's. As from the middle of the XVIIIth Dynasty the contrary was true: any face taken separately would have passed for that of a woman. The art of the New Kingdom was a feminine art.

This did not harm the grandiose creations of architecture in any way. No complete temple of any size dating from before the New Kingdom has survived in Egypt. It is impossible to attribute this total disappearance to the depredations of the Hyksos, particularly in the south of Egypt where their domination never seems to have been effective. It is more reasonable to suppose that the weak Theban kings had let these edifices, whose upkeep was too costly, fall into ruins. When the liberation came, all the temples in Egypt had to be reconstructed.

Egyptian art of the XVIIIth Dynasty

The pharaohs of the XVIIIth Dynasty tackled this task to the best of their ability. In the first place they wished to thank the national divinities whose assistance had enabled the head of the dynasty to eject the foreigners from Egypt and who were to continue to give his successors victory in their Asiatic campaigns which were an extension of the eviction of the Hyksos. The pharaohs also wished to ensure their authority in the eyes of a deeply religious people by demonstrating their piety. Nevertheless, these temples also suffered almost complete destruction. A thousand years later, the Persian invasion had the same disastrous consequences for the Egyptian temples as had the inroads of the Hyksos. Like the kings of the XVIIIth

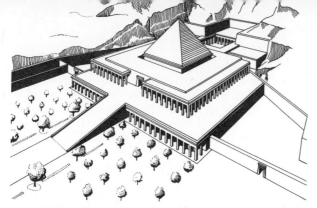

209. EGYPTIAN. Reconstruction of the funerary temple of Nebhepetre Mentuhotep.

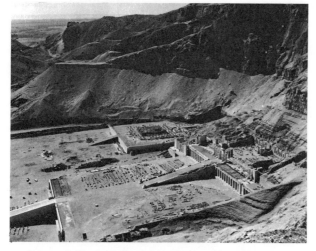

210. View of the temple of Queen Hatshepsut, at Deir el Bahari. XVIIIth Dynasty.

Dynasty, the Ptolemies pulled down what remained of the ancient sanctuaries in order to replace them with new ones. Fortunately, except for minor repairs, they did not touch the religious edifices of Thebes. The town, sacked in 663 B.C. by the troops of Assurbanipal, was never rebuilt; it no longer had any political importance. The Ptolemies were not interested in it. If they had followed the same programme of reconstruction as at Edfu or Denderah, the whole architectural past of Karnak and Luxor would have been wiped out. Today we would only know the art of the builders of the New Kingdom by ruins—imposing enough in themselves it is true—of the funerary temples of the kings and by a few forgotten edifices in distant Nubia.

In the form it took in the XVIIIth Dynasty—and nothing entitles us to believe that it was not in pursuance of a more ancient tradition—the Egyptian temple was a rectangular edifice with a flat roof and sloping walls with no outside openings. In front of the building there were two tall pylons, between which was a monumental entrance gate whose gorge was occupied by a gigantic image of the winged solar disc. Once past this gate, the worshipper was in a court with porticoes. This was the public part of the temple. The secret part of the temple, which could only be entered by the officiating priests, began at the end of this court. It consisted of a hypostyle hall, then a vestibule, and, at the far end, a sanctuary which contained the ritual image of the god. First built of limestone, as in the Middle Kingdom, then, as from the time of Tuthmosis III, more often of Nubian sandstone, the Egyptian temples were decorated with bas-reliefs both inside and outside. In the public part and on the outsides of the walls the decoration of the temple took as themes the great

military achievements of the king who built it, the panegyrics peculiar to the temple and scenes of adoration before its divinities; inside the secret part each room was decorated with scenes of the ceremonies which were practised in them. Daylight, which fell from lofty bays fitted with stone screens or from holes in the ceilings, was regulated so as to produce an impression of growing mystery. It became more and more subdued as one advanced into the temple until it changed to pitch darkness in the sanctuary, where lamps had to be lit to celebrate the service.

This was the simple schema recurring in the additions to the main building which, two hundred years after the beginning of the XVIIIth Dynasty, had already made Karnak a colossal huddle of a temple, difficult to understand at first sight. In contrast with this plan, which was complicated by additions, that of the temple at Luxor, the southern part of which was built at one time by Amenhotep III, is balanced and lucid. Another famous achievement of the architects of the early XVIIIth Dynasty was the funerary temple of Queen Hatshepsut, at Deir el   210
Bahari, built at the foot of the gigantic desert cliff on to which it is joined; access to the sanctuary carved out of the cliff is through three courts on different levels, lined with colonnades. No other temple in Egypt exhibits such a plan; the architect was Senenmut, partisan and favourite of the queen.

In the Old Kingdom the funerary temples of the kings were placed with their backs adjoining the eastern sides of the pyramids in which the monarchs were buried. At the beginning of the XVIIIth Dynasty, separation had already taken place. The bodies of the kings all reposed in rock-cut tombs on both sides of a valley, the famous Valley of the Kings, which penetrated into the mountainous part of the desert on the west side of the Nile facing Luxor. It was dominated by a peak which rose 900 feet above the plain and gave the impression of a natural pyramid. Separated from the Valley of the Kings by the screen of a rocky chain, the royal funerary temples, most of them destroyed today, were aligned facing west on the desert platform which bordered on the cultivated countryside. The reorganisation of the old institution of the royal necropolis left the siting of private individuals' tombs free of rules. They were concentrated in those free places left from which there was a view of the funerary temple of the king. At that time they consisted of a chapel carved out of the rock, which gave on to an open-air court at the end, preceded by a small pylon of sun-dried brick. The flat roof which covered the chapel was generally crowned with a small pyramid of the same material.

It was in the ornamentation of this architectural framework that the new taste which we have mentioned made itself felt, timidly at first, but eventually becoming completely dominant. At first the auxiliary features of the architecture remain the same as those used in the Middle Kingdom, in particular the square pillar and the faceted 'proto-Doric' column. But Amenhotep III favoured the   257
clustered papyrus column; he enlarged this until it was of truly colossal dimensions and used it almost exclusively in his temple at Luxor. The effect is both grandiose and incomparably elegant.

The bas-reliefs of the royal temples, designed after traditional models, at first only reflected the new aesthetic in the elegance of the shapes and the preoccupation with

137

charm. The decoration of private tombs followed quite a different course. In them, fashionable costumes and hair styles, rich jewellery, bouquets of plants often acclimatised from Asia, gardens lined with marshes teeming with birds—the whole of that world which ancient art had transported rather than represented—appeared, especially in the growing number of chapels in which painting was substituted for bas-relief as being cheaper and more flexible. A number of *ostraka,* or potsherds, of this epoch have been found on which the artists have made sketches from life with wonderful skill and a keen sense of humour.

New types of statuary appeared with the changing circumstances. First came the kneeling man holding a stele in front of him on which a hymn to the rising sun was engraved. Statues of this kind were placed facing east in niches cut in the sides of the pyramids of sun-dried brick which surmounted the funerary chapels. There was also the crouching man wrapped in his cloak, the blockstatue and the kneeling or upright personage who clasped either an effigy of the divinity or a ritual object. Such statues were placed in the temples. In fact, after the disappearance of the royal necropolises with their services of offerings for the benefit of those admitted to them, the pharaohs had to find another means of guaranteeing their courtiers the subsistence due to them in the hereafter. This was done by authorising them to place in the temples of certain divinities a statue before which a daily offering was made of an agreed portion of the remnants from the royal altar. At the same time these figures, kneeling or wrapped in their cloaks as if in meditation, which occupied the porticoes of the temple and the bays of the hypostyle hall, constituted for the god a court in perpetual adoration—in that silent contemplation which was the ideal of Egyptian piety.

Although former epochs may have known colossal statues, these were never, it seems, used as frequently as in the New Kingdom. The extraordinary dimensions of the new temples demanded them. The most celebrated of these colossi are those of Memnon, which still tower over the Theban plain with the 58 feet remaining to them now that their crowns have fallen. In their time they ornamented the pylon which Amenhotep III had built in front of his funerary temple, which has now disappeared. In works of this size the subtleties of the new taste are not noticeable, not even in the official statuary which conformed to the rules of traditional protocol. The masterpieces—the statue of Tuthmosis III from Karnak, in schist, with the profile which is both so fine and so imperious, and the impressive statue of Amenhotep, son of Hapu, as an old man, among others—only allow a glimpse of the new style. But in lay sculpture, in particular in the small wooden statuary intended to decorate houses and in the trinkets, of which the toilet accessories—jewel boxes, and ointment boxes such as those of the 'swimmer' type—provide the most beautiful specimens, the new taste inspired the most exquisite creations.

Babylon, the Hittite confederation and Mitanni

While Egyptian art was experiencing this revival as a consequence of the expulsion of the Hyksos, the art of Asia Minor, whose countries had not experienced similar vicissitudes, was fairly static. Old Sumerian art had, throughout the basin of the Tigris and the Euphrates and in the neighbouring countries, sunk roots so deep that in spite of the arrival of new political powers the old themes continued to be used.

Even at Babylon, where two hundred years earlier a Kassite dynasty had implanted itself, artistic production was, it seems, scanty and rarely surpassed the mediocre. Mesopotamian art of this epoch was primarily represented by the *kudurru.* These were natural blocks of hard stone,

211, 280

212

213
215

208

216

211. Fowling in the Marshes. Tomb of Nakht at Thebes. Mural. XVIIIth Dynasty.

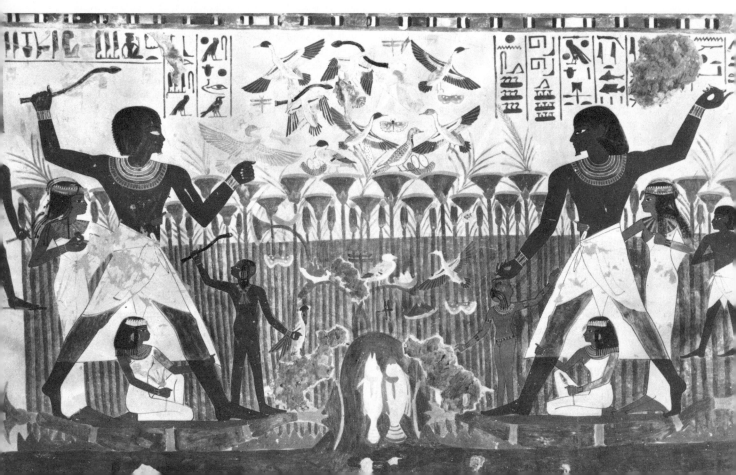

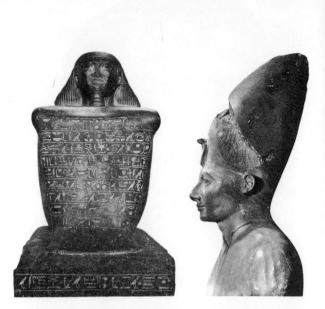

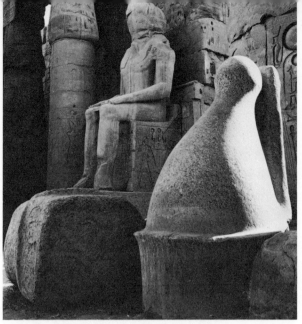

212. EGYPTIAN. Block-statue of Senenmut. *British Museum*.

213. Profile of statue of Tuthmosis III. Schist. XVIIIth Dynasty. *Cairo Museum*.

214. Colossal statue of Ramesses II at Luxor.

215. Statue of Amenhotep, son of Hapu, in his old age. Black granite. XVIIIth Dynasty. *Cairo Museum*.

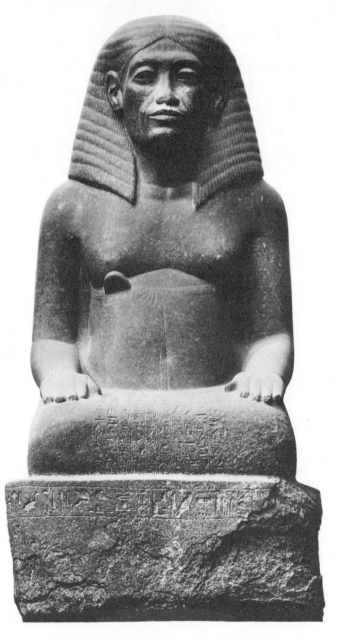

often given an imperfectly regular shape, which bore as decoration texts in cuneiform of the donations of land made to the temples by the kings and also bore images of the divinities standing as guarantors and protectors of the undertaking. This sort of carved 'boundary stone' was placed in the temples, on benches which ran the length of the sanctuary walls. The style of their carvings is clearly defined and is noble but uninspired. Together with the glyptics of the same period, the *kudurru* show Babylonian art as restricted and never inspired by everyday life. They also indicate—by the rarity of their representation —the repulsion the Semites felt for the nude and the low esteem in which they held women. What remains of the brick temples of this period are long halls, necessarily narrow to admit of roofing without the help of columns, which the Babylonians did not use. The façades exhibit a decoration of moulded bricks, such as that of the temple at Warka (ancient Erech) reconstructed in the Baghdad Museum. On it, in the steps which served as niches, divinities hold vases, spouting water, against their chests. This method of decoration, common at this epoch in the Babylonian sphere of influence, recurs at Susa, from where the Louvre possesses bas-reliefs in the same technique. Before the idea of glazing these bricks occurred, this was the germ of what was later to become the decoration of the Assyrian palaces, and, at Babylon itself, of the Ishtar Gate.

276

While the Sumerian tradition was more or less static at Babylon and in its feudal regions and was taking a more original turn in Elam, a new art grew in Anatolia in the service of the dynasties of the great Hittite confederation. Compared with the arts of Egypt and Babylonia, this art may seem crude and even barbarous, but, diffused by the extension of the Hittite power, it was to act as leaven to all the arts of the Asiatic Near East. The apogee of Hittite art, born of the transformation of Sumerian art under Asiatic influence, was to be in the second half of the 2nd millennium, with the monuments of Boghazkoy, Yazilikaya and Alaca Huyuk in Asia Minor, and, in northern Syria, with the earliest sculptures excavated at Malatya, Carchemish and Sinjerli. It was a coherent art which demonstrated its unity in its choice of themes and

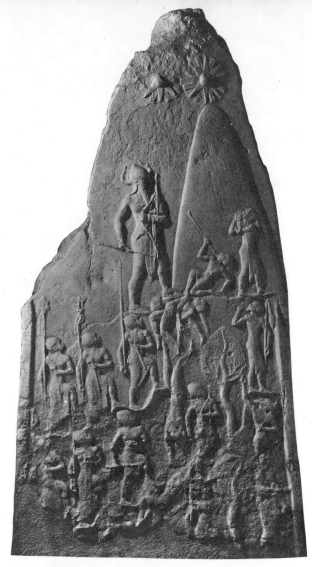

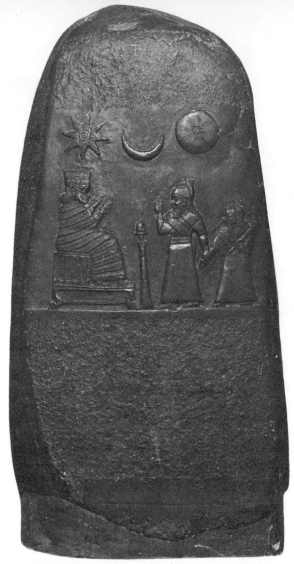

216. KASSITE. *Kudurru* with bas-relief depicting King Melishipak II presenting his daughter to the goddess Nanai. End of the 2nd millennium. *Louvre.*

217. Stele of Victory of Naram Sin. Middle of the 3rd millennium. *Louvre.*

its way of treating figures. The Anatolian school, closer to the Aegean, excelled more in the naturalness and elegance of attitudes; the art of northern Syria was influenced more by Mesopotamia.

What is known of Hittite art, apart from the rock sculptures for which they seemed to have a predilection, is mainly represented by the sculptures on ogival gates embedded in the cyclopean ramparts of the towns, and by the smallish upright slabs (orthostats) which adorned the bases of the walls of the halls and corridors of palaces. The gates have yielded lions and sphinxes in the round, at least as regards their forequarters which supported the posts; the orthostats are bas-reliefs showing kings, divinities, religious and military processions, chimaeras, bulls facing the sacred tree and war, hunting and banquet scenes. Stone bases covered with bas-reliefs or carved in the form of animals must have supported wooden columns. The art of which the majority of these works provide evidence is in no way comparable with the refined and united arts of Egypt and Mesopotamia. It reflects the political decentralisation which was characteristic of the Hittite confederation. In each centre, however unimportant, the different influences made themselves felt to a varying degree. At first, until they formed a school, the locally recruited artists were probably no more than craftsmen, skilful at making jewellery or furniture, who had been promoted to the role of palace decorators. They

did their best, if it was clumsy, to accomplish a task which was above their capacities. Compared with the sculpture of Egypt and Mesopotamia, these works often produce, unless they are of the very first order, the impression of figures clumsily executed by school children. Nevertheless, here and there they show proof of a force of personality and an acute sense of animal art which excuses their lack of refinement. Sometimes—and this is the case with the so-called 'king' (in reality the god Teshub) from the gate of Boghazkoy—they attain an evocative power and a technical perfection which, had it been general, would have made Hittite art the most expressive of all the arts of the ancient East.

Hittite influence was mainly spread at the end of the 15th and during the 14th centuries B.C. through the intermediary of Mitanni. This ephemeral state, which for a century and a half united Mesopotamia north of Babylon and northern Syria as far as the Orontes, was responsible for an important stage in the production of art for this area. It gave permanence to and amalgamated, in its palaces—of which, incidentally, little remains—the various artistic currents circulating in its mixed population, and thus opened the way for the synthesis which Assyrian art formed after it. In the carvings of the tablets from Nuzi, which derive largely from Mitannian art, a certain Egyptian influence, undoubtedly transmitted by the Phoenicians, is shown by the presence of the winged disc.

The Minoan influence came through in the frescoes of the palace at Nuzi and in the ceramics discovered there. It is undoubtedly to this pottery, brought to Egypt on the occasion of the marriages of the Mitannian princesses with the pharaohs of the middle of the XVIIIth Dynasty, that we owe the reproduction of Mitannian motifs on the ceilings of certain Theban tombs of that epoch.

The artistic revolution of Akhenaten and the end of the XVIIIth Dynasty

The new taste which appeared in Egypt towards the middle of the XVIIIth Dynasty had scarcely begun to infiltrate the country's official art when political events gave the movement a sudden impetus.

From the beginning of his reign, Amenhotep IV, who as soon as he was crowned changed his name to Akhenaten, made no secret of his reforming intentions. A convinced monotheist, he meant, by the suppression of all other cults, to restore religion to solar monotheism, of which the dogma of Heliopolis seemed to him the most ancient form and therefore the purest. He proscribed all the other gods, particularly Amon, the Theban god, whose name he had chiselled off the monuments. In the field of art he rejected the official mannerism—which hardly ever represented people except as young and beautiful—in favour of truth and sincerity. Setting an example, having even abandoned Thebes to transfer his court to Tell el Amarna, he had built, to the east of the temple of Amon at Karnak, an open-air esplanade for the new religion; in front of each of the square pillars of the outer porticoes 219 of this edifice is carved a colossal king depicted according to the new conceptions. This was the sign manual of what was henceforth to be official art. Not only did Akhenaten's physical blemishes appear in his portraits, but they were emphasised with a cruelty which could be called 220 caricature if the works themselves were not profoundly serious.

At the same time, while proclaiming himself the only son and prophet of the one divinity, Akhenaten demanded, in the name of the same principle of sincerity, that he be represented in the common acts of life in which, out of respect, there had been no question until then of showing kings: taking his meals in the privacy of the family circle; embracing his wife Nofretete; playing with his children. The idyllic charm of scenes of this type should not make us forget their revolutionary intention.

This ultra-realistic art, commanded and controlled by the king (some bas-reliefs show him visiting the sculptors' workshops, in company with his queen), was at its strictest at the time of the court's installation at Tell el Amarna in the sixth year of the reign. It was the art of the royal monuments, of stelae erected on the boundaries of the new capital and of tombs prepared for high officials in the desert near el Amarna.

But even for a ruler as determined as Akhenaten, it was impossible to stem the rising tide of a whole people's taste for charm. Docile at first, the artists of el Amarba rapidly modified of their own accord the extravagances imposed by the reform. They retained scarcely more than its general characteristics: the excessively tall and thin necks and the exaggeratedly elongated heads. Having made this sacrifice, they felt that they had complied with the king's demands. The pieces found in the workshops of the city, abruptly abandoned with the sudden death of

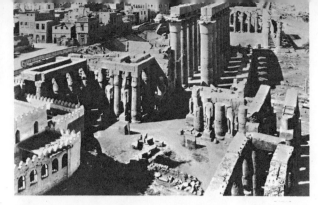

218. View of Luxor.

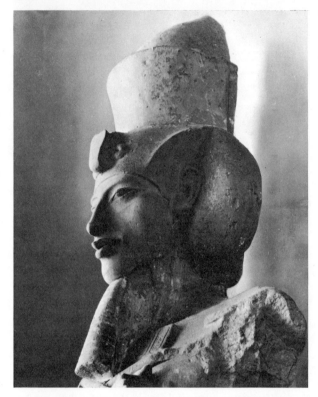

219. Colossal head of Akhenaten, found at Karnak. XVIIIth Dynasty. *Egyptian Museum, Cairo.*

220. EGYPTIAN. Akhenaten seated on a chair beneath the sun disc. *British Museum.*

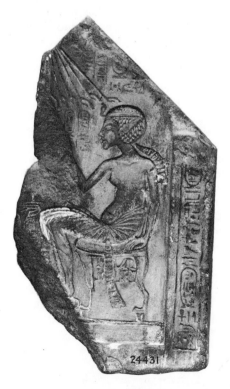

24431

141

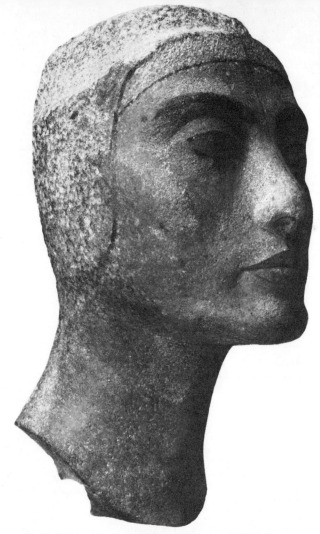

221. Unfinished portrait of Queen Nofretete. XVIIIth Dynasty. *Egyptian Museum, Cairo.*

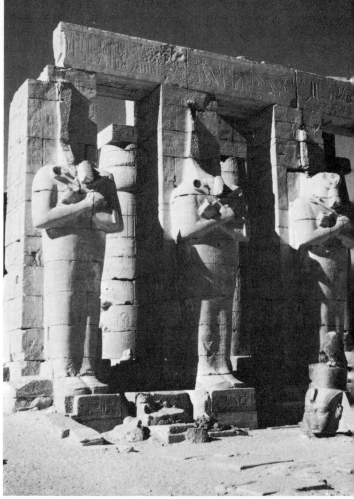

222. The Ramesseum, funerary temple of Ramesses II, at Thebes. XIXth Dynasty.

Akhenaten and the return of Tutankhamen to Thebes, are evidence of the failure of the king's original intentions in the field of art. In the famous bust of Queen Nofretete in the Berlin Museum, and also in the unfinished head of 221 the same queen, done in crystalline orange-coloured sandstone, in the Cairo Museum, the radiant and subtle charm predominates. Even in the limestone bust of Akhenaten himself, in the Louvre, we are far from the confession of human imperfection which the pharaoh had wanted the portraiture of his time to make.

Also, although Egypt was then more avid for novelty than was the rest of the Near East, artistic circles there were not really capable of creating the free and sincere art which Akhenaten expected of them. Relying, until then, on traditional schemas and canons, and using such skill as they possessed to adapt these to the tastes of the royal court, the majority of the artists of el Amarna were at a loss under Akhenaten's régime, especially when it came to human representation. We can see the proof of this in the extreme rarity of lay statues, of which only two examples have so far been found. The high dignitaries had no desire to have themselves portrayed according to the new principles, nor did the artists show any anxiety to portray them. The only human types who were carefully studied, by order, in the sculptors' workshops were those of the royal family: Akhenaten, Nofretete and the little princesses. These studies were intended for the royal monuments and were also intended to meet the many orders for statuettes which the lords of the régime ranged in their houses in honour of the royal

family and as a form of flattery. Thus when it came to representing private individuals—mainly in the bas-reliefs of their tombs—it was found simplest to apply the king's conventions to them: pointed heads, exaggerated necks, swollen stomachs, frail limbs. At all epochs, the representation of the sovereign influenced that of private individuals. This custom flourished more than ever during the royal court's twelve-year stay at el Amarna.

Nevertheless we should not think that his twelve-year period in the history of Egyptian art was an episode without a future, for it broke away from the rigid and stultifying conventions of official art. The best achievements of the next epoch were only possible because el Amarna had opened up the road. The carved reliefs on the pylons of Ramesses II's temple at Luxor and of the Ramesseum at Thebes resembled the decorations of certain tombs at el Amarna, where each wall was conceived as a large picture and the use of superimposed bands to break up the composition was only subsidiary. The powerful Ramesside columns were the heritage of the stocky 222 column of el Amarna, itself a transformation of the clustered column of Amenhotep III, given a more massive outward curve to balance the lightness of the surrounding decoration with its heaviness. Lastly, in painting, the palaces at el Amarna gave artists the chance to surpass themselves in modernity. If we admit that the painted stucco pavement of the main palace, discovered as long ago as 1891 by Sir Flinders Petrie, is a masterpiece, with its representation of a pool surrounded by clumps of flowers in which birds are sporting and calves are gambolling,

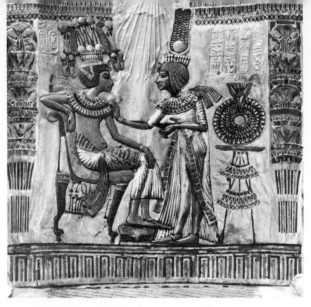

223. Back of the small throne of Tutankhamen, glazed in brilliant colours. XVIIIth Dynasty. *Egyptian Museum, Cairo.*

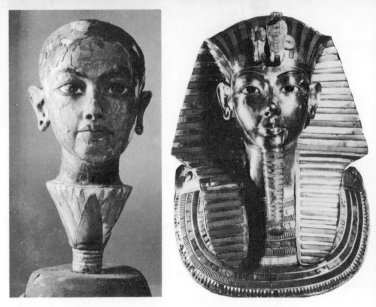

224. *Above.* EGYPTIAN. The young Tutankhamen. XVIIIth Dynasty. *Egyptian Museum, Cairo.*

225. *Right.* EGYPTIAN. Gold mask of Tutankhamen. XVIIIth Dynasty. *Egyptian Museum, Cairo.*

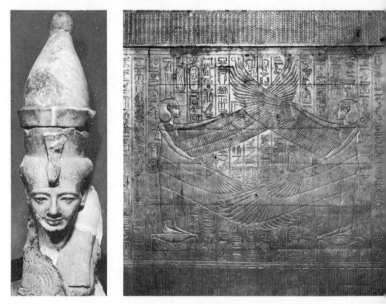

226. Head of a colossal statue of the goddess Mut. XVIIIth Dynasty. *Egyptian Museum, Cairo.*

227. Sarcophagus of Tutankhamen (detail). XVIIIth Dynasty.

284 what are we to say of the frescoes of the Green Room in the North Palace, excavated in 1924 by Francis Newton? The luxuriance of the papyrus thicket full of beautiful birds and brightened up here and there by blue lotuses is spellbinding, and its composition is an example of the highest art.

The return to Thebes of Tutankhamen and his reconciliation with the clergy of Amon resulted in the resumption of the artistic tradition broken by Akhenaten. There is no doubt that such was the young king's intention. The statues he consecrated at Karnak to commemorate the return, which portray him in the costume of the high priest of Amon, presented by the god as his beloved son and head of his cult, are of the strictest classicism. But taste had developed conspiciously since the time of the rupture. The incomparable treasure found intact in the tomb of Tutankhamen includes some pieces made at el Amarna during the king's childhood. Some of them, such as the great throne, bear the image and the legends of the heretical god; the Theban clergy who controlled the funeral ceremony evidently did not take exception to them. Other pieces inspired by el Amarna, such as the big chest with plaques of ivory, with its charming scenes of conjugal intimacy, have simply had their inscriptions modified slightly. In fact, the art of el Amarna, freed of the extravagances demanded by Akhenaten, was the art of the day. One of the most orthodox objects, the Canopic chest, owes the grace of the goddesses surrounding it to el Amarna. We should also credit the legacy of el Amarna with the dreamy and rather melancholy sweetness which we find in the statues of Tutankhamen coming from the Theban workshops after the return to the capital.

The melancholy expression in the portraits of kings during and after the Amarna period disappeared with the advent of Harmais, whose art utterly rejected the morbid stylisation imposed by Akhenaten. Let us take in particular the face of the colossal statue of the goddess 226 Mut. This face has a charming and healthy realism with its sweet, slightly mocking smile and its dreamy eyes. We can imagine that the artist was really happy to feel himself free from the evil spells of el Amarna.

Egyptian art of the XIXth Dynasty

In order to appreciate the difference which separates the arts of the XVIIIth and XIXth Dynasties, we have only to compare the court added by Ramesses II to the temple of Luxor with the court of Amenhotep III.

In the latter the predominance of vertical lines in the clustered columns produces, in comparison with the rest of Egyptian art, something like the impression made by the pointed arch in Western art. In contrast with them, the heavy columns of the court of Ramesses II, with smooth shafts covered with inscriptions and pictures and with the intercolumniations filled with upright colossi, seem like a pompous demonstration of power. This style, which stems from the architectural creations of el Amarna, had, in a lighter form, already been used by Seti I in his funerary temple at Abydos. But there the delicacy of the bas-reliefs on the columns lent a certain grace, where excess could have left an impression of affectation.

On the columns in his own court, Ramesses II applied a decoration which reinforced its opulence. In order to speed up the restoration of all the temples in the country after their abandonment during the el Amarna episode,

143

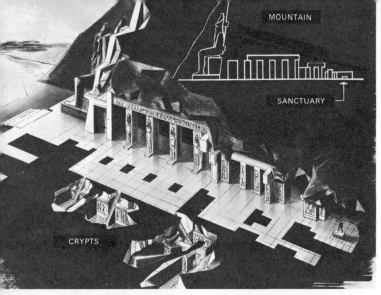

MOUNTAIN

SANCTUARY

CRYPTS

228. Plan and section of the temple at Abu Simbel.

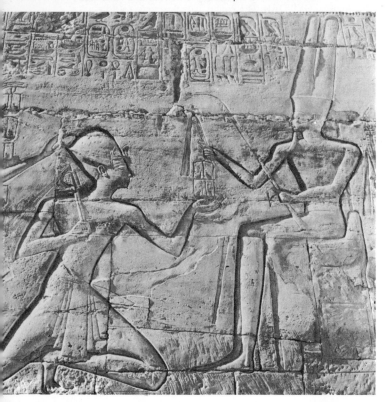

229. Ramesses II before Amon, replacing a bas-relief usurped by Seti I. XIXth Dynasty.

230. EGYPTIAN Diorite statue of Ramesses II. XIXth Dynasty. *Turin Museum*.

he used everything which was still serviceable: columns, lintels, architraves and, especially, the colossi of his predecessors, substituting his own name for theirs. He hoped to protect his own memory from similar usurpations in the future by inaugurating a way of engraving hieroglyphics deeply enough to discourage the slightest desire to erase them. Filled with shadow in this way, which silhouetted its signs in black, hieroglyphic writing, ornamental in itself, became an increasingly important element in Ramesside decoration. The bas-reliefs of the heavy walls were adapted to this style. The scenes, covered with inscriptions, were kept from appearing heavy by the adoption of even taller and slimmer human body forms. Aridity was avoided through a profusion of picturesque details—draped clothes, ribbons flying in the wind and an abundance of flowers—which give the whole a rich and crowded aspect. This was the grandiose style which Ramesses II used for the execution of various monuments of which the principal edifices still extant are the first court and the pylon at Luxor, the hypostyle hall at Karnak, the Ramesseum and the rock temple of Abu Simbel. The most astonishing of all is undeniably   228 the hypostyle hall at Karnak, with which the king filled the space between the pylon recently built by Harmais and the pylon of Amenhotep III. It is a vast edifice, some 380 feet broad by about 180 feet deep, with a central walk whose roof is supported by a double row of columns, 69 feet high and 12 feet in diameter. On either side of this central avenue, into which the light fell through openings placed just below the ceiling, are two side avenues, somewhat lower than 36 feet, each one having sixty-two columns. Those of the central avenue have capitals representing open papyrus umbels; the shorter ones, of the side avenues, have capitals of closed papyrus buds. The effect sought was not so much that of a genuine hall which could never be embraced in its entirety by the eye, as that of an immense and mysterious papyrus thicket. It was the translation into colossal architecture of the little Green Room of the North Palace at el Amarna.

Ramesses II usurped so many of his predecessors' statues that his iconography is rather bewildering to establish at first sight. The most genuine piece in this respect seems to be the alabaster statue in the Turin   230 Museum. Recently it has been suggested that this was a portrait of Seti I appropriated by his son; however this is by no means certain, and we must await more convincing proof than facial resemblance before questioning the evidence of the inscriptions and accessory figures, which do not appear to have been added later. The king, whose energetic features, softened to meet contemporary taste, are sculptured here by a master hand, is represented clothed in ample draperies of pleated fabrics and is wearing sandals. This had been the normal costume in Egypt since the time of Tuthmosis III, but while the fashion had advanced rapidly in private statuary, royal statuary had not accepted it at first. The official artists continued to represent kings in the simple garb of the pharaohs of the Old Kingdom and possibly of an even earlier epoch. Once again it was Akhenaten who, here as elsewhere, rejected tradition and had himself represented, in the name of sincerity, in his everyday clothes, like his subjects. This triumph of realism was to be lasting. In the bas-reliefs of the Ramesside temples, the kings appearing in public, whether going to war or to the temple or officiating in their public capacities, were henceforth depicted in long garments. Only in the interior of the sanctuary, where this costume undoubtedly had remained obligatory by tradition, were they depicted wearing the short, ancient loin-cloth.

The tradition of charm, to which this statue of Ramesses II testifies, must have remained dear to the artists of the following reigns. The pink granite sarcophagus which was sculptured for Merenptah but left unused by him and employed later by Psusennes, stems from this tradition. The gentle expression of Merenptah, successor to Ramesses II, whose head is surrounded by the protective arms of Isis, still retains the qualities of the best sculptures of Seti I, whose likeness it perpetuates.

The impetus given by the artists of the XVIIIth Dynasty survived in the painted tombs of the Theban necropolis, but it was slowly dying out. Scenes from everyday life became rarer and less rich in original and enjoyable observation. A wave of prurience suppressed the representations of dancing girls previously so highly prized, and artists even went so far in a tomb of the XVIIIth Dynasty (used again in the XIXth) as to dress those girls who were too naked. Religious scenes tended to predominate, and there was a new and pompous classicism, as in the official art of the temples. Far away from the Theban priesthood a different tradition seems to have been perpetuated in the necropolis of Memphis. The bas-reliefs from the funerary chapels of Sakkara are good examples. The influence of el Amarna made itself felt there longer, with its small figures, its freedom of movement, and its scenes from everyday life.

The decline of the Hittites; Phoenician eclecticism

During the 13th century B.C., the Hittite confederation halted the warlike expansion of Egypt by signing a peace treaty with Ramesses II and sealing this by giving him in marriage a daughter of the Boghazkoy dynasty. The building and decoration of palaces continued in Anatolia at Arslantepe and Malatya, and, in northern Syria, at Sinjerli and Carchemish. The art of this epoch, however, had lost much of the brutality which had stamped its earlier achievements with personality. It lapsed into the hackneyed, except for some exceptional works such as the basalt statue, found at Carchemish, of a bearded god holding a mace and a double-headed axe, seated on a throne supported by two roaring lions. The effect of formidable power is striking.

268

The Anatolian centre of the Hittite confederation was destroyed by the invasion of the Peoples of the Sea whom Ramesses II had halted at the gates of Egypt in 1191. But the Hittites, although weakened, maintained their political cohesion in the north of Syria and Canaan. Carchemish became their capital. In that town, in Sinjerli and in other feudal towns the sculpture attributable to the times demonstrates a progressive watering down of the once-vigorous national art, and a tendency to imitate Assyrian art baldly without so much as reforming its clumsiness of expression. This was the case at Tell Halaf, where the earliest sculptures, akin to Mitannian art, are crude but powerful and show an exaggeration of the ethnic type. The procedure, more obvious there than elsewhere, of breaking up the flat outlines of the figures in relief by a kind of champlevé and by engraving on them the internal details, adds further to the rustic

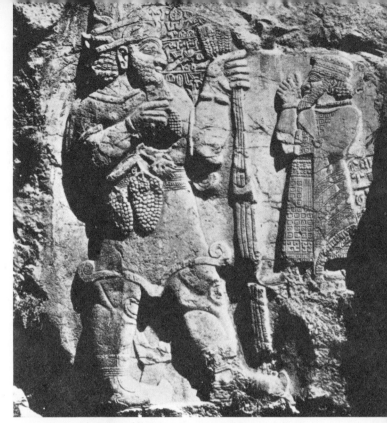

231. SYRO-HITTITE. King Warpalawa worshipping the god of vegetation. Bas-relief from Ivriz. (*After* Le Monde des Hittites, *Editions Correa*.)

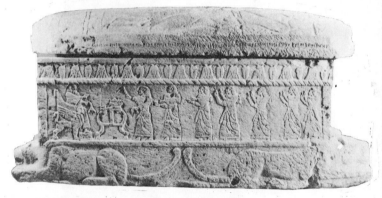

232. PHOENICIAN. The sarcophagus of Ahiram, king of Byblos. 2nd millennium. *Beirut Museum*.

effect of these works, whose barbarous aesthetic recalls that of the Luristan bronzes. In its decline, Hittite art could still produce powerful works such as the rock relief at Ivriz, beyond the Taurus, whose god, having the 231 colossal stature of 16 feet, bears grapes and grain and is of a spellbinding truculence. Like all the arts in the ancient East, Hittite art was bound up with the fortunes of political power and could not decrease and disappear with them. This is what must have happened in 717 B.C., when Carchemish was taken by the Assyrians.

For their part, the peoples of the eastern coast of the Mediterranean were never sufficiently strong to form themselves into kingdoms independent and lasting enough to establish a clearly defined artistic style in the service of the royal courts, which would have controlled its homogeneity and given it permanence. Situated at the point where three civilisations—Egyptian, Mesopotamian and Aegean—met, the eastern Mediterranean peoples felt the influences of those empires as circumstances or—since they, especially the Phoenicians, were traders—the taste of their current customers willed it.

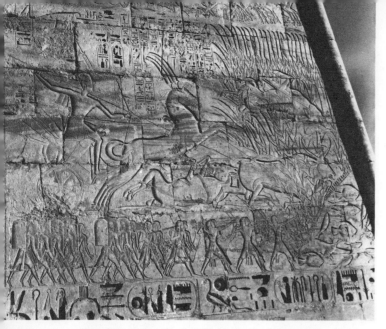

233. Bull hunt at Medinet Habu. Bas-relief on the first pylon of the temple. Time of Ramesses III, XXth Dynasty.

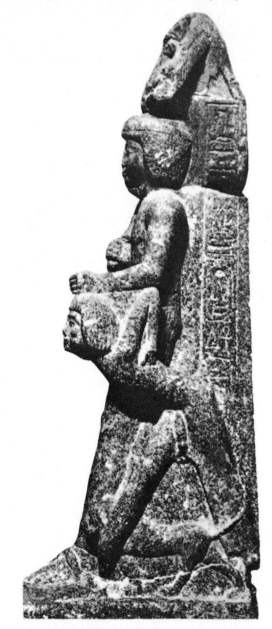

234. EGYPTIAN. Triumphal statue of Ramesses IV in granite. *Cairo Museum*.

At the beginning of history Phoenicia, in which Byblos formed an Egyptian protectorate, had adopted the art of the Nile valley wholesale, its workshops copying Egyptian models slavishly, although with a faint exotic note. When they became more autonomous, the Phoenician towns managed to slacken the Egyptian influence, but without ever completely freeing themselves of it. Their divinities in bronze or bas-relief, however pronounced their Semitic type in other ways, always preserved the short garment of the Egyptian gods. But the most ancient monument of Phoenician art in the strict sense of the word, the sarcophagus of Ahiram, king of Byblos and 232 contemporary of Ramesses II, reflects the influence of Hittite art in the country. Its sides are decorated with scenes having originality but handled in the Egyptian manner of the king receiving the homage of his servants and female mourners. Below a frieze of alternating lotus buds and blossoms, the figures are dressed in the Egyptian fashion of the XIXth Dynasty. The corners of the sarcophagus rest on four lions, like those on the gate-posts of Hittite towns and palaces, their forequarters projecting in the round and the rest of the body in bas-relief.

In the 9th century the Phoenician ivories from the bed of Hazael (king of Damascus) discovered in the palace at Arslan Tash exhibit another mixture, which is also a reflection of the times. Some are frankly Egyptianised, composed of Egyptian elements used for their decorative value, to which are added the Assyrian shell-shaped wings and the exaggerated proportions of the heads of the goddesses, remains of the old Sumerian canon. Others show Egyptian griffons with rams' heads framing the Assyrian sacred tree, while still others are openly Assyrian in style. The same holds true for the gold and silver dishes of which the Phoenicians were always the great suppliers in the ancient East.

Among the last discoveries of C. Schaeffer at Ras Shamra are two panels which undoubtedly ornamented the foot of a couch; they are of a much earlier epoch, recalling the period of Akhenaten; Egyptian and Aegean influences dominate in them but are assimilated by the Phoenicians.

The XXth Egyptian Dynasty and the appearance of the Assyrians

The pharaohs of the XXth Dynasty maintained the traditions of the monarchs of the XIXth. The funerary temple of Ramesses III at Medinet Habu and the ones he had built at Karnak (the temple in the court of the great temple and the temple of Khons) are the masterpieces. They have an undeniable majesty, but the typical heaviness of the XIXth Dynasty monuments is accentuated in them. Deep inscriptions cover all the free surfaces and make them look something like a printed page, as in the second pylon at Medinet Habu. Within this heavy, cramping framework, the old Egyptian verve, revelling in the picturesque and in free detail, still comes through in places: for example, in the bull hunt—so full of movement 233 and sensitivity in the detail of the bulls dying in the midst of waving rushes—which is found on the back of the south wing of the first pylon at Medinet Habu; in the illustration of the victory of Ramesses III over the Peoples of the Sea on the northern façade of the same temple, which recalls the battle of Kadesh on the pylons of Luxor and the Ramesseum, from where it may possibly have drawn its inspiration. The royal statuary of the XXth Dynasty also developed towards the grandiose. We need only compare the triumphal granite statue of Ramesses IV with the statue of Tuthmosis III in schist, which we mentioned earlier. In the latter all is simplicity: the triumphal character is only indicated by the fact that Tuthmosis III is trampling underfoot nine bows, symbols of foreign countries; in the former statue the composition is frankly theatrical.

Private statuary of the same period is generally weak and impersonal, although still graceful. New types of sculpture, such as the granite statue in Cairo entitled Priest with Monkey, did appear from time to time.

In western Asia the outstanding event of this epoch was the appearance of Assyrian art with the growing power of Assur. At the beginning of history the art of this country was identical with Sumerian art, which was transformed later by that of Babylonia. Various influences met in this region and produced an art characterised by a general tendency towards greater simplicity and clarity in the Babylonian sense, in spite of some reversions to Sumerian complexity. The rare works of art of this epoch found on Assyrian soil are evidence of this evolution, which three centuries later was to result in the art of the time of Sargon and his successors.

Egyptian art in pre-Saite times

Nearly all the stone monuments of Egypt from the XXIst to the XXVth Dynasties have vanished today, no doubt because they were mainly built in the Delta, where the pharaohs of those dynasties established their residences. But recent finds are a warning that it would be rash to conclude that these four centuries were artistically barren. At Tanis, in the tombs of the sovereigns of the period, 235–237 treasures of goldsmiths' art have been unearthed whose beauty, richness and technical perfection are quite the equal of the wonders of the Tutankhamen finds. Moreover, the few extant works of art of this period support this evidence. The statuette nielloed with gold and silver of Queen Karomama, in the Louvre, or the one of the 238 Lady Takushit, a century later, show no signs of decadence in the modelling or the metalsmiths' work. The now isolated column of Taharka in the first court at Karnak bears witness to the elegance, boldness and polish of Egyptian architecture on the eve of the Assyrian invasion. Lastly, if the famous alabaster statue of the divine worshipper Ameneritis, in the Cairo Museum, is a little weak in 239 treatment, the statues of Mentuemhat, which we must link with this period because of their style, give an excellent idea of lay sculpture; one of the latter—of which only the bust remains, with its powerfully modelled face defying all the conventions of beauty—is a masterpiece worthy of the great periods of Egyptian art.

Before these discoveries at Tanis, scholars were prone to imagine that the art of the Saite epoch came about suddenly, as a reaction against the Assyrian domination, out of a desire to restore to Egypt the art of the age of the pyramids, free of all foreign influence. It was supposed to be an art which was both nationalistic and archaeological, but without genuine roots in the contemporary taste of the country. The finds at Tanis tend to modify this conception. The objects of art found in the royal burial places spring from two opposite tendencies. One of these is the Rameside tradition, with its richness of colouring, its

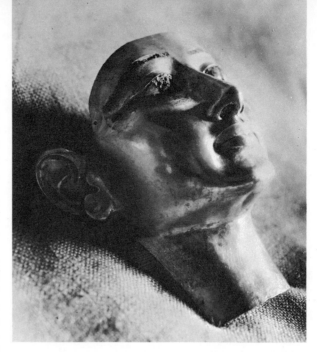

235. Gold mask of Undebunded, head of Psusennes' armies. XXIst Dynasty.

heavy shapes and its overloaded ornamentation; the other leans towards elegance and simplicity of line. The first was on the decrease; the second produced such works as the gold carafe from the tomb of Psusennes. It was the 236 beginning of the art known as Saite. In fact, the works we have just mentioned are more closely connected with the Saite than the Theban aesthetic. That is why they are rightly entitled 'pre-Saite'.

But this shows that Saite art, although circumstances made it reactionary and nationalistic, was nevertheless the product of a spontaneous purifying of Egyptian taste. The artistic flowering of the New Kingdom, in short, had been no more than an epiphenomenon in the general development of Egyptian art, a brilliant episode stimulated by military successes abroad, the ostentation of an opulent court and the rivalry created among the artists. But it had never completely satisfied the Egyptian people's innate taste for the pure, calm lines of which the monuments of the Old Kingdom, still standing at Memphis and in the Delta, were models. When the royal courts emigrated to the Delta, with the XXIst Dynasty, the Theban influence persisted for some time. Eventually,

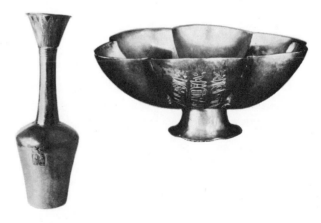

236. *Left*. Gold carafe belonging to Psusennes. XXIst Dynasty.

237. *Right*. EGYPTIAN. Gold cup given to Undebunded by Psusennes and the queen mother. XXIst Dynasty.

147

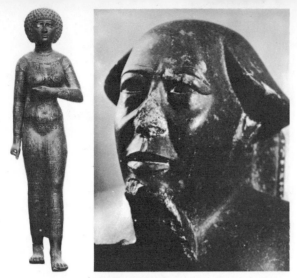

238. *Left*. EGYPTIAN. The Lady Takushit. Bronze statuette. XXVth Dynasty. *Athens Museum*.

239. *Right*. EGYPTIAN. Mentuemhat, prefect of Thebes. Pre-Saite period. *Egyptian Museum, Cairo*.

however, the forces of reaction were loosed. From the XXIst to the XXVth Dynasties they sapped the artistic heritage of Thebes, and slowly but surely they prepared the way for the advent of Saite art.

The apogee of Assyrian art and the neo-Babylonian succession

While Egypt, tired of the excesses and exaggerations of Theban art in its decline, was moving towards a renaissance, the growing Assyrian power had created a new artistic formula for building and decorating the palaces of its kings.

The oldest definitively established evidence of Assyrian art is the palace at Nimrud, built to the south of Nineveh and enlarged by the Assyrian kings of the 9th and 8th centuries, from Assurnasirpal to Tiglath Pileser III. As was usual in the art of western Asia, sculpture in the round continued to play a minor role. The rare examples unearthed appear to be products of the sculptor's assistant rather than the genuine artist. Fresco painting was known —black outlines heightened by a few colours—but surviving examples are very rare. On the other hand, the art of bas-relief can be seen at its best. Orthostats were used to ornament the long narrow halls opening on to an interior court which made up Assyrian palaces.

If this art (as we are entitled to believe) had precedents,

240. ASSYRIAN. Assurnasirpal hunting the lion from a chariot. Bas-relief. 9th century. *British Museum*.

they have not yet been discovered. Under Assurnasirpal, a very mature art developed in the palaces. We find winged bulls and roaring lions (akin to the Hittite lions) executed partly in the round and partly in bas-relief on both sides of the doorways; pairs of winged djinns frame these. In the halls there are series of narrative bas-reliefs. The general theme of these is the glorification of the king. We see him protected by djinns or at his most glorious occupations—court ceremonies, receptions of ambassadors, wild-animal hunts, expeditions of war. With rare exceptions these pictures were composed by assembling extremely stereotyped elements. The general effect is usually serious, with an occasional note of fantasy but never with the good nature or humorous detail which enlivened Egyptian bas-reliefs. Under Assurnasirpal the human figures, executed in rather pronounced relief, were stocky, with heavy shapes. The hunting scenes, 240 undoubtedly more closely observed from life, have more vitality and personality than the battle scenes.

Progress is visible in sculpture under the subsequent kings. The bas-reliefs on the four sides of the Black Obelisk of Shalmaneser III are remarkable for the simplicity and clarity of the scenes as well as for the faithfulness of the rendering of costumes. In the bas-reliefs of Tiglath Pileser III, we find, in the scene of the assault on a town, its sack and the deportation of its inhabitants, a new concern with originality and local colour. In the thick-set figures there is a last trace of Sumerian influence. This was finally shaken off in the time of Sargon II and his successors.

Assyrian art reached its apogee in the gigantic palace at Khorsabad, built by these monarchs. This palace, of which one hundred and eighty-six halls have been uncovered, rested on a terrace which had an area of about 25 acres. In addition to the halls and chambers reserved for the service of the king and his court and for their servants, this palace included temples for the king's domestic worship and a ziggurat. The buildings were of brick, decorated mostly on the inside either with paintings on whitewash or with a facing of glazed bricks. In the main halls, plaques of gypseous alabaster were applied on the lower parts of the walls. These were not like the short orthostats of the Hittite palaces, but were large panels capable of producing a genuine decorative effect. The great doors, with semicircular arches, were flanked by winged bulls executed with a technical ease and skill 242 hitherto unknown. The themes exploited were still the same: stories of mythical heroes, such as the fabulous

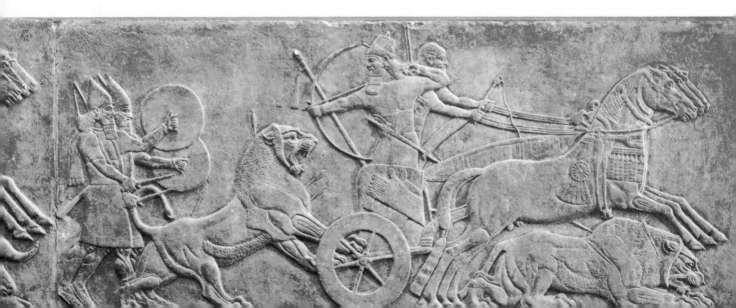

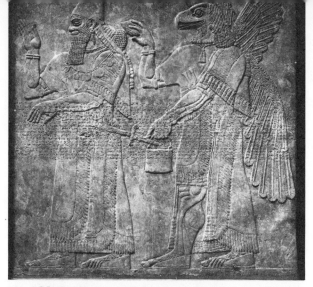

241. ASSYRIAN. Assurnasirpal and a djinn bearing offerings before the sacred tree. Bas-relief. *British Museum.*

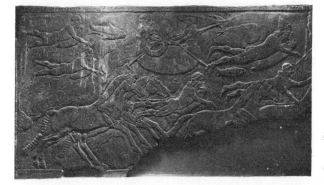

243. ASSYRIAN. Bas-relief from Nimrud, part of which shows soldiers on a river in a boat. 9th century B.C. *British Museum.*

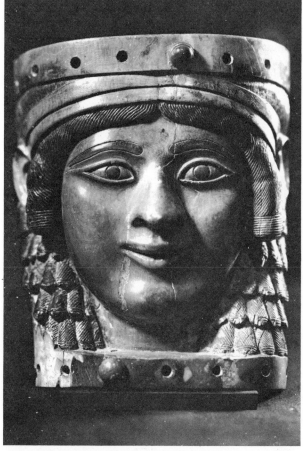

244. ASSYRIAN. The Lady of the Well. Ivory head found at Nimrud. 8th century. *Iraq Museum, Baghdad.*

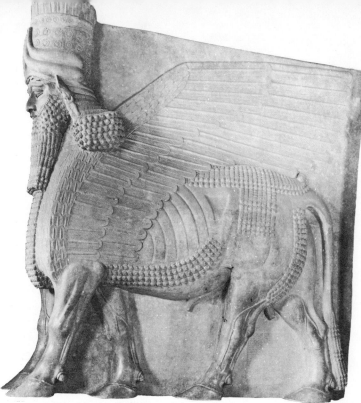

242. ASSYRIAN. Winged bull with human head, from Khorsabad. 8th century. *Louvre.*

Gilgamesh, or scenes glorifying the king. The latter included the monarch's banquet, the procession of his tributaries and his military expeditions. Here the Assyrian sculptors, after more than a century's training, had reached an undeniable mastery.

From the time of Sargon, certain scenes of boats on the sea were depicted on backgrounds covered with striations and scrolls to evoke the turbulent surface of the water. This may be the source which inspired artists in the service of Sennacherib with the idea of applying the same procedure to landscapes—arranging their figures against a continuous background carefully chiselled with rocks, trees and rivers. Although this convention, peculiar to Assyrian art, made possible the organisation of larger compositions, it led to a reduction in size of the human figures, and the scenes which were subject to it lost one of the essential characteristics of their decorative value. Sennacherib's buildings and his capture of Lachish in Palestine were represented in this style on the walls of his palace at Nineveh.

243

Esarhaddon, the next king, left his palace at Nimrud unfinished and built another one at Nineveh which is still incompletely explored. Assurbanipal also built his palace at Nineveh. Under this king, Assyrian art reached its greatest perfection. Continuing the convention which appeared in Sennacherib's time, bas-relief sculptors chose to organise large general pictures by reducing the sizes of the human figures and increasing the number of superposed registers (wherever they still used them). The sculptors worked with such a feeling for clarity that they avoided falling into the same trap as the decorators of the preceding reign. The bas-reliefs which immortalise the victories of the king in Elam and the festivities which followed are handled in this improved style. The principal examples of this sculpture, and, indeed, of all Assyrian sculpture, are the lion-hunting scenes, which show an animal art of a very high order.

The Assyrian bas-reliefs synthesise all the other arts,

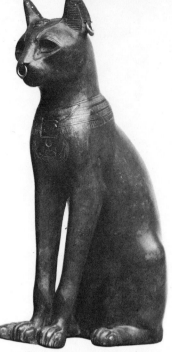

245. EGYPTIAN SAITE.
Bronze cat. *British Museum.*

which, naturally, went hand in hand with them. The minor arts, more particularly furniture and goldsmiths' work, have left irrefutable testimony of the refined taste and the virtuosity of the Assyrians, especially in the carved ivories and the dishes of precious metals. The painting which, in the absence of bas-reliefs, decorated provincial palaces such as Til Barsip and the secondary chambers of the great palaces at Nimrud, Khorsabad and Nineveh, were actually a kind of illumination, a drawing minutely executed in black line and heightened by the application of flat colours. Its repertory was the same as the reliefs, and, undoubtedly, cartoons of the reliefs were used.

Assyrian art disappeared at the very moment when it had reached its maturity, after three centuries of slow but constant progress, with the capture of Nineveh in 612 B.C. by the rebel leader Nabopolassar.

The neo-Babylonian empire, which took over the hegemony of the Eastern world from Assyria from 612 to 538, increased its power by putting an end to Egyptian aspirations in Syria and by definitively destroying what remained of the Hittite confederation at Carchemish. Nebuchadnezzar then wanted to give his empire a capital which would surpass the magnificence of the Assyrian palaces. He therefore began a programme of public works at Babylon; the legend of the hanging gardens is still remembered, and their imposing remains bear witness to a gigantic undertaking. But although this was a period of great brilliance, we have discovered very few of its works of art as yet. Particularly worthy of mention is the **276** Ishtar Gate, entirely encased in glazed bricks which formed a sumptuous decoration. Borders of white rosettes emphasise its architectonic elements, in particular the semicircular arch. The areas inside these borders are taken up with rows of reliefs of bulls and dragons passant. The old Mesopotamian technique of moulded brick united with that of glazing, which had been developed by the Assyrians, made it possible to cover large surfaces. Nebuchadnezzar, and, after him, Nabonidus, had barely time to complete these projects; in 538 their empire and its art disappeared under the assaults of the Persians.

Saite art: the last great Egyptian art

In spite of the desire in the Saite period to revert to Old Kingdom prototypes, Saite art was never more than a sickly pastiche of the earlier art. This was because the aesthetic had changed since the time of the pyramids, and the acquisition of a feeling for 'prettiness' in the New Kingdom had become permanent. The Saite artists, in imitating the works of the Old Kingdom, made them 'pretty' without realising it, and their works never have the vigour and the virility of their models. They were elegant, sometimes of an exquisite purity of shape, but always comparatively cold and formal. Unfortunately nothing remains of the temples which, according to Herodotus, the pharaohs of the XXVIth Dynasty built in the Delta. We have to form an idea of them from the remains of the buildings of the XXXth Dynasty and of the Ptolemaic temples, which continued the Saite tradition. Simplicity of plan, regularity of shapes and scrupulous care in construction seem to have been their characteristics. It also seems probable that we should go back to these Saite kings for the date of the reintroduction of the palm **258** capital, which had fallen into disuse since the Old Kingdom, and of the invention of the composite capital, a **262** combination of papyrus umbels and buds.

Private tombs of this period derive from several styles. They are often gigantic holes at the bottom of which is the funerary cave in the shape of a vaulted chapel, decorated internally according to some archaic formulas borrowed—a sign of the times—from Old Kingdom sources. The Saite statuary also sought its models in the works of the Old Kingdom as regards both attitude and costume. It was the end of the long pleated garments of the Theban epoch. The men had themselves represented in the short loin-cloth and their wives in the clinging sheath of the ancient times, which they would not have worn in everyday life. This was a deliberate anachronism, showing the artificial nature of this art. But instead of limiting themselves to soft limestone and granite, as in the past, the sculptors strove to use hard stones with a fine grain—basalts, breccias, serpentines—which allowed **246** more accurate execution but gave the finished work a cold and studied aspect. When they are not official portraits the faces of statues are gay and trivial; and official portraits show that the sculptors' skill had by no means degenerated. The sculptors had a predilection for the physiognomies of mature or old men, in whose portrayal they excelled.

The Saite bas-reliefs, like the statuary, were mostly characterless imitations of Old Kingdom works. Nevertheless, one series escapes this charge—the one to which the famous bas-relief 'Lily-gathering', in the Louvre, belongs. All the bas-reliefs of this kind are archaistic, but some of them do represent contemporary clothing in the ancient manner. In contrast with the general austerity of human representation, they show a preference for the plump shapes which were to become the fashion in the bas-reliefs of the Nectanebos and the Ptolemies.

Persia's attempt at synthesis

When Egypt, freed of the Assyrian yoke, was recapturing a style and trying to provide herself with an art which truly expressed her age-old culture by calling on the traditions of her most remote past, a new art was developing at the other side of the Near East, in Persia. It will actually be studied in Chapter 5, but it concerns us here because of the efforts it made to effect a synthesis of the arts whose development we have just followed. It fused the arts of all the countries subjected to the domination of Cyrus and Cambyses, including Egypt, which was conquered by Cambyses in 525. It was the first time that an attempt of this kind and scope had been made. It must be admitted that it was successful. The architects who built the palaces at Persepolis and Susa created a new style composed of elements borrowed from various countries which had become satrapies of the empire. From Egypt they took the gate with the winged solar disc; from Assyria, the winged bulls posted on either side of the outer gates, the braids of rosettes framing the decorated surfaces, and, in bas-relief, the method of rendering human shoulders; from Babylon, the process of decoration with moulded glazed bricks in relief; from the Syrians, who preserved the Hittite traditions, the lions supporting architectural elements; from the Ionians, the ovolo and dentil mouldings, and, in bas-relief, the method of draping the folds of garments flat. The whole was blended into a composite formula whose general style was akin to the art of the Sargonids.

The architects of the palaces of Darius and his successors were able to give their new style a personal stamp by the use of the column, the introduction of windows in façades and the character of the decoration.

Although the column had been used in Egypt from the remotest times, both as ornament and as support, the same was not true in Mesopotamia. Neither the Babylonians nor the Assyrians, forced to build in brick, had utilised it generally. Only the Hittites, who built in stone, had used wooden columns, of which we have found the carved stone bases. They were used not only to support the ceiling but also to decorate the façades of buildings and to support the porch roofs. This type of construction, whose Babylonian name of *bît hilâni* perhaps suggests that it also included windows, may have supplied the Achaemenian architects with the first idea for their 'apadana', or columned reception hall, which was also preceded by a peristyle. However that may be, the very tall, slender, fluted shaft of the Persian column certainly derives from a wooden prototype. Its bell- and cushion-shaped bases are akin to Hittite models. As for the capital, it is an original and decorative creation. The forequarters of two kneeling bulls, joined at the waist, bear on their backs the rafters and on their heads the joists of the ceiling. But their origin is still unknown.

Assyrian and Babylonian buildings had no windows. In these two countries, with their intense light, the doorways provided enough illumination for the rooms. The Egyptians, in both lay and religious architecture, were acquainted only with clerestories of pierced stone which let in diffused light from above. According to their name, the Hittite *bît hilâni* may have included windows (possibly from an Aegean influence). However that may be, the Persians were the first people in western Asia to use them as a decorative element by surmounting them with Egyptian cornices. The ornamentation of the Achaemenian palaces, Oriental in its exuberant richness, drew its inspiration from the old Assyrian motifs, simplifying them at the same time. Sculpture, apart from the violent hunting and battle scenes, consisted almost entirely of scenes glorifying the monarch, and processions of warriors or tributaries. The figures, whose musculature was no longer exaggerated, stood out against a plain background with no hint of a landscape. There was no detail to

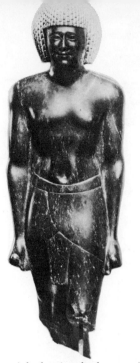

246. EGYPTIAN SAITE. Basalt statuette. *Former Dottari Collection.*

enrich the simple, harmonious folds of their garments.

The tombs of the Persian monarchs also combined the two great traditions of the East: the Egyptian, because they consisted of hypogaea carved out of mountain-sides; the Asiatic, because the entrances were decorated with a large panel of rock sculpture.

However eclectic the art built up by the Achaemenians may have been, it had deep roots in the artistic tradition of western Asia, of which it was the last flowering after Assyrian art. It is significant that the palaces of Pasargadae, Persepolis and Susa were built, like the Assyrian palaces, on vast platforms, whereas the nature of the soil in Persia did not call for such a precaution, and that the masonry of their great works continued to be of brick, although stone was abundant in the country. For the same reason, the majority of the rooms were built on an Assyrian plan, without using the column whose employment was reserved for the apadana which had a new and totally different plan.

The efforts made to spread this art throughout the conquered countries (mainly proved by the discovery at Sidon of a capital with the forequarters of bulls, and by the presence of a representation of another of the same style in the tomb of Petosiris in Upper Egypt) do not appear to have been successful outside the field of the minor arts. 247

The major arts of the various countries, closely bound up with the national religions, were not affected by this effort. But the same feeling which checked the expansion of Achaemenian art throughout the empire, worked in its favour and ensured it a long career in Persia. Linked with the Zoroastrian religion, it perpetuated itself in Parthian and Sassanian art and, through these, eventually influenced Byzantine art.

Moreover, the wise policy initiated by Darius of having the conquered countries governed by their own kings and according to their own traditions also had the effect of slowing down the diffusion of Achaemenian art. Thus, the temple built by Darius I in the Khargah Oasis was in the purest Egyptian style and fitted smoothly into the Saite tradition. The colonnade with which Nectanebo II completed it after the liberation belongs to the same vein of inspiration. It demonstrates the continuity of the tradition of Egyptian art at this epoch.

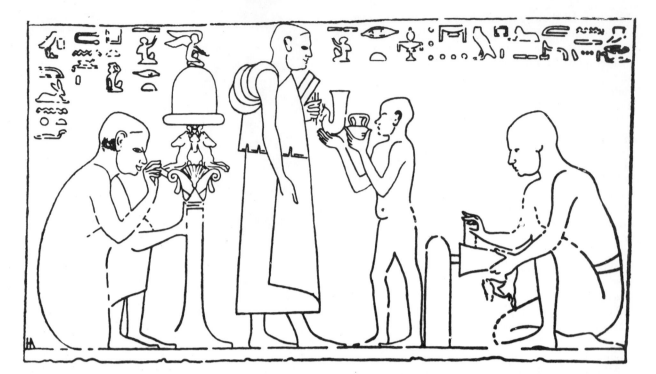

247. EGYPTIAN. PTOLEMAIC. Detail from the tomb of Petosiris, showing a goldsmith at work. *(After Gustave Lefebvre.)*

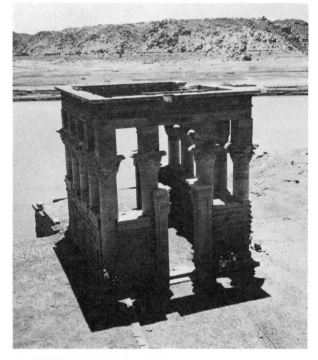

248. EGYPTIAN. ROMAN PERIOD. Part of the temple at Philae.

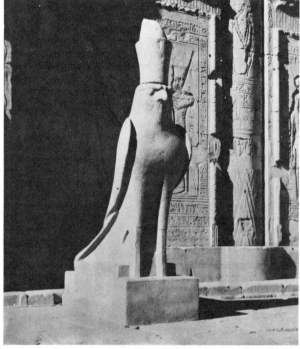

249. EGYPTIAN. PTOLEMAIC. The falcon of Horus, in the court of the temple of Horus at Edfu.

The final phase and the decline of Egyptian art

Scholars have been too ready to denigrate the style of the edifices built in Egypt by the Ptolemies, of which the temples of Philae, Edfu, Esna, Kom Ombo and Denderah are the masterpieces. Under close scrutiny their decoration does not bear comparison with that of the temples of former epochs. There is generally a great deal of ornamentation, which gives the impression of overcrowding. Bas-reliefs fill in the traditional contours (made to be left plain) with models intended to be realistic but managing only to appear bloated. But if we examine the general effect we cannot but admire the noble simplicity of the architectural distribution, the richness of the colonnades, the elegance and diversity of the capitals, the accuracy of the stone-dressing—in short all the qualities of Saite art which the Ptolemies, with improved means at their disposal, continued. Another feature of the decoration of the epoch was that stucco intended to receive polychrome treatment formed a light impasto over the reliefs. This was perhaps to prevent their being swamped when artists began to

248–250
252

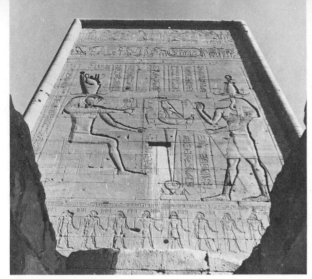

250. EGYPTIAN. PTOLEMAIC. Detail of the pylon of the temple of Horus at Edfu.

exaggerate the modelling.

The great problem when dealing with the art of the Ptolemies is that of its relations with Greek art, which was the art of the dynasty whose new capital, Alexandria, became from its foundation, as we shall see later (Chapter 6), the most active centre of diffusion of culture in the world. At first an attempt at compromise was made. The high priest of Thoth at Hermopolis, the sage Petosiris, had, in the chapel of his tomb, works inspired by Greek art wherever his religion did not insist on the use of traditional imagery. A colossus of Alexander Aigos bears a Greek face on an Egyptian-type body. But after a few attempts, a fusion between the two arts appeared impracticable, for there was no common measure of expression between them and every mixture resulted in a bastard creation. So the two arts reigned side by side on Egyptian soil, each in its own field, with private life as Greece's sphere and religion as Egypt's.

Until the reign of Ptolemy VI, there were scarcely any signs of decadence; bas-reliefs were still lively enough to incorporate and assimilate new themes: for example, the long procession of gods and priests on the steps of the temple at Edfu (imitated later at Denderah) carved nearly life-size and at eye-level, was in the manner of the processions which deported Egyptians could have contemplated three centuries earlier in the palace of the Achaemenian kings at Persepolis. But from the middle of the Ptolemaic period and for the next four centuries Egyptian art declined. The advent of Christianity as the state religion gave it the death blow.

However, it was not Christianity but Hellenism which put an end to Egyptian art. After the conquest of Alexandria, in which the Egyptians at first could see no more than liberation from the hated domination of the Persians, the Nile valley became Hellenised in its everyday life at an increasing pace, which the religious monuments do not show us but which the necropolises, such as that of Tunah el Jebel, near Hermopolis, reveal. The majority of the clergy, living their private lives in the Greek manner like all their contemporaries, finally began to think in the Greek way and to hold no other art but Greek art in esteem. Their ancestral art, although bound up with their religion, then seemed as outmoded and even as barbarous to them as, later, medieval art seemed to the ecclesiastical humanists of the Renaissance, who scornfully named it 'Gothic'. Then pharaonic art was virtually dead, undermined from within.

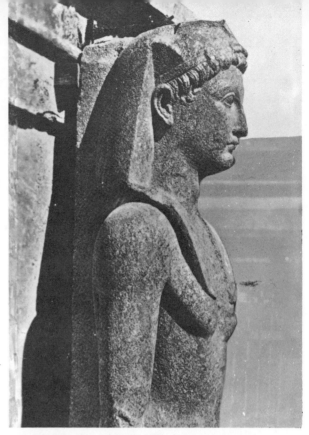

251. EGYPTIAN. PTOLEMAIC. Statue of Alexander Aigos from Karnak. *Egyptian Museum, Cairo.*

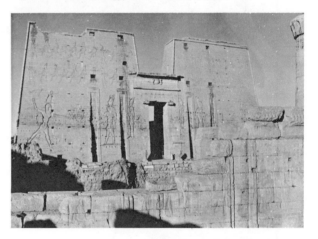

252. EGYPTIAN. PTOLEMAIC. Pylons of the temple of Horus, Edfu.

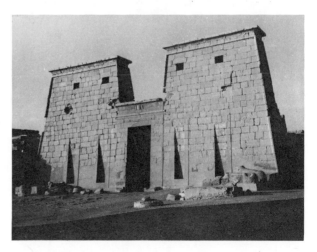

253. EGYPTIAN. NEW KINGDOM. Pylons of the temple of Khons, Karnak.

HISTORICAL SUMMARY: The Agrarian empires

EGYPT

Archaeology

Scientific knowledge of ancient Egypt dates back about a century and a half, owing to the work *Description de l'Egypte* (1809), by Bonaparte's scholars. In it was published the Rosetta Stone, discovered in 1799, whose tri-lingual inscription enabled J. M. F. Champollion (1790–1832) to solve the mystery of the hieroglyphs (1822), in spite of the mixture of phonetical signs—syllabic and alphabetic—with figurative and symbolical signs. Egyptology was established. The opening of the first intact royal tomb, that of Tutankhamen in 1923, then the discoveries at Tanis, marked an epoch.

Chronology

For a long time, scholars began with the concordances noted by the Egyptians between the dates of the civil year and the heliacal rising of Sirius (Sothis). The beginning of the Ist Dynasty was thus fixed at 3197 B.C. But the synchronisms observed between the protohistory of the Nile and Mesopotamia, particularly between the Ist Dynasty and the end of the Jemdet Nasr period, led archaeologists to bring the date forward; A. Scharff has placed it recently at 2850 B.C. As regards the remote epochs of the Near East, scholars are divided into partisans of the

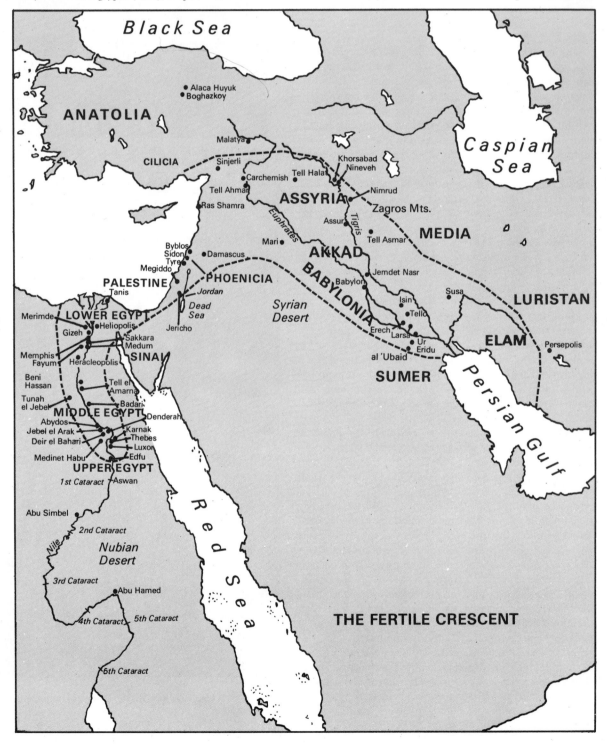

THE FERTILE CRESCENT

154

'long and short' chronologies, the latter two hundred years later. We shall adopt the latter. Manetho's division of the pharaohs into thirty dynasties has been kept.

HISTORY

The pre-dynastic period and the Old Kingdom.

At the end of the Chalcolithic, Egypt was divided into two kingdoms, composed of nomes or provinces. According to tradition, the monarchy of the north conquered the southern one. A new division ended in the hegemony of the Scorpion King of the south, and was completed by the legendary king Narmer, often compared with Menes, first mythical king of Upper and Lower Egypt (towards 2850). His capital was at This, hence the name Thinite monarchy.

The invention of hieroglyphic writing at this time marks the beginning of Egyptian history.

The Old Kingdom or Memphite period begins with the IIIrd Dynasty and Zoser who transferred his capital from Abydos to Memphis in the south of the Delta, about 2650. His minister and architect, Imhotep, was deified in later times. Egyptian grandeur was already asserting itself. In the IVth Dynasty, Sneferu, conqueror in Nubia and Libya, inaugurated the tradition of the great builders, whose pyramids remain. The first three kings of the Xth Dynasty supported the solar worship of Ra, which gave growing power to the priests of Heliopolis.

Commercial and warlike relations with Syria increased, and timber was imported via Byblos: mainly Lebanese timber, pine far more than cedar. The expeditions of the pharaohs, chiefly against invading nomads from the east, were commemorated on the faces of the rocks at Sinai and other places. Expeditions against the land of Punt (Somaliland) procured perfume, oil, incense and ivory.

The VIth Dynasty lapsed into feudalism, then into anarchy. At Sakkara several pyramids were built in addition to that of Zoser; those of Teti and of Pepi I are particularly important. The weakening of the royal authority coincided with the religious and social reform of universal admission to funerary privileges, reserved in the past for the kings.

At the end of the VIth Dynasty, towards 2190, the First Intermediate period began, lasting until the XIth Dynasty and almost until the year 2000.

The Middle Kingdom.

Internal dividing up and rivalry between the king of Heracleopolis in the north, who defeated the Asiatics in the Delta (Xth Dynasty), and the confederation of southern princes, ended in the victory of the sovereign of Thebes, Mentuhotep II. Amenemhat I founded the XIIth Dynasty shortly after 2000. The Theban monarchy marked a high point in Egypt. Trade developed with Byblos, Crete, Nubia and Arabia. The influence of Babylon, where Hammurabi ruled, increased. Literature and art went through a classical phase.

The Second Intermediate period.

Growing pressure from Asia was felt after Aryan invasions in Babylonia (mid-18th century). In 1792, the Pharaohs of the XIIIth Dynasty transferred their capital to Tanis. But towards 1700 the Hyksos invaded Lower Egypt. This victory was gained by the iron weapons and war chariots used by these barbarians, who came from Mitanni with Hittites and Hurrians, bringing Semites and Canaanites with them as well.

For nearly a century and a half the 'shepherd kings', at Avaris in the east of the Delta, tried to enslave their feeble Egyptian rivals in the south. The Theban kings paid tribute. But Ahmose, founding both the XVIIIth Dynasty and the New Kingdom in 1580, drove the invaders towards Palestine.

The New Kingdom.

Ahmose conquered Syria and advanced as far as the Euphrates. He subdued Nubia. Syria, Babylonia and Crete were brought into the orbit of international trade. Egypt then became a powerful and influential empire. From about 1500 Tuthmosis III, in the course of a long reign, dominated Nubia and almost all the Near East from the coast to the Euphrates. The children of vassal kings were brought up in Egypt. A hundred years later Amenhotep III, seeing the growing power of the Hittites in Cappadocia and of the Assyrians, formed an alliance with the Mitanni, masters of the routes from Babylon to the Mediterranean and the route to the Caucasus. The Nile was connected with the Red Sea and Memphis received from Arabia, as well as Phoenicia and Crete, ships coming not only from Greece but also from the Adriatic and even the Black Sea littoral.

The pre-eminence of Amon Ra, the great dynastic god, did not wipe out the mystical and popular worship of Osiris, but the victories gained by the king, with the god's protection, gave his priests excessive wealth and power.

In order to safeguard his power and provide the various peoples who had been conquered with a god they could recognise, Amenhotep IV (Akhenaten) gave preeminence to the solar disc Aten, thus giving open expression to the hidden monotheism of Egyptian religion, but at the same time creating a schism. Akhenaten left Thebes for a capital which he founded in Middle Egypt at Tell el Amarna. On the king's death, the young Tutankhamen, under the ascendancy of the triumphant priests of Amon, re-established the god's sovereignty and returned to Thebes. Protégé of the last pharaoh of the XVIIIth Dynasty and scion of a powerful military family, Ramesses I founded the XIXth Dynasty about 1314. A treaty of non-aggression was signed between Ramesses II and Hattusilis III, king of the Hittites, in 1278. Egyptian influence spread in Syria as far as the Orontes. Tanis, which may have been the king's birthplace, became the capital. Towards the last years of the 13th century Egypt was on the point of being invaded by peoples (possibly Aryans) moving from east to west: the Peoples of the Sea. In 1211 Ramesses III saved Egyptian civilisation by defeating them at sea at the entrance to one of the mouths of the Nile and on land towards the eastern frontier. But feudalism recurred, and the power of the priests of Amon finally opposed that of the pharaoh. The decadence of the Rameside kings was such that towards 1090 the high priest Herihor was the equal of the pharaoh governing the Delta.

Late periods.

Then began a confused epoch in which Libyan and Ethiopian dynasties succeeded each other. Egypt seems to have been divided: the north came under the royal authority; the south was subject to the high priest of Amon. Local dynasties sprang up; confusion reigned. In 671 Egypt was invaded by the Assyrians.

The advent of Psamtik I in 663, prince of Sais, founder of the XXVIth Dynasty known as the Saite, was needed to re-establish the country's unity and restore something of its former brilliance. His son Necho rebuilt the canal linking the Nile with the Red Sea and commissioned an expedition which circumnavigated Africa. But his ambitions in the east were halted by the Babylonia of Nebuchadnezzar.

Soon Persia was in the ascendancy, and Cambyses overthrew the XXVIth Dynasty. After a later brief period of independence, Egypt was conquered by Alexander in 332. His successors, the Ptolemies, governed until the death of Cleopatra (30 B.C.). Then came the Roman domination. It was followed by the rule of the Byzantine empire (in the 4th century A.D.) and the Arabs (640). The latter put an end to three centuries of Christianity and succeeded in blotting out the ancient civilisation.

ARCHITECTURE

Funerary architecture.

All that remains of the royal burial places of the

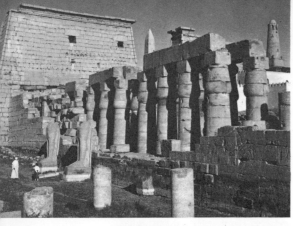

254. View of the temple at Luxor.

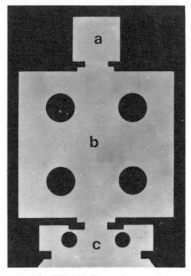

255. EGYPTIAN. Plan of a hypogaeum. Showing: a. serdab, b. court, c. entrance hall.

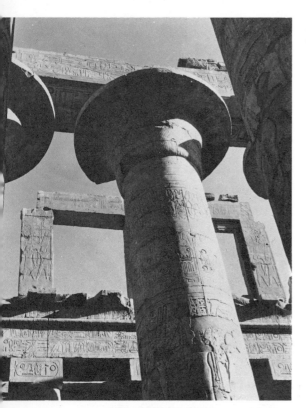

256. EGYPTIAN. Columns of the temple at Karnak.

kings of the Ist and IInd Dynasties near Abydos are brick vaults, access to which was by stairs and, later, by an inclined plane. The addition of chambers for furniture and funerary offerings transformed these tombs into funerary apartments. The whole of such a tomb was covered with fragments of stone and sand disposed in a rectangular mass held up by four sloping brick walls.

The pyramid appeared with the Old Kingdom. The first was built at Sakkara by Zoser's architect Imhotep. Stepped, as if by the superimposition of mastabas of decreasing size, it occupied the centre of a precinct enclosing several chapels with their courtyards. It was the first stone architecture, a faithful translation of earlier wooden constructions.

From the IVth Dynasty onwards the royal funerary architectural complex included a reception temple where the mummy received the ritual purifications. This was connected by a covered rising walk with the funerary temple built on to the east side of the pyramid which covered the burial chamber (the most important pyramids are those of Cheops, Chephren and Mycerinus).

High officials had mastabas built for themselves. The vault and its vestibule, carved out of the rock, were connected by a shaft (afterwards filled in) with the roof of the rectangular mass. The brick outer walls were sloping and stepped and bore symbolic decorations. The inside walls also exhibited a certain battering, but had smooth sides if they were built of limestone blocks. On the eastern façade were two niches. One of these was a false door; a table of offerings for the soul of the deceased stood at its foot. The false door was moved to the west wall when the niche grew into a chapel. The statue of the dead person was in the serdab, a redoubt sunk into the mound. The chapel was decorated inside with very low bas-reliefs of scenes relating to the offerings.

In the Middle Kingdom the royal pyramid was of cheaper material (brick) under a facing of limestone. The mastabas, small and without side chapels, were grouped around the pyramid, as in the Old Kingdom. The narrowness of the Nile valley necessitated that tombs be carved out of the cliffs (the rock-cut tombs, or hypogaea). The typical tomb plan is found in these as in the pyramids: the court, the hall, the sanctuary, the concealed corridor with its slope of varying steepness, and the shaft leading to the vault [**255**].

In the New Kingdom the necropolis of the pharaohs was situated to the west of Thebes, in the Valley of the Kings. The fundamental elements of the royal funerary complex of the Old Kingdom became separated.

A broad causeway connected the reception temple with the funerary temple. The latter, built near the rocky cliff, was completely separated from the tomb, which was not placed in the pyramid but was at the far end of a hypogaeum. This was composed of long corridors with staircases and antechambers leading to the hall containing the sarcophagus. The royal funerary temple of the New Kingdom consisted of two courts; in front of the first of these was a pair of pylons. The courts led to a hypostyle hall. Generally three sanctuaries (one of which was consecrated to the worship of the dead king), preceded by antechambers and surrounded by chapels, formed the secret part of the temple.

Important people had their hypogea carved out in the region of the royal necropolis. Certain tombs, half embedded in the cliff, had their antechambers crowned by a small brick pyramid (Deir el Medineh). As in both the Old and Middle Kingdoms, painted bas-reliefs were used in the decoration.

In the late period, as recent excavations at Tanis show, the modest funerary chapels and vaults of the kings were in the precincts of the temples. A high official was interred in a large sarcophagus placed in a burial chamber situated at the bottom of a deep pit. The superstructure had disappeared.

Religious architecture. First we note the open-air sun temples. At Abu Gurob (Vth Dynasty) the temple was composed of a surrounding wall enclosing a rectangular area in the southern part of which stood a stocky obelisk, the sun symbol, on a high base. At its foot was the table of offerings. It was united by a covered causeway with the portico, which was situated in the actual town. To one side, outside the temple buildings, a solar barque was constructed in an oval pit. The XVIIIth Dynasty temple built by Akhenaten at Tell el Amarna was much more complicated than this. No remains from the late period have yet been discovered.

The cult temples appeared from the beginning of the historical period. The temple of Kasr el Sagha, possibly from the IIIrd Dynasty, appears as a rectangular façade pierced by a door opening on to a lateral court giving access to seven contiguous chapels. In the Middle Kingdom only the temple of Medinet Madi still remained. It was dedicated to a divinity worshipped in the Fayum.

Description of a typical cult temple of the Middle Kingdom. A canal led to an unloading quay from which ran a broad avenue lined with sphinxes. At its far end, the gate of the temple, flanked by two trapezoid towers (the pylons), was preceded by two obelisks

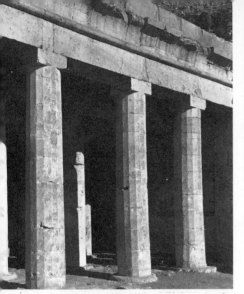

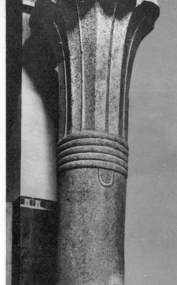

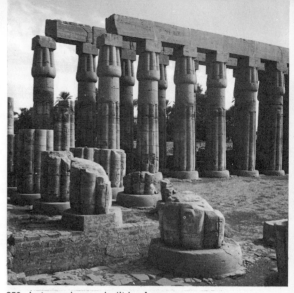

257. Proto-Doric columns, temple of Hatshepsut. XVIIIth Dynasty.

258. Palm capital, temple of King Unos at Sakkara.

259. Lotus columns, built by Amenhotep III at Luxor. XVIIIth Dynasty.

and by statues of the king. This gate opened on to a court lined with lateral porticoes. Via a few steps it led to a hypostyle hall with three central aisles, its ceiling supported by clustered papyrus columns (Karnak: 134 columns, maximum height 69 feet).

Then came the chapel, its antechambers, sacristies and warehouses, then the pro-sanctuary, with the door to the sanctuary containing the divine statue. This typical plan was complicated by architectural additions due to the piety of successive monarchs, as at Karnak and Luxor. Some of these temples were carved out of the mountain (Abu Simbel [228]).

Domestic architecture. As the buildings were constructed of light materials, only rare examples are left from the Old Kingdom; only the foundations of houses (Sakkara and Hierakonpolis, IIIrd Dynasty). In the Middle Kingdom, the new towns exhibited a quadrilateral town-plan. We must wait until the New Kingdom and el Amarna to form some idea of the rich dwellings built in gardens with ornamental lakes. Working-class houses usually comprised one living room, one bedroom and a kitchen (e.g. village at Deir el Medineh). All these types of houses seem to have been continued in the late periods. Few traces remain of the palaces. There was a palace in the middle of the first court of the mortuary temple at Medinet Habu. At el Amarna there are some ground-level remains of the royal and private palaces with their gardens and dependencies.

Military architecture. At Hierakonpolis a fortification consisted of a double wall divided by an artificial ditch. This arrangement was retained in later fortifications.

Columns. The columns used as supports in the buildings around the pyramid of Zoser recall bundles of reeds; they were surmounted by a flat moulding. The 'proto-Doric' column

[257] seems to have been transitional between the post and the column; then, as from the Vth Dynasty, we find the classical types: the palm-type column [258] with a slender shaft; the lotus column [260] (rarely used in stone architecture) whose shaft reproduced a group of several stems, surmounted by a capital of closed lotus buds; the papyrus column [260] whose shaft was also clustered, but with stems of ogival section and the capital in the shape of closed umbels, or open umbels (bell column [261]). In the Middle Kingdom the Hathor-headed column [263] appeared, the capital of which showed the head of the goddess under the models of the birth-house of Horus. In the Ptolemaic period the composite column appeared [262].

Sculpture

After the small ivory statuettes of the first dynasties and the stone statues, still stiff and awkward, sculpture developed rapidly in the IVth Dynasty. The royal statues still showed an ideal image of the sovereign: that of the god to which he was assimilated. Lay statues and 'replacement heads', both of them intended to act as substitutes for the body if it happened to be destroyed, were also idealised. Among the best-known masterpieces are the Sheikh el Beled (in wood) in the Cairo Museum (Vth Dynasty [200]) and the Seated Scribe, in the Louvre (Vth Dynasty) [191].

In the Middle Kingdom the Memphite style, more academic and with an elongated canon (Amenemhat III from Harawa), was distinguished from the Theban style in which an extreme realism appeared; the pharaoh's face is marked by age and worry (Mentuhotep III from Deir el Bahari; Sesostris III from Medamud; Amenemhat III from Karnak). Small statuettes were carved out of granite or schist, or in ivory or wood. In the XIIIth Dynasty there was a decline in sculpture. It

became cold, dry, academic. Always traditionalist, statuary at the beginning of the XVIIIth Dynasty still preserved certain Old Kingdom characteristics which had persisted through the Middle Kingdom. Sweetness and elegance were accentuated and, at the same time, luxury in clothing showed the influence of Asia (larger loincloths; finely pleated garments of transparent linen; embroidery and jewellery). Nevertheless, a growing stylisation and academicism soon appeared.

The New Kingdom seemed only to have to unite and accentuate the features of the two preceding schools: realism and idealism; but the revolution accomplished by Amenhotep IV (Akhenaten) introduced a new aesthetic, in which the accentuation of physical characteristics became almost caricature-like, only to be rapidly watered down into idealism [220, 219].

Even when the failure of this revolution brought art back to the time-honoured traditions, something of the

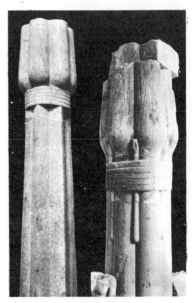

260. *Left*. Lotus column.
Right. Papyrus bud column.

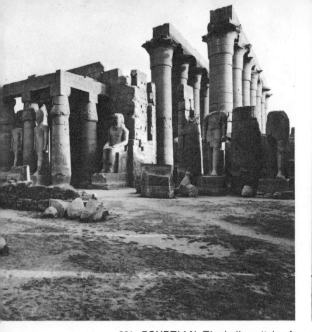

261. EGYPTIAN. The bell capitals of the Luxor temple.

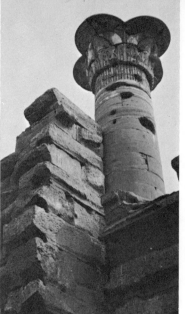

262. Composite capitals. Temple at Medinet Habu.

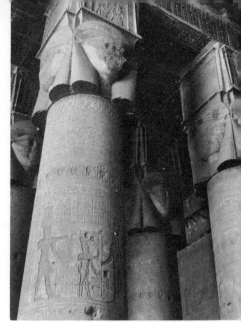

263. Hathor-headed capitals. Temple of Hathor at Denderah.

new spirit survived, particularly a certain charm and delicacy. In lay statuary new forms, such as the block statue, made their appearance.

The return to the past which marked the pre-Saite period inevitably imposed on sculpture an archaism, corrected by a more developed technique and a more profound knowledge of anatomy. At the same time, the quest for grace which came from the preceding period resulted in the 'Saite smile', and in the elongation of the body.

Even if foreign influences showed themselves to be slight, we cannot deny the effect that Greek sculpture had on these last centuries of Egyptian art. The Greek and Roman conquests even resulted in an abortive attempt to reconcile the two styles.

Animal sculpture, encouraged by the religious iconography, always held an important place.

From the Ist Dynasty on steles [179a], and from the Old Kingdom in the decoration of the walls of temples and tombs, the Egyptian adopted a low bas-relief with modelling of great delicacy which was both supple and accurate. The themes, aimed at evoking the preparation of the offering and the life of the dead, are handled with a stylisation which nevertheless allows for flexibility and a diversity of attitudes.

Painting

The low bas-relief and the use of colour on it sometimes lead us to confuse it with painting. The pictorial decoration of walls [225], which had a precedent from the proto-dynastic period in the frescoes of the tomb at Hierakonpolis (themselves inspired by the decoration of Naqada pottery) was apparently, from the IIIrd Dynasty, a substitute for bas-relief, whose conventions it adopted (tomb of Hesy-ra at Sakkara).

In the Middle Kingdom the walls of tombs were plastered and then painted.

The earlier themes were enriched with new details, while others appeared, handled with greater freedom of execution than in the Old Kingdom. Domestic animals, such as the cat and the animals of the desert (Beni Hasan) were rendered with an acute sense of observation.

In the New Kingdom there was a further enrichment of themes: the quest for charm and for beauty of line, attitude and colour reached its highest point. Decoration grew complicated in the late periods, at the same time that a certain affectation of attitude verging on mannerism appeared.

The fragments of pottery (ostraka) or limestone which the artists used for their rough sketches reveal the spontaneity of their art.

The minor arts

In prehistory, jewellery (gold, ivory and flint), decorated toilet accessories and slate palettes foreshadowed the shapes, decoration and techniques of the later periods.

From the Ist Dynasty, both in the decoration of furniture and of jewellery, we note the use of inlays, either with coloured pastes (mural decoration, such as the geese from Medum) or semiprecious stones (jewellery).

The metal-work was mostly in gold, rarely in silver, and sometimes in copper (diadems). Necklaces were made of various dressed and threaded stones.

Goldsmiths' work rose to the level of sculpture (falcon's head from Hierakonpolis).

The jewellery of the Middle Kingdom was some of the loveliest known (pectorals of Sesostris II and Sesostris III; diadems of Ita and Khnumet).

Cloisonné work and milling appeared in Egypt at this time.

With the New Kingdom pastes of coloured glass were substituted for precious stones in jewellery. Flasks of various shapes, made of coloured glass and fashioned by hand and decorated by a very special technique, appeared.

Furniture, richly painted (chest of Tutankhamen) or of valuable woods inlaid with ebony, ivory or coloured glass, had many shapes according to the materials and the use for which the objects were intended [267].

The late periods were essentially characterised by excessive ornamentation.

New techniques were developed, such as filigree in goldsmiths' work and *millefiori* in glassmaking. Blown glass did not appear until the Coptic period. *Information compiled by Marie-Louise Tisserant and Guy Gaudron, under the direction of Christiane Desroches Noblecourt.*

THE LAND OF CANAAN

Geography. Canaan is the region to Palestine and Phoenicia (Lebanon). Located at the tip of the 'Fertile Crescent', this corridor was dominated in turn by Egypt and the Mesopotamian states, and was often the victim of raids by desert nomads.

Civilisation. The important role played by these regions in the first spread of metal techniques earmarks them for special study in the next chapter (see Summary in Chapter 4). But their position at the junction between Egypt and Mesopotamia obliges us to examine their other activities here. From their beginnings, all the towns were fortified because of the threat of raids; stone, which was abundantly available, was used for this. Wood from the forests was frequently employed for joist-framing and for columns.

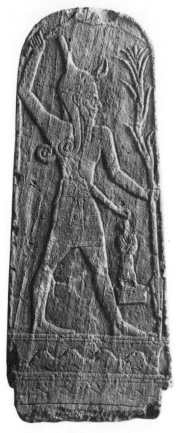

264. SYRIAN. Baal with a lance, from Ras Shamra (Ugarit). Beginning of 2nd millennium. *Louvre.*

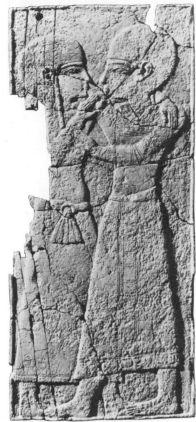

265. SYRIAN. Royal couple. Carved ivory.

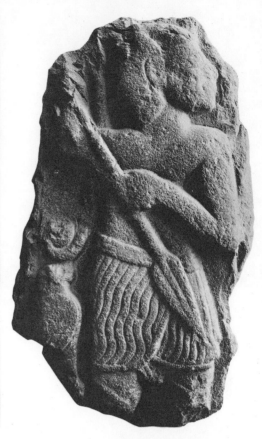

266. PALESTINIAN. CANAAN. The Stele of Moab. 9th century. *Louvre.*

In Palestine the strongholds such as Jericho, Gezer, Ophel (Jerusalem) and Megiddo had fortifications which consisted of enormous stone walls crowned with brick towers at more or less regular intervals. The Hebrews, after their invasion towards the beginning of the 2nd millennium, preserved the same system. Hydraulic works were improved. Palaces had a central court, as in Mesopotamia.

In Phoenicia there were many coastal towns, of which the principal, Ras Shamra (Ugarit), Byblos and Tyre, were ports. They were strongly fortified and carefully planned.

Art. There was no indigenous art in Palestine; the art of the region was composed of Egyptian, Mesopotamian and Cretan influences. There were some notable works: the Stele of Moab (Louvre, 9th century B.C.) representing a god holding a lance pointing to the ground [266]; carved seals; the 'Hyksos' scarabs; ivories, particularly those which decorated furniture and weapons, and ivory statuettes. Palace walls bore painted or carved geometrical motifs.

In Phoenicia, the temples were built around two rectangular or square courts surrounded by thick walls and many rooms; an altar was in the centre of the largest court. Funerary architec-ture consisted of vaults dug below the dwelling; access to them was by a staircase. The sarcophagi were of stone and were often large, such as that of Ahiram, king of Byblos, which has two recumbent figures in low relief on its lid; it is supported by four lions with forequarters carved in the round [232].

Egyptian influence is very noticeable in the sculpture. Work in the round was rare; there were many bas-reliefs. We may mention a stele from Ras Shamra (Louvre) showing the god Baal holding a lance with its shaft turning into a branch and pointing to the ground [264]; on another, later, stele he is shown upright on a lion, threatening a second lion with his lance.

In Phoenicia, too, ivory was very much in favour [265]. There were the plaques from Arslan Tash (about 840 B.C.) ornamenting the bed of Hazael, the king of Damascus, and the works from Ras Shamra: the big panel, found in 1952, decorated with episodes from the king's life; the large hunting-horn carved out of an elephant's tusk; the lid of a box (Louvre), showing the goddess of fertility.

THE HITTITES

Archaeology. Not until 1914 did excavations in Anatolia throw light on the Hittite civilisation; shortly afterwards E. Forrer and B. Hrozný unravelled the secret of their language and were able to decipher the enormous archives of Boghazkoy (formerly Hattusas).

History. An Asian people, possibly descended also from Indo-European conquerors, the Hittites occupied the centre of Anatolia (east of the Kizil

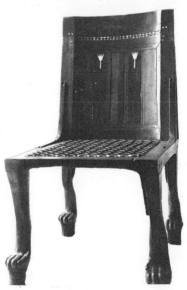

267. EGYPTIAN. Chair of ebony and ivory. New Kingdom. *Louvre.*

159

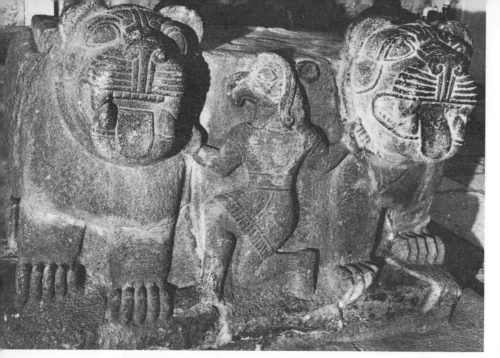

268. HITTITE. The base of the throne of the god Adad. *Ankara Archaeological Museum.*

269. HITTITE. Royal gateway at Boghazkoy. Middle of the 2nd millennium.

270. MESOPOTAMIA. A possible reconstruction of Khorsabad, showing the ziggurat. 8th century B.C.

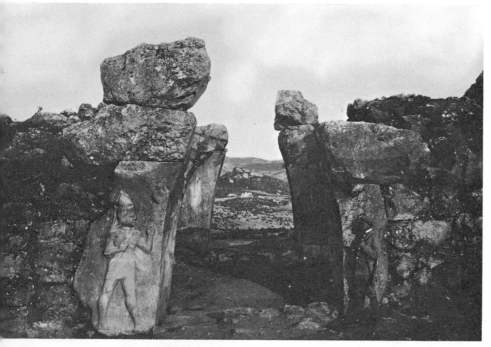

Irmak, formerly the Halys), under the kings Anitta (about 2000 B.C.), Mursilis I and Telepinus. They formed an empire with Hattusas as its capital; under King Suppiluliumas it extended as far as Syria (about 1300). With the events at the end of the 2nd millennium, this empire disappeared. Subsequently the Hittites formed a confederation of several small kingdoms with important centres such as Sinjerli and Carchemish; this confederation disappeared in its turn beneath the attacks of the Assyrians.

Hittite art, which was closely akin to Mesopotamian art, was nevertheless distinguished from it by a certain originality.

Architecture. Stone was widely used. One of the main features of the architecture was the wooden column resting on a stone base.

In the centre of the town, which was divided into fortified quarters, was the *bît hilâni*, or palace, built on a terrace to which a flight of steps gave access. From the building's broadest façade a covered vestibule opened, its roof supported by wooden columns; the rooms were situated behind it. The gates [269] of the towns possessed both an external and an internal opening.

Sculpture. The bas-reliefs include many important works: the rock carvings of Yazilikaya, showing the god of the storm clad in a brief loin-cloth and the earth goddess clad in a long pleated robe (13th century B.C.); those on the gates of the town of Alaca Huyuk of an eagle with two heads, and those from Boghazkoy showing a god clothed in a short loin-cloth and wearing a horned helmet, whose eye, remarkably enough, is represented not frontally but in profile; numerous steles, one of which (in the Louvre) represents the god of the storm wearing a short tunic and brandishing an axe and a trident (2nd millennium); the bas-reliefs which have been found at Malatya (9th century, Louvre); many scenes found at Carchemish of warriors.

A few works of sculpture in the round have come down to us, notably the statue of the god Adad, his head covered with a sort of fur bonnet, wearing a long robe: this statue is on a base composed of two lions [268].

In glyptics, the Hittites preferred using the ordinary seal, decorated with spirals, two-headed eagles, etc. The neo-Hittites employed cylinders, often of haematite, with such scenes as the god of the atmosphere, a goddess disrobing, processions of animals and gods mounted on animals.

The minor arts. Their pottery consisted of vases of elegant shape ornamented with stylised designs, some in the form of animals.

MESOPOTAMIA

The metal arts will be dealt with in Chapter 4.

Archaeology. The excavations by the French consul P. E. Botta, at Khorsabad and Nineveh, brought Assyrian art to light in 1842; the excavations by E. de Sarzec at Tello introduced us to the Sumerians (1877). Cuneiform writing was deciphered in the middle of the 19th century (Sir H. Rawlinson). Recent excavations have thrown special light on the more remote epochs (Sir Leonard Woolley at al 'Ubaid and Ur, and others).

History. The transition from prehistory to historic times was made with the Jemdet Nasr period.

Painted pottery, with heavy shapes, was polychrome; the cylinder seal replaced the ordinary seal. The other arts improved on the style of Erech. The science of numbers developed.

The end of this period coincided with a series of floods, about 3500 B.C. (the biblical Flood), of which traces have been found.

After the Jemdet Nasr period, we enter on historic times (about 3000). There were then two distinct peoples in southern Mesopotamia: in the south and the neighbourhood of the Persian Gulf were the Sumerians, an Asian people with a language of the agglutinative type, initiators, it is believed, of civilisation in the region; in the north were the Akkadians, a Semitic people, whose language exhibits all the characteristics of Semitic languages. It seems that the Sumerians installed themselves in the region first, followed by the Semites, but that at the beginning of the historical period they were one and the same civilisation. They were settled peoples, living by stock-farming and by an agriculture which they developed by means of ingenious irrigation systems. They were familiar with writing, which was linear before becoming cuneiform. This civilisation was divided into several city-states (each composed of a town and its territory), independent of and often at war with each other. At the head of each of them was a king or 'lugal', or a prince-priest or 'patesi' of the city's guardian deity. The priests, who were very strong owing to the wealth of the temples, sometimes seized power.

In the beginning the Sumerians seemed to be dominant; certain of their cities, first Erech, then Ur, exercised a sort of hegemony; at Ur a powerful dynasty was maintained for some time (Ist Ur Dynasty, about 2800–1600 B.C.). After its fall, Lugalzaggisi, a ruler of Umma, another Sumerian city, founded a Sumerian empire reaching to the Mediterranean. After some twenty years the Semites, under the leadership of the king of Akkad, Sargon, overthrew this empire and enlarged it, extending it to the Mediterranean, to Asia Minor and to Elam (a country situated beyond the Tigris to the southeast of Mesopotamia and peopled by Asians who were Semiticised at an early date and had a civilisation closely akin to the Mesopotamian). The successors of Sargon, Naram Sin and Manishtusu, managed to retain their power, but, sapped by internal revolts, this empire eventually collapsed and was invaded by the Guti, barbarians from the Zagros Mountains. After dominating the country for a time, they were finally driven out.

The Sumerian monarchs of the IIIrd Ur Dynasty, firstly Ur-Nammu (about 2382–2311), succeeded in establishing their hegemony; the Sumerian cities, more or less ruined by preceding events, became prosperous again; they developed the arts and trade. Such was the case with Lagash (now Tello) under the leadership of its patesi Gudea.

This dynasty was succeeded by a Semite dynasty at Isin, and another Elamite one at Larsa, which fought each other. Larsa won the day, but succumbed to the attacks of Hammurabi (about 2003–1961), king of Babylon, a hitherto secondary city which then became the capital of a unified state covering the whole of Mesopotamia, north Syria and Elam. Agriculture, trade, law and the arts flourished; it was the golden age of Mesopotamian civilisation; but, like the other empires, it did not last very long. Like Sargon's empire it was ruined by internal revolts and incursions by the mountain dwellers. The invading Hittites were replaced by other barbarians, the Kassites, who succeeded in founding at Babylon a dynasty which ruled for several centuries (about 1746–1171). The 2nd millennium was an extremely disturbed period. Migrations of peoples took place; the Hyksos invaded Egypt, the Indo-Europeans Asia Minor. The Elamites sacked Babylon and dethroned the Kassite dynasty.

Mesopotamia experienced the repercussions of these upsets, and its civilisation came close to disappearing. It managed to survive, but in the 1st millennium the power passed into the hands of a people hitherto held in subjection, the Assyrians, whose capital was successively Assur, Nimrud and Nineveh; they established a great empire owing to their energetic rulers, of whom the outstanding ones were Assurnasirpal (884–859), Shalmaneser III (859–824), Tiglath Pileser III (745–727), Sargon II (722–705), Sennacherib (705–681), Esarhaddon (681–669) and Assurbanipal (668–626). These monarchs relied on well-organised armies, but their methods had a cruelty to which their monuments testify. In addition to the whole of Mesopotamia, the empire embraced Syria, Palestine, Cilicia, Cyprus, and even Egypt; this empire ended in the same way as those which preceded it: the subject peoples rose up, and some mountain dwellers, the Medes, of Indo-European race, allied with the Persians of the same race, and a ruler of Babylon, Nabopolassar, took Nineveh in 612.

The neo-Babylonians then replaced the Assyrian power. They dominated Mesopotamia, as well as Syria, Palestine and Asia Minor; the new power flourished, especially under Nebuchadnezzar. But the Persians, who had previously subdued the Medes, seized Babylon in 539; henceforth Mesopotamia followed the destiny of the Persian empire; Mesopotamian civilisation shone in many fields, but it left its most visible, if not its most glamorous, imprint on art, which was essentially religious.

Architecture. Mesopotamian buildings had thick walls of sun-dried brick or, occasionally, fired brick, and were long and narrow so as to enable the beams, which were made from palm-trees, to support the roofs. The house, which might include an upper storey, was built around a square or rectangular court with a single door on the outside; all round it were the rooms. The palaces were built on the same plan, but were of considerable size and included several courts. They had hundreds of rooms and chapels. Important remains have been found at Tell Asmar (IIIrd Ur Dynasty), Mari (2nd millennium), Nimrud (Assyrian period) and Khorsabad, which was the summer residence of the Assyrian king Sargon.

The temples, such as those at Assur, Khafaje, Mari and Tell Asmar, were modelled on ordinary dwellings. Later they were composed of a square or rectangular building preceded by a cella; it was in a court. Around the building were several rooms for the priests and for various religious accessories. Buildings of this type were found at Eshnuna (IIIrd Ur Dynasty), Khorsabad (8th century) and Babylon (neo-Babylonian period). Next to the temple rose the ziggurat or multi-storeyed tower [**270**], made of a number of square or rectangular buildings each smaller than the one below; a chapel stood on the topmost terrace. Remains of ziggurats have been found in the White Temple at Warka (Jemdet Nasr period), at Ur (IIIrd Dynasty), at Khorsabad (8th century) and at Borsippa.

Every Mesopotamian village was

161

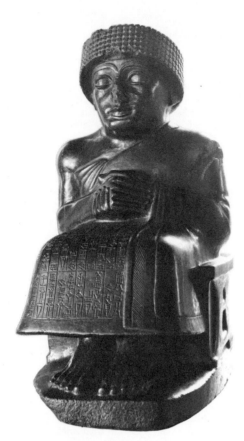

271. NEO-SUMERIAN. The seated figure of the patesi, Gudea. End of the 3rd millennium. *Louvre.*

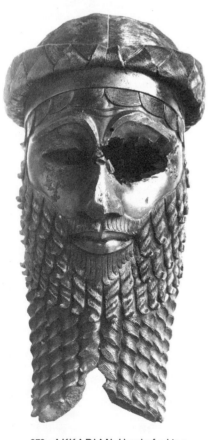

272. AKKADIAN. Head of a king, from Nineveh. 3rd millennium. *Iraq Museum, Baghdad.*

surrounded by ramparts of great technical perfection (especially in the Assyrian and neo-Babylonian periods), reinforced by quadrangular towers and pierced by strongly fortified gates, as at Khorsabad.

Babylon was embellished by the famous hanging gardens on terraces of remarkable technical accomplishment. Funerary architecture was by no means as advanced as Egypt's: the vaults were made of untrimmed blocks of stone like the royal tombs at Ur, where we find rudimentary arches, which were unknown in Mesopotamia. In the Assyrian period the use of the stone sarcophagus spread, but more frequently coffins or large terra-cotta jars were used to bury the dead.

Sculpture in the round. This underwent less development than in other ancient civilisations. Large statues are rare, as are representations of nudes and of women. There were certain rigid conventions including the law of frontal depiction. The legs are generally separated and the feet at rest, one of them slightly in front of the other. The upper arms are held tightly to the bust and the forearms brought together across the chest. The expression of the face is nearly always serious, even severe. Inscriptions in cuneiform characters were often engraved on the clothes.

Noteworthy among the outstanding works of the archaic Sumerian period are male or female statuettes of fine limestone with straight limbs and protruding eyes simulated by white shells (Tell Asmar). For the neo-Sumerian period we have an alabaster statuette of Gudea as a young man and the series of statues of him (ten in the Louvre) seated or standing, all but two of them headless; the figure is clothed in a fabric bordered with braid, the feet slightly apart; on each of the surviving heads is a sort of turban of a woolly cloth, and the face is hairless [**271**]. From the Assyrian period there exists a large-scale statue of Shalmaneser III (8 ft 6 in.) in the Istanbul Museum. There are also some caryatids of divinities holding vases from which water is spouting (Baghdad Museum).

Sculpture in relief. This was very much used in all periods and obeyed the same conventions as sculpture in the round. In the Jemdet Nasr period we may mention the Warka vase, as well as the large goblet of fine limestone (Baghdad Museum) on which a scene of offerings to the fertility goddess is represented on four registers. A stele from the same source represents a lion hunt. In the dynastic period, numerous small square plaques (so-called New Year plaques) represent banquet scenes. The 'genealogical' bas-reliefs of Ur-

Nanshe, ruler of Lagash, which were pierced with holes so that they could be hung up, show the dynast accompanied by his family in various religious scenes. The Stele of the Vultures [**167**] commemorates the victory of Eannatum, king of Lagash, over the king of Umma. On one side, the guardian god of the town, Ningirsu, brings down his mace on one of his enemies caught in a net; on the other the king advances at the head of his troops, and vultures, or rather eagles, tear the enemies' bodies to pieces. From the Akkadian period is the Stele of Victory of Naram Sin [**217**]. At the head of his troops, he is climbing a mountain whose summit, in front of him, is crowned with symbols of the divinities: his enemies litter the ground or flee. From the neo-Sumerian period, a stele shows Gudea with a palm on his shoulder presented by his personal god Ningizzida to Ningirsu (Berlin Museum). A fragment of a vase showing a musical scene also dates from this period, as does the stele of Hammurabi's legal code [**273**]; in the latter the king is seen above, praying before the god Shamash, while below is the text of the code. From the Kassite period several boundary stones have survived on which are engraved, on one side, an act of donation and, on the other, emblems of the gods. The Elamite period produced a stele of King Onntash-Gal and his wife, accompanied by djinns holding vases from which water is pouring. In the Assyrian period the number of bas-reliefs is considerable. The 9th century produced reliefs of two djinns adoring the sacred tree; of King Assurnasirpal holding a bow and two arrows, followed by a djinn asperging him with lustral water; and of the interior of a fortified camp with scenes of cooking and animal-slaughter or horses being groomed [**199**]. There is also the Black Obelisk of Shalmaneser III, illustrating his conquests. In the 8th century there were reliefs of King Tiglath Pileser III shooting an arrow at a town, and of the winged bulls with human heads which guarded the entrance to the palace of Sargon II at Khorsabad. There were also numerous bas-reliefs representing the campaigns of Sennacherib, in particular the one showing the interior of a fortified camp with tents depicted in sections. The 7th century produced a stele representing Esarhaddon holding two conquered enemies on a leash, and numerous scenes representing the campaigns of Assurbanipal, especially the one he conducted against Elam. From the same reign many hunting scenes are to be found.

Glyptics. This branch of art was greatly stimulated by the use of written contracts which meant employing stamps and seals. From historical times, cylinder-seals [**171–173**] of finely engraved stone or hard paste were used. Until the Akkadian period they were decorated with animals in single file, with fantastic animals (Ur) or with scenes of feasts and of men and animals fighting (Lagash). In the Akkadian period the motifs were comparatively varied. In the neo-Sumerian period the favourite theme was that of a member of the faithful being presented to a god by a divine intermediary. At the time of the first Babylonian dynasty the motif was more often that of a devotee praying before a god or group of gods. In the classical period it was the image of a divinity, as it was in the Assyrian period. In the neo-Babylonian period the theme was often Gilgamesh mastering the bull.

Moulded clay. In order to economise on stone, clay was used very frequently in the form of glazed bricks during the neo-Babylonian period. From the Kassite period there have been finds of the decorative elements of the façade of a temple at Warka, representing figures of gods and goddesses (reconstruction in the Baghdad Museum). From the Elamite period, at Susa, there are motifs for a religious building representing a djinn hugging a palm-tree; from the same site there is also the clay head of a man of a markedly Asian type. At Babylon, the Ishtar Gate and the processional way were ornamented with brightly coloured bricks in relief representing animals standing out against a dark blue background.

Terra-cotta statuettes. These were widespread. The archaic period had figurines of snake-headed women breast-feeding children. In the Sumerian period the figurines were of women without arms or feet, with bound ankles. The neo-Sumerian, Assyrian and Babylonian periods produced figurines of nude women with their hands brought up towards their breasts; others represented ithyphallic figures, dancers, musicians and games.

Painting. Decorative painting, much employed on palace walls, has hardly survived owing to its fragility. On a coat of lime, it was composed of flat tints in which whites, blues, reds and blacks predominated; perspective and shading were not used. The best collection comes from the palace at Mari (2nd millennium), with its geometrical motifs and large compositions. One of them has been reconstructed in the Louvre: it shows the king of Mari before the goddess Ishtar, as well as animals, plants and djinns. In the Assyrian palaces decoration consisted of rosettes, squares with concave sides and scenes similar to those of the bas-

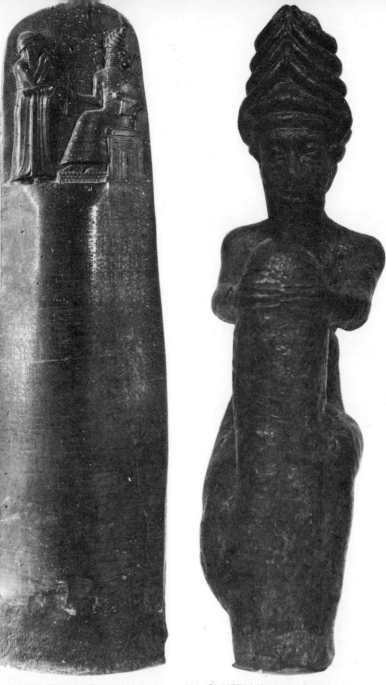

273. BABYLONIAN. Stele of Hammurabi. Beginning of the 2nd millennium. *Louvre.*

274. SUMERIAN. Votive figure dedicated by Gudea. *c.* 2400. *British Museum.*

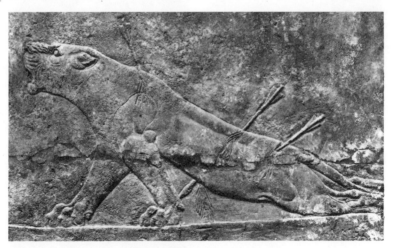

275. ASSYRIAN. Wounded lioness. Bas-relief from Nineveh. 7th century. *British Museum.*

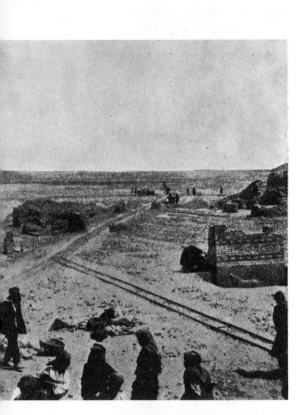

reliefs. Quantities of small objects in various techniques have been found in the excavations: alabaster vases ornamented with or shaped like animals; stone or alabaster animals; inlays such as the mosaic Standard of Ur, made with tiny plaques of mother-of-pearl, cornelian and lapis lazuli embedded in bitumen (these little plaques were engraved in the same way as the front of the harp found in the royal tombs of Ur); and Gudea's libation vase in the shape of a truncated cone (about 10 in. high), ornamented with two intertwined snakes and two dragons.

Metal arts. Governed by the same conventions as sculpture in the round and bas-relief, these arts had a great vogue in Elam; copper and bronze were used, more rarely gold and silver. In the Sumerian period there were foreparts of lions and statues of bulls in copper (site of al 'Ubaid, Ist Ur Dynasty, like the majority of the large-scale works). There were also funerary objects from the royal tombs of Ur, including ornaments, weapons, musical instruments, notably harps, ornamented with gold bulls' heads, items of harness, goldsmiths' work, *ex votos*, such as the statuette of a ram upright against a tree, of gold and silver embellished with lapis lazuli. The Akkadian period produced a copper head with a long beard (Nineveh). In the neo-Sumerian period there were many statuettes with animal or human shapes, which were buried when the temples were constructed.

Dating from the 2nd millennium at Elam there exist the headless statue of Queen Napirasu, cast in one piece by a remarkable technique; bronze gates cast in one piece, and many gold and silver statuettes of devotees. The Assyrian period produced a bronze weight in the form of a recumbent lion with a ring on its back; bronze facings of columns, imitating the bark and leaves of palm-trees, found at Khorsabad; and numerous amulet-statuettes representing djinns.

Pottery. In the Sumerian period pottery was scarlet and decorated with animal or plant motifs evoking fertility. At Susa, it had a red and black decoration on a buff-coloured ground; later it degenerated and became clumsier. In the Elamite period glazed ceramics decorated with rosettes and torsades were produced.

Philippe Jean

276. MESOPOTAMIAN. The excavations at Babylon showing, on the right, part of the Ishtar Gate.

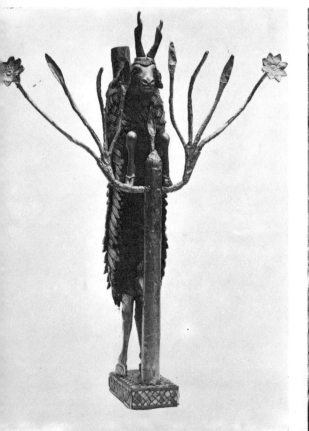

277. SUMERIAN. Goat caught in thicket. *British Museum.*

278. ASSYRIAN. Assurbanipal in his chariot. 7th century. *Louvre.*

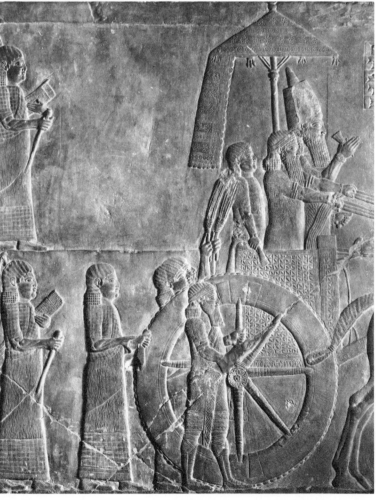

4 THE METAL CIVILISATIONS

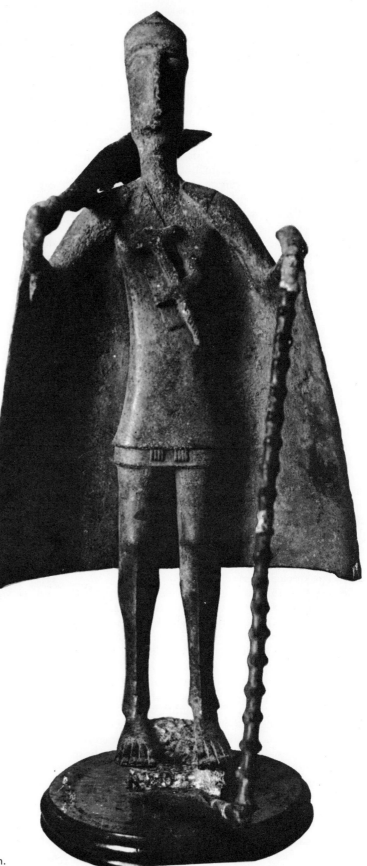

279. SARDINIA. Nuragic bronze of a tribal chieftain.
10th–5th centuries B.C.

ART FORMS AND SOCIETY *René Huyghe*

It was not the discovery of metal as such which changed the world. It had long been known, because it is found in its natural state. The Eskimo for example knows how to hammer meteoric iron; Neolithic man used gold, silver and especially copper. What transformed man and his ways of living, thinking and acting were the new techniques. With metallurgy, the art of treating ores, smelting and making alloys, a new world was born.

The character of the metal arts

Theoretically three stages succeeded each other: hammer-wrought working, then the smelting of metal in its crude form, and lastly the alloying of copper and tin, or copper and antimony, creating bronze, a material harder than stone; only then were the traditions handed down since the beginning of the Neolithic overthrown.

Later iron, when man knew how to prepare it, once again effected a tremendous advance, by providing a material which was simultaneously light, tensile, malleable and strong.

It seems certain that bronze and bronze-working originated in the Near East, where Anatolia and Armenia were mining regions. It was probably four or five centuries later, towards the middle of the 3rd millennium, that the Anatolians, following the law which drives the rough mountain-dweller to swoop down on the plain and plunder the farmer, descended on the 'Fertile Crescent' from the north. It is possible that they were encouraged in their raids by the exhaustion of their resources of ore, and also by the earthquakes of which traces have been found.

The eastern Mediterranean, like the whole Aegean area, was at the Neolithic stage. Then metal helped to advance peoples who were backward in relation to others so that they suddenly subjugated their civilised neighbours. In effect, metal provides its users with weapons which give them superiority in warfare. It projects them into the vanguard of evolution at a time when they are ill-prepared for it. Therefore it speeds up history and completely upsets its expected course.

So first the Achaeans, the 'bronze men' of about 2000, and then the Dorians, the 'iron men' towards 1200 came to transform the Greek world with their attacks. Thus in western Europe, a region still savage in relation to the empires, the Celts asserted themselves as their formidable rivals.

Another effect of metal appeared from the very beginning. It so speeded up the course of history that it initiated the acceleration of the rhythm with which man developed. This speeding up has gone on ever since. It counterbalanced the stabilisation imposed by agriculture which naturally led men to settle. The metal user subsists on the resources of the earth like the farmer, but whereas the latter fructifies land which is living and renews itself, the former exploits land which exhausts itself. Thus in a new way he returns to the migratory life of prehistory. Either he intensifies commercial relations by ranging the world in search of raw materials and also to distribute his manufactured products, or moves on as he exhausts local supplies of mineral resources.

Consequently the metal arts most frequently have a characteristic which seems peculiar to nomads. Not greatly attracted by realism, the patient and emotional observation of nature, at which sedentary man often arrives, they like abstract shapes, the ones which proceed from purely intellectual invention, from the resources of the human brain rather than attentive contact with one's surroundings. At the most the animal, the nomad's companion, animated the play of lines with its presence, although this was more particularly in the art of the steppes, inheritor of the Mesopotamian themes. But the Iron Age, from the Hallstatt to the La Tène periods, mainly concerned itself with patterns. Another concrete factor can be added to these psychological ones: peoples who move from place to place can only possess valuable objects which are transportable; weapons, goldsmiths' work and items of harness held the first place. Practical functions could only just make room for decoration, mainly for ornamental combinations of lines to which colours were freely added. This is true of the art of the barbarians, the ultimate outcome, even in the 5th and 6th centuries A.D.

Metal art had a considerable area of diffusion. It propagated its shapes and themes over unlimited distances. Architecture, sculpture and mural painting can do no more than affect the traveller by leaving him with a blurred memory. Metal objects, on the other hand, were available everywhere as an easy model to copy. The agrarian civilisations had little more than cloth, much harder to preserve, to play the same role.

THE AEGEAN WORLD

The first metal workers discovered the inexhaustible copper of Cyprus near the coast. The local Neolithic peoples had had only the faintest idea of its existence. But their need for tin was to carry them on the quest which Claude F. A. Schaeffer will retrace further on.

The role of the maritime peoples

From then onwards, the cooperation of the metallurgists and the seafaring peoples was inevitable, and they gave the art of navigation a fresh stimulus in exchange for the services they demanded. The Aegean Sea, dotted with islands, had stimulated maritime relations and commercial exchanges from the dawn of civilisation. We know the price which was set on the obsidian of Melos before metal. Very soon the Aegean was in contact with the coast of Asia Minor and through it with the caravans of the hinterland; we know that the rare metals from the Caucasus were bartered for the copper and lead ores of the islands, Seriphos or Amorgos, for example. Contact was rapidly made with Egypt, herself equipped with a remarkable fleet and capable of undertaking some of the boldest expeditions in antiquity. Lastly, routes were even established towards the North Sea in the middle of the 2nd millennium, for its amber which was so precious at the time.

Until about 2500, the ships of the Cyclades predominated; but towards 2000 Crete was already exporting its remarkable pottery. However, their successors the Phoe-

294
298

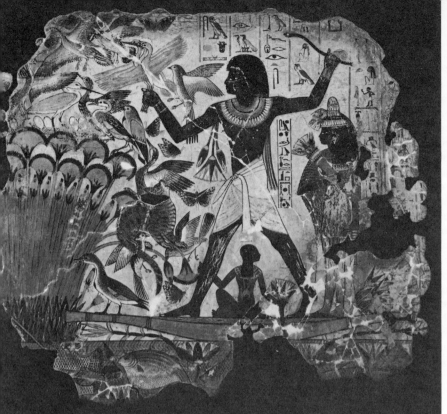

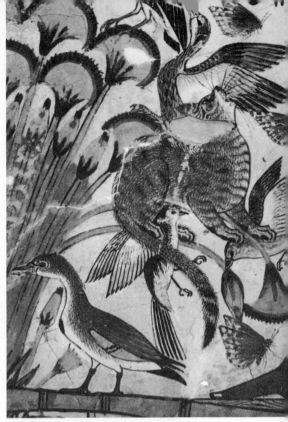

280. EGYPTIAN. Fowling in the marshes. Theban tomb painting. XVIIIth Dynasty. *British Museum. Right:* Detail.

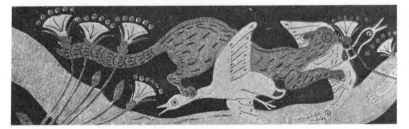

281. CRETAN. Detail of a decorated dagger from the royal necropolis at Mycenae. About the middle of the 2nd millennium.

Whatever novelty it contributed, the Cretan civilisation is linked up in many regards with the civilisation of the agrarian empires, especially Egypt. Exchanges with that country were particularly in evidence at the time of the XVIIIth Dynasty. Both show the same feeling for life and the animal and plant kingdoms, although the conventions of the law of full-face representation were preserved [280, 282].

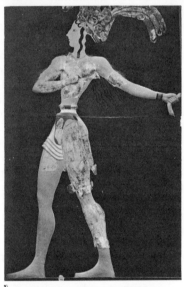

282. CRETAN. CNOSSUS. The Prince with Lilies. Late Minoan I. *Herakleion Museum.*

284. EGYPTIAN. Kingfisher in the papyrus thicket. Fresco in the Green Room of the Palace at Tell el Amarna. XVIIIth Dynasty.

283. CRETAN. CNOSSUS. Blue bird among wild roses, lilies and other flowers. Wall painting. Middle Minoan III to Late Minoan I.

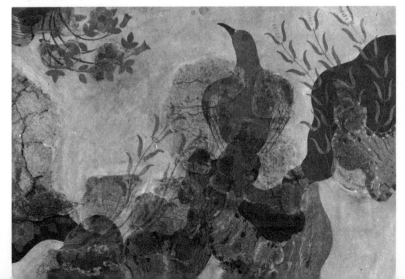

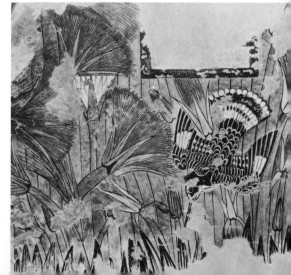

nicians were launching into their role of middlemen and navigators; they were no more than that, and their art was always limited to manufacturing objects in which heterogeneous influences were combined in a practical way, so as not to run the risk of surprising and putting off their customers by personal stylistic creations.

This was not so with the Cretans, who were isolated, thus developing an independent art and civilisation, and yet played the role of turntable of the Mediterranean by their geographical situation. The requirements and potentialities of metal gave their fleet an extraordinary impetus, as it did later to the Phoenicians. They profited by it to extend the field over which their personal creations were diffused. When the Achaean invaders, who also progressively became rival navigators, had defeated and ruined Crete towards 1400 and succeeded to it both at sea and in the field of art, it seems that they increased the scope of their excursions ever further; they never stopped doing so during the four centuries when they were masters of the situation before succumbing in their turn to the Dorian invasions, coming from the same northern source as themselves.

Cretan at first, then Mycenaean, it was however the same art which for a millennium sent its works for considerable distances. It seems that we find echoes of it as far as the other end of the Mediterranean in Spain.

Via the mouth of the Danube and also the upper end of the Adriatic, Aegean culture advanced to make contact with the terminus of the land and sea routes which led to the tin of Bohemia and the Scilly Isles, or even the amber of the Baltic. The most striking find has been that of a Mycenaean dagger in a Bronze Age tumulus at Delynt in Cornwall. The repertoire of decorative shapes of Scan-
293 dinavian metal-work shows singular resemblances with
292 that of the Aegean Sea. We only need to follow the adventure of the Silk Route, which later carried the precious material from China to the Mediterranean, to conceive what distances luxury objects could traverse by successive transmissions. With them went the forms which fertilised distant horizons.

Crete and its relations with the agrarian peoples

But what was this Cretan art composed of? Basically the civilisation of the island was of the agrarian urban type elaborated and diffused by Cilicia from the 5th and 4th millennia onwards. It exhibits all the same characteristics: a religion primarily devoted to a mother goddess, connected with the idea of fecundity, and inherited undoubtedly from the peoples who inhabited the island in the 4th millennium; her worship was celebrated by priestesses. The matriarchal civilisation of the beginning of the Neolithic therefore has its prolongation there. Nevertheless the sometimes densely populated towns (Sir Arthur Evans put the population of Cnossus at 80,000) reveal the authority of the sovereign as in Egypt or Mesopotamia, although it may have been more flexible. In their immense store-houses, the prince accumulated provisions, treasures in kind, constituting the social surplus which he used to pay the craftsmen and officials directly with the products of the soil, grain, oil, wine, etc. contained in enormous
322 jars (pithoi). At first sight, then, one would be tempted to classify Cretan civilisation among those which have been studied in the last chapter, and it must be admitted that in many ways Cretan art has the same characteristics.

However it holds its position mainly by its innovating features coming from commercial and maritime life, simultaneously with those due to metal techniques. Shortly after 2500 came the introduction of bronze; and later in the Greek tradition, Crete remained renowned as one of the great centres of iron manufacture.

Socially, too, Crete was more developed: the sovereign no longer had, it seems, the superhuman character he always preserved in Egypt and Mesopotamia. It has justly been pointed out that, in distinction to the arts of the agrarian empires, the art of Crete did not hierarchise the 217 figures by making the most powerful of them, kings or princes, of a larger size. Born and developed very much 331 later than that of its powerful neighbours, the Cretan civilisation, although the agrarian basis remained alive there with its consequences, deserves therefore to be studied here along with the metal civilisations.

The Cretans' very ancient relations with the coast of Syria and via her with Mesopotamia and Egypt (which they also reached directly with their ships) constantly confirmed the contacts they kept up with the empires. Very soon, the Cretan ports, the ancient Kamo for example, exchanged their jars of oil and wine, their cattle even, for the vegetables, cereals and fabrics which the Delta supplied. They also received objects of art, ivories, blue earthenware and scarab seals. Later they supplied the Nile valley with copper retransmitted from Cyprus, which also became a Cretan protectorate as from the middle of the 3rd millennium, as well as the tin and amber brought back from the distant lands of central and northern Europe.

Relations were particularly close with the XVIIIth Dynasty. It is even probable that, if the new characteristics of the art of el Amarna were stimulated by a religious revolution, they were also strengthened by the example of Cretan art, already removed from all the hieratic traditions and orientated towards the bold facing of life. Through this reverse influence Crete paid off a part of the considerable debt she owed Egypt.

The origins of an art of life

In fact, the singularity of Cretan art is that, although it was the product of a people who owe everything to Asia Minor, it constantly evinces much deeper affinities with its elder brother of the Nile valley. Admittedly, a good deal came to it from Anatolia, if it was only the example of patterns and metal which inspired the pottery with flame-like decoration of Early Minoan II. Metal techniques soon came from the same source. After that, Crete made an advance which clearly proves its wider contacts with the developed peoples. As for the architecture of the first fortified palaces at the beginning of the 2nd millennium, it proclaims its debt to Akkadian, Sumerian or Hittite models. But the actual spirit and the style come from their Egyptian counterparts; they cultivate and develop the feeling of life caught in the intensity of the action it expresses and the impression it gives. Because of the relations of Egyptian art with the funerary cults, it is too often thought that it was essentially hieratic and funerary. In fact, the frescoes and statuettes which kept the spectacle of earthly life in front of the mummy caught it in all the vivacity of its dynamism. Now Crete was linked with Egypt from the time of its first maritime relations.

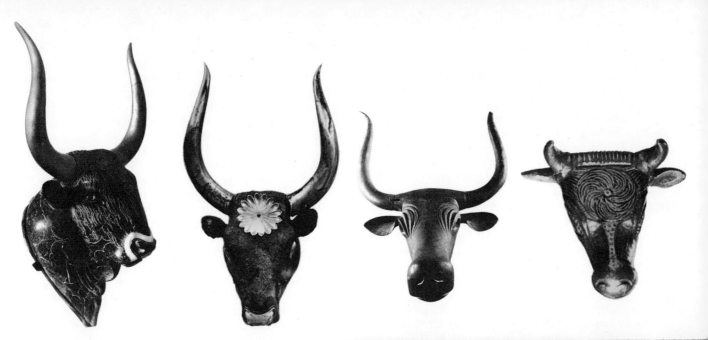

285. *Left*. CRETAN. Rhyton (drinking vessel) in the form of a bull's head. Steatite. Cnossus. Late Minoan I.

286. *Left centre*. MYCENAE. Silver rhyton in the form of a bull's head. *Athens Museum.*

287. *Right centre*. BALEARIC ISLANDS. BRONZE AGE. Bull's head in bronze. *Archaeological Museum, Barcelona.*

288. *Far right*. THRACIAN-GETAEAN WITH SCYTHIAN INFLUENCE. Bull's head in silver gilt found at Craiova, Roumania. *c. 300*B.C. *National Museum, Bucharest.*

THE SPREAD OF CRETAN ART

Thanks to its maritime trade, the essentially pioneering Cretan civilisation had a far-reaching influence, both in the north-east as far as the Black Sea [288] and in the west to the far end of the Mediterranean [287]. The spread of the Minoan bull, sometimes accompanied by the solar disc, is eloquent testimony of this. At the same time, the repertory of forms was enriched. We see the spread of dynamic patterns: scrolls, whorls and spirals which sometimes link up and carry the eye on from one to another. Consecutive spirals running in opposite directions form a favourite decorative theme, probably originally of symbolical significance, perhaps fire or lightning. A legacy of the Cycladic Neolithic, they are found both in Egypt [289], and among the Celts.

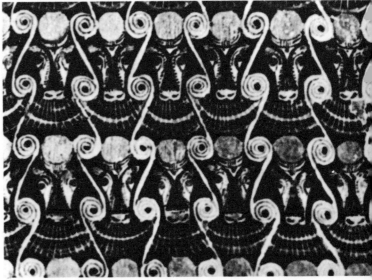

289. EGYPTIAN. Detail of a fresco with the two motifs, the bull's head and the successive reversed spirals. Ceiling in the palace of Amenhotep III at Thebes. XVIIIth Dynasty.

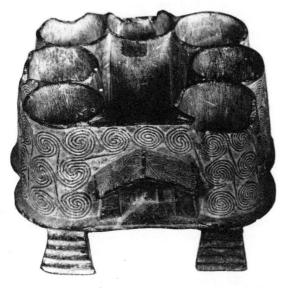

290. CYCLADES. Neolithic model of a house from Melos. *Antikensammlungen, Munich.*

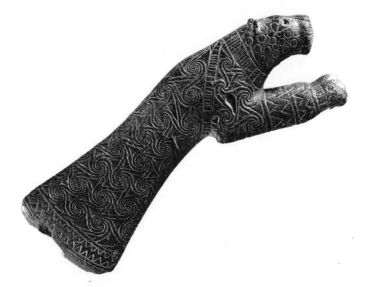

291. CRETE. MIDDLE MINOAN III. Panther-shaped axe-head from Mallia. *Herakleion Museum.*

So the masterpieces of Cretan painting remind one of Egyptian painting: far more than by the conventions (full-face views, different colour schemes for male and female bodies) or the identicality of certain gestures, it is in the gift of seizing the essential of an attitude in action. The simple comparison of the celebrated Prince with Lilies, (Herakleion Museum) with, for example, the funerary painting representing a wild goose hunt (British Museum, XVIIIth Dynasty) or the cat and birds, as they are represented in Crete and Egypt, brings the evidence together. These kinships were especially marked at the time of Crete's repercussions on the Egypt of Amenhotep IV. The mocking humorous air that the Cretans added and which is almost without analogy except in the art of ancient Peru—so different from tragic Mexico—was not even totally unknown to Egyptian art.

Crete went further than Egypt in the quest for capturing and rendering the fleeting moment; it even tried to create forms suggestive of movements in the geometry of decoration. In this, Cretan art shows a further development than the art of the agrarian empires on which fidelity to original traditions weighed heavily.

And Crete's gaze was now solely turned in this new direction. It did not invent the spiral which had existed since the Neolithic and was taken from the older ceramics of the Cyclades; the latter incidentally seem to have borrowed it from Danubian pottery via Thessalian Neolithic, especially that of Dimini. But Crete made it its favourite shape and diffused it wherever it exerted influence, even indirectly. Admittedly, it is found on Egyptian scarabs, mainly spread by the Hyksos kings, but is it not a borrowing from the Aegean?

Even the natural shapes, such as the lily for example, when they show traces of scrolling become an excuse for multiplied spirals. One has the impression that certain themes were borrowed from nature (octopuses, to quote one case) mainly because they lend themselves so wonderfully to moving undulations and loops. Friezes with spiralled elements occupied the place which was held by the angular zigzag in the Neolithic.

The simple spiral suggests its multiplication, in particular the shapes like double springs which knot and unknot, seeming to spout forth from one another, as on the panther-shaped axe from Mallia. There we see the birth of a system of patterns which was to flourish prodigiously in the metal arts and shine again in Celtic art more than a millennium later; it was to form the triskele ('three-legged') pattern characteristic of this decoration. After over another millennium, it crops up again in that supreme flowering of Celtic art produced by the Irish as from the 7th and 8th centuries. We are thus dealing with an essential, lasting contribution to the history of decorations.

A new vision and conception of art

We now have to ask ourselves what could have stimulated this tendency which until then had been no more than latent in the artistic 'capital' of Egypt; we must seek out what made it almost the predominant motif. There is no doubt that the reason is contained in two new characteristics by which the Cretans were separated from the strictly agrarian civilisations: they became established in the 3rd millennium with the advance of the use of metal coming from Asia Minor; they developed at the moment when bronze became widely used; and the Mycenaean civilisation which succeeded them coincided with the great phase of the diffusion of bronze from east to west, before iron, in about 1100, came to play the lead in its turn. Consequently, the destiny of the Mycenaeans was bound up with that of metal.

It was equally bound up with the sea: the Cretans were the great navigators of the Mediterranean in the 2nd millennium. If the landsmen and farmers seemed to be obsessed by the problems of the regular and stable division of space, after the manner of their fields, the seafarers were steeped in a quite different sort of experience: that of the endless moving of continuous forces blending into each other, which was suggested by the sea. Seeing successive spirals running one behind the other round the side of a vase, we cannot help thinking of stylised waves pursuing each other. The same theme was to assert itself in Scandinavian art down to those great navigators the Vikings. In the same way, the living forms of the depths, from the octopus to seaweed, are flexible and indeterminate, lending themselves to scrolls; the shell, for its part, sometimes exhibits the most classical realisation of a spiral to be found in nature.

But if the sea helped the Cretans, by the visual experience it provided, to conceive their technical repertory, manual experience may have contributed to it even more forcefully. Stone and wood are dressed in facets which are rounded off in the finishing to a greater or lesser degree; potter's clay tends to the spherical shape and its softness. As for metal, it is malleable when melted in the mould; prepared by the cire perdue process, it presupposes a model in which the kneaded paste is often shaped in coils. It frequently gave rise to threads and bands whose extremities it was necessary to soften down by a final scrolling which was in effect a spiral. The S-shape is one of the most spontaneous creations of metallurgy; it is the one which was very soon associated with the lightning which Hephaistos-Vulcan later forged for Zeus-Jupiter; it still recurs in our own day in iron garden railings.

The refined Cretan producer of valuable easily transportable objects was a goldsmith even more than a metallurgist. There again, damascening, which he practised so skilfully on his daggers, was a metal thread technique lending itself to undulation and scrolling. The same thing held good for filigree work. Metal, the more so when worked in thin sheets as is the case with goldsmith's work, demands threadlike outlines and their tendency to curves and whorls.

Thus the 'visual' and the 'manual' were yoked together to give the Cretan a new conception of form. The mental process in its turn lends itself to this conception: the seafarer who is led to make perpetual comparisons between beliefs, manners and arts is much less attached to the maintenance of tradition than the farmer. The Egyptian had a fleet, but he was not a sailor: therein lies the difference. Those islanders, the Cretans, found themselves in the perpetual school of renewal.

At the same time they put an end to the belief that the image has the value of a magical double. It seems that with them it even lost at an early stage the symbolical—hence prophylactic—value which remained so tenaciously attached to decorative shapes in particular.

As they had everywhere else, the usual forms must have had a religious origin in Crete. The bull, symbolised by the curve of his horns, was the god of subterranean

280–282

283, 284

290

326f

291

326

335

285

170

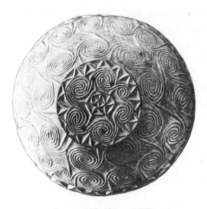

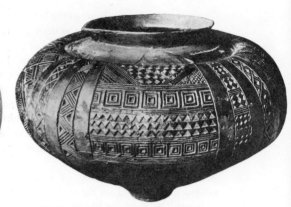

292. CRETE. Lid of a stone vessel from a burial cave in Maroneia. Early Minoan II.

293. DENMARK. Bronze plaque with spirals. Scandinavian Bronze Age V. *Stockholm Museum.*

294. EARLY IRON AGE (HALLSTATT). Funerary urn found at Sternberg. *Antikensammlung, Stuttgart.*

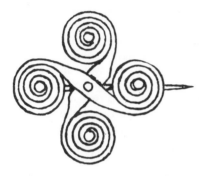

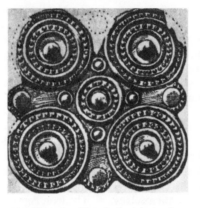

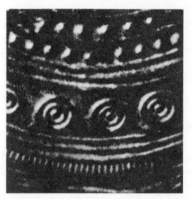

295. EARLY IRON AGE (HALL-STATT). Bronze brooch from Italy.

296. Brooch with a design derived from the four spirals. *Württemberg.*

297. BRANDENBURG. Detail of a gold vessel from the Eberswald treasure. 700 B.C.

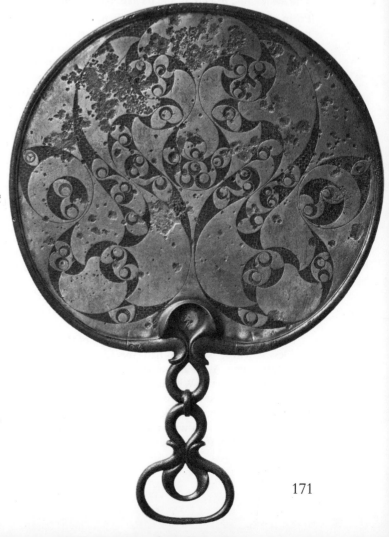

The Cretan theme of successive spirals [292], finally simplified into a sort of Vitruvian scroll, spread everywhere with the advent of bronze, from the Black Sea to the Baltic [293].
The First Iron Age (Hallstatt) marks a total reaction in favour of rectilinear and discontinuous geometrical forms (predominance of parallelograms, angular forms, etc. [294]. This tendency is so strong that the spiral scrolls of the first pieces using metal threads [295] were transformed into concentric circles [296] which were to become a current ornament [297]. However, with the Second Iron Age (La Tène), which corresponds to the flowering of the Celtic and Gallic civilisations, there was a revival of dynamic, continuous wave and spiral patterns.

298. GREAT BRITAIN. Engraved bronze mirror, known as the 'Desborough Mirror'. Beginning of the Christian era. *British Museum.*

171

forces; he lived in the heart of the labyrinth, which seemed to lend itself to the idea of the descent into the bowels of the earth and of which the spiral is perhaps the stylised image. It may also have been in correlation with snakes, also animals of the underworld which were associated with the worship of the mother goddess. In the same way, the double reversed spiral is often connected with lightning, also represented by the double-headed axe, just as in Brittany the polished stones which recall this primitive weapon still bear the name of 'thunder stones'. But these were merely survivals. For the Cretans, the image hardly had any magical meaning or religious background; it ceased to be sacred, as the most seductive reproductions of life still were in the Egyptian tombs: its value was only in what it was, what it showed. It was a spectacle for the eyes, a visual pleasure. Let us take careful note: a primitive era of art is over: it assumes a meaning hitherto unknown which it is not to lose again.

By thus conferring autonomy and the feeling of pleasure it procures on art, the Cretans prepared the way for Greece, which nevertheless accomplished one step further; it began to think out this pleasure, to analyse it, to seek it less in the evocation of what was depicted than in the way it was represented and in its beauty.

EUROPE

Thus the fleets of the Mediterranean effected the liaison between the first metal-producing civilisations and the barbarian peoples in Europe who owned the ores indispensable for its manufacture, although they themselves were still vegetating in a more primitive state.

The awakening of Europe and its geometrical traditions

From the beginning of the 2nd millennium, there appeared a movement converging on the vast reserves of ore formed by the 'metallic mountains' in the north of Hungary, then those which encircle the Bohemian plain to the north and south-west. Their copper and tin could be reached either from the north of the Aegean by reaching the Danube and sailing up it, or by attaining the central Danube from the upper end of the Adriatic and by way of tributaries like the Sava or the Drava. Daggers and pottery recalling Cypriot art have been found at this end of the Adriatic, which was reached from before 2000. About the same time, Cretan ships probably reached Sardinia and even Spain, since at Los Millares the influence of the Aegean and the tholoi (round buildings) seem to appear at the beginning of the 2nd millennium.

The spread of metal, superimposing a Bronze Age I on older cultures, was ensured from the Danube basin throughout the European world by routes which had already been tried in the Neolithic age: in the same way, via the rivers, ribbon pottery had spread towards the Baltic, mainly by the Oder, and towards the North Sea, by the Elbe.

Then came the disappearance in Europe of the fertility goddesses whose worship had spread everywhere in Neolithic times. Art was reduced to the ornamentation of metallic objects. Within these shifting, confused, obscure cultures we see two styles emerge, which alternated according to time and place: one rectilinear, the other curvilinear, both with their roots in the Neolithic. But their different sources seem to correspond to the two points through which Europe must have learnt the art of agriculture: one in the south-west, in Spain, under North African influence, the other in the east, by the Danube, from Asia Minor.

The first zone seems to have cultivated and diffused the old Neolithic repertoire, the themes of parallels, checks, angles and serrations, while the second created for different technical reasons the whole gamut of combinations of spiral scrolls and whorls diffused by ribbon pottery and which would have probably been wiped out with it if the Cyclades and especially Crete had not very early on absorbed, fructified and spread abroad the lesson, as we have just seen.

The decoration of European metal is divided between these two types. The first, rectilinear and severe, prolonged during the Bronze Age and the beginning of the Iron Age at Hallstatt the pre-eminence it had acquired in the Neolithic; it was to have an unexpected expansion with the Villanovans who introduced it to north Italy, and in Greece with the Dorians, with whom it probably inspired the geometric style at the beginning of the 1st millennium; the second, increasingly leaning towards the whirlwind of sinuosities and spirals, was handed down to Bronze Age II by the Aegean example and, via the amber route, as far as Scandinavia where it became implanted. We should not be surprised at this when we note that the trade of the time carried products from Egypt, such as blue faience pearls, as far as England, reached by both Atlantic navigation and exchanges with Scandinavia.

The Iron Age created a new state of affairs. That metal, also coming from Asia Minor, had given a fresh impetus to European industry especially in the central basin of the Danube. It ensured the sudden promotion of the hitherto outcast and backward peoples of Europe and their revenge on the pre-eminence of the Mediterranean, where the empires were soon attacked by them. This first upset, from the beginning of the 2nd millennium, was one of the causes of the Dorian expansion and the rising tide of the Peoples of the Sea, reaching as far as Egypt, while the Hittites were collapsing and the Mesopotamian order was dislodged. Later the Celts moved off from the Danubian regions and spread into northern Italy and Gaul. A second expansion led the Gauls to Italy in the 4th century and into Greece in the 3rd century; they seized Rome and Delphi; a setback carried them to Asia Minor where they founded Galatia.

The first Iron Age, called after the settlement of Hallstatt in the Austrian Tyrol, marks a parallel reassertion, in the first half of the 1st millennium, of the old European decorative heritage, with the predominance of triangles and lozenges, rows of zigzags hatched with criss-cross striations parallel to their sides; as a survival of bronze and its solar worship, it mingled with them some stylised animals with a religious role, such as the horse and the swan, which symbolised their beliefs about death and the last journey. The spiral, which had spread along with bronze, was as it were reabsorbed and gave way to the regularity of concentric circles, with solar significance, even where technical needs, the scrolled ends of metal threads, would lead one to expect it. Thus we see the brooches with four branches rolled up into spirals change into a quadripartite assembly of closed circles.

In the same way, in the decoration of belts, for ex-

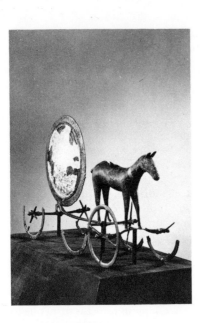

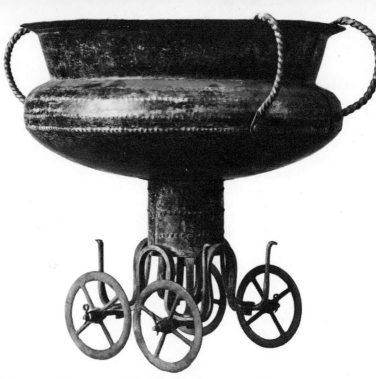

299. DENMARK. The sun chariot from Trundholm. About 1000 B.C. *National Museum, Denmark.*

300. BOHEMIA. BRONZE III. Cauldron of Milavec, a smaller version of the big processional chariots.

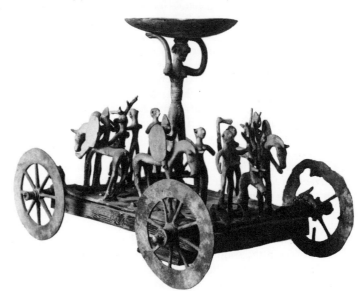

301. STYRIA (AUSTRIA). Hallstatt chariot with bronze figures, from Strettweg. *Graz Museum.*

Through their art the metal civilisations reveal a religion in which fire played a large part, as was natural for iron-smiths. The sun, which is an integral part of it, was represented by circles and discs; it was associated with lightning, represented by S-shapes, and thunder, which was perhaps evoked by the rolling of the ritual metal chariots. Ever since the spread of the Indo-Europeans, the sun appears in art from India to Scandinavia, connected with the horse during its journey through the heavens, and with the swan during its return through the underworld on the river/Ocean [in the same way the Greeks were familiar with Apollo's chariot and the rivans of 'hyperborean' Apollo]. The Scandinavian 'razors' are decorated with a solar wheel, a horse, or a swan. The same associations are found among the Villanovans and the Etruscans. They are stylised and, too, employ the S-shape. But the two animals linked to the chariot or the solar banque are used for the funerary voyage towards the west, beyond the ocean, both in Crete at the end of the Minoan, and in the northern countries. The wild boar, like the stag, seems to be connected with the hereafter.

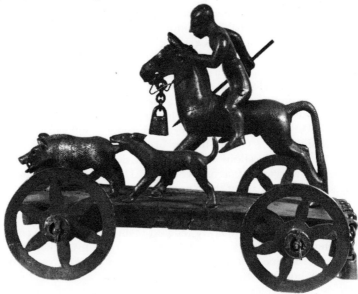

302. SPAIN. Cult chariot: hunter and hound pursuing a wild boar. Found at Merida. End of 1st millennium. *St Germain Museum.*

ample, where damascening or chasing would have seemed to encourage, by their ease of working, series of spirals rolled up end to end, like those of the handsome bronze Scandinavian bucklers, the Hallstatt craftsman preferred the repoussé technique or embossing with a point: the latter tended to make him work in lines and dots and therefore led him to juxtapose squares, rectangles or simple circles.

This was a renunciation of the open shape which gave a sense of movement to decoration; it was a return to the closed, immobile, hard, static shape. Should we be surprised then to see the rebirth of those alternations of squares and parallel lines, which, from the Neolithic, evoked for us the future metopes and triglyphs of Greek temples? Must they have engendered the latter, by way of the Dorians? It looks very much as if the peoples of the north were making a vast effort to reinvigorate the most archaic traditions at the same time as their power was growing.

Celtic art, a return to the dynamic style

The second Iron Age, known as La Tène, from the name of a settlement on the lake of Neuchâtel, inaugurated Celtic art in the strict sense of the word shortly after 500. But henceforth the eclipse of the Mediterranean was over; what have been perhaps rather exaggeratedly called the 'Greek Middle Ages' came to an end. The remains of the old Creto-Mycenaean civilisation, driven from the west, emigrated to the east coast of the Aegean Sea, where Ionia was to become such a brilliant centre of Greek thought and art in the great periods. Then continental Greece, especially Attica, acquired a growing brilliance. And yet again the European metal arts experienced the prestige of the Mediterranean; once more rigid shapes carried on from the Neolithic became more flexible by contact with examples from the south-east.

As early as the Hallstatt epoch the northern iron provinces, in contact with the Mediterranean by the Adriatic route, showed Ionian influence. The foundation of Marseille about 600 in the south of Gaul, in Liguria, created a considerable centre for diffusion, at first in the lower Rhône valley, then beyond it. Spain in her turn was open to influences from the East, Ionia, soon from classical Greece, as well as from Phoenicia, which was to be succeeded by Carthage.

There even resulted a quite unexpected effort by the Europeans to translate the human figure into sculpture in the round; in Spain, the statues of Cerro de los Santos and the famous Lady of Elche were, with their own special accent, nearly equal to their models. In Mediterranean Gaul and incidentally in the valley of the Neckar, i.e. at the points most receptive of influences, sculptures, torsos or heads, whose very theme had hitherto been unknown to northern art, made their appearance; however they submitted their Greek, Iberian or Etruscan models to radical simplifications which restored them almost to the stylised world of decorative shapes. This is what has made people talk about their 'modernity'.

Coins show even more clearly that when the Celts, particularly the Gauls, were inspired by Mediterranean, that is humanist, themes, they quickly reduced them to geometrical abstraction.

But the art of La Tène, if it agreed to share Hellenic suggestions, took hold of them definitively the better to assert its opposite nature, stimulated perhaps by the pressure coming from the steppes. Nothing is more symptomatic than to follow the transmutations it imposed on the Greek palm-leaf or again on the association of human and plant elements, as exhibited by late Greek art. In both cases, we could say that the dynamic spirit of the Cretans, quite forgotten by their successors, revived with unexpected vehemence. Everything is brought back in varying degrees to the simple or double scrolled S-shape, i.e. to the evocation of a whirlpool or a spring ready to uncoil.

The Cretans had already originated this. The art of La Tène added one stage more; it excludes everything which could fix the shape, enclose it in a definition by an outline, immobilise it by a symmetrical axis to such an extent that it is not content to suggest movement; it forces it to pass by imperceptible transitions from one part of the design to the next. It seems to be devoted to the illusion of perpetual motion which runs through all the outlines, linking them, taking its impetus from one to slide into the next one and confuse the whole in an incessant 'transformation'. For example, in the bronze rings from a Celtic chariot preserved at Saint-Germain-en-Laye, the human masks which seem to be interspersed with the ornamental motifs can no longer be distinguished from them; they are confused with the stream of alternating scrolls and lose themselves in it without any clear boundary.

Art not only portrayed the spectacle of life and its movement; it became life and movement itself. It forced the eye to follow its linear play and left it no rest or stopping point with its rebounding whirls. Using terms which only came into use later, one could say that Celtic art is the baroque form of the dynamism of which Crete had created the classical expression.

Art therefore no longer only presents images, charged with magical power, of a religious symbol, of a narrative sense or even of a simple visual pleasure as it had done more or less continuously until now; now it demands the participation of the spectator; it imposes a rhythm on him, it acts on his sensibility and carries him along with its impulse. It is no longer a simple spectacle put at man's disposal; it begins to exert a hold on him. Thus a new enrichment of artistic possibilities is acquired, admittedly in a still unconscious but nevertheless effective manner.

THE STEPPES

This characteristic does not belong exclusively to Celtic art; it is found in another metal art, the art of the steppes. For many years the agrarian lands of the Danube had been in contact with the border of the steppes and their nomadic populations. As from the La Tène epoch, the influence of the latter made itself constantly felt on the 'barbarian', i.e. non-Mediterranean, metal arts of Europe.

But the art of the steppes opened up to them unexpected prolongations which could not even have been suspected. A nomad art, confining itself to weapons or items of harness, working gold or bronze, it ranged over an immense area, from the Carpathians to China. Via the south it even came into contact with other arts, taking from them themes and features which it absorbed and used to express its own conceptions; via the Black Sea, it had access to the Greek world; via the Caucasus it reached Iran and the Mesopotamian civilisations, from which it harvested many animal themes. Luristan is a curious half-way house where the symmetrical feeling of the Chaldeans was married to the bold stylisation of the nomads (see p. 219).

This art reached in the west as far as the Danube, Hungary, Bohemia and even the Lusatian cultures; but, via the peoples of the Ordos plateau in the curve of the Yellow River, it insinuated itself at the eastern extremity into the Chinese world.

Towards 700 the Scythians passed through southern Russia to reach Bulgaria and introduced the animal style among the Europeans. Here once again art showed a gift for staying on the borderline which separates the still recognisable evocation of visible realities, in this case animals, and the purely linear combinations in which the curve, the scroll, the continuous imperceptible passage from one shape to another, predominate; this strange

insistence on transformation results in the tail of a beast ending in a lion's head, or the horns of a stag in the heads of birds of prey.

The role of the nomad was to be a vital one, for in the rivalry between the Mediterranean and the barbarian arts they formed an unassailable artistic reserve. Greece and then her heir Rome could formulate their conceptions more and more clearly, then imperiously impose them progressively on peoples faithful to what could be called the metal aesthetic; Magna Graecia and the Roman Empire were able to extend the limits of their sphere of influence; Gaul and England were able to follow in the wake of the conqueror. But from the day Rome cracked and collapsed, the barbarian hordes only reintroduced to Europe the art which had been stifled there for so long. They brought it with them from the steppes to re-integrate it with the Western tradition and so prepare the way for the new phenomenon of the Middle Ages.

EUROPE IN THE AGE OF METALS

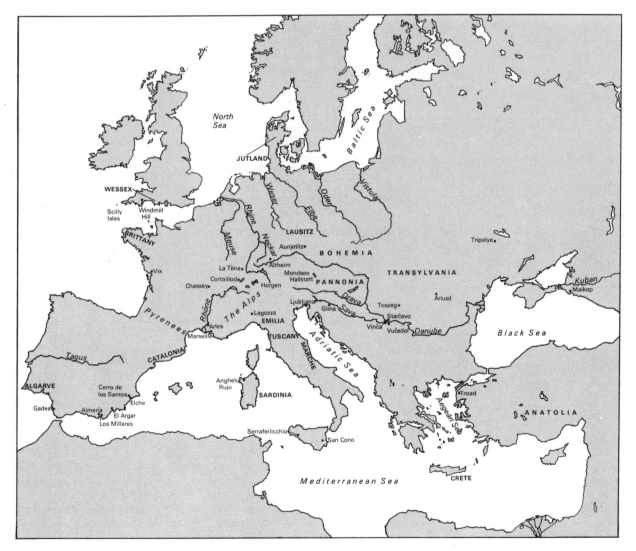

THE APPEARANCE AND SPREAD OF METAL *Claude F. A. Schaeffer*

The major innovations and profound changes in art, especially in the brilliant periods, were principally the after-effects of technical discoveries and the consequent social changes. Metal wrought its own artistic revolution. At first it was to spread in a world in which agrarian societies still at the Neolithic stage existed side by side with societies already at the urban and organised stage. Claude Schaeffer, whose excavations in Cyprus and at Ras Shamra have done so much to clear up these problems, here sets forth the general views on the diffusion of metal which he was the first to formulate.

The great agrarian and monarchical societies of the ancient Orient, dependent on the fertile alluvial soil of the Euphrates and the Nile, developed in their valleys as if in a gigantic cradle. Their adolescence in the 4th millennium and at the beginning of the 3rd passed through a series of crises caused principally by increasing populations. In Egypt and Mesopotamia they entailed dynastic changes and agrarian reforms, then quietened down without having shaken the administrative organisation of those vast empires.

The 3rd millennium: the birth of metallurgy

Between 2400 and 2300 B.C. a general unrest occurred, shaking all the civilisations in western Asia, from the northern Caucasus to the valley of the Nile in the south.

Throughout this vast zone, signs of upheaval can be seen in the strata of the middle of the 3rd millennium. What was the nature of the events which caused such severe destruction in Anatolia and Syria-Palestine, the fall of the ancient Egyptian empire, the upheavals in Cyprus and Mesopotamia, and whose repercussions reached Persia and the countries of the Caucasus? As far as we can interpret the traces of the Early Bronze Age, it seems as if we must seek the major cause of these troubles in an ethnic disturbance in the mountainous zone and in pressure from the north on the civilisations established in Syria-Palestine, Cyprus and the valleys of the Euphrates and the Nile at the extremities of the 'Fertile Crescent'. In its broad scope, its north-south direction and its termination in Egypt, this disturbance resembles the invasion of the Peoples of the North and of the Sea who put an end to the civilisations of the ancient Orient towards 1200 B.C.

It is probable that natural causes contributed to and even unleashed this pressure. The homogeneity of the weapons used by the ethnic element which later installed itself at Ras Shamra and in the majority of the other big sites explored in Syria-Palestine is an indication; this vast movement of peoples seems to have been accompanied if not led by a warlike element which was able to extend its conquests to the huge areas of western Asia and beyond. In fact, after the fall of the VIth Dynasty, Egypt went through a long period of instability when the Delta was occupied by the Asiatics. At the other tip of the 'Fertile Crescent', the precarious situation of the empire bequeathed by Sargon I to Naram Sin was the consequence

of rebellions between 2340 and 2300. In the time of his successor Sharkalisharri, the Guti and other invaders descended into the valley of the two rivers and created a state of anarchy which lasted until about 2100 when the IIIrd Ur Dynasty began.

During the corresponding period, the situation in the north was quite different. Between 2300 and 2000 is the period of the powerful prosperous countries in Asia Minor. We find the treasures and the surrounding walls, 39 feet thick, of Troy III; level I B, so rich in finds, at Alishar; the layers at Tarsa between 29 and 33 feet, whose richness was clear after the first borings; the royal tombs of Alaca Huyuk, full of gold plate, bronze and even iron weapons, the first sign of this metal which was still precious at the time. Everywhere the newcomers installed themselves among the ruins and ashes of cities and buried their exceptionally rich treasures and funerary furniture in them. They seem to have benefited by the changes which had taken place. Still farther north, in the Caucasus, the wealth of the kurgan (sepulchral barrow) at Maikop, near the Caspian Sea, of the tomb of Astrabad and the treasures of Hissar III dazzle us with their profusion of precious metals. Nothing comparable from this period has been found in contemporary sites to the south of the mountainous zone, in Syria-Palestine, Egypt and Mesopotamia, countries all traditionally rich.

The archaeological materials and cuneiform texts so far known do not entirely clarify this situation. However it is accepted that it coincided with the first development of the bronze industry in the mining regions of Anatolia and her neighbour, Persian Armenia. The use of pure copper as from the end of the 4th millennium and at the beginning of the 3rd had hardly brought any advantages over Neolithic implements. Only the invention of bronze and the birth of metallurgy capable of compounding the alloys and changing the properties of simple metals slowly led to the relinquishing of the traditional stone weapons and implements. Existing evidence sends us towards the mining regions to the north of the 'Fertile Crescent' in our search for the original home of metallurgy and the first spread of bronze. The discovery of this alloy of copper and tin, or other metals such as antimony, was conditional on the presence of their ores, rarely proved in Anatolia and Armenia. Was bronze discovered by the chance geographical fusion of a mixture of copper and tin ores? Such accidental or spontaneous bronze seems to have been known to the Egyptians under the name of 'Asian copper', which is found in inscriptions from the end of the VIth Dynasty, about 2300.

Nevertheless, bronze, relatively rare until the end of the 3rd millennium, was only adopted very gradually in Egypt and other countries far from the Anatolian and Armenian centres. In the valley of the Nile, conservative religious traditions seem to have slowed down the adoption of the new metal.

At the height of the 14th century, we still find more copper than bronze objects among the treasures of the tomb of Tutankhamen.

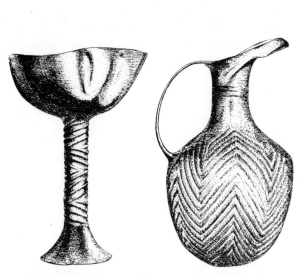

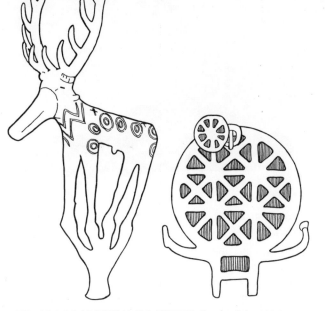

The revolution of the metallurgical and mining industry at the beginning of the 2nd millennium

In both north and south, the end of the 3rd millennium was marked by new disturbances. They resulted in a different distribution of riches in the two zones. This time, the civilisations of the north, which suffered especially, exhausted their power of expansion and had to limit themselves to their own resources. To the south, over the whole extent of the 'Fertile Crescent', once the damage at the end of the 3rd millennium had been made good, stability returned towards about 2000 and Middle Bronze had a brilliant development there.

We have seen that the prosperity of the civilisations to the north of the 'Fertile Crescent', between 2300 and 2000 in round figures, was demonstrated by the profusion of metal objects. Gold and silver abounded; the quantity of bronze with an already remarkably high tin content is impressive. Undeniably the countries of the Caucasus, Asia Minor, Armenia and western Persia knew how to make the most of their mineral wealth. Their mining and metallurgical experience was unique at the time. Nowhere else in Asia, including Egypt, have there been finds
303 comparable to the treasures of Maikop, Alaca Huyuk, Astrabad and Tepe Hissar.

While the scarcity of iron still aroused the envy of the powerful pharaohs of the XVIIIth Dynasty, as shown by their correspondence with the northern kings, the members of the reigning dynasty at Alaca Huyuk, between 2300 and 2000, placed iron weapons of remarkable dimensions in their tombs. And Anitta, the conqueror of Hattusas in the 20th century, boasted of possessing a throne made entirely of iron and a sceptre probably of the same metal. The bronze sword fitted with a tang for attaching the handle which only appeared after 1700 in the south of Asia Minor and protohistoric Europe, was known in Anatolia five hundred years earlier.

Thus the manufacture of bronze and even more of iron remained a monopoly of the metallurgists of the mountainous zone of western Asia until practically the end of the 3rd millennium. Then from the 21st century, fairly suddenly, the metallurgical industry spread to the south. The discovery of bronze objects, sometimes unfinished and accompanied by fragments of crude metal and moulds, attest to the activity of metallurgists in numerous Syrian and Palestinian sites. One of these centres has been discovered at Byblos, near where copper- and tin-bearing

303. ALACA HUYUK (ASIA MINOR). Some of the objects found in the treasure of Alaca Huyuk. About 2500 B.C. Tomb BM: (1) Cup; (2) Jug; (3) Figure of a stag. Tomb MA (a): (4) Perforated insignia plaque.

304. RAS SHAMRA (UGARIT). Torques, bi-conical beads and a club-like pin. 21st–19th centuries B.C.

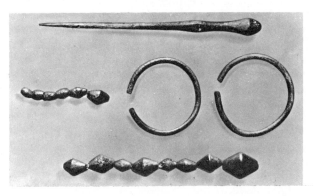

ores must have existed, apparently long since exhausted or forgotten. Bronze manufacturing processes had spread further south, at the same time as prospecting for mineral deposits. This was undoubtedly as a result of the arrival of northern bronze-founders and miners, for in all the ancient urban centres of Syria, we find traces, before and after 2000, of foreign ethnic elements generally native to Asia Minor.

Yet why did they leave their countries? Turkish and American archaeologists have noted that very violent earthquakes destroyed many towns in Asia Minor at this period and wiped out the brilliant civilisation of which the treasures of Troy III and the sumptuous offerings from the tombs of the chiefs of Alaca and from the Caspian region in Persia are the most impressive evidence. However the principal reason for the exodus of miners and craftsmen in metal from Asia Minor and the regions south of the Caspian was probably the progressive impoverishment of the tin and copper deposits exploited from the end of the 4th millennium onwards; hence the regression of the bronze industry in Asia Minor, after the end of the 3rd millennium, and the monotony of strictly Anatolian production during the major part of the 2nd. As for the transfer further south of the principal centres of bronze production, it is explained by the discovery of virgin deposits in those regions, where

177

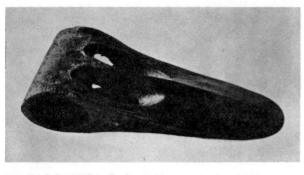

305. RAS SHAMRA. Perforated bronze axe-head. 19th century.

émigré miners and metal-workers became the initiators of the industry's prodigious development from about 2000 onwards. Copper-bearing deposits were then discovered in the island of Cyprus. Thus by prospecting ever further, the men of the metal age developed the roaming habits they preserved for so long.

On the tracks of the Torque Bearers

At Ras Shamra (the Ugarit of Antiquity) a particular type
304 of bronze pin with its swollen head resembling a club has been found in the tombs of Middle Ugarit I (2100 —1900) and in the corresponding layers. Four other types of bronze ornament generally accompany it: open torques with their extremities flattened and scrolled, bracelets, also open, parts of necklaces shaped like stoned olives, often mixed with cornelian or quartz beads, and lastly spring-shaped spirals of bronze wire.

These ornaments are characteristic of a population I shall call the 'Torque Bearers' who settled at Ugarit towards 2000 during a period distinguished by ethnic movements. The ashes on which the layers containing their remains rest confirm that their arrival did not take place without violence. As from Middle Ugarit II (1900 —1700) there are only scattered traces of their existence at Ras Shamra, notably some thin, rather 'effete', club-type pins, found in the burial places. They disappear before the middle of this period; the Torque Bearers had already merged with the indigenous Semitic population by then.

Their installation had coincided with a sudden increase in the production of bronze objects, as the numbers of moulds and remains of workshops bear witness. Three types of weapon introduced by them—the triangular
305–307 bladed dagger, the perforated axe and the lance with a dowel—also disappeared with them. The perfection of these weapons is proof of an advanced and mature metallurgy. Their chemical analysis reveals, side by side with pieces in which the copper contains minor natural impurities (lead, iron, zinc, arsenic, nickel and sulphur), bronzes with a tin content as high as 18 per cent. This content seems to indicate the existence of mines situated in Syria and Asia Minor, later exhausted and forgotten.

A hiding-place in the neighbourhood of the temple of
308 Baal, at Ras Shamra, contained two silver statuettes ornamented with gold torques. Stratigraphy places them between 2000 and 1800. They are therefore contemporary with the Torque Bearers, whose characteristic ornamentation moreover they are wearing. The summary treatment of the body, the disequilibrium of the proportions and the crude modelling of the figures reveal an artist

unskilled in rendering the human body. The god is tall and slim, his impressive breadth across the shoulders implying a muscular strength belied by the thinness of his limbs. The goddess is also lissome, but of smaller stature. The antero-posterior flattening of the skull, revealing extreme brachycephalism, and the receding forehead prolonged by an enormous nose, obviously did not shock the patron who had gone to the considerable expense of commissioning two silver statues weighing nearly two pounds, dressed in loin-cloths of laminated gold. Undoubtedly these physical characteristics were those of the ethnic group to which both creator and patron belonged.

In Syria, the crossroads of the Near East, where populations mingled at a very early stage, the interpretation of physical characteristics is risky. However when they are so clear-cut, it is permissible to take them into account. Now, they recur in the Egyptian and Syrian representations which show the mountain-dwellers of northern Syria and Asia Minor. The statuettes therefore must represent two divinities, perhaps the principal ones of this rough people of metal-workers. Their ornamentation confirms that we are dealing with the Torque Bearers.

We also find them in the region of Carchemish, at Tell As and Hama in the Orontes valley, and especially not far from Beirut at Byblos, now Jebeil, another important bronze centre. There they offered their characteristic ornaments to their divinity in their hundreds, placing them in jars buried beneath the paving of the town's principal temple.

Their traces recur, although less distinctly, in Palestine, at Gaza, Megiddo and Jericho (about 2100–1900). Their most southerly and also the latest evidences of them were discovered at Kahun, in the Nile valley, in the workers' quarter near the pyramid of Sesostris II (about 1906–1888). One of these torques was found there, together with tools for working bronze and a mirror in mint condition.

The discovery of Europe and its mineral wealth by the Torque Bearers

The group of ornaments which we have just enumerated (the open torque, the club-shaped pin with pierced neck and the spring-shaped spiral) were worn at the beginning of the Bronze Age by a population of a markedly intrusive nature which placed its dead in the Alsatian and Swiss tumuli of the upper Rhine, or in stone chests (cists) in subterranean tombs. It is possible to argue that bronzes of the Oriental type were distributed in Europe via the metal trade; but when a group of several ornaments, without losing its unity and character, moves from Syria to the banks of the Rhine, it is difficult to deny that the transfer of individuals or whole ethnic groups was involved.

How did the Torque Bearers, after traversing the 'Fertile Crescent', reach the Rhine, across pre- and proto-historic Europe and how was the knowledge of metal spread with them? There were two principal routes of penetration. One, known as the western route, after skirting the Mediterranean coasts and islands from east to west, led to western Europe and the Atlantic coasts, as far as the British Isles, then to the shores of the North Sea. The second, the eastern route followed the Adriatic, crossed the Balkans to reach the Danube and then extended along the valleys of the great rivers (the Rhine, Weser, Elbe, Oder and Vistula) to the Baltic and Scandinavia, where it rejoined the western route. It was not by chance that the two routes led at the same time to the mining centres then essential: on the western route, the tin-bearing deposits of Spain, France and the British Isles, and on the eastern route, the tin and copper mines of the 'metallic mountains' of Saxony and Bohemia. Therefore the spread in Europe of the first types of bronze went hand in hand with mineral prospecting. We have admitted that they were carried by Etruscan or Phoenician traders, but, given the complexity and difficulty of the crafts involved, it has been suspected that specialists from the south must have accompanied the new inventions. Acting as advisers to the Neolithic Europeans, they at the same time stimulated the quest for minerals. In fact, side side with the first European bronze ornaments and weapons with Eastern prototypes, variations reflect indigenous traditions going back to the Neolithic. Chemical analysis confirms that the first exploitation of the European mines dated from the 19th century B.C.

In their hundreds and thousands, the torques and spirals accompanied by club-shaped pins and often triangular bladed daggers have been collected from deposits in Hungary and Bohemia, as well as from those which signpost the natural routes of penetration into Italy, Germany and Scandinavia. The number and weight of some of these torques lead us to think that they were used as ingots. However the placing of necklaces in the tombs of central Europe, as in those of Ras Shamra in Syria, confirms their use as ornaments.

In the present state of research, we have to admit that

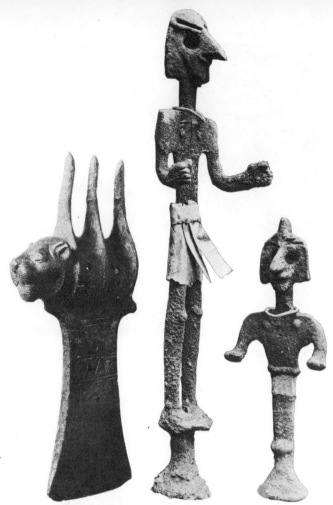

306. RAS SHAMRA. Bronze axe-head ornamented with a lion's head. 15th-14th centuries B.C.

308. RAS SHAMRA. Silver statuettes of two cult figures decorated with gold torques. 20th-18th centuries B.C.

the Torque Bearers were very unlikely to have used the land bridge formed by western Asia Minor and the Balkans in order to pass from Syria to Europe. Nevertheless some pins with pierced necks have been found at Troy. The Torque Bearers must have travelled by sea, via the southern coasts of Anatolia, the Aegean islands and the shore of the Adriatic in order to advance directly to central Europe where they caused the prodigious development of the beginning of the Bronze Age in Hungary and Bohemia. Consequently, other types of bronze originating in the Orient, especially axes of the Syrian type, were transferred to the north of Albania and into Dalmatia without leaving any intermediary traces. So it is difficult not to believe in the journeys of these Syrian and proto-Phoenician metal artists, miners and prospectors towards prehistoric Europe.

Metal's contribution to civilisation and art

To what extent do these considerations about the origin of metallurgy in the ancient Orient and its subsequent diffusion concern an over-all picture of the problems involving art and man? Not only did the invention of bronze constitute a prodigious technical advance; it also put at man's disposal a hitherto unknown material, with unsuspected properties and potentialities. It freed the craftsman and the artist from the heavy primitive materials of clay and stone, with which they had had to be satisfied since the beginning.

The metal, at the same time supple and strong, made

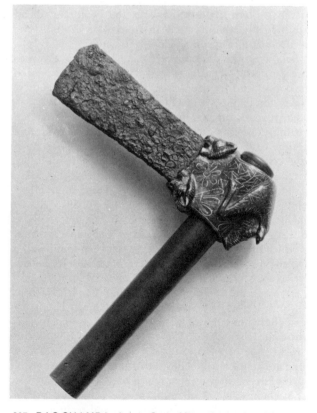

307. RAS SHAMRA. Axe in Syrio-Mitannian style, with copper damascened with gold. The blade is of case-hardened iron and protrudes from two lions' heads. A wild boar straddles the shaft. 15th-14th centuries B.C.

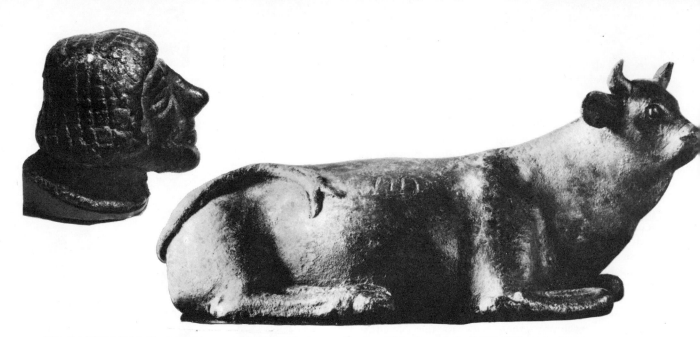

309. RAS SHAMRA. Two weights, one in the form of a human head and the other of a bull. 15th–14th centuries B.C.

possible the creation of more manageable implements, lighter receptacles and figurines with brand-new shapes, bold angles and thin gleaming sides which invited the caress of more refined hands. Perhaps even more important and richer in consequences than this aesthetic revolution was the shock which the invention of metal produced on the hitherto essentially conservative mentality of the agrarian societies of the ancient Orient.

Born of the cooperation between the prospector discovering the ores and the metallurgist with his knowledge of alloys and smelting, the difficult art of metal-working carried man outside the traditional limits of his existence as a labourer bound to the soil and a flock-keeper subject to transhumance or a nomadic existence.

The prospector rapidly established the first international, and later the intercontinental, exchanges. Metallurgists and bronze-founders, whose complicated trade required a long apprenticeship, formed the first corporations of specialists who as from the middle of the 3rd millennium introduced a more marked division of labour in the eastern civilisations. Experts with jealously guarded professional secrets, they penetrated hitherto ethnically homogeneous groups and although marked with the sign of Cain were tolerated by them as foreign but indispensable members of the community. This was the beginning of a sort of social and industrial revolution which coincided—and it was scarcely a coincidence—with the invention and spread of writing.

Agrarian humanity accordingly suddenly found itself in a world which called for greater mobility, an accelerated rhythm of life, a livelier curiosity and a constant effort to master new techniques. Admittedly art had not awaited the invention of metal to blossom. But it was with the development of metallurgy that art and the products of the craftsman, hitherto almost exclusively reserved for the worship of the dead, penetrated the intimate side of men's lives and began to win the respect and interest of the masses whose existence they soon transformed and enriched.

The Mediterranean Near East's appetite for metal was soon so great that the richest and most accessible Anatolian and Armenian deposits as well as those which had been more particularly explored by the Egyptians in the Sinai peninsula showed signs of exhaustion. Towards the end of the 3rd millennium, prospectors crossed the strait bordered by the Anatolian and Syrian coasts to Cyprus whose mountains, visible on the horizon on a clear day, sheltered abundant deposits barely touched by the island's Neolithic population. Others, pushing further west by skirting the southern coast of Asia Minor, arrived opposite the Aegean islands where bold navigators, of whom the best known to us are the Cretans, were able to provide them with transport. Further north, it must have been equally easy for them to cross the Bosphorus or the Dardanelles. But their prospecting carried them mainly to the western countries. It was the beginning of an astounding adventure: the discovery of protohistoric Europe and its mineral wealth.

Following the example of these experienced prospectors, European Neolithic men everywhere began to search for copper and tin deposits and, from the 19th century, to develop their own metallurgical centres.

However, along the lengthy route between their Syrian starting-point and the top of the Adriatic, the Torque Bearers have left no signs of their passage. They must have crossed the Mediterranean. Which sailors did they rely on? Various data enable us to guess that they were the Phoenicians, the same navigators whose ships, a few centuries later and from before 1500, put into all the Mediterranean ports. Legends and myths also attribute to them the invention and spread of alphabetic writing, of which the oldest evidence has in fact been found in the two most ancient centres of the Torque Bearers on the Syrian coast: Ras Shamra (Ugarit) and Byblos.

So strong and so lasting was the impression left by these bold prospectors that in some regions folklore still remembers, after thousands of years, these strange Phoenicians who came from overseas loaded with Oriental objects. On a rocky side of Mont Saint-Odile in the Rhine valley popular tradition still believes that it can see the traces of a pair of mysterious rings to which they were supposed to moor their ships. With them at the beginning of the 2nd millennium the art, imagination and techniques of the Near East began their penetration of the West from which the shadows of barbarian ignorance were finally driven away after long centuries.

HISTORICAL SUMMARY: The appearance of metal

Archaeology. Until the end of the last century only the classical Phoenician civilisation was known (evidence from Greek authors and the expeditions of E. Renan and the Turks Hamdy and Makridi Bey). Research at Sidon (1919 and 1920) first came across traces of the end of the Bronze Age in Phoenicia. During the French Mandate in Syria and Lebanon, excavations uncovered two vital sites: Byblos (digs by Montet and Dunand starting in 1921) and Ras Shamra with its port Minet el Beida (digs by Schaeffer and Chenet starting in 1929) as well as those in the Orontes valley. In Anatolia, the pioneer was Schliemann, the discoverer of Troy at Hissarlik, from 1870 to 1890. After him, Winckler discovered the capital of the Hittite empire at Boghazkoy in 1906. But the first systematic excavations in Anatolia only took place from 1927 onwards at Alishar and from 1935 at Alaca (a rich pre-Hittite royal necropolis) where the art of metalworking flourished at an early date. Further east, near Mesopotamia, important explorations were made at Carchemish (1876–1920), Tell Halaf (1911–1929) and Tell Asmar (1927–1928), the ancient Til Barsip. The Swedes, French and Cypriots have done much to throw light on Cyprus and its very mixed civilisation at the centre of the main maritime exchange routes. The capital of the island in the 2nd millennium was at Enkomi, opposite Syria.

Geography. The regions which concern us here are bounded in the north by the chain of the Caucasus and the Black Sea, to the east by Mesopotamia, to the south by Arabia and Egypt, and lastly to the west by the eastern Mediterranean and the Aegean Sea: in short they are the present day territories of Turkey (Anatolia), northern Syria, Lebanon, Israel and Cyprus. Situated at the crossroads of the great empires (Egyptian, Mesopotamian and Aegean), these countries have had a lively history, closely linked with that of their powerful neighbours, except for Anatolia which remained apart for longer.

Artistic History. The artistic history of the vast countries which saw the birth of bronze, and later iron, metallurgy fits quite naturally into that of neighbouring empires whose influence was often of capital importance. Three great periods when art was at its zenith are distinguished: 1. the age of treasures (probably 18th–16th centuries), especially in Anatolia; 2. the age of the Torque Bearers, in Syria (Phoenicia) under the Egyptian Middle Kingdom

(20th–19th centuries); 3. the golden age of Ras Shamra (Ugarit), centre of international exchanges, under the Egyptian New Kingdom (15th–14th centuries) and the Hittite empire. Thus these two last periods coincide with the apogee of neighbouring civilisations (Egyptian, Anatolian and Aegean), whereas the first corresponds to their temporary eclipse (First Intermediate period in Egypt, Guti (?) invasion in Mesopotamia).

Architecture. In the age of treasures architecture was primarily military and powerful: fortress towns surrounded with solid defence walls reinforced with towers, pierced with a few gates and carefully fortified in depth. Troy provides the best example. Inside, the palaces are of the 'megaron' type; at Alaca, at the same time, the elaborately constructed tombs comprised spacious chambers with flat roofs of beams and joists placed on the lateral walls. In Phoenicia at Byblos, architecture was directly inspired by Egypt (temples). But the Torque Bearers, expert bronze-founders, apparently had little architecture. At Ugarit, as for the other arts, the great epoch in architecture corresponds roughly to the 14th century (from the previous period the temples of Baal and Dagon, founded under the Middle Kingdom, should be noted). The royal palace and the great family funerary vaults were the masterpieces of this beautiful architecture of dressed stone which, with its embossments, recalls that of the Crusades in the Middle Ages. In Cyprus, the great residence of the princes of Enkomi is of the same style and has some interesting peculiarities. At Atchana, the palace of King Niqmepa has a colonnaded entrance akin to that of the palace of Ugarit, where porticoes with wooden columns are frequent; this indicates the influence of the Cretan palaces, especially that of Cnossus.

Sculpture. In the age of metal, sculpture was the peak of achievement in the plastic arts. However monumental sculpture in various media remained in the background, except in Egypt and Mesopotamia, whose sculpture, together with their other arts, has been studied in the previous chapter. Here we are dealing mainly with metal.

The minor arts. From the age of treasures, the funerary furniture of the pre-Hittite necropolis of Alaca yields numerous pieces of gold and silver work, cups with tall pedestals, pitchers with geometrical repoussé decorations, bowls inlaid with stones, ewers, diadems with pendants, bracelets, pins

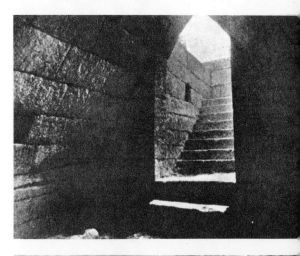

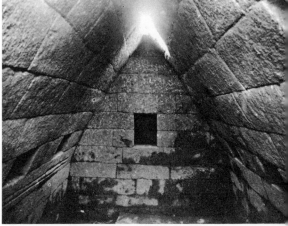

310. RAS SHAMRA. Stairway and interior of tomb I.

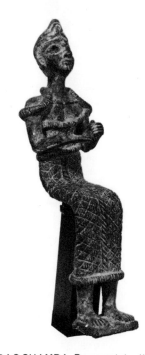

311. RAS SHAMRA. Bronze statuette.

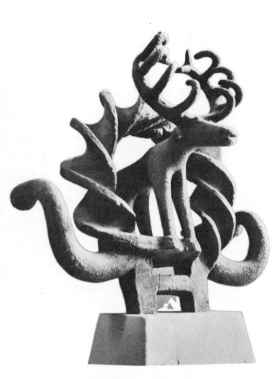

312 Copper stag of the type from the royal tombs at Alaca Huyuk. End of the 2nd millennium. *Ankara Museum*.

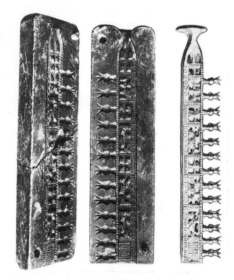

313. RAS SHAMRA. The cast and mould for precious metals, perhaps of a diadem pendant. 14th century B.C.

with ornamented heads, etc.; statuettes mounted on a shaft, of stags or bulls, are of copper inlaid and plated with electrum; female idols and figurines of plated copper or silver. Lastly strange perforated pieces, of copper or bronze with a geometrical lattice-work pattern, rest on a base recalling the outspread horns of a bull; variants show a group of members of the deer tribe surrounded by a plait on the same base; these enigmatic emblems have been named 'solar discs' or 'wheels'. All these works of varying artistic merit

nevertheless demonstrate at the end of the 3rd millennium a mature technical skill in the arts of metal-working comparable with Sumerian goldsmiths' work.

Later in the 2nd millennium the tombs of Alaca Huyuk yielded goldsmiths' work in which the statuette of a god wearing a bonnet, short tunic and pointed shoes stands out. The famous but wrongly-named 'Treasure of Priam', which Schliemann discovered at Troy, apart from numerous bronze weapons, included silver vases and cups, a gold sauce-boat unique of its kind and a variety of jewellery.

Less famous are the curious objects taken from the kurgans of the province of Trialeti in Transcaucasia, to the north-east of Anatolia: of a rather crude and archaic decorative style, they are unlikely to be earlier than the 16th century. They include a silver bucket set in gold, one gold and one silver goblet, both ornamented with figurative scenes, genuine forerunners of the cauldrons of the Early Iron Age in Italy.

On the Phoenician coast, subject to Egyptian influence since the Old Kingdom, Byblos, about 30 miles north of Beirut, the port from which the cedars of Lebanon were exported, emerged towards 2000 as an important metallurgical centre where the torque-bearing bronze-founders played an essential role. In addition to numerous bronze objects which were found in jars, there was the discovery in the sarcophagi of the kings of Byblos, in the 19th century, vassals or allies of the pharaohs of the XIIth Dynasty, of silver vases shaped like teapots with long spouts and ribbed bellies, a bronze scimitar with a gold uraeus inlaid on the blade, a knife showing one of the most ancient examples of damascening (gold threads on nielloed silver and gold), a dagger decorated with a scene in repoussé work on the blade, and a gold sheath.

At Ras Shamra (Ugarit), 7 miles north of Latakia in northern Syria, the Torque Bearers were also real introducers of bronze metallurgy at the end of the 3rd millennium. Working metal rapidly became an essential activity there, but although there are statuettes of the greatest interest dating from the beginning of the 2nd millennium [308], the golden age of the metal arts comes later, at the time of the Egyptian New Kingdom and the Mycenaean expansion in Syria (also true of ivories and architecture). The town, then at the height of its fame, was extraordinarily prosperous, owing to its position as an international market place where Mycenaean, Egyptian, Mitannian and Hittite products changed hands. While the kings enlarged and embellished their palaces, the rich inhabitants constructed

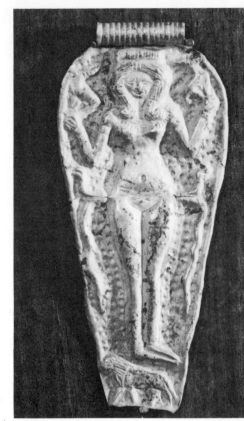

314. RAS SHAMRA. A gold pendant of the goddess Astarte. *Louvre*.

splendid tombs with vaults resting on corbels. In spite of its undeniable cosmopolitanism, Ugarit reflects in its art a living expression of its refined civilisation. Confronted with predominantly but not exclusively Egyptian influence, the genius of its artists created, especially in the 15th and 14th centuries, an original style, although it contained an intimate blend of Creto-Mycenaean and Mitanno-Hurrian tendencies. The following are the principal metal objects from this time: a gold patera of Egyptian shape, ornamented with a royal hunt from a chariot; a gold cup of the involved composite style which foreshadows the series of 7th-century Phoenician pateras diffused from Nimrud to Preneste. Among the bronzes: a statuette of the god Baal, plated with gold; a falcon with a uraeus, with plumage inlaid with gold; two battleaxes with dowels ornamented with lions' and boars' heads; a tripod with pomegranates as pendants.

From Enkomi, in Cyprus, comes a superb silver cup, masterpiece of the Mycenaean style which shows us the importance of the role of Mycenaean exports in the eastern Mediterranean, confirmed by the abundant ceramics and the famous ivory of the mother goddess from Minet el Beida, port of Ugarit.

Jacques-Claude Courtois

THE AEGEAN WORLD *Pierre Demargne*

Crete, in the centre of the eastern Mediterranean, was the ideal stepping-stone for the technical and commercial exchanges produced by the invention of metallurgy. She was the first to build up a civilisation which, freed from the agrarian stage, produced an art new in aspect and spirit; her ships, and later those of her Achaean successors, distributed it, especially among the societies in the process of formation. Pierre Demargne, who has devoted himself to the study of this civilisation and made excavations in Crete, discusses the nature and scope of her art.

Geography and ethnology are the only disciplines capable of endowing pre-Hellenic civilisation and art with meaning, of making us understand its profound originality and the links which connect it to the great civilisations of the Orient.

The Aegean is an insular world surrounded by continents whose coasts share an identical civilisation easily transmitted from one shore to the other via the islands. Among these islands, the central Cyclades (Paros, Naxos, Syros, Melos) are the ones where a human civilisation first awoke. The north coast of the Aegean remained barbarian for a long time, but the two eastern and western shores, the shores of Greece and Asia Minor, have had their lively centres of civilisation since prehistory. From Cythera to Chalcidice, Laconia, the coasts of Argolis and Attica, those of Boeotia and Thessaly were abundantly populated from the Neolithic onwards; the whole of this eastern coast of Greece, tremendously indented, must have been open to remote influences at an early date: the Saronic Gulf, for example, seems made to welcome them and bring them to the Isthmus of Corinth,

so rich in prehistoric sites. The interior of the country and the Adriatic coast were only civilised indirectly and later, but already travel along the Pindus Mountains was incessant, and in any case the Greek peninsula was connected with the Balkans and beyond them with central Europe which was gradually emerging from the barbaric stage. Civilisation advanced from south to north, but it was from north to south that the invasions came which from one age to another were to people Greece.

Together with the large islands along it, the west coast of Asia Minor from Troy, the barrier of the Dardanelles, to Smyrna and Miletus forms the Aegean façade of an immense hinterland: long caravan routes connected the Aegean, from the most remote times, not only with central Anatolia and the Caucasian region, cradle of all the metal arts in the Near East, but also with Mesopotamia, a land of urban civilisation from the 4th millennium, as well as with Cilicia and Syria, crossroads between Asia Minor, western Asia and Egypt.

The fourth and southern side of the Aegean rectangle is only half closed by the large island of Crete and by Rhodes at the point where Asia Minor turns east.

Although Crete was still only one centre among many in its Neolithic infancy, pre-Hellenic art and civilisation towards the 3rd millennium reached a higher point there than elsewhere and were of an extraordinary originality. The geographical reasons for this advance stand out as soon as one looks at the map. Not only does Crete shut off the Aegean world to the south; she also forms the centre of a greater world, that of the eastern Mediterranean, half-way, or very nearly so, between the Balkan and African coasts, and between Syria and Sicily. If the

THE AEGEAN WORLD

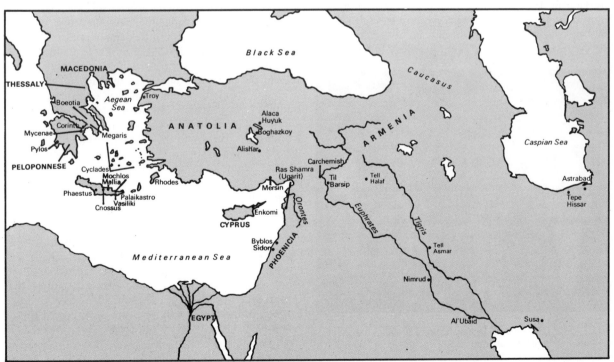

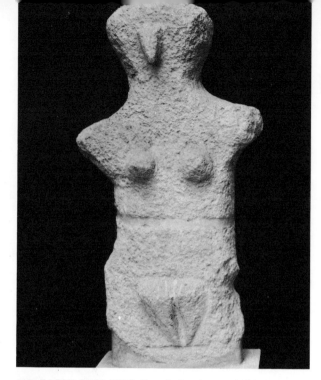

315. EARLY CYCLADIC. Female figurine, probably a primitive fertility goddess. *British Museum.*

ports of Asia Minor received caravans, Crete welcomed the ships which must very early have visited the ports from the Nile to Byblos, to Cyprus—the main stepping-stone between Asia and the Aegean—and lastly to Rhodes and Crete; little later the crossing was made directly. Both by land and more conveniently by sea routes, the contributions of the older civilisations of Egypt and Asia were able to fertilise a world which was still very young, hitherto ignorant of the refined techniques of the metallurgist and the architect, of the mythologies and iconographies, and lastly the writing produced by the historical civilisations.

So geography invites us never to isolate the Aegean civilisation from its neighbours. The ethnographical factor remains much more uncertain, at least as long as the pre-Hellenic languages keep their secrets. Their deciphering is only just beginning and is as yet only applicable to the latest documents. However it is highly probable that the Aegean world as we have described it formed an

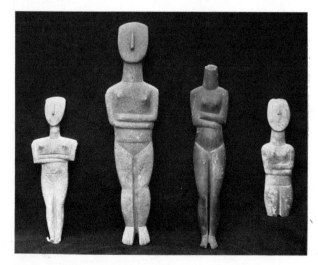

316. EARLY CYCLADIC. Female figures, showing the stylised heads placed on long necks, and the arms folded across the torso. *British Museum.*

ethnical and linguistic, as well as a geographical, community in the 3rd millennium and perhaps even earlier: it is styled Asianic or Mediterranean; let us merely accept that it is neither Indo-European nor Semitic. The element which may pass for pre-Hellenic in the Greek population and language is in fact akin to one of the peoples and tongues of Asia Minor. Scholars have even held the theory that this Graeco-Anatolian community was more widely connected with a pre-Indo-European and pre-Semitic stock which we come across here and there from the Syrian coast to Sumerian Mesopotamia, Caucasian Anatolia, Iran and pre-Aryan India. This would account for the common features which have been mentioned between the art and religion of Crete and those of the Indus civilisations (the iconography of the bull, for example). It is a simpler explanation than that which commercial relations over such vast distances would require.

The Neolithic and the appearance of metal (Early Bronze Age)

Although a few traces of the Upper Palaeolithic have recently been found in central Greece, it is at the Neolithic stage that we begin to understand the Aegean 315 civilisation. Even if Crete remains a centre of its own, the population was continuous on the Greek mainland from Macedonia to the Peloponnese with its principal centres in Thessaly (Sesklo, then Dimini) and around Corinth. In the Aegean world as elsewhere, the Neolithic is the age of agriculture and settled dwellings, and soon of nascent towns. Everywhere in Thessaly artificial hills are made of debris accumulated in the course of life in the rectangular houses of the villages. Idols of naked women, first ex- 316 amples of the plastic arts, are probably the images of a primitive fertility goddess of ample proportions: they recur from one end of the Aegeo-Anatolian region to the other. Simply polished and incised in Crete, pottery is painted in Thessaly. It is only a few years ago since an attempt was made to connect the Neolithic centre of Thessaly and Greece with the Asian regions which earlier, in the 5th and 4th millennia, saw the same types of civilisation appear, with similar painted pottery (civilisations of al'Ubaid and Tell Halaf in Mesopotamia, and of Mersin in Cilicia). If Cyprus has a Neolithic civilisation akin to the preceding ones, intermediate stages are still lacking in Asia Minor which has been so little excavated. But we can immediately link with the first Asian civilisation that of prehistoric Greece, which in its turn gradually acquired the rural way of life and painted pottery of European cultures such as that of Starčevo in Serbia. This advance from south to north does not exclude some influence in the opposite direction, if it is true that the second Thessalian civilisation, that of Dimini, owes to the Danubian regions the beautiful whorls of its spirals which 317 it gave to the Cyclades and to Crete.

The introduction of copper implements into this Neolithic civilisation does not seem to have constituted a revolution: the appearance of bronze had a far greater effect. Once again it was in Egypt and Asia that copper first appeared, perhaps through contacts with eastern Anatolia. Copper, in the form of short weapons, appeared simultaneously in Cyprus, Troy and Crete, about 3000–2700, according to the chronologies used; between 2500 and 2000 it reached Russia, central Europe and Spain. A few centuries were still to pass before bronze made with tin asserted itself in the Aegean, between 2300 and 2000. This last third of the 3rd millennium was an age of considerable transformation, the age of treasures, in the Caucasus (Maikop), in central Anatolia (Alaca), in the Aegean (Troy II, Mochlos in Crete), for gold and silver were as commonly used for vases and jewellery as bronze. It was also the age of the first fortress towns (Troy II) and the first political organisations.

The rich and powerful civilisation of the pre-Hittites of central Anatolia, as revealed by Turkish excavations at Alaca and Alishar, is more appropriately taken into the margin of the Aegean world: then the power of Troy at the converging point of the routes from Asia becomes more intelligible; Troy III, especially, with its first megaron, a rectangular hall preceded by an antechamber, with its copper and bronze weapons, its so-called 'Treasure of Priam', its pottery with Anatolian shapes, readily copied from metal utensils, transmitted the influence of Asia both to the islands and to continental Greece.

Cyprus, for its part, very closely linked with Anatolia at the time, enriched by its copper mines, developed an extremely prosperous civilisation from the Early Bronze Age. It is primarily distinguished by astonishing carved vases, by representing whole scenes complete with figures on the hollow of a plate, and stags or snakes on the belly of a vase.

In this same period the Cyclades played an important intermediary role between Asia Minor, with Crete, and the Greek mainland. The idols showing what Greek plastic art would one day become are of Cycladic marble; they are mainly nude female figures built up by the superimposition of geometrical decoration: a stylised head, round or elongated at the top of a long neck, and with a strong nose, a trapezoidal torso on which the arms are crossed, broad flanks, strictly parallel legs. The types themselves are almost unvaried; sometimes a woman carries a child in her arms or on her head, a man plays the harp or the flute. But these are examples of a very stylised form of sculpture, derived from Neolithic plastic art, and one which was to perpetuate itself parallel with the very different aesthetic which Creto-Mycenaean art was to develop in the 3rd millennium. Pottery is polished with incised decorations, also from Neolithic traditions: the spiral-shaped decoration was borrowed from Balkan pottery via the Dimini culture.

The Cyclades of the 3rd millennium served as a relay station between Asia Minor and the rest of the Aegean world. But, while the 'Helladic' civilisation of the Greek continent still remained very poor, Crete at the same period (Early Minoan) showed signs of the richness to come: undoubtedly she did not confine herself to exploiting the common Anatolian repertoire, but also had a direct relationship with the Egypt of the Old Kingdom and with Syria. In two of her provinces, especially around the Gulf of Mirabello to the east and in the plain of Messara to the south, there are small towns, each with its own necropolis: among the latter, the most curious are the large tholoi of Messara, communal burial places with a circular plan, covered with false vaults.

Side by side with painted pottery with an essentially geometrical decoration, polished ceramics with incised decoration continued, and we must single out an extremely strange pottery with flame-like decoration, formed by

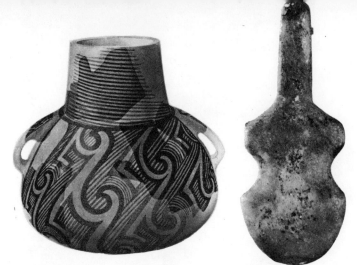

317. NEOLITHIC. SECOND THESSALIAN PERIOD. Pottery with black spirals on a red ground. *(After Wace-Thompson.)*

318. EARLY CYCLADIC. Idol in the form of a violin. *Louvre.*

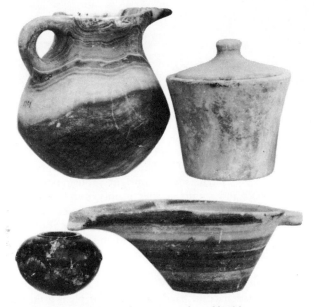

319. EARLY MINOAN II. Stone vases from Mochlos. *Herakleion Museum.*

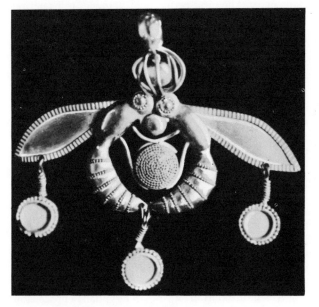

320. CRETE. Pendant representing two bees with a honeycomb. Found in the cemetery of Mallia. *Herakleion Museum.*

315, 316

317

185

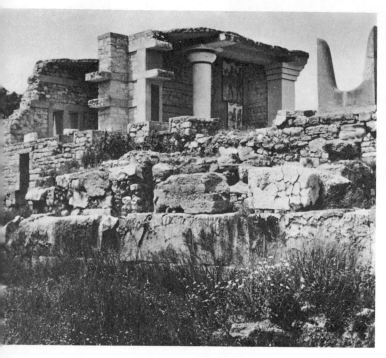

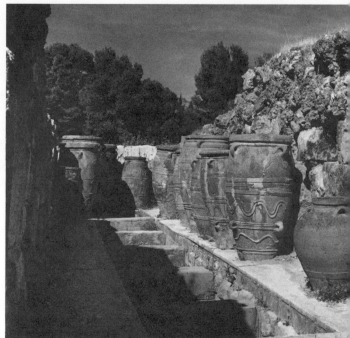

321. CRETE. Anterooms of the palace of Cnossus. Middle Minoan II.

322. CRETE. Storerooms in the palace of Cnossus. Middle Minoan II.

patches of brown, red and black colour arising from accidents in the firing. The shapes tend to be exaggerated (see p. 189): pitchers with upright spouts, pots with long necks and spouts, shapes plainly borrowed from examples in metal from Anatolia. Cretan metallurgy at the time was reduced to a few pure copper tools and weapons, which became more solid and more elongated in the last period of Early Minoan when tin was alloyed with copper.

The treasure of Mochlos comprises, instead of silver objects, diadems and bandeaux made of plain gold leaf cut up and worked in repoussé, pins, simple frail stems spreading out into flower petals: the technique remains elementary. The most perfect achievement of this period 319 is certainly the collection of stone vases from the necropolis at Mochlos. The choice of materials and colours obviously preoccupied the artist and they still attract us today. Side by side with the pale green, grey or black steatite, use was made of breccia of all colours, grey and white marble, alabaster and limestone; Cretan art was already showing its liking for polychromy. But even if the technique of making these polished stone vases was probably taken from the Egyptian Old Kingdom, only a few shapes seem to have been imitated; the majority are specifically Cretan or Anatolian and have their counterparts in the kindred arts of clay- and metal-working.

In the same way, the collection of engraved stones shows that borrowing from foreign techniques was by no means a substitute for originality. In stone, bone and ivory, the seals of the times show, like so many seals throughout the Middle East, a predilection for animal shapes—monkeys, sheep, birds. But local animals tend to take the place of Asian ones. Most often also the decoration is of Asianic inspiration rather than Egyptian: a procession of animals around scorpions which form the centre of the seal, or a potter working on his vases. But the decoration quickly became specifically Cretan; the taste for a vivid

scene or a concrete detail is shown more than in any other art of the period: a fisherman catches his fish, a man sits under a tree and plays chess. A whole world of images is established, from which a rudimentary form of writing was to emerge.

Towards 2000 the Aegean world came to the end of a long period which directly prolonged the Chalcolithic metallurgical heritage of the Anatolian bronze-founders. Crete alone formed relations with more developed civilisations. During this time the Aegean continued to play its role as an intermediary, transmitting to the Balkans and central Europe the new techniques, and above all those of metallurgy.

The period of the first Cretan palaces (Middle Bronze Age)

A new age began about 2000 B.C. The Indo-European migration, to both Greece and Asia Minor, goes back roughly to this date (actually it can be broken down into successive waves before and after 2000). The appearance of the Indo-European element did not totally transform the previous culture. The Hittite civilisation, for example, borrowed many features from the pre-Hittites of the 3rd millennium. In the same way the undoubtedly very primitive Achaean invaders preserved many features of the preceding civilisation, although they destroyed a great deal. The 'Middle Helladic' civilisation, even if it resembles neither the culture of the preceding age nor that of the first Cretan palaces, nevertheless seems to be related to pre-Hittite Anatolia, and, on the other hand, to have no connection with the contemporary civilisation of continental Europe. The problems posed by the Indo-European migration still remain obscure. Only one fact is certain: the continental civilisation, linked with Crete until then, was separated from it for a time.

Between these two worlds, the role of the Cyclades is not clear, perhaps for lack of excavations in recent years.

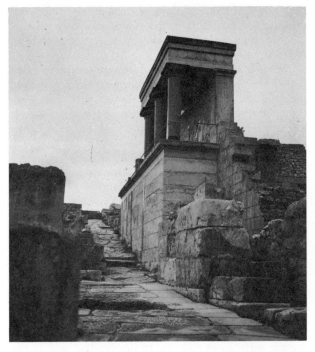

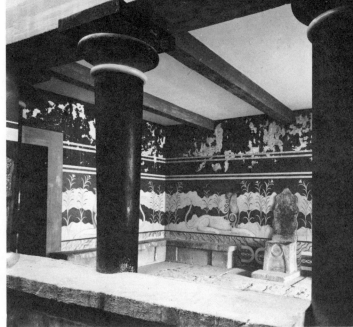

323. CRETE. Palace of Cnossus. North entrance with a guard tower.

324. CRETE. Throne room of the palace of Cnossus, showing the griffon fresco. Late Minoan II.

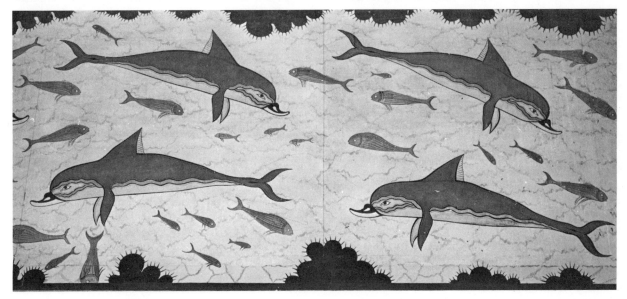

325. CRETE. Palace of Cnossus. The dolphin fresco in the bathroom. Late Minoan II.

Except at Milo which rapidly found itself in the Cretan zone of influence, we do not know whether the civilisation of the preceding age continued more or less as before in the islands, or whether it had a tendency towards the continental culture or the Cretan. In any case, Crete was henceforth to play the leading role in the Aegean world. The flowering of its civilisation, as from this first phase (called the age of the first palaces) is one of the great achievements of Aegean protohistory. A civilisation of small towns was succeeded by a palace civilisation; that is, by one with a certain political, religious and economic power, no doubt relying on an administration possessing a system of writing, and lastly one in which the works of the craftsman gave way to those of the artist. This extremely rapid development can only be explained by the relations—already established, as we have seen, at the end of the preceding period—with Egypt of the Middle Kingdom and the first Babylonian dynasty. The territorial expansion of Egypt in Asia and the thrust of Babylonian influence towards the Mediterranean made the rest of the Phoenician coast, particularly the ports of Ugarit and Byblos, into centres of art and trade where the Cretan sailors could learn how a civilisation could progress to the conscious and refined use of techniques after a mere acquaintance with them. Egypt and Asia possessed organised palaces, luxury jewellery, an iconography and a system of writing before 2000. Even in the absence of direct relations between Egypt and Crete, these Phoenician crossroads provided the necessary contacts for the progress of Cretan civilisation.

The Middle Minoan civilisation probably arose from Early Minoan in the east of Crete—and it is easy to see why. The palace of Mallia at that time must have been a sort of provincial capital dominating the small eastern towns, hitherto flourishing and independent. Cnossus and Phaestos, in the centre and south of the island, seem to have asserted themselves later, but, being less handicapped by the traditions of the preceding age, they pushed the new refinements even further with 'Kamares' ware which in fact only appeared in these parts. Elsewhere a simpler style continued.

How are we to define these artistic advances of Middle Minoan in relation to the preceding period? It was the period when large towns corresponding to a centralised power were organised for the first time. They consisted of a palace surrounded by houses with their necropolises. They lasted from about 2000 to 1750; there followed a period of crisis, after which they were reconstructed. It was therefore a new period which was opening for the Aegean world. Both at Cnossus and at Phaestos, the only remains of these first palaces are a few ruins underneath the later ones, although we can assume that even if the palace of Mallia was built later, it preserves the simple lines of the first period. The precinct here is magnificently built, in the west at least, of well trimmed blocks, the placing of which emphasises the projections and recesses; it is the first example in the Aegean world of an architectural art as opposed to a mere building technique. A chequer-board of quarters separated by corridors was placed around a central courtyard lined on two sides with porticoes. Some of them, such as the store-houses in the east wing, remained of a simpler type, just a ground floor between the courtyard and the outside wall, divided into elongated cells opening on to a common corridor with walls of sun-baked brick covered with stucco along which the storage vases were ranged on benches. Other quarters of the palace were undoubtedly more complicated: from the time of the first palace, there must have been another storey above the west wing reached by large staircases leading from the courtyard, but this part was certainly altered during the following period. A hypostyle hall on the north side of the courtyard, if it dates back, as we may believe, to the time of the first palaces, is evidence that the Cretans borrowed from Egypt the plan of a hall with columns, most frequently those isolated supports which are still employed here with considerable clumsiness, although a little later Cnossus was to use them with extraordinary architectural skill.

Both the houses and the necropolises of Middle Minoan are still very imperfectly known; however the discovery at Mallia of the royal necropolis of Chrysolakkos, near the cliffs on the coast, shows us that, within an exterior similar to that of the palace, it enclosed only simple funerary chambers built like a house. Throughout, with the exception of the exterior, the walls are made of shoddy materials covered with stucco.

In the palaces of the Middle Minoan, Cretan metalworking was to reach in Crete the level which had already been attained in the great civilisations of the Orient; we have only to remember the jewellery from the necropolis at Ur of the Chaldees. At Mallia itself we find, preserved in a bronze-founder's workshop inside the palace, moulds of schist which were used to cast double-headed axes, mirrors and tools of various kinds, such as awls, scissors and scrapers. Quite close by, the same level has yielded a sword three feet long, with a limestone handle covered with gold leaf and a pommel of rock crystal. Before this discovery, it was thought that a long sword could only date from the period of the second palaces or even from Mycenaean times.

The making of jewellery followed the progress of metallurgy; on another sword of similar size is preserved the gold leaf which covered the lower part of its bone pommel; the figure of an acrobat on it is treated in repoussé work, already foreshadowing the taste of the following period for living scenes.

The rare jewels which escaped destruction in the necropolis of Chrysolakkos illustrate another aspect of the same art. The decoration of a gold pendant does not seek to reproduce reality: the joined bodies of two highly stylised bees form a circle whose centre is marked by the honey- 320 comb suspended between their legs; on each side, a large wing ensures the jewel's horizontal axis. We can appreciate the advances then made in the jeweller's technique since the very simple jewellery of Mochlos; undoubtedly these advances must be attributed to knowledge of subtler jewels, the products of Syrian, Mesopotamian and Egyptian art; rough areas, whose very regular graining appears for the first time in Crete, are contrasted with smooth, shining surfaces. In addition to the pendant, a gold pin blossoms, at the top of a massive heavy stalk, into a corolla of delicate, solid petals. Plain sheets of gold leaf are decorated with scrolls which foreshadow those of Mycenaean jewellery. We are at the start of a great metal age.

The same decorative spirit characterises the pottery of this time, which was still without fine painted decoration. Undoubtedly eastern Crete and Mallia itself confined themselves to simple products, combining red and white on a black ground, with very ordinary geometrical ornamentation, sometimes enlivened by stylised plants or flowers; or they imitated metal vases, which have vanished today, by covering the whole vase with black slip with glints of violet, by fluting the lip and by sharpening the line of the belly. But the craftsmen of the palaces of Cnossus and Phaestos were to introduce extraordinary refinements, helped incidentally by inventions such as the potter's wheel which enabled them to make the ultra-thin sides of the famous 'eggshell ware'. This pottery, called Kamares ware, made use of four colours, white, red 326 and yellow on a black ground; it combined spirals and scrolls, stars and suns, leaves and flowers, without any desire to render reality accurately but with a taste for and enjoyment of creating a rich and flexible decoration for the spectator's visual pleasure. It was certainly the first time that a civilisation introduced so many refinements to ornament the humble pottery of everyday life. The pharaohs of the XIIth Dynasty, and the princes of Ugarit and Byblos, as well as the Achaeans, were fond of acquiring fine examples of it, as their descendants were to do later with Attic pottery.

The aesthetic of the Cretans was far more successful in design and colour than in plastic art. They had no equivalent to the great statuary of other countries. The hatchet from Mallia, which ends in the foreparts of a pan- 291 ther, is a vigorously stylised royal or religious emblem; the tiny statuettes from Petsofa are no more than amusing silhouettes with a strangely modern dress. The artists liked working within the small framework provided by seals. Glyptics from the first palaces are a continuation of those of Early Minoan, but, as in all the other fields,

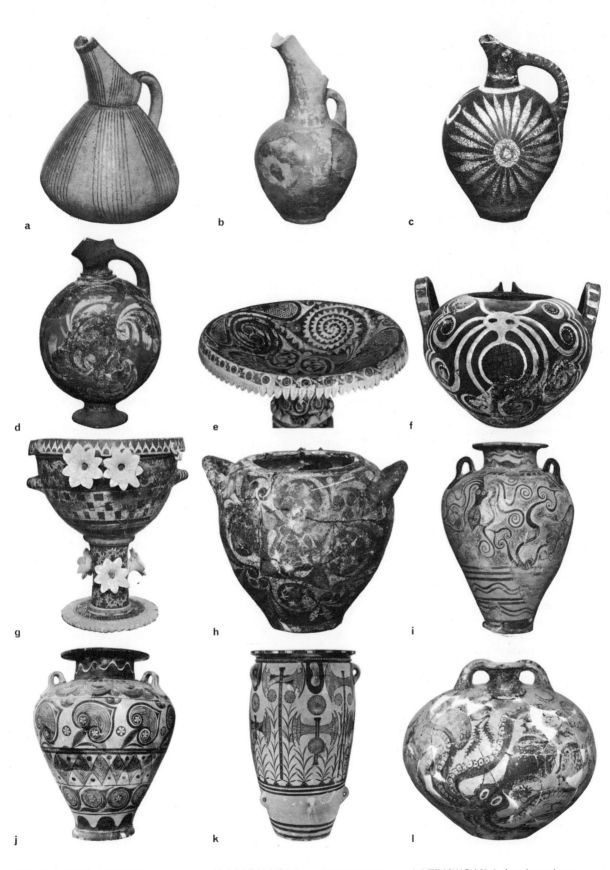

326. CRETAN CERAMICS.
EARLY MINOAN: a Jug with linear decoration. b. Jug with spout.

MIDDLE MINOAN: c. Black jug with white plant decoration. Kamares style. d. Jug with plant motif. Kamares style. e. Lamp decorated with black and white scrolls. f. Pot with stylised octopus decoration. g. Vase decorated with flowers. h. Kamares style vase.

LATE MINOAN: i. Amphora decorated with stylised octopus. Palace style. j. Amphora with stylised flowers. Palace style. k. Jar with double-headed axes, rosettes and stylised foliage. Palace style. l. Amphora decorated with octopus. Palace style.

they made use of technical advances for highly artistic refinements. Harder stones, such as cornelian, chalcedony or jasper, needed more accurate engraving. The shapes of seals lose their rather barbarous and Oriental appearance; nothing is more elegant than the beautiful prismatic shapes of Middle Minoan or the seal with its handle in the shape of a ring. The stylised scenes show us the life of the period: a boat with fishermen casting their nets, a hunting scene, or again two genuine portraits, perhaps of a prince and his son. Sometimes these scenes are no more than images, but sometimes they have become signs and acquired a phonetic value in the 'hieroglyphic' syllabary which was created at the time in imitation of the Egyptian system. The glyptics, which still have rather a primitive character at Mallia, as had the pottery, acquired an unequalled elegance at Cnossus. The East must have furnished models in the past which we can still guess at; the Cretan art of the first palaces stamped them with its own spirit and conferred on them the originality of a great civilisation.

The period of the second Cretan palaces (Late Bronze Age)

The transition from the civilisation of the first palaces to that of the second corresponds to a similar development in Egyptian history; it was the time of the domination of the Hyksos (about 1730–1580). Nevertheless civilisation in Crete continued unbroken on the same lines, but with transformations which we are still unable to explain very satisfactorily. Undoubtedly there were natural catastrophes, such as earthquakes, one of which put an end to the first palaces towards 1750; and the other, around 1570, was perhaps accompanied by raids made by the continental Achaeans, who took to Mycenae the Cretan jewels discovered by Schliemann in the shaft graves. This extremely brilliant new Cretan civilisation lasted until 1400; then the palaces were finally destroyed by the attacks of the Achaeans. We may suppose that Cnossus made its authority, embodied in the person of the Minos of tradition, increasingly felt, and that its influence spread to hitherto autonomous provincial centres. The number of sites, towns or country villas is evidence of the general prosperity in Crete at this time.

By comparing the architecture of the second palaces with that of the preceding period, we can see that the difference lies not so much in the proportions as in a more intensive organisation; even if the system of isolated blocks or blocks connected by simple corridors is retained on the ground floor and in the secondary quarters, the residential quarters and reception rooms, on the other hand, are skilfully planned. As regards elevation the use of light shafts high up in the ceilings produced alternate patches of light and shade; in the same way, the types of hall were made more varied and refined in plan by the increased use of supports, columns, pillars and jambs. It is our belief that this elaboration is purely Cretan. Far from receiving an Oriental influence, these palaces must have exerted their influence on the Egyptian and Syrian ones. The best example, in the palace of Cnossus, is the domestic quarter of several storeys lodged in the east hill. Scholars have been too quick to say that Minoan Crete never conceived grandiose architecture; both in plan and elevation, this is a great over-all work such as neither Greece nor the Orient possessed.

At the same time, the royal tombs became more monumental. The temple-tomb discovered to the south of the palace still belongs to the 16th century: the funerary chamber with a central pillar, hollowed out of the rock, is behind a crypt with two pillars and a hall giving on to a paved courtyard which serves as a light shaft. On the first storey there would have been a sanctuary of the goddess who presided over the funerary rite. This tomb was built in the same spirit as the palace.

Other tombs, on the contrary, which belong to the end of the 15th century, show signs of new spirit; the best known is the one between the palace and the sea at Isopata, which has yielded magnificent Egyptian alabaster vases. This time the tomb, of rectangular plan, is built in a hollowed-out hill and the main chamber has monumental dimensions, almost twenty-six by thirty-two feet in plan, with a height which must have been in proportion. In front of this chamber is a vestibule to which a corridor gave access.

In this connection it is impossible not to bring up the problem of the relationship between Crete and the continental tholoi, especially since a circular tomb resembling them was discovered in the same region in 1938. It is highly probable that the continental tombs were earlier and were imitated in Crete where this monumental type does not fall into line with the general architecture of the palaces.

Side by side with architecture, great painting was one of the most extraordinary revelations of the Cretan excavations. The themes of painted decorative work are infinitely more varied than we should expect and much less utilitarian than in Egypt or Asia: even when the fresco has a religious nature, the figures have a freedom which is found nowhere else; on the other hand, man who was to be most successful on his own in Greek painting is here set in a natural background. The Cretan preferred the play of spontaneous colours to the truth of actual colours. These painters did not paint like sculptors as the Greek painters did, nor did they aim at accuracy like the Egyptians; they preferred to capture the appearance of movement rather than anatomical exactness. To tell the truth, their figures have neither bone structure nor musculature; they are only outlines with free vivid movements. So scenes of plant or animal life are common: hoopoes and partridges flit about in the bushes, a blue bird and a blue monkey frolic in the Cretan countryside; violent blues and reds contrast with soft pinks and greens. A wild cat crouches to spring on a pheasant in a briar bush: this time the scene is treated in brownish tones on the uniform background used in pottery. The life of the court also has its place in this decoration, as do the rites of a religion closely bound up with games and the open air. The miniature frescoes seethe with a strange and charming life: in the courtyard of the palace or under the neighbouring olive-trees, crowds are assembled to watch a show; the ladies of the court surround the queen or priestess on a dais, chatting to each other with affected gestures. Bullfights and acrobatic performances form part of this patrician life which is both courtly and religious, and not without affectation. Large solemn scenes contrast with freer ones: on the walls of the great west corridor the bearers of gifts walk in procession; elsewhere the 'Prince with Lilies' may be taking the head of a similar procession: in the throne room, griffons in red and black frame the royal throne.

Nothing can help us to recapture the atmosphere of Cretan civilisation at its height better than these frescoes from Cnossus: they are the product of an absolutely original civilisation. Even if we do find, at Beni Hasan in Egypt for example, models for the Cretan birds, they seem more like a stiffly accurate zoological plate, whereas the others are free and natural. It needed Cretan art to exercise in its turn an influence on the Egypt of Amarna for Egyptian painting to experience the freer atmosphere of Cretan landscapes.

326   As for pottery, it continued in the same spirit, but with deliberate limitations. The decoration was painted in dark brown, often rather carelessly, on a plain ground; the potter had entirely given up the polychrome patterns of the preceding period; if we did not know the frescoes from the same time, we should think that the artist was insensitive to colour. In the same way, large-scale painting only shows an interest in animal and human life. Decoration with plant motifs is predominant in the pottery, handled in a simple naturalistic way; the adaptation of decoration to shape has rarely been so happily effected as in the vases simply decorated with lilies or palms rising from the ground and blossoming out at the top of the belly. Marine motifs, octopuses, fish, seaweed and shells, are also easily adapted to the curve of the vase.

Some scholars support the theory that the Cretan artist, pre-eminently a painter, did not have a very developed sense of sculpture. But here we must distinguish between work in the round and in relief. There is a total absence in Crete of the major plastic art which Egypt and Mesopotamia had known for so long and in which the Greeks were to excel. The reason the Cretans did not imitate the Egyptian statues, which reached them nevertheless, was that they had little liking for translating forms into volumes. They restricted themselves to works

329 of small dimensions such as the goddesses with snakes, with no plastic qualities of their own. The feeling for the right outline and movement, translated into a lively naturalism, appears particularly in a series of small

328 bronzes, 'worshippers' in the attitude of prayer, the 'flute
327 player' with arched torso, or the famous ivory 'acrobat' extended in his leap over the bull.

Most often the Minoans were satisfied with sculpture in relief, which is closer to painting. Every type of material was used, particularly stone and metal. The three black
331 steatite vases from Hagia Triada are well known. The
332 Harvesters' vase is the most significant; it conveys the atmosphere of a rustic procession with all its familiarity and good humour. Two figures stand out from the serried ranks of the crowd, the leader of the procession and the choir master who has his mouth wide open. Under the forest of forks or poles, the farmers sing gaily as they march; in one part of the procession, they are well aligned, while, in another, movement is created by the fall of one of the harvesters. It is a triumph of vitality and movement, with a tendency to happy caricature. Plastic art in bronze and gold certainly also existed at Cnossus, but it was in a royal tomb at Vaphio in Laconia that dig-
333 gers found two gold cups decorated in repoussé work, marvels of Cretan art which had been taken there by pillage or trade. These two goblets form a pair: on one, bulls are being caught in nets; on the other, domesticated, they are pulling a plough: a scene of violence on one,

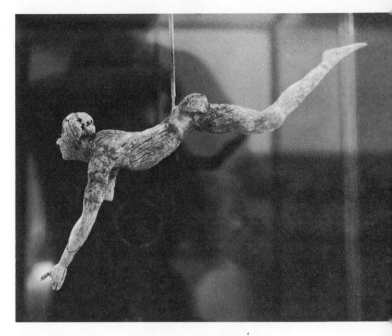

327. CRETE. Ivory figurine of an acrobat from the palace at Cnossus. Late Minoan I.

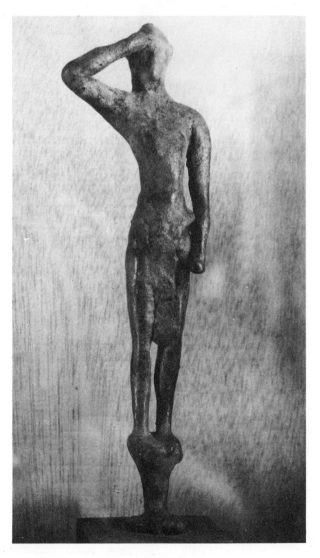

328. CRETE. Figurine of a worshipper with one hand raised to the forehead in adoration. Late Minoan I.

191

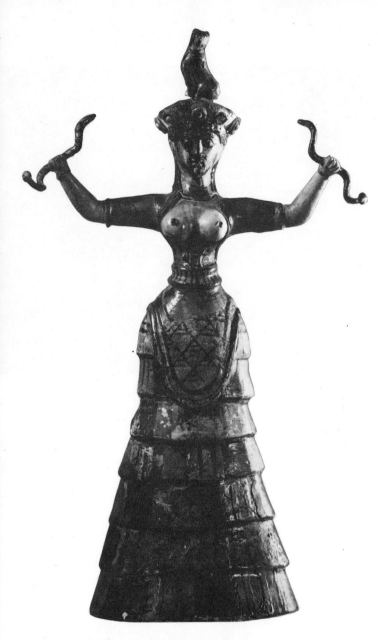

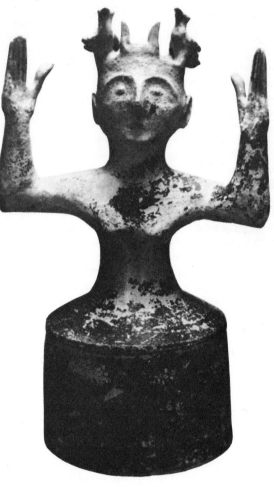

Cretan iconography is associated with the survival of the Neolithic mother goddess (see p. 58), symbol of fertility with her bare breasts, the serpent, the bull's horns, which recur in the architecture [321], and the bird, which precedes the dove of Aphrodite.

329. CRETE. MIDDLE MINOAN III. Snake goddess (faience). Treasure of the Sanctuary of Cnossus. *Herakleion Museum.*

330. CRETE. Terra-cotta goddess with horns and doves on her head. Sub-Minoan.

a rustic idyll on the other. Preoccupation with composition is carried to great lengths here, as is also the desire to represent the contrast between the two scenes.

As in the period of the first palaces, it is the art of engraved stone which offers us the most varied examples of decoration in relief. The hardest stones were used; the shape of seals no longer presents any interest, but only the flat or slightly convex field. The principal of decoration changes; written signs disappear, to be replaced by an image. Henceforth Minoan life in its entirety appeared on glyptics, a veritable microcosm in which everything the Minoans loved is shown to us: plants and trees, animals and their combats, family scenes, religious rites with officiating priests and devotees, for example that of
334 the offering to the goddess seated under a tree. The Cretan artist fulfilled himself within this reduced framework without any inconvenience. His gift for observation, his exceptionally sensitive feeling for outline and his keen sense of movement are emphasised here, concealing his genuine lack of plastic feeling and his dislike of accurate anatomy.

In short, from one art to another, the same aesthetic qualities and the same technical procedures reappear, as is natural. The artist's vision is rapid, shrewd and unthinking; he prefers the fantasy of creation to careful realism. Minoan architects followed the same principles; they used an imaginative approach to building at the expense of rigid planning and orderliness. Nothing could be more unlike the principles of Greek and of Mycenaean architecture.

Mycenaean art and civilisation, and the end of Cretan art

Mycenae and Mycenaean art were known before Crete and Cretan art, but cannot be explained by them. In its first two phases (Early and Middle Bronze) the continental or Helladic civilisation never passed a fairly primitive stage. It is only around 1600 that it suddenly started to progress, no doubt under the influence of Crete.

While the tombs of the Middle Helladic are poor, the shaft graves discovered by Schliemann at Mycenae contain the most beautiful treasures of Cretan art: the famous damascened daggers, seemingly painted in gold, 335 silver and bronze, showing scenes, handled in the purest Cretan style, of lion hunts, hunting water-fowl in the marshes which must be those of the Nile. Throughout the 16th and 15th centuries (Late Helladic I and II) the objects found in the tombs (for we know of no palaces or houses during this time) give us the same impression: it was the Spartan royal tomb at Vaphio which yielded up the Cretan gold goblets we have already mentioned. A few fragments of frescoes make use of the same themes as those of Cnossus; the pottery is closely akin to the Cretan, to such an extent that it is sometimes impossible to state the origin of the vases. Only funerary architecture contributes a very individual note: the tholoi, large circular tombs vaulted by means of corbels, afford us the first example of a monumental conception which seems most un-Cretan.

So scholars have been led to consider more closely the products of this first Mycenaean art and to single out the features which are peculiar to it and those which might be attributed to the Indo-European element in this people. Thus the kings who owned those markedly Cretan daggers were themselves covered with thin sheets of gold in their tombs, a fashion which can be called barbarian: the famous gold masks provide the most striking evidence of this. The quest for what is actually Mycenaean in Mycenaean art is one of the current problems in this field; another, closely linked with it, is that of relations between Crete and Mycenae. Was Crete's undeniable artistic influence on Mycenae connected with political domination? Was the Mycenaean world of that time a vassal of Crete, as Evans thought, basing his argument on the legend of the Athenian tribute paid to Minos? Or, on the contrary, was Mycenae at this time in a commanding position which relegated Crete to the background and gave the continent a sort of monopoly of relations with foreign civilisations? These are the two extreme positions and we believe it is possible to adopt a solution midway between them. Crete was undoubtedly shaken by devastating earthquakes around 1600; profiting by them the Mycenaeans were able to carry out raids from which came the treasures of the shaft graves. Equally certainly Crete subsequently recovered her power and her maritime supremacy: the richness of the second palaces, the representations of Keftiu on the walls of Egyptian tombs and, lastly, Greek tradition all prove this. But the politically autonomous Mycenaean world must have progressively competed with Crete, if we are to trust the finds of Mycenaean objects from then onwards in Syria and Egypt.

The discovery of a trading warehouse at Rhodes enables us to be more precise about this point: around 1450 we see very clearly that Mycenaean imports are taking over from Cretan ones. Towards this date, Mycenae began to exhibit a marked superiority and this would account for a noticeable development in Cretan art itself, which then became more monumental, in the spirit of its pottery (palace style) and in the plan and elevation of a tomb such as that of Isopata, which probably imitates Mycenaean tholoi. It would also explain why the tablets of the last period of the palace of Cnossus were written in Greek like those of Pylos, at least if we accept the deciphering proposed in 1953. It would therefore be towards the middle of the 15th century that Achaean influence asserted itself in Crete, fifty years earlier than had been believed hitherto.

339

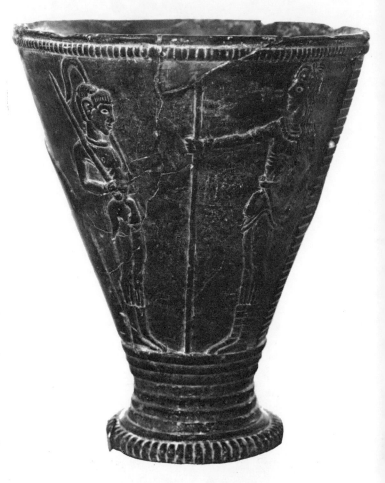

331. CRETE. MIDDLE MINOAN III. The Chieftain's vase. Black steatite. Hagia Triada. *Herakleion Museum.*

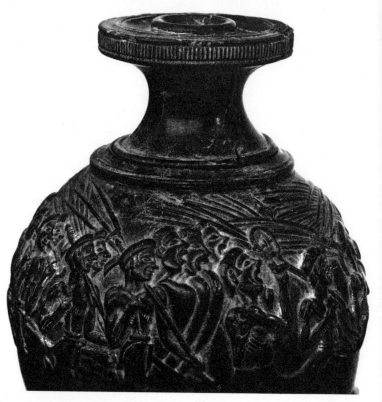

332. CRETE. LATE MINOAN I.
The Harvesters' vase. Black steatite.
Herakleion Museum.

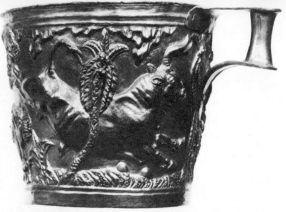

333. CRETAN. Cup, found in the royal tomb at Vaphio, Sparta. Gold. Late Minoan I. *National Museum, Athens*.

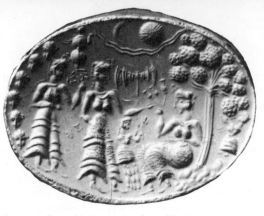

334. Imprint of a gold signet ring from Mycenae showing a religious scene. *Louvre*.

335. Mycenaean. Damascened bronze dagger, showing a lion hunt.

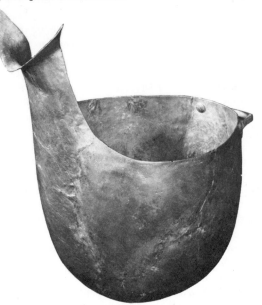

336. Early Helladic gold vessel. *Louvre*.

In fact, the Cretan palaces were destroyed about 1400 and except at Hagia Triada were only reoccupied on a very reduced scale. From 1400 to 1200 or 1150, during the final phase of the Bronze Age (Late Minoan III), the Cretan civilisation gradually fell into decay, at the same time that it succumbed to the Mycenaean civilisation of the same period; the continental megaron (main room) appeared at Hagia Triada, pottery decoration became stylised and small plastic works reverted to primitivism.

We must not believe that Crete no longer played any part at this time: it still preserves its importance in Homeric tradition, in the powerful Achaean myth of Idomenaeus. But henceforth the continent has the upper hand. Argolis remained in control: the sites there are 340–342 more numerous and richer than anywhere else (Tiryns, Argos, Dendra and especially Mycenae). But these archaeological centres, which were also the Homeric centres, multiplied everywhere: Pylos in Messenia, Sparta, Athens, Thebes and Orchomenus in Boeotia.

A veritable Mycenaean empire was established, far exceeding the Minoan empire in size. Provinces, which had remained on the fringe of the Helladic world, the Ionian islands, kingdom of Ulysses, Thessaly and Macedonia, opened their doors to Mycenaean civilisation. By this route, the Mycenaeans were to accelerate the development of the European Bronze Age. The Cyclades, previously in the hands of the sons of Minos, were henceforth Mycenaean, as were the islands off the coast of Asia, from Rhodes to Lesbos. On this coast traders and even settlers

were to install themselves in such towns as Troy, even before the conquest, and Miletus, over which the Achaean kings came into conflict with the Hittite kings, if we are to believe one of the tablets of the archives of Boghazkoy. At the same time settlers established themselves in Cyprus, where Enkomi was their capital. Cyprus, which became Mycenaean but was rich in an old native tradition and open to the near-by influences of Asia, was to develop a curiously mixed art, a sort of Levantine civilisation. From it, Mycenaean traders spread their products more widely than the Cretans had done, not only on the Syrian coast, at Ugarit and Byblos, but also inside Syria and Palestine, in Egypt (Lower Egypt and Amarna, as well as Upper Egypt). At the other extremity of the eastern Mediterranean basin, the pottery finally reached Tarentum and Syracuse, although the *Odyssey* suggests that daring navigators sometimes penetrated into the western basin.

The problem of relations between Cretan and Mycenean art arises: the latter derives from Crete in nearly every sphere, but it evolved towards stylisation. Thus the pottery of Late Helladic III, technically perfect, tends towards linear and abstract decoration, and at the same time incorporates themes or motifs previously rejected, such as human figures, animals and processions of chariots. Painting, still Cretan in its techniques, made use of the more violent themes of war and hunting. The minor arts, jewellery and seals, developed in the same direction as 334–336 pottery; in sculpture large numbers of idols of barbarous

SUMERIAN. Statue of Gudea, governor of Lagash. Diorite. End of the 3rd millennium B.C. British Museum. *Museum photograph*.

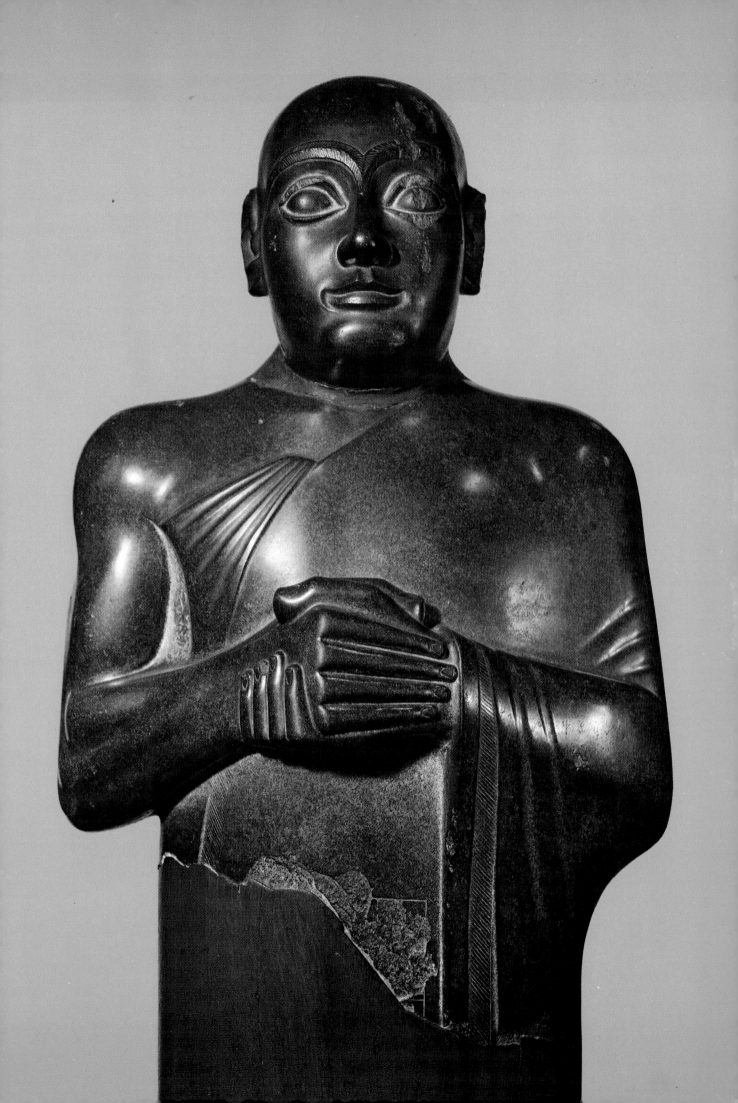

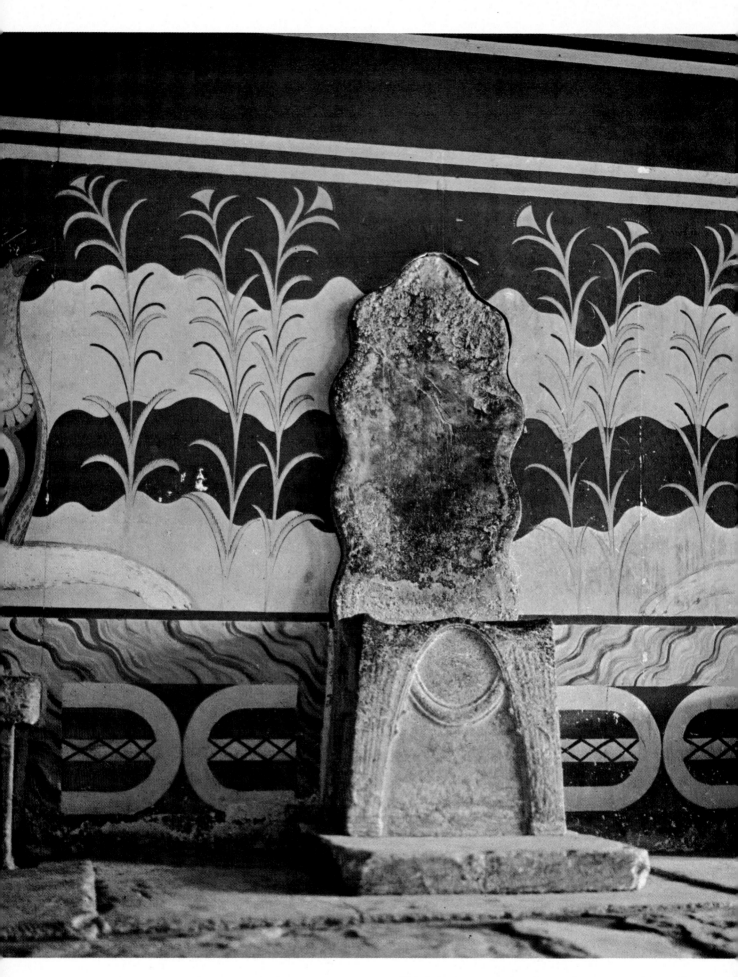

CRETE. Throne room of the palace. Cnossus. Late Minoan II.
Photo: D. Hughes-Gilbey.

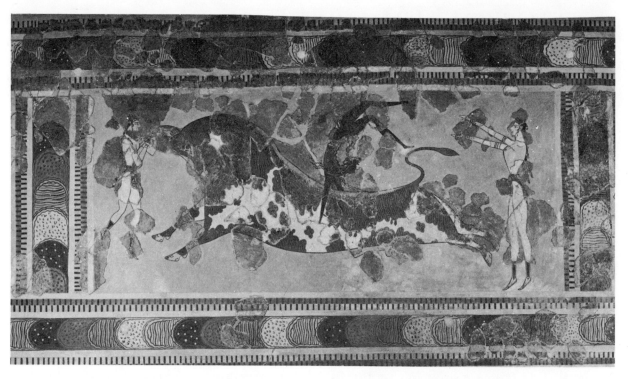

337. CRETE. LATE MINOAN I. Restored fresco from Cnossus showing either a bull-fight or acrobats performing somersaults over a bull. *Herakleion Museum.*

338. CRETE. LATE MINOAN I. Painted figure of a woman in profile, known as 'La Parisienne'. Fragments of a mural from Cnossus. *Herakleion Museum.*

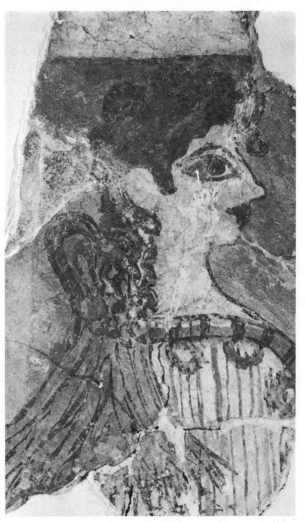

design were produced. But this internal revolution is not enough to explain Mycenaean art at this time: the new spirit is certainly due to ethnic changes. Moreover the architecture of the palaces that we know at this period, in particular the disposition of the megaron with a central hearth, but also the increasingly grandiose construction of the tholoi, shows that the aesthetic had changed, at least on this point: nothing could be more unlike the architecture of the second Cretan palaces.

A second problem is posed by the increasing contacts with the Oriental civilisations. To what extent was the Mycenaean world influenced by Syria or Egypt, either directly or via Cyprus, whose mixed character we have mentioned? Conversely, to what extent were the civilisations of the Syrian towns, of the Egypt of Amarna and the XIXth Dynasty, accessible to Aegean influences? There has even been talk of the birth of a common civilisation. But this is too sweeping, for the original organisation of each civilisation was in no way modified. However it is illuminating to study the traces left by these contacts. As the Mycenaean civilisation comes to an end, amid the turmoil and migrations of the 12th century, when iron was appearing, a final problem is posed. Was there a transition from pre-Hellenic art to the Greek art which was coming to life? It seems unlikely that an increasingly stylised naturalistic art, such as Mycenaean, finally gave birth, without the intervention of new factors, to the protogeometric art of the 11th and 10th centuries, and the geometric art of the 9th and 8th centuries. Even if the so-called 'sub-Mycenaean' phases, of extreme mediocrity, were prolonged in remote regions, especially Crete, I do not believe that an art so full of vigour and so charged with promise for the future as geometric art could have been grafted on to an effete civilisation.

HISTORICAL SUMMARY: The Aegean world

Archaeology. Until 1870, the origins of Greek civilisation before 800 were lost in legend; all that was known came from Greek tradition, particularly Homer. Between 1860 and 1870, strange pottery was discovered at Thera, Melos and Rhodes, but scholars did not know to whom this should be attributed. Between 1870 and 1890 excavations of Schliemann at Troy (from 1870), at Mycenae, Tiryns and Orchomenus (from 1874) revealed the extraordinary Mycenaean civilisation and the more ancient one of Troy. Scholars were struck by the similarity between the Mycenaean and Homeric civilisations. Egyptologists (Sir Flinders Petrie) showed that Mycenaean art was contemporary with the Egyptian New Kingdom (about 1550 to 1150): Mycenaean ceramics were found in Egypt and Egyptian objects at Mycenae.

It is still not certain whether the origin of the Mycenaean civilisation was Eastern or Western. From 1890, Greek archaeologists uncovered a Cycladic civilisation parallel with the Trojan civilisation; A.J. Evans collected engraved stones in Crete and proved that prehistoric Crete had had several systems of writing (hieroglyphic at first, later linear). In 1896, the Austrian linguist Kretschmer produced the theory of the Asian languages, neither Indo-European nor Semitic: languages of Asia Minor, such as Lycian, Carian and the pre-Hellenic tongue which served as a constituent element of Greek.

Between 1900 and 1920, the discovery of Cretan art by A. J. Evans at Cnossus enabled him to describe this amazing civilisation, to show that it preceded and explained the Mycenaean period. In 1905 he put forward a proposal for the chronology of what he called the Minoan civilisation. Excavations on the mainland, in the Mycenaean region and Thessaly, enlarged our knowledge of Greek prehistory which henceforth extends from the Neolithic to the beginnings of the Iron Age. Studies were made of the relations between the Aegean world and the Egyptian, Babylonian and Hittite civilisations, which were becoming better and better known.

Between 1920 and 1939, knowledge of the pre-Hellenic cultures broadened and also became more detailed. In Crete, provincial variants were studied (French excavations at Mallia). Deep digs were made on the mainland: Wace and Blegen discovered a pre-Mycenaean Helladic civilisation, whose relations with Crete they studied. The Americans (Blegen) resumed excavations at Troy (1931–38), the Swedes created Cypriot archaeology: Troy and Cyprus were the meeting places between Asia and the Aegean. In Asia, owing to parallel discoveries in Phoenicia, Syria and Asia Minor, relations between these civilisations and the Aegean world were more clearly defined (the Achaeans were mentioned in the Hittite archives). The Germans for their part studied the relations of the Aegean world with the Balkans and central Europe (the Indo-European character of the Mycenaean civilisation); Kretschmer from 1925 accepted the presence of Indo-European elements in Asian languages.

Since 1939, work on systems of writing and languages resulted in some decipherments, one by Hrozný which was a failure, the other by Ventris and Chadwick (from 1953), favourably received. Linear B at Cnossus and Pylos (the last system of writing) is presumed to be a transcription of a primitive form of Greek. Continued during the war in Cyprus, excavations were resumed everywhere else immediately after hostilities ceased.

HISTORY

Palaeolithic. A few traces in central Greece (Megaris and Boeotia).

Neolithic. It appeared in the course of the 4th millennium, if not earlier, and lasted until about 2700 in Crete, until about 2500 on the mainland.

The main centres were on the one hand in Crete (polished pottery, incised decoration); on the other hand, on the Greek mainland from Macedonia to the Peloponnese, mainly in Thessaly, central Greece and around Corinth (painted pottery, with linear decoration); a Neolithic II developed towards the end but only in Thessaly, around Dimini (spiral-shaped decoration). In the Greek islands, there are only traces of the Neolithic.

The Cretan centre remained isolated. Today the tendency is to connect Neolithic I on the mainland with the older one in Asia (Susa, al 'Ubaid, Tell Halaf, Mersin); the go-between was Cyprus where the Neolithic was very important. Emphasis is also laid on the liaison between Greek Neolithic and that of the Balkans, the civilisation

339. GREECE. Gold funeral mask. *Athens National Museum.*

340. Gallery and casemate of the east bastion of the fortress of Tiryns.

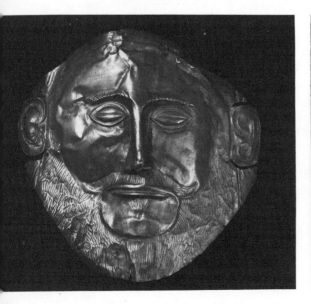

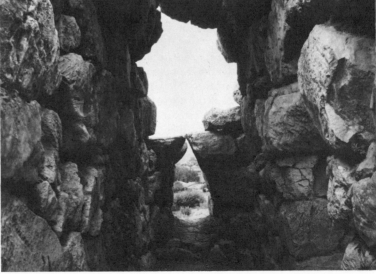

196

advancing from south to north. Nevertheless by a repercussion the Neolithic of Dimini is assumed to derive from that of the Danubian regions.

Chalcolithic and Early Bronze Ages. About 2700–2100 in Crete and the Cyclades; 2500–2000 on the mainland. Copper implements appeared progressively and without interruption from the Neolithic onwards; bronze was unknown until the last phase, from about 2300.

Crete (Early Minoan). The principal centres were in the east, around the gulf of Mirabello, and in the plain of Messara to the south. At Palaikastro, Mochlos and Vasiliki civilisation evolved more quickly (polished pottery, inherited from Early Minoan I; pottery with flame-like decoration and painted pottery, dark on light, in Early Minoan III) and more brilliantly (stone vases, treasure of Mochlos) [**319**].

Early Cycladic. A highly original civilisation (marble statuettes and vases) in close contact with Anatolia developed in all the islands.

Early Helladic. A rather poor civilisation undergoing latterly the influence of the Cyclades and Crete; polished lustre pottery (*Urfirnis*); painted pottery.

The Early Bronze Age of the Aegean was closely dependent on pre-Hittite Anatolia (Alishar, Alaca Huyuk) via Troy whose prosperity was very great (especially Troy II at the end of the 3rd millennium). Mesopotamian influences could also reach it by way of Asia Minor. Early Minoan III established direct relations with Cyprus and possibly Syria; the influence of the Egyptian Old Kingdom was noticeable at Mochlos and in Messara. The Aegean played the part of an intermediary in the propagation of metals in Europe.

Middle Bronze Age. About 2100 to 1600 in Crete; 2000–1900 or 1600 on the mainland.

Crete (Middle Minoan). The civilisation of the first palaces was very brilliant: palatial architecture, a considerable development of metallurgy and jewellery; highly decorative pottery, light on dark; a hieroglyphic system of writing. It is probable that this civilisation first appeared in the east (Mallia), but it was less developed there. At Cnossus and Phaestos, it was particularly refined in the phase of Middle Minoan II or Kamares (a style rather than a period unknown in the east). During the last phase (Middle Minoan III) the palaces were destroyed (in about 1750): Evans's Middle Minoan IIIb belongs to the period of the second palaces (from about 1700).

Middle Cycladic. Except at Melos, where Cretan influence asserted itself, this phase in the Cyclades is not very well known.

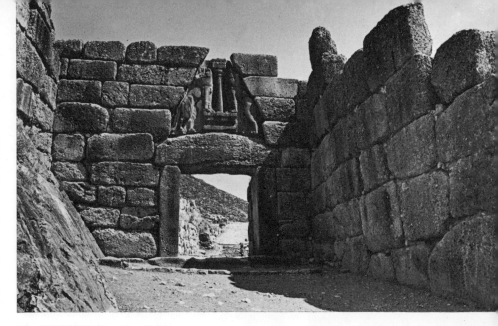

341. MYCENAE. The Lion Gate.

CRETAN CHRONOLOGY

Neolithic	before 2700	
Early Minoan I and II	about 2700–2300	Chalcolithic
Early Minoan III	about 2300–2100	1st Bronze Age
Middle Minoan I	about 2100–1900	
Middle Minoan II	about 1900–1700	1st Cretan hegemony and beginning of Mycenaean
Middle Minoan III	about 1700–1600	2nd Cretan hegemony: Cnossus
Late Minoan I	about 1600–1450	
Late Minoan II	about 1450–1400	Palace style
Late Minoan III	about 1400–1200	Achaean hegemony

NOTE: The dates, especially the oldest ones, are still controversial.

Middle Helladic. The arrival of bands of Indo-Europeans (Ionians or Achaeans) about 2000–1900 cut the continent off from the islands and Crete; relations were resumed on the coast towards the end of this period (Middle Minoan III). The civilisation remained poor, and is difficult to interpret (Minyan pottery, simply polished; pottery painted in flat colours).

Crete already had maritime supremacy and was in close contact with Cyprus, the Syrian coast (Ugarit and Byblos), Mesopotamia, via Mari, and the Egypt of the Middle Kingdom; she exported her Kamares pottery everywhere and in return she received from these more advanced civilisations contributions still unknown to the Greek mainland. Anatolia, in the hands of the Indo-European Hittites, remained apart; Troy lost its importance.

Late Bronze Age. 1600–1200 or 1150. Iron became widely known during the 12th century.

Crete (Late Minoan). The civilisation of the second palaces began about 1700, underwent a crisis towards 1600, then shone again: its palatial architecture was increasingly original. The arts developed in a naturalistic spirit. Linear A was the system of writing used. The cultural and probably the political influence of Cnossus dominated the island. Towards 1450 it seems that Cnossus began to come under the influence of the mainland (palace style;

linear B). However, the palaces were only destroyed about 1400. Crete, in the last phase (Late Minoan III), was in a state of comparative decadence and came under the 'Achaean' influence of the mainland.

Late Cycladic. The Cyclades were divided between the influences of Crete and the mainland; the latter finally predominated.

Late Helladic (Mycenaean). Between 1600 and 1400, the influence of Cretan civilisation was predominant but without any political links: period of the shaft graves (Late Helladic I), period of the tholoi [**342**] (Late Helladic II). In Late Helladic III, the Mycenaean civilisation asserted itself, mixing Indo-European elements with the basic Cretan strain, and spread throughout the eastern basin of the Mediterranean: Mycenaean palaces (the continental megaron). The naturalistic art tended to stylisation; the writing was linear B.

The contacts between the Aegean civilisations and the world outside have already been studied, but let us remember that Crete, Rhodes and Cyprus became Achaean at that time.

The transition from bronze to iron. The 'sub-Minoan' periods in Crete, 'sub-Mycenaean' elsewhere, were transitional phases (12th and 11th centuries). Iron appeared; new invasions (Dorians) changed the ethnical situation. Civilisation grew poorer, and some techniques seem to have been lost.

197

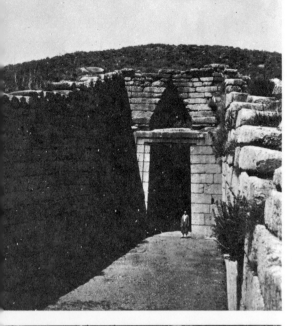

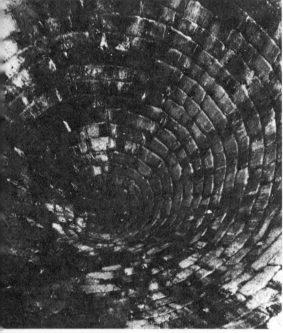

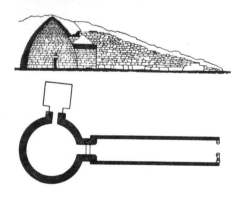

342. MYCENAE. The Treasury of Atreus. a. The façade. b. The dome. c. Section and plan. (*After Perrot and Chipiez.*)

ARTS AND TECHNIQUES

Architecture. In the Neolithic, the cave was replaced by the rectangular house, without a clear-cut plan, but with several rooms and a permanent hearth. On the mainland, the houses were apsidal; from Troy I the megaron appeared, an elongated hall with a central hearth, with a vestibule in front. The appearance of the Cretan palaces is an important development; already grouped around a central courtyard, the quarters remained isolated; the use of columns for supporting the roof was still rare, and contemporary houses were still unplanned. The second Cretan palaces, highly original creations characteristic of the Cretan aesthetic, influenced private houses at least in Crete. Unlike the other arts, the architecture of the mainland hardly owes anything to Crete (except undoubtedly the terrace roof); it developed the ancient tradition of the axial megaron with a central hearth.

Funerary architecture did not exist until the Late Bronze Age except in the tholoi of Messara. Caves, holes in the rock, chambers built like the rooms of houses, pits or cists, jars or sarcophagi were used. Even in the time of the first Cretan palaces, there seem to have been only the necropolises, which were without grandeur: e.g. the precinct of Chrysolakkos at Mallia enclosing simple chambers. More elaborate royal tombs appeared in Crete only during the 15th century: temples, the rectangular tomb of Isopata, with an antechamber and an entrance corridor. The influence of the continental tholoi, genuine architectural creations, can probably be seen here.

Sculpture. In the Neolithic and Early Bronze Ages, sculpture in the round was highly stylised, and reached its height in the Cyclades; at the same time Cyprus and Crete showed a great liking for vases with carved decoration. This stylised aesthetic did not result in a classical art; Cretan sculpture of the following periods is very lively. Small-scale Mycenaean sculpture ended in stereotyped stylisation, the lower parts of the body becoming completely rigid. A sculptural tradition never asserted itself in the Aegean.

Quite the opposite is true of works in relief: the advances in seal-carving prove this. In the Early Bronze Age, the decoration was geometrical; in the Middle Bronze, decorative ornamentation did not inhibit the animated character of the scenes; in the Late Bronze Age the seals were the most lively and varied in the Near East.

During the same period all the arts in relief developed, using the most varied materials, including steatite and precious metals. Mycenaean reliefs for long followed the same aesthetic, and then evolved towards stylisation.

Painting and Pottery. In the Neolithic, pottery was polished, with incised linear (Crete) or painted decoration (Thessaly, Greece). In Thessaly, Neolithic II had a variety with spiral-shaped decoration. The polished pottery, black or red with incised decoration, remained the same as at the beginning of the Early Bronze Age throughout most of the Aegean world; Cretan 'flame' decoration is only a variant. Painted pottery predominated during the Early Bronze Age, purely linear in its decoration, brown (or black) on a pale polished ground (clay or slip), or white on dark glaze. Middle Minoan saw a great development in pottery: polychrome decoration (white, red, yellow) was used on a dark ground; themes based on plant life came into the repertoire, while scrolls proliferated. Kamares ware was a particularly refined variety unknown on the mainland where polished Minyan and flat, purely linear painting were produced [**326**].

The Late Bronze Age saw the simultaneous appearance of great painting, the most original and lively of all the painting in the Near East, and the transformation of ceramic decoration, painted in dark on a light ground, and limiting its repertoire the better to adapt it to the shape of the vase (themes from plant life and the sea). Mycenaean pottery was based on the Cretan but developed towards stylisation.

The metal arts. A very simple range of copper implements ensured the smooth transformation of the stone civilisation into a metal one. During the last third of the 3rd millennium bronze containing tin was widely used, and gold and silver were employed for vases and simple jewellery (cut out leaves). Metallurgical techniques had an influence on the shapes of pottery from the end of the Early Bronze Age [**319**]. During the Middle Bronze Age in Crete, the metal arts made tremendous progress not only in the size of weapons, and in abundance of bronze vases and implements, but also in the delicacy of the jewellery. The Late Bronze Age has left large numbers of deposits of bronze objects; the numerous jewels and pieces of goldsmiths' work, especially on the mainland, are often of Cretan origin; it was the highest point reached by technical methods and aesthetic refinements (damascening) [**335**]. Iron, sometimes used as a rare metal in the Mycenaean period, became more abundant in the 12th century, when most of the Bronze Age techniques disappeared.

Pierre Demargne

THE RISE OF EUROPE *Christopher Hawkes*

At the end of the 3rd millennium, when brilliant civilisations were being developed in the Mediterranean basin, the rest of Europe was still in the Neolithic period. The appearance of metal precipitated its evolution until finally with the Gauls it became a force which threatened Italy, Greece and even Asia Minor. Christopher Hawkes gives perhaps the first methodical, comprehensive and clear summary of this confused period of 2,000 years which has only recently been properly studied.

THE EARLY BRONZE AGE AND ITS NEOLITHIC BACKGROUND

The Europe of Palaeolithic and Mesolithic prehistory received the earliest elements of civilisation in the cultures of the Neolithic. Those elements, from their Asiatic lands of origin, were carried gradually westward by the coasts and islands of the eastern Mediterranean, and by Anatolia, first of all to the regions of the Aegean and the Balkans. Of the zone of Neolithic peasant cultures thus established by colonists in Greece and Macedonia, the northern periphery was next extended into the basin of the Danube. Perhaps as early as the 4th millennium, certainly in the early and middle centuries of the 3rd, when the Aegean was already receiving the fresh cultures of its Early Bronze Age, Neolithic peasants were on both sides of the Danube not only below but also above the Iron Gates, and giving rise to regional groups spread in several directions. With a material equipment of stone and other tools and ornaments, the traditions of their culture prescribed a plastic art of clay or stone figurines, and a ceramic in which coarse pottery is accompanied by fine, with decoration variously incised or painted, in designs including a repertory of spiral motifs. This, prominent first in the Balkans, was developed later also in Transylvania, in the Ariusd or Oltenian culture of the valleys within the Carpathian mountains, as well as in the more extensive Tripolye culture farther east. But before those had arisen, the earliest settlements on the Danube about Belgrade, as at Starčevo, had been extended northwards, in what is called the Körös culture, into Hungary.

The Körös was succeeded there by the culture named after the river Tisza; this, with the parallel culture of Lengyel, formed the substratum for all later developments on the Hungarian plain, and its material shows clear Anatolian or Balkan features. Indeed, all these early cultures of south-east Europe show more or less clear affinity to the Balkans and beyond, and continued in parallel with the continuing Balkans groups, that of the Drava, that of Vinča near Belgrade, etc. But west and north of the middle Danube, beginning in west Hungary and Moravia, the primary Neolithic peasantries were those Danubians who made linear-ornamented 'band' or ribbon pottery; with them, the basic Neolithic culture passed into a more distinctively European embodiment.

The Danubians attained a great extent, to the Oder and Vistula and to the Rhine and Meuse, covering all the loess plains of central Europe. Parallel, but distinct, was the Bükk culture of north Hungary. While in many regions they continued, forming groups distinguished by 'stroke-ornamented' and other varieties of pottery, there arose 'secondary Neolithic' cultures beside them, as the Rössen in Germany and the Aichbühl in the eastern Alps. Away to the north, there arose obscurely the first Neolithic culture of the north European plain, extending thence to Denmark. Meanwhile, around the upper Danube, there appeared fresh groups related to the Hungarian. To the south, a current from here passed into north Italy, and others, from Greek and Balkan sources, crossed to peninsular Italy, especially to Apulia, whence influence reached Sicily and the adjacent islands. These currents impinged upon an older culture, distinguished by impression-ornamented pottery which represents an earlier colonisation from the east, spread by sea not only to Italy and Sicily, but gradually all round the western Mediterranean. That, however, had been purely Neolithic.

The appearance of metal in central Europe

The parts of Europe most directly accessible to the Early Bronze peoples of the Aegean and Anatolia were still those of the south-east, nearest to the Balkans. And it was this way, apparently, that the interior of the continent first became acquainted, during these same centuries, with metal. At first the evidences are rare, consisting of small objects made of copper. But when the Tisza culture was followed by that named Bodrogkeresztur, probably within the last one or two centuries of the 3rd millennium, these became less rare and more significant. A third period of Danubian development has begun, in effect a 'Copper Age' under a primary impulse directed across the Balkans from the metal-using lands beyond. This impulse, in part at least, was probably borne by immigration.

Macedonia now had an Early Bronze culture, parallel to the Early Helladic and Cycladic of Greece and the Aegean islands, but with Anatolian relationships, more particularly with Troy. It seems to have been carried across the Balkan mountains by migration, superseding the older Neolithic, and bringing in stone axe-hammers or battle-axes, and two-handled and especially high-handled vessels of leathery-looking pottery, all with counterparts in Macedonia or Anatolia. Bubanj in Serbia shows this well, and similar traits appear over a wide area west and north of the middle Danube, from west Hungary to Austria and beyond, in what is named the Baden culture. The same culture even reached Poland, and Bohemia and Moravia, where it shows contact, as does the Jordansmühl culture of Silesia, with the Neolithic of the north.

Throughout these regions also, there are now signs of a more important contact, with peoples of eastern Europe. It is well known that elements of Asiatic civilisation were transmitted during the 3rd millennium by the Caucasus to dwellers in the Kuban and the south Russian plain, who thenceforward appear as warlike and pastoral folk, burying their dead individually under tumuli. Repercussions of this, discernible in Anatolia, at Troy and again in Macedonia, are repeated variously in the lower Danube and Carpathian regions (Glina, Schneckenberg), and in north Hungary. Moreover, peoples with the same rite of single burial under a tumulus, using stone battle-

68

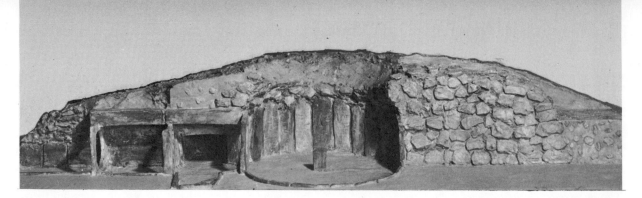

343. SPAIN. The latest reconstruction of the dolmen at Los Millares. *Archaeological Museum, Barcelona.*

axes and the pottery known as 'corded', appear not only further east, but spread across Poland to the north German plain, entering Saxo-Thuringia, joining the area of the Baden culture towards the middle and upper Danube, and reaching west to Switzerland and the Rhine, and south to the eastern Alps and to Slovania. With them, too, must be grouped the 'single-grave' invaders of the Baltic regions.

Another group, distinguished by 'globular amphora' pottery found from Poland to central Germany, has perhaps its own connections with south Russia; and although the corded pottery seems in general to be native to the eastern and north-eastern borders of central Europe, it is sometimes found not only in the Baden culture but also further south-east, in the Carpathians and even occasionally in Macedonia and Greece, at the same time as stone battle-axes. Since in Greece these intrusions accompany the destruction of the Early Helladic culture, around 1900 B.C., and its replacement by the Middle Helladic, whose bearers certainly spoke Greek, this whole complex of movements can be identified, more securely now than formerly, with the primary diffusion of Indo-European languages and institutions. It is thus a matter of the origin not only of the Greeks, and of the Hittite conquerors of Anatolia, but of Thracians and Illyrians, and even Slavs; farther west, of the Celts, and further north, of the Germanic peoples.

Gradually, the various groups created by the turmoil of this period became more settled. Demand and opportunity for metal-production was thus enhanced. The original south-eastern impulse to metal-working gradually spread, round the Danube basin from the Balkans to the Transylvanian and Slovakian mountains enclosing Hungary, and then on to Bohemia and central and south Germany. Between the Danube and the Adriatic, lastly, we have again early metal-working, within the probable homelands of the Indo-European immigrants into Italy.

The Mediterranean countries and Aegean influences

Italic origins in these regions may be connected with several groups accompanying or following those that brought Baden or corded pottery and stone battle-axes among the Neolithic peasantries of the eastern Alps. At the Mondsee and elsewhere in Austria, round Ljubljana in Slovenia, and at the Slavonian site of Vučedol on the Drava, were peoples using locally-worked east Alpine copper. The rhomboid daggers, and the pottery with 'excised' ornament, call to mind the Early Bronze Age of Cyprus; if the metal industry here was started by venturers from there, sailing up the Adriatic, the date would hardly be after 2000. But the peoples themselves had clearly been formed by the same process of admixture

that we have seen at work all over Danubian and central Europe. The evidences include again stone battle-axes, and these appear also in north and central Italy. There, the cultures of Remedello and Rinaldone have otherwise a somewhat different aspect, but they too worked copper. Daggers, not only rhomboid but also square-tanged like those of Early Minoan Crete, suggest metallurgy here started by Cretan venturers, again hardly after 2000, who may also have discovered the tin of north Etruria (Monte Bradoni). On the north Italian lakes, lastly, arose the culture named Polada, which had a long duration, benefiting from traffic with central Europe over the Brenner Pass. Metal was nowhere yet abundant—thus, the dagger-forms were much imitated in flint—but a beginning had been made, and in these European-Oriental minglings lie the cultural roots of Bronze Age Italy.

Eastern initiative in this direction had already been focused on Sicily. Here, beside the Neolithic culture now locally developed (San Cono), the period somewhat before and after 2000 brought incomings first perhaps from western Greece (Serraferlicchio), next from some Aegean-Anatolian source (S. Ippolito), and lastly, to initiate in the south-east of the island the culture of Castelluccio, a people knowing copper and having painted pottery with both Early and Middle Helladic features, who made large cemeteries of rock-cut chamber-tombs for collective burial. Forms of collective tombs appear thereafter in the continuing Neolithic of north-west Sicily; collateral, yet unique, is that of the Maltese islands, where the long history of the famous 'temples', their cult somehow related to that expressed in general by collective tombs, had already, it seems, begun. The plastic art of their many figurines, above all of women, suggests an initial inspiration from those of the Early Cycladic culture; indeed, people from the Cyclades may well have joined in the opening-up of the western Mediterranean. In Sardinia, after poor Neolithic settlers, there appears a culture practising collective burial in rock-cut chamber-tombs, which by their form and surviving contexts indicate colonisation, by seekers and workers of the island's metals, coming westward from homes either in the Cyclades (pottery-forms, and again figurines), or in Minoan Crete; among the most elaborate, grouped together at Anghelu Ruju, some have been sculptured with low reliefs of high-prowed ships and the heads of bulls. There are also stone-built tombs of gallery and simpler forms, and the culture had a long-continued development, but its origin at this time is confirmed by pottery and ornaments showing connections with other west Mediterranean coasts.

The Neolithic settlers who had brought impressed pottery to those coasts have already been noted; in addition, there had arrived others with plain smooth pottery, the originators of what may be called the Western Neolithic. This culture was gradually spread, by further

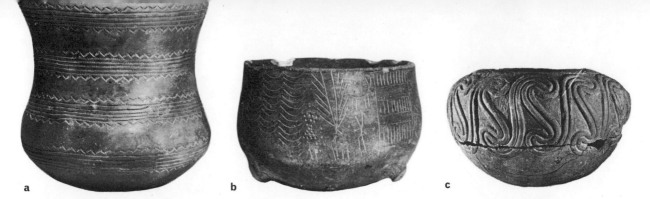

344. POTTERY. a. Bell-beaker found at Los Millares.
Ashmolean Museum, Oxford. b. Decorated bowl found at
Los Millares. *Ashmolean Museum, Oxford.* c. Nebo vase found
at Bila (Bosnia). Butmirian type. *Sarajevo Museum.*

colonisation, over all western Europe: France and the
western Alps (Cortaillod, Lagozza), the British Isles
(Windmill Hill), and Spain and Portugal. From its connections on the Italian side, there spread in it later a convention of pottery-ornament in scratched designs (Camp
de Chassey), and farther west also one of incised grooves
or 'cannelures'. This seems related somehow to the
incised or impressed pottery now made by the natives
of the interior of Spain and North Africa, in the 'secondary' Neolithic culture to which these now had taken,
designated Hispano-Mauretanian.

But in Spain the western culture with plain pottery—
distinguished also by fine flint-work and named Ibero-
Saharan from its possible African connections—was the
more progressive. Tombs lined with stone slabs are found
in it, and in the probably secondary culture derived from
it in Portugal these are 'dolmens' built of slabs enclosed
in mounds. Though its main diffusion seems wholly
Neolithic, its primary Spanish home in the south-east
(Almería) was very early concerned with metal-working
and after a time this became suddenly the scene of a fresh
burst of colonising and industrial energy. Fortified settlements, of which the best known is Los Millares, appear
343 together with fine stone-built chamber-tombs, of the
cupola-roofed tholos type, of which the prototypes seem
east Mediterranean or Aegean and perhaps more particularly Cretan, whose contents include objects certainly
exotic. The date is not yet precisely fixed, but lies without
doubt in the first centuries after 2000.

Metal in western Europe

Thus it is seen that the enterprise of the civilised Orient
in opening up central and western Europe had now two
fronts, one across the Danubian regions, the other along
the coasts and islands of the Mediterranean. And on both
it had to do with the discovery and working of materials,
metals first of all, in regions already colonised by Neolithic
settlers. Yet to the formation of our Early Bronze Age
there is still a third element to add. Over much of central
Europe there are found of this period flat graves (and
some settlements) distinguished by caliciform or bell-like
beakers or goblets with impressed ornament horizontally
arranged; analogues in south-west Europe, to these and
the associated archer's equipment and copper daggers,
344 have suggested the arrival thence of a 'beaker people'. In
Bohemia and near by in Germany, this element entered
into the formation of the Aunjetitz or related culture of
the Early Bronze Age. In the Rhineland, however, it
combined with that of the corded pottery and single-grave
tumuli already mentioned. From there, and from the
Netherlands, crossings were made to Britain, where a

further combination was soon made with single-grave
tumulus people coming over the North Sea; though metal
daggers are less common than flint, and than stone axe-
hammers, this culture began the submergence of the
British Neolithic.

Meanwhile on the continent, the Western Neolithic
outgrowth named the Michelsberg culture had spread
between the Upper Rhine, Belgium and Bohemia, and
round the Seine, Oise, Marne and Meuse there persisted
a secondary Neolithic culture which, although its Swiss
province (Horgen) and its south German neighbour
(Altheim) were now penetrated by corded-pottery people,
allowed little contact to the bell-beaker elements. It did
adopt collective burial, in stone-lined 'covered gallery'
tombs (in the Marne, chalk-cut grottoes) which have
more splendid analogues in Provence round Arles; but an
avenue for 'beaker people' up the Rhône, past the Neolithic Chamblandes culture of the south-west Alps, is hard
to prove. One across the eastern Alps from north Italy
could be easier: the Remedello culture there includes
beaker graves like many in central Europe. But the col-
lective-burial rite did not so travel: its association with
beakers is mainly confined to the west Mediterranean
(Provence, Sardinia, north-west Sicily), south and west
France, including Brittany, and the Iberian Peninsula.
This association is seen at its fullest in the cemeteries of
rock-tombs round the mouth of the Tagus in Portugal
(Palmella, etc.); an exotic 'beaker people', of origin yet
unknown, but with knowledge of metal presumably from
the Mediterranean, could have begun a European diffusion there. But even in the Peninsula the association is
not found everywhere; beakers occur sometimes in
simple graves, and in collective tombs sometimes with
secondary burials only.

In all the south-west, in fact, the spread of metal-using
culture was probably begun by the builders of collective
tombs who are seen at Los Millares, and thence westwards to their distinct province in the Algarve; the
element represented by the beakers is comprised among
them sometimes and sometimes not. In Catalonia and the
Pyrenees, the collective tombs assume the gallery form,
and here and in all south-west France was established a
culture destined for a long survival, including the beaker
element and using some metal, but still much stone (hence
called 'Chalcolithic'), and with stone-built tombs often
reduced to simple 'dolmen' forms. From here to the
Atlantic coasts, to Brittany and to the British Isles, other
forms of collective gallery-tomb suggest diffusions by sea,
in which metal seems absent; the earliest long cairn and
long barrow tombs here belong wholly to the Western
Neolithic cultures. This appears still true of those of the
Loire and the Severn where the gallery can have transepts,
forming in effect a chamber; and again, when true
chamber-tombs with entrance-passage are introduced,
showing that south Spain and Portugal were now contri-

201

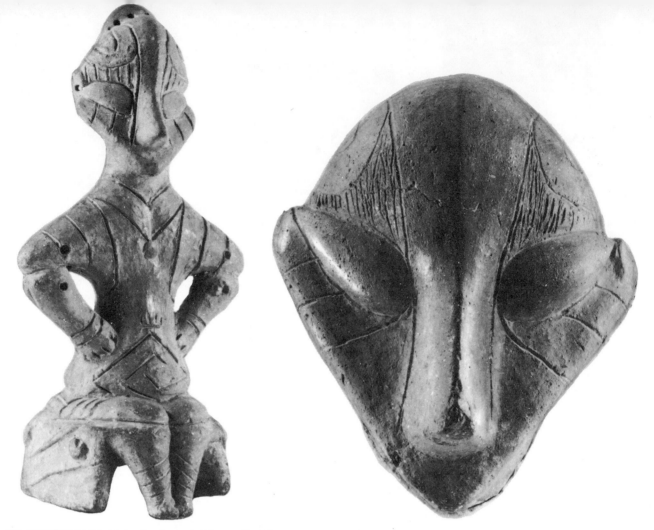

345. YUGOSLAVIA. Statuette of a seated figure. Neolithic deposit of Prishtina (Serbia). *Prishtina Museum.*

346. YUGOSLAVIA. Stone head from the Neolithic deposit of Prishtina (Serbia). *Prishtina Museum.*

buting to the Atlantic diffusion, metal is not yet attested.

Yet in these ventures from the south there was probably prospecting for it, which will have led to discovery of the metal-bearing districts of Atlantic Europe, from northwest Spain to Brittany, and in western Britain and Ireland. Industries in copper, soon also in tin to alloy it for bronze, and even in gold, made their appearance in the second quarter of the 2nd millennium. And when the Seine-Oise-Marne culture spread also to Brittany, with its distinctive gallery-tombs (whence some would derive the wedge-shaped tombs of Ireland), and when the British Isles were invaded from the south-east by the Rhineland beaker peoples described above, these western regions were put in contact not only with Iberia and the Mediterranean, but with central Europe too, and also with the north, where collective passage-tombs had already been adopted (following the local northern 'dolmen') before the arrival of the 'single-grave' invaders, mentioned earlier.

The Early Bronze Age in central Europe

And now we must turn back to review the situation in central Europe, from the margins of the north European plain whence those 'single-grave' invaders came, to the Rhine and upper Danube and the Alps, and to Bohemia, Hungary and the margins of the Balkans. We have seen the beginning of metal-working in these regions, already under impulse from the civilised Orient. Now, in the early centuries of the 2nd millennium, we find cultures of full Early Bronze Age character: in southern Hungary and by the modern Rumanian border, as at Perjamos; farther

north on the Hungarian plain, as at Nagy Rev and Toszeg; and then at the heart of Europe in Bohemia, where the culture is named from the great cemetery at Únětice (Aunjetitz) near Prague, and came to extend, at its broadest, into central Germany, Silesia and Moravia, and over the borders of Bavaria and Austria. These cultures of the plains, raised upon prehistoric Danubian traditions enriched by the incomings of the foregoing centuries, show us settled agricultural life combined with the beginnings of a commercial wealth, above all in bronze. And their distinctive penannular neck-rings, used in commerce as standard ingots of the metal, their triangular daggers, and their pins looped or pierced for cord-fastening, repeat or recall so closely forms found now in the Orient—variously in Anatolia and Cyprus, and in Syria most notably in the French excavations at Byblos and Ras Shamra—that the changes and innovations of the **304** period around 2000 there, which brought important advances in bronze technology, must clearly have affected also central Europe, and emphasise with a new force the Oriental connections of what was now its standard bronze production.

Moreover, around the cultures of the plains there were those of the hills and of the marginal lands between them. As well as those of Rumania and Transylvania, there was the extensive Slavonian culture of the Sava and Drava, together with those of Slovenia and the eastern Alps already noted; in north Hungary, in west Hungary and Slovakia, in parts of Austria and in south Bohemia, there were groups whose share in Early Bronze culture was

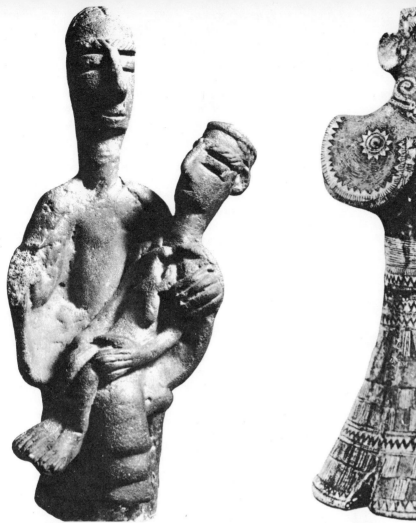

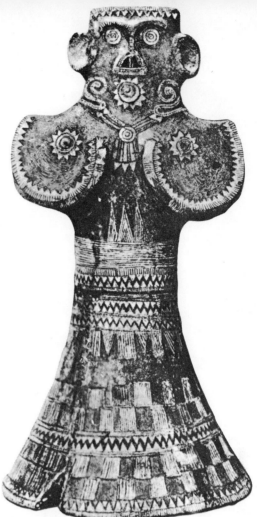

347. SARDINIA. Nuragic bronze figure of mother and child strangely reminiscent of Christian Madonnas.

348. YUGOSLAVIA. BRONZE AGE. Terra-cotta idol from Klicevac. After a drawing. *Belgrade Museum*.

combined with other traditions, of the preceding centuries of the Baden culture, and those of the tumuli and single graves, corded pottery and stone battle-axes. In south Germany, there were continuations from these and from the local Neolithic and beaker cultures, producing that of the Adlerberg on the Rhine, neighbour to the Early Bronze culture of Straubing on the Bavarian plain; in central Germany, the tumulus people of Saxo-Thuringia adopted the Únětice type of Early Bronze culture in a version of their own, its distinctiveness emphasised by the growing wealth of its warlike chiefs, and reflected soon towards the Lausitz, Silesia and Brandenburg. It was from extensions this way, down the Elbe and Oder, that bronze culture was finally transmitted to northern Europe. Moreover, there were oversea connections here with the west, where the beaker and other single-grave invaders of Britain could now command metallic wealth from the west of their country and from Ireland, and where Brittany also, about this time, was invaded by similar bronze-using folk. Thus, all the leading centres of north-west Europe became linked with the northern and western quarters of the great central European province. And along the Alps, Switzerland can show not only an extension of culture from south Germany, but also one from the Danubian-Hungarian direction, whence a distinct Early Bronze culture arose on the upper Rhône. Lastly, the circle is completed by the equally distinctive Early Bronze groups of northern Italy.

It remains to ask what these peoples of the Early Bronze Age can show us in the domain of art. In the traditions of the Neolithic, both in central Europe and in the west, artistic impulse had been manifest in three forms. First, there had been a plastic art of figural representation, primitive and crude, serving the religion of fertility which in one form or another animated all these early communities of cultivators. Essentially, this had been introduced into Europe by the first Neolithic colonists from the Orient; their images of human, mainly female, and animal figures, usually of clay and sometimes reflected in the modelling of pottery, were not much transmitted from their south-eastern and Balkan homes far into central Europe. Similar Neolithic imagery in the west, as well as entering from the Balkans into the conventionally elaborate handle-forms of pottery in Italy, is more explicitly manifest in religious association with collective tombs. In the limestone sculptures of the Maltese sanctuaries, it attained an isolated and unique magnificence; from Sicily westwards, its expression was more narrowly stylised, perhaps especially through contact with the local survival of the prehistoric rock-painted art of south-eastern Spain, in schematic forms normally of animals. These may appear in the tombs on pottery, as may the pair of eyes seen equally among the traits which schematise the female form on idols—hair, necklaces, breasts—whether of bone or stone plaques in the Peninsula or in the larger-sized sculpture of the menhir statues and tomb-carvings of France. In this art, axes, daggers and other weapons, and even ships or other subjects, appear likewise schematically represented; and in remote places, notably the Ligurian Alps, the art lived on to

345, 346, 348

203

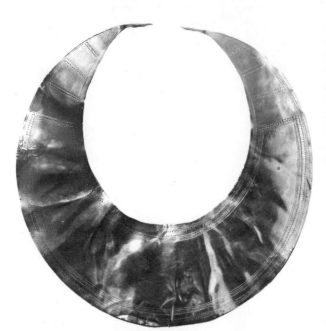

349. IRELAND. Irish gold lunula found at Llanlyffini, Caernarvonshire. *British Museum*.

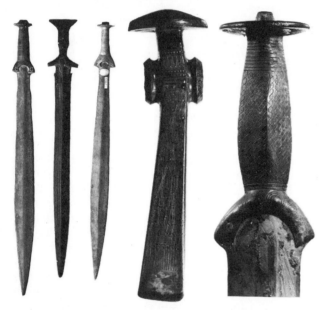

350. CENTRAL EUROPE. BRONZE AGE. Swords. The centre one is from Corcelettes, Neuchâtel, the others from Zsujta, Hungary. *British Museum*.

351. CENTRAL EUROPE. BRONZE AGE. Decorated bronze battle-axe. *Ashmolean Museum, Oxford*.

352. CENTRAL EUROPE. BRONZE AGE. Decorated bronze sword hilt. *Ashmolean Museum, Oxford*.

figure the plough-team and other scenes of full Bronze Age life. But in the geographic extension of that life, this is an art of the peripheries of Europe, not of its central focuses.

It is the same with the second of our prehistoric art-forms, the abstract designs which in the west almost annihilated figural representation, giving us the enigmatic pock-and-ring rock-markings spread from Spain to the British Isles, as well as the linear and hatched patterns of the Irish copper and bronze flat axes, and the channelled and scratched conventions still sometimes continuing on

33

pottery. In central Europe, such abstract designs had made the meanders and spirals of the Danubian Neolithic; now, in the east in Rumania, they continued among the Carpathians, and in the south, they made the concentric and other elaborate patterns of the Alpine and Slavonian pottery and its Italian counterparts. But in all the central regions the tradition of smooth pottery, already established on the plains, prevailed in the Bronze Age absolutely; exuberance of abstract design became peripheral, east and south of the Danube and its plains. In metal-work, the spiral might indeed persist in the elegant coiling of bronze wire ornaments, but the abstract designs applied to metal surfaces, when they were applied at all, were disciplined into exact but monotonous patterns of line and hatching. As for the third form of artistic expression, textiles and basketry no doubt continued their Neolithic conventions; ceramic ornament derived from renderings of them remains in the Bronze Age equally peripheral, as in parts of Spain and Portugal, and in the incised and cord-ornamented pottery of the British Isles. It is in the excellence of form given to the objects of man's material equipment—preserved to us above all in pottery and metal—that the craftsmanship typical of the Early Bronze Age asserted itself most effectively. Weapons, tools and pots had first of all to be well formed for their purpose; decoration was secondary to that, and the artist showed himself most in the technician.

We stand now fifteen or sixteen centuries before Christ, and before the Roman Empire of Augustus. In these next fifteen or sixteen centuries, the West was gradually transformed by civilisation; yet it contributed much that was its own to the transforming, and the individuality of its provinces remained.

THE BRONZE AND IRON AGES: CIVILISING INFLUENCES AND NATIVE TRADITION

The tendency to make all art schematic and conventional, to accept technical creativeness but to distrust organic, was more deeply rooted among the European barbarians. The more naturalistic art of earlier prehistory was now far away; and it was not from indigenous traditions that artistic consciousness was to be further aroused, but from the higher civilisation now extended from the Orient to the Aegean. The story of the Aegean bronze civilisation is told elsewhere; but the conjunction, beginning in the 16th century B.C., between the Minoan culture of Crete and the Greeks of the mainland centred on Mycenae has a significance which carries far into our barbarian regions.

The evolution of Europe

Central Europe continued its trading with the Near East: around the middle Danube now, a by-product of it is seen in a distribution of beads of probably Egyptian faience, and soon also of blue glass; conversely, through the northern connections now established, there began a southward traffic in the amber of Jutland, which appears both in central Europe and in the tombs of Mycenaean lords. Since the connections extended also westwards, it is found likewise in Britain: in the tumuli of Wessex, complex necklaces of amber, such as farther north were made of British jet, appear along with ornaments in gold brought from Ireland—where gold 'lunulae' resembling 349 the necklaces were also made and exported—and with signs of a distant contact with the Mycenaean-Minoan world, including again beads of Egyptian faience, which occur here and there in France and Spain too (El Argar culture). But, although this western contact lasted till the 14th century and even later, it was that with central and northern Europe which had the more significant results.

The bronze industry of Transylvania and Hungary began now to produce and export axes, rapiers and orna-351ments decorated with motifs strongly recalling Mycenaean, not only semi-naturalistic foliation and scrolls but also meanders and above all spirals, which, whatever their relation to those of the Balkan and Danubian Neolithic, show here a counterpart to their widespread adoption in the art of the Aegean and east Mediterranean lands—reflected too in Malta—and of Egypt. In central Europe the chronology of all this is that of the transition from the Early to the Middle Bronze Age, which in Hungary was a continuous development, marked also by an increasingly ornamental pottery, but which further west shows the receding of the Únětice type of culture before the growth of the tumulus cultures, originating in the hilly country districts as above explained, into new wealth and prominence. Their commencement shows the full effect, at least as far as Alsace, of the Oriental connections of the Early Bronze industry already noticed, but soon they were taking part in the amber trade with the south, for the same elaborate amber necklaces were worn by women buried in south German tumuli as have been found exported to Greece, associated in a Mycenaean tomb at Kakovatos with vases of the 15th century. Thereafter, the decorated Transylvanian-Hungarian bronzes inspired new schools of such work both in the north and in central Europe, where weapons passed from daggers to rapiers and then to true swords: among these, the series with massive hilt, of section at first oval and then octagonal, shows rich decoration in a style more geometric than the Hungarian, but still honouring the spiral, which also forms itself in the rolled terminals of many ornaments for personal display.

In the west, meanwhile, the transition from Early to Middle Bronze brought improvements in the practical rather than the ornamental arts. In religious symbolism, it brought no direct sequels to the great schematic 353 sculptures of the Irish passage-tombs—not even to the 354 renowned spirals of New Grange; and, while in Britain the chalk baetyli of Folkton show a related art, suggesting Mediterranean connections, throughout the north-west the ornamenting of surfaces remained monotonous in pottery, and in metal became rare, to be replaced in part only by a new goldsmithery of ear-rings and torques of twisted stem, based on far-off east Mediterranean prototypes. The ceremonial architecture of standing stones, of prehistoric origins in part connected with the megalithic tombs, in part independent but still obscure, in the British Isles never surpassed the unique lintelled structure of Stonehenge, completed towards the end of the Early Bronze Age (as the newly found dagger-carvings on its stones, one resembling a Mycenaean weapon, lead us to believe), nor, in France, the circles of Er-Lannic and the alignments of Carnac. Conservatism, again, even stagnation, appears in much of the Iberian Peninsula, where significance is confined to the culture of Al Argar, based on the Mediterranean coast, agricultural and metallurgist,

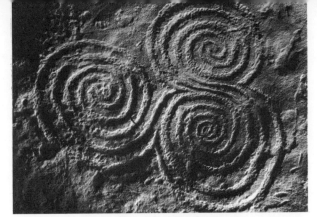

353. IRELAND. Spirals engraved on stone. Tomb at New Grange.

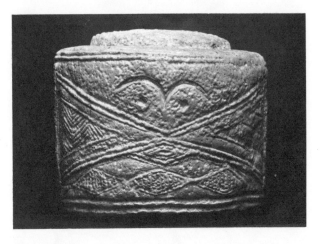

354. ENGLAND. Baetylus (sacred stone in which a god is presumed to live) of hard chalk. Folkton tumulus, Yorkshire. *British Museum.*

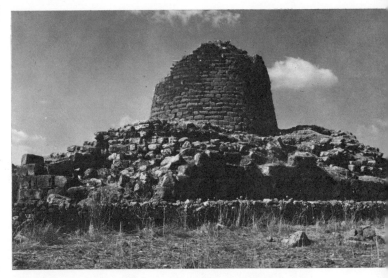

355. SARDINIA. A 'nuraghe' or stone tower.

and with some few foreign connections. That, with the Balearic Islands, shows them still prolonging the traditions of megalithic building and the collective tomb; nevertheless even there, and more clearly in copper-rich Sardinia, rare finds indicate contact with the world of the Aegean or beyond, as occasionally too on the mainland coasts, leading to the Atlantic and Britannic lands beyond, with their copper and precious tin. In the interior, indeed, the bronze culture of the Rhône kept to its continental character; in the Maritime Alps, the Ligurian rock-carvings remained distinctively indigenous. For a direct

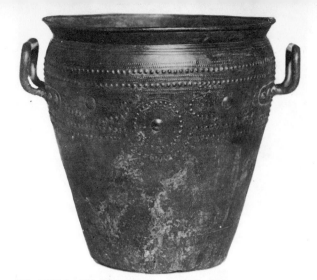

356. HUNGARY. Decorated bronze bucket from Hajduboszormeny. *Budapest Museum.*

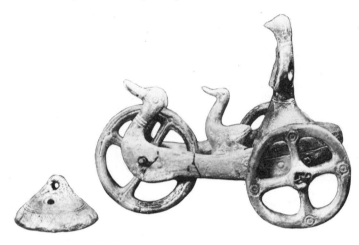

357. YUGOSLAVIA. Votive chariot from Duplaja. *Belgrade Museum.*

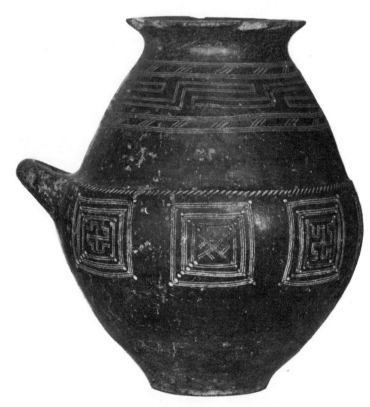

358. ITALY. VILLANOVAN CIVILISATION. Decorated sepulchral urn. *National Museum, Copenhagen.*

link with the Mycenaean world we must turn to Sicily: to the progressive Siculan bronze culture of the east of the island. There, in its large cemeteries of rock-cut chamber-tombs, with an excellent though monochrome native pottery, appear imported painted vases which, with the accompanying ornaments and bronze weapons, declare direct trade and even colonisation from the Mycenaean Greece of the 14th century. The Lipari Islands have also important evidences in this regard, as have both of the coasts of southern Italy.

Italy as a whole, however, remained little affected by civilising penetration. Its connections were always primarily with the Balkans across the Adriatic; and this is true both of the south, where the bronze culture continued into that of the fosse-graves of the Iron Age, and of the long stretch of the Apennines, where the evidence of the bronzes and the ornamental pottery shows a like persistence, with north Balkan connections by the coasts about Rimini and Ancona. In the north Italian plain, lastly, among a scatter of settlements reaching to the lake dwellings of the Alpine margin, and connecting with the more easterly Alpine lands and with Istria, the agricultural villages called 'terremare' have often been claimed for invaders from the Danube region, but in fact seem to make a consolidation of the same Italo-Balkan character as the Apennine culture, succeeding to their country's tradition of bronze metallurgy, and related with central Europe by commercial and cultural connections which might modify, but did not upset, an individuality already founded.

Beyond the north Balkan and east Alpine regions with which Italy was thus related, Hungary continued to develop its Middle Bronze culture, rich not only in bronzes but in a pottery various in its incised, fluted, and boss embellishments. Hungarian influence extended west and south-west and also north-west, to the northern neighbours of the Únětice culture in Silesia and the Lausitz. Then, not later than about the 14th century and inspired apparently from Anatolia and the Troad, the Hungarian populations began the adoption of a new and uniform funeral rite of cremation and urn-burial, which replaced their cemeteries by 'urnfields'. The whole Hungarian and north Balkan area thus came to show a range of assorted urnfield groups; and, with the diffusion of the rite northwestward, there emerges a distinctive urnfield culture in the Lausitz region beyond the Bohemian mountain border, which spread widely not only in east Germany and Poland, but southward into the Bohemian-Moravian country itself; it set in motion new westward currents too.

The Late Bronze Age

The last quarter of the 2nd millennium, indeed, opens with movements and turmoil throughout the territories peripheral to the ancient Near Eastern centres of civilisation. We see the fall of the Hittite empire and the attacks of the Peoples of the Sea on Syria and Egypt, the tumults round the Aegean which included the war of Troy, the appearance of the Phrygians and Thracians, and the crisis of the Mycenaean civilisation which led to its rapid decline and to the Dorian invasion of Greece from the north, and, farther off, the repercussions of this to the west, in Sicily where the culture of Pantalica shows the Mycenaean tradition barbarised, and in Sardinia, where the stone towers called 'nuraghi', and the long-lived 355 culture which they sheltered, represented in art by the bronze statuettes to be noted again below, may be due to Oriental arrivals of this time. Changes both in Italy and the Balkans, and in central Europe beyond, may denote repercussions also up the Adriatic, as well as movements within and around the Danube basin. Urnfields of the cremation rite thence appear among the terremare and elsewhere in north Italy, next in the Marche round Ancona, and then farther south, until all northern and west-central Italy had adopted them, in consequence of pressures working across and round the Adriatic from the Balkan and Alpine margins of the Danubian plain. These stages of fresh culture-formation in Italy will carry us into the Iron Age; but the time of initial impulsion, both on the Adriatic and within the continent, came in the 12th and 11th centuries, together with the Mycenaean collapse. This is the Late Bronze Age, and its transformation of all Europe went on far into the 1st millennium.

Our cultures of the Late Bronze Age can be viewed in three main groups: those of east-central Europe, of the Adriatic and Italian regions, and of the west. In east-356 central Europe, the urnfield cultures centred culturally upon Hungary, succeeding to the Middle Bronze Age developments there noticed previously, show us not only a thriving agricultural population, in villages of which the urnfields are the cemeteries, but also advances both in metallic and in plastic art. Already in the time of the turmoil in the Orient towards the end of the 2nd millennium, the bronze equipment of all this quarter had begun to show a distinctive character, in part reflecting Oriental influences, but in its totality strongly European. The new slashing swords, daggers and knives, with distinctive grip-tongue (languette), appear also in the Adriatic-Italian and the Balkan-Aegean regions. In vessels of sheet-bronze, also, central Europe as well as the Orient had its own industry. Copper mining in the eastern Alps, and probably in the other metalliferous mountains, now greatly increased its output; bronze became everywhere abundant. The barbarian world was reacting to the stimulus of Oriental and Mycenaean civilisation, by a progress of its own. North of the middle Danube, from the March to the Oder and from the Elbe to the Vistula, it was achieved by the folk of the Lausitz (Lusatian) culture; beyond again, by those of northern Europe, whose sources of metal, and of cultural influence, lay in central Europe. Plastic art, which contributed a great deal of pottery, variously incised, fluted and embossed in ornament, owes a particular debt to the Danubian-Balkan borderlands, peripheral to the Aegean world and retaining through the 348 Bronze Age their Neolithic tradition of figurines. The 357 Klicevac idol and that of Duplaja, in his wheeled chariot, drawn like Apollo by water-birds, stand at the source of new forms of imagery, accompanying the urnfield rite, 356 and superseding the spiraliform art of the Middle Bronze Age. The birds, above all, become a ubiquitous element of symbolic decoration, often combined—especially in the convention of a bird-headed boat—with a solar disc; other schematic forms, humans, animals, wheels, are common too, and the art spread as far as Italy.

From Bohemia and Moravia, the urnfield culture was established now in the Tyrol; at the Italian end of the Brenner, the old pile-dwelling people were formed into a further province, Peschiera. It is the country of the Veneti, separated by the Po from the region of the terre-

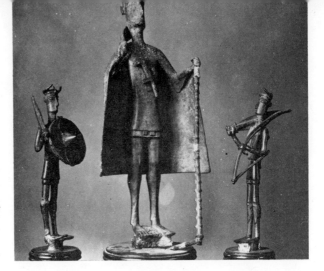

359. SARDINIA. Nuragic bronze figures of a chief and warriors. *Cagliari Museum.*

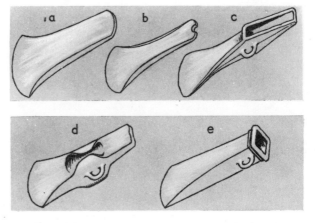

360. BRONZE AGE. Types of axes. a. Flat axe (Bronze I); b. Winged axe with straight sides (Bronze II); c. Axe with stop-ridge (Bronze III); d. Axe with medial wings (Bronze III); e. Axe with dowel (Bronze IV).

mare and of the Ancona urnfields. But these last had their source across the Adriatic in the north-west Balkans; from there, moreover, movement passed still further into Italy, southward through the Apennine peoples down the Tiber, to form them into the new cremating culture named the Villanovan, which was to spread over Tuscany 358 and the Lazio, and north also to Bologna. Meanwhile, the south Italian peoples of the fosse-graves, beside their distinctive neighbours in Sicily, and the still more distinctive Sardinians, continued undisturbed, to meet the recommencement of visits by mariners from the Orient and the Aegean, which led to the Greek colonisation.

In the western province, north of the Alps, urnfields appear first in Bavaria, and soon spread over south Germany from Swabia to the Main, and from the Middle Rhine to Switzerland, where the pile-dwellers of the lakes thus entered on their 'bel âge du bronze'. West and northwest of them, there had been groups of the Middle Bronze Age with tumuli, having, like their British and Irish counterparts, their own bronze industries and distinctive gold-work. But now began penetrations by urnfield peoples from the upper basin of the Rhine. Gradually over several centuries, these came to stretch from Burgundy and the Massif Central to the coast of the Languedoc, and to the basins of the Seine and Somme and of the Moselle, Meuse and lower Rhine. There is everywhere pottery related to that of central Europe more or less; the western bronze industries, however, were comparatively little affected by the central European

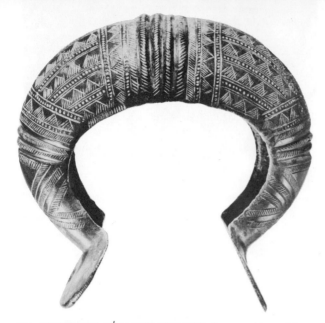

361. BRONZE IV. RÉALLON (FRANCE). Engraved bracelet. *Musée de St Germain.*

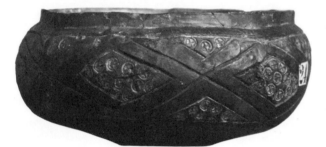

362. GERMANY. HALLSTATT PERIOD. Decorated pot from Gegenfeld. *British Museum.*

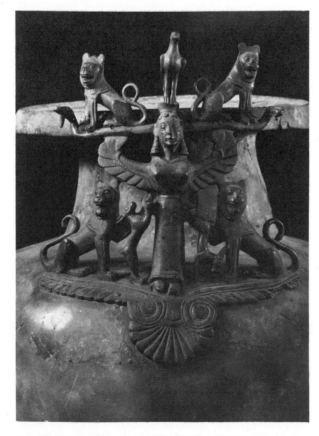

363. SWITZERLAND. HALLSTATT PERIOD. Detail of the Graechwyl hydria. *Berne Museum.*

artistic development, with its birds and other figurations, fibulae and elaborate ornaments. Instead, we find strictly geometric styles, best represented among the Swiss pile-dwellers, who were great exporters of bronze merchandise of all kinds—their distinctive axe with wings, contrasting with the socketed axe of the northern and British prov- 360 inces, borrowed independently out of eastern Europe.

From eastern Europe also by this time, the Danubian basin had been penetrated by nomad warriors, drivers and riders of horses, whose connections run from the invaders of the Orient in the late 2nd millennium to the Cimmerian conquerors of Anatolia in the 7th century. Their characteristic bronze horse-gear shows the spread of their influence throughout the east-central province of the urnfields, promoting the rise everywhere of a warlike aristocracy, strong in horses and chariotry. To the social and economic solidarity of the urnfield peoples there was thus added a new barbaric vigour. And at the same time, in the 8th and 7th centuries, the westward seafaring of the civilised peoples of the Levant and Aegean had begun the further transformation of Europe from the side of the Mediterranean. Its beginnings, often attributed to the Phoenicians, are yet obscure. But their evidences may perhaps extend beyond Sicily, and the domain of the Ausonian culture lately explored in the Lipari Islands, to Sardinia. If so, they can bring more light upon the Sardinian 'nuragic' culture: its remarkable bronze statuettes, of chieftains and warriors, women, animals and boats, show a rare artistic spontaneity, transcending the Oriental inspiration which has sometimes been credited to the Peoples of the Sea of the late 2nd millennium.

The Early Iron Age: Hallstatt

On the Italian mainland among the Villanovans, we can discern first in the 8th century the presence of a ruling class, based upon maritime Tuscany—the Etruscans. The tradition of Antiquity, and now philological and perhaps other evidences, would derive them by sea from Asia Minor; in any case, their rise to prosperity, shown soon by rich tombs of the 7th century, brought busy trade with the Levant, and above all with the Greeks, from whose influence they took so much. From the second half of the 8th century beside the Greek colonies of the Sicilian and south Italian coasts, we can see the natives with their traditions of village and tombs, pottery and metal-work, and the Etruscans with their own monumental sepulchres and their emerging cities. But the native arts were not simply subjugated by the foreign. While, for example, the native geometric art was indeed influenced by the Greek, the meanders of the Villanovans 358 are not mere copies; the rich variety of the native fibulae is essentially Italian; moreover, the influence of central Europe continued strong, and is seen especially in bronze vessels with the ornaments of birds and sun discs, which remind us of Italy's continental connections no less than do the 'hut-urns' of the Lazio cemeteries, with their counterparts. However, the civilised colonists introduced the use and working of iron. And, whether this passed inland into Europe first from Italy, or was already infiltrating from the Aegean region through the Balkans, it was certainly implanted in the metalliferous eastern Alps scarcely later than 700.

The 7th century was a time of great activity and movement. In the west, urnfield people had reached north-

208

east Spain, and related newcomers from the north-west were now reaching the south-west, where their coming was still remembered when the first Greek merchants in 638 discovered the kingdom of Tartessus on the Guadalquivir. Here, already, was the meeting of Mediterranean with Atlantic trade-routes reaching to the Loire and Brittany, Ireland and Cornwall, while from the Aude and the eastern Pyrenees the same coasts were being attained by land across the south-west of France, and the Irish bronze cauldrons now inspired by the Greek *dinos* remind us that Greeks were already crossing the mouths of the Rhône. And inland, throughout the great series of the urnfield cultures, there began rapidly to spread the dynamic repercussions of the new culture of the Early Iron Age now established in and around the eastern Alps—the culture of Hallstatt. Its arrival in Languedoc and north Spain was the rapid sequel of its conquest of the
363 Franche-Comté and Burgundy. It reached the Swiss
362 plateau and Alsace from south Germany, and then the Hunsrück-Eifel province, Belgium and North Brabant; besides its spread across central Germany, the provinces named from Bylany and Platenice took it across Bohemia to Silesia, and from it the use of iron was adopted by the last generations of the Lusatian culture, deep into Poland. And to the south-east were vigorous Illyrian groups, stretching from Slovenia far into Bosnia. The head of the Adriatic, meanwhile, was dominated by the Veneti now centred upon Este; they, with the Villanovans of Bologna, increasingly influenced their more barbaric Hallstatt neighbours.

In the easterly regions of Hallstatt Europe, from the Alpine and Bohemian provinces to the Illyrian and to the Middle Danube, much of the old symbolic art of the
301 urnfield cultures lived on. The Illyrian 'cult-waggon' of
357 Strettweg, with its menacing figures in the Duplaja tradition, is only the most striking example of east Hallstatt iconography. But west and north from the cemetery of Hallstatt itself (in Austria near Salzburg), figural art remained still uncommon, and the west Hallstatt provinces—for the most part the domain of Celts—are distinguished rather by pottery with excised and inlaid work, red ochre paint and graphite, and by bronzes often rich in geometric patterning. Everywhere, however, with its new mastery of iron, the Hallstatt culture throve. The tombs of chieftains in their four-wheeled chariots are particularly impressive in their material, and in the Late Hallstatt culture of the 6th and 5th centuries this strong internal development was quickened by stronger influence from the south.

In Italy, the Etruscans crossed the Apennines to a new city at Bologna; fine bronze-work with reliefs in their
364 Orientalising style (situlae), came with them, and the abundance of all metal-work, down to the innumerable
365 fibulae, was quickly reflected among the Hallstatt peoples. In the south of France, the Greek colonisation now had its centre at Marseille, whence it stretched down the Spanish coast, to be cut off only towards 500 by the rising power of Carthage, based on Gades and the Balearics. From the Ebro to the Riviera, and across the Alps from Italy and the Adriatic port of Spina, Hallstatt Europe lay open to southern merchant enterprise. While in its peripheries it was still extending itself—in Celtic immigrations into Spain, the south-west and north-west of France, Great Britain and the Low Countries—its

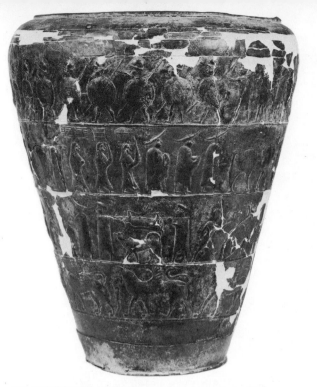

364. ETRUSCAN ART. Bronze situla decorated with figures. *Bologna Museum.*

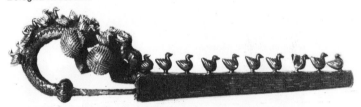

365. ETRUSCAN ART. The gold 'Corsini' fibula found at Marsiliana d'Albegna. *Archaeological Museum, Florence.*

central provinces were being progressively transformed. Soon, Hellenic vases were reaching the French and the Swabian Jura; and today the discoveries of the Heuneburg settlement are matched by those of the Mont-Lassois, and surpassed by the astonishing revelation of the treasure of Vix that the finest products of Greek artists of the early 367 5th century could make the journey to the Seine.

Eastern Europe, meanwhile, had been invaded once again by horse-nomads, more formidable this time than before. The Scyths, Iranian warriors from the Pontic steppe, came west to assail both the north European plain, where they brought ruin to the Lusatian culture from the Vistula to Brandenburg, and also Transylvania and central Hungary whence their further assaults, indicated on both sides of the middle Danube, brought them against the Celtic provinces of the Hallstatt culture. On the borders of east-central and west-central Europe, the potent influence of their decorative art, the Scythic animal style with its vivid schematisations, crossed that of classical Italo-Greek art coming northward across and round the Alps. The result, towards the end of the 5th century and the beginning of the 4th, was the creation, among the Celts of the west-central region, of the first style of the art that is named La Tène—compounded of eastern, southern and old Hallstatt elements, but essentially the original creation of the Celtic genius, now for the first time so displayed.

The Late Iron Age: La Tène art

This La Tène art is magnificently represented in the rich chieftains' graves on both sides of the middle Rhine,

209

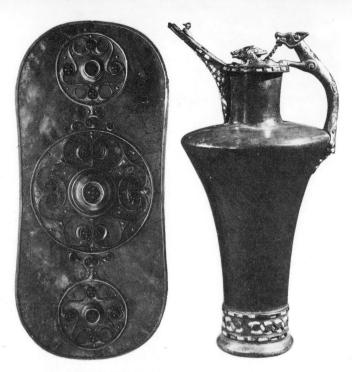

and the art and whole culture are soon found spread to the Marne and the Meuse, Burgundy and the Jura, central Germany and Bohemia; meanwhile southwards, the Celts descended upon north Italy, whence they assailed Etruria and Rome, and eastwards pressed down the Danube, reversing the Scythic incursions by overrunning both Pannonia and the Hungarian plain. From Italy, later in the 4th century, their art drew fresh elements to form its second style, that of Waldalgesheim, further advanced in curvilinear abstraction; in Hungary and Switzerland, in the middle of the 3rd century, arose the still more free arabesques of its third style, while a fourth style, of plastic relief, appears beside this. In the west, while the Aquitanian region and the Celtic tracts of Spain still kept Hallstattian traditions, the La Tène culture spread elsewhere in France, while its greatest centre remained on the Marne, focal point for the whole northern half of the country, between Brittany, the Hunsrück and Eifel, and Belgium. Into Great Britain, the gradual entry of La Tène elements were hastened by fresh invasions. From the 3rd century to the 1st, this insular extension created new art forms in which curvilinear abstraction

366. GREAT BRITAIN. Celtic buckler from Battersea, decorated with enamel, in British style, contemporary with Augustus. *British Museum*.

368. FRANCE (BASSE-YUTZ, MOSELLE). LA TÈNE I. Celtic bronze wine vessels ornamented with coral and enamel. *British Museum*.

367. FRANCE. Detail of the Vix krater. End of the 6th century B.C. Probably of Greek origin, the decoration recalls the figurative vases painted on the walls of Etruscan tombs. *Châtillon-sur-Seine Museum*.

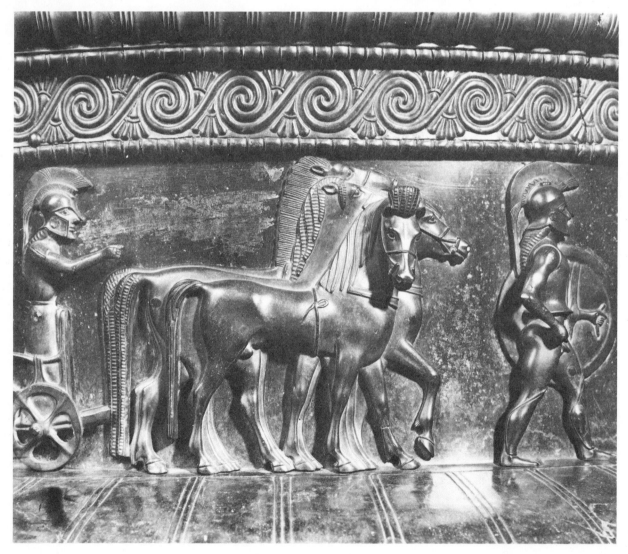

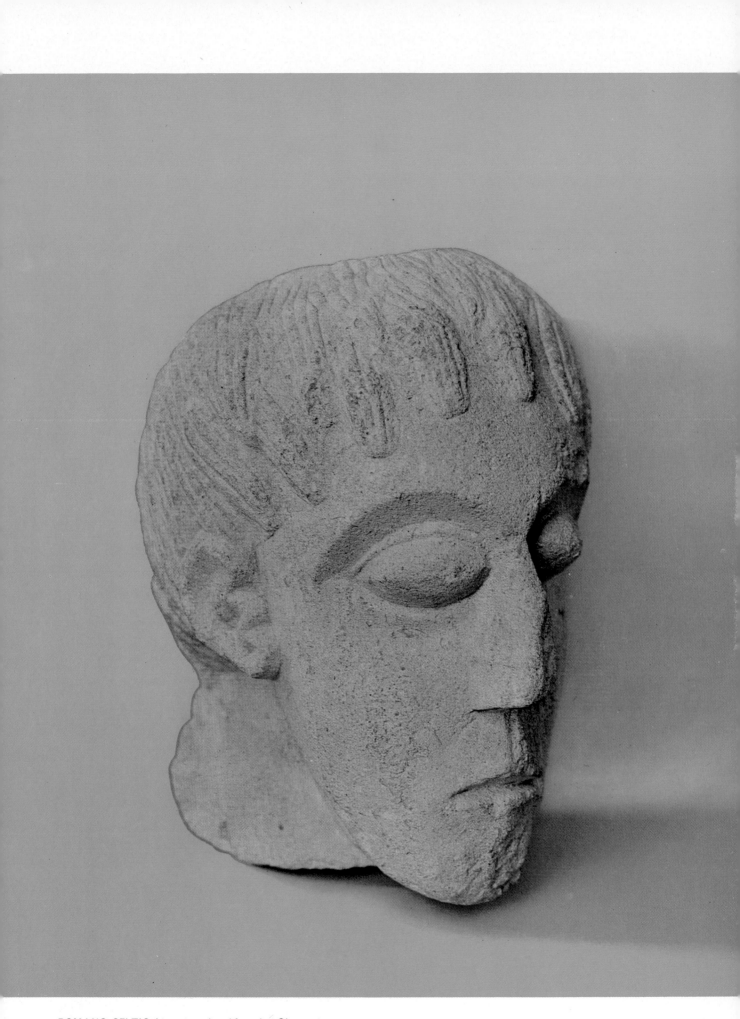

ROMANO-CELTIC. Limestone head found at Gloucester.
Mid 1st century A.D. Gloucester City Museums. *Museum
photograph.*

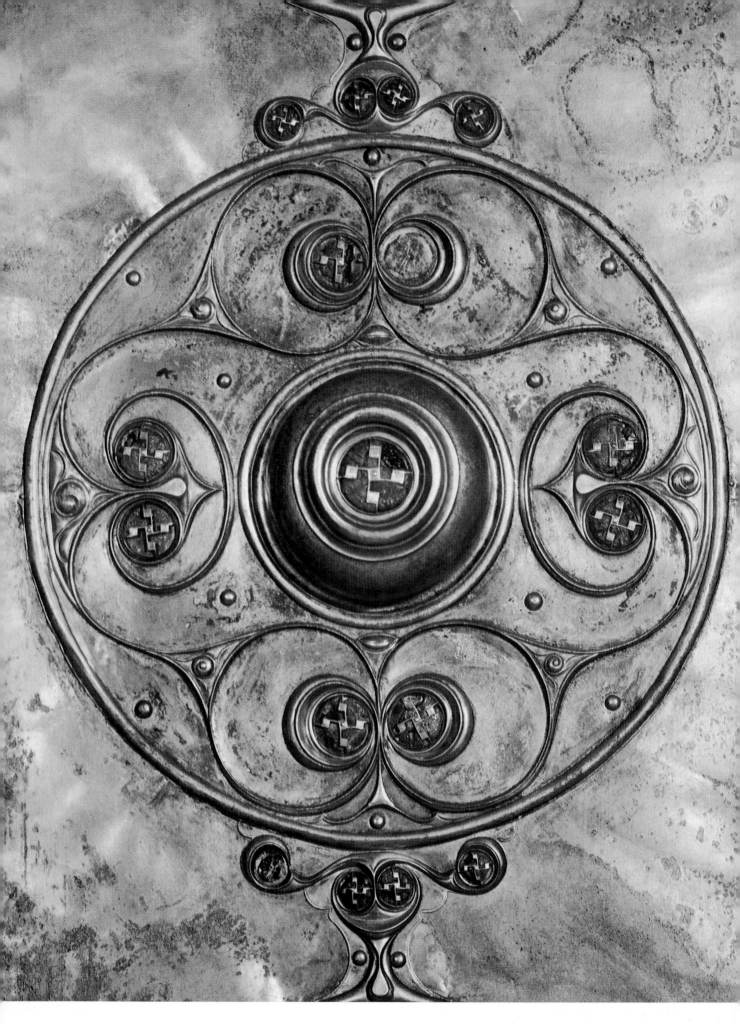

CELTIC. Shield found in the Thames at Battersea (detail).
25 B.C. – A.D. 50. British Museum. *Museum photograph*.

was carried even further, so that a piece such as the Wandsworth shield-boss is followed by the plaque of Llyn Cerrig, and finally by the series of engraved mirrors, leading to those of Desborough and Birdlip. Ireland, invaded in its turn, became a still further province, in part distinctive, in part related to the northern regions of Great Britain, where movement into Scotland and its islands was hastened finally by fresh entries into the south. For meanwhile the Celts of the continent had begun to feel the expanding power of Rome.

Long engaged with their peninsular neighbours and with the Celts of north Italy, the Romans' great struggle with Carthage brought them west into Spain. There, the native Iberians of the east and south had matured their own iron culture, rich in metal-work assured by their mineral wealth, and developing a painted pottery unique in its decorative and figured designs, and a sculpture, indebted both to Punic and Hellenistic influences, whose most famous monuments are the reliefs of Osuna and the Lady of Elche, both of an advanced date. In Celto-Ligurian Provence, the sculptures of Roquepertuse and Entremont show classical influence turned to a new barbaric grimness; and after its conquest by Rome in the late 2nd century the climax of continental La Tène art is perhaps seen best in the designs of the Celtic coinages, instituted from Hellenistic models but rising sometimes to masterpieces of indigenous style. (For the north of Europe and the cauldron of Gundestrup, see pp. 214 and 215). However, these last phases of independence were short. The wars of Julius Caesar and their sequels under Augustus set the impress of Roman provincial culture to work upon the continental Celts; and while Great Britain, among the Belgae who had conquered the south-east, and among their various neighbours, maintained its own forms of Celtic art and culture to the last, the Roman Empire finally left unconquered only the north, with Ireland, to keep a slender continuity alive between the world of La Tène and the world of the Middle Ages.

Thus our whole panorama of these centuries shows us artistic impulse aroused first in the regions of Europe closest to the civilised Near East and Aegean. While what the north took from this it did not retain, the process became effective in the west only after the spread of the urnfield cultures, and after the Mediterranean colonisations had extended the limits of civilisation, while the nomad invasions had driven fresh Eastern impulses in by land. Yet in the end one can declare, surveying their culture record up to these culminating achievements of the Iron Age, that the ancient Europeans did not simply remain passive recipients. Their reactions were spontaneous, sometimes truly creative, and their cultural originality always kept somewhere the capacity for survival and for resurgence.

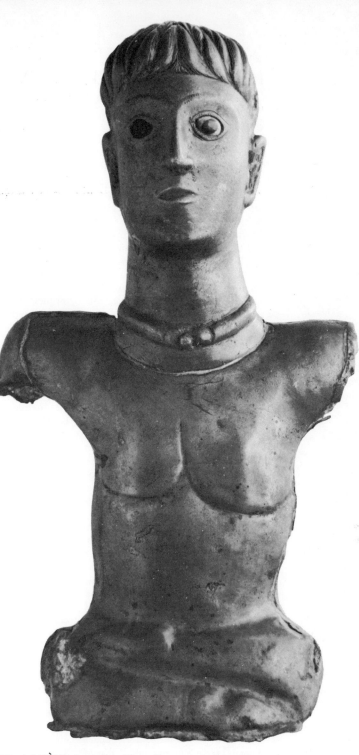

369. LA TÈNE. Seated god from Bouray-sur-Juine (France). Sheet-iron repoussé.

370. LA TÈNE. Coins. The repetition and stylistic transformation of a theme, originally Greek, enable us to follow the change from Mediterranean realism to Celtic abstraction. *British Museum*.

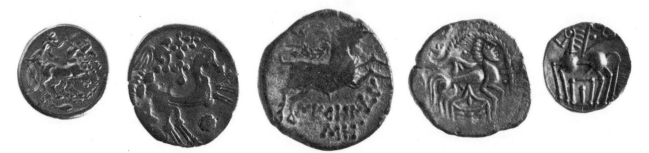

211

HISTORICAL SUMMARY: Metal in Europe

COPPER AND BRONZE

The spread of copper and especially of bronze in Europe remains obscure; details of the routes and methods of penetration and of the reciprocal influences are still unknown.

Origins. However it is quite certain that the knowledge of metal in Neolithic Europe came from the precocious civilisations of the Near East: Egypt, Mesopotamia, Syria (Phoenicia). Cyprus and Crete played a fundamental role as a maritime half-way house, more perhaps than the famous fortress of Hissarlik (Troy), prehistoric key to the straits and link between Asia Minor and the Balkans.

The paths by which metal was diffused were not new: they followed the routes existing from Neolithic times between the Near East and western Europe.

For lack of an accurate date, we can place the appearance of metal in Europe at about 2000 B.C., taking into consideration that it was a progressive penetration starting from the southeast, close to its Oriental sources.

Apparently copper and bronze were not spread by exactly the same routes. Copper seems to have been used very early in Hungary and Spain, countries which were remote but possessed abundant deposits of copper ore. Its spread in Europe was probably connected with the migrations of nomadic tribes with surprisingly homogeneous ways of life from their point of departure in the south of Spain to central Europe and the British Isles. Characterised by their bell-shaped goblets or beakers [**344**], pottery ornamented with engraved decoration or imprinted with linear geometrical motifs in spaced-out horizontal bands, their short copper daggers, their buttons with V-shaped perforations and their enigmatic rectangular 'brassards', they certainly contributed also to the spread of gold throughout western Europe.' The eastern limit of their migrations (according to their traces) lies in three different regions but ones where copper was already known beforehand: Hungary, northern Italy and Sicily. However, copper was unable to disrupt the Neolithic economy; in fact, flint remained superior to it, because of its resistance to wear.

The qualities of bronze as an alloy caused the first industrial revolution in Europe, where it seems to have been introduced by founders or prospectors who had left Asia for the West in search of tin, a comparatively rare precious metal, but essential for the manufacture of bronze. Indeed the Near East only had limited resources of tin-bearing ores, all the more rapidly exhausted as the technical methods of extraction and prospection were elementary. It is difficult to trace the itinerary taken by the Torque Bearers [**308**] between Syria and central Europe, the initiators of the first European bronze metallurgy, for they must have travelled by sea, but the striking resemblances between the torques, daggers and ornaments discovered in these two zones are too close to be the result of pure chance or coincidence.

The role of central Europe. The Torque Bearers sailed up the Adriatic and reached central Europe by crossing the passes of the eastern Alps (mainly the Brenner). Very soon a brilliant Early Bronze civilisation flourished there, especially in Bohemia, Bavaria, then central Germany, eastern Switzerland and Hungary. Starting from these first centres, bronze spread towards Italy, France, Spain, the British Isles, Scandinavia and Poland. Rivers served as natural routes for this general diffusion contemporary with the extraordinary growth of the trade in amber, taken from the shores of Jutland in Denmark. In the same way, the fashion for gold entailed a traffic with Ireland which seems to have been its first exporter. Thus the Bronze Age inaugurated long-distance trade in hitherto unknown materials. Central Germany grew in importance as a stepping-stone between the Nordic regions and the Mediterranean: the richness of its civilisation is explained both by this transit trade and by the metallic resources of Saxony, added to the traditions of a prosperous Neolithic culture. Gradually new metallurgical centres developed in Transylvania, Switzerland, Italy (Emilia, the Marche, Tuscany), Spain (El Argar), Brittany and Great Britain.

The Sardinian bronzes. If the most characteristic civilisation of ancient Sardinia took its name from the 'nuraghe', the massive stone tower-cum-fortress shaped like a truncated cone, the approximately four hundred bronze statuettes and figurines are the best interpreters of the aesthetic tendencies of nuragic art. Essentially religious, this art, whose finest flowering was probably between the 8th and 6th centuries, shows us numerous deities, primarily the mother goddess, sometimes carrying baskets of fruit or a pitcher held on her head with both hands, sometimes bearing on her knee the apparently inanimate corpse of a young god. The divinities often appear as armed warriors [**359**], sometimes wearing helmets or tiaras with horns, a strange reminder of their Mesopotamian ancestors. Among the sacred animals represented in the round in a primitive style which recalls the most ancient Anatolian art, we notice bulls, cows, rams, stags, goats, wild sheep, doves, cocks and even monkeys. As for the bronze funerary ships, whose prows terminated in the foreparts of a stag, a bull or an antelope, their fame spread as far as contemporary Etruria: these votive vessels are by no means among the least suggestive artistic evidence of this curious but most attractive proto-Sardinian plastic art.

The routes of penetration. The growing importance of amber was due to the very heavy demand for it in Mycenaean Greece and the islands, as well as by the new aristocracies resulting from the economic revolution. The finds of beads and pearls starting from the coast of Jutland signpost two almost parallel routes, following respectively the Weser and the Elbe with its affluent the Moldau to join up in the valley of the Adige and reach the Adriatic at the spot where later Venice was built. The last long lap was by sea to the Peloponnese and Crete.

Westwards, another route (Holland and the Channel) supplied the Early Bronze civilisations in Brittany and Wessex with amber. The increase in trade brought with it progress due to the contacts with the Creto-Mycenaean world.

Civilisations. Europe very soon freed itself from its preceptors and began to create original works of art in its own proved techniques: as from the Early Bronze Age and the tumulus cultures, a series of remarkable all-bronze daggers—both blades and handles—ornamented with a sober engraved decoration, conforms to the fundamental geometrism of bronze art which recurs in the pottery. They are found in Italy (Castione), the Rhône valley, Switzerland (La Bordonnette), Bohemia and Germany, and quite exceptionally elsewhere (Spain, Normandy). From Ireland came the famous gold lunulae and the bronze axes, also engraved with linear geometrical designs [**351**]. Lunulae reached western France and even Hanover in Germany, a fresh proof of the long-distance trade in precious objects.

Then in the Saxe-Thuringian region the production began of a new weapon, the halberd, often made wholly of bronze. The halberd had a certain

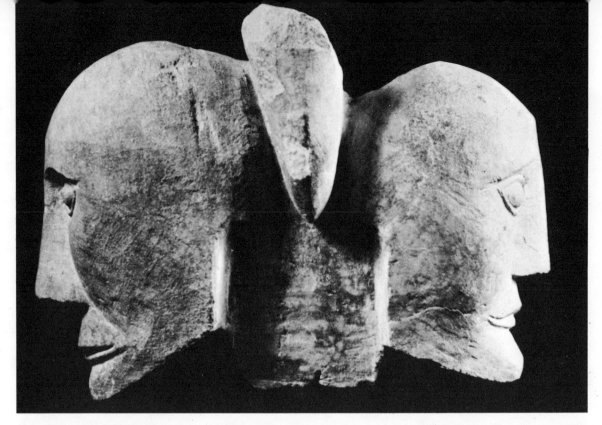

371. FRANCE. Two-headed Hermes from the portal of the sanctuary at Roquepertuse (Bouches-du-Rhône). 3rd–2nd centuries B.C. *Borély Museum, Marseille.*

amount of success in Ireland and Spain (El Argar), another case of very wide distribution. Thus the progress of European metallurgy rapidly made itself felt towards the middle of the 2nd millennium.

After the tumulus cultures there began a new period, that of the urnfield cultures, with a new funerary rite, cremation. Henceforth military equipment and weapons were of nearly every kind and scarcely varied any more. Swords [352], pins, bracelets and ornaments were of a real technical and sometimes artistic skill. In spite of the monotonously dominating use of spirals, they were often combined in such variety as to achieve a beautiful effect by the very austerity of the means. However, there was also a more lively motif in the stylised animals, especially swans, notably on the bronzes of north Germany and Scandinavia. The fibula, invented at the end of this period of the Bronze Age, did not become generalised until the Iron Age.

IRON

The Iron Age in Europe began in the 8th century and is traditionally divided into two periods: that of Hallstatt (8th–5th centuries), and that of La Tène (5th–1st centuries).

Civilisations. Two great civilisations flourished at the time: the Etruscans had their centre in central Italy, and the Celts in southern Germany, eastern France and Switzerland. Bronze was then in great favour for luxury objects: Etruria is extraordinarily rich in cauldrons, situlae [364], mirrors, statuettes and ornaments [365]. In spite of the hitherto unequalled skill of its bronze-founders, it brought the prototypes of Italian bronze plate from central Europe.

The Celts perhaps had their origin in the tumulus culture which grew up at the beginning of the 2nd millennium and had united, by the end of the Bronze Age, all central Europe from Belgium and eastern and central France to Austria and Czechoslovakia. The urnfield culture seems to have marked the first high point of the Celtic world. Towards the end of the 2nd millennium, advances by the Germanic peoples, possibly a reaction to movements from the Russian steppes, sent the Celts moving back westwards. At this time the beginning of the first period of Celtic art is marked by the development of the Hallstatt culture, extending from southern Germany to central France, before reaching the Garonne and Mediterranean. As Germanic pressure increased, Celts reached southern England and possibly Ireland.

In Hallstattian and Celtic Europe, to the north of the Po, geometrism continued to predominate with a tendency to an almost baroque luxuriance. The fresh motif gave new life to symmetrical ornamentation consisting of dots or bosses repoussé in the metal. Naturalism appeared only occasionally with bronze vases, owing nothing to Celtic models, imported from Greece or Italy as a result of growing trade, for example at Graechwyl [363] (Switzerland), Heuneburg (upper Danube) and Vix [367] (upper Seine). But the utilitarian objects, pottery, weapons, fibulae varied shapes, were characteristic.

During the 5th century, the La Tène civilisations mixed growing Mediterranean influences with local traditions. To chequer patterns, undulations, zigzags, circles and serrations were added palmettes or scrolls of Hellenic inspiration. The exuberance of an asymmetrical decoration left only a minute place for the representations of living beings and contrasts with the relative monotony of the Hallstatt period.

Pottery was varied, its shapes frequently imitated from metal; its decoration consisted mainly of geometrical or plant motifs painted in red or brown on a pale ground. The second period saw the appearance of two great innovations: the minting of Celtic coins, stylised and diverging from their Hellenistic models; and the appearance of figurative sculpture in the round: at first two-headed Hermeses, in the tradition of the menhir statues, especially in the sanctuaries of the south of France (Roquepertuse [371] and Entremont), then stone busts of warriors (Sainte-Anastasie and Grézan in the Gard) or statuettes (bronze god from Bouray, Seine-et-Oise) seen full-face in the archaic style.

However, realism predominated in Etruscan art, in both painting and sculpture, at least from the 6th century. Although she provided the connection with the Celtic world, Etruria herself was linked with the classical civilisations and led the way to the formation and expansion of Roman civilisation (see the end of Chapter 5).

Jacques-Claude Courtois

213

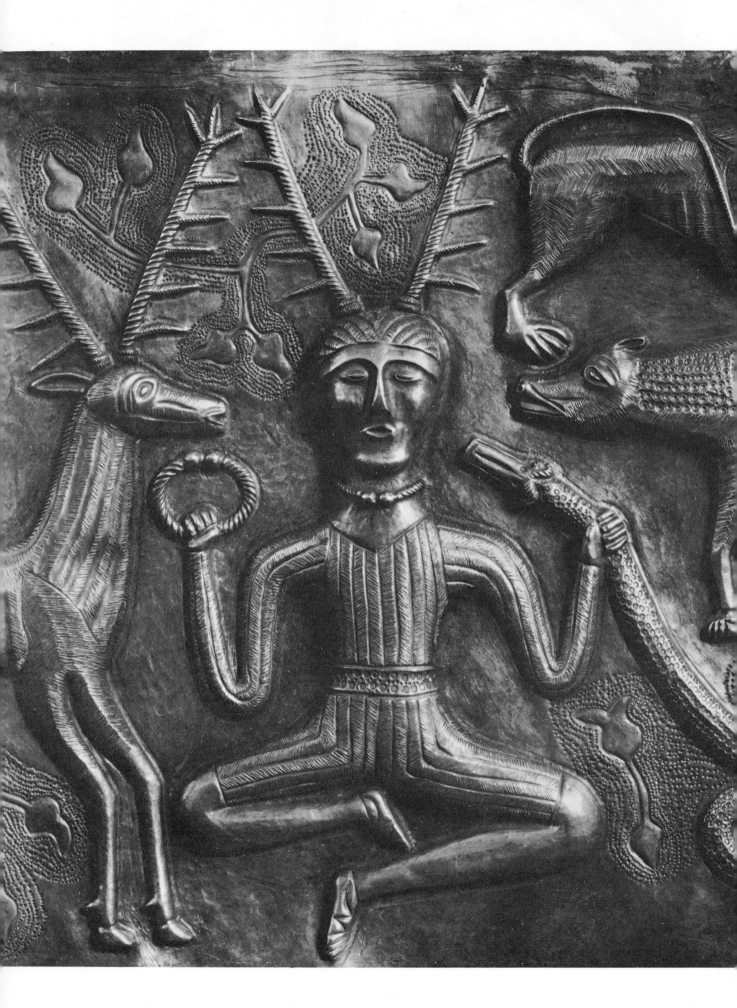

214

NORTHERN EUROPE

*A special place must be reserved in the far north of Europe
for Scandinavia which was to establish one of the most
typical and brilliant Bronze Age civilisations, normally
neglected in general histories. Far from being isolated,
as we might suppose, it received and transmitted the remotest
influences from the Mediterranean, central Europe,
Ireland and Russia. Lasting for centuries and renewed
by the Vikings, it continued until the Middle Ages.*

The settlement of Mesolithic men in Scandinavia between
10,000 and 8000 B.C. stimulated an art of hunters and
fishermen preoccupied with their vital relations with
animals, an art recalling the finest cave art. The amber
373, 374 sculptures and bone engravings of Danish Maglemosian
ended their northern expansion in a late survival in the
extreme north where hunting and fishing were long the
only source of subsistence. The rock carvings of elk,
whales, etc. are sometimes mixed with rough meanders
undoubtedly derived from the first plaiting work.

Towards 5000 the Ertebølle culture, on the Danish
coasts, marked the establishment, helped by the improve-
ment in the climate, of the fishermen living on shellfish.
The age of the *kökkenmödings* (kitchen middens) had seen
the appearance of pottery for cooking, impossible previously with leather receptacles; the shapes recall those of
Spain and even of the African coast as far as Egypt. Many
of the shapes of the Neolithic vases are admirable. A brief
look at the Skarpsalling vase is enough to show that it was
the product of a refined taste. The instruments used for
ornamentation were simple: a pointed bone, a shell and
a thin reed. But the results are astonishing. An imaginative
design with fine, sometimes undulating lines on many
Neolithic battle-axes is equally remarkable.

The north was to establish closer and closer relations
with the more developed southern civilisations: towards
3000, two thousand years later than in the Near East,
the first Neolithic settlers from the southern Baltic area
began deforestation and agriculture. Then, side by side
with former survivals, a new civilisation grew up in which
megaliths and communal tombs with a round chamber
and, later, corridors, initiated the worship of the dead;
the 'missionaries' of this cult came from western Europe
via the Atlantic. Scandinavia made a notable entry into
the interplay of European relations with the amber trade
of Jutland: it reached the British Isles and Iberia by sea
and central Europe by the river routes. It was inevitable
that Scandinavia would in return be affected by the metal
civilisation developed elsewhere. And in fact, knives of
chipped flint, then at its height, began to imitate the
shape of copper daggers and later of Bohemian bronze
ones; sometimes even small-scale amber objects resembled
the double-bladed Minoan axe, the *labrys*.

Towards 2000 immigrants arrived to compete with the
megalithic people and to bring a new simple method
of burial in the earth, as well as new pottery and the
use of the horse in agriculture. Nomads and warriors,

they belonged to the battle-axe civilisation propagated
with the appearance of the Indo-Europeans.

Nevertheless in the first half of the 2nd millennium,
bronze products began to be imported, sometimes in the
form of ingots; master smiths very soon arrived from
Europe or the British Isles, and the Scandinavian Early
Bronze Age had begun.

Meantime rock carvings had also developed in the **375, 378**
south, but differently from their precursors in the north:
the Palaeolithic hunter had given way to the Neolithic
farmer. As crop growers, they depended on the sun and
rain, and the rock carvings certainly had their place in
the ceremonies for invoking the type of weather desired.
There was a spread of various symbols and objects connected with fertility rituals.

The numerous ships, familiar to the Scandinavians
with their maritime trade, are certainly connected with
the same cult, especially when they appear engraved on
the razors of the Bronze Age tombs which were supposed **376**
to serve for the dead man's toilet. The ship, like the
aquatic bird, especially the swan, so common in the later
Western metal arts, refers to the dead man's last voyage
towards the setting sun.

With the introduction of cremation in imitation of the
urnfield cultures of central Europe and more remotely
from Asia Minor, the coffin, and later the wooden, bronze
or clay urn, was placed next to the funerary ship which
was represented by a construction of stones in Gotland.

The horse held a high place in religious and funerary
beliefs; in the Early Bronze Age a horse's head was sometimes engraved in the blade of a razor. The horse was
associated with the sun, and in the famous example from
Trundholm it is pulling the sun chariot. A graceful and **299**
subtle animal, it has a long slender neck, finely decorated,
and wide-open astonished eyes.

Bronze Age art also reflects the importance of natural
phenomena in this religion: there exists, for example, a
ritual metal drum fitted with solar wheels (unless accord- **381**
ing to a more recent theory they represent thunder, as
the processional axes of Bronze II and III may do, or
lightning).

To this repertoire was added the tradition of the Neolithic mother goddess whose role we have seen in the
Mediterranean: a statuette still shows her pressing her
breasts. At Fardal, in Denmark, a small bronze goddess **379**
has been discovered with gold eyes, clad in a skirt of
string (similar to the original piece discovered at Egtved
in the famous tomb). She carries an object in her right
hand, perhaps an implement for controlling the snake
which accompanies her, as it did in Crete, but which is
here given a horse's head. Among the bronze statuettes,
certain ones representing an acrobat and small helmeted
men armed with axes show us, as does the Kivik tomb,
that art was used for religious ends. There is no doubt
that they represent participants in curious ceremonies in
which there were processions, horse-races, etc. Thus this
art at the height of the Bronze Age is also of historical
interest.

The Bronze Age, in spite of the many discoveries which
have been made, is little known. We need still more dis-

372. DENMARK. GUNDESTRUP. Silver cauldron. Detail.
National Museum, Copenhagen.

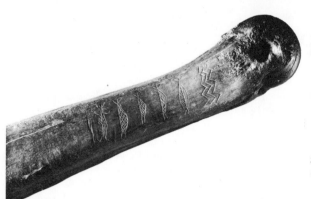

373. SCANDINAVIA. STONE AGE. Figures incised on the bone of an aurochs. *National Museum, Copenhagen.*

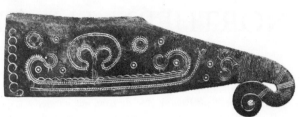

376. SCANDINAVIA. BRONZE AGE. Bronze razor ornamented with a boat design.

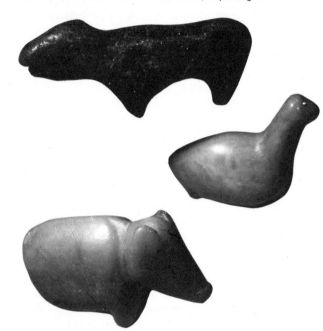

374. SCANDINAVIA. STONE AGE. Bird and bears carved from amber. *National Museum, Copenhagen.*

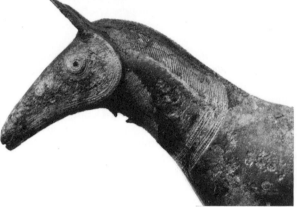

377. DENMARK. Head of the Trundholm horse. *National Museum, Copenhagen.*

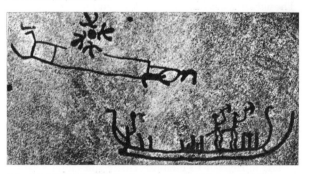

378. SCANDINAVIA. Rock engraving at Tanum, Sweden, showing warriors with axes and swords in a boat.

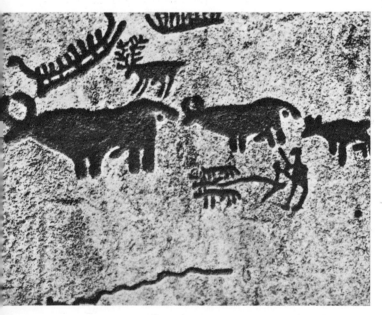

375. SCANDINAVIA. Detail of rock engraving at Aspeberget, Sweden. About 11th century B.C. Notice the boats, and the man ploughing.

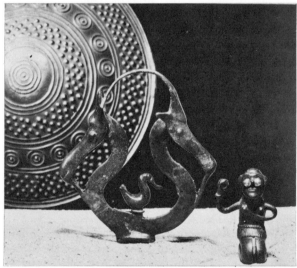

379. DENMARK. LATE BRONZE AGE. A woman with eyes made of gold and with one hand on her breast. Behind her is a two-headed animal with a bird on its back; in the background is part of a buckler. *National Museum, Copenhagen.*

216

coveries of remains of houses, for example, for a better understanding of life in this period. The bronze masterpieces, jewellery and weapons, whose metallurgical perfection especially in Bronze IV and V was only surpassed by Crete, have geometrical designs from Bronze II, the culminating period, onwards which are interesting in the history of decorative forms. In them we notice once again the impeccable spiral scrolls of Creto-Mycenaean origin: they had reached the Baltic from the Adriatic via the amber route. These exchanges were at their height in the middle of the 2nd millennium. Ornamentation was engraved and cast with remarkable precision. The large bronze plaque from Langstrup has arabesques and spirals running one behind the other, a wonderful work of accuracy and clarity. The same taste is shown in the swords and implements, which were certainly owned by the aristocratic class of the Scandinavian people. Bronze and gold were scarce and expensive, and there is no doubt that craftsmen were equally in great demand.

But as from Bronze III, the decorative repertoire changed, and in Bronze IV the predominating element was the star, which was not animated and dynamic like the spiral, but static. Perhaps relations with the Mediterranean by way of central Europe, and, via the Oder and the Vistula, with Russia, the Caucasus, Persia and Siberia, had something to do with this.

However, Bronze V, which was once again an outstanding period, saw a return to free, wavy, flowing lines.

But after Bronze VI, when exaggerated forms led to a decline in the decorative quality, a profound change took place in the middle of the 1st millennium. A cold rainy climate increased the number of marshes; agriculture deteriorated; the beginning of the Iron Age was marked by an artistic gap of several centuries. Iron had already been known at the end of the preceding age; a new development, perhaps following on the arrival of new immigrants, probably did not take place until the 2nd century B.C. It was at this time that Scandinavia came into the Celtic sphere of influence, and some Celtic masterpieces, for example the cauldrons from Gundestrup, Rynkeby and Brå, have been found in Denmark. There are also examples of indigenous art, showing curious links with Celtic art. The bronze horse's head found in the great peat bog in north Jutland clearly follows the tradition of the Trundholm horses; it has the same rather impersonal flexible curves, one of which connects the head with the neck. But the Iron Age head is distinguished by its large eyes and more lively expression, two features inspired by Celtic art as we can see from the Brå cauldron.

After this time, the Cimbrians and the Goths were to burst out of Scandinavia from the shores of the Baltic or from Jutland towards the south. They made their way to the Black Sea via the Vistula. Thus they prepared the way for the invasions of barbarians who, under pressure from the people of the eastern steppes, were to throw Europe into confusion and bring about the Middle Ages. The British Isles were directly assaulted by the Angles coming from Scandinavian soil in the 5th century A.D. where at the same moment the Vikings started to develop, until about 1000 A.D., a new civilisation. During this period the whirlwind spiral style, already so striking in bronze, was to flourish once again.

The text compiled with the cooperation of Ole Klindt-Jensen.

292, 293

380

372, 382

377

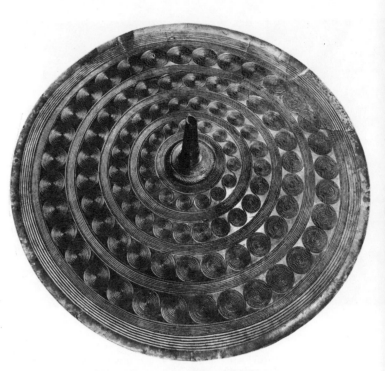

380. EARLY BRONZE AGE. LANGSTRUP (DENMARK). Bronze belt boss with spiral ornamentation.

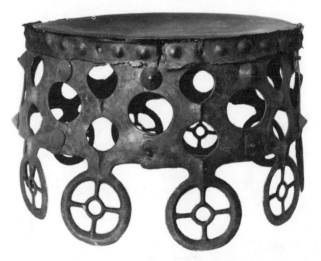

381. SCANDINAVIA. EARLY BRONZE AGE. Bronze ritual drum with solar wheels. Found in Scania (Sweden). *Stockholm Museum.*

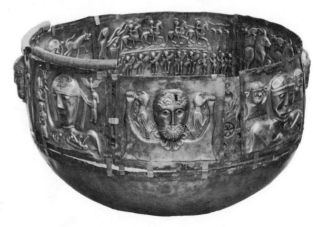

382. DENMARK. GUNDESTRUP. Silver cauldron. *National Museum, Copenhagen.*

217

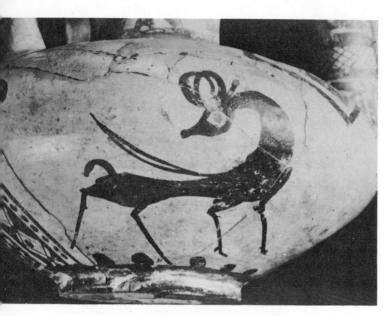

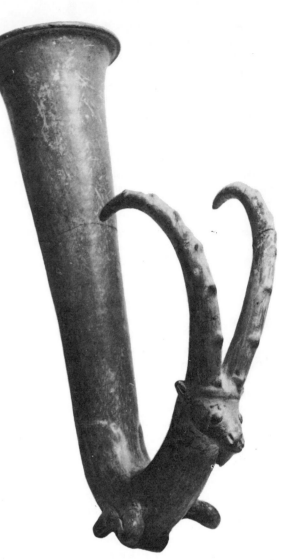

383. SIALK. Detail of a painted pottery vase. About 11th century B.C. *J. Coiffard Collection*.

384. LURISTAN. Handle of a bronze grinder surmounted with a head of a member of the goat family. End of the 2nd millennium B.C. *Musées Royaux d'Art et d'Histoire, Brussels*.

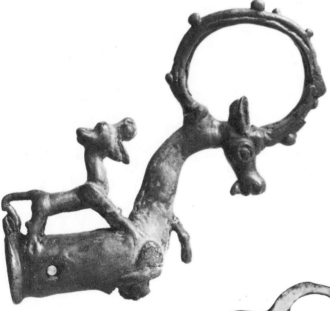

385. LURISTAN. Bronze bit decorated with ibexes. End of the 2nd millennium B.C. *J. Coiffard Collection*.

Throughout Eurasia with its varied arts we find, across the centuries, the same animal themes: horses and game.

386. LURISTAN. Terra-cotta rhyton decorated with an ibex head. *Teheran Museum*.

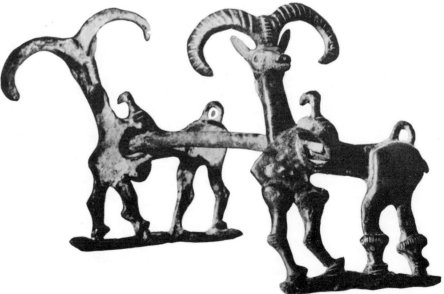

EURASIA AND THE EAST *Vadime Elisseeff*

At this time when civilisations were on the move not only because of the trade stimulated by the discovery of metal but also because of the migration of nomadic peoples, it is impossible to separate Europe from Asia. The horsemen of the steppes carried and amalgamated the contributions of the most varied cultures, from the regions close to the Caucasus where metal had its ancient roots to China, in one direction, where a superb bronze art was to arise, and to the Germanic and Danubian countries in the other. This art was to penetrate even further into the West with the invasions just before the Middle Ages. The exceptional erudition of Vadime Elisseeff has produced an authoritative picture of the discoveries being made about this period of tumult and confusion.

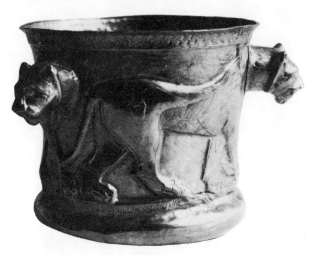

387. KALAR-DASHT (MAZANDERAN). Gold goblet decorated with lions. 11th century B.C. *Teheran Museum.*

LURISTAN AND IRAN

At the end of the Neolithic, after the flowering of the great Mesopotamian civilisations and the tremendous strides made by the farmers in all the cultures with painted pottery from Tripolye to Susa and from Turkestan to China, the Bronze Age was to reverse the roles and give the mountain-dwellers pride of place. The spread of pottery techniques had now opened the routes to potters and bridged the gaps between the big centres of the plains. From now on the mountain-dwellers were no longer mere intermediaries, but sought-after producers of metal. Smelters and bronze-founders, jealous of their knowledge, covered Eurasia and drew the bonds between their various clients closer. Metallurgy was to create two worlds: a new, cruder, and more realistic element was added to the old artistic formulas; to the themes of monsters and fantastic plants was added the theme of ordinary domestic animals and the forest and steppe landscapes of peoples devoted to stock-farming.

Bronze flowed down from the Anatolian massifs and the Iranian plateaux towards the border plains and transformed the life of the farmers of southern Russia to give birth there to the catacomb culture (20th–14th centuries) and the timber-frame culture (16th–12th centuries) in the northern Caucasus. This route through eastern Anatolia was to rejoin, on the banks of the Dnieper and the Danube, the western route bringing Aegean products from the south and thence to carry the new formulas into Europe.

In the Orient, bronze was to give birth, south of the Aral Sea, to the Tazabagiab culture (14th–10th centuries); in Kazakhstan it was to reunite the pastoral tribes in the Andronovo culture (16th–10th centuries). Still further east, at Lake Baikal, the Glaskovo culture (17th–13th centuries) was to transmit the secret of bronze-casting to the China of Shang Dynasty (17th–11th centuries).

In ten centuries bronze from the ancient East conquered the Eurasian economy. It took the same length of time for the formulas peculiar to the art of bronze, supported by old Irano-Anatolian traditions, to cross the same continent in the opposite direction and to found the barbarian art of the Middle Ages, thanks to the cultures of Karasuk (13th–8th centuries) near Minusinsk, and the Scythians (7th–2nd centuries).

If the art of painted pottery is one of geometrical decoration, the art of bronze is that of animal decoration. Animal art is thus a realistic Bronze Age art progressively stylised by the peoples inhabiting the steppe zone, from the Hungarian plain to the Yellow River. For some ten years now a mass of work comparable with that done on Western cultures has enabled us to catalogue, enumerate and characterise the cultures of central Asia and Siberia. These purely archaeological studies have established that the bronze cultures did not develop by following a fixed route, but they were diffused by a series of bilateral exchanges in which all the carriers of Early Bronze Age cultures participated. The works of art are few in number and are sometimes neglected by reports of excavations devoted to stratigraphical or typological problems. Social and economic history is therefore built on solid foundations, but the history of art has not yet been revised in consequence. So we must make our comparisons with great care. The interplay of differences in style is only perceptible over vast periods of time. But even so, this study can provide us with interesting observations.

The origin of animal art

The earliest evidence of animal art is in the arts of Sumer, Susa and Syria. According to M. I. Rostovtzeff, the last-named region shows a style directed towards realism rather like pre-dynastic Egypt, while the other two centres preferred stylisation. There is no doubt that Hittite art derives from the confluence of two streams flowing from these artistic centres. Other currents covered the whole of Eurasia; at the height of Elamite art, for example, the influence of Susa spread far to the west and carried the rhyton in particular as far as Crete. However, the origin 286 of this form should not be attributed to the Sumerians or the Babylonians but to a few northern tribes of the Iranian plateaux; this was undoubtedly one of the first of the northern influences which were to appear more and more and which the Assyrians emphasised until Achaemenian art made it pre-eminently Persian. This northern influence seems to correspond to the invasion by the Kassites from the Caspian regions (18th–12th centuries) who

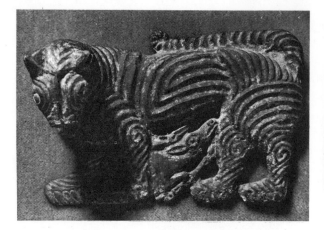

388. CHINA. SHENSI. Bronze applied ornament. 8th–3rd centuries B.C. *Cernuschi Museum, Paris.*

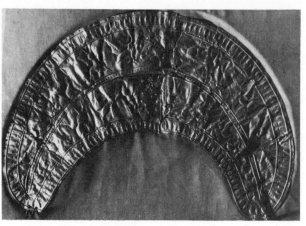

389. IRAN. Sakkez treasure. A gold pectoral. *Teheran Museum.*

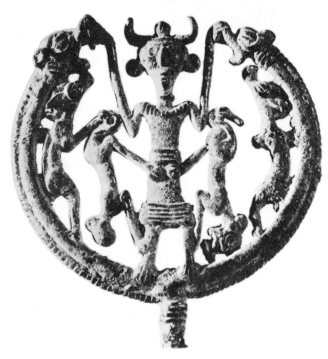

390. LURISTAN. Head of a bronze votive pin. End of 2nd millennium B.C. *N. Heeramaneck Collection.*

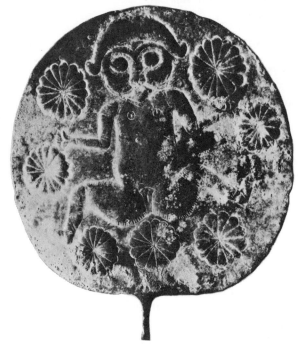

391. LURISTAN. Head of a bronze votive pin. End of 2nd millennium B.C. *Y. and A. Godard Collection.*

conquered Babylonia, introducing the use of the horse, adopting the hero Gilgamesh and skilfully exploiting the local artistic formulas. According to some, a purely animal art of northern inspiration with traces of Assyrian influence must have succeeded to the Mesopotamian art of the Kassites from the 9th to 6th centuries. To the heavy forms of Babylonian art, the art of the Kassites brought a new sensitivity which it owed to the traditions of some of the Caspian peoples. This Kassite art, known as the art of Luristan, has been divided by C. F. A. Schaeffer into three stages, Early, Middle and Late Bronze, corresponding to stratigraphic sequences. Our concern is with Late Bronze which lasted from 1500 or 1200 to 1000 or 800 and which was continued by the Iron Age. The first characteristic piece, still attributed to the end of Middle Bronze, is the handle of a grinder surmounted with the 384 head of a member of the goat family. We shall often see this motif in China, Mongolia and Siberia. Its slenderness is traditional in the art of the Iranian plateau in the form

in which we have it on the Sialk pottery (about 11th 385 century). We see it, undoubtedly nearer its country of origin, ornamenting an 11th-century vase from Kalar-dasht. There too, on the edge of the Hittite country, various cultures met, and Hittite influence is clearly visible in the gold goblet decorated with three lions whose 387 bodies are engraved and repoussé on the surface and whose heads protrude from the side. The same formula recurs much later in the Shensi bronzes. 388

The ibex as a decorative theme

The motif of an ibex with crescent-shaped horns fre- 383 quently decorates the objects found in Luristan. The 386 horns are either of circular cross-section or flat; the heads preserve a normal position and seem, from their style, to adapt traditional Iranian forms. There are two other types. The first is a head with horns in spirals which seems to be a replica of the pins from Koban (beginning of the 1st millennium); the second is the motif of an ibex 392a

220

with elongated head, the horns curving back to join the body again and the ear projecting into the space thus delimited. The last motif seems to have Far Eastern origins: we find it at An-yang at the end of the 2nd millennium, and in Siberia at the beginning of the 1st.

About the year 1000 the western motif of an ibex with horns in a spiral and the eastern one of the ibex with an elongated head met in Luristan. Having left their original regions at the same period they arrived to enrich the undoubtedly earlier formula peculiar to the Iranians which we have already seen. The magnificent Luristan pins are very closely akin to those from Koban. But their decoration often consists of a religious scene taken from local or Babylonian tradition, while those from Koban use only stylised motifs. Pins of a second type are surmounted with a perforated plaque on which we find the habitual themes of the Tree of Life and the horse-tamer. The workmanship is very close to the belt-plates from the Caucasian regions of Colchis in the first half of this 1st millennium.

The weapons from Koban are often of the same shape as those of the region of the Talyche. The marked indentation on the lower edge of the blade is often also found on the Luristan axes. To judge from its animal representations and especially from its weapons, the Talyche seems to have been the centre of diffusion for the Kobanian style. It is therefore probable that the same region formed a source of inspiration and importation for Luristan. The pieces from the Talyche have been dated from the second quarter of the 2nd millennium. Their influence on the north was primarily felt three centuries later and doubtless the same holds good for the south. Whatever the chronologies proposed for the cultures of the border countries, it is certain that Luristan's affinities in the north are closer to the cultures from the beginning of the 1st millennium than to those which preceded them. The Kubanian culture of the beginning of the 2nd millennium shows marks of Babylonian influence but no trace of Iranian influence proper. The fact that archaeological factors enable us to date the earliest shapes of weapons to the end of the 2nd millennium does not prejudice the spread of works from Luristan. Their artistic flowering is to be placed about 1000 and their development continued during the first 300 years of the 1st millennium. These three centuries definitely produced a finished art which must have radiated out and modified the plastic formulas of neighbouring centres. It is quite conceivable that one of the sources of Scythian art was in these regions, so fertile in animal decoration. The recent discovery of the treasure of Ziwiye contributes a new factor to the problem of the origins of Scythian art. A gold pectoral and various pieces of goldsmiths' work are ornamented with Assyrian motifs which it has been possible to date from the reign of Assurnasirpal II (883–859). To these Assyrian elements were added Assyro-Scythian ones, purely local elements from the Manai region, such as the scenes on the gold belt, and lastly purely Scythian elements, such as the motifs of members of the stag tribe in the typical crouching position. We have therefore a purely Scythian motif a century before the appearance of the Scythians. In this case the Manai area probably originated an art which the Scythians subsequently borrowed. In the same region, to the south of Lake Urmia, rhytons have been discovered which

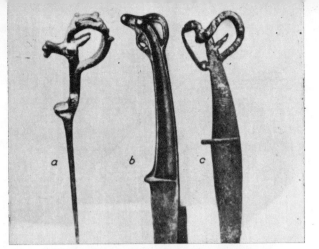

392. a. LURISTAN. Bronze awl. End of 2nd millennium B.C. *J. Coiffard Collection*. b. KARASUK REGION (SIBERIA). Bronze knife. End of 2nd millennium B.C. *Cernuschi Museum, Paris*. c. AN-YANG (CHINA). Bronze knife. 14th–11th centuries B.C. *Lord Cunliffe Collection*.

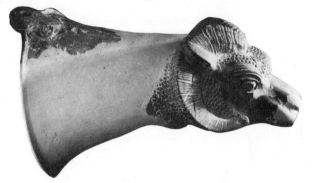

393. IRAN. ZIWIYE. Terra-cotta rhyton. Beginning of 1st millennium B.C. *Teheran Museum*.

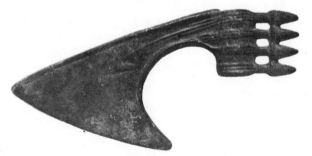

394. LURISTAN. Bronze axe-head. 2nd millennium B.C. *Teheran Museum*.

foreshadow Median art and explain how the borrowing operated. Roman Ghirshman proposes a more recent date, the 7th century, for these objects.

From then onwards, it was probably the Scythians carrying their own art who effectively influenced the countries they passed through and gave rise to a Scytho-Manaian art. The fact that the origin of these typical motifs is attributed to the Scythian people entitles us to seek the sources of this art in some other more ancient culture of the East. The Iranian plateaux, domain of the northern stock-farmers, were steeped in the traditions of the great agricultural civilisations of Eurasia. Nevertheless they still preserved a love for animals which the new-comers from the fertile land were not able to suppress.

CHINA FROM SHANG TO HAN TIMES

The origin of the founders of the Shang-Yin Dynasty still remains a mystery. At the end of the 2nd millennium,

221

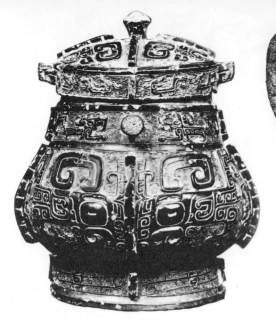

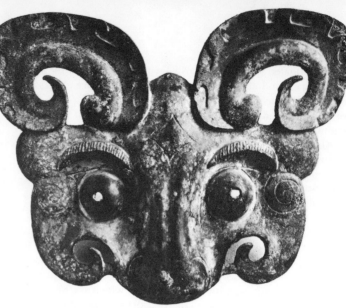

395. SHANG BRONZE. Ritual wine vessel (yu). 14–11th centuries B.C. *C. R. Holmes Collection.*

396. SHANG BRONZE. Applied ornament. 14th–11th centuries B.C. *Dugald-Malcolm Collection.*

their culture was superimposed on that of the painted pottery. The bearers of this pottery had scarcely ever used animal figures on their vases as had the farmers of Sialk or Susa. Animals suddenly appeared in Chinese ornamentation, but the first examples we have, dating from the three great centuries which saw the zenith of the luxurious court of An-yang, already show a wide range of possible treatments from the most realistic to the most stylised.

The only link so far found between Neolithic pottery and the archaic bronzes is the black pottery with fine incisions, and even more the white pottery. In the decoration of the latter the meander plays a vital role: it unfolds in a broad zigzag round the vase, forming a succession of waves over the whole body of the receptacle. The archaic bronzes were to use the same decoration, henceforth with the head of a beast projecting from it, undoubtedly the mask of the ancient witch-doctors, the *t'ao-t'ieh*. Its design is dominated by the eyes. They 395 appear in relief on the side of the vase surmounted by two 396 very shaggy eyebrows. Two horns, often in the shape of dragons, complete the top of the mask. A ridge representing the nose separates the two eyes and terminates in broad nostrils; on either side two coils represent the curled upper lip, often with a pair of protruding fangs. The absence of the lower jaw leaves the monster's mouth gaping. These masks with their well balanced elements produce a terrifying impression which is further enhanced by the staring eyes, the wrinkles accentuating the mouth and widely flaring nostrils. They often cover the whole surface of the vase and give it the high relief which characterised the works of the Yin style from the 14th to the 11th centuries.

Consequently we have at this time a series of decorative motifs, such as the meanders and spirals, and a series of stylised ornaments, such as that of the *t'ao-t'ieh*. Today the interplay and successive preponderance of these series of elements are the subject of more detailed studies.

Realism versus stylisation

In the art of the archaic bronzes, we can distinguish a Yin I phase in which the realistic ornamental motif of 395 the mask predominates over the whole body of the vase, and a Yin II phase, possibly later, in which the decorative

motifs have absorbed the *t'ao-t'ieh* mask to the point of 404 making it completely abstract. The 'Yin-Chou' period continued the preceding Yin style except in a few details, and carried it through to the subsequent Chou Dynasty, whence its name. The transition from realism to geometrisation suggested by Professor B. Karlgren is disputed by Professor M. Loehr. This 'development in reverse' has the single advantage of making a better link between the end of the Shang style and the following Middle Chou style (10th–7th centures) in which the forms are clearly defined.

The great problem thus posed by the traditional classification is the sudden appearance of a finished naturalistic plastic art and the development of a progressive stylisation which suddenly gave way to a new realistic art. 398–40 Reversing this evolution, we may suppose that the first bronze-founders tried, as the decorators of the painted pottery had done, to give a meaning to the geometrical representations by bringing out beasts which were only hinted at.

These figures gradually became more marked by differences in the surfaces and decorative motifs. They then appeared in high relief, covered with distinct ornaments, 392 before actually assuming the shape of a vase or breaking away from it altogether to take on an individual value. So we see small deer-like animals dressing the hair of the guardian goddess of the clan or terminating the handles of daggers. Thus, as early as the 12th century, we have a motif long considered as characteristic of the art of the steppes. The animal has completely lost its former graphic quality; the shapes in relief of the *t'ao-t'ieh* mask have been treated more coherently, and the face of the monster 396 has also become detached from the whole. It has taken on a character of its own and becomes at the beginning of the Chou period (11th century) the ornamental mask, whose realism exceeded even contemporary work in the round.

The Chinese artists of this period did not devote themselves solely to bronzes. They also knew how to do perfect work in wood, stone and jade. In each of these materials we come across the same motifs as those used by the bronze-founders. The most beautiful achievements are undoubtedly the jade objects. Much appreciated in China as a precious material, jade in those remote times was considered as the symbol of purity, virtue and royal

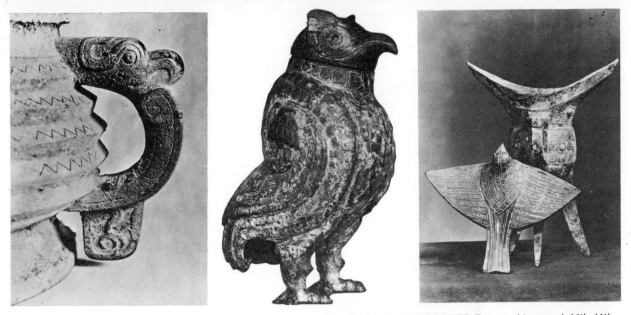

397. MIDDLE CHOU. Detail of bronze ritual vessel (*kuei*). 8th–6th centuries B.C.

398. *Centre.* SHANG BRONZE. Zoomorphic vessel. 14th–11th centuries B.C. *Victoria and Albert Museum, London.*

399. SHANG BRONZE. Bronze ritual vessels. 14th–11th centuries B.C. *Chen Collection, Hongkong.*

power. It occurred in Neolithic times, but it is primarily in An-yang from the 14th century that we see the growth of the circular symbols of heaven (*pi*), the square tubes symbolising the earth (*ts'ung*) and various ornaments. The style is parallel with that of the bronzes; like it, it was markedly realistic and had a vast repertoire of engraved or incised geometrical motifs.

At the beginning of the 1st millennium the Shang and Chou artists were already able to develop an animal art which was peculiar to them. The style of Middle Chou (10th–7th centuries) is generally considered to have lost the brilliant character of its predecessors. Admittedly, political upheavals modified the religious requirements and taste of former times, but we find in it the same arrangements of motifs beneath a greater simplicity; and even if realism seems to give way before a resurgence of geometrisation, it is undoubtedly only a new balance between these tendencies, for the treatment is totally different from the first efforts of the preceding period. The work is less affected, more open; the thick ribbons which figure in the decoration still preserve the finger marks of the craftsman who worked on the wax.

In the following period of the Warring States (5th–3rd centuries) Chinese art was undoubtedly influenced by the art of the steppes. A clearer separation between plastic decoration and ornamentation appeared. The ornaments consist of ribbons, either flat or in bas-relief, and finely engraved spirals and triangles, the same motifs which once decorated the bottoms of vases. But their curves and knots form easily recognisable *t'ao-t'ieh* patterns, giving the vase a vibrant seething quality which is enhanced by extremely vivid animals on the handles and covers. This mixture of ornamentation and naturalism characterises the style of the Warring States, in which one can already foresee the end of a technique menaced by affectation and decadence in spite of the beauty of the ornamentation and perfection of the plastic art.

The humanisation of animal art

Until the 3rd century everything seems to contribute to the substitution of an increasingly animal art for the old geometrical decoration. Around the beginning of the Christian era, with the Han arts, this trend was continued by a humanisation of the animal decoration. Under the

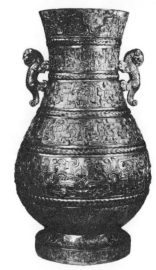

400. WARRING STATES. SHENSI. Bronze ritual vessel (*hu*). 5th–2nd centuries B.C. *Private Collection.*

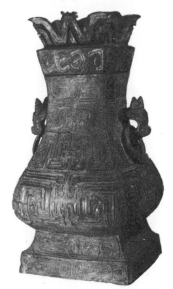

401. MIDDLE CHOU. Bronze ritual vessel (*hu*). 8th–6th centuries B.C. *Musée Guimet, Paris.*

401

400

405

223

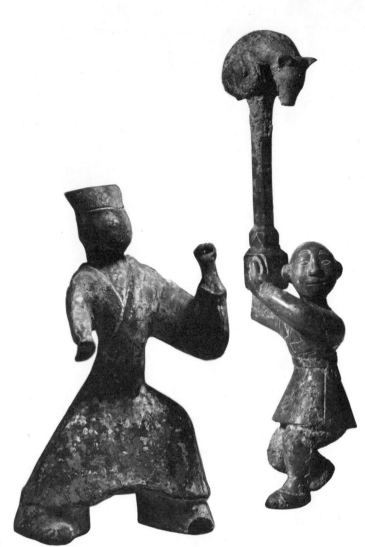

earlier Hans (3rd century B.C.–3rd century A.D.) we still sense the persistence of some geometrical elements. The dragons, which before stood out in flat ribbons cut out against a background of finely engraved spirals and lozenges, then tended to become entangled. Under the later Hans this entanglement became fragmentary, and we see the beginning of scenes which emerge from a background of landscape. The vases were decorated with fine nielli and rich inlays. Pottery in the Late Bronze Age is mainly known for funerary statuettes which show a genuine discovery of human plastic art. At the end of the Chou, human figures appear increasingly often and some 403 of them already reveal a remarkable stylisation. But we must look to the Han for the moving series of dancers and 402 witch-doctors whose silhouettes are so accurately caught in their movement, and for the figures of various animals belonging to the dead man, pigs, ducks, horses and dogs, which join animal art to the art of the engraved portrait. A whole living world animates the walls of the funerary caves and chambers on which are engraved, imprinted or painted the moral or mythological scenes. All the elements of Chinese art are contained in Han art, the great dynasty which founded an academy, inaugurated examinations for public office and restored the Confucian classics to a place of honour.

The southern and eastern expansion

Annam, Chinese under the Han, had already had bronze for some centuries. The diffusion throughout south and central China from Ch'ang-sha had reached the whole of south-east Asia. The same figures of witch-doctors, the same evidences of everyday life are found on drums, weapons and ornaments. The style is different from the northern style; more affected, it takes into full account the luxurious life led by the barbarians of the Chu and Yueh kingdoms—barbarians no doubt, but equipped richly and with fleets which could carry to the river-dwellers of the southern seas all the formulas of an art 407 profoundly adapted to their folklore. 406

In Japan, metal arrived via Korea which exported mirrors and weapons of Chinese origin. Its adoption was slow, and only in the 7th century is Japanese archaic plastic art worth noticing. Many geometrical decorations

402. HAN. Funerary terra-cotta figure.
3rd century A.D. *Cernuschi Museum, Paris.*

403. CHOU BRONZE. Statuette in two parts: the figure of a man with upraised arms, and a bear crouched on top of a square pole the lower end of which fits over the man's right arm. 6th–5th centuries B.C. *Freer Gallery of Art, Washington.*

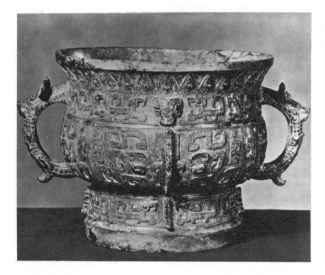

404. SHANG. Bronze ritual vessel *(kuei).* 14th–11th centuries B.C. *Chen Collection, Hongkong.*

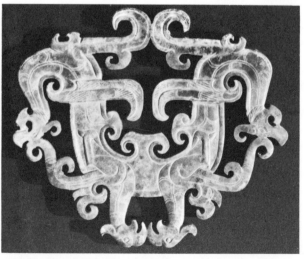

405. WARRING STATES. Jade pendant. 5th–3rd centuries B.C. *W. Rockhill Nelson Gallery of Art, Kansas.*

seem to be original; others seem to follow Chinese models interpreted to meet native taste. Such without doubt are the motifs which ornament the bowls of the Kamegaoka culture and recall the highly stylised motifs of certain Chinese mirrors. It is certain that bronze did not reach Japan solely via Korea and we are inclined to think the countries of Wu and Yueh, famous for their mirrors and swords must have played a vital role which would confirm the importance attached to these two objects in Japanese mythology. The study of the Bronze Age in south-east Asia will be sure to provide new evidence about the introduction of bronze to Japan.

At the other end of the world, Chinese traditional art of the first millennium B.C. developed similarly to that of the West. It developed geometrical and animal formulas, starting from the symbolic and the general and ending in the realistic and the particular. Each great period brought a new tendency to stylisation, undoubtedly showing the assimilation of northern elements from the steppes which, as we shall see, were to give as much to the plains as they took from them.

THE ART OF THE STEPPES

An enigmatic art

The term 'art of the steppes' is one of the most puzzling in our history. Sometimes it is what an expert has seen fit to define as the 'daring art of the Scythians'; sometimes it is an ill-defined art covering everything not included in one or other of the main cultures. It is as difficult to speak of the art of the steppes as it is to speak of the art of the forest or the plains. Admittedly the name defines a world with clear boundaries. Owing to its vast extent it can be made to serve as the place of origin of every elusive art. Everything which does not fit into the framework of the Western, Indian and Chinese worlds is attributed to the peoples of the steppes. To lend them definite characteristics may seem as questionable as to define the art of the Mesopotamians from the Nile to the Euphrates and from the Indus to the Yellow River.

However we must admit that these two worlds do have preoccupations which were usually characteristic of them: nomadic or sedentary ways of life, stock-farming or agricultural economies, oral or written traditions.

The art of the steppes pushed at the frontiers of nearly all the ancient cultures; only Egypt and India perhaps were unaffected. If the steppes had their own culture, if they contributed to the fusion of all the tribes in these immense spaces and launched them throughout Asia, they remain none the less a world as split up as the ancient Orient and only our ignorance prevents us from distinguishing their multiple components equally clearly.

It is only a few years since these immense territories which follow the existing frontier of the U.S.S.R. have been the subject of systematic excavations. The ancient peoples emerge as bearers of local cultures, and even if their territories and chronological limits are vague we have at least an adequate notion of their distribution. Bronze invaded two geographical areas in succession, first southern Russia and western Siberia, then the mountainous zone of the Altai range and the Minusinsk basin; on either side, the plateaux of Iran and Ordos played the part of expert intermediaries between the civilised and the barbarian peoples.

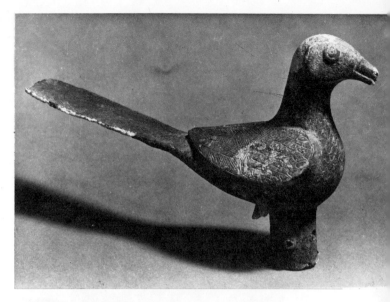

406. INDO-CHINA. Bronze ornament. End of the 1st millennium B.C. *Cernuschi Museum, Paris.*

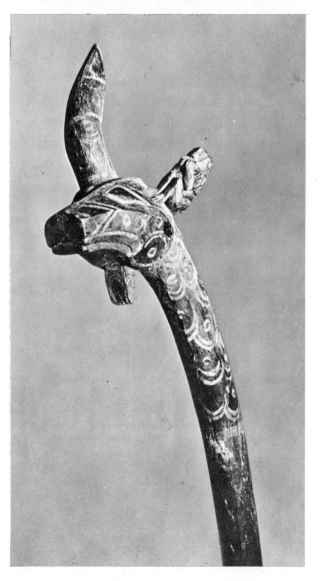

407. CHINA. CH'ANG-SHA. WARRING STATES. Head of a crook in painted wood. 5th–3rd centuries B.C. *Formerly Komor Collection.*

225

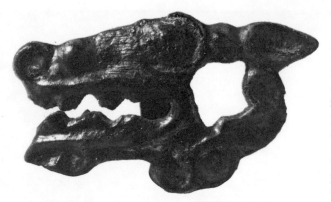

408. URAL MOUNTAINS. Bronze ornament in the shape of a wolf's head. 5th–3rd centuries B.C. *Cernuschi Museum, Paris*.

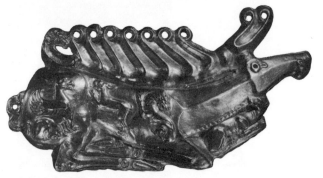

409. KUL-OBA (CRIMEA). Gold ornament for a shield. 5th century B.C. *Hermitage, Leningrad*.

The peoples on the shores of the Caspian and the Black Seas

At the end of the 2nd millennium the timber-frame culture flourished in southern Russia. It was in contact with the Caucasian culture of Koban to the south, with the Kazanian culture to the north, with the Caspian culture of Khvalinsk to the east and the Ukrainian culture of Volynia and the Dnieper to the west. By and large, then, this culture occupied the space controlled by the Cimmerians before the arrival of the Scythians.

Strictly speaking there is no such thing as a Cimmerian art, but on the other hand there is proof that these peoples contributed largely to the spread of metal and the exchanges between their country and central Europe, especially as regards horse-breeding. With their help, the Thraco-Cimmerian zone was in direct contact with the Caucasus; many forms of weapons, implements and ornaments were common to both countries. The cultures of Lausitz and Hallstatt were in close relations with Thrace and via the Danube with Kobanian, Kubanian and Caucasian cultures. Before the arrival of the Scythians, their chosen land shows the influence of the Aegean and Anatolian cultures of the 2nd millennium and of the Hallstattian, Kubanian and Kobano-Colchidian cultures of the beginning of the 1st millennium, which constituted an artistically rich substratum continually renewed by the many cultural streams which flowed across it. It was in such a framework that in the 8th century the Scythians, of the same origin as the Iranians, decided to leave the regions north-east of the Caspian and to install themselves as masters in every province of southern Russia. Archaeological material shows us that far from bringing a uniform culture with them, the Scythians developed and made

wide use of the local institutions: so much so that often it is necessary to distinguish between the Ukrainian Scythians and the Volgan Scythians, just as we speak of Graeco-Roman and Graeco-Iranian. The works of art have the same mixture of elements and this makes it difficult to define Scythian art. For our part, we consider it as the art which exploited to the best advantage certain plastic themes such as those of the lion, the ibex and fighting animals.

The most typical objects are those from Kul-Oba in the Crimea, Kelermes and Kostromskaya, which should probably be placed in either the 7th–6th or 5th–4th centuries. One of the earliest forms is a wolf's head 408 which has something of the harshness of the steppe itself and in which we find the style of certain pieces from the northern cultures of the Volga. In the more classical pieces, such as the stag from Kul-Oba, we can feel the 409 Iranian character, due to the common origins of the Scythian tribes from Eurasia and the Iranians and to the strong Mesopotamian and Iranian influence in the Caucasus. To this Iranian character a clear-cut Hellenic element was added. From the 7th century onwards craftsmen of Olbia, Panticapaeum and the many Greek trading posts on the southern Black Sea were inspired by the old artistic traditions of their country, including that of overloading their art with animals. The happy use of mixtures of traditions is the lifeblood of Scythian decoration. In its stylisation the animals do not have the stiff poses used by the southern cultures; instead they are much more dynamic. This tendency appears clearly in the Hungarian piece from Zöldhalompuszta, so much 410 more animated than the pre-Scythian piece from Turócz. 411 These two examples better than many others enable us to understand the new contributions made by Scythian art and to what extent it influenced the griffon in the treasure 412 of Ziwiye. For the elements of a decoration may be borrowed and returned, but the stamp of individual workmanship is the artist's genius. If the griffon resembles the Hungarian stag, is Ziwiyan art Scythian or vice versa? To the quality of movement is added a marked decorative feeling in which each element keeps its own characteristics, as witness the ornament on the quiver from the Seven Brothers' barrows. Many motifs from Nordic and 413 southern bestiaries recur there in a fantastic composition. An animal with a wolf's head and a swan's neck bears wings which represent the reversed head of a griffon: four beasts are merged into one without the monstrous whole seeming artificial. A lively sense of composition is the other masterly quality of Scythian art.

Eastern animal art

The influence of Scythian art made itself felt in the East as far as the Minusinsk basin, all the more easily because instead of meeting entirely different cultures as in the West it was welcomed by the bearers of a civilisation akin to that of its Scythian ancestors. In the time of the Cimmerians the culture of Karasuk (1200–700) which followed that of Andronovo (1700–1200) occupied by and large the present-day region of Kazakhstan and the Altai mountains. In the north it had as neighbours the Uralian culture of Chigir (2nd millennium–6th century) and that of Ob (16th–8th centuries); to the east was the Baikal culture of Chivera (1300–900) and in the south the culture of Tazabagiab (1500–1000). Carved stone pillars repre-

SCYTHIAN. Vase handle in the form of a wild goat. Silver. 5th century B.C. Part of the Oxus treasure. British Museum. *Museum photograph.*

226

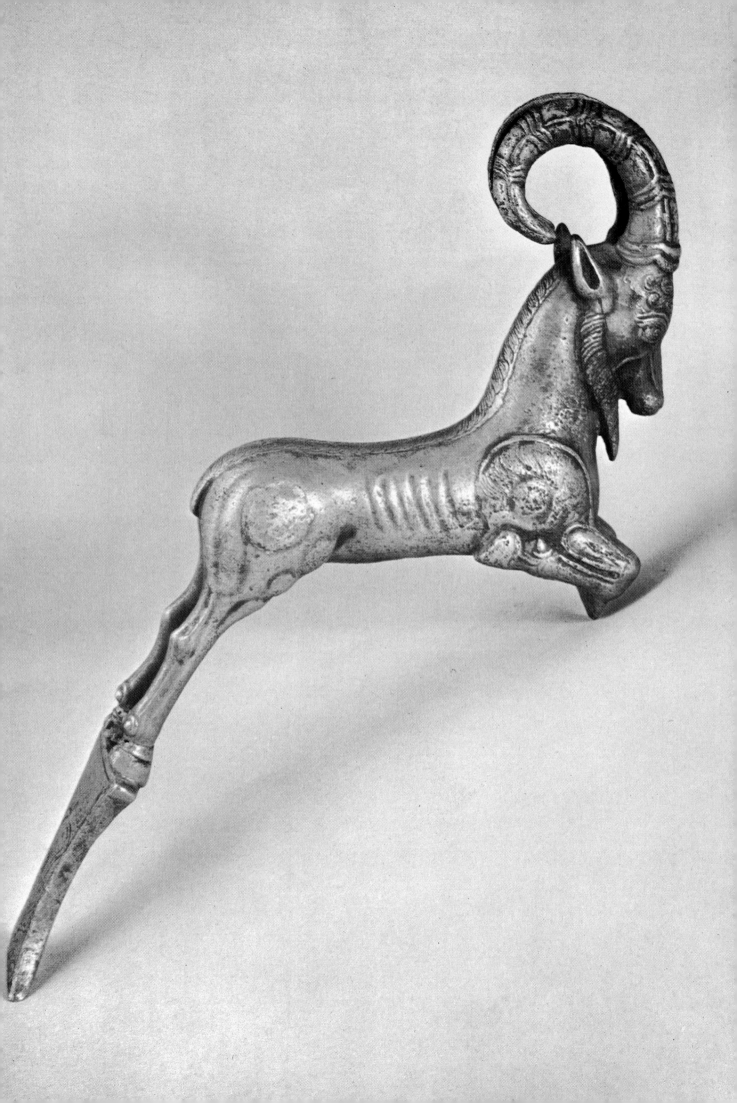

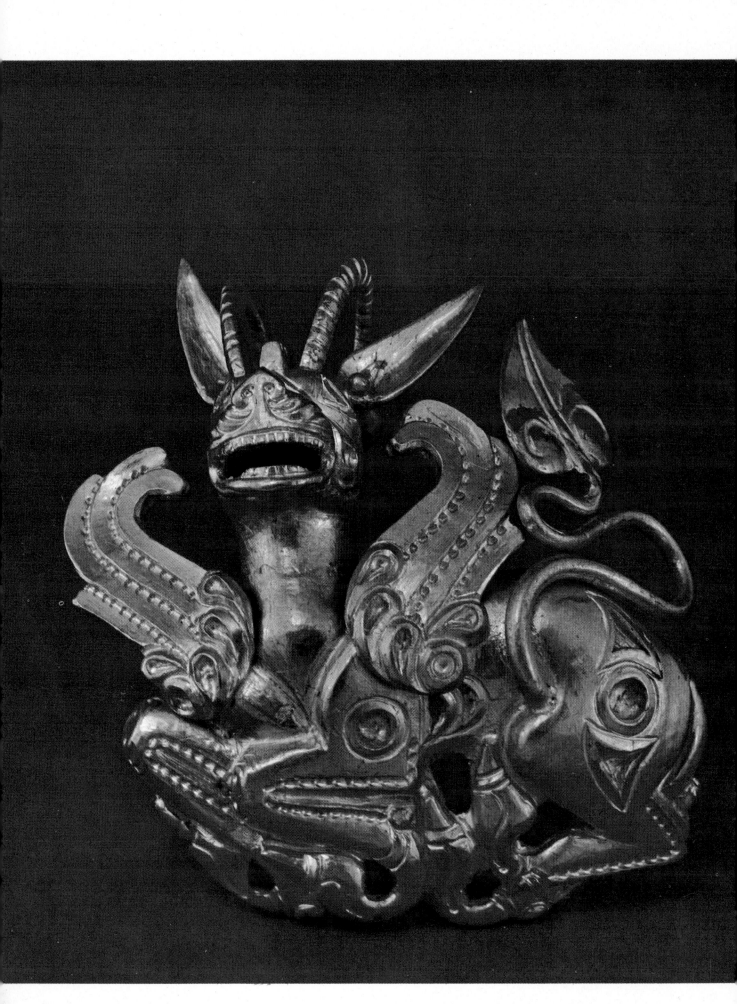

SCYTHIAN. Lion-griffon. Gold. 5th–4th centuries B.C. Part of
the Oxus treasure. British Museum. *Museum photograph*.

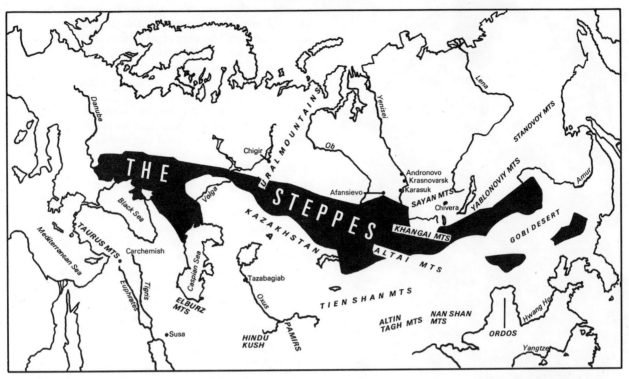

senting bears or rams discovered on the banks of the
Yenisei are stylistically similar to the decorated knife-
handles which this culture has bequeathed to us: heads of
stags, cattle and horses treated in the round like those of
their Chinese neighbours. Unlike the recumbent stags
which made Scythian art famous, the animals of Karasuk
and Tagar are standing up. The motif therefore is completely different and, after comparison with the earlier
Chinese bronzes of An-yang, it shows that even if the
Minusinsk basin gave metallurgy to the Chinese it took
from them in return its style in the art of metal. So the
Karasuk culture formed its animal art independent of the
West. Nevertheless, having replaced the Andronovo
culture which was more interested in geometrical ornamentation than animal decoration, it remained in contact
with the cultures of eastern Europe and the ancient Orient.
But even though the latter transmitted prototypes of
weapons and tools by way of Seima, Chigir and Krasnoyarsk, no animal art was sent in return from west to
east. In the West, Scythian art was grafted on to a geometrical art; in central Siberia its contemporary, the art
of Tagar, found numerous precedents to exploit in order
to establish an art of equal brilliance in its turn.

392b

416

417

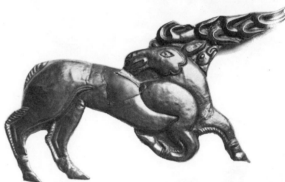

410. HUNGARY. ZÖLDHALOMPUSZTA. Gold stag. Middle
of the 1st millennium B.C. *Budapest Museum.*

Scythia, Tagar and the Ordos

As Ghirshman has pointed out, it is tempting to seek the
point of departure of Scythian art in the Karasuk area,
since it is impossible for us at the present time to show
it rising from a predominantly geometrical culture. Thus
Scythian art (8th century) would be the third stage of
Chinese animal art (14th century) transmitted via the
art of Karasuk (10th century). In the Tagar period (700–
100) the Minusinsk region saw the development of an
animal art following the same rules of evolution as
Scythian art; a certain monumentality gradually gave
way to a more flexible plastic art which concerned itself
with rendering swift movements. In spite of the definite

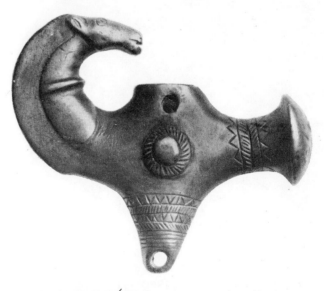

411. HUNGARY. TURÓCZ. Bronze ceremonial axe. Beginning
of 1st millennium B.C. *Storno Collection.*

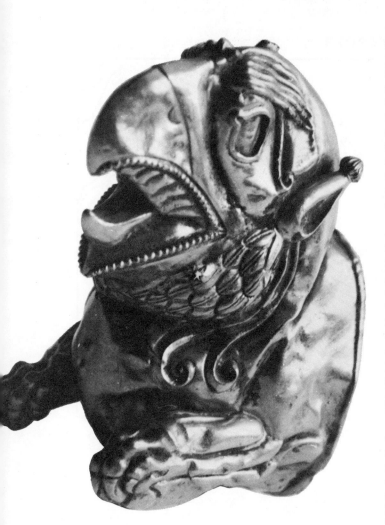

412. ZIWIYE (IRAN). Griffon's head in gold. Beginning of 1st millennium B.C. *Teheran Museum*.

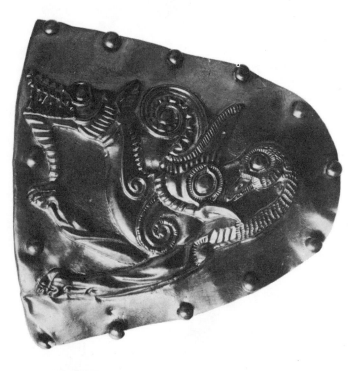

413. SEVEN BROTHERS' BARROWS (KUBAN). Harness ornament, gold appliqué. 7th–3rd centuries B.C. *Hermitage, Leningrad*.

relations which existed between the two cultures, their parallel development does not necessarily seem to have included interdependence. But although their development is independent, exchanges of formulas existed none the less. Side by side with upright animals in the Karasuk tradition there was an abundant production of rampant and galloping beasts like the Scythian animals. Knives and 418 small bells were the favourite objects, to which were added belt-buckles and belt-plates with skilfully worked 415 decoration. On them beasts fight to the death, animals confronting each other stand out against the silhouettes of trees, branches envelop the groups and their foliage serves as a framework for the scene. It is difficult to attribute an origin to these plates: they formed part of the nomads' dress and were very much in fashion in the following period over the whole area of the steppes. Round buckles twist the animals into concentric circles, others turn them back into an S-shape. The first are 414 undoubtedly of Scythian inspiration, but the latter are influenced by China. Since the beginning of the Bronze Age, the Chinese artist was fond of twisting animals in order to give an S-shape. These animals with reversed paws spread to the whole art of the steppes and, side by side with the inlays which were inspired by the ancient East, they formed one of the principal characteristics of barbarian art.

The art of Tagar had as wide a diffusion as Scythian art; it undoubtedly transmitted to the West via the Ana-nino culture (8th–3rd centuries) the knives with animals facing each other of which the Scythians made two rings, and it must also have contributed the constituent elements of the art of the Ordos. The latter, whose origins may go back to the 8th century, was born of the conjunction of Tagar art and Chinese traditions making up the trio of the art of the steppes together with Scythian art. But although the art of the Ordos had at first a modelled 419 plastic art which it handed on to the styles of the Warring 420 States, thus strengthening the internal development of archaic bronzes, it subsequently followed Chinese art in its graphic tendency which gradually overcame Tagar art and which was undoubtedly, owing to the Huns, a strong element of the evolution from Scythian to Sarmatian art.

Huns and Sarmatians

Up to the 4th century there were established in the steppes clearly differentiated cultures which were grafted on to local traditions and which benefited by reciprocal influences. We have discussed their differences, but we must also emphasise their homogeneity beside the unity of the art of the ancient East or that of China. After the Karasuk culture, initiator in the west of the animal arts of the steppes, the Tagar culture was to be the pivot of cultural relations between those two great neighbours, Iran and China. The transportable nature of all the objects played its part in creating a certain unity among all these cultures, which was to be even further consolidated by the appearance of the Huns and the Sarmatians. At present the way in which these people arrived is obscure; undoubtedly new Iranian thrusts similar to those by the Kassites or the Scythians created a vacuum which the turbulence of the nomads was always ready to fill up; the same phenomenon was produced in the 4th century B.C. with the barbarian invasion. As with the Scythians, a movement of peoples unleashed a disturbance which altered the balance of power, and a new tribe gave its name to the reigning aristocracy. The numerous bronze pieces which we possess from this period rarely come from scientific excavations. Their geographical attribution is difficult and those which do not have clearly defined characteristics are usually called Scytho-Sarmatian.

The art of the Huns is better known from the magnificent excavations at Pasyryk, Chibe and Noin-ula in the Altai range. At this time, the Huns formed the strongest confederation of tribes in the eastern steppes. They undoubtedly owed much of their power to their stock-raising and agricultural economy, but a greater part of it was due to the fact that they could easily raid the convoys prospecting for gold in the region and the even richer convoys from the wealthy deposits of northern Kazakhstan. Forming a stage on the gold route coming from China, the Huns found themselves well placed to make use of it in passage. Their richness shows in the brilliance of their tombs, in which the great number of objects reflects their taste for luxury, from the elaborate ornamentations and polychrome inlays to the multicoloured appliqué work. Western influence made itself felt in many details: palm-leaf motifs resemble the horns of stags, and heads of Iranian griffons ornament metal parts of saddlery.

But although numerous elements betray the influence of the west, the workmanship of the objects remains supple and the treatment of bodies is always in the round. The Huns learnt the skilful twists of the Chinese, the entangled compositions which the art of the Warring States used, but they preserved a realism which their western neighbours would no longer understand. A very marked difference separates them. The objects with the most purely ornamental effects belong to the groups from southern Russia. The latter group includes ornaments such as the famous buckles from Maikop or those of Bulgaria with rich inlay which show an exaggerated taste for decoration. The first group on the other hand are astonishingly lively. The formulas of realistic stylisation

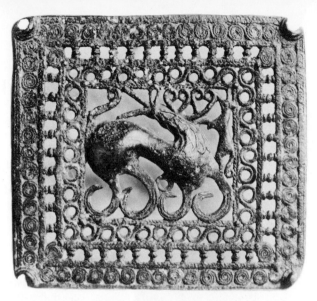

414. CAUCASUS. Bronze belt plaque. 8th–3rd centuries B.C. *Mme Feron-Stoclet Collection.*

preserve the modelling of the body; the compositions sketch skilful geometrical lines, but the movement and the tension never disappear from these works which are strangely reminiscent of the Caucasian belt-plates.

In the Ordos, the works of the Huns underwent a similar experience: they were overcome by a graphic quality distinct from geometrisation. These treatments in bas-relief managed to retain a typical Chinese vitality. Whether it is some trivial pendant or an important ornamental plaque, all the forms have an animated line. One could say that the art of the Ordos is the last outpost of animal art, which thus returned to die where it was born.

The great religious upheavals in Europe around the beginning of the Christian era and the philosophical movements in China were henceforth to transfer the emphasis to man himself. All over Eurasia animal art was to dry up and move into the background.

Nevertheless it did not disappear completely. Avar and Gothic craftsmen bequeathed elements of it to the late Middle Ages. The swords of the Vikings and the niches of the cathedrals, thanks to the Huns, were to preserve traces of it for a long time to come.

415. SIBERIA. Bronze belt plaque. 5th–3rd centuries B.C. *Hermitage, Leningrad.*

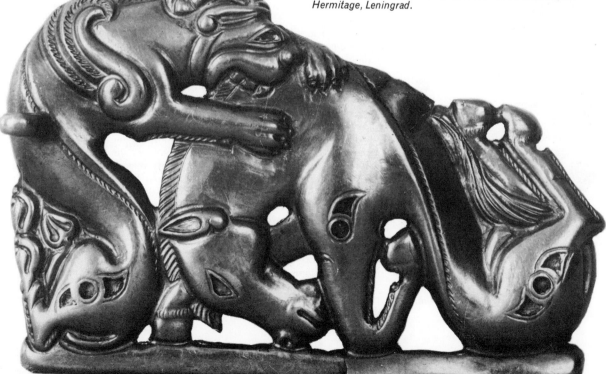

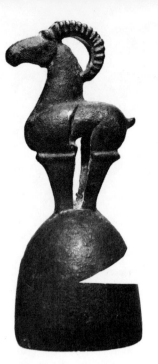

416. SIBERIA. MINUSINSK. Stave head in bronze of Tagar II style. About 6th century B.C. *National Museum, Helsinki.*

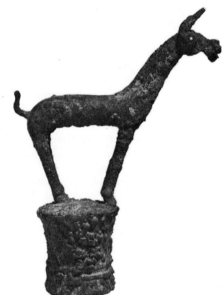

417. AN-YANG (CHINA). Shang bronze shaft-head. 14th–11th centuries B.C. *Pillsbury Collection, Minneapolis Institute of Arts.*

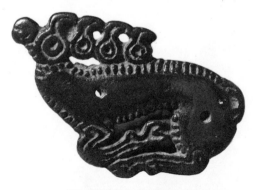

418. SIBERIA. MINUSINSK. Bronze stag of the Tagar period. 8th–3rd centuries B.C. *Cernuschi Museum, Paris.*

HISTORICAL SUMMARY:
Eurasia and the Orient

The height of the Bronze Age came in the 2nd and 1st millennia in Eurasia. It is illustrated to the west, in the southern steppes, by the cultures of the Cimmerians, the Scythians and the Sarmatians; in central Asia by the cultures of Andronovo, Karasuk and Tagar; and in the east by the Chinese Shang and Chou cultures.

The southern steppes. In this zone, the timber-frame culture (1600–800), characterised by dowelled axes, daggers with leaf-shaped blades, bill hooks, and pottery with a flat ground hardly differs from the preceding catacomb culture. Stock-raising remained pastoral, and agricultural activity went on as long as nomadism was not predominant. The bearers of this culture were the Cimmerians, mentioned in Assyrian texts of the 8th century, who may possibly be akin to the Sinds of the Sea of Azov and the Thracians of the lower Danube.

In the 8th century the Scythians replaced them. Speaking the Iranian language, they have not yet been clearly defined and in fact four related cultures are grouped under the name Scythian:

1. The culture of the tribes of Moldavia and the Ukraine, inhabiting the forest zone of the steppes, which together with the Lithuanian tribes made up a part of the elements of the Slavic group.

2. The Scythian culture, in the strict sense of the word, of the nomads and farmers of the lower Bug, the lower Dnieper and the Sea of Azov. These peoples, distinct from the Slavs, belonged to the group of northern Iranians. Their culture can be seen in the sumptuous necropolises of the Crimea (6th century).

3. The culture of the Sindo-Meotic tribes in the Kuban, the bearers of which were in contact with the groups of the forest zone and the northern Caucasus. From the 3rd century onwards, this country underwent transformations owing to penetration by Sarmatian elements.

4. The culture of the Sarmatian tribes of the Volga basin and the Ural steppes which shows many affinities with the cultures of western Siberia.

The elements common to these four groups are weapons and items of harness decorated in an animal-style art in close relations with the eastern cultures of central Asia. The most original character of this culture undoubtedly existed in the art of Pasyryk which in the 4th century exhibits elements of stylisation distinct from those of the Black Sea and the Far East.

Central Asia. The Andronovo culture (1700–1200) succeeded to the culture of Afanasievo. Its area was more extensive and it covered a vast territory bounded by the Urals and the Minusinsk basin. This culture is characterised by pottery with a flat ground and vases of the type of the timber-frame culture; the people raised cattle, sheep and horses. The creators of this culture were Europoids whose patriarchal life was divided between the pastures and crop growing and whose metallurgy remained very primitive. It is highly improbable that this culture transmitted the technique of bronze to China, and there is no doubt that we must seek the spread of this metal along the future Silk Route directly linking China to Iran via the Tien Shan range.

To the south, the Andronovo culture had as neighbour the Tazabagiab culture (1500–1000), under a matriarchal régime, with an agriculture using the hoe, and to the east the Glaskovo cultures of Baikal, still at the Neolithic stage.

The following stage, that of Karasuk (1200–700) saw a great change in the life of Eurasia. A new element of Chinese origin reached the area previously occupied by the Andronovo culture as far as Kazakhstan and the Altai range. An animal style, peculiar to the Shang-Yin Dynasty (1300–1028) spread as far as the Semiretchie.

The complexity of relations between the Chinese world and Siberia at the end of the 2nd millennium has so far prevented us from establishing how they operated.

In the following centuries, the horsemen of the steppes united all the cultural groups from the Danube to the Yellow River. There was a universal tendency for the stock raisers to become nomads and their contacts conferred uniformity on animal art, giving the bronzes of the whole of Eurasia that family resemblance which is so confusing to us and which foreshadows the unity of barbarian art.

China. While these great nomadic empires were being founded, China developed a brilliant sedentary culture. The Shang Dynasty, in 1300, installed its capital at An-yang and built there vast palaces decorated with marble; its sovereigns practised divination and its high officials regulated the calendars in order to coordinate the harvests and

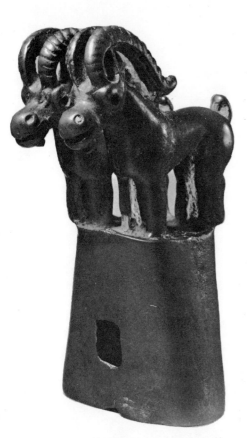

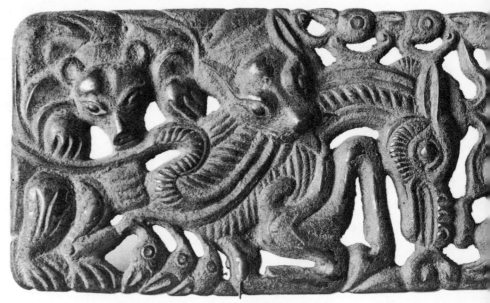

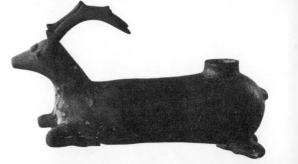

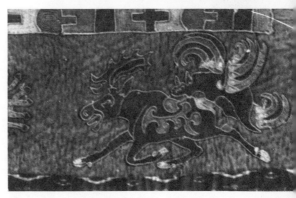

419. ORDOS. Bronze shaft-head. End of 1st millennium B.C. *Far Eastern Collection, Stockholm.*

420. MONGOLIA. HAN BRONZE. Belt plaque showing a horse attacked by two bears. 3rd century B.C.–3rd century A.D. *Metropolitan Museum of Art (Fletcher Fund, 1924).*

421. IRAN. KALAR-DASHT. Vessel in red terra cotta. 11th century B.C. *Teheran Museum.*

422. NOIN-ULA (MONGOLIA). Border of a woollen carpet. About the beginning of the Christian era. *Hermitage, Leningrad.*

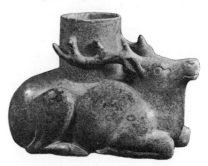

423. CHINA. WARRING STATES. Bronze stand. 5th–3rd centuries B.C. *Art Institute, Chicago.*

work in the fields.

In 1028 the princes of the border countries (Shansi) swept down on the capital and installed the Chou Dynasty (11th–3rd centuries). Pursuing the enlargement of their territory as well as fighting against the nomads of the north, the Chou kings also grew crops sacrificed to the earth and the sky and worshipped their ancestors and the sun god. From the 8th century territorial expansion led to the establishment of powerful rival principalities. This was the troubled period of the Warring States which in the 5th century saw the golden age of Chinese philosophy, with the Taoist philosophers such as Lao-tse and the classical sages such as Confucius.

In the 3rd century, the house of Ch'in eliminated its rival and founded the first united Chinese empire, which the succeeding Han Dynasty moulded into the form it was to keep for more than twenty centuries.

Japan. Chinese culture introduced bronze to Japan via Korea. The new Yayoi culture (about 2nd century B.C.) was superimposed on the old Jomon culture. The former developed the growing of rice, at the same time living by hunting and fishing. Large patriarchal families were formed from the 4th to the 7th centuries A.D. Soon they

organised themselves into rival clans, the strongest of which, in Yamato, wiped out the culture of the tumulus builders (4th–7th centuries A.D.) to found the first Japanese state.

Indochina. In Indochina, the influence of Chinese culture permeated by the bronze creations of the southern centres (Ch'ang-sha, 5th–3rd centuries B.C.) gave birth to the Dong-son culture (5th–3rd centuries). Diffusion from these centres contributed to the establishment of the foundries of southern Asia. They were in contact with the nomads via northern China and they developed many themes common to both East and West, so much so that certain authors have seen the influence of Hallstatt in them.

Thus three great creative centres emerge for the whole of Eurasia: the western centre in which Iranian, Oriental and Greek contributions predominated; the Chinese centres which embrace Japanese and Indo-Chinese bronze; and the centres of the Altai range, which transmitted many formulas and contributed in their turn the original spirit which, via the Scythians and the barbarians, was to distinguish the whole of the European Middle Ages.

Vadime Elisseeff

231

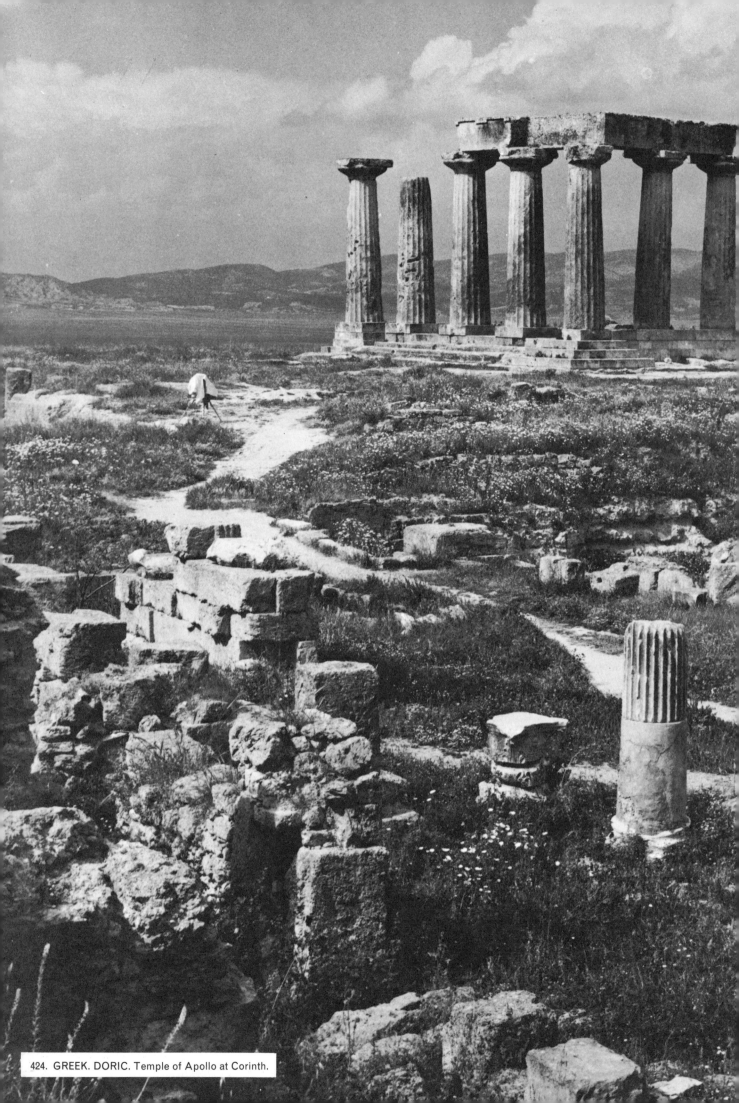

424. GREEK. DORIC. Temple of Apollo at Corinth.

5 THE EARLIEST CIVILISATIONS
OF ANTIQUITY

ART FORMS AND SOCIETY *René Huyghe*

The reputation of Greek art and culture has passed through a critical period, and this is not one of the least signs of the present weakening in Western civilisation. It is not only possible, but essential, to continually expand and enrich the legacy we have inherited from Greece. To repudiate it would be to condemn the basis of our *raison d'être*, to condemn ourselves through a disturbing form of intellectual masochism. If that devaluation corresponds to a necessary reappraisal of our beliefs, all is well. But if it is the sign of a genuine abandonment, then we are already beginning to drift. Is it not symptomatic that André Malraux, that penetrating commentator on modern taste, in his *Musée imaginaire de la sculpture mondiale*, should have devoted only 31 plates to the plastic arts of classical Greece, from Phidias to the Hellenistic age (until only recently considered the supreme examples of perfect beauty), with an additional 15 plates on Rome, while the so-called primitive civilisations of America, Africa and Oceania received 82 plates?

This is only the final episode in a struggle which the present chapter will describe by contrasting Greece and Persia, opponents in historical, but also symbolic, terms. We have reached the stage where the great civilisations were firmly 'in place'. A conflict arose between the attitudes they represented: between the West, since the time of ancient Greece both positive and rational, and the East which was more receptive to subtle influences. It was the start of an ever fruitful debate and of a frequently violent contest.

The roots of Greece

The origin of Greek civilisation begins to grow clearer. A short while ago oversimplified opinion held that the Creto-Mycenaean collapse was followed by a period envisaged, like the Dark Ages in Europe, as a black night from which sprang the rising sun of the 'Greek miracle' created out of a void. Another equally simplified and not entirely disinterested view attributed this collapse and revival to the Dorian invasion from the north and the influx of barbarian blood. The 'Greek miracle' then became merely a miracle of pan-Germanism.

The invasions and infiltrations began in the 15th century, grew more marked in the 13th, and became decisive in the 11th century. They spread from the north, probably from Illyria, to reach first Thessaly and then the Peloponnese a century later. There they destroyed Achaean supremacy which, too, had been established (by about the year 2000) by Indo-European migrations. Through another connection with that first wave of invasions which had founded the Hittite empire in Asia, they, too, concentrated their force in the eastern Mediterranean in a movement that was to cause the collapse of that same empire, whose downfall corresponded to the Achaean overthrow; these attacks had repercussions as far as Egypt, where they caused the onslaught of the Peoples of the Sea, just as the Hyksos invasion in the 18th century had done. This renewed pressure on the part of northern peoples, following, perhaps, attacks further north, was the consequence of the barbarians' increased power produced by the introduction of iron, whereas in the

first case it followed the introduction of bronze. But while the Achaeans had allowed themselves to be absorbed into Cretan civilisation, the Dorians proved to be unshakeable. They remained themselves. It would be too easy to imagine that they therefore destroyed everything which had existed before them. In fact, by the violent infusion of a radically different spirit, they were to bring about one of those clashes, one of those forceful and conflicting mixtures, whose final synthesis has always proved to be one of the most dynamic causes behind human progress.

Both the Greek spirit and Greek art were to be born of this uneasy marriage of rebellious elements. It was to be the source of their new-found richness. Whether as in the past, one inflates, or as today, deflates, the importance of the Dorian contribution, one cannot but observe that the geometric style which was to emerge from the protogeometric style between the years 1000 and 800 took almost the opposite course from the flexible, curvilinear, plastic naturalism of the Cretans. This style only magnified an Achaean tendency which even at that time had introduced into the Creto-Mycenaean complex a reaction against imagination and realistic flexibility in favour of monumental discipline and an abstract severity. ³²⁶

It is still more interesting (to confine ourselves to a review of style) to estimate how much the new artistic repertory, presumed to be of Dorian origin, owed to the decorative spirit which had found a tentative expression in the Palaeolithic and was formulated in the Neolithic. This spirit had, throughout the whole of Europe, replaced the curvilinear spiraliform style which had spread with the influence of the Danubian civilisations from Butmir towards the Adriatic, to Cucuteni and Tripolye, and from there to the Russian steppes. This repertory of angular, strict, rhythmic, arbitrary and simplified forms was in direct contrast to the dynamic freedom which had flourished in the spiraliform elaborations, spread by the Creto-Mycenaeans, that survived solely in the Scandinavian Bronze Age and was later revived and developed by the Celts. It had dominated the early stages of the European metal ages until the changes of the La Tène period. One cannot help, consequently, putting it down to the account of the Indo-European invasions. But, as Charles Picard proves in his authoritative essay, Creto-Mycenaean colonisation could not be cancelled out at a single blow. Everywhere, rooted in the indigenous population, it remained just below the surface. It must not be forgotten that certain districts, Arcadia, for example, and particularly Attica, which were to play so decisive a part, went almost unscathed, their poverty proving to be their protection.

It is the later splendour of Athens which too often makes us forget that a Greece, nurtured on a pre-Hellenic civilisation of a lasting and tremendous importance, survived; this was the Greece of Asia Minor. It is hardly conceivable that the Cretans, those adventurous seafarers, should never have thought at the time of their collapse (that is, from 1400) of seeking refuge in places along the Asian coast. Their conquerors and old Achaean followers, when they in their turn took to the sea, adopted this

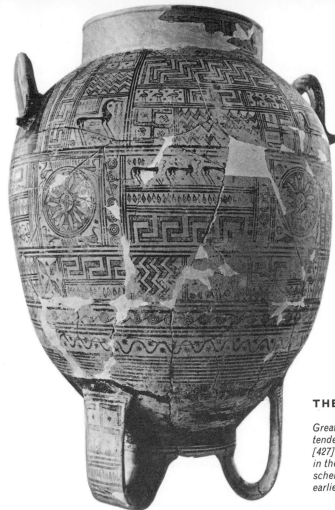

425. GREEK. Geometric vase. Beginning of the 7th century B.C.

THE DORIAN SPIRIT

Great arts often bring about the union of previously contrasting tendencies; the rectilinear stylisation of Hallstattian Europe [427], which the Dorians probably brought with them, is echoed in the geometric style Greek vases [425], where even the schematic outlines of the horse and bird recur, and in the earliest architecture with its powerful and austere feeling [426] ...

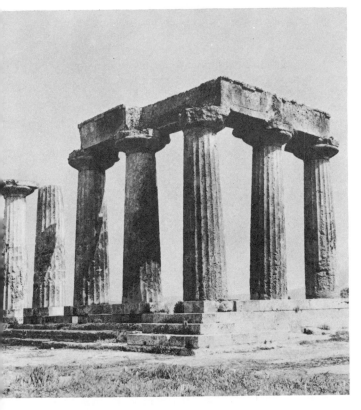

426. GREEK. DORIC. Columns of the archaic temple of Apollo at Corinth.

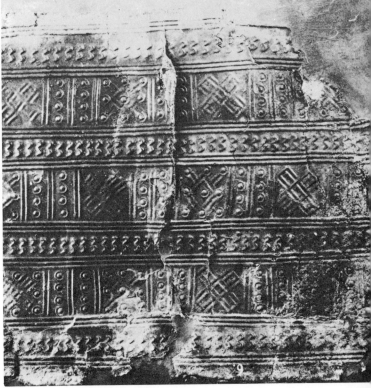

427. EARLY IRON AGE (HALLSTATT). Bronze plaque. *Haguenau Museum.*

same coast, especially to the north and south of Ionia, for colonisation. The Hittites, if we are to believe their archives which have come to light in recent years, maintained relations with the Achaeans of the coast, in Lycia and Cilicia, during the 14th and 13th centuries. This civilisation of Asia Minor had a great bearing on Greece as a whole. It was there, especially in the 7th and 6th centuries, that philosophic thought first made its appearance. Thales, Anaximander and Anaximenes came from Miletus, the strongest of the Greek coastal cities. Persian ambition led to the conquest of Ionia as early as 546, and the Persians destroyed the town in 494. Soon afterwards, following an attempted revolt, the whole region was finally enslaved. At this time there were still thinkers born on this soil who were to form, in Magna Graecia (the Greek colonies in southern Italy) and Sicily, the second phase of Greek philosophy. Pythagoras, born in 570 in Samos, settled in Croton; Xenophon, born in Colophon, went to Elea, an Ionian colony founded about the year 540, and when Heraclitus remained in his native town of Ephesus, it was only to watch the triumph of the Persians.

All this shows us the third element in the make-up of the Greek genius: the influences from the East, which were to make such a powerful contribution to the advance from the more typically European geometric style towards a growing naturalism. The Hittite archives provide evidence of Achaean trading relations with Assyria carried on through the medium of Syrian ports. The Greeks of Asia Minor, by virtue of their very position, were unable to avoid some contact with the Oriental world, with its cloth, ivories, and bronzes, which helped to spread the lesson of realism. This realism, already anticipated by the Cretans and as yet at an immature stage, was to be brought by the Greeks to its final perfection. It has often been pointed out how the Hellenes, starting with the xoanon, the early wooden statue still 442 so like the original tree-trunk, caught up with that stage in sculpture (where the Egyptians had stopped) in which the artist could carve the left leg of a statue poised as though it were about to take a step forward, how with the archaic smile, which soon appeared on the lips, they 443–447 were to progress, stage by stage, towards that living perfection which no people before them had been able to attain. But before a new art could emerge, composed of these three elements (Creto-Mycenaean survivals, the barbaric Dorian contribution and the lessons learned from the ancient Assyrians and Egyptians), Greece had to enter a new phase of human society.

A new social environment: the democratic and trading city

The great agrarian empires of Egypt and Mesopotamia had maintained, virtually unchanged, their thousand-year-old social system. Rigidly hierarchical, headed by a leader who governed by divine right with the co-operation of the priests, it was a system which Persia was to strengthen and uphold and which was to flourish anew in Rome and then in Byzantium—in both cases where the East again had the opportunity to become a living example. Crete, about which so little is known through lack of adequately deciphered written records, had pointed the way to a change. Resources, more maritime and mercantile than agricultural, the position occupied by metal in the economy and the division of land had

certainly weakened the monarch's position; the palace was firmly entrenched within the city; even visibly, the king was coming nearer to the people.

On the other hand the arrival of the Dorians introduced into the Mediterranean world an entirely different organisation, in which the passive and conservative peasant who had toiled on the land, his back bent beneath blows, gave way to the soldier, who only occasionally turned his hand to farming, and a nomadic soldier at that: 'the iron man'. Stress has been put on the probable similarity between these shifting communities subject to a military leader, and, for example, the Bedouins, among whom the position of sheikh is still controlled by public opinion. Fritz Schachermeyr, in particular, has emphasised that with a transitional period of an aristocratic warrior society, of which the Achaean lords had already provided a kind of feudal picture, there was, here, a step towards the democratic city-state, the Greek *Polis*. It was a great deal that the new social structure should be established in a richer and more urban civilisation. Power passed from the absolute monarch to the leader-prince with limited authority, and from him to the citizen king.

We must not, however, be led astray by the term 'democracy'. The city-state—and Athens is the outstanding example—which from the 5th century had become the centre of civilisation, was, indeed, to be governed by its citizens, once the age of tyrants which flourished particularly in Asia Minor and Magna Graecia was over. But it hardly corresponds to our idea of 'the people'. In Athens scarcely one tenth of the inhabitants possessed full civil and political rights. Leaving aside all those who were debarred from their rights as citizens, slavery produced a large class which provided the privileged with a life of leisure reserved up till that time for princes. Nausicaa had already declared to Ulysses that he would find her mother 'sitting by the fireside with her waiting-women behind her, while my father, his chair in the flickering light, slowly sips his wine, like a god.'

Man was no longer dependent upon mysterious powers which were beyond his grasp and which kept him in awe, nor on their mediators. He lived by himself and for himself; he devoted himself to the living of life. He felt responsible both for himself and for the city-state. His essential aim in life was no longer the service and glorification of a supreme power. In an organised, free society where religion offered everyday contact with gods who were not unlike himself, the citizen found his justification in pleasure, and so in the refinements of life. The freedom of time, industry, and capital which royal art had produced was to permit the growth of civic art. This was to be art that had almost nothing to do with its original magic function, an art which was used sparingly for religious purposes and which was intended essentially to embellish everyday life.

This was a decisive step forward. Art suddenly became free and independent, and with the classical era, the idea of beauty—which up till this time had been only a part of the creative instinct and which was now seized upon by philosophers—took shape. In the Athens of the 5th and 4th centuries, philosophers and artists kept company. Plato, supposed to have been a painter in his youth, points this out in his *Dialogues* in regard to Socrates who was said to have been a sculptor. Art ceased to be exclusively functional; it even went beyond the stage of a

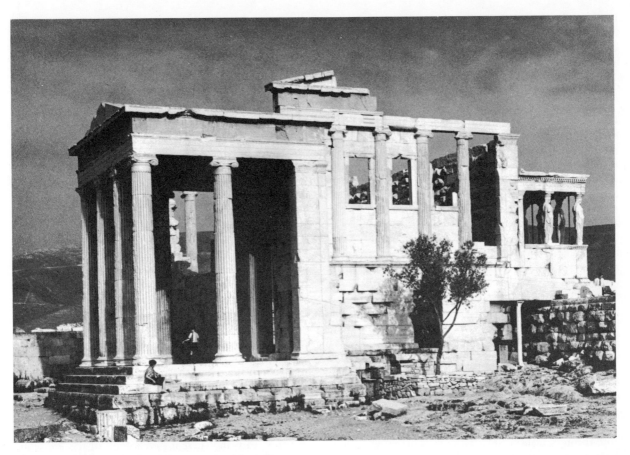

428. GREEK. IONIC. The Erechtheum on the Acropolis, Athens. Beginning of the 5th century B.C.

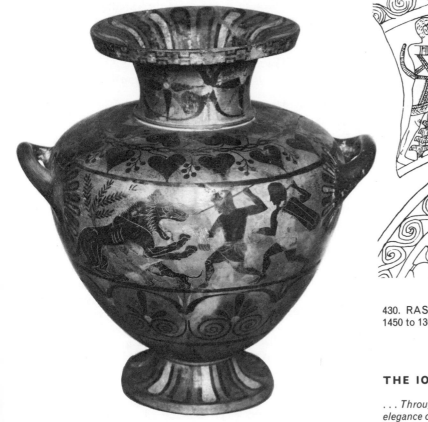

429. GREEK. Hydria from Caere, Ionian style. *Louvre.*

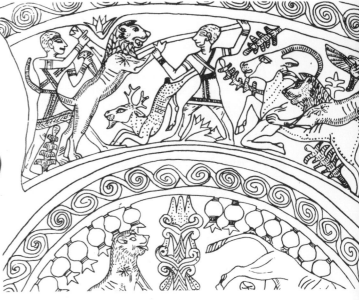

430. RAS SHAMRA. Detail from a drawing of a gold cup. 1450 to 1365 B.C.

THE IONIAN SPIRIT

. . . Through the Ionian Greeks something of the flexible elegance of Asia [430] and its vivid hunting scenes [429, 430] was absorbed, and the Ionians, too, were responsible for the introduction of voluted palmettes and capitals [428].

237

luxurious art dedicated to a diety or a monarch to discover that it could be enjoyed for itself. Democritus had already called to mind the pleasure produced by looking at works of art, and Aristotle was to say more explicitly: 'The beautiful is that which is desirable *in itself*.' For this reason alone Greece would have opened a new era.

515, 519 Pericles was aware of its potential danger and abuse. He only attached so much importance to the Panathenaea so that beauty should once again be made to serve the religious and civic ends of the community. After him, Plato was worried by the appearance of the 'dilettantes': we would call them 'aesthetes'. 'These people who have a passion for fine music and plays,' he wrote in the *Republic*, 'eagerly go in search of beautiful voices, colours and form, and all works of art in which these elements are present.' It is why, in his idea of 'the beautiful in itself' interdependent with 'the good', in his concern to teach men to perceive its real nature and conform to it, he showed his anxiety to check the rise of artistic pleasure as an end in itself, cultivated solely for the enjoyment it gave and released from all religious and moral obligations. This reaction can be compared to the attack on the Sophists who held, in the sphere of philosophy, that thought, similarly, was an end in itself.

Art in accord with reality

Greek art, from this time, was to be essentially and consciously conceived with the idea of giving 'delight' to the spectator and was to seek to stimulate this delight both through realism and harmony. Whether we turn to Plato or Aristotle, or later to Xenocrates of Sicyon, the 3rd-century sculptor who wrote a treatise on painting and sculpture which remained, it seems, of basic importance for the Romans, we are struck by the root nature of the idea that art is above all the skill to render the visual appearance of things. Mimesis (imitation) is the formative rule both for Plato and Aristotle; but let it be noted that when Plato observes this fact it is only to deplore it, and to see precisely in this the inferiority of art and its inability to achieve true beauty, which is ideal. Anecdotes of the great painters which have been handed down to us are rapturous in praise of their virtuosity in *trompe l'œil* (birds tricked into coming to peck at the grapes painted by Zeuxis, or Alexander's horse neighing in front of its own picture).

François Chamoux recalls later in this chapter how the demand of realism led to elaborate attempts at illusion in the painting of statues whose present-day condition is so far removed from what it once was.

This basic realism was an inevitable consequence of the change in society. The new man, the citizen, was becoming aware of his personal responsibilities. He stopped being the obedient toy of natural forces and human powers which were beyond his grasp and were codified in those rites and traditions which he had had merely to observe year in and year out. He judged and decided for himself. He relied only on himself. That is to say, every known fact came initially through what he perceived and observed, i.e. through his senses. In the 6th century Heraclitus put first-hand investigation in the place of inherited beliefs, and stated, 'the eyes are better witnesses than the ears'. Individual observation, particularly through sight, was after all especially important for a seafaring people continuously forced through unpre-

dictable and urgent events to act on their own initiative.

All this is borne out—since the art and thought of a period are interdependent—by the fact that the first Greek thinkers, the Eleatic philosophers of the 7th and 6th centuries, the real founders of philosophy, were above all natural philosophers who looked for the causes of phenomena by questioning experience and ruling out myth and mystery. On this point they were dependent on those well-known facts which above all they took from maritime and meteorological knowledge, seeking the secret of things in the observation of the familiar world around them—in analogies based on the evaporation of water, on cloud formation, on the lightning flash, etc. The herdsmen and farmers of Egypt and Mesopotamia, in their earliest attempts to gain knowledge, relied on little beyond their observation of the heavenly bodies. Later, in the great urban centres, such as Athens at the time of Socrates, the sense of observation, less concerned with nature than with man, was to turn in the direction of close self-examination arrived at through reflection. Both culture and art came to be based more and more firmly on man's knowledge of himself.

But this man was a citizen and not an isolated being. He was man as a social entity and not yet an individual with all the mystery that this idea was to produce in regard to the uniqueness and peculiarity of the inner being. He was man as a type, classical and average; between him and the modern introvert there is the same gap as that which separates the *Characters* of Theophrastus from the current psychology of the individual being. He felt repugnance towards anything which set other people apart. Without citing the tough collective mould of Sparta, we can recall the distrust and enmity which the Athenean reserved for the exceptional individual. The archons were not elected but were chosen by lot; and exile and ostracism, if not death, were reserved for the man who, like Socrates, distinguished himself from his fellow citizens. Such were to be the greatness and the limitations of man's discovery of man.

Art in accord with reason

But this initial sketch would be lacking in an essential feature if it were not pointed out that the Greeks, whose country provided only moderate resources in the way of hunting and agriculture, were primarily seafaring traders, successors to the Creto-Mycenaeans, competing with the Phoenicians as far afield as—and especially along—the Spanish coast. It was a prologue to the more dramatic struggle which was to take place between their heirs, the Romans and the Carthaginians.

The farmer had his roots in traditions which, like his land, were older than memory itself; the trader was perpetually engaged in human change and exchange. If in addition he was a sailor, his range of rough comparisons was extended. How many Greeks would have been able to say along with Democritus, 'No one has travelled more widely than I, seen more countries or climates, nor heard more conversations from the lips of learned men.' 'Heard,' and consequently compared . . . What weight have myths, and folkways and customs in face of that constant lesson in relativity? The intelligence, continually driven from refuges where it might have grown torpid, surges on and grows sharper. Religion expands, makes itself acceptable and seeks some kind of middle term,

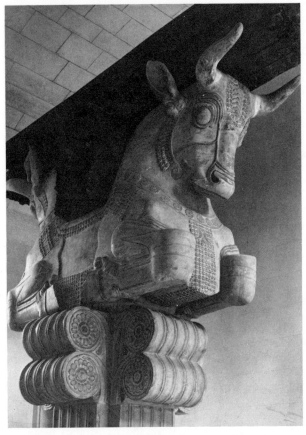

431. PERSIAN. Capital of a column from the palace of Artaxerxes at Susa. 464–358 B.C. *Louvre.*

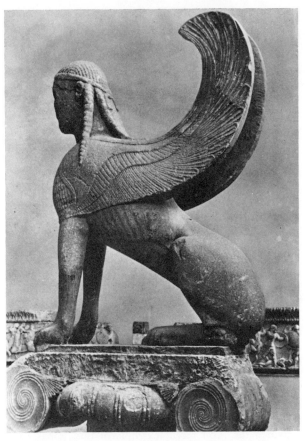

433. GREEK. The great Naxian sphinx. Originally set on a marble column 30 feet high. c. 575 B.C.

HUMANISM AND ANIMAL CULTS

Although the Greeks were strongly aware of Persia and Persian art, they confronted the East with a new spirit, the spirit of the West. The reign of the huge and formidable beast, the embodiment of the forces of terror [431], was over. Now man felt on an equal footing with the world of nature, but no sooner had he won this peace than it became tinged with a gentle sense of sorrow [434]. When the Greeks did adopt Asian monsters [432], copying certain details like the sickle-shaped wings which were to disappear in later years, they could not help making them more 'familiar' by giving them a human face [433].

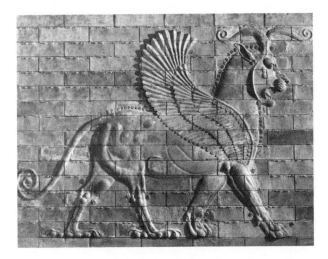

432. PERSIAN. ACHAEMENIAN. Winged lion with horns. Glazed brick from Susa. *Louvre.*

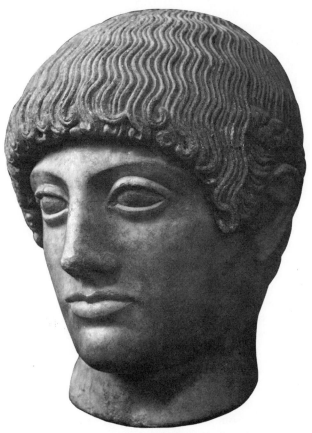

434. GREEK. Head of a youth. 500–490 B.C. *Acropolis Museum, Athens.*

239

some form of syncretism. Very soon there was an attempt to isolate the constant factors in human life, the permanent foundation, and to strip away the emotional elements, in order to uncover a basic ground of understanding. The intellect set out to find the most important common denominators. The Cretans had already progressed from hieroglyphics to linear script; the Phoenicians, who succeeded to their enormous Mediterranean trade, had evolved an abstract alphabet. The Greeks went further, to the very essence of the matter; they stripped down the mental framework to reach the pure, intellectual mechanism common to all men within the outer layer of the local and particular. This was reason, and the laws which governed its working were the rules of logic, which were to find their definitive expression in Aristotle.

In this way the intellectual system was formulated, a system which was to remain fundamental to the West and was to be reinstated in all its power by 19th-century science. (Lavoisier and Auguste Comte cited Aristotle as their authority.) Reason, by applying the permanent laws of logic to material supplied through the senses and constituting the sole experience of objectivity, disentangled the truth. In art this was to be the principle of classicism: to reproduce nature as it appeared, but to correct it in accordance with intellectual standards.

Such an attitude runs a grave risk and invariably ends by falling a victim to impoverishment through a narrow conformity to pattern and to rules. The intellectual aridity of Jacques Louis David and his followers has provided the most recent example of this. It has been called, very unfairly, 'academicism', after Plato's school.

Plato averted this danger by keeping a place for poetry. By ruling out the particular, he renounced the temporal and the futilities of 'not being', in favour of a scale that rose progressively towards Absolute Purity and the Idea; transcending the powers of the senses and even of the intelligence, it laid the foundations for the concepts of the Universal and the Absolute, and thus prepared the way for that of the Divine. For this power to transcend the purely rational and mechanical, he acknowledged the gift of creativity, i.e. inspiration. He invoked it in the name of Eros, Love. In the *Phaedrus* he makes its connection with art more explicit: 'The man who should arrive at the doors of artistic creation with none of *the madness of the Muses*, would be convinced that technical ability alone was enough to make an artist . . . what that man creates by means of reason will pale before the art of inspired beings.' It is true that in Plato there remains a certain longing for mystery and myths which he revived for their power as images; they are like perfume from the East, which he had come so near to visiting on his travels. Later, his successors, the Neo-Platonists, were to adopt this use of myths.

There was no need for art to have risked overstepping the natural boundaries of the Greek genius; the nature of its sensitivity meant that it could reach the level of poetry without abandoning its basic realism. It arrived at that level by the single perfection of harmony.

So Greek art took shape. Based on the idea of accurate truth to appearances, it made them subject to the most subtle rules of rational thought; but more than this, the ideas of verisimilitude and logic were transcended and reconciled in their singleness of purpose: to give pleasure to the eye and the mind.

So it is (to make use once more of an often-quoted example) in the architecture of the Parthenon, where everything is so directly adapted to the building's function and the clear arrangement of its parts that the most important horizontal, the horizontal of the roof, is curved very slightly inwards; it was meant, in this way, to correct the tension of the perspective and to restore the harmony that might otherwise have been jeopardised. In that exquisitely sensitive perception, in its never-satisfied quest for excellence, in its poetry whose substance is neither reality nor reason, lies the unforgettable triumph of Greek art.

The path followed by art

Is it now possible to estimate what progressive stages art went through before it could arrive at that point of understanding and accomplishment, as rational as it was sensitive? Primitive man remained vulnerable in a mysterious world where chaotic forces were at work. He had to divert and ward off the threats of some, inveigle the goodwill of others; in an effective way, he had to impose something of himself in terms of his body, his wishes and intelligence, and by so doing guarantee his life. What we call art was for him a means of ensuring a certain degree of control over forces which eluded his weak and inadequate physical grasp. He could in fact, by making an imaginative representation of these forces, free himself of them for ever, without stress or struggle.

At a very early stage that representation was executed in the two ways open to it: on the one hand by means of a reproduction that was as accurate, as suggestive of visible appearances as it could be, by means of 'likeness'—and this was the path of realism; on the other hand by means of a conventional equivalent, a symbol based on analogy—and therefore something which the mind rather than the eye could understand. This was the stylised, conventional form, but one endowed with a meaning: the symbol, easily converted into a pattern by virtue of its abstract structure and regular simplicity.

The geometric decorative sign, because of the very facility with which it could be produced, was bound to keep its important position among the least skilled civilisations, termed 'barbarian' by the others, and chiefly those civilisations in Europe which had remained prehistoric in spite of the discovery of metals like bronze and iron. The Mediterranean civilisations, proud of their growing technical dexterity, opted rather for realism, which they were continually trying to perfect. While keeping a place for the symbol, which was becoming more a purely linear decoration, Egypt and Mesopotamia, the great agrarian empires, concentrated on the art of the double or replica: the replica of a god in statue form which guaranteed his jealously guarded presence; the replica of the devout man fixed for all eternity in acts of worship or of making an offering, which were thus ensured of being efficacious; replicas of creatures or things without which the dead man would be unable to live happily in the hereafter.

Very soon the sovereigns of these empires (and this extended increasingly to the nobles who surrounded them) discovered a new use for this skill in making replicas. When an event passed away and was lost in time, it could be kept alive in the memory by the making of a picture of it. Commemorative art, the earliest example

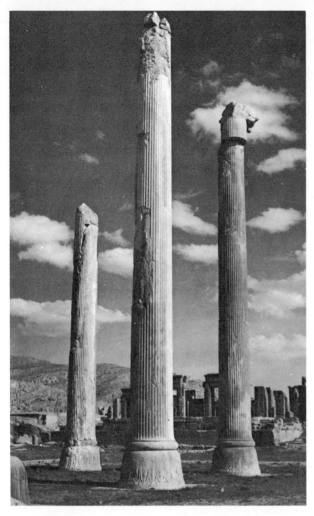

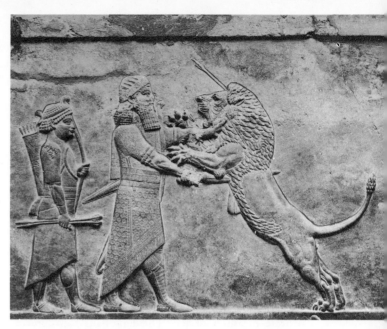

436. ASSYRIAN. Hunting scene, detail from a bas-relief. 6th century B.C. *British Museum.*

GREECE AND PERSIA

Two worlds, two souls: in Persia the vast architectural scale [435] vanishes into the boundless distance, while the disciplined harmony of the Greek temple [437] finds its setting in the countryside's well-defined boundaries; similarly, the bloodthirsty exploits of kings slaughtering wild beasts (at first real and later symbolic), taken from Assyria [436] by the Achaemenian Persians [438], gives place to the quiet meditation of a thoughtful Athena [439].

435. PERSIAN. Ruins of Persepolis. Achaemenian period.

437. GREEK. Detail of columns of the temple of Aphaia at Aegina. *c.* 480 B.C.

438. *Below left.* PERSIAN. ACHAEMENIAN. Darius fighting a monster. Here the king is a 'superman' attacking an evil spirit.

439. *Below right.* GREEK. The Mourning Athena. Before 450 B.C. *Acropolis Museum, Athens.*

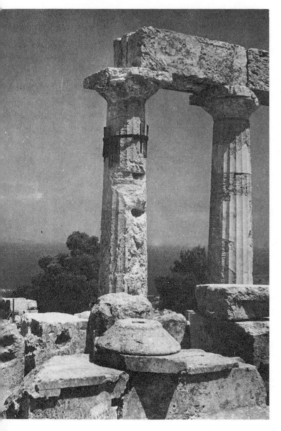

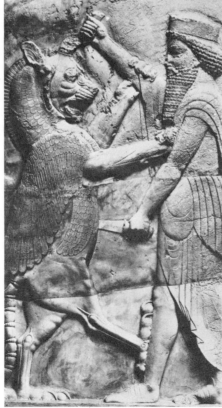

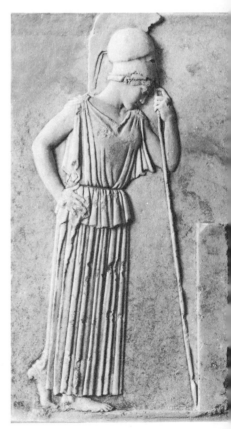

of which is found perhaps in the prehistoric paintings of eastern Spain and of Africa, thus preserved for the future, mostly in the lasting and flexible form of the bas-relief, a particular battle in honour of the king, then, as much for his enjoyment as honour, some hunting episodes recording one of the most memorable pleasures of his life. (It is not, moreover, beyond the bounds of possibility that the struggle against wild animals, like that against men, had been the chief duty of the protector-leader.) So art was learning to immortalise essential human activity, just as literature was turning towards the epic.

But art did not then emerge from the province of those powers; once it had ensnared and tamed them it celebrated 436, 438 them, for war and hunting still represented the practice and intoxicating display of powers that were the prerogatives of men. The highly developed and refined Cretans, following the same path, were to celebrate the more delicate pleasures of life. The Egyptians had depicted these joys in lifelike scenes called for by their funeral rites. The Cretans, increasingly dedicated to pleasure, portrayed the prince holding a lily, walking peacefully among the flowers in his garden. Hedonism was taking shape, the first form of aestheticism, which in the strict sense of the word (Greek aisthetikos: perceptive), describes an 'art of the senses'.

Greek art, reduced under the impact of the Dorians to 425 a form of symbolic stylisation, was, with geometric art, to retrace rapidly the road of representation—initially of magico-religious significance (as François Chamoux will point out, vestiges of this were to survive), later straight-forwardly hedonistic. For the first time man had found a way of life in which he had achieved a balance with the external forces of the universe and had, by explanation, dispersed their oppressive mystery; he had reached the point where the sheer pleasures of being and living could flourish freely. He could, at last, turn nis thoughts towards himself.

Greece and Persia: for and against humanism

So, little by little, man drew back the curtain of threatening shadows and finally came to establish himself as the centre of light and interest. As has often been stressed, the art which appeared in Greece was a humanist art.

It was humanist in subject matter: it put an end to the reign of the animal which had been initiated in the Palaeolithic, in hunting magic. This reign of the animal had continued in the animal totems which, in the Egyptian nomes, became an actual pantheon of gods. It had been kept alive because of the priority of hunting among regal and princely pleasures from the time of the pharaohs and the Assyrian potentates down to the Achaean lords of the period following the Cretan interlude. Man no longer felt obliged to assert himself by demonstrating the superiority of his strength over a defeated animal; he dared to think that it was enough for him to be and to know himself. True, representations of human beings had made their appearance in the Aurignacian, but, mostly depicting the female form, they were merely magic fertility symbols. 434 Now the human being was portrayed for his own sake, for his beauty, which had become art's sole theme.

So here we have the first opposition to Persian art. The 431, 432 Persians had maintained that animal tradition, so meticulously elaborated by the Egyptians and Mesopotamians, which was later to be passed on via Luristan and the

Scythians towards the north and the Asian steppes and from there to be carried eastwards to China, and then into Europe. It finally reached Europe with the great wave of barbarian invasions and eventually pervaded, owing to the link with Byzantium, the entire medieval Christian world with its bestiaries and its collections of Romanesque and Gothic monsters.

Yet Greek art was also humanist in a more fundamental way, because it made man 'the measure of all things', as Protagoras, during the second half of the 5th century, stated in his famous definition. Man became the measure of all things, not in any empirical or practical sense, as in Egypt and Chaldea, but, as it were, in a philosophic sense. It was in relation to man that the world was measured: it was in relation to man that it was explained, and so the universe, freed of everything that was inhuman, mysterious and threatening, seemed everywhere to hold his reflection.

Persian art, on the other hand, sought not to link itself to the human scale but to go beyond it. While Greek art 435 intended to reduce everything complex and confused to an intelligible distinct unity, the former brought into play the idea of the 'innumerable' in order to suggest the feeling of infinity where all thought vanished. So we find the same monotonous figure (such as an archer) repeated 177, 178 inexhaustibly as far as the eye can see, merging bewilderingly into an ensemble to which there seems no end.

While everything for the Greek centred on a rational and unified truth reached through close harmony of body 439 and mind, of the physical and mental working together, the Persian gave to future thought a dualism based on the opposite attraction of poles, the eternal struggle between good and evil and the endless antagonism of spirituality and sensuality which Christianity, through its original connection with the East, was again to take up as the conflict between body and soul.

This desire for unity impelled the Greeks to achieve its visual expression through emphasis on form and therefore on contour, which defines form and brings it into relief. The Persians, however, were bewitched by everything expansive, by the splendour of colour and by gold and light. This contrast has many consequences: form satisfies, strengthens and confirms the intelligence; colour and light, on the other hand, have a mysterious effect on the nervous system and the sensibilities which still remains unexplained. While Greek art, then, aimed to give complete satisfaction to the mind's taste for positive clarity, Persian art opened the way for the disturbing power of suggestion. It would use this power in the service of mystic revelation, which is beyond the grasp of pure intelligence, and later this power would appear in Byzantine art in which the heritages of Greece and the Near East merged. But with Greece and Persia in opposition, we have reached the time when these two basic and incompatible movements, which we shall discover again and again throughout the course of art history, were determined.

The natural environments of these two peoples confirmed them in their vocations. The scale of the Greek countryside, easily encompassed by the eye, and the sea, 437 which was never very far away, undoubtedly helped towards man's smooth establishment of himself at the very heart of things, things which, in future, were to be subordinate to him. The Persian, swallowed up in the

CHINESE. Bronze funerary vessel [yu] representing a man protected by a tiger. Shang Dynasty. Musée Cernuschi, Paris. *Photo: Michael Holford.*

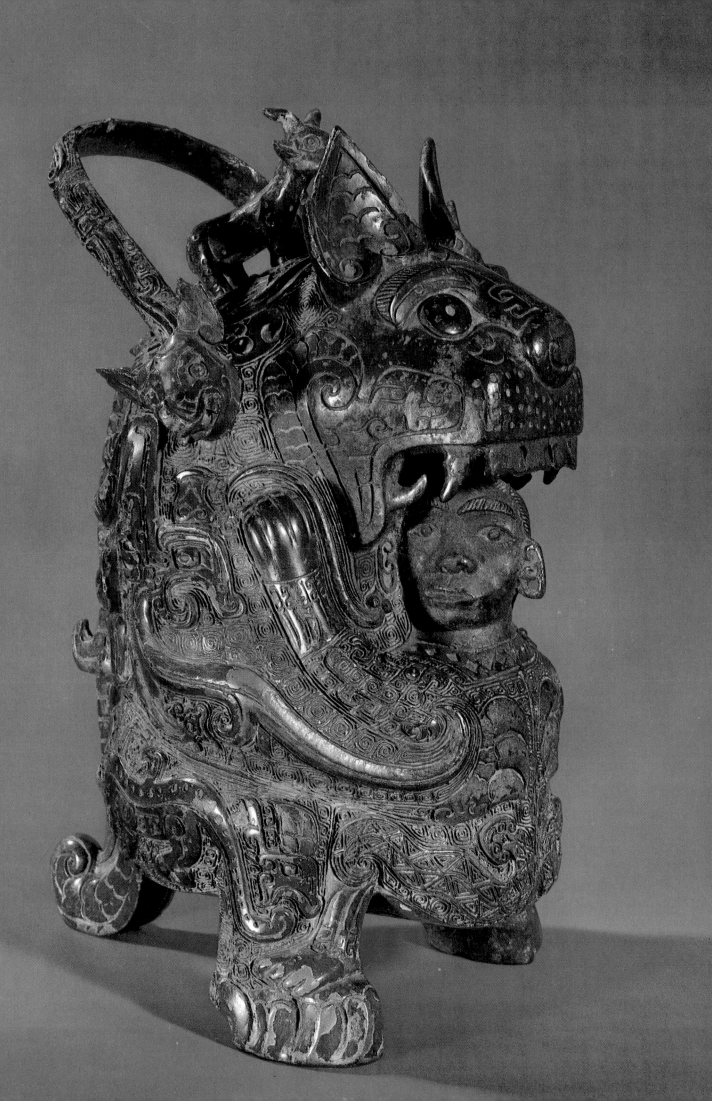

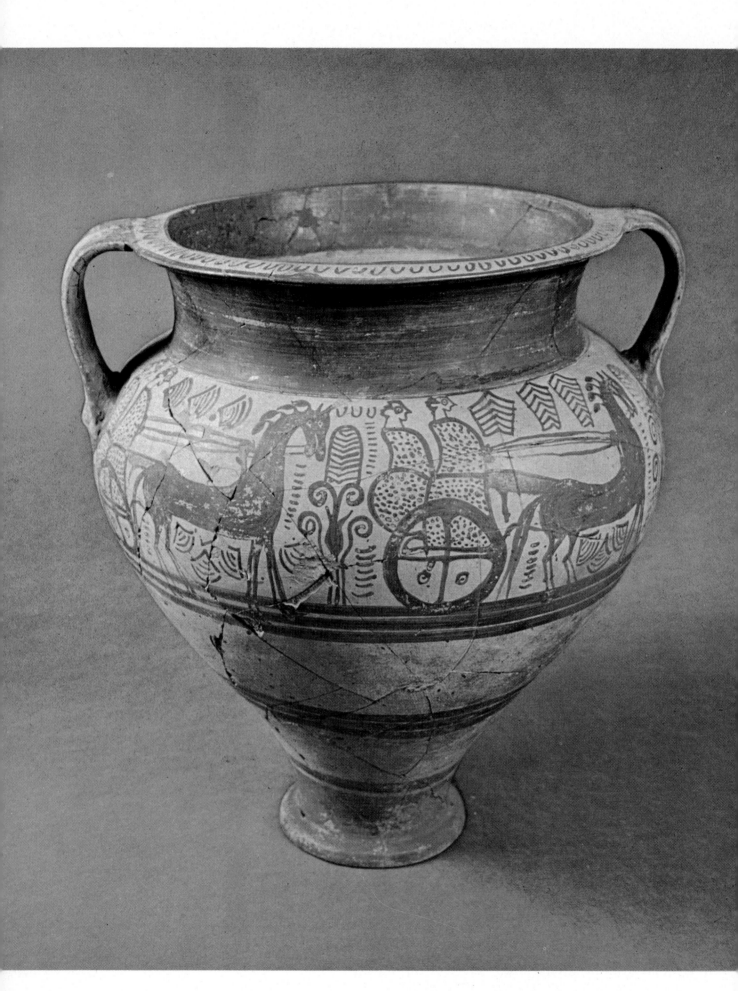

GREEK. Late Helladic krater from Cyprus. *c.* 1350 B.C. British Museum. *Museum photograph.*

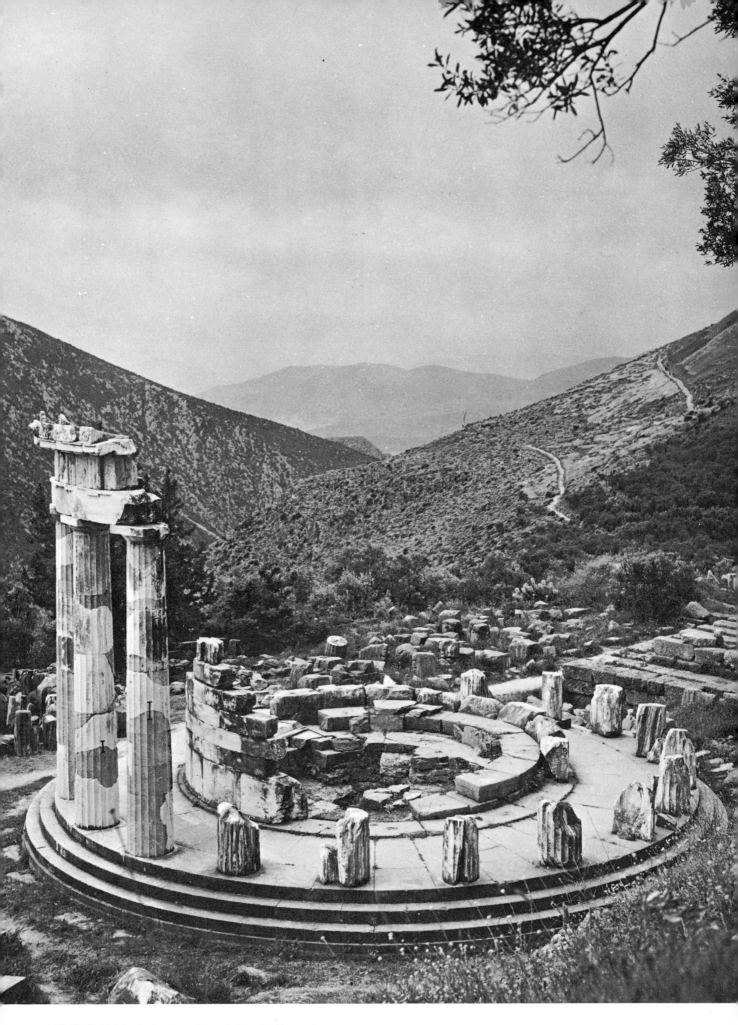

440. GREEK. The tholos (round temple) on the Marmaria
terrace, Delphi.

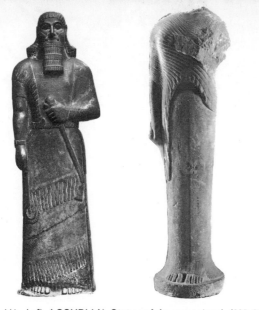

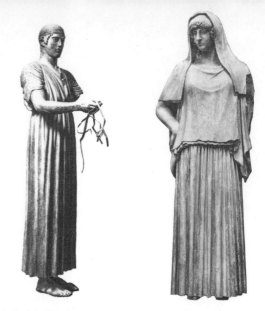

441. *Left*. ASSYRIAN. Statue of Assurnasirpal. (885–860 B.C.)

442. *Right*. Hera of Samos. *c*. 540–520 B.C. *Louvre*.

443. *Left*. GREEK. The Delphic Charioteer. Bronze. *c*. 470 B.C.

444. *Right*. GREEK. Hestia. 460 B.C. Roman copy. *Museo dei Conservatori*, Rome.

vastness of the empire, toiled along roads which stretched from horizon to horizon; he lived his life on the great desert plateaux, but he was almost unaware of where the roads led or of what lay beyond the horizons.

So the Greek, restricted by his natural surroundings, always moved towards a centre of security where he could feel at home. He rejected both the too large and the too small, and this search for the 'middle way', from which the entire Aristotelian ethic was to be drawn, brought him back inevitably to man, since it was only in relation to him that things were judged to be large or small. It was Aristotle himself who thought of applying this attitude to art and to the proportions proper to the sculptor and the architect. The Persian, on the other hand, remained true to imperial megalomania; he never tired of the gigantic, which impressed man because it overwhelmed him and reduced him to nothing. The height and vastness of the Persian palace halls and the inexhaustible repetition of columns aimed to dwarf the person who entered. The dream of Babylon, handed down through the Bible, of a Tower of Babel which would have touched the heavens was the symbol of Persian ambition; the Greek would have been able only too well to accept the moral of its ultimate failure. Is this not the very significance of the Median wars in which that sense of human proportion, dear to the Hellenes, succeeded in destroying the excesses represented by the colossus?

Nature clarified through form

But what Hellenism tried to overcome or to rule out, both in philosophy and art, was the very thing which most eluded man's nature and understanding; it was not solely the infinite and immeasurable but the elusive idea of flux. There lay the world's real mystery, the threshold which human understanding could not cross. Greek art and thought only found a final standpoint in 5th- and 4th-century Attica. Prior to this, the first great Ionian thinkers had grappled with these two troublesome ideas. The problem of the infinite had already been broached by Anaximander and Anaximenes, and that of eternal flux by Heraclitus; until everything whirled and spun, he leaned over that abyss into which, in later years, the Greeks refused to look; he juggled with everything that was most opposed to rational understanding: the coex-

istence of opposites, and the perpetual passing and change of things which by their very nature were unstable and fleeting. None of this was to be followed up, and later generations were to call him 'the obscure one'. Subsequently the sole endeavour of Greek thought, and this affected Greek art, was to make the world intelligible: in other words to make it conform to the laws of reason and to reduce the infinite or unlimited to that order and unity formulated by Plato. We should not, however, forget, at the risk of misunderstanding this early achievement from which this discipline was to emerge, that Plato's master, Cratylus, was thought to have improved on Heraclitus. But Greece's main task lay in another direction. Everything that was not open to definition or analysis was to be steadily ruled out by the exercise of the intellect, so that the mind could have full authority. Aristotle was to come to challenge the idea of eternal flux which Heraclitus had perceived with such intensity. According to Aristotle, every activity moves from an initial state to a perfected state which brings about the actualisation of substantial form which, in its turn, becomes a final cause. In the same way in art movement took second place to form, and thus the mysterious power of the elusive was exorcised. Here began that clarity of thought which, ever since, has been both the prerogative and the aspiration of the West. It was bound to find its essential reflection in art for, as Plato stated in his *Timaeus*, through art 'one is brought, without being aware of it, to move closer to, to love and to be in agreement with, the beauty of reason.'

Art and thought worked along parallel paths. In the sphere of thought, definitions were extracted from the endless and shifting confusion presented by the world: that is to say, ideas which were clear-cut, precise and of lasting value, disentangled from all confusion and, within their own terms, definitive. In the sphere of art, forms were found which answered the same demands. It should not be forgotten that to the Greek the word for 'idea' (*eidos*) had the additional and root meaning of 'image'. We know from texts that the art of painting was primarily a question of delineating contour (the black figures of the vases gain almost their entire effect from the sharp relief of outline), and only after that of applying colour and shading.

435

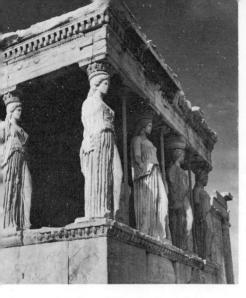

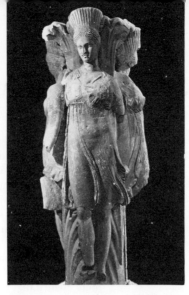

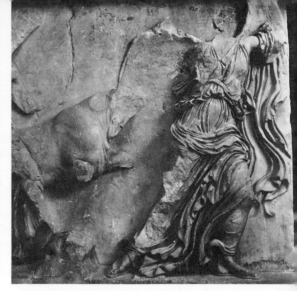

445. Caryatids on the Erechtheum.
c. 440–430 B.C.

446. Dancers from an acanthus
column. Marble. First quarter of the
4th century B.C.

447. Victory leading a bull. Parapet of
temple of Athena Nike. c. 420 B.C.
Acropolis Museum, Athens.

Nature explained through number

But contour, like definition, is limited to making concrete something one wants to grasp; it offers no explanation. It must, therefore, be completed by an analysis of its interior working which should make it appear consistent to reason. The outward investigation initiated by the mind at this early stage was to be completed, therefore, by a more important inward investigation. For the thinker it was instituted by logical analysis and for the artist, by the establishment of a system of relationships and proportions which carried the laws of the intellect within the very framework of the work of art. 'A work of art,' Lucian was to say, 'demands an intelligent observer who would not be satisfied with visual enjoyment, but who would also reason out what he saw.'

513 Polycleitus had written a treatise on his art, devoted to a system of proportions of the human body. Architecture and sculpture soon revealed that their harmony relied on a numerical system of relationships.

We speak of a 'numerical system'. In fact, the artist's attempt to make the accidental appearance of things presented by the chances of Nature conform to the conceptions of the mind was shown in the earliest times through geometric stylisation. We have already noted this stylisa-
9 tion in the Aurignacian Venuses and we shall find it
316 again in pre-Hellenistic art in the Cycladic idols, which
318 were reduced to simplified planes cut into rectangles and ovals. The Greek spirit was not satisfied with this solution. Geometric stylisation could develop only at the expense of realism since it substituted arbitrary abstract form for natural appearance. Now, as we have seen, mimesis was of basic importance in Greek art. How, then, were the Greeks to uphold realism and yet make form subject to intellectual ideas? They did it by substituting mathematics for geometry and by merely regulating the visible appearances by a flexible calculation of relationships, which sprang from the same principle. This attempt was the reflection, in terms of art, of a comparable wish that Greek philosophy had often had, to explain the world by means of a secret arithmetic, to clarify it through numbers.

In the 6th century Pythagoras seemed, in his metaphysical system, to have elaborated those principles which were later to govern art: this involved the transition from geometry to numerical relationships conditioning figures and the introduction of harmonic proportions. It was to introduce into thought, in contrast to the

Ionian attempt to explain the universe with material sense perception as its starting point, the opposing attitude, which made the universe follow from totally abstract, almost mathematical, principles. In fact, Greek philosophy was to waver between these two methods of finding the truth—the one relying on the senses, the other on pure rationalism. There was no attempt to reconcile these two incompatible attitudes until Aristotle stated that the general, logical ideas governing both were arrived at by the activity of the intelligence which itself was based on the initial contribution of the senses.

The Greek philosophers were to overcome this dualism only with great difficulty in the 4th century, but the Greek artists were to make it the very basis of their achievement. This achievement, in fact, came into being through the synthesis of these two attitudes. The convinced realism of Greek art led to an untiring search for more flexibility and refinement with which to reproduce what was seen by the eye; yet the Greek artist reduced that external truth, without any distortion, to an entirely intellectual combination of rhythm and proportion which could be clarified and justified by number. In the same way the architect was concerned with the close reconciliation of what we shall call 'the functional' and with proprotions.

So man, placed face to face with art for the first time, meant to bring it to fruition without ever disclaiming himself; he pursued it in a spirit of truth which held fast to what he had seen with his own eyes, and in a spirit of logical, harmonious unity which was the purest expression of the demands of his reason. While he understood that achievement could only come through transcendence, he did not try to find it in a sphere beyond those solid facts permitted to man, but in an ever growing, ever more exacting perfection, which compelled him not to undervalue himself but to pursue infinitely whatever he possessed only in the shape of desire and potentiality. It was this idea of boundless progress and untiring perfectionism which saved Greek art from the aridity in which many of its imitators have left it, for, to use the language of mathematicians, 'it stretches to infinity', to that infinity which, once discovered, is perfect beauty. 'It is then, if ever, my dear Socrates,' as Plato wrote in the *Symposium*, 'that a man's life is worth living, when he looks on that which is beautiful in itself . . . simple, pure, distinct, no longer tainted by human flesh, by colour and by all these mortal inanities.'

245

THE ORIGINS OF GREEK ART *Charles Picard*

*In years past there was talk of the 'Greek miracle' and
the term remains valid if we are thinking not so much
of the problem of how archaic Greece began but of its
marvellous achievement in the sphere of art. Charles
Picard, one of the greatest authorities on this subject,
analyses the complex factors in the emergence of
Archaic Greek art and shows how it is only in recent years
that the pre-Hellenic tradition, in contrast to the 'barbaric'
contribution of the Dorians, has proved to be
of the utmost importance.*

Dogmatism finds a more fertile ground in which to thrive
in periods which history and art books have mistakenly
ignored throughout the years. It was universally assumed
that primitive Greece only began to stir again with the
arrival of the Dorians. Also, all the claims made to explain
the emergence of the new Greece were tinged with 'to-
talitarian' overtones: everything was put down, for example, to the influence of Crete, or of the Ionians or the
Dorians, according to the whim of the particular modern
commentator. What we shall try to do here is to discuss
impartially the comparative rights and merits of the theories of pan-Cretanism, pan-Daedalism and pan-Hittitism,
as well as those increasingly futile controversies that have
not even put the preliminary pan-Ionian versus pan-
Dorian contest in the background where it belongs. We
must also bear in mind the claims of those people who
are at the moment trying to expand the record of Phoenician trading and extend the activity of this extraordinarily eclectic people to beyond the end of the 2nd millennium and outside the boundaries of the Near East.

The origins of the new Greece

The only real problem is to do our best to avoid the
many forms of uncompromising extremism so as to be
able to restore where necessary to Telepinus as well as
Cadmus and to Dido as well as the Ionian Theseus, the
'law-giver' and lover of Ariadne, and even, indeed, to
Homer, whatever is their respective due. Perhaps the
genus irritabile of scholars and art historians (whom we
sometimes like to look upon as the high priests of modern
times) would have thrown up a less baffling crop of contradictions if only it had been possible—without prejudice
and without losing sight of the everyday life of the tiny
Hellenic nation from its beginnings—to parcel out the
share of influences with a little more wisdom so that we
might have reached a better idea of the different forms of
nascent originality: that delight in living freely and in
looking the world in the face and that new spiritual
potential that first made its appearance in the rather sharp
Hellenic springtime, but so much more forcefully than it
had ever done elsewhere. In this chapter we shall watch it
growing in strength throughout a period of five centuries;
it was never again to disappear from this world in which
we live.

Otfried Müller had the Dorians marching into Sparta,
where he settled them securely all over that large peninsula which Sophocles still insisted on calling the 'Island
of Pelops'. Now Pelops was an Anatolian: true, he had
to stoop to treachery in order to gain favour for himself
as a wealthy foreigner at Pisa-Olympia among the out-
worn privileges and decaying palaces of Oenomaus, who
only with the greatest reluctance consented to become
his father-in-law and died for it. The truth of the matter
was that Hippodamia, the heiress to the palace, impatient
to start living her own life, had secretly favoured their
visitor with her smiles; now, he had probably managed
to secure into the bargain the treacherous servant Myr-
tilus, a local charioteer, as an accomplice to help him put
his underhand plans into effect during the race. It is not
mere chance that this name should be curiously reminiscent of Mursilis, the name of some of the Hittite kings.
Were there not similar connections between the name of
Telepinus and Telephus who returned to Mysia from
Arcadia with his mother, Auge, who later became a
mother goddess in Asia? The mountainous land of
Arcadia, 'as ancient as the moon', was precisely the place
that was supposed to have escaped the elusive Dorians.

As for the Eurotas valley at the foot of the forbidding
Taygetus Mountains, if its countryside and moors had
been able to hold some of the problematical 'invaders'
from the Balkans, it still kept, from Vaphio to Amyclae,
a past that was even more strongly pervaded by the Oriental influences of pre-Hellenic times. Had it not been, at
the time of the Trojan War, the Homeric fief of Menelaus,
the bewildered husband of Helen of Sparta who one day
unconcernedly transferred her household to the palace
of Priam and Paris in Troy? Amyclaean Apollo, helmeted,
horned and bearded lover of the fated Hyacinthius,
showed a kinship with Ionian and Carian Anatolia and
with Cyprus. When the last migrants to arrive from the
north found most of the land overcrowded and set off
once more from the Peloponnese, it was not by pure
chance that they steered towards the Levant, to such
islands as Thera and Rhodes, and to Halicarnassus. This
ethnic movement, undoubtedly less ominous than the
movements that still cause continual earth tremors in the
Aegean, had come to an end by the latter part of the
9th century. But Sparta and Olympia, in any case, had
given up none of the customs during this time of colonising Anatolia. In Laconia it was the practice down to
classical times to celebrate the Lydian procession in the
sanctuary of Orthia-Aotis, the 'Oriental goddess'. The
dances and initiation ceremonies called for by this goddess (so very like the Phrygian Cybele, the great mother
of Ephesus, and Leucophryene of Magnesia) were significantly suggestive of Oriental rites. For many years artists
and poets (Alcman, Bathycles, etc.), brought from Sardis
and Magnesia, did not feel they were living as exiles on
the banks of the Eurotas. The huge altar of ashes was
always kept at Olympia, just like the altars of the Di-
dymaeum at Miletus. The Bronze House at Sparta had
figured revetments that copied the distant gates of the
Balawat temple, the pride of Urartu. We are forced to
admit that there is nothing to be found in the pseudo-
northern contribution that might be brought to balance,
in terms of time and space, these Anatolian influences;
moreover, we should remember that the first examples of
the megaron were found at Troy and the first Mycenaean
tholoi at Arpachiyah a few miles from Nineveh.

Beyond the persistent and surviving traces of Crete and the Anatolian world—from Phrygia to Lycia—where will we find stylistic and artistic principles that might really be part of the contribution of the Dorian conquerors? Almost the only point upon which there is complete agreement is that these nomadic tribes professed contempt for art and that when they armed themselves for their raids they boasted that they could plough only with their spears.

The earliest architecture

After the changes of the year 1200, nothing of the pre-Hellenic past was forgotten in Greece. The Artemisium at Ephesus, built on the Anatolian slopes, with a history that can be traced from at least 800 and to which the Cretan Chersiphron of Cnossus, one of the first-known Greek builders (along with the Samians, Rhoecus and Theodorus) added new features (on the pattern of the Asian megaron), had once been a vast, open-air temenos where the sacred tree was worshipped with dances, incantations and sacrifices. Sacred places at Didyma and Dodona had, like this, originally been set in the open air. The Delphinium at Miletus and the Delium at Paros, as well as many other places of worship, were to remain true in pattern to the temenos—a sacred precinct, of which Plato's Academy in the 4th century was still a classic example, with its Garden of the Muses and its great 448 sepulchres. The plan of the Trojan megaron, which was adopted for roofed temples in Crete and at Mycenae, Tiryns and Eleusis had supporting columns made of wood that were tapered away at the bottom like stakes driven into the ground. This structure is thought to have originated in the north because of the sloping roof (which was gradually replacing the flat roof and which, it was thought, would allow rain water to flow away more easily). But paradoxically it is precisely in the wooded regions of northern Greece that often have sudden showers of torrential rain that this type of megaron is most rare on those very routes supposedly taken by the invaders.

Primitive temples, from Thermos to Delos, that have come to light are mysteriously small, like the Cnossian shrines; this can be seen, for example, at Delos in the Artemisium of the sacred 'treasury' and in the first He- 449 raeum at the foot of Mount Cynthus. The oldest Heraeum, one of the temples in the Altis at Olympia in the Peloponnese, was scarcely any larger. This building had been surrounded by an alsos (a wooden palisade) in the days when the shepherds of Pisatis used to come there to make their pastoral offerings at festival times and camp in their low huts, built with a rear apse. Architecture in the east developed slowly after the old Heraeum at Samos, which, despite its peristyle, is contemporary with the small shed-house of the Heraeum at Argos and the tiny 450 shrine of Hera Limenia at Perachora. Nowadays we are no longer obliged to make do with the old hypothetical plans and introductions of architects of different schools in order to produce purely imaginative, pointless, diagrammatic sub-divisions of megara, either set back to back or coupled together. We know of too many real, quite humble, ruins of small megara which succeeded the Mycenaean sanctuaries: at Thermos, Eleusis, Thasos, Vroulia (Rhodes) and Dreros (the Delphinium) and in Crete. Oval or rectangular in shape and, as a general rule, very elongated, they sometimes had a slender axial colon-

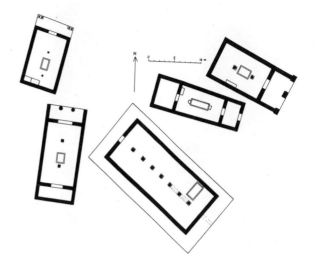

448. Types of megaron temple. The great halls of the Mycenaean palaces. Left to right: Dreros, Thasos, Neandria, Prinias B, Prinias A.

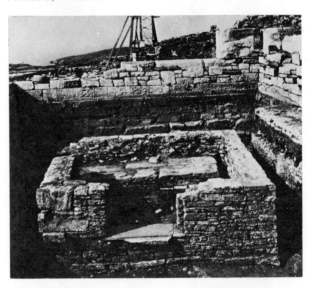

449. Ruins of the Heraeum at Delos. 10th century B.C.

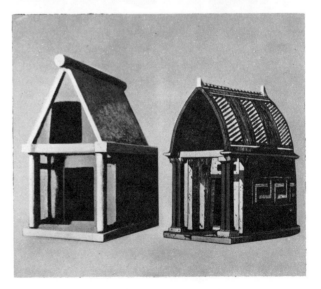

450. *Left.* Model of a shed-type dwelling in terra cotta, from the Heraeum at Argos. *(After Muller.) Right.* Model of a house in the form of a small shrine, from the sanctuary of Hera Limenia at Perachora. *(After Payne.)*

247

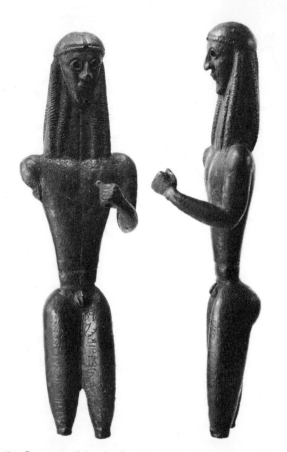

451. Statuette of Apollo (front and side view). Bronze. 7th century B.C. *Museum of Fine Arts, Boston.*

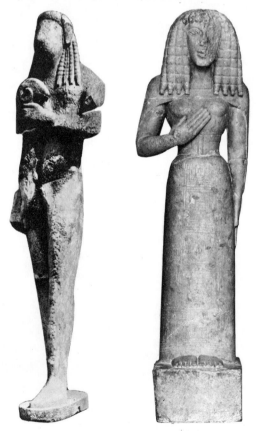

452. Apollo from Thasos. End of the 7th century B.C.

453. DAEDALIC. The Auxerre kore. Last quarter of the 7th century B.C. *Louvre.*

nade that supported a light roof down the centre. They had wall ledges, inside and out, in the Minoan style. Akin to those shrines where sacred objects were kept (treasuries) and usually built close by, they had rather the same kind of decoration, possibly a little less splendid; the holy statue, by sacred prerogative, was set at the far end. The vital, major change in architecture was that these holy places became completely independent of the palaces that had fallen into disrepute. They were moved from the acropolis-citadels and were built apart in the pasture lands of the plains, either within or outside the cities. But they were set, we should remember, in the holiest spots of the countryside. These cultural changes must surely have stemmed from the easily outraged dignity of the new gods whom the patriarchal attitudes of the Indo-Europeans had completely transformed and who had come from the East to settle in Olympus and Olympia. These new gods, like Demeter at Eleusis, sometimes demanded dwelling places built on high ground, above but still in touch with the ordinary mortals. They had left the aristocratic private chapels of the palaces.

The first sacred buildings belonged entirely and solely to the gods themselves; worshippers never went inside to pray but offered up their sacrifices on the outside altar, before the door of the temple. Megaron B at Thermos can be dated about 900 and so helps to establish the dating of certain changes that probably took place about the year 1000. The small Greek temple of this time, in several places, was still suggestive of the Cretan larnakes, the rectangular dwelling-places of the dead; these chests with gabled lids and two end 'pediments' would seem to offer the most certain and direct precedents on a reduced scale of the buildings that were dedicated to the new gods and heroes.

Sculpture before the archaic period

In 1200 the traditional ancestor of Cycladic idols, the xoanon, carved in wood and either left bare or coated with gold leaf, similar to the human figures depicted on the Dipylon vases, was still alive. Sculpture had not yet broken free from its matrix, but its primitive roughness was already vital and exciting. At Samos there were painstaking carpenters who, without any really adequate tools, had already squared up, cut and planed the outer surfaces of planks and beams. Gradually, inert opaque matter was being subjected to human workmanship; man was bringing his imagination to bear upon it.

A continuous progression led up to these first sacred statues that in various places were thought to be alive and revengeful. The xoana before Solon's time were already something more than pictographs of the human body. They had one foot (the left) before the other, in the Egyptian style; shortly afterwards, the arm was lifted from the side and a timid hand was placed on the breast, 451 in the manner of the Auxerre goddess or of one of the 453 female figures of the ivory group in the Pierpont Morgan 454 Collection, Metropolitan Museum, New York. A famous terra cotta from Samos (c. 8th century), provides us with a forerunner of the kouros type. As yet it is far removed from the first Attic kouroi or those of the school of the Dipylon master, and from the more earthy kouroi in the 'Solonian' style with which the over life-size Sunium statues can be grouped. But already it has a burning individuality of its own. A comparison of the earliest bronzes

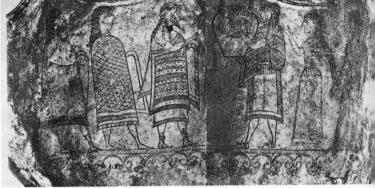

455. Breast-plate (detail) from Olympia. 6th century B.C. (*After Bulletin de correspondance hellénique*.)

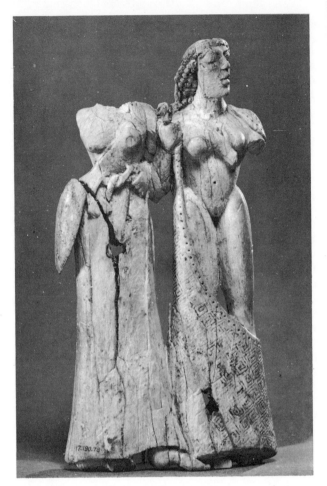

454. Two female figures. Ivory. 7th century B.C. *Metropolitan Museum of Art. Gift of J. Pierpoint Morgan, 1918.*

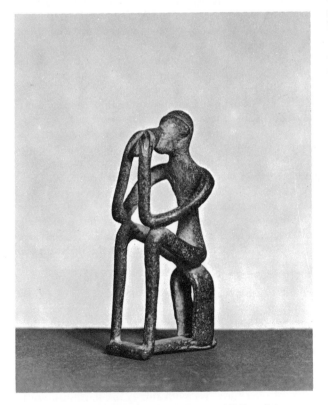

456. Seated figure. Bronze. 8th century B.C. *Walters Art Gallery, Baltimore, Maryland.*

that were produced, from Luristan to Sardinia, should **390–392** shed light on this gradual movement towards the lifelike. We see the earliest signs and the progressive strengthening of pure Greek monumentality emerging slowly from the earliest folk-art productions. These works are enlivened by a feeling of everyday life and, even at this time, are **359** far bolder and more expressive in gesture than classical sculptures.

So a new picture emerges of Greece and her earliest artists, a Greece, moreover, that is usually termed 'barbarian', but this country was always intent upon the voices of the age-old civilisations about her and was beginning to absorb their lessons. When the time came, Greece was to pass on her decorative skill not only to Europe, but also to Iranian Asia under the Achaemenids. This was an effect of the perpetual interchange of influences between East and West, the only one of these movements for which we have sound evidence at this date.

The many foundries set up in all parts of Greece produced works which, a good while before 700, were quite distinctive and individual. At this period we are far from the time when the little bronze *ex votos* in the shape of animals got their conventional form from the tanned skins of beasts, which were stretched out and then folded back along the axis of the spine. The baldric and sling of the Olympian buckler that have been found, with myth- **455** ological ornamentation, could not have been as sophisticated as they were by the 6th century without the progress that had been made in the Argive-Corinthian bronze plaques, for example. Architectural decoration, both within and without, profited from a long line of minor attempts. In the course of five centuries the intelligence was brought to bear upon the basic excitement of visual impressions, and this prepared the way for that archaic art which is so much admired today.

It would be rash to lay down artificial divisions for Greek art in the course of its progress, and to base the stages of historical chronology upon those changes which developed quite independently from the rigidity of the archaic period to the relaxed freedom of later art. There would be too great a risk of hardening the imaginative beauty of archaic art and the earliest Greek sculpture.

At this point it would be both satisfying and completely legitimate to give particular emphasis to those works which are usually called 'minor arts'. A question well worth studying is the relationship between monumental sculpture as it appeared in Greece in the middle of the 7th century and the small bronze, clay and ivory figurines **456, 457** of the previous centuries. These objects are not only curious in themselves but are extraordinarily thin, almost without bodily substance, and are rather like insects of a fantastic size. They help us to solve certain

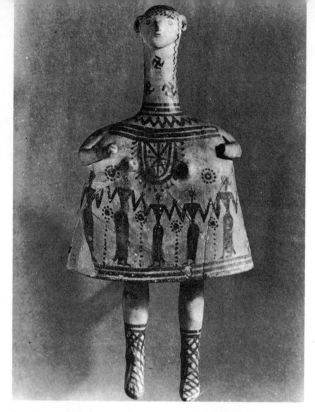

457. Boeotian goddess. Terra cotta. c. 700 B.C. *Louvre*.

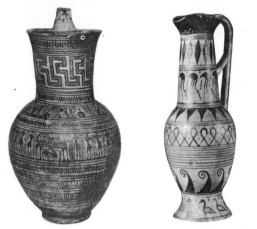

458. *Left*. Geometric Attic vase. 9th-8th centuries B.C. *British Museum*.

459. *Right*. Proto-Attic vase. Early 7th century B.C. *Musée Paul-Dupuy, Toulouse*.

mysteries of an age that was in no way static. In the 7th century Cycladic sailors were considered to be the most skilful seafarers among the Greeks, and they came back laden with foreign cargoes; the many monumental and life-size statues in the islands seem to point to the fact that Cycladic artists and craftsmen drew their inspiration from what they could find to admire in Mesopotamia, Anatolia, Phoenicia and, especially, Egypt, where the Ionians were at a very early date and where, a little later, towards the end of the 7th century, they were to settle and carry on their trade.

The geometric style

Great attention should be paid to this easily overlooked material as well as to metal-work, and to such remains as there are of painting, which was itself a very old art at this time. This should not surprise us, for it is a mistake to think that it had completely disappeared. It continued to be used for the decoration of larnakes and walls long after the time of the lyre player of the Hagia Triada sarcophagus (*c.* 1200) and the paintings in the palaces of Mycenae, Thebes and Tiryns. Votive panels, too, were adorned with paintings, as we should know from the discovery of painted *ex votos* in the Nymphs' Cave at Pitsa, near Corinth.

Some idea of great paintings that have vanished is provided by the wonderful figured vases from Athens and other centres. Attica had from the time of the Achaeans a history that was more accessible and far more complex than that of Orchomenus in Boeotia, plundered by Thebes, or even of the great sub-Mycenaean centres in the Peloponnese.

Until the tyranny of Pisistratus and his sons, who still lived on the Acropolis, the city of Aegeus and Theseus was ruled by kings and by the old aristocratic families whose modest dwellings, huddled together, can be distinguished near the Erechtheum. The legend of the fight against the Dorians and King Codrus' noble sacrifice matched the deep-rooted traditional consciousness of this province that had preserved its autochthony against nomadic tribes and where the present drew continual strength from the past, especially in the arts. The Dipylon vases, 458 covered with triumphant scenes, often glorified the heroes who worked for political unity, the great lords of the Acropolis and the tenacious hoplites, who, step by step, drove back the Eleusinians and the people of Chalcis from Euboea.

From the geometric period to the time of proto-Attic 459 pottery the scenes on these huge vases reveal a far greater sense of continuous history than one might have imagined. In the study of art, to think of these vases as monotonous, as is often done, shows the greatest lack of attention. Those who recently talked of an 'effervescent period' were probably nearer the truth. The artists of the Greek world, not merely in Athens but also in Eleusis, Argos and the Cyclades (Naxos), worked to bring about the vital elegance of archaic art. It was not only Crete in its late period (wrongly termed Daedalic) from which the provinces, enlarged under Theseus, could learn.

Any disparaging undertones in descriptions of geometric Greek art are therefore quite unwarranted since it was probably the most Greek of all the arts, drawing its strength from the logical elaboration of elements that were at root abstract. It might be better to call it 'mathematical', for it achieved its effects by variations on ornamental themes that always retained their simplicity. Take, for example, the meander, the diamond, the zigzag, etc.; they were not the mere husks of natural, living forms. This becomes clear enough if we consider the great feeling for nature and vigorous movement that reappeared with the proto-Attic period, as is shown in the monumental Gorgon Vase from Eleusis.

Greek style emerged on its own, the product of its own internal laws. How else could it have kept its independence, both in motif and style? The artist of these vases was closely bound by the laws of the object he was decorating. He was a dynamic artist who chose discipline and severity of his own accord and who gradually conquered rhythm, proportion and harmony. A disciplined beginning was very necessary for the subsequent development of Greek art; for with this as the starting point it was possible to adapt the patterns which had emerged to the structure of society.

GREEK ART FROM THE SIXTH TO THE FOURTH CENTURIES *François Chamoux*

We can only reach a just appreciation of the importance and nature of Greek art if we reject certain conventional ideas and contemporary prejudices which tend to underestimate it by confusing it with academic classicism. Greek art has in fact kept its place as one of the most vital of all the arts of all time.

By the end of the 7th century Greek expansion throughout the Mediterranean had almost come to an end. For the next three hundred years Hellenic civilisation was to be at its height. The rapid development of economic, social and political organisation within the basic framework of the city-state, which at first grew strong and later disintegrated, encouraged a bold spirit in thought and art.

Greek art

This great creative period has left us an extraordinarily rich literature, as well as a great many significant, if often mutilated, monuments. To further our understanding of this people, who are of supreme importance in our own history, we can make use of both literary and archaeological sources. It follows that the art historian cannot neglect the first to the exclusive advantage of the second; in the sphere of classical Greece the archaeologist must also be a Hellenist.

There is all the more reason for this since the work of art at this time was rarely intended simply for aesthetic enjoyment. The Greeks had almost no idea of a work of art divorced from the practical or religious purpose for which it was primarily designed. The idea of art for art's sake was foreign to the Hellenic way of thinking. The work of art, then, invariably poses a difficult problem of interpretation. It is only after this that the question of an aesthetic judgment can be brought in; otherwise there is danger of serious misunderstanding. Recent studies have provided some fine examples of the important modifications which a new approach can make to the way we appreciate a masterpiece. Today we can no longer think of the Aphrodite of Cnidus as simply a study of a female nude, since it has been shown that Praxiteles' work was conceived in an atmosphere of religious devotion. On the other hand, the famous bas-relief of the Mourning Athena appears in a completely different light as soon as it is recognised for nothing but a victorious athlete's votive offering. We sometimes miss the delightfully tempting speculations which these scholarly commentaries have now replaced with the unadorned truth, but it is up to the historian to understand records, not to encourage flights of fancy.

Classical Greek art is an art charged with meaning that appeals as much to the intelligence as to the sensibility. It has a message that, first and foremost, must be understood. When it comes to the appreciation of a building's qualities, the fact that it may be a temple, a treasury, a propylaeon or a portico is not without relevance. A cult statue followed standards which were different from those of a simple votive offering. The composition of a painting or a bas-relief was governed by religious or moral conventions, determining factors in the way the artist set

about his work. In votive offerings, for example, it was customary to make the gods taller than the worshippers. Although there seems to be a simpler way into Greek art than there is into the art of exotic civilisations, it is nonetheless true that here as elsewhere, to adopt Renan's words, a genuine appreciation is a historical one.

Moreover, an attempted commentary provides an opportunity to counteract the damage which only too often has disfigured works of art and the prejudices which have led to their misinterpretation. Greek architecture and works of art have usually come down to us in such a state of decay that a great deal of research is needed to restore them to their original appearance. Even where, by a rare stroke of fortune, buildings are still standing, like the Theseum in Athens, the 'temple of Poseidon' at Paestum and the temple of Concord at Agrigentum, their interiors have not remained intact and they have lost their extremely rich and colourful exterior ornamentation which must have completely altered their appearance. As for works of sculpture, if by chance they have suffered no serious damage they are usually without any of those surface qualities, especially the vivid colouring which, painted on stone and marble, aimed to complete the lifelike illusion. Finally, we must remember that if we wish to know something of Greek painting, a major art which the ancients ranked along with sculpture, we do not possess one single authentic masterpiece, and it is only in minor works like ceramics, mosaics and frescoes, often separated by a gap of several centuries from the originals, that we must look for a distorted reflection of those vanished marvels. Such are the conditions facing those who wish to learn about classical Greek art. While museums and excavated sites provide relatively easy access to surviving works of art, it is still the mind which must restore, evaluate and understand anything demanding scholarship and explanation.

To reach an understanding of classical Greek art, then, we must first make a resolution to reject both the sentimental charm of ruins and the infinite power of suggestion of broken statues. We must give up the picture of a Greece 'crystallised in Pentelic marble', as misleading in its own way as are the paintings of Jacques Louis David. A good many traditional ideas, forms and emotions to which we are attached must be firmly rejected. In return, we can have a more honest approach to the study of these works of art and, as has been so well expressed by Livy, can create for ourselves an ancient soul by studying the ancient world.

The artist in the city-state

From texts we learn of the Greek attitude to the artist. The few relevant references that exist are all the more precious for their comparative rarity. They show that while the Greeks were enthusiastic admirers of the great masters of form they never accorded the plastic arts those special qualities which were acknowledged in music, philosophy, poetry and the art of rhetoric. The legendary figure of Daedalus undoubtedly occupied an outstanding place in their gallery of great men; Plato quoted Phidias

472
477
530, 535
439

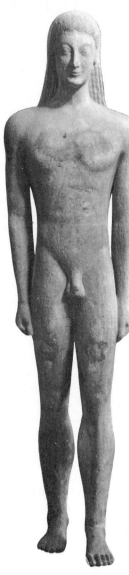

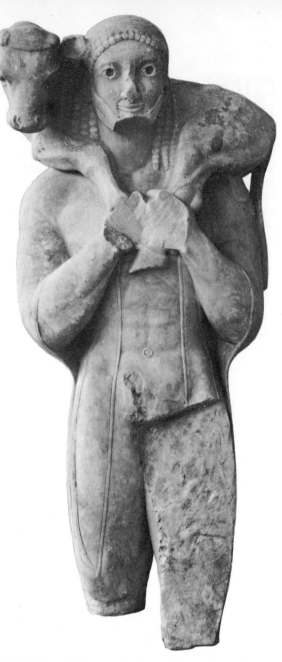

460. IONIAN. Kouros from Melos. Marble. *c.* 540 B.C. *National Museum, Athens.*

461. ATTIC. The Calf-bearer. Marble. *c.* 560 B.C. *Acropolis Museum, Athens.*

462. Head of a kouros, from the temple of Apollo Ptoos. Beginning of the 6th century B.C. *National Museum, Athens.*

463. ATTIC. Head of the Rampin Horseman. Marble. *c.* 560–550 B.C. *Louvre.*

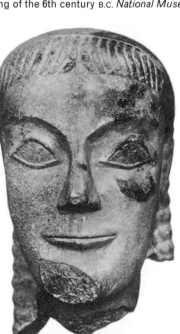

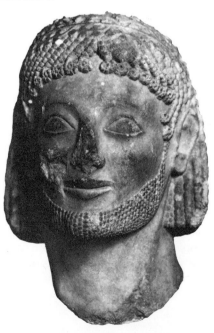

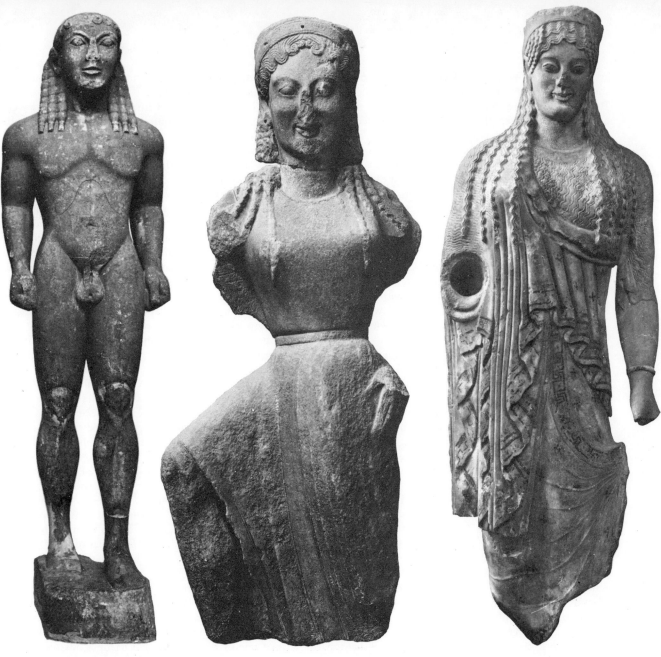

464. *Above.* ARGIVE. Statue of Cleobis. Marble. Beginning of the 6th century B.C. *Delphi Museum.*

467. Kore 674. Marble. 525–500 B.C. *Acropolis Museum, Athens.*

465. *Above, centre.* Winged Nike. Marble, found at Delos. After 570 B.C. *National Museum, Athens.*

466. *Above, right.* Euthydicos kore. Marble. *c.* 500 B.C. *Acropolis Museum, Athens.*

468. Attic kore. 510–500 B.C. *Acropolis Museum, Athens.*

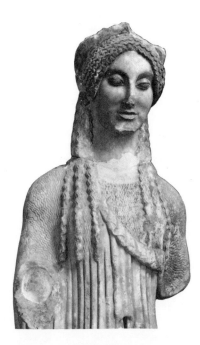

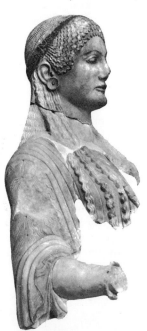

253

and Polycleitus with considerable respect; Alexander showered honours on Apelles, Lysippus and Leochares. But people living at the time of these masters never for a moment supposed that they were possessed of the divine inspiration that musicians, philosophers and poets were credited with. They were ready enough to surround themselves with real or imaginary portraits of Homer, Pindar, Euripides and Demosthenes but it did not occur to them to add a sculptor's or painter's portrait to the collection. Of all the nine Muses, not one was the patroness of the plastic arts. Such omissions are significant. In the eyes of the classical Greeks (and the idea was to persist for a very long time) the artist was essentially a good craftsman, an artisan who worked with his hands, a *banausos*. Art, then, was thought of in terms of technique and the artist was regarded as a man with a thorough knowledge of his craft. Classical Antiquity was unaware of the split between art and craftsmanship which our age so readily proclaims.

The fact that craftsmanship was of prime importance explains the outstandingly high technical quality characteristic of Greek works of art of the so-called 'Golden Age'. This is certainly not to say that all artists in Greece at that time were masters of perfection; to look through the unexhibited works stored in the National Museum of Athens or in less important museums, like the one at Piraeus and those in the provinces, is enough to prove that works of undisputed excellence are in the minority among a crowd of mediocre productions. The same observation could be made of pottery collections. But, for all that, the average standard remains astonishingly high by reason of the extreme care taken over execution. In the modelling of terra cottas, in the decoration on vases and in the carving on metopes or votive bas-reliefs there is often a skilful assurance which baffles us today and which proves that even the artist and craftsman of the second rank had a sure grasp of his medium.

We must add that the factor of time meant almost nothing. That a certain method was slow or difficult was not enough to condemn it if the result showed that it had been worth the trouble. The columns of a building were fluted only after the drums had been put up and the shaft was in place; this can be seen clearly in the temple
470 at Segesta, on which, through unforeseen circumstances, work was never completed.

Imagine the difficulties facing the mason who, in these circumstances, set about carving those fine stone ridges! But this was how he achieved that perfect regularity of fluting, running from top to bottom of the column, which gives the Doric shaft its disciplined nobility. Similarly,
443 a study of the great bronzes, like the Delphic Charioteer, shows that after the statue had been cast the sculptor painstakingly set to work to remove the tiniest defect caused by air bubbles or dross and to bring out details of modelling with minute burin-work. Painters have never been more highly prized for their purely technical achievements, as, for example, the illusion of transparency, in which some of them were thought to excel; much was made, for instance, of a certain allegorical figure of Drunkenness (*Methe*), whose face Pausias had painted as seen through the glass cup from which he was drinking. Even as early as the 6th century there was a sense of technical achievement when beneath the marble
433 Naxian sphinx, four times larger than life, the inscription

proudly declared: 'I have been carved, statue and base, from a single block of stone.'

The Greeks, then, loved fine workmanship and were unconcerned by the amount of time that might have to be spent upon it. They had, too, a kind of team spirit, and each member willingly adapted himself to the general outlines laid down by the craftsman in charge. Hence we have so many examples of great architectural works produced by a team of craftsmen, on which the acumen of archaeologists has been exerted without success to try to distinguish the work of different hands, for example: in the temple of Zeus at Olympia, under the direction of 487 an unknown master; in the Parthenon, under Phidias 488 (pp. 276–77); in the Mausoleum of Halicarnassus, under 536 the guidance of four master-craftsmen, Scopas, Leochares, Timotheus and Bryaxis. It was because they thought of art as a craft in which collaboration was often necessary that these masters buckled down to the demands of a joint undertaking. The sculptor had to call on various assistants to produce the large gold and ivory statues, masterpieces of a refined and complex technique. Phidias had Paeonius the painter and Colotes the goldsmith and carpenter working for him. Praxiteles entrusted the painter Nicias with the task of painting his marble statues. Artists, moreover, never limited themselves to a single field: Phidias was well known both as a painter and a goldsmith, and his work on the Acropolis shows that he was also a competent architect. Polygnotus, the great painter, was a sculptor as well. A similar versatility of talent was to recur among the Renaissance masters. But this is more than an indication of gifted versatility; it is a proof of the thorough technical training that these men received in the workshops. In order to meet with his patron's wishes the *banausos* learned to cope with the most complex tasks.

Such is the picture we have of the Greek artist: a craftsman above all else; a lover of fine workmanship, shaped by a long training in the traditions of his masters. Two Argive sculptors of the late 6th century who inscribed one of their statues at Olympia boasted specifically of the fact that they had learned their art from their forerunners. When ancient authors mention an artist, they like to tell us whose pupil he was. The artist, then, was directly related to his social environment. Just like any other craftsman, he had a part to play in the life of the city; he was respected for his technical ability; he was in no sense an eccentric or a rebel. He was well suited to give full expression to the feelings and aspirations of a society in which he naturally had a place.

ARCHITECTURE

These initial considerations which we have stressed, on one side the importance of the practical and religious purposes of Greek art, and on the other, the artist's dominating concern with his craft, explain why it would be artificial to try to trace the development of architecture and figurative art in the same section. One is the science of purely decorative mass and any scenes taken from life are only incidentals, whereas the other is essentially devoted to the human figure and all it can express. Without forgetting that the Greeks on occasion had with great effect combined the two, we shall nevertheless study them separately.

254

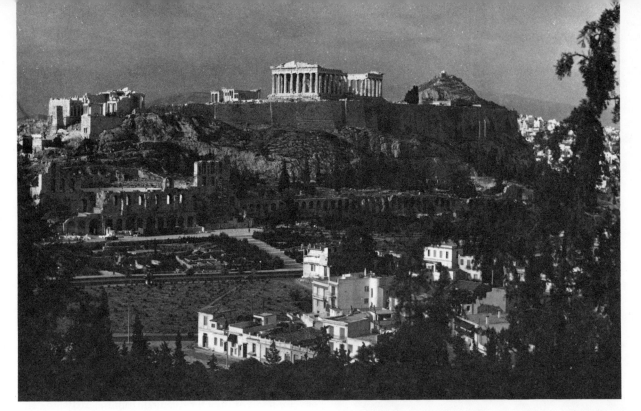

469. The Acropolis, Athens.

Masonry

Greek architecture was essentially a stone architecture. The Greek builders knew of sun-dried brick and used it a great deal, especially for houses, but ashlar construction was usually preferred for public buildings. The Greeks more than any other people could appreciate stone walls whose beauty lies in their masonry. This varied according to the epoch, the method used, and, of course, the function the wall was designed to fulfil. In the 6th century for supporting walls (very common in this mountainous country) and fortified walls the builders preferred polygonal masonry, where each block had its own particular shape, the whole wall forming a perfectly assembled jigsaw puzzle. The masterpiece of this kind is the well-known polygonal wall at Delphi where, as if to add to the difficulties, the adjoining edges are all curves. Although in later years rubble work had not completely disappeared, the Greeks of the classical period preferred regular courses, as used for temple walls, where from one course to another the joints alternated according to a regular pattern (isodomic masonry). In the 4th century several imaginative features were introduced into this strict pattern: diagonal joints (trapezoidal masonry); vertical contrasting bands within the same course. There was certainly a practical reason behind these elaborate contrivances. They were first and foremost employed to strengthen the wall's resistance, but the architects, making a virtue of necessity, thereby produced fine aesthetic effects. Recent research has made a study of these various kinds of masonry and their dates.

For public buildings, both civic and religious, the architect used an even more elaborate technique. The blocks of stone were fitted together without mortar and held in place with metal clamps. The joint facings were treated in a special way which ensured a perfectly firm hold. This method is known as anathyrosis. In the most carefully finished buildings, especially where marble was being used, the walls were scraped with a chisel from top to bottom, to rid them of any blemishes; at the same time,

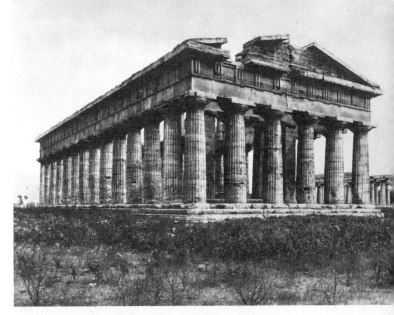

470. MAGNA GRAECIA. Temple at Segesta (Sicily). Doric Order. *Below:* Detail of the entablature of the temple.

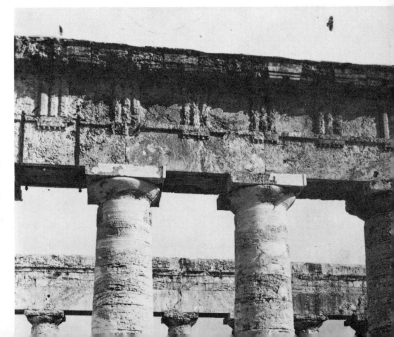

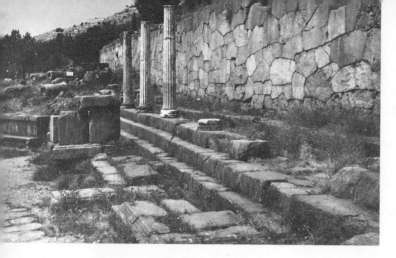

471. Detail of polygonal wall, Delphi.

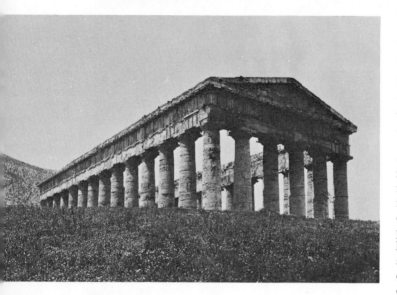

472. MAGNA GRAECIA. DORIC. 'Temple of Poseidon', Paestum. c. 460 B.C.

473. DORIC. Superimposed colonnades, temple of Aphaia.

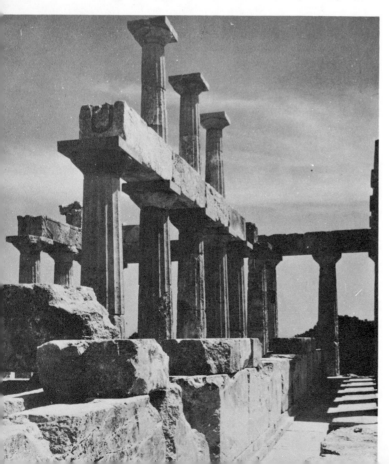

the projections which had been used to shift the blocks into position were removed. The regular stone courses and perfect joints helped to give the wall a kind of rhythm. This is true of the main Periclean monuments of the Acropolis and of the completed parts of the Propylaea, where we have an interesting contrast from some walls which never received the final scraping treatment.

The Doric and Ionic Orders

The same concern for technical perfection appears in the other essential features of building: the column and the entablature. And it is here, in particular, that those rules called Orders (Doric and Ionic), which govern Greek architecture, are brought into play. The Orders, relating to the plan, scale and ornamentation of a building's principal parts, established themselves very rapidly and were already clearly defined by the 6th century. In later years they were hardly ever disregarded and this comparative stability is a good illustration of the way in which the Greek artist accepted the traditions of his craft. Some variations were certainly introduced during the course of the years: we can trace the very nearly uninterrupted development of the Doric capital from the early 6th century down to the middle of the 4th century. Such observations can help us to date buildings, but they also illustrate the builders' loyalty, throughout changing fashions, to traditional ideas. The most remarkable innovation was the invention in the second half of the 5th century of the Corinthian capital which can possibly be put down to the credit of the sculptor Callimachus or, as has recently been suggested, to Phidias. But this was only a matter of a variation in ornamentation, which, although of great importance, was confined within the Ionic Order of which the other features remained unaltered.

To a certain extent, as their names imply, the two Orders predominated in different areas of the Hellenic world. The great Ionic structures, like the Artemisium at Ephesus and the Heraeum at Samos, were in Asia Minor. The Doric Order was much more widespread, both on the mainland and in the Greek colonies; fine examples, like the temple at Assos, are, however, to be found in Asia Minor. Architects at a very early date, and without disregarding local tradition, realised that the two Orders were equally valid modes of expression which, when required, could be employed in the same building; as early as the 6th century an Ionic colonnade made its appearance in the large hall of the Doric temple of 'Ceres' at Paestum. Subsequently the more slender Ionic Order was often preferred for the interior of a building as, for example, in the Periclean Propylaea on the Acropolis. The first Corinthian capitals are also found inside: in the temple of Apollo at Bassae in Arcadia, in the tholos at Delphi, and, at a later date, in the tholos at Epidaurus, the masterpiece of Polycleitus the Younger, built in the middle of the 4th century. Athens, which was in a good position to bring about a union between the Dorian culture of the mainland and the Ionian contribution from the islands and Asia Minor, encouraged a felicitous mixture of styles: in the Parthenon the continuous frieze along the top of the cella walls portraying the Panathenaic procession, introduces a typically Ionic feature into a Doric building. Yet no one censured Phidias or Ictinus, the architect, for having failed to keep the Orders distinct. It is evident that despite certain particularist ideas the

426, 472
475
474
476

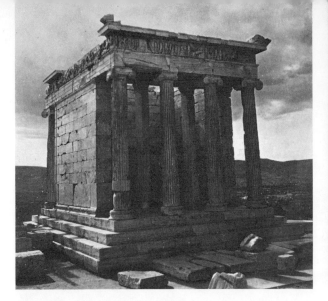

474. IONIC. Temple of Athena Nike, on the Acropolis, Athens. 420 B.C.

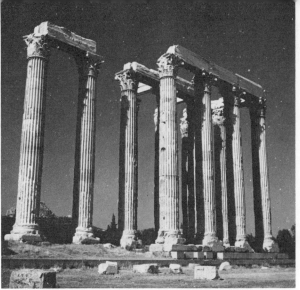

475. CORINTHIAN. The Olympieum at Athens.

Greeks were conscious, in architecture, of Hellenic unity at a very early date.

Town planning

Both Orders were used in the construction of every kind of public building. We shall not stop to look at private houses which, at this period, we know almost nothing about except what we have from the excavations at Olynthus, a town destroyed in 348. The Greeks preferred to spend their time out of doors, in the streets and the market-places where their public monuments stood, rather than in their houses which, modest in size and comprising a few rooms grouped around a central court, were without luxury and were unimpressive to look at.

Of all public buildings it is the temples which have received the most attention, to the neglect of the rest. For a very long time Greek architecture was thought of essentially as a religious architecture. In recent years, however, several books have been devoted to public buildings and the principles of town planning in Greece. We now have a fuller knowledge of those buildings designed specifically to house assemblies, councils and tribunals. In the 6th and 5th centuries the Greeks developed, both for religious and civic purposes, a rectangular hall with tiers of seats on three sides, of the pattern seen in the British House of Commons.

The Mediterranean climate encouraged open-air political meetings; in order to give these meetings proper settings, architects gradually fixed on certain new types of structures which marked off the seats of the assembly while affording various advantages to the spectators. In this way the stoa, which had certainly been known before in the East and in the Aegean world, developed. The Greeks, by erecting these in their public squares, put them to an entirely new use. These open-fronted roofed walks, with their colonnades, which plainly called for the use of the Orders, provided shelter for walkers and merchants. Sometimes the stoas were built with wings slightly projecting from the centre, and they then provided an ideal setting for public meetings of fairly limited size, such as tribunal sessions. The most characteristic example is the Royal Stoa in the agora at Athens, which was built in the second half of the 5th century. Town planners, by making flexible use of these stoas, gradually set the pattern for the four-sided public square flanked with covered walks which was later copied by the

Romans in the imperial forum.

This development brings out very well an essential feature of Hellenic art—the way it could adapt itself to the object in hand. When in the 5th century Ionian architects such as Hippodamus of Miletus recommended that towns should be laid out on an orthogonal pattern, they were thinking primarily of what the founders of new cities would find practicable. When it came to putting theory into practice, as Hippodamus did in Piraeus, they were able to adapt their rigid quadrilateral plans to suit the site; modern Athens with its absurd grid of straight streets at right-angles to each other, which was laid down by a Bavarian architect, has, unhappily, disregarded the example set by its ancestors.

In the archaic and classical periods architectural planning was in no way stiff or artificial. Too much symmetry in perspective must have appeared uninspired and limited. What better example can we find of this, in the light of recent study, than the Acropolis? The great flight of steps leading up to the entrance is a Roman addition; Pericles' architects had deliberately preserved the ancient winding ramp which was the old way into the Propylaea. The Propylaea, one of Mnesicles' masterpieces, **476** was wholeheartedly admired in Antiquity because the architect had turned a difficult site to extraordinary advantage, not by disguising the nature of the uneven, sloping ground but by making this serve his purpose. Today we can no longer believe the well-worn story of an original, perfectly symmetrical, plan which Mnesicles was unable fully to put into effect. The actual asymmetry is an essential feature of the building. Modern commentators have made the same mistake in regard to the Erechtheum, which staggered them with its unusual **479** design; here again, we now know that this complex structure was quite consciously planned by an architect who was trying to take into account not only the unevenness of the ground but the needs of a particular form of worship, which was a leading consideration. His strength lies in the fact that he was apparently undeterred by the task he was presented with, and the bold choice and the unity of the ornamentation of this building produced a supremely neat solution to a difficult problem. We know what subtle steps were taken by Ictinus and Callicrates to correct optical illusions in the Parthenon itself, but, **480** as has recently been shown, they had also foreseen that the visitors' first sight of the building would be from

257

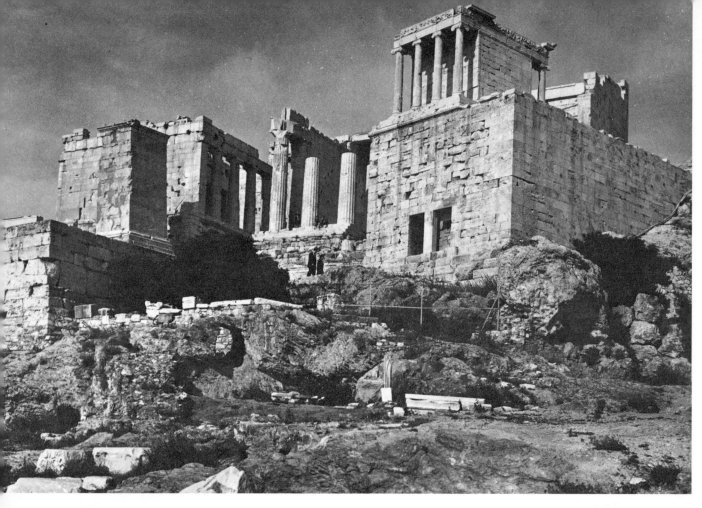

476. The Propylaea, gateway to the Acropolis, Athens.   477. Temple of Concord at Agrigentum, Sicily. 5th century B.C.

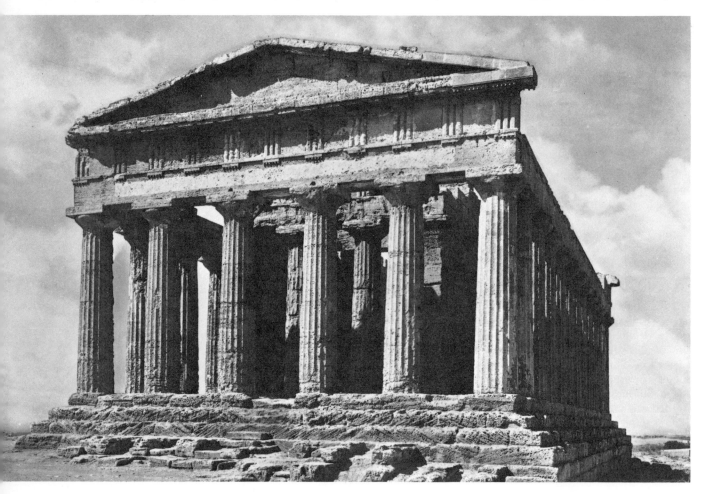

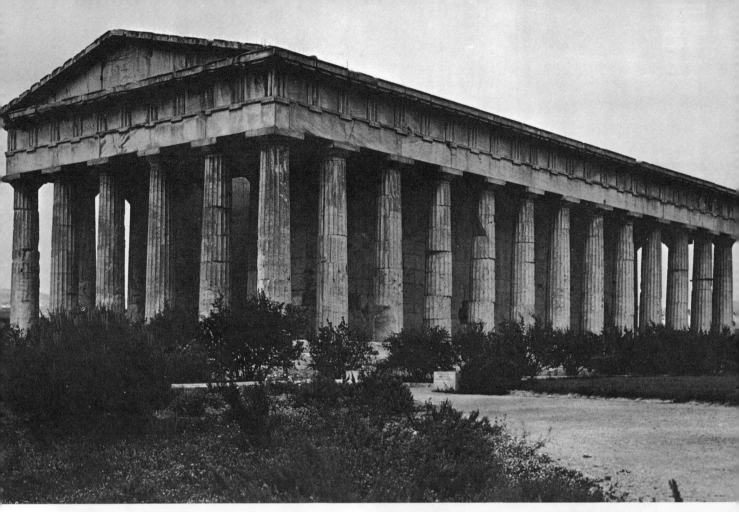

478. Temple of Theseus, Athens, sometimes called the Hephaestus. 5th century B.C. The metopes represented the exploits of Hercules and Theseus.

479. The Caryatid porch on the Erechtheum. Acropolis, Athens.

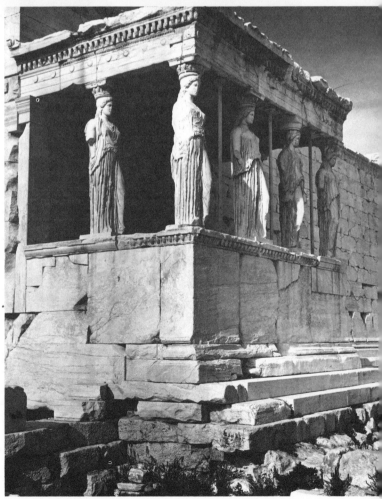

behind, looking three-quarters on from an oblique angle. Here again the work of architecture was a spatial conception, a living reality and not a coldly irrelevant blue-print.

Yet mathematics forms the essence of architecture and this the Greeks never forgot. They certainly delighted in working out proportions; there is scarcely a building of any pretension where the experienced archaeologist has not managed to find the module which was used to determine scale. If we are to follow the attractive suggestions made in a recent study of the subjects, some architects took the science of numbers even further. At times they related the very proportions of their buildings to the concerns of certain mathematical schools of the day: the squaring of a circle, the three-fold division of an angle and the numerical value of π. At least, this is what seems to be shown by the graphic restoration of the treasury built by the town of Cyrene at Delphi in the middle of the 4th century. Calculations of a similar kind have been recognised in another architectural work dating from the same time as this treasury—the famous theatre at Epidaurus, for which Polycleitus the Younger was responsible.

498

The Greek Temple

These studies help us to picture the buildings of the classical period as they were designed by their architects. How different they must have looked in those days compared with what we see now! When any part of a temple is still standing, it is usually the damaged colonnade.

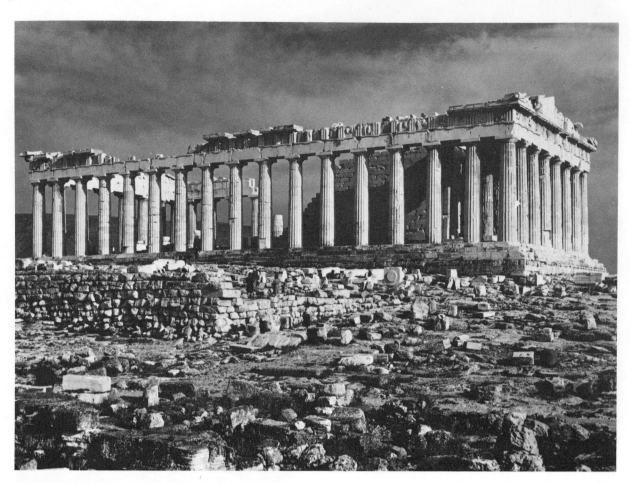

480. The Parthenon on the Acropolis, Athens. 450–430 B.C.

CLASSICAL GREECE

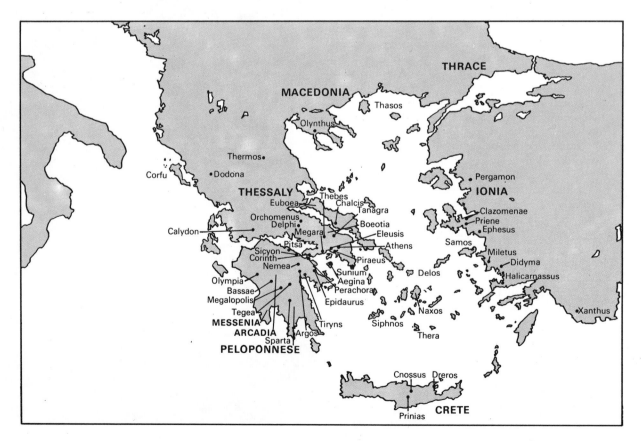

Naturally we are led to think of the columned portico which surrounded the temple as its chief feature—a romantic and mistaken conclusion. The Greek temple was the house of a god, where he dwelt in image form. The principal part, the *sine qua non* of the building was the hall (cella) which housed the cult statue. Whether this hall was entered by a porch or an antechamber or both, whether for the sake of symmetry a false porch (opisthodomos) was added on to the rear of the cella, whether the building was surrounded by a single or a double colonnade, these were only accessories; the cella remained the essential feature. Today the cella has, in most cases, disappeared, and where a few traces of it survive it is difficult for us to make any certain and detailed restoration of what it was like inside. And yet it was here that the architect had to show all his skill. In the large temples a two-tiered colonnade, supporting the roof, divided the spacious hall into three aisles. At the far end of the central aisle the cult statue loomed out of the shadows, for the only light came through the door. Votive offerings covered the walls and crowded the paved floor. Any person entering must have experienced a strong feeling of being in the presence of a god. Some writings, like the descriptions of the traveller Pausanius from the 2nd century A.D., help to give us a picture of the cella as it was in some of the great classical temples like the temple of Zeus at Olympia and the Parthenon.

From the earliest archaic times the design of temples had been undergoing a development tending towards the reduction of length in relation to breadth. Since it had become common practice to surround the building with a colonnade, this ratio became that of the number of columns along the façade to the number along the side. (The corner columns, in this case, are counted twice.) It varied from 6:11 to 6:17, but there were exceptions. There were usually not more than six columns along the façade, except in the large temples which generally had eight; this is the case with the Parthenon (mid 5th century). These buildings usually measured about 95 by 190 feet. These measurements were exceeded only in the case of buildings of unusual type, like the Artemisium at Ephesus, the Heraeum at Samos, the temple of Olympian Zeus at Agrigentum and Temple G at Selinus, gigantic buildings which were more than 300 feet long by 150 feet wide. The interiors sometimes had no roofs and were more like courtyards than halls. Seen from outside, the classical temple, set on a stylobate (the topmost step of the base) gives an impression of power and balance. The colonnades are arranged in accordance with a simple rhythm in which the functional quality of the supports and roof is clearly brought out. The eye delights in this pure geometry which masks calculations of a more refined kind like the delicate curve of the stylobate, the subtle variations of the intercolumniations and the slight upward tapering of the columns. But here we only grasp the abstract essence of this art; the visual effect which it was trying to create eludes us.

By an effort of imagination, based on scholarship, let us try then to restore something of the colour and the wealth of adornment which profoundly altered the temple's appearance. When, as was usually the case, some material other than marble was employed, the columns had none of that fine russet or grey patina which we nowadays find so attractive. White stucco, of which there are still

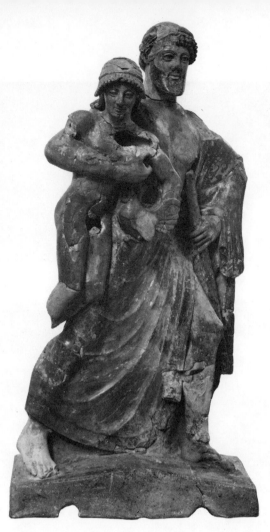

481. Zeus carrying Ganymede. Acroterion from the Gelan treasury (?). Terra cotta. Beginning of 5th century B.C. *Olympia Museum.*

occasional traces, was employed to imitate the look of marble. The entablature was daubed with bright, strongly contrasting colours: blue or red panels with yellow or green details. The cornice, made of stone or terra cotta, was lavishly and colourfully decorated with ornamental foliage; palmettes and lions' heads served as gargoyles. From the tiled covering of the roof, erect, multi-coloured tiles, the antefixes, projected. Lastly, from the three corners of the pediment the acroteria rose up against the sky—bronze, marble or terra-cotta motifs of tremendous **481** variety of shapes and colours: shields; fantastic animals; the figures of gods or heroes; groups in which the figures were depicted in animated and even violently contrasting poses. Here there was obviously a certain preference for scenes showing abduction or flight. These acroteria originally served to attract a kind of magic protection for certain vulnerable parts of the building. But as far as the eye is concerned they establish a kind of interval between the building's tight composition and the surrounding countryside.

Decorative themes

Archaic and classical temples sometimes had other sculptural decorations apart from the acroteria. These were restricted to certain selected parts of the building: pediments and metopes in the Doric Order and the frieze in the Ionic Order. Any attempts made to expand or to modify the use of figurative decoration were few and short lived. A place apart must be given to the figured

261

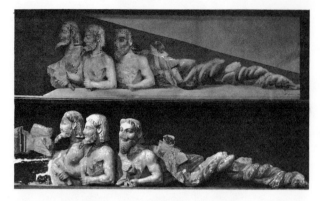

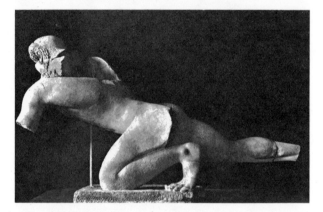

482. 'Bluebeard' pediment. c. 570 B.C.

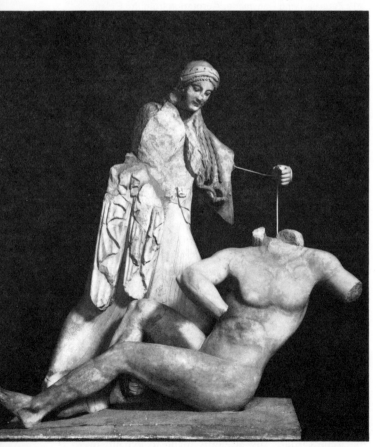

483. Fallen giant. Marble. From a temple on the Acropolis. c. 520 B.C.

484. Athena and Enceladus. Pediment of the Hecatompedon. Marble. c. 520 B.C. *Acropolis Museum, Athens.*

and ornamented cornices which were popular in the Greek cities of Asia Minor during the archaic period. An original and felicitous invention which was destined for success was the column-statue or caryatid, created by 445 Ionian artists and employed for the treasuries at Delphi from the end of the 6th century.

There were complex reasons which led the Greeks so to restrict the use of sculpture in their buildings. Some were of a practical nature: in wood or brick structures, which generally preceded stone structures, the upper parts of the building, being more exposed in bad weather conditions, needed special protection which was provided in the form of figured revetments such as slabs of terra cotta. The sculptured ornamentation of classical buildings would have been an echo of that early necessity. But there must also have been religious reasons, comparable to those which hold good for the acroteria: it must originally have been thought that a series of figurative scenes high up on the walls or on the pediment would secure some kind of magic protection for the building, more or less related to the nature of the scene depicted.

The pediments

The triangular pediment is one of the instances where the collaboration between architect and sculptor can best be grasped. A complex composition had to be arranged, within this very individually shaped framework, that could bring into play many figures, varying in pose according to the decreasing height of the sloping sides, from 482 the apex to the extreme angles. Both religious convention 483 and practical convenience were in agreement that the central position should be given to figures of the gods; so the image of the deity worshipped within the sanctuary often appeared in glory at the crowning point of this temple. This figure replaced those traditional motifs which archaic art in its earliest stages had taken over from the East: animals set face to face like heraldic beasts, Gorgon masks and other themes imbued with magic symbolism. In the centre of the early 6th-century pedi- 486 ment from Corfu, the Gorgon with her terrifying mask is portrayed in full length between two huge felines which glare at the spectator, but already making a rather timid appearance in the two extreme corners of the pediment and unrelated to the central group are two legendary scenes—Zeus' battle with the giant and an incident from the capture of Troy.

These mythological themes quickly took hold, at first on the pediments of small buildings which were less subject to the forceful traditions of great architecture and then on the large temples themselves. From the end of the 6th century all sculptured pediments illustrated or narrated a story. Sometimes obvious trouble has been taken to find relations and contrasts in façades of the same building: on the third temple of Aphaia at Aegina, which dates from the early part of the 5th century, the two pediments were decorated with battle scenes, in both cases arranged around the central figure of Athena. Sometimes we find a peaceful and solemn scene on the pediment of the main façade contrasted with a violent or animated scene on the rear pediment. This is so, for example, in the temple of Apollo at Delphi, built at the end of the 6th century, the temple of Zeus at Olympia, dating from a little 487, 488 before the middle of the 5th century, and the Parthenon itself.

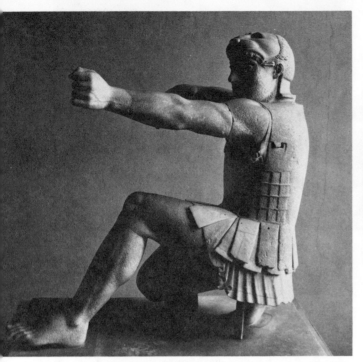

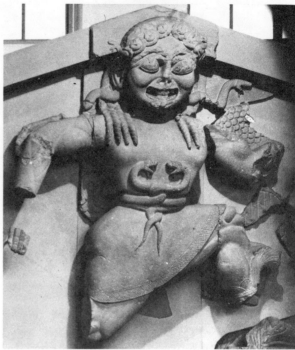

485. Trojan bowman from the eastern façade of the temple of Aphaia, Aegina. Marble. 490–480 B.C. *Staatliche Antikensammlungen, Munich.*

486. Medusa from the temple of Artemis, Corfu. *Corfu Museum.*

So the work of the sculptor came to be deliberately included in the architecture of the building as a whole.

The frieze

The same was true of the ornamentation of both Doric and Ionic friezes. In the Doric frieze barred triglyphs alternated with the smooth slabs of the metopes. Their only adornment was usually a simple colour-wash. But the rectangular framework of the metope, occupying such a splendid position, was naturally bound to tempt painters and sculptors: it was admirably suited to take scenes comprising one or two figures, and, besides this, the large number of metopes along a single side of a building (as

487. Eastern pediment of the temple of Zeus at Olympia showing preparations for a chariot race between Pelops and Oenomaus. *Olympia Museum.*

a rule two to every intercolumniation) meant that an action made up of several episodes could be described. This was the reason for the popularity of the figurative metope, either painted (on stone or terra cotta) or, more often, sculptured and embellished with colour. The deeds of Hercules and Theseus were among the favourite subjects. Similarly, the great battles of mythology such as the struggles between the gods and the giants, the Lapiths and the Centaurs and the Greeks and the Amazons, were very well adapted to the ornamentation of the Doric frieze: they were easily broken up into a series of single combats. Occasionally the artist set out to combine figures appearing on several successive metopes into a single action, but the Doric frieze was ordered in such a way that each metope was relatively self-contained and therefore discouraged such combinations, which disregarded the laws proper to architectural decoration. The rarity of

488, 490

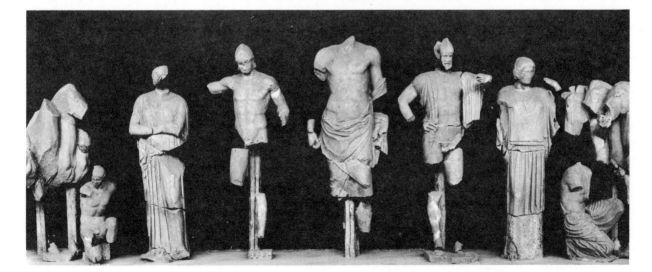

263

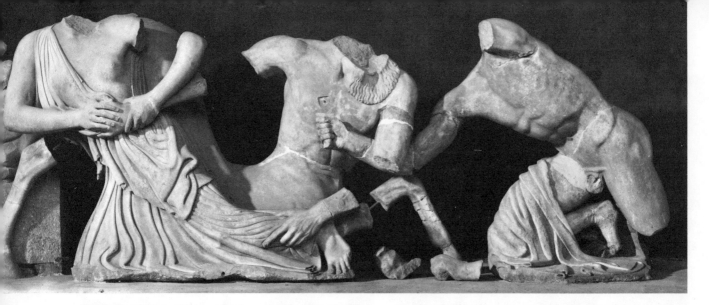

488. Battle of the Lapiths and Centaurs, west pediment of the temple of Zeus at Olympia. Marble. *c.* 470–455 B.C. *Olympia Museum.*

these attempts shows that the Greeks had a sound understanding of these laws.

The artist enjoyed a greater freedom with the continuous frieze above the architrave, which is found in the Ionic order. Here the difficulty was not so much to cover an area without transgressing the limits of the framework but to take a continuous action along the whole length of a building's side without breaking the natural unity of architectural line by coming to an untimely stop. Movement had to be sustained but, at the same time, monotony had to be avoided. Therefore, they made free use of processions, lines of soldiers, hunting scenes, chariot races, battles, banquets—all of which, through the frequent repetition of the same motif combined with the necessary variations, were particularly suitable.

The art of the frieze lay in the skilful handling of the relationship between the rhythm of the action and the rhythm of the building. This can be seen in the Siphnian treasury at Delphi (second half of the 6th century), where the frieze along the façade links three chariots (two of which have survived). On the long northern side the frieze, running along the top of a bare wall, gets its vitality from an uninterrupted movement which begins in the extreme left-hand corner and continues unchecked throughout the whole of the scene depicted (the gods'
496 struggle against the giants), accompanying the triumphant progress of the immortals in the direction of the façade.

This concern for the perfect integration of the movement of the frieze with the building's design was taken even further by Phidias in the Parthenon, while, at the same time, he managed to endow it with the full religious significance. Along the top of the temple wall he portrayed the procession which once every four years brought the traditional offering of a ceremonial robe to the goddess
515 Athena. The marble procession includes several hundred
519, 520 figures. Starting at the south-west corner, it moves round the building, running parallel with the route taken by the real Panathenaic procession along the near-by Sacred Way. The artist portrays the procession with an assured grasp of rhythm, with the necessary rests but without repetition or slackening of tempo until the solemn moment when, on the main façade at the climax of the ceremony, the bearers of offerings arrive in the presence of the assembled Olympians. By creating the close union of architecture and figurative scenes Phidias had achieved a miracle—the

miracle of effecting an imperceptible transition between the world of men and the world of the gods.

Greek architects perfected, in addition to figurative ornamentation, mouldings and purely decorative motifs which had a lasting popularity.

The profiles and enrichments of mouldings have been dealt with in detailed studies which have revealed a certain development in the way they were used. It is to the artists of the archaic and classical periods that we owe the bands of egg-and-tongue, leaf-and-dart, astragals, palmettes, rosettes and scrolls of foliage which are still part of our decorative repertory today. On many and particularly on Ionic buildings these were the only embellishment. The Greek craftsman was so sure of his skill that he could introduce those almost unnoticeable variations which give life to any ornamentation. Modern restorations in their frigid, mechanical execution can be detected immediately when placed beside the genuine thing. At Delphi the 492 visitor can still see the first stone-courses of the Massalian treasury, with its very simple column base, consisting of a large torus with horizontal fluting surmounted by a band of bead-and-reel moulding. It is almost impossible not to reach out to touch it, so perfect is the workmanship, and that bare, deserted ruin still has the power to awaken in us a strong feeling of its former beauty.

Architecture and politics

Vast resources were needed to erect such buildings. Consequently the Golden Age in architecture followed closely upon the material prosperity of the Greek city-states. In the 6th century the largest and richest monuments appeared in those places which had become wealthy through trade and agriculture: Corinth, the principal trading city; Ionia, where a legendary luxury existed until the Persian conquest; the colonies in southern Italy and Sicily, where vast temples like the one at Poseidonia-Paestum are still standing today and where impressive ruins, as at Selinus, still provide evidence of the splendour 489, 491 of the archaic period in the west. A very typical example is provided by the Siphnian treasury at Delphi, a magnificent little building erected on the small Cycladic island of Siphnos which had become enormously rich after the 494–496 discovery of ores in its soil. Political developments of the 6th century which had produced flourishing tyrannical régimes in many Greek city-states encouraged the growth of architecture: the tyrants, wishing to dazzle the people, competed in splendour and extravagance and hoped to embellish the cities over which they ruled. In Samos,

264

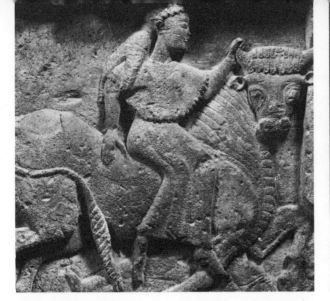

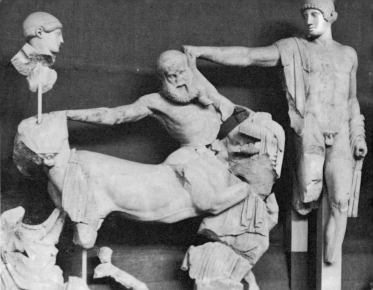

489. Metope from a temple at Selinus, Sicily, showing Europa and the Bull. c. 590–580 B.C. *Palermo Museum.*

490. Part of the west pediment of the temple of Zeus at Olympia, showing Apollo settling the battle of the Lapiths and Centaurs. Marble. c. 470–455 B.C. *Olympia Museum.*

Polycrates undertook one venture after another with the help of architects like the Samians Rhoecus and Theodorus. The Battiad kings in Cyrene adopted a tyrannic form of government and at the end of the 6th century built the temple of Zeus, which remains the largest Greek monument in Africa. Athens took a decisive step forward under the tyranny of Pisistratus and his sons, who put up several buildings of distinction on the Acropolis, such as the old temple of Athena, known as the Hecatompedon. At the same time the Alcmaeonid family, rivals of the Athenian tyrants by whom they had been exiled, secured amazing success for themselves by having the temple of Apollo at Delphi finished in marble instead of stone as had been stated in the specifications; in this way they won the favour of the Oracle, which helped to bring about their triumphant return to their native city. In later years the Periclean buildings on the Acropolis were, in the same way, the symbols of a political system. In the 4th century, when Alexander the Great at the head of a united Greek army regained Ionia from the Persians, he wanted to commemorate his visit by helping to rebuild the Artemisium at Ephesus, which had been destroyed in a fire, started, it was said, by Erostratus on the very night of the conqueror's birth. Architecture was the outward expression of the changing fortunes of political, social and economic history in the Greek world.

We have an even better idea of the close connection between the buildings and the life of the city-state from inscriptions which provide us with accounts and specifications. Chance excavations have given us, in a more or less dilapidated state, quite a large number of these engraved records. So we possess, for example, a section of the accounts for the Parthenon and the Erechtheum, full accounts for the temple of Asclepius at Epidaurus (first half of the 4th century), accounts relating to the restoration work carried out on the sanctuary at Delphi following the disaster of 373 and a very important building specification for the arsenal at Piraeus (second half of the 4th century). Other records, such as inventories, can supply us with valuable information; research is being carried on at the moment which, by working from the position of offerings, may make clear the interior design of the buildings which housed them at Athens and Delos.

Lastly, we should not forget that Greek architects liked to engage in intellectual discussion about their art and,

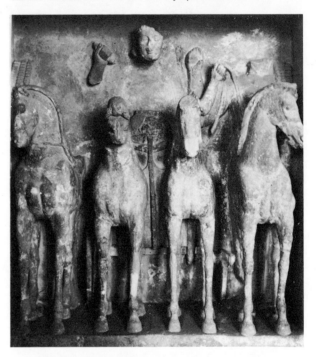

491. The quadriga of Apollo. Metope from Temple C at Selinus, Sicily. 560 B.C. *Palermo Museum.*

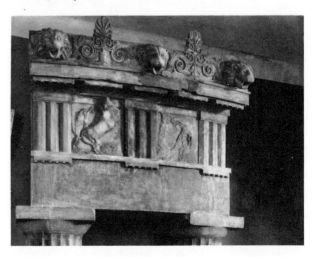

492. Metopes and triglyphs from the tholos on the Marmaria terrace, Delphi. Early 4th century B.C. *Delphi Museum.*

265

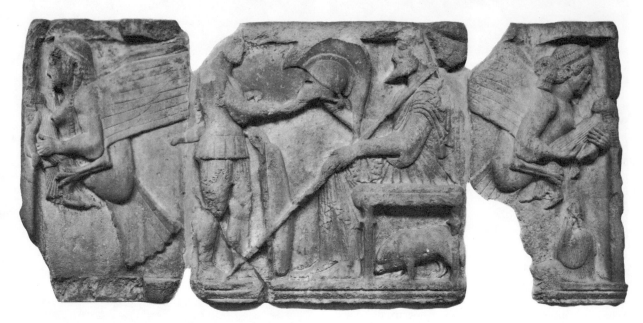

493. Tomb of the Harpies. Funerary cult scenes. *c.* 500 B.C. *British Museum.*

occasionally, from the archaic period on, wrote treatises containing comments on their own work. In the middle of the 4th century the Cretans Chersiphron and Metagenes, who designed the Artemisium at Ephesus, and Theodorus of Samos, who built the Heraeum for his native city, all wrote such works. We know that Ictinus, the architect of the Parthenon, established a school to which we should probably link Theodorus of Phocaea who, in the 4th century, wrote a monograph on a tholos at Delphi. The designer of the arsenal at Piraeus also wrote a commentary on the principles from which he had worked. All these treatises, no longer extant, were known to Vitruvius, the architect of the Augustan age whose Latin work *On Architecture* we still possess, written, it is true, very much under the influence of the theorists of the Hellenistic era. It is through Vitruvius, who was studied with such enthusiasm by Renaissance artists, that the legacy of the Greek architects of the Golden Age, has, in large part, come down to us.

FIGURATIVE ART

The late 7th century and the early 6th century mark an important turning point in the sphere of Greek figurative art. From this time, what we can call decorative art—vase painting, all types of relief (in stone, marble, bronze, metal and ivory), metal and terra-cotta figurines—gave the foremost place to the human figure, relegating other kinds of ornamentation to a secondary position. On the other hand, something of supreme importance had just occurred; this was the appearance of large-size sculpture which in its early stages experimented with over life-size works, as the Sunium statues show. In this large sculpture, too, the human body (and the nude male figure in particular) was the principal subject.

Naturalism and abstraction

Greek art, then, had by the beginning of the 6th century already started out along the path it was to travel—the path of humanism. It was naturally carried in this direction by the anthropomorphic polytheism from which it

drew its inspiration.

To portray gods in human form the human model necessarily had to be studied. This is why a continuous progression can be traced, from the stiff figures of the early archaic period, akin to geometric pictographs, right down to the end of the 4th century, which led Greek plastic art to find a solution to all the problems it would encounter—in the study of anatomy and of how to render movement, in the expression of emotion and the sense of individual likeness and in the rendering of perspective and the organisation of complex groups.

But the imitation of nature did not remain a superficial concern; it led to a step forward in consciousness which made claims to understanding as well as observation. Consequently, reproduction of reality was often more a question of reconstruction, for it was based on numerical relationships which the mind thought it could recognise in things: hence the importance of canons in Greek art. The rhythms springing from these calculations show the organising intelligence for ever at work, ruling and guiding the hand. Greek art, even at its most realistic, is steeped in intellectual activity. As these two qualities cannot be reconciled without a high degree of technical accomplishment, it is understandable that the all too rare surviving masterpieces should still stir us with a sense of their perfection.

Technique and art forms

There are two types of records which provide us with especially valuable evidence: sculpture and vases. Their study forms two separate branches of archaeology, each with its own tools for the job and its own individual working methods. The very large number of vases discovered in excavated sites has enabled considerable progress to be made in the classification of production centres, workshops and even individual painters, while chronology has become so exact that for the period from the 6th to the 4th centuries a fragment of figured pottery can, with a fair degree of certainty, be dated to within twenty years. Signatures and other inscriptions that are quite often found on vases have been a great help in this work. Collected together in specialist publications, these ceramic documents contain a mine of precious information on the

266

life and beliefs of the ancient Greeks. In their shapes and materials and in the fineness and colour of the clay and the splendour of the black glaze they are also invaluable works of art. But most of all the scenes portrayed on the majority of these vases are of inestimable interest, for they have preserved for us a reflection of vanished major works of painting from which vase painters drew their inspiration. In this respect texts are quite categorical: the Greeks admired painting just as much as sculpture, and Polygnotus, Zeuxis and Apelles were ranked as the equals of Phidias, Polycleitus and Praxiteles.

Most surviving sculpture is in stone, more specifically in marble. Not that Greek artists were more ready to work with a chisel than a burin; on the contrary, they had a particularly high regard for bronze statuary. But very few large bronzes have survived. We still have, on the other hand, an impressive number of marbles unearthed by chance excavations, even though the vast majority have vanished into lime kilns. Unfortunately they have usually suffered severe damage, and, above all, they have lost all the colouring which once gave them life.

The role of polychromy

All Greek stone sculpture, whether in the round or in relief, was polychrome; this is, in fact, a point of prime importance which cannot be overemphasised. In this we have quite definite information from texts. On the other hand, some monuments retain very distinct traces of their original polychromy: when the famous female statues from the Acropolis were brought to light again at the end of the last century the colouring on several of them had been partly preserved. Not only were garments, hair, eyes and lips adorned with vivid colours, but certain details like embroidery and various accessories of the robes, instead of being carved, were picked out in paint. Even the flesh was specially treated with a clear wax foundation. We can have a very good idea of just how different a Greek marble must have looked in those days compared with how it appears today. That rich polychromy made the work of plastic art both more gay and more striking; it brought out its realistic nature and established a close bond between sculpture and painting, techniques which we are accustomed to think of in separate compartments. From sculpture in the round to the fresco, from the bas-relief to the incised stele, each and every work was painted, and this was why the same artist was often both a painter and a sculptor.

Bronzes have undergone an equally considerable change in appearance. On discovery they are always heavily oxidised and totally covered by a verdigris deposit ranging in colour from azure blue to dark green. As long as this patina has not hardened into a thick, light green crust (known as the 'bronze disease'), art lovers take great delight in it and do their utmost to preserve it. It was not unknown in Antiquity, as a famous passage in Plutarch shows where he talks of Lacedaemonian votive statues at Delphi, but they knew it was the work of time and not of men. Far from encouraging its formation, they took steps to prevent its growth by frequent cleaning. The truth of the matter was that for them the great disadvantage of the patina was that it concealed beneath the oxidised deposit one of the features which they prized above all else in bronze statues: the carefully detailed burin-work which was done after the statue had been cast.

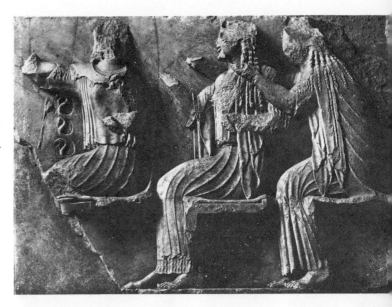

494. Seated gods. Detail of the frieze from the Siphnian treasury at Delphi. 550–525 B.C. (Cast.) *Louvre*.

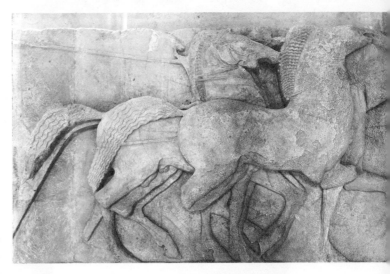

495. Detail of the frieze from the Siphnian treasury at Delphi. *c.* 525 B.C. (Cast.) *Louvre*.

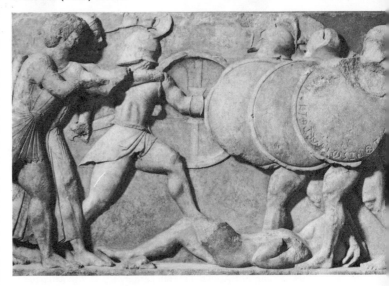

496. The battle of the gods and giants. Northern frieze, Siphnian treasury. *c.* 525 B.C. *Delphi Museum*.

267

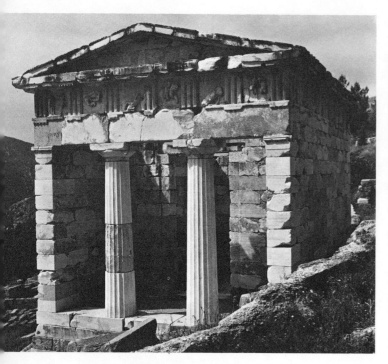

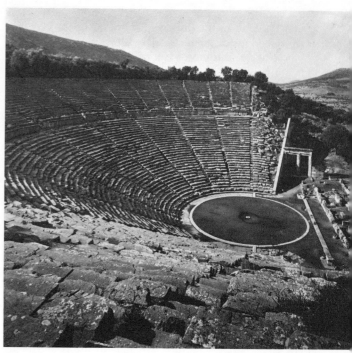

497. The Treasury of the Athenians at Delphi.

498. The theatre at Epidaurus. 4th century B.C.

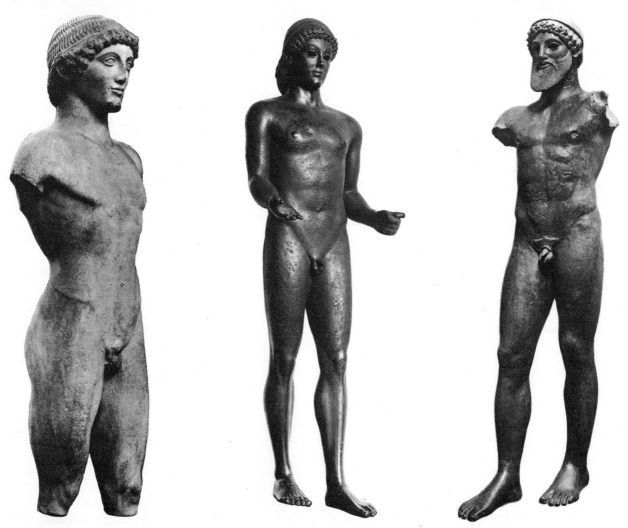

499. Strangford Apollo. Late 6th century B.C. *British Museum*.

500. The Piombino Apollo. Bronze. *c.* 500 B.C. *Louvre*.

501. Bronze statue of Poseidon, found in Boeotia. Beginning of the 5th century B.C. *National Museum, Athens*.

This can be clearly seen when an object undergoes a process to get rid of the patina; it turns an unpleasant black colour, but in cleaning all the fine chisel-work which was blurred over by oxidisation is revealed. In fact the real colour of Greek bronzes, which they had when they were taken from the mould, was the colour of a shining metal, like gold. So they would have glistened in the sunlight, standing in the sanctuaries. The eyes of these statues were set with coloured stones or green paste, the lips were covered with a plate of copper and the teeth were often represented by a small band of chased silver slipped between the parted lips; the many details of anatomy and dress, inlaid with metal of a colour contrasting with bronze, were similarly emphasised. Usually all these effects have now vanished.

Precious metals

The gold and ivory statues (called chryselephantine) were looked on by the classical Greeks as the very pinnacle of art. We know from texts how much these people admired these technically complex masterpieces, for which Phidias was especially renowned. A fortunate find at Delphi has given us several fragments of small chryselephantine statues—unluckily severely damaged by fire—which date from the 6th century. These specimens confirm what was already known of the methods employed by sculptors: the statue was made from wood and overlaid with thin plates of chased gold to represent clothing and with carved ivory plates for the naked parts of the figure. In the case of colossal images, like the Zeus at Olympia and the Athena in the Parthenon (Athena Parthenos) which could be anything up to 40 feet high, the body of the statue was no longer made of solid wood but of slats arranged around a structural framework. In the paved cella floor of the Parthenon a hollow can still be seen in which the beam serving for the spine of Phidias' Athena was embedded. To fit the ivory and gold plates over the carved wooden body was a task demanding the finest skill on the part of the carpenter and goldsmith. The statue was also incrusted with precious stones (to represent the eyes, for example), and parts were even painted, probably on wood: thus the concave face of the Athena Parthenos' shield was adorned with a painted composition showing the gods' struggle against the giants, while the convex face bore gold bas-reliefs depicting the Amazons' attack on the Acropolis. Inside the temple there was no light other than the daylight which streamed through the door, and in the shadows these statues must have been even more impressive as their reflections were mirrored in a wide, shallow pool set before the sacred image; into this, water and oil were poured, primarily intended to prevent the atmosphere from becoming too dry (which would have been injurious to these wood, ivory and gold structures). But the double image of the idol, reflected in this mirror set before it on the ground, must have had a striking effect on the imagination. It would be a great mistake to think of an art as somewhat barbarian just because of its bold combination of so many precious materials. To the mind of the classical Greek there was nothing incompatible between these statues and the restraint and austerity of other contemporary works of art. His taste did not find it difficult to reconcile such contrasts: an everyday simplicity was appropriate for a sepulchral stele because it helped to keep alive the memory of the dead person, but for a cult statue, which had to make divine majesty a tangible reality, nothing could be too lavish or too splendid.

Greek art, then, at the time of its dynamic growth and in its full maturity was a rich and vividly coloured art. One must be careful not to look at it exclusively from the point of view of a single technique. It is undoubtedly true that, for convenience of study, specialist research must be carried on, but this deliberate restriction should never cause us to forget the basic unity of Greek art—an art which in all its various spheres was always part of the same movement. An intaglio, a piece of jewellery, a fragment of painted pottery and a mirror-back are justifiably considered as records with as much to say about the history of Greek art as a bas-relief or a large bronze. We learn from ancient writings, moreover, that the most renowned artists did not look down upon the minor arts: Phidias was supposed to have carved fish, cicadas and bees, and the lamp which the sculptor Callimachus made for the Erechtheum was one of his most highly prized works. The story of Polycrates' ring as told by Herodotus, and Cicero's *Verrines*, shows us how much jewellery and gold and silver plate were enthusiastically admired by lovers of art.

THE 6TH CENTURY: THE CLIMAX OF ARCHAIC ART

In the early 6th century Greek art emerged from the Oriental influence which had deeply affected it in the preceding period.

Vase painting

There was a particularly marked development in the field of painted vases, of which there are a very great number of surviving examples. During the first half of the century there was a definite increase in the number of vases using the human figure as part of their ornamentation, while the importance of purely decorative motifs was weakening. Attic pottery already set the tone: well prepared for the task by the masters of the previous century, it was Attica that provided the first artist of importance by whom we possess signed works; this was Sophilus. His earliest works still rely on friezes of animals set face to face: sirens, sphinxes and other fabulous beasts which had been used so freely in the period of Oriental influence. But in his later works, first place was given to legendary scenes, like the wedding procession of Thetis and Peleus and the funerary games held in honour of Patroclus. Even as early as this, these images are striking in their accurate and vivid observation; take, for example, the stiff formality of the mother goddesses who file past so sedately in the procession.

The same qualities can be noticed in Corinthian ceramic art, which was then at the peak of its power. Tradition was undoubtedly stronger there than in Attica, and the more common Corinthian works remained faithful, right to the last, to the old Oriental motifs. But the largest and finest vases were decorated with scenes taken from life: on a famous krater the painter depicted the feast Eurytius gave for Hercules, which became the pretext for portraying a vividly observed banqueting scene. Even militarist Sparta, which for the next three-quarters of a century was still open to outside influences, took part in this

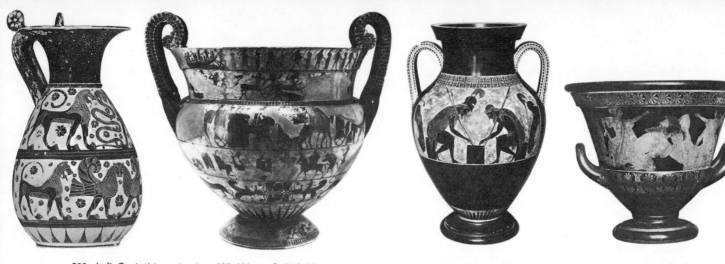

502. *Left*. Corinthian wine jug. 625–600 B.C. *British Museum*.

503. *Right*. The François Vase. Middle of the 6th century B.C. *Archaeological Museum, Florence*.

504. *Left*. Amphora by Exekias. The decoration shows Achilles and Ajax playing dice. Second half of the 6th century B.C. *Etruscan Museum, Vatican, Rome*.

505. *Right*. Red-figure krater by Euphronius. Fight between Hercules and Antaeus. End of the 6th century B.C.

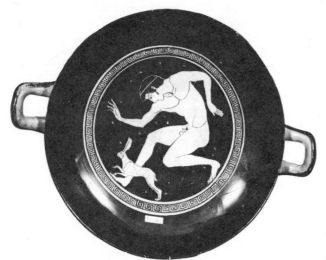

506. *Above*. Attic kylix. The decoration shows a youth chasing a hare. c. 500 B.C. *British Museum*.

507. *Left*. Detail of an Attic amphora with figure of Artemis in red and black. 530–500 B.C. *National Archaeological Museum, Madrid*.

508. *Right*. Detail of an Attic amphora with red and black figure of a Maenad, painted by Psiax. 530–500 B.C. *National Archaeological Museum, Madrid*.

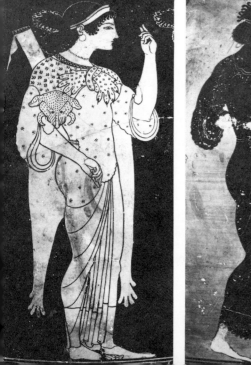
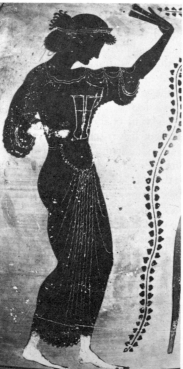

movement towards artistic freedom. At this time she began to export ceramics with figurative scenes which took their inspiration mainly from legend or from the everyday life of the time. Inside a bowl we see a line of Lacedaemonian soldiers marching, bearing on their shoulders the bodies of their dead comrades brought back from the field of battle. On another we are carried to a foreign land—to distant Cyrene, linked to Sparta by ancient ties of friendship; here we watch the weighing of a tribute raised by the natives for King Arcesilaus II, who is identified by an inscription. The tribute, made up of tubers of silphium, a much sought-after plant, is being placed in sacks and stored in the royal cellars. How strange it is to watch that historic scene, dating from 570–60, which seems to bring us into closer familiarity with a sovereign whom we know only from texts. The Laconian painter who produced it has thereby left us outstanding proof that Greek art from this time on was able to draw its inspiration from real life.

At about the same time, in Athens, Ergotimos the potter and Klitias the painter produced the monumental krater known as the François Vase, which is a fine ex- 503 ample of the new trend in painting during the first half of the 6th century. Of six decorated bands which divide up the area between the base and mouth of the vase, there is only one, the least obvious, which still has a place for traditional animals and monsters. The other five bands are devoted to various legendary scenes, among which can be recognised certain subjects already treated by Sophilus but executed with more imagination and refinement than can be found in his works. It is evident, in any case, that vase painters drew upon a repertory of subjects taken over from the mainstream of painting. Of this we can have some idea from the small painted wooden panels discovered at Pitsa, near Corinth; with a richer variety of colour (blues and greens are added to black and reddish-purple), they can be very well compared in drawing, composition and choice of subject to vase painting of the time.

Sculpture

We find that plastic art in the course of the first half of the 6th century followed the same road as painting. Religious convention was almost certainly responsible for the fact that symmetrically arranged animal groups—lions devouring bulls, felines staring hypnotically at the spectator, etc.—continued to appear on the pediments of some temples. Yet we have seen that, in the early part of the century, in the corners of the Corfu pediment, a place was made for legendary scenes comparable to those appearing in vase painting. During the first half of the 6th century several buildings on the Athenian Acropolis had pediments ornamented with the same subjects as can be found on painted vases of the time, such as the labours of Hercules and incidents from the Trojan War. Sculptors at first found some difficulty in organising scenes clearly taken over from friezes within the triangular framework of the pediment, but they came to learn how to make better use of the angles; they turned the Triton's twirling tail to good purpose.

Bas-reliefs, too, lend themselves to comparison with vases. A metope from a Sicyonian building erected at 510 Delphi about 570–60 depicts the ranks of the Dioscuri and their attendants driving before them oxen captured in a raid. The sculptor has taken great pleasure in increasing the number of planes by presenting the oxen in strict alignment one behind the other, just as painters, portraying processions on vases, had treated four horses pulling a chariot as an arrangement in depth.

Sculpture in the round presented other problems: there was not so much freedom to express movement. Tradition had laid down stereotyped poses for sacred statues, and with votive or sepulchral images of human beings, conventional ideas of decorum restricted individual originality. A good illustration of the strength of belief which attached to these simulacra is the written inscription which for a long time adopted the formula, 'I am so-and-so,' implying that the statue and person portrayed were actually identified.

In the wealthy Greek cities of the Anatolian coast, directly influenced by Oriental civilisations, preference was given to the seated male figure clothed in a long robe which disguised the forms of the body. This shows one of the strong tendencies of archaic art, that of Ionian art of Asia Minor, which had become slack and heavy and was not concerned with details of anatomy. The Cycladic Islands and the Greek mainland were, on the contrary, taken up with the nude male figure, and in this they broke away from Eastern tradition which was extremely prudish on this point. The customary athletic games most certainly had a great deal to do with this taste. After the impressive statues from Sunium, which belong to the end of the 7th century, the chief interpretations of the 462 kouros type, that is, the naked athletic youth, are adequately embodied in a small number of typical examples: the two statues of Cleobis and Biton in Delphi—the work of an Argive sculptor, the Theran kouros and lastly 461 the famous Calf-bearer in Athens. The two Argive statues, powerful, thick-set, even slightly crude, with the forms of the body accentuated in their strong stylisation, are typical examples of Peloponnesian art. The Theran kouros, his face already radiant with the celebrated archaic smile, is more slender and relaxed but has also been more slackly treated: he conforms to the ideal of Cycladic art. The Calf-bearer has a sharp face; the forms of the body are both elegant and solid and show a close observation of anatomy—all of which reveals in the artist an acute feeling for discipline and structure. With its refinement of execution, this study is characteristic of Attic art.

These four main trends—Anatolian Ionian art, Pelo-

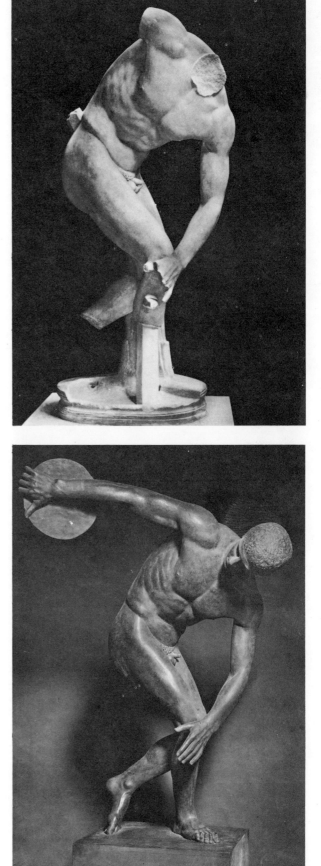

509. a. The Discus Thrower, by Myron. c. 450 B.C. Marble copy. b. Reconstruction of the Discus Thrower taken from many replicas. *Terme Museum, Rome.*

271

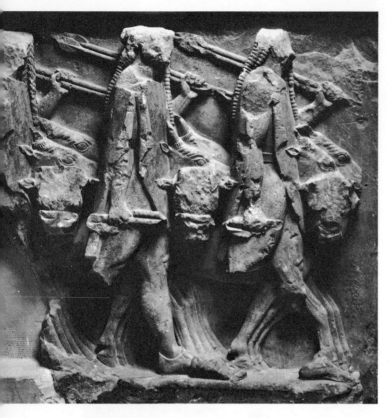

510. Raid by the Dioscuri. Metope from the Sicyonian treasury. *c.* 560 B.C. *Delphi Museum.*

ponnesian art (traditionally called 'Dorian'), Cycladic Ionian art and Attic art—are virtually the only valid lines along which sculpture can be classified. For a long time modern scholars have been trying to differentiate between theoretical local schools in questions of detail. Just as the various pottery-producing centres can be distinguished, they would like to be able to separate the sculpture of Naxos, Paros and Delos, or of Corinth and Sicyon. They are still hoping to identify specifically western characteristics in the fine compositions on the archaic metopes discovered at Selinus or, in more recent years, at the mouth of the Silaris near Paestum. This research, conducted with the utmost care and subtlety, has added to our knowledge on a number of points, but it has not managed to establish any undebatable classifications.

But rather than poorly defined schools it is individual artists that one would like to know more about. For Hellenic art from the earliest period never appeared as an anonymous, collective art but (and this is one of its basic characteristics) very much as the work of individuals who stamped it with the mark of their own genius. The Greeks were fully aware of this fact; witness the importance they attached to the legendary figure of Daedalus. In the early 6th century there were still sculptors who freely proclaimed themselves as the disciples of this master; such, for example, were the Cretans Dipoinos and Scyllis and their pupils Tectaios and Angelion who produced a celebrated Apollo at Delos. Unfortunately, we possess only the faintest trace of their work: from written descriptions we can just about recognise the Delian Apollo in its crudely sketched outline which appeared on late Athenian coins. We can take this opportunity to point out that recent work has brought to light everything which can properly be

extracted from numismatic examples, which, especially in the Hellenistic and Roman periods, took their inspiration from works of sculpture that have since disappeared.

The frequent occurrence of signatures is another sign of the Greek artist's sense of individuality. Sculptors, like painters and potters, like to sign their work. We have a great many inscribed signatures from as early as the 6th century, and they are often names of which no mention is made in any of the extant literary texts. A whole branch of Greek epigraphy is devoted to the study of these records. They implement the information supplied by the traveller Pausanius who in the 2nd century A.D. included in his *Guide to Greece* highly detailed descriptions of works of art which could still be seen in his day.

In this way an important fact can be established: from the archaic period the artist travelled freely throughout the Greek world. As his fame spread, more and more commissions flowed in from far afield and he went to carry them out on the spot. In this way the Cretans Dipoinos and Scyllis travelled all over the Peloponnese. Theodorus of Samos, the renowned sculptor who lived in the middle of the 6th century, did not confine his activity to his native island: there is evidence that he visited Sparta and Ephesus. Smilis, an artist from Aegina, was, on the other hand, summoned to Samos to make the cult statue for the temple of Hera. In the second half of the century the Lacedaemonians invited Bathycles of Magnesia, an Ionian from Anatolia, to decorate their national sanctuary at Amyclae, whereas the Ionians had the cult statue for their temple of Apollo carved by a Peloponnesian artist, Canachus of Sicyon. This perpetual circulation of artists from one region to another, regardless of native country or language, explains why it is virtually impossible to establish any definite classifications of local schools. Besides, everything gave encouragement to interchange of influences. The great sanctuaries like those at Olympia and Delphi attracted pilgrims from all over **487, 488** who there dedicated votive offerings produced by the widest variety of artists; this provided an endless opportunity for different styles to be brought together. Maritime trading established economic relations between cities, which increased the circulation of manufactured products such as pottery, small bronze objects and jewellery. Even objects of considerable size could be transported to very distant places: witness the monumental Vix krater, a late **367** 6th century Greek work, which was recently discovered in a Gallic tomb in Burgundy.

The advance towards naturalism

A good judge, then, has been able to say that in archaic art a general advance towards naturalism is far more apparent than are any well-defined regional characteristics.

It was a very rapid advance and one which we cannot possibly attempt to go over here. But with the help of detailed studies, we can follow its development towards a finer rendering of the human body both in the drawing of the vase paintings and in the modelling of the anatomy in the nude male statues. By the end of the century the kouros type had achieved a kind of perfection: such is the case with the superb marble sepulchral monument of a certain Aristodicos, discovered a short time ago in the small Attic market town of Anavyssos. In all the fullness of its supple and controlled strength it is a wonderful evocation of the aristocratic youth of Athens in the years before the Median Wars. The progress from the Theran kouros of three-quarters of a century earlier is tremendous.

442 The draped female figure, or kore, made the same rapid progress. About 570, the famous Hera of Samos was carved in the hieratic style, the body sheathed in the unrealistic folds of a robe that was both rigid and insubstantial. Thanks to the splendid series of korai from the Acropolis, we can see how sculptors very quickly began to take an interest in both the forms of the female body,

466–468 which became increasingly perceptible beneath draperies which moulded them, and in the almost architectural treatment of folds. The korai lent themselves to infinite variations, and, with the enigmatic charm of their faces matched by the grace of their draped bodies, we can still fall under their spell. These statues, sometimes quite small in size but of very polished workmanship and of great beauty, reveal a minute attention to the decorative arrangement of costume and head-dress. They conjure up a civilisation which loved luxury and a life of grace and refinement. Such works as these are excellent testimonials to Athenian life in those times.

The supremacy of Athens

Most of the korai come from Athens, where their survival was due to extraordinary circumstances: they were buried after the buildings and statues on the Acropolis were burned and destroyed by the Persians in 480. There are many other records which show that Attica, inhabited by an artistically gifted people with many ancient traditions to draw upon, began to take a leading part in Greek civilisation from the second half of the 6th century; despite political strife, Pisistratus and his sons provided the impulse in Athens for a period of extraordinary economic prosperity which was accompanied by thriving artistic activity. At that time Athens did not occupy the unchallenged first place which it was to hold in the following century, but through the high quality and abundance of works of art being produced it already stood out from the other city-states; and in the years ahead this applied both

504 to pottery and sculpture. In a few years Attic vases came
507, 508 to dominate the market. This achievement was due in large part to the fact that Corinth, Athens' greatest rival in this sphere, was now concentrating on the manufacture of metal objects, for which it was renowned. But Attic pottery deserved its victory because of its technical perfection—the high quality of the red clay, the unequalled splendour of the black glaze and the supple and unerring draughtsmanship. At this time first rank masters like

504 Exekias painted superb vases on which black figures stood out in silhouette on a red clay ground. Their sometimes noble, sometimes mundane, inspiration occasionally achieved a sublime lyricism, as on the famous cup which shows Dionysus lying in a boat which sails over a sea where dolphins play, while from the bottom of the mast springs a great vine that shelters the god beneath its sweeping branches.

In the last quarter of the century vase painters replaced the black-figure technique by the reverse process, known
505 as red figure, in which the figures appeared in red clay and stood out against a black-glazed ground. Detail, instead of being engraved with a pointed tool, was now painted in. The more flexible red-figure technique was to

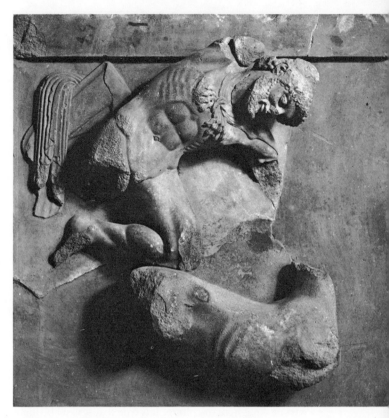

511. Scene from the exploits of Hercules and Theseus. Metope from the treasury of the Athenians at Delphi. 500–495 B.C. *Delphi Museum.*

enable Attic potters to make even further advances. At the end of the 6th century this is exemplified in the work of painters like Euphronius. In these works, which contained a number of allusions to everyday life, the aristocratic and cultured society of Athens before and after the fall of the Pisistratids comes to life for us with all its delight in athletic sports, its reverence of Homer and enthusiasm for Anacreon and its passionate love of youth and beauty. Vase painters often wrote on the sides of vases the admiring comment, 'So-and-so is fair.' Sepulchral stelae never depicted the old man, weary of life, but the man he had been at the peak of his strength and youth. It was a prosperous time for artists, who were sometimes linked to the political fortunes of a great family like the sculptor Antenor who worked for the Alcmaeonids. But the sons of these luxury-loving men, so proud of their curling hair, were to be able to withstand the Persians at Marathon. Sometime before this battle, about the year 500, they lauded the deeds of Hercules and the 511 Athenian Theseus on the metopes of the treasury at Delphi: these supple yet disciplined compositions, carved in marble by an exacting hand, represent the finest flowering of Attic archaic art.

THE 5TH CENTURY: THE FIRST CLASSICAL PERIOD

Early in the 5th century the Persians swept down over Greece. Athens, which was severely hit by the invasion, found a new strength in this ordeal and immediately after it built up a considerable empire which was, however, not to last long. During the 5th century the city-state of Themistocles, Cimon and Pericles came to play a leading

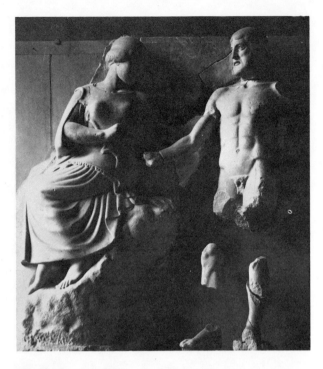

512. Metope from the temple of Zeus at Olympia. Hercules giving Athena the birds from Lake Stymphalus. 470–455 B.C. *Louvre.*

part in the sphere of culture. It is true that several brilliant individual artists, among them Polycleitus of Argos, managed not to come under Athens' sway; but as soon as Phidias' genius had made itself plain, the progress of Greek art for the next fifty years was to be the progress of Attic art. In contrast to the expansiveness and creative freedom typical of the preceding century, the 5th century—the age in which the first form of classicism took shape and came to maturity—for all its wealth, presents a great degree of unity. It can be divided into two main phases: the period of Phidias' forerunners and that of Phidias and his followers. We shall look at each of these in turn.

The transitional style

The period of the transitional style stretches from about the beginning of the 5th century to the appearance of Phidias' earliest works (*c.* 460). After the studied refinement and elaboration of the metopes from the Athenian treasury at Delphi (dating from the period immediately preceding Marathon) sculptors and, to a lesser extent, painters began to aim at a greater simplicity and even at a certain ruggedness. The ideal physical type changed: in face, the chin became broader and more prominent, the forehead more square, the eyes were no longer almond-shaped, the nose was shortened and the smile— that enchanting, enigmatic, archaic smile—completely vanished. The pleasantly cheerful expression which never left the faces of heroes or goddesses, even when they were under the most violent strain or involved in deeds of extreme cruelty, was replaced by an expression of sober serenity that is not without a certain coldness; here, too, neither emotion nor strain could disturb the expression. Theseus continues to smile from the Athenian treasury with a strange tenderness while in the act of striking down the Amazon; forty years later the Lapith woman from the temple of Zeus at Olympia, clasped by a Centaur in a rough embrace, maintains an expressionless face.

Sculptors adapted themselves superbly well to this new style. But here we meet with a difficulty which only grows worse as we go on. Contemporary literary texts and inscriptions give us quite a lot of information about the great masters, but surviving works are generally without any authenticated status. The fame of certain statues, moreover, meant that they came to be copied by artists of the Roman period, sometimes with accuracy but more often with alterations of varying importance. Many of these late copies (often in marble where the original was bronze) have passed into our hands. The archaeologist must, therefore, use texts and figurative records to arrive at some reconstruction of works no longer in existence. This problem does not arise with the archaic period, for although archaic works were imitated, they were not, strictly speaking, copied. On the other hand, for the transitional period, a critical assessment of copies presents many often insoluble difficulties.

At this time there were great artists like Onatas, Pythagoras, Kritios, Calamis and Myron who were greatly esteemed. They mostly seem to have worked in bronze, the potentialities of which they wanted to exploit to the utmost in order to express movement. The time of the rather stiff stance of the archaic kouros was well and truly over. Even when he portrayed a figure in a relaxed pose, the sculptor of the transitional period endowed it with a living rhythm which the eye took for potential movement. This was Kritios' way, who, along with Myron, is the one artist of this group of whom we have some small knowledge. In the marble 'Kritian Boy' in the Acropolis Museum, which is attributed to him, the planes of the legs, hips, shoulders and face are delicately pivoted on a vertical axis, giving the body a slight twist and so breaking with the archaic frontal attitude. The same rhythm, but slightly more stressed, appears again in the Delphic Charioteer, a bronze original which has **443** many features in common with Kritios' statue. It is the only surviving figure from a votive group which portrayed the victorious chariot in a race and shows the driver with the reins still quivering in his hands. It conveys a feeling of controlled strength, of mental and muscular tension held in check by a clear effort of the will and a self-confidence, a sense of being secure in the gods' favour. Its rich expressiveness is based on the combined use of simple numerical, geometric schematisation, which analysis brings out without difficulty, and a high degree of realistic observation which in the treatment of detail gives variation and life to the mathematical rhythm from which the work as a whole takes its solidity.

Sculptors of the transitional period, then, showed their virtuosity by capturing in bronze the isolated, fleeting moment. This is also true of the statuettes of Zeus hurling a thunderbolt and of Hercules about to strike a blow with his club, as well as of larger pieces of sculpture, like Myron's Discus Thrower, of which we possess several **509** copies. Realistic observation of nature always supplied the basic elements which were then reorganised by the intellect and so became more real than reality. At times, the artist managed to combine in one work a forceful attitude with a calm godlike majesty: such is the case with the Poseidon from Histiaea, his trident poised behind **514** him, ready to strike—a vivid plastic translation of Aeschylus' lines describing 'the god who rules the seas and wields the unerring spear'.

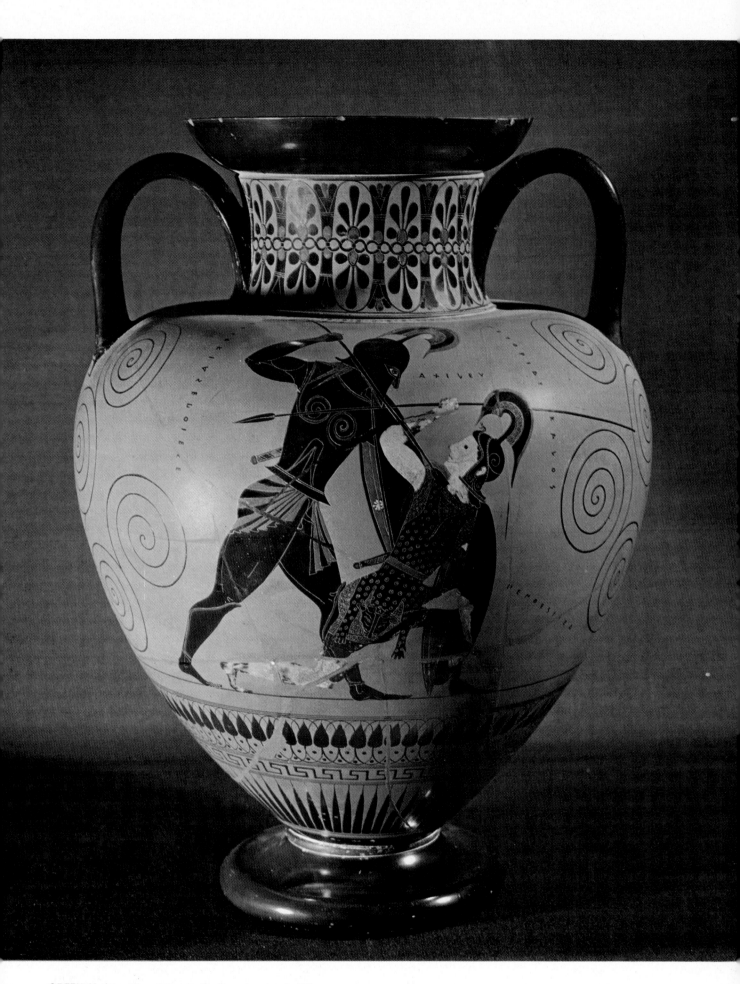

GREEK. Hydria with painting by Exekias showing Achilles
slaying Penthesilea. *c.* 530 B.C. British Museum. *Museum
photograph.*

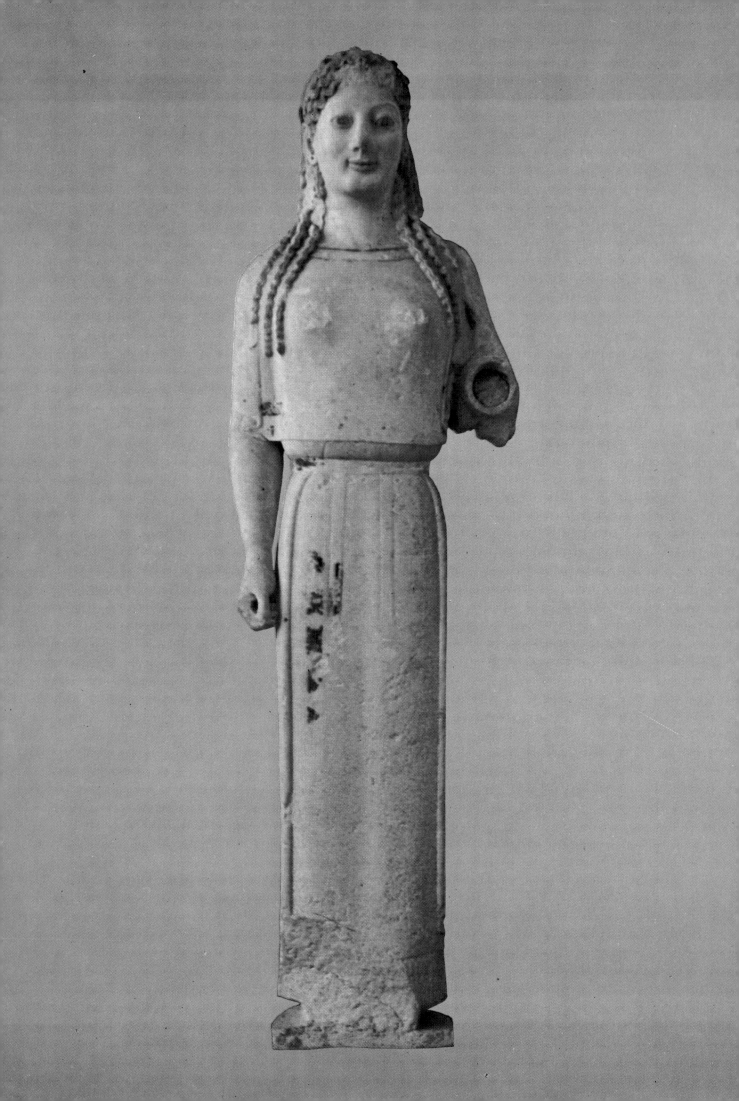

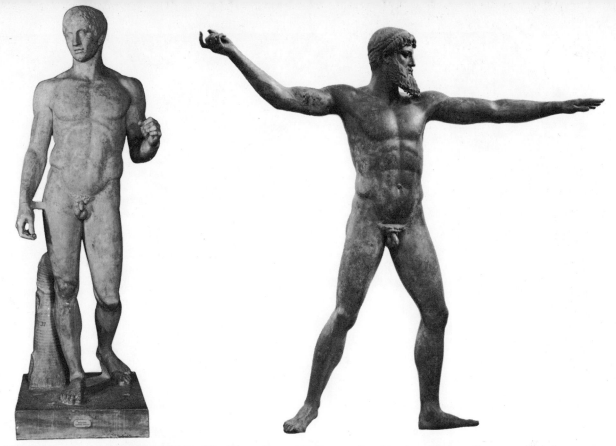

513. The Doryphorus, by Polycleitus. Middle of the 5th century B.C. Roman copy of a bronze original. *Naples Museum.*

514. Zeus or Poseidon from Histiaea. Bronze attributed to Calamis. *c.* 470 B.C. *National Museum, Athens.*

If these works of the transitional period make us think spontaneously of some line of poetry it is not accidental. The generation that fought at Marathon and the one that came after it had Aeschylus and Pindar as poets. Pindar sang of the Greek city-state, triumphant over the barbarians and loyal to its gods, while Aeschylus gave voice to the aristocratic ideal and the great ancestral myths.

If Aeschylus throws light on the Poseidon from Histiaea, the themes of Pindar seem to find an extraordinary echo in the sculpture on the temple of Zeus at Olympia, executed about 460 by an unknown artist. The metopes illustrate the labours of Hercules, who was helped in his trials by his protectress Athena. These concentrated, powerful and expressive compositions achieve their force by a simplicity of line and by clearly stressed verticals and sweeping diagonals. They come to life by a variety of delicate touches: a young, unhelmeted Athena, seated, like a shepherdess, on a rock, accepts Hercules' offering of the birds from Lake Stymphalus; elsewhere, in the Atlas episode, sympathetically and unobtrusively she helps her favourite to bear the weight of the heavens. On the rear pediment, above the frantic confusion of struggling Centaurs and Lapiths (with a rhythm springing from subtle relationships between the groups), towers the supremely calm and detached presence of Apollo. On the east façade we watch preparations for the chariot race to be run between Pelops and Oenomaus, a local myth here very much in its right place: Zeus stands at the centre, presiding over this scene which is peaceful yet charged with an atmosphere of foreboding. There is no other plastic composition which so well conveys a feeling of the unseen hand of destiny.

Another artist who loved scenes which struck a similarly tragic chord was the painter Polygnotus of Thasos, whose works are known to us only by descriptions and references made by ancient authors but who played such

a decisive part in the development of art. He was the first to arrange figures on several levels, which he did in his large frescoes and painted panels, through the invention of a mountainous landscape. He thus created a kind of perspective which gave his works depth and made them very different from the earlier frieze compositions. At the same time he set about trying to express emotion, not merely through stance and gesture, as in the earlier manner, but by portraying individual faces, realistically observed. In this he was ahead of his time and so prepared the way for the art of the 4th century. These innovations which were ascribed to Polygnotus recur in vase painting around 470–60 and give a clear picture of the relationship between vase painting and painting proper.

At this time there was a close kinship between different art forms: a profitable comparison can be made between the profile of the Delphic Charioteer, the head of Orpheus from a white-ground cup and the Apollo of Catanian coins. The stylistic unity apparent in all media reigned, from one end of the Greek world to the other: the noble gravity stamped on the features of a marble goddess found at Cyrene can be discovered, some twenty years later, in the faces of gods from the metopes of Temple E at Selinus.

Phidias and the mature classical style

Phidias' art was shaped by the discipline of the transitional style which he took over; in stripping this of its excessive austerity, he brought it to full maturity. One of his contemporaries, Polycleitus, had a considerable influence in his own way by his modification and codification of a system of proportions of the human body and his creation of an idealised type having a harmony that was pleasing to the eye and mind alike. This was the canon embodied in the statue of the Doryphorus, or the Lance-bearer, of which we have a number of faithful copies. But this perfection of form was, it would seem,

487, 488

512

513

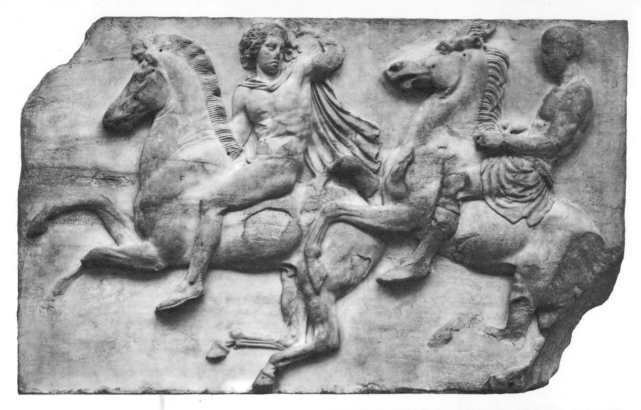

515. Horsemen. West frieze of the Parthenon. 440–437 B.C.
British Museum.

516. Horse's head. East pediment, north-east corner of the
Parthenon. 440–437 B.C. *British Museum.*

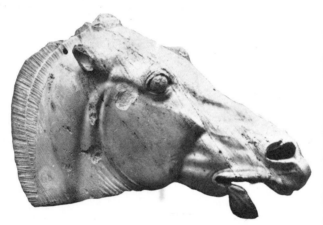

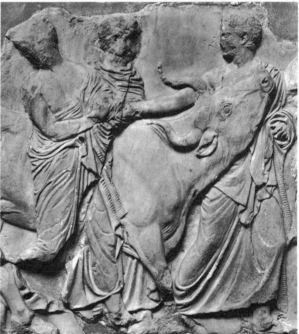

517. Heifers being led to sacrifice. South frieze of the
Parthenon. 440–437 B.C. *British Museum.*

518. The Three Fates. East pediment of the Parthenon.
446–437 B.C. *British Museum.*

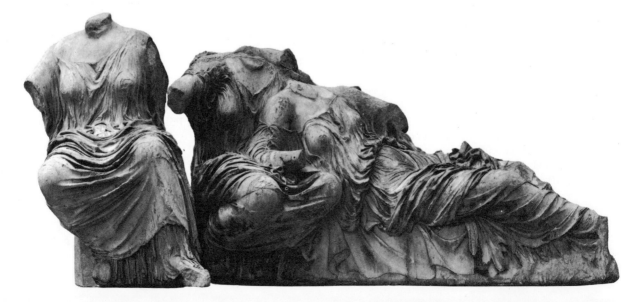

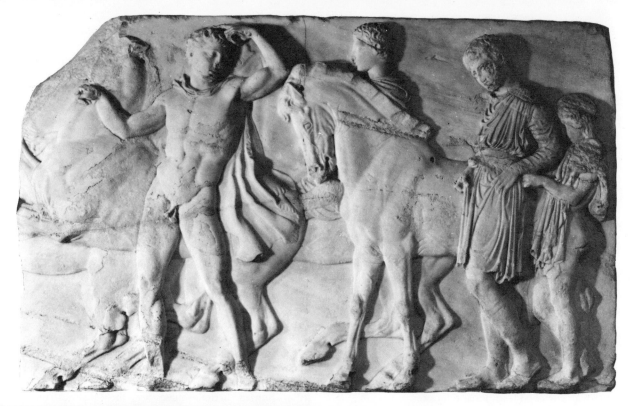

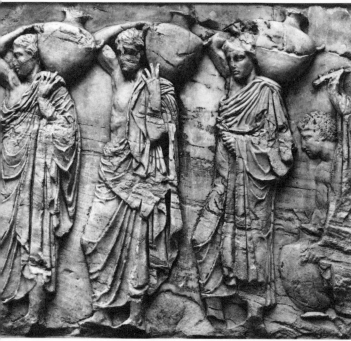

519. Youths and horsemen. North frieze of the Parthenon. 440–437 B.C. *British Museum*.

520. Men carrying water jars. North frieze of the Parthenon. 440–437 B.C. *Acropolis Museum, Athens*.

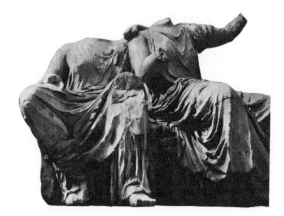

521. Demeter and Persephone. East pediment of the Parthenon. 440–437 B.C. *British Museum*.

522. The Ilissus. West pediment of the Parthenon. 440–437 B.C. *British Museum*.

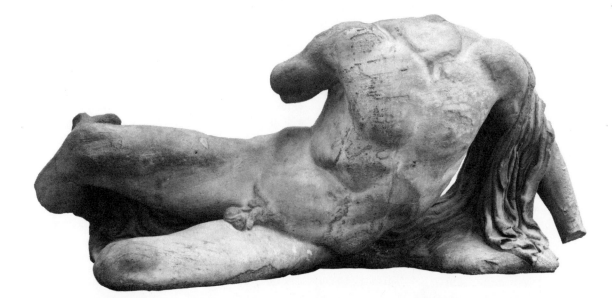

without soul, and the Greeks, alive to beauty but alive also to spiritual inspiration, were very quick to feel it.

Whatever their admiration of Polycleitus their regard for Phidias was on a completely different plane. Sculptor, painter, goldsmith, architect, Phidias not only exploited all the resources of art to the full with complete mastery, but he was able to express in his works, more powerfully than anyone had done before him, a religious and patriotic conception whose nobility still fills us with wonder. Never had the Greek idea of the immortals been more finely embodied than in the chryselephantine statue of Zeus at Olympia, which Phidias completed about the year 448 and which won him his glorious reputation. It was said that the god's majesty had been revealed to him by a line from Homer. If it is worth little else, the story is, at least, a reminder that the two great figures behind the elaboration of Greek religion were the poet and the sculptor, the one who set down the great stories of mythology and the other who gave the gods a concrete shape. In a cultural tradition which was closely bound up with religious images, the artist's role was obviously of prime importance: when Phidias as an artist expressed his sublime idea of the gods, as Quintilian put it he in some way enriched traditional religion.

Today we have only an imperfect appreciation of this religious and cultural contribution, from Pausanius' descriptions which, together with a few pictorial records, mostly mediocre and dating from a later period, allow us to form a very inadequate idea of the two great cult statues, the Zeus at Olympia and the Athena from the Parthenon. But the sculptured decoration from the Par- 515–522 thenon, a large part of which has been preserved, is more immediately illuminating. The work's unity, questioned for a good many years, has after detailed study finally been established. Emphasis has been put on the way Phidias contrived to relate the decoration of the temple to that of the cult statue. Some examples are particularly meaningful: on several occasions one finds that a scene from mythology is set between the two celestial deities of the sun and moon, showing that whatever was taking place was part of the vast cosmic rhythm.

Phidias brought a plastic imagination of astounding fertility to work in the service of a powerful idea. So forceful was this imagination that although there was a whole army of craftsmen working under him (except in the metopes which were the earliest part of the work) there are no signs of individual divergences. Even more than in the nude male figure, his genius truly came into its own in the treatment of the draped figure. Previously there had still been something slightly frigid and rather stylised about the treatment of drapery. Phidias gave it a fresh, rich fullness, a new eloquence, his inexhaustibly fertile imagination organising the abundance of voluminous folds without allowing them to detract from the solid structure and the balance of the figures. From the superb head on Metope I on the southern side, which was probably Phidias' own work, to the pure faces of the Ergastinae (maidens who had woven the peplos), from the tense, highly mettled, fiery horses to the gods and goddesses of the east pediment seated in relaxed poses, Phidias created a whole world which sprang to life under his genius. He fulfilled Pericles' dream and created a monument which men throughout the ages were to admire.

Even after his trial and death, no cloud could cover the radiant inspiration of his work. Not only sculptors but painters, too, came under his influence. A whole period of Attic ceramic art is called after him. In Sicily the engravers Eucleidas and Evainetos produced admirable coins showing close affinities with the Parthenon figures. But most appealing of all perhaps for us today are those white-ground vases (called lekythoi) which were set as 524 offerings on tombs, and the sepulchral stelae. They convey with an extraordinary delicacy what the Greek of the classical period felt on the death of someone dear to him: religious reverence is mingled with human love. In these 'family gatherings' set, as it were, out of time, the dead man appears in the midst of his close relations and in no way set apart from them. A sense of reflective peace and quiet sorrow pervades these scenes which are profoundly moving in their wordless eloquence.

So it is that figurative art can let us penetrate to the very core of a people. This nobility and love of man turn our thoughts to the tragedies of Sophocles, a contemporary of Phidias, who was shaped by the same disciplines. A trust in mankind and a belief in human dignity which the intangible framework of city-state and religion held secure, a desire for order which directed, but did not stifle, human action—these are the qualities which 5th-century classicism holds up for our admiration. Violent, brute emotion, it is true, was not ignored; vase painters were not afraid to show drunkenness and debauchery, but for the Greeks of the first classical period the animal appetites were mastered by the heroes' manly valour. This valour was backed up by the city-state's traditions, and as these began to crumble away, individual desires began to show themselves more and more plainly. Already in the 5th century the power of this individualism was understood and was conveyed in the rare but expressive character portraits. Whereas Cresilas' Pericles, 523 as it appears in later copies, keeps faithfully to the iconographic pattern of regular beauty, the bust of Themistocles from Ostia portrays the great strategist's features in all their forceful ugliness. It was by developing the idea of the individual—even, if necessary, in the face of the rules of society—that the 4th century injected a new spirit into the classical tradition.

THE 4TH CENTURY

The 4th century, unlike the unified age of Phidias, appears as a time of great diversity. As political and social structures broke up, as religious feeling altered and the influence of the Sophists and Socrates caused men to give up old ways of thinking, art became the expression of the confusion and upheaval of the times.

There were already signs of new trends in the last years of the 5th century, among Phidias' immediate successors: the sculptor Callimachus and his imitators, for 527 example from the drapery of the Parthenon figures, 528 evolved new effects of transparency, of the diaphanous 'wet' drapery which, especially in female figures, revealed the forms of the body. This we can see in the enchanting figures of Victory which adorned the parapet of the tem- 526 ple of Athena Nike on the Acropolis. This refined delicacy had its equivalent in vase painting in, for example, those delightful pictures of Aphrodite surrounded by Loves and Graces which were the crowning achievements of the movement towards the delicately decorative rather

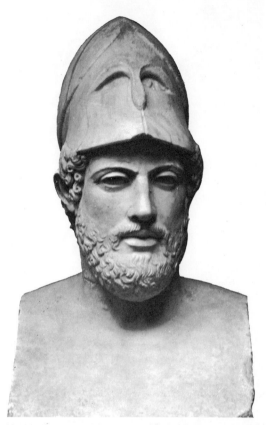

523. Marble bust copied from a statue by Cresilas. 499–429 B.C. *Vatican Museum, Rome.*

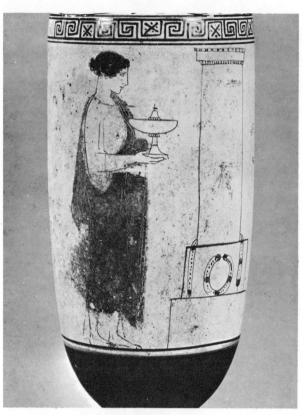

524. Lekythos. Style of the Achilles Painter. Attic white-ground. *Museum of Fine Arts, Boston.*

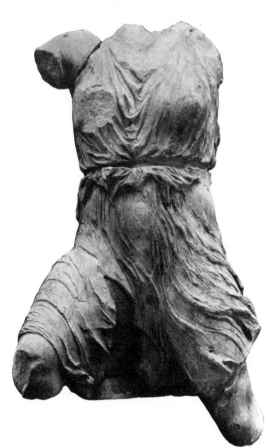

525. Victory from the east pediment of the Parthenon. 440–437 B.C.

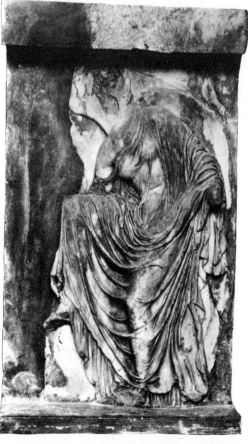

526. Victory removing her sandal. Fragment from the parapet of the temple of Athena Nike. Late 5th century B.C. *Acropolis Museum, Athens.*

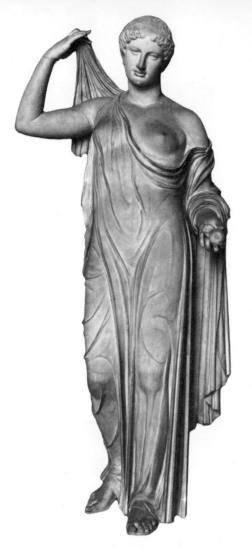

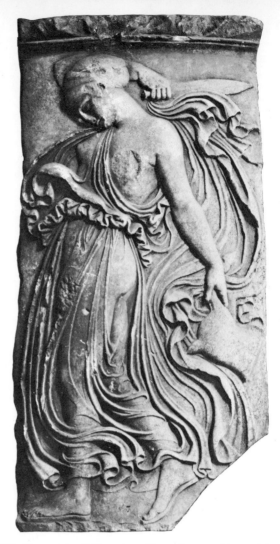

527. Venus Genetrix, attributed to Callimachus. Roman copy. Late 5th century B.C. *Louvre*.

528. Maenad, by Callimachus. 5th century B.C. *Museo dei Conservatori, Rome*.

than the majestic. This florid style was cultivated by the vase painter Meidias, while at the same time major painters, about whom unfortunately we know very little, were making profound changes in their art. Parrhasius was thought to have exploited flexibility and the expressive power of line to the full, while Zeuxis, following up Apollodorus' technical innovations, replaced traditional coloured drawing by a genuine form of painting which utilised the qualities of light and shade.

These technical advances widened the gap which since the time of Polygnotus had existed between painting proper and vase decoration, and from this time we can no longer rely on one form to give us information about the other. We have another source of information, it is true, with the appearance of pictorial mosaics, but we mostly have to turn to late copies such as the paintings and mosaics from Pompeii (see pp. 334–7) to reconstruct something of 4th-century painting. According to texts, Euphranor, Pausias, Nicias, Apelles and Protogenes brought the art of painting to the peak of perfection. They knew how to make the best use of colour, how to graduate and blend it, how to produce transparent effects, how to organise groups of figures in battle scenes and how to express emotion by violent movement, controlled poses and the flash of a glance. They excelled in still-life and landscape as well as historical panel-painting and portraiture. With our scanty sources we can only guess at their paintings, but their variety would seem very typical of the wealth of 4th-century art.

Praxiteles

We know more about the sculptors, even though there is not one definitely authentic work which can be attributed to the most renowned of their number, Praxiteles, Scopas and Lysippus. For a long time it was thought with complete certainty that Praxiteles was the artist of a statue of Hermes found in the exact place where Pausanius had 529 referred to a Hermes by Praxiteles, but in the last few years such serious doubts have been expressed that we can no longer hold this assumption, and, in fact, it is quite probably only a very finely finished copy. The great numbers of Roman copies and imitations enable us, in the absence of authentic works, to form some appreciation of the styles and personalities of these three sculptors. Their work is highly individual, and, in all three cases, their own genius counts for a great deal more than the specific tradition which shaped them.

It makes virtually no difference that Scopas came from Paros and Lysippus from Sicyon; where they came from merely explains, to a certain extent, why Scopas liked to work in marble while Lysippus preferred bronze. Undoubtedly Praxiteles, an Athenian and the son of a sculptor, must have benefited from his father's guidance and the favourable artistic climate which he found in his native city, 'the school of Greece'. His subtle and refined art is very much a part of the mainstream of Attic tradition. But he often worked outside Athens, mostly in Asia Minor and the Peloponnese, and his work has a quality which belongs to him alone.

280

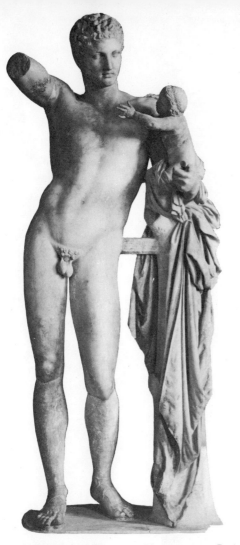

529. Hermes and the Infant Dionysus. 4th century B.C. Perhaps Roman replica of a work by Praxiteles. *Olympia Museum.*

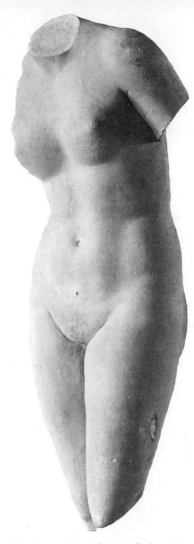

530. Torso of the Aphrodite of Cnidus. Before 350 B.C. Roman replica of a work by Praxiteles. *Louvre.*

His favourite subjects were taken over from the traditional Olympian stock for he still worked in the service of a religion, but his gods and goddesses were very unlike those of the previous century. Praxiteles saw them as beautiful nude young women and finely shaped youths: Aphrodite, Eros, a young satyr or a boy Apollo. Even the strong and manly Hermes and the chaste Artemis conformed to this elegant pattern. The artist loved youthful bodies in slightly languid poses, and his chisel was particularly skilful in interpreting the softness of flesh. He brings us to a world of carefree leisure, an idealised and protected world: a half smile plays about the lips of his statues, and the eyes have a remote dreaming expression while the fingers toy absent-mindedly with something. His gods are not remote, but they have a pleasant air of indifference which would keep ordinary mortals at their distance. It would be wrong to make too much of their realistic nature, for Praxiteles, in this way faithful to the example of his predecessors, was able to transform his models. If his mistress, the beautiful Phryne, posed for the Aphrodite of Cnidus, we can be quite sure that the finished work was only a faint reflection of the courtesan's real body. It seems rather that the artist, in his awareness of Platonic teaching, sought for a pattern of idealised beauty, along very different paths from Phidias but with great spiritual effort which went unrecognised for a long time. His reputation, not less considerable than the acclaim which had surrounded the Parthenon master, can be explained not only by the excellence of his statues but

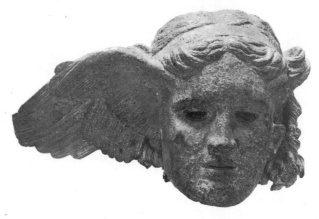

531. Head of Hypnos. Bronze. Early 4th century B.C. *British Museum.*

also and most especially because these were the magnificent embodiments of the human longing for calm sensuality. Even more than Plato's philosophy, it was the 'quiet hedonism' of Aristippus of Cyrene which Praxiteles seems to have understood.

From Scopas to Lysippus

How different Scopas appears—a burning, tormented artist who seems to speak for the troubled mood of his age. We have but a slight first-hand knowledge of this sculptor and architect, from some excessively mutilated pediments from Tegea in Arcadia on which he directed work. Several heads have, despite the ruin of time, kept

281

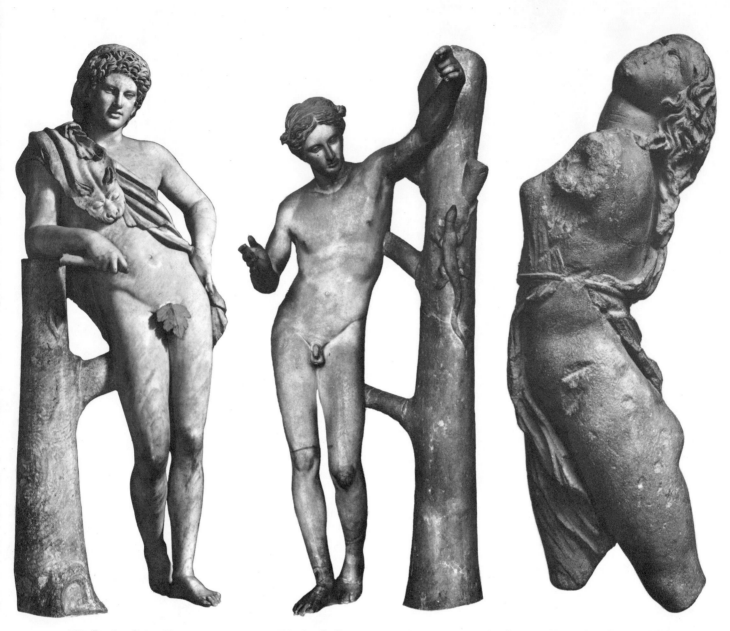

532. Resting Satyr. 4th century B.C.
Roman replica of a work by Praxiteles.
Capitoline Museum, Rome.

533. Apollo Sauroctonus. Middle of the
4th century B.C. Replica of a work by
Praxiteles. *Louvre.*

534. Dancing Maenad, by Scopas. Marble
from Sicyon. *c.* 450 B.C. Roman replica.
Dresden Museum.

their expression of moving intensity which comes largely
from their shadowy deep-set eyes, turned upwards beneath heavy slanting eyebrows which are drawn together
in a frown. This is a recurring feature in surviving statues
534 by Scopas. Some, like the famous Meanad, writhe in
orgiastic frenzy, moved by violent ecstasy. A mood of
languor pervades others, such as the personification of
Longing. The artist particularly chose to portray tragic
537 and fated characters, like Meleager, Hercules and Niobe.
This highly individual and masterly sculptor, with his
acute feeling for the beauty of form, translated all the
yearning and rapture of a mysterious, impassioned nature
into marble. Already sculpture had come a long way from
the serenity of Praxiteles.

Lysippus, who was younger than the other two, was
very much aware of their contribution. His Hercules has
the expression of one of Scopas' heads, and when Lysippus
carved a nude Aphrodite he remembered the Aphrodite
of Cnidus. But essentially his genius was bent in another
direction. A master in bronze, he concentrated largely on

statues of athletes. He went back to Polycleitus' system of
proportions, but by modifying it he introduced a new
and more slender canon which was extremely popular in
later years. He broke with the last traces of the frontal
attitude; his figures were no longer conceived with the
idea that they should be viewed from a special angle; on
the contrary, he tried to make them effective from whatever view they were looked at. Thus he came back to the
experiments carried out by sculptors of the transitional
period more than a century earlier. We have a fine copy
of the Apoxyomenus, the statue of an athlete with his 540
arms stretched out before him, scraping himself with a
strigil; for a full appreciation of its plastic qualities it must
be looked at from every side. Lysippus, lastly, excelled in
portraiture, and in this he was a man of his time—an age
in which realistic portraits were becoming increasingly
popular. He was the official portraitist of Alexander the 546
Great, and by immortalising his features the artist helped
to build up the heroic and superhuman character which
the conqueror had to preserve before the dazzled eyes

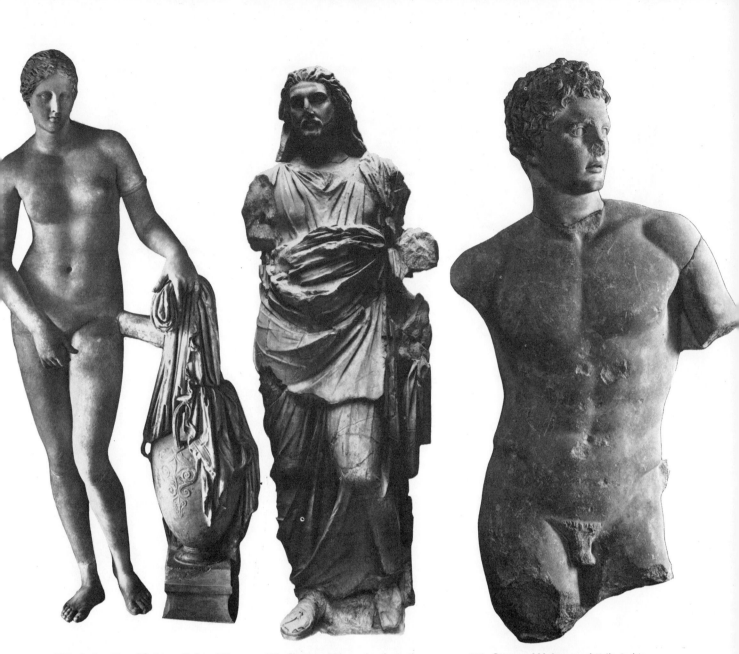

535. Aphrodite of Cnidus. Before 350 B.C. Roman copy of a work by Praxiteles. *Vatican Museum, Rome*

536. Statue of Mausolus from the Mausoleum at Halicarnassus. School of Bryaxis (?). c. 350 B.C. *British Museum.*

537. Statue of Meleager. Attributed to Scopas. First half of the 4th century B.C. *Fogg Art Museum, Harvard University, Boston.*

of his subjects. By this very fact Lysippus brings us to the Hellenistic world.

If we were to look no further than these few great names in painting and sculpture we should have a totally false estimation of 4th-century art. There were many artists who followed close after the above men, each one of whom deserves careful study.

Aristides of Thebes, Pamphilus, Pausias and Nichomachus, among the painters, all enjoyed a quite considerable renown, and of the sculptors we know quite a lot about Timotheus who adorned the temple at Epidaurus, and Bryaxis and Leochares who worked with Scopas and **536, 538** Timotheus on the sculptures for the Mausoleum at Halicarnassus. Silanion produced a famous portrait bust of Plato and possibly the fine bronze Wrestler from Olympia. We know about many others from inscriptions and writings. Lastly, there are anonymous works like the delightful 'Marathon Youth' and the dignified Demeter of Cnidus.

The minor arts also bring us very close to the Greeks

of the 4th century. It is true that there had been a decline in ceramics, but as has been recently illustrated, they still have interesting information to offer. Terra-cotta statu- **539** ettes from Tanagra and elsewhere, had, on the other hand, never been more enchanting. Small bronzes are often of outstanding quality: Lysippus himself was not too great to make one for Alexander. Silver and bronze mirrors and vases were in no way inferior to the great **541** works of sculpture. Coins and engraved gems show a fine and assured craftsmanship which can still give us pleasure.

The art of this century had a rich variety which must never be lost sight of and which defies any attempt at generalisation. There is significance in its very diversity. It helps us to a better understanding of the sometimes contradictory sides of the Greek mind in this age of restless inquiry and peaceful pleasure, with its love of things archaic and its desire to make new discoveries— an age that was cosmopolitan and inquisitive yet true to the ancient gods.

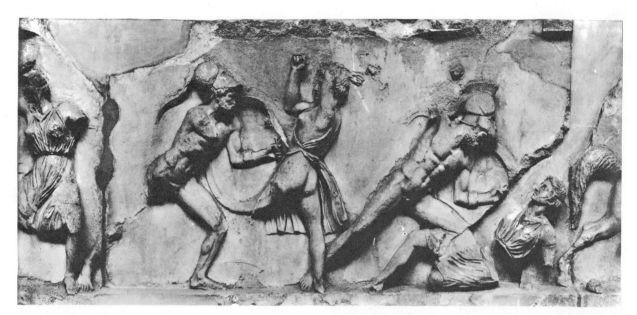

538. Battle of the Greeks and Amazons. Frieze from the Mausoleum at Halicarnassus. Workshop of Scopas. Marble. c. 350 B.C. *British Museum.*

540. *Right.* The Apoxyomenus, by Lysippus. Roman copy. Third quarter of the 4th century B.C. *Vatican Museum, Rome.*

539. Aphrodite and Eros; terra-cotta group from Cyrene. First half of the 4th century B.C. *Louvre.*

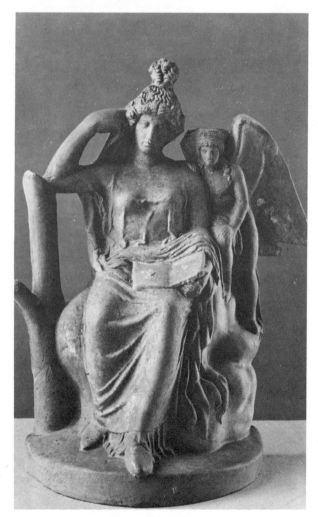

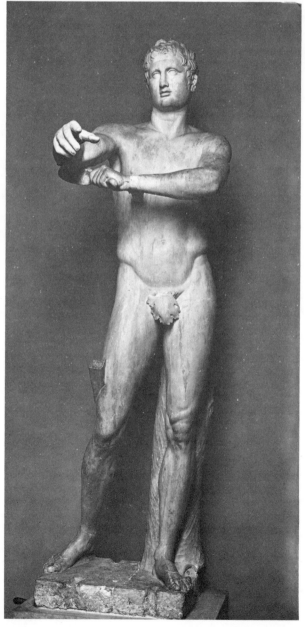

HISTORICAL SUMMARY: Greek art

The development of Greek and Roman archaeology.

Although an interest had been taken in Greek and Roman art since the time of the Italian Renaissance, it was not until the 17th century, with the Marquis de Nointel and a painter in his service who made drawings of the Parthenon sculpture (1674) that any real beginning was made in the study of archaeology. In the 18th century excavation was begun on the sites of Herculaneum (1719) and Pompeii (1748), while at the same time travels in the East and the written accounts of these journeys became increasingly popular. The Count de Caylus in France and Winckelmann in Germany promoted studies in the history of art. At the beginning of the 19th century the first systematic excavations were begun in Greece on the temples at Aegina (1811) and Bassae (1812); in 1829 the Archaeological Mission, attached to the French Expeditionary Force in the Morea, explored the Peloponnese, and the German Hyperborean Society in Rome was converted into an institute for archaeological publications. The French School in Athens was not formed until 1846, though this preceded the German, British, American and Italian Schools, and at this time the major sites of excavation were opened up: in Greece, at Athens, Eleusis, Delphi, Olympia and Epidaurus; on the islands, at Thera and Delos; along the Ionian coast, at Pergamon, Miletus and Ephesus. In 1870 Heinrich Schliemann started excavating and discovered the Homeric civilisation at Troy. Then in 1900 Sir Arthur Evans' work on the palace at Cnossus brought Cretan civilisation to light.

During the 20th century an increasing number of sites have been excavated in Greece and Italy and throughout the Roman world, and great improvements have been made in exploratory technique and the examination of archaeological specimens by the use of exact scientific methods.

HISTORY

In the centuries immediately following the Trojan War, the Greek world was divided into many small kingdoms ruled over by kings who were the objects of both public and family cults in which their authority was vested. This society lasted a very short time as almost everywhere the landed aristocracy came to power.

Alongside a ruling minority (oligarchy) controlling all sources of wealth, there was an expanding population living in poverty: from the 8th century and even earlier enterprising Greeks went abroad in search of fertile lands, to the wheat-growing regions around the Black Sea and in Thrace, to Magna Graecia, Sicily, Gaul, Spain and Cyrenaica. These settlements had strong religious and political ties with their parent city-states and so created the cultural and spiritual unity of the Greek world.

Towards the end of the 7th century money first made its appearance. There was a growth of manufacturing and mercantile prosperity which led to violent class struggles; these were mostly brought to a stop by the intervention of a strong leader—Gelon in Syracuse, Cypselus in Corinth, Polycrates in Samos—whose rule or tyranny was, in most cases, replaced by a government of the people, or democracy. By the end of the 6th century the democratic city-state of Athens and the aristocratic city-state of Corinth were ready to play important political roles.

5th Century.

In 499 the Greek cities in Ionia, supported by Athens, rebelled against Darius, the Persian king; by 493 he had managed to check this revolt and then determined on a war of retaliation against the Greeks who had helped his vassals. In 490 he was defeated at Marathon by the Athenians led by Miltiades. He died in 486, but his son Xerxes, with guarantees of the neutrality of Magna Graecia and the collusion of Thessaly, reopened the fighting.

In 480 the Lacedaemonians were routed at Thermopylae. Athens fell, but with her navy reorganised by Themistocles she inflicted a crushing defeat on the Persian fleet at Salamis. In the following year the Persians were beaten both on land and sea, at Plataea and Mycale.

Gelon of Syracuse had won a victory in 480 against the Carthaginians led by Hamilcar. Both in the east and in the west the Greeks were driving back the barbarians, and Athens emerged from this conflict a great power.

The régimes of Themistocles, Aristides and Cimon prepared the way for the age of Pericles. Depending on the maritime alliance of the Delian confederacy, Athens was still chasing her dream of leadership despite the bitter opposition of Sparta, Corinth and Boeotian Thebes. Pericles made peace with the Persians (c. 448) and secured a thirty-years' truce with Sparta, but he was unable to prevent the outbreak of the Peloponnesian War in 431. He died in 429, and in spite of the precautionary

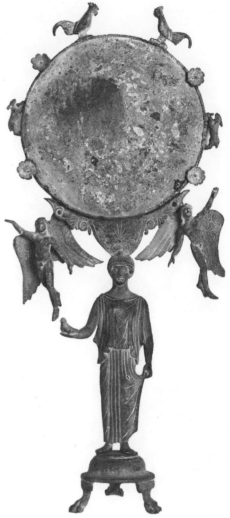

541. Bronze mirror. Corinthian or Sicyonian (?) workmanship. 5th century B.C. *Louvre.*

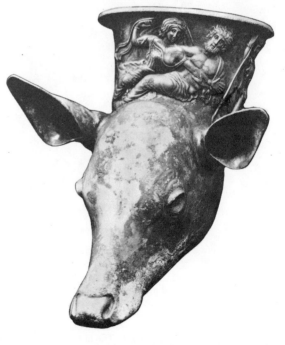

542. Silver rhyton. Late 5th–early 4th centuries B.C. *Trieste Museum.*

285

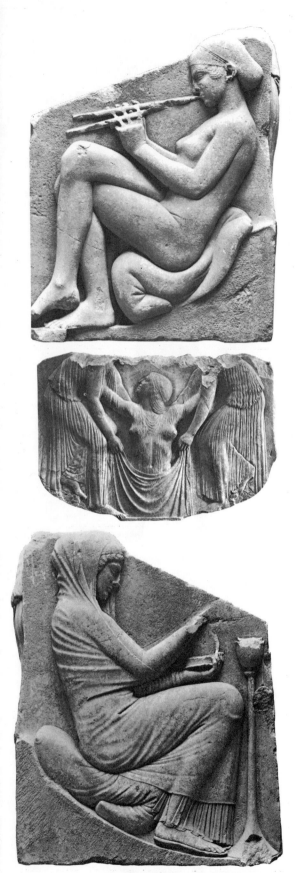

543. The Ludovisi Throne. Three-sided marble relief showing Ionian influence, probably carved in southern Italy. *c.* 470–60 B.C. *Terme Museum, Rome.* a. Nude woman playing a double flute. b. The birth of Aphrodite. c. Veiled woman burning incense.

step of the Peace of Nicias (421), the collapse of the Athenians in Sicily, at Syracuse in 414, led to a further outbreak of fighting and to Athens' defeat in 404.

4th century. Although it was not long before Athens recovered again and built up another Delian confederacy, having no real political leader she was never to regain her supremacy. Sparta and Thebes competed for this position: Sparta was defeated at Leuctra in 371 and Thebes at Mantinea in 362. With all its strength exhausted, Greece was at the mercy of Philip, king of Macedon, who used the Sacred War between Delphi and Phocis as an opportunity for intervention. In spite of Demosthenes and his *Philippics*, the Greeks did not unite soon enough and were defeated at Chaeronea, in 338. Using the Corinthian confederacy as his tool, Philip became ruler of Greece, and it was only his assassination in 336 that prevented him from involving Greece in another war with the Persians.

ARCHITECTURE

The early period. Remains of a few buildings supply details of how the Greek temple originated. There are two types: one is of very elongated design, with or without an axial colonnade, a pteron and an apsidal nave (Megaron B at Thermos, 10th century; temple of Artemis Orthia at Sparta, 9th century; Heraeum at Samos, 8th century). This type, a survival of the Late Helladic period, was probably at the root of the design of classical temples. The other type is a rectangular cella (hall) sometimes entered by a porch (prodomos), with a gabled roof (temple of Apollo at Dreros, 8th century; Heraeum at Delos; Heraeum at Perachora; terra-cotta models of buildings). This was to be the pattern of the treasuries; the presence of a ledge running around the walls which held cult objects recalls the Cretan palace shrines.

7th and 6th centuries. Temples were still being built in the 7th century made up of a simple cella (temple at Prinias in Crete) without a peristyle and sometimes with an axial colonnade (Neandria); but during the latter half of the century, on the Greek mainland, the classical Doric temple came into being, erected on a stylobate made up of steps and comprising a cella with a pronaos and opisthodomos (rear false porch) with a surrounding peristyle. It was still of elongated design (Heraeum at Olympia) with slender column shafts, and painted terra-cotta decorative facings (metopes and acroteria) were still frequently used (Thermos, Calydon, Larisa-on-Hermos). During the 6th

century certain municipal undertakings were carried out (planning of Syracuse, aqueducts at Megara and Samos and fountains in Athens). Work was started on great sanctuaries all over the Greek world from Ionia to Sicily; these were planned with a surrounding wall which enclosed treasuries and smaller buildings, stoas, theatres and stadia. A series of tufa temples was built on the Athenian Acropolis; the old tholos on the Marmaria terrace [**492**] and the Sicyonian treasury [**510**] were constructed at Delphi; in Magna Graecia and Sicily, temples were often on an extraordinary scale with elaborate ornamentation (Selinus: Heraclaeum, temple of Demeter and temple of Poseidon; Syracuse; Artemisium; south Italy: small sanctuary of Hera, at the mouth of the Silaris).

In the latter half of the 6th century the Doric Order began to take on its classical form (temple of Apollo at Delphi—the Alcmaeonid temple, 548–510; temple of Apollo at Corinth, 540) with reduced proportions (6 by 15 columns along the sides), shorter, more solid shafts and broader, heavier capitals. Many treasuries were built in the sanctuaries at this period (Cnidian and Siphnian treasuries at Delphi [**495**] with a caryatid order; Massalian treasury at Delphi, etc.). Only traces remain of the two great Ionic temples built at this time in Asia Minor, the Artemisium at Ephesus and the Heraeum at Samos, both with western orientation, which were built on a vast scale with extremely ornate decoration. Building continued at the same pace in Magna Graecia and Sicily, with many survivals of the proto-archaic period in the design of roofs and the shape of entablatures, pediments and cornices (the so-called 'Basilica' at Paestum; the Apollonium and Artemisium at Selinus). Sicily provided the first example of the Corinthian capital in a pilaster capital.

5th century. During the first half of the century, architects gave all their concentration to religious buildings in attempts to perfect the Doric Order and solve problems arising from the interrelation of architectural features. In Greece the Athenians built the first Parthenon on the Acropolis, a tholos and two stoas in the agora, and a small Doric treasury (489–485) at Delphi. The temple of Aphaia at Aegina [**473**] was begun in 500. But the great architectural achievement of this period was the temple of Zeus at Olympia, designed by the Peloponnesian architect Libon of Elis, and built of local limestone between the years 472 and 456; it was one of the supreme examples of the Doric Order, with stuccoed columns, marble roofing and rich

286

sculptural decoration.

In Magna Graecia and Sicily, which were unaffected by the Persian invasion, work was started on a number of temples: at Paestum the great sanctuary of Hera was built at the mouth of the Silaris (480) and the so-called 'temple of Poseidon' (460) in the town itself; at Selinus, the Olympieum was built on the Acropolis and the Dionysium on the Marinella plateau; the temple of Athena was constructed at Syracuse. The temple of Olympian Zeus at Agrigentum was a building of revolutionary plan with an unroofed cella, a pteron (external colonnade) of engaged half-columns embedded in the walls, and an entablature supported by colossal male figures.

From about 450, expanding public and private resources led to the growth of civic architecture—private houses, buildings in the agoras, stoas, odeons, theatres—while at the same time work was started on several temples. In Athens, Pericles was responsible for the plan to rebuild or restore the Acropolis buildings destroyed by the Persians, and Ictinus the architect, who was already well known for his work on the Telesterium at Eleusis, was commissioned in 447 to build a new Parthenon in collaboration with the architect Callicrates. This was a temple in the Doric Order but very unusual in plan (being 8 by 17 columns), elevation and sculptural decorations. In 437 Mnesicles began work on the Propylaea, made up of two Doric porches backing on to each other, but they were never completed as they had originally been planned. The small Ionic temple of Athena Nike was erected in 425 on a westerly spur of the Acropolis [**469**], while the Erechtheum, begun in 421, was built on a terrace higher up; the peculiar plan of this Ionic temple was determined by considerations of a religious nature, and it also had an extremely ornate decoration; it was completed in 405. In the town below, on a hill overlooking the agora, the temple of Hephaestus (the so-called 'Theseum') was built between the years 450 and 440.

Ictinus was summoned to Bassae to build the temple of Apollo; the exterior was built in the Doric Order, but the interior wall of the cella was surrounded by an engaged Ionic colonnade with Corinthian capitals crowning the three end columns. The temple of Poseidon at Sunium and the temple of Apollo at Delos (not finished until the 3rd century) were built during this period.

In Sicily architectural activity was greatly slowed down by political events. There are definite signs of Ionian influence in the finely built Doric temple at Segesta which was left unfinished in 425 and the 'temple of Concord' at Agrigentum which was begun in 440.

4th Century. Athens made a courageous recovery after the defeat of 404 and completed much of the building work which had been started in the 5th century; several monuments in the agora were rebuilt (temple of Apollo Patroos); the temenos (sacred precinct) of Dionysus Eleutherus on the south slope of the Acropolis was planned. Restoration of the wooden theatre was begun, using stone, in 400, and was not finally completed until the time of Lycurgus which was also the time when the Sacred Way was opened. This was lined with monuments erected by the winning choragi, such as the Choragic Monument of Lysicrates, in the Corinthian Order. In Piraeus, the military port, the arsenal was replanned by the architect Philo who, at the end of the century, also completed work on the Telesterium at Eleusis. The Alcmaeonid temple of Apollo at Delphi, destroyed in 373, was rebuilt on the same pattern between 370 and 330. In the early part of the century Theodorus of Phocaea, a pupil of Ictinus, designed the tholos on the Marmaria terrace at Delphi with a very slender Doric pteron and an interior employing half-columns and Corinthian capitals.

But the most important work of this period was being carried on in the Peloponnese. The sanctuary of Asclepius at Epidaurus drew together some of the finest architects of the 4th century; the temple, a Doric peripteral building with an adytum (back room behind the cella) was built between 380 and 375. Polycleitus the Younger, grandson of the 5th-century sculptor, designed the tholos at Epidaurus in 360, which rivalled the perfection of that at Delphi, and in 330 he also built the theatre at Epidaurus, which is one of the best preserved and probably the finest of all Greek theatres. At Tegea, Scopas was responsible for the rebuilding and decoration of the temple of Athena (between 350 and 340), a Doric peripteral building with an engaged Corinthian Order inside, and in all likelihood considering similarities of plan and style, he was also the architect of the temple of Zeus at Nemea. The Thersilium (hypostyle assembly hall) was built in 370 at Megalopolis and, later in the century, the largest Greek theatre was constructed there. The Philippeum at Olympia, an Ionic tholos, was started by Philip of Macedon shortly after 338 and provides yet another example of the Corinthian capital used inside the cella wall.

The 4th century in Asia Minor was notable for a great architectural revival, characteristic of which was the wide-

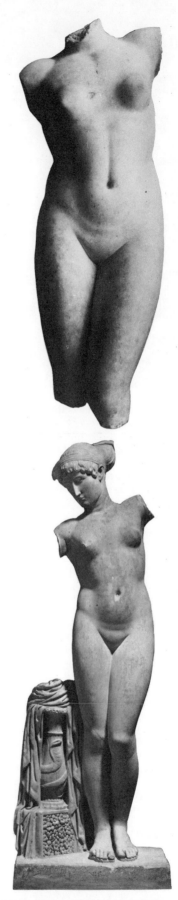

544. a. The Esquiline Venus. Roman copy. c. 460 B.C. *Louvre.* b. Another version of the Esquiline Venus. *Museo dei Conservatori, Rome.*

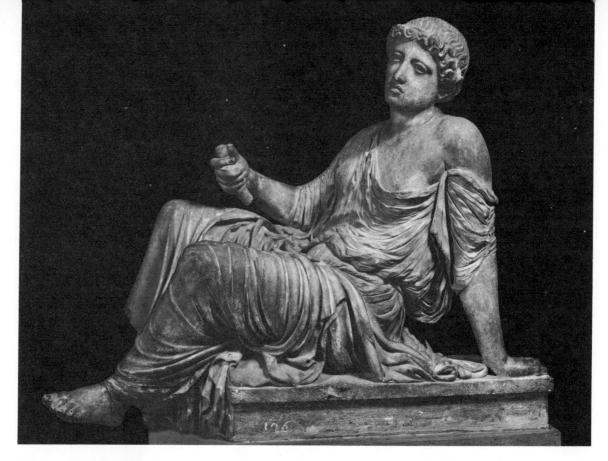

545. A suppliant. End of the 5th century B.C. *Barberini Palace, Rome.*

spread use of the Ionic Order, a taste for buildings on a colossal scale and lavish sculptured ornamentation. Ephesus: following the fire of 356, the Artemisium was rebuilt on the same pattern as before, also with column bases adorned with sculpture. Didyma: the temple of Apollo was begun in 333 by Paeonius of Ephesus and Daphnis of Miletus. Priene: the temple of Athena Polias, begun in 335, was built by Pythius, one of the Mausoleum architects. Halicarnassus: the Mausoleum, built for Mausolus, the Carian king, on which work began shortly before 353, was a temple-tomb which combined a pteron and a steep base with a funerary chamber.

Finally, the Greeks began to give some attention at this time to domestic architecture: excavations at Olynthus have brought to light about a hundred of these houses, built in light materials on a square plan, with a paved court and a deep porch opening off the main room of the house. These dwellings were decorated with mosaics and stucco-work.

SCULPTURE

The early period. The earliest specimens of plastic art of the geometric period are small ivory *ex votos* (Dipylon, Sparta, Ephesus and Delos), bronzes (shields from Mount Ida and statuettes of men and animals from Dodona, Delphi, Athens, Perachora, Argos, Sparta and Olympia) and terra cotta (chariots and horsemen, and bell-shaped idols from Boeotia).

7th and 6th centuries. In the 7th century certain differences became apparent between the various art centres, which were to become completely individual during the 6th century. Crete was a very active centre in the 7th century (statuettes from Dreros; frieze from the temple at Prinias; the Auxerre goddess [**453**]), but by the 6th century it had virtually fallen into oblivion. The Peloponnesian group, to which the workshops of Magna Graecia and northern Greece can be linked, was, on the other hand, very productive at this time; there are examples of Corinthian art on the east pediment of the temple of Artemis at Corfu (580) [**486**], and of Sicyonian art in the sculptures from the Sicyonian treasury at Delphi (560). At Mycenae there were sculptures on the metopes and pediment of the 7th-century temple of Athena; at Olympia we have a carved head of Hera from the Heraeum (7th century) and the pediment of the Megarian treasury. From northern Greece came the series of kouroi from the temple of Apollo Ptoos (Boeotia) [**462**] and the kouros of Orchomenus. Magna Graecia had a centre near the mouth of the Silaris which was responsible for two series of highly original metopes. Another group includes sculpture from the Ionian coast and the islands (carved bases of the columns of the Artemisium at Ephesus; seated statues from Miletus; statues from Samos such as the Hera from the Louvre and various sepulchral groups. There was also the sculpture from the Cnidian treasury at Delphi and the Harpy tomb, Xanthus (*c.* 500). Fragments of ivory statues found beneath the Sacred Way at Delphi came from an Ionian work-shop (first half of the 6th century). Delos, Naxos, Siphnos and Thasos all had fine centres of sculpture.

But Athens still had the most active school and took the lead in the development of architectural sculpture, in the treatment of the nude male figure and the draped female figure and in the rendering of movement and expression. There are three main groups of sculpture:

1 Pediments: Hydra pediment; Red pediment; earliest pediment from the Hecatompedon, 585–60; pediments from the new Hecatompedon, 520 [**483**, **484**], which show how much progress had been made; Antenor's pediments on the Alcmaeonid temple of Apollo at Delphi (510).

2 Kouroi: from the Dipylon and Sunium kouroi to the Rampin horseman [**463**] and the first group of Tyrannicides (attributed to Antenor).

3 Korai: from kore No. 589 (second quarter of the 6th century) to the korai of the first decade of the 5th century.

5th century: transitional period (500–450). There were three chief spheres of influence during this period:

1 Athens: late kouroi and korai; the work of the artist Calamis to whom the Zeus from Histiaea and the metopes of the Athenian treasury at Delphi [**497**] are attributed. At Aegina the sculptures of the three pediments (one of which is a restoration) of the temple of Aphaia (500–480) were still fairly crude. Workshops in the islands and northern Greece were linked to the Attic centre.

2 Magna Graecia and Sicily: There has been an attempt to reconstruct the work of Pythagoras, a Samian artist who had made his home in Rhegium at the time of the Persian invasion and who was interested in the problems of rhythm and realistic detail. The school of Locri produced the Ludovisi Throne [**543**] and Esquiline Venus [**544**]. From the school of Selinus came the metopes from the Dionysium.

3 The Peloponnese: Experiments were made with the striding kouros type in Corinth, Sicyon and Sparta and with the draped female figure (wearing the peplos) in Argos. The temple of Zeus at Olympia [**487**, **488**] was virtually the manifesto of this school, being built and ornamented by Peloponnesians; the influence of Pindar is evident in the choice of subject and that of Polygnotus of Thasos, the painter, in the geometric yet harmonious compositions. On the east pediment are preparations for the chariot race between Pelops and Oenomaus. On the west pediment is the battle of the Lapiths and Centaurs. Zeus and Apollo preside serenely over the fates of heroes and mortals on the metopes, with subjects taken from the labours of Hercules; the actual or implied presence of the goddess Athena enables the hero, representative of civilisation, to triumph in the face of all adversities.

First classical period (450–400). The idea of a centre or school was being replaced by the conception of the individual artist who travelled from one art centre to another. Myron of Eleutherae (Boeotia), who worked in the second third of the 5th century was a student of movement (Discus Thrower [**509**], Ladas, Athena and Marsyas group). Polycleitus of Argos carried on Peloponnesian traditions and tried to establish a reconciliation between the athletic masculine body in repose and a structure that developed on an architectural ideal, the canon; the Cyniscus, the Doryphorus [**513**] and the Diadumenus, along with a Wounded Amazon made for the Ephesus Artemisium and a gold and ivory statue of Hera (Argos), mark the progressive stages in his researches.

Phidias, born in Athens around the year 490, was in Olympia before 455 where he produced the statue of Zeus; in 450 he was summoned to Athens in order to take charge of the sculpture on the Parthenon [**480**] and to make the cult statue of Athena which was unveiled in 438. We know nothing about his life after he stood trial for impiety in 432. Besides the Parthenon sculp-

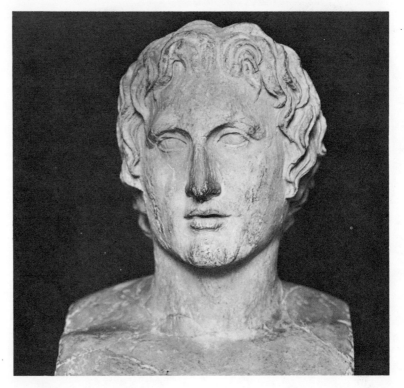

tures, there have been attempts to identify a large number of works as his by comparing them with the Parthenon frieze, e.g. the great relief from Eleusis, the original of the Mattei Amazon, the Demeter from Cherchel and the Albani kore. Something is known of the Athena Promachus and the Athena Lemnia which once stood on the Acropolis, but as for the Parthenon Athena, we have only copies of this statue and interpretations in works of minor art. The traditional view which sees Phidias as the overseer of the Parthenon decoration is borne out by the unity of inspiration and even of style, despite certain dissimilarities in execution due to the large number of sculptors who collaborated on the undertaking. The work consisted of the metopes, the pediments and the frieze. The metopes add almost nothing new to the stock of decorative themes, with a Gigantomachy on the east side, an Amazonomachy on the west side, a Centauromachy and the birth of Erichthonius on the south, and the fall of Troy on the north side. The pediments were dedicated to the glory of Athena and Athens (east pediment: the goddess' miraculous birth; west pediment: Athena and Poseidon contending for the ownership of the Acropolis, watched by members of the Attic royal families). Lastly, the frieze around the outer wall of the cella depicts the Panathenaic procession, in the presence of an assembly of gods who thus come to be closely associated with ordinary mortals.

There are signs of Phidias' influence in several architectural sculptures of the

546. Alexander the Great (?). Roman copy of the original (4th century B.C.) attributed to Lysippus. *Louvre.*

same period, such as those from the Metroum (temple of Cybele) at Athens and the Athenian temple of Apollo at Delos. His influence is also apparent in such works as the Athena of Velletri, the Medici Torso and the Erechtheum caryatids. Against this, the influence of Ionian art and a certain reaction against Phidias' idealism are evident in the frieze from the temple of Apollo at Bassae, the statues of Victory from the parapet of the Athena Nike temple on the Acropolis, the Nereid Monument from Xanthus, and some isolated works like the Barberini Suppliant [**545**] and the Wounded Niobid in the Terme Museum, as well as in the works of certain artists of the end of the century, e.g. Cresilas, Alcamenes, Callimachus.

4th century: second classical period. This was distinguished by a revival of art in the Ionian cities, where their great architectural schemes attracted the finest sculptors and craftsmen in bronze. Scopas, architect and sculptor [**534**], was born in Paros and worked in Sicyon (Maenad, in Dresden), Rhamnus and Samothrace before he was summoned to Asia Minor to collaborate on the ornamentation of the Mausoleum at Halicarnassus and the Artemisium at Ephesus. On his return to Greece, he built and decorated the temples at Tegea and Nemea. Leochares and Bryaxis, who also collaborated on the Mausoleum, were to work for Alexander.

289

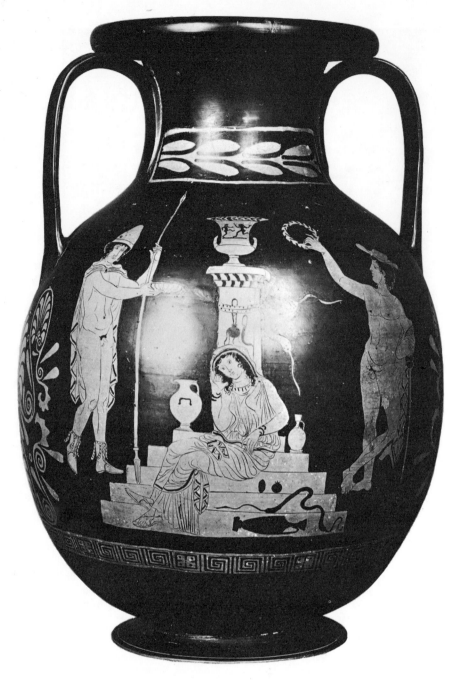

Praxiteles from Attica preferred to work in marble which was afterwards painted by Nicias; he, too, made a journey to Asia Minor (*c.* 350) during which he helped on the ornamentation of the altar of the Ephesus Artemisium and carved an Aphrodite for the city of Cnidus. To his earlier period belong the Satyr Pouring Wine, the Satyr Resting, the Apollo Sauroctonus and the Aphrodite of Arles, known only from Roman copies. The Hermes at Olympia may also be a Roman copy. Later works such as the Artemis Brauronia show more religious maturity.

Lysippus, a painter and a sculptor in bronze, served his apprenticeship in Sicyonian workshops and was an innovator whose experiments were concerned with movement, the role of light, and the individual personality of his models. He evolved a new canon of more slender proportions (the body eight heads high), and his works are the reflection of an ideal far removed from those of Scopas and Praxiteles (Agias; Apoxyomenus). Appointed Alexander's official sculptor, he followed him on his travels and created many portraits of him (Azara Herm). After the emperor's death he made many journeys from Greece to Sicily and produced a large number of statues of gods (Eros of Thespiae, Hercules of Tarentum and Hermes tying his sandal).

Scopas and Praxiteles had a powerful influence on the sculpture of their time in sepulchral stelae and in the many versions of Aphrodite and Demeter.

PAINTING

Although no frescoes or paintings have survived it is possible with the help of written descriptions, painted vases and painting and mosaics of the Roman period to trace the development of this art in which the great masters were every bit as famous as the sculptors.

7th and 6th centuries. The Greeks believed that this art had been first evolved and perfected in Corinth and Sicyon, and several records seem to lend weight to this supposition: the

547. Red-figure amphora in the South Italian style. First half of the 4th century B.C. *Louvre.*

548. Principal types of Greek vases.

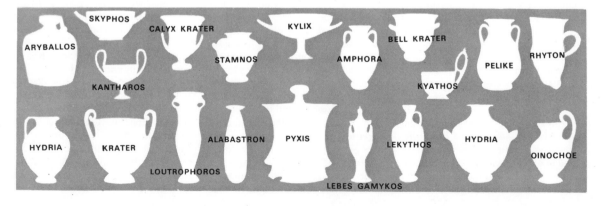

GREEK. Head of a victorious athlete. Bronze. End of the 5th century B.C. Louvre. *Photo: Giraudon.*

290

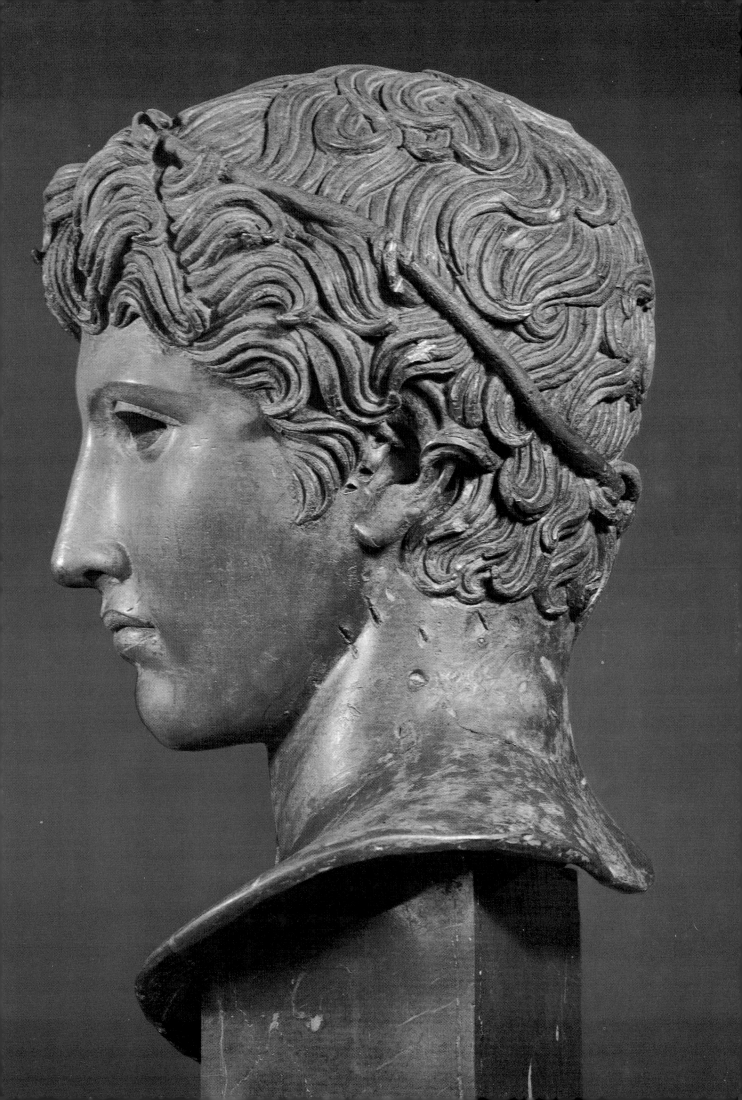

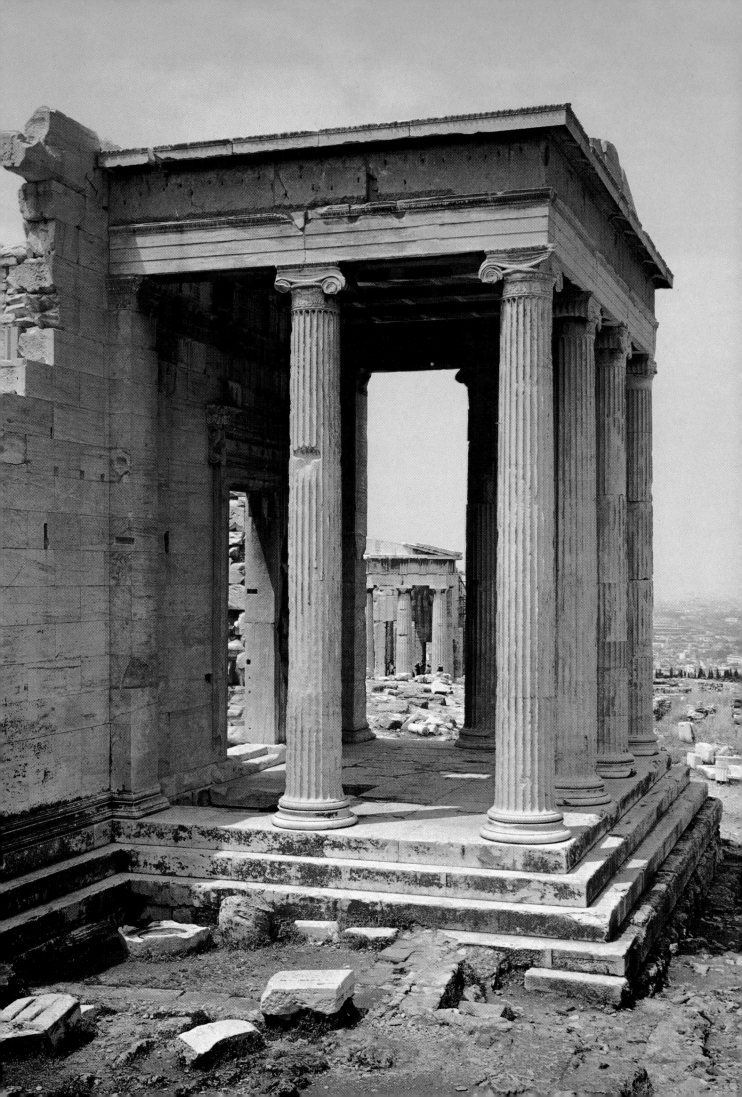

metopes from Thermos (650–630) and Calydon (600–580) are of Corinthian workmanship, while the earlier painted wooden panels were discovered in the Cave of the Nymphs at Pitsa (latter half of the 6th century). There was also a thriving Attic school by the end of the 6th century, where Cimon of Cleonae worked, who was credited with the various advances made on archaic painting, such as foreshortening, rendering of anatomy and drapery and of expression, advances which can also be found in vase painting of the time.

5th century. When the painter Polygnotus of Thasos arrived in Athens in 470, painting came to have a greater importance, not only on vases but also on sculpture. He was commissioned to decorate the Lesche of the Cnidians in Delphi and the Stoa Poekile in Athens and drew his inspiration from Homeric literature (fall of Troy; scenes from the Odyssey). He was renowned among his contemporaries for his balanced compositions, his attention to perspective and landscape and the moving expressions he gave to faces—all qualities which can be found, for example, in the Orvieto krater. Later 5th-century painters, Parrhasius of Ephesus, who decorated the new Dionysium in Athens, and Xeuxippus, revealed a new, less disciplined, spirit.

4th century. Our sources of information, though few and far between, enable us to glimpse something of the leading position of painting among the arts of this period and its growing influence, and also the fact that there were regional schools. One of the most famous of these was the Athenian school to which Nicias, Praxiteles' painter, belonged—copies of three of whose paintings are possibly preserved in frescoes at Pompeii and Rome. The school of Sicyon was scarcely less renowned, with pupils like Pausias, who worked on the Tholos at Epidaurus, Lysippus who, like Phidias, was also a painter, and Apelles who was to be Alexander's official painter. His portraits and allegorical pictures were typical of contemporary trends.

CERAMICS

The early period. This period takes its name from the geometric decoration so very characteristic of vase painting of this time, which constitutes the most important archaeological material. Excavation of vases and pottery in Athens has enabled the geometric style to be definitely dated, and the comparative study of ceramics has made clear different trends in vase production: protogeometric (10th century), still an offshoot of pre-Hellenic pottery (Salamis, Tiryns, Athens); severe style geometric (9th–8th centuries); pictorially decorated amphoras of the last quarter of the 8th century; subgeometric, overlapping into the proto-Attic of the early 7th century.

Vases from Crete and Thera generally have linear decoration, while those from Boeotia tend towards plastic ornamentation; Attic workshops specialised in colossal vases known as Dipylon vases, on which human beings and animals were depicted [**458**].

7th and 6th centuries. With the growth of trade between Greece and the Oriental world, certain changes became apparent in the shape and ornamentation of vases; Rhodes, Samos, Melos and Corinth were producing vases with 'Orientalising' decoration, adorned with real and fabulous animals and with plant motifs. Vase painters in the Attic workshops soon gave first place to the human figure and began to use brighter colours. In the early 6th century there were still flourishing workshops in Corinth, Cyrene, Chalcis and Clazomenae, but by 575 Athens had taken the lead with black-figure pottery and it became virtually the only centre producing vases in this style. After Sophilus and Lydus, the most famous vase makers and painters were Amasis, an Ionian, and Exekias, who is representative of the Dorian stream. Towards 530 experiments made by Nicosthenes and Andokides under the influence of major painting resulted in the replacing of the black-figure technique by the red-figure one [**549**].

5th and 4th centuries. 510–460 was the great period of red-figure vases; the artists were Euphronius, Douris, Hieron and his painter Macron, Brygus and Sotades (the great master of the whiteground ware). Large vases were decorated with mythological and Homeric themes, while cups and small vases bore scenes taken from everyday life and the activities of youth; the influence of Cimon and Polygnotus is perceptible in draughtsmanship and technique. Later, the free style (460–430), of which the Achilles painter was a master, shows the influence of painting giving way to that of Phidias and sculpture; but the former influence was to return with the ornate style (late 5th and early 4th centuries), which was also affected by the drama. Meidias was the last of the great vase painters, and in the 4th century there was a steep decline in painted pottery, except possibly for the series of vases in the Kerch style.

THE MINOR ARTS

Domestic articles and small *ex votos* in bronze, terra-cotta figurines and reliefs, silver work, jewellery, coins, engraved gems and mosaics all come

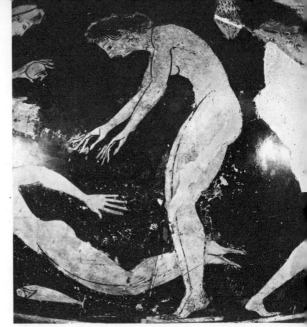

549. Women bathing. Detail of an amphora by the Andokides painter. *c.* 540–525 B.C. *Louvre.*

under the convenient heading of the 'minor arts'; but they show all the technical skill and feeling for beauty of the Greek tradition, and they are important reflections of the major arts.

6th century. The bronze workshops of Corinth and Sicyon exported kraters, tripods and mirrors with stands [**541**] throughout the entire Greek world. The ivory workshops which produced the chest of Cypselus (Sicyon) and the small ivories from the Delphic treasury were in the Peloponnese. Terra-cotta figurines were of local manufacture, but special mention must be made of the Boeotian workshops (Thebes and Tanagra) and of those at Rhodes and Corinth. Gold and silver coins from Athens and Sicily were of outstanding aesthetic and technical quality.

5th century. Although Corinth was still supreme in bronze craftsmanship, Athens was also manufacturing fine mirrors, with handles made in the form of a statuette, which were replaced in the 4th century by box-mirrors with relief ornamentation and vases depicting mythological themes. Terra-cotta figurines (from Boeotia, Attica and the Peloponnese) reflected trends in sculpture, and some acroterial figures (from Olympia) were completely dependent on major plastic art. Fine terra-cotta reliefs were made at Locri and Melos.

4th century. Attic workshops were producing bronze household objects, vases and rhytons embossed with silver and decorated with reliefs [**542**], cinerary urns and jewel boxes. There were thriving workshops producing small clay figures in Boeotia (Thebes and Tanagra) and Tarentum as well as flourishing engravers' and goldsmiths' workshops; it was also at this time that the first figurative mosaics appeared.

Simone Besques-Mollard

GREEK. North porch of the Erechtheum on the Acropolis, Athens. Beginning of the 5th century B.C. *Photo: A. F. Kersting.*

THE PERSIAN EMPIRE *Marguerite Rutten*

Greek civilisation owed a great deal to that of Asia Minor; at a very early date, contact between the two was established along the shores of the Aegean. This lasting contact developed, little by little, into a formidable struggle against the Persian empire, whose history was closely linked with an Oriental civilisation that the West was for ever to be confronted with and that it was never able to escape.

The Medes and Persians were part of the tide of Aryans who, taking advantage of the upheaval produced by the Indo-Europeans throughout the entire ancient world, came to settle on the Iranian plateau. The Medes, like both the Cimmerians—who came from Thrace and Phrygia—and the Scythians, were a race of horsemen possessing no other riches beyond objects that could be carried with them, such as weapons, metal vessels and ornaments. Median art, of which the Sakkez treasure is the main example, combined the influence of the Medes' northerly neighbours the Scythians with that of their opponents the Assyrians.

The Persians, who settled farther south, spent some time, however, in northern Iran where they came under Median domination. Their art, consequently, from the time they were firmly established on the Persian plateau presents an everlasting dualism springing from this mixture of influences, from the north and from the south with its echoes of Mesopotamian traditions. The union

of these two basic factors was strengthened by the marriage of the Persian king Cambyses to the daughter of the Median king. It also incorporated elements of foreign arts in the expansion of that vast empire that one day was to extend from the Indus to the Nile; thus a composite art was created which was typically Achaemenid but of which only a few works, created for the court, remain.

The Achaemenids—the builder-kings

When Cyrus captured Babylon in 538 and the Achaemenid Dynasty took the place of Babylonian rule, the capitals of the new empire were brought farther east to the Persian plateau and to Susa, bordering on the plains of lower Mesopotamia, thus reducing the great cities of the Tigris and Euphrates basin to the state of mere satellites. This kind of upheaval was inevitably bound to carry the art of this region in new directions.

We should always take into account the factors at work in the creation of every art: that is, on the one hand the world of reality, and on the other the world of suggestion. The first is influenced by physical environment and conditions: climate and materials; the second is bound up with society, religion and social customs. The nature of the country is of vital importance in its influence on an emerging art. The country of Sumer was entirely without stone or any wood really suitable for building, and it made up for this by the use of clay on a large scale, which gave its architecture a massiveness that had profound effects on every interdependent art. But the Persian plateau offered quite different opportunities: there was no shortage of stone (of a slightly softer variety than that

550. ACHAEMENIAN. Persepolis. Ruins of the palace, showing the double stairway leading to the esplanade.

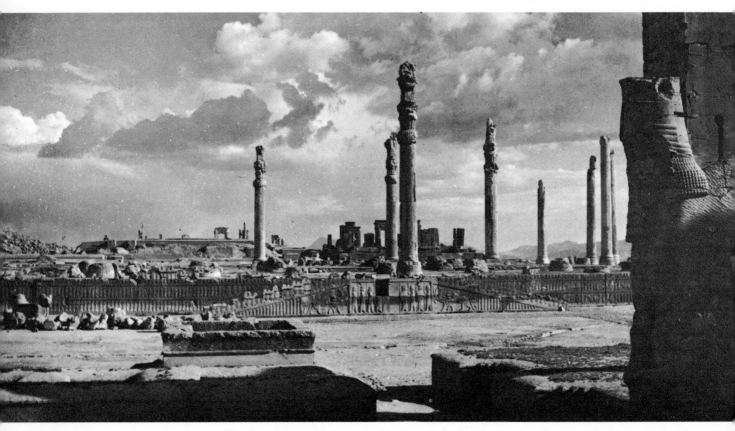

used for the decoration of the Assyrian palaces). This completely changed architecture. Building in clay would have been as difficult in this area as building in stone in the Tigris-Euphrates basin. While they were in the north, in Urartu, the Persians learned how to build surrounding walls intended to protect the villages and the chiefs' residences against the raids of mountain peoples, who were notorious brigands; the man-made terrace backing on to the mountain near Masjid-i-Sulaiman represents an earlier stage in technical progress than that shown by the building of Pasargadae. Incidentally, there is still disagreement over the etymology of the word 'Pasargadae', read by some as 'Parsagadae', which would mean 'camp of the Persians' and would tie in very well with this type of town.

Achaemenid architects were to build 'royal cities', just as the Assyrian kings, like Sargon II at Khorsabad, had done before them; but the Achaemenian cities were to be on a grandiose scale worthy of a monarch who ruled from the Indus to the Nile, and the decorative artists, in their turn, were to try to provide him with fitting surround-550 ings. Persepolis is the supreme example of a royal Achaemenian town. There we are really faced with a state art, created for the court.

There is a kind of disconcerting effrontery about this art where architects showed no hesitation in building a forest of colonnades against a mountain-side which was quite overwhelming in comparison. It is a bewildering sight, this architecture, with its columns with slender seventy-foot-high shafts topped with colossal capitals—an architecture so unrelated to human proportions that men were to wander like dwarfs at its feet. It was an art that was not on a human scale. Nowhere else had this ever found such complete expression. But by the early days of the empire architectural design had been settled once and for all and was to remain unchanged: the column, the chief feature in building and the one which inspired the audience chamber or apadana, was to become an obsession. The Persian era was the time when the column, from Greece to Asia, reigned supreme, but the Achaemenids were particularly extreme in their use of it, which they carried even to Delos in the Thesmophorium which Charles Picard has compared in design to Darius' Tachara (composed of a central chamber with three rows of four columns and two matching rooms with two rows of four columns). At Persepolis all the halls and chambers had columns (like the audience chamber or apadana), and when we think of the staggering number of more than 550 columns erected in that limited space, we inevitably react against such an excess. We cannot assimilate this extreme profusion, but we must remember that to all Oriental minds it is entirely acceptable. Persian artists wanted to achieve a majestic grandeur and could only do this by impressing the mind with the repetition of a single motif, something that we shall find again in their ornamental sculpture.

Art and symbolic meaning

When we come to consider the number of columns generally used in buildings we find that it is always connected with the number 4 and its multiples: 4, 8, 12, 16, 36, 72, 100. It could very well be that here as in Mesopotamia we are faced with a law that obeys the 'symbolism of numbers'. From the very earliest times, the Sumerian goddess Nisaba was thought to be versed in the meaning of numbers, and the Tower of Babel and the Great Temple provide us with typical examples of the architectural application of sacred numbers. Although the decimal system of numbering was known in Mesopotamia, the sexagesimal system was the one mostly used. The preponderance of the number 4 at Persepolis corresponds to some new conception; did it perhaps symbolise the four elements of fire, air, water and earth? The number 12, that was soon to be endowed with a quite special significance, was also used a great deal. In more ways than one the influence of Europe was already making itself felt among the Persians. This is borne out if we look at certain themes such as the king battling with a fantastic beast, **438** where it is now no longer a question, as it was with the Assyrian king, of exalting his bravery in a hunting exploit: the king is at grips with a demon, plunging his dagger into its body. Now it has become a conflict between the spirit of good (Ahura Mazda) and the spirit of evil (Ahriman). This theme came to symbolise the victory of the Aryan god of light, who was depicted in the act of killing a dragon. It seems likely, nevertheless, that the Persians were responsible for the introduction of a new type—the 'horseman-god'—who became an accepted iconographical figure; he recurs in Egypt in Coptic art with the god Horus on horseback (in Christian iconography identified with St George) crushing the crocodile. This conception of the conflict between good and evil was developed and spread by the Persians. Before this, it seems to have been touched on in Babylon with the victory of the god Marduk over Tiamat—the victory of order over chaos, an idea which might possibly stem from

551. PERSEPOLIS. Lion attacking a bull. Marble. Darian epoch. (521–486 B.C.)

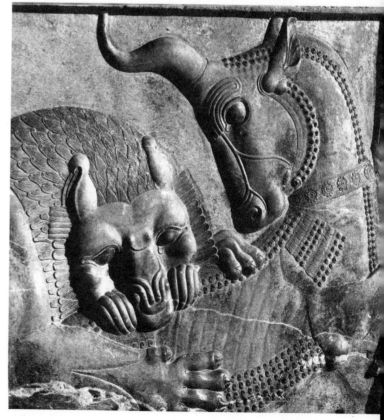

293

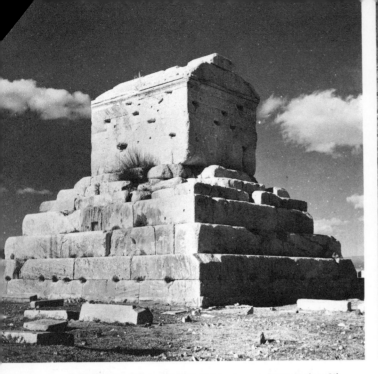

552. Tomb of Cyrus II (557–529 B.C.), near Pasargadae. 6th century B.C.

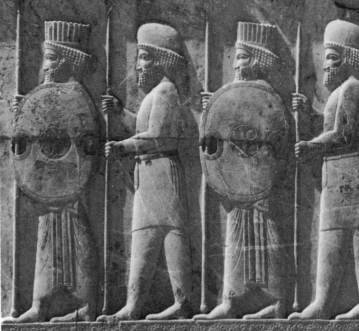

553. PERSEPOLIS. Detail of a stairway leading to the apadana. Soldiers carrying spears. Darian epoch. (521–486 B.C.)

an earlier period.

Persian religious thought, governed by the idea of the polarity of good and evil, penetrated the entire ancient world of that time. Mostly artists drew upon local portrayals of gods and malevolent or guardian djinns. They dominated a people who went on seeing them as they had always been, and the Persian artist, using scenes that were already well known, elaborated them not only in the way they were depicted but also in the purpose for which they were intended. Their treatment is disturbingly cold and detached, and the protagonists seem totally unconcerned with whatever they are doing. On the other hand, if we look at these scenes from another point of view we shall see that the artist invariably produced set pieces that were extremely fine as architectural ornamentation, as, for example, the motif of the lion attacking a bull, which had possibly been chosen because it could symbolise one of the religious themes that was later to take root: Mithra the sun god slaying the bull.

It was at this time that the idea of survival after death, and the mediation of a spirit or a god that was the guide of souls, took a firm hold. Royal tombs, far from being concealed as they had been in Babylonia or in Egypt, stood proudly beneath the sky like the mausoleum thought to be the tomb of Cyrus. The royal rock-tombs at Naksh-i-Rustam and Persepolis were very well known, a fact which explains why they were plundered. On the tomb at Naksh-i-Rustam the king, standing on a dais, towers above a façade (carved out of the rock) in imitation of his earthly home; he is alone before a fire altar under the protection of the god Ahura Mazda whose face, surrounded by a circle (symbol of eternity), hovers above. We have seen that the Persians readily took over the religious symbols of neighbouring peoples, but it appears that the Egyptian winged sun-disc (set in the uraeus), adopted in the Near East (with the exception of Babylonia) during the 2nd millennium, was altered in Persia and became a disc set in a circle. This emblem was already known to the Persians, as it was used in Assyria for the god Assur. It seems, then, very likely that the Persians did not think of portraying their god in image form before they had

come into contact with the peoples around them, but we should remember that the ancient Mesopotamians, too, never made a figurative representation of their great god of heaven An or Anu.

The splendour of Persian art

The artist had also to create for the world some impression of that vast state which was the Persian empire and of the tens of thousands of subjects living under its sway. This he tried to do in the bas-reliefs which adorned the palaces, exploiting to the full all the splendour and magnificence of the court and the surroundings in which the king lived. The Assyrian kings had surrounded themselves with scenes of atrocious barbarity, like the banqueting scene where Assurbanipal and his queen feast before the head of a defeated enemy that hangs from a hook, the bas-reliefs showing heaps of enemy heads cut off at the neck and meticulously counted by the scribes, the impaled bodies standing out against the landscape (a universal reminder of the fate awaiting rebels), battle scenes with their horrifying confusion of mangled bodies and appalling atrocities, and, lastly, the hunting scenes which acclaimed the courage of the king. The Persians portrayed nothing like this on their palace walls. The stairway balustrades, like the palace halls, were decorated with great ornamental friezes whose chosen theme was a feast where a crowd of courtiers press round the king to pay him homage while a line of tribute-bearers approaches.

The artist was able to produce a series of the most vivid tableaux, fascinating in the variety of people and tributes depicted, that far and away surpassed King Shalmaneser's timid attempt on the Black Obelisk at Nimrud.

The figures grasp each other by the hand; some turn to talk to the person behind, or hold the shoulder of the man in front, just as in some fabulous procession which at night by the flickering light of torches could leap into life on the walls. But finally we are overcome by a feeling of weariness and monotony when faced with these scenes which recur in every one of the palaces and sometimes even several times over in the same palace. We must set aside, then, our own opinions if we are to understand

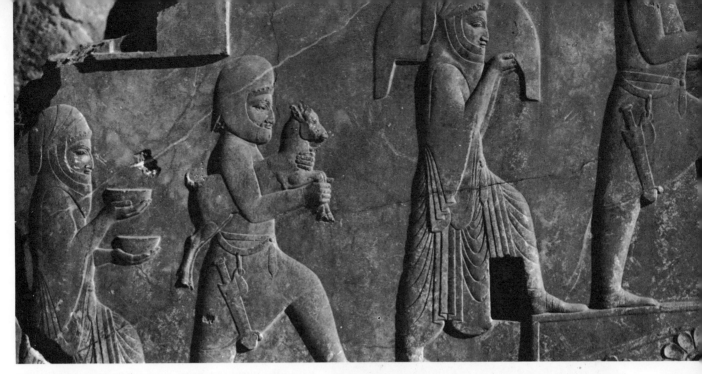

554. PERSEPOLIS. Frieze showing tribute-bearers. Darian epoch. (521–486 B.C.)

this art that does not fit in with Western attitudes, for a Persian artist, if he had not penetrated to their deeper significance, could make just the same complaint of our cathedrals with their Nativities and Crucifixions. What the Persian artist wanted to produce was a great, uniformly decorated, frieze. We watch a procession in stone where almost all the figures are shown strictly in profile, standing out from the wall.

Light and colour

It is when we come to Susa, the ancient Elamite capital which became a royal city, that we begin to realise the importance of the physical environment and the pervading influences shaping an art. The absence of stone, which had to be transported at great expense, and the closeness of Mesopotamia were both factors that gave Susa its unique and individual character.

At Susa we are no longer presented with sober processions as we were at Persepolis; here we are spectators in a fairyland of light and colour. The walls of the palace—on which we find episodes from the story of Esther—are decorated with iridescent and lavish colour; they are 432 adorned with glazed brick, with archers and fantastic animals springing from the same root as the naturistic ideas that were fundamental to the Asian religions. Babylonian artists, some time earlier, had been unrivalled in the way they managed to produce harmonious forms from these heterogeneous creatures evolved from the combination of features from different species during the course of thousands of years.

The fantastic colours used by the artists for the bodies and wings of these djinns, possibly with some magical purpose, seem to have been inspired by a world of dreams where fancy rules supreme: such, for example are the 176 glazed panels where we see two sphinxes turning their heads backwards towards the doorways (for they were set between the entrances so that no person coming in could pass unnoticed before their brown, inscrutable, mysterious faces). Similarly, the innumerable archers at the king's side had a magic significance, almost a security against any possible desertion on the part of the actual

guard, who had, in fact, given the monarch such poor protection. At Susa, as at Persepolis, there are friezes wholly devoted to lines of guards, but in glazed bricks, 178 vivid and glowing warmly in this light, with all the rich ochres and yellows and, as in Babylon, invariably standing out from a blue ground, the forerunner of the incomparable blues of the Ispahan mosques. The artist has paid attention to racial differences among the archers by distinguishing the swarthy complexioned southerners from the fair-skinned men of the north. The lavish magnificence of their embroidered silk robes appears to be exactly matched by the description of the immortals crossing the Dardanelles by a bridge of boats, crowned with flowers and with myrtle branches beneath their feet; and we can understand how these archers, though of unsurpassed skill as marksmen, should have been so hampered by their clothes when it came to a hand-to-hand tussle with the well-armed Greek infantry. It is not difficult to imagine the envy of the Greeks, a young and poor people then, as they gazed at the splendour and wealth of Asia.

The cosmopolitan empire

Persia then appeared to be the country that was potentially a centre for every kind of activity: in 512 Darius ordered Scylax of Caryonda, the Carian captain, to sail down the Indus. The Greek doctor Ctesias lived at the court of Darius II, and Telephanes of Phocaea worked for the King of Kings for the greater part of his life. This in part explains the infiltration of Greek and other foreign influences, along with the use of foreign labour with which the foundation charter of the palace of Darius at Susa (translated by Father Scheil), is very much concerned; this charter is, in this respect, one of our most useful and instructive sources. There the king lists all the materials required, from India to Greece, for the building of his palace: they came accompanied by craftsmen experienced in working with these materials.

Cedarwood was brought from Lebanon; brick walls were built by Babylonians. There was continual contact between all the different regions of the empire and the neighbouring countries; ambassadors, scholars and artists travelled from one country to another and the fame and

295

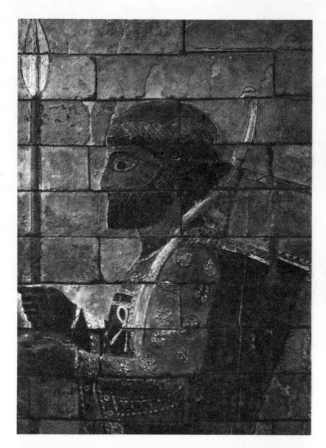

555. SUSA. Detail of an archer. Glazed brick. *Louvre.*

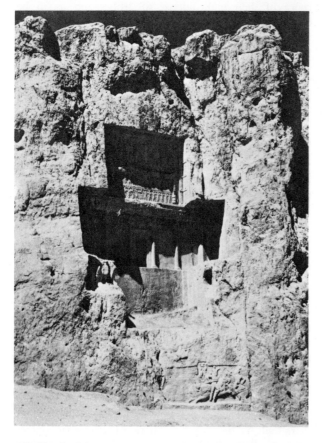

556. Tomb of Artaxerxes II (404–358) at Naksh-i-Rustam. The façade represents that of a palace. At the base is a Sassanian bas-relief of Shapur I.

reputation of the East, with the Persians as its representatives, spread far and wide. So the Greeks came to be acquainted with the sciences of ancient Babylonia (handed down by initiation ceremonies) and it has been pointed out that Pythagoras' headgear was, in fact, that worn by the initiated. But these interchanges often produced clashes. Trade was made considerably easier by the adoption of the daric (which can be traced back in origin to Croesus) and was backed up by the great banks established in Babylonia by Murashu and his sons. The ancient great highway—the old Semiramis road—was extended to Susa, and at intervals along it monuments were set up in honour of the King of Kings, like the Behistun rock where it was a feat of daring for sculptors to climb up (and this was repeated in modern times by archaeologists) and to carve bas-reliefs to the glory of Darius and engrave his address from the throne in three languages (Babylonian, Elamite and Persian). The fact that the Achaemenids were compelled to make use of other languages besides Persian in order to communicate with all the subject peoples of the empire has enabled scholars to decipher cuneiform script—with the help, too, of a successful reading of an Egyptian cartouche on an oil-bottle where the name of Xerxes appears.

When they came to power the renown of the Persians spread throughout the ancient world; before this, Nabonidus had been told by the god Marduk, who had appeared to him in a dream, of Astyages' downfall and the coming of Cyrus. We have a typical example of the infiltration of Medo-Persian influence in Babylon, where Nebuchadnezzar II had built the hanging gardens, to delight his wife Amytis, the grand-daughter of Astyages, who remembered with longing the gardens or 'paradises' which were part of every Achaemenid palace, those gardens that are still part of Iran's enchantment today. Even in Babylon buildings were to be found termed 'appa dana'. A palace in Sidon (then a Persian capital), burnt during the insurrection of the satrapies (362), illustrates well enough how the Persian style, both in dress and architecture, had everywhere taken root.

The magnificence of the King of Kings

Many new characteristic features came into being under Persian rule. After the Sumerian patesis, the viceroys of the gods, after the rulers of Babylon and Assur, kings of 'everything that was', the Persian king appeared as something quite different; from now on, royal protocol conferred upon him the title of King of Kings. He was created by Ahura Mazda to govern that vast land, entrusted by him with that great kingdom with its fine warriors and 'excellent horses', in recognition of the fact that his forebears had been a race of horsemen. Now this was no longer an art like that practised in Assyria, exclusively dedicated to the honour and praise of a military leader's courage, nor like that of Babylon put at the service of a devout king intent upon the worship of his god, but an art which celebrated the 'superman', a conception that is a very early foreshadowing of Nietzsche's ideas.

But even more than this, the ruler was not a monarch whom the gods had made an instrument of fear, as he had been in Assyria, but a righteous king, elected by all the gods. The prophet Isaiah was to be able to write: 'Thus spake the Lord to his anointed, to Cyrus whose right

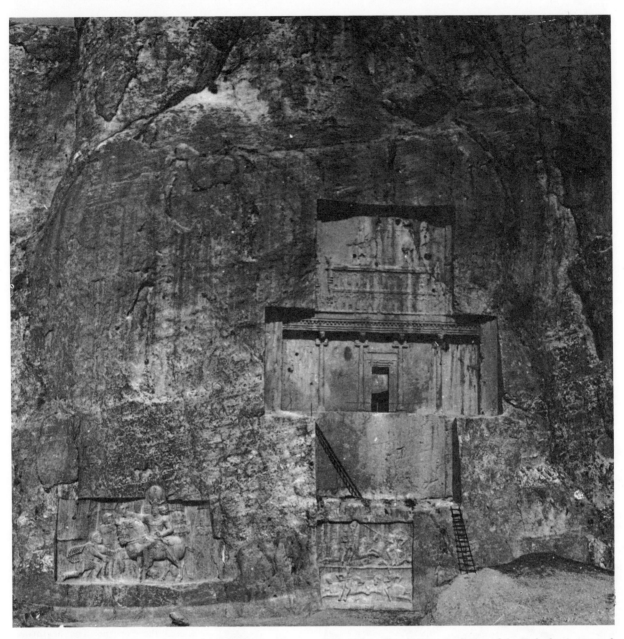

557. ACHAEMENIAN. Tomb of Darius I at Naksh-i-Rustam. At the base of the tomb are two reliefs of the Sassanian epoch. 5th century B.C.

hand I have holden . . . to subdue the nations before him . . . I will go before thee that thou mayest know that I am the Lord which calls thee by thy name; I have surnamed thee though thou hast not known me . . . I am the Lord and there is none else . . . I form the light and create darkness . . .' (Isaiah 45, 1–7). We could imply, it seems, from this, that it was, in fact, precisely the God of Light whom Cyrus worshipped and it shows what links there were between beliefs at this time. This same king Cyrus speaking to the Babylonians tells them on his cylinder: 'The god Marduk considered all the countries of the earth. He scanned them in search of a righteous king . . . whom he would lead by the hand. He called his name "Cyrus, King of Anshan" . . . The god Marduk looked with pleasure upon his pious acts and his righteous heart . . . and like a friend and companion, he walked by his side.' Cyrus concludes with these words: 'The god

Marduk inclined the great heart of the Babylonian people towards me . . . and each day I remembered to pay it homage' (Cylinder of Cyrus V. R. 35, 11–25).

The Achaemenid kings had filled their palaces full of treasures, and Plutarch tells how ten thousand mules and five hundred camels were employed by the Greeks in the sack of Persepolis. The Greeks carried off from Susa about forty-nine thousand gold and silver talents, which, considering the value of gold at this time, would nowadays represent an impressive sum of several millions.

Texts and monuments alike have nothing to say of the Persians' religion, which we can only begin to appreciate by its contribution to culture—so unlike anything that happened in Greece—as its light shone throughout the ancient world long after the collapse of the Achaemenid empire. Crystallised within the Persian civilisation was an Oriental civilisation many thousands of years old; but a new spirit had swept across the great plateau in the tracks of those audacious horsemen, and when Alexander embarked on his conquest of Asia he followed the routes taken before him by the Kings of Kings.

HISTORICAL SUMMARY: Persian art

Archaeology. Surviving remains of ancient Persia were first brought to notice by Rabbi Benjamin of Tudela in the 12th century, and subsequently by Sir John Chardin (17th century), Karsten Niebuhr (18th century), Sir Henry Rawlinson and Sir Henry Layard (19th century) and by the many travellers to Persia. E. Flandin and P. Coste were commissioned to make drawings of these remains in 1839. Investigation began only in 1884–86, when M. and Mme M. Dieulafoy settled in Susa (identified by W. K. Loftus) where J.

558. Plan of Persepolis.
1. Terrace stairway.
2. Propylaea of Xerxes.
3. Apadana of Xerxes and Darius.
4. Hall of the hundred columns.
5. Tachara of Darius.
6. Palace of Artaxerxes III.
7. Hadish of Xerxes.
8. Tripylon.
9. Harem.
10. Treasury.
11. Part of the fortified wall (where the Elamite tablets were found).
12. Tomb of Artaxerxes II (or III).

de Morgan began systematic excavations in 1897; this work was carried on by R. de Mecquenem and later by R. Ghirshman, while the Oriental Institute in Chicago and the Department of Iranian Antiquities concentrated their efforts on Persepolis.

Geography. Persia assumed the name of Iran under the Sassanids. It is bounded by Armenia, the Caspian Sea and Russia to the north, Afghanistan to the east, the Persian Gulf to the south and Iraq to the west. The country is made up of a very high plateau with a central salt desert. To the west this plateau runs into the mountains of Armenia and, along the eastern side of Mesopotamia, matches the plateau of Asia Minor which borders Mesopotamia to the north-west. These two plateaux, cut by small valleys, form the extreme edges of the central Asian plateau known as the 'great steppes'. The empire of the Achaemenid Persians extended far beyond these boundaries, stretching from the Indus to the Aegean Sea and the Nile.

History. Civilisation grew up in this part of the world at a very early date. Its existence in the Neolithic, and possibly from the 5th millennium, is borne out by the excavated sites at Tepe Hissar, Tepe Sialk (pre-'Ubaid culture) and, a little later, at Tepe Giyan ('Ubaid culture). The excavation of Susa, the capital of the country of Elam bordering on lower Mesopotamia, has shown that the growth of this civilisation was to be closely dependent on the development of Mesopotamian civilisation.

The great Indo-European migrations of the 3rd millennium brought Aryans, on their way to India by way of Turkestan and the Caucasus, to the Iranian plateau. Some of them intermarried with the people of the Zagros Mountains (modern Luristan), where they took control; soon after, they swept down into Babylonia, and this was the beginning of the Kassite domination that was to last almost until the end of the 2nd millennium. The Assyrians, in a few centuries, were to reverse the situation. The Medes, a young Iranian warrior tribe like the Scythians and brought up in their tradition, had selected Ecbatana as their capital, while the Persians, members of the same race, descended the slopes of the Iranian plateau.

About the 9th century B.C. the Assyrians began to move southwards and came into conflict with the Medes and Persians in the Zagros Mountains; in the 8th century Sargon smashed the alliance of Median leaders. Phraorte then became the leader of the Medes, Mannaeans and Cimmerians, and conquered the Persians. The Scythians, who had taken control of Media, were governed by Cyaxares; he reorganised the army and, following his alliance with Nabopolassar, founder of the Chaldean dynasty in Babylon, and with the help of nomadic tribes, he destroyed Nineveh in 612, thereby avenging the Assyrian sack of Susa in 640.

Prior to the Scythian invasion the Persians had established a sovereign state under Achaemenes, which was to be reunited under Cambyses I; his marriage to the daughter of the Median king produced Cyrus, who conquered Media in 555, then Lydia in 546 and lastly, in 538, Babylon. He was succeeded by Cambyses in 529. Cambyses had his brother Smerdis put to death, conquered Egypt and proclaimed himself king and conquered Ethiopia, but because of the Phoenician sailors' lack of cooperation, he was unable to reach

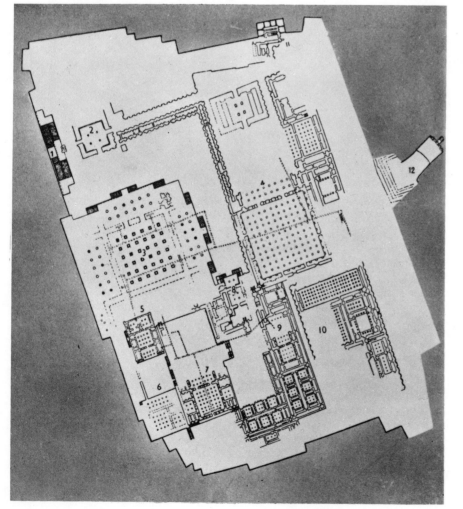

Carthage. On his death a pretender claiming to be Smerdis stirred up the people. Darius I deposed the usurper, crushed the rebellion and launched out to conquer India (512). Later, turning to the north and Europe, he marched as far as the Danube. The rest of the story belongs to Greek history: the Ionian rebellion, the burning of Sardis (499), the fall of Miletus (494) and finally the first Persian War and the battle of Marathon (490). Darius, who had recognised his son Xerxes as heir to the throne, died at the age of thirty-six. None of his successors came near to matching his greatness, with the exception of Artaxerxes II (Mnemon) who signed the peace of Antalcidas (387), a compensation for Marathon and Salamis. He was the last of the great kings; Artaxerxes III (Ochus) and Darius III (Codamannus), the ill-starred opponent of Alexander, were both unfit to rule.

Early art. Little has survived of the art of the Medes, and the most important remains come from the Sakkez treasure found to the south of Lake Urmia. It could just as well be the treasure of a Scythian king. The objects belonging to it can be divided into four groups which reveal the various influences affecting Median art: in the first group can be put a typically Assyrian bracelet adorned with lions carved in relief; the second group, identified as Assyro-Scythian, includes a breast-plate on which a procession of animals and djinns is making its way towards a cluster of stylised Sacred Trees. In actual fact, except for one or two animals in the Scythian style, this shows entirely Assyrian influence. The last two groups are Scythian (scabbard and dish decorated with Scythian motifs, notably the lynx) and native (which can be related to bronzes like those from Luristan).

There are two conflicting theories regarding the various features of this treasure. Godard dates the Assyrian objects from the reign of Assurnasirpal (9th century) whereas Ghirshman attributes them to the time of Esarhaddon (7th century). According to the first theory the objects must be attributed to local Mannaean workshops, and it must be assumed that while the Scythians were in this area they adopted certain features out of which they developed their own style. If we follow Ghirshman's idea, these specimens can be properly attributed to 7th-century Scythians and would thus be the first known examples of their work.

Achaemenian art, the youngest art of the ancient Orient, covers two centuries (from the middle of the 6th to the middle of the 4th). Examples can be seen in the ruins of Pasargadae, Persepolis and Susa.

Architecture. *PASARGADAE.* This was the first settlement on the plateau for which Cyrus was responsible. The palace and various other buildings were set among gardens, and the many columns, surmounted by bulls' heads, show that the ideas behind the apadana were already in full force. Pasargadae can be described as the forerunner of Achaemenian architecture, but the terrace near Masjid-i-Sulaiman, with its gigantic walls and the ten flights of stairs leading up to it, can be attributed to the Persians and to a period prior to the building of Pasargadae and Persepolis.

Fire Temples. At Pasargadae there is also a fire temple. These temples were square towers, built of well-bonded stone with mock loopholes and windows in dark materials; inside, the sacred fire was kept alight by the Magi, who belonged to a Median tribe specially trained in the study and practice of religious ritual. At one time these buildings were thought to be 'towers of silence'. Similar structures can be found near Persepolis and at Naksh-i-Rustam, along with four-sided monuments having ornamental bas-relief battlements, that have been identified as fire altars.

Tombs. Not far from Pasargadae, at Meshed-i-Murgad, stands the tomb of Cyrus [**552**], a rectangular building set on a base of seven stone-courses, with a gabled roof made of flat stone slabs. It can be compared with monuments in Asia Minor.

At Naksh-i-Rustam, near Persepolis, are the royal rock-tombs standing one beside the other [**556, 557**]. The tomb of Darius Codamannus at Persepolis was never finished. The tombs are hollowed out of the rock on the pattern of the tomb of Da-u-Dokhtar in the province of Fars. The architects carved from the rock itself an imitation of a palace façade with four engaged columns, crowned by 'kneeling bull' capitals which support an entablature decorated with a Greek moulding; above this is carved a line of bulls and lions, on which rests a dais held up by Atlantes; the king, turning towards a fire altar, stands on steps beneath the emblem of Ahura Mazda whose face is inside the circle.

Private tombs have been discovered (like the one at Susa) in which a woman of high rank, adorned with jewels, was laid in a bronze receptacle.

PERSEPOLIS. It was here that the Achaemenian genius developed to the full. The barracks and citadel were built on a mountain overlooking a wide plain in the direction of Shiraz. The lower slopes were levelled off for an esplanade on which a virtual city of palaces was built [**435, 550**]. Although

excavations have now uncovered almost all the buildings, we still have no very clear idea of the purposes for which they were intended, although it would seem that the buildings in question are almost exclusively state or ceremonial edifices. From the walled esplanade a great stairway with a double ramp leads down into the plain; opposite the highest landing are the propylaea of Xerxes, a massive four-sided structure open at each end and along the sides and decorated with colossal human-headed winged bulls [**560**]. Around the entrance, spaces left empty with regular hollows cut out of the rock were intended for terrace gardens.

What is left of the palace is a veritable skeleton structure of doors and windows hewn from great blocks of stone that served as supporting props for walls that have long since vanished [**179c**]. Here the Egyptian gorge was used, and the king was portrayed on the lateral blocks of stone inside the doorways. On the right side a stairway, decorated with bas-reliefs, led to the apadana of Darius and Xerxes. The

559. PERSEPOLIS. Relief showing the king seated on a throne.

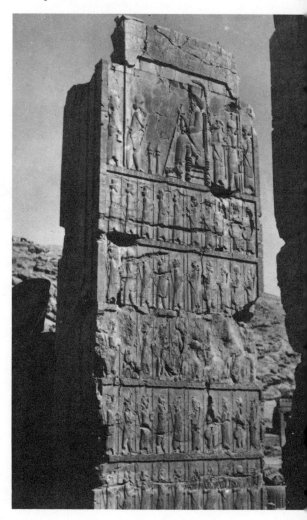

299

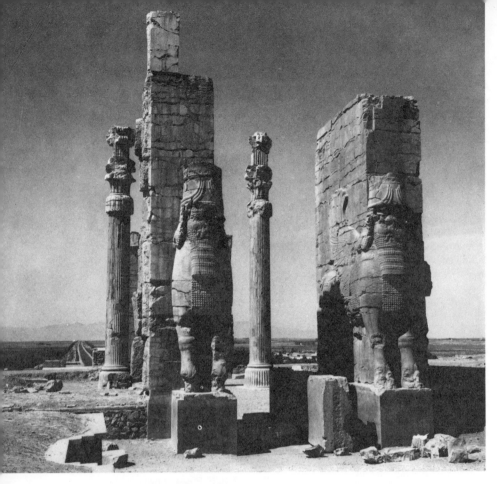

560. PERSEPOLIS. Winged human-headed bulls. Propylaea of Xerxes I (485–464).

561. PERSEPOLIS. Throne of Xerxes I. In the relief on the lower half representatives of the satrapies support the royal throne.

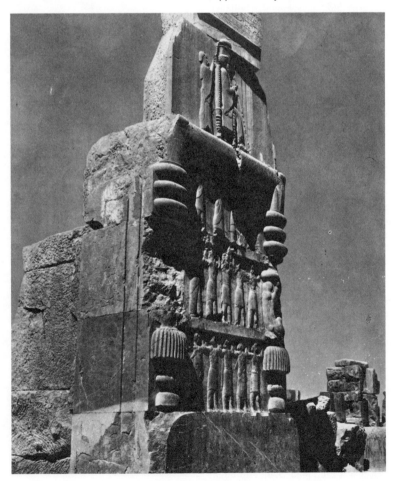

apadana, used as an audience chamber, was a typically Achaemenian structure. Its roof was supported by columns about seventy feet high—fluted, slender shafts that were mostly set on a bell-shaped base and were crowned by typically Achaemenian capitals like the one from Susa which is now in the Louvre. The lower part of these eighteen-foot-high capitals was made up of volutes, like C's set back to back, which supported the main part of the capital —the forequarters of two kneeling bulls, joined together [431]. Beams rested on the saddle and in turn supported the larger beams of the roof so that some weight was taken by the bulls' heads. The apadana at Susa had thirty-six columns and covered an area of almost two and a half acres. This chamber at Persepolis had the same number of columns and was surrounded by a single peristyle that had two rows of six columns on three sides.

SUSA. The old royal cities continued to be important alongside the new capitals. At the ancient Elamite capital of Susa, on a hill, Darius I built his winter residence, with its vast apadana which was restored by Artaxerxes II (Mnemon). It was explored by M. Dieulafoy, who retrieved some of its glazed ornamentation, and then by J. de Morgan in 1908, who uncovered the building's plan by tracing cuttings in the ground pavements (made of a sort of concrete composed of chalk and pounded baked clay) which corresponded to the baked-brick walls dating from 440. The palace was planned on similar lines to the one in Babylonia, with chambers arranged around a rectangular court.

Plastic arts. The plastic arts were primarily devoted to the ornamentation of the palaces.

Bas-reliefs formed the main part of the Persepolis ornamentation: the double stairway which led on to the terrace and into the palace chambers was decorated with two kinds of bas-relief. The motif of the lion attacking a bull [551], a familiar device since the earliest period of Mesopotamian art, appeared on the triangular panels of the balustrades; elsewhere, the king 'in majesty' was found. On a dais shaped like a throne, a colossal prototype of the royal Persian throne (the Peacock Throne), the king sits in a great chair [559]. Beneath the dais, lines of figures are carved, whose dress indicates that they belong to the various satrapies. The second type of bas-relief depicts processions of guards, courtiers and tribute-bearers [553, 554]. The artist has taken immense trouble to differentiate the characteristic features of their dress. The Persians wear a single or embattled tiara and long robes whose

300

wide sleeves are adorned with symmetrical folds in imitation of drapery (a concession to Greek influence) but of a completely uniform treatment. Over one shoulder they carry a quiver holding a bow and arrows. The Medes, wearing caps, have a short tunic, and trousers, entirely free of folds, caught in at the ankle. They carry daggers with scabbards of the same shape as those of Scythian origin. The tribute-bearers are distinguished more by the nature of their gifts than by their costume and are preceded by a chamberlain.

Along the great routes of the empire, even in the most outlying regions, artists carved bas-reliefs in the king's glory, like the one carved on the rock at Behistun, which accompanies Darius' proclamation and portrays him as a conqueror in an already familiar pose, with the defeated enemy beneath his foot.

Graeco-Persian reliefs from the end of the 5th century have been discovered in the region of Dascyleium in Bithynia, depicting a procession of men and women on horseback and a Persian sacrifice with two priests (Magi), the lower half of their faces veiled, carrying a mace in their hands, nearing an altar, with the heads of a ram and a bull on a brushwood stake at their feet.

At Susa, glazed bricks [555], copied from Babylonia, took the place of the marble ornamentation of Persepolis. The Achaemenians, however, used a different method from that of their teachers. Instead of clay they used chalk and sand. The bricks were first baked in a moderate heat and then the outline of the figures was added in blue glaze and the bricks were returned to the oven; finally the areas outlined in blue were filled in with chosen colours and received one last baking to complete the process.

The ornamentation of the staircase balustrades at Susa drew its inspiration from the Theban tombs with their superimposed lotus flowers, and from Aegean art with its alternating volutes.

The gates were adorned with lions, their coats dappled grey-green or blueish, set in a framework of zigzags and palmettes interspersed with scallops and rosettes. The palace walls were embellished with mythological beasts, whose origins can be traced back to Babylonia, with scallop-edged wings and breasts coloured alternately yellow and green [432]. Elsewhere, as at Persepolis, there were robes of lavish embroideries on material of white or yellow ground, adorned with three-towered castles and eight-pointed stars, the folds indicated in dark colours; these garments had wide yellow or purplish-brown sleeves; the shoes of the guards were yellow, their quivers

made of panther skin and their hair held back by a bandeau [178]. Between the gateways sat sphinxes wearing the horned tiara headdress, their heads turned to look behind them in an inscrutable attitude but one which adds a great decorative appeal to this motif [176], which recurs on the seal of Darius' chancellery, where the sphinxes turn to face towards each other.

Minor arts. Metal-work, of the utmost importance to an equestrian people, suffered no decline under the Achaemenids. Bronze was used for the facing of certain parts of buildings, such as doors.

For work in gold and silver an especially elaborate technique was employed, with silver dishes in repoussé (foreshadowing Sassanian plate with its rosette and boss-beading ornamentation), angled rhytons whose bases are formed by the head of a goat or an ibex, vases with handles ending in an animal's head or else made to represent an animal's body (like the two handles of the same vase, one of which is in Berlin and the other in the Louvre [562], depicting a winged silver ibex incrusted with gold), a triangular stand from Persepolis composed of three roaring lions, the realistic treatment of which contrasts with that of the bronze lion found at Susa [564], comparable in pose to the lion from Khorsabad but far more stylised and suggestive of the monsters of the Far East.

Jewellery shows a wide variety of influences. Some ornaments from the Oxus treasure in the British Museum—gold plaques, bracelets and rings—indicate the same Scythian influence that can be found in other treasures. Gems from the Susa sepulchre—crescent-shaped earrings decorated with coloured stones set in gold, and bracelets with no clasp but tipped with a lion's head chased and incrusted with turquoise and lapis lazuli, illustrate a technique which was to be adopted by the 'barbarians'.

Achaemenian glyptics surpassed in refinement anything hitherto known: one of the finest intaglios shows the king in his chariot out hunting with bow and arrow, his horses at full gallop. A plaque used as a mould for inlaid gold leaf has been found, as well as a small head of extraordinary delicacy —all that remains of a statuette, for after the looting by Alexander's soldiers statuary, like everything else, survived, if at all, only in a mutilated condition.

On the obverse side of the gold coins called darics, the Achaemenid kings, kneeling on one knee, are depicted as archers.

Marguerite Rutten

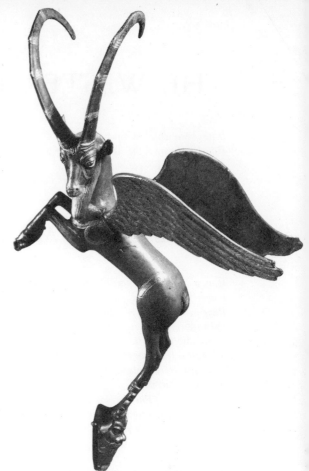

562. Winged silver ibex incrusted with gold. Graeco-Persian. 4th century B.C. *Louvre.*

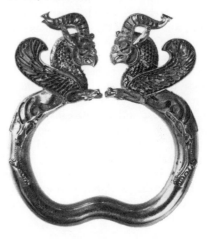

563. Amulet decorated with griffons, from the Oxus treasure. 5th century B.C. *British Museum.*

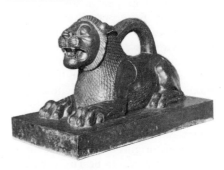

564. ACHAEMENIAN. Bronze lion from Susa. 6th–5th centuries B.C. *Louvre.*

THE WESTERN MEDITERRANEAN

It has been usual to think of the art of Antiquity, before Rome arrived on the scene, as being involved almost entirely with Greece and the Aegean. The western Mediterranean was something more than a mere passive

mirror for Hellenism: it served as a link with Europe, whose economic importance we have looked at in an earlier chapter, and it was the scene of commercial competition and military struggles that held back the development of art.

I. THE CARTHAGINIAN WORLD *Gilbert Charles Picard*

If we pass over the part played by Cretan sea power from the 2nd millennium, we find that it was the Phoenicians who, from the beginning of the next millennium, were responsible for carrying the ancient world into the western Mediterranean basin and who, in the 5th century, managed to get as far as Finistère. They in their turn were replaced by Carthage, an offshoot of the parent nation, which continued the uninspired eclectic tradition of the Phoenicians but, for all this, helped to produce a more original art in Spain. Gilbert Charles Picard, for thirteen years, until 1955, Director of Antiquities in Tunisia, describes this little-known art.

Standard histories concentrate almost exclusively on the study of the eastern Mediterranean basin until the decline of the Hellenistic world; only then are we brought back to ancient Italy in order to explain the origins of Roman power which by late Hellenistic times was capable of taking control of all the countries surrounding the Mediterranean. Gaul, Spain and North Africa are completely ignored except by specialist archaeologists who methodically examine their earliest artifacts, and philologists who analyse their languages. Yet from the beginning of the Bronze Age the growth of the brilliant civilisation of the Near East and the Balkans depended to no mean extent on the material contributions made by an as yet barbarian West which also offered the vast resources of its practically virgin lands to the overflow of Hellenic and Asian peoples. The position occupied by these new countries of the West offers an interesting analogy with America's position in relationship to Europe from the 16th to the 19th centuries in our era.

The maritime power of Tyre

It was only from the 4th century B.C. that the West rebelled against its passive role, and this can largely be explained by the economic and maritime control which from the end of the 2nd millennium had been in the hands of a people who were not disposed to let anyone else profit from the benefits of their discoveries. Certain archaeological discoveries, in the light of recent interpretations of Greek history, are now bringing us round to see that Mycenaeans, and possibly even Cretans, had penetrated into Italian and Sicilian waters. The growth of Etruscan civilisation—no matter how one explains its mysterious origins—implies that there were close links between what was to be Tuscany and Asia Minor from the end of the 9th century. When Aegean maritime power declined, the seafarers of Tyre seized the opportunity to take over the exclusive trading monopoly in the southern

half of the Hesperian basin and to snap up all the profits attached to its Atlantic outlet. From the 13th to the 10th centuries, under pressure from the Greek settlers, the Phoenicians were forced to be content with the conquests they had already made, but there was no serious threat of encroachment.

This outcome was vital from the trading point of view, and this was the only one that really mattered to this nation in which 'merchants were princes and traders were the great men of the land' (Isaiah 23, 8). From the beginning of the 2nd millennium, southern Spain (present-day Andalusia) had become one of the greatest producing and trading centres in the world. Its influence extended as far as Britain and Ireland in the north and at least as far as Sardinia to the east, and with this as a stepping-stone, most probably to the Aegean. The Phoenicians made their fortune by establishing the first direct and close trading relations between Tarshish (Tartessus, near Cadiz) and Asia. This trade was being carried on in the time of Solomon (*c.* 970–33), and the Bible bears out that Phoenician ships from the high seas were called the 'navy of Tarshish' (I Kings, 9, 28).

It was obviously unavoidable, considering sailing conditions at that time, to have trading settlements and ports of call along a route which would take several years to travel; besides, these settlements could only have been very modest and were probably inhabited by a floating population. The absence to this very day of any archaeological discoveries which can be dated from the early part of the 2nd millennium should not lead us to doubt the traditional date given for the foundation of Gades (Cadiz), Lixos in Morocco and Utica (11th century).

At the end of the 9th century the growing Assyrian threat obliged the Phoenicians to find a more secure headquarters than Tyre. Yet Cyprus was too close and Tarshish too distant and over-populated. The new capital, Qart Hadash, was therefore founded in 814 half-way along their route, near Utica. In 1947 a hoard of votive vases was discovered which would seem to indicate that in the latter half of the 8th century a cult had existed on the shore near Carthage, probably dedicated to Dido, the city's founder, who had willingly sacrificed herself. It was around this holy place that the Tophets grew up, the sanctuaries where children were sacrificed, which, along with the necropolises, remain the chief sources of archaeological documentation.

The growth of Carthage

The history of Carthage falls into four periods. During the first (8th century and first quarter of the 7th century),

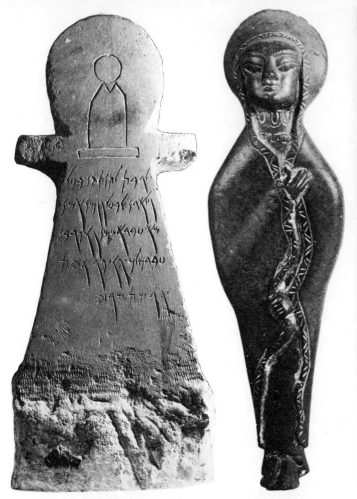

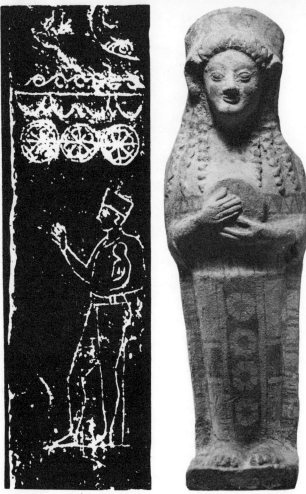

565. CARTHAGINIAN. Stele carved in the shape of the symbol of Tanit and engraved with the bottle symbol. 4th–3rd century B.C. *Bardo Museum, Tunis.*

566. IBERIAN. Woman wearing a cloak. Bronze *ex-voto.* Middle of the 1st millennium. *Archaeological Museum, Madrid.*

567. CARTHAGINIAN. Stele of a priest and child. Bas-relief in the Orientalised style. Late 5th–early 4th centuries B.C. *Bardo Museum, Tunis.*

568. GREEK. Statuette of a goddess wearing an embroidered robe, found at Carthage. 6th century B.C. *Bardo Museum, Tunis.*

the colony was still only a trading settlement with few inhabitants, probably slightly more important than the others and closely dependent on Tyre. In the second period (*c.* 675–450) Carthage set out to check the advance of Greek colonisation. In the third period (450–300) the defeat of Carthage by the Greeks at Himera, dating from the same time as the Persian wars, forced the Carthaginians (now surrounded by the Greeks and cut off from the East) to fall back on the resources of the West-Barbary, Negro Africa and the Celtic world. In the last period the Phoenicians in the west found it necessary to become part of the Hellenistic world, and with the decline of the Greeks in the west and the economic resources of their own empire they could have held one of the foremost places in this world had not Rome broken up their hegemony before destroying Carthage (147) to prevent it from becoming the capital of a Libyo-Carthaginian realm.

Leaving aside the first phase, about which very little is known, each of the other three periods coincides with independent cultural development. In the 7th and 6th centuries Carthage was still tied to a form of civilisation shaped in the parent-city from a combination of national characteristics and Egyptian, Mesopotamian and Aegean influences. Egyptian influence was the most apparent, both in architecture (of which we can have some idea thanks to the votive *cippi* in the shape of shrines and tombs) and in gem engraving, with its characteristic signet scarabs. The Hellenised Aegean seems to have had an

effect not so much with its painted vases (which were without influence on the heavy, clumsy local pottery) as with its clay modelling where the Carthaginian sacred prophylactic masks drew their inspiration from both Ionian kouroi and korai and the scowling, diabolical figures of which something of the same sort has been found in the Spartan temple of Artemis Orthia.

All this was cut short in the middle of the 5th century by a strict puritan reaction which established Tanit as the supreme deity and overthrew the old forms of worship (and, as a quite natural consequence, the conditions in which art had developed). The stopping of imports put an end to Egyptian and Greek influences. An abstract geometric style gathered inspiration from the revival of very ancient Aegean symbols: the 'symbol of Tanit' was **565** derived from the idol with outstretched arms and the 'bottle symbol' came from the Cycladic violin-shaped idol. A few reliefs show that Mesopotamian tradition was kept alive in the portrayal of deities. Metal crafts, however, which along with sculpture developed rapidly at this time, continued to copy archaic Greek models but, aware only of earliest stages of archaic Greek art, the craftsmen made no similar progress.

But in the early 4th century Hellenism won out. The adoption of Greek gods (Demeter in 396) and their images, and their alliance with the Carthaginian gods, caused the most fanatical defenders of national tradition to accept this form of iconography. *Ex votos*, and especially

303

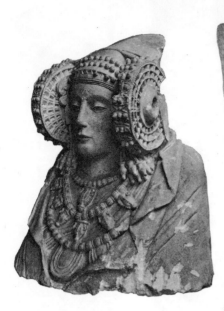

569. IBERIAN, showing
Greek influence. The Lady of
Elche. Painted sandstone
Early 5th century B.C.
Archaeological Museum, Madrid.

570. GRAECO-CARTHAGINIAN
ART OF THE HELLENIS-
TIC PERIOD. Shrine of Demeter
discovered at Thurbudo
Majus. *Bardo Museum, Tunis.*

571. *Top right.* CARTHAGINIAN. Small prophylactic mask,
very much enlarged, of a bearded man. Late 3rd or early 2nd
century   *Bardo Museum, Tunis.*

572. Right ear pendant of Phoenician workmanship,
decorated with lotus flowers, palmettes and birds. Found in
the treasure of Aliseda. (Cáceres, Spain). Middle of the 1st
millennium. *Archaeological Museum, Madrid.*

3rd-century sanctuaries and houses, brought to light by
excavation, show that religious and domestic architecture
had become a purely provincial variant of the Hellenistic
dialect. In the decoration of stelae and sacrificial knives,
as well as in gem engraving, an increasing number of
motifs of Greek origin were interwoven with Carthaginian symbols. The history of Carthaginian art, then, from
beginning to end, is almost entirely a history of the influences it came under. This creative impotence was a characteristic of the Phoenician people as a whole, whose
inward-looking natures, when not entirely taken up with
tasks of a practical kind, seem to have found freedom and
fulfilment only in theological speculation and in the poeti-
cal expression of these reflections. Except in the sphere
of agriculture Carthage, lacking any spirit of inquiry,
made very little progress even in technical matters. This
inability to find a concrete means of outward expression
for their inner life, undoubtedly stemming from a philosophical attitude, meant that the Carthaginians, unlike
the Etruscans, could not even take full advantage of their
adopted foreign models. The only art forms in which
they were able to produce works worthy of interest were
those which suppressed, as far as possible, the importance
of materials and space. Their engravings and bas-reliefs
are superior to their sculpture in the round, and in their
choice of decorative devices abstract motifs—geometric
signs, palmettes and stylised foliage—were invariably
preferred to naturalistic motifs. Even the human body
was treated as a symbol.

Carthaginian influence

So this explains the seemingly paradoxical fact that the
best examples of Carthaginian art have been found in the
overseas provinces, primarily in Spain which, apart from
specifically Carthaginian settlements like Ibiza in the
Balearics, must be thought of as a province apart that took
a great deal from Carthage but was never entirely subject
to her. Nothing could be more foreign to the Carthaginian
spirit than the Lady of Elche; her heavy head-dress was 569
probably the work of a Phoenician craftsman but it frames
a face treated in the manner of the Greek transitional
period, a style which Carthage always refused to follow.
Numidian art developed as Carthaginian artists immi-
grated to Masinissa's kingdom after the fall of Carthage,
but it was only in the 1st century A.D., when the artistic
traditions of Carthage had finally dried up, that it was
able fully to realise its potentialities. Carthaginian architects also built the Dougga Mausoleum and the Souma
at Kroub in the 2nd century, and, probably, a little later
in Algeria, the tomb known as the Medracen and the
Tombeau de la Chrétienne. The Ķbor Klib, a monumental
altar built on Zama territory about the middle of the 1st
century A.D., is purely Hellenistic in style. On the other
hand, the artists who decorated the Ghorfa stelae, working
in the 2nd century A.D., treated their subjects (which
stemmed from Phoenician theology, with elements taken
over from Greek philosophy) with a luxuriant inventiv-
ness as far removed from Carthaginian sterility as from
the rationalism and naturalism of classical Greece.

II. SICILY AND MAGNA GRAECIA *Gilbert Charles Picard*

The Graeco-Persian struggle in the east was complemented by the fierce conflict between the Greeks and the Persian allies the Phoenicians, and later their Carthaginian successors, in the west. The Greeks settled in southern Italy and Sicily and from there founded Phocaean Massalia (Marseille) a convenient gateway to southern Gaul and the Spanish coast. With them went their art, so much so that some of the most characteristic examples of Greek art have been taken from Sicily, but here we shall look at the independent development of Magna Graecia.

Western Hellenism was in direct opposition to Carthage; its productivity was in contrast with Semitic paucity, and its period of political and cultural expansion coincided exactly with periods of Phoenician decline, and vice versa. This was why Hellenism became firmly entrenched in Sicily in the interim between Tyre's domination of the sea and Carthage's hegemony. The very recent discoveries made by F. Villard and G. Vallet confirm that there was a definite break in continuity between the voyages of Mycenaean sailors of the 14th and 13th centuries and the colonisation of the 8th century. The traditional idea which has come down from Thucydides and which makes the Phoenicians the chief link between Sicily and the west at the beginning of the 2nd millennium, seems to be borne out by the presence of native pottery of Cypriot influence in archaeological strata dating from a time prior to the arrival of the Greeks.

The Doric style in Sicily

The Greek colonists who poured into Sicily and southern Italy in the latter half of the 8th century and throughout the 7th century, came first from Euboea and later from the Isthmus of Corinth and from Rhodes and Crete; the Dorian element soon took control, and the earliest works of art, dating from the beginning of the 7th century, are notably Doric in spirit. Temple architecture without exception was strictly Doric, and architectural sculptures from these buildings are the oldest records we have of the plastic arts in this area. The series of metopes from Selinus and from Paestum enable us to follow the progress of a style through three main stages (600–580–540). Initially it was clumsy and unsophisticated, largely subordinated to its geometrical framework and, like the first Romanesque sculpture, more akin to the minor arts (repoussé metal and ivories). Then we find less static, more dramatic compositions, and, finally, the great epic subjects. A preference for warlike themes and the exaltation of a quietly confident male strength was the expression of the ideal of a young nation engaged in a relentless struggle against a race enemy. The feeling for discipline and order which had been the strength of the Dorian armies appears in the strict symmetry that gives balance to the figures. Yet often some fine picturesque detail, like the wavy mane of Europa's bull, breaks through that heroic severity. The Youth from Selinus and the one from Agrigentum, the oldest surviving statues, do not date from before the late 6th century. These works, also strictly governed by Peloponnesian canons, contain echoes of old

masters known to us through literary texts: Perillus of Agrigentum who cast Philaris' Bull and Learchus of Rhegium.

In the early 5th century this heroic phase was followed by a mood of optimism, brought about by the victory at Himera. Sicily had then reached the peak of her strength and prosperity. All over the country the most imposing temples ever conceived by the Greek genius were erected **576** in thanksgiving. In Agrigentum, according to Pindar the most beautiful of those ill-fated cities, Carthaginian prisoners were set to build the temple of Olympian Zeus, its entablature supported by colossal Atlases, captives in **574** stone. On the eastern hill of Syracuse a group of three temples was erected and, it is nowadays thought, dedicated to Apollo, Artemis and Dionysus. The metopes from the last of these, dating from about 460, represent the finest work of architectural sculpture ever achieved by the Greeks in the west. Four of them depict battles fought by the gods and the punishment of various impieties which in their very enormity point to the crimes of the recently defeated barbarians. In one sweeping rhythm Hercules strikes down an Amazon while Athena slays Enceladus; Actaeon is torn to pieces by his hounds while Artemis looks on unmoved. A taste for pathos is apparent in these works, which was as yet unknown in Greece proper—a kind of expressionism which has enabled people to talk of the anti-classical quality of Sicilian sculpture. Violence gives way to serenity on the best known of these slabs, now identified as the Mystic Marriage of Persephone and Dionysus—Hades in the underworld. The Persephone's draperies recall the delicate workmanship of the robes of the Ionian korai. And it was in fact true that with the extraordinary economic development that had followed victory, western Greece had become a centre of attraction for artists from all regions, and its sculpture was no longer dominated by Peloponnesian influences alone. Pythagoras of Rhegium, born, like his philosopher-namesake, in Samos and like him, too, an exile in the west, was counted by his contemporaries among the great masters. He was wonderfully skilled in detailed renderings of the human body which he was able to enhance with movement, yet preserving the symmetry and order dear to the Dorian schools.

His best-known work, a statue of the wounded Philoctetes, has probably been partially preserved in a Roman copy. Sicilian archaeologists ascribe to his school a small bronze from Syracuse of a man pouring a libation, as well as the now strangely bald acrolith of Apollo Alaeus from Crimisa. The Delphic Charioteer, an *ex voto* of the **443** Sicilian town Gela, was once thought to be from his school, but it has once again been claimed to be of Attic workmanship. In compensation, Magna Graecia can still boast the Ludovisi Throne, the relief triptych dedicated **543** to the birth of Aphrodite in whose sensuous grace seems to linger something of the refined civilisation for which Sybaris has become a symbol.

The minor arts were also affected by this revival of activity. Whereas ceramics continued to be dominated by Attic competition, artists who had supplied the ordinary people with small clay models as votive offerings (twelve

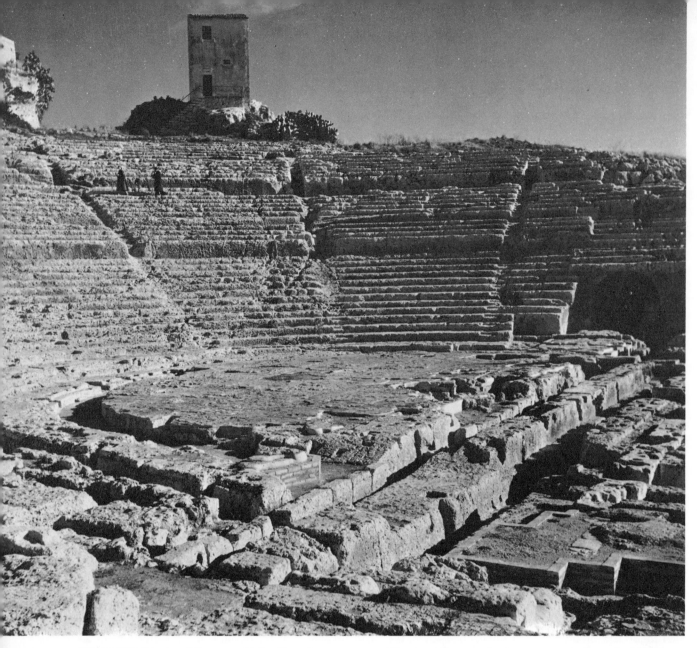

573. GREEK. Theatre at Syracuse, Sicily. 4th century B.C.

thousand statuettes were found at Selinus in the sanctuary of Demeter alone) now turned their hand to large statues; the powerful and calmly majestic busts of Demeter made for the city of Agrigentum are in no way inferior to the most perfect 5th-century marbles. This same goddess, the patroness of Sicily, appears also on coins made by Eumenes, Evainetos and Cimon (430–360), whose craftsmanship was never anywhere to be surpassed. These artifacts circulated freely and did more to spread Hellenism than either architecture or sculpture. At the time that Segesta—the capital of the Elymians, the loyal and ancient allies of the Carthaginians—entered the Athenian confederation, its people had already begun a Doric temple and a Greek theatre. But the temple was never finished; the Hellenisation of Sicily was violently interrupted in 409 by the Carthaginian counter-attack.

Syracuse and the decline of Sicily

The damage inflicted on Selinus and Segesta enables us to assess the gravity of the blow struck against civilisation by the savage onslaught of Carthaginian mercenaries; it was undoubtedly a disaster of far greater consequence to the Western world than was the total destruction of

Tyre's settlements in the west a century and a half later.

Syracuse was saved by the exertions of Dionysius I, but it was a city that had never equalled the great centres of the south in the sphere of culture. Besides, all its potentialities were taken up by the war; the fortifications of Euryala were most certainly works of art in their own way. But B. Pace, who has listed forty-six temples built in Sicily before 409, has found only four belonging to the subsequent period. Down to the end of the 4th century coins, it is true, preserved a high standard, but we have lost a great many bronzes—notably the statues of tyrants from the Syracusan agora, which were melted down on the orders of the well-intentioned but tiresome Timoleon. We have to wait till Hellenistic times when the Carthaginian clash had abated before we see a revival of the arts (given impetus by Hiero II). A fine bust from Volubilis discovered only a short while ago, which once formed part of Juba II's collection, may be a portrait of the Sicilian king. Finally, with the Roman conquest and the two centuries of ruthless exploitation that followed, Sicily's economic and cultural collapse was complete.

The Greeks in the west

The Greeks in Italy were engaged in a desperate struggle with the native inhabitants. This state of affairs did little

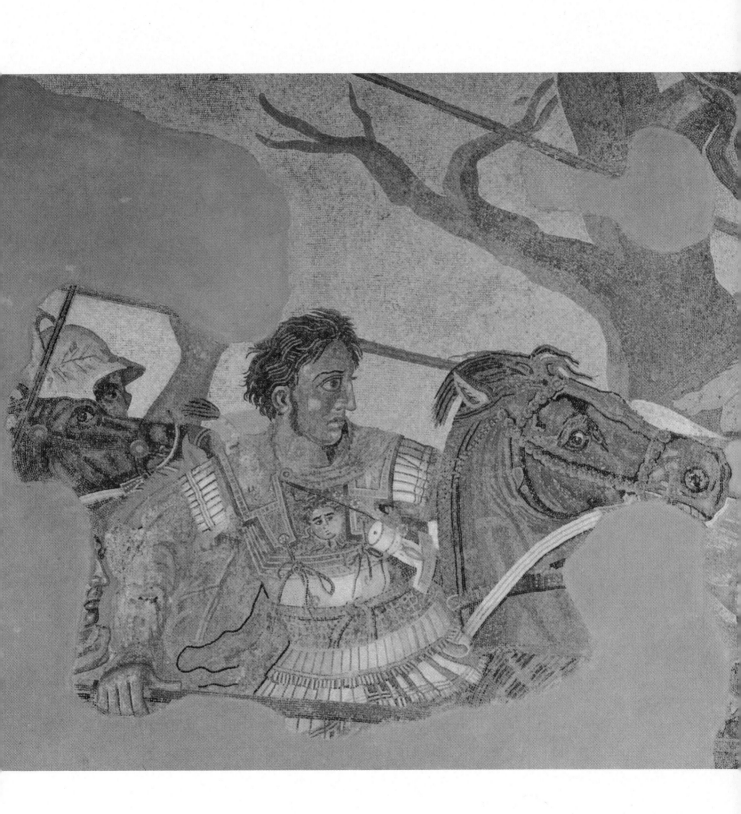

GREEK. The Alexander mosaic (Battle of Issus). Detail.
2nd century B.C. Believed to be a copy of a 4th-century painting.
National Museum, Naples. *Photo: D. Hughes-Gilbey*.

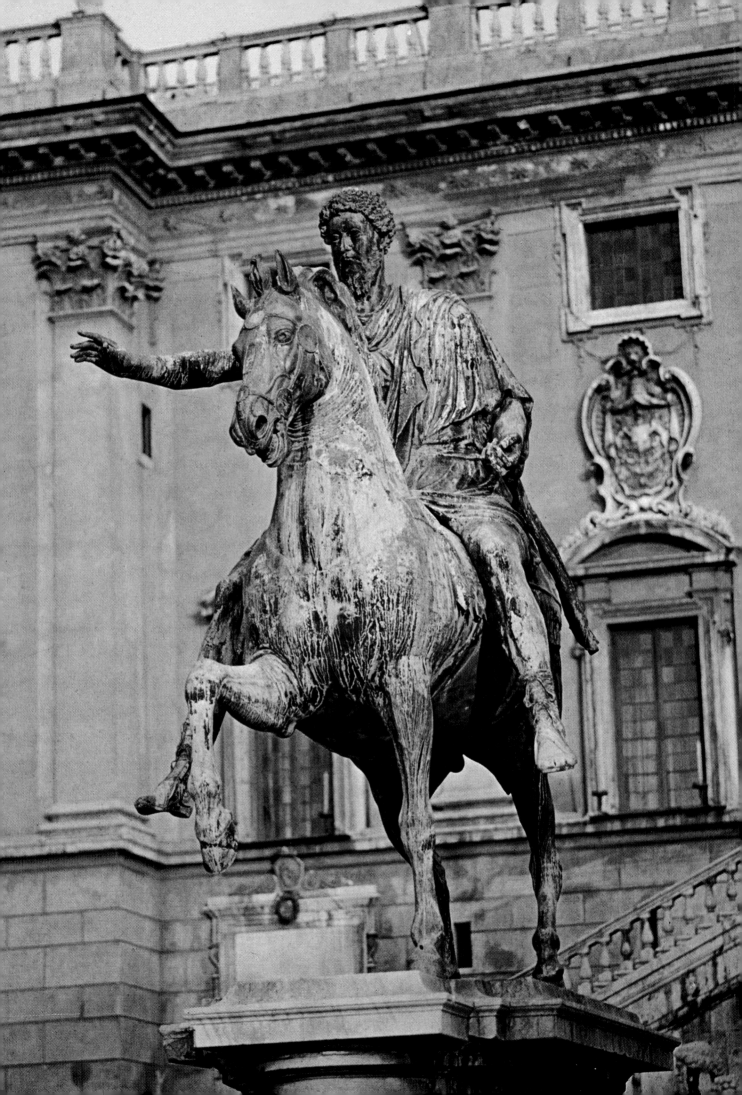

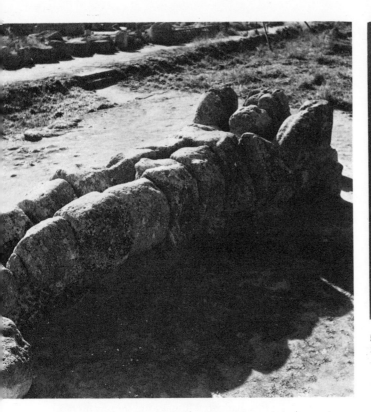

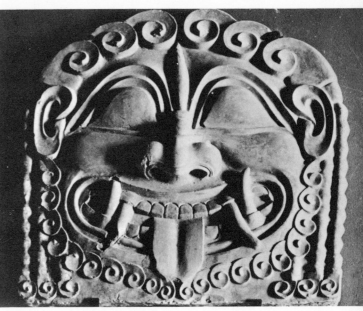

575. *Above*. GREEK. Head of Medusa. Terra-cotta antefix. Second half of the 6th century B.C. *Syracuse Museum*.

574. *Left*. GREEK. Atlas from the temple of Zeus at Agrigentum, Sicily. 5th century B.C.

to encourage the growth of artistic activity; we have almost no sculpture from this area after the group from Locri (*c.* 420) which portrays dead heroes carried by tritons to the Isles of the Blessed. But against this, domestic arts prospered. In the 4th century southern Italy became one of the chief pottery producing centres in the Mediterranean, but even here its work became increasingly commonplace and was soon taken over by the Italians. After the expedition of Pyrrhus, who dedicated a trophy-bearing Nike, probably of Oriental workmanship, in Tarentum, it could be said that true Greek art had ceased to exist in the peninsula.

At an even earlier date among the other Greek settlements in the west, for example with the Phocaeans of Marseille and Spain, isolation and the difficulties of life where barbarians were a continual threat had exhausted artistic activity or reduced it to the artisan level. So colonial life, on the whole, did not favour the growth of art. Sicily had become the seat of a school about the year 500 through a series of extraordinary circumstances and, in fact, it never really managed to free itself entirely of metropolitan influences. Rather than enriching their own culture, the vital work of the Greeks in the western Mediterranean had been to pass on to the barbarians something of the civilisation they had brought with them.

The western Mediterranean basin, then, was not the centre of an original artistic development. The areas between the Hellenic and Celtic spheres of influence fall into two cultural divisions: the north-east, which was soon controlled by the Greeks, and the south-west, which, at a distance, followed the aesthetic development of western Asia. The Roman conquest was to bring some kind of unity, at first only by the exclusive emphasis on a debased kind of Hellenism; but subsequently it encouraged the emergence of more original, sensitive art forms whose part in preparing the ground for medieval art has often been underestimated.

ROMAN. Marcus Aurelius. Bronze. A.D.161–180. Piazza del Campidoglio, Rome. *Photo: Michael Holford*.

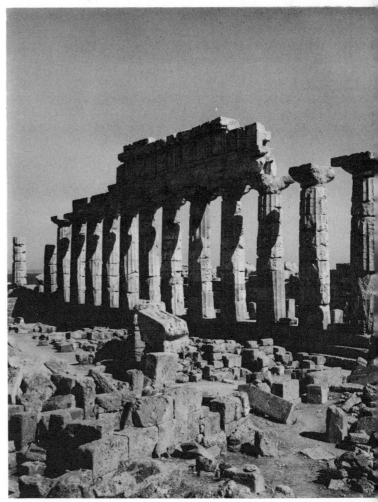

576. GREEK. Ruins of the Doric temple of Hercules at Selinus, Sicily.

307

III. THE ETRUSCANS *Raymond Bloch*

We have seen, in Chapter 4, the emergence of Etruscan art in the context of the European metal civilisations, and it was not long before the Etruscans began to take part in the Mediterranean conflict. Although they had sided with Carthage against the Greeks, they came more and more under Hellenic influence; but they maintained a strongly independent spirit which is mirrored in their art—some features of which were to be developed by the Romans, who conquered the Etruscans and all other rival nations and so came to make the Mediterranean Mare Nostrum.

For many years the question of Etruscan art's proper position among all the other Mediterranean arts has given rise to heated discussion. In 1879 J. Martha wrote: 'The one great misfortune of Etruscan art was that it never had time to take shape.' Modern critics have reached the conclusion that this art shows a complete lack of originality and represents nothing more than a totally provincial output, a mere reflection of Greek art on which it modelled itself. Another equally extremist point of view maintains, just as confidently, the complete independence of the art of ancient Tuscany. Both attitudes, I believe, go too far, and so in many ways are quite mistaken. If we are to get at the truth we must take a less extreme and dogmatic view. It is quite true that Etruscan art was continually and beneficially influenced by artists from Greece and Magna Graecia. Unless the profound 583 effect of the Greek workshops is taken into account, Etruscan art cannot begin to be understood. But the work of the Etruscans was not merely a slavish imitation without a genuine identity of its own. It was the outcome of the abilities, taste and spirit which were the individual characteristics of this people who, from the 7th century down to the beginning of the Christian era, were able to develop an original civilisation in Tuscany.

One of the most important characteristics of this civilisation was the leading part played by religious doubt and the concern with the after-life. Their gods were of a mysterious and cryptic nature, and men had a profound dread of the fate awaiting them after death. It would seem that the idea of death was ever present to the Etruscan mind. In this context it is understandable that their art 582 was primarily an art of the tomb. A kind of magic survival had to be secured for the dead in their final resting-place

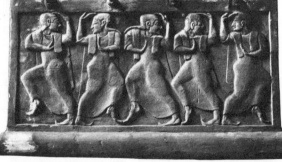

577. ETRUSCAN. Cinerary sarcophagus, decorated with a relief of dancers. From Chiusi. *Archaeological Museum, Florence.*

and then, according to later belief, in the shadowy world of Hades. This funerary cult was observed with the minutest attention to detail, and Etruscan art itself seems to have had no other end in view. The portrait immortalised the dead man's features and so wrested him from the powers of darkness. Here we have the reason for the creation and continuing popularity of the Tuscan portrait out of which, in its turn, the Roman portrait was to 581 emerge. On a burial urn from Chiusi we can see that in the earlier period a faithful copy of the dead man's face, in the form of a bronze mask, was affixed to the vessel. 579 Later, the head was carved and took the place of the urn's lid. Eventually this heterogeneous creation gave way to a real statue. Similarly, the frescoes which covered the 578 damp walls of the Tuscan hypogaea (subterranean burial chambers) are important as religious symbols. They depict the funeral feasts; they also portray the occupations and pleasures of his earthly life, and most of all they give concrete shape to his life in the next world.

This clears up the apparent contradiction of a sepulchral art infused with an ardent and vigorous feeling of life. To the mystic souls of the Etruscans the life of this world merely foreshadowed the more significant and infinitely more permanent destiny awaiting them after death. Consequently they paid less attention to the adornment of their towns than to their tombs which were built of solid stone or hollowed out of the same material—dwelling places intended to defy time.

This life is depicted in its own individual and concrete form. Unlike the Greeks, the Etruscans never tried to create types; their sole interest was in the individual and in the reality of everyday life. The Etruscan artist, apparently, felt nothing but contempt for formal beauty— that is for the beauty and harmony of different parts of his work. Guided by religious considerations which demanded a realistic likeness, he exaggerated his model's traits, beautiful or ugly, even to the point of caricature. 581 It was the bas-relief and the fresco rather than sculpture 577 in the round, and it was clay, bronze and colour rather than marble and stone which in Tuscany most successfully conveyed the rhythms of movement and the pulse of life. The creative personality in all fields was to show a deep-seated preference for simplification and stylisation, for the evocative rather than the realistic line. Detail was deliberately eliminated to emphasise contour and mass.

This natural talent for draughtsmanship shines out of their marvellous achievements in the minor arts and especially in engraving on precious metals and bronze. It was probably in the field of plate and jewellery that the Etruscans exploited their technical skill and decorative taste to the utmost. Treasures from the tombs of the 'Orientalising' period have a characteristic richness and elaboration, and some Etruscan jewellery of the 7th and 6th centuries truly represents a high-water mark of art.

So with all these contradictions (more apparent, it is true, than real), with its inequalities and its many failures, but with its exquisite achievements as well, Etruscan art is visually appealing and unusual. Very often it presents a curiously modern side, and the present age has at times found in it hints of some of its own trends and tastes.

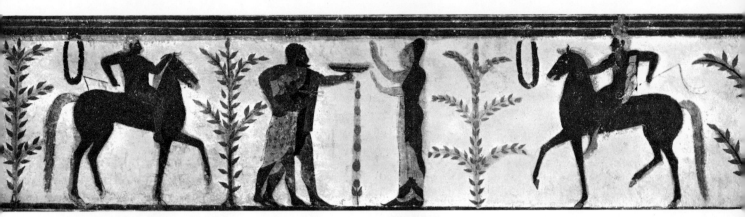

578. ETRUSCAN. Fresco from the so-called Baron's Tomb. Side wall. 510–500 B.C.

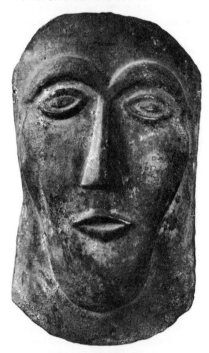

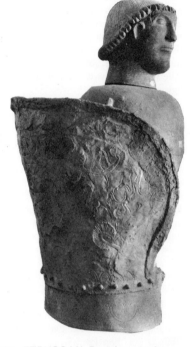

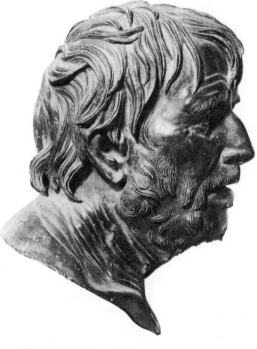

579. ETRUSCAN. Bronze death-mask affixed to a burial urn. From Chiusi. First half ot the 7th century B.C.

580. ETRUSCAN. Burial urn in the shape of a head on a seat. Sarteano. Late 7th century B.C. *Archaeological Museum, Florence.*

581. ROMAN. The Pseudo-Seneca. 1st century B.C. *National Museum, Naples.*

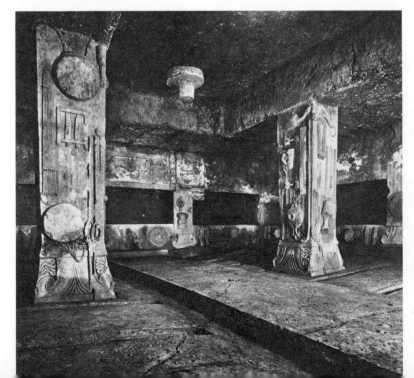

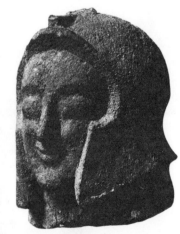

583. ETRUSCAN. Colossal head of a warrior. Characteristic of Ionic-Etruscan sculpture. Found at the necropolis at Orvieto. 530–520 B.C. *Archaeological Museum, Florence.*

582. ETRUSCAN. Funerary chamber in the Tomb of the Reliefs. Cerveteri Necropolis.

HISTORICAL SUMMARY: The western Mediterranean

CARTHAGE

History. Carthage was founded in 814 B.C. by Phoenicians from Tyre; it adopted the colonising system of its parent city and from the 6th century established trading settlements throughout the western Mediterranean. The Roman annexation in the early part of the 3rd century of southern Italy, an area ringed by Carthaginian settlements in Sicily and Sardinia, sparked off the Punic Wars (264–241, 219–201, 149–146). In spite of a stubborn resistance, Carthage was defeated; the city was razed and its inhabitants massacred.

Architecture. Very little is known about Carthaginian architecture, but

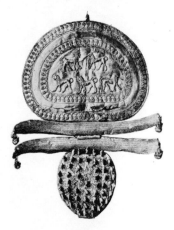

584. ETRUSCAN. Gold fibula with discs. Cerveteri Necropolis. c. Middle of the 7th century B.C. *Etruscan Museum, Vatican, Rome.*

585. ETRUSCAN. Capitoline She-wolf. 5th century B.C. (The twins are modern.) *Museo dei Conservatori, Rome.*

writings and the few remaining ruins show that their architects used both bonded construction and rubble work and cement, often decorated with painted stucco and with sculptures. Sanctuaries were of the Canaanite type with a holy precinct, sacrificial altars, memorial stelae and bowls for lustral water. From the 7th century, tombs were often well-built subterranean chambers.

Sculpture. The Carthaginians were traders, and consequently their sculpture, of which few examples of any outstanding quality have survived, reflects the influences of Egypt, Cyprus and Greece (sarcophagi ornamented with figures in relief and sarcophagi in the shape of the human body). The memorial stelae [567] and funerary reliefs are mostly decorated with religious symbols.

The minor arts. The many influences and the lack of individuality are reflected in all those objects—weapons, pottery, toilet articles, glassware and ivories—which were found in large quantities in tombs; only certain masks in terra cotta and glass [571] and some jewellery show any spirit of originality.

Expansion. Carthaginian trading settlements in North Africa and the Balearics (Ibiza) and along the southern coast of Spain show the same artistic characteristics. Figurines and masks from sanctuaries and tombs in Ibiza are similar to those discovered at Carthage except that, as with the Cerro de los Santos sculptures, there are signs of original native traits. The Lady of Elche [569] is the best-known example of Spanish sculpture under the Carthaginians.

Lydie Huyghe

MAGNA GRAECIA AND SICILY

(See Summary, page 286)

THE ETRUSCANS

In the 8th century an Italic civilisation, the Villanovan, grew up in Tuscany, and in Latium a form of art developed which served as a kind of prologue to Etruscan art.

Etruscan civilisation emerged about the year 700. There are several conflicting theories on the origin of the Etruscans. According to ancient tradition, which goes back to Herodotus, the Etruscans came by sea to Italy from Lydia. Some modern scholars have a theory that they were of northern descent, and, finally, certain authorities, taking up a statement of Dionysius of Halicarnassus, view them as an autochthonous people. In actual fact it must be a question of an ethnic complex in which a variety of elements were intermingled including, in all probability, a nucleus of Asian immigrants. The 'Orientalising' period of Etruscan art extended roughly from 700 to 575. The ruling influences until about 625 were Phoenician and Cypriot. From 625 to 575, Greek influence had the upper hand, and larger works of sculpture and mural painting made their appearance. Throughout the archaic period the effect of Ionian and then Attic art ruled supreme. Greek artists worked in Etruria. The large terra-cotta statues from Veii produced in the workshop of Vulca, a sculptor of genius and the 'master of the Apollo of Veii', mark the finest achievement of Etruscan art.

In 474 the Etruscan fleet was defeated by the Syracusan Greeks at the battle of Cumae, and this marked the start of a political and cultural decline. Hellenic classicism remained alien to Tuscan temperament. It was only in the 4th century that there was an increase in the number of works drawing on classical inspiration; the Mars from Todi is one of the finest examples.

In the 3rd century the taste for the picturesque and for the realistic, which was spreading through the Hellenistic schools, accorded with the natural aptitude of the Tuscans, whose creative genius flourished till just before Christ.

Raymond Bloch

586. *Opposite.* ROMAN. Statue of Augustus, known as the Prima Porta Augustus. Early 1st century A.D. *Vatican Museum, Rome.*

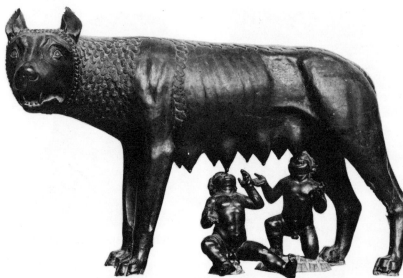

6 ANTIQUITY AND THE SHAPING OF THE MODERN WORLD

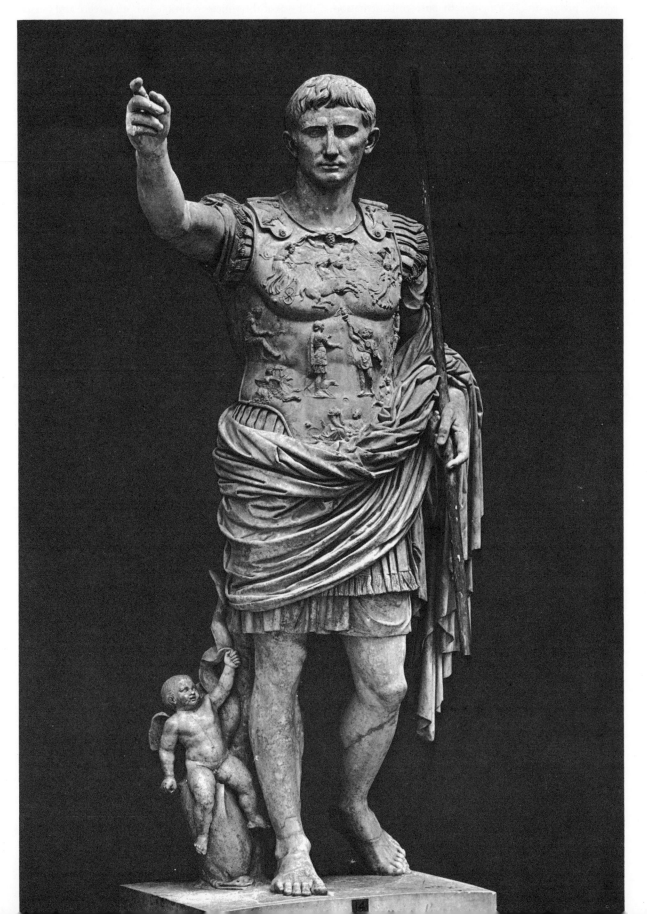

ART FORMS AND SOCIETY *René Huyghe*

Art, from the earliest times, had always been related to the beliefs and rites of a specific human group: the Palaeolithic hunter's magic, the Egyptian's guarantees of a life after death, etc. Even decorative art, which had become progressively a matter of pure ornamentation, kept for a long time traces of the protective-magical and religious qualities which had once served as its justification. As to artistic beauty, if its creation and appreciation were instinctive, it was in all probability the product of a still very confused idea of what constituted achievement and technical accomplishment.

From universalism to imperialism

By the middle of the 1st millennium Greece had taken an enormous step forward: for one thing, instead of being restricted to the more or less obscure feeling that something was beautiful, the Greeks had come to think of beauty as a spiritual reality, existing in itself, as an ideal to which every artist had, as far as possible, to approximate. 'I am not asking you whether something is beautiful or not; I ask you what is Beauty?' Thus Socrates posed the question in terms that were to be taken up once more by Father André in the 18th century. For another thing, to make beauty an absolute truth in this way, the Greeks had set it beyond all the variations and incidental peculiarities of men and circumstances. Not only did beauty exist, but it existed universally.

Following on from this, man at the same time was beginning to discover what was also universal in himself. Previously his consciousness had been restricted to that of his community; he was blindly committed to beliefs and forms of worship without any suspicion of their fortuitous causes and ephemeral significance. And then quite suddenly he broke through the barriers confining all those more or less limited, self-contained communities. The only limits the Greeks came to recognise were those of the whole of mankind, before one last effort was made to transcend limitations by reaching out towards the divine. Consequently the Greeks came to rely on what is least subject to change and variation between man and man, that is to say on the reason, which, by definition, is fundamentally the same in all men, whereas sensibility depends on the nervous make-up of each individual and so must inevitably vary from person to person.

In the conservative and autonomous empires of Egypt and Mesopotamia, art had been the reflection of a particular stage in social development and was limited to their geographical frontiers. Except in influences of a superficial kind, their art, unlike the art of the Greeks, could not be taken over by any other civilisation. This is evident when Egyptian art, towards the end of its history, was confronted with the very elastic art of its new Hellenistic masters: it was unable to blend with the new art, condemned as it was by its own nature to maintain its purity. The metal age was responsible for the transition from this self-centred traditionalism to the universal solution proposed by Greece; it was the time when for economic reasons nation began to make contact with nation, no longer merely through migrations, but on a stable and relatively regular basis. We have already seen

the diffusion of art forms which was the consequence of this new contact.

This movement to make art, as it were, international, came to maturity in the middle of the 1st millennium, and if it was at this time perceptible in both Greece and Persia there was, however, an enormous difference between the rational solution proposed by Greece and the completely empirical answer provided by Persia. Persia, in fact, anxious to find a principle in art which could unify all the different peoples encompassed by the Empire, sought to reconcile these widely varying traditions not so much in universalism as in mutual 'give and take'. All the peoples of the Empire, from the Hittites to the Assyrians, have a greater or lesser place in Persian art. Purely mercantile civilisations—Syrian, Phoenician and, later, Carthaginian—faced a similar problem: to boost the sale of their wares they had to make a successful effort to find an artistic common denominator from among all the conflicting elements with which they came in contact. How far the Greeks' intellectually bold solution was revolutionary and creative can be judged by comparison.

At all events, this impulse to expand art so as to make it acceptable to a heterogeneous community invariably ends in the adoption of one of two methods: the first way taken by Persia, self-absorbed and enclosed, was destined, in return for compromise, to centre everything on the monarch and the capital city; the second was the way of Greece, open and outgoing, which aimed at finding, beyond the incidental, individual distinctions, a ground of understanding based on the intellect reduced to its root principles, the most basic of all common attributes.

It would be interesting to trace what became of these two different methods. Very much later, with the Renaissance, neo-classicism and the 'Age of Enlightenment', there was an attempt to restore the Greek method in all its integrity. But then in the 19th century it became clear that it had been superseded and had become increasingly incapable of encompassing all those human elements, enriched through the centuries, which had been notably deepened and expanded. Even in the ancient world it soon degenerated under the contaminating influence of Persia whose political, 'imperialistic' example was to have a profound effect on the centuries to come. From this time on, empire supplanted empire, each with the ambition to encompass the entire known, civilised world, the *orbis terrarum*. Persian imperialism, shattered against the Greek world, was succeeded by Greek, or at least Macedonian imperialism which, after Alexander, was to engender the Hellenistic world and all the bitter struggles of those competing for power. Cities, confederacies and kingdoms vacillated between Egypt and Macedonia, the two leading powers. Finally Roman imperialism took control and swallowed up the rest.

Superficially Greece had got the better of Persia, first by the defeat inflicted on their kings, and second by Alexander's revenge which completed the reversal of the situation. But the Greek spirit was defeated by its own victory. To overcome imperialism, Greece had to adapt itself to it, had to cope with the same administrative problems and inevitably slid, little by little, into accepting

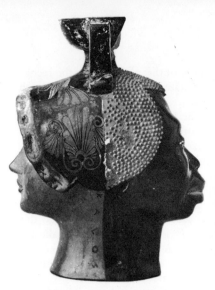

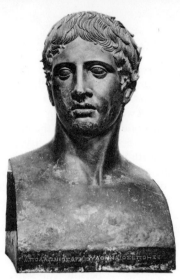

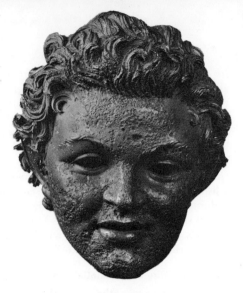

587. The two faces of Greek art: idealism and realism. Vase of the end of the 6th or beginning of the 5th centuries B.C. *Louvre.*

588. GREEK. Head of the Doryphorus by Polycleitus. Roman copy of the bronze original. *Naples Museum.*

589. HELLENISTIC. Head of a satyr. Bronze. *Glyptothek, Munich.*

HELLENISTIC ART AND THE COLLAPSE OF HUMANISM

This vase with contrasting sides [587] could be the symbol of the two ideas on which Greek art was based: the imitation of nature and the creation of an ideal beauty. But for a long time it had been able to unite them by seeking beauty through an 'improved' reality. This harmony and balance that produced humanism (taking nature and adapting it to the demands and laws of human reason) disintegrated during the later centuries: the peaceful serenity of the great classical works [588] gave way to the observation of life in action [589]; there was a taste for rough, striking details like the boxer's cauliflower ear and scars [591, 592] which even came to include representations of deformity [593]. The golden rule of the mind had been ousted by the chance oddities of the body; and as humanism faded, there appeared the mask with its grotesque grimace [590].

593. HELLENISTIC. A dwarf. Bronze. *Louvre.*

590. LATE HELLENISTIC, Pillar depicting a comic actor. *Istanbul Museum.*

591, 592. HELLENISTIC. Seated boxer by Apollonius. 1st century B.C. *Terme Museum, Rome.*

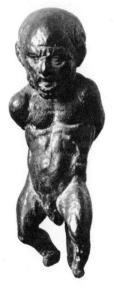

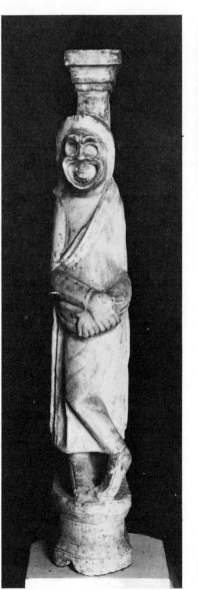

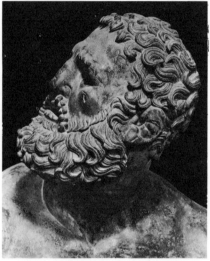

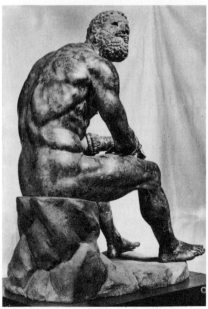

its solutions. By the 4th century Greek universalism already had less lofty ambitions and was gradually turning towards the idea of unification. When Rome came to take its place in the 2nd and 1st centuries, its only concern was to create the outward appearance of a common bond; Roman art, deprived of any ideal, was ultimately to become nothing more than a repertoire of forms. With its spiritual strength so dissipated, Graeco-Roman universalism was to be defenceless in the face of those communities, and in particular the religious communities, that wished to remain within its framework but autonomous. Of these, Christianity, which was culturally and intellectually the richest, was to shatter this empty shell.

The 4th century and Aristotle's new conception of art

We still have to trace the stages of this development and see how art reflected and joined forces with this movement. Whenever we attempt to interpret a work of art there is always the danger that we are forcing it to take on a meaning it may not have had. The study of parallel developments in thought can therefore be an important check. The preoccupations of the period seem clear and unambiguous, and all the more so since by this time there was a bedrock of philosophy.

Let us go back to the end of the 5th century to see whether changing ideas can give us any clue to the alterations that were to come. First and foremost in the sphere of thought there was a dangerous and increasing scepticism, and soon a total repudiation of reason and ideas of the absolute that it had brought with it, of the very things, in fact, that had made an intellectual universalism possible. For Plato, ultimate truth lay beyond all human contingency and imperfection, enthroned in the magnificence of Ideas: the Beautiful, along with the Good and the True. He died in 347. Aristotle, his rebellious pupil, was already coming to the fore; the son of a doctor, brought up in close contact with the world of facts, ideas to him were nothing more than generalisations elaborated by the mind, working from evidence provided by the senses and therefore based on that physical and concrete reality which Plato was seeking to leave behind and which he acknowledged only as a mere semblance of existence. This use of the senses was to give more weight to realism. Although the Macedonian philosopher's book on beauty has been lost, we do know that he stressed the basic role of imitation, mimesis, in art ('All art is imitation', he had stated), whereas Plato, rather scornfully, merely accepted it as an inevitable fact.

As a parallel to this, realism was making tremendous progress in Hellenistic art. It had even taken its place in architecture where the Corinthian capital was being increasingly used, its ornamental foliage in direct contrast to the abstract decoration of the Doric and Ionic capitals. Realism was no longer solely concerned with human beings, nor even with animals, but was coming to concentrate on nature and landscape which, virtually ignored in the earlier period, were to become the main features 608 of Alexandrian art. From this art Rome copied the large ornamental painted panels that became so popular, in which the *trompe l'œil*, that trick verisimilitude, led the eye 'through' the walls of rooms into landscapes or architectural perspectives.

Aristotle indirectly encouraged naturalism by thinking that the aim of art was to give pleasure to the spectator and that the chief element of this pleasure was the recognition of the thing imitated. For, he observed, such pleasure existed even when the subject represented was something repellent. The logic of mimesis led Aristotle to justify the imitation of ugliness in art.

Universality, at the same time, was beginning to crumble with the rise of individualism. The ground had been prepared by Aristotle who had made all truth stem from material sense perceptions. Consequently he came to reject the absolute nature of general ideas and so to prompt the repudiation of the security and stability which this had brought, reflected in classical art with its unshakeable faith in perfect proportion. A man for whom ideas count 513 more than anything else forgets his individuality, but the person who will only trust first-hand evidence, what he perceives and sees for himself, is brought back to himself and his own personal way of feeling. So he becomes increasingly aware of the differences between him and other people, conscious, in fact, of his own individuality. 595

When Aristotle rid the idea of its transcendental nature and stressed the empiricism of the senses, he put the expression of feelings in the place once held by the application of principles. In fact, as soon as we talk of the 'senses' we are already talking of sensibility. Where can the line be drawn between a perception claiming to be objective and an individual way of feeling and experiencing this perception? Aristotle himself managed to overcome this difficulty by emphasising the part played by *catharsis* (the purging of the emotions) in art. It is true he still thought the turmoil aroused by the emotions should be got rid of, but it was to art that he appealed to give people this liberation; it was for this reason that he wanted to make art both the expression, and draining away, of the emotions. He showed how the person listening to music shares 'feelings which have such a powerful effect on certain souls'. Along with the ugly, the emotive was establishing itself in the realm of art. 590

And lastly, the central point of this philosophy was that form is created from the union of active energy and matter, and this obviously had an immediate application in terms of art; the unchanging serenity of classical per- 588 fection was forgotten in the search for passion and intensity.

A romantic tendency

Such an all-embracing philosophy with such important implications does not merely reflect, but adds to and speeds up the development of ideas. It is not surprising that from this time Greek art very quickly lost the balance and stability of the great classical period and became increasingly interested in physical movement and even physical strain of the kind that Myron had already tried to render in his celebrated Discus Thrower, whose face, 509 however, still kept the customary unmoved expression. The great generation of sculptors born at the beginning of the 4th century were to go further: Lysippus, who travelled with Alexander throughout the future capitals of the Hellenistic world, was to be, as Charles Picard has succinctly put it, 'the sculptor of the strong man in action'. In the attempt to go further and further, the idea of proportion was soon forgotten, an idea to which Aristotle had been deeply attached and which he had upheld as a basic sign of beauty. This taste for movement allied to energy was to become, then, a desire to outstrip human limits, to celebrate the hero, the 'superman' as he was

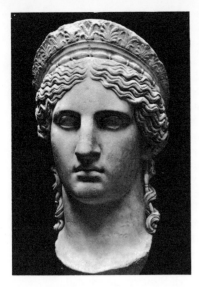

594. ROMAN. The Ludovisi Juno.
2nd century A.D. Copy of Greek bust.
Terme Museum, Rome.

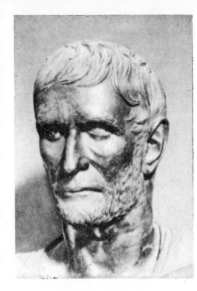

595. HELLENISTIC. ALEXANDRIA.
Ptolemy I (323–283), King of Egypt.
Ny Carlsberg Glyptotek, Copenhagen.

596. ETRUSCAN. Bronze statue said
to be of Brutus, founder of the
Roman Republic. Near Chiusi. 3rd
century B.C. *Capitoline Museum,
Rome.*

ROMAN PORTRAITURE AND ITS ORIGINS

*If, on the one hand, Roman art followed
Greek art in its cultivation of a symmetrical
beauty until it became merely an artistic
convention [594], it even more eagerly
followed the example of Hellenistic realism
[595] and Etruscan naturalism [596] that
appealed more to Roman temperament.
The custom of making lifelike ancestor
portrait-busts developed a firsthand and
individualised treatment of the human
face which in painting and mosaics even
[598] heralded the illusionistic Romano-
Egyptian portraits [597 and colour plate
opposite p. 144].*

599. *Right.* ROMAN. Patrician with
portrait-busts of ancestors. Marble.
Republican period. *Barberini Palace,
Rome.*

597. EGYPTIAN ART OF THE
ROMAN PERIOD. Painting of the 3rd
century A.D. *Staatliche Museen, Berlin.*

598. ROMAN. Portrait of a poetess.
Mosaic of the 1st century A.D. *Naples
Museum.*

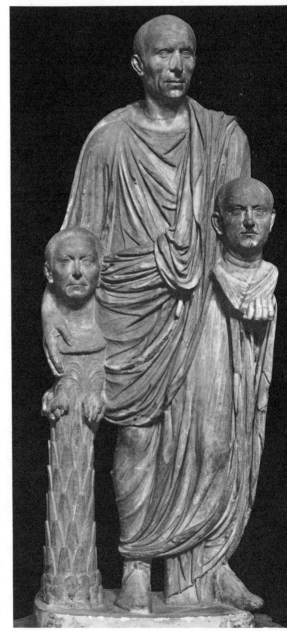

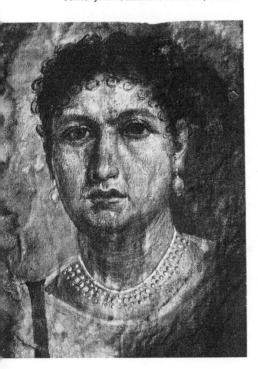

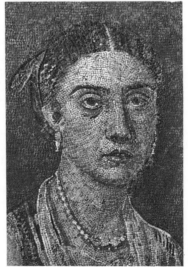

315

546 later to be called. And Alexander was the living example of this dream. Now art was concerned solely with colossal epic battles; the Amazonomachy which Scopas sculpted on the mausoleum in Asia Minor was to prepare the way for the massive struggle of gods and giants of the Gi-
613 gantomachy at Pergamon. The gods on a colossal scale which Lysippus had produced at Tarentum and elsewhere formed a prologue to this love of the huge. Hellenic art had passed into Hellenistic art.

All the seeds had been sown in Alexander's dazzling generation. The inclination to display powerful strength in action could not find full expression in the body alone; the inner life, the soul, offered a far wider field, but before it could be approached the carefully worked out fixed boundaries of reason had to be left behind for the exciting regions of the sensibility. The facial expressions on Lysip-pus's statues represent the first attempts to convey physical
618 strain. And later, in the contorted features of Laocoön, physical tension became the means of conveying moral tension. Before this, Socrates, championing psychology, had laid down that 'the sculptor should give concrete form to the workings of the soul.' In fact, M. Fougères has pointed out, it was in the 4th century that eyes began to show expression. In the first half of the 3rd century Xenocrates, the sculptor and critic, was to praise Aristides of Thebes for being the 'first to paint the soul by expressing its affections and passions'. Scopas' romantic sorrow had been left behind. Classical, stoical indifference had become inflamed rhetoric.

More than this, gone was the time when man was 'the measure of all things'. Alexander's generation, now that it had lost its old ancestral fears, began to take a new interest in the animal kingdom; Scopas had already de-picted human figures accompanied by some creature, a kid, a goose or a goat, and plant life also appeared with them. Lysippus was just as interested in a deer, a horse or a dog as he was in the athletic body which had once been virtually the sole theme of Greek art.

By turning towards his inner life, man learned not only the language of emotion and passion, already so far removed from the pure voice of the Idea. He soon en-countered something that eluded his lucid intellect, some-thing beyond its grasp: after the nebulous, inarticulate, indefinable feelings which had clouded Scopas' faces with
537 a sorrowful dream-like expression, suddenly there were the first quivering signs of a religious, and sometimes ecstatic, note, a prelude to the return of Asian influence with its feeling for mysticism which had been banished by the Greek intellect. The ancient classical building was breaking up, and through the widening cracks a breath of life was beginning to blow. The Stoics were representa-tive of 3rd-century thought and, whereas most of them in any case came from Asia Minor, two of them, Diogenes of Babylon and Apollodorus of Seleucia, were, as their names show, Chaldeans. This whispered warning sig-nalled the tide which, with Christianity, was to sweep over the old Mediterranean world.

From the individual to the human condition

The rise of individualism seems to be the most immedi-ately fruitful consequence of the intellectual transforma-tion of which Aristotle was the manifestation.

The major problems of the new philosophies were to be concerned with the moulding of the personality by education and the ideal way of life in which it might fully mature. This was the sole aim of Epicureanism and Stoicism, the two great philosophies being taught by Epi-curus and Zeno in Athens at the end of the 4th century and which were to dominate everything that survived of the ancient world. Both were based on Aristotle's idea of the reality of sense perceptions: man's first knowledge was a knowledge of himself. As W. Tarn has pertinently summed it up, 'both were the product of the new world created by Alexander and, primarily, of the feeling that man was no longer just part of a city but an individual, and as such had need of new rules by which to live.' The whole aim of this life was happiness, whether it was sought in the most refined pleasures as Epicureanism recommended or in that unshakeable resolution reaching out after perfection which Stoicism demanded.

It is hardly surprising that this age first introduced the idea that every great artist should have his own charac-teristic approach and style. Never had there been more regard for the creative artist's ability to stamp his work with the mark of his individual personality. Xenocrates always set out to define, as he said in his remarks on Apelles, 'the characteristic and unique beauty' of a specific painter or sculptor. In Rome, Cicero was to be more definite when he observed that although 'there is only one art of sculpture and of painting, great artists are all different from each other. But, for all that, you would not have any one of them untrue to himself.'

As individuality asserted itself in style, it also expressed itself in the choice of subject: the portrait, which crystal-lises a person's characteristic traits, became increasingly important. The artist was turning away from the elabora-tion of neutral types in which the average man could recognise his idealised face. Lysippus had become famous for his portraits of Alexander and Aristotle. A new genre was taking root which was to have its greatest vogue in Rome. As the individual was magnified, he inevitably became sceptical of the worth of common ground and common bonds between men, apart from the personal and emotional impulses which unite similar people.

The various opposing schools of philosophy which came after Plato and Aristotle have, in fact, nothing but doubt or antipathy for the two strongest points upon which a universal intellectual system had been based; namely, the exact sciences, or quite simply, knowledge, and the organisation and rules of society. Diogenes (413–327) with his Cynicism founded the most typical of these new schools of thought. Pyrrhon of Elea in the 4th century even went so far as to suspend all formal judg-ment, to repudiate the exact sciences, and so became the founder of Scepticism.

And yet a generalised system was reappearing, of a far more nebulous kind and this time based on love, with the belief that everything in the world was united in an inescapable sympathy, taking breath from a single Being. Zeno, born in Cyprus and therefore a native of the eastern Mediterranean that was to see the rise of Christianity, thereby once again gave meaning to the brotherhood of man. As Plutarch put it, he taught that 'men should not group themselves into cities which all made their own particular laws, for all men are fellow citizens since life and the order of things is the same for each and every one.' And Plutarch remarks that Alexander had made this dream a reality by bringing together 'all peoples of the

316

THE DISAPPEARANCE OF HUMANISM

Whereas in the Republican period plant ornamentation was still subordinate to geometrical patterns [600], it began to develop its own naturalistic tendencies [601], became elaborate and heavy [602] and finally ended in a riotous profusion of extravagant detail [603]. Animals, like plant life, came to have an increasing importance in Rome, whereas there had been no place for them in Greek humanism, whose disappearance paved the way for the most anecdotal, and sometimes most mundane, forms of verisimilitude [604].

whole world, as though in a vase; he ordained that everyone should regard the earth as his native land.' This explains the apparent contradiction that might have been found between the trend towards individualism and the movement towards a world-wide internationalism, that were both characteristic of the new age.

Men no longer put their faith in reason nor in its universal application; often they did not even believe in patriotism, but they were moving towards the idea of the solidarity of all peoples of the civilised world. Similarly art paradoxically combined the most detailed and individualised kinds of observation, as for example in the portrait, with the conviction that the same forms and language were bound to exist everywhere.

It was to form an artistic repertoire that was drawn upon throughout the length and breadth of the civilised world, but its growing reputation and popularity helped to turn it into a widespread iconographical and stylistic convention. Even less important cities were filled with works of art: Philip V discovered two thousand statues in Thermos and the Romans found one thousand in Ambracia. But there was danger in sheer routine, a danger that was to be increased by Rome and its mania for replicas, and carried to such lengths that with the Cossutii it became an actual business venture, setting out to multiply the number of workshops in Greece which could mechanically turn out articles in answer to that enormous demand; here were the seeds of academicism.

Whilst remembering that forms, in an uncreative and mediocre way, remained faithful to Greek prototypes of the 5th century, art lapsed into its former narrative function. This was so in Alexandria, delicate, dazzling, lost in fantasy; and in Rome, tough, forceful and weighty.

Rome and realism

Rome was only a Mediterranean nation involved in the vast Hellenistic community but one which, unlike the others, managed to secure the leadership and build up once more an empire comparable to Alexander's. Roman art, like the art of all other Hellenistic provinces, is a mixture of characteristics which all held in common and of trends peculiar to itself. Its primitive Italic basis, rural and thereby hardly inclined towards refinement, offers comparisons with Etruscan art, at least in its sense of mystery and the supernatural. Similarly, its original language was quite unsuited to abstract generalisations and these loan words were taken only from Greek sources.

The period of assimilation was quickly over but was not entirely free from resentment. National prejudice was very much aroused when Livius Andronicus staged at the Roman Games in 240 B.C. the first play to be translated from an Attic source. Leaving aside Cato's reputed hostility, we should remember that two Epicurean philosophers were expelled from Rome in 173 B.C. and two

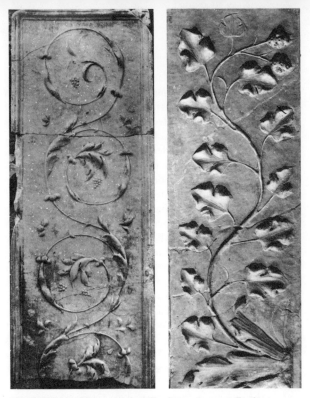

600. ROMAN. Stone relief of the Augustan era. Emilian Basilica. *Roman Forum.*

601. ROMAN. Marble relief of ivy imitating stucco. Beginning of the Imperial period. *Lateran Museum, Rome.*

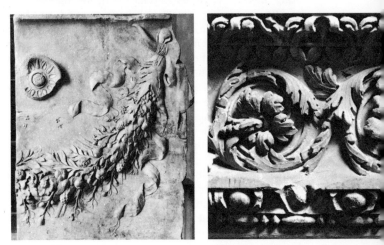

602. ROMAN. Part of the frieze of the Ara Pacis Augustae. 9 B.C. *Terme Museum, Rome.*

603. ROMAN. Detail of carving in the Forum at Rome.

604. ROMAN. Mosaic called the 'unswept dining-room'. Beginning of Imperial era. *Lateran Museum, Rome.*

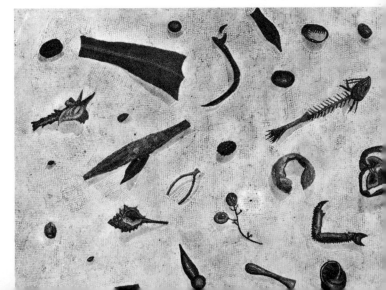

years later the city was placed out of bounds to rhetors and philosophers, the apostles of the new spirit. For a long time the down-to-earth Romans made a show of being completely unaffected by the renown of theorists and artists; at the height of the classical period, Cicero in the *De Signis*, out of deference to this atavistic distrust, was to pretend that he had never heard of Polycleitus.

Such an attitude is good enough proof that Rome wanted to maintain her individual spirit despite the hoard of Greek art treasures that she had acquired, mostly through pillage, and despite the fact that she relied on 'imported' artists whom she encouraged to settle in the country. It was a spirit naturally inclined towards realism with its dislike of subtle delicacy that was considered to be without vigour, and its roots in rural soil that gave it a fundamentally factual bias. Roman art was irresistibly drawn towards nature which it treated in a more direct, less sophisticated way than the Alexandrian school, in spite of certain similarities which political circumstances served to emphasise. The Roman spirit was almost entirely uninventive: it turned to Alexandria because it could learn nothing about landscape from Greek models, and, in the same way, it continued the Bronze Age animal tradition, notably through Etruscan art, of which the 585 She-wolf of the Capitol is the most outstanding example.

The development of ornamentation is similarly illuminating. In Greece, purely abstract motifs like the meander and 'wave', dating from the geometric period, had been kept in use; Rome set the highest store by the foliated scroll which could more easily be adapted to suggest the waving movement of a leafy bough, with the alternating sweep of its branches to left and right. Examples of this were found in the cities of the Near East like Baalbek and Palmyra. The vine branch motif which figured on 648 Alexander's Sarcophagus, dating from about 300 B.C., had spread with the popularity of the Hellenic Dionysiac cults. Long before it was adopted by Christianity for its symbolic value, it was taken over by Rome along with the Bacchanalian garlands and thyrsi. Thus it was through ornamentation that they returned to the world of nature, 600 of flowers and plants. This realistic foliage initially embellished the dominant line of the pattern, but this gradually 602 vanished beneath its increasing elaboration until in the 603 last phase the entire area was covered by a profusion of vegetation. This same naturalistic impulse to copy foliage with detailed accuracy, even on precious metals, can be found in their gold and silver plate.

But realism was to produce the most outstanding results in the field of portraiture; consequently, despite the fact 595 that it had been developed in the Hellenistic period, it has often been thought of as essentially Roman, almost a national invention. Significantly enough, the fine portrait 620 of Antiochus III, King of Syria from 223 to 183, was for many years admired and taken for a head of Julius Caesar. Such mistakes, if they impress upon us the need for caution, should not make us forget the Italic character of 596 this form of art, probably an off-shoot of Etruscan art as the archaic bronze Brutus in the Capitoline Museum seems to prove. The accurate, individualised copies of the human face had been encouraged from a very early date 599 by the custom of ancestor portraits, *imagines majorum*, done in wax to make them appear more lifelike, which were carried in procession at the funeral of any of the *gens* and were normally kept permanently on show in the atrium. Living members of the family, in exceptional cases, were granted the right to add their own portrait to the family collection. But as the supply of wax could not keep pace with the demand (according to Pliny, the makers of these images would often melt them down) stone sculpture was adopted. Sepulchral monuments of the 1st century show impressive lines of highly individualised figures. Hence there was a natural development which culminated in statues where the copying of an individual's features was of prime importance, in contrast to Greek 586 sculpture, which, it should be remembered, had originated in the celebration of victorious athletes and which had, therefore, the quite different purpose of celebrating the beauty of the human body rather than of catching an individual likeness.

The Empire and narrative art

The foundation of the Empire was to give a new justification and a fresh impetus to the Roman tendency to view everything in a positive, factual way. The imperial idea, we should recognise, was distrusted, and even opposed, by the old Roman establishment, embodied in the Republican Senate, and it really seems to have been supported only by the greed of businessmen. The traditional Roman felt that his country was bound to lose some of its best and even some of its most independent characteristics. And in fact, when Rome began on her conquest of the known world, she realised, as Hellenism had previously done, the basic necessity of the use of art as a universally understood language to bring the legends and beliefs upon which Rome rested to the notice of the community; it was the official version of the facts.

As soon as personal power replaced the Republic, there was a revival of those ideas which had been the concern of the earliest Egyptian and Mesopotamian empires, namely, the celebration of the monarch and propaganda for his deeds and victories. Roman realism, once turned in this direction, and already based on the clarity of form belonging to the Greek tradition, was bound to develop towards narration. The bas-relief then came to be pre- 606 ferred to statuary, which was so much a part of Hellenic tradition, as an art form far better suited to portray complex and animated incidents, a reason which had also been behind its increasing popularity since Alexander's time. It was possibly at this time that there had been a movement towards the example set by Egyptian and Mesopotamian bas-reliefs which had probably become 605 widely known through figured and embroidered materials and ivories. It is even possible that, long before this, they had been at the root of Greek painting, especially vase painting, with its active and lively subjects and many attitudes and gestures long absent from sculpture in the round, which had itself evolved from Egyptian sculpture. Similarly the Ionian frieze, stemming more directly from these Eastern roots, had provided the first examples of narrative description and, although initially it concentrated solely on mythology and stories of the gods, it progressed through the Parthenon frieze and the Per- 612 gamon Altar, finally culminating in Augustus's Ara Pacis. 633 When a series of military conquests in the Near East once more brought them into direct contact with the original artistic roots, this tradition was converted into the tall cylindrical columns built in honour of Trajan and Marcus 632 Aurelius, on which, as in the early Mesopotamian proto- 605 types, figures are portrayed in action, set among military structures and representations of rivers, hills and trees.

Rome, it is true, was naturally predisposed towards these anecdotal visual records, and stage plays were often turned into lavish and spectacular pageants. In one of his letters Cicero tells how in *Clytemnestra* the citizens were able to watch a procession across the stage of six hundred mules laden with booty seized at the capture of Troy, and how the *Trojan Horse* was a pretext to show three thousand vases and, 'in a battle scene, all the trappings of the infantry and cavalry'. Here already was something akin to Trajan's Column, but it no longer had anything to do with Homer, Greek tragedy or Greek art.

First signs of a revolution

Yet another excuse to move away from pure Greek tradition was provided by the extraordinary importance attached to bas-relief technique: there was a shift away from the sculptural, through which the Greeks had tried to isolate beauty of form and proportion, towards the pictorial, which was more suited to the realistic *trompe l'œil* and to the sensuous rather than abstract effects that could be achieved through shading, colour, etc. Earlier on, the Egyptians in particular had found no difficulty in passing from relief to painting on their tombs. The popularity of stucco work, so widespread among the Alexandrians, expressed the desire for flexibility and minute detail for which hard stone was quite unsuitable. Sculptural technique gives an intellectual reminder of basic structure; pictorial technique dissolves it in the varying tones of light and in chiaroscuro effects that the bas-relief was beginning to introduce. Linear patterns and sharply outlined black and white shapes appeared on Greek mosaic pavements; Roman mosaic made increasing use of ducks, fish, shells, which in regard to materials, colouring and detail were depicted with staggering skill. This development, already anticipated in the Hellenistic world, had been noted by Dionysius of Halicarnassus: 'In ancient painting the method of colouring was extremely simple . . . and line was rendered with complete perfection . . . Later this purity of draughtsmanship was lost and its place was taken by a more subtle technique, a more delicate variation of light and shade and all the resources of rich colouring.'

Surely here was the collapse of the Greek spirit, behind all the outward pretence of preserving it intact. The repertoire of forms, it is true, went on being mechanically repeated but a gradual deterioration was setting in as it does in any language of too widespread and persistent usage; soon nothing was left but a hollow façade. Greek forms implied the existence of a pure beauty conceived beyond chance and incidentals; Roman forms merely used the same language, which eventually lost all meaning. When a foreign and fertile germ, bursting with potential growth, penetrated this decaying, shell-like body, it took hold and spread through every part that still had some life left in it. The Roman Empire, as it advanced into the countries of the Near East, could not avoid picking up this destructive but revitalising germ.

Now, it was in the Near East that all those things that were helping to break down specifically Greek characteristics were strong and thriving; the ancients had recognised the Asian origin of the pursuit of rich materials and colour which, unlike the study of form, appealed more

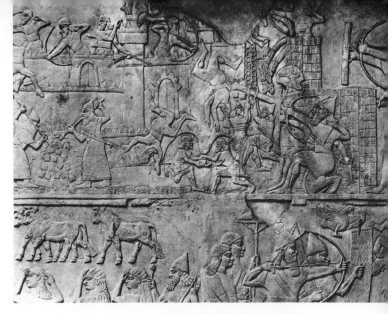

605. ASSYRIAN. Detail of a cast of a bas-relief at Nineveh, showing the capture of a town. 8th century B.C.

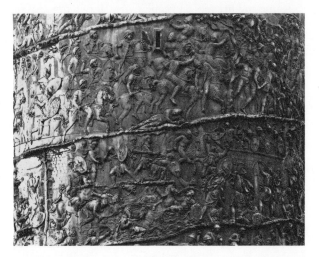

606. ROMAN. Detail from Trajan's Column. A.D. 113. *Trajan's Forum, Rome.*

607. ROMAN. Woman leaning on an amphora. Bas-relief in marble. 1st or 2nd centuries A.D. *Louvre.*

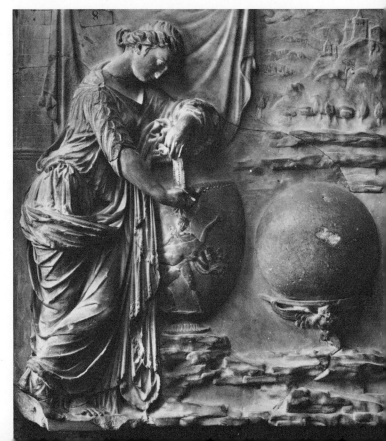

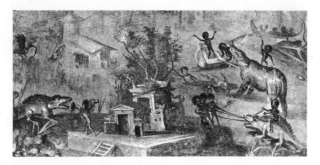

608. ROMAN. Pygmies hunting on the Nile. Mural painting from Pompeii, showing in the subject its Alexandrian inspiration. *National Museum, Naples.*

led Augustus to order the closure of all the temples that had been dedicated at this time to Nile deities. The importation of Asian cults and mysteries had begun at the end of the Republican era, but by the 3rd century A.D. they constituted a formidable opposition to the official state religion.

This contact often led to the copying of strange and unfamiliar styles, but besides this it had a more profound effect: the robust Roman taste for facts was transformed bit by bit until it disappeared altogether. The love of fantasy and imagination had spread with Alexandrian art: decors were ornamented with representations of buildings of a flimsy and improbable kind; this taste was to grow with the 3rd and 4th Pompeian styles, the start of a long tradition through the Raphael Loggia to Audran's arabesques. Their improbability outraged the solid good sense of Vitruvius who pointed out that it was impossible for a reed to support a roof or for candelabra to take the weight of a temple's dome. The Stoics and Epicureans had reduced the value of mimesis by insisting on 'the emotive and irrational nature of art', in the words of Lionello Venturi, who has also provided us with some of the earlier and most characteristic quotations. The idea was gradually emerging that the true business of art was not so much to copy and represent as to stimulate emotion, to open doors on to a dream world, to reveal something intangible, something that eluded the grasp of logic. These were the first signs of that radical upheaval that was to be completed by Christianity and under which the aesthetic ideas of Greece, or rather what remained of them, were to lie buried for many long centuries. The East, the age-old enemy of Greece, was to take its revenge by injecting into the Western world radically new values, thus overturning that collection of ideas, feelings and forms which go to make up an art and determine the direction it will take.

to the senses than the intellect. It was noticed by Pliny 'in these days when India sends us the silt of her rivers and the blood of her dragons and elephants'.

Rome and her subject peoples were drawn towards the East not only because it offered a sensuous satisfaction of a less austere kind than that provided by Greek rationalism; they also thought it could appease that hungering after sensibility and the inner life that an empire, reduced to a mere form of administration, and an art that was nothing but an academic convention could no longer disguise. Rome was established in Egypt at Alexandria in the 1st century. But it was not long before the legions were pressing on into Mesopotamia and Iran, occupying an area from Syria to Egypt that had always been the spiritual home of the Semitic races in particular. Consequently the first influences to make themselves felt were of a religious nature; moving from one frontier to another, the legions carried with them and spread various exotic cults—Mithras of Persian origin, Attis and Cybele from Phrygia, Isis and Osiris, as well as Serapis, from Egypt. It was probably his anxiety in face of this new threat that

609. ROMAN. Stucco from a villa discovered in the Farnesina Gardens. End of the 1st century B.C. *Terme Museum, Rome.*

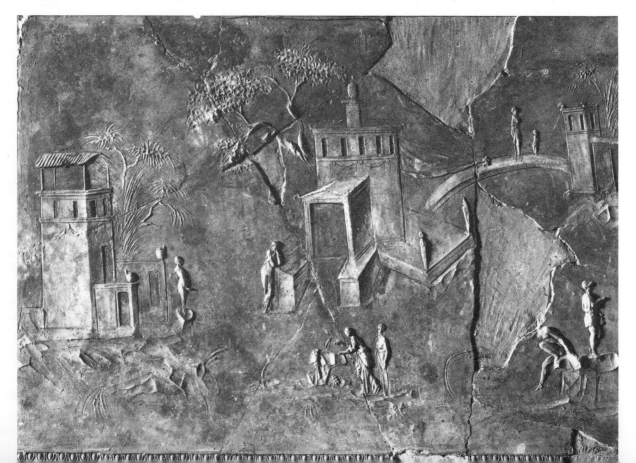

THE HELLENISTIC WORLD AND ROME
BEFORE SULLA (330–88 B.C.) *Charles Picard*

It is usual nowadays to find Rome placed immediately after classical Greece, but this is to overlook the importance of the Hellenistic world which formed a bridge between the two. Rome's chief concerns, in the days before conquest, were to learn from Hellenistic culture, and then, as the supreme power, to stamp the Hellenistic world with the mark of Rome. It was in no way a barren period but one in which there was a resurgence of activity, an age which produced some of the most famous masterpieces of Antiquity and some of the most profitable artistic innovations which Rome later exploited; furthermore, it was an era when, for the first time, literary and artistic life became predominant.

610–611 The Battle of Issus, as it appears in the mosaic in the Casa del Fauno at Pompeii, after the mural painting by Philoxenus of Eretria, would not have won its dramatic reputation, which it kept not only in Roman Italy but right down to the Renaissance, if it had not presented the symbolic outcome of a clash of arms which ruled the fates of two worlds. There we see the tense-faced Macedonian prince bearing down upon Darius's chariot among the uproar of the final, and by this time disastrous, mêlée. A dead, branchless tree sticks out against the sky; a sudden shower of long javelins hovers in the air, like the fate of the battle, one might think. But the fate of Persia was already decided: from this encounter, where the indomitable horsemen of the West clashed with the age-old, lax civilisation of Asia, a cosmopolitan world was to emerge once more.

A cosmopolitan renaissance

Could anyone have prophesied, from the changes that so quickly became apparent, the advent of an already modern aesthetic, combining the extremes of reason and mysticism, dogmatic authority and free experimentation, the spark of the Greek genius and the still unconscious, latent, absorbent wealth of the Levant that had lain dormant for so long and had been only spasmodically productive? Past and future were kneaded together and barbarism was mixed with a rationalist classicism which was already turning towards doubt and extremism in philosophic thought. The popular gods of the day, like Tyche and Dionysus, were backed up by the concept of chance or by orgiastic frenzy, as well as by the widespread insecurity and sense of weariness in which people lived among the dangers and crises of the disjointed world of the Near East. It was then that those profound and misleading words, humanity and brotherhood, began to be whispered abroad. People gave themselves up to an emotional form of mysticism in a world that was becoming more and more concerned with the human condition, torn between tradition and discovery, anguish and hope, an age that knew the limits of what it wanted and was beginning to deny the limits of human nature. There is no period to compare with the Hellenistic age in its dreams of Eternity and its quest after the earthly paradise.

The great mistake (and until now an almost universal one) would be to see nothing but decadence here, at the dawn of a period which, as Aldous Huxley has remarked, is, at least in certain ways, awkwardly like our own.

It is, at all events, the most 'accessible' period in the ancient history of the Mediterranean. All round the *Mare Nostrum* from east to west it built up a civilisation concerned with the pursuit of poetry, religion and knowledge; and with the civilisation Rome managed to associate herself in the victorious days before Augustus, when she had become the greatest of all Mediterranean cities. Without it, Rome could not be explained.

It would be wrong to belittle Athens' continuing part in this real Hellenistic 'Renaissance', far-reaching and so often misunderstood. The teachings of Plato and Aristotle had fallen on good ground. When Heracleides Criticus in the 2nd century went to Greece, visiting every city, he still talked with emotion of that citadel of the mind and sovereign lucidity which would never grow old, where statues mounted an eloquent guard about the past.

True, Athens at this time was surrounded by a number of rivals, the most formidable being Alexandria in Egypt. The tragedy of this great city-port, built near the Pyramids and Memphis by the Ptolemies in record time, was that it was looted and plundered more than any other ancient city of the Near East.

How aptly might one say, *etiam periere ruinae*! The Lighthouse, the Regia, the Library, the Serapeum, the round temple of Tyche, the Eleusis quarter, they have all, in varying degrees, vanished from the earth. Even the necropolises have disappeared. But definite and distinct traces of Alexandrian architecture are scattered far and wide, in Syria, in Nabatene, in Greece, in the Cyclades (at Delos, for example), in the islands of the Thracian Archipelago, Samothrace, Thasos; and moreover, not just in the hypostyle buildings where they tried to imitate the Egyptian structures so popular in the capital city of the Delta. Everywhere, as we can see, Hellenistic architecture laid down rules relating to the use of materials, polychromy and architectural ornamentation. The links that have been established between Al Khazna at Petra (Nabatene) and certain villas in the Campagna, like the Villa of P. Fannius Synistor for example, are very significant; but unfortunately, virtually everything, and not just temporary ceremonial buildings, has vanished from the local places of origin.

More and more, on the other hand, we must consider what can be learnt from the art of Cyrenaica. Prior to the year 96 B.C. when, at the time of the Roman wars against Mithridates, the last Ptolemy, King of Cyrene, had bequeathed his kingdom to the Romans, this region was famed for its art. In Cyrenaica, connecting link between Ptolemaic Egypt and Carthage, sanctuaries, private residences and mausoleums were built in the best Lagidian style. Not only 'the Palace of Columns' at Ptolemais, with capitals adorned with the figures of gods, but also the great provincial tombs reveal an architectural and sculptural splendour from which Rome learned much.

As for the Seleucids, they had had to rearrange and

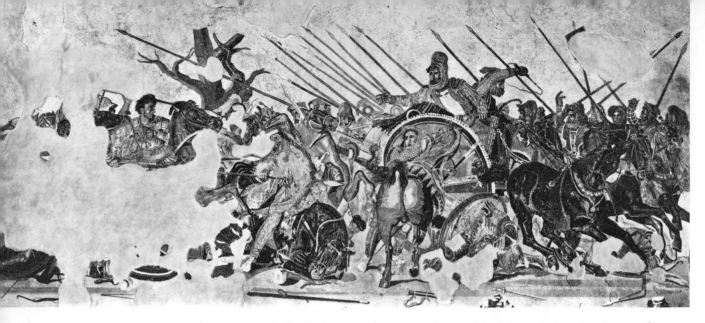

610. ROMAN. Darius and Alexander at the Battle of Issus or Gaugamela. Mosaic of the 2nd–1st centuries B.C. from the Casa del Fauno at Pompeii, after an early 3rd-century Greek painting commissioned by Alexander's generals. *Naples Museum.*

firmly cement an unstable, heterogeneous mosaic of semi-barbarian peoples who, in the first wave of defeat, had been subdued but who remained, at heart, rebellious.

For the entire period prior to the Persian conquest, very little remains of the arts—sculpture, painting, metal-work—that were being produced locally in Asia at the time of these Macedonian princes. At the moment, we have more definite information from texts than from archaeological finds. The magnificent procession organised by Antiochus IV Epiphanes at Daphne in 166 B.C., as described by Polybius and by Athenaeus after him, had been a complete revelation. The Daphne Apollo, a colossal work by Bryaxis, called for a setting of splendour; there exists a dazzling account of the wealth of precious gifts offered at every festival—purple cloaks embroidered with gold and drawings of animals, statues, sculptured groups, priceless vases, luxurious palanquins.

The example of Pergamon

In the vast Hellenistic cosmopolis where there were inevitable and continual attempts at political fragmentation, one of the most typical examples is provided by the Kingdom of the Attalids: it originated in 287 with the rebellion of Philetaerus, son of Attalus and one of Lysimachus's officers.

In later years, through their competition with the Seleucids, the Attalids gradually abandoned the political cause of Hellenism; in this region on the banks of the Caicus, it seems that nothing fermented without a leaven of treachery.

In 133 B.C., under the will of Attalus III, the kingdom of Pergamon also passed into the hands of the Romans; the history of this kingdom, one could say, was encompassed between two acts of betrayal. At all events between the years 282 and 133, a young city grew up on the slopes of the usurped fortress of Mysia; it was a city of the new rich, lavishly equipped and planned to stretch up the hillside. From the reign of Attalus I, the great-nephew of Philetaerus, the slopes of the Mysian stronghold were adorned with sacred and secular buildings built in picturesque terraces. For more than a century the princes of this land benefited from Roman favour which helped them to extend their territories in Thrace and Anatolia at the expense of the Seleucids.

Pergamene sculpture carries the stamp of local economic prosperity with its sometimes excessive and even brash ostentation, in which there was a certain jealousy of the glorious past of the Greek mainland. For all the efforts made by the kings to live only on a bourgeois scale in small palaces that adhered quite intentionally to the pattern of the houses built near the top of the hill close to their arsenals, the position and status accorded on the Acropolis to the cult of Zeus and Athena Nikephoros, Bringer of Victory, is extremely revealing. It was all a question of imitating and outclassing the Athenian Acropolis and even of making it appear a thing of the past. The sanctuary of the father of the gods and his warrior daughter contained, in fact, the monumental Altar of the 612 Gigantomachy; early Christians who saw it more or less 613 intact believed it to be the 'throne of Satan'. The altar had been dedicated by Eumenes II (197–159) who had also been the main figure behind the planning of Pergamon; he had also had superb porticoes and halls built in a Library of Arts and Sciences intended to rival the Athenian Lyceum, set up by Aristotle, Theophrastus and Demetrius of Phalerum and even the Museum at Alexandria. Below these lofty halls of learning descended the wooded, flower-covered terraces of the city where spacious gymnasia and temples were built on many different levels, one of which, the temple of Demeter, quickly grew to be an important cultural and intellectual centre.

Eumenes' engineers had paved the way for the future when they produced their scheme which combined the sanctuary of Athena Nikephoros, set on the highest point overlooking Pergamon, with the great Altar of the Gigantomachy on the terrace immediately below.

The altar, on which work had begun a few years after the Peace of Apamea, somewhere around 185–180, shows the same orientation as the temple of Athena which dates from the 3rd century. The colonnades surrounding the terrace where the altar was built were set out virtually in the same direction: if it had been possible to adapt the colonnades of the temple terrace to the governing idea, it would certainly have been done, for it was undoubtedly thought of; we would then have the first known attempt to design a great work of religious architecture according to a preconceived vertical outline.

The Pergamene Acropolis is a fine example of what

ROMAN. The Colosseum, Rome. A.D. 72–80. *Photo: A. F. Kersting.*

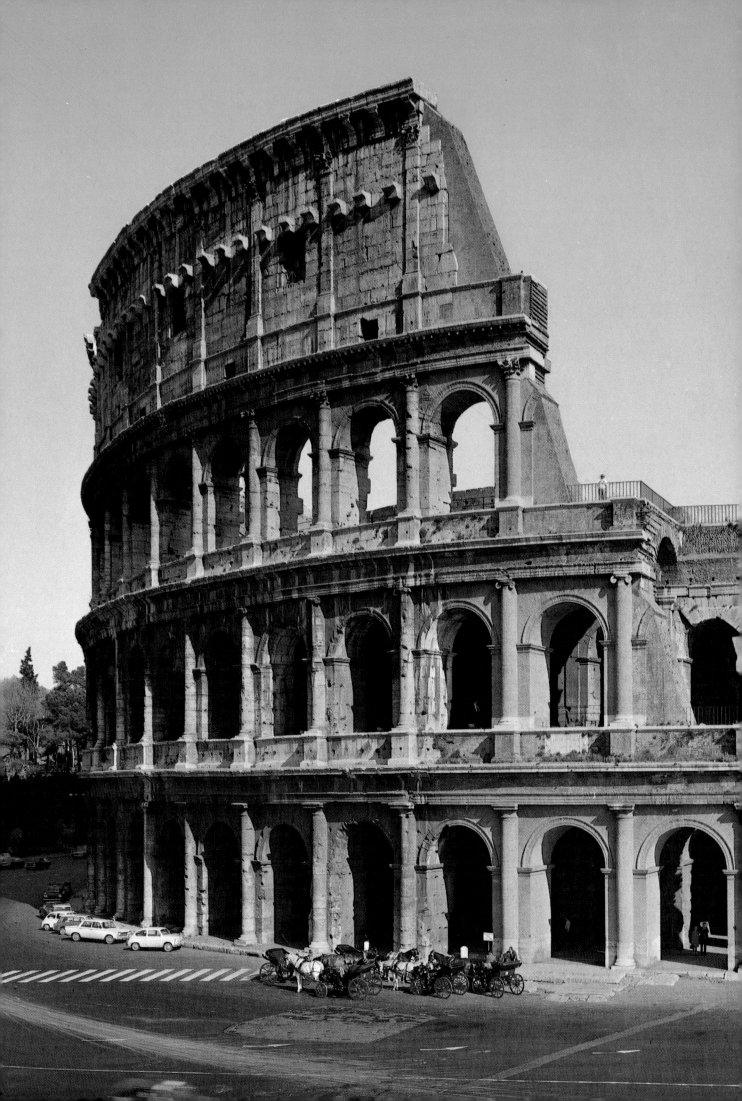

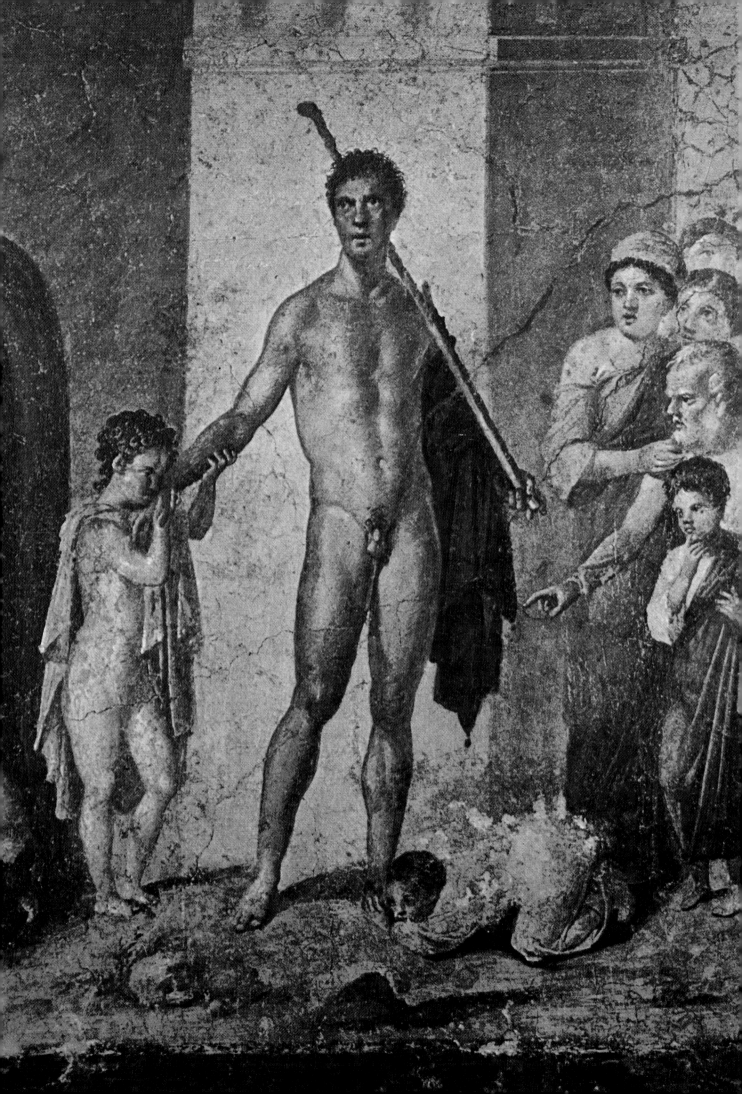

Hellenistic engineers and architects (already working in partnership) were adventurous enough to produce in the new capital cities, even in the West.

The architects of Rome, Preneste, New Carthage, and, in Gaul, of Lyon, Vienne and Orange were given a great deal to think about by this new type of city, built vertically and thriving on the credit from Roman banks.

Hellenistic influence on Rome

Where, if not at Pergamon, could we find a place more apt in which to repeat the famous line: *Graecia capta ferum victorem cepit ('Defeated Greece triumphed over the barbarian victors')*?

The treasures that were to pour into Rome as a part of their legacy after 133 B.C. dazzled the greedy eyes of the Romans and gave them a taste for splendour mixed, however, with all the decadence of the old way of life of the Latin peasantry in the true Cato style. Most of the first artists in Pergamon had come from Athens and central Greece and, for a good price, they introduced into Mysia the still modern technical teachings of classicism and filled the Pergamene religious buildings with images of the Greek gods. The Attalids paid handsomely for the commissions they gave to sculptors like Niceratus and Phyromachus of Athens and Antigonus of Carystus as well as painters who created the wide variety of themes that were later carried into the cities of the Campagna. At one time, they came from Mysia to carry out commissions in Greece, to restore the Delphic frescoes for instance.

Both Rome and Pergamon experienced, at different times, the 'great fear' which the migrations and raids of our warlike ancestors inspired, throughout the ancient world. Epigonus, the first real Pergamene sculptor, carved nothing but Celtomachies. But Rome's greatest trial of strength was the duel with Carthage. We should not forget the mixed emotions of horror and sullen fear which Hannibal's Carthaginians, no less than Brennus's Gauls, left behind them in Italy. Carthage had virtually no effect on Rome except in this humiliating panic which, one day, was to be avenged when the Romans defeated the rival city and destroyed it with their own hands. Nothing was left of Dido's capital and the ritual curse was intended to ensure that Carthage would never rise again; it was forbidden to use its soil even for the burial of the dead. And so Carthage, which had been influenced by the East and Sicily, perished without producing any great art because it had been the relentless enemy of everything that was to triumph with the Latin spirit (see Chapter 5).

Hellenistic Sicily, a great but surprisingly underrated centre of the arts, almost never receives enough attention in books. The Nymphs of Syracuse, who inspired Virgil, do not deserve this slight. In literature, from Theocritus to the Mantuan poet, all the known sources are recalled often enough but we should see to it that they are not neglected in the arts. Southern Italy, meaningfully called 'Magna Graecia', and Sicily were conquered in the 3rd century before the Greek mainland was occupied or the lands of the Hellenised East were divided up into Roman provinces.

The first art treasures that conjured up the Eastern mirage on the banks of the Tiber came to Rome, in the days before Pergamon, from Sicily and Magna Graecia. A monarch like Hiero II of Syracuse, who had rallied to

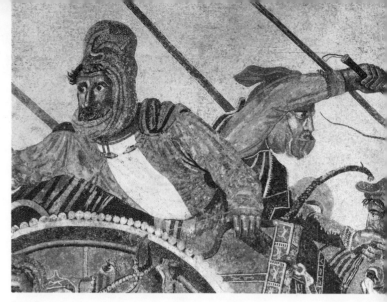

611. Detail of the mosaic shows Darius' head.

the Roman cause and was one of the first civilised rulers in a West that was gradually being taken over by the force of arms and possessions, proved to be a lover of the fine arts; he encouraged Theocritus and invited to his court Micon, coin engraver to Queen Philistis and the son of the great Attico-Pergamene sculptor, Niceratus. Between the 3rd century and the last decisive Roman conquest, Sicily and Magna Graecia produced works of painting and sculpture which show both the persistence of the finest traditions and new trends in sensibility. One would like to establish the history of the works of this period in more detail for it seems that they were like an autumn flower in full bloom, growing in a still favoured corner of the earth. The museums at Syracuse and at Palermo with the Aphrodite Landolina and famous Ram, to mention only two of a host of masterpieces, and the museums at Taranto, Lecce, Bari and Reggio possess many treasures whose worth has never really been fully appreciated; the priceless silver plate from Canosa and Taranto shows that the art of metal engraving was very highly prized in southern Italy at that time, just as it was in Sicily, and the looting of Sicily by Verres, the Roman proconsul, is not the only thing to bear this out.

When Pyrrhus, King of Epirus, who claimed to be the descendant of Achilles, attacked Roman Italy in 272–270 with half-hearted support from Tarentum, he was hardly considering the interests of his kingdom, and his defeat showed this well enough. It was far from certain whether the oracles of Dodona had influenced and indeed governed the ventures of Alexander the Molossian. In any case, after Pyrrhus' venture the Roman conquest of the peninsula went ahead with greater speed and led fairly soon to the decay of the group of free cities in Magna Graecia. These were unforgettable facts of history that had a profound effect on the religious, intellectual and social outlook of the Romans of the Republican period. Emphasis had recently been put, on the other hand, on the possible part played by the 'new Achilles' in the growth of the mythological theme of Trojan Rome. The famous legend that the Romans originated in Ilium—circulating in Italy at the time of the Etruscans, if not before—had at some earlier period received at the very least a fresh impulse, and now from this time, as we know, settled on the banks of the Tiber and there flourished; in the reign of Caesar, the city of Romulus and Remus and the she-wolf linked its fate to Venus-Aphrodite and the East. From the time of Sulla, other combinations of Roman ideas and elements of

ROMAN. Theseus Triumphant. Fresco. 1st century A.D. National Museum, Naples. *Photo: D. Hughes-Gilbey.*

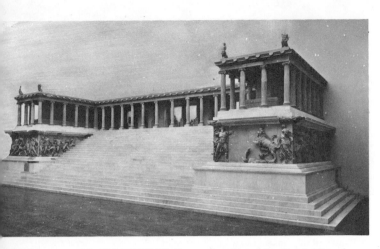

612. HELLENISTIC. Reconstruction of the Great Altar of Zeus at Pergamon. *Staatliche Museen, Berlin.*

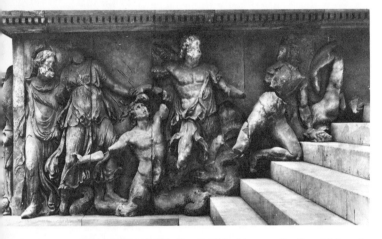

613. HELLENISTIC. Detail of the frieze on the Great Altar of Zeus at Pergamon. Carved between 197 and 159 B.C., it depicts the battle of the gods and giants and symbolises the victory of the kings of Pergamon over the Galatians. *Staatliche Museen, Berlin.*

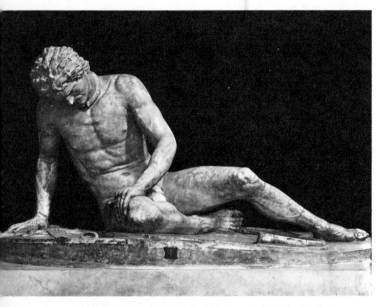

614. HELLENISTIC. Dying Gaul, called the Capitoline Gladiator. Roman replica after the original from the first Pergamene school (2nd century B.C.), a votive figure dedicated by Attalus I to commemorate his victories over the Gauls. *Capitoline Museum, Rome.*

Greek art and religion were gradually evolved which were to remain fundamental for many centuries. As far as the nature and success of these mixtures is concerned, it hardly matters that almost all the painters, sculptors and indeed architects in the Latin country came from Greece. It was only to be expected that when victorious Rome became the new centre of the civilised world in place of the defeated Hellenistic kingdoms it would attract all the talent and rivalry in the artistic field. The endeavour on the part of the Roman nobility to imitate the splendour of Alexander's Diadochi had immeasurable consequences that were particularly beneficial to the arts.

The contribution of Hellenistic architecture

There can be absolutely no doubt that architecture in the Hellenistic age profited from the classical heritage. Here we need only say that, by and large, it kept the three Greek Orders and the taste for clear cut, linear designs. But the search to find the most ingenious solutions to new problems, great and small, went on. In the new towns there was, on the other hand, a considerable and significant increase in privately commissioned building—palaces and more luxurious houses. Architecture, which had become more cosmopolitan, had to be made to match in this way the scale of the Oriental empire conquered and reformed by Alexander since Greece was suddenly confronted with the age-old treasures and chaos of the oldest civilisations of Babylonia, Egypt, Syria, etc. Greek art, with its love of proportion, had then to compete with this past that had been acquired, a past that stretched back for thousands of years, with an inexhaustible stock of traditions. When the Macedonian conquerors, moreover, settled in Asia and in almost all regions founded their cities, they were faced with the task of peopling, equipping and defending them. It is true that very few names of outstanding or commendable architects have come down to us from this period. Beyond Decimus Cossutius, who, it seems, was a Roman freedman, virtually the only ones we can find to mention are Hermogenes, a Greek who designed the temple of Teos and others in Anatolia, and Sostratus of Cnidus who produced the Alexandrian lighthouse in the reign of Ptolemy II. We also know of Apaturius of Alabanda, and possibly one or two more.

But lack of information should not make us underestimate an age which, under the worst possible material conditions, was able to transform so many art forms and erect in all countries the most impressive buildings. The small island of Delos alone, one of the Cycladic islands, seems to be a kind of museum of Hellenistic inventions with Demetrius Poliorcetes' Neorium its hypostyle Hall (210 B.C.), its Dodecatheon, etc. The cities spread out through Asia Minor were open to a wide variety of influences that came from farther afield, for this was the period which produced many of the Seven Wonders of the World, the oldest of which were the Halicarnassus 538 Mausoleum, the Hephaestium at Babylon, the Ephesus Artemisium, the Colossos of Rhodes and the Alexandrian lighthouse and, later, the great altar at Pergamon which 612 was begun somewhere around 185–180 and finished a few years after 160. No matter what is said, Greek architecture had never been the slave of alignment and symmetry, nor even paid it lip service. Now, it was in the Hellenistic period that the *hiera* (holy places), more strictly planned on the main axis of a rectangle, were first being developed: the Metroön at Mamurt Kaleh near Pergamon, and the temple of Asclepius at Cos. It was the Hellenistic period, too, which first saw the growth of public squares with colonnades, generally quadrangular, which, taking the place of the almost religiously respected, overladen disorder of the archaic and classical market places and civic assembly halls, were the only real architecturally planned agoras. It is ironic that the agora only reached its finest form, which was to be adopted in the forums of the West, immediately after the battle of Chaeronea had sounded the knell for the idea of the free city with an independent public life; this is not often noticed.

The cosmopolitanism of the Hellenistic age—a period of middle class opportunism and royal patronage—was also, generally speaking, notable in the field of architecture for its progressive building schemes, far more varied than ever before: in the first place, they were not only building sanctuaries, temples and altars but a great many theatres, gymnasia, assembly halls, buildings where people could pass their leisure hours or that would be of practical service to them, government offices and, above all, fine comfortable houses with peristyles that were gradually beginning, even at this time, to be built several storeys high (for instance, the 'Maison de l'Hermes' at Delos). The Roman villa could never have been what it was—a combined temple, museum and residence—if it had not learnt from the houses at Priene and at Delos, for example, where it was not only the theatre which made this island a 'museum of innovations', as it has been called.

On the other hand, buildings were being built on a larger and larger scale, the expression of royal achievement and the arrogant temptations of grandeur. All in all, there was an attempt to add to the height of Greek architecture and, by so doing, to make it less solid and heavy. Let us take a look at the architectural history of Delos where a start has been made on the detailed and general study of its many varied innovations: hypostyle halls, skylights, even the use of false, hollow pediments and pediments without a base that belong to Hellenistic and Roman architecture, which for much too long were mistakenly looked upon as stage contrivances or purely picturesque inventions, taken over and used in the Campagna and in Rome. There were other original features relating to the design of piers, the fashion for pilasters and vaults (for example, the cistern in the theatre at Delos), the round arch, of which the Romans never grew tired and whose role they would not have developed so rapidly had they not been able to take advantage of their long apprenticeship in Hellenistic Greece and in the Near and Middle East.

There was competition to produce a wide variety of effects in the new buildings; the use of marble was continued and although some materials that were much sought after in earlier periods were bypassed, after 250, in favour of others of little value, the Romans used, apart from slabs of very dull colour, famous marbles of a bluish-grey colour, with and without veining, for the sake of their fine translucent effects. At Antioch, in the temple of Apollo of Daphne, and in the magnificent chambers of the royal state barge (*thalamegos*) built for Ptolemy IV Philopator at Alexandria after 221, there were attempts to produce many other kinds of rich polychrome effects. One can also see the beginning of a freer use of granite, poros, diorites, aragonite, alabaster, etc.

The marvels of the East

At the same time, toreutic art was coming to be used in architecture with its sumptuous floral glories covering the tops of walls and sometimes even the whole area between ceiling and floor. It was in Syria and Alexandria that these displays of gold plate, silver and bronze had first compelled the Romans' admiration. They were not only used as ornamental features in themselves; their lustre added to the variegated colours of certain hard and precious stones, the dull gleam of ivory, the glittering gems, pearls of India that people have wrongly tried to pretend were first used by the very much later Sassanians. The model for the ornamental plant motifs of the Ara Pacis and city gateways was first found in Alexandria and Pergamon. **602**

Once Rome had defeated the Hellenistic kingdoms, it was the newly wealthy West that increasingly began to set the pace, thanks to the means at its disposal and its ambitions, thwarted for so long. Sulla, Pompey, Caesar, Augustus—one after another, once they had returned triumphant from the East, they all worked to make a future for their country along Hellenistic lines and to make Rome a metropolis of art, worthy of the supreme wonders of the East. In this way they hoped to promote and gain ground for their secret imperial ambitions. After Sulla, who became dictator in 82 B.C., the Oriental-Anatolian-Syrian pattern was imposed more and more upon the old Rome, built of brick and now dissatisfied with the rural austerity of its old self—a poor city which, Augustus in his turn was to say, had been waiting for him to come. Bit by bit, Magna Graecia was ousted by an even greater Orient.

At Nimrud-Dagh, Antiochus I of Commagene had in fact had the entire summit of a hill transformed into a royal mausoleum for himself, which he thought extremely impressive. Something of its ostentatious design is today being brought to light. Terraced town-planning on a colossal scale, a taste that had also gained ground in Gaul and in the new Carthage, was not the only thing with which they were concerned: at the same time, research was being fruitfully carried on relating to the symmetrical planning of large areas.

Already in Egypt, since the time of the Old Kingdom, sanctuaries had had to be planned symmetrically with their various features grouped and developed around a central axis. In Greece and Ionia, neither in the very early stages nor for a long time afterwards, was there very much concern with this excessively ordered utilisation of space. Greek temples had remained self-contained works of architecture, entirely unrelated to each other and to the surrounding wall which marked off the boundary of the ground on which they stood. The same was true of the altars, except in Ionia and Sicily during the archaic period. Hellenistic architects, on the other hand, were very much interested in the problems and discipline of design and, besides, they could not discount buildings like the temple of Horus at Edfu in Egypt.

We can find much the same thing in the field of town-planning: we can find no starting points at either Priene or Delos, in spite of the influence of the Italian agora. The truth of the matter is that Roman town-planning in its early stages was centred in the East, with all its love of regularity and with the *cardo* and *decumanus* (see p. 348) intersecting at right angles. Latin engineers, acclaimed in Greece and Asia, only in later years worked for their own

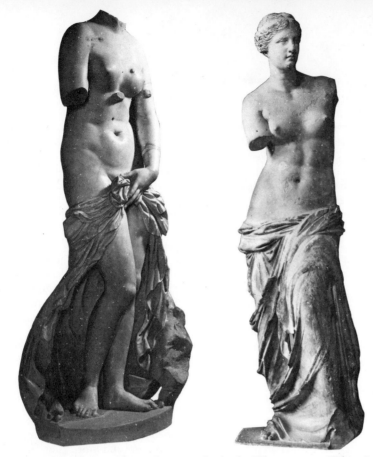

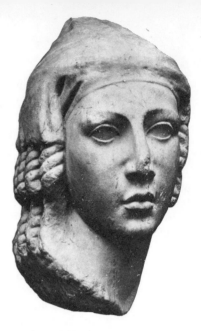

615. HELLENISTIC. Aphrodite of Syracuse. Marble. 3rd century B.C. Roman copy. *Syracuse Museum*.

616. HELLENISTIC. Aphrodite known as the Venus de Milo. 2nd century B.C. *Louvre*.

617. LATE HELLENISTIC. Head of a woman. *Alexandria Museum*.

cities and for the temples and sanctuaries in the West.

The vital importance of Syrian influence, for example, in Roman and Hellenistic architecture would have had more recognition if it had only been borne in mind that, from the time of the Olympieum of Antiochus IV at Athens (164 B.C.), the capitals of the Augustan era or the capitals at Baalbek, dating from the time of Nero, have unchanged and virtually similar specific features. The axial principle had been completely accepted by Latin taste. But it was not a Western invention.

Wide variety of sculpture

Hellenistic sculpture, or as it is sometimes wrongly called 'Graeco-Roman' sculpture, of the period before Sulla, has not yet received all the attention it deserves, in matters of both technique and inspiration. In general studies of the period, essays have been written on 'Late Greek Sculpture' as if it had appeared in the exhausted, last days of the age and was one of the signs of a creeping decay. So in all the talk of 'rococo' and 'baroque', both meaningless terms in this context, the entire emphasis is put on the continuing and 'sterilising' traditions of the great 4th-century schools, while everything alongside them that was new is entirely overlooked. Thus it is difficult, in theory, to account for the unflagging prestige of the plastic arts, producing an exciting and astonishingly complex body of works which, if in fact it helped, as has been said, towards the vulgarisation of Greek art, at least never stopped being a source of constant wonder all over the world. And above all, it can hardly be said that it allowed itself to become vulgarised. 'I hate every thing that is popular,' wrote Callimachus, the great inspiration behind the art of his age.

The processional displays as described by Callixenes of Rhodes and Polybius show how Hellenistic sculptors—from Madeconia to Alexandrian Egypt and to Antioch—were able to create and supply priceless, vivid and ingenious masterpieces, durable or fragile.

When Lysippus sculpted the dying Alexander, struck down at the peak of his glory, making him only a very human figure, very much of this world, he managed to keep at bay (almost until the Byzantine period) the imminent danger of the 'theocratic' royal portrait which Byzantium was to develop in later years.

Yet the gods were far from being forgotten in this age of adventure in which it would only be absurd to see a universal waning of religious faith. Religions, both national and foreign, were thriving. People have commented on the lack of calm, supposedly stemming from the general insecurity of the period. The truth of the matter is that emotion was the thing most sought after in this cosmopolitan age, looked for in the pointed or sentimental inflation of basic feelings: never had the sensual beauty of Aphrodites, Erotes and boy Bacchoi been dwelt upon with more satisfaction; never had more honour been paid to the carefree sport of these eternally youthful gods and those spirits, created to hover between heaven and earth, with which Praxiteles had already peopled his world of fantasy. The religious and aesthetic changes, which had made the lords of Olympus, and more especially those upon whom salvation after death depended, far more familiar figures, and which exalted piety on earth, everywhere produced, with varying success, something new in the art of sculpture which was now inspired by a more human faith and more tormented by the thought of life after death.

Besides this, at the opposite end of the scale of everyday life, poor labourers were also raised to a more noble level in the art of Pergamon, Smyrna, Tarsus and Alexandria: bent and emaciated peasants, unsteadily leading their young mules; watchful fishermen on the riverbank; old, bony peasant women on their way to market: from Rome to New York, there are many examples to be found of these spirited and extraordinary portraits of ordinary, humble people. And as if this all-inclusiveness —which had been more or less held in check by the remote nobility of classical art—were not enough, Alexandria produced fairyland countrysides and landscapes, along with that 'Raumpoesie' that German art critics have rightly commented upon and which was responsible for introducing the picturesque into reliefs: in Athens, Asia Minor and Pergamon, plant-life came into its own. But let us make no mistake; Greek art, for all that is said, had never turned its back on nature. But exactly coinciding with Theocritus' *Idylls*, the Alexandrian landscape reliefs, at the origin of not only the Ara Pacis but the entire art of modern relief, undoubtedly broadened and deepened an awareness that has never disappeared; with a few statuettes and with a ruined *tempietto* or a country shrine, they introduced and asserted all the reverence that was due to the cosmos and to the sovereign forces of change in nature and human beings, and the stubborn hope of a life after death that is a source of compensation to all outcasts of fortune.

In the space available here, we must unfortunately restrict ourselves to pointing out the way some of these new endeavours were going, without daring to tackle any definition or detailed account of these new schools which, in creative genius, were in no way inferior to the schools of the preceding period. But it is just as well to emphasise the place that was kept, or perhaps restored, to over life-size statuary; this is borne out by the Helios of the port of Rhodes, one of the Seven Wonders of the World, and the group from Lycosura in mainland Greece. One should also note the fashion for sumptuous statues adorned with precious metals. The colossal works by Bryaxis—for instance, the statue of Daphne in the temple of Serapis at Alexandria—combined the polychrome splendour of metal work with purely plastic effects; this conscious magnificence helped to strengthen the new religious beliefs, since it had to be able to uphold the magical *mana* of the gods. The whole succession of Hellenistic statues of Zeus, Poseidon and especially the series of Apollo and the youthful or infant Dionysus, the many versions of Aphrodite—these magnificent nudes set a radiant example from Melos to Syracuse. With the statues of Hercules, standing ready to do battle or bent beneath his club as if under the heavy memory of too many exhausting labours, they form an inexhaustible and original collection of gods and heroes that can be returned to again and again: these works did not betray the noble precepts of the past and in no way do they appear decadent. The recent finds made at Memphis and in Alexandria itself, with limestone and marble architectural sculptures from the Memphis Serapeum and the Regia quarter of Alexandria, and the superb exploitation of regional iconography of which the portrait-bust of a woman in the Graeco-Roman Museum, Alexandria, is a fine example, have exposed the injustice of trying to pretend that the new art of the Delta cities had nothing to offer but 'minor' works. This view has been taken to such lengths that there has even been a certain amount of quibbling about the origin of the pictorial bas-relief!

615
616

617

Development of Hellenistic sculpture

If Hellenistic sculpture, from Anatolia to Italy, is ever to be properly understood, each one of the great centres must be examined in turn, with careful attention to chronology in order to clarify its development. We have to reconsider three centuries of art, from roughly the beginning of the

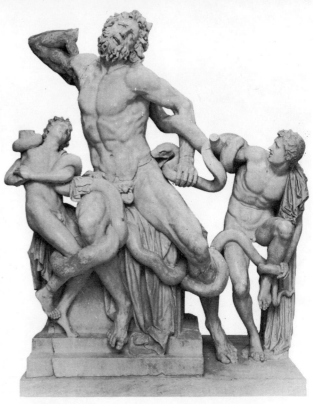

618. HELLENISTIC. Laocoön and his sons. Marble. About 50 B.C. *Vatican Museum.*

3rd century to the end of the 1st century (Principate of Augustus). During the whole of this period, Asia, Greece, Africa and the Italic West reveal the same artistic fashion; allowing for inevitable differences between individual artists, the same themes, both old and new, Gigantomachies and Galatomachies, for example, were treated over and over again. We can learn a great deal here by noticing how different centres were able to produce their own variations on a single theme. The succession of Celtomachies echo the invasions from the west in Italy, Greece and Anatolia. Pergamon and Cyzicus, more than anywhere else, set out to immortalise, both realistically and symbolically, the battles fought against the western areas. Mysia gave the finest form to a heroic theme that was to be taken up and repeated by the entire ancient Latin world: it was here that the heroic Galatian type was evolved. He is sometimes depicted as a defeated figure, collapsing upon his shattered weapons; sometimes he stands upright, ready to take his own life, having first killed his wife so that he should not have to see her captured as a slave. Such is the Dying Gaul by Epigonus, misrepresented by Lord Byron who gave it the name of Gladiator, and again the impressive Ludovisi Gaul with his noble love of freedom that does not falter at the sacrifice of life.

A study of dates proves that the Galatian themes preceded the Gigantomachy subjects: to the 3rd century belongs Epigonus of Mysia, who was working just a very short time after Niceratus and Phyromachus, the Athenian artists summoned to Pergamon by Philetaerus; Epigonus worked for Attalus I. Next came the group of Rhodian and local sculptors and the others (a team of forty artists from every country) who produced the Gigantomachy of the Great Altar. It is not surprising that Rhodes, which in the 3rd century had at first commissioned foreign artists, one of whom was Phyles of Halicarnassus, should have managed to create by the 2nd century an original school of their own whose works were

327

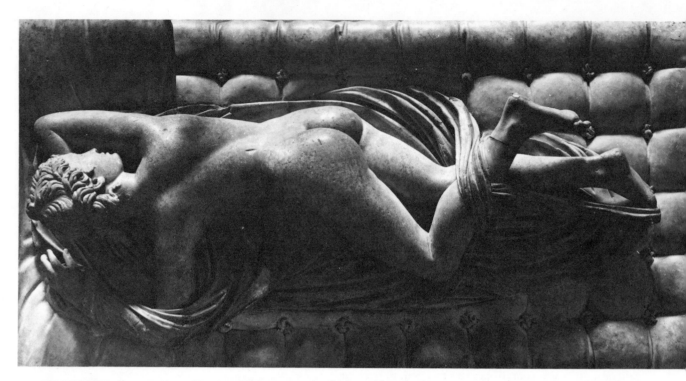

619. HELLENISTIC. Sleeping Hermaphrodite. Antique copy of an original of the 3rd century B.C.. The mattress was added by Bernini. *Louvre.*

chiefly concerned with the expression of pathos. The
650 Victory of Samothrace was the work of a Rhodian sculptor who skilfully and dramatically revived a theme that had been quite common at the time when the coins of Demetrius Poliorcetes were being minted and, so it seems, in the period of the Delian Neorium. At the other end of the Hellenistic period we have the overrated group
618 of Laocoön and his two sons, writhing so conventionally in the encircling coils of monstrous serpents, which was to set Michelangelo a dangerous example. It merely illustrates, along with the later versions of the Pergamene Gigantomachy, the extremist trends of Anatolian art. But we should bear in mind, on the other hand, another extremely turbulent composition in the form of a pyramid, the Punishment of Dirce, usually known as the Farnese Bull. We next return to more classical effects in the work of the school of Aphrodisias in Caria which provided Rome with generations of artists, who were, it is true, more skilful than inspired, and with the first examples of realistic ornamental foliage that was in use until the time of Severus and even indeed, in many places, right down to the Renaissance.

It has recently been pointed out how the pictorial works of Protogenes of Caunos, the young rival of Apelles, and those of Aetion, Nicomachus, Athenion of Maroneia, Antipholus, Theon of Samos, Theorus, Aristides II, Demetrius, son of Seleucus, and Philoxenus of Eretria, could perhaps be, if not brought to light, at least deduced with reasonable accuracy from the many different copies of them that were made soon after, in all regions from the East to the Latin West.

On the whole, the best Hellenistic painting—evidently highly appreciated by the Macedonian monarchs, the Lagidae and Seleucids, since they paid higher prices for it than for sculpture and it was later haggled over and paid

for in gold in the Roman *atria auctionaria*—must certainly have been a great art, but unfortunately, like painting of every age, unable to withstand the passage of time and therefore largely unknown to us today.

Toreutic art and metal crafts produced especially fine work throughout the Hellenistic period: in Alexandria, Pergamon, Syria (helmet from Emesa), the Greek mainland and Italy. The pictures of religious processions on vases made of precious metals, and the lists of plunder captured by victorious generals, both show the lavish abundance of objects that were being produced in the workshops of the time, in the cities and provinces alike. It was these workshops that were responsible for the work that can be found in central Egypt, in the reliefs of the tomb of Petosiris (*c.* 300 B.C.) at Hermopolis, and of which we are now beginning to discover products that were exported to Scythia (Chertomlyk vase), to Begram in the heart of Asia as regards the East, and elsewhere, to Bernay, to Glanum, in Germany and even as far away as the British Isles in the West. The recent chance discovery of nine gold vases at Panagyurishte in the Balkans is of great significance: the patera from Aquileia shows that the same fashion existed in Italy. All these precious vases that T. Schreiber assumed must still be in existence are gradually coming to light and presenting us with their richly lifelike ornamentation and a wealth of information: a profusion of ornamental plant motifs, the persistence of religious and mythological life, borrowings from the old legendary epics with occasional evocations of the literary life of the time, showing playwrights, famous men of letters, poets and scholars at home in their studies or at the theatre, watched over by their benevolent muses. Nothing is better suited to recreate something of the atmosphere of the 'museums' and great libraries that were built in every Hellenistic capital.

Naturally, painted pottery, highly prized in the archaic and classical periods, from this time suffered a decline. It no longer matched the tastes of a world of luxury and splendour where the favourites of fortune, not knowing

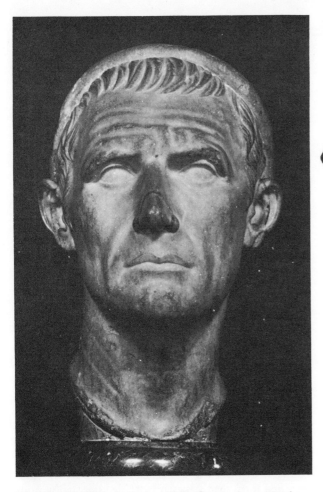

620. HELLENISTIC. Antiochus III the Great, who restored Seleucid power. Antique copy of 3rd-century B.C. original. *Louvre.*

what the morrow would bring, loved to feast and drink their Falernian wine out of gold cups. Although in all regions the production of clay vases continued, they were beginning to make use of borrowed ornamentation which grew increasingly schematised all the time. For less wealthy customers there was pottery with a relief decoration that imitated metal ware (Megarian, Samian, Aretine, etc.).

Terra cotta was merely at this period a poor man's substitute that could not stand up to the competition of glass. Only the small terra-cotta figurines were still able to hold their own. This art in the Hellenistic period produced some real masterpieces, on the Greek mainland in Boeotia (notably at Tanagra), in Asia Minor (Myrina, Smyrna and almost everywhere) and especially in Alexandria. It has been proved that in Hellenistic Italy, a country in which *statuaria*, the art of terra cotta, had always been highly prized, they were also still being produced at Paestum, the Silaris workshops and at Locri.

Cameos, intaglios, glassware and coins all reveal the highest qualities and contribute to a Hellenistic art, very far from being 'minor', drawing inspiration from religion and culture and adding to the collection of antique masterpieces. Just think, for example, of the coins bearing the heads of the beautiful Ptolemaic queens or those from Sicily, engraved with the image of Philistis. The entire achievement of this period, sometimes so staggeringly neglected, compels our admiration.

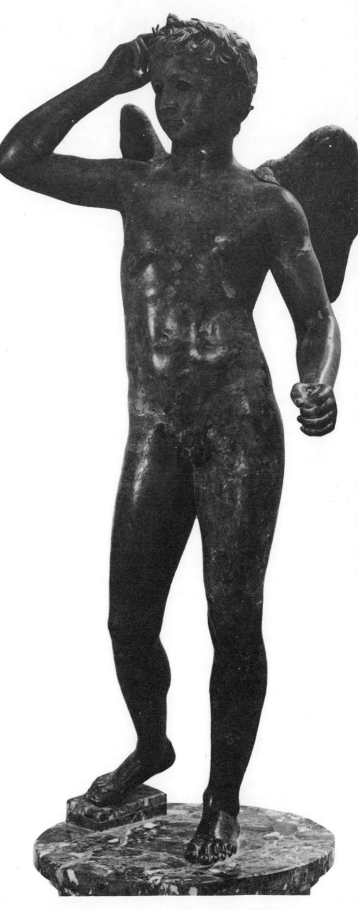

621. HELLENISTIC. Bronze Eros found in the sea off Mahdia, Tunisia. The influence of Praxiteles and Lysippus is visible. 3rd century B.C. *Alaoui Museum, Bardo, Tunisia.*

329

THE ROMAN WORLD FROM SULLA TO SEVERUS (1st century B.C. 3rd century A.D.) *François Chamoux*

By the 2nd century B.C. Rome had become the centre of the ancient world. Roman art, bit by bit, was ousting Greek art and spreading a fixed vocabulary of plastic forms throughout a still strongly united world. Nowadays it is only through Roman art that we can rediscover Antiquity but opinion is divided as to its real worth. Was it simply a conventional, academic art taken over from Greece or, as is now being maintained, original and creative? The distinguished Hellenist, François Chamoux, counteracts the extremism of this last theory by stressing the part played by Greek influence, though he does not deny that specifically Roman trends carried it in new directions.

Greek history, strictly speaking, for most historians closes with Mummius' capture of Corinth in 146 B.C. This important political event does, in fact, mark the victory of the Latin West over the Hellenised East. Subsequently the ancient world was no longer centred on the eastern Mediterranean basin but on Italy. The conquerors grew rich on the spoils of the Hellenistic kingdoms and booty pillaged on a staggering scale from captured cities. While works of art were pouring into the country, there was also an influx of artists—architects, sculptors, painters— who arrived in large numbers from the East, either as slaves or of their own free will. They were drawn to Italy by the new Roman patrons who had grown rich from the profits of conquest and wanted to surround themselves with all the refinements that their forefathers had never known.

Is there a Roman art?

The important economic aspect of Rome's victory, therefore, had a considerable effect on the development of ancient art. Alongside well-established workshops and studios and the ever prosperous centres in Athens and the Greek cities of Asia Minor, other workshops were set up in Italy and the western provinces in order to answer the considerable increase in demand. We know, it is true, very little about these artists' workshops; the odd mention by an ancient writer tells us something of a master of a school, like Pasiteles who was very popular in Rome at the time of Sulla. But it is obvious from surviving monuments that the *Pax Romana* encouraged a traffic in artists and works of art. Whole shiploads of statues and even parts of buildings, marble columns for instance, were crossing the sea; such was the famous galley ship-wrecked off Mahdia in Tunisia in the early part of the 1st century A.D.

Never had cultural unity been more apparent than it was in the Mediterranean basin during the first centuries of the Empire. Monuments which survive from this time form part of what is called Roman art.

What exactly is meant by this adjective 'Roman'? Down to the end of the 19th century, scholars used it merely to describe works dating from a certain period. Without question, they accepted what was said by the Romans themselves, who for all their acute sense of national pride, nonetheless proclaimed, through the mouths of Horace and Virgil, their greatest poets,

Greece's supremacy in the realm of art. Roman art, then, was thought of only as the last embodiment of Greek art. This interpretation went with a certain scorn for works of the late period, considered to be far inferior to those of the classical period that were the only ones allowed to belong to the 'Golden Age'. As a reaction, some critics began to stress those features of 'Roman' works of art that seemed to them to be outside the Greek artistic tradition: they then asserted that there was, in the full sense of the word, a Roman art and set out to analyse its original characteristics. Although this thesis encountered opposition, it has on the whole held its own, and it has now, in fact, become a commonplace to contrast Greek and Roman art.

That, however, is not the final and complete solution to the problem. Recent research has brought out the leading part played by Greek artists in the Latin world. And in addition a fuller knowledge of Greek art and more especially of the long neglected Hellenistic art has enabled us to see in them the signs of certain trends that all too readily were assumed to be the exclusive prerogative of 'western' art. It is just as well then to take another look at these dogmatic assertions and hasty generalisations. Probably years of detailed study and microscopic examination are still needed before we can hope to arrive at a thesis which is genuinely based on the true facts. The view expressed in this article, in an extremely concentrated form that makes any detailed illustration quite out of the question, should be looked upon as a provisional opinion that I, as a Hellenist and therefore more alive to the Greek contribution in this field, have been brought to hold after a series of studies relating to a wide variety of monuments.

The Greek artist and the Roman art lover

The first point to consider is the racial origins of these artists. It has been said, it is true, that Roman art, in contrast to Greek art which abounds in celebrated names, is an 'art without artists'. This merely means that texts have left no mention of great artists worthy of a place in the front rank. Neither the sculptor Arcesilaus who was commissioned by Caesar to carve the statue of Venus Genetrix, nor the painter Ludius whose landscapes adorned with architectural motifs were made so much of, nor the architect Apollodorus of Damascus, the designer of the Column of Trajan, could be put on the same plane 632 as Polygnotus, Ictinus or Praxiteles. Of this the ancients themselves were very much aware: authors like the scholarly Pliny the Elder or the much travelled Pausanius, who at the time of the Empire were writing about the arts, have virtually no interest except for the 'masters of bygone days' and very rarely mention the name of an artist of a later age.

Information from literary texts is too meagre in this matter to be of any help, but fortunately we have at our disposal a quantity of epigraphic sources, such as the signatures of sculptors, architects, mosaicists and gem engravers. The name of the artist is sometimes accompanied by an 'ethnic' adjective which indicates his native city. The systematic study of these inscriptions is far from complete but it has already gone far enough to allow us to draw certain conclusions.

The outstanding fact about these signatures is that the large majority are written in Greek. The only group which forms an exception is that of sigillated pottery where the potters' signatures are in Latin, but this group comes more under the heading of artisans' work than art proper. In all other cases writings in Greek far outnumber the others even in Italy. So it is clear that in Rome as well as in the East, Greek was the usual language spoken by artists. Besides, the very names prove that we are dealing with Greeks or Hellenised Orientals. Whenever we come across a Latin name it is usually accompanied by a Greek cognomen which shows that the man was either a foreigner who had been granted the freedom of the city, or a freedman. It is only in rare cases that the artist can be assumed to be a Roman by birth.

This observation need not surprise us for it corresponds to what we know of Roman attitudes. They were passionate lovers of art but, as has recently been emphasised, they would have thought it a profession beneath the dignity of a man of good family. This manual work was willingly left to foreigners and slaves. This is what is really meant by the famous passage in Virgil's *Aeneid*, Book VI, where Anchises prophesies to Aeneas: 'There will be others, at least so I believe, far abler than you to breathe life into bronze and carve living faces from marble . . . but remember, Roman, your art will lie in governing the nations, in keeping true peace, in sparing the humbled and crushing the proud.' As he gives his sanction to other men, that is to the Greeks, to become masters in the plastic arts so that the privilege of governing should be kept for his fellow countrymen, the Latin poet displays more pride than humility. If some emperors, like Nero, Hadrian and Marcus Aurelius, took up painting and sculpture, it can only be viewed as a princely whim; they would have no more thought of practising art seriously than of teaching grammar.

The only claim made by the Roman, then, in the field of art, was that he had taste and appreciation. He had more appreciation for works of art than for the artist as a person. And ancient works of art gave him more pleasure than anything else; in this he was following the example of his Greek masters. Consequently the incessant imitation of classical masterpieces was a characteristic feature of Roman art. Statues of Athena after Phidias, of Hermes after Alcamenes, of Aphrodite in the manner of Praxiteles were produced in their hundreds by expert craftsman. The work of the finest copyists displays a strict attention to detail and, with the help of mechanical devices and casting, could reproduce with complete accuracy the proportions and size of the original, to the extent that in modern times it has sometimes been possible to complete a damaged replica by adding pieces from another cast copy. Good fortune in excavating has sometimes enabled us to compare the copy with its original, as happened recently when faithful copies of the Erechtheum Caryatids were discovered in the ruins of Hadrian's villa at Tivoli. These copies bear the sculptor's signature with no mention of the artist of the original; he was quite aware that the discriminating Roman art lover was unlikely to be duped. Similarly the Capitoline Amazon, in imitation of Polycleitus' work, is signed by the sculptor Sosicles.

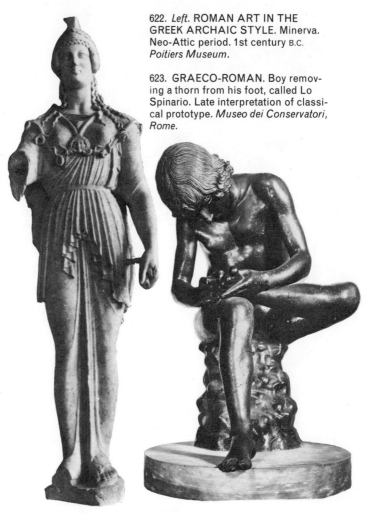

622. *Left*. ROMAN ART IN THE GREEK ARCHAIC STYLE. Minerva. Neo-Attic period. 1st century B.C. *Poitiers Museum.*

623. GRAECO-ROMAN. Boy removing a thorn from his foot, called Lo Spinario. Late interpretation of classical prototype. *Museo dei Conservatori, Rome.*

The same was true of the painters responsible for the ornamentation of the houses in Pompeii who drew freely upon the Hellenic repertoire. It is quite usual to find several frescoes that have taken their inspiration from the same earlier Greek painting. This is one of our most valuable sources of information concerning an art of which none of the masterpieces has survived.

The Roman art lover's taste for things ancient led to the flourishing production of pastiches as well as copies. There is a whole class of sculptures which imitate the Greek archaic style and which, carried out in a way that could not possibly deceive the trained eye, are nevertheless significant. The archaicising Minerva from Poitiers shows 622 how this method gained ground even in the remotest provinces. The *pasticcio* technique was also employed which consisted in combining, with varying degrees of success, a head and body that were modelled on different styles. The torch-bearing Dionysus from Sakha has a Hellenistic head set upon a body obviously inspired by Polycleitus. Other well known works, like the Spinario 623 and the Esquiline Venus, were very probably the result 544 of similar mixtures, which still survive to perplex modern archaeologists.

This period, however, was far from concentrating absolutely on the past. If a large part of their inspiration was derived from the classical repertoire, the artists who worked for the new masters of the world also had new problems to cope with and were able, at times, to give their works an original flavour. The vital part of their

530

331

THE HELLENISTIC WORLD

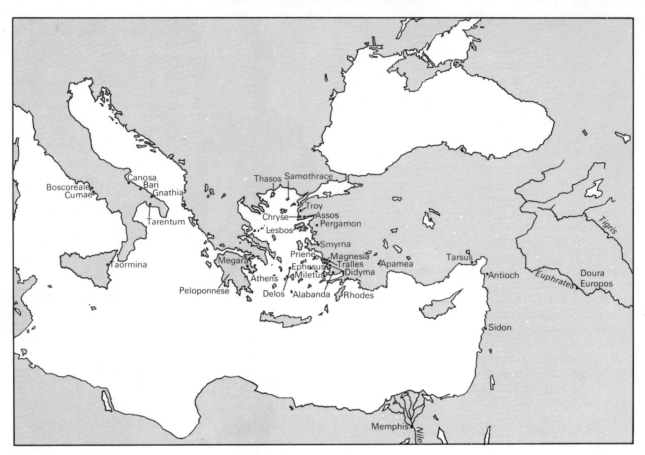

Boscoreale
Cumae
Canosa
Bari
Gnathia
Tarentum
Taormina
Megara
Peloponnese
Athens
Delos
Thasos
Samothrace
Chryse
Lesbos
Troy
Assos
Pergamon
Smyrna
Priene
Ephesus
Miletus
Magnesia
Tralles
Didyma
Alabanda
Rhodes
Apamea
Tarsus
Antioch
Euphrates
Tigris
Doura
Europos
Sidon
Memphis
Nile

THE ROMAN WORLD

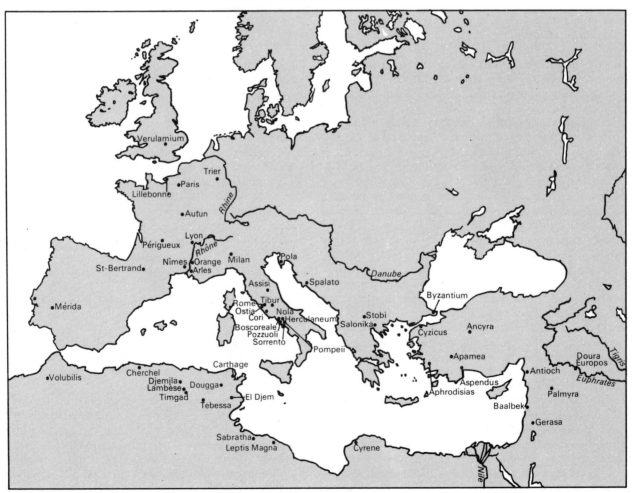

Verulamium
Trier
Paris
Lillebonne
Autun
Lyon
Périgueux
St-Bertrand
Nîmes
Orange
Arles
Rhône
Rhine
Milan
Pola
Danube
Byzantium
Mérida
Assisi
Tibur
Rome
Ostia
Cori
Boscoreale
Pozzuoli
Sorrento
Nola
Herculaneum
Spalato
Stobi
Salonika
Cyzicus
Ancyra
Apamea
Doura
Europos
Antioch
Euphrates
Tigris
Pompeii
Volubilis
Cherchel
Djemila
Lambese
Timgad
Tebessa
Dougga
El Djem
Carthage
Aspendus
Aphrodisias
Palmyra
Baalbek
Gerasa
Sabratha
Leptis Magna
Cyrene
Nile

332

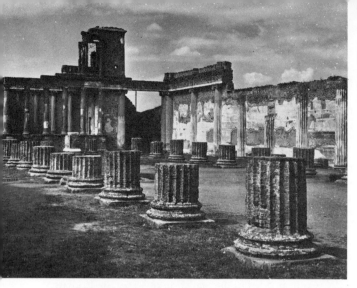

624. ROMAN. Ruins of the Basilica at Pompeii. Probably 2nd century B.C.

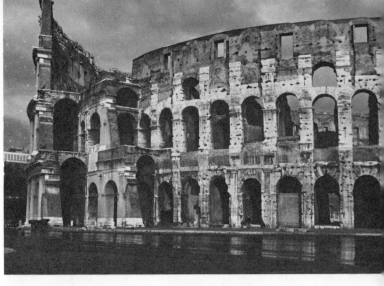

625. ROMAN. The Colosseum or Flavian amphitheatre. Started by Vespasian in A.D. 72 it was completed by Titus in

contribution can be studied under two main headings: firstly architecture, in which many important innovations were made, and secondly the plastic arts, which were especially productive in the field of historical subjects, picturesque landscapes and portraiture. We shall look at both in turn.

New techniques in building

The Romans were great builders. Impressive ruins that have survived fire the imagination with Rome's erstwhile greatness. But it is a fact that the architects of these buildings were for the most part Greeks and Hellenised Orientals. This is acknowledged in a letter from Trajan to his friend Pliny the Younger and is completely borne out by the names of architects that have come down to us. Cicero employed a Greek to build his villas. The archway at Verona bears the signature of Cerdo, a freedman. Apollodorus, who worked for Trajan and was possibly the most outstanding individual artist of the Antonine age, was a Greek from Damascus. When the Roman Vitruvius wrote his famous Latin treatise *On Architecture* in the reign of Augustus, he was still largely dependent on Greek sources and especially on the theorist Hermogenes who lived in the late 3rd and early 2nd centuries. In the art of building the Romans carried on the unbroken traditions of Hellenistic architecture.

But once this continuity is recognised, it is important to realise how far methods and technique were changing under the influence of fresh social and economic conditions. Concrete and brick were in widespread use by the early days of the Empire and led to innovations of the greatest importance which enabled sounder and larger structures to be built with greater speed. Building with blocks of stone in the Greek tradition was not given up, for in travertine the Romans had an excellent building material. It was used for the most carefully worked public buildings, like the Theatre of Marcellus and the Colosseum. Marble was employed for some temples built in imitation of Greek temples as, for example, the temple of Venus Genetrix in the Forum of Caesar and the temple of Castor and Pollux in the Roman Forum. Arches and vaults were not unknown to the Greeks, but it was not until the Roman period, in the great buildings demanded by the new way of life, that they were fully developed.

In fact, these technical advances were conditioned by the demands of the new society. Tenement houses, several storeys high, of the kind brought to light by the excava-

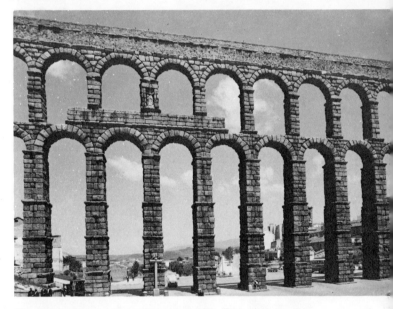

626. ROMAN. Aqueduct at Segovia, built in Trajan's reign (96–117). With 128 arches it is about half a mile long.

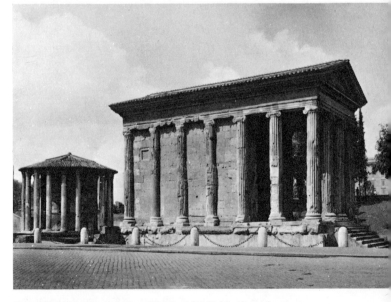

627. ROMAN. The 'temple of Fortuna Virilis' built in about the 1st century B.C. There is still some doubt as to its identification. In the background the temple of Vesta dating from the time of Augustus or earlier.

333

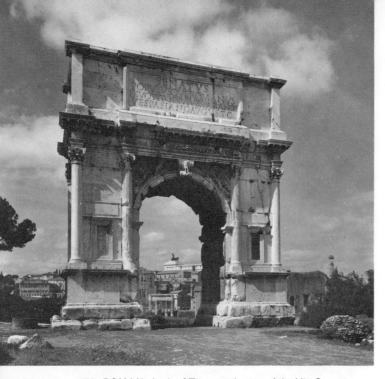

628. ROMAN. Arch of Titus, at the top of the Via Sacra. Erected to commemorate the victories won by Titus and Vespasian in the Judean War. A.D. 70.

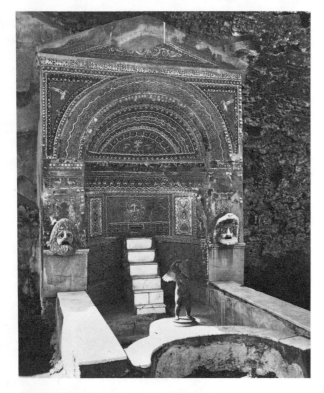

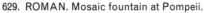

629. ROMAN. Mosaic fountain at Pompeii.

tions at Ostia, were needed to accommodate the increased populations of the large towns. They also needed spacious
624 porticoes with several aisles, called basilicas, where tribunals sat or those with nothing to do could pass the time
625 of day; colossal theatres that could hold the tens of thousands of spectators that came to watch animals or gladiators fighting; the lofty vaulted thermae which housed
626 public swimming baths and libraries; aqueducts with hundreds of arches which brought water from the mountains. So architecture was the expression of a new social and economic phenomenon—a population concentrated in towns and cities—which Rome developed to an un-

precedented point in the ancient world.

Besides this, architects working for Rome had to meet religious requirements unlike those that had existed in Greece. The Roman temple derived its high stone podium from the Etruscan temple which, unlike the Greek ones, had steps only up to the entrance façade. It also kept the deep porch leading into the cella which, as a rule, was without a surrounding colonnade. Various changes and adaptations therefore had to be made to features of Hellenic architecture. The outcome was, at times, a building of a very significant, heterogeneous kind. The very widespread pseudo-peripteral type, for example, consisted of a false continuous colonnade running round the outside of the cella (in fact a whole section of the 'colonnade' was imbedded in the walls); in this way the Roman temple, without making alterations to its original plan, came to look like a Greek temple from the outside. Such is the case with the 'temple of Fortuna Virilis' in Rome 627 and the Maison Carrée at Nîmes. It is a fine example of one of the essential characteristics of the art of this period —its intelligent adaptation of traditional forms to new needs.

The Roman aesthetic in architecture

The taste of the age inclined towards elaboration and even extravagance; thus it was that the Ionic Order, the most ornate in the Greek decorative repertoire, predominated over the more austere Doric, and similarly the Corinthian capital in its most lavish form was preferred to the Ionic capital. Mouldings and ornamentation became more and more elaborate; free use was made of rosettes, foliage, garlands and bull's-head reliefs. The Romans did not hesitate to combine several Orders in the same building, as the classical Greeks had already done, and even on the same façade which was something new: the Theatre of Pompey, built in 55 B.C., may be the first example of the superimposed use of all three Orders, with the Doric Order on the first level, next the Ionic and, at the top, the Corinthian. Far greater attention was being given to making a deep impression on the imagination and less to the balance and harmony of form and mass.

Architecture, then, in the Roman world was drawn in two opposite directions: there was the engineer with a purely functional end in view, and the educated, cultured architect engaged on academic pastiches. Its very finest achievements were the outcome of the first where, as in the arena at Nîmes or the Pont du Gard, the structure was perfectly suited to its purpose. When, on the other hand, architects found themselves in the position of applying Greek aesthetic ideas to a monument of an original type, they sometimes managed to produce successful combinations, the most outstanding of which was probably the triumphal arch. These impressive, vaulted gateways 628 were originally intended to be used as pedestals for groups of sculptures or trophies and were thus similar in function to the pillars and double-columned monuments that it had been the practice to erect in Greek sanctuaries. But it was not until the 2nd century B.C. that the idea was evolved in Rome of setting these pedestals on two tall piers joined by a vault, thus making them span a public highway. The idea was so successful that it was at once accepted and has remained in use till modern times.

Lastly we come to Hadrian's Pantheon built in Rome to take the place of the temple constructed by Agrippa in the reign of Augustus, and which, still standing today, has the oldest domed roof to have survived from the ancient world. Its architectural beauty stems not so much from the materials used, nor their pattern and rhythm but from the sheer size and proportions of the space spanned and enclosed. Few buildings have played such an influential part in the history of architecture.

So we see that Roman architecture emerged from a synthesis. Men bred upon the aesthetic traditions and techniques of Greece had to find an answer to those unexplored problems presented by the new Roman society. They used their imagination, as well as the many technical advances, to produce new forms which they were always concerned to incorporate into traditional Hellenic forms. The path they chose often strikes us with its modernity, but the great attention to ornamentation, characteristic of their building, shows that they were never aware of any break with the past. In this way they are a doubly fruitful example for us today, for they show quite clearly that a spirit of adventure and a respect for tradition are in no sense incompatible.

The plastic arts under the Empire

We find the same complexity in the field of the plastic arts: remarkably strong traditions, still rich in creative qualities, were sometimes brought in to serve new ideas. But here technical progress played nothing like the part it had done in architecture towards the formation of a new style. The painter, sculptor, goldsmith and engraver carried on, unchanged, the old working methods. Only one technical innovation should be pointed out: about the time of Hadrian, sculptors began to use purely plastic techniques to obtain certain effects which, until this time, had been rendered with the help of paint. Hair and beards were deeply under-cut to bring out dark shadows, and the pupils of the eyes were shown by an incision or by a ring carved in relief; flesh parts of a statue were given a more highly finished, lustrous polish. This was probably the first sign of a reaction that was to grow steadily against polychromy, the first split between painting and sculpture. As if they were now relying on materials alone to produce those polychrome effects for which the brush had been rejected, we can see about this time the increasingly extensive practice of using several differently coloured stones in the same statue—white, black and yellow marble, porphyry and red granite.

Apart from this one instance it is only in the minor arts that technical developments had any perceptible influence: in ceramics, where the generalised use of sigillated ornamentation was one of the reasons for its decline; in glassware, where from this time craftsmen had the materials 629 to produce masterpieces; and in mosaics, which now reached a peak of technical refinement. In all other fields technique changed hardly at all; it was aesthetic ideas alone which developed.

A conspicuous fact is that this development took the same course throughout the entire Empire. The strong centralisation of the Roman world with its political and economic unity helped to establish a uniform catholic civilisation which, in the realm of art, was conveyed by a common body of plastic themes. Greek art had conquered Rome and everywhere it imposed its own traditions and methods. Attempts to distinguish provincial styles have met with no success. It was hoped to find, for

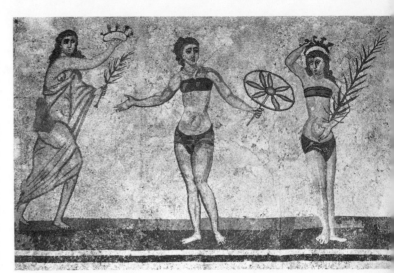

630. ROMAN. The 'Ten Girls' mosaic pavement. 3rd century A.D. Piazza Armerina, Sicily.

example, a 'linear' bias, basically opposed to the spirit of Graeco-Roman plastic art, in the monuments of Gaul, Germania and the Danubian countries. But these analyses are misleading; the argument depends on features which have nothing to do with the innate aesthetic bents of a particular people, but which are common to all unskilled sculptors from no matter what country. From Belgium to Syria, from Spain to Cyrenaica and including the provinces of the Greek mainland, we can discover sculpture less modelled than cut away in sharp and peremptory lines. In face of the modern taste for primitive art, we must be careful not to mistake crudity for style.

There was a still more obvious kinship between first-class works, no matter where they came from; so much so that we can talk of a universal artistic language, an artistic koine, as it is called, in the Roman world. The Gallic sculptors who decorated the buildings at Saint-Rémy-de-Provence were intimately acquainted with the plastic themes laid down by classical Greek painters and sculptors so that the large bas-reliefs of the mausoleum are virtual patchworks juxtaposing many extracts taken from Greek masterpieces, now transformed into artistic conventions. It is surprising to find on several Gallo-Roman monuments that Gauls are portrayed in a way which is more in line with the traditional Galatian type evolved by Pergamene artists than with contemporary reality. On trophies celebrating Rome's conquest of Gaul appear weapons and arms like the double-headed axe and the crescent-shaped shield that were attributes of the Amazons and obviously directly borrowed from the classical repertoire. Even in the provinces, then, art was closely dependent on Greek traditions, so powerful was the example that radiated out from Rome, Athens and the Greek cities of Asia Minor.

It can reasonably be assumed that collections of plastic themes circulated among studios and workshops; they are what are called 'pattern books'. In any case, artists themselves travelled a great deal: signatures of a great number of Athenian artists have come to light in Italy, like a certain Cleomenes who carved the fine prince as Mercury, now in the Louvre, and recent research has emphasised how extremely widespread are the signatures of artists from the Anatolian town of Aphrodisias in Caria

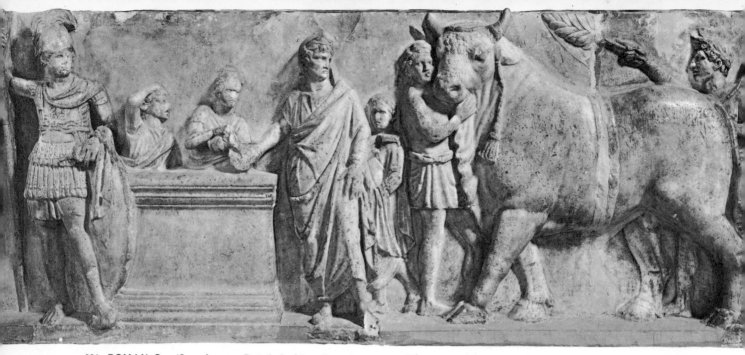

631. ROMAN. Sacrifice of a ram. Detail of a frieze from the 'Altar of Domitius Ahenobarbus'. Late 1st century B.C. *Louvre*.

during the first two centuries of the Christian era.

What was Rome's essential part in all this? Rome created the political framework within which all this intensive activity could go on, and, too, Roman taste and temperament helped to direct artists towards certain subjects and to strengthen certain trends in the development of style. These subjects and trends were not unknown in Greek art, especially in the Hellenistic period, but the wishes of Latin patrons had a great deal to do with the way this art was transformed in later years.

The vogue for history

So it was that these patrons undoubtedly encouraged the fashion for historical themes in architectural decoration. The Romans, of a factual turn of mind and aware that they were making history, loved to have their triumphs celebrated in the most minutely detailed descriptions. Greek artists had no difficulty whatsoever in satisfying this desire; Hellenic art is not without representations directly inspired by an actual event, from the Arcesilaus
610–611 Cup down to Alexander's Victory, preserved at second hand in a mosaic from Pompeii. When the Greek sculptor depicted the Battle of Pydna in a bas-relief treatment on the column of Lucius Aemilius Paulus at Delphi, he had no need to make innovations. But the Romans were especially fond of these pictures; when Roman generals made their triumphal entry, they had paintings of their victories carried in their procession. Although these paintings have disappeared we still have a series of bas-reliefs which evoke the glory of the legions and their leaders.
631 Even as early as the 1st century B.C. on the 'Altar of Domitius Ahenobarbus', armed legionaries watch a sacrifice which in ritual is specifically Roman. Under the Empire, artists liked to show the imperator either in the pose of the magnanimous conqueror, like Augustus on the silver vase in the Rothschild Collection, or in the heat of action, leading on his army to crush the enemy, as he appears on the frieze dating from Trajan's time which was later transferred, piece by piece, to the Arch of Constantine. The ideal outlined by Virgil was ever present: *'sparing the humbled and crushing the proud'*.

These martial scenes could be developed into epic narratives recording all the vicissitudes of a campaign. This is known as the continuous style in which the same figure, mostly the Emperor, appears several times in successive episodes. Apollodorus of Damascus was probably the first to think of unfolding a lengthy narrative in relief around a gigantic column. He designed the hundred-foot Column 606 of Trajan on which the expedition against the Dacians 632 was described in a full account lacking neither purely picturesque details, anecdotes nor even unnecessary repetition. It served as the pattern for the Column of Marcus Aurelius erected in the last quarter of the 2nd century. Sculptors did not make use of classical models for these long pictorial sequences: naturalistic elements, the result of first-hand observation, naturally came to play a more important part than ever before.

On the other hand when artists were dealing with religious or civic ceremonies, triumphal entries, processions, sacrifices, solemn assemblies of the people or the Senate, where the prince in all his majesty was revealed, they liked to mingle human and mythological figures, either gods or allegorical personages. On the Altar of Domitius 631 Ahenobarbus, the god Mars in person stands close by to watch the sacrifice. On the frieze of the Ara Pacis, built by Augustus between 13 and 9 B.C., a procession of priests, members of the imperial family and high dignitaries is set alongside a personification of Tellus, fruitful Mother 633 Earth. The famous cameo, the Gemma Augustea from 634 Vienna, shows Augustus and the goddess Roma seated side by side and surrounded by a group of various allegorical figures with Tiberius and Caius Caesar who were at this time (7 B.C.) the prince's appointed heirs. On the Arch of Titus, where the prince's triumphal entry is depicted with an obvious attention to realism (the seven-branched candlestick brought back from Jerusalem in the procession), the Emperor is nonetheless accompanied by a figure of Victory who crowns him while the goddess Roma rides at the head of the triumphal quadriga. The Cancellaria reliefs from the reign of Domitian and the Arch of Benevento from the reign of Trajan several times show the Emperor and his high officials at the side of figures like Apollo, Diana, Hercules and personifications of Honour and Valour. In keeping with Greek tradition, there was an easy interchange between the world of mortals and the world of gods. Consequently the apotheosis of a prince, a frequently treated subject, appeared as a natural occurrence.

It would therefore, be a mistake to dwell overmuch on Roman realism. Then, as before, artists were almost unable to think of the lofty style without some transmutation of reality; they continued to rely largely on myth. Purely realistic scenes belong mostly to folk art: they are found on sepulchral and votive bas-reliefs; similarly, in Greek art they appear primarily on painted vases. Roman taste, if it helped to steer artists in this direction, led to no decisive break with the past.

Landscape: nature and artifice

The growth of landscape painting is also usually ascribed to Roman influence. At this point let us recall that at heart the Romans had remained a nation of peasants, deeply imbued with an ancient, rustic atavism. The *Bucolics* and *Georgics* strike a chord even in our memories. The *Odyssey* paintings from the Esquiline, the frescoes from Livia's House on the Palatine, the stuccoes in the
609 Palazzo Farnesina, the pastoral decorations of the Pompeian houses, the so-called 'picturesque' bas-reliefs, can all these works be put down to the Roman's love of nature? They, in fact, all have a part in the most firmly established Hellenistic tradition. Plato, at a much earlier date, had referred to landscape paintings. Well known stories relate how Apelles and Protogenes liked to paint still-lifes with fruit and flowers in which they achieved highly successful illusionistic effects. Houses at Delos had been ornamented with painted garlands, anticipating
602 those produced by Augustan sculptors for the Altar of
633 Peace. The brilliant naturalism of these sculptures, like
635 that of the frescoes from Rome and Pompeii, was not, then, in any way an innovation. But here again it is true that the predominantly urban civilisation, as it existed in Rome from the 1st century A.D., fostered the desire for a
607 kind of escapism into nature. Rustic ornamentation and 'picturesque' reliefs were, in this sense, catering very much to the same needs as Virgil and Horace when they sang of the Mantuan countryside and the cool shades of Tibur. They reveal all the artifice of pastoral literature. Far from creating an accurate image of the Italian countryside, they are in fact works of the imagination, dream landscapes, sometimes even stage sets. These landscapes are dotted with statues, benches, shrines and tombs, and here and there spring up light and flimsy constructions of the kind that no architect has ever dared to build. The invention, towards the end of the 1st century A.D., of landscapes where the green countryside was adorned with colonnades was attributed to a certain Ludius about whom nothing definite is known. Although these landscapes have no more genuinely rural realism than a typical French garden, we can at least recognise the charm of these fantasies.

Similarly, when sculptors carved on those small marble plaques a peasant with his cow or a lioness with her cubs, the setting was always a conventionalised landscape: thus a genre was revived for Rome's benefit which may have been Alexandrian in origin and which, at all events, was Hellenistic. As a parallel to this, some of the fine silver
636 cups found at Boscoreale and Bernay, which have been assigned, probably correctly, to the time of Augustus, take up once again naturalistic, decorative motifs which the 4th-century Greek masters had painted so freely and

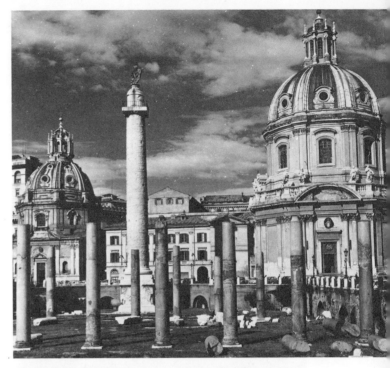

632. ROMAN. Trajan's Column in Trajan's Forum.

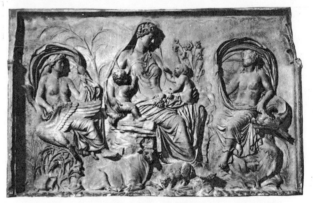

633. ROMAN. Relief from the Ara Pacis Augustae, Rome, depicting the three peaceful elements, air, earth and water. 13–9 B.C. *Uffizi, Florence.*

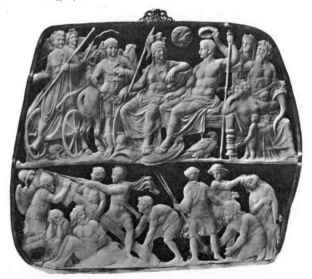

634. ROMAN. The Vienna Cameo, probably executed by the Greek engraver Dioscorides. 1st century A.D. *Bibliothèque Nationale, Paris.*

337

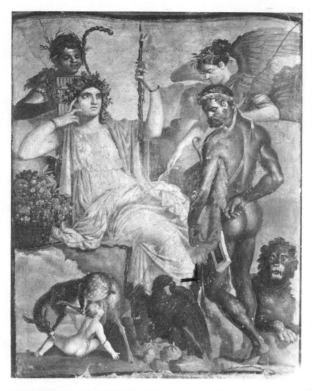

635. ROMAN. Allegorical painting, personifying Arcadia. End of 1st century A.D. *Naples Museum*.

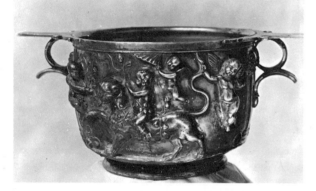

636. ROMAN. Bacchus goblet. Silver. Boscoreale Treasure. Late Augustan period. 1st century B.C. *Louvre*.

637. ROMAN. ARLES. Arena (2nd century A.D.) and theatre (1st or 2nd centuries A.D.).

which, if we are to believe Theocritus, the goldsmiths of his day were already able to chase on the sides of vases. So here once again, as in the case of the bas-relief, the Romans did not introduce anything really new: chiefly they comprised a wealthy and easily satisfied market for a traditional feature of Greek art and thereby gave it a fresh lease of life.

Did Rome invent portraiture?

We are left, then, with the problem of portraiture, the main stronghold of those who uphold the originality of Roman art. There is a well known, classic distinction between the Greek portrait, which tried to attain to a universal truth by transcending the individual, and the Roman portrait, whose sole aim, through photographic observation, was to catch an individual likeness. Once more the Roman realist and the Greek idealist are contrasted and once again we need to take a subtler view of the facts. Recent research has given us a more complete knowledge of the 'Republican' portraits, of those highly 638 individualised men with clean-shaven, deeply lined faces and stern expressions. We now know that their dates must be moved forward and that, for the most part, they cannot belong to a period before the reign of Sulla at the earliest. Their appearance, then, coincided with the large-scale arrival of Greek sculptors who, trained in Hellenistic traditions that had produced expressive heads and even 595 caricature, were well equipped to make realistic portrait 593 busts and were thus able to carry out the wishes of Roman families, eager to add to their collections of ancestor portraits. Roman Republican portraits were therefore the result of a combination of the technical abilities of Greek artists and the demands of Roman patrons. Hellenistic art had had little more to discover in the way of realism and physical likeness but favourable social and cultural conditions gave them more rein to develop.

It was not long, moreover, before Greek sculptors, following their models, returned to a conception of portraiture that was more in keeping with classical practice. Whereas the recently identified bust of Antony still shows signs of an automatic and rough realism, the face of Caesar, on the contrary, is imprinted with a more than human majesty, and the portraits of Augustus, allowing 586 for their necessary iconographical conformity, soon acquire the stature of a type, that of the magnanimous, enlightened prince. Greek art, which had previously given

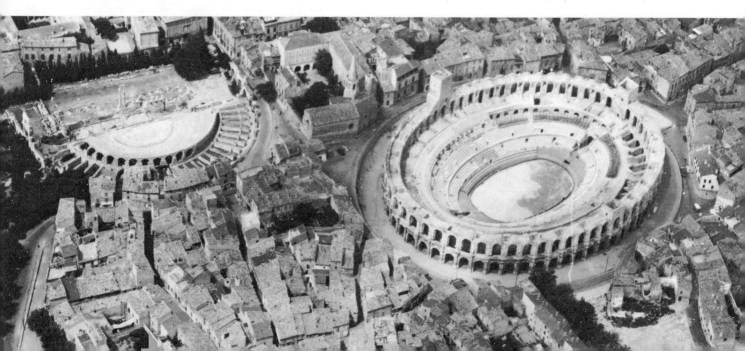

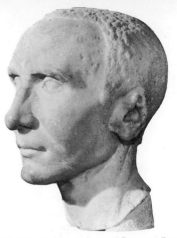

638. ROMAN. Head of an unknown Roman. First half of 1st century B.C. *Louvre*.

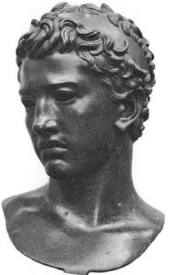

639. HELLENISTIC. Bust of Hiero II, King of Syracuse. 2nd century B.C.

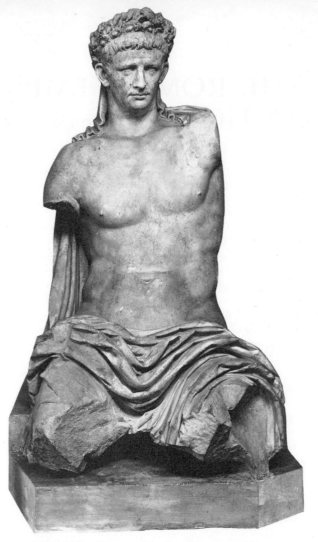

640. ROMAN. The Emperor Claudius (10 B.C. – A.D. 54). *Lateran Museum, Rome*.

expression to the divine nature of the Hellenistic monarch, had no difficulty in official portraits in marking out the progressive stages of a development which was gradually bringing the Emperor to the level of a god. The religion of the Empire and the mood of adulation was responsible for the increasing popularity of these portraits. Not only the Emperor but members of his family were portrayed without restraint: scholars today are trying to identify these busts with the help of textual allusions. Thus sculpture and engraved gems provide vivid commentaries to Tacitus and Suetonius; they give us, for example, the faces of Agrippa and his sons, the features of Germanicus and his wife Agrippina, as well as the distrustful mask of Claudius and the monstrous appearance of Nero. Some of these portraits are staggering psychological documents. Their creators have shown themselves to be worthy of the great Greek tradition of portraiture: they have not only preserved for us the outer facial expression or a passing mood but they have captured some profound truth about the man himself. Even with Tacitus to guide us, the imperial portraits remain remarkably revealing documents; they speak to us, unambiguously, of Hadrian's dilettantism, of the high-minded Marcus Aurelius and Caracalla's relentless cruelty.

This short description has been able to give only a partial idea of an art which was able to meet the needs of an entire world. We must remember the leading part which Greek artists played in it. Horace was right to say that Greece in defeat had won a victory over her untutored conqueror. Rome did not argue about Hellenic superiority in this realm. She provided Greek artists and craftsmen with wealthy and passive patrons whose wishes they could satisfy while educating their taste. Rather than a Roman art, then, it would be more meaningful to talk of Greek art in the service of Rome. It was a direct continuation of Hellenistic art and neither side was aware of any break. And this is important, for it enables us to see Greek art as a continuous development from the archaic period down to the time of the Byzantine Empire.

The art of the Roman period, viewed in this way, can be appreciated in a more legitimate fashion. Like every post-classical art, it was the trustee of a heavy load of traditions and knowledge by which it appears occasionally to have been overwhelmed. It has been called a decadent art as well as a lifeless, academic art. Yet if it did often preserve forms inherited from the past, they were frequently used to express new ideas. Now, in understanding the purpose for which they were intended, we come to appreciate the works themselves. When Franz Cumont's authoritative study demonstrated the symbolic qualities of the sarcophagus sculptures, he, at one and the same time, made a whole class of sepulchral monuments the subject of a passionate interest, that previously had been thought to be extremely dull. We should learn from this example and try to glean from the art of the Roman world all the evidence it has to give us of the society of which it was such a faithful reflection: we shall find that it offers as much enjoyment to the art lover as interest to the scholar.

339

THE ROMAN EMPIRE AND LATE ANTIQUITY *Ernest Will*

Although by the 3rd century A.D. *Roman art seemed to have reached its definitive form and was accepted, without protest, throughout the entire Empire, Roman territories covered such a vast area that inevitably provincial tendencies began to assert themselves, particularly in the East and above all in Mesopotamia which had been annexed at a later date. The 'barbarian' peoples that had been absorbed were exerting a growing influence which had an increasingly undermining effect. Hellenistic traditions, which as we have seen in the previous article played such a vital part, were now becoming more original, but Christianity was to appear and alter the entire course of art. It was the end of the ancient world.*

Art under the Severus Dynasty seemed, in its most outstanding characteristics, to be the natural development of the art of the preceding periods; the Parthian war depicted on the Arch of Septimius Severus in the Roman Forum is in the tradition of the Columns of Trajan and Marcus Aurelius, and its luxuriant, decorative style marks a return, possibly a conscious one, to the works of the Flavian era. But the discovery of monuments dating from the Severian period in the Emperor's native town of Leptis Magna in Tripolitania has cast some doubt on the validity of this view.

A new style

The large panels adorning the upper part of the four-sided archway at Leptis Magna reveal a completely unfamiliar style noticeable, for example, in the monarch's triumphal procession. The unrelated arrangement of figures, their almost rigid, frontal attitudes, the absence of perspective, particularly striking in the carving of the chariot, and of any feeling for depth, shown in the vertical treatment of the two rows of figures, and the decorative and graphic design of drapery betray ideas at work that were entirely alien to all those traditions that Rome had inherited from Greece. What is more, some of the ornate pilasters on this arch and in the city's basilica, while developing an already conventional ornamental motif of well established origins, are related to this same style in which decorative line, the interplay of light and shade and carving technique had ousted any feeling for modelling and organic form.

Byzantium does not seem very far away and it is obvious, in fact, that these monuments must have had connections with one of the sources on which the future Eastern capital was to draw. On analysis, we find that the ideas behind this style belong to 'Graeco-Mesopotamian' art, very well known nowadays, that was flourishing on the banks of the Euphrates in the first centuries of the Christian era. A work like the fresco of the tribune Terentius at Doura Europos makes the common source of inspiration very apparent. There was absolutely no reason why the Emperor, closely linked to Syria by his marriage to Julia Domna, should not have summoned Eastern artists to his native city, if not to the capital. Thus for the first time the provincial centres showed their

importance. If we take this opportunity to point out that these were the stylistic principles that were to come, slowly but surely, to dominate the art of Late Antiquity, it will be understood why the development of Roman art after a certain date should have appeared to be governed by a foreign influence, and more precisely, by the Eastern influence that was also the spirit behind Graeco-Mesopotamian art. The disturbing case of Leptis Magna, then, obliges us to take a look at some of the works of art that were being produced in the Roman provinces.

Rome's place in imperial art

This problem has bearings on the very definition of Roman art. Should we understand by this term an original contribution dependent on Rome's existence and produced in the city of Rome itself? Or should we widen it to cover the artistic output of the Mediterranean world unified under the Roman Empire, even though each province retained its individuality and even though it was left to Greece, or at least the Hellenised East, to give concrete expression to the aspirations of the new masters of the world? We can only try, faced with an unusually intricate set of facts, to isolate the major points of a complex phenomenon in the hope of arriving at a clear picture of its chief features.

There can be little doubt that the capital of the Empire formed an unrivalled artistic centre; the unique opportunities it offered and its social and intellectual ethos could hardly have helped producing a 'Roman' art. The existence of a Roman architecture, original in pattern, design, technique and ornamentation, is hardly debated. Rome is credited with the invention of the political and historical relief which in inspiration and treatment (notably the rendering of space) made a contribution that was not only new, but specifically Roman. There would be little point in denying that Rome depended continually on artists from the great defeated cities of the Hellenised East— Alexandria, Antioch, Pergamon—but it is also worth noticing that these uprooted artists should have achieved so little in the field of sculpture (which had been, after all, Greece's unsurpassed triumph) and so much in everything that catered to Roman taste. Rejection by Rome of the Greek heritage was never to be seriously considered, but it is nonetheless true that she needed to experiment with new ideas of which the most original were developed in the workshops and studios of the capital itself. A legitimate admiration for Greece should not prevent us from talking of the European Renaissance or of European classicism even though they both stemmed from the imitation of Hellenic ideals.

What is more difficult to appreciate is the influence that radiated from the capital as a centre of the arts. All the evidence compels us to distinguish between the Western and Eastern halves of the Empire, between barbarian provinces without any artistic traditions of their own and the ancient centres of the civilised world. In the West, in Gaul, Britain, Spain, North Africa and the lands bordering on the Rhine and the Danube, the many amphitheatres, theatres, baths, triumphal arches, bridges, villas, capitols and forums enable us to trace without difficulty the growth of an irresistible and radical process of Romanisation. From the time of Augustus, these monuments, like the temples of Gallia Narbonensis, show the direct influence of Rome. It is undoubtedly true that, here and there, some local centres of art were established. Thus it is that the numerous arches built in Gallia Narbonensis at the beginning of the Empire are clearly distinguishable, in details of architectural ornamentation and the place set aside for trophies and figurative scenes, from their Italian counterparts of the same date; but the idea, design and structure of this type of monument, nevertheless, stemmed directly from Rome.

There are other pointers, however, that encourage us to take a less simplified view. The Empire was crossed by military and trade routes which, despite the proverb, did not all lead to Rome. This explains why the type of mausoleum of which there are many examples in Syria and which was equally widespread in Roman North Africa and Spain, and even in north-west Gaul, appears to have been completely unknown in Rome and Italy. In the same way, the sepulchral pillars from Belgium and Germania which prove, right down to the middle of the 3rd century, that there was an especially active team of sculptors working in the provinces, show certain details of design and decoration which lead us to suspect that there was direct contact with some centre in the Hellenised East, in Anatolia or, more likely, in Syria. What in one case is an assumption, in another becomes definite fact. From the 2nd century, richly ornate sarcophagi were being used and their popularity was spreading. Working from differences in structure and ornamentation, modern experts have little difficulty in distinguishing the products of the main workshops whether Roman, Attic, 'Asiatic' (Anatolian) or Syrian. Now, it has been shown that the Hellenised East, Greece and Anatolia produced works largely for export and despatched them throughout the entire Empire, to Rome, Italy and the provinces. We also know that local production, especially on the Rhine and Danube, was more readily inspired by these Eastern models than by those from Rome, and that in fact Rome's influence outside Africa and Spain was only very weak.

641–643

The part played by the Hellenised East

It is not surprising to find that the Hellenised East, with an influence that extended even into the Western provinces, not only remained more true to its own traditions, whether Greek, Hellenistic or Eastern, but was also more conservative in face of specifically Roman innovations. True, certain functional buildings like the thermae achieved a popularity of unexpected permanence, and similarly Roman theatre design, with its monumental stage wall, was also adopted. But the East was to give only a very lukewarm reception to the historical and political relief and the triumphal arch. Generally speaking, vaults and arches, so typical of Roman architecture, were to come into conflict with Greek building principles; in contrast to the monumental gateway at Ephesus, which can be traced back to the Roman arch, stands a long list of traditionally Hellenic propylaea.

The complex relationship between the two halves of the Empire can perhaps be better illustrated, and Rome's exact part in it more clearly shown, by following through

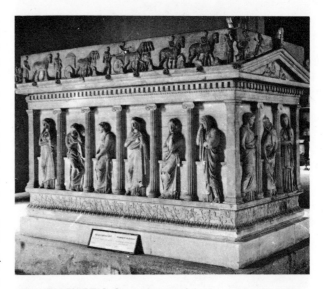

641. HELLENISTIC. Sarcophagus of the mourning women from Sidon. *Istanbul Museum.*

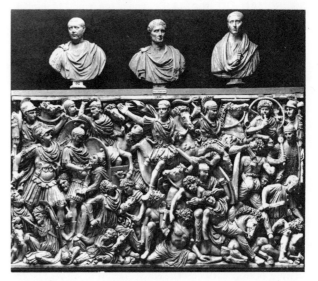

642. ROMAN. The 'Ludovisi' sarcophagus showing a battle between Gauls and Romans. 2nd–3rd centuries A.D. *Capitoline Museum, Rome.*

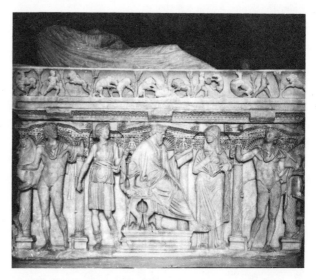

643. ROMAN FROM ASIA MINOR. Front of the Sidamara sarcophagus. 3rd–4th centuries A.D. *Istanbul Museum.*

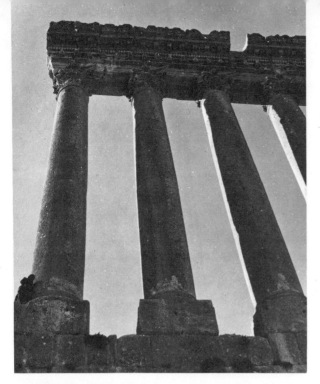

644. ROMAN ART IN ASIA. Column of the temple of Jupiter Heliopolitanus at Baalbek (Lebanon). Originally there were fifty-four columns, which at 65 feet high are among the tallest in the world. 1st–2nd centuries A.D.

the development of Syrian architecture. Thus Baalbek 644 (Heliopolis), which became a Roman colony under Augustus, is adorned with impressive temples that betray the hands of architects and decorative artists from Rome. Again, quite recently, sculptured ceilings have been found from the monumental altar of the courtyard of the Great Temple, which in ornamentation seem to be related, at least in part, to the work of artists engaged on the Ara Pacis. Elsewhere in Syria we find that, after the imaginative features and heterogeneous forms of the Hellenistic age, a standardised imperial style came to be established that was supposed to be a re-adoption of pure Greek 645 traditions. In a town like Palmyra this trend towards 'regularity' was growing steadily stronger in the intervening period between the consecration in A.D. 32 of the temple of Baal, a building still imbued with the Eastern

645. ROMAN ART IN ASIA. Monumental archway at Palmyra (Syria). About A.D. 200.

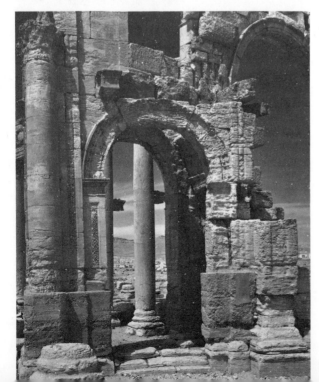

spirit, and the last building to be erected in the city. It is tempting to put this development down to the unifying influence of Rome which in every field secured a victory for Hellenism in the East. However, this imperial style was not the one used in Rome but that produced in the workshops and studios of Antioch, the ancient metropolis of Syria.

But if in discussing the Empire one at times makes more of a plea for specifically Roman impulses, and at others concentrates more on Hellenic traditions, the basic unity and regular rhythm of development of this art are nonetheless obvious; after all they were based on the same admiration of Greece and a uniform way of life under the aegis of Rome. It was only in later years that the latent opposition between the Eastern and Western halves of the Empire was to become an actual breach and it is not to this that we can look for an explanation of the appearance of a new art, the art of Late Antiquity.

Where, then, must we look to find the discordant voice in this choir that was singing in almost perfect unison? An eminent authority once maintained that the increasingly marked weakening of classical tradition was due to the overwhelming influence of the East, and the discovery of Graeco-Mesopotamian art has given weight to this theory. It can almost be seen as a foreshadowing of Byzantine art and, in any case, as an art essentially opposed to the Greek spirit, the spirit that had conquered Rome. It is a non-illusionistic art, concerned more with making things understood than with making them felt, an abstract art which ignores the diversity of nature and substitutes instead the uniformity of conventions, especially the convention of the frontal attitude where figures are always viewed full-face. It is an intellectual art, preferring graphic expression, the vocabulary of the relief or painting, to the reality of plastic form. And, lastly, it is a spiritual art in which the human body does not appear as the chief wonder. Thus the aspirations of the rising East shine powerfully through the faces of the Doura Europos frescoes.

Graeco-Mesopotamian art, an art in which the East built up a new form of expression after the death of its ancient arts, probably emerged in one of the great cities of Mesopotamia and existed in isolation on the outskirts of the Empire where its works were preserved in the cities of Palmyra and Doura Europos. There are no signs that it had any extensive influence outside its native country; Leptis Magna is without parallels elsewhere.

But as a matter of fact the main characteristics as we have analysed them are not uniquely the property of Graeco-Mesopotamian art; an abstract, non-illusionist, intellectual impulse and the use of conventions like the law of frontality are features common to a whole group of arts as well as to children's drawing and are therefore related to a stage of individual and collective development. Consequently, a theory of internal development seems preferable to a theory of foreign influences. It has, in fact, been possible to discover the expression of similarly 'primitivist' trends in the Western provinces of the 646 Empire and even in Rome itself in works, like sepulchral reliefs, that can be attributed to ordinary artisans. The problem takes on a new aspect: it seems that barbarian peoples in the East and West alike, emerging from the shadows, grew from subjects into citizens and took a decisive part in the Empire's history; and that, as the ideal

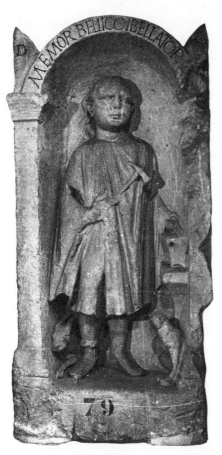

646. GALLO-ROMAN. Stele of the 3rd century A.D. *Sens Museum.*

of the ruling class changed, the antique vision of the classical world was doomed.

The 3rd century: crisis and transition

There was no more critical century in the history of Rome than the 3rd century A.D.—critical in the economic, political, military, as well as the intellectual and moral spheres. The Empire all but collapsed in the face of internal strife and outside pressures. It was the century in which Gaul, Anatolia and Syria were devastated, in which Dacia was evacuated and Palmyra destroyed. It is hardly astonishing that works of art are rare and that any great architectural achievements belong to the arts of war, like Aurelian's wall surrounding Rome. Otherwise there are only two kinds of work, sarcophagi and portraits, which enable us at the very least to understand something of the way in which art was developing. In the field of portraiture this grim age speaks with eloquence. The head of Septimius Severus with its wavy hair, curling beard and smooth skin was followed by the lined, haggard, clean shaven faces and close cropped heads of the military Emperors; the pleasure loving Africans had been succeeded by the austere Illyrian. The ruthless severity of a whole era is expressed in the Republican portrait's apparent return to realism. In the case of sarcophagi, the tension and trouble of the time was conveyed by pathos of expression and violence of movement, drawn from earlier 'baroque' tendencies, as well as by the use of the favourite lion-hunt theme.

One generation, it is true, is not like another; and as a general rule imperial art from the time of Augustus showed an alternation between Roman pathos and realism and Hellenising classicism. It was the latter that was behind the 'renaissance' in the reign of Gallienus, the Emperor-philosopher and friend of the great Plotinus: in his face one can recognise a conscious attempt to revive the Greek ideal.

But all this was really only a ripple on the surface that had no effect on the basic development of the period. Two examples will demonstrate this quite adequately. Take the monumental Ludovisi Sarcophagus on which a **642** battle between Romans and barbarians is depicted. This frantic tangle of writhing bodies, with faces distorted by pain, at first impressed itself as an extreme example of the 'baroque' style that had been taken over from earlier centuries. But we cannot avoid noticing the absence of any landscape features that might have given the figures a realistic, spatial setting, the compression of figures, all squashed into the foreground and arranged on the same plane. The word 'tapestry' would not be out of place in describing the general effect of the gilt and painting that had adorned early monuments. Later we find artificial compositions, noticeable in the way the victorious Romans at the top are separated from the defeated barbarians below, and in the central place given to the dead hero in the role of a conquering general; portrayed in a frontal pose and as the supreme master of the situation, he is set apart from all the incidental happenings going on around him and directs a compelling stare at the spectator. Now the work no longer pretends simply to narrate an exploit but, by using an almost theatrical technique, presents the spectator with an object of reverence and admiration. It is a long way from the Alexander of the **610** celebrated Naples mosaic.

Another sarcophagus from the reign of Gallienus has a characteristic theme—a meeting of philosophers. Violent movement has given way to the peace of metaphysical reflection; there is no mistaking the breath of a Hellenic spirit, dedicated to gravity, lucidity and lofty moral discipline. But in every other way there is the same axial composition related to a central figure, the same frontal pose and the same didactic purpose. There is the same two-dimensional vision as well: for the first time a Roman relief offers us the front view of a seated figure, but the foreshortening technique needed to depict the thighs has been derived from painting, not from sculpture.

Everywhere there were signs of this decaying plastic sensibility. Production stopped in the workshops of sculptors and copyists that had once been so busy; temples were no longer filled with statues of gods and heroes. Paganism, which might seem the stronghold of Graeco-Roman tradition, had in fact discovered new gods and new forms of worship. Philosophico-mystical sects, Eastern religions, mystery cults, astrological speculations, all were working in their own way, every bit as much as militant Christianity, for the victory of the abstract. Even in the realist portraits of the early part of the century, it is their powerful expressions that most impress us, expressions that lay bare the state of the soul.

The East made its most powerful and decisive contribution to this course of development, by spreading abroad its ideas and beliefs. Plotinus, the most representative mind of the age, formulated the principles of a new aesthetic that have been shown to conform absolutely to the ideas behind the art of Late Antiquity. An

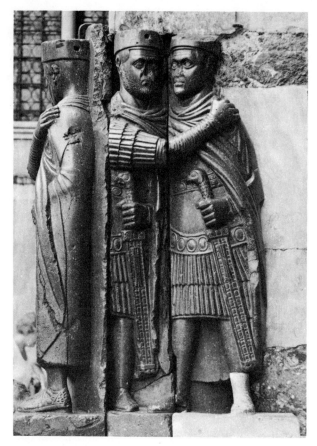

647. LATE ROMAN. The Tetrarch Group in the facade of St Mark's, Venice.

avowed follower of Plato, he was already a Byzantine Greek, in whom the old ideal of the harmonious union of body and soul was forgotten before the sovereign importance of the mind.

If we are to judge the age by what it produced, then our assessment will be largely a negative one; by the end of the century it seems nothing will stop the decay. Not a single new formula has emerged from the encounter of all the diverse and antagonistic forces that were brought together. One watches the world built by Greece crumbling away, the decay of Greek sensibility, the death of its artistic vision, and we find no clear signs of an approaching spring.

Diocletian and the beginning of Late Antiquity

There were good reasons why it was proposed to date the beginning of Late Antiquity in art from Diocletian's accession to the throne (A.D. 284); the close of this era was to be marked by the invasion of the Lombards in the West (568), and in the East by the death of Justinian (565). We do not need to go as far as that, but can close our enquiry with the disappearance of one of the major factors in the ancient world, namely paganism, overthrown in the reign of Theodosius (379–395).

Diocletian's political and military achievement in consolidating the Empire and, as it were, reshaping it was matched by a revival in the realm of art. Many different tendencies, some of which came from the provinces, were to vie with trends stemming from the classical heritage and called attention to the great diversity which was finally acknowledged by the Emperor when he estab-

lished the Tetrarchy. Here again any attempt at reunification was left until the reign of Constantine, when a mode of expression in keeping with the spirit of the age was found, of course in new formulas, certainly, but also in respect for tradition. For there could be no question of a break; Late Antiquity carried on the work of Antiquity.

Work under the Tetrarchy, then, was primarily concerned with restoration. The great Roman Emperors were builders, and neither Diocletian nor Constantine proved an exception to the rule. In the meantime, before Constantinople became the new Rome, great cities were built throughout the Empire: Milan, Trier, Salonica, Nicodemia. Very little of this tremendous activity has survived the ravages of time. It is likely, however, that architects of this period had neither lost the bold spirit of their predecessors, nor forgotten the example they had set. The Thermae of Diocletian in Rome shows only the persistence of tradition, and one of the most impressive buildings of this period, the Basilica in the Roman Forum, started by Maxentius, very far from anticipating the Christian type of basilica, presents one last victory for the Roman arcade and vault. Were there signs of a new inspiration in the palace where the master of the world resided? Diocletian's palace at Spalato (Split in Yugoslavia) appears to be traditional in details of design, a villa on the usual pattern, a conventional type of temple and an octagonal mausoleum of a form that was not without precedents. If the architect and craftsmen came from the Hellenised East, as the ornamental features seem to indicate, the East had not advanced decisively.

New forms were to emerge from new schemes and ventures; the Christian architect's great triumph was to be the creation of the basilica and the development of the shrine, a two-fold invention in which the supreme importance of architecture in Rome has always asserted itself, just as the supreme importance of Rome in architecture has of course always asserted itself.

We find the same monumental tendencies in the revival of the historical and political relief, well established in Roman traditions; a whole group of monuments, from the base of the *Decennalia* in the Roman Forum to the Column of Arcadius at Constantinople, illustrate the final flowering of this state art. The same time-hallowed subjects appear again and again and in decorative motifs one frequently comes across old, worn out clichés. Even in style, the monuments of the Tetrarchy have no distinctive originality and always exhibit a marked weakening of plastic ability and a bias in favour of frontal attitudes and axial composition. The Arch of Galerius at Salonica, built on Greek soil by Greek artists, has one new feature that was to be used again on the Column of Arcadius. Adopting an ancient Eastern formula, scenes are arranged in superimposed friezes; but what really strikes the attention is the complete disregard for the architectural structure that the use of this method reveals.

In the Arch of Constantine in the Roman Forum, the new trends reach an unexpected peak. The structure itself continues the purest Roman traditions; moreover, a whole sequence of figured panels are borrowed from 2nd-century monuments—only the heads of monarchs are, as it were, brought up to date. But there are some small narrative friezes that recount the victories of Constantine and his deeds of chivalry, and here we seem to be carried into another world. Figures stand out in flat relief and are hardly modelled at all; details are emphasised by cutting away, and it is more a matter of draughtsmanship than sculpture. The frontal orientation, the axial and symmetrical composition focus attention upon the main figure. There is a lack of sophistication about these scenes and a certain incompetence in execution (with a kind of simple vitality, it should be said) which lead one to suspect a Roman workshop working in the traditions of folk art.

In later years, this primitivist folk trend was never again to find such full expression; the base of the Obelisk of Theodosius in Constantinople shows a return to classicism, perceptible in a style that was both more monumental and more elaborate, but it was a return that allowed for the pictorial treatment of scenes and the victory of the law of frontality and intellectual composition, the victory, in short of all those non-illusionist ideas that form the essence of Late Antique art.

Portraiture and the rise of a new spirit

This development described above becomes much clearer if we follow the development of portraiture. By the reign of Diocletian, portraits were beginning to show signs of the great changes that were to come. After the head of Gallienus, striving after Greek beauty, we come to the porphyry group from St Mark's in Venice where we feel we have been carried right into the Middle Ages, and yet this work represents a group of Tetrarchs. We have seen the last of Hellenic beauty with its rounded forms, subtle modelling, soft lines and its inimitable knowledge of the human body. Now the human figure is short and stocky, stiffly posed, and limbs are roughly shaped. Even more striking is the way the head is treated: a solid mass, nearly square in shape with the features of the face looking almost as if they have been added afterwards, drawn in and entirely dominated by the staring expression of the eyes. It is a barbarian work, perhaps, but one with an assured unity of conception and of unarguable power. Not all the works produced under the Tetrarchy were of this kind. A head in the Doria-Pamphilii Palace, for example, probably of Diocletian himself, makes certain concessions to tradition in order to tone down the geometric, abstract effect. But dissimilarities of this kind can be accounted for by the existence of different studios; the head of Diocletian just mentioned and others like it are Roman works, while the Venetian group, the best known of another series, was produced by provincial artists, by Orientals who were virtually unhampered by Greek traditions.

Popular folk art and provincial arts—these, in fact, were the sources with the power to rejuvenate decaying classical traditions. No original way of uniting the old and the new was to be found until the reign of Constantine. But this did not happen all at once. On the Arch of Constantine, the heads of the Emperor included in the 2nd-century panels seem to us to be inspired with a spirit different from that which pervades the small friezes; these vivid, life-like heads appear to give full expression to classical traditions. Yet, although the colossal head in the Forum basilica has adopted from Greece the rounded forms and attention to the organic structure, it nonetheless remains an abstract, intellectual work; the real life of this face lies in the huge eyes with their remote, imperious expression, eyes that command the spectator's respect and reveal to him the superhuman qualities of the new *dominus* at the head of the Empire.

But in that age, dedicated to a quite different ideal, a loyalty to the perfection of Greek forms was to produce works of art in which a great variety of elements were subtly blended. Sometimes, as in the period known as the 'Theodosian renaissance', stress was put on the beauty of form and purity of line while less emphasis was given to the statue's subject as an ideal; the head of Valentinian II from Aphrodisias in Caria is an example. Sometimes, on the other hand, and especially in portraits of private individuals, the spirit of the age was revealed more openly. If the head of Valentinian reminds us in a certain way of archaic Greek works at the time of their decline, other statues from the reign of Theodosius have prompted the term 'Gothic': the elongated face, the extremely delicate features and the detached, reflective expression give these figures an ethereal, remote appearance.

This was, indeed, the perfect expression of the new ideas and beliefs that upheld the superiority of mind over matter and the soul's transcendence over the body. The power of this form of idealism explains the decline of sculpture; it still survived in reliefs which were linked to state propaganda and in the portrait-statue; but the sarcophagus-producing workshops that had flourished for two centuries were at a standstill by the end of the 3rd century and it was only the elaborately figured Christian sarcophagi that, for propagandist reasons of another kind, were to have one last period of prosperity in Rome, Italy and Gaul. The decline of the major arts of the classical period—with the exception of architecture—was symptomatic; their place was taken by arts that until this time had been regarded as less important. Sculpture was replaced by painting and above all by mosaics, which were destined for a brilliant future; as the appreciation of plastic qualities decayed, the love of everything decorative and ornamental blossomed.

Consequently, the so-called minor arts flourished too. We have a number of cameos from this time devoted to the glorification of the monarch. Then there was the development of ivories, diptychs and triptychs, with a popularity that was to last for a very long time, the fashion for which was originally connected with the appointment of high officials. They are works, too, that have a great deal to do with the end of a long struggle that the last representatives of paganism, notably members of the Roman aristocracy, had waged against the protagonists of the new religion. These ivories seem to have caught the last dying rays of ancient and classical grace, ivories that bear the names of members of the Symmachus and Nicomachus families, and the one which probably provides us with a portrait of Claudian, the last pagan Latin poet and possibly the last great poet of Antiquity. To these one could add the ornate figured gold and silver plate of which we still have some idea from official records, like the missoria, and from private treasures that have come to light, mostly in the West.

Spiritual and artistic development at this point again caught up with social development. In the 4th century we watch the victory of the class of great landowners and high dignitaries, in Rome and throughout the Empire.

It was in this parade of ornate extravagance that the taste and the arrogance of these feudal lords found expression, in this ethos of ostentation and splendour with which we still associate the term Byzantine.

HISTORICAL SUMMARY: Hellenistic art

ARCHAEOLOGY

See beginning of Historical Summary for Chapter 5 (p. 285).

HISTORY

In 336 B.C. Philip was succeeded by his son Alexander who first dealt with an attempted revolt in Greece and then declared war on the Persians. He defeated Darius III at the battle of Granicus in 334 and the battle of Issus in 333, liberated the Ionian Greek cities, conquered Syria and seized Egypt where he founded the port of Alexandria. In 331 after the battle of Guagamela (Arbela) he marched into Babylon, Persepolis and Ecbatana, married a Persian princess (Roxana) and in 327 embarked on the invasion of India. He got as far as the Ganges but did not continue his march of conquest and on the return journey, at Susa in 323, he died.

His successors, the Diadochi, involved themselves in ruthless struggles for the control of the world empire, all of which ended either in defeat or in their death; in 301 at the battle of Ipsus and 281 at Corupedium, Ptolemy, the son of Lagos, came to power in Egypt, Seleucus in Asia, and Antigonus Gonata in Macedon, while the Attalids made Pergamon one of the capitals of the Hellenistic world. In the West, from the end of the 3rd century Rome was beginning to annex Greek territories; first Magna Graecia was occupied and then Sicily in 322 at the end of the Punic War and despite Pyrrhus' intervention. After the defeat of Philip V at Cynoscephalae (197) and Perseus at Pydna (168), Macedon became, in 149, a Roman province. In the East the Treaty of Apamea (188) completed the Seleucids' overthrow; in 133 Attalus III bequeathed the kingdom of Pergamon to the Romans who in turn annexed Cyrene (96), Cyprus, and following Sulla's victory (86) over Mithridates, King of Pontus, occupied Greece.

ARCHITECTURE

A large number of temples were either built or reconstructed. In Greece, the Doric Order was virtually abandoned except for reconstructions (third temple of Apollo at Delos) and small temples of the distyle in antis type (temples of Asclepius at Agrigentum, of Serapis at Taormina, of Isis at Delos). It was used more frequently in Asia Minor but with modifications relating to design,

proportion, treatment of columns and mouldings (temples of Athena at Troy and at Pergamon). The Ionic Order underwent similar modifications; the temple of Apollo at Didyma, which in large part dates from this time, kept a classical appearance. Changes made their appearance in a second period (temples of Apollo Smintheus at Chryse in Troada, and of Aphrodite at Messa in Lesbos). The rules of this Order were codified in the 2nd century by the architect Hermogenes who made considerable modifications both to proportion and ornamentation (temples of Dionysus at Teos [193], of Artemis at Magnesia-ad-Meandrum, the altar of Athena Polias at Priene [168–156]). The inspiration for the temple of Apollo at Alabanda in Caria was drawn from these principles. The Corinthian Order was established at this time as a real Order, illustrated by the temple of Olympian Zeus at Athens which was begun in 164 by Cossutius, architect to Antiochus IV. Similarly in Asia Minor the late 2nd-century temple of Hecate at Lagina in Caria was built in the Corinthian Order.

Monuments appeared at this time of a type later to be developed by the Romans: the Rotunda of Queen Arsinoe at Samothrace and the Doric Cabirion with its long narrow nave culminating in an apse; the sanctuary of the Bulls (3rd century) and the Pillared Hall at Delos (208–207).

One remarkable feature of Hellenistic architecture was the progress it made in town planning both in rebuilt ancient towns and in the new ones. More and more roads, intersecting at right angles, were lined with colonnades (Priene, Antioch, Apamea); porticoes were increasing in number: the 'winged' stoa like the porticoes of Antigonus (c. 254) and Philip V (212–205) at Delos, and the Pergamene stoa, modelled on the one surrounding the temple of Athena Polias (250), as seen in the porticoes of Eumenes II and Attalus II in Athens. Design of market places was becoming regular (Ephesus, Miletus and Magnesia-ad-Meandrum) with buildings designed for popular assemblies (Bouleuteria at Priene, Assos, Thasos and Miletus) and citizen bodies: Italian Agora, the buildings of the Poseidoniastae at Delos (110).

Theatres were greatly altered as a result of the disappearance of the chorus and the increased importance of dialogue: the parascenia vanished, the proscenium was enlarged with an elaborately decorated back wall (theatre

at Athens, which was rebuilt in 150, and those in the Peloponnese, at Priene, Assos and Ephesus). The Hellenistic dwelling house was of unpretentious size but becoming increasingly luxurious. In the 3rd century (Priene) the central part of the house was still the megaron with a prodomos leading on to a large courtyard and completed by smaller rooms and outbuildings. In the 2nd century (Delos and Rhodes) rooms were arranged around a central courtyard with a Doric peristyle and a central pool, and were adorned with stucco-work, paintings and mosaics.

SCULPTURE

Classical traditions. In 3rd-century Athens the masters in the classical tradition were Cephisodotus and Timarchus, the sons of Praxiteles, who produced a statue of Menander in 293–292, probably the prototype of the Medici Aphrodite and the original of the Medici krater; the Cupids, Satyrs and Aphrodites illustrate Praxiteles' continuing popularity, while the influence of Scopas is apparent in several emotive heads (Pourtales Apollo, Castellani Apollo, the Dying Alexander). Portraits of statesmen and philosophers (Polyeuctus' Demosthenes, 280–279) and statues of athletes took their inspiration more from the tradition of Lysippus which was kept alive by his sons at Sicyon. This school produced Eutychides, the creator of the Fortune of Antioch, Chares of Lindos who made the Colossus of Rhodes. Attic influence was also strong in Thasos (Choragic Monument).

In the 2nd century, Delos was open to every kind of influence: the presence of classical tradition is plain from certain copies and interpretations (Polycleitus' Diadumonos, Cephisodotus' Eirene). In the Peloponnese, Damophon of Messina produced an over life-size group for the sanctuary of Lycosura; the Aphrodite of Melos (Venus de Milo [**616**]) also dates from this time.

In the 1st century, Athens was the centre of the 'neo-Attic' revival, which drew its inspiration from archaic as well as classical works: Apollonius (the Belvedere Torso) and Glycon (the Farnese Hercules) went back to the tradition of Lysippus. Pasitiles claimed to be of the Peloponnesian school, while sculptors of the archaising style imitated 6th-century sculpture (the Poitiers Minerva [**622**] and the Munich Athena). Decorative vases (the Bor-

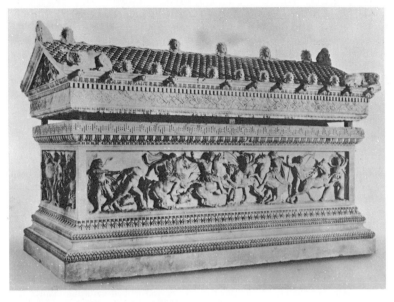

648. HELLENISTIC. The Alexander
Sarcophagus. Last quarter of 4th
century B.C. *Istanbul Museum.*

ghese krater and the Sosibios amphora)
and votive reliefs also belong to this
period.

Classical tradition made its appearance in the 3rd century at Pergamon in copies and through the visits of Greek artists like Niceratus, Phyromachus and Antigonus of Carystus. This school's first original contribution was the votive offering of Attalus I erected in 228 to commemorate his victory over the Galatians, of which a smaller copy was made for Athens in 201. The Galatian figures of the sculptor Epigonus probably set the pattern for all the 'dead' or 'dying' Gauls of the Hellenistic period [**614**].

Its second contribution was the Great Altar of Zeus and Athena Nicephorus (197–159) dedicated by Eumenes II (197–159); a Gigantomachy was depicted on the main frieze, over four hundred feet long, in very high relief, and the legend of Telephus, more pictorially, on the interior frieze.

There were thriving workshops in other Ionian cities: Doedalsas of Bithynia (3rd century) was the creator of the crouching Aphrodite type, while Boethus of Chalcedon (2nd century) produced the Boy with a Goose. In the 2nd century, Myron of Thebes was the leader of the Smyrna school; Agasias, son of Dositheus and creator of the Borghese Gladiator, came from Ephesus, as did Agasias, son of Menophilus, who produced the Dying Gaul for the Italian Agora at Delos. Tralles was the centre of a great variety of trends—classical (over life-size Apollo, Youth in Repose), archaicising (Caryatid), and Pergamene (picturesque reliefs and the Farnese Bull by the brothers Apollonius and Tauriscus, 2nd century).

Rhodes, like Delos, was affected by a

probability a Rhodian master who, in the 2nd century, created a Victory standing on the prow of a ship for the sanctuary of the Cabeiri at Samothrace [**650**]; in the 1st century Agesander, Polydorus and Athenodorus were the creators of the Laocoön group in the strictest Pergamene tradition [**618**].

Syrian works are often of only mediocre standard; there are some sarcophagi from Sidon (the so-called Alexander Sarcophagus [**648**] and the Aphrodite from Doura Europos, and the Aphrodite, Pan and Eros from the buildings of the Poseidoniastae at Delos.

The Alexandrian school remains comparatively unknown despite recent discoveries (statues from the temple of Serapis at Memphis). Certainly a large part of its earliest works were of Egyptian deities, Amon, Isis, Serapis and the Nile god, in the Greek style. Originally, too, it produced realistic types—old men, dwarfs, Negroes and Semites, as well as extremely fine portraits of Ptolemaic and Nubian princes. Pictorial reliefs [**609**] also owe their popularity to this school. In Cyrene, classical tradition and the style of Praxiteles remained strong.

PAINTING

The attempt to reconstruct what painting at this time was like must, as for earlier periods, be made with the help of descriptions, a few paintings and Italian mosaics. The Pergamene school drew its inspiration mostly from history and mythology, the Alexandrian school from the Aphrodite and Eros legends. The mosaic in the House of the Faun at Pompeii is probably a reasonably faithful copy of an early 3rd-century painting by Philoxenus of Eretria of a scene from the Battle of Gaugamela [**610**].

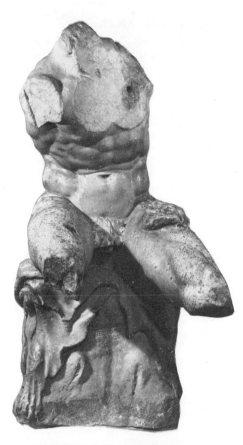

649. HELLENISTIC. Belvedere Torso,
signed by Apollonius. Marble. 1st
century B.C. *Vatican Museum.*

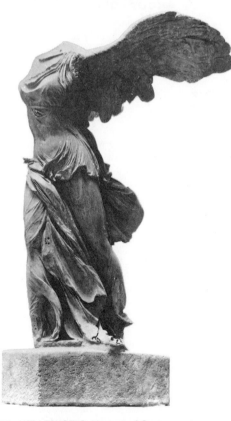

650. HELLENISTIC. Victory of Samothrace. *c.* 200 B.C. The left wing, right
breast and square pedestal are
modern. *Louvre.*

347

MINOR ARTS

The popularity of metal vessels increased: to the objects of the Tarentum treasure should be added a cup from Bari, some vases of the Boscoreale and Hildesheim treasures, and bronze cinerary urns [636].

It was, too, the great period for terra-cotta figurines: the craftsmen of Tanagra (late 4th–2nd centuries) became the acknowledged masters in the production of statuettes of women and children. There must have been workshops in all the artistic centres of Asia Minor but it is those at Myrina, Tarsus and Smyrna that are especially well known with their collections of grotesque figures and copies of famous works. Painted terra-cotta vessels had not altogether disappeared (vases from Gnathia) but vases with relief ornamentation were coming to be preferred (dishes from Megara, vases from Cumae and Canosa).

The Hellenistic period was also outstanding for its many coins, occasionally of high quality, the advent of cameos (Vienna Cameo [634], Gonzaga Cameo) and for jewellery which in its showy workmanship and lavishness sometimes lapsed into poor taste.

Roman art

ARCHAEOLOGY

See beginning of Historical Summary for Chapter 5 (p. 285).

HISTORY

According to legend, Rome was founded in the middle of the 8th century B.C. A manufacturing and trading city governed by the *rex* and Senate, it grew rapidly despite the defensive wars which it was forced to wage against the Gauls (390), Samnites (343–341; 328–312; 311–280) and the Tarentians who had united with Pyrrhus, King of Epirus (281–270). Once in control of Italy, Rome clashed with Carthage which was defeated in the course of two Punic wars (264–241; 219–201). From this time onwards Rome embarked on wars of conquest, against Macedon and Syria in the east and against Spain in the west.

But serious changes resulted from these wars: the growth of large estates, the waning of the middle class, an increasing urban plebeian population and the formation of a professional army brought about an economic crisis followed by civil wars, hatched by ambitious men like Marius, Sulla, Pompey and Caesar; the latter, however, after his conquest of Gaul (58–51) and victory over Pompey (48), used his dictatorial powers for the common

good, and the rule of Octavius Augustus (30 B.C.–14 A.D.), his adopted son, opened up a period of prosperity, the age of the *Pax Romana*.

The ambiguity of imperial power was to govern Rome's fate: this power, which, in reality, was absolute, had to be granted afresh at the beginning of every reign by a special delegation over which the Emperor, through the practice of adoption, tried to gain some say. But this ambiguity, which was to continue until the reign of Diocletian, led to friction between the Senate and the legions and involved the régime in strife and bloodshed. However, for a long time it had little effect on the prosperity of the Empire and some Emperors were extremely conscientious administrators.

From 14 to 68 Rome was ruled by the Emperors of the House of Augustus; Tiberius, Caligula, Claudius [640], Nero, all jeopardised sovereign authority. In the years 68 and 69 Galba, Otho and Vitellius followed each other in quick succession, and the Flavians (69–96) with Vespasian and his two sons Titus and Domitian (notorious for his Christian persecutions) ended the line of the Twelve Caesars.

The Antonines (96–196) established a line of wise rulers consisting of Nerva, Trajan, his adopted son, whose cousin Hadrian adopted Antoninus, the step-father of Marcus Aurelius. After the murder of his son Commodus came the Syrian Emperors, so called because the first of them, Septimius Severus, had married Julia Domna, a Syrian. His son Caracalla and grandson Heliogabalus reverted to a tyrannical form of rule. The murder of Alexander Severus, the last of this line, opened the period of military anarchy (235–268).

Following this, Claudius II, Aurelian and Probus devoted themselves to combating the barbarian invasions.

Diocletian, with the Tetrarchy of 284, tried to save the Empire: it was divided in two, under an Emperor of the West and an Emperor of the East (in Byzantium) who were aided by two Caesars. But under the continual threat of invasion—from central Europe in the West and from the Parthians, and later the Persians, in the East—the time came when the Western Empire, in the throes of anarchy, could no longer withstand the barbarian hordes. Constantine, in establishing his capital at Byzantium (330), and Theodosius, in dividing the Empire between his two sons Honorius and Arcadius, were only facing up to the actual state of affairs.

ARCHITECTURE

Tufa, perperino and, later, the more durable travertine were initially used

for walls built of rectangular blocks of stone (*opus quadratum*). But from the 2nd century the discovery of cement, where stones were sunk in a mixture of sand and fragments of volcanic rock, made a great difference to building methods, and by the time of Hadrian brick was becoming widespread.

There are few examples of the Doric Order; its place was taken by the Tuscan Order (with a base); the Ionic Order was used less than either the Corinthian Order which had been derived from it or the Composite Order in which the capital combined the Ionic scroll with the acanthus leaves. The Romans, in particular, exploited the possibilities of vaults to the utmost; taken over from the Etruscans, waggon vaulting was used to cover porticoes, passages and stairways, and ribbed vaulting, domes and half-domes for large halls.

Roman cities were usually laid out on a geometrical pattern with a road running north-south (the *cardo*) cutting an east-west road (the *decumanus*) at right angles, with the forum at their juncture. Cities were protected by ramparts, embellished with porticoes, columns and arches, had a water supply from aqueducts and were linked by straight highways. Necropolises built outside the city gates offer a wide variety of sepulchral architecture, from the columbarium reserved for cremated remains to the real temple-tomb.

Most religious and public buildings were grouped around the forum; Roman temples took features from both Etruscan and Greek traditions. Generally of medium size, they were set on a high podium with a flight of steps leading up to a porch one or more columns deep, which led into a simple or complex cella of pseudoperipteral type with columns or pillars.

Basilicas were designed for tribunals, trading markets and meeting places; only much later were they to take on a specifically religious character. In appearance they were of a large rectangular shape divided into aisles by rows of columns, the entrance being placed on the short front facing the apse (Greek style) or on the longer side (Eastern style) [624].

Thermae (baths) were complex structures: they sometimes had separate quarters for men and women and included, besides the actual bath, a *calidarium*, *tepidarium* and *frigidarium* as well as rest rooms, meeting halls, libraries, porticoes and gymnasia.

There was a wide variety of buildings of entertainment: theatres, amphitheatres made up of two adjoining theatres thus forming an oval arena, circuses and hippodromes. Theatres were composed of an auditorium and a semicircular orchestra with a deep stage dominated by a high back wall. The auditorium, sometimes hollowed out of a hillside, was more often built up and supported on vaulted corridors which also served as exits and entrances.

City-dwellers lived in multi-storey tenements, built in *insulae* (blocks) bounded by four roads; the *domus*, country or private residence, included both the *atrium* and *tablinum* of Etruscan houses and the Hellenistic villa's peristyle, and generally had a garden.

Earliest period to Flavian times.

In the 4th and 3rd centuries the great highways out of Rome were planned: the Appian and Latinian Ways (4th century) as well as the Flaminian Way which was begun in 220 by Gaius Flaminius, the consul, who also built the Circus Flaminius.

In the 2nd century the first basilicas were erected—Basilica Porcia, by Cato the Elder (184), Basilica Aemilia, Basilica Sempronia and Basilica Opimia, as well as porticoes, arches and bridges. The round temple near the Tiber is a reconstruction of a temple dating from this period.

The 1st century B.C., with Sulla, Pompey, Caesar, Augustus and his followers, was an important time for Roman town planning. Sulla built the Tabularium (where the archives of ancient Rome were kept), Pompey the first stone theatre, Caesar was responsible for a forum, Augustus for the theatre of Marcellus, a second forum and his mausoleum; Agrippa planned the Campus Martius, Tiberius' successors built the circus and baths named after Caligula and the Porta Maggiore basilica; Claudius erected an aqueduct and redesigned the port of Ostia; and Nero built his Golden House on the Palatine.

There are many remains of temples of the period: the temple of Fortuna rebuilt by Sulla at Preneste on the site of the ancient temple which had had ten superimposed terraces; the round temple of Vesta in the Corinthian Order at Tibur (Tivoli) and the nearby Ionic temple; in Rome, the temple situated near the Tiber also dates from this period. The temple at Cori is one of the few examples of Roman Doric. The temples of Minerva at Assisi and Pola are both in the Corinthian Order and date from the reign of Augustus. The temple of Venus Genetrix built by Caesar, Augustus' temple of Apollo Palatinus, Agrippa's Pantheon and the temple of Mars Ultor are all of the Latin type. Tiberius restored the two Corinthian temples of the Magna Mater and of Concord, and started work on the temple of the deified Augustus which was dedicated by Caligula.

From the Flavian Emperors to the end of the Empire.

The face of Rome was considerably changed both by the large scale enterprises which followed the fires of 191 and 283 and by the trend towards everything lavish and colossal, well illustrated by the Flavian amphitheatre, opened by Titus in the year 80. Domitian commissioned Rabirius to build the Domus Flavia on the Palatine, the Forum Transitorium dedicated by Nerva and baths which were completed by Trajan. In the reign of Trajan, the architect Apollodorus of Damascus designed a forum with markets, the Basilica Ulpia and Trajan's Column in memory of the Dacian campaign. The Thermae of Caracalla were begun by Septimius Severus who was also responsible for the Septizonium (or Nymphaeum) and the restoration of the Vestals' Portico.

The Baths of Diocletian, built by Maximian, the latter's palace at Milan and the former's palace at Spalato, all show signs of the influence of Oriental architecture. Maxentius commenced the basilica which Constantine dedicated in 310; Constantine also built baths, an archway, the Lateran Palace and the Mausoleum of Helena, and set out, along with his successors, to enhance the beauty of Constantinople with the Theodosius Obelisk, the Columns of Theodosius and Arcadius, and the Imperial Palace.

Domitian completed work on the

651. HELLENISTIC AND ROMAN. The ruins of Cyrene (Libya).

temple of the deified Verpasian and Titus, decorated with a strange frieze of priestly symbols, and built a temple of Serapis and another of Isis. Hadrian, the architect Emperor, rebuilt the Pantheon in the shape of a rotunda with a magnificent domed roof, and also erected the temple of Venus and Rome made up of two cellas joined at their apses. Under the Antonines there was a return to classical forms in the temple of the deified Hadrian, the temple of Antoninus and Faustina; Septimius Severus restored the temple of the Vestals, Caracalla built a temple to Serapis, while Heliogabalus and Aurelian erected temples to the sun god, the last sanctuaries of paganism.

The Roman provinces.

Towns in Gaul and North Africa were built on the Roman pattern; in Syria they were often built upon Hellenistic foundations but have all the characteristics of a Roman city: geometrically planned, surrounded by ramparts, main streets lined with porticoes and with archways and town gateways with four arches. Outstanding are the municipal enterprises—roads, bridges, aqueducts, fountains—many of which are still in use.

Public buildings were like those in Italy: basilicas were either on the Oriental pattern (Trier, Tebessa, Leptis Magna) or the Greek pattern (Arles, Aspendus, Djemila) or both combined (Timgad). There are large numbers of thermae, usually well built, both in towns (Paris, Aphrodisias, Gerasa, Lambèse, Volubilis) and in the sanctuaries

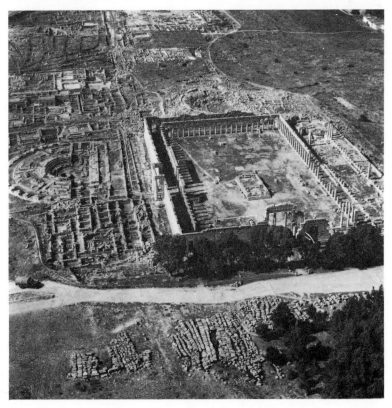

349

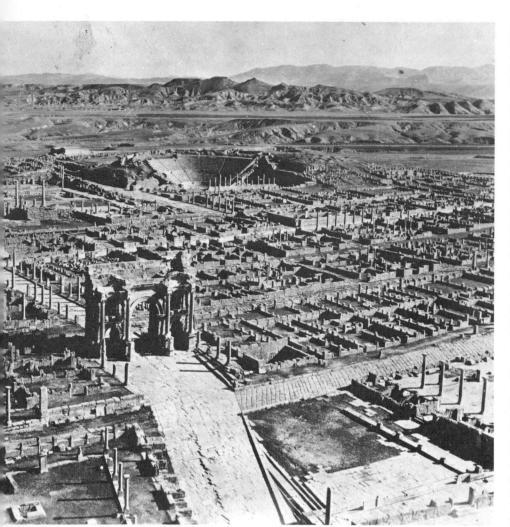

652. ROMAN ART IN AFRICA. Ruins at Timgad (Algeria). Foreground: the Arch of Trajan. Background: the Theatre. 2nd–3rd centuries A.D.

of gods with healing powers, as at Nîmes, which were adapted to suit the local climate. Each town had its theatre and sometimes two, as at Lyon; they are generally in the Roman style (Orange, Aspendus, Apamea, Timgad, Sabratha) but sometimes have regional variations (Lillebonne, Paris, Verulamium, Stobi in Yugoslavia). Many towns also have an amphitheatre (Nîmes, el Djem).

Commemorative columns and a good number of archways are fair proof of the architectural knowledge possessed by Roman architects and their pupils.

Sacred buildings generally show signs of the religious traditions of the province; in Gaul, alongside temples of Roman type, there are also temples of a native pattern (Périgueux and Autun in France, Petinesca in Switzerland, and Trier). Temples in Asia Minor and Syria tend to be on a colossal scale with sumptuous decoration using the Corinthian and Composite Orders, statue columns, sculptured pediments, etc.

(temples at Ancyra, Aezani, Termessus, Baalbek, Palmyra, Gerasa). There are temples of unique design in Syria (temple of Mithras and temple of Adonis at Doura Europos) and likewise in Africa (temple of Tanit and Saturn at Dougga), but sanctuaries in North Africa are mostly of pure Roman type.

SCULPTURE

Some of the outstanding points of Roman sculpture were the lack of any great individual artists, the part played by royal patronage, the rarity of statues of gods, the abundance and high quality of portraits, and the historical nature of reliefs. In the early stages this sculpture was almost purely Etruscan but it was affected by Greek influence which first came through the cities of Magna Graecia, then through the many Greek artists living in Rome and finally by the arrival of many works of art plundered from Greek cities, copies of which were to adorn both private residences and princes' palaces.

From the early period to the Flavian era. Few works of sculpture can be dated from before the Republican

period; from the 3rd century almost nothing can be mentioned other than a Marsyas from the Forum. The Republican portraits, the Orator and the Brutus [**638**, **653**], are really Etruscan works; the trend towards Greek idealism first appeared with the portraits of Caesar and is even more apparent in portraits of women and the young Octavius. This tendency grew more marked in the statues of Augustus [**586**], depicted as a naked heroic figure (Louvre), wearing a breast plate (the Prima Porta Augustus), clad in a toga (Louvre and Via Labicana), and in the statues of his contemporaries and successors (Agrippa, Livy, the seated figure of Tiberius in the Vatican, the Louvre Caligula, and the Vatican Claudius). The varied and numerous portraits of unknown Roman men and women make up a collection of an often breathtaking forcefulness of style coupled with striking psychological penetration.

Similarly, reliefs show how Hellenic forms and techniques were adapted to specifically Roman themes; the Altar of Domitius Ahenobarbus (Louvre and Munich) [**631**] combines a Roman sacrifice with a procession of Amphitrite and Neptune; the Ara Pacis Augustae [**633**] blends a Roman procession with scenes inspired by Greek tradition (the Mother Earth relief). The altar from Carthage, reliefs from Pozzuoli, Sorrento and Nola, the decoration of the temple of Augustus and Rome at Ostia, the Britannicus Arch, sacrificial panels (Louvre, Villa Medici) and some pictorial reliefs form an achievement of high technical and aesthetic merit.

Last stage of Roman art. Some portraits of Nero had shown a return to realism and this grew more marked in portraits of Vespasian, Titus and Domitian. Greek influence became once again powerful under Trajan and especially Hadrian (portraits of Sabina and Antinous) and it was at this time that over life-size statues (the Vatican Nerva) and ethnic portraits first made their appearance. These tendencies became even more firmly entrenched in the Antonine age (the equestrian statue of Marcus Aurelius on the Capitoline) and under the Severus dynasty (the Naples Heliogabalus, Maximinus of Thrace); it was a trend which reached a climax in portraits of the last Emperors (the Conservatori Constantine, Constantius II and Valentinian I from Barletta). Eyes and mouths have soft, pathetic expressions which tone down the strict formal symmetry (the Antiquario Probus, the Tetrarch group from the St Mark's pillar, the head of Theodora in Milan).

The distinguishing features of reliefs

of the Flavian era were experimentation in perspective, the relationship of light and shadow (Arch of Titus [**628**]), boldness in composition and technique (Domitian medallions on the Arch of Constantine, reliefs from the Palazzo della Cancelleria and the Forum of Nerva). Whereas the decoration on the Trajan Column was still Roman in style and spirit, Greek influence was evident in the Forum friezes and in the sculptures on the arch at Benevento and grew even more marked during Hadrian's reign (Isis relief in the Louvre, battle scenes on the Arch of Constantine) even where purely Roman subjects are treated (Louvre Sacrifice). It was the period of mythological reliefs inspired by the Alexandrian school (Perseus and Andromeda, Sleeping Endymion, Ariadne with the Stag) and the first sarcophagi to use relief ornamentation.

The Antonine age was a flourishing period with excellent sculpture (Hadrianum, temple of Antoninus and Faustina, Aurelian Column, panels now in the Conservatori Museum); the first Mithraic reliefs and sarcophagi with niches (Melfi Sarcophagus) belong to this period.

In the reign of Septimius Severus the influence of Oriental art, with its bias towards the frontal attitude and formal, loaded and anecdotal compositions, was becoming apparent (reliefs from the Palazzo Sacchetti, capitals from the Caracalla thermae, sarcophagi of the Sidamaran type [**643**]); the sculpture of the time of Galerius (arch at Salonika), reliefs on the Arch of Constantine and the base of the Theodosius Obelisk in Constantinople are part of the same stylistic conception and foreshadow the art of the Middle Ages.

The Roman provinces. Even if it was no part of Rome's plan to enforce her own aesthetic ideas on the provinces, they made themselves felt to a degree that varied with the cultural development of the country.

In western Europe where there were centres with a distinct culture of their own, rich in Celtic traditions or Greek influences, native art flourished alongside imperial art: sculptures from Orange, St Rémy, the district around Lyon, portraits and reliefs from the Rhine district, sculpture of the period of Augustus and Hadrian from St-Bertrand-de-Comminges and Spain (Mérida) are only a small part of a large output which still awaits study.

On the Greek mainland, works of the Roman period, except for a few portraits, were of indifferent quality, but there was a real revival in Asia Minor where cities, profiting from the *Pax Romana,* were maturing—Ephesus,

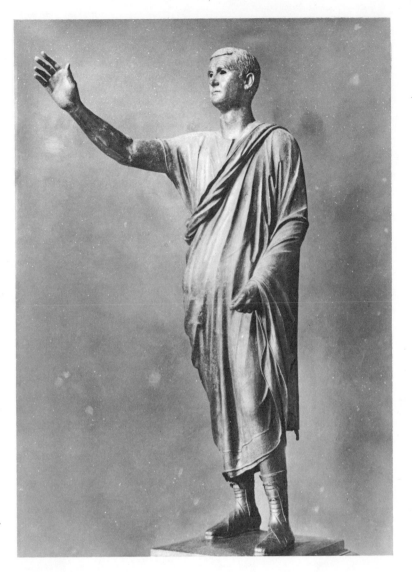

653. ETRUSCAN. The 'Arringatore' (Orator). Bronze. 1st century B.C. *Archaeological Museum, Florence.*

654. ROMAN. The House of the Vettii at Pompeii.

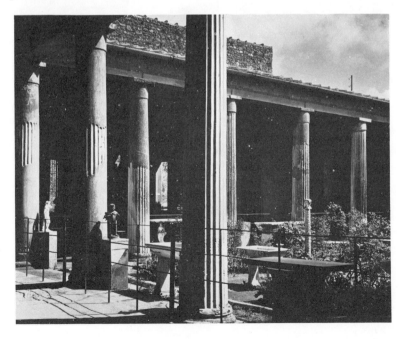

351

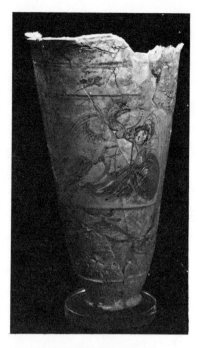

656. ALEXANDRIAN. Painted drinking vessel with a scene from the Ganymede story, found at Begram (Afghanistan). About 2nd century B.C. *Musée Guimet, Paris.*

655. ROMAN. A street in Herculaneum.

Lagina in Caria, and especially Aphrodisias where Antonianus, Aristeas and Pappias worked.

Baalbek in the Lebanon (frieze from the temple of Bacchus) and Palmyra in Syria (sepulchral portraits) continued to be active centres. In Egypt, artistic output was usually on a surprisingly low level and the same would be true of North Africa with certain exceptions (the Cyrene Jupiter, Carthage Apollo) if it were not for Juba II's discriminating but catholic taste which turned Leptis Magna, Volubilis and Cherchel into virtual museum-cities.

PAINTING

Painting, with mosaics, took pride of place in the decoration of Roman buildings and from the 5th century was to occupy the position previously held by sculptured reliefs. No easel paintings have survived, but many frescoes, often bordered with gilded stucco-work, can be found in Roman houses and tombs.

The earliest paintings go back to the beginning of the 3rd century (Esquiline tomb), and in the latter part of the 2nd century painted decoration made its appearance, imitating the polychrome effects of marble plaques (House of Sallust); then about the year 70 (2nd style), walls were divided up into separate panels by architectural motifs which framed landscapes containing real or mythological figures (Esquiline House, House of Cleopatra built by Caesar, House of Livia built by Augustus; Villa of the Boscoreale, Villa of Mysteries at Pompeii, Villa of Livia at Prima Porta). Finally in Nero's time (3rd style) mythological paintings and family portraits were set in a framework of 'fantastic' architectural devices (Houses of the Vettii and of the Cithara-player at Pompeii, Nero's Golden House).

From the 2nd century, tomb decoration was largely concerned with religious themes (the Pancratii and Valerii tombs on the Via Latina, 2nd-century tomb of the Nasonii on the Via Flaminia and the 3rd-century tomb of the Aurelii) while domestic painting took its inspiration from the 2nd Pompeian style (Villa of the San Sebastiano Basilica, Palatine House). As far afield as Syria (2nd-century tomb of the Palmyra gods at Doura Europos) and in Egypt (the Fayum portraits, 2nd–3rd centuries) many excellent works show the vitality of this art form, which was to reach new heights in the 4th century (tomb of Trebius Justus).

MINOR ARTS

Both in Italy and in the provinces, mosaics were to be extremely popular, consisting mainly of interpretations of famous paintings (Alexander Mosaic [**610**]), of landscapes, and of portraits framed by elaborate decorative motifs; supremely beautiful work was still being produced in the 5th century (Phoenix Mosaic in Antioch). Metal craftsmanship, using bronze for household utensils, furniture and weapons, silver for plate, gold for jewellery and medals (Aboukir medallions), and crafts using semi-precious stones were both flourishing throughout the entire Roman period: the treasures of Boscoreale [**636**], Marengo, Hildesheim and Berthouville include many objects from the time of Augustus and Tiberius. on the Hellenic pattern but with Roman ornamentation. Of the large number of cameos, we must mention the 'Grand Camée de France', the Vienna Cameo [**634**] and the Blacas Cameo.

Lastly we must include sigillated ware, known as Aretine pottery, with its bright red glaze and relief patterns, which was imitated by Auvergnat potters of Graufesenque and Lezoux right down to the 4th century and was exported as far as the East where it was especially popular in Syria and Egypt.

Simone Besques-Mollard

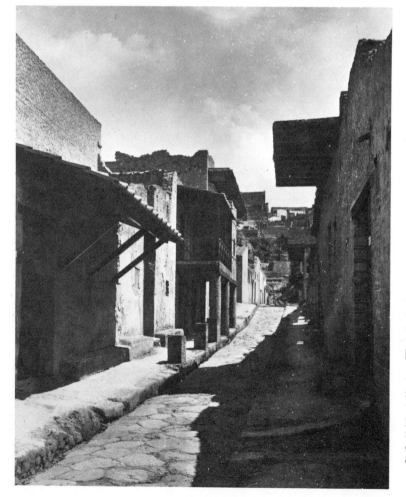

TOWARDS THE FAR EAST *Jeannine Auboyer*

Greece and Rome had brought unity to an ancient world that was still centred on the Mediterranean. But through the contact not only of war, but of trade and culture too, new inroads were being made into Asia. Chapter 7 is concerned entirely with Asia, but it is important in relation to Antiquity to show here how these connections with India, China and Japan came about, connections that were to have such profound consequences. Buddhist thought had imposed some kind of unity on the East which, in turn, was to infiltrate the West, carrying new ideas of a more religious nature that hastened the end of Antiquity.

THE ARTS OF THE SILK ROUTE

Just before the beginning of the Christian era and in the following centuries one of the most exciting encounters in history took place in the very heart of Asia: the Hellenic, Iranian, Indian and Chinese worlds came together and established contact.

This came about on account of the parallel growth of the great civilising blocs which, at this time, shared the control of the Eurasian continent between them. In both the East and the West, they had reached a stage in development which, in retrospect, appears to have been not so much a dramatic and sudden flowering but a kind of Middle Ages, seething with contradictions and rich variety. There is, in fact, no period to match this one for violent adventures, colossal fortunes lost without ceremony and swiftly made again, and mighty undertakings in the commercial, as well as the religious and intellectual spheres. Mutual curiosity born of a spirit of adventure, common interests bound up with the expansion of 'international' trade, the certainty of financial gain for the

ruling classes—these were the chief motives that urged on the caravans, pilgrims, ambassadors and travellers of every description. These regions of the Asian plateau, crossed at intervals by trade routes that linked Rome to China and India to Iran, were to be the area chosen to receive the overflow of all this widespread activity.

Buddhism had a potent effect on this general ferment; it travelled like a great wave along the caravan routes and brought to wandering adventurers and settled farmers alike the peaceful comfort of its teaching with the hope that all human actions would be justly rewarded.

It was in this area of central Asia, criss-crossed by trade routes and dotted with oases, that the cosmopolitan throng of Eurasia travelled around, settled, moved off again and returned. Hellenic influence, carried by the merchants of Iran, penetrated this region and was grafted on to purely Oriental styles. In this territory, geographically a single unit but so widely diverse in culture, there grew up a genuine artistic tradition. In the field of art history, it is the ideal place to study the working of cultural influences; as a result of political and cultural factors, central Asia became a melting-pot in which influences from the great civilisations of East and West fermented and combined to produce new repertoires and new styles that Western Asiatic studies have labelled as Graeco-Buddhist, Irano-Buddhist, Central Asiatic, etc. These complex artistic styles, of a hybrid character as their names show, can help to evolve a system of study.

Comparisons, if they are made with great prudence, can help us to distinguish several classes of influence. There was in the first place the direct influence stemming from the actual example of imported objects or else from objects produced by foreign craftsmen living in the

657. GRAECO-BUDDHIST. Head of a woman worshipper found at Hadda (Afghanistan). Moulded stucco. 4th–5th centuries A.D. *Musée Guimet, Paris.*

658. GRAECO-BUDDHIST. Head of Buddha from Gandhara (India). Schist. About 3rd–4th centuries A.D. (?). *Musée Guimet, Paris.*

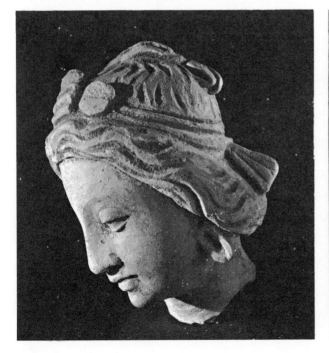

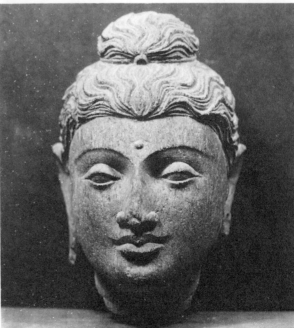

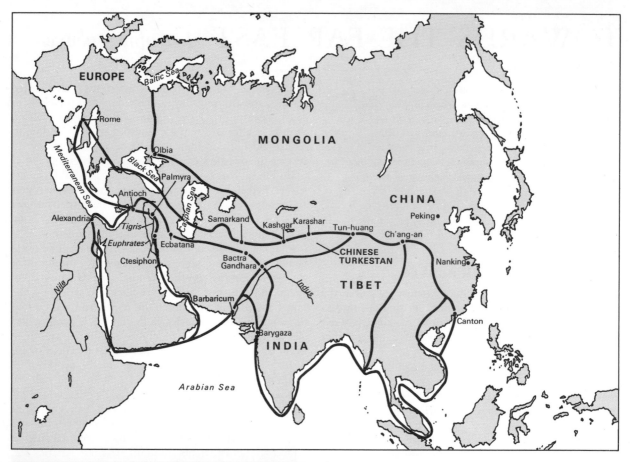

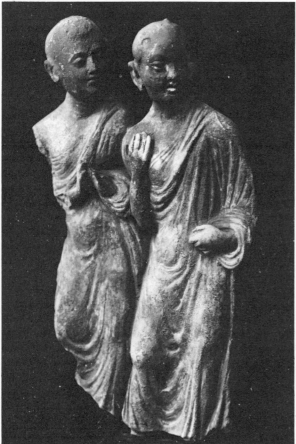

659. GRAECO-BUDDHIST. Two young Buddhist monks.
Moulded stucco from Hadda (Afghanistan). 4th–5th centuries
A.D. *Musée Guimet, Paris.*

district. It had a counterpart in a whole stock of themes
retailed by the traders in luxury articles who had selected
the characteristic or most valuable products of each
country and who usually restricted themselves to the
kinds of objects that could be easily carried: statuettes
made in many different kinds of material, domestic
articles, bronze, alabaster and porphyry vessels, glassware
and glass trinkets, jewellery, ornaments, cloth, weapons,
ivory chests and furniture etc. Besides this, mention must
be made of the effect produced, as we know from the
literature of the time, by itinerant troupes of entertainers,
like the group from Khotan who were particularly
famous and the band of acrobats who were supposed to
have come from Rome, as well as by the trade in horses
from Turkestan, etc. Just how real this trade was in the
realm of the plastic arts has been shown by excavations
both in Afghanistan, with the finds of J. and R. Hackin at
Begram, and in Chinese Turkestan (Sassanian cloth at
Tun-huang, Roman lamps, etc.). These admired and
coveted objects certainly played an important part in the
formation of a new local repertoire; the study of these
problems, still far from complete, will, when more progress has been made, enable us to reach a more definite
estimate of the importance of this part.

Also in this group of influences we can include works
of art produced locally under the rule of various 'occupying powers': there is, for example, the mural painting
discovered at Dokhtar-i-Noshirwan, at this time an area
under the protection of Iran, which portrays an Iranian
governor with all the pomp attaching to his high position.
To this group also belong the gift-bearers depicted on the
banners and frescoes at the frontier town of Tun-huang;
they are really nothing but Chinese officials and settlers
who, as Buddhist converts, wanted in some way to

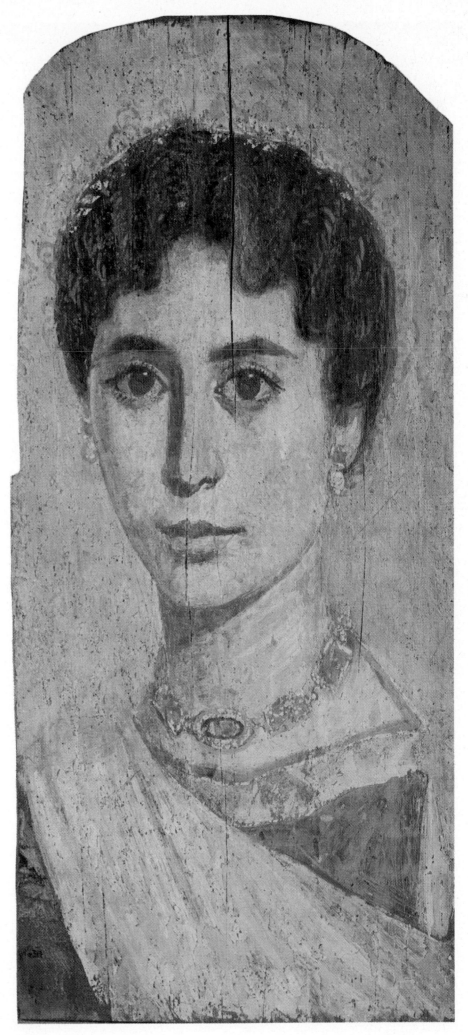

ROMAN. Mummy-portrait of a
woman. Coloured wax on wood.
Found at Fayum, Egypt. Second
half of the 2nd century A.D.
Graf Collection, British Museum.
Photo: Paul Hamlyn Archive

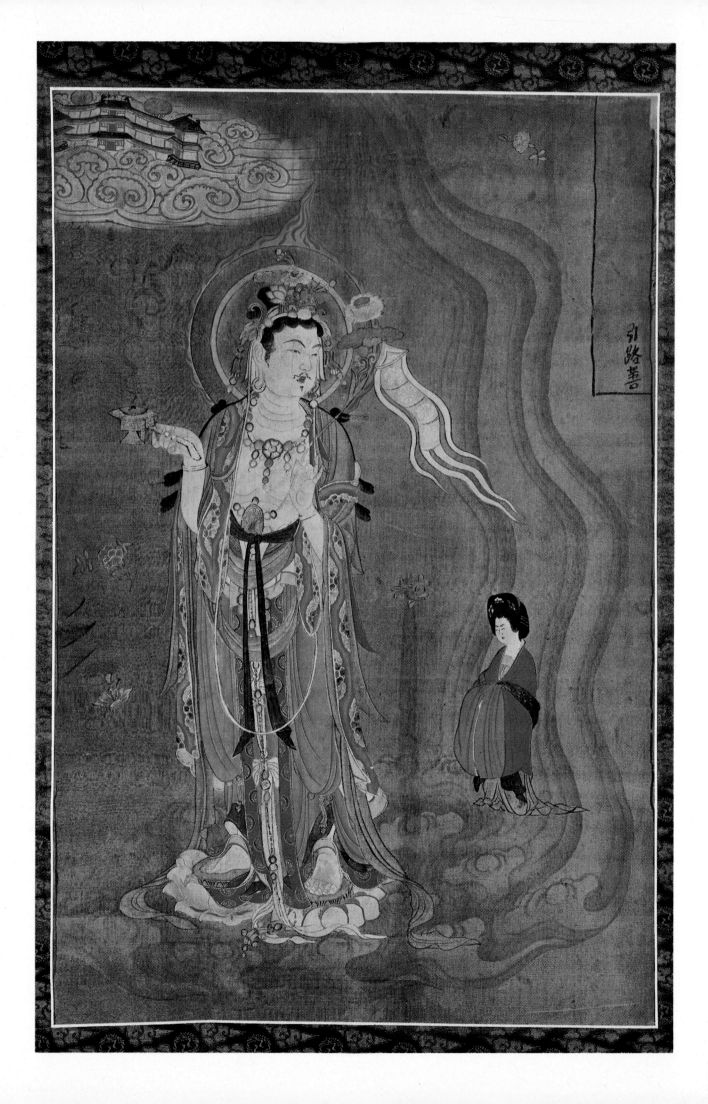

guarantee their life in the next world. The whole group of works at Tun-huang, moreover, is a direct manifestation of China under the T'ang Dynasty and is purely Chinese both in subject-matter and the supple draughtsmanship of the paintings. Cloth was also responsible for the spread of certain motifs, and here the influence of Iran, with its cloth trade of world-wide renown, was the strongest; Sassanian medallions adorned with a boar's and a bird's head were found on the ceiling of Cave D at Bamiyan, on fragments of material dug up from the burial ground at Astana, and in the mural decoration of Toyuk Mazar and Idiqutshari (Ruin K).

Next we come to influences of an indirect kind; they are more difficult to disentangle, for there were factors at work making their effect different in every case. They were responsible for those strange juxtapositions and mixtures with which the arts of the Silk Routes are saturated. All these routes led into central Asia which acted like a mirror reflecting all the artistic styles of neighbouring lands; many different forms were yoked together with a kind of audacity that sometimes seems the result of ignorance, and straightforwardly Western features were combined with others that were typically Oriental. It is no longer a question of indirect influences but of continual borrowings that were pieced together to form a very complex puzzle. Thus it was that the domes made up of beams set at angles to form a squinch (originally an Iranian idea) came to be used in the Afghan caves along with painted and modelled ornamentation which included Syrian, Iranian and Indian elements. There were, too, the Corinthian capitals of Graeco-Buddhist art, sheltering a statuette of the Buddha among their ornamental foliage, as well as the figures portrayed in Graeco-Buddhist art that have the regular profile, well-defined, swelling lips and hair falling into symmetrical waves, all features taken from Greece, combined with the Oriental fleshy, oval face, heavy-lidded protuberant eyes and elongated ear lobes weighed down with jewellery. We can also find Buddhist monks with cloaks falling into 'transparent' folds in the classical style, Iranian men and women, wearing fitted, well-cut, stitched clothes as they mingle in the throng of bare-chested Buddhist worshippers, and the horsemen and demons dressed for battle, again in the Iranian style, which were to become so much a part of Buddhist iconography in Chinese Turkestan. And lastly there were techniques, stemming recognisably from India—the contrast of light and dark flesh tints and many other details.

Persistence of indirect influences

That there should have been so many influences, both direct and indirect, was only to be expected in such a cosmopolitan environment; what was truly remarkable was their abundance and rich variety which in central Asia reached a point unmatched by any other civilisation. But another phenomenon grew out of these specifically heterogeneous styles. Influences of an indirect kind that had developed on their own, uprooted from their place of origin and closely bound up with other foreign elements, began gradually to lose some of their former power until their effect was evident only in a single detail of another tradition. They followed a kind of pattern: in the first place these indirect influences seemed to persist longer than others for no apparent reason and, secondly,

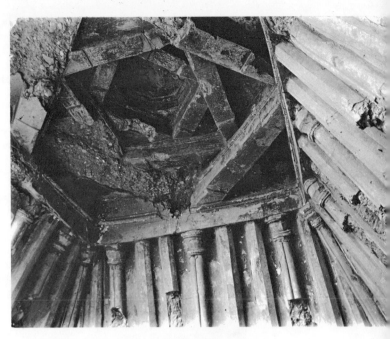

660. AFGHANISTAN. Ceiling of Cave 15 at Bamiyan. About 5th century A.D.

a single feature often became smaller and smaller in size.

Now we are dealing no longer with influences but with the far more difficult question of unconscious memories. So we must be doubly cautious and try to track down these motifs in their travels without allowing deceptive similarities to mislead us; in this, careful and detailed observation is not good enough but must be supported by a knowledge of historical facts and the routes followed. There are surprises in store as one watches a stylistic theme making its way from its place of origin to its final destination. Not only is it possible to re-establish all the stages of its route but we can also gauge the astonishing slowness with which it travelled—and its even more astonishing persistence. There are outstanding examples to illustrate this and one of the most typical is that of the crescent head-dress: it originated in Iran (2nd century) where the ornamental features (crescent and ball shapes) were large in size; it next passed into the Buddhist repertoire in Afghanistan (4th–5th centuries), Chinese Turkestan (8th century), and China (6th century), finally reaching Japan (8th century); in the course of this progress, its ornamental features became very much smaller. The same thing happened with the cape worn by Greek and Roman soldiers (comparable to the way the hooded cloak of medieval monks in Europe was gradually reduced to a scapular) when, in the form of a mantle that grew increasingly smaller, it was carried into Afghanistan (Hadda and Bamiyan), Gandhara, India (6th century), Chinese Turkestan (8th–10th centuries) and lastly into Japan (8th century). Many other features made their way eastwards, including the Phrygian cap which appears in Cambodia in the 7th century, and the boots of the god Surya, all that remains in India of the full soldier's outfit seen on figures of Surya in Iran.

Decorative motifs succeeded where armies had failed: they were still making their way along the routes to the East long after the civilisations where they had originated had disappeared, and it was primarily Buddhism that established contact between them.

CHINESE. Kuan-yin guiding a soul. T'ang Dynasty painting. British Museum. *Museum photograph.*

HISTORICAL SUMMARY: The Silk Route

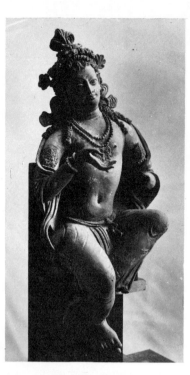

661. GRAECO-BUDDHIST. Terracotta Devata. 7th century A.D. Fondukistan (Afghanistan). *Musée Guimet, Paris.*

662. IRANO-BUDDHIST. High relief of dried clay from Tumshuq (Chinese Turkestan). 6th–7th centuries A.D. *Musée Guimet, Paris.*

GEOGRAPHY

The general name 'Silk Route' is given to a group of caravan routes which, possibly from prehistoric times, linked the countries of Europe to central Asia and China. For merchants who had come by land and sea, from the Baltic, southern Russia, Rome and Alexandria, these routes left Antioch, Tyre and Sidon, crossed Iran or Mongolia, and Chinese Turkestan, linking up again at Tun-huang, a Chinese frontier town.

Branching off from these main routes were many minor ones leading to Gandhara and India, linking central Asia with the numerous ports of the Bombay coast, going to Ch'ang-an, Yunnan and Burma or towards Canton and Tonking. Luxury merchandise, traded between the East and West, of which silk was obviously the most important, was carried over all these routes.

ART

In the realm of art this led to the growth of many styles, governed alternately by Hellenic, Indian, Iranian and Chinese influences, styles which were to be continued until the climax of the T'ang Dynasty (618–906). Buddhism, being spread by missionaries from India and establishing itself in the 'Holy Places' of central Asia, acted as a unifying agent for this wide variety of artistic forms.

Graeco-Buddhist style. It mostly took root in the region of Peshawar (Gandhara) and in Afghanistan (Hadda, Qunduz, etc.) where it was developed from the latter part of the 1st century B.C. to the 7th century and continued down to the 9th century; its finest period coincided with the reigns of Marcus Aurelius and Septimius Severus.

The most important features of religious architecture in this style were the shrines (stupa) and monasteries (vihara) which, except in their sculpted ornamentation, were scarcely any different from those of India. This ornamentation, made of schist or stucco, was characterised by a great many Hellenic motifs incorporated into themes taken over from Buddhist tradition and by the development of certain types of which the Buddha is especially important, being until this time (about 2nd century) portrayed only by symbols.

The Graeco-Buddhist Buddha is a heterogeneous creation in appearance: a straight nose which in profile continues the line of the forehead, a boldly chiselled mouth, waving hair, a robe with concentric, diaphanous folds covering the shoulders—all features which were part of the classical repertoire; the fleshy oval face, protuberant eyes and elongated ear lobes were Oriental characteristics. The canonical symbols (*lakshanas*) exemplifying the figure's outstanding holiness were first formed at this time. Schist sculpture tended to be conventionalised, while stucco sculpture was very much more free and reflected, in the same way as the Tanagra figurines, all the rich variety of contemporary society (those from Hadda in particular, about 3rd–8th centuries).

The Graeco-Buddhist style had very important repercussions: by way of the Silk Routes, it penetrated Chinese Turkestan and then China whence some elements were carried into Japan; it was passed on from one settlement to the next along the Spice Routes, and reached some parts of Indo-China. The more ancient classical formulas were blended with features of Syrian influence (Palmyra, Doura Europos, Baalbek) of which there are very clear traces in the Miran mural paintings (about 2nd century) and in the architecture and sculptural ornamentation of Bamiyan (5th century).

Jeannine Auboyer

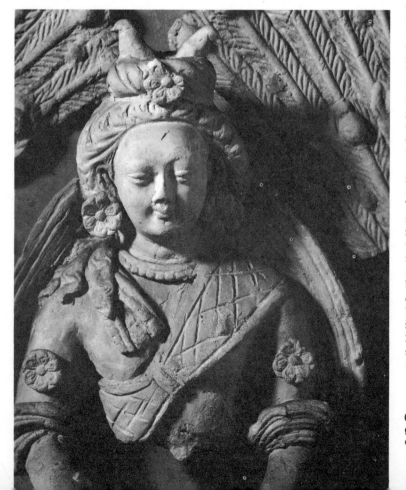

663. *Opposite.* **INDIAN.** Northern gateway of Stupa 1 at Sanchi. 1st century A.D. (?)

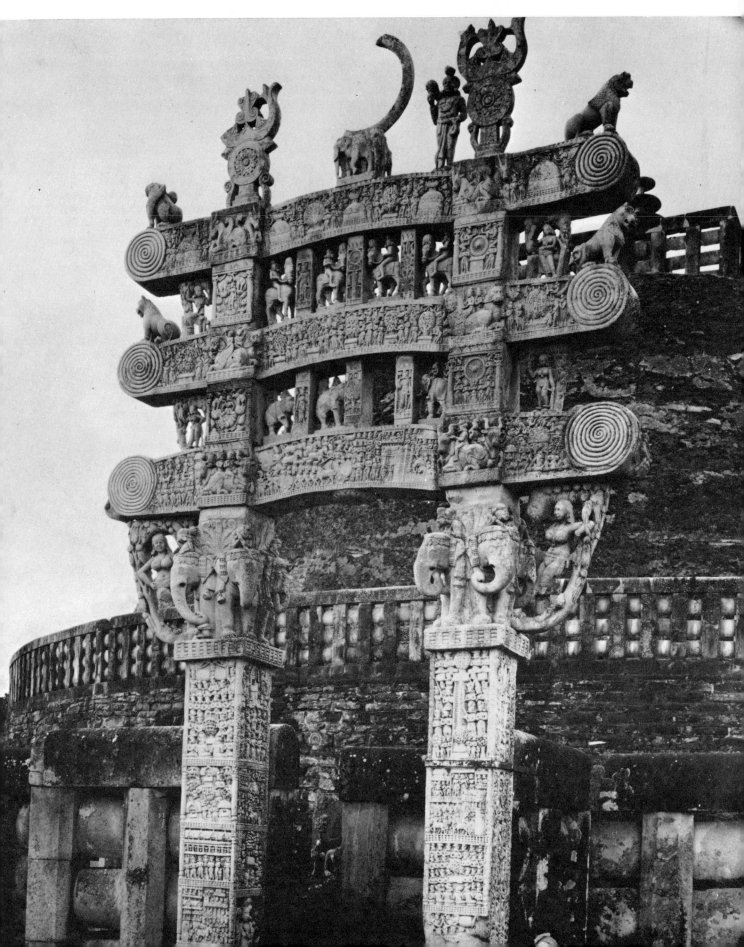

ART FORMS AND SOCIETY *Philippe Stern*

The newcomer to the arts of southern and eastern Asia—of India, China and Japan—often tends to be put off by their strangeness and impenetrability. He is instinctively afraid that religions and thought so different from his own would cause the arts they engendered to remain for ever inaccessible to him. Not infrequently, moreover, through an association of ideas, recollections of old adventure stories or recent films surge into his mind, evoking repulsive or caricatural images—perhaps of terrible, grimacing gods with multiple gesticulating arms, looming in the dark caverns and temples of India, China or Vietnam; or perhaps of corpulent Chinese grotesque figures of mirth. Are these entirely false images? Not altogether. They are, however, highly exaggerated and correspond to only one aspect of these arts—an extreme, exceptional and decadent aspect which generally speaking manifested itself at a relatively recent date. The best in the arts of southern and eastern Asia is, in fact, often much more closely related to Western art (and especially when inspired by analogous ideals) than to these fictitious images.

These unpleasant evocations sometimes give rise to the impression that there is a definite unity between the arts that flourished from India to Japan—a fallacy due, perhaps, to the fact that with the propagation of Buddhism these divinities with their multiple arms were diffused throughout the Far East. That which is most characteristic of Indian art has, however, nothing in common with that which is most characteristic of the art of China, and indeed, the differences between Indian and Chinese art would seem to be far more strongly marked than those between corresponding stages of artistic development in Asia and the West. Contrary to what might be supposed, there is no screen separating the East from the West, and, although an understanding of the religions and thought of India and China certainly leads to a deeper insight into their arts, a susceptibility to the common human element in all forms of traditional religious arts would seem to be of far greater value. The 19th-century man, who considered that art began in Italy with Raphael and who rejected anything that did not constitute an exact copy of reality, was much further removed from the hieratic Romanesque art than this Romanesque art is from certain aspects of the art of China and Japan.

667, 668

AN APPROACH TO THE ARTS OF SOUTHERN AND EASTERN ASIA

Rather than make a direct attempt to pierce their surface strangeness, we propose to approach the arts of Asia in a roundabout way, through the aspects which relate them to Western art and through the corresponding rhythms and tendencies which relate widely divergent arts and which cannot be explained either by contact or by reciprocal influence. Let us begin, however, by analysing the significance of the arts of the Orient and by establishing the various points of view from which we shall discuss them.

While the aesthetic and human value of Oriental art is indisputable, a quasi-superstitious and artificially religious veneration automatically accorded to all that comes from India or that is otherwise occult or remote may at once be discarded, as may any preconceived ideas tending to a rejection of anything that is not European as inferior: we have no use for either attitude here. As scholars have expressed it, in the arts of all parts of the world there are occasional masterpieces, many mediocre works, a few culminating points, periods of decadence and even frequent instances of downright bad taste. Thus it is with the arts of Asia.

Having accepted this premise we can wholeheartedly rejoice in the fact that our recent acquaintance with these arts has infinitely widened our aesthetic horizons. Indeed, it is only in our time—a fact too often forgotten—that the camera and tape recorder have allowed us to capture the most varied arts in one particular place and at a given moment in time. Before, the furthest and the most frequent journeys did not permit of such numerous and constant comparisons. And it is the arts of Asia, particularly the earlier manifestations of these arts, that have chiefly benefited from these new possibilities. Documents and studies have enriched our perceptions and opened up new perspectives.

Turning to the various headings into which we shall divide our discussion of the arts of Asia, under that of evolution we shall find seemingly confused and disparate elements falling into a pattern similar to that of the growth of a living being: continuity, development, achievement, decline and revival.

Running parallel to the caprices and contrasts manifest in evolution, may be discerned the tenuous thread of certain constants.

Then, in the Far East as elsewhere, there is a definite correspondence between the visual arts (sculpture, painting, architecture and the decorative arts) and the other arts (music, literature, the theatre, etc.), and also between the visual arts and religion, philosophy and contemporary thought. As we shall see, this correspondence sometimes came about through parallel evolution and sometimes through reciprocal influences.

We have already seen how the migrations of peoples brought about the spread of motifs, techniques and even styles in art, sometimes to regions separated by vast expanses. Whether this spread was rapidly effected and due to a small group of travellers, a band of pilgrims or just one man, or whether, as seems more probable, it represented a gradual process, it took place along a great network of sea and overland routes which covered an immense part of Eurasia.

Quite apart from this network of sea and overland routes, we shall encounter similar tendencies and rhythms of evolution in arts so widely separated, not only in space but also in time, that it seems impossible that either direct or indirect contact could have taken place between them. It is due only to our recently acquired knowledge of the arts of Asia, which has enormously expanded our range of comparisons, that we are now able to attempt an analysis of these tendencies and rhythms. Further on we shall also go more deeply into the common elements already mentioned, for it is these, together with an even more deep-

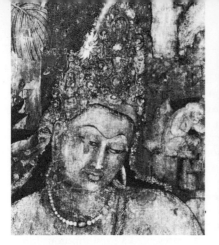

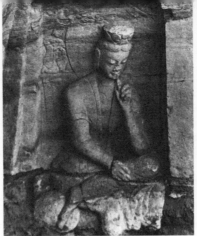

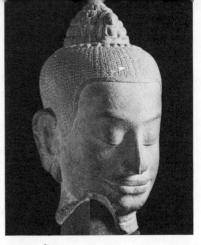

664. INDIAN. GUPTA. Head of a Bodhisattva. Detail from a mural at Cave 1, Ajanta. *c.* beginning of 6th century A.D.

665. CHINESE. Bodhisattva. Bas-relief in Cave G at Yun-kang. End of first half of 6th century A.D.

666. KHMER. Head of a Buddha, Bayon style. End of 12th–beginning of 13th centuries A.D. *Musée Guimet, Paris.*

SPIRITUAL UNION

The corresponding air of tranquil meditation, serene introspection, and grave tenderness, and the smile of communion with all humanity, which relate the arts of eastern Asia to each other and to Egyptian and Graeco-Etruscan art, spring not from any communication between them but from the fact that all expressed the same fundamental ideals.

OTHER CORRESPONDING TENDENCIES

French Romanesque art [667], and Japanese art inspired by that of 7th-century China [668], show the same elongated, immobile and erect hieratism, modified by a certain suppleness and even something bordering on affectation.

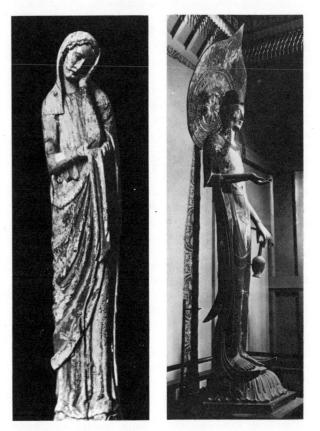

667. FRENCH. Virgin of Verneuil-sur-Avre. Polychromed wood. 13th–14th centuries.

668. JAPANESE. Kudara Kwannon in the Horiyuji, near Nara. Wood. 7th century A.D.

rooted tendency towards unity—inherent in all art—which form a link between Oriental and Western art. Meanwhile, it is on the basis of these elements that we shall conduct our study of the arts of Asia, and first of all from the point of view of tendencies and rhythms.

TENDENCIES AND RHYTHMS COMMON TO ASIA AND THE WEST

It is our belief, and the main theme of an aesthetic conception which we shall elaborate as we proceed, that all arts, however diverse or widely separated in time or space, are basically akin. Behind the multiple tendencies whose interplay and accentuation constitute the countless different forms of beauty in art, there is a spiritual relationship which unites their most diametrically opposite manifestations. A family likeness lurks beneath totally divergent outward appearances. This basic affinity is mainly recog-

664–
666 nisable in representations of the human face and the rigid

or relaxed attitude of the human body. There are faces wrapped in meditation and tranquillity, whose gaze, transcending space and present time, is far removed from its immediate environment; and there are faces in which sorrow, compassion and tenderness lie in the mobility of the mouth and chin and in the ineffable smile that often plays over them. A smile is infinite in its variety: while it may reach the extreme of superficiality in the mundane smile of polite society, it may also reach the ultimate in depth, intimacy and intensity. It may express absorption and detachment and yet contain a compassion for and communion with all humanity: the dominant accents of Buddhism, in which lie the essential qualities of the arts of India and China. It is this smile that we find in the faces at Angkor (Khmer art, Cambodia, end of the 12th **666** century A.D. or beginning of the 13th), in that of a Chinese **665** figure (Yun-kang, 5th or 6th century A.D.), in those of the Bodhisattvas at Ajanta (first half of the 6th century **664** A.D.), in which it is suggested rather than apparent and, as the expression of rather different ideals, in arts which, though geographically closer to us, are far more ancient: Egyptian art of the XVIIIth Dynasty (14th century B.C.) and Greek and Italian art of the beginning of the 5th century B.C. (Hermes of Veii). Here we can indicate no more than a few of the countless examples.

Of a far more superficial nature is the tendency, common to both the East and the West, to emphasise certain aspects at the expense of others, such as the hieratic aspect of rigid, immobile grandeur—a sort of suspension of eternity. Hieratic statuary, with its extreme vertical elongation accentuated by the stylised folds of the drapery, sometimes attains to a tenuous refinement which, though almost unbearable in its tension, is moving in its very majesty. It is this quality that lends such charm to Japanese art imitating and exaggerating the hieratic elongation of Chinese Northern Wei art (Kudara Kwannon, 7th century A.D.), and to French Romanesque art (Virgin of Verneuil-sur-Avre, probably a 13th-century survival of Romanesque art, and more supple than the statues in the royal portal at Chartres).

A tendency towards dynamic tension is characteristic of youthful arts and often manifests itself in the representation of fantastic animals, which disappear as an art matures and the tendency is outgrown. This process is noticeable on Greek vases during the period of transition from archaic to so-called Golden Age art, and on capitals in France at the time when Gothic superseded Romanesque art. Although fantastic animals were certainly transmitted from one art to another, the analogy between the Red Bird of the South (China, Han period) and the griffon of Angoulême (France, 12th century A.D.) would seem, since no similar intermediaries are known to exist, to be a case but of analogous tendencies towards linear inflection, intense vivacity and grandeur.

As an art evolves it tends to become steadily more refined until it reaches the point of equilibrium, beyond which mannerism sets in and gradually destroys the existing harmony. However, it is often at this crucial moment in its evolution, when affectation adds spice to refinement but without predominating, that an art produces some of its most unusual and, though perhaps exaggerated, most charming forms. This 'affected refinement' appears at the same point in their evolution in the art of both India (towards the 6th century A.D., post-Gupta figures at Badami) and Egypt (during the 14th century B.C., Daughters of Akhenaten, from el Amarna).

The superficiality and the excess which pervade an art that has evolved beyond the point of equilibrium bring about a cleavage between the two opposing tendencies— tension and relaxation—which were previously united in harmonious balance. These tendencies when accentuated inevitably become dissociated: dynamism and vigour are exaggerated on the one hand, refinement and mannerism on the other. It is a recurrent rhythm of evolution which merits far more abundant illustration than the two examples, taken from Greek and Chinese art, that must here suffice. In Hellenistic art we have such forms as the Laocoön and the Pergamon figure on the one hand, and the Myrina statuette on the other, while in Chinese T'ang art (7th–9th centuries) we find, for example, the Lokapalas (guardians of the cardinal points of the world) and the Dvarapalas (guardians of the gates) as well as such statuettes as the funerary terra cotta of a foreign dancer.

Thus, in China as in Greece, the accentuation and subsequent dissociation of opposing tendencies gave rise to correspondingly novel forms, to dramatic, wildly gesticulating figures with excessive musculature and to figures that were all refinement and manneristic affectation.

As this dissociation progresses, the dramatic and violent element often takes on a horrific aspect—a phenomenon that may still be observed today. At corresponding moments in their evolution beyond the point of equilibrium India and the medieval West found an analogous image for the expression of horror, the exposure of entrails. While Indian art represented a presumptuous king being disembowelled by Vishnu in the form of a man-lion (Pala-Sena period), French funerary sculpture portrayed the disintegration of the human body after death (Jeanne de Bourbon, beginning of the 16th century).

The comparison of all these works, separated sufficiently by time and space to rule out both the possibility of any sort of transmission of influence or actual motifs and the existence of any sort of intermediary between them, would thus seem to prove one initial theory, namely, that certain general tendencies are common to all arts. It also proves that the arts of Asia do not form a world apart.

RICHNESS AND DIVERSITY OF EVOLUTION

Our discussion of tendencies and rhythms has shown how numerous are the points of similarity existing between widely separated arts. When we come to consider the evolution of the arts of various civilisations we shall see that pronounced contrasts frequently coexist and persist within any given art. However, the successive stages of development in the life span of an art are so many and so varied that it would be impossible fully to trace the evolution of any art within the limited space allotted to us here. The few and often arbitrarily chosen indications to which we must restrict ourselves are aimed solely at giving an idea of the richness and diversity of certain arts and at providing a bird's-eye view of the marked differences between the most characteristic periods in their development. Since the changes wrought by time (evolution) in any given art are generally far more pronounced than either the regional differences between various schools or the differences between types of subjects represented (in India, for instance, where Buddhism and Hinduism flourished side by side, Buddhist and Hindu subjects were often simultaneously represented), we shall stress the point of view of evolution.

India

Our subject in this chapter will be the evolution of the arts of India and China up to the 10th century. As far as the art of India is concerned, we shall momentarily exclude the Indus valley civilisation (we return to it later, on page 365, and consider only Indian art proper, which, founded on Sanskrit culture, appeared towards the 3rd century B.C. and continues to this day.

Throughout the early period of Indian art, lasting until about the beginning of the Christian era (early style at Sanchi, and Maurya and Sunga periods), the artist remained a close observer of nature. He showed a remarkable talent for the portrayal of the animal world and an affectionate interest in the realities of daily life, without lapsing into any of the dry and precise realism, devoid of

substance, which is typical of decadent arts. Female
673 forms were full and rounded just as were those of the
695 stupas—religious monuments whose vast rotundity closed
upon itself. The Buddhist gentleness without insipidity,
and the understanding and love of ordinary life and living
things which characterised this art in its initial stages, gave
no hint of either the violent tension or the dynamic
vigour that were to come.

These qualities were perpetuated in northern India in
683 the Mathura style (*c.* 2nd century A.D.), with its rounded
figures, its love of the ordinary and a sensual coquetry
which gradually became idealised. The contemporary
though longer lasting Amaravati style (*c.* 2nd–4th centuries) in south-eastern India, showed a break with the early
style. Although the naturalism of the early period was
basically maintained, sexual preoccupations appeared, the
forms became elongated and idealised and the composition grew intensely mobile. The result was sometimes an
intimate and perfect union of contrasting elements, as in
681 the medallion from a stupa, showing the raising to heaven
of the Buddha's begging bowl. Despite the frenzied vitality
which dominates this circular composition, an effect of
homogeneity has been achieved through the organised
pattern of double concentric circles from which the bearer
of the bowl emerges and stands out; in the midst of so
much unbridled movement and of such varied almost
contorted attitudes, a harmony has been preserved through
the skilful balancing and interweaving of the forms into
a compact whole. While this Amaravati style tended in its
early stages to sacrifice harmony for intense movement,
in its decline it often succeeded in tempering movement
with harmony—though the female figures remained
elongated, restless and sexually provocative throughout,
and frequently of an incredibly sinuous suppleness.

Meanwhile, in the north-western confines of India
(West Pakistan and the eastern part of modern Afghanistan—ancient Gandhara and Kapisa), quite another style
687 was developing—a style known as Graeco-Buddhist
which, aesthetically, was merely the offshoot of the contemporary Graeco-Roman art, furthest removed from its
source. However, since the Graeco-Buddhist artists revo-
lutionised the Buddhist iconography by being the first
to dare to represent the Buddha himself, we cannot afford
to ignore this style. Through its iconographic innovation
this extremely original influence spread throughout India
and was soon assimilated and Indianised. Moreover, the
internal evolution of this short-lived Graeco-Buddhist
style is extremely curious in itself; it developed, so to
speak, from back to front, becoming younger and fresher
in appearance as it matured in age. Evolving from an
amalgam of motifs which through constant circulation
throughout the contemporary Graeco-Roman world had
become drained of substance, it revived and revitalised
them with the stimulus provided by the young and
exuberant Buddhism. Indeed, in this respect a comparison
of the same motif in Roman and in Graeco-Buddhist
art is most revealing, for the Graeco-Buddhist motif,
although certainly of later date, is less cold and less
academic and appears to be the earlier of the two.

The Gupta art of India (*c.* 5th–6th centuries), like the
Mathura style, derived its tendency towards idealisation
and its type of Buddha from Graeco-Buddhist art. However, having completely assimilated and transformed this
somewhat inferior Graeco-Buddhist contribution, it

achieved a rare degree of intimacy and perfection. The 688
clinging drapery, with or without supple concentric
folds, that enveloped and framed the Blessed One became
increasingly transparent, enhancing at once the majestic
stiffness and the idealisation of the figure and vibrating
around the sensitive modelling of the body surface. The
head was framed in a large decorated halo, and the features,
which at first presented the somewhat cold appearance of
the Graeco-Buddhist images, gradually assumed an expression of infinite warmth. This style reached its apogee,
and a harmonious balance of essential opposites, in the
great Bodhisattvas at Ajanta, whose faces express the 664
ineffable serenity and tranquillity acquired through patient meditation and the sacrifice of self out of compassion
for all suffering humanity. Raised to the level of mystic
introspection, these qualities correspond to the modesty
and desire, the introversion and amorous lassitude of the
female figures in Sanskrit painting and the heroines of the
Sanskrit theatre. The bodies of the Bodhisattvas have at
once a majestic fullness and a supple slenderness in keeping
with their beautiful faces, and a subtle languor and
refinement emanates from these frescoes at Ajanta.

Despite the continuity of evolution, the post-Gupta
style (6th–9th centuries) showed a reversal of certain
tendencies. Hinduism, with its cosmic intensity and
violence, gradually superseded and eliminated Buddhism
and, although the introspective qualities remained for a
time, new tendencies appeared (the dancing Siva at
Elephanta, etc.). We pass from the static, at first very
pronounced in this theme (Cave 14 at Ellura), to an equilibrium between the static and the dynamic (Cave 15 at 694
Ellura), and then we see the triumph of the latter (Cave
16 at Ellura). The point of equilibrium was overshot, and
the breach caused by the disruption of the balance between excessive movement and mannerism was filled by
the element of horror. Sanchi seems remote indeed!

China

The most characteristic examples of early art in China
are the bronzes. It must be remembered, however, that
our study of ancient Chinese art is based entirely on the
ritual objects pertaining to the funerary cults; other art
objects have disappeared. The strong harmonious forms
of the early style (end of the Shang-Yin and beginning of
the Chou Dynasties, 14th–11th centuries B.C.), ranging
from the most powerful and ruggedly massive and masculine to the most delicate and feminine, are covered with
geometric motifs and with meanders and spirals. Highly
stylised forms, sometimes made up of composite elements,
lend a dynamic vigour to the decoration; among these
forms are the animal head known as the *t'ao-t'ieh* (merging 396
into and emerging from the over-all design), the filiform
dragon in profile, and the wide, almost square, open
volute, an ornament which, sometimes flat, sometimes in 395
relief, is often interwoven with the fantastic animal forms.
This early style was succeeded by a series of important
styles. Let us consider a characteristic feature in the
evolution of the bronzes, which continued through the
Middle Chou period to that of the Warring States 401, 400
(5th–3rd centuries B.C.). This feature could be described
as a sort of realism within the fantastic. The handles and
lids of certain bronzes were modelled in the form of
fantastic animals with long, taut bodies—animals which
look as though they are about to leap into the air. The

period of the Warring States, which included more elaborate and more delicate and graceful ornaments, produced the first wholly realistic imitations of nature which were to thrive and to reach their full development during the Han epoch (2nd century B.C.—2nd century A.D.).

With the growth of realism, representations of everyday life and activities, which had hitherto been extremely rare, began to appear in great abundance. A narrative style developed, which portrayed history and legends with the same dynamic vigour as the preceding styles had portrayed animals. Indeed, despite a certain majestic stiffness, these narrative works give the impression of the impetuous fury of a whirlwind. Brush-and-ink painting also appeared about this time, and figures were captured with a few skilfully graduated open strokes of the brush (tiles in the Museum of Fine Arts, Boston). The Han epoch, in fact, constituted a sort of turning point in the development of Chinese art, a period which witnessed the decline of the past and the birth of new trends and techniques.

After a rather less vigorous prolongation of Han art, the spread of Buddhism to China gave rise to the Northern Wei style (c. 5th–6th centuries), which rapidly and radically transformed the outside influences which had penetrated with Buddhism. The dominant characteristic of this style was a hieratism, which, expressed in the static and frozen majesty of the figures and the almost schematic stylisation of the folds of the draperies, corresponds to that of Romanesque art. Among much that was mediocre, we find a few figures from this period which have the depth, the serenity and the introspection peculiar to Buddhism, and which display the ineffable smile.

Politically and economically China reached its height during the T'ang Dynasty (7th–9th centuries), but whereas Chinese painting and ceramics were to become fully developed during a later period, T'ang sculpture shows all the signs of an art that has reached the limits of its power and equilibrium and is on the decline. The tendency towards naturalism remained, but it was marred by too much attention to detail (horses of the Emperor T'ai-tsung, 7th century). We also find this tendency in the religious statuary of both China and Japan, but, while draperies remained stylised, these statues are so unctuously realistic that they leave one with a disagreeable impression of affectation. Moreover, as we have seen, the gulf between studied refinement on the one hand and profuse gesticulation and ostentatious musculature on the other became increasingly wider, until the menacing attitude and expression of the guardian divinities in both China and Japan reached the peak of exaggeration.

Chinese art now evinced a richness and diversity which became fully manifest in Sung painting and ceramics.

CONSTANTS

Constants are the qualities in an art which continue unchanged through the sometimes markedly mutating stages of its evolution. Since these constants may persist for a very long time, they are of inestimable value for the identification of the art in which they are found. However, let us beware of the all too common error of mistaking for constants those artificially or intellectually fabricated qualities which, under the names of 'basic personality', or *genius loci*, correspond to elements common to every art.

Generally speaking, the constants in an art are far outnumbered by the mutations.

India

A sensual quality has persisted through all Indian art proper (as apart from the Indus valley civilisations) from the 3rd century B.C. until the present time. It is an aesthetically valid sensuality which is much more than mere sexuality and which is manifest in the triple flexion (tribhanga) so often displayed by the figures. Together with a fullness of the breast and hips, the tribhanga is ubiquitous throughout the art of India, and its changing aspect reflects the diversity of the succeeding stages of evolution. Tranquil at first (early styles, from the 3rd century B.C. to about the beginning of the Christian era), it gradually became provocative (Mathura, c. 2nd century A.D.), and then tense and restlessly challenging, somewhere between naturalism and idealism (Amaravati, c. 2nd–4th centuries). With the Gupta period the triple flexion relaxed into a languorous, idealistic surrender of self (Ajanta, towards the beginning of the 6th century), only to be whipped up anew by the cosmic power that characterised the post-Gupta style (Siva's dance, 6th–8th centuries). Finally, while retaining its aesthetic value, it assumed either a contorted and rather manneristic aspect (particularly in the art of northern and eastern India, or south-east India right up to the present time). But through all these changes this sensual quality persisted and was moreover perpetually reinforced by what might be called a negative constant, the total absence of impassibility in Indian art, at least until a comparatively recent date. As scholars have pointed out, there is nothing austere, nothing that is the opposite of sensuality, and the tension in this art is almost always dynamic. The rigid hieratic quality (suspended tension) which is a characteristic feature of almost all religious arts is noticeably absent from the art of ancient India during the first ten centuries of its existence.

China

Chinese art at first glance appears to have no constants. However, it must be remembered that it covers an immense period of time of over three thousand years. If, therefore, we make a distinction between early Chinese art (up to about the first centuries of the Christian era) and 'recent' Chinese art, from the beginning of the T'ang period (7th century), two constants are discernible which seem to persist for about a thousand years.

The first is an almost violent energy and a balanced cosmic symbolism (probably the equilibrium between *yin* and *yang*) associated with the perennial representation of fantastic monsters and animals—a constant which doubtless appeared with the first bronzes (between the 14th and 11th centuries B.C.). In any case, it persisted up to the Christian era and did not disappear even then, though it was thereafter perpetuated through conscious imitations rather than spontaneous creations.

The second constant, which appeared early in the T'ang and became dominant during the Sung period (10th–13th centuries), is an ultra-refined taste. This taste, which stemmed from the traditions of calligraphy and brush-and-ink painting and from the development of ceramics, tends at times to smack of dilettantism and literary preoccupation. It is manifest in the at once delicate and sober

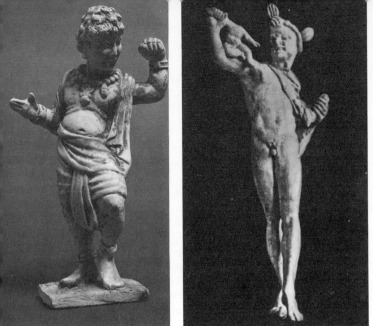

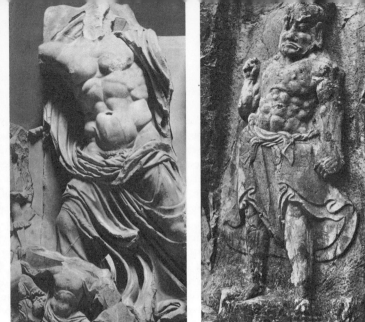

669. *Left*. CHINESE. T'ANG. Foreign dancer. Funerary terra-cotta figurine. *Cernuschi Museum, Paris*.

670. *Right*. GREEK. HELLENISTIC. Terra-cotta figurine from Myrina. *Louvre*.

671. *Left*. GREEK. HELLENISTIC. Detail from the frieze on the Great Altar at Pergamon. 2nd century B.C. *Berlin Museum*.

672. *Right*. CHINESE. T'ANG. Dvarapala (guardian of the gates). Rock carving at Lung-men (Honan).

painting, usually monochromatic, on silk or fragile paper, and in the ceramics (white, celadon, blue-grey, etc.), to which the same descriptive terms could be applied. Though it persisted long after the Sung, it steadily deteriorated, deviating further and further from its original monochrome subtlety to become pedantic, precious and superficial, with an almost excessive use of colour.

THE ARTS AND THOUGHT

The spiritual affinity between the visual arts and music, drama, literature, religion and philosophy goes far deeper than any palpable similarities of outward form. Indeed, though the environmental conditions under which an art develops also determine its orientation, aesthetic, religious or philosophical factors seem, in fact, to be far more influential and also infinitely more revealing.

India

Since the art (founded on Sanskrit culture) which appeared in India towards the 3rd century B.C. was pre-eminently Buddhist, it unmistakably reflected Buddhist ideals. We know that Buddhism generally emphasises compassion for all humanity and that early Buddhism in particular, reacting against the intellectualism of metaphysical preoccupations and the often extreme nervous tension caused by the excessive austerity of Brahmanism, stressed 'the middle way'. These ideals are incarnate in the art of Sanchi, which radiates a tranquil and confident affection for the things of everyday life, for the immediate environment and for the animal world. The ideals of later, Mahayana, Buddhism (Buddhism of the Great Vehicle) which, while permeated with outside elements, is also more elaborate and profoundly mystic, are in their turn

664
666 reflected in the Bodhisattvas of Ajanta (and in the Khmer smile of Angkor), who express at once the contemplative detachment and the compassion for humanity and its suffering that characterise mature Buddhism and its

CORRESPONDING EVOLUTIONS OF RHYTHM

Similar excesses of violence (gesticulation, musculature [671, 672]), and refinement [669, 670] may be observed in Chinese art and Greek art when they overstepped the point of equilibrium in their evolution.

673. *Left*. INDIAN. Tree divinity. Sculpture on eastern gate of Stupa 1 at Sanchi. 1st century B.C.–1st century A.D.

674. *Right*. INDIAN. LATE PERIOD. Female divinity. Bronze. *Madras Museum*.

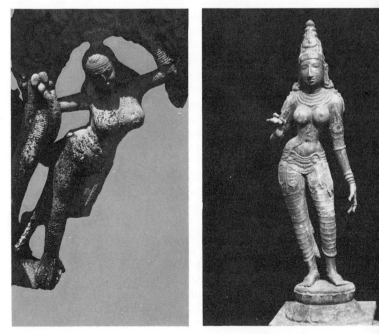

Bodhisattvas. This same expression was even perpetuated for a time in the predominantly Hindu art of the post-Gupta period.

We have had occasion earlier to mention the relations between the frescoes at Ajanta (first half of the 6th century) and Sanskrit theatre. There are also possibilities of reciprocal influences. In the first place, there is a striking correspondence between the Sanskrit language and the composition of the frescoes. According to the laws of euphony governing the Sanskrit language, contiguous words are united to form extended words and long, unbroken phrases punctuated only by the rebounding of the accents and rhythms. In the same way the frescoes along the walls at Ajanta, which unite figures and scenes in a continuous uninterrupted flow, at first appear confused and overfilled. (However, they are thus devoid of the harshness of, for example, Italian frescoes, which are brutally cut up by the straight lines separating the various scenes represented.) Like the accents in a Sanskrit phrase, the figures in Indian painting, by their position or the direction of their gaze, delimit the different scenes without interrupting the continuity of the composition as a whole. The analogy between Indian painting and Sanskrit theatre is not limited to this one point. Sanskrit theatre is essentially plastic, the plays generally being acted out in long, static scenes which constitute a succession of living tableaux of communicating figures. The characters are always idealised, heroes, heroines, etc., and sometimes they are described in poetic stanzas before they appear on stage. The duality and the contrasting emotions expressed by the female figures in the frescoes constantly recur in Sanskrit theatre and often in the stage directions—'with a mixture of desire and modesty' or 'of modesty and love', etc. Thus although the frescoes at Ajanta represent exclusively religious subjects they also unconsciously reflect court life and the idealised sexual love portrayed in Sanskrit theatre.

The subsequent (post-Gupta) period witnessed a complete change in trends and attitude, not only in the visual arts but also in literature and religion. The tone of cosmic exaltation and the violent and horrific elements which gradually pervaded both religion and the arts, while generally absent from Buddhism, are characteristic of Hinduism (worship of Vishnu and Siva). In fact it was during this period that Hinduism gradually came to replace Buddhism as the dominant religion of India. Was it the change in taste that brought about the change of religion, or was it the religious change which led to the change in taste? It is impossible to say—it may have been reciprocal action. In any case, the changes seem to have come about simultaneously in the visual arts, in literature and in religion. An extremely curious testimony of this transition has survived in a work of the Sanskrit theatre, the *Nagananda* (*The Joy of the Serpents*), which reflects the new trend. It shows as well the link between religion and profane literature. The first half of this play shows the usual mild flirtations between amorous couples, typical of Sanskrit theatre during the preceding (Gupta) period with its Buddhistic overtones and consistently gentle atmosphere devoid of violence. The second half, however, while maintaining the Buddhist tradition of charity (demonstrated in the self-sacrifice of the hero), has all the accents of Hinduism in its most exaggerated form, accents which in turn correspond to certain aspects of post-Gupta

art, horror, bloodshed and repugnant tragedy. These images, which are totally absent from only slightly older texts, reflect the new (almost Surrealist) trend in both the literature and the art of this period.

China

In China a connection is immediately apparent between the monochrome painting of the 7th and the 13th centuries A.D. Moreover, there is a definite relationship with the fantastic animals and the cosmic symbolism of an earlier period. The animals of the four cardinal points were constantly reproduced during the Han period, the Red Bird of the South, the Green Dragon of the East, the White Tiger of the West and the Black Warrior of the North, this last represented by a tortoise combatting a serpent. These same colours were apparently worn by the emperor when he symbolically journeyed, four times a year, to the four cardinal points to regulate the seasons and to ensure the harmonious balance of the principles *yin* and *yang*. Indeed, the alternation of these two principles seems to have constituted the basis of the Chinese concept of the world.

723

COMMUNICATIONS: THE GREAT MARITIME AND OVERLAND ROUTES

What most impressed scholars forty years ago was the then comparatively recent revelation of the great network of maritime and overland routes which had existed throughout Eurasia from earliest times. The many discoveries of objects and the steady widening of the field of historical knowledge have enabled our generation to reconnoitre vast spaces and to gain some understanding of seemingly inaccessible arts. However, a great deal of prejudice and misplaced chauvinism has still to be overcome if we are to reap the full benefit of the new possibilities offered. Only one art can be 'the oldest in the world', and the fact that each art, with the exception of the oldest, has absorbed outside influences does not in the least detract from its value, since the personality of an art is manifest not in its imperviousness to outside influences but in its ability to assimilate and transform these into an original art form. The world's greatest arts have all been influenced by their predecessors or contemporaries: Egyptian art by Mesopotamian art, Cretan art by Egyptian art and Greek art and European medieval art by the art of the Near East. As for India, the Indus valley civilisation was probably influenced by ancient Mesopotamia; Achaemenian Persia and the Hellenised Near East influenced the early style of Indian art proper (up to the beginning of the Christian era); Graeco-Roman art influenced the Graeco-Buddhist style, and, during a later period, the influence of Islamic Persia became preponderant in northern India—yet India's art has always been one of the most personal and creative. Likewise, Chinese art is no longer the isolated phenomenon it seemed until not so long ago, and Khmer art appears no less independent and original for having made ample use of Indian techniques and motifs, which it radically transformed to suit its own individual needs and taste. The same is true of the other arts in the Oriental world.

Generally speaking, commercial and quasi-cultural exchanges (pilgrimages, voyages in quest of religious information, the conversion of a ruler, etc.) have con-

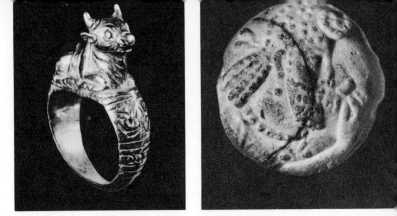

tributed to a far greater extent than conquests (such as Alexander's short-lived expedition) and political factors to the often incredibly far-flung migration and transmission of artistic motifs, many of which were perpetuated long after their significance had been forgotten.

Working on the principle that the course of ancient, overgrown roads can be more easily distinguished from the air, we shall attempt to get, as it were, an aerial perspective on these great migrations, even at the risk of the routes perhaps appearing slightly distorted from a distance. We shall also go back in time, since a brief discussion of the earliest civilisations to appear in the regions we are studying seems appropriate here.

Influences in prehistoric times

Mohenjo-Daro and Harappa are the best-known sites of an ancient civilisation which flourished in the Indus valley and which is generally presumed to date back to about 2000 years before the Christian era. This civilisation would seem, despite several marked differences, to be much more closely related to the vast group of Mesopotamian and neighbouring arts than to Indian art proper, which did not develop until later and to which its resemblance is but slight. An art that succeeds another in the same place need not *ipso facto* have any connection with its predecessor. In Iran, for example, Persian Islamic art shows but little affinity to either early Elamite art or even Achaemenian art (6th century B.C.) though all flourished on the same soil. Whereas the urban organisation of the Indus valley civilisation places it in a class apart, its seals, though differing from Mesopotamian cylinders, were no doubt used for similar purposes. The numerous objects that have come to light, especially local ceramics (among which is a vase with typical Indus valley decoration, found near Kandahar, in Afghanistan, in the spring of 1954), prove that a quasi-civilisation existed throughout the region between the Indus and Mesopotamia, from which emerged limited zones of more advanced civilisation (Mesopotamia and the Indus valley). It is quite possible that Mesopotamian influence, which had already spread to Egypt at a very early date, was later projected in the opposite direction.

85, 86 Probably of a slightly later date, the earliest Chinese Neolithic pottery is not perhaps without some resemblance to Western pottery. While this pottery has sometimes been compared to that of the Caucasus regions, a certain correspondence has also been noted between the motifs on some of the early Chinese vases and Cretan designs, a correspondence which, though far from being sufficiently positive to admit a common ancestor, is perhaps not wholly coincidental. China can no longer be considered an isolated civilisation, since even in its remotest past a corpus of painted ceramics linked it to Europe.

Moreover, thanks to the long and patient research of Vadime Elisseeff, whose ideas we hope we have not misrepresented, new light has been thrown on the spread of the motifs associated with the early bronzes. In connection with this, two images come to mind: the first is that of an arc drawn across the map, representing a road running through southern Siberia and the steppes (which were inhabited by nomadic tribes) from northern Iran (Luristan and the Caucasus) to the China of the Shang Dynasty; but it is possible that a different, more southerly route, the one that was to become the Silk Route, already existed at

675. *Left*. INDIAN. Ring decorated with a bull. *Saigon Museum*.

676. *Right*. IRANIAN. Cameo of Sassanian style. *Saigon Museum*.

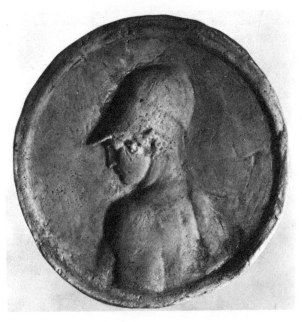

677. WESTERN INFLUENCE. GRAECO-ROMAN. Plaster medallion. 1st century A.D.

THE NETWORK OF COMMUNICATIONS

The diverse origins of objects discovered in one and the same site (at Begram or at Oc Eo for example) prove the existence of an important network of communications across Eurasia during the first centuries A.D.

678. *Left*. INDIAN. Carved ivory plaque. 1st–2nd centuries A.D.

679. *Right*. WESTERN INFLUENCE. GRAECO-ROMAN. Painted glass goblet. 1st–2nd centuries. A.D.

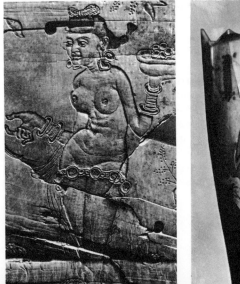

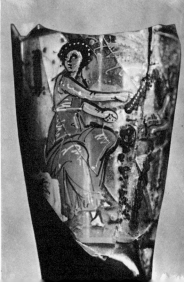

this time. The second image is one that is often encountered in Egyptian tombs, that of two figures facing one another from either end of a composition, each figure holding a vase with liquid spraying from it, the sprays meeting and intersecting. It has been common knowledge for some time that early Mesopotamian and Elamite motifs had long been perpetuated in the Near East and that, through the agency of Luristan and the regions bordering on the Caucasus, these motifs had become incorporated into the animal art known as the art of the steppes. It seems, however, that the motifs which circulated through Shang China (14th–11th centuries) and the other regions at the eastern end of our route were of Chinese origin: hence the probability of a counter-movement from east to west. That southern Siberia and China communicated across the Ordos regions has been conclusively proved, though the nature of this communication is still not completely understood; possibly it was a case of reciprocal influence. The picture is only just beginning to emerge, but already its extreme complexity has become apparent. It seems at present quite certain that the flow and exchange of influences and motifs across northern Asia, between Luristan and the Caucasus and China, was constant throughout the 1st millennium A.D. (see pp. 219–230).

From the Mediterranean to India and beyond

There was doubtless a break in continuity after the Indus valley civilisation, and Indian art proper when it appeared during the 3rd century B.C. had a highly individual style made up partly of local elements (copies in stone of the forms and motifs developed in wood—figures, animals and plants reproduced directly from nature) and partly of imported elements (motifs from Achaemenian Persia and the Hellenised Near East). It was a composite style which demonstrated the relations between different arts, and which persisted in Indian art during the whole of its early period. The capital from one of the Emperor Asoka's columns, found at Sarnath, while it displays Indian animals treated in the Indian manner, has the bell form of the Persepolitan capitals and is surmounted by lions of Hellenic type (as scholars have pointed out). In the same way, the superimposed palaces representing the six nether heavens of the gods, carved on a pillar of one of the gateways of the great stupa at Sanchi (dating from just before the beginning of the Christian era), are of two different types: whereas some have the octagonal columns without capitals or bases, and the high cornice pierced with the ogival arches of local tradition (copied from wooden architecture), others display transformed Persepolitan columns with bell capitals and joined forequarters of animals. Elsewhere we find on one and the same gateway pillars which are adorned with typically Indian motifs (lotus blooms, undulating boughs, etc.) and others which have Western ornamentation (palmettes). The columns in the rock-cut sanctuary at Karli (towards the beginning of the Christian era) combine the octagonal and the sixteen-sided shafts of local tradition with the bell capital and back-to-back animals of Persepolitan art. The juxtaposition of indigenous and outside elements was thus persistent throughout early Indian art.

Even more striking amalgams were to come, most probably due to the expansion of Roman trade and commerce during the first centuries of our era and to the establishment at this time of relations between Rome and China. The effect of Alexander's expedition on art was long overestimated, credited, as it was, with having been the direct cause of the development of the Graeco-Buddhist style, although the latter did not appear until at least four hundred years after Alexander's death. Actually, though in itself of real significance, the expedition had only an indirect, partial and delayed effect on art, and then only in as much as it led to the establishment of Hellenised kingdoms within the confines of India from which Greek culture was, under the Kushan rulers, subsequently disseminated throughout all the border regions. In fact, it would seem to have been the conversion to Buddhism of Kanishka, the most famous of these rulers, which by promoting the spread of Buddhism also promoted that of surviving or reimported Graeco-Roman-Iranian culture. Above all, it was the vast movement of Roman commerce during the 1st century A.D. that we believe provided the stimulus for the development of Graeco-Buddhist art, which appeared towards the end of the 1st century or in the first half of the 2nd century.

The most important archaeological campaigns of recent years in southern and south-eastern Asia, the majority of which have been carried out by the French, have all provided further proof of the manifold communications between these various civilisations. Three of these campaigns marked out the course of the maritime route followed during the 1st and 2nd centuries of our era. The elaborate network of overland caravan routes across Eurasia appears to be of slightly later date.

The expeditions directed by Joseph Hackin in Afghanistan in 1937, 1939 and 1940, brought to light a veritable treasure at Begram, the summer capital of the Kushan sovereign. There, under great mounds of earth in two walled-up rooms, lay many damaged objects from the West, from India and from China—a meeting of three civilisations. Western civilisation was represented by painted glassware, bronzes and the plaster casts of vanished silver plate, offering examples in their most perfect form of themes recurrent in the Graeco-Roman world. Indian 677, 679 civilisation was represented by the fragmentary remains of ivory furniture, revealing the hitherto unknown work of the early Indian ivory-carvers. With the help of drawings, 678 photographs and notes, made during the course of excavation, the archaeologists were able to give some picture of this furniture and its extreme decorative richness. Lacquer being a very fragile material, nothing remains of the objects from China beyond a few traces of their decoration. O. Kurz, V. Elisseeff and the author, who each made a separate study of the objects in this treasure, agree that they would all seem to date from the 1st and perhaps the 2nd centuries A.D. The objects from the West would seem to have been brought by Roman traders following the maritime route and going up the Indus to reach Kapisa.

The excavations started by G. Jouveau-Dubreuil and continued by Sir Mortimer Wheeler and others, at Virapatnam-Arikamedu, near Pondicherry, led to the discovery of numerous fragments of Aretine pottery from Italy, dating from the first half of the 1st century A.D. Commerce of some importance must therefore have linked Rome and India at that time.

Further afield, excavations made at Oc Eo, near Saigon in Indo-China, in 1944, revealed an assortment of

Roman intaglios and two impressions from Roman coins, one of which is dated 152. Small pieces of delicately worked Indian jewellery, some objects of Iranian origin and a fragment of a Chinese mirror were also found here. Thus a Rome-China link by sea was definitely established by the 2nd century A.D., either by Roman traders themselves or by intermediaries. In view of the discoveries made at Begram, Virapatnam and Oc Eo, and considering that the excavations in these regions are only of recent date and limited number, that very few of the objects buried have as yet been uncovered and that the buried objects themselves constitute only a handful of those which circulated in the region, one has the impression that the Roman sea trade at this time must have been considerable.

675, 676

Across central Asia

Overland communications, which did not assume their full importance until a later date, were first established between the Graeco-Roman world and India; subsequently they extended through the oases of central Asia and along the Silk Route to China. The religious upsurges throughout the Near East during the first centuries of the Christian era (Gnostic, Manichaean, etc.) were intense and influential. We are told that during the 3rd century the great Alexandrian philosopher Plotinus and the Iranian religious founder Mani simultaneously accompanied the opposing Roman and Iranian armies, the one to get in touch with the religions of the East and the other to acquire a better knowledge of thought in the West. This may be legendary but it is significant. Mani, the creator of a sect which almost became the nucleus of one of the great religions of the world, preached a syncretism uniting Jesus, Zoroaster and the Buddha. He too had been to India. Indeed, such figures show how accessible was the ancient world at that time to religious penetration and thus to aesthetic penetration, which usually follows. Had Mazdaism (Zoroastrianism) not prevailed over nascent Manichaeism in Iran, thus creating a barrier between India and the West at a time when Mani's disciples were bringing the two worlds closer together, it is possible (according to Alfred Foucher) that Buddhism, instead of branching off towards the East along the Silk Route and reaching China, might have continued on its way northwest and gained Europe before the triumph of Christianity. Had this been the case Indian art, instead of taking the Silk Route to China, might have spread towards the West and reached Europe before the Carolingian renaissance, thus changing the entire course of medieval art.

But we must leave these digressions into hypothetical history and return to authentic facts. Running parallel to but south of the bronze route, and only fully developed after the dawn of the Christian era, the Silk Route traversed the oases of central Asia and joined the overland route linking India to Rome. China had opened up this route in the Han epoch for military purposes and reasons of security (campaigns and supremacy in central Asia). The route then opened to commerce, and new centres of culture arose which subsisted for almost a thousand years and whose role in connection with ancient civilisations had already been discussed in Chapter 6. These centres collected, amalgamated and spread the styles and motifs of the West, of Persia, of India and of China.

Graeco-Buddhist art spread through central Asia to China, where completely transformed Graeco-Buddhist elements constituted the basis of Wei art.

Next came a wave of Iranian influence, which seems to have corresponded to the Sassanian period and which persisted up to the 7th century (Fondukistan, in Afghanistan). It swept through what is now Afghanistan to central Asia (Kizil, etc.), and on as far as the Chinese border, bringing with it a host of Iranian themes (the cut of Iranian dress, head-dresses, armour, etc.). J. Hackin, who indicated the importance of this Iranian influence, proposed that the art in which it predominated should be called Irano-Buddhist, in the same way that a preceding art had been named Graeco-Buddhist.

A third wave of influence came from India, whose art had already intermittently affected central Asia. However, it was not until the great expansion of Indian art, during the 6th, 7th and 8th centuries, that Indian influence really began to make itself felt. Painted Buddhas in three-quarters view and figures in the Gupta style, bent in the Indian fashion, are to be seen at Ajanta (India), at Bamiyan and Fondukistan (in present-day Afghanistan) and in central Asia (Kizil and Dandan Uiliq). The Indian elements eventually reached China (T'ien-lung Shan) and even Japan (frescoes at Horyuji).

Finally, Chinese influence was felt which at its peak not only affected Tun-huang, on China's borders, but also penetrated to Astana and even beyond, though its force diminished as it went farther afield.

The Indian and Chinese influences met in Tibet, whose history and art commenced with its conversion to Buddhism during the 7th century. The first great Tibetan ruler successively married an Indian and a Chinese princess, an authentic fact which would seem to be symbolic of the two currents that dominated Tibetan art; these two princesses are represented by the Green Tara and the White Tara. Although none of the works known at present are particularly ancient, Tibetan art is so traditional that even recent works preserve details which appear to have been imported from India during the 7th and 8th centuries.

In Tibet as elsewhere successive waves of outside influence would appear to have left their mark on painting and bronzes, though we have not yet been able to define accurately the various foreign elements. In painting, the composition, the figures, the iconography and certain rather precious attitudes seem to derive from Indian art, while the architectural representations and landscapes in painting, and certain unusual attitudes noted among the bronzes, appear to be attributable to China. Added to these Indian and Chinese influences we find certain local elements (such as architecture and decoration) and, perhaps, a slight admixture of Iranian influence of a much later date than that which inspired Irano-Buddhist art.

Parallel to these great overland routes, the maritime route, opened up by the Roman traders, was of a very special importance to art. Indeed, it was in the Hinduised kingdoms along this route that new arts flourished which, though born of Indian influence, rapidly developed individual and original styles. Although their rise was contemporary with the third wave of influence that spread overland through central Asia—the Indian expansion of the 6th–8th centuries—usually these new arts did not reach maturity until after the 10th century.

INDIA AND ITS CULTURAL EXPANSION UP TO 1000 A.D. *Jeannine Auboyer*

India, whose Indus valley civilisation had had some links with the civilisations of the Near East, was henceforth to assert its own individual personality. As the birthplace of Buddhism, India was to be the founder of a tremendous religious movement whose eastward expansion was to revolutionise the art of the Far East and bring about a certain cultural unity in Asia.

The art of India long remained unknown to the West; since only the lamentable products of contemporary artisans found their way into the hands of Western collectors, it is hardly surprising that India's artistic abilities met with little appreciation. For while the monstrous iconography of late debased art doubtless had the lure of singularity, it gave but a pale reflection of the Indian artist's real gifts. The West saw only figures with grimacing convulsed faces and multiple gesticulating arms, pyramids of more or less repulsive heads, and human figures with the heads or bodies of animals—all of them garishly coloured—works of a cheap and sentimental tastelessness, rendered grotesque through exaggeration, which, unfortunately, are still being sold to both tourists and pilgrims. Yet these same collectors, even after devoting three quarters of a century to cataloguing the art treasures of India, may still be guilty of having overlooked a few of the masterpieces which place India among the greatest artistic civilisations of all time. With their purity of line, simplicity of modelling, sober grace of attitude and balanced composition, these masterpieces are able to satisfy even the most intransigent 'classicists'.

Thanks to the above-mentioned inventory it is now possible to survey the panorama of Indian art in its entirety. It stretches from about the 3rd century B.C. to the present day and may be divided into distinct if not clearly delimited periods, one of the most important of which was the period of the nationalist and imperialist Gupta Dynasty. However, the earlier period had hardly run its course before a new and entirely different era opened, between the 10th and 11th centuries, at a time when the earlier styles were beginning to be transformed by new concepts which reflected the increasing taste for the monumental—a taste which had existed previously but had been differently expressed.

The obscure origins of Indian art

The art of India as we know it today sprang suddenly into being between the 3rd and 2nd centuries B.C., apparently out of nothing. Indeed, neither the terra-cotta figurines nor the few remains of the foundations of the palace at Pataliputra, dating from the 4th century, suffice to explain the magnificent flowering of the 2nd century; they merely reveal the powerful influence of Achaemenian Persia—while the small terra cottas only remotely suggest the monumental sculpture which was to come. To expect to find any correspondence between early Indian art and the far more archaic pieces which came to light during the excavations at Mohenjo-Daro and Harappa would be still less feasible: related to the Mesopotamian or Mediterranean civilisations, these latter bear no stylistic resemblance whatsoever to Indian art proper. However, though no traces of its genesis remain (India has a formidably destructive climate) we may safely assume that Indian art went through a long period of gestation during which only perishable materials were used. For when the architects and sculptors of the early period learned to fashion stone, they faithfully copied the techniques of carpentry and of wood and ivory carving. The **680** Indian artists' first works in stone have disappeared along with their perishable prototypes; by the time the earliest of the surviving stone monuments appeared—those at Bharhut and other early decorated caves—the period of apprenticeship, to judge by the consummate execution, was long past.

Since no trial pieces have been found, it is tempting to suppose that stone carving was taught the Indians by foreigners who had already perfected the art, like the Iranians with whom India had commercial relations and who also had sanctuaries hewn out of rocky cliffs. However, there is nothing to justify such a supposition; on the contrary, the integral transposition into stone of the motifs and techniques used in wood carving and wooden construction work leads to the conclusion that the Indian worker in stone must at first have been associated with the workers in heavy timber, and must have learned the technique of building on the spot. The application of this technique to a completely different material must have created many problems: trying to assemble stone uprights and cross-pieces by means of tenon and mortise seems a hazardous process; nevertheless, this was the method **693, 697** that prevailed for four or five hundred years, a fact which is extremely revealing, for throughout its evolution Indian architecture was to remain, at least in spirit, far closer to sculpture than to a genuine architecture.

The face of Indian art

Though the evolution of architecture in India is tremendously interesting, it is the sculpture and mural paintings that provide the best material for the study and definition of the Indian aesthetic. The sculptured images represent its most formal aspect, while the relief carvings and narrative frescoes betray a more uninhibited, everyday vein. It is in these frescoes that the descriptive and narrative qualities so typical of Indian literature, whose fables have inspired both East and West, are expressed with wonderful spontaneity. At first glance, mystic or religious undertones are hardly discernible; the art of India is essentially a sacred art, yet it is the profane aspect in the scenes depicted which is the most striking: a wealth of precise detail faithfully reproduces the public and private life of the time, and even the subjects themselves would appear to have been taken from everyday life; nothing in the early iconography distinguishes a god from a man. Moreover, the artist's delight in the human body, **673, 674** which he depicted in lascivious, languorous or dynamic attitudes, further heightened the impression of profanity made on the uninitiated. This impression, however, is

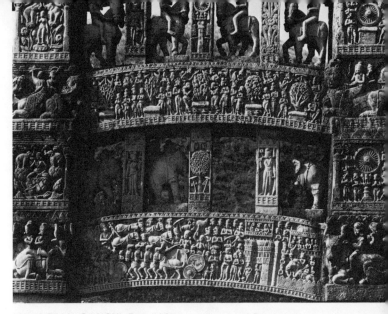

illusory, and is no more than a literal translation into visual terms of Indian life, in which things sacred are in fact so intimately linked to things profane—and especially during these early periods—that the miraculous appears natural. As in the time of the pilgrims of Emmaus, any man encountered along the road could turn out to be a god incarnate, while the hooked fish or snared hind might well be some holy man temporarily obliged to assume animal form. It is from this viewpoint, based entirely on the principle of the transmigration of souls or *samsara*, that the scenes of the early period should be approached.

During the twelve or thirteen centuries which constitute the first phase of India's artistic development, as much progress was made in the mastery of technique as in the style as a whole. As the proficiency of the painters and sculptors increased, the compositions became more sophisticated. At first only the protagonists of the story were represented, but later the number of human figures was greatly increased to symbolise the Asiatic crowd, always dense and always abreast of every major or trivial event; the scenery, at first indicated by a single element (a tree for a forest or a building for a town), was soon evoked with a wealth of a detail as decorative as it was valuable for archaeological study; the groupings became 680 more complicated as a result of the artist's search for conventions which would enable him to reproduce any scene within a given form. The whole became increasingly complex, and the Oriental taste, with its tendency to fill every last space with decoration, asserted itself to the full. The human body came to play an increasingly important 681 part in the pattern of the compositions. The arts of relief carving and mural painting began to interpenetrate; the carvings were polychromed and the painted forms were raised with slight modelling. This convergence, though no longer apparent today (the carvings having lost their colour), is in itself highly significant, since it explains the similarity in character between the narrative and decorative forms and the fact that the two used identical formulas.

From its beginnings the art of India had its own definite personality: it was naturalistic and depicted nature in an idealised way. Old age and deformity were never portrayed, except in cases of absolute necessity. Heroes were shown as young and virile; heroines were women in all the fullness of their youth. Of all the arts of Asia, this is the one most directly comprehensible to Western eyes and is the living embodiment of the definition 'Indo-European', applied to Indian civilisation. While China was orientated towards the Pacific, India's history was marked by contacts with the Near East, and, beyond it, with the Mediterranean world; it was no chance affinity that linked India to the West, but direct influence. The bulk and the most effective of the motifs Indian art received from outside were those which came with the variety of styles, collectively called Graeco-Buddhist, which reached India by way of the Indo-Greek satrapies of Afghanistan and Gandhara. A lesser though more constant influence was that of Iran, which increased during the period of the Indo-Scythian or Kushan supremacy throughout northern and central India (from the 2nd century B.C. to the 2nd century A.D.) and which was continually renewed by the political, commercial and intellectual exchanges that went on over the centuries that followed. These motifs—which all seem to have

680. INDIAN. SANCHI. Detail of the north gate of Stupa 1, with scenes from the Buddha's previous incarnations.

reached India by way of the north-western overland routes—were at first adopted more or less unchanged by the Indian artists, though, eventually, few actually remained in the Indian repertory. Those that did, became totally assimilated with the Indian formulas and were endlessly reproduced and transmitted together with more essentially Indian motifs.

A further two distinguishing features complete the 'physical' portrait of Indian art. The first is an almost total anonymity, due to the fact that Indian art is a religious art and also that it reflects an ensemble of distinct beliefs. The second is its equal mastery of the representation of either animal or human forms, a mastery which 691 revealed itself in the earliest works and which has been maintained to this day.

Indianity and Brahmanism

Though the art of India is relatively simple in appearance, and though it is possible to define its aesthetic principles and trace its decorative evolution, it is not enough to

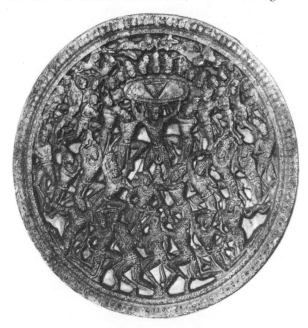

681. INDIAN. AMARAVATI. The elevation of the Buddha's begging bowl. Medallion decorating a balustrade of the stupa. 2nd–3rd centuries A.D. *Madras Museum.*

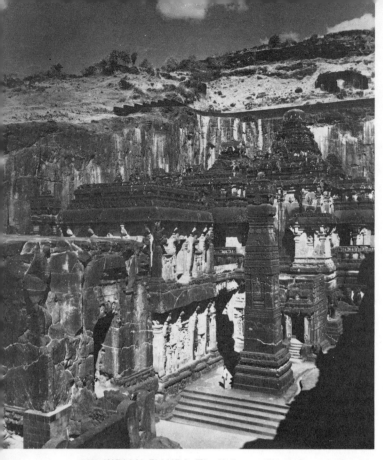

682. INDIAN. ELLURA. The Kailasanath temple, entirely hewn out of the rock. 8th century A.D.

appreciate merely its simple outward form, for beneath this lies all 'Indianity', with its millennia of traditions, its beliefs, its symbolism, its way of life and its thoughts and feelings. The least of its expressions has a profound reason; there is not a single early work that is not subject to its laws. Perhaps no art so faithfully reflects the civilisation that produced it.

What, then, is India, and what is meant by Indianity? In truth, such a definition is fraught with pitfalls and is inevitably of a somewhat arbitrary nature; one must take into account not only the immensity of India, which is a veritable subcontinent, but also the contrasts which characterise it throughout; it is a vast triangle bordered by the sea and by a wall of almost impassable mountains, an extravagant land vacillating between extremes of climate and grooved by gigantic rivers whose flow is irregular and whose course is changeable. Its climate runs the gamut from the Indus desert through the sumptuous palm-groves of Malabar, the humid tropical zone, and from the bleak savannahs of Bengal to the luxuriant flora of the Himalayan forest. The diverse regions are very unevenly populated, and the people range from purest white with aquiline noses to negroid elements and types akin to those of Indo-China and Malaya. In certain coastal regions a wide variety of cross-breeding has taken place over the centuries between Portuguese, African Negroes, Ethiopians, Jews and Arabs; elsewhere, colonies were established such as those of the Parsees who had fled from persecutions in Iran. In short it is a land of opposites and contrasts, of fabulous riches and sordid misery, and yet it forms an integrated whole.

Despite the instability and political disintegration which have often been the rule throughout its history, India seems to possess a mysterious power to transform the peoples and individuals who settle on her soil—a sort

of magnetism which Indianises them, binds them together and renders them an integral part of the immense Indian community. Thus the extremes of geographic diversity and ethnic variety are offset by a certain coherence which maintains the balance of the colossus. This diversity and fundamental unity are simultaneously reflected in the art of India, and there is nothing more revealing in this connection than a comparison of contemporary schools. Whereas the styles differ to the point of being distinguishable one from another at first glance, the details are of the period: the shape of a turban, a piece of jewellery or a chair is more often than not identical from one region to another; only the aesthetic expression differs. Northern art is drier, more rounded and stocky, southern art more supple, manneristic and exuberant.

The principal factor in this unity is undoubtedly Brahmanism, which appears to be not only a religion or philosophy, but also the very basis of Indianity. With its roots reaching back to protohistoric times, when the Aryans inhabited Avestic Iran and invaded India, Brahmanism is in effect the sum of knowledge as much as a ritual technique, and it embraces practically every individual and collective activity of Indian society. Perceptible throughout an astonishingly copious literature, in which the esoteric is coupled with magical recipes of the utmost banality and the metaphysical with rules of military strategy, is the intense pulsation of an organised world, rich in traditions and endowed with an exceptional sense of the divine. This world, a world to whose laws both gods and men alike are subject, is based on a rigid hierarchy. Society, divided into four main castes and innumerable sub-castes, is subject to the authority of the two ruling castes, that of the Brahmins, or priests, and that of the Kshatriyas, or warriors; the whole system is built on the principle of a sacrosanct aristocracy, and although the Brahmin caste is superior to the Kshatriya, in the final analysis it is of necessity from the latter caste that the king or emperor is recruited, and it is he who is in fact the keystone of the social edifice. The ideal and perfect example of the noble warrior, he is by definition endowed with all the qualities of the hero: he is a skilful archer and swordsman, a consummate horseman, a shrewd diplomat, a wise administrator, an experienced and successful player of games and a man as deeply versed in the arts and sciences as it is possible to be. In all things he is the first among his subjects; he is moreover their mandatory and their protector.

The status of the artist and the state of art

The status of the artist and artisan in this society seems to have been variable, and it is impossible to make any definite pronouncements on the subject. During the early period the painter or sculptor was regarded as a domestic; later, he was assigned to the caste of the Sudras or cultivators; he must in any case have become fairly prosperous, since it is recorded that around the 9th–10th centuries he paid his debts in gold. To judge from Indian literature, however, it would seem that guilds and corporations were the prevailing system and that villages were inhabited entirely by one or other of these corporations whose members observed certain rules or customs which tended to set them in a class apart within the social hierarchy: artistic production would thus have been a matter of teamwork or of ateliers.

683

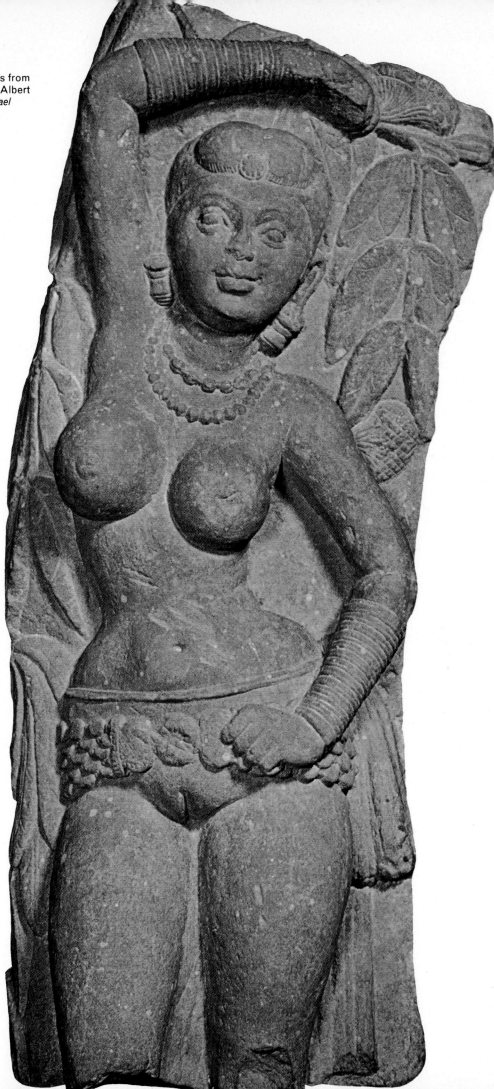

INDIAN. Tree goddess from Mathura. Victoria and Albert Museum. *Photo: Michael Holford.*

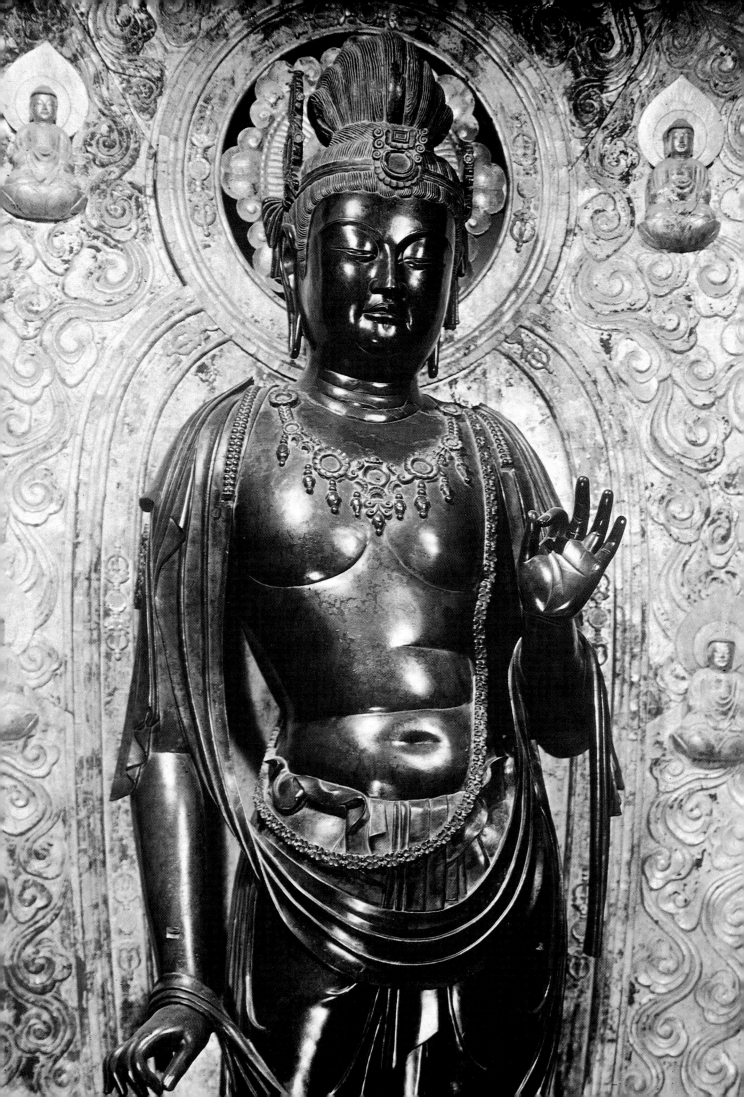

This, however, excluded neither the existence of the isolated artist nor the practice of the visual arts by the superior castes. During the classical period, in particular, the king would have been the first to take up painting; he generally owned a gallery of paintings which were the pride of the kingdom, and, what is more, it was he who was the principal promoter of the great religious foundations in which sculpture and mural painting flourished. Following the monarch's enlightened dilettantism, the rich landowners each had their own goldsmiths and participated in the erection of monuments and statues; they even practised certain arts themselves, and a painting kit was the recommended gift during the 3rd and 4th centuries for a young girl to give to a young man. Carved boxes containing brushes, and gourds for colours, figure also among the gifts presented in the 5th century.

The majority of the great works of art which have survived were the result of collective labour, probably directed by a foreman whose presence would explain their uniform character.

This is only the practical aspect of the matter, and, in reality, it is the least important, for Indian art being essentially a religious art exists solely in the service of a vast cosmological and symbolic concept, fostered by Brahmanism but also considerably exploited by Buddhism. This cosmology, certain details of which were perhaps derived from Babylonia, closely associates the human world to the divine world: both have oceans, mountains, rivers, palaces, a hierarchic population and a supreme ruler. Everything in these two worlds is founded on analogies and obeys joint schemes which correlate and coordinate their different elements on various levels. Both are subjects to a code which justifies, from the Indian point of view, the establishment of castes, and which determines the incorporation of art into the domain of ritual technique. The whole mechanism which governs art is hereby explained: the temple or statue cannot be just any work of art, a thing beautiful for its own sake and an expression of the artist's personal concept and love of beauty; it must fulfil minutely the religious function for which it is created, obeying the precise and inexorable rules laid down in aesthetic treatises; the artist must scrupulously follow these rules, on pain of otherwise producing an imperfect work. Behind all this there is in fact a quasi-magical law which it would be dangerous to transgress: if the work does not conform in every last detail to the canonical principles, it runs the risk not only of failing to benefit either its author or its viewer, but also of being the cause of certain disaster.

The symbolic character of the temple

The symbolic value attached to the temple or statue is in fact fundamental and is rooted in thousands of years of tradition: as in prehistoric times, the work is the equivalent of the cosmos. The temple is therefore a replica of the divine residence, the world mountain which is the central pivot of the universe. Among the various architectural forms devised for the symbolic portrayal of this mountain the most explicit is that of a temple with a pyramidal roof corresponding to the different storeys which in the divine cosmology support the dwellings of the gods. The temple is a veritable microcosm, its every part a parallel of those of the divine world. The theoretical plan of an Indian temple (put into practice far more often in Cambodia

684
682

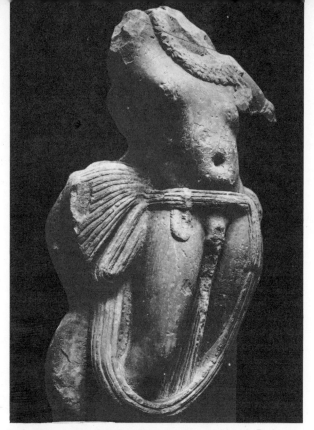

683. INDIAN. MATHURA. Nagaraja (serpent-king). Red sandstone. 2nd century A.D. *Musée Guimet, Paris.*

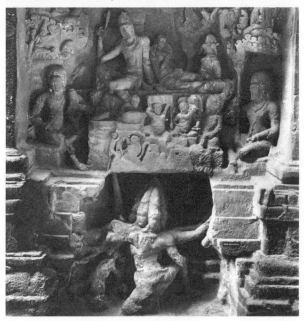

684. INDIAN. ELLURA. Representation of Mount Kailasa, the summit of which is the residence of Siva and his sakti, Parvati; the demon Ravana tries to lift the divine mountain. Carving in high relief from the Kailasanath. Kashtrakuta style. 8th century A.D.

than in India itself) consists of a vast quadrangular enclosure with concentric enclosures, also quadrangular. The walls are pierced with monumental portals; there is a central sanctuary, and there are numerous buildings within the enclosures. This disposition is an intentional reproduction of the imagined shape of the world, which, according to Indian tradition, resembles an immense quadrangle bordered by oceans (the artificial lakes encircling the temple), surrounded by chains of mountains (the enclosures) and supporting in its midst the world mountain, the habitat of the divinity (the sanctuary). The

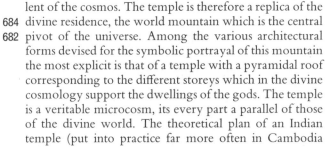

JAPANESE. Gakko Bosatsu, one of the attendants of the Yakushi Buddha. Detail. Bronze. *c.* 720. Yakushiji, Japan. *Photo: Sakamoto.*

disposition is also that of the magic diagrams (*mandala*) which in Buddhism are used in initiation and as an incitement to prayer.

This plan corresponds to the plans (also wholly theoretical) of the standard town and of the family dwelling, which embody the same idea of a more or less inaccessible centre surrounded by courtyards and enclosures and hidden, as it were, within successive layers of wrappings in the manner of an embryo.

Where the palace contained the throne of the monarch, the sanctuary held the statue, the symbol of the god. There was thus an analogy between the god and the monarch, which the latter sought, by various ritual means, to emphasise: the statue might reproduce the monarch's features, or its weight or proportions might correspond to those of the king's person, while a double name, his own coupled with that of the god, might be conferred upon the king at his consecration. This identity was still further accentuated by the fact that the statue was surrounded by the same attentions as the monarch: it was fanned, bathed, anointed, clothed and adorned. It received offerings of food, it was carried about in a litter and, on certain occasions, was even pushed in a swing.

The temple resembled a town not only in plan but also by reason of its multitude of residents, visitors and tradespeople; besides the passing pilgrims, there were the priests who officiated in the chapels and the sanctuary, the temple servitors whose multiple functions were enumerated in the acts of foundation, the sacred female dancers for the god's entertainment, the musicians, the motley crowd out of doors of beggars and vendors selling garlands of flowers and pious objects of every sort. According to texts, the most active temples thus maintained an establishment of from 10,000 to 20,000 people; supplies and manufactured articles for them all reached impressive figures which could not be met entirely out of the establishment's own resources, though these were sometimes considerable since the temple owned enormous agricultural concerns (200 villages or more, exempt from tax because of their sacred character). The often very substantial subsidies came from royal donations and gifts from rich and devout merchants; moreover, the monarch periodically donated food and clothes, and the more solemn of these almsgivings, which took place every five years, emptied the royal treasury for the benefit of both the religious bodies and the common people.

The religious mission of the artist

The art of India derives its quality of nobility from its sacred function of reflecting a composite world in which animals, men and gods constitute integral parts of the same cosmic whole. The architect and the sculptor therefore have a superior mission, which they cannot adequately fulfil unless they possess the required technical skill and the necessary erudition to make complete artists of them, and also the moral qualities to maintain them in a kind of state of grace: in order to perform the ritual (*puja*), which precedes the creation of a work of art, they must be pure in heart. When the work is finished, the priests perform a ceremony of consecration which confers a divine nature on the sanctuary or image. By 'opening the eyes' of a statue —that is, by simulating the insertion of its pupils—and by giving it a name (*nama*), the priest effectually gives it life, for a name creates form (*rupa*); the name is that of the donor coupled with that of the divinity, the two being thus identified.

The anonymity of the Indian artist seems to spring largely from this concept of art: the architect or sculptor is effaced before his work, which is endowed by the priest who consecrates it with an independent and sacred life of its own while the artist is merely the superior instrument through whose agency it came into existence. Few works are signed, but the names of a few artists have been transmitted by tradition. In fact, the artist would have little reason to desire to be remembered by posterity, since the belief in the transmigration of souls renders the vanity of individuality obvious and leads the believer to aspire instead to break the bondage such vanity constitutes. This belief also explains the contempt for dates and history sometimes shown by the Indians of early times; to a people who lived in the hope of a cessation of the continuity of rebirths, time—in the rationalist Western sense —was of no more account than individuality.

Relying on ritual and tradition, the idea of 'art for art's sake' never occurring to him, and only accounting himself glorious in the realisation of the ideal of a perfect canonical work, the Indian artist contributes anonymously to the collective work which constitutes the grandeur of Indian art. This collective character stands out in the art of all the schools it has been possible to distinguish; there is, indeed, such cohesion that it requires all the art historian's perspicacity to trace the evolution of the style in any given region. Each school in fact forms a separate entity in which a few individual concepts are allied to traditions common to all the different schools. Whereas iconographical requirements and certain decorative motifs constitute a strong link between the schools, their styles differ radically; it is by comparing these styles, with the aid of a few dates (more often than not inaccurate, unfortunately), that we have been able to reconstitute the evolution of Indian art.

The Buddhist tradition in art

A major problem arises in connection with this evolution: that of the divergence or collusion between Buddhist art and art influenced by Brahmanism. Their common characteristics are *a priori* undeniable, but here again we are confronted with the paradoxical attitude typical of Indian history. Throughout several centuries Buddhism alone made use of the visual arts for religious purposes; yet Buddhism was a latecomer compared to Brahmanism which, originating from the Vedism of early India, was far older and had by this time become an abstract religion: founded strictly on sacrifice, it limited its teachings to the initiated, who required neither icons nor imagery to illustrate the symbolism of the ritual. Buddhism, in contrast—a moral code illustrated with fables, as a reaction to the stultifying laws imposed by Brahmanism— was endowed with a missionary and didactic spirit and regarded this imagery as a powerful means of acting upon the receptivity of both neophytes and devotees. Furthermore, whereas Brahmanism, which is an individual religion, was content with an ephemeral and diminutive altar, Buddhism, which is essentially a community religion, raised vast and permanent edifices for meeting and communal prayer. These various factors doubtless determined the flowering of a Buddhist art long before the appearance of an art based on Brahmanism. But this

Buddhist art, original though it may have been, inevitably derived its inspiration from existing traditions—that is, from the traditions of Indianity; it thus started off dependent upon the formulas adopted by Brahmanism, since the latter was the very embodiment of Indianity at this time.

The most striking example of this process is the stupa, the most typical of Buddhist edifices (though also adopted by Jainism), which in its most archaic form derived its shape from that of the Vedic tomb (that is, from an ordinary tumulus). A relief carving of one of these tombs, 685 on the eastern portal of Stupa 1 at Sanchi, is most revealing: it shows a hemispherical dome (egg, or *anda*), composed of layers of bricks or stones and surrounded by a balustrade. This simple and unadorned structure, divested of its funerary role and given the status of a monumental memorial, was subsequently embellished with various elements upon which the Buddhist texts soon conferred a symbolic or legendary significance: the 695 solid, hemispherical dome was placed on a square base and surmounted by a balcony-like structure (*harmika*), with a balustrade (*vedika*) around it, from which rose a shaft bearing umbrellas (*chatra*). Finally, as with the tomb represented on Stupa 1 at Sanchi, the whole thing was surrounded by a balustrade having entrances which were oriented according to the cardinal points and were often 663 adorned with tall ornamental gateways (*torana*) with 680 carved lintels. Whereas early Buddhism regarded this disposition merely as the translation into architectural terms of the Buddha's begging bowl turned upside down on his folded robe and pierced through with his mendicant monk's staff (an explanation at least plausible), mature Buddhism read an elaborate symbolism into it, whose elements can readily be traced back to Indian cosmology: the umbrella shaft, deeply embedded in the dome of the stupa, would correspond to the central pivot of Hindu mythology; the dome itself would represent the cosmic receptacle of the universal embryo, etc. Be this as it may, the stupa has remained the most specifically Buddhist work of architecture and has been transmitted to the whole of Asia.

Outstripping Brahmanism and boldly innovating, Buddhism developed a rich iconography. Though there are perhaps a few examples of Brahmanic sculpture more or less contemporary with the first Buddhist works in stone, they are so small in number that during the first four centuries of its evolution Indian art may safely be defined as Buddhist. As a precursor in art, Buddhism had to build up its own iconographic repertory and probably even draw up the aesthetic laws best suited to express this repertory. Buddhism brought to its art the peaceful quality of its doctrine and the immense compassion which it extended to all creation.

Sculpture and painting have set down Indian society for posterity. They have also given us a whole assortment of real and fantastic creatures whose forms the Indian artists have always excelled at reproducing.

However, the principal personage did not figure in these scenes until the end of the 1st or the beginning of the 2nd century: the presence of the Buddha was merely suggested by a few symbols readily understood by the faithful: this lacuna did not in the least mar the composition or the animation of the scenes, but when eventually the Buddha's image was introduced, the composition

686. *Right*. Buddha of the Mathura school, from northern India. Red sandstone. 2nd century A.D. *Musée Guimet, Paris.*

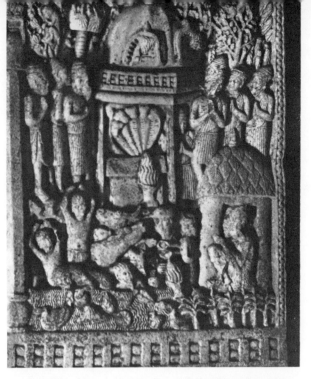

685. INDIAN. Representation of an archaic stupa. Detail of a relief from the eastern gateway of Stupa 1 at Sanchi.

tended to become more rigorously symmetrical. The representation of the Buddha constitutes the highlight of the iconographic and aesthetic evolution of Buddhism, though its origin is still a moot point. It may have originated from Gandhara, the profoundly Hellenised 658, 687 province of north-western India, or from the Mathura 686 school of 'Indian' India, and it would seem to have come in response to a growing need of the faithful to worship something more concrete than mere symbols; it might also be the sign of a decline in the faith of the first centuries of Buddhism, or perhaps merely the result of the abrogation of certain laws against the representation of the sacred. The fact remains that at one point Buddhist art received a host of motifs originating from the Hellenistic repertory; though the majority of these motifs did not survive in the aesthetic tradition of India itself, Buddhism nonetheless derived great benefit from these valuable acquisitions. The most complete and detailed illustrations of the Buddhist legends were developed in Gandhara and transmitted, with Buddhism, to all the regions along the Silk Route.

Buddhist art maintained its lead up until the Gupta period. Enjoying the patronage of the Buddhist rulers or benefiting from a wide tolerance on the part of the Hindu

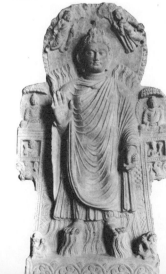

687. *Below*. Buddha in the Graeco-Buddhist style, from Paitava. Schist. 3rd–4th centuries A.D. *Musée Guimet, Paris.*

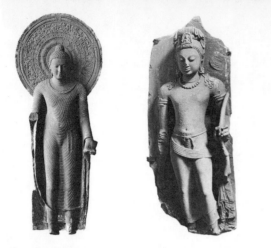

688. *Left*. Buddha in the Gupta style, from Mathura. Red sandstone. 5th century A.D. *National Museum of India, New Delhi*.

689. *Right*. Avalokitesvara, Bodhisattva of Compassion. Northern school, Gupta style. 5th century A.D. *Indian Museum, Calcutta*.

monarchs, and enriched materially by the generous contributions of its wealthiest zealots and spiritually by the piety of its monks, Buddhism attained its apogee during this time; more and more sanctuaries, richly decorated, were built; enormous universities grew up, of which that at Nalanda, receiving several thousand students each year from all over Asia, was one of the most famous. Buddhist activity continued to spread far and wide: all along the Silk Route and throughout south-east Asia its monks preached, settled, made converts and created Buddhist colonies.

Later trends in Buddhism and the rise of Brahmanism

Meanwhile, Brahmanism (which henceforth took the name of Hinduism) was soon to assert itself. Not that anything in the nature of a religious war took place: apart from a few outbreaks of violence, the process was far more one of slow osmosis. In effect, Buddhism was far from having maintained its early emphasis on moral conduct rather than belief; from the beginning of the Christian era it had undergone a schism which had brought about profound changes in its concepts and which led an increasing number of its adepts to practise an emotional, even mystic, religion and to adopt a continually expanding pantheon; this new form of Buddhism was called Mahayana. A sort of fusion subsequently took place between Mahayana Buddhism and Hinduism, from

690. BARABUDUR. CENTRAL JAVA. Bas-relief showing the future Buddha deciding on the life of an ascetic. He removes his jewels and cuts off his hair, which the gods gather up to take to the heavens. 9th century A.D.

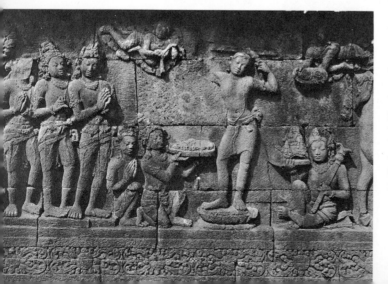

which there developed a separate religious form called Tantrism that combined the extravagant characteristics of late Buddhism with a number of Hindu themes. From then on, the simple and straightforward spirit of early Buddhism foundered on a formalism in which nothing mattered any more except detailed attention to ritual.

Whereas there is no doubt that this religious evolution influenced both iconography and the aesthetics, most studies of the evolution of Indian art tend to disregard the religious distinctions: we have been misled as much by the often extremely close affinities of style as by the uniformity in the choice of materials, in the use of techniques and in the application of aesthetic principles. However, if we stop to look for the most personal elements that each religious movement may have transmitted through its artistic expressions, we shall perceive, beneath this very real stylistic unity, the presence of diverse tendencies which doubtless sometimes also reflect the taste of the period. Thus early and classic Buddhism constantly retained its highly developed narrative quality, and to it we owe the majority of the infinitely precious illustrations of the Buddhist legends (the life of the Buddha, his previous incarnations or Jatakas, edifying stories of avadanas, etc.), which were one of its principal means of teaching. From the earliest carved or painted images to the celebrated frescoes at Ajanta, which con- 664 stitute both its aesthetic apogee and its swan song, Buddhist art built up a continuous tradition characterised by a joyous and graceful simplicity with undertones of a charming gravity, a predilection for picturesque detail and the things of everyday life, a warm humanity and absolutely nothing excessive.

Hinduism never managed to produce the same verve in the illustration of its own legends and always inclined towards the fantastic rather than the realistic. This was probably because for 'primitive' Buddhism the Buddha himself was a man and not a god, whereas Brahmanism was endowed with somewhat artificial deities who, though they could and did become incarnate at will, nevertheless remained within the realm of mythology. In this connection, schismatic Mahayana Buddhism and Tantrism present the same peculiarity which, in both cases, may be ascribed to the influence of Brahmanism: they filled their pantheon with abstract divinities who were acceptable for their symbolic virtues but were far removed from the natural concepts of early Buddhism; they, too, generally avoided narrative imagery and, if and when they resorted to it, limited it to episodes with little or nothing picturesque about them. This narrative quality of early Buddhism, which was transmitted throughout Asia by missionary activity, gave rise to remarkable masterpieces, such as the relief carvings at Barabudur in Java 690 and the mural paintings in the caves of central Asia; though inspired by Mahayana Buddhism, these retained —allowing for the lapse of time—the qualities of the early Buddhist imagery.

To Buddhism's achievements must be added the adaptation of the architectural forms of timber-work to stone, and their gradual transformation in accordance with its own concepts and needs—a process of adaptation which was practically one of veritable creation: its drive, whether directed towards stupas, sanctuaries or monasteries, gave rise to a magnificent flowering of monumental art. Starting from a simple tumulus, the stupa gradually became an imposing edifice surrounded by ornamental balustrades and faced with slabs of carved stone; it sometimes attained considerable dimensions, as, for example, at Amaravati. As to its construction, bricks were used for the foundations and stone of good quality (marble or sandstone) for the facing; the balustrades and gateways, generally of carved stone uprights and lintels, were assembled by means of tenon and mortise, a process which doubtless demanded a labour of the utmost precision; finally, the whole was covered with a layer of polychromed and gilded stucco. The sanctuaries and monasteries, which were direct adaptations of the technique of timber-work, also betray the attempt to achieve a grandly conceived and brilliantly executed balanced disposition. Their columns were ever more richly adorned, often with motifs inspired by jewellery, and the capitals—which betray the influence of Achaemenian Persepolis—were surmounted with carved groups; the sanctuaries were ornamented with high friezes, their walls, pillars and ceilings were covered with paintings and their façades embellished with sculpture in high relief. Thus the transition from the early sanctuaries, with their sober, even austere style, to the temples and monasteries of the classical and post-classical periods, which though covered with decoration yet preserved a setting worthy of the masterpieces, was imperceptibly effected.

693, 697

The construction of monumental icons, of which the most celebrated examples are the colossal Buddhas of Cave 26 at Ajanta (6th century) and those at Bamiyan, in what is today Afghanistan (4th–5th centuries), must also be attributed to Buddhism. As we shall see, this taste for the colossal had its influence on Hindu art.

However, with the development of Mahayana a different spirit seems to have grown up in the very midst of Buddhism. The icon assumed paramount importance at the expense of the whole narrative repertory; this change is already perceptible in the Theravadin Buddhism of the Gupta period: it produced (perhaps under the influence of Mahayana Buddhism and contemporary Brahmanism) both ultra-severe images, classical to the point of frigidity, and veritable 'litanies in stone', in which the same personages were endlessly repeated, without the slightest regard for aestheticism (7th–8th centuries). This tendency became more and more accentuated with the rise of Tantrism and under the increasingly powerful pressure of iconographic laws, which, by laying down a whole vocabulary of gestures and attributes, progressively sapped the vitality of Indian art and reduced it to a quasi-mechanical production.

688

Dynamism and the colossal in Hindu art

The exuberance, dynamism and extravagance of Hinduism gradually prevailed over the Buddhist gentleness and equilibrium. During the Gupta and post-Gupta periods, however, the Buddhist rhythm persisted in Hindu art, which maintained the same tranquil, even slightly academic aestheticism; in fact, its images differed only in iconographic detail from those of Buddhist art. Thus the Pallava style, particularly well illustrated at Mamallapuram (7th century), produced a beautiful array of sculpture in high relief which, with its purity of line, elongated forms and balanced attitudes, to some extent perpetuated the Buddhist aesthetic. Above all, this Pallava style retained something of the narrative quality that

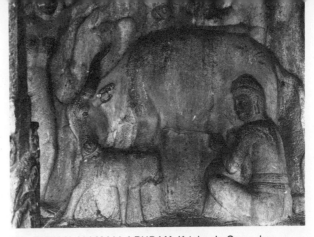

691. INDIAN. MAMALLAPURAM. Krishna's Cows, bas-relief in Krishna's Cave. Pallava style. 7th century A.D.

was totally absent from the majority of the Hindu works of this period: it is manifest in the pastoral in Krishna's Cave, with its charming details—the cows being milked; 691 the mother with her child; the flautist—and especially in the remarkable composition the Descent of the Ganges. Whereas this latter composition is pervaded and sustained by an epic vitality, the direct observation of nature adds a note of meditative sympathy closely akin to that which constituted the charm of the preceding Buddhist art.

In fact, though, this is not the true character of Hindu art. Two other tendencies appeared, both of which culminated between the 6th and 8th centuries, and both of which developed in response to the need felt by Brahmanism to emphasise the cosmic grandeur of the divinity: a taste for the colossal, and a dynamism of form. By aiming at the colossal, Hindu art was, one might think, perhaps merely following the example of Buddhism: however, though it derived its inspiration from gigantic Buddhas which enjoyed a well-deserved reputation in the Buddhist world, it turned out to be itself a past master in this field. One of the earliest examples, the striking Vishnu Varaha of Udayagiri, dates back to the 5th century: the amenable and benevolent majesty of Buddhism is paralleled by the overwhelming impression made by the disconcerting and implacable Hindu deity. This impression is perhaps most powerful, in the realm of sculpture, in such works as the celebrated Saivite Trinity at Elephanta (6th century); this colossal bust, which one can make out in the gloom of a partially subterranean sanctuary through columns with massive shafts and enormous capitals, is certainly calculated to strike terror into the beholder. In less grandiose compositions the same taste for the cosmic and colossal is betrayed by a certain artifice, which consists in establishing a total disparity between the protagonist, who is immense, and the participants, who are dwarfed in com- 684 parison; Buddhist art had resort to this same device during the post-Gupta period.

At the same time, Hindu art produced compositions dominated by diagonals, in which movement sometimes attained to frenzy. The static quality of the god Vishnu, who personified tranquillity, peace and patient anticipation, was counterbalanced by the god Siva, master of the cosmic dance, and, for the representation of the latter, plastic art achieved—as, moreover, did literature—a magisterial note. The most beautiful examples are the sculptures in the caves at Ellura (7th–8th centuries); here again the god is portrayed with cosmic grandeur and his movements have the infallible balance which is the heritage of all Indian art and which we also notice

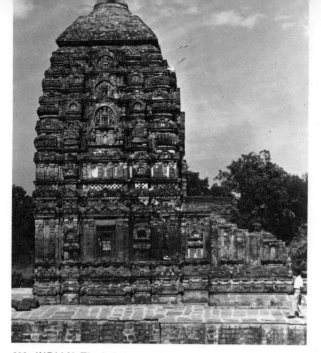

692. INDIAN. The Lakshmana temple, at Sirpur. 6th century A.D.

be traced. The culminating point was reached only with the monumental architecture of the medieval period.

The other types of temple were governed by the same laws: above a square substructure rose a pyramidal roof whose corners curved progressively inwards and were adorned with a vertical succession of quoins in the shape of bulbous pillows, called amalaka, after the name of **692** a fruit; above a rectangular substructure the roof retained the barrel form, as in the rock architecture of the earliest Buddhist sanctuaries; up to about the 7th century this barrel form was curved at one end to form an apse; later, **693** the apsidal form was maintained only in the roof while the substructure itself remained angular. For both types of building the elevation of the monument was obtained through the intercalation of an ever increasing number of cornices between the body of the edifice—the cella of the early period—and its roof: a polygonal cupola above the square substructure and a barrel roof above the elongated substructure.

India transmitted this process to the overseas territories to which its influence extended. Thus, from the time it penetrated the various Indianised kingdoms of the Indo-Chinese peninsula and the Sunda Islands, their brick and stone architecture followed the same process. The Khmer prasat, the Champa kalan and the Javanese candi are all composed of a square cella supporting a pyramidal roof whose various storeys are adorned with small replicas of buildings. Each was elaborated from the same basic elements and subsequently assumed an individual aspect corresponding to the genius of the country: thus in central Java, which was essentially Buddhist during this period, the small replicas were of stupas. Although numerous variations on the Indian prototypes were produced in these territories, all preserved the same symbolism as in India. In effect, India exported not only its aesthetic and sacred forms: the temple was generally identified with the celestial habitation of the gods, the sacred mountain which, translated into architecture, took precisely the form of the stepped pyramid, as is confirmed by numerous documents and in particular by the tympanum of the Khmer temple at Banteai Srei (third quarter of the 10th century).

Under the impetus of local architects and sculptors, a whole series of styles developed which, while related to those of India, had an original accent—the style of central Java, imbued with Buddhist serenity and equi- **690** librium; the Khmer style, which reached its peak during the 12th and 13th centuries; the Champa style, which represented Indian culture's most easterly advance in Indo-China; the hybrid styles of Burma, Thailand and the Malay peninsula.

Thus Indian culture constituted a vast ensemble which, gradually building up in the course of centuries, has spread far beyond the confines of India itself but has nevertheless managed to preserve its coherence and unity, thanks, no doubt, to India's individual concepts, according to which art is an integral part of a spiritual, religious, sociological and even political whole, without—as in the West—any division into compartments. Indian art, mirror of Indian civilisation, is an all-embracing art: in order to be a painter or sculptor one must be versed in the laws of choreography, hence in those of music, itself related to words and to sound, a concept which dates back to the beginning of time.

694 in certain Vishnuite compositions, such as that representing the fight between the presumptuous monarch and the god Vishnu in the form of king-lion. This dynamism remained characteristic of Hindu art, and, after the 'medieval' period, it passed into popular iconography.

Hinduism and architecture

Hinduism made its mark equally on architecture, for which, not unnaturally, it drew its inspiration from earlier formulas which Buddhism had adapted to stone edifices. Of these, it rejected the stupa, which remained characteristic of Buddhism and Jainism, but retained the square cella with a peristyle and the elongated edifice covered with a barrel roof. The square cella seems to have appeared during the Gupta epoch and to have been adopted indiscriminately by both Buddhism and Hinduism; it is to be seen in its simplest form at Sanchi (Temple 17), where it is of diminutive size, is covered with a flat roof and has a front porch with columns. It was, however, to become a sanctuary of more ample proportions, with the roof as the centre of interest. Following the system of evolution which Indian art has never ceased to obey, the architects in effect raised successive cornices above the cella proper, which, disposed like stepped pyramids, formed a corbelled roof over the edifice. Small replicas of the temple itself were placed on the cornices. Though these storeys were at first of a limited number, as in the small temple represented in one of the frescoes in Cave 1 at Ajanta (6th century), they were continually multiplied, and thus developed the elevated roof of mature Hindu architecture.

This process constitutes one of the most typical features of the laws of Indianity, and it reappears under different aspects in various fields; it probably springs from the Indians' deep respect for tradition and for the observance of those treatises the majority of which are regarded as part of the ritual and of the revealed texts. The prolific multiplication of an element and the persistent repetition of a motif bring to mind the litanies which ceaselessly recur in sacred or canonical literature. Through a period of slow gestation, this process gradually modified the outline of the temples and resulted in an entirely new form whose succeeding stages of development can each

HISTORICAL SUMMARY: Indian art

INDIA UP TO 1000 A.D.

History. Of the long period lasting from the disappearance of the Indus valley civilisation, around 1500 or 1200 B.C., until the 3rd or 2nd century B.C., no positive artistic examples are at present known. It was probably during this period that the Aryans who had long inhabited Iran, slowly spread into India, establishing an already matured civilisation closely related to that of Iran and summed up in the *Vedas*, a vast literary compilation that has constituted the basis of the whole of the subsequent evolution of Indian culture.

During the 6th century B.C. a great religious movement spread through Aryan India; two new religions appeared, Jainism and Buddhism. The latter—founded at Magadha by a prince of the family of Sakyas, who came from the borders of Nepal—was the first to produce works of art, thus providing the stimulus for the development of other religious arts. However, its artistic manifestations only date from about the 3rd century B.C., the period in which, a few years after Alexander the Great's passage through the Indus region, the first imperial dynasty of India, that of the Mauryas, was founded. It was thanks to the patronage of Asoka, the most famous of the Maurya emperors (274 or 268–

237 or 232 B.C.), who became converted to Buddhism, that the first Buddhist monuments were built. When this dynasty broke up, around 184 B.C., the political power was again divided though the artistic tradition was maintained, first by the Sungas and then by the Kanvas.

A new and fertile period, lasting from about the end of the 1st century B.C. until the 4th century A.D. witnessed a fever of commercial activity which opened up the way for cultural and artistic exchanges between East and West. The political situation at this time was somewhat confused: in the north-west the Greek conquerors, organised in satrapies, had largely been replaced by Scythians; in the south-east an indigenous kingdom, that of the Andhras, was set up. In the course of the 1st and 2nd centuries A.D. a powerful empire was established by a profoundly Iranised people who had originally come from Mongolia; the imperial Kushan Dynasty reigned from the Oxus to the Ganges plain, residing at Mathura and at Kapisa. Its greatest emperor, Kanishka, who became converted to Buddhism, gave a tremendous impetus to Buddhist art. It was at this time that Western influence—Roman and Iranian—most forcefully asserted itself, giving rise to, among others, the Graeco-Buddhist and Irano-Buddhist

styles, whose schools have been located in Afghanistan and Chinese Turkestan (see Chapter 6). Meanwhile, the Andhras had created a southern Buddhist style which also showed traces of Roman influence, due to the existence of commercial centres on the south-eastern coast.

The Gupta Dynasty, the second indigenous and imperial dynasty of India, was founded in about 320. It came to an end in about 470, after having given such an impetus to Indian culture in all its branches that the latter continued to flourish long after the Gupta Dynasty itself had disappeared, engendering successive Buddhist and Brahmanic styles up to 1000 A.D.: the Pala-Sena style of Bengal (8th–12th centuries) and the Maharastra (6th–8th centuries), Pallava (7th century) and Chalukya (7th–8th centuries) styles, etc. All had tremendous repercussions on the countries of south-east Asia, and their traces are to be found from Indo-China to the East Indies as far as Borneo.

The invasion, during the 5th century, of the Huns, who penetrated as far as the Ganges basin, had put an end to the hegemony of the Guptas and had caused a fresh crumbling of the local

693. INDIAN. AJANTA. Interior of Cave 26. 6th century A.D.

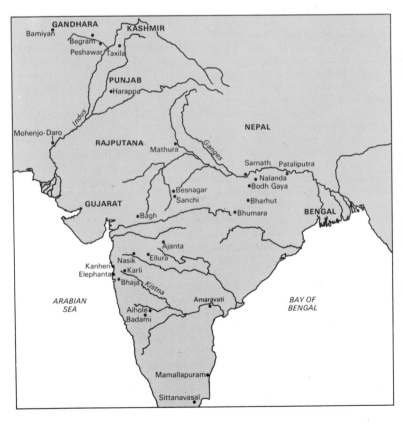

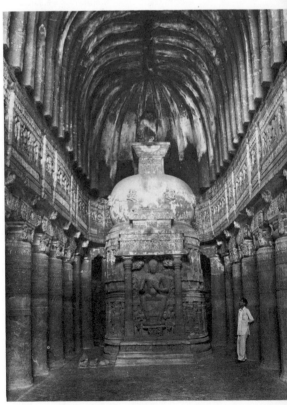

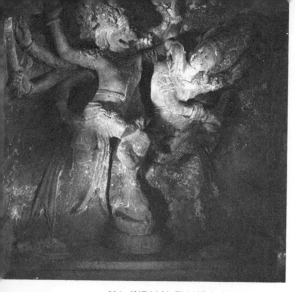

694. INDIAN. ELLURA. Vishnu in the form of a man-lion fighting the presumptuous monarch. Chalukya style. 7th century A.D.

dynasties; that of the Moslems, who appeared at the north-western frontiers at the beginning of the 8th century, heralded a progressive disintegration of the indigenous power. Gradually gaining all the northern provinces, the advancing Islamic wave drove Indian tradition to the south, where it continued an almost sealed-off existence; its internal evolution resulted in the development of various new styles which became manifest as from the beginning of the 11th century.

Architecture. From the appearance of the first monuments in durable materials during the 3rd and 2nd centuries B.C., it may readily be inferred that the previous architecture was essentially the technique of timberwork in rock; the caves which were converted into sanctuaries thus perpetuated, to the supreme good fortune of the archaeologist, the aspect of perishable and probably earlier constructions. This rock architecture was of two principal types: the sanctuaries or chaityas and the monasteries or viharas. The former—which are apparently the older —were characterised by a façade pierced by a vast horseshoe-shaped arch, and by a nave in the form of an apse lined with columns [693]. The monasteries were square, with cells and one or more chapels opening out around them and with a columned porch in front. These two architectural types slowly evolved; the horseshoe arch (kudu) was modified and transformed, becoming stylised, and the columns and the friezes above them were gradually covered with decoration [693, 697]. Supported on a bulbous base, the columns had bell-shaped capitals which were probably of Persepolitan origin and which, from about the 1st century B.C. onwards, were surmounted by a group of two animals back to back, a motif that was perpetuated throughout several centuries.

Towards the 4th century, that is, with the development of the Gupta style, free-standing architecture was no longer executed only in wood, but also in brick and stone; rock and wooden architecture continued to coexist and to evolve. Although perpetuated as late as the 8th century (it is still to be seen at Mamallapuram) the apsidal plan had become almost an archaism by this time and was only rarely used for stone buildings; it was soon completely abandoned, but its barrel roof was retained and adopted, during the following period, for the monumental gateway-towers (gopura) of certain temples.

The square plan underwent an infinite number of variations, determined by the period and region, and, having been used in numerous sanctuaries in India [682], was diffused throughout south-east Asia, serving as the prototype for the great Khmer, Champa and Javanese temples. Between the 6th and 8th centuries a pyramidal roof with inward-curving corners appeared, also above a square substructure [692]; this type underwent an incredible development during the medieval period and, like the storeyed pyramid type, reappeared in Java and in the Indo-China of the Khmers.

There is one special type of monument: the Buddhist and Jain stupa, derived from a funeral mound, started out as, and remained until about the 2nd century B.C., a simple brick dome placed on a square base. The most famous stupas are those at Bharhut, Sanchi and Bodh Gaya. During the time of the Kushams and Andhras, from the 1st and 2nd centuries, they sometimes covered a considerable surface area: that at Amaravati was over 1600 feet in diameter. The outline of the stupa became modified in the course of the centuries: the hemispherical dome tended to assume a globular form while the base was progressively elevated; during the 3rd and 4th centuries the vertical elongation of the monument was accentuated, and it gradually lost its original aspect. The building was bulbous or campaniform from the Gupta epoch onwards, and it was under this aspect that it was transmitted to south-east Asia, where it assumed the shape of a tower surmounted by a high spire which may be regarded as a multiplication of the unique umbrella which had once surmounted the pavilion on the dome. The stupa also arrived under a deformed aspect in the regions along the Silk Route and in Tibet, where it continued its evolution and where it has been perpetuated to the present day [685, 695].

Sculpture. The role of sculpture is paramount in the art of India, and we may even go so far as to say that, in the case of rock architecture, it took the place of architectural technique. Generally executed in stone—though sometimes also in terra cotta, wood, metal or ivory—it can be divided into two main categories: sculpture in the round for the icons in sanctuaries or other consecrated buildings and for the images of the most important divinities; relief carving, which was used to illustrate the innumerable pios legends.

The sculpture in the round of the Maurya period, apart from a few quite distinctive statuettes, was characterised by the ponderosity of its form, the stiffness of its outline and the massive aspect of the personage represented; though the understanding of the third dimension was still rudimentary, the regard for detail already foreshadowed the consummate finish which was subsequently to reach the height of perfection; huge statues of male and female figures, found at Parkham, Mathura and Besnagar, were produced, together with representations of animals, the latter already equally those of later epochs.

From the 2nd century B.C. on wards, noticeable progress was made: though the pose remained rigid, the outline softened and the modelling became more fluent in the rendering of the suppleness of flesh; the decorative sense became accentuated, especially in the narrative relief carvings. The latter, which were entirely Buddhist during this period, mainly adorned the balustrades and gateways of the stupas; their perspective was still somewhat elementary, consisting of a vertical superimposition of the different planes, but they were rich in descriptive verve. The best style of this period was that of Bharhut, in which—despite the stylisation of the animals, the simplicity of the gestures and the homeliness of the scenes, the mastery over the material is manifest. From this style developed that of Stupa I at Sanchi (c. 1st century A.D.), better composed and with more skilful perspective, in which the different planes were made to overlap to give the impression of depth [680]. In round sculpture, the artists were still hesitant about the rendering of profile, but were soon to become perfectly able to make their figures 'revolve' in space.

This art reached maturity during the period of transition (2nd–4th centuries) which followed and which was represented by three main Buddhist schools, clearly contemporary, but with divergent 'climates': in the north-west, the Graeco-Buddhist style; in the north, the Mathura school; in the south-east, the Amaravati school.

Graeco-Buddhist (Gandhara) art, located in the Punjab, in Afghanistan and in Turkestan, but flourishing particularly in the Peshawar region, represented a marginal manifestation of Indian art proper (see Chapter 6). Appearing about the 1st century A.D., it seems to have survived as late as the 7th or 8th centuries in certain regions, notably in Kashmir. It is perhaps to this school that we owe the first representation of the Buddha. Strongly marked by Hellenistic influence, Graeco-Buddhist art developed an abundant iconography on the literary themes of Buddhism, together with a type of symmetrical composition, both of which were adopted by contemporary Indian art.

The Mathura school (1st–3rd centuries) had more charm: instead of the bluish or greenish schist of Gandhara, it worked in the local reddish sandstone; the acquisitions of the Bharhut and Sanchi styles were not forgotten: the balance of the volumes, the harmony of line, the suppleness of the attitudes and gestures and the youthfulness of the subjects all derived from previous experience; this school was characterised by the fullness of its female forms, the robust but flexible grace, the modelling simplified but without conventionalism, the joyous expression of the faces, and, here and there, the unmistakable traces of lasting Iranian influence [**683, 686**].

The Amaravati school (2nd–4th centuries) revealed a very different spirit which, with an effervescent quality that sometimes bordered on decadence, already foreshadowed the Gupta aesthetic. The compositions were mannered: the use of the circle and of diagonals attests to an advanced science of schematic design. The forms were elongated and were animated by a balanced dynamism and a graceful languor.

This transitional period showed variety not only in its aesthetic aspects but also in the materials used and in the dimensions of the art which was produced: the latter ranged from the extreme refinement (and yet power) of the ivories unearthed at Begram, the ancient Kapisa [**678**], to the monumental rock-carvings in high relief at Karli and Kanheri.

The Gupta style (4th–5th centuries) represented a sort of completion of the preceding evolution, a halt in classicism. Brahmanic art, which had appeared during the 1st or 2nd century, became a rival to Buddhist art but adhered to more or less the same aesthetic. Its icons constituted its most academic expression and were, at the same time, a synthesis of the plastic qualities of the period; the often exquisite lines of the bodies, the softness of the modelling and the balance of the

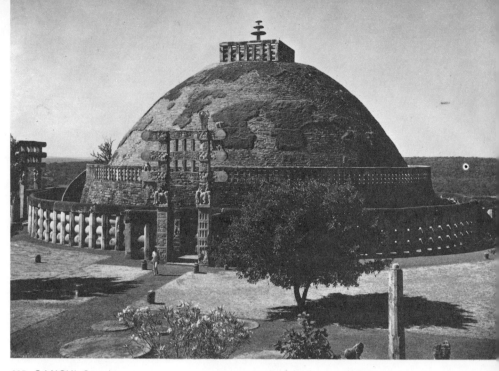

695. SANCHI. Stupa 1.

movements gave the figures a somewhat frigid aspect which was redeemed by the youthful and charming smile. The monastic simplicity of the Buddhas [**688**] contrasted with the princely costumes and jewellery of the Brahmanic divinities [**689**], which were henceforth as numerous as the divine beings of Buddhism. A very different spirit emanates from the relief carvings, in which the narrative verve of the previous periods was perpetuated; however, the taste for picturesque detail gave way before a more highly developed sense of composition: the sculptors had become increasingly aware of the monumental and architectural role of the decorative relief carving. This tendency was to be masterfully expressed during the following period, particularly at Mamallapuram and Ellura.

The post-Gupta style, perpetuated long after the disappearance of the dynasty, did not maintain quite the high standard previously attained; the forms became ponderous, and the artistic production as a whole was heavy. However, a genuine grandeur emanates from the vast mural compositions, executed principally at Ajanta, Elephanta, Mamallapuram and Ellura (6th–8th centuries): the potentialities of the monumental relief carving, which was more specifically a product of Brahmanic art, were exploited to the full. One of the most beautiful examples is the celebrated Descent of the Ganges, at Mamallapuram (7th century), in which the Pallava aestheticism, heir to that of the Gupta period, recaptured all the narrative verve of past epochs [**691**]. The cold elegance of this style was offset by the art of the Chalukyas at Ellura (7th–8th centuries), which developed an astonishing energy and

yet preserved a perfect equilibrium [**694**]. Meanwhile, Buddhist art slowed down in development and became confined to the north-east (Bengal), where it was to be an art more of virtuosi than of creative artists; it steadily degenerated, and it was no longer produced in India after the beginning of the 13th century.

Painting. Apparently contemporary with the earliest monuments of historical India, mural painting was already at an advanced stage by the time the art of relief carving was beginning to develop at Bharhut and Sanchi (2nd century B.C.–1st century A.D.). As far

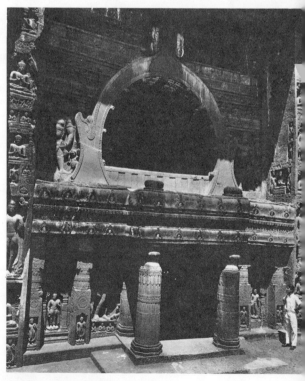

696. INDIAN. AJANTA. Façade of Cave 19. 6th century A.D.

379

as one can judge, its progress over the centuries paralleled—perhaps even led—that of relief carving, as is amply proved by the frescoes contemporary with the Amaravati style (*c.* 2nd century), found at Ajanta (Cave 10). It reached the most beautiful stage in its development during the Gupta and post-Gupta periods, in the outstanding series at Ajanta (Caves 1, 2, 6, 9, 10, 11, 16, 17, 19 and 22), which constitutes the culminating point of mural painting in India. With the subtlety of the compositions, the precision of line, the beauty of the forms and the patent mastery and inherent refinement it betrays, it remains a universal masterpiece [**644**]. Composition tends to be circular; in it, under a highly elaborated form, is visible the form of composition which has constantly prevailed in India and whose mystic significance can be traced back to the *mandala*, or magic diagram, which was assigned a place of honour in evolved Buddhism. In the complex perspective used at Ajanta, an extremely subtle compromise is reached between normal optic distortion and the empirical knowledge of objects;

there is, however, nothing in the way of a perspective foreshortening of distant objects, and the aspect of profusion that characterises these compositions, in which the hierarchic importance of the figures outweighs all other considerations, is thereby accentuated.

Paintings of the same period are to be found on other sites: Sigiriya (Ceylon, 5th–6th centuries?), Bagh (Gwalior, 6th century?), Sittanavasal (eastern Deccan, 6th century), Badami (Maharastra, 7th century?), etc. Each site presents a different style, generally less elaborate than that of Ajanta.

The technique applied in these mural paintings resembles that of tempera; when the fresco was completed, the mural was gone over *a secco* (further colour was applied to the set plaster); the different stages were carried out in more or less the same order, but the ingredients used (composition of the mortar and the plaster, and vegetable colours which ill withstood the chemical precipitate of the wall preparation) were defective. The outline was traced with a piece of charcoal on the dry

plaster and gone over with a paintbrush dipped in red ochre; in some cases the technique of pouncing was used, but more often the composition is marked by great freedom. The actual painting began with a white or green undercoat over which the final colours were applied, while the details were added *a secco* at the end. The painters' palette varied from place to place; that of Ajanta was the richest and included yellow and red ochre, pigments ranging from bistre to black, an opaque white, several greens, blue and violet. The brushes were made of animal hair, which varied according to their thickness. This art of mural painting seems to have been at its most beautiful between the 5th and 7th centuries, after which it deteriorated.

Minor arts. Both metal-work and carving in wood and ivory have always enjoyed a great vogue in India. From before the Christian era, Indian ironwork had a reputation which spread to Iran, Greece and even Egypt; by about the 4th century this technique had attained such a high degree of perfection that the Indians were able to work volumes of iron greater than any European foundry could have handled before 1850. As to precious metals, proofs of the gold- and silversmiths' skill in transforming these into jewellery [**675**] and such objects as statuettes, reliquaries, imperial plate, etc., abound, those of the Gupta epoch being particularly elegant. The Kushan and Gupta coins are beautifully minted.

Wood, as we have seen, was the basic material for architecture and its decoration; though the Indian climate has destroyed all the originals, the copies in stone attest to the continued use of wood for building. A few rare specimens have, however, survived, such as certain wooden structures still adhering to the walls of various rock sanctuaries.

Ivory, which was much sought after, was incorporated into the decoration of furniture and even into monumental sculpture. The existence as early as the 1st century of guilds of ivory-workers has been established, and the mirror-handle found during the excavations at Pompeii would seem to prove that their skill was widely recognised outside India. J. and R. Hackin's discovery at Begram (ancient Kapisa) in 1937 and 1939–40, of wooden chairs and stools inlaid with plaques of carved and engraved open-work and painted ivory, has enabled us to judge, piece in hand, the accomplishment of the technique and the beauty of the workmanship [**678**]. This art has continued in the different regions of India to this day.

Jeannine Auboyer

697. INDIAN. AJANTA. Interior of Cave 1. 6th century A.D.

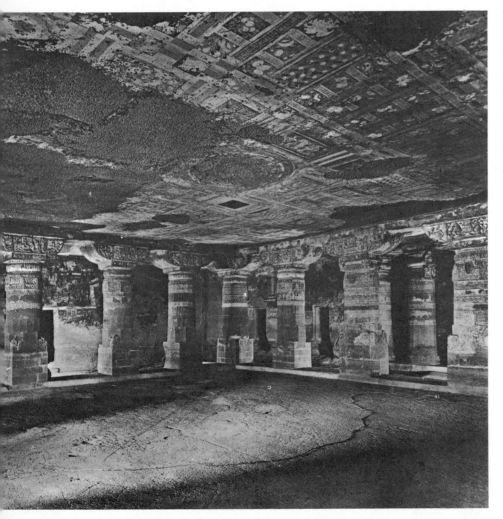

CHINA AND ITS DEVELOPMENT FROM THE HAN TO THE T'ANG DYNASTIES

Madeleine Paul-David

With the Han Dynasty China forcefully renewed its own culture, laying the definitive foundations of its art and crystallising its concept of and outlook on the world. The arrival of Buddhism, which came from India by way of Turkestan and later continued on to Korea and Japan, resulted in close relations with India.

THE BIRTH OF HUMANISM

In the 1st millennium B.C. there was a continuation of the slow colonisation which would bring the Chinese from the banks of the Huang Ho (the Yellow River) to the Mongolian plateau and southern Manchuria, as well as to the Yangtze and to the Canton region beyond.

The evolution of Chinese civilisation

Chinese civilisation, which had its beginnings on the borders of the high loess plateaux and the great northern plain, gradually spread beyond its narrow boundaries and radiated over vast expanses, becoming enriched with a variety of extraneous elements on its way.

Towards the 5th century B.C., through Chinese contact with the nomads of the north, the animal motifs which around the year 1000 had spread from An-yang as far as southern Siberia, were reintroduced into China in the elaborated form they had evolved under Western influence—especially that of the Siberian art of Tagar.

During its progress towards the south, Chinese civilisation encountered local cultures from which it adopted new elements that it rapidly transformed. This is an aspect of Chinese civilisation that has long been neglected due to the absence of archaeological documentation. Research carried on over the past few years in the southern provinces has, however, revealed the importance of their contribution to the common heritage. Hitherto unknown techniques subsequently appeared in northern China, such as the use of lacquer and precious materials—ivory, pearls, silver and wood, which abounded in the Chou country on either side of the Yangtze and in the opulent Wu and Yu kingdoms established along the littoral, whose fleets traded with south-east Asia. The Chinese horizon was widened by the discovery of this new world, and the magic and religious practices of the populations newly drawn into its orbit were not unrelated to the remarkable development of Chinese thought between the 6th and 3rd centuries B.C.

Likewise from the beginning of the 5th century, relations with the West were established for the first time in north-western China. The Achaemenid empire was then consolidating its supremacy over the eastern Iranian peoples and expanding southwards to the Punjab, in India, and northwards to Sogdiana and Bactria—territories which had constituted the easternmost limits of Alexander's conquest, during the 4th century B.C. From this time on, caravans began to transport merchandise through the Tarim basin as far as Liang Chou, the doorway to China and the terminal point of the Chinese

boat traffic on the Yellow River. Along this forerunner of the Silk Route, the Indian merchants transmitted Western techniques to China (that of glass-making, for instance, which was practised from the 5th century onwards), and would subsequently introduce Buddhism; in particular, they brought to China their crude and often fanciful knowledge of the geography of western Asia and of the roads leading to it, but also more precise information, needed by travellers, on astronomy (or astrology), and, after the beginning of the 4th century, following the Hellenic advance, the rudiments of mathematics and geometry. This new knowledge, which the Chinese assimilated and compared with their own ideas, awakened them to an awareness of the universe and led them to define their often very ancient and still vague concepts in a more systematic fashion. It was during this period that the space-time relationships were established around the five elements (water, fire, wood, metal, earth), to which, in turn, were associated the five directions (north, south, east, west, centre), the four seasons, the five notes of the scale and the five colours. It was also at this time that a definition was established of *yang* and *yin*, ancient terms rich in diverse associations, male and female principles, darkness and light, and moisture and dryness, whose alternation created the Tao, the universal rhythm.

While speculations on the universe constituted the main theme of the thinkers' inquiries, the study of man as such and of man in relation to society was also beginning to take shape. From the 8th to the 3rd centuries B.C. the rival lords fought to establish their hegemony and to oust the house of Chou, whose authority was weakening. They were on the lookout for any systems or recipes which would guarantee them victory. How should a ruler comport himself? In accordance with the dictates of reason and the rites whose efficacy, proved by long usage, would procure the satisfaction of heaven, the supreme arbiter, and the favourable progress of terrestrial affairs, replied Confucius; with the saintliness obtained through perfect communion with the Tao through the contemplation of and concentration on self which enable man to dominate the universe, said Lao-tse and Chuang-tzu; in accordance with the law and by the equitable distribution of rewards and punishments, declared the legalists who helped the Ch'in state to consolidate its power and triumph over its rivals. That which befits the ruler equally befits the subject—a social animal for Confucius, an individual isolated in the midst of the universe according to Lao-tse; and the precepts for good government thus rapidly became philosophical systems and methods of education.

The joint discovery of the world and man and of their mutual relations explains on the one hand the birth of humanism and on the other the part played by the natural elements in the poetry and art of China.

The fundamental role of the Han Dynasty

With Ch'in Shih Huang Ti, the first August Emperor, the turbulent and fertile period of the Warring States came to an end. In the place of local diversity he created a united China and laid the foundations of the vast empire of the eighteen provinces, whose boundaries, established by his offices, would henceforth remain immutable, despite the transient encroachments of 'barbarian' usurpers. A great empire-builder, Ch'in Shih Huang Ti has remained, in the eyes of the traditionalist Chinese, the standard type of iconoclast. In order to consolidate his work of unification he had to battle with the forces of retrogression and the partisans of archaic rites, and he therefore ordered the destruction of every book, with the exception of technical works, intending by this means to sever the new China from a past which he wished to see ended. His death led to the rapid downfall of the first imperial dynasty; however, after some years of struggle Liu Pang, a soldier of fortune of peasant origin who founded the Han Dynasty and resumed the work of his predecessor with a little more leniency, ensured the 'recreated' empire four centuries of peace (206 B.C.–220 A.D.).

With law and order re-established, the new power had to be endowed with a spiritual and intellectual framework, and the Chinese proceeded to an inventory of their cultural riches. In this work of reconstruction the lion's share fell to the disciples of Confucius, who, in rewriting the classics, adapted the master's teaching to their own ideas and created Confucianism. Educators by tradition, it was also they who were called upon to direct the great imperial university, where they dispensed the education necessary to a respectable man: the scholarship required

698, 699. The Search for the Tripod of Yu; *Below*. The World of the Airs. CHINESE. EASTERN HAN. Carved stone slabs from the tomb of Wu Liang Tzu.

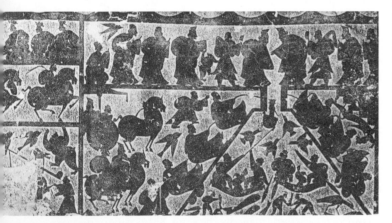

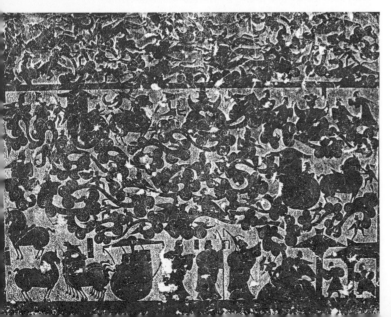

for the examinations which were the means of access to the service of the state. Thus a new class arose—that of the scholars who, regardless of which dynasty was in power, were to preside over the destiny of the empire right up to its fall. Not only the classics, but geography with the *Shan Hai King*, history with the *Annals*, edited during the 2nd century B.C. by Ssu-ma Ch'ien, and poetry, enriched with the *fu* (the elegy), created during the 4th century B.C. in the Chou country, assumed their definitive forms during the Han epoch—forms that were to remain the models from which later writers drew their inspiration. The culture of this period, which reconciled a past that was in fact largely misunderstood with the ideas newly acquired over the preceding centuries, has remained the basis of all Chinese thought up to modern times.

What is true of Han culture is also true of Han art, which, proceeding directly from the style of the Warring States, played a double role. In the first place it transmitted to posterity the heritage of the past, a heritage whose significance had been more or less forgotten by this time but which, from a formal point of view, had retained such power that it has been perpetuated in the decorative repertory to this day. Secondly it created, with the help of elements collected from all over the empire, a style which has constituted the solid framework for all subsequent developments. In this synthesis are reflected the cosmological, philosophical and religious ideas which, as we have seen, had taken shape in the course of the preceding centuries. Like the decoration of medieval cathedrals, Han art was a summing-up: an encyclopedia of time and space, a mirror of history and nature; as E. Chavannes put it, abandoning the abstract forms which had dominated Shang and Chou art, it took its symbols from reality. Thus, the four cardinal points were represented by the White Tiger of the West, the Green 723 Dragon of the East, the Red Bird of the South and the Black Warrior of the North, the last a tortoise fighting with a snake. These symbols were portrayed on mirrors, outlined on funerary stones and magnificently carved on the pillars in front of the sepulchres in Szechwan province.

A mirror of history, the art of the Han epoch set out, in accordance with the principles of Confucianist ethics, to encourage virtue by illustrating the noble deeds of the men of ancient times and to render vice odious by evoking their crimes. These were the chosen themes of the paintings that adorned the imperial palaces and of which only the texts have preserved any record, though they are echoed in the carved stone slabs of the funeral chambers set up before the tombs of important personages in Shantung and Honan. The Search for the Tripod of Yu, 698 the palladium of the house of Chou, which was thrown into a river after the downfall of the dynasty, is a good example of these edifying representations: the tripod, emerging from the water, immediately falls back again thanks to a dragon who comes up out of the river and cuts the cord holding it. This miraculous intervention proved the unworthiness of Ch'in Shih Huang Ti, who had ordered a search for this treasure whose possession would ensure his power; by depriving him of it, heaven was manifesting its disapproval of this man whom the Confucianists regarded as a usurper.

A mirror of nature, art drew its inspiration from popular imagination and from the Taoist legends. In the World of the Waters, superimposed registers of fishes undulate amid waves; in the World of the Airs, divinities personifying the forces of nature are outlined amid clouds.

The art of the Han epoch thus reveals the two aspects of Chinese art that spring from the twofold tendency which animates Far Eastern thought: the Confucianist tendency, which is edifying, moralistic and founded essentially on man, and the Taoist tendency, which is mystic and poetic and is associated with magic and the phenomenal and which gave birth to Chinese landscape painting. In the still fluid society of the new empire these two tendencies intermingled and overlapped, the edifying tendency being manifest mainly in official art, which can be reconstituted from contemporary texts, and the mystic and magical tendency showing up mainly in decorative art, preserved in the tombs whose interior ornamentation and furnishings recreate the life of the period.

Although resolutely realistic and narrative, the Han style did not evade the laws which seem to have governed the art of China from its inception. The tendency towards abstraction and stylisation of forms, only the essential lines of which are retained, pervades it throughout. But the forms are animated by a new vitality, the very keen sense of cosmic movement, basis of the unity of creation, expressed in the concepts of the period. Both man and animals are captured in the attitude that best conveys their being, and the supple and undulating line describing them is part of the rhythm of life. This trend had already been apparent in the art of the period of the Warring States, in which two styles are distinguishable. The one displays motifs inherited from the past: beribboned dragons with heads of felines or birds, and spirals dominated by an extremely forceful rhythm which twists the forms into a subtle pattern of curves and counter-curves. However, alongside these stylised motifs more realistic forms appeared; as we have already noted in Chapter 4, the animal suddenly made its appearance in Chinese art, replacing the fantastic beast. Goats and felines engraved in relief were distributed in superimposed registers over the bronze ritual wine vessels known as *hu*. All alternation of curves and counter-curves is gone from their impetuous round, which is dominated solely by the internal rhythm of the diverse animal forms. It was this second style that became general in Han times.

The new iconography: man, animals and landscape

The practical nature of the Han artists is attested by the fact that animals, whether mythical or real, always have a realistic appearance and that the supernatural world seems to participate in everyday life.

The differentiations are mainly inherent in the different techniques, as is evident from a comparison of a horse which stands at the tomb of Ho Ch'u-ping (who died in 117 B.C.), whose form barely emerges from the stone, with the same animal cast in bronze. Both are of the squat Mongolian breed, with short, broad heads; both have been treated in the same style: the volume is dealt with as a whole without regard for detail or the accidental, and the different planes are melted into a harmonious mass—a synthetic form, but one which expresses the animal's very essence. While the first horse is heavier and reveals a still tentative craft, the second is the product of a venerable technique in which the Chinese were past masters. The silhouetted form has, however, always remained more vivacious: carved in stone, modelled in

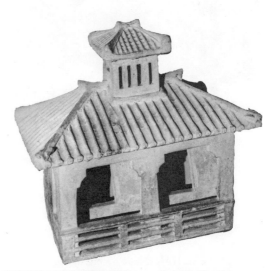

700. CHINESE. EASTERN HAN (A.D. 25–220). Pleasure pavilion. Funerary terra cotta. *Cernuschi Museum, Paris.*

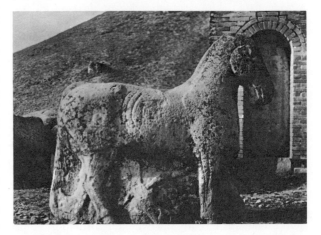

701. CHINESE. HAN. Stone sculpture from the tomb of Ho Ch'u-ping (d. 117 B.C.) in Shansi: horse trampling a barbarian. *Musée Guimet, Paris.*

clay, engraved in bronze or painted on lacquer, it expresses, through the sheer power of line, the intimate knowledge of the animal world that characterises Han art. Indeed, in this form lay the germs of the master qualities which would make painting, still in its infancy during this period, the Chinese art *par excellence*.

On the bronze vases of the period of the Warring States, man is shown participating in the saraband of the wild beasts, whom he combats, and pursues in a four-horse chariot, but this nude hunter is barely distinguishable from the animal world around him.

Humanity, which thus made its début in Chinese art, took a prominent place in the Han style, determined by Confucianist concepts and also by the funerary customs. In fact, the deceased was attended in his tomb by small terra-cotta replicas of the people and the things that had constituted the surroundings of his earthly life (houses, farms, domestic animals, etc.). These funerary figurines (*ming-ch'i*) betray the potters' greater familiarity with the animal form than with that of the human being, which they experienced a certain amount of difficulty in rendering. Some, awkwardly hunched up under robes with voluminous sleeves, are stiff and flat; others, like the statuette in the Hashimoto collection at Kyoto, with its hair falling over its shoulders and its tiny waist offsetting

383

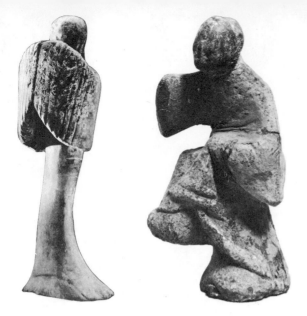

702, 703. CHINESE. HAN (206 B.C.–A.D. 220). Terra-cotta funerary figurines.

703
402 a wide flared skirt, are quite elegant. In contrast, the acrobats and dancers, often modelled in planes, reveal a brilliant science of movement.

The representation of the silhouetted form without any attempt at individualisation seems equally to have been the intention of the stone-cutters who engraved or incised the stone slabs for the funerary chambers and the potters who produced the stamped tiles constituting the inner walls of the tombs, works which must be considered in conjunction with the few rare paintings found in these tombs. The figures in these two-dimensional compositions move with a supreme ease, their profiles in stone being almost as supple as the continuous lines describing painted figures. At the same time, the painted tiles in the Boston Museum of Fine Arts and the portrait of an
704 official that was recently discovered in a tomb in Hopei show an attention to the rendering of faces and great skill in the treatment of folds, with thick or fine strokes of the brush.

The figures on the funerary slabs are arranged in superimposed registers, and the horizontal division of the composition is often accentuated by frontally represented buildings of several storeys, with large trapezoidal roofs supported on columns. In certain scenes, however, there is a noticeable desire to express the relationship in space between the different figures: those in the background are

704. CHINESE. EASTERN HAN (25–220 A.D.). Portrait of a high official. Mural decoration recently discovered in a tomb at Wangtu (Hopei).

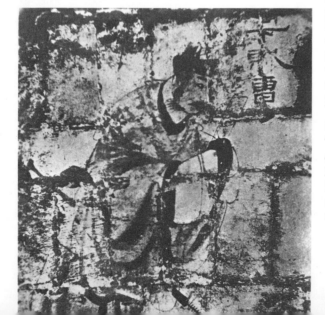

of lesser size and are placed above those in the foreground, while the musicians are arranged in diagonal and parallel lines. Indications of locality are summary and are given only when their presence is necessary to the understanding of the subject (the banks of the river in the Search for the Tripod of Yu).

Nature hardly even figures in these representations. In the World of the Airs, in the Wu Liang Tzu tomb (146 A.D.), the personified natural elements move amid clouds and waves. In this way art seems to have lagged some way behind pottery; by the 4th century B.C., with the poets K'iu Yuan and Sung Yu, a great school of nature poetry had sprung up in the Chou country, a region of beautiful scenery which has been a constant source of inspiration to Chinese painters. The Chou elegies became official literature during the Han epoch, and the world of nature has occupied an important place in Chinese poetry ever since.

The art of landscape gardening also started during the Han period. The imperial palaces were surrounded by immense parks, game reserves for the imperial hunt, in which rockeries, representing the Taoists' beloved Isles of the Blessed, rose in the middle of artificial lakes.

Mountains and rivers have always been regarded as sacred in China. Classifications of them had been established which were the starting point for geographical study, and the ideas from the West gave a new relevance to these ancient traditions. Mount Meru, the sacred mountain of India, became the Kun-lun, habitation of the goddess Si Wang-mu. There is, therefore, nothing surprising in the fact that the mountain soon became an important theme in decoration and that, with the atmosphere, symbolised by cloud, it was one of the first natural phenomena to be represented in a more or less realistic manner. The decorative art of the Han epoch abounds in examples of this subject, whose treatment varies according to the techniques applied, though one technique influenced another. In the absence of accurately dated and sufficiently localised documentation, it is at present impossible to determine precisely the general pattern of the elaboration of this treatment. Of the various forms distinguished, some were inherited from the period of the Warring States, others came from the west and the north and still others were local creations, certain of which must have originated in the south.

Debating the origins of landscape painting, specialists have emphasised sometimes the outside factors and sometimes the Chinese contribution proper. However, they all agree that there was still nothing in the way of landscape painting as such during this period; rather there was a localisation in space of the living forms expressing cosmic vitality, the universal rhythm that penetrates all things, animate or inanimate. The interpretations of this rhythm varied: some were realistic, while others, springing from the tendency towards abstraction that is one of the permanent features of Chinese art, were linear.

Nature and the new forms of decoration

The new forms of decoration that came in during the Han epoch were inspired by the legend of the Isles of the Blessed; the *po-shan lu*, a bronze or earthenware incense-burner, was mounted on a stand with a broad base and surmounted by a conical cover designed to resemble mountains emerging from waves; a round terra-cotta 706

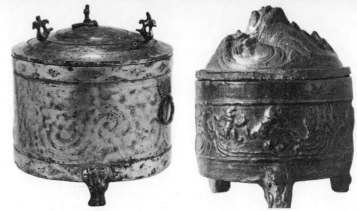

receptacle had a cover of similar design. The mountains, surrounded by turbulent waters, were sometimes formed of successive planes with regular outlines, like flat, superimposed compartments; on other examples, they were made up of irregular undulations, emphasised by secondary lines that ran parallel to the main outline and overlapped one another. Silhouetted slightly in relief on the flat panels and among the waves are running or fighting animals and mounted hunters in the flying gallop, carrying bows and with their heads turned back to front to take better aim at their prey—motifs whose Nordic origin is indubitable. The round receptacles are also adorned with a band, in which the same animals figure not on a plain surface, as during the period of the Warring States, but amid series of parallel lines which follow the lower contour of the band and undulate to form alternate peaks and valleys, the animal forms thus being more or less framed within and governed by these spatial delimitations. According to A. A. Soper, this sort of compartmentation, appearing in diverse forms, was probably transmitted across central Asia from Iran, where it is to be seen on Sassanian metal-work of later date.

Let us investigate the appearance of this motif on the bronzes of traditional form. The spiral, which during the period of the Warring States had been used mainly for bases and borders, was transformed into a cloud or a mountain and became one of the principal elements of the décor. Undulating lines, forming mountainous peaks adorned with spirals, alternate with dragons on the back of a mirror in the Lagrelius Collection, attributed to the 2nd century B.C., while on a gilt-bronze cosmetic box in the Pillsbury Collection, the spiral turned cloud, its contours bristling with irregularly distributed curls, fluently frames engraved animals incrusted with silver. It has replaced the dragon of the preceding period, but it is no longer dominated by the alternation of curves and counter-curves. The bronze tube enriched with gold, belonging to the School of Fine Arts in Tokyo, has a design of undulating and intersecting mountains bordered with fine vertical striations and crowded with animals climbing their slopes or perched on their summits. Another bronze tube, in the Hosakawa Collection, incrusted with plaques and threads of gold and silver, shows the same animals disporting themselves among mountains which are drawn with thick lines and organised into a pattern of irregular arches, and whose peaks are composed of two joined triangles divided by a vertical line that tapers off into two outward-twisting spirals: a flamboyant and baroque motif that, as Mrs Prudence Myers has pointed out, finally became split into two parallel elements on the fragment of embroidered silk discovered at Noin-ula, in Mongolia, in the tomb of a Hun chieftain.

The spiral as cloud or mountain is the object of infinite variations on the lacquerware discovered at Lo-lang, a Chinese military outpost in North Korea, and at Ch'angsha in Hunan province. The curls integrated at random into its contour have transformed it into an abstract motif. Displayed in a regular design on the lids of round boxes, it forms three compartments into which fantastic creatures are inserted; it stiffens and assumes a geometric aspect; it tapers off into the head of a feline or a bird; it sometimes even turns into a stilt bird, or it splits up into distinct elements and alternates with figures of animals instead of framing them. The tendency towards abstrac-

705. *Left*. CHINESE. HAN. Gilt-bronze cosmetic box, inlaid with silver. *Pillsbury Collection, Minneapolis Institute of Arts.*

706. *Right*. CHINESE. HAN. Jar with lid in the shape of a mountain. *Museum of Fine Arts, Boston.*

tion seems to have prevailed over realistic representations.

However, between the 2nd and 3rd centuries A.D., a new trend appears in a fresco adorning a tomb at Liaoyang in southern Manchuria, showing two horsemen passing in front of a hill 'shaped like a camel's hump', behind which emerges the outline of a tent, while a stamped tile from Ch'eng-tu (Szechwan) shows overlapping and superimposed mountains of the same shape, each one forming a frame around a scene. In both these examples the mountains serve to give the impression of depth, a specifically Chinese solution to the problem of rendering space and one which reappears.

The spread of Han art

The unification of the empire had promoted the formation of an official art which, via the imperial workshops, spread beyond the frontiers of China itself.

The need to resist the pressure exerted by the Huns along the northern and north-western frontiers had led to the occupation of southern Manchuria and North Korea in the east, and to the conquest of Kansu and the establishment of bases inside Mongolia in the west. Central Asia was thus opened up to the Chinese armies and merchants. The old commercial routes, rendered safer under military rule, became the Silk Routes, along which rich materials were transported as far as present-day Afghanistan: these materials eventually reached Iran and the Mediterranean basin, and their fragmentary remains have been found at Kerch and Palmyra. Commercial and diplomatic relations led to the exportation of other luxury articles, and pieces of lacquerware made in the imperial workshops in Szechwan province have been found among the treasures of a Kushan ruler at Begram and also in the tomb of a Hun chieftain at Noin-ula. However, it was on the Far East that Chinese civilisation made its most powerful impact. From North Korea, where it had established the important military outpost of Lo-lang, it penetrated to South Korea where, in conjunction with elements transmitted from southern China, it transformed a Neolithic culture by introducing the use of iron and bronze.

The Japanese islands, whose people were still divided into a large number of clans, were also affected, though more gradually, by a double wave from Korea and southern China which caused them to pass from a Neolithic stage straight into the bronze and iron ages. Chinese weapons and mirrors were copied, and, in the north of Kyushu and the south of the large island of Honshu *yayoishiki*, pottery made on a wheel after the forms of

385

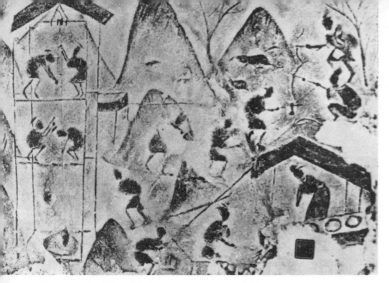

707. CHINESE. EASTERN HAN. Tomb tile with stamped decoration, from a suburb of Ch'eng-tu (Szechwan).

Han vases, replaced the *jomonshiki* of the preceding period. This continental influence steadily increased, preparing the way for the massive introduction of Chinese culture during the 6th century.

Finally, in Tongking and northern Annam, colonised between the 2nd and 3rd centuries A.D., a whole collection of objects, of local origin but inspired by Chinese forms and particularly by those of southern China, was discovered in the tombs studied by the Ecole Française d'Extrême-Orient.

CHINESE TRADITION AND BUDDHISM

Dark days and the religions of salvation

In 220, with the downfall of the Han Dynasty, the empire disintegrated and chaos reigned supreme.

By the beginning of the 4th century the whole of the north had fallen into the hands of the barbarians. The T'o-pa, under the Chinese name of Northern Wei, ruled it from 398 to 550 and were then supplanted by two other, already strongly Sinicised, barbarian families, the Northern Ch'i, who ruled Honan from 550 to 579, and the Northern Chou, who held Shansi from 557 to 580. In the south, six Chinese dynasties succeeded one another at Nanking between 317 and 580. Northern and southern China were thus separated throughout over two centuries and evolved along different lines. Whereas the north, which continued to have access to central Asia, received numerous outside influences, the south remained more faithful to the exclusively Chinese traditions.

Dark days had come upon China, and the Confucian moral code lacked the necessary qualities to alleviate the anxiety and suffering of a people in a disorganised society. Thus it was this period of affliction that saw the triumph of Taoism, a religion of salvation, which promised men accession to immortality through the observance of magic practices and dietetic rules. In its most elevated, mystic and individualistic form, Taoism also attracted the élite, who, like the Seven Sages of the Bamboo Grove, had withdrawn into a world of their own and leaned towards hedonism, devoting their time to meditation and the study of poetry, aesthetics and art.

Under cover of Taoism, whose vocabulary it had borrowed and of which it was long thought to be a foreign offshoot, Buddhism also made rapid progress. It, too, was a religion of salvation and brought the faithful the promise of a better world. It had been introduced into China as early as the 1st century, by Indian merchants who came either overland through the Tarim basin, or by sea to the south. The barbarian rulers in the north, who had nothing but their ancient shamanism to offer in its stead, had accorded it official status by the middle of the 5th century. In the south, where Taoism had become firmly established, Buddhism, though flourishing, did not obtain the imperial patronage until much later.

The barbarians of the north transmitted Buddhism to the Tungusic rulers of Koguryo (who had driven the Chinese out of Lo-lang in 315), with whom they had established relations. South Korea was divided into two kingdoms, Paekche in the west and Silla in the east. An original civilisation had sprung up in Korea, where large tumuli, in the form of a single or double calabash, have yielded up numerous engraved and filigreed gold objects: crowns, earrings, and belts adorned with magarama (ornaments of hard, ovoid stones). The pottery betrays the influence of southern China. The northern part of Kyushu and the southern part of Honshu, in Japan, seem to have shared in this new culture; the funerary objects in their vast tombs or *ko-fun*, though not as rich as those of the peninsula, include Chinese mirrors. Brought to Yamato, a small plain in the north of Osaka, by the clan from which the imperial house of Japan would spring, this culture was transformed by the advent of Buddhism at the end of the 6th century and became for a time completely Chinese.

The role of Chinese tradition

Fleeing from the barbarian hordes, part of the Chinese aristocracy had taken refuge in the south. In this for them new region, far removed from any official duty, were many gentlemen scholars who led a roving life or, following the example of the Taoist sages, lived in intimate communication with nature in the depths of some solitary retreat. Thus, admiring the rich countryside where, in contrast to the sandy expanses of the north, trees and greenery abounded under misty skies, they came to discover the beauty of nature. The contemplation of natural forms seemed to them to be a new way of attaining to that intimate understanding of the universe at which the sages and the virtuous arrived through reasoning. Great poets such as T'ao Yuan-ming and Hsieh Ling-yun celebrated the steep valleys and the wild, uncultivated hills. What the poets were able so aptly to describe, the painters, in their turn, sought to render into visual terms, and thoughts and forms were expressed with the same instrument: the paintbrush. Calligraphy and painting were thus closely related, and both developed in the aristocratic and refined milieu of the gentleman scholar. The latter devoted innumerable treatises to painting, especially to landscape painting, in which aesthetic, religious and technical considerations were closely intermingled. Ku K'ai-chih, a famous portraitist of the end of the 4th century, emphasised the necessity of transcending all form, whether human or taken from nature, since a mere faithful reproduction does not suffice to render the 'divine spirit' and the 'vital movement': the given forms must be thought out afresh and animated with new life. Furthermore, a rigorous selection of the most representative features of the subject must be exercised in order to individualise it. In another text, in which he discusses the ideal representation of a Taoist theme, the Mountain

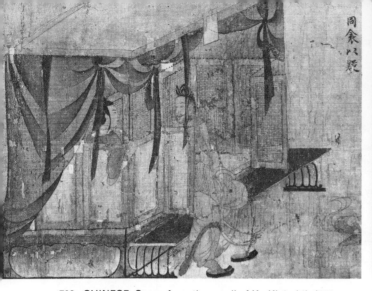

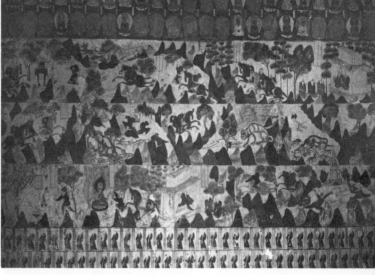

708. CHINESE. Scene from the scroll of Ku K'ai-chih (344–406). Painting in colours on silk (copy attributed to the T'ang period). *British Museum.*

709. CENTRAL ASIAN. NORTHERN WEI. Detail of a mural painting in Cave 135 at Tun-huang (Kansu): scenes from the Jatakas. 398–550 A.D. *Musée Guimet, Paris.*

of the Terrace of Mists, the artist seems to be concerned mainly with the harmonising of the different parts of the composition, the uniting, by superimposition, of the different planes and the ensuring of an exact relationship between the proportions of the living forms and those of the mountains in the background.

Tsung Ping (375–443) and Wang Wei (415–443) also did not seek to individualise their forms but rather emphasised the unity between man and the rest of creation. Wang Wei already saw in natural forms a symbolic language with which the rhythm governing all life might be expressed. Finally, in the 5th century, Hsieh Ho made a synthesis of all these different views in the Six Principles, which have remained the dogma of all the painters and critics of China since. He regarded the capture of the vital rhythm (*ch'i-yum*) and its expression by means of essential lines, the harmony between lines and colours and the balance between space and volume as the basis of all pictorial composition. The doctrine was now firmly laid down, but whether or not it was immediately applied is hard to tell. Of all the works emanating from the aristocratic circle in the south, only the celebrated scroll in the British Museum, a T'ang copy of a painting by Ku K'ai-chih, has come down to us. It illustrates a poem by Chang Hua, *Admonitions of the Imperial Preceptres*, in nine scenes which alternate with passages of text. Eight of these

708 show figures in action, moving in barely indicated surroundings; the figures are drawn with fine lines reminiscent of those of the preceding period, but due to a skilful balancing of figures and space the groupings are more coherent. The ninth scene is a landscape: a precipitous mountain flanked by a hunter and a tiger; with its complex construction in planes, it is far removed from the representations by parallel and superimposed lines of the Han epoch, but its proportions bear no relation to those of the man and the animal. The progress of technique does not appear to have kept pace with that of theory. It has been suggested that the introduction of Buddhist art, by drawing the artist's attention towards other problems, retarded the development of landscape painting.

The artisans in the north, who decorated the great tombs of the rulers of Koguryo, effortlessly resumed the themes already illustrated under the Han Dynasty. The mountains in the hunting scenes, treated in bird's-eye perspective, continued to be represented by parallel undu-

lations, and no attempt was made to coordinate their proportions with those of the figures and animals. On the lantern-shaped ceilings (a feature derived, as we shall see, from central Asia) flying djinns with undulating scarves and animals of all kinds prance amid clouds and flowers. The most striking quality of this décor is its movement: all the motifs appear to be caught up in a whirlwind. The bird's-eye or panoramic perspective reappears in the Buddhist frescoes at Tun-huang, a rock 709 sanctuary founded in 366 on the Chinese border, at the terminal point of the two Silk Routes. The illustrations of the Jatakas (tales of previous incarnations of the Buddha) in Cave 135, attributed to the Northern Wei period, are set out in broad, superimposed registers in which the different episodes are framed and bounded by chains of uniformly drawn mountain peaks whose alternating light and dark tones give a certain illusion of depth. This development of the use of compartments, already noted in Han art, represents some slight progress; the juxtaposed mountain peaks are either placed in the foreground or in semicircles around each scene, this latter disposition issuing, it would seem, from the disposition of rows of figures in parallel diagonals during the Han epoch. In Cave 120N the registers have disappeared and the much more extensive scenes are bounded in a less symmetrical fashion. Finally, in the Sacrifice to the Tigress (represented on the Tamamushi shrine) which has been preserved at the Horyuji in Japan since the 7th century and which appears to be of Korean or Chinese origin, the Buddha, who closely resembles the flying djinns at Koguryo and the apsaras (flying deities) at Tun-huang, is shown casting himself headlong into the depths of an abyss, defined by an eroded rock of baroque design; this latter, which was thought to be of Indian origin, would in fact seem to have issued directly from the flamboyant mountains on the lacquerware and the incised bronzes of the Han period.

The beginnings of Buddhist art: Turkestan

We have already traced the origins of Buddhist art in India and the creation, almost simultaneously in Gand- 658 hara and at Mathura, of the Buddha's image. 686, 687

The establishment of the Kushan empire (1st–3rd centuries) hastened the spread of the new beliefs and forms throughout central Asia. The Tarim basin, bounded to the north and south by almost impassable mountains,

387

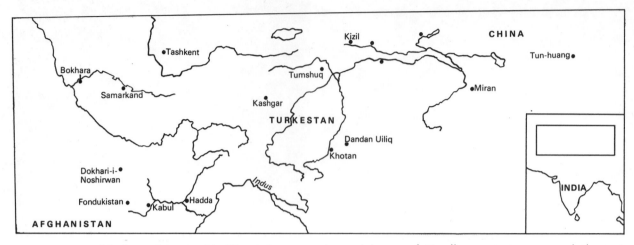

was most accessible from the west side. The easiest way to reach it from India was to go through Kapisa, the heart of the Kushan empire, and, more specifically, through the valley of Bamiyan. In this important stopping place along the route between Peshawar and Bactria, the Kushan rulers had founded numerous religious establishments: rock sanctuaries copied from those of India and adorned, like the latter, with paintings or sculpture executed directly on the rock face. For almost a thousand years (1st–8th centuries) Bamiyan remained the centre of the elaboration of themes and motifs which, through the agency of the merchants, missionaries and, later on, pilgrims from the Far East who came to visit the Buddhist shrines in India, were transmitted to the oases of central Asia, and from there to China, Korea and Japan. Unlike the reddish sandstone of Mathura and the blue schist of Gandhara, the stone of this region does not lend itself to fine sculpture; at Bamiyan, in order to hide this defect, the forms blocked out in the rock were covered with a thick layer of mortar in which the detail was modelled (Buddhas 175 feet and 115 feet high), while at Hadda stucco figurines reveal a realistic art excelling in portraiture and caricature. The early style at Bamiyan (2nd–3rd centuries) was inspired by that of the Hellenised Near East, but, by the end of the 3rd century, after the founding of the Sassanian empire, Iranian themes began to appear in the medallions of the painted décor (boars' heads, winged horses, joined pigeons, their heads facing forward, and birds with pearls in their beaks), and, by the end of the 4th century, in the iconography as well (the lunar divinity in the apex of the niche of the 115-foot Buddha). The Irano-Buddhist art which thus developed is explained by the presence of Dokhtar-i-Noshirwan, the easternmost Sassanian site, about 60 miles north of Bamiyan. During the 5th and 6th centuries this style underwent further developments, determined by the local taste, which resulted in a superabundance of jewels and ornaments. At the end of the 7th century, after the Arab occupation of Iran had left Bamiyan isolated, the monks turned to India, where they found a fresh source of inspiration in Gupta art. It is these different formulas, mixed with elements of diverse origin, that reappear in the oases to the north and south of the two routes skirting the Taklamakan Desert in the direction of China.

Graeco-Buddhist influence seems to have penetrated at an early date along the southern route; a small wooden frieze (2nd–3rd centuries) found at Liu-lan (a Chinese outpost in Lob-Nor), adorned with figures under arches,

657, 659

is reminiscent of Gandhara art; tempera paintings at Miran, attributed to the 4th century, show scenes from the Jakatas treated in a style closely resembling that of Doura Europos. Finally, a little clay Buddha of the Mathura style, found at Aq-terek, reveals the direct penetration of Indian influence, which is confirmed by the appearance in the Khotan region, during the 7th and 8th centuries, of forms inspired by the Gupta and post-Gupta styles and which were probably transmitted through the Gilgit region.

The Ming Oi (Thousand Caves) at Kizil in the north, followed the architectural formula elaborated in Kapisa province: square sanctuaries with ceilings composed of false corbelled beams under a cupola, a formula which was transmitted to Tun-huang and which also appeared in the tombs of the Koguryo kings in North Korea. The painted decoration (c. 450–650), which was also inspired by Bamiyan, is strongly marked by Indian influence: the figures are modelled with shading and sketched with more or less accentuated lines, but Sassanian motifs appear alongside them (ducks carrying pearls; boars' heads), and the donors display Iranian costumes. In the middle of the 7th century shading was abandoned in favour of a linear treatment, while the subtle colouring (grey, bistre and light green or brown) gave way to harsh tones dominated by lapis lazuli. At neighbouring Qumtura and at Bezeklik the Indo-Iranian style became permeated, during the 7th and 8th centuries, with the T'ang influence: the schematisation of the forms, the apsaras swathed in floating scarves and the stylised clouds are of Chinese origin. The same amalgamation of diverse influences may be observed in the clay figurines of Tumshuq and Chortchuq where, as at Fondukistan (between Bamiyan and Kabul), the Hadda tradition, transformed by Gupta art, gave rise to an Irano-Gupta style of elegant figures whose preciosity was accentuated by a profusion of jewellery. Between the 8th and 9th centuries rather less elegant representations appeared at Tumshuq, where the Chinese physiognomy replaced the Indo-Greek features.

660

662
661

Buddhist art in China

As Professor S. Mizuno has pointed out, early Buddhist art in the Far East remained completely Chinese, since the Buddha's image seems to have crept almost surreptitiously into the Taoist mirrors, where it replaced the 'sage', from whom it is distinguishable only by a circular halo. The oldest mirror of this type bears the date 240; other examples enable us to trace the evolution of this image right up to the beginning of the 5th century; the Gandharan features gradually prevailed over the Taoist theme, and the Buddha was finally represented on a throne, surrounded by apsaras. The oldest dated statue has the same Chinese appearance: the gilt-bronze Buddha in the Brundage Collection, Chicago, is dated 338 and comes from north-western China. Its Graeco-Buddhist robe has been clumsily reproduced with series of parallel folds whose mechanical aspect, like the hair drawn with fine incisions, is reminiscent of the treatment of the Taoist mirrors (2nd–3rd centuries) and the incised stone slabs of the Hans, on which various parts of the costumes were outlined with short, parallel striations. The Buddha of 437 (at Kyoto) and that of 451 (in the Metropolitan Museum of Art), both from southern China, are in the same vein and attest to a certain unity of style between the north and south, but their treatment is more elegant and their faces are more refined. They are, in fact, a Chinese bronze-caster's interpretation *à la chinoise* of a foreign theme.

The standing Buddha in the Matsumoto Collection and the Bodhisattva in the Fujii Yurikan at Kyoto, both probably dating from the beginning of the 5th century, would seem to furnish proof of the Chinese bronze-caster's talent for copying Gandhara prototypes. The identity of style is indeed so perfect that some people regard these two pieces as having originated from Turkestan, while others ascribe them to the group of copies made, during the T'ang period, after relics brought back from India by Chinese pilgrims.

In 336 an important series of models, the dates of which have still not been ascertained, is supposed to have been made available to Chinese artists by the founder of the Temple of the Thousand Buddhas at Tun-huang. Experts are still wondering whether or not Caves 3 and 3A, considered to be the oldest of an ensemble that covers several centuries, are earlier than those at Yun-kang. The clay reliefs at Tun-huang are in fact an offshoot of the art of central Asia, a Graeco-Buddhist art tinged with Gupta influence.

The five earliest caves at Yun-kang (Caves 16–20, according to O. Sirén's numbering), founded between 460 and 480 by an emperor of the Northern Wei Dynasty, are cut entirely out of the rock and contain neither clay reliefs nor painted decoration; moreover, instead of the lantern ceilings of Tun-huang, these caves have ceilings decorated with rosettes in the form of lotus blooms. As 710 for the great standing or seated Buddhas, they seem, with their massive forms enveloped in draperies with rounded and fluted folds, to be a distant reflection of the colossal images at Bamiyan, while their high foreheads, straight, narrow noses and inexpressive eyes are reminiscent of the Gandharan images. At the same time, haloes of incised flames are visible behind these exotic forms, and dragons and phoenixes are associated with scrolls of acanthus leaves and with Corinthian capitals in the decoration of the caves. The Chinese stone-cutter had forgotten neither the traditional technique nor the traditional motifs, and, by the end of the 5th century, he had adapted the forms of the Western divinities in accordance with his own ideas. While the body is still suggested under the draperies in Cave 8, this is no longer the case in Caves 5 and 6, in which a new style may be seen to be developing: the bodies have become elongated and flat and are completely

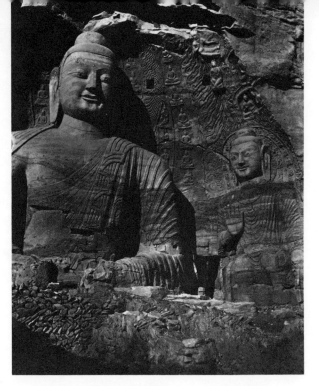

710. **CHINESE. NORTHERN WEI.** The Great Buddha in Cave 20 at Yun-kang (Shansi). Second half of the 5th century A.D.

disguised by the draperies, whose folds are assuming increasing importance; the neck has become thinner and the face narrower, with high, prominent cheek-bones. Moreover, the veiled eyes disappear behind drooping lids and an ineffable smile plays over the lips. China, with its mystic impulse, has transcended the Apollonian Buddha derived from degenerate Greek art; it has deprived the figure of its plastic qualities but has endowed it instead with an intensity of spiritual expression which those of us who have learnt to love Romanesque art appreciate highly. For the next forty years the emphasis was entirely on the faces and the draperies, in which Chinese graphism allowed itself free rein. In their monumental work on Yun-kang, Professors Mizuno and Nagahiro note that the 665 costume of the divinities also became Sinicised. The Buddhas and Bodhisattvas displayed the layers of different robes which were worn by the Chinese aristocracy and which, in 486, became the official dress of the Northern Wei court.

In 495, on the occasion of the transfer of the Northern Wei capital to Lo-yang, a new rock sanctuary was founded, at Lung-men. It was here that the last Yun-kang style, better known as the Lung-men style, became fully developed. In the Ku-yang cave (*c.* 500) the robes of the seated Buddha are draped over the pedestal to form a cascade of tubular folds ending in sharp points, while the skirts of the seated Bodhisattvas form a series of fin-shaped folds on either side of their crossed legs; the shawls enveloping the shoulders of the standing Bodhisattvas cross at the waist and, passing over the shoulders, fall in superimposed streamers on either side. In the Pin-yang cave (505–525) the outline of the folds becomes rounded in the form of a 'keyhole' and, though fuller and less nervous in movement, still remains highly graphic. The Lung-men models spread throughout northern China, to Kunhsien in Homan as well as to P'ing-ling Ssu and Mai-chi Shan in Kansu, sites recently studied by Chinese archaeologists; innumerable stone stelae and gilt-bronze 711 statuettes, in which the treatment of the folds has assumed a singular sharpness, attest to this diffusion, which

389

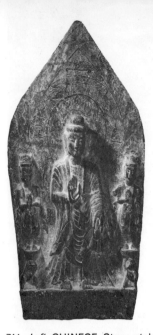

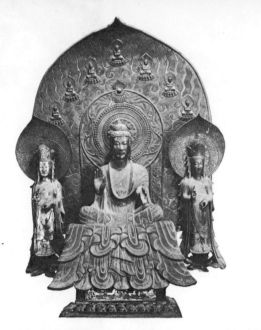

711. *Left*. CHINESE. Stone stele showing the Buddha between two attendants. 520 A.D. *Rietberg Museum, Zürich*.

712. JAPANESE. The Buddha Sakyamuni. Gilt-bronze triad at the Horyuji, near Nara 623 A.D.

713. JAPANESE. ASUKA. The Yumedono Kwannon. Wood statue at the Horyuji. End of the 6th century A.D.

apparently also affected southern China. This unity of style is apparent in a gilt-bronze figurine found in the Paekche kingdom (Korea), where the penetration of southern Chinese influence is attested by ancient texts and would seem to have been confirmed by Chinese archaeologists' recent investigations in the region of Nanking.

Between 560 and 572, however, a reaction to the exaggerated graphic style of the sculpture at Lung-men set in at the Pin-yang cave and became accentuated in Caves 2 and 3 at T'ien-lung Shan on the border between Hopei and Honan. This period of turmoil, which witnessed the splitting up of the Northern Wei Dynasty into two branches that would subsequently be replaced by the Northern Ch'i and Northern Chou, was one of the greatest periods in the development of Chinese sculpture. The draperies became softer, assuming a less graphic and more natural outline; the bodies became more substantial and began to stand out more from the wall, while the faces became rounder and the shoulders broadened. A tranquil and simple harmony emanated from these less ethereal figures which began to assume a more human aspect. This change perhaps reflected the growing popularity of the cult of Amitabha, the metaphysical Buddha (Dhyani-Buddha), who promises salvation and access to the paradise of the Pure Land to all who repent. Whereas in the past experts were inclined to attribute this transformation to a fresh influx of Gupta influence, they now tend to regard this return to weight and solidity as the result of an internal evolution of Chinese plastic art.

The introduction of Buddhism into Japan

The gilt-bronze statuettes, being easy to transport, seem to have contributed towards the propagation of the Buddha's message beyond the Chinese borders. Northern Wei art was thus transmitted to Korea, where it was to be perpetuated during the 7th century, and it was by way of the peninsula that the Buddhist writings and images penetrated to Japan together with the art and civilisation of the continent. The adoption of Buddhism by the Yamato court was a political move accomplished by Prince Shotoku, who acted as regent during the reign of his aunt, the Empress Suiko. Bonzes and artisans from

Paekche, where this conversion had originated, presided over the building of the temples founded by the imperial family. Though the Horyuji was rebuilt perhaps a century 724 later, its early symmetrical plan was retained, and the pagoda, built on a stone platform and with its multiple roofs supported on brackets in the form of frogs' legs, resembles those represented on the walls at Yun-kang and Lung-men. In China the traditional architecture had been adapted to meet the requirements of the Buddhist ritual; the pagoda, the Chinese interpretation of the stupa, was a tower of the Han period, only distinguishable from the latter by the *sorin*, a metal spire surmounted with discs recalling the umbrellas that crowned the reliquaries of India. The main sanctuary in the Horyuji, the Golden Hall (Kondo), is a Chinese pavilion. 724

Through Buddhism, the architecture of the continent, with its spreading tiled roofs supported on wooden columns, imposed itself on Japan; although these formulas actually came from Korea, China itself must have contributed actively to this first wave of influence, for the inscription on the gilt-bronze trinity at Horyuji indicated 712 that the piece was completed in 623 by Tori, the grandson of a Chinese immigrant. Contemporary with the T'ang Dynasty (618–906), this work was executed in the severe, angular style of the Ku-yang cave at Lung-men, as is evident in the importance of the heads, which are quite out of proportion to the rest of the body, in the elongated, smiling faces and in the treatment of the drapery in 'keyhole' folds. Whereas the Yumedono Kwannon (Ava- 713 lokitesvara, the Bodhisattva of Light—the Chinese Kuan-yin), a magnificent wooden idol crowned with a diadem of precious metal, is executed in the same frontal style, accentuated by the rigorous symmetry of the superimposed scarves, other works of the Asuka period reveal the diverse origins of the influences which penetrated to Japan at this time. The forty-eight gilt-bronze statuettes, treasures of the imperial palace, now preserved in the Tokyo Museum, and the numerous images preserved in the temples around Nara attest to the variety of these outside elements, among which the transitional style of the Northern Ch'i Dynasty is by no means poorly represented. The Kudara Kwannon (so called because it is 668, 716 presumed to be a Korean piece) at Horyuji is not as flat as

the Yumedono Kwannon, its flexible body being somewhat fuller. Another type which seems to have been very popular and which also originated from Yun-kang but was elaborated in Korea, as is proved by the beautiful gilt-bronze in the collection of Prince Li at Seoul, was the Buddha Maitreya (the Buddha of the Future) in meditation, sitting with one leg down and the other folded across him and his head resting on his raised hand. No continental representations of this figure achieved the
714 grandeur of that at Chuguji (known as the Nyoirin
715 Kwannon) or the elegance of those at Koryuji. All three are seated in the same position, have the same slender torso and the same draperies treated in subtly graded folds. At the same time, each has a personality of its own: the Bodhisattva at Chuguji is austere and remote, that at Koryuji simple and unaffected, and the third, which is unjustly ignored beside the other two, has a disdainful expression and a rather precious elegance. It seems that these variations on the same theme were in fact portraits; the characteristic tendency towards individualisation, which, despite their obvious affinity, always distinguishes a Japanese work from its Chinese model, was already manifest.

The universality of T'ang art: sculpture

In 589 Yang Chien, the founder of the Sui Dynasty, united northern and southern China; the Sui reign was, however, short lived and by 618 had been replaced by the T'ang Dynasty. The T'ang emperors resumed the expansionist policy of the Hans; circumstances were favourable for such an enterprise, which the uniformity of belief further facilitated. It was over a Buddhist world that China exerted her influence at this time. Masters of central Asia, whose princelings had recognised their suzerainty, masters of Korea, where, thanks to their support, the Silla Dynasty had established its hegemony, the Chinese emperors were the arbiters of the whole of Oriental Asia.

In 645 Japan replaced her still primitive clan organisation by a centralised administration run on Chinese lines and, through annual embassies that included bonzes and students, remained in close contact with Ch'ang-an, the great metropolis and the meeting-place of diplomatic and trade missions. Kyongju, the residence of the Silla kings, and Nara, the first fixed capital of the Yamato emperors, were Chinese cities whose chequerboard plan was inspired by that of Ch'ang-an; not only their palaces and temples, but also their painted and carved divinities, their materials, their dress and their luxury articles were Chinese. In central Asia, the Chinese graphic style began, as we have seen, to wither the Indo-Iranian forms, while pilgrims like Hsuan-tsang brought sacred texts and images all the way back from India. Interpreted and elaborated in China, the mystic idealism of Asanga and Vasubandhu and the theories of the metaphysical sects—who identified the sum total of phenomena with the 'absolute nature', the soul of the Buddhas and the worlds—contributed towards the formation of a Chinese Buddhism, distinguished by the cult of Vairocana, the great illuminator, who had come to personify a metaphysical concept. Renascent Confucianism (the classics, which had become the basis of the entrance examinations to government service, had once again been collected together) also played its part in this intellectualisation of Buddhism. It was at this time, moreover, under the Northern Ch'i and

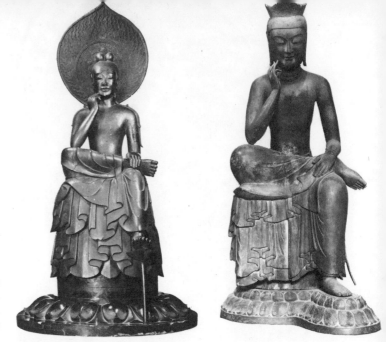

714. JAPANESE. ASUKA. Nyorin Kwannon. Wooden statue at Chuguji, near Nara. End of the 6th century A.D.

715. JAPANESE. ASUKA. Miroku, the Bodhisattva Maitreya. Gilded and lacquered wood statue from Koryuji, near Kyoto. Beginning of the 7th century A.D.

the Sui Dynasties, that the Buddha's image became completely impersonal and, as V. Elisseeff has observed, assumed the solemn aspect of an official that it has retained over the centuries.

A new realism appeared as Chinese plastic art progressed. The Sui artisans, who had sought above all to render the volume of their forms, had produced an abundance of stocky, rigid figures with ovoid and rather severe heads. To volume, the T'ang sculptors allied modelling and movement. Experts have tended to regard these innovations as the fruit of Gupta and post-Gupta influence, reinforced by the images brought from India by Buddhist travellers. This influence is undeniable at T'ien-lung Shan (middle of the 8th century), where figures of semi-nude Bodhisattvas, their limbs moulded by clinging draperies, are governed by the tribhanga, or triple flexion, of Indian statuary. However, as Elisseeff has pointed out, in the movement that animates the T'ang statues it is not the hip but the stomach that protrudes; this feature, already foreshadowed in the Kudara Kwannon at Horyuji, becomes pronounced in the high-relief carvings at Pao-k'ing Ssu (7th century), where the light 718 plays in patterns over the softly modelled forms. The latter's serene equilibrium reappears in the eleven-headed Kuan-yin of the Sokkulam temple, near Kyongju, and in the bronze Sho Kwannon of the Yakushiji at Nara, while the austere majesty of the Maha Vairocana, emerging from the rocky wall at Lung-men, is reflected in the Yakushinyorai of the Yakushiji. Having overcome all the technical difficulties that had shackled them up to this time, the Chinese took up the study of musculature: the Lokapalas (temple guardians) at Lung-men writhe in 672 violent *contraposto* with a brutal realism that becomes mere caricature in the wooden images at Tun-huang. The tendency towards exaggeration of form and pose, which rapidly degenerated into pretension and vapidity, had already begun to manifest itself in China.

Japan maintained more equilibrium in her treatment of this theme; her figures were more tense and nervous,

391

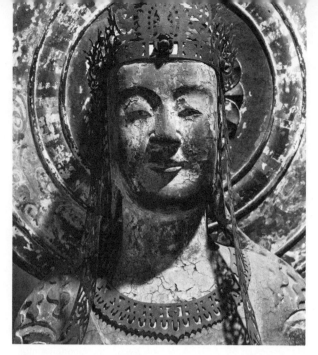

716. JAPANESE. ASUKA. Head of the Kudara Kwannon. Wood statue at thr Horyuji. End of the 6th century

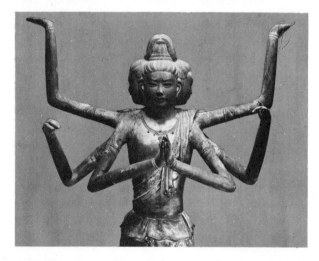

717. JAPANESE. TEMPYO. Asura, from the Kofukuji, Nara. Middle of the 8th century A.D.

718. *Left*. CHINESE. T'ANG. Kuan-yin with eleven heads. Relief carving from Pao-k'ing Ssu (Shensi). *Museum of Fine Arts, Boston.*

719. *Right*. JAPANESE. TEMPYO. Clay statue in the Todaiji, Nara. 8th century A.D.

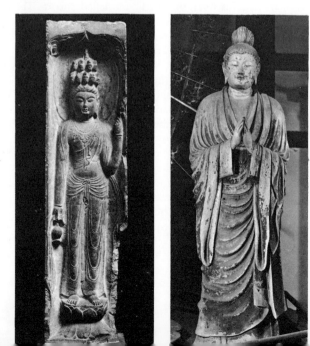

and her artists continued to devote their attention to line rather than to volume. In bronze, wood, plaster or dry lacquer, the sculptors of the Tempoyo period proved themselves worthy emulators of their T'ang masters, but their less intellectual art remained more instinctive.

From the Asura, or from the Twelve Disciples of the Koryuji, to the Bonten from the Todaiji and the portrait of Ganjin the blind Chinese bonze, a fresher and more acute sensibility emanates from the Japanese faces. 717 719

The development of painting

Thus, between 550 and 750, Chinese sculpture reached the height of its development and thereafter ceased to be renewed. However, lest it be thought that a parallel evolution is to be observed in pictorial art, we hasten to say that in China the different art forms did not develop according to the same rhythm. Whereas it promoted the progress of sculpture, Buddhism seems to have somewhat retarded the development of painting by introducing outside elements into it, which, for a time, diverted it from its original course. Not a trace remains of the great Buddhist paintings that adorned the walls of the temples at Ch'ang-an and of which the frescoes at Tun-huang are but a provincial reflection.

It was only in Japan that a magnificent example of this official style could be studied—up until 1949, when it was destroyed by a disastrous fire—in the mural paintings of the Kondo at Horyuji. Here, four paradises had been the setting for harmoniously grouped and richly attired Buddhas and Bodhisattvas, whose faces and bodies were treated in 'spot-lighting', which, as Jean Buhot has expressed it, is a sort of 'inwardly sensed modelling' that 'has nothing to do with the natural play of light and shade'; it was a practice foreign to Chinese art but well known to central Asia. Art historians were struck by the 'exotic' aspect of the paintings at Horyuji, which they compared to the frescoes at Ajanta. The affinity, however, was superficial, and although the experts were able to prove that all the iconographic and decorative detail was of central Asiatic origin, they recognised in these works the grandeur and rigidity of a purely Chinese style. The treatment of the forms on a piece of embroidery—also Chinese—preserved in the Kajuki at Uji confirms the validity of this conclusion. The use of 'spot-lighting' seems, moreover, to have been reserved for religious subjects and, as is attested by the Scroll of the Thirteen Emperors, a work by the court painter Yen Li-pen (d. 673), the figure painting had remained in the tradition of Ku K'ai-chih; at most, a greater attention to detail is perceptible in the faces. 720

According to the texts, Wu Tao-tzu (first half of the 8th century), with his vigour and the variety of his brushwork, gave new life to this style. His work has completely disappeared, and the rather sugary charm of the female figures in the Screen of the Beauties under the Trees, or in the extremely fragmentary painting found in the cemetery at Astana (near Turfan), whose replete and portly forms can be ascribed to the middle of the 8th century, betrays nothing of this great master's influence.

At the end of the 7th century, Li Ssu-hsun, another court painter, had become famous for the brilliant colouring of his landscapes. A work of his son and pupil, Li Chao-tao, preserved in the Peking Museum, shows a panoramic view in which the horizon is placed very high up and the mountains in the background are picked out in deep blue with their jagged contours outlined in gold. These compositions, with, in the foreground, palaces and terraces traced with a ruler and picked out in red and gold, have an enchanted air. However, Li Ssu-hsun's mountains remain close to the traditional motifs, which he merely enlarged upon, and they reappear, arranged in four masses and alternated with clouds, figures and trees, on the beautiful bronze mirror inlaid with gold belonging to the Shoso-in at Nara.

Wang Wei, a contemporary of Wu Tao-tzu, was a member, with Li T'ai-po and Tu Fu, of the group of sublime poets who delighted the court of Hsuan-tsung (middle of the 8th century). He was interested in painting and is supposed to have originated the monochrome landscape. If tradition is to be believed, he is also supposed to have written that a landscape should be thought out before being painted, but his writings are of as doubtful attribution as his paintings. The monochrome style already existed, and a landscape done in ink on canvas is to be seen in the Shoso-in. Its atmosphere is very different from that of the fantasies of Li Ssu-hsun and his school: a winding river, a few trees and a fisherman perched on a rock in midstream. With its few rapid but sensitive notations, this simple sketch already foreshadows the masters of the Sung period.

The heterogeneity of T'ang art

669 The funerary figurines, a motley assortment of female dancers and musicians, court ladies, warriors, mountebanks and travellers, reflect the cosmopolitan crowd at Ch'ang-an, the rallying point of Asia, where bonzes, tribute bearers and merchants rubbed shoulders with Indians, Iranians, Sogdians and Arabs. From the west came horses, carpets and objects of precious metal; to the west went silks and ceramics, remains of which have been found as far away as Samarra.

All these contacts left their mark on T'ang decorative art. In ceramics, forms inspired by those of Iran appeared as early as the Sui period: amphoras with handles transformed into dragons, and ewers imitating Sassanian gold and silverware. The white porcelains extolled by the Arab travellers, and the earthenware vessels with shot-coloured lead glazes, which the Iranian potters were to imitate in their turn, were inspired by Western prototypes and adorned with Western motifs: rosettes, palmettes, floral fields and pearled medallions.

During this same period the whole decorative repertory of Iran was introduced into China. The Shosoin at Nara—in which the Emperor Shomu's collections have been preserved since 755—contains an inexhaustible store of material for the study of this aspect of T'ang art: painted or inlaid laquerware, mirrors adorned with vine motifs and inlaid with mother of pearl or tortoise-shell, diversely woven silks and metalware with guilloche (cable pattern) ornamentation and inlaid with gold and silver are among the examples of a rich, precious and exotic official art, which betrays the tendency towards baroque exuberance that becomes manifest in Chinese art whenever an influx of outside elements upsets its delicate balance.

The Sung period saw the Chinese refining this rather abundant decoration and, at the same time, witnessed the birth of true Japanese art at Kyoto.

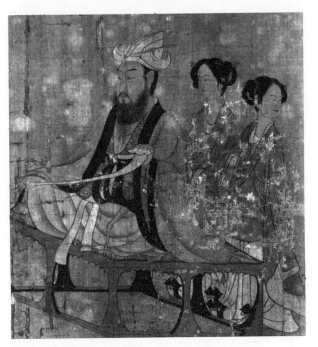

720. CHINESE. Portrait of the Emperor Wen-ti, of the Ch'en Dynasty. Detail from the Scroll of the Thirteen Emperors. Painting on silk, attributed to Yen Li-pen (d. A.D. 673). *Museum of Fine Arts, Boston.*

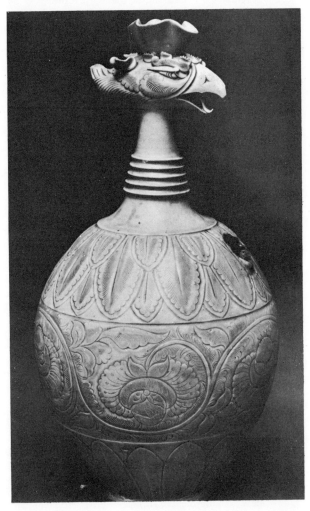

721. CHINESE. SUNG. Ting ware ewer. *British Museum.*

HISTORICAL SUMMARY: Far Eastern art

CHINA FROM THE HAN TO THE T'ANG DYNASTIES

History. The advent of the Han Dynasty in 206 B.C. put an end to the sanguinary disorders that followed the break-up of the empire created by Ch'in Shih Huang Ti.

An era of peace opened with the Hans; China's powerfully protected frontiers were extended by conquests in Chinese Turkestan, in Tongking and at Than-hoa (northern Annam). Except for an interlude between 9 and 22 A.D., due to the usurpation of Wang Mang, the Han Dynasty, established at Lo-yang, ruled for over four centuries; for the first time in its history China came into contact with the West, through the protectorate she had established in central Asia: the Silk Route linked her directly with the Syrian markets. The Han Dynasty's military power, the rise of a new society eager for luxuries, the development of trade and the westward expansion, all contributed towards the formation of a vigorous and sumptuous art.

However, the Han Dynasty collapsed (220 A.D.), undermined by palace intrigue and weakened by peasant revolts. The period of chaos that followed saw the country divided into three kingdoms and invaded by the Huns and the proto-Mongols, who settled in the north, causing the legitimate rulers to take refuge in Nanking, where five dynasties succeeded one another; meanwhile another family, of Turkish origin, seized power in the north under the name of Wei (398–550). Unity was finally re-established in 589 by the Chinese house of Sui, whose reign was short-lived (618) but whose labours bore fruit.

The Sui Dynasty was replaced by the powerful T'ang Dynasty (618–907), who continued the reforms started by the house of Sui and under whom Chinese civilisation reached its apogee. With the unity of the country secured, the T'ang Dynasty extended its conquests farther than its predecessors and pursued a policy on the scale of the contemporary world. A cosmopolitan spirit developed, making China accessible to outside influence which penetrated chiefly through the channels of trade and of Indian-born Buddhism. Everything circulated along the Silk Route and reached China in the wake of the merchants and missionaries: ideas, religious beliefs, art forms, techniques and decorative motifs. As a result, Chinese art underwent a complete transformation; nevertheless, it stamped each new formula it adopted with its own personality. Despite the vicissitudes suffered by the T'ang Dynasty from the end of the 7th century onwards, its impetus had been such that the T'ang style had an immense influence throughout all the regions within the political sphere of China.

Architecture. Owing to the destruction caused by the revolts that brought about the downfall of the Han Dynasty, virtually none of the civil, military or religious monuments of this period have survived. It is only in the funerary art that certain architectural forms have been preserved; for the sepulchres more or less imitated the habitations of the living and contained a whole assortment of miniature furniture made of terra cotta, bronze and lacquered wood. The tomb itself—and especially the imperial tomb—was set up under a tumulus raised in the middle of a funerary enclosure, which was approached by a road called the Spirit Road; this was bordered on either side by rows of animal statues, while high pillars marked its entrance. This arrangement, which probably crystallised under the Han Dynasty, was continually improved upon and lasted until the downfall of the Ch'ing Dynasty. The subterranean architecture of the tomb imitated civil architecture, numerous terra cotta models of which have been found not only in China but also in Korea and at Than-hoa: overhanging tiled roofs resting on walls that widen out towards the ground, columns with brackets, and ridgepoles decorated with ornamental birds or animals—formulas which have all remained in the architectural repertory up to modern times [**700**]

When Buddhism was introduced, the same formulas were applied to religious buildings; the stupa typical of Indian Buddhism became a brick or stone pagoda in China, a sort of square tower of superimposed storeys and roofs [**722**]. Following the example of India, Kapisa (Afghanistan) and Chinese Turkestan, China produced rock sanctuaries as from the 5th century, in the frontier town of Tun-huang, at Yun-kang, at Lung-men, at T'ien-lung Shan, in Shantung, etc. However, their importance lies in their painted or carved decoration rather than in their architecture, which, compared to that of India, is virtually without interest.

Sculpture. Although related to the style of the period of the Warring States, which it continued, Han sculpture represents a novelty in its return to stone, a material which had not been used since the Shang period. It was summed up in the funerary relief carvings, the mythological subjects of which, then in process of elaboration, were later to be incorporated into official Confucianism and Taoism. An astonishing vitality emanates from these compositions despite the simplicity of the means employed: the surface, on which the internal detail is incised, is outlined against a plain or striated background—a technique closely resembling that of decorated bronze. The human figures, the animals and the elements of architecture, are endowed with an extraordinarily dynamic power (Hsiao-t'ang Shan, 1st century B.C.; Chu Wei, c. 50 B.C.; Wu Liang Tzu, 147–167 A.D., etc. [**698**, **699**]. This art was perpetuated in the stamped tiles of Szechwan (1st–2nd centuries), which give a powerful feeling of synthesis [**707**]. Sculpture in the round was still limited to funerary statuettes [**702**, **703**] and to the animal statues that lined the roads leading to the tombs, all of which manifest the same stylisation and the same tendency towards simplification of volume.

The rise of Buddhist art brought about a transformation not only in the iconography but even in the spirit of Chinese sculpture: though deriving its inspiration from the art of Kapisa, it retained a Chinese accent which became steadily stronger [**710**]. The Northern Wei style (middle of the 5th–middle of the 6th centuries), developed a very personal aestheticism [**710**, **711**]. This style is noted for its extremely elongated forms enveloped in draperies which are arranged in a series of angular pleats, for the touching and mysterious spirituality that radiates from the slightly smiling faces and for the subjection of the whole to a 'graphism' that has prevailed throughout the evolution of Chinese art, but which was modified through contact with the arts of central Asia and India: under the Northern Chou Dynasty, though rigorous frontality remained the rule, the forms all became rounded and supple (T'ien-lung Shan 10 and 16, in particular).

These new tendencies were worked out during the T'ang epoch, a period which was particularly rich in sculptural works. A fresh wave of Indian influence from the Gupta and post-Gupta styles swept across central Asia and superseded the outside influences (Graeco-Roman and Iranian) which Buddhism had attracted to China earlier on. Ponderous, hieratic and completely clothed figures gave way to softly modelled, inflected, supple and almost languorous figures, with skilfully indicated fluid and gossamer draperies, and torsos bared in the Indian fashion. For representations of temple guardians or warriors, movement was whipped into violence and musculature inflated beyond all proportion to heighten the impression of strength [**672**]. The celebrated caves at Lungmen (Cave of the Thousand Buddhas; Cave of the Lions) and T'ien-lung Shan offer perfect illustrations of this Indianised aestheticism.

The same mastery is manifest in the animal art, which reached its apogee during this period. The funerary statuary [**669**] deserves special mention: generally of small dimensions, executed in terra cotta and polychromed, it manifests the naturalistic taste of the period: personages of all races and all the strata of society—court ladies, female dancers and musicians, mountebanks, foreigners—flank pawing and wheeling horses, camels and buffaloes, presenting a particularly lively picture of the cosmopolitan society of the time. These qualities did not survive the downfall of the T'ang Dynasty and the decline of Buddhism (which was brutally persecuted in 845).

Painting. The examples of painting surviving from the Han epoch are rare; however, a few painted tiles and mural compositions [**704**] and a large quantity of lacquerware found in Korea suffice to show that the Chinese painters had attained a high degree of skill and technical ability by this period. The extremely subtle handling of line already foreshadows the qualities that were to constitute the glory of the Chinese artists. There is no doubt that painting was highly appreciated as from this time; during the 5th century a portraitist by the name of Hsieh Ho formulated the Six Principles of Painting, which, in a laconic form, perhaps inspired by that of Indian treatises, have remained fundamental to this day.

A work of the first great artist on record has been preserved in a copy, attributed to the T'ang epoch, in which the style of the original is perhaps modified: the celebrated scroll of Ku K'ai-chih (344–406), the Admonitions of the Imperial Preceptress; this work reveals a subtle sense of grouping which tends towards a pyramidal arrangement, a refined taste and the importance already accorded to landscape [**708**].

The destruction of untold masterpieces at the time of the downfall of the T'ang Dynasty has deprived us of those produced by the greatest artists, which we only know through tradition or the testimony of later copies. However, certain works have been preserved outside China, such as the mural com-

positions adorning the numerous Buddhist caves at Tun-huang [**709**] in Chinese Turkestan and the paintings that could be admired in the Kondo of the Horyuji at Nara (Japan, 8th century) until they were destroyed by fire in 1949. All the same, these are only provincial works which do not bear the mark of genius. They reveal the increasing importance of landscape, which was already conceived in such a way as to give the feeling of the infinity and grandeur of nature, but their line is rather inexpressive, and it has been proved that the technique of pouncing was used. Of the great masters whose names have been handed down to posterity the following should be cited: Yen Li-pen (d. 673), of whom an original work is preserved in the Boston Museum; it manifests the qualities noted in Ku K'ai-chih's scroll, despite the restorations that have impaired it (Scroll of the Thirteen Emperors [**720**]). Li Ssu-hsun (c. 650) is credited with the creation of panoramic landscapes in stylised colours enhanced with touches of gold, which the northern school was to repeat *ad infinitum*. His son Li Chao-tao is supposed to have added to his father's manner the practice of drawing buildings with the aid of a ruler and with fine regular lines, which practice was also adopted by the northern school. The brushwork of Wu Tao-tzu (first half of the 8th century), the greatest painter of this period, is particularly vigorous and varied. Wang Wei, his contemporary and a poet as well as a painter, is regarded as the founder of the southern school, since his monochrome landscapes inspired the style for which the greatest painters of the Sung period became famous.

Portraitists, animal painters and flower painters were also well represented.

Minor arts. The Han epoch, a period of luxury-loving parvenus and adventurers, produced metalware of a signal

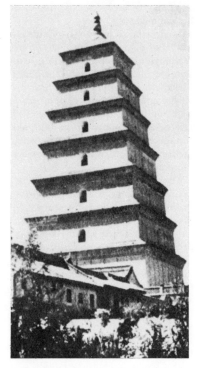

722. CHINA. T'ANG. The Tayen pagoda at Ch'ang-an.

splendour: bronzes were inlaid with gold, silver, turquoise, malachite, jade and glass paste; ritual bronzes deteriorated, but the clasps, belt buckles, mirrors, weapons, harness and carriage pieces and innumerable small bronzes attest to the popularity of metalware [**705**], which betrays the probable influence of the animal art of the steppes [**723**].

During the reign of the Wei Dynasty, this predilection was diverted, under the influence of Buddhism, towards pious imagery: gilt-bronze statuettes and shrines imitated the style of the large stone images, thus creating

723. CHINESE. HAN. The White Tiger of the West. Jade. *Musée Guimet, Paris.*

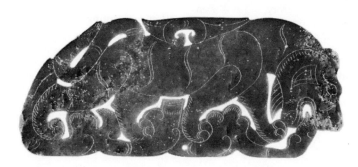

a miniature sculpture of the very highest quality.

Under the T'ang Dynasty, metalware and gold and silver objects were of a previously unsurpassed refinement. Outside influence added tremendous variety to the production, which included gilded objects, objects inlaid with mother-of-pearl and amber and filigree and granular work; the gold and silver plate, imitating similar work of the Sassanians, was also extremely sumptuous.

The silks, ceramics, furniture and lacquerware objects were all equally magnificent. By the 2nd century B.C., silk-weaving (damask; polychrome silk serge) had reached a high degree of perfection, and, through Chinese commercial activity, its reputation spread throughout the entire Eurasian world. Under Iranian influence the T'ang weavers adopted Mediterranean techniques, of which that of Gobelin weaving was the most important, and Iranian motifs became so fashionable that they were faithfully reproduced in both Chinese and Japanese fabrics.

Ceramics, which were to become one of the glories of the Chinese artisans, were in an experimental stage under the Han Dynasty and still imitated bronze forms [**706**], but, according to an ancient discovery, they were baked at a high temperature (from 2200° to 2400° F); a greenish stoneware appeared, which was to develop into the celadon. Having become part of the increasing trade under the T'ang Dynasty, they were designed to suit the taste of customers, and that of Iran in particular, whose forms, colours and decorative motifs they imitated; the monochrome pieces—so highly appreciated under the Sung Dynasty—also became very popular at this time [**721**].

Jeannine Auboyer

KOREA FROM THE 2nd CENTURY B.C. TO THE 9th CENTURY A.D.

History. Korea made a relatively late appearance in history and was mentioned for the first time in the *Annals* of the Han Dynasty. In the year 108 B.C., the Han emperor Wu Ti established four command posts in North Korea, the most important of which, Lak-liang (Lo-lang in Chinese, Rakuro in Japanese), existed until the 4th century A.D. Chinese culture thus penetrated to North Korea and gradually spread to the south, where it appears to have become mixed with other elements originating from southern China.

During the 4th century the peninsula was divided into three kingdoms, of whose origins little is known: the north was ruled by the Koguryo Dynasty, of Tungusic stock, which was in close contact with the Northern Wei Dynasty and which became converted to Buddhism; the Paekche kingdom in the south-west established relations with the Chinese dynasties at Nanking and, having received Buddhism from the latter, in turn transmitted it, in the middle of the 6th century, to the Yamato court of Japan; the Silla kingdom in the south-east, isolated by a barrier of mountains from the rest of the peninsula, developed an original civilisation which seems to have been in contact with southern China and to have had a certain amount of influence on protohistoric Japan. During the 6th and 7th centuries these three kingdoms entered into rivalry.

After the reunification of the Chinese empire, the Sui rulers (589–618) made a vain attempt to conquer the neighbouring peninsula. Their successors, the T'ang rulers, supported the Silla Dynasty, which then succeeded in establishing its hegemony over the whole of the peninsula (668) and, in return, recognised the suzerainty of China. This dynasty ruled Korea until the year 936.

THE ART OF THE CHINESE COMMAND POSTS

(End of the 2nd century B.C.–4th century A.D.)

The excavations carried out by Japanese archaeologists on the site of the ancient city of Lo-lang have brought to light important funerary complexes which have furnished interesting complementary information on Han art. Among the large amount of funerary furniture discovered were numerous pieces of inscribed and dated laquerware from the imperial workshops in Szechwan, in the west of China.

THE ART OF THE THREE KINGDOMS

(4th–9th centuries)

Koguryo. The tombs of the Koguryo rulers were studied by Japanese archaeologists. The earliest were situated not far from the Yalu, on the northern frontier of Korea; others were grouped around the site of the ancient city of Lo-lang, on the Ta-t'ung river. They consisted of one or two stone funerary chambers, covered with a corbelled vault forming a 'lantern'. This type of roof, unknown in China, is found in the rock sanctuaries of central Asia. The walls and ceilings of these chambers were adorned with frescoes inspired by Chinese painting: representations of the four cardinal points, hunting scenes, court ladies, etc., which, because of the disappearance of décor of this type in China itself, are of inestimable value for the study of Chinese painting during the period of the Six Dynasties.

The remains of Buddhist art are small in number, although a few surviving gilt-bronze statuettes reveal the influence of Northern Wei art (Yun-kang and Lung-men), which persisted until late in the 6th century.

Paekche. Little remains of the Buddhist art, but the first temples and the earliest sculpture in Japan have preserved the memory of an art that is almost non-existent today.

Silla. *Protohistoric period (4th–6th centuries).* The royal tombs, single or double mounds in the form of a calabash, have yielded an important assortment of funerary furniture.

Chased and filigreed gold objects: crowns, earrings, and belts adorned with pearls and magatama (ornaments in the shape of a bear's or tiger's claw) were valued for their magic properties. Numerous examples of these last have also been found on protohistoric sites in Japan.

Ceramics: numerous bowls and vases on open-work bases, adorned with incised or stamped geometric designs. They appear to be related to the samples of black pottery found in the region of the lower Yangtze, and they were the forerunners of certain Japanese protohistoric ceramics.

Historic period (6th–9th centuries). During the 6th century Chinese influence began to penetrate to the Silla kingdom, which became converted to Buddhism. During the 7th century the capital, Kyongju, was rebuilt on the chequerboard plan of Ch'ang-an. The royal tombs were laid out like those of the Chinese emperors and were preceded by stone figures of animals and people.

A few examples of Buddhist architecture have survived: Queen Syontok's stupa (7th century), which is square, and the stone stairway of the Pul-kuk-sa (8th century).

The relief carvings in the artificial cave of Sokkulam are excellent examples of T'ang Buddhist sculpture.

Numerous decorated tiles have also been found.

JAPAN

History. During the first centuries of our era, the influx of numerous continental elements gradually transformed the Japanese culture, which had remained very primitive until then.

Agriculture and the use of metal and of the potter's wheel were introduced. During the 4th century, a clan came from the southern island of Kyushu to settle on Yamato, a small plain north of Osaka, and began to acquire increasing political importance. The great tombs (*ko-fun*) of its chiefs, surmounted by circular mounds, and their funerary furniture (crowns; weapons; magatama; ceramics), show an affinity with the protohistoric culture of Silla in south-eastern Korea. Through the agency of Paekche, another Korean kingdom, the Yamato received Buddhism in the middle of the 6th century. This religion was officially adopted by Prince Shotoku, who acted as regent under his aunt, the Empress Suiko (593–629). Since then the evolution of Japanese culture has never slowed down. The Yamato adopted Sino-Korean civilisation and, in 645, the ancient clan organisation was replaced by a centralised administration of Chinese type. Nara, the first fixed capital,

724. JAPANESE. ASUKA. The Kondo (Golden Hall) of the Horyuji, near Nara. End of the 6th century–beginning of the 7th century A.D.

was built on the chequerboard plan of Ch'ang-an, the metropolis of the T'ang Dynasty, whose prestige was steadily increasing. Official embassies were sent to the Chinese court, and the culture of the empire became the model which the Japanese sought to emulate in the course of the 8th and 9th centuries. The early Buddhist art in Japan was entirely continental.

Architecture. The earliest religious foundations, such as the Horyuji, remain the venerable examples of an architecture that has completely disappeared from the country where it originated: wooden architecture mounted on stone terraces, with columns coated in red plaster and surmounted by brackets supporting heavy, overhanging tiled roofs [**724**]. At the end of the 7th century and during the 8th century, the temples at Nara (Yakushiji; Shin-Yakushiji; Todaiji) imitated the T'ang temples.

Sculpture. The earliest religious images, of gilt-bronze or wood, were inspired by the style of the Six Dynasties, to which Korea long remained faithful. By the beginning of the 8th century, the influence of T'ang sculpture was in the ascendant, and the

Buddhist statues in the temples at Nara (in bronze, lacquered wood and polychromed plaster) are magnificent examples of faithful Japanese copies of Chinese sculpture [**712–717**, **719**].

Painting. The few surviving paintings betray the same sources of inspiration: the style of the Six Dynasties in the celebrated Tamamushi shrine, preserved at the Horyuji; the official T'ang style in the frescoes of the Kondo or Golden Hall of the same temple, in which the traditional Chinese motifs were associated with elements of central Asiatic origin.

Minor arts. Numerous artisans from Korea and China introduced the most varied techniques to the court, and ambassadors brought a wealth of objects back with them from China. The Shoso-in, which has housed the collections of the Emperor Shomu (presented to the Todaiji by his widow) since the middle of the 8th century, possesses a superb assortment of T'ang objects: mirrors inlaid with mother-of-pearl and amber, musical instruments and furniture adorned with paintings, silks, screens and ceramics.

Madeleine Paul-David

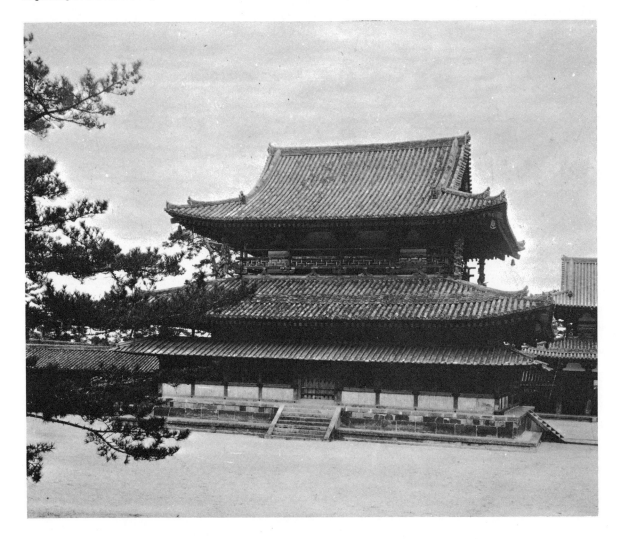

CONCLUSION: THE AESTHETICS OF INDIA AND CHINA *Jeannine Auboyer*

*Though India and China, the great Asiatic partners, may
differ from one another, they hold a concept of art that
is opposed to that of the West where realism, the external
likeness of art to the physical world, remains the essential.
Jeannine Auboyer, with her profound knowledge of the arts
of Asia, underscores the factor common to the Orient:
the material reality of an object is used to communicate
its invisible spiritual truth.*

India and China constitute two distinct civilisations,
whose traditions, ideas and forms stem from the mentality
peculiar to each. To say that their aesthetics are opposed
would doubtless not be quite accurate; they are, however,
sufficiently different, if not in principle then at least in
expression, for a comparison between the two to reveal
a genuine divergence in the processes of their thought.

A comprehension of this thought is essential to an
'inside' understanding of the works of their artists. It is
also extremely important, since India and China between
them shared the whole of southern and Far Eastern Asia,
in which they created well-defined spheres of influence
that persist to this day.

Visual reality and spiritual reality

Their point of departure rests on the quasi-necessity of
faithfully representing nature, and on a profound knowledge of the latter, founded on a mental operation tending
to transpose it to a philosophical or symbolic plan. At a
fairly early date each country realised the necessity of
condensing its aesthetic theories into a laconic form,
subsequently glossed *ad infinitum*. India seems to have
taken the initiative in this, a fact which, considering the
trend of her particular codification, is not surprising. A
comparison will suffice to reveal the analogies between
the two; first there are the Six Rules (*Shadangga*) of India,
which are anonymous and which, it seems, may be
attributed to the 3rd century A.D.: (1) science of forms
(*rupa-bheda*); (2) feeling for the exact correspondences or
measurements (*pramani*); (3) influence of sentiment on
form (*bhava*); (4) feeling for gracefulness (*lavanya-
yoganam*); (5) comparisons (*sadriçyam*); (6) science of
colours (*varnika-bhagga*). The Six Principles of China
were laid down by the Chinese portraitist Hsieh Ho and
date back to the 5th century; we give Alexander Soper's
version: (1) animation through spirit consonance (*ch'-yun
sheng-tung*); (2) structural method in use of the brush;
(3) fidelity to the object in portraying forms; (4) conformity to kind in applying colours; (5) proper planning
in placing (of elements); (6) transmission (of the experience of the past) in making copies.

Although there is no similarity of either order or
wording between these two sets of rules,' they may
readily be compared; for both attest to an attentive
observation of the problems of plastic and pictorial art.
However, whereas India gives pre-eminence to accuracy
of form and mensuration, including sentiment (*bhava*)
only in third place and the science of colours last, China
stresses above all the principle of animation by the spirit

of the form represented, and is careful to ensure the
transmission of masterpieces through 'copies' as a last
rule. Since the innumerable commentaries that have
attempted to explain the hidden meaning behind these
enigmatic formulas are distributed over the centuries up
to the present day, they offer an excellent picture of the
reaction of the Indian and Chinese mentalities to these
problems, as well as this evolution. Without them,
Western critics would be obliged to give hypothetical
interpretations of the principles.

However, it is hard to determine the chronological
order of these reactions: the commentary of the *Shadangga*
has been undertaken again in our time by the most
eminent Indian poet, Sir Rabindranath Tagore; the *Ku
hua p'in lu* of Hsieh Ho has remained the golden rule for
Chinese artists to this day, after having inspired all the
methods and the treatises on aesthetics of the Ming epoch.

The explanation given by the Indians of the *Shadangga*
is most instructive, since it shows that India not only took
a precious stand in the controversy between objective
and subjective art, but that she also approached a number
of theories carried to their extreme consequences by
modern Western research. Thus *rupa*, form, is not—in
the view of Indian artists—the natural aspect of an object
but is essentially the aspect produced: that which the
artist represents is not an object 'seen', but an object
'known'; far from making a servile copy of nature, the
Indian artist works after a mental prototype that represents an ideal selection among a series of real objects of
a determined category. The object is therefore not represented for its own sake nor to the life, but is endowed with
all the potential of evocation that its category may contain. For *rupa* signifies at once tangible form and mental
form; it implies analysis and synthesis of forms by the
senses and the spirit. 'The outward appearance alone
reveals neither the spirit nor the soul enclosed within the
material . . . To depend solely on the outward appearance,
neglecting the spirit, is to limit oneself to seeing and
painting only the superficial aspect of a form. In order to
acquire true knowledge of a form, we must illuminate all
things with the rays of our soul, and be receptive to the
light which emanates from all things visible and invisible'
(R. Tagore).

The same conviction is apparent in the commentary on
the first principle of Hsieh Ho: the term *ch'i-yun*, variously
interpreted by the critics, signifies the rhythm of the
spirit, creator of life movement; it is the quality inherent
in the true artist who, having acquired the necessary
virtuosity, expresses the nature of his model with appropriate lines and colours. Here again, forms without spirit
are of no value. In fact, this had, originally at least, to do
with a magic obligation to endow a representation with
life; to this end—as in India—the representation had to
conform rigorously to its subject, and it is for this same
reason that India, in her turn, was so insistent upon the
importance of exact measurements. Although this magic
obligation was gradually eclipsed by considerations of an
aesthetic nature, it long persisted as an undercurrent in

both Indian and Chinese art. This conformity is not what the West understands by this term: it has nothing to do with 'photographic' art, but with a process of synthesis designed to sift the ideal forms of the visible world, discarding all that is accidental; it is an act of recreating, whereby the artist sets down that which is permanent in a durable manner. In this effort at synthesis every feature has its own significance, consecrated by the canonical laws, a significance of such importance that, in Chinese portrait painting (in which the term *ch'i-yun* is replaced by the term *ch'uan-shen*), the artist, with great subtlety, represents his subject at successive moments of time; it is in fact impossible, as the Chinese artists observe, to take 728   in the whole face at once: thus, the expression of the right eye (the one first seen by this people, accustomed to read from right to left) precedes that of the left eye, the mouth following, and slightly modifying the expression of both eyes.

Technique and the power of suggestion

It would seem *a priori* that *bhava*, sentiment, placed third in the Indian rules, ought to be closer to the term *ch'i-yun* than *rupa*. However, the Indian concept is rather different and perhaps more artificial; in modern times the idea of *rasa*, quintessence of taste, has been added to it. These two notions, which are extremely closely related, correspond to two different mental attitudes: that of the artist, who must be capable of evoking them, and that of the spectator, in whom they must vibrate in such a way that he is under the impression that he feels them spontaneously. This process is true of all artistic expression, including dancing and music. The action of 'making live' is as much a recreation as *ch'i-yun* or *ch'uan-shen*, and, as the Chinese selected and catalogued the traits that would translate the *ch'i-yun* into painting, so the Indians minutely codified the forms and gestures that would bring about the *bhava* and the *rasa*: that which was at first perhaps only the result of very attentive observation became in both countries a series of technical formulas for the attainment of perfection. However, all agree that even the most proven formulas cannot give a work of art its full power of evocation if the artist is incapable of endowing it with that mysterious life which animates every masterpiece. But the contrary is equally true: life will be conferred on a work of art only if the technique, perfectly mastered, permits of its being expressed in all its intensity.

It is for this reason that India and China accord such importance to the purely technical aspects of painting and 727   sculpture; India stresses accurate proportions, appropriate colours and the comparisons which are a peculiarity of her own. China advocates a perfect knowledge of the laws of composition, the study of forms based on the observation of their structure and, naturally, a discerning use of colours. Whereas both envisaged these problems from a theoretical point of view, each nevertheless proposed its own solution: India proceeded by comparisons, China by analogies. The Indian science of comparisons (*sadrí-çyam*) led to experiments very similar to those of Surrealism: it is a transposition of the attributes of an object, or else more or less systematised parallel images, associations of ideas which, while assuming an aspect strange to a Western mind, always remain, from a formal point of view, within the natural order of things, since India never ventured beyond the borderline into absurdity. In this

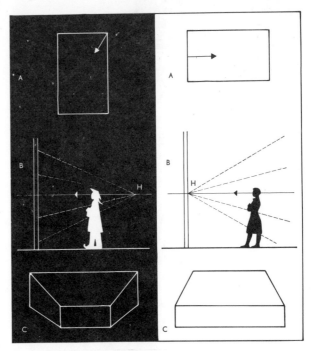

725. CHINESE. Diagram showing the principles of Chinese perspective as compared to that of the West. (A) In China the eye is directed from top to bottom and from right to left; in the West the eye travels from left to right. (B) In China the horizon line (H) is placed behind the spectator; in the West it is placed before him. (C) A dais drawn according to Chinese and Western perspective.

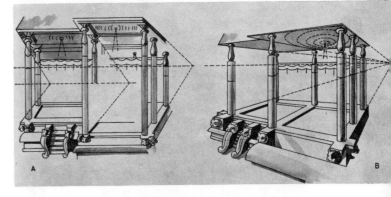

726. INDIAN. Diagram comparing the perspective at Ajanta (A) with Western perspective (B).

realm belong the colour symbolism and the vocabulary of gestures (*mudra* and *hasta*) and facial expressions. Thus divine personages have serpent necklaces, display a crescent in their hair or hold a bounding hind on their outstretched fingers. The green or blue flesh-colour given to certain divinities defies the laws of nature but is in accordance with modern symbolism, in the same way as are the colours given to each letter of the alphabet in the *Tantra* (sacred books), a practice that curiously foreshadows Rimbaud in his poems 'Voyelles' and 'Alchimie du verbe'.

China, on the contrary, remains within the natural order of things—except in certain categories of paintings of Buddhist inspiration, for which she adopted India's repertory of comparisons. This naturalism, however, is anything but objective, at least during the period that is most representative of Chinese painting, the Sung epoch,

399

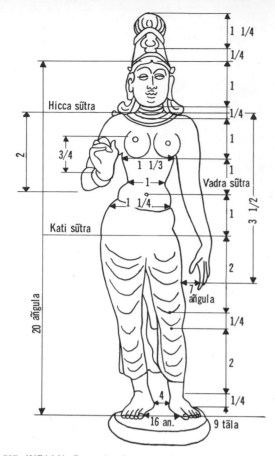

727. INDIAN. Example of canonical measurements for a statue. (After Gangoly.)

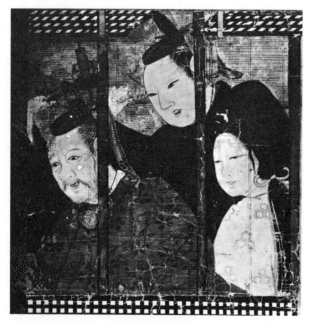

728. JAPANESE. Spectators behind a blind. Part of a screen, gouache on silk. c. 1600–1610. *Musée Guimet, Paris.*

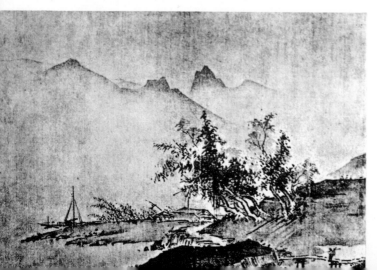

which witnessed the magnificent flowering of the monochrome landscape in ink; it is in fact a purely subjective art, in which the elements of nature serve as pretexts for the interpretation of the painter's mood and symbolism is used merely to establish an analogy—even an identity—between the quality of the landscape and its components and the passion, peace, nostalgia and other sentiments felt by the artist.

Divergences of shadows and perspective

Two other essential differences should be noted between Indian and Chinese aesthetics: one has to do with shadows, the other with perspective. It is perhaps these two points that most clearly reveal the extent to which India is decidedly a part of the Indo-European world while China is resolutely Oriental. In India, the body is modelled with discreet shadows which accentuate the roundness of its form but do not correspond to any specific source of light. In China, shadows are unknown; in any case, they belong in the category of things accidental and are therefore rejected. As for perspective, that at Ajanta—which 726 appears to be the outcome of trial and error—approaches European perspective but is more subtle: like the European painter, the Indian painter uses a horizon line, though on it he projects not one vanishing point, but several; sometimes he even multiplies the horizon lines in a scene. This is yet another phenomenon due to the fact that the artist does not work from nature but from a mental image conceived to illustrate a specific subject. The spectator is not, as in Western painting, thought of as standing immobile outside the picture but is introduced into it by the artist, who causes him to revolve inside it, simultaneously showing him the façade of a building and its receding side as he would actually see them were he himself to walk the length of a building. It is the most subtle application of so-called rotary perspective ever realised, and it is also a process which, carried to its extreme consequence, could have resulted in the modern science of simultaneity.

The Chinese approach is totally different. The spectator 725 is accustomed to read from right to left and from top to bottom; his eye thus automatically travels diagonally, from the upper right-hand corner to the lower left-hand corner. This conditions the whole composition which, moreover, is often panoramic and in bird's-eye view. According to Chinese theory, the horizon line is not placed in front of the spectator, as in Europe and as at Ajanta, but behind him; thus the vanishing points, converging towards the horizon, are projected on to the picture already diverging into the distance, a practice which is in complete contrast to the law that traditionally governs the Western eye. The consequence of these two concepts of perspective, Indian and Chinese, is extremely significant: while India uses the whole surface and fills up the horizon with elements of landscape or any other sort of combination, China gives concrete value to space 729 and opens the horizon on to infinity.

We thus have two different worlds, one linked by many characteristics (and probably also due to the influence it underwent in the course of its history) to the West, the other resolutely abiding by its own formulas and transmitting them eastwards, in particular to Japan, where they laid the foundations for the greatest decorative art ever known.

729. CHINESE. Landscape by Hsia Kuei. Ink on paper. c. 1180–1234. *Iwasaki Collection, Tokyo.*

INDEX

Figures in bold type refer to illustrations

A

Abelam 92
Abomey 87
Abri Poisson 48, **50**
Abstract art 18, 19, 20, 86, 166, 204, 210, 211, 222, 245, 266, 342, 383, 384, 385, **63**
Abu Gurob 156
Abu Hamed 154 (map)
Abu Simbel 144, 154 (map), 157, **228**
Abydos 143, 154 (map), 155, 156
Abyssinia 50
Achaean 59, 166, 168, 183, 186, 188, 190, 191, 194, 196, 197, 234, 236, 242, 250
Achaemenes 298
Achaemenian 136, 151, 153, 219, 220, 249, 292, 299, 300, 301, 364, 365, 366, 368, **432, 435, 438, 550, 557, 564**
Achaemenids 249, 292–3, 296, 297, 298, 300, 301, 381
Acheulian 28–9, 41 (chart), 43
Achilles Painter 291, **524**
Acropolis, Athens 250, 254, 256, 257, 265, 269, 271, 273, 278, 286, 287, 289, 322, **428, 469, 474**; see also Parthenon
Acropolis, Pergamon 322, 323
Addaura 50
Adad 160, **268**
Adige 212
Adlerberg 203
Admiralty Islands 92, 96
Adonis 350
Adriatic 59, 155, 168, 172, 174, 175 (map), 179, 180, 183, 200, 206, 207, 209, 212, 213, 216, 234
Aegean 24, 66, 135, 140, 145, 146, 151, 166–72, 174, 175 (map), 179, 180, 181, 183 (map), 183–98, 199, 200, 201, 204, 205, 206, 207, 208, 211, 219, 226, 246, 257, 292, 298, 301, 302, 303
Aegeus 250
Aegina 260 (map), 262, 272, 285, 286, 287, 288, **437**
Aeschylus 274, 275
Aetion 328
Aezani 350
Afanasievo 68, 227 (map), 230
Afghanistan 298, 354, 355, 356, 361, 366, 367, 369, 377, 378, 385, 388 (map)
Afontova-gora II 68
Africa 20, 22, 27, 30, 35, 36, 42, 43, 45, 50–1, 68, 74, 76, 77, 78, 81–8, 89 (map), 116, 155, 183, 242, 303, 327; bas-reliefs 85; bronzes 77, 85–6, **102, 107, 111, 112**; Bushmen 20, 30, 51, 74, 78 (and map), 79, East 51, 81, **94**; jewellery 85, 86; North 26, 50, 54, 57, 78, 172, 201, 215, 302, 310, 340, 341, 349, 350, 352; rock art 50–1, 74, 81, 116, **31**b, **36, 56, 57**a, **57**b; sculpture 83, 84, 85, 86, 87, 88, **106, 110, 116**; South 22, 32, 34, 35, 38, 51, 81; statuettes 85, 86, 87, 88, **119**; see also Sahara
Agasias 347
Agesander 347
Agias 290
Agoras 287, 325, 326, 346, 347
Agrigentum 305, 306; temple of Asclepius 346; temple of Concord 251, 287, **477, 478**; temple of Olympian Zeus 261, 287, 305, **574**
Agrippa 334, 339, 349, 350
Agrippina 339
Ahaggar 51
Ahiram 146, 159, **232**
Ahmose 155
Ahriman 293
Ahura Mazda 293, 294, 296, 299
Aichbühl 199
Ainus 78
Ajanta 359, 361, 362, 363, 364, 367, 374, 375, 376, 377 (map), 379, 380, 392, 400, **664, 693, 696, 697, 726**
Akhenaten 141–2, 143, 144, 146, 155, 156, 157, 170, 360, **219, 220**
Akkad, Akkadian 63, 123, 128, 133, 134, 154 (map), 161, 162, 163, 164, 168, **272**
Al Khazna 321

Alabanda 324, 332 (map), 346
Alaca Huyuk 154 (map), 160, 176, 177, 181, 182, 183 (map), 185, 197, **303, 312**
Alaska 40, 98 (map), 104, **93**, 101
Albacete 38, 50
Albani-kore 289
Albania 179
Alcamenes 289, 331
Alcmaeonids 265, 273, 286, 287, 288
Alcman 246
Alexander the Great 155, 254, 265, 282, 283, 290, 291, 297, 299, 301, 312, 314, 316, 317, 318, 324, 326, 336, 343, 346, 352, 365, 366, 377, 381, **546, 610, 648**
Alexander sarcophagus 318, 347, **648**
Alexander Aigos 152, **251**
Alexander Severus 348
Alexandria, Alexandrians 152, 153, 317, 318, 319, 320, 321, 322, 325, 326, 327, 328, 329, 337, 340, 346, 347, 351, 354 (map), 356, **656**; lighthouse 321, 324
Algarve 175 (map), 201
Algeria 304
Aliseda 572
Alishar 176, 181, 183 (map), 185, 197
Almería 38, 59, 175 (map), 201
Alps 40, 41, 43, 175 (map), 199, 200, 201, 202, 203, 204, 205, 206, 207, 208, 209, 212
Alsace 57, 178, 205, 209
Altai Mts 225, 226, 227 (map), 230, 231
Altamira 19, 34–5, 37, 48, 49, 52 (map), 116, **28, 29**
Altars 99, 106, 246, 318, 322, 325, 327, 336, 337, 342, 346, 347, 350, **612**
Altheim 175 (map), 201
Altin Tagh Mts 227 (map)
Altis 247
Amaravati 361, 362, 375, 377 (map), 378, 379, 380, **681**
Amarna, Tell el, see Tell el Amarna
Amasis 291
Amasis 291
Amazon 98 (map), 103, 107, 108, 111
Amazons 59, 269, 274, 335
Amazonomachy 263, 269, 289, 316, **538**
Amber 166, 168, 172, 204, 205, 212, 213, 215, 216, 396, 397, **374**
Ambracia 317
Ambrym 92
Amenemhat II 134, 155
Amenemhat III 157
Ameneritis 147
Amenhotep III 135, 136, 137, 138, 142, 143, 144, 155, **215, 259**
Amenhotep IV, see Akhenaten
Amitabha 390
Amon 141, 143, 155, 347, **229**
Amon Ra 155, see Amon
Amorgos 166
Amphitheatres 341, 350
Amphoras 200, 291, 347, 393, **326, 504, 507, 508, 547, 548, 549**
Amratian 61, 65, 116
Amri 62
Amu Darya 68
Amur 227 (map)
Amurru 114
Amunenchi 135
Amyclae 246, 272
Amytis 296

An, Anu 294
Anacreon 273
Anahuac 105
Ananino 228
Anasazi 104
Anathyrosis 255
Anatolia 30, 53, 59, 139, 140, 145, 154 (map), 159, 166, 168, 175 (map), 176, 177, 178, 179, 180, 181, 182, 183 and map, 184, 185, 186, 197, 199, 200, 202, 206, 208, 212, 219, 226, 246, 247, 250, 271, 272, 322, 324, 325, 327, 328, 329, 341, 343
Anau 68
Anavyssos 272
Anaximander 236, 244
Anaximenes 236, 244
Ancash Andes 110
Ancona 206, 207
Ancyra 332 (map), 350
Andalusia 38, 302
Andes 99, 100, 103, 108, 109, 110, 111
Andhras 377, 378
Andokides 291, **549**
Androvono 219, 226, 227 (and map), 230
Angelion 272
Anghelu Ruju 175 (map), 200
Angkor 359, 363, 364
Angles-sur-l'Anglin 48, 52 (map)
Angola 87
Angoulême, 360
Animal representation 166, 172, 175, 182, 186, 203, 209, 212, 213, 219–21, 226–7; African 85, 87, 88; Assyrian 148, 149; cave and rock art 20, 21, 24, 30, 34, 50, 51, 59, 76; Chinese 222, 223, 224, 225, 228, 231, 361, 364, 381, 383, 385, 387, 394, 395; Cretan 190, 193, 194; Egyptian 61, 116, 118, 120, 128, 146, 158, 170, **242, 245**; Etruscan 318; Greek 270, 291, 316; Hittite 140, 145, 148, 160; Indian 360, 366, 369, 378; Mesopotamian 64, 66, 67, 128, 163, 164, 242, 366; Persian 242, 299, 300; pre-Columbian 100, 101, 102, 104, 108, 109, 111; Roman 317, 318; Sardinian 212; Scandinavian 215, **269**; Scythian 209, 227, 299; steppes 228, 229, 230, 366, 396
Anitta 160, 177
Annam 224–5, 386, 394
Antalcidas 299
Antarctic 96
Antenor 273, 288
Antigonus of Carysus 323, 346, 347
Antigonus Gonata 346
Antilles 98 (map), 107, 108
Antimony 176
Antinous 350
Antioch 325, 326, 332 (map), 340, 342, 346, 347, 352, 354 (map), 356
Antiochus I 325
Antiochus III 318, **620**
Antiochus IV 322, 326, 346
Antipholus 328
Antonianus 352
Antonine 333, 348, 349, 350, 351
Antoninus 349
Antoninus, temple of 351
Antony 338
An-yang 221, 222, 223, 227, 230, 381, **392**c, **417**
Anyathian 68
Apadana 151, 293, 299, 300
Apamea 322, 332 (map), 346, 350
Apaturius of Alabanda 324
Apelles 254, 267, 280, 291, 316, 328, 337
Apennines 206, 207, 209
Aphaia, temple of, Aegina 262, 286, 287, 289, **437, 473, 485**
Aphrodisias 328, 332 (map), 335, 345, 349, 352
Aphrodite 192, 278, 281, 282, 290, 305, 326, 327, 331, 346, 347, **539, 543, 615, 616**
Aphrodite Landolina 323; of Arles 290; of Cnidus 251, 281, 282, 290, **530, 535**
Aphrodite, temple of, Messa 346
Apis 116

An, Anu 294

Apollo 275, 281, 289, 322, 327, 336, 346, 347, 352, **451, 452, 490, 491, 499, 500**
Apollo, temple of, Alabanda 346; Antioch 325; Bassae 256, 260 (map), 285, 287, 289; Corinth 286, **424**, 426; Delos 272, 287, 289, 346; Delphi 262, 286, 287, 288; Didyma 265, 288, 346; Dreros 286; Ptoos 288, **462**; Syracuse 139, 305
Apollo Alaeus 305; Palatinus 349; Patroos 287; Sauroctonus 290, **533**
Apollo Smintheus, temple of, Chryse 346
Apollodorus of Damascus 280, 330, 333, 336, 349
Apollodorus of Selencia 316
Apollonius 346, 347, **591, 592, 649**
Apoxyomenus 282, 290, **540**
Appian Way 349
Apulia 199
Aq-terek 388
Aqueducts, Roman 344, 349, **626**
Aquileia 328
Aquitania 210
Ara Pacis 318, 325, 327, 336, 337, 342, 350, **602, 633**
Arabia, Arabs 155, 181, 370, 388, 393
Arabian Sea 67, 377 (map)
Aral Sea 53, 219
Aralo-Caspian Lake 40 (map); Sea 68
Arawaks 107, 108, 111
Arcadia 234, 246, 256, 260 (map), 281, **635**
Arcadius 348
Arcadius, column of 344
Arcesilaus II 270, 330
Arcesilaus cup 336
Arches, Roman 325, 334–5, 336, 340, 341, 344, 348, 350, 351, **628, 645**
Architecture 24, 57, **59**, 118, 120, 166, 181, 182, 184, 188, 190, 198; Carthaginian 303, 310; Chinese 390, 394; Egyptian 120, 122, 123, 124, 136, 137, 138, 143, 151, 155–7; Graeco-Buddhist 356; Greek 245, 247–8, 251, 254–6, 286–8, 289; Hellenistic 257, 314, 324–6, 333, 346; Hittite 160, **269**; Indian 368, 371–3, 374, 376, 378; Japanese 390, 391, 397; Korean 397; Mesopotamian 66, 67, 120, 123, 124, 134, 161–2; Minoan, 190, 192; Mycenean 193, 195; Oceanic 96; Persian 293, 299–300; Phoenicians 159, 181; pre-Columbian 104, 105, 108, 110; Roman 257, 325, 326, 333–5, 340, 341, 344, 345, 348–50; Sicilian 305; Syrian 324, see also palaces, temples, tombs
Arctic 44, 51, 53, 68, 96, 104
Ardèche 47, 57
Arezzo 329, 352, 366
Argentine 22, 98 (map), 103, 110, 111
Argolis 183, 194
Argos, Argive 194, 247, 249, 250, 254, 260 (map), 271, 273, 288, 289, **464**; Heraeum 247, 289, **450**
Ariadne 246
Ariège 37
Aristeas 352
Aristides 283, 285, 316
Aristides II 328
Aristippus of Cyrene 281
Aristodicos 272
Aristotle 238, 240, 242, 244, 245, 314, 316, 321, 322
Ariusd 175 (map), 199
Arizona 104
Arkansas **144**
Arles 175 (map), 201, 290, 332 (map), 349, **637**
Armenia 166, 176, 177, 180, 183 (map), 298
Arpachiyah 66, 246, **80**
Arsinoe 346
Arslan Tash 146, 159
Arslantepe 145
Artaxerxes **431**
Artaxerxes II 299, 300, **556, 558**
Artaxerxes III 299, **558**
Artemis 281; temple of, Corfu 288, **486**; Magnesia-ad-Meandrum 346; Sparta 286; Syracuse 305
Artemis Brauronia 290; Orthia 286, 303
Artemisium, Delos 247; Ephesus 247, 256, 261, 265, 266, 286, 288, 289, 290, 324;

413